FINANCIAL AND MANAGEMENT ACCOUNTING

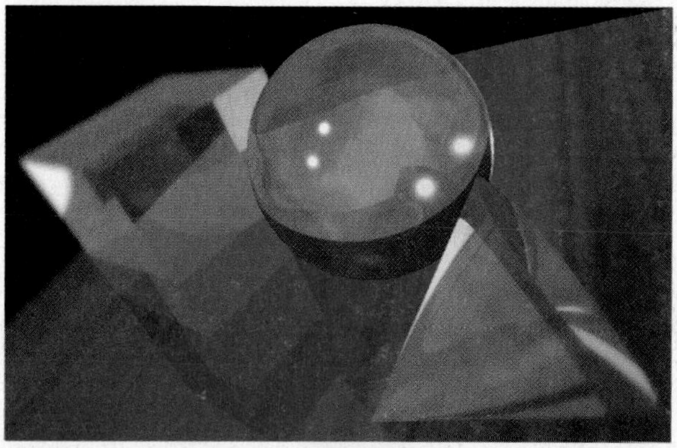

Michael A. Diamond
University of Southern California

Don R. Hansen
Oklahoma State University

David S. Murphy
Oklahoma State University

COLLEGE DIVISION South-Western Publishing Co.
Cincinnati Ohio

Sponsoring Editor: David L. Shaut
Developmental Editor: Linda A. Spang
Production Editors II: Sharon L. Smith and Nancy J. Ahr
Production Editor I: Jackie Myrick
Production House: Litten Editing and Production
Designer: Joseph M. Devine
Marketing Manager: Michael J. O'Brien

AB68AA

1 2 3 4 5 6 KI 9 8 7 6 5 4

Printed in the United States of America

Library of Congress Cataloging-in-Publication Data

Diamond, Michael A.
Financial and management accounting / Michael A. Diamond, Don R. Hansen, David S. Murphy.—1st ed.
p. cm.
Includes index.
ISBN 0-538-82532-4
1. Accounting. 2. Managerial accounting. 3. Corporations—Finance. I. Hansen, Don R. II. Murphy, David S., 1952– . III. Title.
HF5635.D5143 1993 93-31905
658.15'11—dc20 CIP

I(T)P

International Thomson Publishing
South-Western is an ITP Company. The ITP trademark is used under license.

PREFACE

Financial and Management Accounting is designed for use in the first-year undergraduate or graduate accounting course that covers either two semesters or three quarters. It presumes that the student has no previous exposure to accounting.

The early 1990s is the beginning of a period that has already seen and will continue to see important changes in accounting education. These changes are being fostered by the dynamic changes in the way enterprises conduct business. These changes, in turn, are affecting the role of accounting within organizations. In response, the accounting profession and accounting educators have joined in partnership and created the Accounting Education Change Commission (AECC) to encourage revisions in the traditional accounting curriculum. These changes, now being implemented in a number of colleges and universities throughout the country, focus on teaching students of all majors to recognize accounting issues and problems facing organizations, to develop alternative solutions to these problems, and to communicate these solutions to internal and external decision makers. This book is written in response to these changes and is based upon the AECC's philosophy that:

The primary objective of the first course in accounting is for students to learn about accounting as an information development and communication function that supports economic decision making. The knowledge and skills provided by the first course in accounting should facilitate subsequent learning even if the student takes no additional academic work in accounting or directly related disciplines. For example, the course should help students perform financial analysis; derive information for personal or organizational decisions; and understand business, governmental, and other organizational entities.[1]

1 *Accounting Education Change Commission,* "The First Accounting Course," Position Statement No. 2, June 1992.

INNOVATIVE FEATURES

With the changes suggested by the AECC and other accounting educators in mind, the important innovative features of this text include:

- An increased emphasis on accounting concepts and analysis and the role of accounting information in decision making.
- A greater emphasis on management accounting than found in traditional principles texts, including coverage of conventional and new manufacturing environments.
- Information systems concepts integrated throughout the text.
- A corporate setting and emphasis of contemporary business, accounting, and ethical issues facing business people and other users of accounting information.
- A complete and integrated student learning package.

An Increased Emphasis on Accounting Concepts and Analysis and the Role of Accounting Information in Decision Making

Financial and Management Accounting emphasizes the analysis and decision-making concepts important for all members of today's complex international business community. Therefore, this book is written to meet the needs of a wide range of students with varying interests and goals. For potential accounting majors, a solid foundation in financial and management accounting concepts and practices is important so that they can apply that knowledge in the various careers. Students choosing other majors need a basic knowledge of accounting to assist them in the many financial and managerial decision-making situations they will encounter in their future professional careers.

The organizational structure of this text, especially the financial chapters, is designed to facilitate this emphasis on concepts, analysis, and decision making. Traditional principles of accounting and financial/managerial textbooks have taken a balance sheet approach to organizing the financial accounting material. That is, after discussing the accounting cycle, the table of contents basically works its way down the balance sheet causing students to view each chapter as completely independent of other chapters. This makes integrating the material and making logical conceptual connections difficult. This text is organized in a completely different manner. First, the student is introduced to accounting and financial reporting issues including the basic accounting model and transaction analysis. Included in this first part of the book is a unique chapter entitled Management Controls, Fraudulent Financial Reporting, and Accounting Information Systems.

As noted, the accounting information system is covered in Part 1. Students are introduced to the accounting cycle without being burdened by unnecessary procedures. Parts 2, 3, and 4 are organized to match the structure and format of the statement of cash flows. That is, these three parts cover operating, investing, and financing activities. Following the introduction to Part 3, a module introduces students to present value techniques and applications, thus allowing ease of inclusion or omission according to the needs of each school's curriculum. Part 5 concludes the primarily financial accounting section with the interpretation of financial information. In a sense, Chapter 14, The Statement of Cash Flows and Financial Statement Analysis, is in the nature of summary and review of the financial accounting information covered in the preceding chapters. For example, material on the statement of cash flows is introduced in Chapter 1 and discussed in more detail in Chapter 5. Financial statement analysis and the use of accounting information for decision making are stressed in all previous chapters.

In the remaining three parts, management accounting is emphasized. The parts correspond to the three objectives of a cost management information system: (1) product costing, (2) decision making, and (3) planning and control. Each part covers both traditional and advanced cost management concepts.

To further provide students with a strong conceptual and analytical background in accounting, the least important procedural material is omitted or covered only briefly. For example, such topics as bank reconciliations, petty cash funds, worksheets, and specialized journals are not covered. Essential procedures, however, are presented in a concise and relevant manner and used to enhance student understanding of a particular concept or accounting standard. Chapter 10, for example, fully explains the concepts behind operating assets and depreciation before it illustrates the various depreciation methods.

A Greater Emphasis on Management Accounting

Financial and Management Accounting emphasizes to a greater degree management accounting than do current principles textbooks. Twelve chapters are devoted to management accounting concepts and practices.

Unlike other financial/managerial textbooks, this text is more than a mere combination of separate successful financial and managerial books. Special attention is made to integrate managerial topics into appropriate financial chapters. Chapters 7 and 8, covering the revenue and expenditure cycles respectively, discuss budgeting for cash receipts and expenditures. Chapter 9, Inventory Valuation, introduces the student to manufacturing inventories. Chapter 10, on operating assets and intangibles, contains a brief introduction to capital budgeting. This approach enables students to better integrate financial and managerial topics and to recognize the broad role accounting plays in organizations.

Coverage of management accounting includes the conventional and new manufacturing environments. The changes taking place in management accounting necessitate coverage of new developments such as activity-based costing, JIT and its effect on management accounting, strategic costing, quality costing, productivity accounting, activity-based responsibility accounting, and life-cycle costing.

Integration of Systems Concepts

This book adopts a systems orientation to fulfill the AECC's prescription that "students completing the first course in accounting should understand the basic features of accounting and reporting by organizations, including the principles underlying the design, integrity, and effectiveness of accounting information systems."[2] Chapter 2, Accounting As an Information System, introduces the student to the systems theory and basic systems concepts. Additional systems concepts, such as transaction cycles, systems tools, systems analysis and design, internal control, and data bases, are introduced in subsequent chapters. These modules are short, basic introductions to critical accounting information topics and are supported by questions, exercises, and problems at the end of each chapter.

A Corporate and Contemporary Setting

Again, unlike most principles of accounting and financial/managerial textbooks, *Financial and Management Accounting* adopts a corporate setting. A corporate setting makes it easier to integrate management accounting topics in appropriate financial accounting chapters. It also facilitates the integration of financial statement analysis concepts into individual chapters. Most importantly, the use of a

2 Ibid.

corporate approach allows us to include numerous quotes from business publications, such as *Forbes* and the *Wall Street Journal*, to add realism and spark student interest. In addition, the financial statements of Albertson's, a large retail grocery chain, are used as an integrating force throughout the financial accounting chapters of the text.

Further, a corporate approach and the coverage of contemporary topics allow the use of financial and managerial case studies and scenarios to catch the students' attention and emphasize that what they are studying relates to actual business decisions. The objective is to provide evidence that accounting is useful for all functional areas of business. Finally, ethics is stressed throughout the book so that students, early on, understand the importance of ethics in business decisions. Each chapter includes at least one discussion problem presenting an ethical dilemma for the student to interpret.

A Complete and Integrated Learning Package

This text and the complete student's and instructor's support packages have been designed as an integrated unit.

PEDAGOGICAL FEATURES

We have gone to great lengths to design a pedagogically sound textbook. Each chapter contains an **opening scenario** to relate the chapter material to real world situations. A concise set of action-worded **learning objectives** is also presented at the beginning of each chapter. These objectives are repeated in the margin of the text where the related material is presented and are summarized at the end of the chapter. In addition, specific learning objectives are identified for each end-of-chapter exercise and problem.

Throughout each chapter, **key terms** are presented in the text margin where they are introduced. The terms are listed, with page references, at the end of the chapter. A complete **glossary** of key terms appears at the end of the book.

At the end of each chapter, one or more **review problems** emphasize key points in the chapter. These problems are followed by detailed solutions, so that students can compare their solutions with the correct one. Many review problems contain notes that anticipate student questions or areas of difficulty. Each part of the text concludes with one or more **comprehensive cases** that review the major points of the chapters within each part.

End-of-Chapter Assignment Material

The text contains a varied set of assignment materials. **Questions** relate to the major concepts and key terms introduced in the chapter. **Exercises** involve single concepts and provide the student with practice in applying those concepts. The end-of-chapter **problems** are more complex and often cover several related topics. The exercises and problems contain short captions describing their content.

At the end of each chapter, we have included a section entitled Discussion and Interpretation Problems. These problems are of four types. Problems in **understanding financial statements** ask students to interpret and analyze information from financial statements of real domestic and, where appropriate, foreign companies. **Financial and managerial decision cases** place students in the role of decision makers and ask them to analyze and interpret financial and/or managerial and other quantitative data. **Research assignments** are short cases that require students to use outside sources available in university and college libraries. They ask students to extend the material introduced in the text. These research assignments are ideal for individual and group written and oral presentations. **Ethical issues** are problems and cases that ask students to face and respond to realistic ethical dilemmas. Many of these cases require the student to reason through situations that do not have one "correct" solution. Again, these cases are ideal for individual and group written and oral presentations.

The Discussion and Interpretation Problems are a response to the AECC's view that beginning accounting students should have experience in solving unstructured problems. Again, in its Position Statement No. 1, the AECC states that the first course in accounting should "enhance students' analytical skills by presenting them with unstructured problems that yield to decision-making skills—that is, problems with more than one defensible solution."[3]

The Student's Support Package

The Study Guide, prepared by Donna K. Ulmer of Southern Illinois University, Edwardsville, provides a detailed review of each chapter and allows students to check their understanding of the material through a Key Terms Test, a Chapter Quiz, and Practice Exercises. Answers are provided for all self-testing material.

The student support package also includes partially completed **Working Papers** for end-of-chapter assignment material. They are designed to reduce the amount of nonproductive pencil work required of the student.

The Instructor's Support Package

A two-volume **Solutions and Instructor's Manual** contains detailed solutions to end-of-chapter assignment material. These solutions have all been independently verified. The manual also provides a set of lecture notes for each chapter, designed to reduce class preparation time for the instructor.

Solutions Transparencies are available from the publisher to adopters of the textbook. These acetate transparencies have been prepared in oversized type for easy readability.

The **Test Bank**, prepared by Donna K. Ulmer, includes fill-in-the-blanks, multiple-choice questions, short problems, and essay questions. Solutions to all questions are provided, along with explanations and computations where appropriate. Test bank chapters contain enough material to prepare several exams without repeating questions and problems. The test bank is available in both computerized and manual versions.

Template Diskettes, prepared by John H. Palipchak of Pennsylvania State University-Harrisburg, are used with Lotus 1-2-3[4] for solving selected end-of-chapter problems, which are identified with a diskette symbol in the margin. The template diskettes are provided free of charge to instructors at educational institutions that adopt this text.

Several video supplements are available to text adopters. A Financial Accounting Video contains five segments in which business managers and accountants discuss financial accounting and its function in the workplace. A Management Accounting Video features segments that follow the production process through three different manufacturing companies and a segment that highlights work flows in two service organizations. Other videos focus on JIT, ABC, and total quality control.

Updated **Annual Reports** for Albertson's, Inc., are free to text adopters who request them from South-Western Publishing Co.

3 Ibid.

4 Lotus and 1-2-3 are registered trademarks of the Lotus Development Corporation. Any reference to Lotus or 1-2-3 refers to this footnote.

Acknowledgements

We wish to express our appreciation for all who have provided helpful comments and suggestions. Feedback from the following reviewers was invaluable in developing this text.

Mark Bettner
Bucknell University

Sandra Byrd
Southwest Missouri State Univ.

Judy Cook
Grossmont College

Rosalind Cranor
Virginia Polytechnic Institute

Lyle Dehning
Metropolitan State College

Cynthia Edmonds
Univ. of Alabama-Birmingham

Katherine Beal Frazier
North Carolina State University

Gary Freeman
University of Tulsa

Shirley Friar
Howard University

Vincent Guide
Clemson University

Abo Habib
Mankato State University

Nabil Hassan
Wright State University

Emin Hussein
Nassau Community College

Antoine Jabbour
California State Polytechnic University-Pomona

Stanley Jenne
Illinois State University

Roxanne Johnson
University of Baltimore

Kumen Jones
Arizona State University

Vern Jorgensen
Southwestern College

Amy H. Lau
Oklahoma State University

Linda Lessing
SUNY College of Technology

Johanna Lyle
Kansas State University

Ronald Mannino
University of Massachusetts

Robert Maust
West Virginia University

Richard McDermott
Weber State University

Paul Mihalek
University of Hartford

William Mister
Colorado State University

Daniel O'Mara
Villanova University

Jeffrey Phillips
University of Dayton

Robert Rouse
College of Charleston

Robert Ruland
Northeastern University

Victoria Rymer
University of Maryland

Edward Schwan
Susquehanna University

Kenneth Sinclair
Lehigh University

Janice Smith
Bryant College

Murat Tanju
Univ. of Alabama-Birmingham

Vajana Tongtharadol
Univ. of Wisconsin-Eau Claire

We would like to thank Cathy Xanthaky Larson, Middlesex Community College, who served as verifier for the solutions, test bank, and study guide. Her careful editing helped us produce a high-quality text and ancillary materials.

Appreciation is extended to Donna Ulmer for her preparation of the Test Bank and Study Guide and for granting us permission to use the case she created. We would also like to acknowledge Professor Mark Defond of the University of Southern California for assistance during this project and for allowing us to use several of his cases in the text. We also appreciate Albertson's allowing us to use a large portion of their annual report for illustrative purposes.

We also want to express our appreciation to the American Institute of Certified Public Accountants for permission to use questions and unofficial answers from past CPA examinations and to the Institute of Management Accountants for permission to use questions and unofficial answers from past CMA examinations.

Finally, this project would never have been completed without the help of the outstanding editorial staff of South-Western Publishing Co. A special note of thanks goes to our families who gave up valuable family time to allow us to complete this project.

Notwithstanding the assistance of all of these individuals, we are solely responsible for the final product. Any suggestions for improvement would be greatly appreciated.

Michael A. Diamond
Don R. Hansen
David S. Murphy

CONTENTS

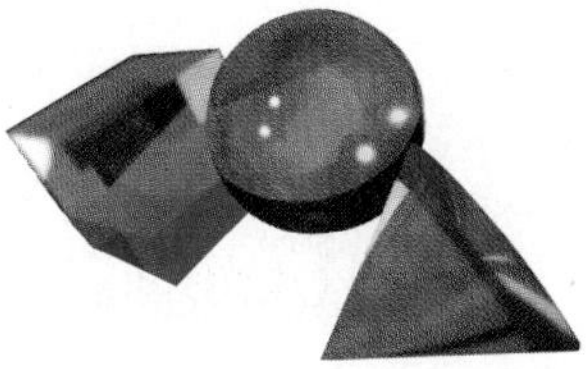

PART 3
INVESTING ACTIVITIES

Present Value Module 444

10 Investments in Operating and Intangible Assets 461

11 Investments in Debt and Equity Securities 515

PART 1

INTRODUCTION TO ACCOUNTING AND FINANCIAL REPORTING

Many students enter an accounting course with the preconceived notion that it will be difficult and somewhat boring, requiring aptitude at numbers and a willingness to memorize many dry procedures and techniques, but not really calling for any originality or judgment.

This notion of accounting is just not correct. As you will see in this course, accountants must fully understand the economics and finance of business and be able to deal on a daily basis with ambiguity and unstructured problems. You will quickly learn that when accountants prepare financial statements they are not simply following steps in a cut-and-dried process but must make many judgments and estimates that can profoundly affect the results.

Part 1 provides an introduction to the role of accounting in business organizations and begins the discussion of the accounting system, and the set of methods and procedures used to record, classify, and summarize financial information that is distributed to interested users in the form of financial statements. The accounting system is part of a firm's broader information system which provides relevant information to management and others responsible for the operations of the enterprise.

The accounting procedures we will discuss in Chapters 2 through 4 have their roots in the Middle Ages. An Italian monk, Luca Pacioli, is credited with inventing in the 1490's what has become the basic accounting equation and the set of procedures to record financial information. However, historians have traced what appears to be early accounting tablets to 3000 B.C.. Those interested in accounting history have also traced early accounting records to the Incans, an Indian tribe in South America in A.D. 1100.

Chapter 5 introduces you to the financial statements of Albertson's, a large retail grocery chain with stores in many localities. Chapter 6 drives home the importance of ethics in the accounting profession and describes some unfortunate instances of fraudulent financial reporting. In sum, Part 1 sets the stage for a more detailed analysis of the important financial accounting issues presented in Parts 2 through 5.

CHAPTER 1

ACCOUNTING: ITS NATURE AND FUNCTIONS

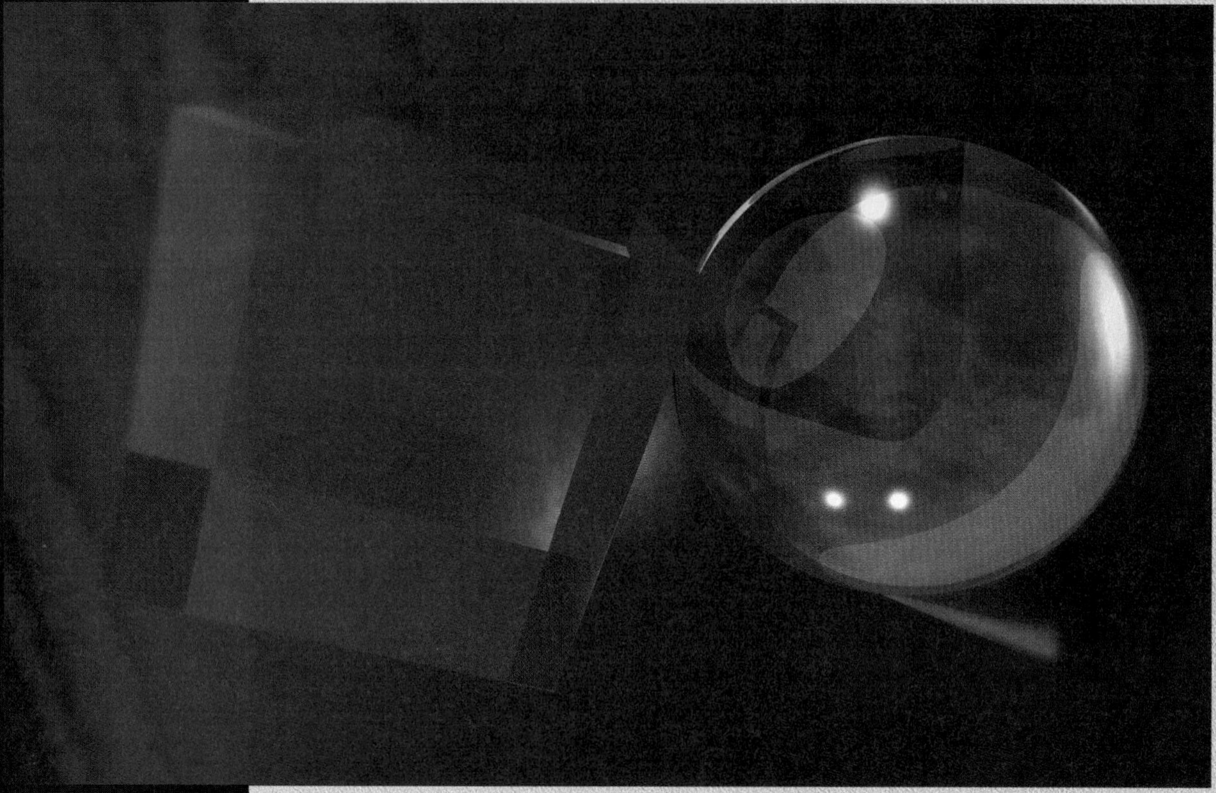

LEARNING OBJECTIVES

After studying this chapter, you should be able to:

1. Define accounting and discuss its functions.
2. Explain the relationship between accounting and different forms of business enterprises.
3. List the primary users of accounting information.
4. Describe the work of accountants.
5. Explain the importance of ethical behavior for accountants and managers.
6. Describe and prepare the primary financial statements: balance sheet, income statement, retained earnings statement, and statement of cash flows.
7. Describe the codes of professional conduct for public accountants and management accountants (Appendix).

Scenario

Today's business world can be baffling if you are not familiar with the language and concepts of financial accounting. Almost every day you read newspaper headlines that require accounting knowledge to understand. For example, what do the following statements mean?

- Matsushita, the Japanese conglomerate, purchased MCA, the parent company of Universal Pictures.
- RJR/Nabisco was the target of one of the largest and most controversial leveraged buyouts ever attempted.
- A commissioner of the Securities and Exchange Commission questions whether U.S. companies are at a competitive disadvantage vis-á-vis non-U.S. companies because of our financial accounting and reporting requirements.
- Regulators estimate that it will cost between $300 and $500 *billion* to bail out the savings and loan industry.
- General Motors manufactures automobiles in Hungary.
- A company you know is the target of a hostile takeover.

Each of these events illustrates an organization using or discussing accounting concepts to improve its own, or the nation's economic health. The language of business is accounting. During a weekday lunch hour you could walk into almost any restaurant in the U.S. or another industrialized country and hear business professionals discussing accounting-related issues. You might hear a stockbroker tell a colleague, "My clients are a retired couple looking for companies that pay a regular dividend. Because they need a steady income, I need to find stable companies with good earnings potential and low risk of financial problems."

At another table, you might hear a commercial loan officer advise a client: "Although you can provide me with good security, I need your first year's budget, your projected cash flows from operations for the next three years, and copies of your financial statements for last year. I need this information to analyze the financial strength of your company and provide the loan committee with data on how your company compares to others in the industry."

Across the room the treasurer of an airline could be discussing the potential effects of lowering ticket prices with her staff. "Profits are down because of intense competition. Our marketing VP claims that if we reduce airfares by 20 percent and spend $500,000 more in advertising, we can increase our passenger load 20 percent and still be competitive. Is this true? Also, there are new accounting rules relating to frequent flyer programs. I am concerned that these rules could have a substantial negative effect on our profits."

And near the window, the recently elected state insurance commissioner is trying to deal with a rash of applications from insurance companies for significant rate increases. These companies are claiming that under current regulations they are not earning enough profit on their assets and are threatening to discontinue writing automobile insurance in the state.

In these cases, knowing financial accounting concepts enables:

- Stockbrokers to spot a company's strengths and weaknesses.
- Loan officers to determine quickly a client's financial strength, thereby making it easier for the client to borrow money and develop a business.

- Company treasurers to make good decisions and recommendations.
- Regulators and elected officials to make crucial decisions regarding the economic climate in their states.

The message is clear. No matter what your profession, the more you know about accounting, the easier it will be to understand and solve business problems, understand daily financial news, and respond to the dynamics of a corporate world that affects the lives of all of us.

Accounting was practiced in ancient societies, such as Babylonia and Assyria. Then as now, accounting not only helped individuals manage their businesses but also served a broader social function by facilitating the development of commerce. Today, accounting plays a central role in our day-to-day economic activities. As highlighted in the opening scenario, whether you decide to become a stockbroker, a loan officer, or a company treasurer, you will use accounting data. Even if you decide not to enter a business field, instead choosing a career in engineering or professional sports, knowledge of accounting will help you manage your everyday affairs and understand the economic environment in which you live. For example, understanding domestic and international mergers and acquisitions such as the Matsushita purchase of MCA or the leveraged buyout of RJR/Nabisco, requires a basic knowledge of accounting. Indeed, accounting is the language of business, and fluency in this language is needed in today's world. The purpose of this chapter is to introduce you to that language and to the nature and functions of accounting.

ACCOUNTING AND ITS FUNCTIONS

Objective 1
Define accounting and discuss its functions.

Accounting is, in part, a function of a specific country's economic, political, and social systems. Accounting is a cultural phenomenon, much like language and law, and is used as a tool in understanding economic events. Because accounting has been created for economic purposes, it tends to evolve and adapt to changes in its environment. For example, modern accounting has its roots in the fourteenth century but has been able to adapt and cope with the relatively new phenomenon of multinational firms, such as IBM, ITT, Mitsubishi, and Grand Metropolitan. Thus, despite its use of numbers, accounting is not a natural science, and unlike mathematics, does not consist of a system of numbers that, once proven, does not change. Rather, accounting is dynamic; it changes over time according to economic needs.

accounting

Traditionally **accounting** has been defined as a system of providing "quantitative information, primarily financial in nature, about economic entities that is intended to be useful in making economic decisions."[1] Its primary functions are to record, classify, and summarize in a significant manner and in monetary terms transactions of a financial character. This information is used by groups such as

1. American Institute of Certified Public Accounts, Accounting Principles Board, Statement No. 4, Basic Concepts and Accounting Principles Underlying Financial Statements of Business Enterprises (New York: AICPA, 1970), par. 9.

accounting system

the firm's managers and external parties to make a variety of decisions about an entity. The **accounting system,** part of the overall information system in an organization, is the set of principles, methods, and procedures used to record, classify, and summarize the financial information to be distributed to users.

The Record-Keeping Function

transactions

All organizations that engage in economic activities need a method of keeping track of their transactions. **Transactions** are the business events of a particular enterprise that are measured in money and recorded in its financial records. Except in the smallest enterprises, failure to record sales or the purchase of goods or services systematically would lead to confusion.

Classifying and Summarizing Transactions. Transactions must first be classified into similar categories so that they can be meaningfully summarized. For example, all of a firm's sales during a certain period are aggregated to determine total sales. Likewise, all of the transactions affecting cash are aggregated to determine the amount of cash on hand at any point in time, as well as to analyze how the cash was received and used.

Large firms enter into hundreds of thousands or even millions of transactions each year. This data must be summarized into accounting reports that are presented in useful formats so that the information can be used by decision makers. These reports are called *financial statements* and are the primary way in which financial information about an enterprise is communicated to external users.

financial statements

Financial statements are concise reports that summarize specific transactions for a particular period of time. They show the financial position of the firm as well as the results of its activities. The four primary financial statements are introduced later in this chapter.

A Broader View of Accounting

Many people find this definition of accounting rather limited, too process oriented, and not robust enough to meet the needs of a changing economic world. They feel that accounting broadly viewed involves (1) the observation, selection, and identification of significant variables about the activities of an organization, (2) the measurement of these selected variables, (3) the analysis and processing of data to identify relevant information for long-term and operating decision making, and (4) the disclosure of the information to the various decision makers. In this context, accounting is seen as a "broad economic information development and distribution process, based on the design, implementation, and operation of multiple types of information systems."[2]

Observation and Selection of Events. The important words in this expanded definition of accounting are *observation, selection, measurement, analysis,* and *disclosure.* Accountants must observe economic events and select the ones to be measured, analyzed, and disclosed. Selection is particularly important because it determines what will be communicated to users through a firm's financial statements.

2. Adapted from "Future Accounting Education: Preparing for the Expanding Profession," The American Accounting Association Committee on the Future Structure, Content, and Scope of Accounting Education, *Issues in Accounting Education,* Vol. 1, No. 1, Spring 1986, pp. 168-193.

Accounting usually has focused only on economic events involving monetary transactions, that is, transactions that are quantified in dollars or other currencies. However, monetary transactions represent only one type of event about which accountants and decision makers must be concerned. For example, decision makers are interested in variables such as market share, employee turnover, sales backlogs, and currency exchange rates. These kinds of data traditionally have not been reported in firms' published financial statements. However, because these data are important in determining the future prospects of the enterprise, they are often included in internal management reports. Accountants need to understand what information various decision makers need and how they make decisions so that the accounting system can provide relevant and reliable information. Throughout this book, we will discuss how variables relevant to financial decisions concerning an enterprise can be observed, measured, and disclosed in the accounting information system.

Measurement. Accounting measurement includes two activities: identifying what the accountant should measure and selecting the most appropriate measurement technique. For example, assume you purchased a plot of land several years ago. Do we want to measure its current value, what you paid for it several years ago (i.e., its historical cost), or what you could sell it for in a forced sale, auction, or liquidation? Each of these attributes is likely to yield quite different information. Later you will see that accountants have focused primarily upon measuring the historical cost of an item.

In addition to deciding which attribute of an item to measure, accountants also must decide how to measure the attribute. For example, there are different measurement scales. In some cases, accountants just classify items into categories such as current or short-term versus noncurrent or long-term. Accountants usually use numerical scales such as dollars to measure financial statement items. Single item measurements are used, rather than intervals or ranges. For example, the market value of securities might be disclosed as $145,000 on a financial statement. If exact market values are not available, however, it might be more appropriate to use a range between $142,000 and $146,000. Nonetheless, accountants decide upon a single figure, lets say $145,000 in this case, to represent the dollar amount of the securities. The measurement of financial statement items is a topic we will refer to frequently in future chapters of this book.

Analysis and Disclosure. Financial analysis is the process of examining and understanding the significance of important relationships between elements of financial data. Information that is likely to affect an individual's decisions should be disclosed, even if the information is usually not included on a financial statement. This book will describe how financial statement disclosures have expanded and how internal and external decision makers use these expanded disclosures to make better use of accounting information.

Accounting and Decision Making

This expanded view of accounting emphasizes providing information that is useful in decision making. The accounting information system identifies and measures relevant variables, analyzes that information, and distributes it to interested users inside and outside the enterprise. It is applicable to governmental and not-for-profit organizations such as museums, zoos, and religious organizations, as

Exhibit 1-1
The Preparation and Dissemination of Accounting Information

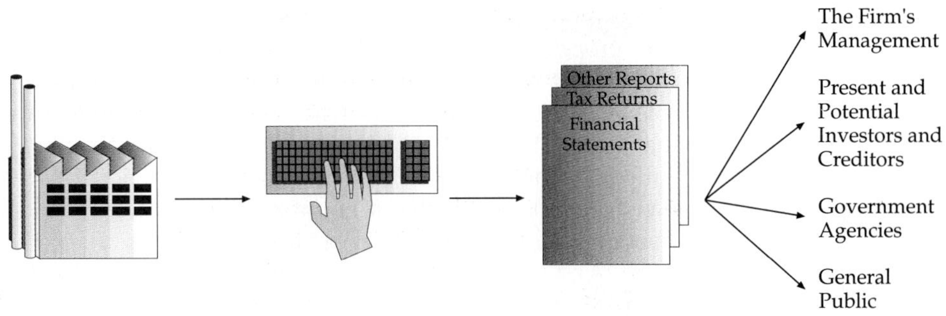

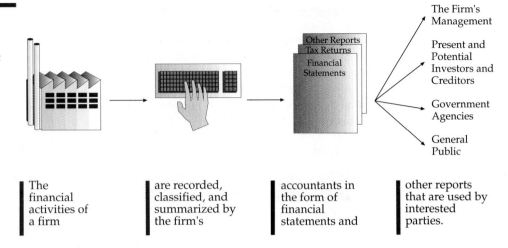

The financial activities of a firm | are recorded, classified, and summarized by the firm's | accountants in the form of financial statements and | other reports that are used by interested parties.

well as to business enterprises and to those who have to make decisions about those enterprises. In this book, the primary concern will be the role of accounting in business enterprises, especially corporations.

Exhibit 1-1 illustrates the relationships on which this book will focus. The corporation, the most important form of business organization in the United States, is central to this discussion. The primary users of corporate financial information are the firm's management, present and potential investors and creditors, government agencies such as the Internal Revenue Service, and the general public. The information needs of these user groups will be examined later in the chapter. First, however, we will discuss the important characteristics of corporations and other forms of business enterprises.

ACCOUNTING AND FORMS OF BUSINESS ENTERPRISES

Objective 2
Explain the relationship between accounting and different forms of business enterprises.

The three major types of business organizations are (1) the sole proprietorship, (2) the partnership, and (3) the corporation. Good accounting practices are necessary to each form of business organization. Most of the accounting concepts and practices you will learn in this course are applicable to all three forms of business organizations. However, each type of business organization does have some unique features that are important to understand early in your studies.

Sole Proprietorships

sole proprietorship

A **sole proprietorship** is a business entity owned by one individual. The business may employ few or many people, but there is only one owner, who realizes the profits or the losses of the business. The major advantages of a sole proprietorship are their ease of establishment, low organization costs, and, in many cases, limited legal and regulatory requirements.

business entity

In accounting theory and practice, a business and its owner are different entities. A **business entity** is a distinct economic unit whose transactions are kept separate from those of its owners. As a result, the scope of accounting for the sole proprietorship is limited to the transactions of the business and does not include the owner's personal transactions. Despite this accounting treatment, a sole proprietorship and its owner are not independent legal entities. This means that legally the sole proprietor is personally responsible for the debts and obligations of the business. The accounting distinction between the business and its owner demonstrates that accounting is more concerned with the economic substance of an event than with its legal form.

Partnerships

partnership

A **partnership** is a business entity that is owned by two or more individuals, but which is not legally independent of the owners. Like a sole proprietorship, a partnership may employ few or many people. Some partnerships, such as the large international CPA firms, have hundreds or even thousands of partners. There are different types of partnership agreements. Individuals may be equal partners or have unequal interests in the partnership's profits and losses. Some partners might be actively involved in managing the business, while other partners contribute funds to the enterprise but take no part in management. Formation of a partnership does not require the formal approval of a state or other governmental agency. A partnership can be formed with an oral or written agreement among the individuals or entities who are to be partners. The partnership agreement should identify the terms and conditions for the admission and withdrawal of partners, distributions of profits and losses, and settlements in the event of illness, incapacity, or death of a member.

From an accounting perspective, a partnership is an accounting entity distinct from its owners. Each individual partner has a predetermined interest in the enterprise's profits or losses; as with a sole proprietorship, the partners and the partnership are legally one entity.

Corporations

corporation

A **corporation** is a business entity that is viewed legally as separate and distinct from its owners, who are *stockholders*. In the United States, a business may be incorporated in any one of the 50 states. To incorporate, an application must be filed with officials of the state in which incorporation is desired. If approved, the application becomes the articles of incorporation. The articles of incorporation include the corporate name, principal location of business, and the number of shares of stock that are authorized for sale. Ownership in a corporation is designated by stock certificates. Each share of stock represents a proportionate share of the corporation. State laws govern the sale or transfer of corporate stock from one stockholder to another.

Because a corporation is legally a separate entity, its owners have limited liability. Thus, unlike owners of sole proprietorships and partnerships, stockholders are not personally responsible, as individuals, for the debts incurred by the corporation beyond the amount that they have invested in the corporation.

limited liability

This **limited liability** feature of corporations enables them to obtain funds from many individuals who want to become part owners of the business, but who may not wish to participate actively in the operations of the enterprise nor be personally liable for its debts. Therefore, corporations, especially large ones, usually employ professional managers. The stockholders elect a board of directors, who may or may not be owners. The board, in turn, appoints the officers of the corporation (president, vice-president, treasurer, secretary, etc.) to manage the business.

publicly owned corporations

Many large U.S. corporations are **publicly owned corporations,** which means that a corporation's stock is bought and sold by the public. Many stocks are traded (bought and sold) on large exchanges such as the New York or American Stock Exchange. Through these and other smaller exchanges, individuals can easily buy or sell shares of the stock of corporations. As a result, large publicly held corporations have hundreds of thousands or, in some cases, over a million shareholders.

Not all corporations are publicly held. Some corporations are owned by families, a few shareholders, or a single individual, and the stock in these closely held corporations is not traded publicly. During the late 1980s, many publicly held corporations went "private" through what is called a *leveraged buyout.* In these cases, management or others borrowed large amounts of money to repurchase all the corporation's stock. The purchase of RJR/Nabisco, mentioned earlier, is an example of a leveraged buyout.

The role of accounting becomes critical in corporations because of the separation between ownership and management. Owners require financial reports to evaluate management's performance and to decide whether to retain, sell, or add to their investment in the corporation. Accounting data is equally important to managers, who need this information to help them manage the enterprise.

PRIMARY USERS OF ACCOUNTING INFORMATION

Objective 3
List the primary users of accounting information.

The primary users of accounting information can be divided into two major categories: external users and internal users. External users are decision makers outside the organization. Major external users are present and potential investors and creditors, government agencies, and the general public. Internal users are decision makers within an organization. The firm's management represents the primary internal user of accounting information.

External Users of Accounting Information

financial accounting

Financial accounting is the study of the concepts, standards, and procedures used to prepare financial information distributed to external users. The definition of external users, however, is broad indeed. Almost all of us are users of accounting information. For example, voters use accounting information to analyze many issues and propositions on state and local ballots. Fully understanding the insurance initiative placed on a recent ballot in California required a working knowledge of the accounting rate of return (a concept to which you will be introduced in Chapter 5). For ease of explanation, external users can be divided into present and potential investors and creditors, government agencies, and the general public.

Present and Potential Investors and Creditors. Present and potential investors use financial statements and other information about an enterprise to make decisions about increasing, decreasing, or maintaining their investment in the entity. These same financial statements are used by creditors to evaluate whether the corporation can repay its debts or obligations. For example, a bank will analyze a company's financial statements to determine whether to make a new loan or to extend a current loan. One of the primary objectives of financial reporting is to

. . . provide information that is useful to present and potential investors and creditors and others in making rational investment, credit, and similar decisions. The information should be comprehensible to those who have a reasonable understanding of business and economic activities and are willing to study the information with reasonable diligence.[3]

Government Agencies. Government agencies are another major user of financial information about a firm. For example, the Internal Revenue Service uses some of the information contained in financial statements to help determine the amount of taxes due to the government. Other federal agencies, such as the Interstate Commerce Commission and the Securities and Exchange Commission, use the firm's financial statements in their regulatory activities. The Resolution Trust Agency, which was set up by Congress to oversee the resolution and bailout of the nation's troubled savings and loans, has become an important user of accounting information in recent years. State agencies, such as public utility commissions and insurance commissions, use financial statements and other accounting information in setting and/or approving utility and insurance rates. In many circumstances, this information is based on the same accounting principles that govern the financial statements presented to investors and creditors. However, it does not necessarily have to be the same, and in some cases there are significant differences. The concepts, standards, and practice of accounting as it relates particularly to government organizations is called **governmental accounting.**

governmental accounting

The General Public. Many of us, whether investors, creditors, or just citizens, are interested in the activities of business entities. The affairs of large corporations affect individuals throughout the world. For example, IBM's decision on whether to manufacture computer components in the United States or abroad affects the employment and income of U.S. residents as well as residents of other countries. The public often relies on the financial information that is summarized in financial statements to evaluate the actions of IBM, Toyota, and other firms. Society uses a vast quantity of financial information in assessing its economic well-being.

Other External Users. There are also other external users of accounting information. For example, labor unions use financial statements to help them assess a company's ability to increase wage payments to employees. The financial information contained in a firm's financial statements is often used in negotiations. In recent years, labor unions have also considered the purchase of certain businesses. For example, the unions at United Airlines and TWA attempted to purchase their respective airlines in 1990. Obviously, accounting information played an important role in determining what price the unions were willing to offer for the airlines. Potential employees may use financial information to evaluate the long-range prospects of the firm before deciding to accept an employment offer.

External Users' Need for Generally Accepted Accounting Principles. External users must rely on others to prepare reliable financial information for their use. Accountants have developed what are referred to as generally accepted account-

3. Financial Accounting Standards Board, Concepts Statement No. 1, Objectives of Financial Reporting by Business Enterprises (Stamford, Conn.: FASB, November 1978), par. 34.

generally accepted accounting principles (GAAP)

ing principles to guide them in preparing financial statements and related information for use by external parties. **Generally accepted accounting principles (GAAP)** represent the consensus at a particular time on how accounting information should be recorded, what information should be disclosed, how it should be disclosed, and which financial statements should be prepared. These principles range from broad assumptions about the economic environment to specific methods of accounting for certain events. In effect, these principles provide a common financial language that enables informed users to read and interpret financial statements.

The development of GAAP is a complex process involving a mixture of theory, governmental regulation, and conventions derived from actual practice. It is impossible to specify one source of GAAP or one book that codifies all of the accounting principles.

Chapter 5 contains a detailed discussion of how accounting principles and standards are set. At this point two important groups are briefly mentioned; The American Institute of Certified Public Accountants and the Financial Accounting Standards Board. The **American Institute of Certified Public Accountants (AICPA)** is the professional body of CPAs. Throughout the years various committees of the AICPA have played a role in setting accounting standards by issuing research statements and opinions. Many of the opinions of the AICPA are still in force and will be referenced from time to time.

American Institute of Certified Public Accountants (AICPA)

Financial Accounting Standards Board (FASB)

In 1973 the **Financial Accounting Standards Board (FASB)** was created as an independent body from the AICPA to set accounting standards and principles underlying financial reporting. The FASB, now the primary private group charged with setting accounting standards, issues statements of accounting standards and through the spring of 1993 has issued 111 statements covering a variety of accounting issues.[4] Only financial statements prepared using principles and standards sanctioned by the AICPA and FASB are considered based upon generally accepted accounting principles. Thus, external users can rely on the information based upon these standards.

Internal Users of Accounting Information—Company Management

As mentioned before, company managers are the primary internal users of accounting information. Managers need an information system that will identify problems, such as possible cost overruns or a department's inability to implement a plan properly. The selection and implementation of solutions can occur only after problems have been identified. Accounting information is used to pin point problems and to help select appropriate solutions. Managers also use accounting information as they make business decisions. For example, accounting information would be used by a manager deciding whether to reduce airfares and increase advertising to improve profitability, or by a manager deciding whether to automate a production facility. Finally, accounting information can help managers assess organizational performance, such as quantifying the firm's control of costs or evaluating the efficiency of a sub-unit. **Management accounting** is the system and the procedures for providing information for managerial activities.

management accounting

4. As we will see in Chapter 5, the Securities and Exchange Commission, a regulatory body of the federal government, also has substantial influence in the setting of accounting standards.

Management accountants are not constrained by GAAP in developing accounting information to meet their particular needs. Management accountants are free to use principles and standards that meet their particular needs. Nonetheless, when that information is published in the form of financial statements for distribution outside the company it must be based upon GAAP.

ACCOUNTANTS—THE PROVIDERS OF ACCOUNTING INFORMATION

Objective 4
Describe the work of accountants.

Accountants are qualified through education and experience to perform accounting services. Professional accountants may work in public accounting, private accounting, or governmental accounting. In the course of an accountant's career, he or she may work in all three of these areas.

Public Accountants

public accounting

certified public accountant (CPA)

Public accounting is the field of accounting that provides a variety of accounting services to clients for a fee. A professional accountant who works in a public accounting firm usually is a **certified public accountant (CPA).** CPAs are licensed by individual states to practice accounting after having met a number of requirements. All states require that individuals pass the Uniform CPA Examination developed and administered by the AICPA. In addition, the various states have different education and experience requirements for licensing a person as a CPA.[5]

Certified public accounting firms range in size from one-person firms to large multinational firms. Firms with more than one owner usually are organized as partnerships. The large firms have offices in the principal cities in the United States and throughout the world and often have more than 2,000 partners. There are six international accounting firms collectively known as the "Big Six." They are in alphabetical order:

- Arthur Andersen
- Coopers & Lybrand
- Deloitte & Touche
- Ernst & Young
- KPMG Peat Marwick
- Price Waterhouse

audit

audit report

Auditing and Accounting Services. Auditing is one of the main functions of a CPA firm. An **audit** is an objective and independent third-party examination of an organization's financial statements. Publicly held corporations are required by federal securities law to have their financial statements audited. Many privately owned firms have their financial statements audited to satisfy banks and/or owners even when they are not required by law to do so. The auditor evaluates the firm's accounting system, performs tests to determine whether economic transactions have been properly recorded, and gathers other evidence to ensure that all relevant economic events have been appropriately reported or disclosed. After this examination is completed, the auditor evaluates the findings and issues a report. The **audit report** identifies the financial statements audited, describes

5. More than half of the states have passed laws that require an individual to have 150 semester hours of education prior to sitting for the CPA examination. This movement toward 150 hours of education began in earnest when the AICPA passed a measure in 1989 that requires 150 semester hours of education to qualify for membership in the organization beginning in the year 2000.

Exhibit 1-2
Report of Independent Public Accountants

To the Stockholders and the Board of Directors of Delta Air Lines, Inc.:

We have audited the accompanying consolidated balance sheets of Delta Air Lines, Inc. (a Delaware corporation) and subsidiaries as of June 30, 1992 and 1991, and the related consolidated statements of operations, cash flows and common stockholders' equity for each of the three years in the period ended June 30, 1992. These financial statements are the responsibility of the Company's management. Our responsibility is to express an opinion on these financial statements based on our audits.

We conducted our audits in accordance with generally accepted auditing standards. Those standards require that we plan and perform the audit to obtain reasonable assurance about whether the financial statements are free of material misstatement. An audit includes examining, on a test basis, evidence supporting the amounts and disclosures in the financial statements. An audit also includes assessing the accounting principles used and significant estimates made by management, as well as evaluating the overall financial statement presentation. We believe that our audits provide a reasonable basis for our opinion.

In our opinion, the financial statements referred to above present fairly, in all material respects, the financial position of Delta Air Lines, Inc. and subsidiaries as of June 30, 1992 and 1991, and the results of their operations and their cash flows for the periods stated, in conformity with generally accepted accounting principles.

Arthur Andersen & Co.

Arthur Andersen & Co.
Atlanta, Georgia
August 14, 1992

auditor's opinion

the nature and scope of the audit, and expresses the auditor's conclusion. This conclusion, called the **auditor's opinion,** states whether the financial statements present fairly the firm's financial position, results of operations, and cash flows. An audit report for Delta Air Lines is reproduced in Exhibit 1-2. This report is called an unqualified report because the auditor did not express any qualifications about the fairness of the presentation of the financial statements. CPAs are licensed by their respective states to perform audits and to express opinions on financial statements. External users of financial statements can rely on this opinion, because the CPA must be independent of the firm it is auditing.

Many businesses, especially smaller ones, may not need or desire to have their financial statements audited. However, they often need some review of their records or help in preparing their financial statements. As a result, CPA firms also provide such accounting services, called reviews and compilations.

Tax Preparation and Planning. Tax preparation and planning is another function of a public accountant. CPAs often are asked for advice about the possible tax consequences of a particular decision because tax factors are important to most major financial decisions. CPAs are also often asked to prepare income tax returns. Almost all CPA firms derive fees from tax services.

Management Advisory Services. Increasingly, accountants are called upon to provide information and formal business advice. In fact, the accountant is often considered the primary business adviser to executives of smaller companies. To better serve their clients' needs, CPA firms of all sizes have established management advisory service departments in addition to their audit and tax departments. Individuals who provide management services do not have to be CPAs or even accountants. Frequently, they are individuals with broad business education and backgrounds.

Today, management advisory services are among the fastest-growing practice areas in accounting firms. In fact, Arthur Andersen started a separate organization, Andersen Consulting, to conduct this part of its business. In addition, many firms are expanding the traditional bounds of consulting services to include such areas as financial planning and life insurance analysis.

Management Accountants

management accountant

A **management accountant** works for a single firm, such as McDonald's or General Motors, and is responsible for collecting, processing, and reporting information. Accountants who work for individual firms are employed in a variety of capacities. For example, the chief accounting officer for a private enterprise typically is known as the controller, and the head financial officer is often called the treasurer. Other individuals working in accounting departments perform such tasks as determining the cost of items produced by the firm, budgeting, internal auditing, taxation, and financial reporting.

Institute of Management Accountants (IMA)

Certified Management Accountants (CMA)

A number of certification programs have been developed to provide professional recognition for individuals who work in private accounting. For example, the **Institute of Management Accountants (IMA),** the professional organization for management accountants, offers a program that allows accountants to become **Certified Management Accountants (CMA).** To obtain this designation, a person must pass the CMA exam and satisfy certain other key requirements (e.g., experience).

One of the main purposes of the CMA was to establish management accounting as a recognized, professional discipline, separate from the profession of public accounting. Since its inception, the CMA program has been quite successful. For many in the industrial world, the CMA has gained a reputation rivaling that of the CPA. Many firms now sponsor and pay for classes that prepare their management accountants for the qualifying examination, as well as providing other financial incentives to encourage their employees to obtain the CMA.

internal auditors

compliance audits

operational audits

Certified Internal Auditors (CIA)

Some management accountants perform an audit function within their companies. These specialized management accountants, known as **internal auditors,** audit the fairness of the presentation of financial information, as do public accountants. However, internal auditors also perform compliance audits and operational audits. **Compliance audits** determine whether employees are following management's policies and procedures. **Operational audits** assess the efficiency and effectiveness of operations within an organizational unit. Internal auditors can become **Certified Internal Auditors (CIA)** by passing an examination and meeting the requirements of the Institute of Internal Auditors.

Governmental Accountants

As noted, most governmental agencies use accounting information in completing their regulatory tasks and are large employers of accountants. In addition, individual states, cities, counties, school districts, and other governmental bodies employ accountants for a variety of functions.

Accounting as a Career

Accountants today are information providers, system designers, auditors, and business advisors to a variety of clients and employers. The profession has become a leader in the use of technological innovations. The accounting profession offers a multitude of career paths to well-rounded students who have a strong background in liberal arts, good oral and written communication skills, and strong analytical abilities, as well as an in-depth knowledge of accounting. Individuals who began their careers as accountants have gone on to serve in such capacities as chief executive officers of major corporations, mayors and legislators, and even novelists and television comedians such as Bob Newhart.

ACCOUNTANTS AND ETHICAL BEHAVIOR

Objective 5
Explain the importance of ethical behavior for accountants and managers.

All across our country, there is evidence of a deterioration of ethics. Nowhere is this decline greater than in the world of business. Honest, caring, rational individuals seemingly have come to check their values at the door when they enter the office. The attitude in many businesses appears to be profit at any cost, especially if a company's gains can be at the expense of a competitor—and sometimes even if it is at the expense of its customers.
Kenneth H. Blanchard
Chairman, Blanchard Training and Development[6]

Unfortunately, many people feel that Blanchard's comments correctly depict the state of American business ethics. Although he limits his criticism to U.S. business, recent scandals in the securities markets in Japan and the collapse of the Bank of Commerce and Credit International (BCCI) indicate that the deterioration of business ethics is a worldwide concern.

What Is Ethical Behavior?

Ethical behavior involves choosing actions that are "right" and "proper" and "just." Our behavior can be right or wrong, it can be proper or improper, and the decisions we make can be fair or unfair. People often differ in their views of the meaning of the ethical terms cited; however, there seems to be a common principle underlying all ethical systems. This principle is expressed by the belief that each member of a group bears some responsibility for the well-being of other members in the group. Willingness to sacrifice one's self-interest for the well-being of the group is the heart of ethical action.[7]

Although it may seem contradictory, sacrificing one's self-interest for the collective good may not only be right and bring a sense of individual worth, but it may also be good business sense. Ethical behavior may pay in real economic terms. There is some empirical evidence that companies with above-average ethical standards outperform the stock market average.[8] The market may therefore reward integrity and ethical conduct.

It is very important to recognize that ethical norms may be affected by cultural factors and, as such, may vary across national borders. For example, a study

6. W. Steve Albrecht, *Ethical Issues in the Practice of Accounting*, Cincinnati, Ohio: South-Western Publishing Co., 1992, p. 170.
7. For a detailed discussion of ethical behavior, see LaRue Tone Hosmer, *The Ethics of Management*, (Homewood, Ill.: Irwin, 1987).
8. John R. Shad, "Ethics Should be Added to the Business Curriculum," *Rocky Mountain News*, July 29, 1987, p. 49.

was conducted comparing the perceptions of U.S. and Taiwanese accountants concerning ethical business practices. The authors found that U.S. accountants focused on the legal ramifications of unethical business practices, while Taiwanese accountants differentiated among unethical business practices on the basis of which groups were affected.[9] Other studies have found that students from various countries have differing views of the appropriateness of bribes. Thus, norms of ethical behavior may vary across different cultures, and, as a result, the professional conduct of the accountant may vary considerably from one culture to another.

Accountants' Ethical Responsibilities

Accountants have a significant ethical responsibility because they supply accounting information to a variety of users who make important economic decisions. Confidence in the reliability and integrity of the accounting information supplied to users is absolutely essential for our day-to-day economic activities to function efficiently. Unfortunately, opportunities for manipulating and abusing accounting information for personal gain do exist.

For example, senior executives at General Dynamics improperly assigned $63 million of expenses to defense contracts from 1979 to 1982.[10] Managers of the now defunct brokerage firm, E.F. Hutton, used bank overdrafts to obtain interest-free use of approximately $250 million. This action cost the affected banks nearly $8 million. Fraudulent transactions and reporting by Lincoln Savings and Loan almost ruined the entire savings and loan industry and has had a devastating effect on the U.S. economy.

Implications for Public Accounting. The combination of business failures, greater incidence of fraudulent financial reporting, and ethical questions has increased scrutiny of the accounting profession. Recently, the U.S. General Accounting Office charged the accounting profession with poor-quality audits of many savings and loan institutions that have gone bankrupt. The revelation that a CPA participated with management in the fraudulent financial reporting of a major client he was auditing has caused many to question the ethical standards of the accounting profession. Lack of confidence in the profession can have far-reaching consequences for our economic system. This was clearly spelled out by Joe Conner, former head of Price Waterhouse, when he stated:

Confidence in business and confidence in the accounting profession are inseparable. The profession's primary role is to help sustain confidence in our business and economic system by ensuring the integrity of financial information. When the public's faith in our effectiveness in carrying out that role wanes, so does faith in the system itself.[11]

Implications for Management Accounting. One of the major goals of management accounting is to help managers increase the profitability of their organization. Because of this profit orientation, numerous opportunities exist for managers to manipulate accounting data or use it to justify increasing profits in an

9. A. J. Karnes, R. Sterner, R. Walker, and F. Wu, "A Bicultural Study of Independent Auditors' Perceptions of Unethical Business Practices," *International Journal of Accounting*, 1989, Vol. 24, pp. 29-41.
10. Roger Bennet, "Profile of Harry Crown, Founder of General Dynamics, Inc.," *New York Times*, June 16, 1985, p. 26.
11. Ralph Walters, "Operation Highroad: A Plan to Restore Confidence and Balance," *Ethics in the Accounting Profession*, (May 1986), p. 69.

unethical or illegal way. The opportunity for the abuse of accounting information exists, as does the legitimate use of this information. Clearly, the management accounting system should not be used to justify and support unethical behavior. Furthermore, if at all possible, the evaluation and reward system should be designed to discourage unethical behavior. Essentially, the management accounting system should not be used in isolation, divorced from ethical issues. In planning, controlling, and making decisions, managers should always consider the impact of their actions on others, both within the organization and without. Answering the question "Is it right?" should always be part of the managerial process.

Managers and management accountants should not become so focused on profits that they develop a belief that the *only* goal of business is maximizing the firm's net worth. Yet in most business textbooks, including those that discuss management accounting, the examples and problems essentially convey the message that profit maximization is the sole concern of managers and organizations. In reality, the objective of profit maximization should be constrained by the requirement that profits be achieved through legal and ethical means. While this has always been an implicit assumption of the management accounting methodology, the assumption should be made explicit. To help achieve this objective, many of the problems in this book require explicit consideration of ethical issues.

Ethical Standards for Accountants. Organizations commonly establish standards of conduct for their managers and employees. Professional associations also establish ethical standards. In fact, one of the hallmarks of a profession is its ethics. The accounting profession is no different. For example, both the AICPA and the IMA have established ethical standards for accountants. These codes of professional ethics and behavior, which provide important guidelines for professional accountants, are discussed in the Appendix to this chapter.

The two codes of ethics presented are important, and it is commendable that the accounting profession creates these codes to emphasize the importance of ethical behavior. Codes of ethics alone, whether on the national or international level, will not ensure ethical behavior; it depends on the individual actions of all of us. As stated so eloquently by Ed Kangas, co-managing partner of Deloitte and Touche, "Ethics must begin with one's individual commitment to doing what's right."

FINANCIAL STATEMENTS AND THEIR ELEMENTS

Objective 6
Describe and prepare the primary financial statements: balance sheet, income statement, retained earnings statement, and statement of cash flows.

Financial statements are one of the primary means of communicating economic information about a firm to both external and internal users. The four main financial statements are the balance sheet, the income statement, the retained earnings statement, and the statement of cash flows. These statements summarize the many inputs into the accounting system and present them in a form that is useful to decision makers. Financial statements communicate information on a firm's financial position, its profitability, and significant changes in its resources and obligations.

Balance Sheet

balance sheet

A **balance sheet** presents the financial position of a firm at a particular point in time. The balance sheet is often called the statement of financial position because it shows the financial resources the firm owns or controls and the claims on those

Exhibit 1-3

Carson Corporation
Balance Sheet
January 1, 1995

Assets		*Liabilities and Stockholders' Equity*		
Cash	$ 40,000	Liabilities		
Accounts receivable	75,000	Accounts payable		$ 96,000
Inventories	155,000	Notes payable		40,000
Supplies	30,000	Other payables		79,000
Land	130,000			
Plant and equipment	115,000	Total liabilities		$215,000
		Stockholders' equity		
		Capital stock	$270,000	
		Retained earnings	60,000	
		Total stockholders' equity		330,000
Total assets	$545,000	Total liabilities and stockholders' equity		$545,000

resources. One of the primary purposes of a balance sheet is to help users assess the financial strength of a firm. A balance sheet is prepared at least yearly and, in many cases, more frequently.

The balance sheet for Carson Corporation is presented in Exhibit 1-3. The heading at the top of each financial statement identifies the name of the enterprise, the title of the statement, and either the period of time the statement covers or the date of the statement. A balance sheet is dated as of a certain date because it reflects the resources and obligations of the enterprise as of that date. The body of a corporate balance sheet contains three major categories or elements: assets, liabilities, and stockholders' equity. By convention, assets are listed first, then liabilities, and then stockholders' equity. This particular example shows the **account form of balance sheet,** in which assets are listed on the left and liabilities and stockholders' equity on the right. A balance sheet may also be prepared in a vertical format, with the liabilities and stockholders' equity listed below the assets. This format is called the **report form of balance sheet.**

account form of balance sheet

report form of balance sheet

Assets represent the economic resources of the firm. **Liabilities** are the financial obligations of a firm to its creditors. They represent creditors' claims against the assets of a firm. **Owners' equity** is a general term used to specify the owners' residual interest in the assets of a firm. The residual interest is usually viewed as the assets that remain after all the liabilities have been paid. Because Carson Corporation is a corporation, its owners' equity is specified as **stockholders' equity.**

assets
liabilities
owners' equity
stockholder's equity

The Accounting Equation. The total assets of the enterprise equal its total liabilities and owners' equity. These relationships can be expressed through the basic **accounting equation:**

accounting equation

$$\text{Assets} = \text{Liabilities} + \text{Owners' Equity}$$

The balance sheet is a detailed version of the accounting equation.

The two sides of the accounting equation must always be equal because they are two views of the same accounting entity. The left-hand side of the equation shows the economic resources controlled by a business, and the right-hand side shows the claims against these resources. Another way to view this equality is that the firm's assets must have sources, and the right-hand side of the equation shows the origin of these resources. Using the data from Carson Corporation in Exhibit 1-3, the accounting equation can be stated as follows:

$$\text{Assets} = \text{Liabilities} + \text{Stockholders' Equity}$$
$$\$545{,}000 = \$215{,}000 + \$330{,}000$$

The term *stockholders' equity* has been used in this accounting equation because the firm is a corporation. In this case, the corporation has assets totaling $545,000. The creditors have claims against those assets of $215,000, and the stockholders' residual interest is $330,000.

Sometimes the accounting equation is stated in the following form, which emphasizes that the owners' claims are secondary to those of the creditors:

$$\text{Assets} - \text{Liabilities} = \text{Stockholders' Equity}$$
$$\$545{,}000 - \$215{,}000 = \$330{,}000$$

Assets. Assets are the firm's economic resources. They are formally defined by the FASB as "probable future economic benefits obtained or controlled by a particular entity as a result of past transactions or events."[12] An item is considered an asset when it: (1) results from a past transaction, (2) has a historical cost, (3) is expected to provide future economic benefits, and (4) is owned or controlled by the enterprise. It is important to understand that, from an accounting perspective, a firm need not legally own an item for it to be considered an asset of the firm. All that is necessary is control. For example, in many states, if a firm purchases an automobile and finances that purchase through a bank loan, the bank will retain ownership of the automobile until the loan is paid off. However, the automobile is considered an asset of the firm because the firm has control over its use.

A business may have several different types of assets. Some assets have physical substance, including items such as cash, inventory, property, plant, and equipment. Other assets have no physical substance and represent legal claims or rights. They include such items as receivables and patents. Receivables are claims to future cash, and patents are the exclusive right granted by the federal government to make a product or to use a process. Assets are generally listed on the balance sheet in the order of their **liquidity,** which is the ease with which an item can be turned into cash. As a result, cash and items that can be turned into cash are listed first. Items such as supplies and equipment that are used in the operations of the business are listed next. Exhibit 1-4 lists and describes some of the common assets found in many businesses.

liquidity

Liabilities. The FASB formally defines liabilities as the "probable future sacrifices of economic benefits arising from present obligations of a particular entity to transfer assets or provide services to other entities in the future as a result of past transactions or events."[13] Simply put, liabilities are the economic obligations of an enterprise. They consist of the money or services that the accounting entity owes to its creditors.

12. Financial Accounting Standards Board, *Concepts Statement No. 6,* "Elements of Financial Statements" (Stamford, Conn.: FASB, December 1985), par. 25.
13. Ibid., par. 35.

Exhibit 1-4
Common Assets and Liabilities

Assets

Cash: Includes such items as coins, currency, money orders, drafts, and checks.

Marketable securities: Includes such items as investments in stocks and bonds of other companies.

Notes receivable: Written promises from others to pay a specific amount of money at a specific time in the future. Notes receivable usually contain an interest element.

Accounts receivable: Accounts receivable arise from sales on credit and represent future cash collections.

Inventory: Inventories represent items held for resale.

Prepaid expenses: Includes items such as prepaid insurance, licenses, and prepaid rent, all of which represent payment for goods or services that will be used in the future.

Property, plant, and equipment: Assets such as land, buildings, equipment, furniture, and fixtures that provide long-term benefits to a firm, but that, except for land, usually wear out over time.

Liabilities

Accounts payable: Accounts payable arise from the purchase of goods and services from vendors and suppliers for which the firm has not yet made payment.

Notes and Loans Payable: Notes and loans payable generally result from cash borrowings from banks and other creditors. Like notes receivable, they usually have an interest element.

Other liabilities: Other short-term payable accounts arising at the time expenses are incurred, including taxes payable, interest payable, and salaries payable.

Liabilities are often sources of assets to a firm. For example, businesses frequently buy goods for resale (inventory) on credit rather than paying cash, and this creates the liability called *accounts payable.* In addition, businesses often borrow money from banks and other lenders for various purposes, such as purchasing land, new machinery and equipment, or additional inventory. These debts are *notes payable,* which are formal written promises to repay the lender at a certain time in the future. Notes payable may be short-term (less than a year) or long-term, and unlike accounts payable, they require the payment of interest to the lender. Other liabilities result from incurring expenses that are yet to be paid in cash, such as wages payable and interest payable. Liabilities are generally grouped on the balance sheet according to their due dates with short-term liabilities listed first.

If a business fails to pay its obligations, the law may give creditors the right to force the business to sell some assets to satisfy their claims. Similarly, if a business is dissolved, its creditors legally must be paid first, with anything left over going to the owners. This is why creditors have a primary claim on the assets of a business and owners have a residual, or secondary claim on its assets. Exhibit 1-4 also lists and describes common liability accounts.

Owners' Equity. The owners' equity in a business enterprise is "the residual interest in the assets of an entity that remains after deducting its liabilities."[14]

14. Ibid., par. 49.

This definition emphasizes that creditors legally have first claim on the assets of a business. The term **net assets** is often used to refer to owners' equity, because it also equals assets minus liabilities. For example, the owners' equity of Carson Corporation (its net assets) is $330,000 ($545,000 minus $215,000).

net assets

Owners' equity is increased when the owners of a business invest assets in the firm. It is also increased when the firm is making a profit, because profitable operations add to the firm's net assets.

Owners' equity is decreased when the firm distributes cash or other assets to its owners. This distribution is called a *dividend*. Essentially, the firm is returning to its owners part of the investment they made in the company or is distributing the assets earned through profitable operations. Owners' equity is also decreased by unprofitable operations, because a net loss decreases the firm's net assets.

As noted earlier, the owners' equity section of a balance sheet for a corporation is called *stockholders' equity*. The stockholders' equity section of Carson Corporation balance sheet in Exhibit 1-3 on page 18 consists of two components: capital stock and retained earnings.

Capital Stock. When the owners of a corporation invest cash or other assets in the business, they receive **capital stock** in exchange. Thus the amount of capital stock on the balance sheet represents the amount invested by the owners. In the case of Carson Corporation, the owners have invested $270,000 in the business.

capital stock

Individual units of capital stock are called *shares*, and someone who invests in a corporation receives a stock certificate or certificates for the number of shares purchased. The more shares of stock owned, the greater the proportionate ownership interest in the corporation. Shares of stock in a publicly held corporation are easily transferable. It is important to note that once it issues and sells its shares, the corporation is not affected by subsequent sales of these shares to others.

To illustrate, assume you invested $10,000 in a travel agency started by your friend. In exchange you received 1,000 shares of capital stock—this makes the purchase price of the stock $10 per share. Other individuals also invested in the travel agency, and a total of 10,000 shares were issued. Thus, your 1,000 shares represent a 10% interest in the business. A year later, you decide to sell half of your shares to your brother at $14 a share. This is a transaction between you and your brother. The corporation is not affected by the transaction because the same total number of shares is in the hands of the owners. The only result is that you now own 500 shares and your brother owns 500 shares. The corporation also is not affected by the fact that you were able to sell your shares for more than you paid for them. Again, this is a personal transaction between you and your brother. The corporation receives only what the original investors paid to the corporation for the shares. However, the corporation updates its list of stockholders so that its records indicate that you and your brother each now owns 500 shares of its stock.

Retained Earnings. The other component of stockholders' equity is retained earnings. **Retained earnings** represent the portion of stockholders' equity (resulting from the cumulative profitable operations of the corporation) that has not been distributed as dividends to the owners. Thus, each year that the firm earns a profit its retained earnings are increased by the amount of the profit minus whatever dividends are distributed to the owners. In effect, when a firm is profitable, its net assets increase, and this increase is assigned to the retained earnings

retained earnings

component of stockholders' equity. Retained earnings are reduced by the amount of any loss that a firm suffers. Carson Corporation had retained earnings of $60,000 as of January 1, 1995. The term *retained* is used because the firm decided to keep $60,000 of its total lifetime earnings in the business instead of distributing them as dividends in the form of cash or other assets. Carson Corporation has been in existence for some time, and its total lifetime earnings exceed the amount reported as retained earnings; the $60,000 represents just the portion retained that has not yet been distributed to shareholders.

Concepts Related to the Balance Sheet. There are a number of important concepts related to the content of all financial statements. Two important concepts—the historical cost convention and the going concern assumption—are particularly relevant to the balance sheet.

historical cost convention

Historical Cost Convention. Under the **historical cost convention,** assets and liabilities are initially recorded in the accounting system at their original or historical cost and are not adjusted for subsequent changes in value. Thus, the attribute that accountants measure is historical cost. For accounting purposes, an asset's historical cost is the consideration given at the time of its acquisition. If cash is given as consideration at the time of purchase, the asset will be recorded at the amount of cash paid. If an asset other than cash is given in exchange, the asset received will be recorded at its cash-equivalent value. That is, what the asset would have cost if purchased for cash. Liabilities are also recorded in accordance with the historical cost convention which means they are recorded at their current market values at the time the corresponding resources were received.

Assets and liabilities are normally shown on subsequent balance sheets at historical cost. For example, Carson Corporation purchased land for possible future use as a building site and paid $130,000 for the property. The land was recorded at its cost of $130,000 when it was acquired. Although the market value of the land might increase to $300,000, the land will continue to be shown on the balance sheet at its historical cost of $130,000. The main reasons for this are the objectivity of the original cost and the going concern assumption.

objectivity

A major advantage of historical cost is its **objectivity.** Historical cost is objective (not subject to different interpretations) because it is reliable and verifiable. For example, owners, real estate brokers, and tax collectors might appraise the market value of a piece of land quite differently. Once purchased, its subsequent actual value cannot be objectively determined until the land is sold. Therefore, external users can best rely on the financial statements if assets and liabilities are recorded at the objective measure of historical cost.

Going Concern Assumption. Another reason for using historical cost when recording and valuing assets and liabilities is the going concern assumption. To illustrate, when a firm purchases assets such as plant and equipment, it does so with the intent of using these assets to help produce revenues for the firm by providing infrastructure necessary to make sales. Plant assets are used in the operations of the business and usually are not held for the purpose of resale. Furthermore, it is assumed that the firm will be in existence long enough to use these assets and derive their benefits. This is known as the **going concern assumption.** Unless there is evidence to the contrary, it is assumed that a particular firm will continue to operate indefinitely. This does not mean that the firm will be profitable indefinitely, but only that it is expected to continue to operate. Thus, the current liquidation value of these assets generally is not important unless the firm is about to sell all of its assets.

going concern assumption

This is not to say that accountants ignore obvious indications that a firm is not a going concern. For example, it was clear for at least a year before its bankruptcy that Pan Am was not likely to continue as a going concern. Under circumstances like these the accountants' opinion will be modified to indicate this fact.

Income Statement

income statement

One of the primary objectives of any business enterprise is to earn a profit. The profit earned by an enterprise is a yardstick that managers, investors, and creditors use to evaluate the future prospects of the business. Many people consider the **income statement** the primary financial statement because it provides information concerning the firm's profitability.

An income statement for Carson Corporation is shown in Exhibit 1-5. The heading identifies the name of the enterprise, the title of the statement, and the period of time the statement covers. Because income is earned over a period of time, the heading of an income statement must identify the period covered by the statement, not just a single date. For Carson Corporation, the period is one year, although income statements are usually prepared more frequently.

The body of the statement appears below the heading. The income statement for Carson Corporation contains four major elements or categories: revenues, expenses, income before taxes, and net income. By convention, income taxes are shown separately from the rest of the expenses. Specific items are listed within each category. The detail contained within each category is determined by the information needs of the intended users. For example, income statements prepared for management are likely to be more detailed than those prepared for external users.

Exhibit 1-5

Carson Corporation
Income Statement
For the Year Ended December 31, 1995

Revenues		
Sales	$620,000	
Rental revenue	10,000	
Total revenues		$630,000
Expenses		
Cost of goods sold	$370,000	
Salary	80,000	
Office rental	50,000	
Supplies	25,000	
Repairs and maintenance	10,000	
Utilities	7,000	
Interest	3,000	
Total expenses (other than taxes)		545,000
Income before taxes		$ 85,000
Income taxes		40,000
Net income		$ 45,000

revenues

Revenues. **Revenues** are the price of goods sold or services rendered by a firm to others in exchange for cash or other assets or to satisfy liabilities. In effect, revenues represent the inflows of resources resulting from the firm's operations and generally result from completed economic exchanges. A firm receives an asset when it sells its product or renders a service to another entity. Often the asset received is cash, but if a sale is made on credit, an account receivable is created. An account receivable is a promise of cash to be received in the future. *Accountants do not differentiate between sales made or services rendered for cash and those made or rendered on credit.* Both represent revenues to the firm at the point of sale, regardless of when the cash is collected.

The firm recognizes revenue as a result of these exchanges of goods and/or services for cash or receivables. The amount of revenue recognized is equal to the cash or the cash equivalent of the receivable and/or other resources received at the time the sale is made or the service is rendered. For retail firms such as Safeway Stores or manufacturing firms such as General Motors, sales are the major source of revenues. For service firms, such as law or accounting firms, fees earned are the major source of revenues. Other sources of revenues include interest, rentals, and investments.

expenses

Expenses. **Expenses** are the resources used up by the firm during a particular period of time in the process of earning revenues. Expenses represent the efforts of the enterprise and generally result from completed transactions. A firm must expend some of its resources to earn revenues. In some situations, expenses involve the immediate payment of cash or the use of another asset. In other cases, the payment of cash or the use of other resources is made after the expense is incurred by the firm. In this sense, *incur* refers to the time the firm receives the service or other benefit. The expense is recorded on the income statement in the period in which it was incurred, even though it may be paid in cash during a subsequent period. For a retail or manufacturing firm, the major expense is cost of goods sold, which is the cost of the items sold to customers. Other expenses might include salaries, utilities, rent, interest, repairs and maintenance, and various taxes.

net income (net loss)

Net Income. **Net income** or **net loss** is the difference between revenues and expenses. Net income results when revenues exceed expenses. On the other hand, a net loss results when expenses exceed revenues. Revenues increase a firm's net assets or stockholders' equity (assets minus liabilities), and expenses use a firm's net assets. Therefore net income of $45,000 for the year caused an increase in Carson Corporation's net assets. The firm's net assets increased by $45,000 during the year because of profitable operations. This $45,000 increase in net assets resulted in a corresponding increase in the retained earnings portion of the firm's stockholders' equity. In Chapter 3 we will see how the actual recording of these types of transactions increases the firm's net assets.

Retained Earnings Statement

retained earnings statement

The **retained earnings statement** for Carson Corporation is presented in Exhibit 1-6. The purpose of this statement is to explain the changes in the retained earnings account over a specified period. The statement begins with the retained earnings balance at the beginning of the period. Balance sheet amounts at the end of an accounting period become the beginning balances for the next period. Net income from the income statement for that period is added to this beginning

Exhibit 1-6

Carson Corporation Retained Earnings Statement For the Year Ended December 31, 1995	
Retained earnings, January 1, 1995	$ 60,000
Add: Net income for the year	45,000
Subtotal	$105,000
Less: Dividends declared	5,000
Retained earnings, December 31, 1995	$100,000

retained earnings balance. A net loss would be subtracted from the beginning retained earnings balance. Any dividends declared during the period will also reduce retained earnings. *Dividends declared are not expenses but are direct deductions in the earnings kept in the company.* The result is the end-of-the-period retained earnings amount that will be reported on the December 31, 1995 balance sheet.

The beginning retained earnings balance in Exhibit 1-6 of $60,000 on January 1, 1995 is taken from Carson Corporation's January 1, 1995 balance sheet (Exhibit 1-3). The net income of $45,000 comes from the income statement for the year ended December 31, 1995 (Exhibit 1-5). Dividends are a direct deduction from retained earnings. The ending balance in retained earnings on the retained earnings statement for the year ended December 31, 1995 and on the balance sheet at December 31, 1995 is $100,000 (see Exhibit 1-8, page 27).

Statement of Cash Flows

statement of cash flows

The **statement of cash flows** for Carson Corporation is presented in Exhibit 1-7. The purpose of this statement is to provide relevant information about the cash receipts and disbursements of an enterprise during a period. It helps statement users determine how a firm generates cash and for what purposes this cash is used. It is a very important statement because ultimately for a firm to stay in business it must generate cash flows from its operations.

A firm can obtain its cash from three primary sources: operating activities, investing activities, and financing activities. As indicated in Exhibit 1-7, Carson Corporation's operating activities for the year provided a $15,000 source of cash. *Net cash flow from operating activities is not equal to net income for the year.* This is because net income includes revenues that have yet to be collected in cash (sales made on account for which the entire amount has not yet been collected) and expenses incurred for which the cash has not yet been paid. Conversely, cash flow includes cash received from current period revenues less cash paid for current period expenses, plus cash received during the current period on outstanding accounts receivable recorded in earlier periods less cash paid currently on outstanding accounts payable recorded in earlier periods. Thus, cash flows from operating activities include only revenues and expenses received or paid in cash. In the Carson Corporation example, net income equals $45,000 (see the income statement, Exhibit 1-5), but cash inflow from operating activities equals $15,000.

Investing activities relate primarily to the receipt and payment of cash from the sale or purchase of property, plant, and equipment, other productive assets, and long-term investments. Carson Corporation entered into two transactions that would be classified as investing activities: the $45,000 purchase of land and the $25,000 purchase of plant and equipment. The total cash outflows from investing activities amounted to $70,000.

Exhibit 1-7

Carson Corporation Statement of Cash Flows For the Year Ended December 31, 1995		
Cash flows from operating activities		
Cash revenues	$570,000	
Cash expenses	(555,000)	
Net cash provided by operating activities		$15,000
Cash flows from investing activities		
Purchase of land	$ (45,000)	
Purchase of plant and equipment	(25,000)	
Net cash used by investing activities		(70,000)
Cash flows from financing activities		
Issuance of note payable	$ 40,000	
Issuance of capital stock	30,000	
Payment of dividends	(5,000)	
Net cash provided by financing activities		65,000
Net increase in cash		$10,000
Cash balance, January 1, 1995		40,000
Cash balance, December 31, 1995		$50,000

Financing activities have to do with obtaining resources from owners, paying dividends, and borrowing and repaying money to creditors on long-term debt. As shown in Exhibit 1-7, Carson Corporation had two sources of cash inflows from financing activities: $40,000 received from issuing a note payable and $30,000 received from issuing capital stock. The $5,000 of dividends paid represents a cash outflow from financing activities. The net result is a $65,000 increase in cash flows from financing activities.

At the end of the period, the firm's cash inflows exceeded its outflows by $10,000. When this is added to the beginning cash balance, the ending cash balance of $50,000 is obtained. This is the amount shown on the balance sheet of December 31, 1995 (see Exhibit 1-8).

Relationships Among the Financial Statements

articulation

The balance sheet, income statement, retained earnings statement, and statement of cash flows all are related to one another. This relationship is referred to as **articulation,** which means that the four financial statements all tie in with one another. The balance sheet at the beginning of the period describes the firm's financial position at that particular time. This financial position changes because the firm enters into various transactions. The firm's financial position is strengthened when a profit is earned and is weakened when a loss occurs. These transactions are summarized on the income statement. The net effect is shown on the retained earnings statement as well. Thus, the income statement and the retained earnings statement provide a link between two consecutive balance sheets and show how net assets have increased or decreased from operations.

A firm enters into a variety of investing and financing activities, including the borrowing and repayment of loans, the purchase and sale of noncash assets, and the issuance of capital stock. Though many of these activities do not affect

Exhibit 1-8
The Relationship Among Financial Statements

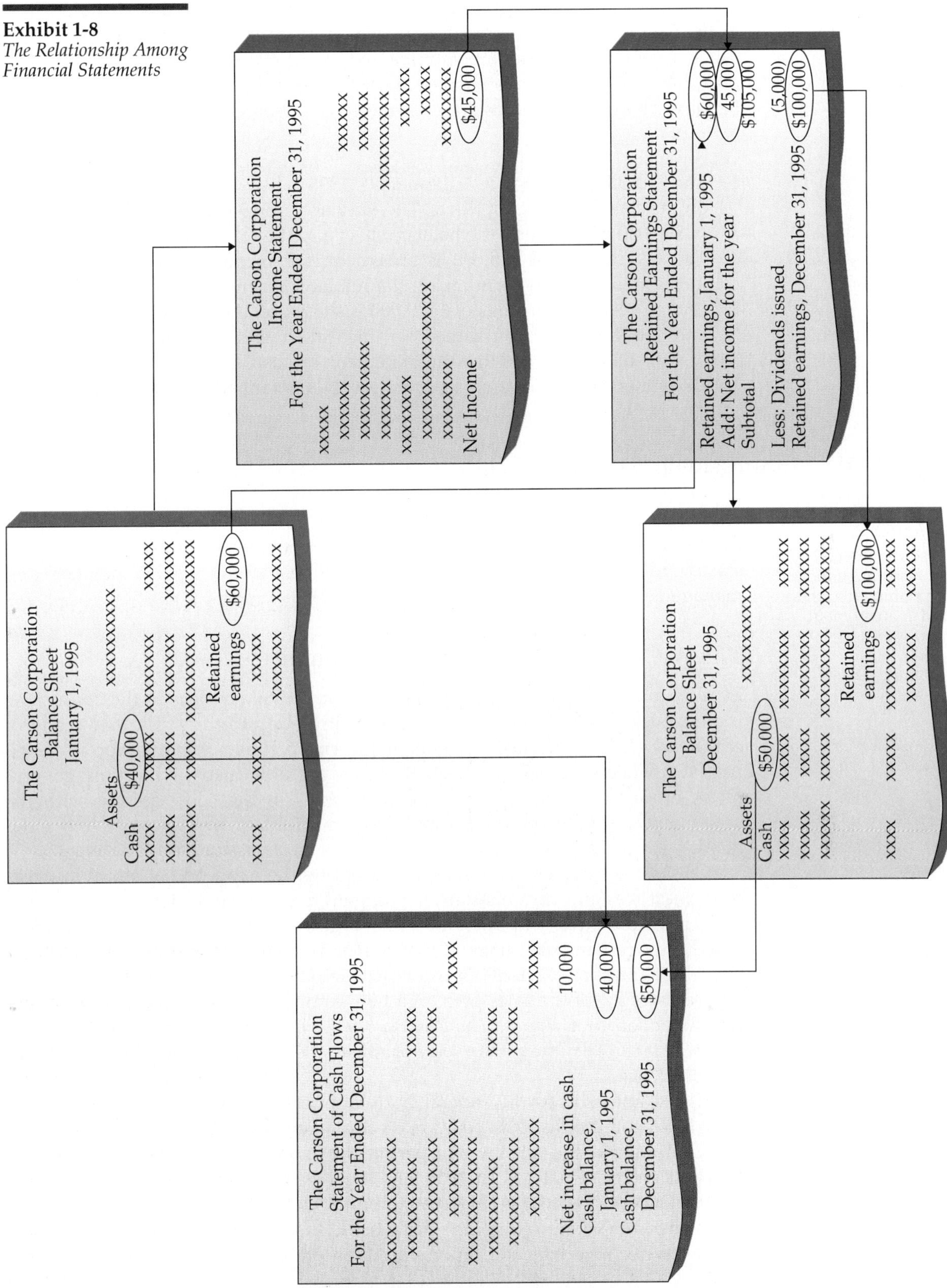
The Carson Corporation
Income Statement
For the Year Ended December 31, 1995
Net Income
$45,000
The Carson Corporation
Retained Earnings Statement
For the Year Ended December 31, 1995
Retained earnings, January 1, 1995
$60,000
Add: Net income for the year
45,000
Subtotal
$105,000
Less: Dividends issued
(5,000)
Retained earnings, December 31, 1995
$100,000
The Carson Corporation
Balance Sheet
January 1, 1995
Assets
Cash
$40,000
Retained earnings
$60,000
The Carson Corporation
Balance Sheet
December 31, 1995
Assets
Cash
$50,000
Retained earnings
$100,000
The Carson Corporation
Statement of Cash Flows
For the Year Ended December 31, 1995
Net increase in cash
10,000
Cash balance, January 1, 1995
40,000
Cash balance, December 31, 1995
$50,000

net income during the current period, they change the amount and composition of the firm's net assets, especially its cash. Such transactions, as well as changes due to operating activities are summarized on the statement of cash flows, which also links two consecutive balance sheets by detailing changes in a firm's cash balance. These relationships are presented for Carson Corporation in Exhibit 1-8. Note that:

1. The $40,000 cash balance at **January 1, 1995** is listed on the balance sheet and on the statement of cash flows. The **January 1, 1995** retained earnings balance of $60,000 is shown on the balance sheet and the retained earnings statement.
2. The net income of $45,000 is shown on the income statement and as an increase in retained earnings on the retained earnings statement.
3. Ending retained earnings of $100,000 is shown on the **December 31, 1995** balance sheet and on the retained earnings statement. The ending cash balance of $50,000 determined on the statement of cash flows for the year ended December 31, 1995 is also reported on the December 31, 1995 balance sheet.

APPENDIX—Professional Codes of Conduct

Objective 7

Describe the codes of professional conduct for public accountants and management accountants.

This appendix introduces you to the AICPA Code of Professional Conduct and the Standards of Ethical Conduct for Management Accountants. These are specific rules and codes that guide the ethical behavior of AICPA members and management accountants.

The AICPA Code of Professional Conduct

In 1988, in response to the many changes that had taken place in the accounting profession, the AICPA completely revised its code of ethics. The new code of ethics, which is reproduced in part at the end of this appendix, applies to all AICPA members regardless of whether they are in industry, education, government, or public practice. There are six articles in the code dealing with the accountant's responsibilities, the public interest, integrity, objectivity and independence, due care, and the scope and nature of the accountant's services.

One of the troublesome issues addressed by the new code of ethics involves contingent fees and commissions. Contingent fees are based not on the value of the service provided, but on some other event (for example, a fee arrangement based on a certain percentage of a tax refund). Commissions are fees based on the sale of goods or services (for example, a fee arrangement whereby the accountant receives 5% of the sales price of a new computer system that the accountant recommended to a client). The AICPA has always opposed these fee arrangements, as it feels they may compromise the accountant's objectivity and independence.

After complaints by the Federal Trade Commission and a threatened law suit, the AICPA compromised its position on contingent fees and commissions. Under this compromise, the AICPA will permit the acceptance of contingent fees and commissions in situations that do not involve the need to maintain independence. That is, now the AICPA can prohibit contingent fees and commissions only when the client is one for which the CPA firm provides audit services or other services involving the expression of an opinion.

Standards of Ethical Conduct for Management Accountants

CPAs who are members of the AICPA are bound by its code of ethics. However, many accountants are not CPAs or are not members of the AICPA. In 1983, in response to the needs of management accountants, the IMA developed its own code of ethics. This code, reproduced at the end of this appendix, covers such areas as the management accountant's competence, confidentiality, integrity, and objectivity. The code also provides guidance on how to resolve issues involving ethical conflict. Although the two codes of conduct specifically target accountants, the standards of behavior required are typical of the type of behavior expected of any business professional.

To illustrate, suppose a manager's bonus is linked to reported profits, with a bonus increasing as profits increase. Thus, the manager has an incentive to find ways to increase reported profits, including unethical approaches. For example, a manager could increase profits by delaying promotions of deserving employees or by using cheaper parts to produce a product. In either case, if the motive is simply to increase the bonus, the behavior could be labeled unethical. Such actions are not in the best interests of the company or its employees. Yet, where should the blame be assigned? After all, the reward system strongly encourages the manager to increase profits. Is the reward system at fault or is the manager who chooses to increase profits? Or both?

In reality, both are probably at fault. It is important to design the evaluation and reward system so that incentives to pursue undesirable behavior are minimized. Yet designing a perfect reward system is not a realistic expectation. Managers have an obligation to avoid abusing the system. Standard III-3 in Code of Ethical Conduct for Management Accountants makes this clear: "A management accountant should refuse any gift, favor, or hospitality that would influence their actions." Manipulating income to increase a bonus can be interpreted as a violation of this standard. Basically, the prospect of an increased bonus (e.g., a favor) should not influence a manager to engage in unethical actions.

AICPA CODE OF PROFESSIONAL CONDUCT[15]

Composition, Applicability, and Compliance

The Code of Professional Conduct of the American Institute of Certified Public Accountants consists of two sections—(1) the Principles and (2) the Rules. The Principles provide the framework for the Rules, which govern the performance of professional services by members. The Council of the American Institute of Certified Public Accountants is authorized to designate bodies to promulgate technical standards under the Rules, and the bylaws require adherence to those Rules and standards.

The Code of Professional Conduct was adopted by the membership to provide guidance and rules to all members—those in public practice, in industry, in government, and in education—in the performance of their professional responsibilities.

Compliance with the Code of Professional Conduct, as with all standards in an open society, depends primarily on members' understanding and voluntary actions, secondarily on reinforcement by peers and public opinion, and ulti-

15. From American Institute of Certified Public Accountants, *Code of Professional Conduct*. Copyright 1988 by American Institute of Certified Public Accountants, Inc. (New York, N.Y.). Reprinted with permission.

mately on disciplinary proceedings, when necessary, against members who fail to comply with the Rules.

Section I: Principles

PREAMBLE

Membership in the American Institute of Certified Public Accountants is voluntary. By accepting membership, a certified public accountant assumes an obligation of self-discipline above and beyond the requirements of laws and regulations.

These Principles of the Code of Professional Conduct of the American Institute of Certified Public Accountants express the profession's recognition of its responsibilities to the public, to clients, and to colleagues. They guide members in the performance of their professional responsibilities and express the basic tenets of ethical and professional conduct. The Principles call for an unswerving commitment to honorable behavior, even at the sacrifice of personal advantage.

ARTICLE I

Responsibilities

In carrying out their responsibilities as professionals, members should exercise sensitive professional and moral judgments in all their activities.

As professionals, certified public accountants perform an essential role in society. Consistent with that role, members of the American Institute of Certified Public Accountants have responsibilities to all those who use their professional services. Members also have a continuing responsibility to cooperate with each other to improve the art of accounting, maintain the public's confidence, and carry out the profession's special responsibilities for self-governance. The collective efforts of all members are required to maintain and enhance the traditions of the profession.

ARTICLE II

The Public Interest

Members should accept the obligation to act in a way that will serve the public interest, honor the public trust, and demonstrate commitment to professionalism.

A distinguishing mark of a profession is acceptance of its responsibilities to the public. The accounting profession's public consists of clients, credit grantors, governments, employers, investors, the business and financial community, and others who rely on the objectivity and integrity of certified public accountants to maintain the orderly functioning of commerce. This reliance imposes a public interest responsibility on certified public accountants. The public interest is defined as the collective well-being of the community of people and institutions the profession serves.

In discharging their professional responsibilities, members may encounter conflicting pressures from among each of those groups. In resolving those conflicts, members should act with integrity, guided by the precept that when members fulfill their responsibility to the public, clients' and employers' interests are best served.

Those who rely on certified public accountants expect them to discharge their responsibilities with integrity, objectivity, due professional care, and a genuine interest in serving the public. They are expected to provide quality services, enter into fee arrangements, and offer a range of services—all in a manner that demonstrates a level of professionalism consistent with these Principles of the Code of Professional Conduct.

All who accept membership in the American Institute of Certified Public Accountants commit themselves to honor the public trust. In return for the faith that the public reposes in them, members should seek continually to demonstrate their dedication to professional excellence.

ARTICLE III

Integrity

To maintain and broaden public confidence, members should perform all professional responsibilities with the highest sense of integrity.

Integrity is an element of character fundamental to professional recognition. It is the quality from which the public trust derives and the benchmark against which a member must ultimately test all decisions.

Integrity requires a member to be, among other things, honest and candid within the constraints of client confidentiality. Service and the public trust should not be subordinated to personal gain and advantage. Integrity can accommodate the inadvertent error and the honest difference of opinion; it cannot accommodate deceit or subordination of principle.

Integrity is measured in terms of what is right and just. In the absence of specific rules, standards, or guidance, or in the face of conflicting opinions, a member should test decisions and deeds by asking: "Am I doing what a person of integrity would do? Have I retained my integrity?" Integrity requires a member to observe both the form and the spirit of technical and ethical standards; circumvention of those standards constitutes subordination of judgment.

Integrity also requires a member to observe the principles of objectivity and independence and of due care.

ARTICLE IV

Objectivity and Independence

A member should maintain objectivity and be free of conflicts of interest in discharging professional responsibilities. A member in public practice should be independent in fact and appearance when providing auditing and other attestation services.

Objectivity is a state of mind, a quality that lends value to a member's services. It is a distinguishing feature of the profession. The principle of objectivity imposes the obligation to be impartial, intellectually honest, and free of conflicts of interest. Independence precludes relationships that may appear to impair a member's objectivity in rendering attestation services.

Members often serve multiple interests in many different capacities and must demonstrate their objectivity in varying circumstances. Members in public practice render attest, tax, and management advisory services. Other members prepare financial statements in the employment of others, perform internal auditing services, and serve in financial and management capacities in industry, education, and government. They also educate and train those who aspire to admission into the profession. Regardless of service or capacity, members should protect the integrity of their work, maintain objectivity, and avoid any subordination of their judgment.

For a member in public practice, the maintenance of objectivity and independence requires a continuing assessment of client relationships and public responsibility. Such a member who provides auditing and other attestation services should be independent in fact and appearance. In providing all other services, a member should maintain objectivity and avoid conflicts of interest.

Although members not in public practice cannot maintain the appearance of independence, they nevertheless have the responsibility to maintain objectivity in rendering professional services. Members employed by others to prepare financial statements or to perform auditing, tax, or consulting services are charged with the same responsibility for objectivity as members in public practice and must be scrupulous in their application of generally accepted accounting principles and candid in all their dealings with members in public practice.

ARTICLE V

Due Care

A member should observe the profession's technical and ethical standards, strive continually to improve competence and the quality of services, and discharge professional responsibility to the best of the member's ability.

The quest for excellence is the essence of due care. Due care requires a member to discharge professional responsibilities with competence and diligence. It imposes the obligation to perform professional services to the best of a member's ability with concern for the best interest of those for whom the services are performed and consistent with the profession's responsibility to the public.

Competence is derived from a synthesis of education and experience. It begins with a mastery of the common body of knowledge required for designation as a certified public accountant. The maintenance of competence requires a commitment to learning and professional improvement that must continue throughout a member's professional life. It is a member's individual responsibility. In all engagements and in all responsibilities, each member should undertake to achieve a level of competence that will assure that the quality of the member's services meets the high level of professionalism required by these Principles.

Competence represents the attainment and maintenance of a level of understanding and knowledge that enables a member to render services with facility and acumen. It also establishes the limitations of a member's capabilities by dictating that consultation or referral may be required when a professional engagement exceeds the personal competence of a member or a member's firm. Each member is responsible for assessing his or her own competence—of evaluating whether education, experience, and judgment are adequate for the responsibility to be assumed.

Members should be diligent in discharging responsibilities to clients, employers, and the public. Diligence imposes the responsibility to render services promptly and carefully, to be thorough, and to observe applicable technical and ethical standards.

Due care requires a member to plan and supervise adequately any professional activity for which he or she is responsible.

ARTICLE VI

Scope and Nature of Services

A member in public practice should observe the Principles of the Code of Professional Conduct in determining the scope and nature of services to be provided.

The public interest aspect of certified public accountants' services requires that such services be consistent with acceptable professional behavior for certified public accountants. Integrity requires that service and the public trust not be subordinated to personal gain and advantage. Objectivity and independence require that members be free from conflicts of interest in discharging professional responsibilities. Due care requires that services be provided with competence and diligence.

Each of these Principles should be considered by members in determining whether or not to provide specific services in individual circumstances. In some instances, they may represent an overall constraint on the nonaudit services that might be offered to a specific client. No hard-and-fast rules can be developed to help members reach these judgments, but they must be satisfied that they are meeting the spirit of the Principles in this regard.

In order to accomplish this, members should

- Practice in firms that have in place internal quality-control procedures to ensure that services are competently delivered and adequately supervised.
- Determine, in their individual judgments, whether the scope and nature of other services provided to an audit client would create a conflict of interest in the performance of the audit function for that client.
- Assess, in their individual judgments, whether an activity is consistent with their role as professionals (for example, Is such activity a reasonable extension or variation of existing services offered by the member or others in the profession?).

STANDARDS OF ETHICAL CONDUCT FOR MANAGEMENT ACCOUNTANTS[16]

Management accountants have an obligation to the organizations they serve, their profession, the public, and themselves to maintain the highest standards of ethical conduct. In recognition of this obligation, the Institute of Management Accountants has promulgated the following standards of ethical conduct for management accountants. Adherence to these standards is integral to achieving the *Objectives of Management Accounting*. Management accountants shall not commit acts contrary to these standards nor shall they condone the commission of such acts by others within their organizations.

I. Competence

Management accountants have a responsibility to:

1. Maintain an appropriate level of professional competence by ongoing development of their knowledge and skills.
2. Perform their professional duties in accordance with relevant laws, regulations, and technical standards.

16. From Institute of Management Accountants, *Statements on Management Accounting No. 1C: Standards of Ethical Conduct for Management Accountants,* (10 Paragon Drive, Montvale, N.J., 1983). Reprinted with permission from the Institute of Management Accountants.

3. Prepare complete and clear reports and recommendations after appropriate analysis of relevant and reliable information.

II. Confidentiality

Management accountants have a responsibility to:

1. Refrain from disclosing confidential information acquired in the course of their work except when authorized, unless legally obligated to do so.
2. Inform subordinates as appropriate regarding the confidentiality of information acquired in the course of their work and monitor their activities to assure the maintenance of that confidentiality.
3. Refrain from using or appearing to use confidential information acquired in the course of their work for unethical or illegal advantage either personally or through third parties.

III. Integrity

Management accountants have a responsibility to:

1. Avoid actual or apparent conflicts of interest and advise all appropriate parties of any potential conflict.
2. Refrain from engaging in any activity that would prejudice their ability to carry out their duties ethically.
3. Refuse any gift, favor, or hospitality that would influence or would appear to influence their actions.
4. Refrain from either actively or passively subverting the attainment of the organization's legitimate and ethical objectives.
5. Recognize and communicate professional limitations or other constraints that would preclude responsible judgment or successful performance of an activity.
6. Communicate unfavorable as well as favorable information and professional judgments or opinions.
7. Refrain from engaging in or supporting any activity that would discredit the profession.

IV. Objectivity

Management accountants have a responsibility to:

1. Communicate information fairly and objectively.
2. Disclose fully all relevant information that could reasonably be expected to influence an intended user's understanding of the reports, comments, and recommendations presented.

Resolution of Ethical Conflict

In applying the standards of ethical conduct, management accountants may encounter problems in identifying unethical behavior or in resolving an ethical conflict. When faced with significant ethical issues, management accountants should follow the established policies of the organization bearing on the resolution of such conflict. If these policies do not resolve the ethical conflict, management accountants should consider the following courses of action:

- Discuss such problems with the immediate superior except when it appears that the superior is involved, in which case the problem should be presented initially to the next higher managerial level. If satisfactory resolution cannot be achieved when the problem is initially presented, submit the issues to the next higher managerial level.

If the immediate superior is the chief executive officer, or equivalent, the acceptable reviewing authority may be a group such as the audit committee, executive committee, board of directors, board of trustees, or owners. Contact with levels above the immediate superior should be initiated only with the superior's knowledge, assuming the superior is not involved.

- Clarify relevant concepts by confidential discussion with an objective adviser to obtain an understanding of possible courses of action.
- If the ethical conflict still exists after exhausting all levels of internal review, the management accountant may have no other recourse on significant matters than to resign from the organization and to submit an informative memorandum to an appropriate representative of the organization.

Except where legally prescribed, communication of such problems to authorities or individuals not employed or engaged by the organization is not considered appropriate.

SUMMARY OF LEARNING OBJECTIVES

1. ***Define accounting and discuss its functions.*** Accounting has traditionally been viewed as a system of recording, classifying, and summarizing financial information about economic entities that is useful in making economic decisions. However, in recent years the functions of accounting have been expanded so that accounting is now viewed as a broad economic information development and distribution process, based on the design, implementation, and operation of multiple types of information systems. Accounting is a tool created for economic use, and it changes according to the economic needs of society.

2. ***Explain the relationship between accounting and different forms of business enterprises.*** Accounting is used by sole proprietorships, partnerships, and corporations. For all three forms of enterprise, the transactions of the business are kept separate from those of the owners. For a partnership, the accounting system must keep track of the partners' investments. For a corporation, whose stockholders are its owners, there frequently is a separation of ownership and management, with accounting reports used to inform the stockholders about management's performance.

3. ***List the primary users of accounting information.*** The users of accounting information can be divided into two categories: external and internal users. The major external users are present and potential investors and creditors, governmental agencies, and the general public. External users rely on financial statements prepared according to GAAP. The AICPA and the FASB are two of the primary groups involved in setting accounting principles and standards. The internal user of accounting information is the management.

4. ***Describe the work of accountants.*** Public accountants offer their services to the public for a fee and generally perform auditing and accounting, tax preparation and planning, and some management advisory services. Private accountants are employed by a single firm and perform such activities as cost accounting, budgetary planning and control, internal auditing, and financial reporting. Governmental accountants perform various accounting services for federal, state, or local governmental units or agencies.

5. ***Explain the importance of ethical behavior for accountants and managers.*** The accounting information system aids managers in their efforts to improve the economic performance of the firm. Unfortunately, some managers and accountants have overemphasized the economic dimension and have engaged in unethical and illegal actions. Many of these actions have relied on the accounting information system to bring about and even support that unethical behavior. The accounting profession has reacted by placing more emphasis on ethical behavior including the development of new codes of conduct.

6. ***Describe and prepare the primary financial statements: balance sheet, income statement, retained earnings statement, and statement of cash flows.*** The four primary financial statements are the balance sheet, the income statement, the retained earnings statement, and the statement of cash flows. The balance sheet discloses a firms' financial position at a point in time. The income statement shows the results of operations over a period of time. The retained earnings statement explains the change in retained earnings from the beginning of an accounting period to the end of the period. The statement

of cash flows shows the results of operating, financing, and investing activities.

7. Describe the codes of professional conduct for public accountants and management accountants (Appendix). Ethical behavior involves choosing actions that are "right" and "proper" and "just." Both public accountants and management accountants have developed codes of professional conduct to guide their behavior. However, only the individual actions of people can insure ethical behavior.

KEY TERMS

Account form of balance sheet *18*
Accounting *4*
Accounting equation *18*
Accounting system *5*
American Institute of Certified Public Accountants (AICPA) *11*
Articulation *26*
Assets *18*
Audit *12*
Audit report *12*
Auditor's opinion *13*
Balance sheet *17*
Business entity *7*
Capital stock *21*
Certified Internal Auditor (CIA) *14*
Certified Management Accountant (CMA) *14*
Certified Public Accountant (CPA) *12*
Compliance audits *14*
Corporation *8*
Expenses *24*
Financial accounting *9*
Financial Accounting Standards Board (FASB) *11*
Financial statements *5*
Generally Accepted Accounting Principles (GAAP) *11*
Going concern assumption *22*
Governmental accounting *10*
Historical cost convention *22*
Income statement *23*
Institute of Management Accountants (IMA) *14*
Internal auditor *14*
Liabilities *18*
Limited liability *8*
Liquidity *19*
Management accountant *14*
Management accounting *11*
Net assets *21*
Net income (net loss) *24*
Objectivity *22*
Operational audits *14*
Owners' equity *18*
Partnership *8*
Public accounting *12*
Publicly owned corporation *9*
Report form of balance sheet *18*
Retained earnings *21*
Retained earnings statement *24*
Revenues *24*
Sole proprietorship *7*
Statement of cash flows *25*
Stockholders' equity *18*
Transactions *5*

REVIEW PROBLEMS

State whether the following statements are true or false and give your reasons:

1. Both partnerships and corporations are similar in that both partners and stockholders have limited liability.
2. Only corporations are required to have audits of their financial statements.
3. CPAs are licensed to do business by states in which they operate.
4. An audit is an objective and independent third-party examination of an organization's financial statements.
5. Big Six accounting firms only provide audit services.
6. Management accountants must be CPAs.
7. Only small businesses are sole proprietorships.

Solutions

1. False—only stockholders have limited liability. There are some situations in which limited partners have limited liability. However, at least one partner must have unlimited liability.
2. False—only publicly held corporations are required to have audits. Banks and other creditors may require any firm to have an audit.
3. True—CPAs must receive a license to practice and that license is granted by individual states.
4. True—The statement is a correct definition of an audit.

5. False—Big Six, as well as other accounting firms, provide a broad range of services including tax and consulting services.
6. False—Management accountants are not required to be CPAs, although many are. Many management accountants are CMAs, although this is not required.
7. False—A sole proprietorship can be any size. However, the corporate form is most appropriate for large businesses because it facilitates the acquisition of capital.

At the beginning of 1995, Patti Edwards decided to open a real estate firm called Real Property, Inc. The following transactions occurred during the first year of the firm's existence.

Patti invested $100,000 of her personal funds in the business, in exchange for 1,000 shares of capital stock. In addition, some of Patti's friends decided to invest in her business. She issued them 250 shares of capital stock in exchange for $25,000. The firm obtained a $25,000 loan from a local bank to provide additional operating funds. During the year, the real estate agency purchased, for $80,000 cash, a small building to use as an office. The firm purchased some office equipment for $8,000, $2,000 of which was paid in cash, the remainder was to be paid later in the year. Finally, various office supplies were purchased close to the end of the year. The supplies cost $2,500 and were purchased on account. No payments were made on this account during the current year.

The following revenue and expense transactions also occurred during the first year of operations:

a. Commissions earned during the year amounted to $300,000. By year-end, $230,000 of these commissions had been collected in cash.
b. Various operating expenses of $220,000 were incurred during the year. As of year-end, $190,000 of these expenses had been paid in cash.
c. Interest expense on the bank loan amounted to $2,500 and was unpaid at year-end.
d. Taxes of $15,500 were incurred and paid during the year.

REQUIRED: Using the information provided, prepare the following financial statements:

1. An income statement for the year ended December 31, 1995.
2. A statement of cash flows for the year ended December 31, 1995.
3. A balance sheet as of December 31, 1995.

Use the financial statements in the text as examples. Use the following expense categories in the income statement: operating expenses, interest expense, and tax expense.

Solutions 1

Real Properties, Inc.
Income Statement
For the Year Ended December 31, 1995

Revenues		
Commissions earned		$300,000
Expenses		
Various operating expenses	$220,000	
Interest expense	2,500	
Total expenses before income taxes		222,500
Income before taxes		$ 77,500
Income taxes		15,500
Net income		$ 62,000

2

Real Properties, Inc.
Statement of Cash Flows
For the Year Ended December 31, 1995

Cash flows from operating activities		
Cash commissions received	$230,000	
Various expenses and taxes paid	(205,500)	
Net cash provided by operating activities		$ 24,500
Cash flows from investing activities		
Purchase of building	$ (80,000)	
Purchase of office equipment	(8,000)	
Net cash used by investing activities		(88,000)
Cash flows from financing activities		
Issuance of bank loan payable	$ 25,000	
Issuance of capital stock	125,000	
Net cash provided by financing activities		150,000
Net increase in cash		$ 86,500
Cash balance, January 1, 1995		0
Cash balance, December 31, 1995		$ 86,500

3

Real Properties, Inc.
Balance Sheet[1]
For the Year Ended December 31, 1995

Assets		*Liabilities and Stockholders' Equity*	
Cash	$ 86,500	Liabilities	
Accounts receivable	70,000	Accounts payable	$ 32,500
Office supplies	2,500	Interest payable	2,500
Equipment	8,000	Bank loan payable	25,000
Building	80,000	Total liabilities	$ 60,000
		Stockholders' equity	
		Capital stock	$125,000
		Retained earnings[2]	62,000
		Total stockholders' equity	$187,000
Total assets	$247,000	Total liabilities and stockholders' equity	$247,000

[1]The order of the accounts follows typical balance sheet order. Assets are shown first, with cash being the first asset, followed by items such as accounts receivable and supplies. The longer-term assets such as buildings and equipment are generally shown last.

[2]Because this is the firm's first year of operation, there is no beginning balance in retained earnings. In addition, no dividends were issued. As a result, the ending balance or retained earnings equals the net income for the year of $62,000.

QUESTIONS

1. What is your proposed major? How do you see the study of accounting fitting into that major?
2. Describe what have been the primary functions of accounting. Contrast these to the expanded view of accounting described in the textbook.
3. In what ways do you think accounting differs for external and internal users?
4. Identify four outside groups that would be interested in a company's financial statements, and indicate their particular interest.
5. What are the characteristics of the corporate form of organization that would explain its popularity?
6. Identify the three forms of accounting certification. Which form of certification do you believe is best for the management accountant? Why?
7. Firms with higher ethical standards will experience a higher level of economic performance than firms with lower or poor ethical standards. Do you agree? Explain.
8. Describe the role and function of the AICPA and FASB.
9. As the accountant for the DeAngelo Company, you have been asked to prepare the company's financial statements at the end of 1995. Prepare the headings for each of the four statements, and explain their differences.
10. The main elements of a balance sheet are assets, liabilities, and stockholders' equity. Define and give examples of each.
11. Describe the historical cost convention, and explain its use in accounting.
12. If a transaction causes total liabilities to increase but does not affect owners' equity, what change is to be expected in total assets?
13. Assuming you never took an accounting course and were asked to prepare a statement listing your individual assets and liabilities, would you do so at their historical cost or their current value? Why?
14. A company purchased land ten years ago for $250,000. The land has just been appraised at $570,000. When does the accountant recognize the fact that the land has increased in value?
15. List and define the main elements of an income statement.
16. What is the statement of cash flows, and what are its main purposes?
17. The four main financial statements articulate with one another. Explain what this means.

EXERCISES

E1-1
Users of Financial Statements
LO 3

You are currently being interviewed for the position of manager of financial reporting for a large corporation. You have been asked to explain to the chief financial officer, your potential boss, why each of the following individuals or groups might be interested in the firm's financial statements:

a. The current owners of the firm.
b. The creditors of the firm.
c. The management of the firm.
d. The prospective stockholders of the firm.
e. The Internal Revenue Service.
f. The firm's major labor union.

E1-2
Careers in Accounting
LO 4

You have been asked to lecture on accounting careers to a group of prospective accounting students. Describe to them the types of work available in:

a. CPA firms.
b. Private industry.
c. Government.

E1-3
Business Entities
LO 2

Below are statements concerning sole proprietorships, partnerships, and corporations. Indicate whether each statement is true or false; if the statement is false, provide an explanation for your answer.

a. If there are two or more owners of a business, it must be organized as a partnership.
b. In a sole proprietorship, the owner and the business are legally one entity.
c. The sole proprietorship and its owner represent the same accounting entity.
d. Any two individuals, by oral agreement, can form a corporation.
e. The owners of a corporation are not legally responsible for the individual debts incurred by the corporation.
f. In a partnership, the partners and the partnership are legally one entity.
g. All partners in a partnership must share the profits and losses equally.
h. Ownership in a corporation is evidenced by a share of stock.

E1-4
The Accounting Equation
LO 6

Answer each of the following independent questions:

a. The New Company's assets equal $75,000, and its stockholders' equity totals $42,500. What is the amount of its liabilities?
b. The liabilities of the Old Company are $46,200, and its owners' equity is $35,800. What is the amount of its assets?
c. The Rose Corporation has total assets of $77,000 and total liabilities of $35,600. What is the amount of its owners' equity?
d. The Barney Corporation started in July with assets of $150,000 and liabilities of $90,000. During the month of July, stockholders' equity increased by $24,000 and liabilities decreased by $10,000. What is the amount of total assets at the end of July?

E1-5
Recognition of Balance Sheet Items
LO 6

Classify the following items as assets, liabilities, or stockholders' equity. If you do not think that the item would be recognized as any of the above, so state and give your reasons.

a. Cash
b. Notes payable
c. Office equipment
d. Retained earnings
e. Accounts payable
f. Accounts receivable
g. A firm's good management
h. Office supplies
i. Capital stock
j. Notes receivable
k. Land
l. A trademark such as McDonald's golden arches

E1-6
Recognition of Assets and Liabilities
LO 6

Sue Ann Gordard recently opened a unisex haircut store called "Cut Them As You See Them." On opening day she received a framed picture of one her clients, a famous movie star, that she intends to hang on the wall. The store also purchased a $5 state lottery ticket as a good luck charm. Finally, on opening day the store received a $200 utility bill from the local power company for services rendered for the prior occupant of the store.

REQUIRED: Should these items be listed as assets or liabilities of the "Cut Them As You See Them" Company? Explain.

E1-7
Balance Sheet Preparation
LO 6

The following data is available for Igloo's Camping Store as of September 30, 1995.

Cash	$ 9,000
Accounts payable	2,800
Stockholders' equity	?
Office equipment	8,400
Accounts receivable	2,800
Supplies	4,500
Notes payable	4,200
Land	17,000
Taxes payable	3,300

REQUIRED: Prepare a balance sheet for the company as of September 30, 1995 in the format shown in Exhibit 1-3. Show figures for total assets, total liabilities, and stockholders' equity.

E1-8
Balance Sheet Preparation
LO 6

The following data is available for High Tech Inc.

a. The purchase cost of all equipment owned by the store was $40,000. When making the purchase, $12,000 cash and a note for $28,000 were given to the supplier. An additional payment of $2,000 has subsequently been made on the note.
b. Several years ago, the company purchased a plot of land for $125,000 cash, to be used for future store expansion. Although the land has yet to be used, the company still owns it. Recently it has been appraised at $180,000.
c. Supplies on hand cost $12,000.
d. High Tech owed various suppliers $22,000.
e. When the firm was organized, capital stock of $70,000 was issued.
f. Various individuals owed the firm a total of $2,500.
g. Retained earnings amounted to $78,000.
h. The firm had inventory for resale of $13,000.
i. The firm had some cash in a checking account but was unable to determine the amount. All other items have been given to you.

REQUIRED: Prepare a balance sheet for High Tech Inc. as of June 30, 1995, using the format of Exhibit 1-3.

E1-9
Recognition of Revenue and Expense Transactions
LO 6

A summary of the Grant Corporation's transactions during November is reproduced below. State which of the events would be recorded on the income statement for November.

a. The owners needed additional funds, and they borrowed $200,000 from the bank.
b. The firm collected $20,000 on account from a sale made in October.
c. Cash sales during November totaled $5,000.
d. The firm received its November utility bill of $75.
e. The firm paid $40 for October's utility bill.
f. The firm made sales on account in November totaling $7,500.
g. A dividend of $500 was declared and paid in November.

E1-10
Recognizing Balance Sheet and Income Statement Items
LO 6

Review the following items and state whether they are an asset, a liability, stockholders' equity, revenue, or expense account.

a. Salary expense
b. Supplies on hand
c. Land
d. Interest earned
e. Capital stock
f. Accounts receivable
g. Sales
h. Retained earnings
i. Cost of goods sold
j. Salaries payable
k. Repairs and maintenance
l. Patents
m. Investment in XYZ Company

E1-11
Income Statement Preparation
LO 6

Sam Houston, owner of Houston's Fun Ranch, wants to know the bottom line from his 1995 operations. Prepare an income statement using the following information:

a. Salaries and wages expense was $76,000.
b. House rental revenue came to $272,000.
c. Insurance expense was $3,200.
d. Interest earned on invested cash was $800.
e. Rental revenue from horseback riding totaled $17,500.

f. Horse feed and other expenses totaled $21,800.
g. Advertising expense totaled $2,900.
h. Income taxes totaled 20% of income before taxes. (*Hint:* Income before taxes equals revenues minus all expenses other than taxes.)

E1-12
Income Statement Preparation
LO 6

The University Book Store has just completed its busy fall season. Taking the following facts into consideration, construct an income statement for the month ending September 30.

a. Sales, both cash and on account, totaled $1,000,000.
b. Salary and wages equaled 12% of sales.
c. All items were priced to sell at 1.25 times their cost.
d. Insurance expense for the period was $3,100.
e. Miscellaneous expense equaled 1% of cost of goods sold.
f. Advertising and promotion cost 5% of sales but was estimated to have attracted 45% of the current month's sales.
g. Because the store is run by the university foundation, no taxes are levied.

E1-13
Income Statement Interpretation
LO 6

As the accountant for the Software Circle Company, you have prepared the following income statement:

Software Circle Company
Income Statement
For the Year Ended December 31, 1995

Revenues		
Cash sales	$160,000	
Sales on account	240,000	
Total revenues		$400,000
Expenses		
Cost of goods sold	$190,000	
Salary expense	60,000	
Advertising expense	50,000	
Rent expense	30,000	
Supplies used	10,000	
Total expenses		340,000
Income before taxes		$ 60,000
Taxes		5,000
Net income		$ 55,000

REQUIRED: One of the directors of the company, an expert in marketing, knows little about accounting. She asks you the following questions, to which you should make a brief response:

1. If some of the sales made on account will not be collected until the next year, why are they included in this year's income statement?
2. The greatest part of the advertising was based on a promotion undertaken during the last quarter of the year. Although the advertisements ran before the end of the year, the payment to the advertising agency will not be made until early January. Why is the total amount listed on the current income statement?
3. At the end of the year, the firm purchased 100 new computers from AT&T. Why is this transaction not listed on the income statement?
4. The member of the board of directors knows the firm issued a $1,000 cash dividend but she cannot find this amount listed on the income statement. Why?

E1-14
Analysis of Stockholders' Equity
LO 6

When the Calbear Corporation was formed ten years ago, individuals invested a total of $700,000 in the corporation. No additional subsequent investments have been made. Since then the company has been very profitable. At the end of the current year, December 1995, the firm's total assets had grown to $2,900,000. Liabilities were $1,350,000. During the past ten years, the firm has issued dividends equal to 30% of the current (December 1995) balance in the retained earnings account.

REQUIRED:

1. Prepare the stockholders' equity section of the balance sheet as of December 31, 1995.
2. How much in dividends has the firm issued since its inception?
3. Assuming that no dividends have been issued, what would the balance in stockholders' equity have been at the end of 1995?

E1-15
Preparation of the Retained Earnings Statement
LO 6

At the beginning of the current year, January 1, 1995, the stockholders' equity section of the Tracy Golf Store contained the following items:

Capital stock	$350,000
Retained earnings	$540,000

During the year, the following events occurred:

a. The company's net income amounted to $98,000.
b. Dividends issued in cash amounted to $24,000.
c. The firm issued additional capital stock for cash in the amount of $80,000.

REQUIRED:

1. Prepare the retained earnings statement for the year ended December 31, 1995.
2. Prepare the stockholders' equity section of the balance sheet at the end of 1995.

E1-16
Preparation of an Income Statement and a Balance Sheet
LO 6

Several years ago, Ellen Glazerman started an art supply store called Ellen's Art. The store has been very successful, and profits for last year reached a new high. Ellen asks you to help her prepare an income statement and balance sheet for the current year and gives you the following information:

Total sales	$800,000
Cost of goods sold	?
Salaries expense	60,000
Rental expense	40,000
Advertising expense	10,000
Taxes	57,000
Net income	133,000
Cash	25,000
Receivables	40,000
Inventory	?
Land	215,000
Total assets	370,000
Accounts payable	30,000
Salaries payable	10,000
Capital stock	100,000
Retained earnings, January 1, 1995, beginning of period	97,000

REQUIRED: Assuming that all the items are listed, prepare (a) an income statement for the year ended December 31, 1995, and (b) a balance sheet at December 31, 1995. Be sure to determine the missing values.

E1-17
Preparing a Statement of Cash Flows
LO 6

The Olympic Corporation began business at the beginning of 1995. As the accountant, you have been asked by management to prepare a statement of cash flows, for presentation to the board of directors. You obtained the following cash flow data for the year: revenues received in cash, $220,000; cash outflows for operating expenses, $148,000; purchased land and buildings for cash, $165,000; borrowings from a local bank, $50,000; issue of capital stock for cash, $100,000; and the issue of a cash dividend of $12,000.

REQUIRED: Using a format similar to Exhibit 1-7, prepare a statement of cash flows for the year ended December 31, 1995.

E1-18
Relationships Among Financial Statements
LO 6

The income statement for the Telsis Company is as follows:

The Telsis Company
Income Statement
For the Year Ended December 31, 1995

Revenues		
Commissions earned	$700,000	
Rentals	80,000	
Total revenues		$780,000
Expenses		
Salaries expense	$300,000	
Advertising expense	150,000	
Building lease expense	60,000	
Supplies used	30,000	
Total expenses		540,000
Income before taxes		$240,000
Taxes		30,000
Net income		$210,000

Additional information:

a. Twenty percent of the commission revenues have not been collected in cash.
b. All rental revenues were collected in cash.
c. All salaries, except for $10,000, were paid in cash.
d. The supplies that were used in the business were purchased and paid for in late 1994.
e. All other expenses were paid for in cash during the current year.

REQUIRED:

1. Determine the amount of cash inflows or outflows from operations.
2. Explain the difference between net income and cash inflow or outflow from operations.

PROBLEMS

P1-1
Recognition of Events
LO 1, 2

Amy Brooks opened a photographic studio on May 1, 1995. For each transaction that occurred in May, identify which would be recognized in preparing Amy's personal accounts and which would be recognized in accounting for her business entity, Brooks Studio. Some transactions may affect both entities, and some neither. In either case, be sure to so state and explain your reasoning.

a. Amy received $10,000 in termination pay from her previous employer.
b. Of this termination pay, $6,000 was deposited in the Brooks Studio's checking account in exchange for capital stock.
c. Amy personally borrowed $45,000 from the local bank to open the studio. Her home was used as security for the loan.
d. A three-year lease on a small building will be used for a studio. A $2,000 deposit was made by the firm at the time of signing.
e. The $45,000 that Amy borrowed from the bank was invested in the business in exchange for additional capital stock.
f. The studio bought $8,500 of photographic supplies on account.
g. The printing of 10,000 brochures announcing the opening of the studio cost $2,000. None of the brochures has yet been distributed. Amy thinks she has enough brochures to last for one year.
h. Amy hired an assistant at a monthly salary of $1,000. He will start work in June; no payments were made.
i. Several of Amy's friends worked on the weekend, without pay, to help decorate the studio.
j. Amy needed some money for her personal use and withdrew $1,000 of her investment in the form of a dividend from the corporation.

P1-2
Balance Sheet Preparation
LO 6

The balance sheet items for Alfredo's Pizza Parlor at June 1, 1995 were as follows (in alphabetical order):

Accounts payable	$ 8,000
Bank loan payable	4,000
Capital stock	80,000
Cash	8,000
Pizza ovens	12,000
Inventory of food items	15,000
Loan receivable	8,000
Note to insurance company	9,000
Restaurant furniture	60,000
Retained earnings	?

During June, the following transactions occurred:

a. The company paid its suppliers $2,400 on account.
b. Additional food inventory of $2,500 was purchased on account.
c. The loan receivable was from a friend of the store's owner. A payment of one-half of the balance was made to the company.
d. Additional equipment costing $900 was purchased for cash.
e. A soft drink supplier wanted the pizza parlor to stock his brand of drink, so he agreed to sell the parlor 10 cartons of the soft drinks for a total of $200. The normal purchase price of the drinks is $250. The purchase was made on account.

REQUIRED:

1. Prepare a balance sheet as of June 1, 1995. Be sure to determine the retained earnings amount.
2. Prepare a balance sheet as of June 30, 1995.
3. Have the balances in the stockholders' equity accounts changed? If so, by how much? Can you explain the change or lack of change in these accounts?

P1-3
Preparing an Income Statement and Statement of Retained Earnings
LO 6

The following items were taken from the records of the Anasonic Corporation for the month ended October 31, 1995:

Sales revenue	$620,000
Salaries expense	80,000
Capital stock issued	140,000
Cost of goods sold	335,000
Service revenues	55,000
Rental expense	45,000
Repairs and maintenance expense	54,000
Retained earnings, October 1, 1995	230,000
Accounts payable	40,000
Taxes expense	30,000
Dividends declared and paid	13,000

REQUIRED:

1. Prepare in good form an income statement and a retained earnings statement for the month ended October 31, 1995.
2. During the month, the company made sales of $75,000 on credit, which have not yet been collected in cash. Why are these sales included in the October 1995 income statement?
3. Is it accurate to say that when a firm earns net income during the period, its resources increase? Explain.

P1-4
The Entity Assumption and Preparation of a Balance Sheet
LO 6

John Alexander owns a small retail store. He recently approached a bank for a loan to finance a planned expansion of the store. He was asked to submit the latest balance sheet for the store, which he prepared as follows:

Alexander's Rental Outlet
Balance Sheet
For the Year Ended December 31, 1995

Assets		*Liabilities and Stockholders' Equity*	
Cash	$ 4,500	Accounts payable	$ 6,000
Accounts receivable	9,000	Note payable on family car	4,500
Inventory	30,000	Mortgage on house	100,000
Equipment	12,000	Stockholders' equity	105,700
Personal residence	150,000		
Store supplies	2,700		
Family car	8,000		
Total assets	$216,200	Total liabilities and stockholders' equity	$216,200

In addition, John offered the following information:

a. The inventory has an original cost of $25,000. It is listed on the balance sheet at what it would cost to purchase today.
b. Of the cash listed on the balance sheet, $2,500 is in his personal account, and the remainder is in the store's account.
c. The store has a delivery truck that it recently purchased for $10,000. It was financed through a bank loan, and the bank has legal title to the truck. To date, the store has

paid $2,000 on the loan. John did not include the truck or the loan because it is not owned by either himself or the business.

REQUIRED:

1. Identify any errors in this balance sheet, and explain why they should be considered errors.
2. Prepare a corrected balance sheet for the store.

P1-5
The Income Statement and Statement of Cash Flows (Alternative to P1-6)
LO 6

The Ocra Corporation began operations July 1, 1995. During the six months ended December 31, 1995, the following events took place:

a. The owners invested $150,000 cash in exchange for capital stock.
b. Total commissions earned amounted to $300,000, of which $60,000 had not yet been collected in cash by December 31.
c. Total operating expenses amounted to $240,000, of which $35,000 had not yet been paid in cash at December 31.
d. The firm borrowed $72,000 cash from a local bank.
e. Various items of property, plant, and equipment were purchased for $125,000 cash.
f. The firm declared and paid dividends in cash, amounting to $14,000.
g. The firm invested $15,000 of excess cash in a long-term investment.
h. During the six-month period, interest revenue earned on the investments amounted to $1,000, of which $800 was received in cash.

REQUIRED:

1. Prepare an income statement in condensed form and a statement of cash flows for the six months ended December 31, 1995. (Taxes are ignored for simplicity.)
2. What information does the statement of cash flows contain that cannot be learned from the income statement?

P1-6
The Income Statement, Retained Earnings Statement, and Statement of Cash Flows (Alternative to P1-5)
LO 6

The law firm of Scully, Porter, and Drysdale began operations January 1, 1995. During the three months ended March 31, 1995, the following events occurred:

a. The three owners, Scully, Porter, and Drysdale each invested $40,000 cash in exchange for capital stock.
b. The firm borrowed an additional $100,000 from Wilshire National Bank.
c. Legal fees earned for the three month period totaled $125,000 of which $70,000 had not yet been collected in cash.
d. Operating expenses amounted to $132,000 of which $30,000 had not yet been paid in cash as of March 31, 1995.
e. Various items of computer hardware and software was purchased for $40,000 cash.

REQUIRED:

1. Prepare an income statement in condensed form and a statement of retained earnings for the three months ending March 31, 1995.
2. Prepare a statement of cash flows for the three months ended March 31, 1995.
3. Explain the relationship between the three statements.

P1-7
Summary Problem
LO 6

At the beginning of 1995, Jan Ochi decided to open an advertising agency called The Best Agency. During 1995, Jan and her family members invested $320,000 cash in the company in exchange for 3,000 shares of capital stock and a bank loaned the corporation $100,000. Cash from the stock sale and bank loan was used to purchase land for $50,000, a building for $100,000, and office equipment for $80,000. The firm purchased additional office equipment for $50,000 on account, all of which will be paid next year.

The following summary transactions also occurred in 1995:

a. Advertising revenues of $130,000 were earned during the year. By year end, $120,000 had been collected in cash. The firm expects to collect the remaining cash early next year.
b. Various operating expenses of $115,000 were incurred and paid in cash during the year.
c. Interest expense of $1,000 on the bank loan was incurred but remained unpaid at December 31.
d. The corporation declared and paid dividends of $5,000 during the year.
e. Taxes of $2,000 were incurred and paid during the year.

REQUIRED: Using the above information, prepare the following financial statements.

1. An income statement for the year ended December 31, 1995.
2. A retained earnings statement for the year ended December 31, 1995.
3. A balance sheet at December 31, 1995.
4. A statement of cash flows for the year ended December 31, 1995.

DISCUSSION AND INTERPRETATION PROBLEMS

D1-1
Understanding Financial Statements

The following items, in random order, have been taken from a recent balance sheet of Coca-Cola Enterprises Inc. (in thousands)

Investments and other assets	$ 105,637
Intangible assets	3,046,871
Accounts payable	478,161
Loans payable	576,630
Cash	507
Inventories	128,450
Stockholders' equity	1,626,479
Prepaid expenses	69,562
Long-term debt	2,004,318
Income taxes payable	335,008
Property, plant and equipment	1,372,747
Accounts receivable	296,822

REQUIRED:

1. Prepare a balance sheet for Coca-Cola Enterprises at December 31.
2. Describe what each item represents.
3. Why do you think Coca-Cola has such a small amount of cash in relation to the rest of its assets?
4. Evaluate, as best you can at this early point in your studies, the financial position of Coca-Cola Enterprises, Inc.

D1-2
Financial Decision Case

One of your friends is the sole owner of a small company that makes banners. Although the firm has been relatively successful, it has grown little in the last few years. However, recently the company was contracted by an Olympic organizing committee to be the official banner supplier to the Olympics. As a result, the firm is planning to expand and needs funds for the expansion.

Your friend has always prepared his own financial statements. However, in negotiating a bank loan, the loan officer insisted that the statements be audited by a CPA. Because your friend was unfamiliar with the accounting profession, he asked you the following questions:

a. What is a CPA, and what services are provided by CPA firms?
b. The loan officer mentioned an audit. What is an audit, and why would the banker want my financial statements audited?
c. The loan officer mentioned that my financial statements should be prepared in accordance with generally accepted accounting principles. What does she mean? Where can I go to find these generally accepted accounting principles? Who sets these principles?

REQUIRED: Write a brief memo responding to your friend's questions.

D1-3
Financial Decision Case

Ben Racket is considering establishing a pro tennis team to compete in the new World Tennis League. He figures it will cost over $1 million to start up the team. A good part of this will go toward signing bonuses for players. Each of the five players will receive a $200,000 bonus for signing a three-year contract with the team.

Ben also feels that he will need substantial funds after the initial start-up, which will be used to obtain a stadium lease and for general operations. Although Ben will be the sole owner now, he might be willing to take in other investors, especially if he is unable to finance the team himself.

Ben is not very familiar with business practices or accounting and asks your advice on a number of items.

REQUIRED:

1. Ben has heard that he could organize his business as a sole proprietorship, partnership, or corporation. Advise him on his options and which you feel would be best.
2. After making his initial $1.1 million investment in the business, Ben drew up the following balance sheet:

West Panash Aces
Balance Sheet
April 1, 1995

Assets		*Owners Equity*	
Cash	$ 100,000	Owners' equity	$1,100,000
Players' contracts	1,000,000		
Total assets	$1,100,000	Total owners' equity	$1,100,000

Ben never had accounting but looked in a dictionary and noted that it defined asset as any item owned by a person. As Ben had owned the players for three years, he listed their contracts as an asset. Do you agree with his interpretation of assets? Why or why not? How would you account for the players' contracts?

D1-4
Research Assignment

Using the resources in your library find the latest data concerning entry level salaries in accounting. If possible, determine salaries for those entering public accounting and those obtaining positions with private industry. What comparisons can you draw?

D1-5
Research Assignment

Using the resources available in your library or elsewhere find out what your state's requirements are to become a CPA. When did those requirements last change, and how did they change?

D1-6
Research Assignment

Interview an individual who currently works for a CPA firm or is an accountant in private industry. Ask that person the following questions and write up their responses:

a. How long have you been practicing accounting?
b. What is the biggest challenge of your position?

c. What do you like most and least about your job?
d. What advice would you give someone just beginning their study of accounting?

D1-7
Ethical Issues

Assess and comment on each of the following statements that have appeared in newspaper editorials:

a. Business students come from all segments of life. If they have not been taught ethics by their family, by elementary and secondary schools, there is little effect a business school can have.
b. Unethical firms and individuals, like high rollers in Las Vegas, are eventually wiped out financially.

D1-8
Ethical Issues

The Alert Company is a closely held investment service group that has been very successful over the past five years, consistently providing most members of the top management group with 50% bonuses. In addition, both the chief financial officer and the chief executive officer have received 100% bonuses. Alert expects this trend to continue.

Recently, the top management group of Alert, which holds 35% of the outstanding shares of capital stock, has learned that a major corporation is interested in acquiring Alert. Alert's management is concerned that this corporation may make an attractive offer to the other shareholders and that management would be unable to prevent the takeover. If the acquisition occurs, this executive group is uncertain about continued employment in the new corporate structure. As a consequence, the management group is considering changes to several accounting policies and practices which, although not in accordance with generally accepted accounting principles, would make the company a less attractive acquisition. Management has told Roger Deerling, Alert's controller, to implement some of these changes. Deerling has also been informed that Alert's management does not intend to immediately disclose these changes to anyone outside of the immediate top management group.

REQUIRED: Using the code of ethics for management accountants, evaluate the changes that Deerling's management is considering and discuss the specific steps that Roger should take to resolve the situation.

(IMA adapted)

D1-9
Ethical Responsibilities

JLA Electronics is a U.S.-based high-tech company that manufactures and distributes computer and telecommunications equipment. JLA has developed a hand-held, light-weight fax system, Proto-Fax, that will allow the user total freedom in receiving and transmitting information. Marketing research studies indicate that the potential market for this item is large, and immediate action in test marketing the product is recommended.

Despite the fact that JLA has excess capacity at its current manufacturing facility, the company has decided to build a new manufacturing plant to accommodate the Proto-Fax and is in the process of deciding where to locate the plant. The current unionized employees believe this move is being made to eliminate union involvement in the Proto-Fax manufacturing process. The management team that was formed to oversee the site selection process has already received bids from several locales, both domestic and foreign, offering a wide range of incentives to encourage the company to select particular sites.

Some of the incentives are personal in nature such as housing at reduced cost for the selection team, reduced property taxes, open accounts at certain restaurants, and free tickets to local sporting events. Other incentives offered affect corporate profitability and include reduced tax rates, low-interest, or no-interest loans, outright grants, and low-cost property. The marketing research team has reported that product price will have a major effect on the sale of Proto-Fax and recommends that the selection team pick a site that minimizes costs.

REQUIRED:

1. What is meant by the term, "corporate social responsibility?"
2. Should JLA Electronics consider its social responsibility when making the final decision regarding the site selection?
3. Describe the ethical responsibilities of the individuals on the site selection team.
4. Discuss the responsibilities that the union at the current manufacturing facility may have in this situation.

(IMA adapted)

CHAPTER 2
ACCOUNTING AS AN INFORMATION SYSTEM RECORDING BALANCE SHEET TRANSACTIONS

LEARNING OBJECTIVES

After studying this chapter, you should be able to:

1. Explain how accounting functions as an information system, and describe the components of the system and the characteristics of information processed by the system.
2. Explain the effects of transactions on the accounting equation.
3. Detail the components of the accounting system and steps in the accounting cycle.
4. Record balance sheet transactions in the journal and ledger.
5. Prepare a trial balance and describe its uses and limitations.

Scenario

"What do you mean I can't get a loan?" Frank Maas asked his banker with astonishment. "I know I have only been in business for a little while, but these records show that my sales are booming. I am bound to be a success." His banker, Lisa Rios, looked at him thoughtfully. "Frank, I can't tell a thing from this information. The loan committee would never approve a loan with these records. They are going to want to see real financial statements!"

Frank just shook his head in disbelief. After graduating from the local university with a degree in entrepreneurship, Frank opened his first magnet store in a local area shopping center. The store, which sold over 5,000 different varieties of magnets, was an instant success. It wasn't long before he was doing over $1,000 a day in sales and was even considering opening a second store. However, Frank realized that although he had invested $20,000 of his own money in setting up the store, he did not have enough cash to open a second store. That's when he decided to ask his local bank for a loan.

Frank had been using only a checkbook to keep track of the store's sales and expenses. This seemed good enough to him. At the end of each week he would analyze his check register to figure out the store's sales (counted all the deposits) and the store expenses (added up all the checks he wrote). Frank gathered his checkbook, sales slips, and expense receipts and went to see Lisa Rios, the loan officer at Pico National Bank.

After meeting with Frank, Lisa recognized that his store appeared to be a success. She tried to explain to him that, as part of the loan application, he would have to have financial statements prepared. She told Frank that the loan committee would ask for at least a balance sheet and an income statement. "The check register which is part of your checkbook may be good enough to keep track of your personal transactions, but your business needs separate records of its own." She gave Frank the names of three accountants and strongly recommended that he engage one of them to prepare financial statements for his store. She also suggested that he might want to take an accounting course at the local university.

As this scenario indicates, businesses of all sizes need a way to keep track of the various transactions into which they enter. As early as the Middle Ages, individuals had developed a systematic method of keeping track of various economic events so they could prepare reports for their own use and for the use of others. Technology has increased the speed and complexity of transaction processing and reporting. Nevertheless, the methods in use today are similar to those developed much earlier.

This chapter begins our discussion of contemporary accounting systems, the methods and procedures used to record, classify, and summarize the financial information that is distributed to interested users. We begin by discussing the characteristics of an accounting system and we then identify and discuss the economic events that are recorded in the accounting system. This is followed by a discussion of the standard accounting procedures that are used to record, classify, and summarize the information contained in the accounting system.

THE ACCOUNTING INFORMATION SYSTEM

Objective 1
Explain how accounting functions as an information system, and describe the components of the system and the characteristics of information processed by the system.

accounting information system

An **accounting information system** is a system designed to provide financial information about economic entities. All systems have three basic characteristics: (1) objectives, (2) interrelated parts, and (3) processes. To illustrate these basic characteristics, consider an automotive system. The primary objective of an automotive system is to provide safe reliable transportation. Some of the interrelated parts of an automobile are the engine, the drive train, and the electrical system. All of the parts work together so that the objective of providing safe and reliable transportation is met. Each of the component parts performs one or more critical processes. These processes must take place for the car to function and meet its objective.

In the automotive system, combustion is the most obvious process that takes place within the engine. The inputs into this combustion process are fuel and oxygen. These inputs are transformed into energy within the engine. This energy is then used to move the automobile. Thus, the interrelated parts of the automobile system perform necessary processes such as combustion so that the system's objective of safe and reliable transportation is met. Exhibit 2-1 shows how the automotive system transforms inputs into outputs.

Accounting systems follow much the same pattern. The objective of an accounting system is to provide relevant and reliable information to decision makers. This objective is met through the production of financial statements and reports—the outputs of the accounting system. Like the automotive system, the accounting system requires inputs and a process to transform inputs into usable outputs.

Exhibit 2-2 illustrates how the accounting information system transforms raw data into useful economic information. Economic events which the firm enters are inputs to the accounting system. The transformation process is the set of rules and conventions that accountants use to record, classify, and summarize these inputs. The outputs of the accounting system are the accounting reports provided for a variety of users.

financial accounting information system

management accounting information system

Outputs for external users are produced by the **financial accounting information system,** a subsystem of the overall accounting system. Outputs for internal users are produced by the **management accounting information system,** a subsystem of the overall accounting system. Two key differences between the two subsystems should be mentioned. First, for the financial accounting information system, only those economic events which meet certain well-specified criteria set by GAAP become system inputs. The management accounting information system, on the other hand, allows a much broader set of inputs—it is not bound by the formal input criteria of financial accounting. Second, for financial accounting the rules and conventions are set externally by groups such as the FASB, whereas for the management accounting information system they are set internally based on managerial decision making needs.

Exhibit 2-1
The Automotive System

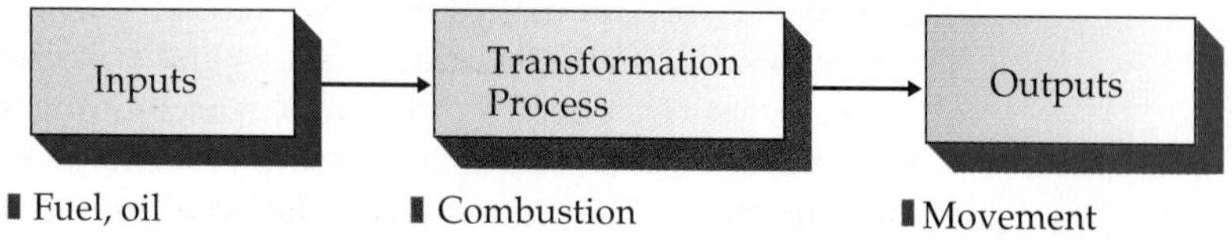

Exhibit 2-2
The Accounting Information System

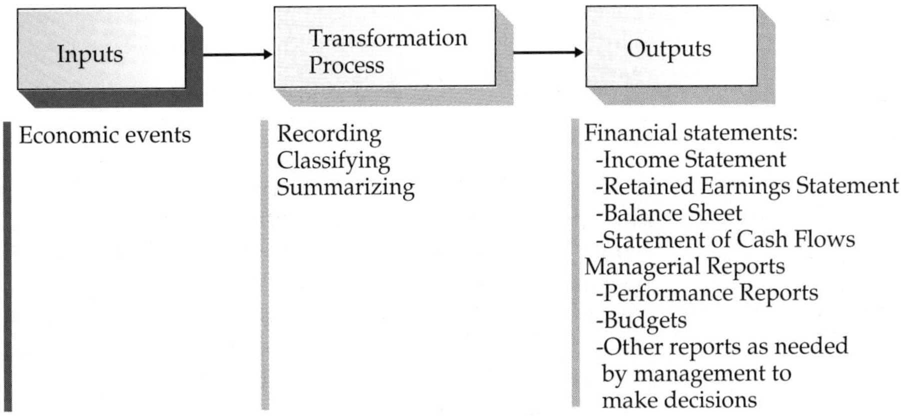

The Information Systems Role of The Accountant

Accountants play three important information-systems roles; they are users, designers, and auditors of those systems. The most obvious information systems role that accountants play is that of the user. In that role, accountants use an accounting information system to provide useful financial information to decision makers. Accountants enter transactions into the accounting system and then use the system to process the transactions and to generate reports and financial statements.

The roles of designers and auditors of information are equally important, however. Because of their in-depth understanding of accounting processes and functions and the uses of information, accountants are frequently involved in the design and development of new information systems. Accountants and other information specialists work together on project teams to design and implement manual and computer-based information systems. The accountant may be involved in the design of input documents and screens, reports and financial statements, files and data bases, and processing functions and controls. This is part of the broad-based management advisory service role of accountants that was discussed in Chapter 1.

Accounting information systems, once they have been implemented, must frequently be reviewed and tested to ensure that the systems are correctly processing transactions and working as designed. Accountants are thus frequently involved as reviewers or auditors of information systems. To be successful in that role, accountants must understand accounting concepts and procedures and the technology used to perform the accounting functions. The auditor role has become very important with the rapid growth of computer-based accounting systems. Computer-based accounting systems are able to process a tremendous volume of transactions very quickly. However, there is always a risk that the transactions will not be processed correctly, and that the resulting errors will not be detected. If this occurs, then the financial statements and reports produced by the system may be misstated. One of the important responsibilities of the accounting information systems auditor is to test information systems and to recommend changes to reduce the risk of errors. The rest of this chapter focuses primarily on the financial accounting information system. Later in this book, we will discuss in detail the management information system. We begin now by providing a simple example so that the systems concepts can be illustrated. Using this example, the input criteria are formally defined and illustrated. The example is also used to define and illustrate the steps in recording, classifying, and summarizing economic events.

An Example: The White-Water Boat Company

A small mail-order company that sells canoe and kayak supplies will be used to illustrate how an accounting information system works. Kim Colby is currently employed as a marketing manager in a large corporation. Kim has always wanted to be self-employed and has decided to start a white-water mail-order company that specializes in white-water canoe and kayak supplies. Initially, Kim will operate the company only on weekends and evenings. The company will take orders from customers and then send them to appropriate manufacturers who will ship the products directly to the firm's customers. Kim also plans to maintain a small in-house inventory of high-volume products that the firm can ship directly to customers. Kim wants to do the first catalog mailing on March 1, 1995 and thus decides to organize The White-Water Boat Company on January 1, 1995 to give himself plenty of time to prepare.

Kim's first step is to form a corporation by filing the necessary forms with the state where he lives and by making an initial cash investment. On January 1, 1995, Kim invests $5,000 in the business in exchange for 500 shares of capital stock. The $5,000 investment is deposited in White-Water's checking account. The new corporation immediately purchases a business license from the city for $200. The corporation then purchases a used computer for $800 and a fax machine for $500 and spends $1,000 on the stock of inventory items to be kept on hand. Throughout January, Kim works evenings on the computer using desktop publishing to design, prepare, and assemble the first catalog.

Kim initially decides to use a checkbook to record the transactions of the firm. All purchases are made by check and all money received by the company is deposited into White-Water's checking account. At first, this procedure seems to be working fine. However, by the end of January Kim realizes that he is not sure how much has been spent on individual inventory items; the checkbook shows only the amounts paid to the different suppliers. Kim feels there must be a better way to keep track of the firm's activities.

If the business grows as expected, Kim will want to work full time for White-Water. He also expects that he will need a bank loan to help finance the firm's activities. Kim knows that the banker will want to see some financial statements before a loan can be granted. The bank will be especially interested in whether or not the firm is profitable once operations begin. Furthermore, Kim remembers taking a few small items from inventory for a recent kayak trip and isn't sure how to account for the items that were taken.

Kim recognizes that the business needs a more complex accounting system and decides to take a systems approach in his design work. The first step is to identify the inputs to the accounting system.

Data Which Can Be Input Into the Financial Accounting System. Only data related to specific economic events can be recorded in The White-Water Boat Company's financial accounting system. These events must be:

1. Transactions for the business entity, The White-Water Boat Company
2. Quantifiable or measurable in monetary terms
3. Verifiable

business entity assumption

Business Entity Assumption. As noted in Chapter 1, an accounting system relates to a particular business entity. This is called the **business entity assumption** of accounting—the concept that the business is independent and distinct from its owners, even though the owners clearly have a residual interest in the net assets of the business.

Because the financial accounting system is intended for a specified business entity, only the transactions and events related to the entity's economic activities should be included in the system. In the White-Water Boat Company example, this means only business transactions, not Kim Colby's personal transactions, should be input into the accounting system. For example, Kim's use of some of the inventory items on a personal kayak trip is not a business expense and should not be recorded as such. The accounting reports produced for The White-Water Boat Company will be distorted if the accounting system fails to distinguish between the firm's expenditures and Kim's personal expenditures.

quantifiability

Quantifiability. Only those transactions that can be represented in numerical (primarily monetary) terms are admitted as inputs to the accounting system. This characteristic is known as **quantifiability.** An event is not treated as an input of the accounting system if it cannot be expressed in numerical terms. For example, Kim has spent considerable time and effort establishing relationships with suppliers and assembling the catalog. Kim wonders whether all this time and effort should be recorded in the accounting system. However, this time and effort cannot be an input of the system unless there is some reasonable way to translate it into monetary terms.

verifiability

Verifiability. In addition to being quantifiable, an economic event should be verifiable before it can be an input of the accounting system. **Verifiability** means that the data pertaining to the transaction or event must be available and that if two or more qualified persons examined the same data, they would reach essentially the same conclusions about the amount at which it should be recorded. Verifiability adds to the usefulness and thus the reliability of the accounting information. For example, assume that Kim could quantify in monetary terms the time and effort it took to develop supplier relationships and the white-water supply catalog. It is doubtful that the resulting figure would be verifiable. It would be difficult for independent parties to verify the amount of time and effort Kim spent developing these relationships and the dollar value of that effort.

The initial events and transactions related to the establishment of The White-Water Boat Company are analyzed in Exhibit 2-3 using these input criteria. Exhibit 2-3 shows that there are three categories of events and transactions:

1. Those that clearly are admissible to the accounting system (3, 5, 6, and 7).
2. Those that are not admissible (1).
3. Those that might be admissible if they can be quantified and verified (2 and 4).

Recognizing Transactions In the System. Accountants not only must decide if an event meets the criteria for input to the accounting system, they also must decide when to recognize or record the event in the accounting records. Accountants recognize transactions in the system only at specified points. For example, assume that White-Water places an order with a wholesaler for 10 pairs of knee pads. The company sends a purchase order, a document indicating what is being purchased, to the wholesale supplier. The knee pads are delivered to the boat

Exhibit 2-3
Analysis of Events and Transactions of The White-Water Boat Company

Events and Transactions	Accounting System Inputs	Explanation
1. Kim's salary as a marketing manager	No	Not related to business entity
2. Space used to store inventory	Maybe	If it can be quantified and verified
3. Kim's initial investment in the business	Yes	Business receives funds
4. Catalog preparation	Maybe	If it can be quantified and verified
5. City license	Yes	Related to business and quantifiable
6. Inventory	Yes	Related to business and quantifiable
7. Computer and fax machine	Yes	Related to business and quantifiable

company a week later, and two days after that the company receives the invoice, or bill. Kim writes a check on White-Water's checking account to pay for the knee pads two weeks after receiving the invoice. Finally, several weeks later, one pair of knee pads is sold to a customer. In this example, there are several distinct events:

1. An order is placed, and a purchase order is generated.
2. The knee pads are delivered.
3. An invoice is received.
4. The invoice is paid in full.
5. Some of the knee pads are sold.

Which of these events, all relating to the purchase of the knee pads for eventual resale, are recognized as transactions in the accounting system? Generally, accountants do not recognize mutual promises to perform. For example, in the first event, the wholesale supplier promised to deliver some knee pads, and the boat company promised to pay, but at that point, neither party had yet performed. Such mutual promises are not recorded as either assets or liabilities until one or both parties perform. Nevertheless, records and documents were generated; the boat company sent a purchase order to the wholesale firm. Kim kept a copy of the purchase order to keep track of the items which were on order and their expected delivery date.

The transaction is first recorded in both the boat company's and the wholesaler's accounting records when the boat company receives the knee pads. Note that at this point the wholesaler has performed its part of the agreement by delivering the knee pads, but the boat company has only made a promise to pay in the future. This obligation is recorded in the boat company's accounting records as a payable and in the wholesaler's records as a receivable, as cash has yet to be exchanged.

Receipt of the invoice does not cause a transaction to be recorded in the boat company's accounting records, because the purchase was recorded when the knee pads were received. However, the invoice does enter the system and generates paperwork that will result in payment of the invoice. The actual payment of the invoice is the second transaction that is recorded in White-Water's accounting system. At that point, the boat company is fulfilling its promise to pay. It is important to keep in mind that the purchase of the knee pads first entered the accounting system at the time the boat company received the knee pads, two weeks and two days before the payment was made.

Business transactions enter the accounting system at their historical cost and are not changed with subsequent increases in value until another transaction has taken place. For example, assume the knee pads cost the boat company $3 per pair, or $30. The boat company records these knee pads as an asset at their historical cost of $30. Regardless of any future price increase, they remain in the system at that amount until they are sold. When one pair of knee pads was sold for $10, the boat company recorded the fact that it gave up an asset that cost $3 and received another asset (either cash or a promise to receive cash from another entity) that has a value of $10. Further, at this point the shop recognizes the $7 profit ($10 − $3) on the transaction.

In order to illustrate the concepts discussed above, we will show in detail how White-Water's transactions are actually recorded in the accounting information system by indicating how they affect the accounting equation introduced in Chapter 1.

EFFECTS OF TRANSACTIONS ON THE ACCOUNTING EQUATION

Objective 2
Explain the effects of transactions on the accounting equation.

Chapter 1 introduced the accounting equation:

$$\text{Assets} = \text{Liabilities} + \text{Stockholders' Equity}$$

This equation, which summarizes the contents of the balance sheet, shows the assets, liabilities, and stockholders' equity of a business at a point in time. The accounting equation is part of the transformation process that converts data into useful information. We return to Kim Colby's new mail order business to see how transactions that are admissible into the accounting system affect assets, liabilities, and stockholders' equity.

account

First, all transactions are recorded in accounts, one of the interrelated parts of an accounting system. An **account** is a record that summarizes all transactions that affect a particular category of asset, liability, or stockholders' equity. Specific accounts are set up by a company, depending on its specific information needs and type of business. Accounts are added or deleted over time as the company grows and changes.

Second, for the accounting equation to remain in balance, each transaction must involve a change in at least two accounts. For example, if an asset is increased by $20, either another asset must be decreased by that amount, or a liability or stockholders' equity account must be increased by $20. Keep this fundamental relationship in mind as the transactions of The White-Water Boat Company are next traced through the financial accounting system.

Kim Colby started the new business by investing $5,000 cash. Kim organized the business as a corporation and received 500 shares of capital stock from the new corporation. The effect of this transaction was to provide the business with cash. The source of that asset was the owner's personal investment in the business. As a result, an asset account, Cash, and a stockholders' equity account, Capital Stock, are both increased by $5,000.

	Assets	=	*Liabilities*	+	*Stockholders' Equity*
	Cash	=			*Capital Stock*
1/1	+5,000	=			+5,000

On January 2, the new company purchased a business license from the city for $200 cash. This transaction resulted in a decrease in Cash, but at the same time a new asset, the license, was acquired. The license is an asset because it will provide the company future economic benefits, the right to conduct business in the city.

	Assets			=	*Liabilities*	+	*Stockholders' Equity*
	Cash	+	*License*	=			*Capital Stock*
1/1	+5,000			=			+5,000
1/2	− 200		+ 200				
Bal.	4,800	+	200	=			5,000
	Total = $5,000						

On January 3, the company bought a used computer for $800 and a fax machine for $500. Both of these assets will be used in the company's office, so Kim decided to include both the computer and the fax machine in one account, Office Equipment. This transaction decreases the asset account, Cash, by $1,300 and increases the asset account, Office Equipment, by $1,300. Note that the amount of total assets is not changed by this transaction. Notice also that each transaction affects two accounts and that the accounting equation remains in balance after each transaction has been recorded.

	Assets					=	*Liabilities*	+	*Stockholders' Equity*
	Cash	+	*License*	+	*Office Equipment*	=			*Capital Stock*
Bal.	4,800	+	200	+		=			+5,000
1/3	−1,300				+1,300				
Bal.	3,500	+	200	+	1,300	=			5,000
	Total = $5,000								

The boat company purchased a variety of items for resale from various manufacturers for $1,000 on January 5. These inventory items were purchased on credit so that the firm could conserve its cash. This transaction resulted in the creation of a liability, Accounts Payable, and a new asset, Inventory. (Kim decided to put all of these items into a single account, Inventory).

	Assets							=	*Liabilities*	+	*Stockholders' Equity*
	Cash	+	*Inventory*	+	*License*	+	*Office Equipment*	=	*Accounts Payable*	+	*Capital Stock*
Bal.	3,500	+		+	200	+	1,300	=			5,000
1/5			+1,000						+1,000		
Bal.	3,500	+	1,000	+	200	+	1,300	=	1,000	+	5,000
	Total = $6,000								Total = $6,000		

Kim soon decided that the used computer did not have enough disk storage and was not fast enough. A friend offered to buy the computer from Kim for $800, Kim's original cost. Unfortunately the friend could only afford to pay $100 per month for eight months.[1] Kim considered the offer and accepted it on January 15. This transaction reduced the balance in the asset account, Office Equipment, from $1,300 to $500, and created a new asset, Accounts Receivable. This transaction did not result in any revenue because the sale of the computer was not related to the main activities of the business. Furthermore, stockholders' equity was not affected because the computer was sold for exactly its cost. Thus, this transaction is the exchange of one asset for another of the same cost. Revenue transactions will be discussed in the next chapter.

	Assets					= *Liabilities*	+ *Stockholders' Equity*
	Cash +	*Accounts Receivable* +	*Inventory* +	*License* +	*Office Equipment* =	*Accounts Payable* +	*Capital Stock*
Bal.	3,500 +	+	1,000 +	200 +	1,300 =	1,000 +	5,000
1/15		+800			− 800	+	
Bal.	3,500 +	800 +	1,000 +	200 +	500 =	1,000 +	5,000
	Total = $6,000					Total = $6,000	

On January 16, the company purchased on credit a larger computer for $1,400. This transaction increased both the asset account, Office Equipment, and the liability account, Accounts Payable.

	Assets					= *Liabilities*	+ *Stockholders' Equity*
	Cash +	*Accounts Receivable* +	*Inventory* +	*License* +	*Office Equipment* =	*Accounts Payable* +	*Capital Stock*
Bal.	3,500 +	800 +	1,000 +	200 +	500 =	1,000 +	5,000
1/16					+1,400	+1,400	
Bal.	3,500 +	800 +	1,000 +	200 +	1,900 =	2,400 +	5,000
	Total = $7,400					Total = $7,400	

On January 31, the boat company paid one-half the amount owed for the inventory purchased on January 5. This decreased both the asset account, Cash, and Accounts Payable, a liability account.

	Assets					= *Liabilities*	+ *Stockholders' Equity*
	Cash +	*Accounts Receivable* +	*Inventory* +	*License* +	*Office Equipment* =	*Accounts Payable* +	*Capital Stock*
Bal.	3,500 +	800 +	1,000 +	200 +	1,900 =	2,400 +	5,000
1/31	− 500					− 500	
Bal.	3,000 +	800 +	1,000 +	200 +	1,900 =	1,900 +	5,000
	Total = $6,900					Total = $6,900	

1. In reality, payments such as this which are spread over a period of time also include interest. That is, some amount of interest would be added to the $100 per month. For simplicity, at this point in the analysis, we are ignoring this interest element.

On January 31, the company also received partial payment of $100 for the computer it had sold. This transaction affected only asset accounts, as Cash increased and Accounts Receivable decreased.

	Assets					= Liabilities +	Stockholders' Equity
	Cash +	*Accounts Receivable* +	*Inventory* +	*License* +	*Office Equipment* =	*Accounts Payable* +	*Capital Stock*
Bal.	3,000 +	800 +	1,000 +	200 +	1,900 =	1,900 +	5,000
1/31	+ 100	−100					
Bal.	3,100 +	700 +	1,000 +	200 +	1,900 =	1,900 +	5,000

Total = $6,900 — Total = $6,900

The chart in Exhibit 2-4 summarizes all the transactions for the month of January. The balance sheet at January 31, 1995 that Kim prepared from that chart is shown in Exhibit 2-5. Note that Kim began the business with a $5,000 investment, so at that time stockholders' equity (assets minus liabilities) was $5,000. As the balance sheet shows, at the end of January stockholders' equity is still $5,000

Exhibit 2-4

The White-Water Boat Company
Summary of Transactions for January

	Assets					= Liabilities +	Stockholders' Equity
	Cash +	*Accounts Receivable* +	*Inventory* +	*License* +	*Office Equipment* =	*Accounts Payable* +	*Capital Stock*
1/1	+5,000						+5,000
1/2	− 200			+200			
Bal.	4,800 +			200	=		5,000
1/3	−1,300				+1,300		
Bal.	3,500 +			200 +	1,300 =		5,000
1/5			+1,000			+1,000	
Bal.	3,500 +		1,000 +	200 +	1,300 =	1,000 +	5,000
1/15		+800			− 800		
Bal.	3,500 +	800 +	1,000 +	200 +	500 =	1,000 +	5,000
1/16					+1,400	+1,400	
Bal.	3,500 +	800 +	1,000 +	200 +	1,900 =	2,400 +	5,000
1/31	−500					− 500	
Bal.	3,000 +	800 +	1,000 +	200 +	1,900 =	1,900 +	5,000
1/31	+100	−100					
Bal.	3,100 +	700 +	1,000 +	200 +	1,900 =	1,900 +	5,000

Total = $6,900 — Total = $6,900

Exhibit 2-5

The White-Water Boat Company Balance Sheet January 31, 1995	
Assets	
Cash	$3,100
Accounts receivable	700
Inventory	1,000
License	200
Office equipment	1,900
Total assets	$6,900
Liabilities and Stockholders' Equity	
Liabilities	
Accounts payable	$1,900
Stockholders' equity	
Capital stock	5,000
Total liabilities and stockholders' equity	$6,900

(assets of $6,900 less liabilities of $1,900). The firm's assets have increased from the $5,000 Kim originally contributed to $6,900. In addition, instead of the assets being all in cash, the business now has a variety of assets. The additional $1,900 in assets was contributed by creditors. Thus, stockholders' equity of the firm did not change in January from Kim's original $5,000 investment.

As previously explained, stockholders' equity is affected not only by what the owners invest, but by the profitability of the business as well. Kim spent the month of January getting ready to sell canoe and kayak supplies, so the company did not generate any revenues and expenses. Thus, an income statement that would show whether or not the firm is profitable cannot be prepared. Transactions for The White-Water Boat Company affecting the income statement are introduced in Chapter 3.

It would be very difficult and costly for a business to prepare a balance sheet or accounting equation after each transaction, as has been done here for purposes of illustration. Therefore accountants have developed a process for storing and classifying transactions so that a periodic balance sheet can easily be prepared. The next part of this chapter, as well as Chapters 3 and 4, show how accounting systems store and classify information for this purpose. This is a part of the transformation process through which large amounts of input data are stored, classified, and summarized into accounting reports.

COMPONENTS OF THE ACCOUNTING SYSTEM

Objective 3
Detail the components of the accounting system and steps in the accounting cycle.

The major components of the accounting system are illustrated in Exhibit 2-6. These components are similar whether the system is manual or computerized. Most transactions are written on business documents, such as sales invoices, purchase orders, cash register tapes, and checks. These documents serve as the source for inputs into the two basic components of any financial accounting system, journals and ledgers.

Exhibit 2-6
Components of the Accounting System

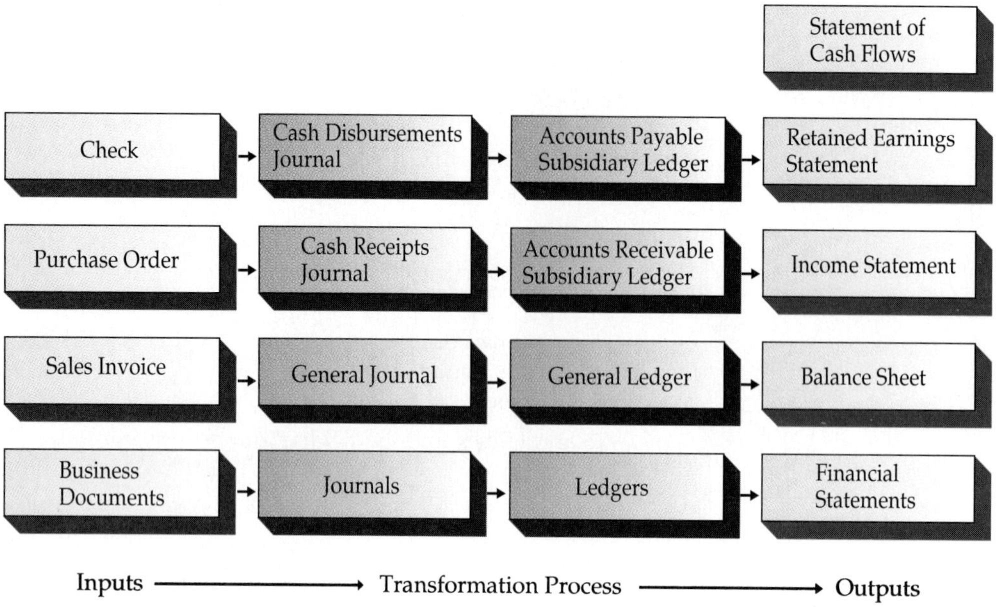

The Journal

journal

Transactions are originally recorded in a book or computerized record called the **journal**. For this reason, the journal is often referred to as the book of original entry. The journal is, in effect, a chronological list of transactions entered into by the firm. There are several types of journals, ranging from a general journal to specialized journals. General journals can be used to record all types of transactions, whereas specialized journals are used to record a specific type of transaction, such as cash receipts and cash disbursements.

The Ledger

ledger

general ledger

subsidiary ledgers

A **ledger** is a book or computerized record of specific accounts; it is the place where the effects of all transactions which affect a specific account are summarized. A **general ledger** contains a specific account for each item listed on the financial statements and shows how each transaction changes the balances of these accounts. **Subsidiary ledgers** contain back-up or more detailed accounts. For example, the primary account, Accounts Receivable, is in the general ledger, whereas the individual accounts for each customer are contained in the Accounts Receivable subsidiary ledger.

Transactions are first recorded in a journal. The recorded information at specific intervals is manually or electronically transferred from the journal to the relevant accounts in the general ledger and, when appropriate, to the related subsidiary ledger accounts. The balances in the general ledger are then used to prepare financial statements.

The accounts used by a particular firm depend on its needs and the nature and size of the business. For example, a large, publicly owned corporation may have hundreds or even thousands of accounts, whereas a small business may

Exhibit 2-7

The White-Water Boat Company
Chart of Accounts

100 ASSETS	400 REVENUES
101 Cash	401 Sales
103 Marketable Securities	405 Other Revenues
105 Notes Receivable	
106 Accounts Receivable	500 COST OF GOODS SOLD
110 Inventory	
115 Office Supplies	600 EXPENSES—SELLING
120 License	601 Salaries Expense
125 Prepaid Insurance	605 Advertising Expense
150 Land	
160 Office Equipment	700 EXPENSES—GENERAL AND ADMINISTRATIVE
165 Buildings	701 Repairs and Maintenance Expense
170 Other Assets	703 Utilities Expense
	705 License Expense
200 LIABILITIES	707 Office Supplies Expense
201 Accounts Payable	711 Insurance Expense
205 Bank Loan Payable	715 Depreciation Expense
210 Salaries Payable	
212 Interest Payable	800 OTHER EXPENSES
214 Taxes Payable	801 Interest Expense
	811 Taxes Expense
300 STOCKHOLDERS' EQUITY	
301 Capital Stock	900 INCOME SUMMARY
311 Retained Earnings	

have a dozen or so accounts. A firm may combine many of its accounts when it prepares financial statements. For example, for internal purposes Ford probably has thousands of different accounts. When preparing financial statements for external use, however, many of these accounts are combined into fewer, more meaningful accounts.

chart of accounts

Firms generally maintain a **chart of accounts,** which is a list of all the accounts that it uses. Accounts in the chart are sequentially numbered. The chart of accounts for The White-Water Boat Company is illustrated in Exhibit 2-7. Notice that there are gaps in the numbering sequence which provide the company the ability to add new accounts as needed.

THE RECORDING PROCESS

Objective 4
Record balance sheet transactions in the journal and ledger.

accounting cycle

Accountants have developed a set of standardized procedures that are used to record economic transactions. These procedures are performed in sequence during every accounting period. Accounting periods can be monthly, quarterly, or yearly, depending on the needs of the business. This set of procedures, generally known as the **accounting cycle,** is outlined below:

During the Period

- Record transactions in the journal.
- Periodically post journal entries to ledger accounts.

At End of Period

- Prepare the unadjusted trial balance.
- Prepare the worksheet—optional.
- Prepare adjusting entries.
- Post adjusting entries to the ledger accounts, balance the accounts, and prepare the adjusted trial balance.
- Prepare the financial statements.
- Prepare closing entries, post to the ledger accounts, and prepare a post-closing trial balance.

The accounting system may be a manual, hand-kept set of records or a complex computerized system. Since the accounting remains the same, the discussion here will be based on a simple manual system. The concepts and procedures that you will learn are equally applicable to computerized systems.

As illustrated, the first step in the accounting cycle is to record transactions in the journal. These entries are then periodically transferred to the ledger accounts. From a learning standpoint, however, it is more effective to start the discussion of the accounting cycle in reverse by explaining how transactions are entered in the ledger. This is because the rules for recording transactions in the accounting records are based on how they affect the ledger accounts. The discussion will then turn to how transactions are recorded in the journal. The remaining parts of the cycle will be covered in Chapters 3 and 4.

Recording Transactions in the Ledger

T accounts

The effect of numerous transactions on specific accounts are accumulated in a ledger. In a manual accounting system, a ledger contains a separate page for each account. Throughout this text, **T accounts**—so named because of their T shape—are used to represent individual ledger accounts. A sample T account looks like this:

Cash	*101*

The account name and account number are written above the T account. One side of the T account is used to record increases in the account balance, and the other side is used to record decreases. *Increases in asset account balances are recorded on the left side of the ledger account, and decreases are recorded on the right side of the ledger account. Conversely, increases in liability and stockholders' equity accounts are recorded on the right side of the ledger account and decreases are recorded on the left side.* These points are illustrated in the following T accounts.

Assets		=	*Liabilities*		+	*Stockholders' Equity*	
Increases +	Decreases −		Decreases −	Increases +		Decreases −	Increases +

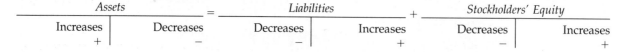

Each time an entry is made on the left side of an account, a corresponding entry or set of entries is made on the right side of another account. This action preserves the equality of the accounting equation. For example, an increase in an asset can come only from a decrease in another asset account or an increase in a liability or a stockholders' equity account. This means that when an entry is made on the left side of an asset account to record an increase in that account, there will be a corresponding entry on the right side of either another asset account to record a decrease, or an entry on the right side of a liability or a stockholders' equity account to record an increase in that account.

This is illustrated in the following two examples taken from the transactions of The White-Water Boat Company. Kim began the business by investing $5,000 cash on January 1. This transaction increases both an asset account, Cash, and a stockholders' equity account, Capital Stock. It results in an entry on the left side of the Cash account, which represents an increase of $5,000 in this account. A corresponding entry is made on the right side of the stockholders' equity account, Capital Stock, which represents an increase in that account. The following T accounts reflect this transaction.

Cash			
1/1	5,000		

Capital Stock			
		1/1	5,000

A second example is the transaction on January 5 when Kim purchases inventory for $1,000 on account. The increase in the asset account, Inventory, is recorded on the left side of the T account, and the increase in the liability account, Accounts Payable, is recorded on the right side of that account:

Inventory			
1/5	1,000		

Accounts Payable			
		1/5	1,000

As indicated in these transactions, the system for recording transactions maintains the equality of the accounting equation:

- For every increase in an asset account, there is a corresponding decrease in another asset account or an increase in a liability or stockholders' equity account.
- For every entry on the left side of an account, there is always a corresponding entry on the right side of another account.

Understanding Debits and Credits

debit

credit

Accountants have developed other conventions to help them record transactions easily and efficiently. Debits, often abbreviated Dr., and credits, often abbreviated Cr., are examples of these conventions. To **debit** an account means to make an entry on the left side of any ledger account. Therefore, a debit increases the balance of an asset account and decreases the balance of a liability or stockholders' equity account. Credits have the opposite effect. A **credit** is an entry on the right side of any ledger account. Consequently, a credit decreases the balance of an asset account or increases the balance in a liability or stockholders' equity account. You should understand that in accounting, the words debit and credit are just shorthand ways of saying that you are making an entry on the debit (left) side or credit (right) side of any ledger account. They have no other meanings and do not imply a favorable or unfavorable condition. These accounting conventions are summarized in the following T accounts:

Assets		=	*Liabilities*		+	*Stockholders' Equity*	
Increases + Debit	Decreases − Credit		Decreases − Debit	Increases + Credit		Decreases − Debit	Increases + Credit

Going back to the previous example, you would debit the asset account, Cash, and credit the stockholders' equity account, Capital Stock, to record the $5,000 cash investment in Kim's business. To record the $1,000 purchase of inventory on account, you would debit the asset account, Inventory, and credit the liability account, Accounts Payable.

double-entry accounting

Debits Must Equal Credits. Correct application of the debit and credit rules ensures that the accounting equation will always stay in balance. For example, if an asset account is increased (debited), there must be a corresponding decrease in another asset account (a credit) or an increase in a liability or stockholders' equity account (a credit). For this reason, this system of accounting is often referred to as **double-entry accounting.** Each transaction will have equal debit and credit effects on the accounting equation. However, the fact that debits equal credits does not necessarily mean that a particular transaction was recorded correctly. For example, Cash could be credited by mistake when, in fact, Accounts Payable should have been credited. As long as equal debits and credits are recorded, the accounting equation will remain in balance.

Balancing T Accounts. After all transactions for a specified period have been entered in the individual ledger accounts, the accounts are totaled and balanced. All of the cash transactions for the month of January for The White-Water Boat Company are shown in the following T account. As indicated, each side of the account is totaled. These totals are referred to as *footings;* in this example, they are marked in color.

Cash

1/1 Beginning Balance	0	1/2 Purchase of license	200
1/1 Kim's investment	5,000	1/3 Purchase of office equipment	1,300
1/31 Receipt of payment on account	100	1/31 Payment on account	500
	5,100		2,000
1/31 Ending Balance	3,100		

The beginning balance plus debits, or increases, equals $5,100, and the credits, or decreases, equal $2,000. Subtracting the decreases of $2,000 on the right side from the total of $5,100 on the left leaves a balance of $3,100. This is the ending balance on January 31 and will become the beginning balance for the period beginning February 1. In future examples, the footings will be eliminated, and only the new balance will be shown. Normally only the date and amount of a transaction are entered in the ledger account. The specific transaction is fully described in the journal.

As you would expect, all asset accounts normally have debit balances.

Remember that debits represent increases in assets, and as a result there are very few situations in which it would be possible to have a credit balance in an asset account because that would represent a negative asset. Liability and stockholders' equity accounts are totaled and balanced in the same way. These accounts normally have credit balances. The T account (with footings omitted) for Accounts Payable for The White-Water Boat Company is:

Accounts Payable

1/31 Payment on account	500	1/1 Beginning balance	0
		1/5 Purchase of inventory on account	1,000
		1/31 Purchase of office equipment on account	1,400
		1/31 Ending balance	1,900

White-Water Boat Company Transactions

The White-Water Boat Company was organized on January 1, 1995. January transactions were discussed in the first part of this chapter. The balances reported on the January 31, 1995 balance sheet (Exhibit 2-5) are the opening balances in the ledger accounts on February 1. Kim continued to organize the business and to prepare for operations to begin on March 1.

During the month of February, the following transactions took place:

- February 2: Some of Kim's friends purchased a total of 3,500 shares of capital stock at $10 per share.
- February 5: The firm purchased land and a small building for $15,000. The land cost $5,000 and the building $10,000. The firm paid cash for both the land and the building.
- February 11: Numerous office supplies were purchased by the firm for cash. The total cost of these supplies was $2,000.
- February 12: The company purchased a variety of office equipment for $8,000; $4,000 was paid in cash and the remaining $4,000 was borrowed from the bank.
- February 18: The firm purchased a comprehensive insurance policy for $1,200 cash. The policy covers a two-year period from March 1, 1995 to February 28, 1997.
- February 27: The company purchased additional inventory for resale for $8,000 on account.
- February 28: The company made a $5,000 payment on accounts payable.
- February 28: Cash of $100 was received for the computer sold in January.

Each of these transactions is analyzed from the standpoint of how it affects various accounts, and then it is entered in the appropriate ledger accounts. You should go through a three-step process as you think about how to record each transaction.

a. Determine the specific accounts that are affected by the transaction and whether they are asset, liability, or stockholders' equity accounts.
b. Decide whether each of these accounts is increased or decreased.
c. Make the appropriate debit and credit entries in the specific ledger accounts.

Analyzing Transactions

1. **Transaction on February 2—Issuance of $35,000 of capital stock for cash.**
   a. This transaction is an exchange of cash for capital stock. Thus the two accounts affected are Cash, an asset account, and Capital Stock, a stockholders' equity account.
   b. Cash is increased by $35,000 (3,500 shares times $10 per share), and Capital Stock, a stockholders' equity account is increased by the same $35,000.
   c. The increase in the asset account Cash is recorded on the left side of the T account as a debit. The increase in the stockholders' equity account Capital Stock is recorded on the right side of the T account as a credit.

Cash			
2/1 Bal.	3,100		
2/2	35,000		

Capital Stock			
		2/1 Bal.	5,000
		2/2	35,000

2. **Transaction on February 5—Purchase of land and building for a total of $15,000 cash; cost of land, $5,000, and building, $10,000.**
   a. The three accounts affected by this transaction are Cash, Land, and Building. All three are asset accounts.
   b. Land and Building are increased $5,000 and $10,000, respectively. Cash is decreased by the total outlay of $15,000. Because more than two accounts are involved, this is referred to as a *compound entry.*
   c. The increases in the asset accounts Land and Building are recorded on the left side of these T accounts as debits. The decrease in the asset account Cash is recorded on the right side of the T account as a credit.

Cash			
2/1 Bal.	3,100	2/5	15,000
2/2	35,000		

Land			
2/1 Bal.	0		
2/5	5,000		

Building			
2/1 Bal.	0		
2/5	10,000		

3. **Transaction on February 11—Purchase of office supplies for $2,000 cash.**
   a. This transaction affects two asset accounts, Office Supplies and Cash.
   b. Office Supplies is increased and Cash is decreased.
   c. The increase in the asset account Office Supplies is recorded on the left side of the T account as a debit. The decrease in the asset account Cash is recorded on the right side of the T account as a credit.

Cash			
2/1 Bal.	3,100	2/5	15,000
2/2	35,000	2/11	2,000

Office Supplies			
2/1 Bal.	0		
2/11	2,000		

4. **Transaction on February 12—Purchase of $8,000 of office equipment for $4,000 cash and a bank loan of $4,000.**
   a. This transaction involves two asset accounts, Office Equipment and Cash, and one liability account, Bank Loan Payable.
   b. Office Equipment is increased, Cash is decreased, and the liability account Bank Loan Payable is increased.
   c. The increase in the asset account Office Equipment is recorded on the left side of the T account as a debit. The decrease in the asset account Cash is recorded on the right side of the T account as a credit. Finally, the increase in the liability account Bank Loan Payable is recorded on the right side of that account as a credit.

Cash

2/1 Bal.	3,100	2/5	15,000
2/2	35,000	2/11	2,000
		2/12	4,000

Office Equipment

2/1 Bal.	1,900		
2/12	8,000		

Bank Loan Payable

		2/1 Bal.	0
		2/12	4,000

5. **Transaction on February 18—Purchase of a comprehensive insurance policy for $1,200 cash.**
   a. The two accounts affected by this transaction are the asset accounts Prepaid Insurance and Cash.
   b. Prepaid Insurance is increased and Cash is decreased.
   c. The increase in the asset account Prepaid Insurance is recorded on the left side of the T account as a debit. The decrease in the asset account Cash is recorded on the right side of the T account as a credit.

Cash

2/1 Bal.	3,100	2/5	15,000
2/2	35,000	2/11	2,000
		2/12	4,000
		2/18	1,200

Prepaid Insurance

2/1 Bal.	0		
2/18	1,200		

6. **Transaction on February 27—Purchase of $8,000 of inventory on account.**
   a. This transaction involves an asset account, Inventory, and a liability account, Accounts Payable.
   b. Inventory is increased, and Accounts Payable is also increased.
   c. The increase in the asset account Inventory is recorded on the left side of the T account as a debit. The increase in the liability account Accounts Payable is recorded on the right side of the T account as a credit.

Inventory

2/1 Bal.	1,000		
2/27	8,000		

Accounts Payable

		2/1 Bal.	1,900
		2/27	8,000

7. **Transaction on February 28—$5,000 partial payment of accounts payable.**
   a. This transaction involves an asset account Cash and the liability account Accounts Payable.
   b. Cash is decreased, and Accounts Payable is decreased.
   c. The decrease in the asset account Cash is recorded on the right side of the T account as a credit. The decrease in the liability account Accounts Payable is recorded on the left side of the T account as a debit.

Cash

2/1 Bal.	3,100	2/5	15,000
2/2	35,000	2/11	2,000
		2/12	4,000
		2/18	1,200
		2/28	5,000

Accounts Payable

2/28	5,000	2/1 Bal.	1,900
		2/27	8,000

8. **Transaction on February 28—$100 received on accounts receivable.**
   a. This transaction involves two asset accounts, Cash and Accounts Receivable.
   b. Cash is increased and Accounts Receivable is decreased.
   c. The increase in the asset account Cash is recorded on the left side of the T account as a debit. The decrease in the asset account Accounts Receivable is recorded on the right side of the T account as a credit.

Cash

2/1 Bal.	3,100	2/5	15,000
2/2	35,000	2/11	2,000
2/28	100	2/12	4,000
		2/18	1,200
		2/28	5,000

Accounts Receivable

2/1	700	2/28	100

Using Ledger Accounts in Practice

T accounts are used throughout this book to represent ledger accounts. In practice, however, more sophisticated account forms are used. The cash account for The White-Water Boat Company in Exhibit 2-8 illustrates what an actual ledger account might look like in a manual accounting system.

This ledger account, often called a *running balance ledger account* because it keeps continuous track of the account balance, is designed for easy cross-reference to the journal where the transactions were recorded initially. For example, the date column is used to record the date on which the actual transaction took place. The same date will appear in the journal. The description column is generally not used unless it is necessary to make an unusual notation. *Ref.* is the abbreviation for reference. This column is used to indicate the page number of the journal where the complete journal entry can be found. In Exhibit 2-8, the entries GJ-1 in the Ref. column indicate page 1 of the general journal. The debit and credit columns are used to record the respective entries, and the balance column is used to keep a running balance.

The accounts in a ledger are arranged in normal balance sheet order, so assets are listed first, followed by liabilities and stockholders' equity. As previously

Exhibit 2-8

The White-Water Boat Company
Ledger Account for Cash

Cash 101

Date 1995		*Description*	*Ref.*	*Debit*	*Credit*	*Balance* Debit	*Balance* Credit
Feb.	1	Bal.				3,100.00	
	2		GJ-1	35,000.00		38,100.00	
	5		GJ-1		15,000.00	23,100.00	
	11		GJ-1		2,000.00	21,100.00	
	12		GJ-1		4,000.00	17,100.00	
	18		GJ-1		1,200.00	15,900.00	
	28		GJ-1		5,000.00	10,900.00	
	28		GJ-1	100.00		11,000.00	
		Balance				11,000.00	

noted, each account is given a specific number for easy identification. The specific numbering system used by a particular firm depends on the company's size and complexity.

Recording Transactions in the Journal

The use of journals and ledgers is interrelated. By first recording an entire transaction in the journal, all the specifics of the transaction are in one place and can be referred to at any future time. Remember that only part of the transaction is recorded in a particular ledger account.

Transactions for the month of February for The White-Water Boat Company are recorded in the general journal (Exhibit 2-9). Although a variety of different journals are used in practice, a standard two-column general journal will be used here and throughout the text. A number of points need to be made regarding how transactions are journalized.

1. The Date column is used to record the date on which the transaction took place. For the first entry in each month, it is customary to record both the month and day. For subsequent entries in that month, only the day of the month is recorded.
2. The Account Title or explanation column is used to record the specific accounts affected by the transaction. A number of conventions simplify the use of the journal:
   a. Debits are always listed first, with the account title beginning at the left margin of the explanation column.
   b. The credit portion of the entry is then recorded, indented slightly.
   c. If the transaction is a compound entry and thus involves more than two accounts, all the debits are recorded before the credits. The entries on February 5 and 12 are examples.
   d. The dollar amounts are inserted in the respective debit and credit columns on the same line as the account titles. No dollar signs are used, because it's understood that all debit and credit amounts are in dollars.
   e. Because a general journal is used for many different types of transactions, accountants generally write a short explanation under the entry. This

Exhibit 2-9
General Journal

The White-Water Boat Company

Date	Account Title	Ref.	Debit	Credit
1995				
Feb. 2	Cash	101	35,000	
	Capital Stock	301		35,000
	To record sale of 3,500 shares of stock.			
5	Land	150	5,000	
	Buildings	165	10,000	
	Cash	101		15,000
	To record the purchase of land and building.			
11	Office Supplies	115	2,000	
	Cash	101		2,000
	To record the purchase of office supplies.			
12	Office Equipment	160	8,000	
	Cash	101		4,000
	Bank Loan Payable	205		4,000
	To record the purchase of office furniture and fixtures.			
18	Prepaid Insurance	125	1,200	
	Cash	101		1,200
	To record purchase of prepaid insurance.			
27	Inventory	110	8,000	
	Accounts Payable	201		8,000
	To record purchase of inventory on account.			
28	Accounts Payable	201	5,000	
	Cash	101		5,000
	To record payment on account.			
28	Cash	101	100	
	Accounts Receivable	106		100
	To record receipt of cash on account.			

makes it easier to recall the specifics of the entry if it is referred to months or years later.

3. The Ref. (references) column is used to cross-reference the journal to the ledger. The number of the ledger account to which the entry is posted is placed in this column at the time the entry is posted.

Posting to the Ledger

posting

Transactions are entered in the individual ledger accounts after they have been recorded in the journal. This process is referred to as **posting.** The size of the company and the volume of transactions usually determine how frequently journal entries are posted to the ledger accounts. Posting can take place daily, semimonthly, monthly, or in rare situations even yearly. If a computer is used to record transactions, posting can be performed instantaneously as the transactions are recorded. For ease of illustration, most of the problem material in this book assumes that entries are posted either monthly or yearly.

There are several things to remember about posting that will help you reduce errors when solving exercises or problems. Each transaction should be posted in its entirety, one transaction at a time. Using the entry on February 2 (Exhibit 2-9) as an example, first post the debit to the Cash account and then the credit to the Capital Stock account before going on to the next transaction. If account numbers are provided, as in this example, place the number of the account to which the posting is made in the reference column in the journal on the appropriate line. For example, in Exhibit 2-9 the account number for Cash, 101, is placed in the reference (Ref.) column on the same line as the account title. If account numbers are not provided, place a check in this column. This will indicate that you have posted the entry. In addition, as shown in Exhibit 2-8, the page number of the journal where the entry is recorded should be placed in the reference column of the ledger account. If T accounts are used, only the date or number of the transaction should be placed beside the dollar amount.

For illustrative purposes, the journal entry on February 11 is posted to the appropriate ledger accounts in Exhibit 2-10. After all transactions for the month

Exhibit 2-10
Posting from the General Journal to the Ledger Accounts

The White-Water Boat Company

Journal — Page GJ-1

Date	*Account Title*	*Ref.*	*Debit*	*Credit*
1995				
Feb. 11	Office Supplies	115	2,000	
	Cash	101		2,000
	To record purchase of office supplies.			

Cash — 101

Date		*Description*	*Ref.*	*Debit*	*Credit*	*Balance Debit*	*Balance Credit*
1995							
Feb.	1	Balance				3100 00	
	2		GJ-1	35000 00		38100 00	
	5		GJ-1		15000 00	23100 00	
	11		GJ-1		2000 00	21100 00	

Office Supplies — 115

Date		*Description*	*Ref.*	*Debit*	*Credit*	*Balance Debit*	*Balance Credit*
1995							
Feb.	11		GJ-1	2000 00		2000 00	

Exhibit 2-11
T Account Summary

The White-Water Boat Company

Cash 101

2/1 Bal.	3,100	2/5	15,000
2/2	35,000	2/11	2,000
		2/12	4,000
		2/18	1,200
2/28	100	2/28	5,000
2/28 Bal	11,000		

Accounts Receivable 106

2/1 Bal.	700	2/28	100
2/28 Bal	600		

Inventory 110

2/1 Bal.	1,000		
2/27	8,000		
2/28 Bal.	9,000		

Office Supplies 115

2/1 Bal.	0		
2/11	2,000		
2/28 Bal.	9,000		

License 120

2/1 Bal.	200		
2/28 Bal.	200		

Prepaid Insurance 125

2/1 Bal.	0		
2/18	1,200		
2/28 Bal.	1,200		

Land 150

2/1 Bal.	0		
2/5	5,000		
2/28 Bal.	5,000		

Office Equipment 160

2/1 Bal.	1,900		
2/12	8,000		
2/28 Bal.	9,900		

Buildings 165

2/1 Bal.	0		
2/5	10,000		
2/28 Bal.	10,000		

Accounts Payable 201

2/28	5,000	2/1 Bal.	1,900
		2/27	8,000
		2/28 Bal.	4,900

Bank Loan Payable 205

		2/1 Bal.	0
		2/12	4,000
		2/28 Bal.	4,000

Capital Stock 301

		2/1 Bal.	5,000
		2/2	35,000
		2/28 Bal.	40,000

have been posted, the T accounts for The White-Water Boat Company will appear as shown in Exhibit 2-11.

THE TRIAL BALANCE

Objective 5
Prepare a trial balance and describe its uses and limitations.

trial balance

The **trial balance** is a list of the accounts in the general ledger with their respective debit or credit balances. It is the third step in the accounting cycle, and is prepared after all transactions for the accounting period have been posted to the ledger. Accounts on the trial balance are listed in the same order as in the general ledger; that is, assets first, followed by the liabilities and stockholders' equity accounts. The trial balance is a check to see whether equal amounts of

Exhibit 2-12

The White-Water Boat Company Trial Balance February 28, 1995		
	Debit	*Credit*
Cash	$11,000	
Accounts Receivable	600	
Inventory	9,000	
Office Supplies	2,000	
License	200	
Prepaid Insurance	1,200	
Land	5,000	
Office Equipment	9,900	
Buildings	10,000	
Accounts Payable		$ 4,900
Bank Loan Payable		4,000
Capital Stock		40,000
Totals	$48,900	$48,900

debits and credits have been posted to the ledger. If this is the case and all accounts have been correctly balanced, then the trial balance will be "in balance." Thus, the dollar amount of the debits will equal the dollar amount of the credits.

The trial balance of The White-Water Boat Company at February 28 is shown in Exhibit 2-12. It is important to understand the uses of a trial balance. If the trial balance is in balance, this tells you that (1) the same dollar amounts of debits and credits have been posted and (2) the accounts have been correctly balanced. However, the trial balance does *not* tell you that each entry has been posted to the correct account. For example, suppose that in the entry on February 11, you posted the $2,000 debit to Office Supplies as a debit to Inventory by mistake. The Office Supplies account is understated by $2,000, and the Inventory account is overstated by $2,000. The errors, in effect, cancel each other in the accounting equation, and no discrepancy would be revealed by the trial balance. The trial balance would be in balance even though it contains an error.

Errors in the Trial Balance

There are a number of reasons why the total of the debits may not equal the total of the credits. Some of the more common errors that may occur in the trial balance include the following:

1. **An addition error was made in totaling the trial balance.**
2. **A debit may have been posted as a credit or vice versa.** If this occurs, the difference between the totals will be twice the amount of the misposted entry. For example, if the credit of $2,000 to the Cash account on February 11 was posted as a debit, the total of the debits would be $50,900 and the total of the credits would be $46,900. The difference is $4,000, or twice the original $2,000 posting error. Therefore, errors of this type can be found by dividing by 2 the difference between the debit and credit column totals and checking for this amount as a debit that was posted as a credit or vice versa. If the error is a debit that was posted as a credit, the credit column total will be larger than

the debit column total. Conversely, if a credit is mistakenly posted as a debit, the debit column total will be the larger one. Finally, if an account balance is listed in the incorrect column on the trial balance, an error of this type will also occur. For example, if the bank loan payable of $4,000 is listed under the debit column, the trial balance will be out of balance by $8,000.

3. **Part of an entry may not have been posted.** If this occurs, the difference in the total of the debit and credit columns will equal the part of the entry not posted. For example, you may have posted the $1,200 debit to Prepaid Insurance in the February 18 entry, but forgot to post the credit to the Cash account. If that had happened, the total of the debits would still be $48,900 but the total of the credits would be only $47,700. The difference of $1,200 is the credit part of the entry that was not posted.
4. **A dollar amount may have been misposted.** Errors in the trial balance are often the result of transpositions or misplaced decimal points. An example of a transposition is posting $56 as $65. An example of a misplaced decimal point is posting $800 as $80. If there is a transposition or misplaced decimal point error, the resulting difference between the total of the debit and credit columns will be *evenly divisible by 9*. In the two examples above, posting $56 instead of $65 creates a $9 difference and posting $80 instead of $800 creates a $720 difference. Both $9 and $720 are evenly divisible by 9.
5. **Other Errors.** Other errors in the trial balance occur when ledger accounts are incorrectly balanced or an incorrect balance is transferred to the trial balance from a ledger account.

The best way to avoid errors in the trial balance is to work slowly and carefully when you are journalizing and posting. However, errors will inevitably occur. When they do, you should work backwards by first checking to see whether you have correctly added the debit and credit columns of the trial balance. The next step is to analyze the difference in the totals of the debit and credit columns, using the techniques just described, in order to try to locate the error. If you still can't find it, check to make sure the balance of each account in the trial balance is the same as the balance in the ledger account, and, if necessary, check the calculations in each ledger account.

If none of these steps uncovers the error, stop your search for a while and do something else. When you resume your search later, you will probably find your error quickly. If the error continues to elude you, however, retrace the entries of each ledger account back to the journal to be sure the posting was done correctly. As a final step, make sure each journal entry balances.

SUMMARY OF LEARNING OBJECTIVES

1. Explain how accounting functions as an information system, and describe the components of the system and the characteristics of information processed by the system. All systems have three characteristics: objectives, interrelated parts, and processes. The objective of the accounting system is to provide certain information about economic entities. Some of the interrelated parts of the accounting system include: (1) inputs, (2) a transformation process, and (3) outputs. Raw economic data are entered into the accounting system where they are stored and classified during the transformation process to produce the outputs of the accounting system—financial reports for management and external users.

Data input into the accounting system must be:

a. A transaction or event of the specified business entity,
b. Measurable in monetary terms, and
c. Verifiable.

Economic events take place continually, and accountants must decide when to recognize and record them in the accounting system. For example, in The White-Water Boat Company example, the purchase of knee pads was not actually recorded in Kim's records until the company received delivery of the purchased knee pads.

2. ***Explain the effects of transactions on the accounting equation.*** All the economic events that qualify as inputs for the accounting system can affect one or more of the three elements of the accounting equation. The purchase of assets for cash, for example, affects only assets, whereas the purchase of assets on account affects both assets and liabilities. Similarly, transactions that result in the receipt of cash owed to the firm affect only asset accounts (cash and accounts receivable), but the payment of a liability affects assets and liabilities (cash and accounts payable, for example). All transactions affect at least two accounts—that is, two assets, assets and liabilities, assets and stockholders' equity, or liabilities and stockholders' equity.

3. ***Detail the components of the accounting system and steps in the accounting cycle.*** The journal and ledger are the two primary components or interrelated parts of the accounting system. The journal is a listing of all transactions in the order in which they occurred. At specific intervals, these transactions are posted to the appropriate accounts in the ledger. A ledger, whether maintained by computer or manually, is a book of all the accounts the company lists in its chart of accounts. The specific accounts used by a firm depend on the nature, size, and complexity of the business.

4. ***Record balance sheet* transactions in the journal and ledger.** The following T accounts summarize the rules for recording changes in the balance sheet accounts:

Assets

Increases	Decreases
+	−
Debit	Credit
Normal Balance	

=

Liabilities

Decreases	Increases
−	+
Debit	Credit
	Normal Balance

\+

Stockholders' Equity

Decreases	Increases
−	+
Debit	Credit
	Normal Balance

5. ***Prepare a trial balance and describe its uses and limitations.*** A trial balance is usually prepared after transactions have been posted from the journal to the ledger. It presents a listing of the dollar balances of the general ledger accounts. If the trial balance is in balance, this will tell you that equal dollar amounts of debits and credits have been posted and that the amounts are correctly balanced. However, errors still may occur if accounts were debited, credited, or posted incorrectly.

KEY TERMS

Account 59
Accounting cycle 65
Accounting information system 54
Business entity assumption 57
Chart of accounts 65
Credit 67
Debit 67
Double-entry accounting 68
Financial accounting information system 54
General ledger 64
Journal 64
Ledger 64
Management accounting information system 54
Posting 74
Quantifiability 57
Subsidiary ledger 64
T account 66
Trial balance 76
Verifiability 57

REVIEW PROBLEM

On January 2, 1995, Bonnie Brinkley, an excellent cook, decides to open her own restaurant, BB's Fine Food. The following events occur during the month of January:

a. January 2: Bonnie invests $100,000 cash in the business by issuing herself 1,000 shares of capital stock.

b. January 10: The corporation purchases a small building, including land, for $60,000 cash. The land has a value of $10,000 and the building a value of $50,000.

c. January 15: The company purchases a variety of restaurant furniture and fixtures for $10,000. The company is able to finance the purchase through a one-year bank loan.
d. January 21: Food and beverages totaling $5,000 are purchased on account. These items are recorded in an account called Food and Beverage Inventory.
e. January 30: The corporation pays $3,500 on the account payable incurred on January 21.

REQUIRED:

1. Record the transactions in the general journal.
2. Post the transactions to the appropriate T accounts.
3. Prepare a trial balance at January 31, 1995.
4. Prepare a balance sheet at January 31, 1995.

Solution 1 Journal Entries

General Journal

Date	*Account Title*	*Ref.*	*Debit*	*Credit*
1995				
Jan. 2	Cash		100,000	
	Capital Stock			100,000
	To record issue of 1,000 shares of capital stock to B. Brinkley for $100,000.			
10	Land		10,000	
	Building		50,000	
	Cash			60,000
	To record purchase of land and building for $60,000.			
15	Furniture and Fixtures		10,000	
	Bank Loan Payable			10,000
	To record purchase of furniture and fixtures through bank loan.			
21	Food and Beverage Inventory		5,000	
	Accounts Payable			5,000
	To record purchase of food and beverages on account.			
30	Accounts Payable		3,500	
	Cash			3,500
	To record payment on account.			

2 T Accounts

Cash

1/2	100,000	1/10	60,000
		1/30	3,500
1/31 Bal.	36,500		

Food and Beverage Industry

1/21	5,000		

Furniture and Fixtures

1/15	10,000		

Land

1/10	10,000		

Building

1/10	50,000		

Accounts Payable

1/30	3,500	1/21	5,000
		1/31 Bal.	1,500

Bank Loan Payable

		1/15	10,000

Capital Stock

		1/2	100,000

3 Trial Balance

BB's Fine Food
Trial Balance
January 31, 1995

	Debit	Credit
Cash	$ 36,500	
Food and beverage inventory	5,000	
Furniture and fixtures	10,000	
Land	10,000	
Building	50,000	
Accounts payable		$ 1,500
Bank loan payable		10,000
Capital stock		100,000
Totals	$111,500	$111,500

4 Balance Sheet

BB's Fine Food
Balance Sheet
January 31, 1995

Assets		*Liabilities and Stockholders' Equity*	
Cash	$ 36,500	Liabilities	
Food and beverage inventory	5,000	Accounts payable	$ 1,500
Furniture and fixtures	10,000	Bank loan payable	10,000
Land	10,000		
Building	50,000	Total liabilities	$ 11,500
		Stockholders' equity	
		Capital stock	100,000
Total assets	$111,500	Total liabilities and stockholders' equity	$111,500

QUESTIONS

1. What are the transformation processes that are performed by accounting information systems?
2. Assume that you are the owner of the small business described in the opening scenario. How could you use your checkbook as a way of keeping track of the company's transactions? Why would this not provide you with all the information you may need to run the business?
3. Explain what factors determine whether an event or transaction will be recognized as an input into the accounting system.
4. On January 20, the Gilbert Corporation enters into a contract to sell 100 dozen footballs to the University of California. The footballs are delivered on February 10 and February 15. The Gilbert Corporation receives full payment from the university on February 21. Which events are recognized in the accounting records of Gilbert and the University of California? Why?
5. What is a chart of accounts? How might a chart of accounts for Carl's Market differ from that of Ohman and Rattan, attorneys?
6. Explain to your good friend, who has no knowledge of accounting, the purpose of a ledger and a journal and how they are related.
7. Complete the following chart by entering either increases or decreases on the appropriate line:

	Ledger Side	
Accounts	*Left*	*Right*
Assets		
Liabilities		
Stockholders' equity		

8. You overheard one of your friends telling another person that all credits must be good because every time she deposits money in the bank, she gets a credit memo. Is her reasoning correct? If not, explain the meaning of *credit* in accounting.
9. Complete the following chart by entering either debit or credit on the appropriate line:

Accounts	*Increase*	*Decrease*
Accounts receivable		
Accounts payable		
Cash		
Inventory		
Wages payable		
Capital stock		

10. Why is it necessary to post journal entries to ledger accounts? What determines how often postings are made?
11. Complete the following chart by indicating whether each account is an asset, liability, or stockholders' equity account and its normal balance (either debit or credit):

Accounts	*Type of Account*	*Normal Balance*
Accounts payable		
Buildings		
Cash		
Taxes Payable		
Prepaid rent		
Land		
Capital stock		

12. Put the following six items into chronological order:
    a. Enter transaction in journal.
    b. Business event occurs.
    c. Prepare trial balance.
    d. Post entries to ledger.
    e. Balance ledger accounts.
    f. Prepare balance sheet.
13. After spending several hours doing her accounting homework, one of your accounting classmates was able to balance the trial balance. Convinced her homework must be correct, she went to bed. Should she be as confident as she is? Explain.
14. The debit and credit column totals of a trial balance are not equal. What are three possible causes of this problem?
15. Explain the four transactions that appear in the following T accounts:

Cash

1)	100,000	2)	40,000
		3)	5,000
		4)	10,000

Prepaid Insurance

3)	5,000		

Land

2)	60,000		

Bank Loan Payable

4)	10,000	2)	20,000

Capital Stock

		1)	100,000

EXERCISES

E2-1
Recognition of Inputs
LO 1

John Brown started his own legal practice on January 2 of the current year. Which of the following events and transactions would be recognized as an input of the accounting system for his business?

a. John invests $60,000 of his own money in exchange for capital stock of the law firm.
b. John receives $4,500 vacation pay from his previous law firm. He deposits the money in his own account.
c. John has a computer that he purchased with personal funds. He gives the computer to his new law firm.
d. The law firm purchases $3,000 of supplies to be paid in February. The supplies are received immediately.
e. The law firm purchases several items of office equipment for $18,000. These purchases are financed by a local bank. Because John's law firm is new, the bank insists that John personally guarantee the loan, which he does.

E2-2
Accounting Systems
LO 1

Identify the important pieces of information, such as customer number, that would be input into an accounting system for each of the following transactions:

a. You go to a convenience store and use your credit card to purchase gas.
b. Semiannual insurance on your car is due so you mail the insurance remittance advice and your check to the insurance company.
c. You drop off your rent check at the apartment manager's office on your way to school one morning.

E2-3
The Accounting Equation
LO 2

At the beginning of January of the current year, the Petini Corporation started out with total assets of $80,000. During January, the firm entered into a number of transactions. State whether each of the transactions increased total assets, decreased total assets, or had no effect on total assets. Also determine the amount of total assets at the end of January.

a. The firm purchased for cash office supplies at a total cost of $7,000.
b. The firm purchased for $12,000 a computer, laser printer, and CD reader for office use. It paid $4,000 in cash and borrowed the rest from a local bank.
c. The firm needed additional cash and found an investor who invested $80,000 in exchange for capital stock.
d. A business license that allowed the firm to operate within the city for the rest of the year was purchased for $500 cash.
e. A three-year business interruption insurance policy was purchased on account. The policy cost $7,200 and took effect immediately.
f. One of the owners of the business withdrew $500 of the original investment she had made.
g. The firm repaid the bank $1,000 of the amount owed from item (b).

E2-4
Analyzing Transactions
LO 2

The O'Hare Corporation entered into a number of transactions during the month. State the effect of each transaction on total assets, liabilities, and stockholders' equity. Use + for increase, − for decrease, and NE for no effect. If a transaction has the effect of both increasing and decreasing an item, use both a + and a − sign. Use the format of the table below, which has been completed for the first transaction.

Transaction	*Assets*	*Liabilities*	*Stockholders' Equity*
a	−	−	NE

a. O'Hare paid a liability.
b. The firm purchased some stationery on account.
c. The firm issued capital stock in exchange for some land.
d. The firm returned some of the stationery it purchased in item (b) because the firm's logo was shown incorrectly.
e. The firm distributed a cash dividend to one of its owners.
f. O'Hare purchased a building by paying cash and issuing a note payable.
g. O'Hare had an account payable to the Midway Co. The Midway Co. agreed to increase the payment period and take a note payable in exchange for the account payable.
h. O'Hare paid in advance for a year's rent.
i. O'Hare collected $1,000 on an account receivable from one of its customers.

E2-5
Economic Transactions and the Entity Assumption
LO 1, 2

Indicate whether the following transactions of the Main Construction Corporation would increase, decrease, or have no effect on the company's total assets, liabilities, and stockholders' equity. Use + for increase, − for decrease, and NE for no effect. It may be that in some cases none of the accounts is affected. Use the format of the table below, which has been completed for the first transaction.

Transaction	*Assets*	*Liabilities*	*Stockholders' Equity*
a	–	–	NE

Transactions

a. The firm purchased land for $200,000, $60,000 of which was paid in cash and a note payable signed for the balance.
b. The firm bought equipment for $60,000 on credit.
c. The firm paid a $15,000 liability.
d. The firm arranged for a $100,000 line of credit (the right to borrow funds as needed) from the bank. No funds have yet been borrowed.
e. One of the investors wanted to make an additional investment in the company and arranged an $80,000 personal bank loan.
f. The firm borrowed $65,000 on its line of credit.
g. The firm issued a $5,000 cash dividend to its stockholders.
h. The individual in item (e) invested the $80,000 in the company in exchange for additional capital stock.

E2-6 Analyzing Transactions
LO 3

In this chapter, we stated that in thinking about how to record transactions, you should go through this three-step process:

1. Determine the specific accounts that are affected by the transaction and whether they are asset, liability, or stockholders' equity accounts.
2. Decide whether each of these accounts is increased or decreased.
3. Make the appropriate debit and credit entries in the T accounts.

Analyze each of the following transactions using the three steps shown above. Example (a) has been done for you.

a. The Fazzi Corporation issued 1,000 shares of capital stock at a total price of $30,000.
b. The firm purchased equipment for $14,000 cash.
c. Inventory of $8,000 was purchased on account.
d. A month's rent of $4,000 was paid in advance.
e. Some of the equipment that was purchased in item (b), at a cost of $3,200, was sold at its cost for cash.
f. Accounts payable of $3,400 were paid.

Example (a):

1. This transaction affects Cash, an asset account, and Capital Stock, a stockholders' equity account.
2. Cash is increased by $30,000, and Capital Stock is increased by $30,000.
3. The T accounts:

Cash			*Capital Stock*		
a)	30,000			a)	30,000

E2-7 Recognition of Accounting Events
LO 1

Crystal Kingdom, owner of Crystal Kingdom's Funland, has asked you to review the following transactions. For each event, state whether the transaction should be recorded on the books of the company, and state why.

a. January 2: The firm places an order for three video games and two pinball machines at a cost of $1,300 each. The machines will be delivered next month.
b. January 3: Three days later, Funland sends a deposit of $2,000 for the machines.
c. February 1: The machines are delivered, and Funland receives an invoice for the balance.

d. February 10: As she does each business day, one of Crystal's daughters, Rainbow, goes to the local bank and exchanges $200 cash for the same amount of quarters.
e. February 12: The balance due on the machines is paid.
f. February 22: The demand to play video games has far surpassed anyone's expectations. As a result, Funland has negotiated a line of credit to expand the business. The line of credit allows Funland to borrow up to $100,000 as the funds are needed. As of this date, the line of credit has not been used.

E2-8
Analysis of the Accounting Equation
LO 2

You have obtained the following data from the Madonna Corporation as of December 31, 1995. However, certain figures were smeared by the duplicating machine, and you are to determine the missing figures.

Madonna Corporation	
Accounts payable	$ 35,000
Accounts receivable	?
Bank loan payable	7,000
Buildings	55,000
Cash	44,000
Inventory	34,800
Land	50,000
Licenses	1,000
Office supplies	1,400
Other assets	200
Prepaid insurance	3,600
Store furniture and fixtures	23,800
Total assets	255,800
Total liabilities	?
Total stockholders' equity	?

E2-9
Making Entries in T Accounts
LO 4

Enter the following transactions in the appropriate T accounts. Label each transaction with the date it occurred, and balance the T accounts.

a. February 1: Chen and Orlando started a software store and consulting service by issuing capital stock to themselves, for a total of $200,000 cash.
b. February 2: They rented a store and had to make a deposit of $2,000, which represented one month's rent. They will move in March.
c. February 10: Supplies of $8,000 were purchased on account.
d. February 15: A number of laptop and notebook computers were purchased for demonstration purposes. The cost was $12,500, of which $5,000 was paid in cash and the remainder borrowed from the bank. Use the account Bank Loan Payable.
e. February 22: The account payable that resulted from the purchase of supplies was paid.
f. February 26: The firm hired two students to work as part-time employees. Both students will begin work in the first week of March.

E2-10
Classification of Accounts and Debits and Credits
LO 4

For each of the following accounts, indicate whether the account is an asset, liability, or stockholders' equity account and whether the normal balance is a debit or credit. Arrange your answers in a table similar to the following:

Account	*Type of Account*	*Normal Balance*
a. Cash		
b. Inventory		
c. Wages payable		
d. Capital stock		

(continued)

Account	Type of Account	Normal Balance
e. Land		
f. Equipment		
g. Investment in ABC Corporation		
h. Patent		
i. Accounts receivable		
j. Accounts payable		
k. Advance fees received from client		

E2-11
The Retained Earnings Account
LO 2

Answer the following questions related to the Retained Earnings account:

a. Should Retained Earnings be classified as an asset, a liability, or a stockholders' equity account?
b. What is the normal balance in the Retained Earnings account? Can you describe a situation in which the Retained Earnings account would not have its normal balance? Describe that situation.
c. What activities cause Retained Earnings to increase and decrease?

E2-12
Journal Entries and Posting
LO 4

The Computer Assisted Drawing Corporation began business on March 1 of the current year. During the month, the firm entered into the following transactions:

a. March 1: Issued capital stock to various investors for $200,000.
b. March 2: Arranged a $75,000 cash loan from the local bank. The cash was received immediately.
c. March 10: Purchased a small building on a downtown corner for $125,000 cash.
d. March 16: Purchased various types of sophisticated computer equipment for $40,000 on account.
e. March 20: Placed an order for $2,000 of various office supplies, including stationery. All supplies will be received next month. However, the stationery store required that the firm pay in advance. Full payment was made.
f. March 25: Paid for equipment purchased on March 16.
g. March 30: Purchased a three-year comprehensive insurance policy for $2,400.

REQUIRED:

1. Make the required journal entries.
2. Create T accounts for each account, and post the journal entries to the ledger T accounts. Balance the ledger accounts.

E2-13
Understanding and Explaining Journal Entries
LO 4

a. State the most reasonable explanation for each of the following entries:

1. Cash	5,000	
Accounts Receivable		5,000
2. Accounts Payable	3,000	
Cash		3,000
3. Inventory	10,000	
Accounts Payable		10,000
4. Accounts Payable	2,000	
Notes Payable		2,000
5. Stockholders' Equity	1,000	
Cash		1,000

b. The following entries are missing information. Complete them with the most reasonable account names.

1. ________________	50,000	
Capital Stock		50,000

2. Loans Payable	1,000	
______________		1,000

3. ______________	12,000	
Accounts Receivable		12,000

E2-14
Trial Balance and Effect of Errors
LO 5

Which of the following posting errors would cause the debit and credit columns of the trial balance not to balance? Briefly explain your reasoning.

a. A receipt of cash from a payment on account was posted by debiting Cash for $2,500 and crediting Accounts Receivable for $25,000.
b. A purchase of inventory on account was posted by debiting Inventory for $1,000 and crediting Cash for $1,000.
c. When the following journal entry was posted, the debit to Accounts Payable was left out by mistake:

Accounts Payable	1,200	
Cash		1,200

d. The purchase of supplies for cash was posted as a debit to Cash and a credit to Supplies for $500, respectively.
e. When the following journal entry was posted, the debit to Cash was actually posted as a credit:

Cash	10,000	
Capital Stock		10,000

E2-15
Correcting Errors in the Trial Balance and Preparing a Balance Sheet
LO 5

The accountant for PEW is having trouble balancing the trial balance and asks your help. You have obtained the following trial balance as well as the additional data:

PEW
Trial Balance
December 31, 1995

	Debit	*Credit*
Cash	$ 5,000	
Marketable securities	1,500	
Inventory	15,000	
Office supplies	2,000	
Prepaid rent	2,000	
Land	20,000	
Buildings	45,000	
Other assets		$ 5,000
Bank loans payable		10,000
Accounts payable		6,320
Mortgages payable		30,000
Capital stock		45,900
	$90,500	$97,220

Additional data:

a. A purchase of marketable securities for $500 was not posted to the account.
b. A cash payment on account of $570 was posted to Accounts Payable as a debit of $750. The credit was correctly posted.
c. The Prepaid Rent account was balanced incorrectly and overstated by $200.

d. When office supplies were purchased for $100, a credit was posted in that amount to the Office Supplies account, as well as the credit to the Cash account.
e. Although the Capital Stock account was correctly balanced at $49,500, it was listed in the trial balance as $45,000.

REQUIRED:

1. Prepare a corrected trial balance.
2. Prepare a balance sheet.

PROBLEMS

P2-1 Accounting Systems
LO 1

The Northwest Passage is a small book store that sells outdoor books. The owner is in the process of implementing a computer-based accounting system.

a. What kinds of transactions should the new computer-based accounting system capture?
b. What data would be input for each transaction?
c. What financial accounting reports or statements should be produced by the accounting system?
d. What management accounting reports would the owner need to effectively manage the book store?
e. Assume that the manager would like a report that will identify books that have been in inventory an unusually long time so that those books can either be returned to their publishers or discounted. Design an appropriate report.

P2-2 Information for Decision Making
LO 1

Accounting information is essential in making economic decisions. For example, if a hospital is considering changing the price of a laboratory test, the following information would be required: labor costs, material and supply costs, equipment costs, and competitors' prices for the same services. For each of the following situations, identify the specific accounting information that would be required before making each decision.

a. A customer has just offered to purchase an expensive mountain bike from the owner of a bicycle shop. The offer is substantially less than the list price for the bicycle.
b. A commercial loan office at the community bank is evaluating a small business' loan application. The business has applied for a long-term loan so that the store-front can be remodeled.
c. You have just inherited $100,000 from your aunt's estate. Under the terms of the will you cannot spend the inheritance, but must invest it until you have graduated from college. A stockbroker suggested that you invest the entire sum in SUNTECK, a one-year-old alternative energy technology firm.
d. The vice-president of marketing for a pharmaceutical firm is preparing formal performance reports for all the regional sales managers so that one of the managers can be promoted to national sales manager.

P2-3 Recognition of Accounting Events
LO 1

The Notre Dame Company entered into the following business events during December of the current year:

a. The firm established a line of credit in the amount of $2 million with State National Bank. The firm paid a $40,000 commitment fee. Currently, the firm has not used any of the line.
b. The company entered into a purchase agreement with Middle East Oil, Ltd. Under this agreement Notre Dame will purchase over the next 12 months 100,000 barrels of oil at

$24 per barrel. Notre Dame anticipates placing the first order for 10,000 barrels within the next month.

c. The firm is in the process of moving its main office, and made a $15,000 downpayment on 50,000 square feet of office space in a building under construction. The building will be complete in about eight months, and Notre Dame expects to move in at that time. Monthly rental will be $7,500.
d. Notre Dame received a purchase order for 100,000 baseball caps, its main product. The caps will be delivered in early January of the next year.
e. The CFO of the Notre Dame Company resigned in a dispute with the president concerning the company's internal control procedures. The firm retained the search firm of Nelson and Ruggles to find a new CFO. Notre Dame gave Nelson and Ruggles a retainer of $5,000.
f. Notre Dame delivered 4,000 baseball caps ordered in early November when a purchase order was received from the South Bend Corporation.
g. The company completed negotiations with Atlantic Health Care to provide health care coverage for its employees. Under the agreement Notre Dame will pay $100 per month for each employee; the employee's contribution will depend on the number of dependents covered. The agreement goes into effect with the pay period beginning January 1 of the next year.

REQUIRED: Indicate for each of the above transactions whether the event would be recorded on Notre Dame's accounting records in December. State your reasons why or why not. If the event is not to be recorded in December, when should it be recorded?

P2-4
The Accounting Equation and Economic Transactions
LO 2

On December 31, 1994, the First In, First Out Hamburger Store had the following account balances:

Cash	+	*Loan Receivable*	+	*Supplies*	+	*Equipment*	=
$6,000		$4,000		$2,000		$10,000	

Accounts Payable	+	*Notes Payable*	+	*Stockholders' Equity*
$7,500		$3,000		$11,500

During January 1995, the following events occurred:

a. Supplies were purchased for $4,800, $2,000 on credit and the rest for cash.
b. The amount of $2,500 was collected on loans receivable.
c. One of the owners of the business contributed a new computer and CD at a value of $4,200 to the firm in exchange for capital stock (use the Equipment account).
d. One of the old computers was sold for its original cost of $1,700, of which $700 was received in cash and the remainder on account. (Use the Loan Receivable account.)
e. Accounts payable of $4,200 were paid.
f. An installment payment of $500 was made on the note payable.
g. The remainder due on the sale of the computer was collected.

REQUIRED: Prepare a chart similar to the one in Exhibit 2-4 on page 62 showing the accounts and their balances at December 31, 1994 as the first line. Use a separate line to show the effects of each transaction on the accounting equation. Total all columns after each transaction.

P2-5
Understanding Transactions
LO 2

The balance sheet of the Star Group at December 31, 1995 is shown below in equation form, followed by January transactions, whose effect on the accounting equation is also shown.

	Cash	+ Accounts Receivable	+ Supplies	+ Equipment	= Accounts Payable	+ Capital Stock	+ Retained Earnings
	$ 5,000	$8,000	$1,200	$17,000	$4,500	$20,000	$6,700
1.	+ 4,000	− 4,000					
	9,000	4,000	1,200	17,000	4,500	20,000	6,700
2.	− 2,000			+ 2,000			
	7,000	4,000	1,200	19,000	4,500	20,000	6,700
3.			− 500		− 500		
	7,000	4,000	700	19,000	4,000	20,000	6,700
4.	− 3,000				− 3,000		
	4,000	4,000	700	19,000	1,000	20,000	6,700
5.	+ 2,500			− 2,500			
	6,500	4,000	700	16,500	1,000	20,000	6,700
6.	+ 5,000					+ 5,000	
	$11,500	$4,000	$ 700	$16,500	$1,000	$25,000	$6,700

REQUIRED:

1. Describe the nature of each of the numbered transactions that would produce the effect shown on the table.
2. Determine the amount of net assets (assets minus liabilities or stockholders' equity) at the end of December and at the end of January after all the transactions have been recorded. How much have the net assets increased or decreased? Can you determine the reason for the change?

P2-6
Recording Transactions
LO 2

On January 2, 1995, Stuart DePino decided to start a business that performed acts at children's birthday parties. The business was called Children Are Fun. The following transactions occurred during the start-up month of January:

a. Stuart invested $70,000 cash in the business, plus toys he had personally purchased recently at a cost of $25,000, in exchange for capital stock. (Record the toys in the Toy Supplies account.)
b. The company leased a small store at an annual rental of $30,000, all of which was paid in advance.
c. Various items of equipment including racks, tables, and an electronic clown were purchased for $14,000; $5,000 was paid in cash, and the remainder was put on account.
d. Additional toys costing $22,000 were purchased on account.
e. The business obtained a $35,000 loan from a local bank.
f. $1,500 worth of toys purchased in transaction (d) arrived damaged. They were returned to the manufacturer, and the firm's account payable was decreased.
g. The remaining account payable from the purchase in transaction (d) was paid by making a $12,000 cash payment and converting the remainder to a note payable.
h. A $7,000 installment was paid on the bank loan.
i. The firm decided to replace the electronic clown it had purchased with a small robot. The clown, which cost $500, was sold for that amount of cash. The new robot was purchased for $3,200 cash.

REQUIRED: Prepare a chart similar to the one in Exhibit 2-4 on page 62 using the following accounts as column headings: Cash, Prepaid Rent, Toy Supplies, Store Equipment, Notes Payable, Accounts Payable, Bank Loans Payable, and Capital Stock. Show the effect of each transaction on the accounting equation. You do not have to give totals after each transaction.

P2-7
T Account Analysis
LO 4, 5

The T accounts for Melissa's Maternity Mart follow, reflecting all the transactions for November. The firm was organized on November 1 of the current year.

Cash

1)	100,000	3)	3,600
10)	2,000	4)	10,000
		5)	240
		9)	400

Accounts Receivable

7)	2,000	10)	2,000

Prepaid Insurance

3)	3,600		

License

5)	240		

Inventory

11)	5,000		

Office Supplies

6)	1,000		

Land

2)	20,000		

Buildings

2)	40,000		

Furniture and Fixtures

4)	10,000	7)	2,000
8)	3,500		

Accounts Payable

9)	400	6)	1,000
		11)	5,000

Mortgage Payable

		2)	60,000

Capital Stock

		1)	100,000
		8)	3,500

REQUIRED:

1. For each of the numbered transactions (1 through 11), make the appropriate journal entry, including a complete explanation of the transaction.
2. Determine the balances of the T accounts, and prepare a trial balance.

P2-8
Journal Entries, T Accounts, and Trial Balance (Alternative to P2-9)
LO 4, 5

Will Miller decided to go into CPA practice for himself after three years of experience with another firm. The following events occurred in September, 1995, the month he organized his business:

a. September 1: Will began his practice with $100,000. A local bank supplied a loan for half of the $100,000, and Will issued himself capital stock for the remaining half in exchange for cash.
b. September 3: Will rented a small office for his practice. In accordance with the rental agreement, he prepaid the first six months at $2,400 per month.
c. September 10: Various word processors, calculators, printers, and other office equipment were purchased for $17,500 on account from a local supplier. (Record all items in the Office Equipment account.)
d. September 14: A two-year liability insurance policy with a cost of $5,400 was purchased for cash.
e. September 18: One of the computers that cost $1,500 arrived damaged. Will returned it to his supplier and received a credit.
f. September 24: Various pieces of office furniture at a cost of $4,000 were purchased for cash.
g. September 29: The remainder of the balance on the purchase of office equipment was paid.
h. September 30: A part-time secretary was hired to begin work on October 1. Monthly wages will be $1,800.

REQUIRED:

1. Make the required journal entries.
2. Set up the required T accounts and post the entries to these accounts.
3. Prepare a trial balance at September 30, 1995.

P2-9
Journal Entries, Ledger Accounts, and Trial Balance (Alternative to P2-8)
LO 4, 5

Sumi Kuramoto decided to open a children's book and record store called The Reading Store. The business was organized in January, 1995, and during that month the following transactions occurred:

a. January 2: Sumi invested $75,000 of her own funds in the business and issued herself capital stock.
b. January 3: Five of her good friends each invested $10,000 in the business and received capital stock in exchange.
c. January 6: The business purchased land and a small building. The total cost was $200,000, of which 65% was applicable to the building and 35% to the land. A 20% down payment was made, and a bank loan was taken out for the remainder.
d. January 11: The building appeared too small for the anticipated operations. The firm contracted with a local builder to add a new wing at a cost of $70,000. The work will begin next month, and the first cash payment is due on February 15.
e. January 16: Sumi bought various books and records to be held for resale at a total cost of $100,000 on account.
f. January 19: Various pieces of store equipment and furniture were purchased for $55,000 cash.
g. January 23: The firm made a $20,000 payment on account for the inventory purchased on January 16.
h. January 24: Sumi decided that she could not use one of the pieces of furniture, which cost $2,200. She sold it to one of her friends on account for that amount.
i. January 29: Office supplies costing $1,200 were bought on account.
j. January 30: Her friend paid Sumi half of the amount due on furniture purchased on January 24.

Sumi decided to use the following account titles and account numbers in the business:

Cash	110	Building	122
Accounts Receivable	112	Store Equipment and Furniture	124
Inventory	115	Bank Loan Payable	230
Office Supplies	118	Accounts Payable	232
Land	120	Capital Stock	340

REQUIRED:

1. Make the required journal entries for January.
2. Post these entries to ledger accounts, using the running balance type form shown in Exhibit 2-8.
3. Prepare a trial balance at January 31, 1995.

P2-10
T Account Analysis
LO 4

Frankie's Fish Hatchery has the following T accounts in its general ledger. (Note that BB indicates beginning balance.)

Cash

BB	14,000	9/1	4,500
9/15	5,000	9/12	3,500
9/20	27,000	9/28	2,460
		9/29	2,662

Supplies

BB	19,200		
9/15	3,750		
9/29	2,662		

Livestock

BB	78,826		
9/10	6,240		

Accounts Payable

9/1	4,500	BB	6,927
9/28	2,460	9/15	3,750
		9/10	6,240

Other Assets

BB	5,600		

Mortgage Payable

9/12	3,500	BB	115,000
		9/25	28,850

Accounts Receivable

BB	10,290	9/15	5,000

Capital Stock

		BB	290,616
		9/20	27,000

Equipment

BB	52,650		
9/26	11,200		

Land

BB	72,100		
9/25	13,250		

Note Payable

		BB	32,700
		9/26	11,200

Building

BB	192,577		
9/25	15,600		

REQUIRED: Provide the following:

1. Ending balance of each account.
2. Beginning balance of assets.
3. Net change in the Cash account for September.
4. Net change in total assets for September.
5. Beginning balance of liabilities.
6. Ending balance of liabilities.
7. Amount of cash paid on mortgage.
8. Amount of net assets at the beginning of September.
9. Amount of net assets at the end of September.
10. Net change in owner's equity for September. Explain the relationship between the change in net assets during September and the change in the Capital Stock account.

P2-11
Preparation of Balance Sheet from Incomplete Data
LO 2

The accountant for Casey Consulting Incorporated attempted to prepare the firm's balance sheet at December 31, 1995, but was unable to complete the job. You have obtained the following data:

Casey Consulting Incorporated
Balance Sheet
December 31, 1995

Assets

Cash	$ 25,000
Commissions receivable	?
Office supplies	?
Prepaid insurance	?
Computer equipment	24,500
Land and building	1,000,000
Total assets	?

(continued)

Liabilities and Stockholders' Equity	
Liabilities	
Accounts payable	$ 46,000
Wages payable	7,400
Property taxes payable	?
Bank note payable	?
Mortgage payable	?
Total liabilities	?
Stockholders' equity	?
Total liabilities and stockholders' equity	$1,400,000

Additional data:

a. Insurance costs are $1,000 per month, and six months have been prepaid.
b. Property taxes owed equal 4% of the balance in the Land and Building account.
c. The balance in the Mortgage Payable account represents 20% of the cost of the Land and Buildings, and the Bank Note Payable represents 15% of the cost of the land and building.
d. All records pertaining to the Office Supplies account were lost. A count of the supplies at December 31, 1995 indicated that supplies that cost $4,500 remained on hand.
e. Computer equipment costing $1,000 was purchased but was never posted to the account.

REQUIRED: Prepare a corrected balance sheet at December 31, 1995.

DISCUSSION AND INTERPRETATION PROBLEMS

D2-1 Understanding Financial Statements

The following accounts have been taken from a recent annual report of Bausch & Lomb, Incorporated. Bausch & Lomb is a leading marketer of health-care and optical products. The accounts have been condensed to simplify the problem. All amounts are shown in thousands of dollars.

Accounts	*Amounts*
Accounts payable	$ 57,774
Accrued liabilities	137,304
Cash	4,670
Federal and foreign income taxes due	21,202
Goodwill	264,085
Inventories	225,914
Long-term debt	262,522
Other assets	103,364
Notes payable	228,166
Property, plant & equipment	351,021
Short-term investments	316,069
Stockholders' equity	721,378
Trade receivables	163,223

REQUIRED:

1. What accounts do you think are included in accrued liabilities? Why do you think that they are not included in accounts payable?
2. Goodwill is considered an asset. What do you think it represents and why is it considered an asset?

3. The firm has almost seventy times as much in short-term investments as they do in cash. Why do you think that this is the case? What does it say about the firm's cash management policies?
4. Assume that the firm used this data to prepare a trial balance. What would be the totals of the debit and credit columns?
5. Prepare a balance sheet from the above data. For purposes of this problem, assume that these figures are as of December 31, 19—.

D2-2
Financial Decision Case

Karen Short, one of your close friends, has decided to open a business that offers accounting and tax courses to teachers and school administrators. These courses are marketed to professional societies and meet the required continuing education requirement of these groups. During the first month of business, the following events occurred:

a. Karen invested $100,000, her entire savings, in the business in exchange for capital stock.
b. The firm, which is called Tax Help, negotiated a line of credit with the bank in the amount of $70,000. Currently, none of the line has been used.
c. After Karen met several times with a number of professional societies, two of them agreed to use Karen's services. In three months Tax Help will put on a seminar in Las Vegas. To obtain the business, Karen agreed to waive any required deposits.
d. The firm made a $6,000 down payment to the Great Sand Hotel for the use of its facilities for the seminar.
e. Karen contacted five associates who were professors at major universities, and they agreed to teach the classes for a fee of $3,000 a week. In order to show her good faith, she sent each of them $500.
f. During the month, Karen worked very hard putting together the tax course. By the end of the month, she had outlined the highlights of individual taxation in over 100 typed pages. She estimates that the purchase price of similar materials would be over $1,800.

Karen was extremely pleased with the progress of her business in the first month of its existence. However, when her accountant prepared a balance sheet, presented below, she became very confused, feeling that the statement did not tell the true story of the business activities during the month.

Tax Help
Balance Sheet
Janaury 31, 1995

Assets		*Stockholders' Equity*	
Cash	$ 91,500		
Deposits	8,500	Capital stock	$100,000
Total assets	$100,000	Total equity	$100,000

REQUIRED: Write a brief memo to Karen explaining how and why the accountant prepared the balance sheet. Be sure to explain which transactions were included and which were not and the reasons for their inclusion or omission. Also, be sure to explain to Karen the accounting concepts involved in this situation.

D2-3
Research Assignment

The chapter discussed what criteria an economic event must meet in order to be admitted into the accounting system. Other than accounting for salaries, benefits, training, and other related employee costs, accountants have not recognized the value and cost of human assets. A field of accounting called "human resource accounting" has developed which calls for giving accounting recognition to human assets. Obtain information from your library and/or other sources and answer the following questions:

a. Briefly describe "human resource accounting."
b. What are some of the more important concepts underlying "human resource accounting"?
c. Do you think that human resources should be considered an asset? Why or why not?

D2-4
Ethical Issues

After receiving a degree in entrepreneurship from a large midwestern university, R. J. News decided to open her own business to counsel students in their first job search. She invested $20,000 of her own funds and asked two of her friends to each invest $5,000 in the business. In addition, the firm was granted a $30,000 line of credit from the local bank. Within the month of opening her business, R. J. decided to purchase a new house for her personal use. Because she was short of funds for the required $15,000 downpayment, she had the firm draw down that amount from the bank line of credit. The $15,000 was first deposited in the firm's bank account, and then R. J. wrote herself a check in that amount from the firm's bank account. She recorded this part of the transaction by debiting Loan Receivables and crediting Cash. The $15,000 was then deposited in her own checking account. As R. J. was the sole owner of the business, she did not feel there was anything wrong with using the firm's funds to make the downpayment. She knew that eventually she would pay the $15,000 back, although she did not actually sign a note recognizing the loan.

REQUIRED: In your opinion, did R. J. do anything that was not ethical in using the $15,000 to make the downpayment on her personal residence? Explain your answer.

CHAPTER 3
MEASURING AND RECORDING INCOME STATEMENT TRANSACTIONS

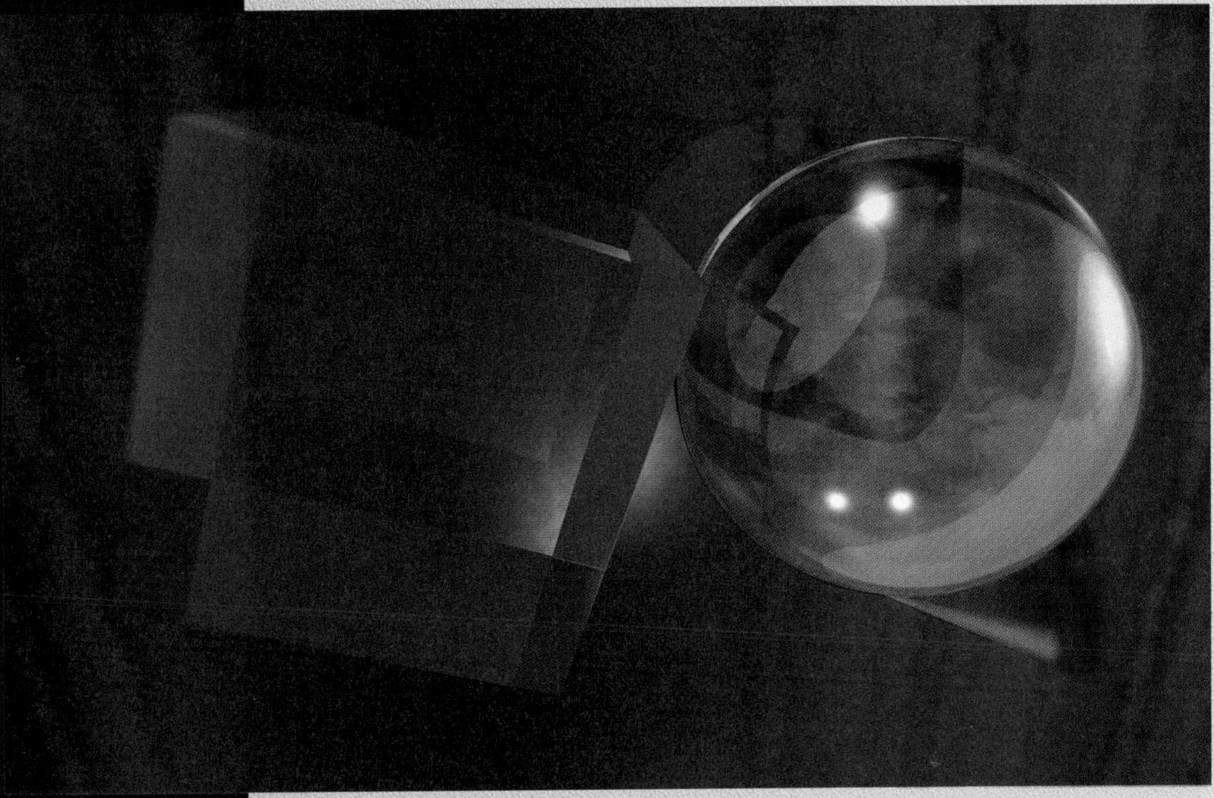

LEARNING OBJECTIVES

After studying this chapter, you should be able to:

1. Describe the transaction processing cycles within a merchandising firm.
2. Describe how accountants measure income including its components: revenues and expenses, gains and losses, and net income.
3. Explain the major concepts in determining net income, and distinguish between the accrual basis and the cash basis of accounting.
4. Describe the revenue and expense recognition principles and identify the different points in the earnings cycle at which revenue can be recognized.
5. Record income statement transactions.
6. Describe the relationships among the balance sheet, income statement, and retained earnings statement.

Scenario

Gary Frazer is chairman of the marketing department in the School of Business at a well known university. Gary's duties, which include faculty and student recruiting, fund raising, and professional and academic committee work, take him on many out-of-state trips. Because of these trips he has accumulated over one million miles on American Airlines' AAdvantage program.[1] Although he has redeemed some of these miles, he still has over 600,000 unused miles available for several free roundtrip first-class trips to Europe, Asia, and Hawaii.

As a marketing professor, Gary understands how these programs create customer loyalty. He was not surprised when other businesses began to imitate the frequent-flyer programs started by the airline industry. In fact, Gary also belongs to the frequent-user programs of a car rental firm, a hotel chain, and a long-distance phone company. However, Gary was astonished when he learned that something close to 5% of all passenger miles flown are due to free travel award programs.

Curious about how the airlines, as well as other firms with similar programs, accounted for these unused miles, Gary looked at the balance sheets and income statements of several airlines and was unable to find any reference to them. Although Gary had taken only two accounting courses many years ago during his graduate studies, he knew that the airlines must account for these outstanding miles somehow. After all, the airlines are obligated to provide free tickets in exchange for these miles. Somehow he felt that the value of these free tickets should be accounted for on the financial statements of the airlines. He was quite sure that these unredeemed tickets represented a dollar amount that might materially affect a firm's financial statements.

Gary decided to ask one of his colleagues, Dan Elnathan, a professor in the accounting department, for some help. Dan explained to Gary that this was really a question of revenue and expense recognition. That is, when the airlines sell a ticket for current travel, they were really selling two items, the current trip and the right to receive part of a future trip. Accountants are struggling with how to account for these items and whether there is some liability for this future travel that should be recognized at the point of the original sale. Dan told Gary that he would have one of his graduate students research the issue and give Gary a brief write-up about the correct accounting for these programs.

The ability of a business enterprise to earn a profit is essential to its continued operation. The profit earned by an enterprise is a yardstick that managers, investors, and creditors use to evaluate the future prospects of the business. Thus one of the most important parts of the accounting process is the recognition, measurement, and recording of those economic transactions that affect the firm's income. These concepts are the main focus of this chapter.

1. AAdvantage is a registered service mark of American Airlines, Inc.

The importance of proper revenue recognition and measurement of revenues and expenses cannot be overestimated. The opening scenario to this chapter briefly introduced the issue of how airlines should recognize and measure revenue related to frequent-flyer programs. Some have estimated that these programs could have a $2 billion effect on the collective financial statements of U.S. airlines. In other situations, the improper recognition and measurement of revenue is one of the primary causes of fraudulent financial reporting cases against publicly held corporations.

TRANSACTION PROCESSING CYCLES

Objective 1
Describe the transaction processing cycles within a merchandising firm.

The volume of revenue and expense transactions processed by modern businesses is tremendous. For example, try to visualize the number of times daily that individuals in the United States purchase gas using a credit card. Each of these purchases must be processed through the accounting information system so that revenue is properly measured and reported. To help achieve accurate measurement and reporting, the term *cycle* is used by accountants to describe the major processing steps that related transactions follow.

Accounting records summarize the financial effects of business events and transactions. These business events usually occur in predictable cycles. For example, when the White-Water Boat Company, introduced in Chapter 2, receives a purchase order from a customer, the order is checked for accuracy and the customer's credit status is verified. The ordered goods are then withdrawn from White-Water's inventory and are then packaged and shipped to the customer. The White-Water Boat Company bills the customer when the goods are shipped and eventually receives a payment from the customer. The sequence of related steps used to process a series of repetitive transactions is called a **transaction cycle.**

transaction cycle

There are two related transaction cycles at all retail firms, such as the White-Water Boat Company. (These firms, which sell goods to the public, are called *merchandising firms.*) These two transaction cycles are the *revenue cycle* and the *expenditure cycle.* The **revenue cycle** is the set of systems and procedures that process transactions related to the sale of goods and services. Thus, accounting transactions associated with the generation of revenue are recorded in the revenue cycle. In the White-Water Boat Company case, revenue-generating transactions are the sales of canoe and kayak supplies.

revenue cycle

The **expenditure cycle** consists of the systems and procedures used to process transactions related to the acquisition and use of goods and services. Again in the White-Water Boat case the purchase of canoe and kayak supplies from the manufacturers illustrates the expenditure cycle. These two transaction cycles are depicted in Exhibit 3-1 and discussed in detail next.

expenditure cycle

Revenue Cycle

Sales and cash receipt transactions are captured, processed, and recorded in the revenue cycle. The revenue cycle has three major subsystems that process transactions: the order entry system, the billing system, and the cash receipts system.

Order Entry System. Revenue transaction processing begins when a customer's order is entered into the order entry system. The *order entry system* validates the order, checks the customer's credit status, and checks inventory quantities to

Exhibit 3-1
Transaction Cycle Diagram

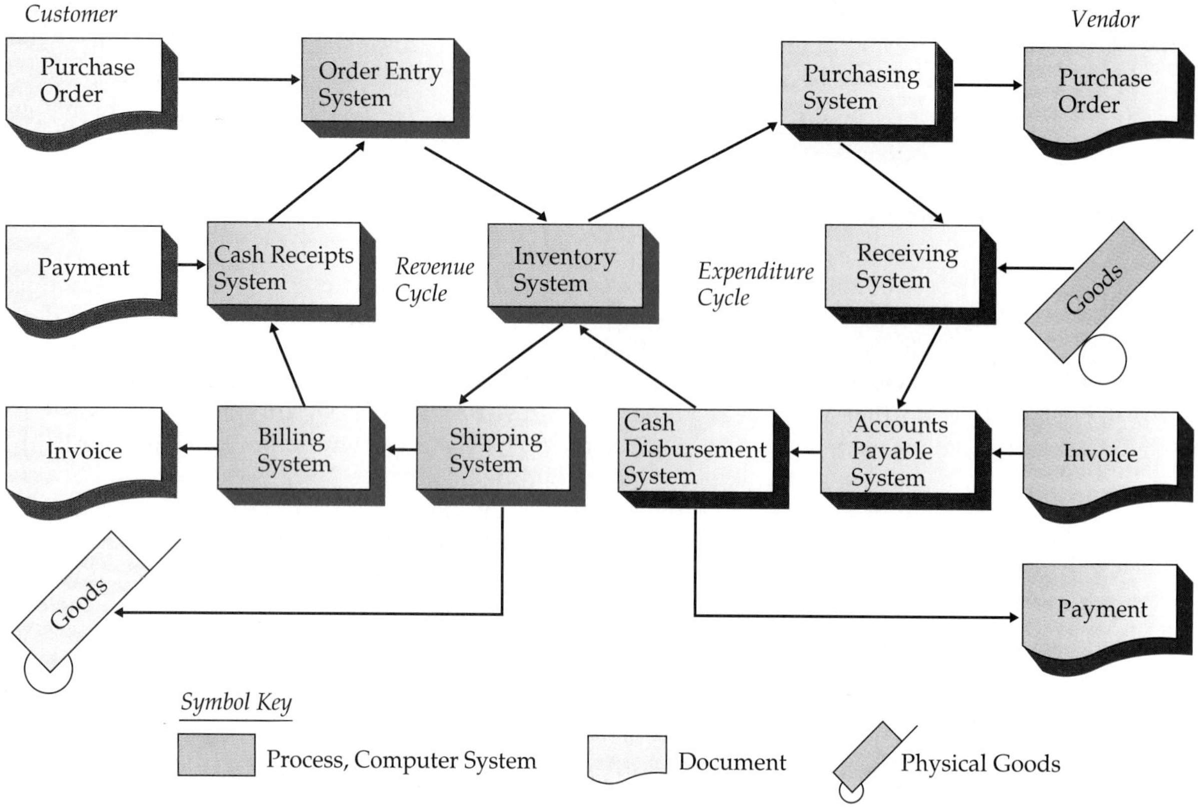

make sure sufficient inventory exists to fill the customer's order. Once the order has been approved, the ordered goods are withdrawn from inventory and are taken to shipping where they are packaged for shipment. A **shipping notice,** which is shown in Exhibit 3-2, informs the customer that the goods have been shipped.

shipping notice

Billing System. A copy of the shipping notice is input into the billing system. The *billing system* records the sales transaction and prepares and mails an invoice indicating how much the customer owes. A sample **invoice** is shown in Exhibit 3-3.

invoice

Cash Receipts System. The *cash receipts system* processes the cash received from cash and credit sales. These cash payments received by the seller (vendor) are processed through the purchaser's cash disbursement system (discussed as part of the expenditure cycle.) To illustrate, when the goods are received the customer compares what was received with a copy of the purchase order. This insures that what was ordered was, in fact, received. Any goods that are back ordered (that were not received) are noted. The goods received are compared with the invoice to make sure the invoice is correct and a check is then prepared and mailed to the seller. The customer's check is processed through the seller's cash receipts

Exhibit 3-2
Shipping Notice

Shipping Notice
Date 03/16/94

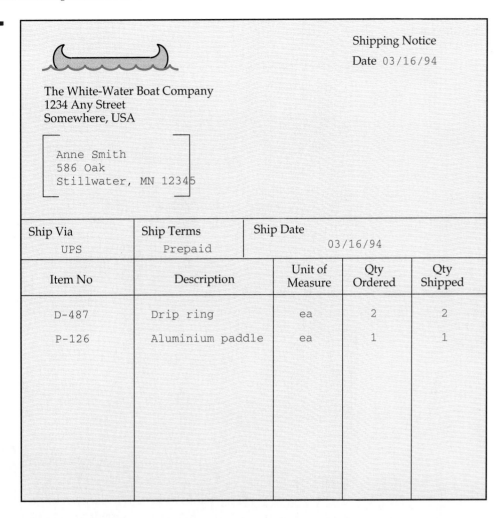

The White-Water Boat Company
1234 Any Street
Somewhere, USA

Anne Smith
586 Oak
Stillwater, MN 12345

Ship Via	Ship Terms	Ship Date
UPS	Prepaid	03/16/94

Item No	Description	Unit of Measure	Qty Ordered	Qty Shipped
D-487	Drip ring	ea	2	2
P-126	Aluminium paddle	ea	1	1

system which records the receipt of the check and reduces the customers outstanding account receivable by the amount received.

Expenditure Cycle

Transactions for the purchase of goods and services are recorded in the expenditure cycle. Like the revenue cycle, the expenditure cycle has three major subsystems: the purchasing system, the receiving system, and the cash disbursement system.

purchase order

Purchasing System. Whenever a firm needs to acquire goods or services, a purchase order is generated by the *purchasing system.* A **purchase order,** illustrated in Exhibit 3-4, is a formal external request for the purchase of goods or services from a vendor. The purchase order, after it has been reviewed and approved, is mailed to the selected vendor. The purchase order is processed by the vendor's revenue cycle systems described above.

Receiving System. Goods received by the purchaser are processed through the *receiving system.* During the process the goods received are counted and com-

Exhibit 3-3
Invoice

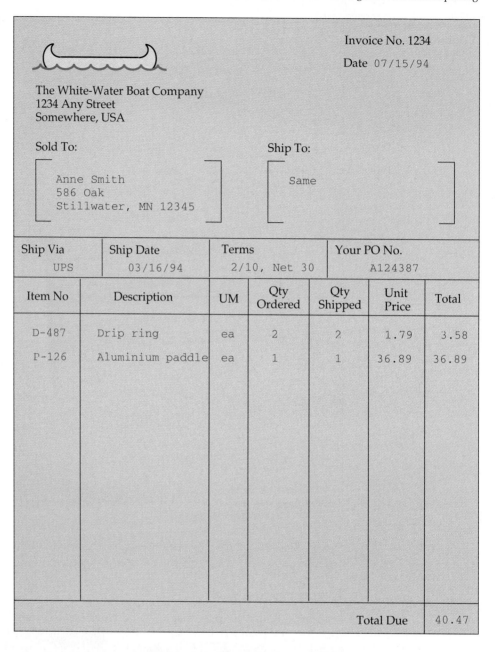

Invoice No. 1234
Date 07/15/94

The White-Water Boat Company
1234 Any Street
Somewhere, USA

Sold To:
Anne Smith
586 Oak
Stillwater, MN 12345

Ship To:
Same

Ship Via	Ship Date	Terms	Your PO No.
UPS	03/16/94	2/10, Net 30	A124387

Item No	Description	UM	Qty Ordered	Qty Shipped	Unit Price	Total
D-487	Drip ring	ea	2	2	1.79	3.58
P-126	Aluminium paddle	ea	1	1	36.89	36.89
					Total Due	40.47

pared with the goods ordered (as shown on the purchase order). This process ensures that no goods which have not been ordered are accepted and/or that back orders noted. A **receiving report** that shows the quantity of goods received is prepared and input to the accounts payable and inventory systems.

receiving report

Cash Disbursement System. The *cash disbursement system* is designed to insure that the liability associated with the purchase and receipt of merchandise is recorded in the purchaser's records and that required payment of the liability is made on a timely basis. Once copies of the original purchase order, the receiving report, and the vendor's invoice have been compared and differences reconciled,

Exhibit 3-4
Purchase Order

Purchase Order No. 4567
Date 03/20/94

The White-Water Boat Company
1234 Any Street
Somewhere, USA

Northwest Manufacturing
1011 S. 15th Street
Renton, WA 99352

Ship Via	Ship Date
UPS	03/31/94

Item No	Description	UM	Qty Ordered	Unit Price	Total
P-126	Aluminium paddle	ea	5	15.95	79.75
P-128	Oak paddle - 6 foot	ea	3	23.95	47.90
				Purchase Order Total	127.65

Authorized By ____ Date ____ Acct # ____

the obligation to pay for goods and services received is recorded as an account payable. At the appropriate time, the liability is paid, and the cash disbursement is recorded.

Revenue and expense transactions are recorded continually by the accounting systems within the revenue and expenditure cycles. These transactions are summarized periodically on an income statement which measures the net income or loss of the organization. The accounting concepts and procedures required to process and record the transactions are illustrated next.

MEASURING INCOME

Objective 2
Describe how accountants measure income including its components: revenues and expenses, gains and losses, and net income.

Net income often is measured by the increase in owners' equity that results from operations. However, accountants, economists, and the Internal Revenue Service all define and measure this increase differently. Income, for financial reporting purposes, generally is recognized when transactions have been completed. The accountant measures and records the transactions that occurred during the period and summarizes them on the income statement. The effect of these transactions, plus additional capital contributions, less withdrawals, is added to the historical cost of net assets at the beginning of the period to determine the historical cost of net assets at the end of the period. Recall from Chapter 2 that assets minus liabilities is equal to owners' equity, or net assets. This approach is illustrated in Exhibit 3-5.

Accountants prefer this method because measurements of completed transactions are objective and verifiable. Thus, the income statement that results from this process is a reliable financial statement that describes in detail the components of income: revenues and expenses, gains and losses, and net income.

Revenues and Expenses

The definitions of revenues and expenses were introduced in Chapter 1. To review, revenues are the prices of goods sold or services rendered by a firm to others in exchange for cash or other assets. Conversely, expenses are the dollar amounts of the resources used up by the firm during a particular period of time in the process of earning revenues. *Both revenues and expenses result from the firm's major operating activities, such as the sale of its goods or services during the period.*

receipts

In accounting, it is important to distinguish between receipts and revenues, as well as between expenditures and expenses. *Receipts* are not the same as revenues. **Receipts** are inflows of cash or other assets and do not always represent revenues. For example, a firm may receive cash from a bank loan or from a customer who is making a payment on account. The cash receipts from a bank loan represent an increase in an asset, Cash, and an increase in a liability, Bank Loans Payable. Similarly, the collection of a receivable represents a cash receipt which is the exchange of one asset, Cash, for another asset, Accounts Receivable. Neither is considered a revenue because stockholders' equity is not affected. On the other hand, receipts of cash or receivables that *do* represent revenues come primarily from products sold or services performed for customers.

expenditures

Expenditures are outflows of cash or other assets or increases in liabilities, and are not the same as expenses. For example, a firm may use its assets to purchase other assets such as buildings, inventories, or supplies. It may also use its cash to reduce liabilities by paying off a bank loan. Such expenditures do not affect stockholders' equity. If, however, an expenditure is made to produce revenues in the current period and does not provide for future economic benefits, it is an expense that reduces the stockholders' equity account, Retained Earnings.

Gains and Losses

gains
losses

Gains are increases in equity (net assets) from activities other than revenues and investments by owners of the firm during a period. Likewise, **losses** are decreases in equity (net assets) from activities other than expenses or distributions to owners affecting the firm during the period. Recall that revenues and expenses are

Exhibit 3-5
Income Measurement

Historical Cost Net Assets Beginning of the Period	±	Income Statement Transactions During the Period	±	Capital Contributions Withdrawals	=	Historical Cost Net Assets End of the Period

directly related to producing and selling goods and services. Gains and losses, however, are not. The sale of an asset, for example a building[2] that was purchased by an enterprise to house the operations of a business, is an example of a transaction that might result in a gain or loss.

For example, assume the Carson Corporation sold some marketable securities at an amount greater than their cost. The securities originally were purchased for $1,800 and were sold for $2,500 cash. The Carson Corporation records this transaction by increasing the asset, Cash, by $2,500, decreasing the asset, Marketable Securities, by $1,800, and recording a Gain on Sale of Marketable Securities for the difference of $700. This gain on sale represents an increase in retained earnings, because the firm received more assets than it gave up. Note that only the net gain of $700 is recorded in retained earnings. That is, the firm does not show revenues of $2,500 and expenses of $1,800 in the way that it does when selling goods and services related to its primary business activities.

Net Income

net income (loss)

Net income or **loss** is the difference between the total of revenues and gains and the total of expenses and losses of a period. Net income results when revenues and gains exceed expenses and losses. A net loss results when expenses and losses exceed revenues and gains. Net income causes an increase in the firm's net assets (owners' equity) during the period, whereas a net loss causes a decrease in the firm's net assets during the period.

Dividends

dividends

Corporations often pay dividends to stockholders. **Dividends** are a return to the stockholders of some of the assets that have increased because of the profits earned. Therefore, dividends generally can be issued only if there is a positive balance in Retained Earnings. If a dividend were issued when there was a negative balance in Retained Earnings (called a *deficit*), the firm would be returning the corporation's original capital to the stockholders. These are called *liquidating dividends* and are issued only in very rare circumstances.

Although dividends can be issued in many forms, cash dividends are the most common. Remember that dividends are not expenses but rather a distribution of assets resulting from the corporation's accumulated profits. Therefore, dividends do not appear on the income statement, but instead are a direct deduction from Retained Earnings on the retained earnings statement.

2. Buildings are not generally purchased by firms, except real estate companies, for immediate resale to outsiders.

MAJOR CONCEPTS RELATED TO DETERMINING INCOME

Objective 3
Explain the major concepts in determining net income, and distinguish between the accrual basis and the cash basis of accounting.

Accountants have developed a number of concepts and conventions to help determine net income. The most important concepts include the time period assumption, the matching convention, the accrual basis of accounting, and revenue and expense recognition.

Time Period Assumption

time period assumption

interim statements

Division of the enterprise's life span into accounting periods is called the **time period assumption.** Users need timely information about an enterprise's financial condition and performance to make informed decisions. Thus the enterprise's life span is divided into time periods, which can be as short as a month or a quarter. At a minimum, firms prepare annual financial statements. Publicly held corporations are required to issue quarterly financial statements, called **interim statements.** Most firms also prepare monthly financial statements for internal purposes.

The Matching Convention

matching convention

The matching convention is the concept that accountants use to guide them in determining the net income for an accounting period. The **matching convention** simply states that the expenses incurred in one period to earn the revenues of that period should be offset against those revenues. Revenues are determined in accordance with revenue recognition principles, and the expenses incurred in earning those revenues during the period are matched with them. The accrual basis of accounting has been developed to provide the best matching of expenses with revenues and the most useful income figure. This is considered to be the generally accepted method of accounting.

Accrual Basis Versus Cash Basis of Accounting

accrual basis of accounting

cash basis of accounting

Accounting information can be presented on either an accrual basis or a cash basis. When the **accrual basis of accounting** is used, revenues, expenses, and other changes in assets, liabilities, and owners' equity are accounted for in the period in which the economic event takes place and not necessarily when the cash inflows and outflows take place. When using the **cash basis of accounting,** revenues and expenses are not recognized until cash is received or paid.

Accrual Basis. As previously noted, the best matching of revenues and expenses takes place when the accrual basis of accounting is used. This means that the financial effects of transactions and economic events are recognized by the enterprise when they occur, rather than when the actual cash is received or paid by the enterprise. For example, sales are recognized as revenues when goods are sold, and services are recognized as revenues when the services are performed. When sales are made or services performed, there is a corresponding right to receive payment regardless of when the cash is actually collected. Thus, a sale on account (that is, a sale for which payment is to be made later) is recognized in the same manner as a cash sale. The only difference is that Accounts Receivable rather than Cash is increased or debited at the time of sale. When the cash from the sale on account is collected, no revenue is recognized. The cash collection is just an exchange of one asset, Accounts Receivable, for another asset,

Cash. The total amount of assets remains the same. The revenue and asset increases were properly recognized at the time the sale took place.

No revenue is recognized under the accrual basis of accounting when cash is received before the actual sale takes place or the service is rendered. Instead, a liability to perform a future service or to deliver a product is recognized at the time of the cash receipt. This liability is usually referred to as an *unearned revenue.* Revenue is recognized and the corresponding liability is decreased when the service is finally rendered or the sale is made. The entries associated with this particular event will be discussed in the next chapter.

Expenses are recognized in a similar manner. That is, expenses are considered to be incurred when the goods or services are consumed by the enterprise, not necessarily when the cash outflow takes place. For example, the Carson Corporation records, as a June expense, the salaries earned by its employees in that month, even though those salaries may not be paid until early July. This is accomplished by recording a liability, Salaries Payable, in June. When June's salaries are paid in July, no expense is recognized. Both Salaries Payable and Cash are reduced at that time, but no expense is involved. The decrease in the firm's net assets and the corresponding expense were recorded in June.

Cash is paid at the same time the expense is incurred in many cases. For example, plumbing repairs may be paid for when the services are rendered. In this case, Repairs and Maintenance Expense is recorded when the cash is paid. However, it is not the payment of cash that triggers the recognition of the expense. The expense is recognized because the plumbing services were received and an obligation to pay was incurred. Finally, no expense is recognized if cash is paid before the expense is incurred. For example, if a firm prepays its June rent in May, the prepayment is considered an asset in May and is not considered an expense until June, when the service has been received.

Cash Basis. Revenue is recognized when cash is received, and an expense is recognized when cash is paid under the cash basis of accounting. Consequently, the cash basis of accounting does not properly match revenues and expenses because the recognition of revenue and expense is contingent upon the timing of cash receipts and disbursements. The expenses of one period could be matched against the sales or services of another period when the timing of the recognition is determined by cash payments and receipts. The cash basis of accounting is not a generally accepted accounting principle for external financial reporting purposes. However, many professionals, such as doctors and lawyers, who prepare financial statements solely for their own use, use the cash basis to simplify their record keeping. In addition, most individuals use the cash basis of accounting for their personal affairs and to determine their taxable income.

An Example of the Cash Versus the Accrual Basis of Accounting. An example of the difference between the accrual and the cash basis of accounting is presented in Exhibit 3-6. This table shows how ten different transactions for the month of May affect accrual basis and cash basis income. As the exhibit shows, total accrual basis revenue is equal to the sum of May cash sales and sales on account. Total accrual basis expenses during the period are equal to the sum of those incurred and paid for in cash during May, and the expenses incurred on credit during the month. Cash basis net income is solely a function of the timing of cash receipts and payments. The accrual basis of accounting is used throughout the remainder of this book unless otherwise specified.

Exhibit 3-6
Comparison of Cash and Accrual Basis

Transactions in May		*Revenue/Expense Amounts Recognized in May* — *Cash Basis*	*Accrual Basis*
1. Cash sales during May	$10,000	$10,000	$10,000
2. Credit sales during May	12,000		12,000
3. Cash collected from May's credit sales	4,000	4,000	
4. Cash collected from April's credit sales	5,000	5,000	
5. Cash deposit received in May for a sale in June	1,000	1,000	
Total revenues		$20,000	$22,000
6. Cash expenses incurred and paid in May	8,000	$ 8,000	$ 8,000
7. Expenses incurred on account in May	7,000		7,000
8. Cash paid on May's expense incurred on account	4,000	4,000	
9. Cash paid in May on April's expenses incurred on account	3,000	3,000	
10. Insurance expense effective June 1 paid on May 17	2,000	2,000	
Total expenses		$17,000	$15,000
Net income		$ 3,000	$ 7,000

REVENUE AND EXPENSE RECOGNITION

Objective 4
Describe the revenue and expense recognition principles and identify the different points in the earnings cycle at which revenue can be recognized.

Although the accrual basis of accounting may seem like a straightforward concept, it has caused many controversies. The opening scenario describing accounting issues for frequent-flyer programs is an example of such a controversy. Other examples of controversies that have arisen over revenue and expense recognition include franchise fees and land sales.

realization principle

Accountants follow the **realization principle** to determine when revenue should be recognized. In short, this principle states that revenue is earned and, therefore, should be recognized when:

1. The earnings process is essentially complete, and
2. There is objective evidence as to the exchange or sales price.

These two requirements can be met at different points in the earnings cycle, depending on a firm's particular business and industry. Exhibit 3-7 depicts the different points at which these events may occur. The earnings process is continuous, however, and for most firms it is difficult to identify the exact point where the earnings process is complete. At each point in the process, some earnings take place as the firm adds value to the products before their actual sale. The White-Water Boat Company provides a good example of this problem. Assume that Kim purchases kayak covers for $10 each. The kayak covers are eventually sold for $25. At what point should Kim recognize the $15 earned from the sale of the kayak covers? Another way of looking at the issue is to ask, "When should the value of the kayak covers be increased from their historical cost of $10 to their sales price of $25?"

Exhibit 3-7
Earnings Cycle

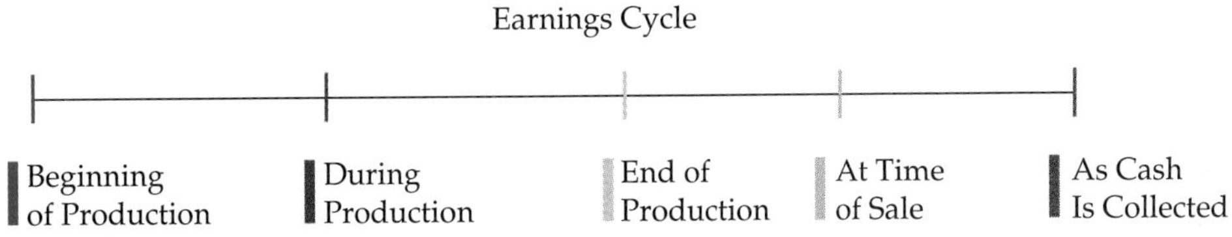

Sale as the Point of Revenue Recognition

The application of the revenue realization principle leads to the conclusion that the point of sale is usually the most realistic point at which to recognize revenue. Thus, in the White-Water Boat Company example, revenue would be recognized when the canoe and kayak supplies are sold. There are two reasons for this. First, at this point an actual exchange takes place which provides objective evidence of the amount of revenue actually realized. That is, the transaction has been completed, and the sale price is known with certainty. Second, most accountants feel that the earnings process is not complete until an actual sale is made. The sale, therefore, represents the culmination of the earnings process; thus revenue should not be recognized before this point. Consequently, the sale is considered to be the critical event in the earnings process.

For a service firm, revenues are normally considered earned when the service has been performed. A firm also earns revenues by allowing others to use its assets. Revenues from these sources include interest, rents, and royalties and are considered to be earned as time passes or as the assets are used. Finally, gains or losses from the disposal of other assets are recognized at the date of sale.

Alternative Revenue Recognition Methods

The diagram presented in Exhibit 3-7 illustrates that there are other times when revenue recognition can take place. Alternative revenue recognition methods are used when industry characteristics make it reasonable to recognize revenue at a time other than the sale. Revenue recognition can take place during production, at the end of production but prior to sale, or delayed until the cash is received. The percentage of completion, the completion of production, and the installment methods are three examples of alternative revenue recognition methods.

Percentage of Completion. Large-scale construction projects can take several years to complete. The primary issue faced by accountants is whether to delay recognizing the revenue from the project until it is complete or to recognize a portion of the revenue in each of the years it takes to complete the project. In the **completed-contract method,** all of the revenue earned from the contract is recognized in the year that the project is 100% completed.

completed-contract method

percentage-of-completion method

The **percentage-of-completion method** is an alternative revenue recognition method. This method recognizes revenue during construction in proportion to the amount of work completed on the project; all revenue from the project is recognized by the end of the project. The percentage-of-completion method should be used only when reasonable estimates of construction progress and future costs can be made because of the reliability principle. This method is widely used by construction companies because these estimates can be made in most situations.

Completion of Production. Revenue recognition occurs in some situations when the production cycle is complete and before a sale takes place. These situations occur when indistinguishable goods are sold in large, well-developed markets. Examples include certain agricultural products, such as wheat, and precious metals. Because the market can absorb all of the production of these products, a sale is ensured at harvest or mining. Further, an objective price can be obtained from the marketplace. Because the sale is ensured, the earnings process is considered complete at the end of production rather than at the point of sale.

Installment Basis. In a few situations, accountants will delay the recognition of revenue until the cash is collected from the sale. These installment sales are long-term payment plans where the buyer makes a relatively low downpayment and the payments are spread over a number of years. In the 1960's and 1970's many companies, such as land development firms, recognized all the revenue from their sales at the time of sale but only collected a small portion of the receivable before the buyer defaulted on the arrangement. As a result, accountants required that the installment method of accounting be used in these special circumstances. Under the installment method, revenues are recognized in proportion to the cash collected. This method is used infrequently, and only when there is a great deal of uncertainty about the collectability of the receivable.

Expense Recognition

Expense recognition is the other essential ingredient of the matching convention. With the accrual basis of accounting, expenses are recognized when they are incurred and matched against the corresponding revenues. This matching is accomplished by relating the expense to either (1) a particular product sold or service rendered or (2) a particular time period in which the revenue is recognized.

Some expenses can be related directly to the product the firm sells or the service it renders. Cost of goods sold is probably the most obvious example. Inventory costs are accumulated in the asset account Inventory. These costs are written off as expenses to Cost of Goods Sold when the merchandise is sold. Sales commissions are another example of an expense that is matched against revenues as the revenues are earned. This direct matching occurs because the amount of the commission is a direct function of the amount of the sale.

period expenses

Many expenses of a business cannot be directly related to a product or service. These expenses, called **period expenses,** are matched against revenues in the period during which the expenses are incurred. Most selling expenses and general and administrative expenses are period expenses. Examples of period expenses include insurance, rent, and salaries other than direct commissions.

RECORDING INCOME STATEMENT TRANSACTIONS

Objective 5
Record income statement transactions.

This section illustrates the proper recording of income statement transactions. Following the pattern of Chapter 2, we will first review the debit and credit rules related to income statement transactions, and then illustrate the actual journal entries. Finally, income statement transactions for The White-Water Boat Company will be analyzed.

Understanding Debit and Credit Rules

The debit and credit rules for income statement transactions are based on the accounting equation and the definition of revenues and expenses. Remember that the accounting equation is

$$\text{Assets} = \text{Liabilities} + \text{Stockholders' Equity}$$

Because stockholders' equity can be classified into two major components, capital stock and retained earnings, the accounting equation can therefore be rewritten as:

$$\text{Assets} = \text{Liabilities} + \text{Capital Stock} + \text{Retained Earnings}$$

One way to interpret this equation is to say that there are several sources of assets: creditors (liabilities), investors (capital stock), and the business itself through profitable operations (retained earnings). Thus, retained earnings represent the increases in net assets contributed by the profitable operations of the business after all dividends have been deducted. Corporations must maintain separate accounts for retained earnings and capital stock because, in most states, dividends cannot exceed the cumulative earnings of the business.

These concepts can be summarized by successively expanding the accounting equation, as shown below. The essential point to remember is how income statement accounts fit into the overall accounting equation. These accounts are summarized through changes in retained earnings and corresponding changes in the net assets (assets minus liabilities) of the firm.

The Expanded Accounting Equation

Assets = Liabilities + Stockholders' Equity

Assets = Liabilities + Capital Stock + Retained Earnings

Assets = Liabilities + Capital Stock + Retained Earnings, beginning of period + Net Income − Dividends

Net Income = Revenues + Gains − Expenses − Losses

Assets = Liabilities + Capital Stock + Retained Earnings, beginning of period + Revenues + Gains − Expenses − Losses − Dividends

Actually, all income statement transactions can be directly recorded in the retained earnings account. However, it would be very difficult to determine the dollar amounts of separate revenue and expense items such as sales and cost of goods sold if this were done. Therefore, accountants capture this essential information in separate revenue and expense accounts during the period. At the end of the period, the net effect of the transactions recorded in the revenue and expense accounts is transferred to the retained earnings account. The separate revenue and expense accounts often are referred to as **nominal** or **temporary accounts** because they are only used during the period and are zeroed at the end of each period. In contrast, balance sheet accounts, including Retained Earnings, often are referred to as **real** or **permanent accounts,** because they maintain a running balance that extends beyond the accounting period.

nominal (temporary) accounts

real (permanent) accounts

The rules for revenue and expense accounts follow the same rules as those for the retained earnings account, which is part of stockholders' equity. These rules are illustrated on the following page.

Debit/Credit Rules for Revenue and Expense Accounts

Retained Earnings

Decrease Debit	Increase Credit

Any Expense Account

Increase Debit Normal Balance: Debit	Decrease Credit

Any Revenue Account

Decrease Debit	Increase Credit Normal Balance: Credit

These rules are interpreted as follows:

1. Revenues represent increases in retained earnings. Increases in retained earnings are recorded as credits on the right side of the account ledger. Therefore, increases in revenues are recorded as credits on the right side of the revenue account.
2. Expenses represent decreases in retained earnings. Decreases in retained earnings are recorded as debits on the left side of the account. Therefore, because an increase in an expense represents a decrease in retained earnings, these increases are recorded as debits on the left side of expense accounts.

Journal Entries

Journal entry rules for income statement accounts parallel the rules for balance sheet transactions. Debits are recorded first at the left margin of the journal, and credits are indented slightly. To illustrate how revenue and expense transactions are recorded, assume that a firm enters into the following eight transactions. The appropriate journal entry is prepared after each transaction. For simplicity, the transaction number is entered into the date column, and the reference column is not used since the transaction has not yet been posted.

1. During the month, the firm made sales of $20,000, including $5,000 on account and $15,000 for cash. The summary journal entry for the month is:

Date	*Account Title*	*Ref*	*Debit*	*Credit*
1	Cash		15,000	
	Accounts Receivable		5,000	
	Sales			20,000
	To record sales for cash and on account.			

The increase in Sales is recorded as a credit because it represents an increase in retained earnings. The increases in Cash and Accounts Receivable are recorded as debits.

2. The firm determines that the cost of inventory sold in transaction 1 is $14,000. The journal entry is:

Date	*Account Title*	*Ref*	*Debit*	*Credit*
2	Cost of Goods Sold		14,000	
	Inventory			14,000
	To record the cost of goods sold.			

The increase in the expense, Cost of Goods Sold, is a decrease in retained earnings and is recorded as a debit. The decrease in Inventory is a decrease in an asset account and is recorded as a credit.

3. The firm's employees earned salaries of $15,000 but will not be paid until next week. The journal entry is:

Date	*Account Title*	*Ref*	*Debit*	*Credit*
3	Salaries Expense		15,000	
	Salaries Payable			15,000
	To record salaries expense incurred but not yet paid.			

Again, the increase in the expense, Salaries, is a decrease in retained earnings; thus it is recorded as a debit. The increase in the liability account Salaries Payable is recorded as a credit.

4. The firm collected $1,000 of the sales made on account in transaction 1. The journal entry is:

Date	*Account Title*	*Ref*	*Debit*	*Credit*
4	Cash		1,000	
	Accounts Receivable			1,000
	To record the collection of accounts receivable.			

This transaction does not involve the recognition of revenue. It is the collection of a receivable that was generated from the sale recorded in transaction 1 and is an exchange of one asset, Cash, for another asset, Accounts Receivable. It is presented to point out once again that revenue and expense recognition is not necessarily tied to cash receipts and disbursements.

5. Expenses of $500 for repairs and maintenance were incurred and immediately paid in cash. The journal entry is:

Date	*Account Title*	*Ref*	*Debit*	*Credit*
5	Repairs and Maintenance Expense		500	
	Cash			500
	To record payment of $500 in repairs and maintenance expense.			

This transaction illustrates the payment of an expense in cash rather than the incurrence of a liability. The increase in Repairs and Maintenance Expense decreases retained earnings and is recorded as a debit. The decrease in Cash is recorded as a credit.

6. The firm paid $15,000 of salaries owed from transaction 3. The journal entry is:

Date	*Account Title*	*Ref*	*Debit*	*Credit*
6	Salaries Payable		15,000	
	Cash			15,000
	To record payment of salaries.			

This transaction does not involve the recognition of an expense. It is the payment of salaries that resulted from the recognition of salaries payable in transaction 3. It is presented to point out once more that revenue and expense recognition is not necessarily tied to cash receipts and disbursements.

7. The firm sold some marketable securities for $1,000 cash that it had purchased for $700 in a prior year. The journal entry is:

Date	*Account Title*	*Ref*	*Debit*	*Credit*
7	Cash		1,000	
	Marketable Securities			700
	Gain on Sale of Marketable Securities			300
	To record gain on sale of marketable securities.			

This transaction shows how to record a gain or a loss. This transaction is recorded net; that is, a revenue of $1,000 and an expense of $700 are not shown. Only the net gain of $300 is shown in the account Gain on Sale of Marketable Securities. This gain represents an increase in retained earnings and therefore is a credit. Conversely, had the sale resulted in a loss the account Loss on Sale of Marketable Securities would have been debited.

8. The firm declares and pays a $5,000 dividend. The journal entry is:

Date	*Account Title*	*Ref*	*Debit*	*Credit*
8	Retained Earnings		5,000	
	Cash			5,000
	To record the declaration and payment of a $5,000 cash dividend.			

The declaration and payment of the cash dividend is recorded directly as a reduction of retained earnings and does not represent an expense to the firm. If the firm desired, the dividend could be debited to a dividends declared account. If this is done, the amount must eventually be transferred to retained earnings as a debit.

In reality, dividends often are declared several weeks prior to their payment. Either the Retained Earnings account or the Dividends Declared account is debited and the liability account, Dividends Payable, is credited at the time of the declaration in this case. When the dividend is paid, dividends payable is debited and cash is credited.

Transactions for The White-Water Boat Company

To illustrate further how to record income statement transactions, let us examine transactions for The White-Water Boat Company's first month of actual operations. Remember that the company was organized in January, 1995 but did not record any sales until March, 1995. The trial balance as of February 28, 1995, developed in Chapter 2, is reproduced in Exhibit 3-8. March transactions are recorded in the general journal, shown in Exhibit 3-9. After the journal entries have been posted to the appropriate accounts, the resulting T accounts are shown in Exhibit 3-10. Finally, the new trial balance as of March 31 is shown in Exhibit 3-11.

Exhibit 3-8

The White Water Boat Company Trial Balance February 28, 1995		
	Debit	*Credit*
Cash	$11,000	
Accounts Receivable	600	
Inventory	9,000	
Office Supplies	2,000	
Prepaid Insurance	1,200	
License	200	
Land	5,000	
Office Equipment	9,900	
Buildings	10,000	
Accounts Payable		$ 4,900
Bank Loan Payable		4,000
Capital Stock		40,000
Totals	$48,900	$48,900

Transactions for the month of March were as follows:

- March 2: The company placed an advertisement in a white-water magazine. A bill of $300, payable within the month, was received from the publisher.
- March 15: Sales of canoe and kayak supplies and accessories for the first half of March totaled $6,000, of which $2,000 was cash and $4,000 was on account.
- March 15: The total cost of the supplies and accessories sold during the first half of the month was $3,500.
- March 16: Salaries of $500 were paid in cash on March 16.
- March 20: The firm made another purchase of inventory of $10,000 on account.
- March 23: Accounts receivable of $3,000 were collected.
- March 24: Repairs and maintenance expense of $60 was paid in cash.
- March 24: The firm paid a utility bill of $100 for the month of March.
- March 29: Accounts payable of $8,000 were paid.
- March 31: Sales of canoe and kayak supplies and accessories for the second half of the month totaled $10,000, of which $7,000 was for cash and $3,000 was on account.
- March 31: The total cost of the supplies and accessories sold during the last half of the month was $6,000.

Two points need to be made about this example:

1. The journal entries represent summary transactions for the month. In practice, journal entries are made daily to record the transactions as they occur. In this example, sales were recorded only twice a month, rather than on a day-to-day basis, to simplify the example.
2. The trial balance as of March 31, 1995 (Exhibit 3-11) illustrates the manner in which the accounts should be listed. Note that the balance sheet accounts (assets, liabilities, and stockholders' equity) are listed first, followed by the income statement accounts (revenues and expense accounts).

Exhibit 3-9

The White-Water Boat Company
General Journal

Date	Account Title	Ref.	Debit	Credit
1995				
March 2	Advertising Expense	605	300	
	Accounts Payable	201		300
	To record advertising expense.			
15	Cash	101	2,000	
	Accounts Receivable	106	4,000	
	Sales	401		6,000
	To record sales during the first half of March.			
15	Cost of Goods Sold	500	3,500	
	Inventory	110		3,500
	To record cost of goods sold during first half of March.			
16	Salaries Expense	601	500	
	Cash	101		500
	To record salaries expense for the first half of March.			
20	Inventory	110	10,000	
	Accounts Payable	201		10,000
	To record purchase of inventory on account.			
23	Cash	101	3,000	
	Accounts Receivable	106		3,000
	To record collection of accounts receivable.			
24	Repairs and Maintenance Expense	701	60	
	Cash	101		60
	To record repairs and maintenance expense paid in cash.			
26	Utilities Expense	703	100	
	Cash	101		100
	To record utilities expense.			
29	Accounts Payable	201	8,000	
	Cash	101		8,000
	To record payment of liability.			
31	Cash	101	7,000	
	Accounts Receivable	106	3,000	
	Sales	401		10,000
	To record sales during the last half of March.			
30	Cost of Goods Sold	500	6,000	
	Inventory	110		6,000
	To record cost of goods sold during the last half of March.			

Exhibit 3-10

The White-Water Boat Company
T Accounts for March 1995

Cash			*101*
3/1 Bal.	11,000	3/16	500
3/15	2,000	3/24	60
3/23	3,000	3/26	100
3/31	7,000	3/29	8,000
3/31 Bal.	14,340		

Accounts Receivable			*106*
3/1 Bal.	600	3/23	3,000
3/15	4,000		
3/31	3,000		
3/31 Bal.	4,600		

Inventory			*110*
3/1 Bal.	9,000	3/15	3,500
3/20	10,000	3/31	6,000
3/31 Bal.	9,500		

Office Supplies			*115*
3/1 Bal.	2,000		
3/31 Bal.	2,000		

License			*120*
3/1 Bal.	200		
3/31 Bal.	200		

Prepaid Insurance			*125*
3/1 Bal.	1,200		
3/31 Bal.	1,200		

Land			*150*
3/1 Bal.	5,000		
3/31 Bal.	5,000		

Office Equipment			*160*
3/1 Bal.	9,900		
3/31 Bal.	9,900		

Building			*165*
3/1 Bal.	10,000		
3/31 Bal.	10,000		

Accounts Payable			*201*
3/29	8,000	3/1 Bal.	4,900
		3/2	300
		3/20	10,000
		3/31 Bal.	7,200

Bank Loan Payable			*205*
		3/1 Bal.	4,000
		3/31 Bal.	4,000

Capital Stock			*301*
		3/1 Bal.	40,000
		3/31 Bal.	40,000

Sales			*401*
		3/15	6,000
		3/31	10,000
		3/31 Bal.	16,000

Cost of Goods Sold			*500*
3/15	3,500		
3/31	6,000		
3/31 Bal.	9,500		

Salaries Expense			*601*
3/16	500		

Advertising Expense			*605*
3/2	300		

Repairs and Maintenance Expense			*701*
3/24	60		

Utilities Expense			*703*
3/26	100		

Exhibit 3-11

The White-Water Boat Company
Trial Balance
March 31, 1995

	Debit	*Credit*
Cash	$14,340	
Accounts receivable	4,600	
Inventory	9,500	
Office supplies	2,000	
License	200	
Prepaid insurance	1,200	
Land	5,000	
Office equipment	9,900	
Buildings	10,000	
Accounts payable		$ 7,200
Bank loan payable		4,000
Capital stock		40,000
Sales		16,000
Cost of goods sold	9,500	
Salaries expense	500	
Advertising expense	300	
Repairs and maintenance expense	60	
Utilities expense	100	
Totals	$67,200	$67,200

Financial Statements

As all the steps in the accounting process are not yet complete, financial statements are normally not prepared at this point in the process.[3] However, in order to emphasize the important relationships among the income statement, the statement of retained earnings, and the balance sheet, preliminary financial statements are illustrated next.

The financial statements for The White-Water Boat Company are shown in the next three exhibits. The income statement (Exhibit 3-12) covers a three-month period ending on March 31, 1995. (Even though sales did not actually begin until March, the firm was in existence for that three-month period.) In this simple example, the expenses are listed with the largest amount first. Expenses could also have been listed alphabetically or by categories, as is usually the case in published financial statements. Income taxes have not been discussed in this chapter. As the next chapter will show, income taxes usually are recorded during the adjustment process.

The retained earnings statement (Exhibit 3-13) covers the same period as the income statement. There is no beginning balance for Retained Earnings because The White-Water Boat Company was formed January 1. The net income of $5,540 increases Retained Earnings. Since the company did not declare any dividends, the balance in Retained Earnings on March 31, 1995 is also $5,540. The retained earnings statement for the next month will show a beginning balance on April 1 of $5,540.

3. Chapter 4 will discuss the remaining steps in the accounting cycle.

Exhibit 3-12

The White-Water Boat Company Income Statement For the Three Months Ended March 31, 1995		
Revenues		
Sales		$16,000
Expenses		
Cost of goods sold	$9,500	
Salaries expense	500	
Advertising expense	300	
Utility expense	100	
Repairs and maintenance expense	60	
Total expenses		10,460
Net income		$ 5,540

Exhibit 3-13

The White-Water Boat Company Retained Earnings Statement For the Three Months Ended March 31, 1995	
Retained earnings, January 1, 1995	$ 0
Add: net income from January 1, to March 31	5,540
Retained earnings, March 31, 1995	$5,540

comparative balance sheet

The March 31, and February 28, 1995 comparative balance sheets for The White-Water Boat Company are presented in Exhibit 3-14. A **comparative balance sheet** is a balance sheet in which data for two or more years is presented in adjacent columns. Except for the retained earnings balance, the amounts for the March 31 balance sheet come from the March 31 trial balance (Exhibit 3-11). The balance in the retained earnings account is taken from the retained earnings statement (Exhibit 3-13). The data for the February 28 balance sheet is from the trial balance as of that date (Exhibit 3-8).

RELATIONSHIPS AMONG THE FINANCIAL STATEMENTS

Objective 6
Describe the relationships among the balance sheet, income statement, and retained earnings statement.

If you compare the stockholders' equity section of the two balance sheets in Exhibit 3-14 you will see that at March 31, Retained Earnings had a balance of $5,540, while at February 28, the balance was zero. The $5,540 represents an increase in the net assets due to the profitable operations of the business. This important point can also be seen by comparing the net assets at March 31 and February 28, 1995:

Date	*Net Assets*	=	*Assets*	−	*Liabilities*
March 31	$45,540	=	$56,740	−	$11,200
Feb. 28	40,000		48,900		8,900
Increase	$ 5,540		$ 7,840		$ 2,300

Exhibit 3-14

The White-Water Boat Company
Comparative Balance Sheet

Assets	*March 31, 1995*	*February 28, 1995*
Cash	$14,340	$11,000
Accounts receivable	4,600	600
Inventory	9,500	9,000
Office supplies	2,000	2,000
License	200	200
Prepaid insurance	1,200	1,200
Land	5,000	5,000
Office equipment	9,900	9,900
Buildings	10,000	10,000
Total assets	$56,740	$48,900
Liabilities and Stockholders' Equity		
Liabilities:		
Accounts payable	$ 7,200	$ 4,900
Bank loan payable	4,000	4,000
Total liabilities	$11,200	$ 8,900
Stockholders' equity:		
Capital stock	$40,000	$40,000
Retained earnings	5,540	0
Total stockholders' equity	$45,540	$40,000
Total liabilities and stockholders' equity	$56,740	$48,900

You should note that the retained earnings balance represents the increase in net assets, not just the increase in cash. In this example, the cash balance alone increased $3,340 ($14,340 – $11,000) during the period. Other assets and liabilities also increased or decreased, causing an overall net increase of $5,540 in net assets.

Recall that accountants use the transaction approach to measure income. That is, accountants measure the revenue and expense transactions that occurred during the period and then summarize them on the income statement. The effect of these transactions, plus any additional capital contributions and less any withdrawals, is added to the historical cost net assets at the beginning of the period to determine the historical cost net assets at the end of the period. Using the diagram from Exhibit 3-5, page 105 and adding data from The White-Water Boat Company gives the following results:

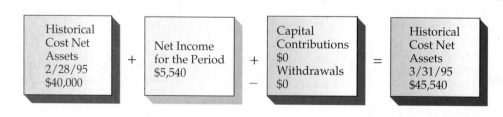

Historical Cost Net Assets 2/28/95 $40,000	+	Net Income for the Period $5,540	+ –	Capital Contributions $0 Withdrawals $0	=	Historical Cost Net Assets 3/31/95 $45,540

This diagram shows how the balance sheet, income statement, and statement of retained earnings are related. Two consecutive balance sheets are, in part, linked by the statement of retained earnings. The statement of retained earnings summarizes the factors that have caused retained earnings to change: net income or net loss and dividends. The income statement explains the change in retained earnings due to the profitable or unprofitable operations. The statement of cash flows, introduced in Chapter 1, further explains changes in the cash account. As noted in Chapter 1, the term *articulation* as used in accounting refers to these relationships among the financial statements.

SUMMARY OF LEARNING OBJECTIVES

1. Describe the transaction processing cycles within a merchandising firm. The two transaction processing cycles in most merchandising firms are the revenue cycle and the expenditure cycle. The revenue cycle processes sales and cash receipts transactions. The application systems within the revenue cycle are the: order entry system, shipping system, billing system, and cash receipts system. The expenditure cycle processes expenditure and cash disbursement transactions. Application systems within the expenditure cycle include: the purchasing system, the receiving system, and the cash disbursements system. The inventory system acts as an interface between the revenue and expenditure cycles. A majority of the journal entries processed by an accounting system originate in these two transaction processing cycles.

2. Describe how accountants measure income including its components: revenues and expenses, gains and losses, and net income. There are various ways to define income. Accountants use a transaction approach to determine income; generally, only completed transactions affect income. Accountants believe that this provides the most objective measure of income. Revenues (inflows of net assets) and expenses (outflows of net assets) result from the primary operating activity of the enterprise. Gains and losses are related to other activities of the firm. Net income or loss is the difference between the total revenues and gains and the total expenses and losses.

3. Explain the major concepts in determining net income, and distinguish between the accrual basis and the cash basis of accounting. Accountants have developed several important concepts or conventions to help them determine income. The need for timely information requires that a firm's continuous economic activities be divided into monthly, quarterly, or yearly accounting periods. The matching convention requires that the expenses for a particular period be matched against the revenues that they helped generate for the period. This is best accomplished by using the accrual basis of accounting.

With the accrual basis of accounting, revenues are recognized when earned and expenses are recognized when incurred. With the cash basis of accounting, revenues are recognized when received and expenses are recognized when paid. The accrual basis of accounting is the generally accepted accounting method because it provides the best matching of revenues and expenses.

4. Describe the revenue and expense recognition principles and identify the different points in the earnings cycle at which revenue can be recognized. With the accrual basis of accounting, revenue is recognized when it is earned. In most cases the point of sale is chosen as the point of revenue recognition. This is because two conditions usually are present at the point of sale.

a. There is objective evidence as to the exchange or sale price.
b. The earnings process is essentially complete.

However, in limited situations, revenue may be recognized:

a. During production, such as the percentage-of-completion method.
b. At the end of production but prior to sale.
c. As the cash is collected (the installment method). Expenses are related to either a particular product sold or a service rendered, or a particular time period when revenue is recognized.

5. Record income statement transactions. Increases in net assets from business activities are assigned to retained earnings and represent increases in that account. Conversely, decreases in net assets from business activities are also assigned to retained earnings but represent decreases. Thus the rules for revenue and expense accounts are the same as for retained earnings, which is a component of stockholders' equity. These rules are illustrated in the following T accounts:

Any Expense Account

Increase + Debit	Decrease − Credit

Any Revenue Account

Decrease − Debit	Increase + Credit

6. Describe the relationships among the balance sheet, income statement, and retained earnings statement. The balance sheet, income statement, and retained earnings statement are related to one another. Two consecutive balance sheets are linked by the retained earnings statement. The retained earnings statement summarizes the factors (net income or net loss and dividends) that have caused retained earnings to change. The income statement details the changes in retained earnings due to profitable or unprofitable operations. The statement of cash flows, which also is linked to the other statements, further explains changes in the cash account. This linkage among the financial statements is often referred to as articulation.

KEY TERMS

Accrual basis of accounting 106
Cash basis of accounting 106
Comparative balance sheet 119
Completed-contract method 109
Dividends 105
Expenditure cycle 99
Expenditures 104
Gains 104
Interim statements 106
Invoice 100
Losses 104
Matching convention 106
Net income (loss) 105
Nominal (temporary) accounts 111
Percentage-of-completion method 109
Period expenses 110
Purchase order 101
Real (permanent) accounts 111
Realization principle 108
Receipts 104
Receiving report 102
Revenue cycle 99
Shipping notice 100
Time period assumption 106
Transaction cycle 99

REVIEW PROBLEM

You are the accountant for Kids Tech, a large retail children's store, and have obtained the following information as of January 1, 1995.

Kids Tech
Balance Sheet
January 1, 1995

Assets		*Liabilities and Stockholders' Equity*		
Cash	$ 5,000	Liabilities		
Accounts receivable	6,000	Accounts payable	$ 4,600	
Inventory	12,000	Salaries payable	1,400	
Office supplies	1,500	Bank loan payable	10,000	
Land	25,000			
Building	45,000	Total liabilities		$ 16,000
Furniture and fixtures	15,000	Stockholders' equity		
		Capital stock	$50,000	
		Retained earnings	43,500	
		Total stockholders' equity		93,500
Total assets	$109,500	Total liabilities and stockholders' equity		$109,500

The following events occurred throughout 1995 and are numbered because they represent summary events for the year.

a. Inventory totaling $60,000 was purchased on account during the year.
b. The firm purchased a two-year comprehensive insurance policy for $3,600 cash. The policy takes effect on April 1, 1995.
c. Sales for the year amounted to $80,000, of which $50,000 was for cash and $30,000 was on account.

d. The cost of the inventory sold amounted to $52,000.
e. Salaries payable of $1,400 were paid at the beginning of 1995; the salaries were earned by employees in 1994.
f. Salaries earned in 1995 totaling $10,000 were paid during the year.
g. Cash collections on account totaled $28,000.
h. Cash payments on account were $52,000.
i. Land that cost Kids Tech $5,000 was sold for $5,200 cash.
j. The following expenses were paid in cash:

Advertising	$1,000
Utilities	750
Automobile expense	2,000
Repairs and maintenance	450

REQUIRED:

1. Make the journal entries to record these events.
2. Post the entries to ledger T accounts, and open new accounts where appropriate.
3. Prepare a trial balance.

Solution 1
Journal Entries

a. Inventory	60,000	
Accounts Payable		60,000
To record purchase of inventory on account.		
b. Prepaid Insurance	3,600	
Cash		3,600
To record purchase of insurance policy that takes effect on April 1, 1995.		
c. Cash	50,000	
Accounts Receivable	30,000	
Sales		80,000
To record sales on cash and credit.		
d. Cost of Goods Sold	52,000	
Inventory		52,000
To record cost of goods sold.		
e. Salaries Payable	1,400	
Cash		1,400
To record payment of the salaries liability from 1994.		
f. Salaries Expense	10,000	
Cash		10,000
To record 1995 salaries paid during the year.		
g. Cash	28,000	
Accounts Receivable		28,000
To record cash collected on account.		
h. Accounts Payable	52,000	
Cash		52,000
To record cash payments on account.		
i. Cash	5,200	
Gain on Sale of Land		200
Land		5,000
To record gain on sale of land.		

j. Advertising Expense	1,000	
Utilities Expense	750	
Automobile Expense	2,000	
Repairs and Maintenance Expense	450	
Cash		4,200
To record various expenses for the period.		

2 T Accounts

Cash

1/1 Bal.	5,000	(b)	3,600
(c)	50,000	(e)	1,400
(g)	28,000	(f)	10,000
(i)	5,200	(h)	52,000
		(j)	4,200
12/31 Bal.	17,000		

Accounts Receivable

1/1 Bal.	6,000	(g)	28,000
(c)	30,000		
12/31 Bal.	8,000		

Inventory

1/1 Bal.	12,000	(d)	52,000
(a)	60,000		
12/31 Bal.	20,000		

Office Supplies

1/1 Bal.	1,500		
12/31 Bal.	1,500		

Prepaid Insurance

(b)	3,600		
12/31 Bal.	3,600		

Land

1/1 Bal.	25,000	(i)	5,000
12/31 Bal.	20,000		

Building

1/1 Bal.	45,000		
12/31 Bal.	45,000		

Furniture and Fixtures

1/1 Bal.	15,000		
12/31 Bal.	15,000		

Accounts Payable

(h)	52,000	1/1 Bal.	4,600
		(a)	60,000
		12/31 Bal.	12,600

Salaries Payable

(e)	1,400	1/1 Bal.	1,400
		12/31 Bal.	0

Bank Loan Payable

		1/1 Bal.	10,000
		12/31 Bal.	10,000

Capital Stock

		1/1 Bal.	50,000
		12/31 Bal.	50,000

Retained Earnings

		1/1 Bal.	43,500

Sales

		(c)	80,000

Cost of Goods Sold

(d)	52,000		

Salaries Expense

(f)	10,000		

Advertising Expense

(j)	1,000		

Utilities Expense

(j)	750		

Automobile Expense

(j)	2,000		

Repairs and Maintenance Expense

(j)	450		

Gain on Sale of Land

		(i)	200

3
Trial Balance

Kids Tech
Trial Balance
December 31, 1995

	Debit	Credit
Cash	$ 17,000	
Accounts receivable	8,000	
Inventory	20,000	
Office supplies	1,500	
Prepaid insurance	3,600	
Land	20,000	
Building	45,000	
Furniture and fixtures	15,000	
Accounts payable		$ 12,600
Salaries payable		0
Bank loan payable		10,000
Capital stock		50,000
Retained earnings		43,500
Sales		80,000
Cost of goods sold	52,000	
Salaries expense	10,000	
Advertising expense	1,000	
Utilities expense	750	
Automobile expense	2,000	
Repairs and maintenance expense	450	
Gain on sale of land		200
Totals	$196,300	$196,300

QUESTIONS

1. What are the transaction processing cycles of a merchandising firm?
2. What systems are found within each of the transaction processing cycles of a merchandising firm?
3. Define revenues and expenses, and explain how they differ from gains and losses.
4. How do the time period assumption and the matching concept relate to the measurement of income for the period?
5. Compare and contrast the accrual basis and the cash basis of accounting. Which method is favored by accountants, and why?
6. A friend of yours was told by his accountant that his business was profitable during the year. However, your friend is concerned because his cash decreased during the year. Explain to him how this can happen.
7. The Pfeifer Corporation sold 100 items for a total of $10,000, $8,000 of which was collected in the current month and $2,000 in the next month. The firm also collected $1,000 during the current month from last month's sales. How much revenue is recognized on the accrual basis? How much revenue is recognized on the cash basis?
8. State the realization rule. Give an example, other than those in the text, of when a firm might recognize revenue at a time other than at the point of sale.
9. You have decided to enter the magazine business. All subscriptions are for two years, payable in advance. You will publish monthly. When should you recognize the revenue from the subscriptions?
10. The text indicated that there are several points in the earnings cycle when revenue could be recognized. These include:
    a. During production
    b. At the end of production, before sale
    c. At the time of sale
    d. As cash is collected

Provide a separate example of an industry or product where you think it would be appropriate to recognize revenue at each of the above points.

11. Why are revenue and expense accounts called temporary or nominal accounts?
12. What happens to retained earnings if there is a loss during a certain period? Can dividends be distributed if there is a loss during the period?
13. Why would a deposit or downpayment received before a sale be considered a liability? Why would a prepaid expense be considered an asset?

EXERCISES

E3-1 Transaction Processing Cycles

LO 1

Identify the transaction processing cycle (revenue or expense) and the accounting system that would be used to process each of the following transactions.

a. Preparation of a purchase order to buy additional inventory.
b. Shipment of goods to a customer.
c. Payment for goods that were purchased on account.
d. Preparation of an invoice to bill a customer.
e. Receipt of a customer's order.
f. Recording the liability for goods that were purchased on account.
g. Receipt of goods that were previously ordered.
h. Recording the asset for goods that were sold to a customer on account.

As an example, item (a) is completed for you below:

a. Expense cycle; purchasing system

E3-2 Recognizing Accounts

LO 2, 4

Examine the following accounts and indicate whether they are asset, liability, stockholders' equity, revenue, or expense accounts. State whether a debit or a credit increases each account.

a. Salary expense
b. Buildings
c. Unearned rent
d. Retained earnings
e. Taxes payable
f. Prepaid insurance
g. Interest earned
h. Sales
i. Cost of goods sold
j. Commissions paid to salespeople

E3-3 Recognition of Revenue and Expense Transactions

LO 3, 4

A summary of the transactions into which the Usher Corporation entered during October and November is reproduced below. State which of the events affected the income statement during the month of October.

a. The company needed additional funds, so the owners made an additional $50,000 investment.
b. The firm collected $40,000 on account from credit sales made during September.
c. Cash sales during October totaled $8,000.
d. The firm paid $40 for some plumbing repairs made in August.
e. October sales on account totaled $10,000.
f. The firm repaid a bank loan. The original amount of the loan, made on October 1, was $5,000. At the end of October, the $5,000 was repaid, plus $50 in interest for the month.
g. A customer placed an order for 50 dozen items at a sales price of $20,000. The order will be shipped in December. No deposit was received.
h. A dividend of $1,000 was declared and paid in October.
i. A dividend of $500 was paid in November.
j. Another customer ordered a special item to be delivered in early January. The customer made a $1,000 deposit in October when the order was placed.

E3-4
Revenue Recognition
LO 3, 4

For many years the Yellow Pages provided an important source of auxiliary income for AT&T. Under the divestiture order, the Yellow Pages became the property of the independent operating companies. The judge's order was based on the presumption that the net profits of the Yellow Pages would help cover local operating cost deficits. Given the regulatory environment and local rate regulation, determining the net profits derived from the Yellow Pages is an important issue.

Revenue from the Yellow Pages is generated primarily through the sales of advertisements. Before the forthcoming issue can be put into production, a significant number of sales must be closed. In some cases, orders must be placed four to five months before the issue date. In some areas of the country, the customer is billed after the sale is made, and a substantial amount of the revenue is collected by the end of the production of the book or shortly thereafter. In other parts of the country, the customer is billed in monthly installments over the 12-month life of the issue.

During the production process, significant costs are incurred. In fact, other than distribution costs, almost all relevant costs are incurred prior to the delivery of the book.

REQUIRED:

1. At what point or points in the yearly production cycle should the Yellow Pages recognize revenue? How should they account for their billings and cash receipts?
2. How should the Yellow Pages account for the costs incurred in the production and distribution cycle?
3. How should these costs be matched against the revenues for the period?

E3-5
Recording Journal Entries
LO 5

The Golden Bear Company, a sporting goods store, entered into the following transactions during November:

a. November 1: Purchased $30,000 of inventory on account.
b. November 3: Placed an advertisement in the local paper for $200. Paid cash.
c. November 16: Paid October's utility bill of $100. This bill was recorded as a payable at the end of October.
d. November 29: Paid salaries of $8,000 for the month.
e. November 30: Sales for the month amounted to $70,000, of which $45,000 was for cash.
f. November 30: Cost of goods sold amounted to $50,000.
g. November 30: November's utility bill of $85 was received. It will be paid in early December. Record in Accounts Payable.

REQUIRED: Prepare the necessary journal entries for the month of November.

E3-6
Income Statement Preparation
LO 5

Sheri Ferraro is the owner of a small computer consulting service called The Professor. She has gathered the following data and asks you to help her prepare an income statement for the year ending on December 31, 1995.

a. Salaries earned by various employees totaled $35,000. At year-end, only $28,000 of this amount had been paid in cash.
b. Office rental expense for the year amounted to $20,000.
c. Consulting fees earned during the year amounted to $100,000. Of this amount, the firm has collected all but 10%.
d. Sheri issued herself a $5,000 cash dividend.
e. The firm sold some marketable securities for $113,000 that it had originally purchased for $20,000.
f. Other operating expenses incurred during the year amounted to $22,000.
g. The current tax rate is 30% of income before taxes.

REQUIRED: Prepare an income statement for the year ended December 31, 1995.

E3-7
Income Statement and Retained Earnings Preparation
LO 5

The MBA Company runs a local news service. At the beginning of the current year, January 1, 1995, the balance in its Retained Earnings account was $45,000. During the year the following events occurred:

a. Total subscription revenues earned amounted to $120,000.
b. Interest revenue earned on investments totaled $4,500.
c. Dividends declared during the year amounted to $7,000.
d. Selling expenses incurred during the year were $75,000.
e. General and administrative expenses incurred during the year amounted to $60,000.
f. The owners made an additional $25,000 investment in exchange for additional capital stock.
g. Interest expense incurred during the period amounted to $5,000.

REQUIRED:

1. Prepare an income statement for the year ended December 31, 1995.
2. Prepare a statement of retained earnings for the year ended December 31, 1995.

E3-8
Income Statement Concepts
LO 3

Match the following statements from Gregory Simpson, president of Efficient Printing Services, Inc., to the relevant underlying accounting concept or concepts. There may be more than one answer for each question.

a. Time-period assumption.
b. Matching convention.
c. Accrual versus cash basis of accounting.

1. "All I want to know is how you can tell me we had income of $32,000 and the bank says we're overdrawn."
2. "Well, I don't care—how about not reporting income this year?"
3. "Shouldn't we wait and pay for the advertising after year-end so that our profits will look better for this period?"
4. "We're doing great! I finally collected on that $4,500 wedding invitation job we completed last year. This will improve current profits."

E3-9
Accrual Versus Cash Basis
LO 3

The Alpine Realty Corporation entered into the following transactions in July. Determine net income on the accrual and cash basis for the month of July.

1. Commissions earned and received in July	$8,500
2. Commissions earned in July but not yet received	4,600
3. Commissions received in advance on sale to close in August	900
4. Cash collected on commissions from May sales	3,800
5. Payment of June's utility and telephone bills	750
6. Payment of rent for six months, July through December	6,600
7. July's salaries paid in August	4,300
8. Received bill from plumber for services performed in July, to be paid in August	80

E3-10
Accounting Equation and Retained Earnings
LO 5

The following data are available for three consecutive years for the Orazco Corporation:

	Year 1	*Year 2*	*Year 3*
Retained earnings, beginning balance	$75,000	$105,000	?
Net income	?	?	$14,000
Dividends	5,000	16,000	?
Retained earnings, ending balance	?	$ 96,000	$98,000

REQUIRED: Complete the chart by filling in the missing amounts.

E3-11
Preparing Financial Statements from Accounts
LO 6

The following accounts were taken from the records of the Hernandez Cellular Telephone Store at December 31, 1995 (all accounts have normal balances):

Cash	$ 10,000
Land and buildings	170,000
Sales	400,000
Accounts payable	8,500
Accounts receivable	12,000
Cost of goods sold	250,000
Inventories	70,400
Selling expenses	40,600
Other assets	70,000
Retained earnings, January 1, 1995	130,000
Notes payable	20,000
General and administrative expenses	135,500
Capital stock	200,000

REQUIRED: Based on the above data prepare:

1. An income statement for the year ended December 31, 1995.
2. A retained earnings statement for the year ended December 31, 1995.
3. A balance sheet at December 31, 1995.

E3-12
Cash to Accrual
LO 3, 5

The following income statement uses the cash basis of accounting instead of the accrual basis. Prepare an income statement using the accrual basis.

Lamb and Wolf Incorporated
Income Statement—Cash Basis
For the Year Ended December 31, 1995

Revenues		
Sales	$357,000	
Interest	47,000	$404,000
Expenses		
Wages	$ 66,500	
Insurance	6,600	
Rent	34,900	
Utilities	13,700	
Office	4,200	
Other	1,200	
		127,100
Net income		$276,900

Additional information:

a. At year-end, 15% of sales had not yet been collected.
b. Lamb and Wolf own land worth $450,000; this was $80,000 more than it was appraised for last year.
c. One month's wages totaling $7,300 have not yet been paid.
d. Three years of insurance was paid this year. One year's worth was considered used in the current year.
e. Thirty percent of the office expense incurred during the year was unpaid at year-end.

E3-13
Error Correction
LO 5

The Murray Corporation made the following errors in preparing its financial statements for December 31, 1995:

a. Failed to record the purchase of supplies on account.
b. Failed to record a sale made on account.
c. Recorded a $500 cash sale as a $5,000 cash sale.
d. Failed to record the payment of a dividend during the year. The company's policy is to record dividends only when paid in cash.
e. Failed to record an expense for repairs incurred but not yet paid.
f. Recorded the purchase of inventory on account as a cash purchase. None of the inventory has been sold.

REQUIRED: Complete the following table using these abbreviations:

+ means the item is overstated
0 means the item is neither overstated nor understated
− means the item is understated

Effect on December 31, 1995	*a*	*b*	*c*	*d*	*e*	*f*
Total assets	____	____	____	____	____	____
Total liabilities	____	____	____	____	____	____
Total stockholders' equity	____	____	____	____	____	____
Net income	____	____	____	____	____	____

PROBLEMS

P3-1
Transaction Cycles and Integrated Accounting Systems
LO 1

Assume that you are employed by a large consulting firm as a staff consultant. You are a member of the project team that is designing an integrated accounting system for M & L Plumbing, a plumbing supply wholesale company. You have been asked to make a presentation to middle managers at M & L to introduce them to integrated accounting systems. Your presentation will include an overview of the transaction processing cycles being developed for M & L Plumbing and a detailed description of the order entry system and the accounts receivable system, the two systems that you have helped develop.

REQUIRED:

1. Identify the transaction cycles and the systems within each transaction cycle that should be developed for M & L Plumbing.
2. Identify the significant input documents, processes, and outputs for the order entry system and the accounts receivable system.
3. Journal entries will be generated by one or more systems in both the revenue cycle and the expenditure cycle. Identify the journal entries that should be generated within each transaction cycle, and the system(s) that would most likely generate each journal entry.

P3-2
Revenue Recognition
LO 3, 4

Following are a number of independent situations relating to revenue recognition principles:

a. The Aloha Company sells prepaid tours to Hawaii. All customers must pay two months in advance of their trip.
b. The Levian Corporation is the world's largest dam construction company. It recently received a $50 million contract to build a dam over the Los Angeles River. It will take five years to complete, but the company feels that it can make reasonable estimates of costs necessary to complete the dam as it is being built.
c. Bumby Aircraft Company recently received an order for 25 of its new generation of turbofan airliners. Each plane will take about 15 months to manufacture and will be

delivered to the purchaser as manufactured. The firm received a $5 million downpayment. The firm estimates that it has received enough orders from all airline companies to make a reasonable profit on the entire turbofan program.

d. ABC Appliance sells a variety of household appliances such as televisions and refrigerators to the general public. Most sales are made for cash, but some on account. The company has a no-questions-asked 30-day return policy.

REQUIRED: For each of the situations above, state when revenue should be recognized. Be sure to give your reasons.

P3-3
Journal Entries
LO 5

The Jaminez Corporation summary transactions for April follow:

a. Paid a property tax bill of $4,800 that was recorded as a payable in March.
b. Paid its monthly rental of $6,800.
c. Sales during the month totaled $75,000; 30% of these were for cash, and the remainder were on credit.
d. The cost of the items sold equaled $44,000.
e. Purchased additional inventory on account for $14,200.
f. Cash collections from credits sales were:

$18,000 from March's sales
$32,000 from current month's sales

g. The following expenses were paid in cash:

Automobile	$2,400
Repairs	2,600
Utility	1,900

h. The firm made a $10,000 payment on the inventory purchases in item (e).
i. The firm sold some rental property that it owned. The land cost $54,000 and was sold for $48,000 cash.
j. Employee wages earned but not yet paid equaled $4,400.
k. Dividends of $2,000 were paid in cash.

REQUIRED: Make the journal entries with appropriate explanations to record each of the transactions.

P3-4
Journal Entries, Posting, and Trial Balance
LO 5

Happy Helen's Hamburger Haven was organized in January 1995. The following events occurred during that month:

a. January 2: Helen organized the business by issuing herself capital stock for the following assets:

Cash	$80,000
Furniture and fixtures	38,000
Office equipment	22,000

b. January 3: The company obtained additional financing by borrowing $25,000 from a local bank for one year. (Ignore interest.)
c. January 5: Various items of inventory were purchased on account for $45,000.

d. January 6: The company rented a storefront in which to conduct business. It signed a three-year lease and had to pay the first (January) and last months' rent of $3,000 per month.
e. January 15: Sales for the first half of the month totaled $34,000, of which $18,000 was for cash and the remainder on account.
f. January 15: The cost of sales was $20,800.
g. January 18: Additional inventory purchased for cash amounted to $23,000.
h. January 19: The company purchased a health license from the county at a cost of $4,800. The license runs from January 1 of the current year for two years.
i. January 20: Cash collections on account totaled $15,000.
j. January 23: A $21,000 payment was made for the inventory purchased on January 5.
k. January 28: The company signed a contract with Creative Ads to do all its local cable television promotions. The contract runs from February 1 for 12 months. The company is committed to purchase $20,000 of advertising time over the 12-month period. In addition, the company must give the agency a $5,000 cash retainer when the contract takes effect.
l. January 30: Sales for the second half of January totaled $40,000, of which $28,000 was for cash and the remainder on account.
m. January 30: The cost of sales was $28,000.
n. January 31: The following expenses were paid in cash:

Salaries	$11,000
Utilities	700
Taxes	2,800
Delivery	2,500

o. January 31: The company received notice that a lawsuit was filed against it in Superior Court for violating the city's sign code. The potential fine is $1,000. The company does not think the suit has merit as it received preliminary approval for the design of its sign from the city in early January.

REQUIRED:

1. Make the appropriate journal entries to record the transactions. If you decide that a particular transaction does not meet the criteria for recognition, please so state and give your reasons.
2. Set up the appropriate T accounts, post the entries to these accounts, and balance the accounts.
3. Prepare a trial balance as of January 31, 1995.

P3-5
Journal Entries, Posting, Trial Balance, and Financial Statements
LO 5

Elaine Jaeger decided to open a travel agency called Four Corners Travel. All the necessary preopening arrangements were made in January, and the doors opened for business on February 1, 1995.

During the month of February the following events occurred:

a. February 1: February's rent of $3,000 was paid in cash.
b. February 2: Anticipating good business, Four Corners Travel purchased on account an additional $7,000 of office furniture and fixtures.
c. February 4: The firm placed an advertisement in the local paper that cost $600 and was paid for in cash.
d. February 15: Commissions earned for the first half of the month totaled $40,000. All commissions except for $5,000 from a large airline were received in cash.
e. February 15: Outside salesperson salaries of $4,500 for the first half of the month were paid in cash.
f. February 16: The firm had some excess cash and invested $14,000 in marketable securities.

g. February 18: The bill for the office furniture and fixtures purchased on February 7 was paid in full.
h. February 24: Cash of $4,200 was received from commissions earned on account.
i. February 25: Marketable securities with a cost of $2,000 were sold for $2,800 cash.
j. February 28: Commissions for the last half of the month were $27,000. All but $8,000 were for cash.
k. February 28: Outside salespeople salaries of $6,000 were paid in cash.
l. February 28: The following expenses were paid in cash:

Office salaries	$9,000
Automobile	2,000
Janitorial service	3,500

m. February 28: The firm received notification from its brokers that it had earned interest of $125 on its investment in marketable securities, to be received next month.
n. February 28: The bank notified the firm that interest of $155 was incurred on the loan during February and was immediately payable. As of the end of February, however, it had not been paid.
o. February 28: Because business appeared to be good, dividends of $1,500 were paid in cash. Record these dividends in a Dividends Declared account.
p. February 28: The firm made a $3,000 payment on the amount due to the Association of Airline Travel Agents.

The January 31, 1995 trial balance is as follows:

Four Corners Travel
Trial Balance
January 31, 1995

	Debit	*Credit*
Cash	$12,000	
Supplies	3,000	
Ticket stock	4,500	
Office furniture and fixtures	17,000	
Computer equipment	24,500	
Accounts payable		$ 9,000
Bank notes payable		10,000
Due to Association of Airline Travel Agents		15,000
Capital stock		27,000
Totals	$61,000	$61,000

In addition, the firm's chart of accounts is as follows:

Cash	10
Investment in Marketable Securities	11
Accounts Receivable	15
Supplies	16
Ticket Stock	17
Interest Receivable	19
Office Furniture and Fixtures	20
Computer Equipment	22
Accounts Payable	30
Bank Notes Payable	32
Interest Payable	33
Due to Association of Airline Travel Agents	35

(continued)

Capital Stock	40
Retained Earnings	42
Dividends Declared	49
Commissions	50
Interest Revenue	51
Gain on Sale of Marketable Securities	52
Advertising Expense	70
Automobile Expense	71
Interest Expense	72
Outside Salesperson Salaries Expense	73
Office Salaries Expense	74
Rent Expense	75
Janitorial Service	77

REQUIRED:

1. Make the required entries to record these transactions in the general journal. Assume the journal starts with page 1 and reference it by using the abbreviations GJ-1.
2. Post all entries to the running balance form of the ledger account. Use the account numbers from the chart of accounts.
3. Balance the ledger accounts and prepare a trial balance.
4. Prepare an income statement for the month ended February 28, 1995.
5. Prepare a retained earnings statement for the month ended February 28, 1995.
6. Prepare a balance sheet at February 28, 1995.

P3-6
Preparation of an Income Statement and a Balance Sheet
LO 5

You have obtained the following trial balance of Drysdale Fashion Designs as of December 31, 1995:

Drysdale Fashion Designs
Trial Balance
December 31, 1995

	Debit	*Credit*
Cash	$ 35,000	
Loans receivable	14,000	
Accounts receivable	31,000	
Inventory	75,000	
Office supplies	2,600	
Prepaid insurance	2,400	
Land held for future plant site	60,000	
Land	75,000	
Building	140,000	
Store equipment	15,000	
Bank notes payable		$ 40,000
Accounts payable		24,800
Wages payable		8,200
Mortgage payable		50,000
Capital stock		100,000
Retained earnings		167,400
Sales		280,000

(continued)

	Debit	*Credit*
Interest revenue		1,500
Gain on sale of equipment		5,000
Cost of goods sold	190,000	
Advertising expense	4,000	
Automobile expense	3,500	
Entertainment expense	1,500	
Interest expense	1,700	
Repairs expense	800	
Taxes expense	5,200	
Wages expense	20,200	
Totals	$676,900	$676,900

The total shown for retained earnings on the trial balance represents the beginning balance at January 1995 minus the cash dividend of $5,000 paid on April 1, 1995.

REQUIRED:

1. Prepare an income statement for the year ended December 31, 1995.
2. Verify that the balance in the Retained Earnings account at January 1, 1995 is $172,400 and that the balance at December 31, 1995 is $227,000.
3. Prepare the retained earnings statement for the year ended December 31, 1995.
4. Prepare a balance sheet as of December 31, 1995.

P3-7
T Account Analysis
LO 5

The following data relate to several accounts. You are to supply the entry that would most likely account for the missing information. Assume that all items are independent.

a. The beginning balance in the Accounts Receivable account is $100,000, and the ending balance is $150,000. Assume that all the firm's sales were on credit and that they totaled $450,000 during the year.
b. The beginning balance in the Land account is $200,000 and the ending balance is $158,000. During the year, the firm sold some land with a cost of $82,000 for $89,000 cash.
c. The beginning balance in the Interest Receivable account is $5,600, and the ending balance is $5,300. During the year, the firm received interest payments of $2,900.
d. The beginning balance in the Retained Earnings account is $57,000. During the year the firm earned net income of $12,000, and the ending balance in the Retained Earnings account is $53,400.
e. The Accounts Payable account has a beginning balance of $24,000. All inventory purchases are made on account and the cash payments for the purchases totaled $103,000. The Accounts Payable account is only used to record inventory purchased on account. The ending balance in the account is $99,000.
f. The beginning balance in the Notes Payable account is $100,000. During the year, the firm borrowed an additional $40,000, and at the end of the year the balance in the Notes Payable account is zero.
g. Wages Payable has a beginning balance of $1,400 and an ending balance of $900. During the year the firm paid $63,500 in wages.

P3-8
Cash Versus Accrual Accounting
LO 3, 5

The C G Ware Corporation was organized at the beginning of 1995 to provide management consulting services. The following represents the summary transactions for the year:

a. The firm was organized when five shareholders each contributed $25,000.
b. The firm rented some office space in a prestigious building. The rent was $8,000 per month for 12 months. In addition, the corporation had to make a $15,000 prepayment, which will be applied to the rent at the end of a four-year lease term.

c. The firm purchased various supplies on account for $6,800. At the end of the year, $1,500 of the supplies remained on hand.
d. Instead of purchasing office equipment and furniture, the Ware Corporation decided to lease them. The total required lease payments for the year were $26,200. However, December's payment was late and was not paid until January.
e. Total billings for professional services were $250,000. However, total cash collections for these services equaled $127,000.
f. Miscellaneous administrative expenses paid in cash were $6,500.
g. Payments on Accounts Payable from item (c) were $6,000.
h. Salaries paid during the year were $98,000. However, $15,000 of that total was a prepayment for services to be received next year. The prepayment was made in order to take advantage of the tax laws.

REQUIRED:

1. Prepare an income statement for the year on an accrual basis.
2. Prepare an income statement for the year on a cash basis.
3. Evaluate the performance of C G Ware Corporation. How much cash was on hand at the end of the year? Which method of accounting provides a better measure of performance? Why?

P3-9
The Earnings Cycle and Revenue Recognition
LO 4

The Ripston Corporation is a major grower of the xedra plant. This plant is produced especially for areas in the United States that receive little rainfall, as it can survive on very little water. You have gathered the following data related to the production and sale of xedras during the past three years:

	Year 1	*Year 2*	*Year 3*
Units produced	3,000	3,200	2,700
Cost per unit to produce	$12	$12	$12
Unit sales	2,400	2,900	3,600
Sales price per unit	$18	$18	$18
Cash collected	$42,000	$49,500	$43,500

REQUIRED:

1. Determine the amount of gross profit (sales less cost of sales) for each of the following revenue recognition points:
   a. At the end of production, but prior to sale
   b. At the point of sale
   c. When the cash is collected
2. Now determine the amount of gross profit for each of the revenue recognition points over the three-year cumulative period. Discuss and explain your results.
3. Name a separate product or industry which would most likely recognize revenue:
   a. During production
   b. At the end of production, but before sale
   c. When cash is collected

DISCUSSION AND INTERPRETATION PROBLEMS

D3-1
Understanding Financial Statements

The following was taken from the notes to the financial statements for the Dean Witter Financial Services Group in the Sears, Roebuck 1991 annual report:

Securities

Client transactions are recorded on settlement date with related commission revenues and expenses recorded on a trade date basis. Proprietary security transactions are recorded on the trade date. Securities are valued at market, and the unrealized gains and losses are reflected in income.

REQUIRED:

1. Comment on the policy of recording securities transactions on the settlement date and recording commission revenues and expenses on the trade date.
2. Dean Witter values securities at market and recognizes unrealized gains and losses. This violates the historical cost principle but is common in the industry. Explain what this means and why you think it is common in the industry.

D3-2
Understanding Financial Statements

The following is taken from the notes to the financial statements in a recent McDonnell Douglas annual report:

Revenue Recognition. *Revenues and earnings on cost-reimbursement and fixed price government contracts are generally recognized on the percentage-of-completion method of accounting as costs are incurred (cost-to-cost basis). Revenues include costs incurred plus a portion of estimated fees or profits . . .*

Revenues are recognized on commercial aircraft programs, including military versions of commercial aircraft, based on sales prices as aircraft are delivered.

REQUIRED:

1. Using McDonnell Douglas as an example, explain the percentage-of-completion method of recognizing revenue. Contrast it to the completed-contract method.
2. Why do you think that McDonnell Douglas uses one method to recognize revenue for military aircraft and a different method for commercial aircraft? Do you think that their choice of recognition methods is appropriate? Why or why not?

D3-3
Financial Decision Case

The president of A&D Associates, an advertising agency, is quite concerned about the financial condition of her business. After reviewing the income statement for the year ended December 31, 1995 and the balance sheets at December 31, 1994 and 1995, she relates the following to you:

"I just don't understand our cash situation. As the years go by, we seem to have less and less cash. I started the business in early 1994 with $100,000 cash and also borrowed $60,000 from the bank. During 1994 and 1995, we were profitable. In fact, our net income in 1995 was 20% greater than it was in 1994. Yet our cash balance has decreased, and retained earnings have continued to increase."

She gives you the following financial statements and asks your advice:

A&D Associates
Balance Sheet

	December 31	
Assets	*1995*	*1994*
Cash	$ 15,000	$ 55,000
Accounts receivable	92,000	60,000
Advertising supplies	38,000	30,000
Prepaids	15,000	10,000
Property and equipment	130,000	90,000
Total assets	$290,000	$245,000
Equities		
Accounts payable	$ 20,000	$ 35,000
Notes payable, due March 1996	60,000	60,000
Common stock	100,000	100,000
Retained earnings	110,000	50,000
Total equities	$290,000	$245,000

A&D Associates
Income Statement
For the Year Ended December 31, 1995

Revenues		
Advertising fees		$250,000
Operating expenses		
Salaries	$100,000	
Advertising supplies used	40,000	
Commissions paid	25,000	
General office expenses	10,000	
Other	5,000	
Total expenses		180,000
Net income		$ 70,000

REQUIRED: Help explain the cash position of A&D Associates to the president by addressing the following questions:

1. Reconcile the change in retained earnings with the net income for the period. What other event appears to have occurred?
2. Explain to the president the relevance of her statement that the company's cash balance has decreased whereas its retained earnings have increased.
3. Explain to her the possible reason for the continued decrease in cash since the inception of the business.
4. What future problems do you foresee for A&D Associates?

D3-4 Research Assignment

The opening scenario raised the question of how best to account for revenues and costs associated with the various frequent-flyer or other frequent-customer programs. In the last few years much has been written on this topic. Using the resources in your library and/or other sources, answer the following questions:

a. What proposals has the accounting profession made to account for revenues and costs of these programs?
b. How has the airline industry reacted to these proposals?
c. Describe the current status of accounting for these programs.

D3-5 Ethical Issues

Leon Jenks is the owner of Jenks' Auto Store, a auto dealership that specializes in luxury domestic cars. As of February 23 of the current year, the firm had 20 automobiles on its dealership floor or lot. The state in which the dealership is located levies a property tax on all such inventories. Any property owned by a firm as of February 25 is subject to the tax. Jenks was very concerned that the tax on the autos the firm was holding for sale would be a substantial amount. He arranged to sell the cars on February 23 to a dealer who had a temporary shortage of cars. Jenks agreed to repurchase, at the original sales price plus 5%, those cars that the dealer was unable to sell between February 23 and March 1. As a result, on March 1 Jenks' Auto Store repurchased 18 of the 20 autos it had sold on February 23.

REQUIRED:

1. If you were the accountant for Jenks' Auto Store how would you handle the sale and repurchase of the autos. That is, would you record a sale in February. If so, for how much?
2. Jenks feels that since he had sold all the cars by February 25 they should not be included in his inventory for purposes of the property tax return. Therefore, he instructs you, his accountant, not to include these cars on the tax return. Would you comply with Jenks' instructions? Why or why not?
3. Do you think that Jenks acted in an ethical manner? Why or why not?

CHAPTER 4
COMPLETING THE ACCOUNTING CYCLE

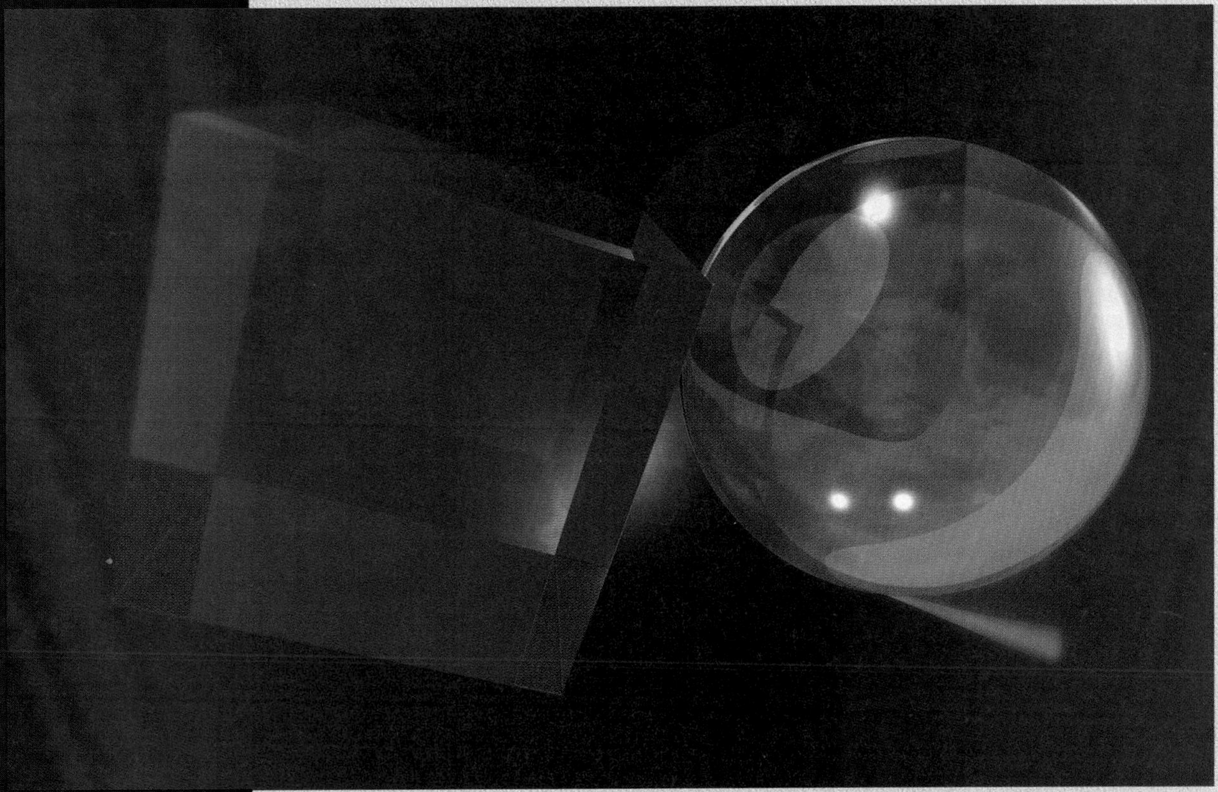

LEARNING OBJECTIVES

After studying this chapter, you should be able to:

1. Explain why adjusting entries are necessary, and describe the major categories of adjusting entries.
2. Complete the remaining steps in the accounting cycle.
3. Describe the flow of transactions through a computer-based general ledger system.

Scenario

Vicki couldn't believe it when her roommate, Lisa, told her how much she was enjoying her accounting course. Lisa had just completed the first few chapters of her introductory financial accounting text, and found the course to be both challenging and interesting. Although Vicki had never taken an accounting course, she had worked as a bookkeeper for a local yogurt store. She had found the time she spent manually recording numerous transactions in journals to be boring and certainly not very challenging.

"Did you ever analyze any accounts, figure out the amount of depreciation expense that should be recorded for a particular period, make adjusting entries, or prepare financial statements?" Lisa asked Vicki. Vicki shook her head. She also admitted to Lisa that she had no idea what adjusting journal entries were or what depreciation was and why it was necessary to worry about these things.

"It sounds to me, Vicki, as though you were just doing bookkeeping—recording transactions and keeping records. That's just one small part of accounting. Accounting includes much more than that. For example, in my accounting course, I am beginning to understand such concepts as accruals, depreciation, and allocations. Did you know, that even though the current market value of a building may be increasing, accountants will make part of the cost of that building an expense every period to reflect the fact the building is gradually losing its ability to produce future revenues? This is really what the concept of depreciation is all about."

Lisa went on to tell Vicki about the chapter she completed in her accounting book that had to do with adjusting entries and the problems accountants encounter as they develop methods to ensure that the firm's financial statements reflect all the events that occurred during a particular period. Finally, with a slight smile on her face, Lisa told Vicki that much of what Vicki had done at the yogurt store could be done by a computer but that the work of the accountant involved judgment, problem solving, and ethical behavior that a computer simply could not handle. "For example, my father's business just purchased a new warehouse for $1 million," Lisa told Vicki. "Part of the work of the accountant was to determine how many years that warehouse will generate revenues and how much of its cost should be allocated each period against the revenues generated."

All this sounded a bit confusing to Vicki. However, she did recognize that her bookkeeping job had only involved her in a small part of the accounting process. Vicki figured that if Lisa could do it so could she. Perhaps she should consider taking an accounting course next semester.

This chapter completes our discussion of the accounting cycle. Balance sheet transactions were analyzed in chapter two and income statement transactions were analyzed in chapter three. The final steps in the accounting cycle are described in this chapter. These steps are preparing adjusting entries, financial statements, and closing entries. This part of the accounting cycle often involves analysis and judgment, and as pointed out in the opening scenario, separates the work of the accountant from that of the bookkeeper.

ADJUSTING ENTRIES

Objective 1
Explain why adjusting entries are necessary, and describe the major categories of adjusting entries.

adjusting entries

Adjusting entries are made at the end of each accounting period to make sure that the financial statements reflect all relevant economic events that occurred during a particular period, and to ensure the proper matching of revenues and expenses. Several types of events are recognized through adjusting entries. All of these events are related to the timing of the recognition of revenues and expenses. Exhibit 4-1 lists the different categories of adjusting entries and provides specific examples of each.

Most of the examples in this chapter will illustrate adjusting entries that involve relatively small amounts, but in the accounting for actual business firms, adjusting entries usually involve only material amounts. For example, a mail order house is likely to use a significant amount of packaging supplies. The amount of supplies used during a particular period would be recorded by an adjusting entry at the end of each period. Failure to expense the cost of packaging supplies used would seriously overstate net income and the net assets of the firm.

Nonmonetary Assets Acquired in One Period and Used Up in Subsequent Periods

nonmonetary assets

monetary assets

Enterprises make cash payments or incur liabilities for nonmonetary assets that affect more than one accounting period. **Nonmonetary assets** are assets that do not represent future claims to fixed amounts of cash. Such assets include prepaid items, office supplies, inventories, buildings, and equipment. (On the other hand, **monetary assets** are cash and the right to receive a specific amount of cash, such as receivables.) Although nonmonetary assets do have economic value, they are used in the generation of revenue and they will not be converted into a known amount of cash at some future date. Nonmonetary assets initially are recorded at their historical cost. This amount represents the future benefits or services that an enterprise expects to receive from these assets. The related cost must be matched against the revenues for the period as these services or benefits are consumed. This allocation is accomplished by making adjusting entries at the end of the period.

Exhibit 4-1

Categories of Adjusting Entries	*Specific Examples*
1. Nonmonetary assets acquired in one period and used up in subsequent period(s)	Supplies, prepaid insurance, depreciation
2. Nonmonetary liabilities recorded in one period with associated revenues earned in subsequent period(s)	Unearned revenue
3. Accruals:	
A. Cash received or receipts obtained after earnings recognized (accrued revenues)	Interest receivable
B. Cash paid in period after benefits received (accrued expenses)	Salaries Payable
4. Estimates of expenses matched with current period revenues	Uncollectible accounts
5. Correction of current and past period errors	Those specific accounts affected

Exhibit 4-2
Allocation Process for Nonmonetary Assets

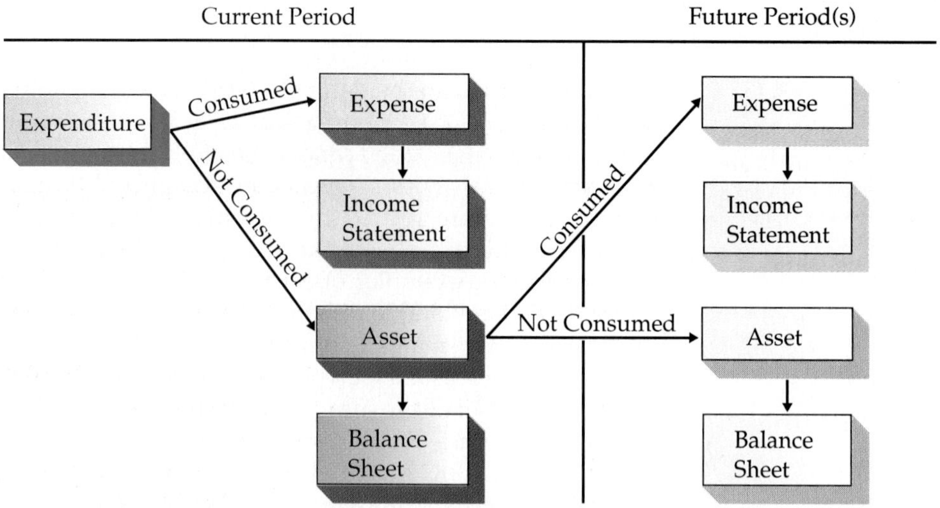

Exhibit 4-2 illustrates this adjustment process. Note that expenditures made in the current period for items having future economic benefits are recorded as assets and are included in the current period's balance sheet. The costs of assets used or consumed in the operations of the business are transferred from an asset account to the corresponding expense account. The unused portion of these assets (representing future economic benefits) at the end of a particular period is included in the balance sheet prepared at the end of the period.

Supplies, prepaid items, and long-lived assets such as buildings and equipment are used in this section to illustrate the allocation process. You should remember, however, that this process can be applied to any similar nonmonetary asset account and its corresponding expense account. The process allocates the portion of total cost that has future economic benefits to an asset account and the portion that has been consumed or used to the appropriate expense account.

Supplies. Firms often purchase supplies at different times during the year. The original debit usually is made to an asset account, such as Office Supplies, when the supplies are purchased.[1] Firms generally do not take time to record the use of office supplies as it occurs. Instead, the cost of the remaining supplies on hand is determined at the end of the accounting period. The cost of supplies used during the period can easily be calculated once the amount of supplies on hand is known. An adjusting journal entry is necessary to record the amount of supplies used.

The calculation of the cost of supplies used is illustrated below. The cost of the supplies used, $1,700 in this case, would be transferred from the supplies account, an asset account, to the supplies expense account.

1. It is possible to record the purchase of supplies by debiting Supplies Expense instead of the asset account, Supplies, for the amount of the purchase. In this case the journal entry would be:

Supplies Expense	xxxx	
Cash (or Accounts Payable)		xxxx

However, the more common practice is to debit the asset account to record the purchase of nonmonetary assets such as supplies and prepaid items. This is the method followed in the text and in the problem assignments.

Computation	*Cost*
Beginning balance of supplies	$ 900
+ Purchases of supplies during the year	1,500
= Supplies available for use	$2,400
− Ending balance of supplies	700
= Supplies used during the period (= supplies expense)	$1,700

The journal entries to record the purchases of supplies on March 14 and September 10 (these are assumed purchase dates), the adjusting entry at the end of the period, December 31, and the appropriate T accounts are shown in Exhibit 4-3. The figures in this example are based on the information just presented and on the assumption that the firm makes adjusting entries only at the end of its reporting year, in this case the calendar year. The balance in the supplies account is $700 after the adjusting entry is posted. This amount represents the cost of the supplies on hand that are available for future use. The balance of $1,700 in Supplies Expense represents the cost of supplies used during the period.

prepaid assets

Prepaid Assets. **Prepaid assets** represent payments made in advance for the right to receive future services or benefits. Examples include prepaid insurance, prepaid rent, and prepaid subscriptions. The rights to these future benefits or services rarely last more than two or three years. The matching convention requires that the costs of these assets be allocated between the current and future periods. The allocation process is related to the term of service because the services to be received are a function of time.

The purchase of prepaid insurance is an example. Assume that the Smith Company, which has a yearly accounting period ending on December 31, purchases a two-year comprehensive insurance policy for $2,400 on April 1. The asset account, Prepaid Insurance, is debited when the insurance policy is purchased. The original journal entry, as well as the adjusting entry and the relevant T accounts, are illustrated in Exhibit 4-4. The asset account Prepaid Insurance is

Exhibit 4-3
Purchase of Supplies

March 14	Supplies	700	
	Cash		700
	To record purchase of supplies.		
September 10	Supplies	800	
	Cash		800
	To record purchase of supplies.		
December 31	Supplies Expense	1,700	
	Supplies		1,700
	To record supplies used during the year.		

Supplies				*Supplies Expense*			
1/1 Bal.	900	12/31	1,700	12/31	1,700		
3/14	700						
9/10	800						
12/31 Bal.	700						

Exhibit 4-4
Prepaid Insurance Entries

April 1	Prepaid Insurance	2,400	
	Cash		2,400
	To record purchase of 2-year insurance policy.		
Dec. 31	Insurance Expense	900	
	Prepaid Insurance		900
	To adjust prepaid insurance for 9 months.		

Amount of journal entry:

$$\frac{\text{Cost of insurance}}{\text{Number of months}} = \frac{\$2{,}400}{24 \text{ months}} = \frac{\$100 \text{ per month}}{\text{cost of benefits received}}$$

Adjusting entry = 9 months × \$100 = \$900

Prepaid Insurance

4/1	2,400	12/31	900
12/31 Bal.	1,500		

Insurance Expense

12/31	900		

reduced by the amount of insurance that has expired as of December 31 because the purchase of the insurance was originally recorded in the asset account. The service represented by the asset expires equally each month in this case. Consequently, Prepaid Insurance must be reduced by $900, or $100 per month, leaving a balance of $1,500. The remaining balance in the account represents the future benefits of the insurance policy. The $900 balance in Insurance Expense represents the amount of expired benefits.

The adjusting entry for prepaid rent and other prepaid assets follows the same process. When you make adjusting entries for prepaid assets, you should follow these steps:

1. Estimate monthly cost of benefits to be received from the asset, using this general formula:

$$\frac{\text{Cost of the asset}}{\text{Total number of months benefits are to be received}}$$

2. Expense the amount of the asset used or consumed, based on the date the asset was acquired and the length of the accounting period. The adjusting entry decreases the asset account and records an expense for the amount of benefits used or expired.

Depreciation. Nonmonetary assets such as property, plant, and equipment are purchased by an enterprise because of the ability of these assets to generate future revenues over a long period of time. For example, a firm might have a computerized molding press which manufactures its main product, plastic key chains. Because of this production process the firm manufacturers a product which when sold produces revenues for the firm. In effect, these assets represent bundles of service potentials that are gradually used up through wear and tear, obsolescence, and other factors. Except for land, which does not lose its future benefits, the matching convention requires that a portion of the cost of these assets be systematically allocated against the revenues generated by the use of these assets. This cost allocation process is called **depreciation.**

depreciation

Although it is more difficult to imagine a building or piece of equipment giving up its benefits than it is to imagine supplies being physically used up or the term of an insurance policy expiring, the concept is the same. As the benefits from these assets are consumed, a portion of their cost should be written off to expense. In this sense, the term *write off* means decreasing the asset balance and increasing the expense account balance by the benefits that have been used or have expired.

Depreciation is an allocation concept rather than a valuation concept. In this sense, allocation means apportioning the cost of the asset to various accounting periods. Accountants allocate the historical cost of an asset to different time periods as the asset gradually loses its ability to generate future operating revenues, even if the asset's current market value is increasing.

A number of acceptable methods to compute depreciation are discussed in Chapter 10. For our present purposes, we will assume that a firm uses the straight-line method. **Straight-line depreciation** assumes that the asset's benefits expire evenly over time and thus allocates an equal amount of the asset's cost to each accounting period during its useful life.

straight-line depreciation

The asset's useful life and residual (or salvage) value must be estimated before depreciation expense can be calculated. The asset's **useful or economic life** is a measure of the service potential that the current user may expect from the asset. That is, it is management's estimate of how long the asset will provide economic benefits to the firm. Useful life is usually expressed in years, but as we will see in Chapter 10, it can also be expressed in expected output such as the number of miles a delivery truck will last. Further, an asset's actual physical life may be many years, but its economic life may be much shorter. For example, a computer may have an actual life of many years, but new technology may make its real economic life much shorter.

useful or economic life

Determining the life of a building or piece of equipment is much more difficult than determining the life or term of other nonmonetary assets. For example, an insurance policy has a fixed term, but there is clearly no fixed life for a building. Management makes a best estimate of the useful life of buildings and other long-lived assets using broad guidelines established by the accounting profession and past experience.

Residual (salvage) value is an estimate of what the asset will be worth at the end of its life. Again, management must make this estimate based on past experience and the asset's economic characteristics. The residual value of an asset is not depreciated. Depreciation is limited to the asset's **depreciable base,** which is its acquisition cost less its estimated residual value.

residual (salvage) value

depreciable base

The following formula is used to calculate straight-line depreciation:

$$\text{Annual Depreciation Expense} = \frac{\text{Depreciable base*}}{\text{Estimated useful life}}$$

*Acquisition cost − Residual value

Residual or salvage value is considered to be zero in many cases. In that case, the depreciable base equals the acquisition cost.

To illustrate these concepts, assume that on January 2, 1995, an enterprise purchases a new piece of equipment for $75,000 cash. The company has a yearly accounting period ending December 31 and makes adjusting entries only at that time. The firm estimates that the equipment has a useful life of ten years and that at the end of the tenth year, the equipment will have a residual value of $5,000. Exhibit 4-5 shows the journal entries to record the purchase of the equip-

Exhibit 4-5
Journal Entries Related to Depreciation Expense

January 2, 1995	Equipment	75,000	
	Cash		75,000
	To record purchase of equipment for cash.		
December 31, 1995, and thereafter through 2004	Depreciation Expense	7,000	
	Accumulated Depreciation—Equipment		7,000
	To record annual depreciation expense of $7,000.		

$$\text{Calculation of annual depreciation expense} = \frac{\text{Depreciable base}}{\text{Estimated useful life}}$$

$$\$7{,}000 = \frac{\$75{,}000 - \$5{,}000}{10 \text{ years}}$$

Equipment

Debit		Credit
1/2/95	75,000	

Accumulated Depreciation—Equipment

Debit	Credit	
	12/31/95	7,000
	12/31/96	7,000
	12/31/97	7,000
	12/31/98	7,000
	12/31/99	7,000
	12/31/2000	7,000
	12/31/01	7,000
	12/31/02	7,000
	12/31/03	7,000
	12/31/04	7,000
	12/31/04 Bal.	70,000

Depreciation Expense

Debit		Credit
12/31 each year	7,000	

ment, the adjusting entry to record the annual depreciation expense of $7,000 each December 31 during the ten-year useful life, and the relevant T accounts.

contra account

Note that the credit entry is made to an accumulated depreciation account rather than directly to the equipment account. Accumulated Depreciation is a contra asset account. A **contra account** partially or wholly offsets the balance in another account. Crediting this account rather than the equipment account allows the accounting system to maintain both the original historical cost of the asset in one account (Equipment in this case) and to accumulate the depreciation-to-date in the accumulated depreciation account. Both of these accounts are shown on the asset side of the balance sheet. The balance in Accumulated Depreciation is deducted from the balance in the corresponding asset account. Going back to the original example, the proper balance sheet presentation of equipment as of December 31, 1995 is:

Property, plant, and equipment	
Equipment (cost)	$75,000
Less: Accumulated depreciation	7,000
Net book value—12/31/95	$68,000

The difference between these two accounts, $68,000, at the end of the first year of the asset's life, is often referred to as the asset's net book value. **Net book value** is the difference between the historical cost of an asset and its accumulated depreciation.

net book value

Like other balance sheet accounts, the accumulated depreciation account has a cumulative balance. At the end of 1996, the balance in that account will be $14,000, and the net book value of the equipment will be $61,000, determined as follows:

Property, plant and equipment	
Equipment (cost)	$75,000
Less: Accumulated depreciation	14,000
Net book value—12/31/96	$61,000

By the end of 2004, the accumulated depreciation account will have a balance of $70,000, and the net book value will equal $5,000, the asset's estimated residual value. Later in this chapter, you will learn how the $7,000 yearly balance in the depreciation expense account is transferred to the retained earnings account at the end of the year.

Equipment was used for the depreciation example. The same concept applies to all operational assets except land, which is not depreciable. Other examples are buildings, furniture and fixtures, automobiles, and machines. Different useful lives and salvage values have to be estimated for each of these assets. In addition, a separate accumulated depreciation account is maintained for each major category. For example, Accumulated Depreciation—Equipment was used in Exhibit 4-5. The contra account Accumulated Depreciation—Buildings would be used with the Buildings account, and so forth.

Nonmonetary Liabilities Recorded in One Period With Associated Revenues Earned in Subsequent Period(s)

The previous section examined the purchase of nonmonetary assets in one period that affect current and subsequent periods. This section will consider transactions in which a firm receives cash or other assets before goods have been delivered or services rendered. The receipts represent revenues that are to be earned in the future. The portion of the receipts that will be earned in subsequent accounting periods is a nonmonetary liability called *unearned revenue.* These unearned revenues are considered **nonmonetary liabilities** because the liability is reduced by the performance of a service or the delivery of goods, not by a cash payment.

nonmonetary liabilities

Unearned revenues arise whenever an enterprise receives cash or other assets prior to a sale or the performance of a service. At the time the firm receives the asset, an obligation (liability) to deliver a product or perform a service arises. Common sources of unearned revenues are dues and subscriptions. An example is a publisher of a magazine, such as *Time,* who collects subscription money before the magazine is delivered.

To illustrate this concept, assume that a firm rents part of a building it owns to others, on a yearly basis. The agreement calls for the tenant to pay a full year's rent of $18,000 in advance, on September 1, 1995.[2] Assuming that the firm is on

2. Receiving a year's rent in advance is not a common situation. It is used in this example as an easy way to illustrate the important concepts.

Exhibit 4-6
Allocation Process for Unearned Revenues

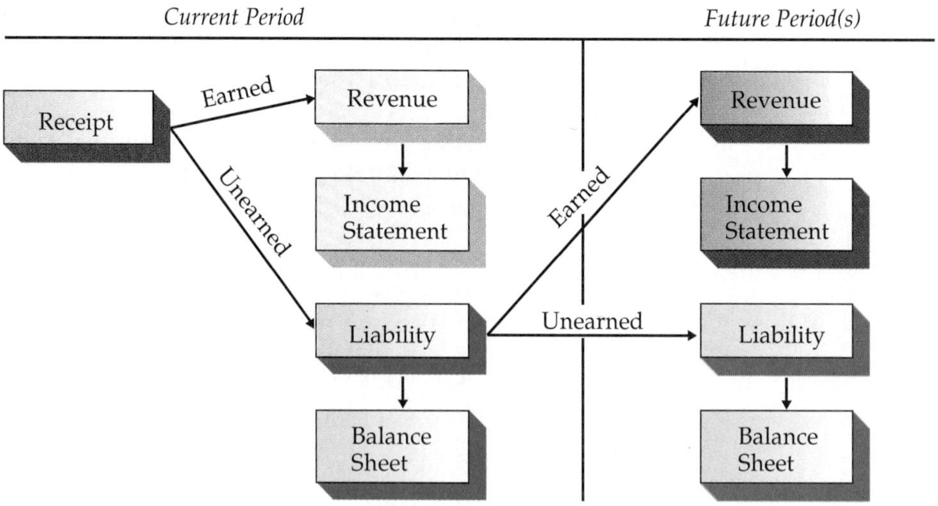

a calendar year, the revenue must be allocated between 1995 and 1996. The portion that is unearned at the end of 1995 must be reflected as a liability.

This allocation process is illustrated in Exhibit 4-6. In reviewing this diagram, note that receipts which have not been earned by the end of the current period are recorded as liabilities and are included on the balance sheet at the end of the current period. The portion of these liabilities that is earned in a subsequent period will be recorded as revenue and reported on the income statement in that subsequent period. The unearned balance at the end of the subsequent period will be reported on the balance sheet as a liability.

Recall that prepaid expenses were initially recorded as assets in a prepaid asset account. In the same fashion, unearned revenues are initially recorded as liabilities.[3] As the revenues are earned, the liability balance is decreased, and the revenue balance is increased. The original entry, the adjusting entry, and the T accounts for the building rental example are illustrated in Exhibit 4-7. The entire $18,000 receipt is originally recorded as a liability. The adjusting entry prepared on December 31 reduces the balance in the liability account and transfers the earned portion of the receipt to the revenue account. Earned monthly revenues total $1,500, determined by dividing the total rental payment of $18,000 by 12 months. The adjusting journal entry for $6,000 ($1,500 per month × 4 months) is necessary to reduce the liability and to recognize the rental revenue earned from September 1 to December 31 (4 months).

Again, it is important to note the end result. The liability account has an ending balance of $12,000. This balance represents the revenues yet to be earned (8 months at $1,500 per month), and the revenue account has a balance of $6,000 representing the 4 months of rental revenue earned by the firm. Although this example concerns rent, other more common unearned revenues, such as subscriptions and dues, are handled in the same manner.

3. Again, it is possible to record this transaction by crediting a revenue account rather than the liability account for the revenue received in advance. However, this would require a change in the way the adjusting entry is made. This text and the problem assignments follow the more common method of crediting the unearned revenue account at the time the asset is recorded.

Exhibit 4-7
Recording Unearned Revenues

September 1	Cash	18,000	
	Unearned Rent Revenue		18,000
	To record receipt of 1 year's rent.		
December 31	Unearned Rent Revenue	6,000	
	Rent Revenue		6,000
	To adjust unearned rent for 4 months of earned revenue.		

Amount of journal entry:

$$\frac{\text{Total receipt}}{\text{Number of months}} = \frac{\$18{,}000}{12\text{ months}} = \$1{,}500\text{ per month}$$

$$\text{Adjusting entry} = 4\text{ months} \times \$1{,}500 = \$6{,}000$$

Unearned Rent Revenue

12/31	6,000	9/1	18,000
		12/31 Bal.	12,000

Rent Revenue

		12/31	6,000

Accruals

accruals

This section will discuss adjusting entries for transactions in which the cash receipt or cash payment occurs after revenues have been earned or expenses have been incurred. These adjusting entries are called **accruals,** and are necessary to record the proper amount of revenue or expense before cash is received or paid.

Accruals recognize that certain expenses are incurred and certain revenues earned over time but are only recorded periodically. Consequently, adjustments must be made for revenues or expenses that are continuously earned or incurred but which have not been recorded because cash has not yet been received or paid. The cash receipt or payment will occur during one or more subsequent accounting periods.

Accruals are a very common form of adjusting entry. Examples of accruals include interest revenue, interest expense, and salaries expense. It is important to note that accruals are made only for revenues or expenses that are earned or incurred in one period and for which cash will be received or paid in a subsequent period. An accrual is not necessary when cash is received or paid in the period the revenue or expense is recognized.

The difference between asset or liability allocation and accruals is illustrated in Exhibit 4-8. The prepaid or unearned portion of assets and liabilities decreases over time as the account balances are allocated to the appropriate accounting periods. This allocation occurs when the assets or liabilities are used or earned over time. Accruals, on the other hand, increase over time as revenue is earned or expenses are incurred.

accrued revenue

Accrued Revenues. Revenue that is earned over time but for which the corresponding cash is received periodically is an **accrued revenue.** Examples of accrued revenues include interest revenue and rental revenue. Adjusting entries must be made for these items to recognize revenue in the accounting period in which it is earned, even though the receipt of cash will take place in following periods. Revenues from these items are earned continuously. However, to simplify the recording process, the revenues are recorded at the end of the account-

Exhibit 4-8
Allocation Versus Accrual

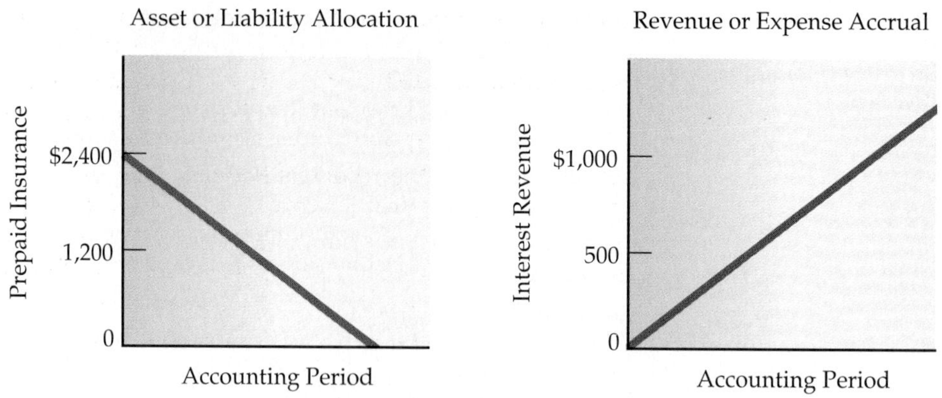

ing period. The adjusting entry recognizes a receivable and a corresponding revenue item.

Accrued Interest Revenue. Interest is payment for the use of money. Most loans are interest bearing and have the following characteristics:

principal (face amount)
maturity date
maturity value
interest rate

1. **Principal (or face amount)**—the amount lent or borrowed.
2. **Maturity date**—the date the loan must be repaid.
3. **Maturity value**—the total of the principal plus interest at the maturity date.
4. **Interest rate**—the percentage rate which is usually stated in annual terms and must be prorated for periods shorter than a year.

In general, interest can be calculated with the following formula:

$$i = p \times r \times t$$

where

i = interest
p = principal of the loan
r = annual interest rate
t = applicable time period in fractions of a year

The following example illustrates the calculation of interest and maturity value. Assume that a firm lends $200,000 to its best supplier at 12% interest for nine months. The loan principal is $200,000 and the annual interest rate is 12%. The maturity value of the loan is $218,000. The maturity value is calculated as follows:

Principal	$200,000
Interest for 9 months	
$200,000 × .12 × 9/12 =	18,000
Maturity value	$218,000

The time period is 9/12 because the loan will be outstanding for nine months of the year (12 months).

To now illustrate the adjusting entries for interest accruals, assume that on June 1, 1995 the Marconi Company lent $10,000 for nine months with a 9% annual interest rate to one of its suppliers. The supplier signed an actual note so the loan will be recorded as a note payable. The note's maturity date is February 28, 1996, at which time both the principal and the total interest will be due. In this situation, 9% represents the interest rate for one year and must be prorated to determine the interest for nine months. (In this example, as well as others, interest is based on 12 30-day months or a 360-day year.)

The Marconi Company started earning interest revenue as soon as the loan was made. However, the revenue is not recorded until the end of the accounting period, in this case December 31, 1995. Waiting until the due date of February 28, 1996 to recognize the interest revenue earned through December 31, 1995 would not be correct because no revenue would be recognized in 1995 and too much would be recognized in 1996. This would violate the matching principle. Although it is possible to record the interest daily, this involves excess record keeping, so an adjusting entry is made before financial statements are prepared at the end of the accounting period.

In this example, the $10,000, 9% note earns interest from June 1 to December 31, 1995 (seven months) which amounts to $525, calculated as follows:

$$i = \$10{,}000 \times .09 \times 7/12$$
$$= \$525$$

The total interest for the nine-month term of the note is $675, or $10,000 × .09 × 9/12. Thus the interest revenue recognized for the seven months in 1995 is $525, and the interest earned for 1996 is $150 (total interest for 9 months of $675 less $525 earned in 1995). These relationships are illustrated on the time line shown below.

Total Interest Revenue

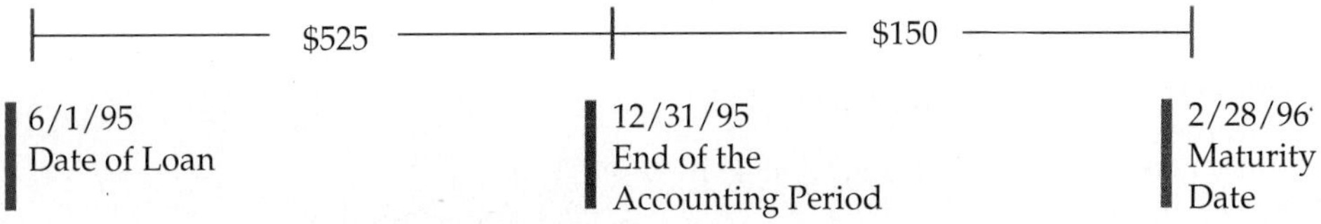

The appropriate journal entries are shown in Exhibit 4-9.

The adjusting entry prepared on December 31, 1995 appropriately recognizes and records the interest revenue earned in 1995. The cash payment for the interest will not be received until the note's maturity in 1996.

At the maturity date, cash is debited for the entire cash proceeds related to the note (the principal plus the interest—in this case $10,675). Interest Receivable is credited for $525, the interest recognized in the prior period but received on the maturity date. Interest Revenue is credited for $150, the interest earned during 1996. Finally, Notes Receivable is credited for $10,000, the principal of the loan.

accrued expenses

Accrued Expenses. **Accrued expenses** are expenses incurred in one accounting period that will be paid in a subsequent accounting period. Accrued expenses include such items as interest expense, salaries expense, tax expense, and rental expense. Adjusting entries must be made for these items to recognize the expense in the period in which it is incurred, even though the cash will not be paid until the following period. Like accrued revenues, accrued expenses occur continuously, but they are recorded only at the end of the accounting period to simplify the accounting process. The adjusting entry recognizes a payable and a corresponding expense item.

Exhibit 4-9
Interest Revenue Accrual

June 1, 1995	Note Receivable	10,000	
	Cash		10,000
	To record issuance of note.		
Dec. 31, 1995	Interest Receivable	525	
	Interest Revenue		525
	To record 7 months' interest on $10,000, 9%, 9-month note.		
Feb. 28, 1996	Cash	10,675	
	Interest Receivable		525
	Interest Revenue		150
	Note Receivable		10,000
	To record payment of principal and interest on note.		

Accrued Interest Expense. The adjusting journal entry for accrued interest expense corresponds to the entry for accrued interest revenue, except that a payable and an expense are recorded instead of a receivable and a revenue. For example, assume that on July 1, 1995, the Dogget Company borrows $10,000 from a local bank at 8%. Both principal and interest are payable in four quarterly installments, beginning October 1, 1995. The series of journal entries through January 2, 1996, including the December 31, 1995 adjusting journal entry, is shown in Exhibit 4-10.

Exhibit 4-10
Interest Expense Accrual

July 1, 1995	Cash	10,000	
	Note Payable		10,000
	To record $10,000, 8% loan from bank.		
Oct. 1, 1995	Note Payable	2,500	
	Interest Expense	200	
	Cash		2,700
	To record first payment of interest and principal.		
	$i = p \times r \times t$		
	$= \$10,000 \times .08 \times 3/12$		
	$= \$200$		
Dec. 31, 1995	Interest Expense	150	
	Interest Payable		150
	To record accrued interest payable.		
	$i = p \times r \times t$		
	$= (\$10,000 - \$2,500) \times .08 \times 3/12$		
	$= \$150$		
Jan. 2, 1996	Note Payable	2,500	
	Interest Payable	150	
	Cash		2,650
	To record payment of second installment of principal and interest.		

The example is slightly more complex than the previous interest revenue example. In this case, the note and the interest are paid quarterly. The interest expense is based on the outstanding principal balance of the note at the beginning of the period. Therefore, on October 1, 1995, interest expense is $200, or 8% of $10,000 for three months. The interest expense for the next quarter is based on the new balance in the Note Payable account of $7,500, which is the unpaid balance after the principal payment on October 1, 1995. An adjustment must be made at December 31, 1995, to record the interest expense that was incurred for the three month period between October 1, 1995 and December 31, 1995 but will not be paid until January 2, 1996. Finally, the journal entry on January 2, 1996 reflects the second payment of principal and interest.

Accrued Salaries Expense. Salaries expense is another example of an accrued expense for which adjusting entries normally are made. An adjustment is necessary when the date that salaries are paid does not correspond to the last date of the accounting period. Therefore accrued salaries expense must be recorded for salaries earned by employees but unpaid at the end of the accounting period.

For example, assume that a firm pays salaries on Friday for the workweek ending on that day. For simplicity's sake, also assume that the firm began operations on Monday, January 1, 1995; the first payday of the year was Friday, January 5, 1995 and weekly salaries total $1,500. After the last full week of the year on December 28, 1995, the salaries T account appears as follows:[4]

Salaries Expense

1/5	1,500	
1/12	1,500	
1/19	1,500	
"	"	
"	"	
12/28	1,500	
12/28 Bal.	78,000	

Because salaries earned for the week beginning Monday, December 31, 1995 are not paid until Friday, January 4, 1996, it is necessary to make an adjusting entry to accrue salaries through December 31, 1995. This requires an entry to debit Salaries Expense and to credit Salaries Payable. In this case, the amount of accrued salaries at December 31, 1995 is for one day's salaries, or $300 ($1,500 ÷ 5 days = $300). The salaries for the next four days of the week, or $1,200, are an expense of the next year, 1996. The time line below shows the total amount of salaries expense for the week ended Friday, January 4, 1996, and how much expense should be allocated between the two years. Finally, the adjusting journal entry at December 31, 1995, the entry to record the payment of salaries on January 4, 1996, and the T accounts are shown in Exhibit 4-11.

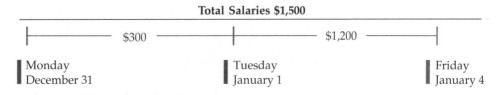

Total Salaries $1,500

$300	$1,200	
Monday December 31	Tuesday January 1	Friday January 4

4. In actuality, the last Friday of 1995 is December 29. We assume it is December 28 in this example to illustrate how to allocate the salaries between the two years.

Exhibit 4-11
Accrual of Salaries Payable

Dec. 31, 1995	Salaries Expense	300	
	Salaries Payable		300
	To record accrued salaries.		
Jan. 4, 1996	Salaries Payable	300	
	Salaries Expense	1,200	
	Cash		1,500
	To record payment of salaries.		

Salaries Expense

1/5	1,500	
1/12	1,500	
1/19	1,500	
"	"	
12/28	1,500	
12/31	300	
12/31 Bal.	78,300	

Salaries Payable

12/31	300	

Cash is credited for the full week's salaries on January 4, 1996 when the salaries are paid. Salaries Payable is debited for the salaries owed at the end of the prior period, and Salaries Expense is debited for the current period's salaries at the same time.

Other Items Requiring Adjusting Entries

Other items may also require adjusting entries. For example, accounts receivable, inventories, and estimated liabilities such as warranties may need to be adjusted to their proper balances. The entry to record federal and state tax expense and taxes payable often is made as an adjusting entry. These items will be covered in later chapters. In addition, bookkeeping errors usually are corrected through adjusting entries at the end of the accounting period.

Adjusting Entries: A Summary

Adjusting entries ensure the proper timing of the recognition of revenues and expenses. Adjusting entries are prepared when cash is paid or received for nonmonetary assets or liabilities in one period but the related expense or revenue will be recognized in future accounting periods. Adjusting entries are also prepared when an expense or revenue is recognized in the current period but no payment will be made or received until a future accounting period. Finally, adjusting entries are necessary to record certain estimated expenses as well as correct errors.

THE WHITE-WATER BOAT COMPANY

Let us now examine the adjusting entries necessary for The White-Water Boat Company at the end of its first (quarterly) accounting cycle. The March 31, 1995

Exhibit 4-12

The White-Water Boat Company
Unadjusted Trial Balance
March 31, 1995

	Debit	Credit
Cash	$14,340	
Accounts receivable	4,600	
Inventory	9,500	
Office supplies	2,000	
License	200	
Prepaid insurance	1,200	
Land	5,000	
Office equipment	9,900	
Buildings	10,000	
Accounts payable		$ 7,200
Bank loan payable		4,000
Capital stock		40,000
Sales		16,000
Cost of goods sold	9,500	
Salaries expense	500	
Advertising expense	300	
Repairs and maintenance expense	60	
Utilities expense	100	
Totals	$67,200	$67,200

unadjusted trial balance

unadjusted trial balance for the company is reproduced in Exhibit 4-12.[5] Assume that the firm's quarterly accounting period ends on March 31, 1995 and that adjusting entries must be made for the three-month period January 1 (the date the firm was organized) through March 31, 1995.

Activities of the firm requiring adjusting entries are enumerated below, and the actual adjusting entries in the general journal are shown in Exhibit 4-13. The number of the adjusting entry is listed under the date column, and the number of the account is listed in the Ref. column.

1. The license purchased on January 2, 1995 has a life of one year. The appropriate amount of expense must be recorded for January, February, and March.
2. A count of office supplies indicated that supplies costing $1,200 remained on hand at the end of March.
3. Prepaid insurance used must be allocated to expense. The policy was purchased on February 18, but it does not become effective until March 1. Therefore, one month's cost must be expensed.
4. Office equipment has an estimated useful life of five years and a $900 estimated residual value. In order to simplify the calculations, the firm will recognize depreciation on the office equipment from the beginning of February.
5. The building has an estimated useful life of 15 years and a $2,800 estimated residual value. Again, for simplicity, the firm will depreciate the building from the beginning of February.

5. Past chapters have referred to the unadjusted trial balance as just the trial balance. However, because it is produced from the general ledger balances prior to adjustments, its proper name is the unadjusted trial balance.

6. The $4,000 bank loan to purchase office equipment has an annual interest rate of 9%. Interest and $1,000 of principal are payable in one year. The remaining $3,000 is payable in $1,000 installments thereafter. The loan was made on February 12. Assume an entire month's interest for February.
7. Salaries expense for the second half of March totaled $800 and will be paid the first day of April.
8. Income taxes payable for the three months ending March 31 amounted to $670. This is based on a combined federal and state tax rate of 20% on $3,350 of income before taxes.

Exhibit 4-13

The White-Water Boat Company
Adjusting Journal Entries
General Journal

Date	*Account Title*	*Ref.*	*Debit*	*Credit*
1	License Expense	705	50	
	License	120		50
	To write off three months, or 1/4 year of the license.			
	$200 × 1/4 = $50			
2	Office Supplies Expense	707	800	
	Office Supplies	115		800
	To write off office supplies used during the period.			
	Beginning Balance $2,000			
	− Supplies on hand 1,200			
	Supplies used $ 800			
3	Insurance Expense	711	100	
	Prepaid Insurance	125		100
	To write off one month of prepaid insurance. Monthly write off = $100 or $1,200 ÷ 12 months.			
4	Depreciation Expense	715	300	
	Accumulated Depreciation—Office Equipment	161		300
	To record two months' depreciation. ($9,900 − $900)/5 years = $1,800 per year or $150 per month, or $300 for two months.			
5	Depreciation Expense	715	80	
	Accumulated Depreciation—Buildings	166		80
	To record two months' depreciation. ($10,000 − $2,800)/15 years = $480 per year or $40 per month, or $80 for two months.			
6	Interest Expense	801	60	
	Interest Payable	212		60
	To record interest for two months. $4,000 × $.09 × 2/12 = $60.			

(continued)

Exhibit 4-13
(continued)

Date	Account Title	Ref.	Debit	Credit
7	Salaries Expense	601	800	
	Salaries Payable	210		800
	To record salaries payable for the second half of March.			
8	Taxes Expense	811	670	
	Taxes Payable	214		670
	To record taxes payable.			

COMPLETING THE ACCOUNTING CYCLE

Objective 2
Complete the remaining steps in the accounting cycle.

Five steps remain in the accounting cycle after the adjusting entries have been recorded in the general journal. These steps are:

1. Post the adjusting entries to the ledger accounts.
2. Prepare an adjusted trial balance.
3. Prepare financial statements:
   a. Income statement.
   b. Retained earnings statement.
   c. Balance sheet.
   d. Statement of cash flows.
4. Make closing entries and post to the ledger accounts.
5. Prepare a post-closing trial balance.

Posting Adjusting Entries to the General Ledger

Like other journal entries, the adjusting entries must be posted to the ledger accounts after they have been recorded in the general journal. The general ledger T accounts for The White-Water Boat Company after the adjusting entries have been posted are shown in Exhibit 4-14. The adjusting entries are posted to the T accounts with a reference A1 through A8.

Exhibit 4-14

The White-Water Boat Company
T Accounts
March 31, 1995, After Posting Adjusting Entries

Cash			*101*	*Accounts Receivable*			*106*
3/1 Bal.	11,000	3/16	500	3/1 Bal.	600	3/23	3,000
3/15	2,000	3/24	60	3/15	4,000		
3/23	3,000	3/26	100	3/31	3,000		
3/31	7,000	3/29	8,000				
3/31 Bal.	14,340			3/31 Bal.	4,600		

Inventory			*110*	*Office Supplies*			*115*
3/1 Bal.	9,000	3/15	3,500	3/1 Bal.	2,000	A2	800
3/20	10,000	3/31	6,000				
3/31 Bal.	9,500			3/31 Bal.	1,200		

(continued)

Exhibit 4-14
(continued)

License 120

3/1 Bal.	200	A1	50
3/31 Bal.	150		

Prepaid Insurance 125

3/1 Bal.	1,200	A3	100
3/31 Bal.	1,100		

Land 150

3/1 Bal.	5,000		

Office Equipment 160

3/1 Bal.	9,900		

Accumulated Depreciation—Office Equipment 161

		A4	300

Buildings 165

3/1 Bal.	10,000		

Accumulated Depreciation—Buildings 166

		A5	80

Accounts Payable 201

3/29	8,000	3/1 Bal.	4,900
		3/2	300
		3/20	10,000
		3/31 Bal.	7,200

Bank Loan Payable 205

		3/1 Bal.	4,000

Salaries Payable 210

		A7	800

Interest Payable 212

		A6	60

Taxes Payable 214

		A8	670

Capital Stock 301

		3/1 Bal.	40,000

Sales 401

		3/15	6,000
		3/31	10,000
		3/31 Bal.	16,000

Cost of Goods Sold 500

3/15	3,500		
3/31	6,000		
3/31 Bal.	9,500		

Salaries Expense 601

3/16	500		
A7	800		
3/31 Bal.	1,300		

Advertising Expense 605

3/2	300		

Repairs and Maintenance Expense 701

3/24	60		

Utilities Expense 703

3/26	100		

License Expense 705

A1	50		

Office Supplies Expense 707

A2	800		

Insurance Expense 711

A3	100		

Depreciation Expense 715

A4	300		
A5	80		
3/31 Bal.	380		

Interest Expense 801

A6	60		

Taxes Expense 811

A8	670		

Adjusted Trial Balance

adjusted trial balance

An **adjusted trial balance** is normally prepared after the adjusting entries have been posted to the general ledger, and thus is a list of all the accounts after adjustments. The adjusted trial balance is used to check for posting errors. The March 31, 1995 adjusted trial balance for The White-Water Boat Company is presented in Exhibit 4-15.

Financial Statements

The income statement (Exhibit 4-16), statement of retained earnings (Exhibit 4-17), and balance sheet (Exhibit 4-18) for The White-Water Boat Company are illustrated next. These three financial statements can be prepared from the adjusted trial balance.

Exhibit 4-15

The White-Water Boat Company
Adjusted Trial Balance
March 31, 1995

	Debit	*Credit*
Cash	$14,340	
Accounts receivable	4,600	
Inventory	9,500	
Office supplies	1,200	
License	150	
Prepaid insurance	1,100	
Land	5,000	
Office equipment	9,900	
Accumulated Depreciation—Office Equipment		$ 300
Buildings	10,000	
Accumulated Depreciation—Buildings		80
Accounts payable		7,200
Bank loan payable		4,000
Salaries payable		800
Interest payable		60
Taxes payable		670
Capital stock		40,000
Sales		16,000
Cost of goods sold	9,500	
Salaries expense	1,300	
Advertising expense	300	
Repairs and maintenance expense	60	
Utilities expense	100	
License expense	50	
Office supplies expense	800	
Insurance expense	100	
Depreciation expense	380	
Interest expense	60	
Taxes expense	670	
Totals	$69,110	$69,110

Exhibit 4-16

The White-Water Boat Company Income Statement For the Three Months Ended March 31, 1995		
Revenues		
Sales		$16,000
Expenses		
Cost of goods sold	$9,500	
Salaries	1,300	
Office supplies	800	
Depreciation	380	
Advertising	300	
Utilities	100	
Insurance	100	
Interest	60	
Repairs and maintenance	60	
License	50	
Total expenses		12,650
Income before taxes		$ 3,350
Income taxes		670
Net income		$ 2,680

Exhibit 4-17

The White-Water Boat Company Retained Earnings Statement For the Three Months Ended March 31, 1995	
Retained earnings, January 1, 1995	$ 0
Add: Income for the period	2,680
Total	$2,680
Less: Dividends	0
Retained earnings, March 31, 1995	$2,680

The income statement is taken directly from the adjusted trial balance with the expenses listed in descending magnitude of their dollar amounts. Except for the retained earnings total, amounts for the balance sheet also are taken directly from the adjusted trial balance. The retained earnings total on the balance sheet is taken from the ending balance on the statement of retained earnings. This is because the retained earnings balance will not reflect any of the income statement transactions until after closing entries are made. Later in this chapter, it will become clear that the journalizing and posting of closing entries to the general ledger makes the retained earnings account balance equal to the ending retained earnings balance presented on the March 31, 1995 balance sheet.

Unlike the other statements, the statement of cash flows cannot be prepared directly from the adjusted trial balance. Cash receipts and disbursements must be analyzed to prepare this statement. Essentially, there must be a conversion from the accrual basis to the cash basis of accounting. This statement is shown in Exhibit 4-19. The source of the data for the statement is presented in Exhibit

Exhibit 4-18

The White-Water Boat Company
Balance Sheet
March 31, 1995

Assets

Cash		$14,340
Accounts receivable		4,600
Inventory		9,500
Office supplies		1,200
License		150
Prepaid insurance		1,100
Land		5,000
Office equipment	$ 9,900	
Less accumulated depreciation	300	9,600
Buildings	$10,000	
Less accumulated depreciation	80	9,920
Total assets		$55,410

Liabilities and Stockholders' Equity

Liabilities		
Accounts payable	$ 7,200	
Bank loan payable	4,000	
Salaries payable	800	
Interest payable	60	
Taxes payable	670	
Total liabilities		$12,730
Stockholders' Equity		
Capital stock	$40,000	
Retained earnings	2,680	
Total stockholders' equity		42,680
Total liabilities and stockholders' equity		$55,410

4-20 on page 163. Note that the final cash balance of $14,340 shown at the bottom of the statement of cash flows agrees with the cash balance presented in the balance sheet (Exhibit 4-18).

Closing Entries

closing entries

Separate revenue and expense accounts are maintained to accumulate information on the details of operations during an accounting period. This information is reported in the income statement at the end of a period. However, the net effect of these transactions must ultimately be reflected in the Retained Earnings account. **Closing entries** are made at the end of the period and are used to accomplish two objectives:

1. Eliminating the balances in the revenue and expense accounts so that the income statement accounts begin the subsequent period with zero balances.
2. Updating the retained earnings balance to reflect the results of operations.

Exhibit 4-19

The White-Water Boat Company Statement of Cash Flows For the Three Months Ended March 31, 1995		
Cash flows from operating activities		
Cash receipts from operations	$12,200	
Cash disbursements from operations	(17,560)	
Net cash used in operations		$ (5,360)
Cash flows from investing activities		
Purchase of office equipment	$ (5,300)	
Purchase of land	(5,000)	
Purchase of building	(10,000)	
Net cash used in investing activities		(20,300)
Cash flows from financing activities		
Issuance of stock		40,000
Net increase in cash		$14,340
Cash balance at January 1, 1995		0
Cash balance at March 31, 1995		$14,340

Closing Revenue Accounts. Revenue accounts such as sales, fees earned, and interest revenue have credit balances. To close these accounts to a zero balance, they are debited for the amount of the ending balance. The credit part of this entry is made to an account entitled Income Summary. The **income summary account** is a temporary holding account used in the closing process. This account does not appear on any financial statements.

income summary account

The White-Water Boat Company has only one revenue account, Sales, that is closed. If several revenue accounts were listed, they could all be debited in one compound closing entry and balanced with a single credit to the Income Summary account.

3/31/95	C-1	Sales	16,000	
		Income Summary		16,000
		To close the revenue account to Income Summary.		

The T accounts appear as follows after this closing entry has been posted:

Sales 401

Debit		Credit	
		3/15	6,000
		3/31	10,000
C1	16,000		
		3/31 Bal.	0

Income Summary 1000

Debit		Credit	
		C1	16,000

Closing Expense Accounts. Expense accounts generally have debit balances. To close these accounts to a zero balance, they are credited for the amount of their individual ending balances. The debit part of the entry is to the Income Summary account. One compound entry is used to close all the expense accounts. The entry to close the expense accounts for The White-Water Boat Company is on the bottom of page 163.

Exhibit 4-20

The White-Water Boat Company
Analysis for Statement of Cash Flows
For the Three Months Ended March 31, 1995

Cash receipts from operations		
Cash received from sale of computer		
January 31	$ 100	
February 28	100	$ 200
Cash sales		
March 15	$ 2,000	
March 31	7,000	9,000
Cash collected on account		
March 23		3,000
Total cash receipts from operations		$12,200
Cash disbursements from operations		
Purchase of license—Jan. 1	$ 200	
Payment on account—Jan. 31	500	
Purchase of office supplies—Feb. 11	2,000	
Purchase of insurance—Feb. 18	1,200	
Payment on account—Feb. 28	5,000	
Payment of salaries—March 16	500	
Repairs and maintenance—March 24	60	
Utilities—March 26	100	
Payment on account—March 29	8,000	
Total cash disbursements from operations		$17,560
Cash flows from investing activities		
Purchase of office equipment—Jan. 3	$ 1,300	
Purchase of land—Feb. 5	5,000	
Purchase of building—Feb. 5	10,000	
Purchase of office equipment—Feb. 12	4,000	
Total cash flows from investing activities		$20,300
Cash flows from financing activities		
Issuance of stock—Jan. 1	$ 5,000	
Issuance of stock—Feb. 2	35,000	
Total cash flows from financing activities		$40,000

3/31/95	C-2	Income Summary	13,320	
		Cost of Goods Sold		9,500
		Salaries Expense		1,300
		Advertising Expense		300
		Repairs and Maintenance Expense		60
		Utilities Expense		100
		License Expense		50
		Office Supplies Expense		800
		Insurance Expense		100
		Depreciation Expense		380
		Interest Expense		60
		Taxes Expense		670
		To close the expense accounts to Income Summary.		

After this entry is posted, the T accounts appear as shown in Exhibit 4-21. The arrows in Exhibit 4-21 indicate the flow of the closing entry that credits the various expense accounts and debits Income Summary.

Closing the Income Summary Account. The next step in the closing process is to close the Income Summary account into the Retained Earnings account. The effects of all the income statement transactions for a period are summarized in the Income Summary account after the revenue and expense accounts have been closed. The Income Summary account will have a credit balance if the firm earned a profit because more credits (revenues) have been transferred into this account than debits (expenses). A debit to Income Summary will be required to close the account into Retained Earnings in this case. The amount of the balancing debit will equal the net income for the period. Conversely, if the firm has suffered a net loss during the period, a credit will be required to close the Income Summary account. This is because more debits (expenses) have been transferred into this account than credits (revenues). The amount of this balancing credit will equal the net loss for the period. The entry to close the Income Summary account for The White-Water Boat Company is as follows:

3/31/95	C-3	Income Summary	2,680	
		Retained Earnings		2,680
		To close Income Summary to Retained Earnings.		

After this entry has been posted to the appropriate T accounts, all income statement accounts have a zero balance, and the Income Summary and Retained Earnings accounts appear as follows:

Income Summary			*1000*
C2	13,320	C1	16,000
C3	2,680		
3/31 Bal.	0		

Retained Earnings			*311*
		1/1 Bal.	0
		C3	2,680
		3/31 Bal.	2,680

Some firms shorten the closing process by not using an Income Summary account and instead making the closing entries directly to the Retained Earnings account. Either method is acceptable; the one chosen depends on the firm's accounting system.

Closing the Dividends Declared Account. If a firm records the issuance of dividends by directly debiting Retained Earnings, a closing entry for dividends is not required. However, if the declaration of dividends is recorded by debiting the temporary dividends declared account (and crediting a dividends payable account) the temporary account also must be closed to Retained Earnings. The White-Water Boat Company did not declare any dividends, so no closing entry is required. However, to illustrate this entry, assume that $1,000 of dividends had been declared, and recorded by a debit to the Dividends Declared account. The following closing entry would be required:

Retained Earnings	1,000	
Dividends Declared		1,000
To close Dividends Declared to Retained Earnings.		

Exhibit 4-21
Expense Closing Entries—T Accounts

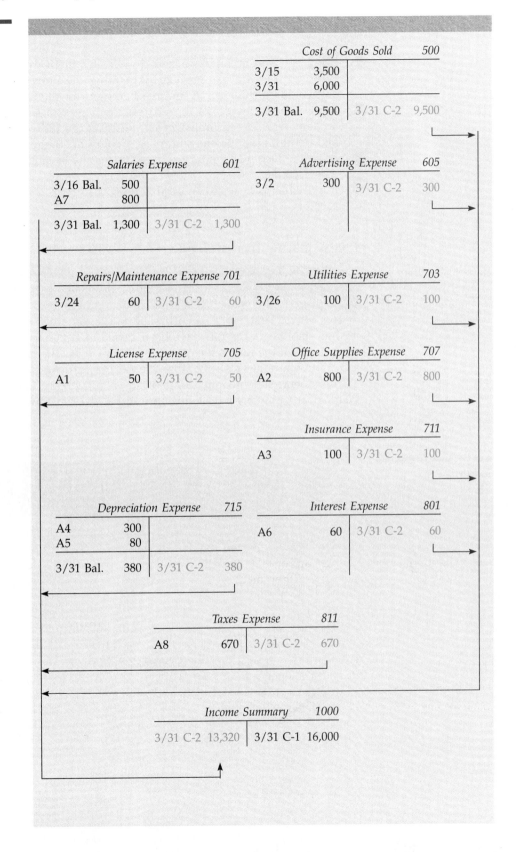

Cost of Goods Sold 500

3/15	3,500		
3/31	6,000		
3/31 Bal.	9,500	3/31 C-2	9,500

Salaries Expense 601

3/16 Bal.	500		
A7	800		
3/31 Bal.	1,300	3/31 C-2	1,300

Advertising Expense 605

3/2	300	3/31 C-2	300

Repairs/Maintenance Expense 701

3/24	60	3/31 C-2	60

Utilities Expense 703

3/26	100	3/31 C-2	100

License Expense 705

A1	50	3/31 C-2	50

Office Supplies Expense 707

A2	800	3/31 C-2	800

Insurance Expense 711

A3	100	3/31 C-2	100

Depreciation Expense 715

A4	300		
A5	80		
3/31 Bal.	380	3/31 C-2	380

Interest Expense 801

A6	60	3/31 C-2	60

Taxes Expense 811

A8	670	3/31 C-2	670

Income Summary 1000

3/31 C-2	13,320	3/31 C-1	16,000

The Closing Process—A Summary. To summarize, the closing process contains four steps:

1. Bring revenue accounts to zero by closing them to the Income Summary account. This is accomplished by debiting the individual revenue accounts and crediting the income summary account for the total.
2. Bring expense accounts to zero by closing them to the income summary account. This is accomplished by crediting the individual expense accounts and debiting the income summary account for the total.
3. Bring the income summary account to zero by closing it to the retained earnings account.
4. If a dividends declared account is used, also close it to the retained earnings account.

Post-Closing Trial Balance

post-closing trial balance

The **post-closing trial balance** is prepared from the ledger accounts after the closing entries have been posted and helps ensure that these entries have been correctly posted. The post-closing trial balance differs from the other trial balances in two ways. First, only balance sheet accounts are included, because all the income statement accounts have been closed to zero balances. Second, as noted, the balance in the retained earnings account is now the balance at the end of the accounting period. This is because the closing entries have recorded the effect of all the income statement accounts on the retained earnings account. The White-Water Boat Company's post-closing trial balance is shown in Exhibit 4-22.

Exhibit 4-22

The White-Water Boat Company
Post-Closing Trial Balance
March 31, 1995

	Debit	*Credit*
Cash	$14,340	
Accounts receivable	4,600	
Inventory	9,500	
Office supplies	1,200	
License	150	
Prepaid insurance	1,100	
Land	5,000	
Office equipment	9,900	
Accumulated depreciation—office equipment		$ 300
Buildings	10,000	
Accumulated depreciation—buildings		80
Accounts payable		7,200
Bank loan payable		4,000
Salaries payable		800
Interest payable		60
Taxes payable		670
Capital stock		40,000
Retained earnings		2,680
Totals	$55,790	$55,790

GENERAL LEDGER SYSTEMS

Objective 3
Describe the flow of transactions through a computer-based general ledger system.

This chapter has introduced adjusting journal entries. Considerable thought and analysis are required to prepare these adjusting entries. However, compared to the volume of revenue and expense transactions processed by an accounting system, relatively few adjusting entries are prepared each accounting period. The revenue and expense journal entries are generated by the transaction processing systems in the revenue and expenditure cycles which were introduced in Chapter 3. A majority of these revenue and expenditure journal entries are generated automatically when a computer-based accounting system is used.

general ledger system

Accountants monitor the transaction processing systems that generate these journal entries and, in a computer environment, are not required to prepare all the high-volume revenue and expenditure journal entries. Adjusting entries and the journal entries generated by the transaction processing systems in the revenue and expenditure cycles are input into a *general ledger system.* A **general ledger system** is a manual or computer-based accounting system that accepts journal entry input and posts those entries to a general ledger. A high-level system flowchart for a computer-based general ledger system is shown in Exhibit 4-23.

system flowchart

A **system flowchart** is a diagram that summarizes the inputs to a system and the outputs generated by a system. Three flowchart symbols are used in Exhibit 4-23: process, on-line file, and document. The process symbol is used to represent computer systems and computer programs. The on-line file symbol is used to represent computer files, such as diskettes, which can be accessed by the program

Exhibit 4-23
General Ledger System Flowchart

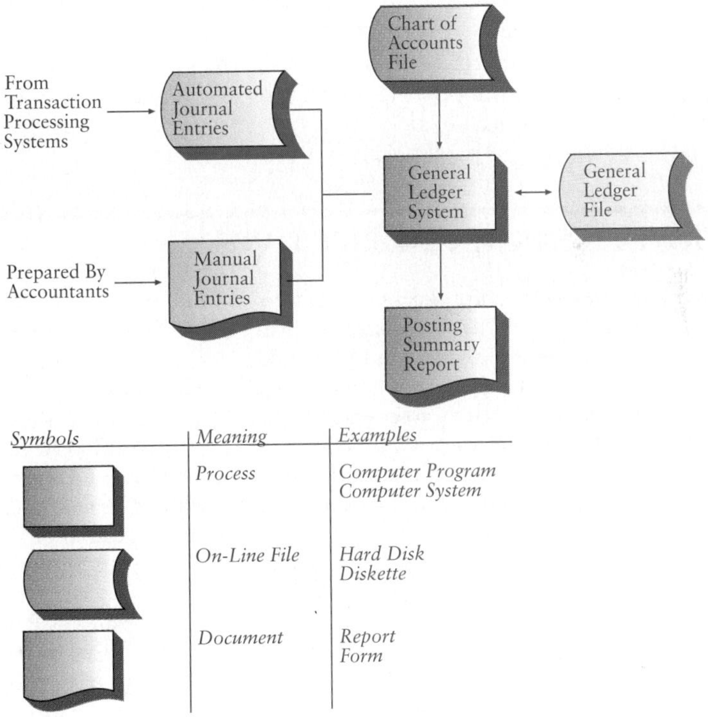

or system. The document symbol is used to represent forms and documents containing data that is input into a computer program or system. The document symbol is also used to represent reports and business documents that are printed by a computer program or system. Accountants and auditors make extensive use of system flowcharts when they are involved in the design and audit of computer-based accounting systems because a system flowchart is a concise and effective communications tool.

The general ledger system in Exhibit 4-23 is represented by the rectangular process symbol. Two sources of inputs into the general ledger system are shown in the exhibit. These inputs include both manual and automated journal entries. The manual journal entries, shown within the document symbol, include all journal entries that are not generated by transaction processing systems. Adjusting journal entries would normally be input as manual journal entries.

The automated journal entries, shown within the file symbol, include all journal entries that are created by transaction processing systems. Revenue and expenditure journal entries to record sales, cost of goods sold, collections and payments on account, expenses and related transactions are usually included in the automated journal entry file. The chart of accounts file, which contains the chart of account information illustrated in Exhibit 2-7 is used by the general ledger system to ensure that all journal entries contain valid general ledger account numbers. The general ledger file is updated by the general ledger system. The general ledger file contains account balance information similar to that contained in a T account or a manual general ledger. A posting summary report, shown in a document symbol, is often printed by general ledger systems. This report is similar to a manual general journal and summarizes all the journal entries that were processed by the general ledger system. A computer-based general ledger system maintains the general ledger by performing the routine recording and posting tasks that are very time consuming in manual accounting systems.

SUMMARY OF LEARNING OBJECTIVES

1. Explain why adjusting entries are necessary, and describe the major categories of adjusting entries. Adjusting entries are made at the end of the accounting period to update various accounts to their proper balances. They result from the need to match economic events with accounting periods. There are several different categories of adjusting entries commonly made by enterprises. These types of entries and the accounts usually involved and covered in this chapter are:

a. Nonmonetary assets acquired in one period and used up in subsequent period(s).
   1. Typical accounts involved
      i. Prepaid assets
      ii. Supplies
   2. Form of the adjusting entry

Expense	xxx	
Nonmonetary Assets or Contra Account		xxx

b. Nonmonetary liabilities recorded in one period with associated revenues earned in subsequent period(s).
   1. Typical accounts involved
      i. Unearned Rent
      ii. Dues and Subscriptions Received in Advance
   2. Form of the adjusting entry

Unearned Revenue	xxx	
Earned Revenue		xxx

c. Accruals—Either (1) cash received or receipts obtained after earnings recognized or (2) cash paid in the period after the benefits received.
   1. Typical accounts involved
      i. Interest Receivable or Payable
      ii. Salaries Payable
      iii. Taxes payable
   2. Form of the adjusting entry
      i. To record accrued receivables

Receivable	xxx	
Revenue		xxx

      ii. To record accrued payables

Expense	xxx	
Payable		xxx

d. Estimates of expenses matched with current periods revenues.
   1. Typical accounts involved include warranties and bad debts.
e. Correction of current and past period errors.
   1. Those specific accounts affected.

2. Complete the remaining steps in the accounting cycle. The accounting cycle includes the following steps:

During the period:

a. Record business transactions in the journal.
b. Post the journal entries to the ledger.

At the end of the period:

a. Prepare the unadjusted trial balance.
b. Prepare adjusting entries.
c. Post adjusting entries to the ledger.
d. Prepare an adjusted trial balance.
e. prepare a worksheet—an optional step.
f. prepare financial statements.
g. Make closing entries and post to the ledger accounts.
h. Prepare a post-closing trial balance.

3. Describe the flow of transactions through a computer-based general ledger system. A computer-based general ledger system accepts journal entry input from two sources. Manual entries, like adjusting entries, are prepared by accountants and input into the general ledger system. Automated journal entries generated by transaction processing systems are also input into the general ledger system. The general ledger system posts the journal entries to a general ledger file and prints a posting summary report.

KEY TERMS

REVIEW PROBLEM

This problem is a continuation of the review problem in Chapter 3. As the accountant for Kids Tech children's store, you have been able to prepare an unadjusted trial balance as shown on page 170. You have also determined the following data:

a. At the end of the year, office supplies on hand totaled $400.
b. The prepaid insurance policy was purchased during the year for $3,600. It became effective on April 1, 1995 and has a two-year term.
c. The building and furniture and fixtures were purchased at the beginning of the year. The building has a useful 30-year life and no salvage value. The furniture and fixtures have a six-year useful life and a residual value of $3,000.
d. Salaries earned but unpaid at year-end were $1,500.
e. The bank loan has been outstanding all year. The interest (12%) and principal are due next year.
f. A December 1995 utility bill for $50 did not arrive until early January. (Note: Although the firm's year-end is December 31, this does not mean that all the steps in the accounting process will take place by that date. Usually it takes a firm at least one month to complete many of the steps and prepare financial statements. During this month, the firm has the opportunity to record transactions such as item (e) that relates to December but for which the paperwork will not be received until January. In many cases, such transactions are recorded as adjusting entries.)

Kids Tech
Unadjusted Trial Balance
December 31, 1995

	Debit	Credit
Cash	$ 17,000	
Accounts receivable	8,000	
Inventory	20,000	
Office supplies	1,500	
Prepaid insurance	3,600	
Land	20,000	
Building	45,000	
Furniture and fixtures	15,000	
Accounts payable		$ 12,600
Salaries payable		0
Bank loan payable		10,000
Capital stock		50,000
Retained earnings		43,500
Sales		80,000
Cost of goods sold	52,000	
Salaries expense	10,000	
Advertising expense	1,000	
Utilities expense	750	
Automobile expense	2,000	
Repairs and maintenance expense	450	
Gain on sale of land		200
Totals	$196,300	$196,300

REQUIRED:

1. Prepare the necessary adjusting entries.
2. Post these entries to the ledger T accounts.
3. Prepare an adjusted trial balance.
4. Prepare an income statement, a statement of retained earnings, and a balance sheet.
5. Prepare closing entries.
6. Prepare a post-closing trial balance.

SOLUTION 1
Adjusting Entries

	Debit	Credit
Adj 1. Office Supplies Expense	1,100	
Office Supplies		1,100
To record office supplies used during the period.		
2. Insurance Expense	1,350	
Prepaid Insurance		1,350
To record insurance used during the period.		
$3,600 ÷ 24 months = $150		
$150 × 9 months = $1,350		
3. Depreciation Expense	3,500	
Accumulated Depreciation—Building		1,500
Accumulated Depreciation—Furniture and Fixtures		2,000
To record depreciation expense for the period.		

Building $\frac{\$45{,}000}{30 \text{ years}} = \$1{,}500$ per year

Furniture and Fixtures $\frac{\$15{,}000 - \$3{,}000}{6 \text{ years}} = \$2{,}000$ per year

4. Salaries Expense	1,500	
Salaries Payable		1,500
To record salaries payable.		
5. Interest Expense	1,200	
Interest Payable		1,200
To record interest payable.		
$10,000 × .12 = $1,200		
6. Utilities Expense	50	
Accounts Payable		50
To record December utility bill received in January.		

2 T Accounts

Cash

1/1 Bal.	5,000	2)	3,600
3)	50,000	5)	10,000
7)	28,000	6)	1,400
9)	5,200	8)	52,000
		10)	4,200
12/31 Bal.	17,000		

Accounts Receivable

1/1 Bal.	6,000	7)	28,000
3)	30,000		
12/31 Bal.	8,000		

Inventory

1/1 Bal.	12,000	4)	52,000
1)	60,000		
12/31 Bal.	20,000		

Office Supplies

1/1 Bal.	1,500	Adj. 1	1,100
12/31 Bal.	400		

Prepaid Insurance

2)	3,600	Adj. 2	1,350
12/31 Bal.	2,250		

Land

1/1 Bal.	25,000	9)	5,000
12/31 Bal.	20,000		

Building

1/1 Bal.	45,000		

Furniture and Fixtures

1/1 Bal.	15,000		

Accumulated Depreciation—Building

		Adj. 3	1,500

Accumulated Depreciation Furniture and Fixtures

		Adj. 3	2,000

Accounts Payable

8)	52,000	1/1 Bal.	4,600
		1)	60,000
		12/31	12,600
		Adj. 6	50
		12/31 Bal.	12,650

Salaries Payable

6)	1,400	1/1 Bal.	1,400
		Adj. 4	1,500

Bank Loan Payable

		1/1 Bal.	10,000

Interest Payable

		Adj. 5	1,200

Capital Stock

		1/1 Bal.	50,000

Retained Earnings

		1/1	43,500

Sales

Debit		Credit	
		3)	80,000

Cost of Goods Sold

Debit		Credit	
4)	52,000		

Advertising Expense

Debit		Credit	
11)	1,000		

Salaries Expense

Debit		Credit	
5)	10,000		
Adj. 4	1,500		
12/31 Bal.	11,500		

Utilities Expense

Debit		Credit	
10)	750		
Adj. 6	50		
12/31 Bal.	800		

Automobile Expense

Debit		Credit	
10)	2,000		

Repairs and Maintenance Expense

Debit		Credit	
10)	450		

Gain on Sale of Land

Debit		Credit	
		9)	200

Office Supplies Expense

Debit		Credit	
Adj. 1	1,100		

Insurance Expense

Debit		Credit	
Adj. 2	1,350		

Depreciation Expense

Debit		Credit	
Adj. 3	3,500		

Interest Expense

Debit		Credit	
Adj. 5	1,200		

3 Adjusted Trial Balance

Kids Tech
Adjusted Trial Balance
December 31, 1995

	Debit	*Credit*
Cash	$ 17,000	
Accounts receivable	8,000	
Inventory	20,000	
Office supplies	400	
Prepaid insurance	2,250	
Land	20,000	
Building	45,000	
Accumulated depreciation—building		$ 1,500
Furniture and fixtures	15,000	
Accumulated depreciation—furniture and fixtures		2,000
Accounts payable		12,650
Salaries payable		1,500
Interest payable		1,200
Bank loan payable		10,000
Capital stock		50,000
Retained earnings		43,500
Sales		80,000
Cost of goods sold	52,000	
Salaries expense	11,500	
Advertising expense	1,000	
Utilities expense	800	
Automobile expense	2,000	
Depreciation expense	3,500	
Repairs and maintenance expense	450	
Insurance expense	1,350	
Office supplies expense	1,100	
Interest expense	1,200	
Gain on sale of land		200
Totals	$202,550	$202,550

4
Income Statement, Statement of Retained Earnings, and Balance Sheet

Kids Tech
Income Statement
For the Year Ended December 31, 1995

Revenue		
Sales	$80,000	
Gain on sale of land	200	$80,200
Expenses		
Cost of goods sold	$52,000	
Salaries	11,500	
Advertising	1,000	
Utilities	800	
Automobile	2,000	
Depreciation	3,500	
Repairs and maintenance	450	
Insurance	1,350	
Supplies used	1,100	
Interest	1,200	74,900
Net income		$ 5,300

At this point, the exact order of the expenses on the income statement is not important. Some firms list them alphabetically or in the order of their magnitude. For simplicity, taxes are ignored.

Kids Tech
Retained Earnings Statement
For the Year Ended December 31, 1995

Retained Earnings—January 1, 1995	$43,500
Plus: Net income	5,300
Less: Dividends	0
Retained Earnings—December 31, 1995	$48,800

Kids Tech
Balance Sheet
December 31, 1995

Assets			*Liabilities and Stockholders' Equity*	
Cash		$ 17,000	Liabilities	
Accounts receivable		8,000	Accounts payable	$ 12,650
Inventory		20,000	Salaries payable	1,500
Office supplies		400	Interest payable	1,200
Prepaid insurance		2,250	Bank loan payable	10,000
Land		20,000		
Building	$45,000		Total liabilities	$ 25,350
Less: Accumulated depreciation	1,500	43,500	Stockholders' equity	
			Capital stock	$ 50,000
Furniture and fixtures	$15,000		Retained earnings	48,800
Less: Accumulated depreciation	2,000	13,000	Total stockholders' equity	$ 98,800
Total assets		$124,150	Total liabilities and stockholders' equity	$124,150

5 Closing Entries

1. Sales	80,000	
Gain on Sale of Land	200	
Income Summary		80,200
To close revenue accounts to Income Summary.		
2. Income Summary	74,900	
Cost of Goods Sold		52,000
Salaries Expense		11,500
Advertising Expense		1,000
Utilities Expense		800
Automobile Expense		2,000
Depreciation Expense		3,500
Repairs and Maintenance Expense		450
Insurance Expense		1,350
Supplies Expense		1,100
Interest Expense		1,200
To close expense accounts to Income Summary.		
3. Income Summary	5,300	
Retained Earnings		5,300
To close Income Summary to Retained Earnings.		

6 Post-Closing Trial Balance

Kids Tech
Post-Closing Trial Balance
December 31, 1995

	Debit	*Credit*
Cash	$ 17,000	
Accounts receivable	8,000	
Inventory	20,000	
Office supplies	400	
Prepaid insurance	2,250	
Land	20,000	
Building	45,000	
Accumulated depreciation—building		$ 1,500
Furniture and fixtures	15,000	
Accumulated depreciation—furniture and fixtures		2,000
Accounts payable		12,650
Salaries payable		1,500
Interest payable		1,200
Bank loan payable		10,000
Capital stock		50,000
Retained earnings		48,800
Totals	$127,650	$127,650

QUESTIONS

1. Give three examples of an expenditure for a nonmonetary asset that is made in the current period but affects both the current and subsequent periods. What is the accounting problem related to these expenditures?
2. Why is it necessary to make adjusting entries? Can you think of a situation in which adjusting entries would not be required?
3. Prepaid insurance amounted to $1,900 at the beginning of the year and $500 at the end of the year. The income statement for the year showed insurance expense of $2,100. How much insurance was purchased during the year?
4. Explain to your friend how a building that has an increasing market value must be depreciated for financial reporting purposes.
5. Several years ago, a piece of equipment was purchased. It cost $180,000 and had no salvage value. Yearly depreciation on the straight-line method was $6,000, and at the end of 1995 the accumulated depreciation account had a credit balance of $36,000. When was the equipment purchased? What is the life of the equipment?
6. Give two examples of receipts received in one period that affect current and subsequent periods.
7. At the beginning of the year, the balance in a firm's Unearned Subscription Revenue account was $1,800, and at the end of the year, it was $750. During the year, the firm received an additional $2,200 in subscription receipts. Supply the missing entry.
8. Jones owns a 12% note receivable that was acquired on January 2, 1995. On September 30, 1995, the interest receivable account showed a balance of $3,600, and there have been no receipts of interest or principal. What is the principal of the note?
9. What is the purpose of closing entries? When are they made? Describe the logic of debiting revenue accounts in the closing process.
10. Describe the difference between an adjusted trial balance and post-closing trial balance.
11. Retained earnings were $85,000 on January 1, 1995 and were $98,000 on December 31, 1995. During that time, the firm issued $30,000 cash dividends, debited to Retained Earnings. Make the entry needed to close Income Summary to Retained Earnings.
12. What are the two primary sources of inputs to a computer-based general ledger system?
13. Describe the similarities and differences between manual and computer-based general ledger systems.

EXERCISES

E4-1
The Accounting Cycle
LO 2

Following is a list of steps in the accounting cycle. Arrange them in the proper sequence by placing the appropriate number to the left of the step. The first step should be numbered 1, and so on.

_________ Preparing financial statements.
_________ Posting journal entries to the ledger.
_________ Recording transactions in the journal.
_________ Preparing an unadjusted trial balance.
_________ Preparing a post-closing trial balance.
_________ Preparing closing entries.
_________ Preparing adjusting entries.
_________ Posting adjusting entries and preparing an adjusted trial balance.

E4-2
Making Adjusting Entries
LO 1

Make the necessary entries for each of the following two independent situations:

a. On April 1, O'Sell Company received $7,200 for a three-year subscription to its political newsletter, which is issued monthly. The firm closes its books once a year, on December 31. Make the entry to record the receipt of the subscription and the adjusting entry at December 31. The firm uses an account called Unearned Subscription Revenue.
b. The Greenwell Company pays its salaries every Friday for the five-day workweek. Salaries of $75,000 are earned equally throughout the week. December 31 of the current year is a Wednesday.
   1. Make the adjusting entry at December 31.

2. Make the entry to pay the week's salaries on Friday, January 2, of the next year. Assume that all employees are paid for New Year's Day.

E4-3
Making Adjusting Entries
LO 1

The Deloitte Company closes its books on December 31 and makes adjusting entries once a year at that time. For each of the following items, make the appropriate adjusting journal entry, if any:

a. At the beginning of the year, the firm had $700 of supplies on hand. During the year, another $3,400 worth was purchased on account and recorded in the asset account Supplies. At the end of the year, the firm determined that $650 of supplies remained on hand.
b. On October 1 of the current year, the firm lent the Rosevsky Co. $15,000 at 12% interest. Principal and interest are due in one year.
c. Three full years ago, the firm purchased a building and land for $600,000. Two-fifths of the cost was allocated to the land and three-fifths to the building. The building has a life of 20 years with no salvage value.
d. On July 1 of the current year, the firm borrowed $12,000 at 10% interest. As of December 31 of the same year, the Interest Expense account showed a balance of $600.
e. On March 1 of the current year, the firm rented to another firm some excess space in one of its buildings. The Deloitte Company received a year's rent, $18,000, at that time, and credited the account Unearned Rent Revenue.

E4-4
Adjusting Entries for Interest
LO 1

On October 1, 1995, the Cooper Company lent $200,000 to Lybrand Company at 14% interest. Both interest and principal are due on September 30, 1996. Both firms have a December 31 year-end and close their books annually at that time. Make the required entries for both firms at October 1, 1995; December 31, 1995; and September 30, 1996.

E4-5
Making and Analyzing Adjusting Entries
LO 1

The Jennings Company opened a news service on January 2 of the current year. The firm's year-end is December 31, and it makes adjusting entries once a year at that time. For each of the following items, make the initial entry, where appropriate, to record the transaction and, if necessary, the adjusting entry at December 31:

a. On March 31 the Jennings Company rented a new office. Before it could move, it had to prepay a year's rent of $24,000 cash.
b. On January 31, the firm borrowed $150,000 from a local bank at 12%. The principal and interest on the loan are due in one year but no interest payments have yet been made.
c. On March 15, the firm purchased $800 of supplies for cash. On September 14, it made another cash purchase of $1,100. During the current year, the firm's accountant determined that $1,400 of supplies had been used.
d. The firm charges its customers in advance for subscribing to its news service. During the year, the firm received $140,000 cash from its customers. The firm's accountant determined that 12% of that had not yet been earned.
e. Before closing its books, the Jennings Company found a bill for $1,800 from a local newspaper for an advertisement that was placed in a November issue.
f. Wages accrued but unpaid at December 31 totaled $4,400.

E4-6
Determining the Ending Balance in Certain Accounts
LO 1

The Dunesberry Company is preparing its September 30, 1995 financial statements. State at what amounts the following assets should be shown:

a. On January 2, 1994, the firm bought a three-year comprehensive insurance policy for $7,200.
b. A piece of equipment was purchased on June 30, 1993 for $125,000. It has a twelve-year life with an estimated salvage value of $5,000. Depreciation is taken from July 1, 1993. Give the proper balance in the Accumulated Depreciation account.

c. On January 1, 1992, the firm bought some land for $650,000, which is currently being used as a parking lot. It expects to sell the land by the end of 1995 and feels it will get approximately $1 million at that time. It recently received a cash offer for $987,000.
d. The firm purchases several types of supplies. During the year, the firm purchased 4,250 boxes of staples at a total cost of $14,875. On September 30, 1995, the firm had 1,200 boxes of staples left.
e. On July 1, 1994, the firm lent $70,000 to one of its best customers at 14% interest for two years. Interest is due yearly, the principal at the end of two years. What amount of interest receivable should be shown on the September 30, 1995 balance sheet?

E4-7
Closing Entries
LO 2

Some of the accounts of the Trezevant Company at the end of the current year are listed below in alphabetical order. All accounts have normal balances, and all adjusting entries have been made.

Accounts	*Amount*
Accounts payable	$ 36,000
Accounts receivable	45,000
Accumulated depreciation—furniture and fixtures	24,000
Capital stock	120,000
Cash	12,000
Cost of goods sold	275,000
Depreciation expense	8,000
Furniture and fixtures	100,000
General and administrative expenses	80,000
Interest receivable	3,000
Interest revenue	5,000
Inventory	90,000
Land	120,000
Gain on sale of furniture	6,000
Retained earnings	176,000
Sales	500,000
Selling expenses	106,000

REQUIRED:

1. Prepare the necessary closing entries at the end of the year.
2. Assuming that dividends of $1,000 were declared and paid during the year, what was the balance in the retained earnings account at
   a. the beginning of the year?
   b. the end of the year?

E4-8
Closing Entries
LO 2

The accountant for the Tuner Corporation made the following closing entries at the end of the firm's year. After reviewing these entries,

a. Discuss the errors, if any.
b. Make the correct closing entries.

1. Interest Revenue	4,700	
Accounts Payable	1,900	
Capital Stock	10,000	
Sales	45,000	
Income Summary		61,600
To close accounts with credit balances.		

2. Income Summary	48,700	
Gain on Sale of Land	3,000	
Cost of Goods Sold		32,000
Accounts Receivable		12,000
Operating Expense		4,200
Other Assets		3,500
To close accounts with debit balances.		
3. Income Summary	12,900	
Retained Earnings		12,900
To close Income Summary to Retained Earnings.		

E4-9
Analysis of the Accounting Equation
Review

For each of the following five independent situations, determine the net income or loss for the period:

a.	Net assets at the beginning of the year	$87,000
	Net assets at the end of the year	92,000
	Dividends declared	0
	Capital stock issued	0
b.	Net assets at the beginning of the year	$54,000
	Net assets at the end of the year	78,000
	Dividends declared	3,400
	Capital stock issued	0
c.	Net assets at the beginning of the year	$36,000
	Net assets at the end of the year	52,000
	Dividends declared	400
	Capital stock issued	8,000
d.	Net assets at the beginning of the year	$ 79,000
	Net assets at the end of the year	128,000
	Dividends declared	17,000
	Capital stock issued	25,000
e.	Net assets at the beginning of the year	$130,000
	Net assets at the end of the year	175,000
	Dividends declared	8,000
	Capital stock issued	70,000

E4-10
The Accounting Equation
Review

Answer each of the following two questions:

a. You have obtained the following information from the USC Company: Total assets at January 1, 1995 were $200,000 and at December 31, 1995 were $240,000. Total liabilities at January 1, 1995 were $85,000 and at December 31, 1995 were $100,000. During the year, the firm's total sales were $510,000. Cost of goods sold was $425,000. Capital stock of $10,000 was issued during the year, and dividends of $4,000 were declared. Determine:
   1. The net income for 1995.
   2. The total of all other expenses excluding cost of goods for 1995.

b. You have determined the following data for the independent situations in the table. Calculate the missing figures:

	Year-end Amounts						
	Total Assets	*Total Liabilities*	*Capital Stock*	*Retained Earnings, Beginning*	*Net Income (Loss)*	*Dividends Declared*	*Retained Earnings, Ending*
a.	$ 80,000	?	$15,000	$22,000	$15,000	$7,000	?
b.	?	$65,000	20,000	?	20,000	5,000	$30,000
c.	120,000	70,000	?	30,000	?	4,000	20,000

E4-11
Accrual to Cash Basis of Accounting
Review

You have determined the following balance sheet data for the Oregon Company:

	1/1/95	*12/31/95*
Accounts receivable	$150,000	$210,000
Supplies	8,000	9,200
Salaries payable	17,000	15,000
Unearned rent revenue	8,200	7,000

The income statement data for the year showed the following data:

Sales—all credit	$660,000
Supplies used	14,000
Salaries expense	56,000
Rent revenue	23,000

You are to calculate the following information:

a. Cash received on account.
b. Cash paid for supplies—all supplies purchased for cash.
c. Salaries paid in cash.
d. Cash collected for rent.

E4-12
Cash to Accrual Basis of Accounting
Review

You have determined the following balance sheet data for the Washington Corporation:

	1/1/95	*12/31/95*
Interest receivable	$6,400	$5,900
Prepaid insurance	2,300	1,400
Interest payable	4,900	5,600
Dividends payable	2,000	1,500

During the year, the company made the following cash payments or received cash related to the items listed above:

Cash received on interest receivable	$ 4,600
Cash paid for additional insurance covering several periods	7,700
Interest paid	3,800
Dividends paid	11,000

You are to calculate the following information:

a. Interest earned during the year.
b. Insurance expense for the year.
c. Interest expense for the period.
d. Dividends declared during the year.

E4-13
Computations and Analysis
LO 1

In doing these computations, be sure to show your calculations.

a. On January 1, 1997, the Fantasy Company received a 12%, $45,000 note receivable. If accrued interest on December 31, 1997, equals $900, through what date was the interest received?

b. On August 1, 1997, the Premier Company received a $24,000 note. At December 31, 1997, the firm had not yet received any interest payments. If Interest Receivable had a balance of $800, what would the interest rate be?
c. The Seaborn Company purchased a large machine on January 2, 1994. It is being depreciated at a straight-line rate of $12,000 per year. At the end of its useful life, it will have a salvage value of $3,000. As of December 31, 1997, the machine has a remaining life of four years. What was the machine's purchase price?
d. The Organization of Travel Consultants owns a small building that is being depreciated at the rate of $7,500 per year. The building has a remaining life of 24 years from December 31, 1997. Assuming that the building originally cost $225,000 and has no salvage value, determine when it was purchased.

E4-14 Net Income and Cash Flow from Operations

LO 2

FAAM Corporation recorded the following entries during May in its general journal:

a. Cash	42,000	
Accounts Receivable		42,000
b. Cash	64,000	
Accounts Receivable	38,000	
Sales		102,000
c. Cost of Goods Sold	76,200	
Inventory		76,200
d. Inventory	75,000	
Accounts Payable		75,000
e. Dividends Declared	12,000	
Cash		12,000
f. Accounts Payable	61,000	
Cash		61,000
g. Various Operating Expenses	27,000	
Cash		27,000

REQUIRED:

1. From the data above determine net income for the month of May.
2. From the data above determine cash flow from operating activities as it would appear on the statement of cash flows.
3. Explain why the two figures differ.

E4-15 System Flowcharts

LO 3

Holly Togs has recently implemented a computer-based accounts receivable system. Shipping notices, which were prepared in the shipping department, are manually entered into the accounts receivable system. The system reads data from the customer master file and prints an invoice, which is mailed to the customer. The system also updates the accounts receivable file and writes journal entries to the automated journal entry file.

REQUIRED:

1. Draw a high level system flowchart to depict the inputs to the accounts receivable system and the outputs generated by the system.
2. Describe the journal entries that are output to the automated journal entry file by the accounts receivable system.
3. Explain how the accounts receivable system should be interfaced with the general ledger system.

PROBLEMS

P4-1
Adjusting Entries
LO 1

The accountant for the Nutro Company obtained the following information while preparing adjusting entries for the year ended December 31, 1995:

a. During the year the company made the following purchases of supplies:

February 23	$4,700
June 14	3,900
November 29	4,500

At the beginning of the year supplies on hand totaled $1,200. At the end of the year, it was determined that $3,250 of supplies remained on hand.

b. The Nutro Company publishes a monthly beauty newsletter. All customers are required to subscribe to 12 issues, or one per month for the entire year. Subscriptions are renewed annually, but the subscribers list is staggered so that one-fourth of the subscribers renew at the beginning of each quarter. The following subscriptions were received during the year and credited to unearned subscription revenue:

Date	*Yearly Subscription*
January 1	$3,600
April 1	2,700
July 1	5,400
October 1	7,200

c. On April 1, 1995, Nutro borrowed $25,000 at 12% from the South City National Bank. The note has a one year maturity. Principal and interest on the unpaid balance are due quarterly on:

July 1, 1995	January 1, 1996
October 1, 1995	April 1, 1996

d. As of January 1, 1995, the balance in the firm's Prepaid Rent account was $16,000 and represented four months of prepaid rent. The lease was renewed in 1995 at an increase of 10% of last year's full rent. The full year's rent was prepaid as of the beginning of the new lease term on May 1, 1995.

e. Land, buildings, and equipment all were purchased at the beginning of 1992. All assets were given a zero salvage value and have the same life, which is longer than four years. As of January 1, 1995, you obtained the following account balances:

Accounts	*Balance*
Land	$95,000
Accumulated depreciation—building	21,000
Accumulated depreciation—equipment	36,000

REQUIRED: Make the necessary adjusting entries at December 31, 1995.

P4-2
Adjusting Entries
LO 1

The accountant for the Wong Corporation obtained the following data as she was preparing adjusting entries for the firm's fiscal year ending June 30, 1995:

a. On July 1, 1994, the balance in the firm's Prepaid Insurance account was $2,600, representing four months of prepaid insurance. When the policy expired, the firm purchased for cash a new three-year policy for $25,200.

b. On July 1, 1994, the balance in the firm's Supplies account was $6,400. In November 1994, $10,600 of supplies were purchased on account. As of June 30, 1995, all of the original supplies had been used, and two-thirds of the supplies purchased in November had been used.
c. The Wong Corporation lent its main customer some needed cash. Analysis of the loans indicates the following:

Date of loan	*Principal*	*Interest Rate*	*Interest Paid Through*
9/1/93	$15,000	9%	9/1/93
11/1/94	12,000	9	4/30/94
3/1/95	50,000	12	5/31/94

All loan due dates are after June 30, 1995. Interest on the September 1, 1993 loan is paid annually.
d. The firm's rental agreement on its office and stores calls for a monthly rental of $7,200 per month plus 1% of the firm's gross revenues. The monthly portion of $7,200 is payable at the beginning of each month. The 1% portion is payable once a year, on July 15, based on the prior year's gross revenues. Gross revenues for the year ended June 30, 1995 were $975,000.

REQUIRED:

1. Make the appropriate journal entries to record the initial transactions between July 1, 1994 and June 30, 1995.
2. Make the necessary adjusting entries at June 30, 1995.

P4-3
Completion of the Accounting Cycle from the Unadjusted Trial Balance (Alternative to P4-4)
LO 2

The bookkeeper of Management Behavior Associates gave you the unadjusted trial balance at December 31, 1995 and the following additional information:

a. The firm was notified by its broker that it had earned interest revenue of $1,050 from various marketable securities.
b. Supplies on hand at the end of the year amounted to $500.
c. Prepaid rent of $900 was used during the year.
d. The building was purchased on January 2, 1993 and has no salvage value.
e. The interest rate on the note is 8%. No interest has been paid on the note since July 1, 1995.
f. Salaries payable at year-end amounted to $2,500.
g. The December 31, 1995 telephone bill of $450 arrived in January 1996 and was not included in the utility expense of $1,000 listed in the unadjusted trial balance. Use the Accounts Payable account.

REQUIRED:

1. Set up T accounts with the December 31, 1995 balances from the unadjusted trial balance.
2. Make the adjusting entries in the general journal. Set up new accounts where appropriate.
3. Post the adjusting entries to the ledger accounts.
4. Prepare an adjusted trial balance.
5. Prepare an income statement, retained earnings statement, and balance sheet.
6. Make the closing entries.
7. Post the closing entries to the ledger accounts.
8. Prepare a post-closing trial balance.

Management Behavior Associates
Unadjusted Trial Balance
December 31, 1995

	Debit	Credit
Cash	$ 8,000	
Investment in marketable securities	10,000	
Accounts receivable	16,500	
Interest receivable	0	
Supplies	2,800	
Prepaid rent	1,400	
Land	25,000	
Buildings	120,000	
Accumulated depreciation—buildings		$ 8,000
Accounts payable		9,400
Bank notes payable		20,000
Salaries payable		0
Interest payable		0
Capital stock		25,000
Retained earnings		35,600
Fees earned		200,000
Salaries expense	90,000	
Rent expense	20,000	
Legal and accounting expense	1,800	
Utility expense	1,000	
Delivery expense	1,500	
Totals	$298,000	$298,000

P4-4
Completing the Accounting Cycle from the Unadjusted Trial Balance (Alternative to P4-3)
LO 2

The unadjusted trial balance for the Oas Accounting Firm for the fiscal year ended October 31, 1995 is presented below.

Oas Accounting Firm
Unadjusted Trial Balance
October 31, 1995

	Debit	Credit
Cash	$ 19,700	
Accounts receivable	23,000	
Note receivable	5,000	
Interest receivable	0	
Office supplies	7,200	
Prepaid rent	12,000	
Prepaid insurance	8,400	
Land	30,000	
Building	70,000	
Accumulated depreciation—building		$ 17,500
Accounts payable		15,000
Property taxes payable		0
Salaries payable		0
Capital stock		50,000

(continued)

	Debit	*Credit*
Retained earnings		41,160
Fees earned		104,000
Interest revenue		0
Insurance expense	0	
Advertising expense	700	
Salaries expense	8,490	
Utilities expense	550	
Rent expense	42,000	
Miscellaneous expense	620	
Totals	$227,660	$227,660

Additional information:

a. The note receivable is a one-year note. The interest rate is 12%, and both the interest and principal are due on February 1, 1996.
b. Office supplies on hand at the end of the year cost $1,600.
c. Twelve hundred dollars of the prepaid rent expired during the year.
d. The prepaid insurance is for a two-year period beginning October 1, 1995.
e. The building has a useful life of ten years with no salvage value.
f. Property taxes are based on the fair market value of the property owned by the firm, at a rate of 15% of its fair market value on July 1, 1995. At that date, the property had an estimated fair market value of $220,000. Property taxes for the year ended October 31, 1995 are payable on November 10, 1995 but are assessed as of October 31, 1995.
g. Salaries earned but not yet paid at the end of the year amounted to $3,100.

REQUIRED:

1. Set up ledger accounts with the October 31, 1995 balances from the unadjusted trial balance.
2. Make the adjusting entries in the general journal. Set up new accounts if needed.
3. Post the adjusting entries to the T accounts.
4. Prepare an adjusted trial balance.
5. Prepare an income statement for the year ended October 31, 1995 and a balance sheet at October 31, 1995.
6. Make the closing entries.
7. Post the closing entries to the T accounts.
8. Prepare the post-closing trial balance.

P4-5
Accrual and Cash Basis of Accounting
Review

The comparative balance sheets for December 31, 1995 and 1994 and the income statement for the year ended December 31, 1995 for the Caster Corporation are presented on page 185.

REQUIRED:

1. Prepare the necessary closing entries.
2. Prepare a statement of retained earnings for the year ended December 31, 1995.
3. Answer each of the following questions:
   a. How much cash was collected from customers on account during 1995? Assume that all fees earned were originally recorded in Accounts Receivable.
   b. If no notes receivable were repaid, by how much did the firm increase its Notes Receivable?
   c. How much cash was paid for rent during 1995?
   d. Assuming that all purchases of supplies were paid in cash, how much cash was paid for supplies during 1995?
   e. How much cash was paid for salaries during the year?
   f. How much cash was paid for interest during the year?

Caster Corporation
Comparative Balance Sheets
December 31

Assets	*1995*	*1994*
Cash	$ 14,320	$ 6,200
Accounts receivable	10,500	3,400
Notes receivable	22,000	10,000
Inventory	32,000	25,000
Prepaid rent	3,400	2,500
Supplies	2,100	4,200
Land	65,000	65,000
Buildings, net of accumulated depreciation	165,600	172,800
Other assets	10,000	10,000
Total assets	$324,920	$299,100

Liabilities and Stockholders' Equity		
Liabilities		
Accounts payable	$ 8,200	$ 10,000
Notes payable	20,000	25,000
Salaries payable	4,700	5,200
Interest payable	820	1,200
Other payables	4,000	0
Total liabilities	$ 37,720	$ 41,400
Stockholders' equity		
Capital stock	$120,000	$120,000
Retained earnings	167,200	137,700
Total stockholders' equity	$287,200	$257,700
Total liabilities and stockholders' equity	$324,920	$299,100

Caster Corporation
Income Statement
For the Year Ended December 31, 1995

Revenues		
Sales	$600,000	
Interest revenue	1,500	
Total revenues		$601,500
Expenses		
Cost of goods sold	$400,000	
Salaries expense	60,000	
Rent expense	25,000	
Depreciation	7,200	
Supplies expense	4,250	
Interest expense	3,500	
Total expenses		499,950
Income before taxes		$101,550
Income taxes		40,000
Net income		$ 61,550

P4-6
Computations and Analysis
Review

Make the necessary computations for each of the following independent situations. In all cases, assume that the year-end is December 31, 1997 and that the firm has made all required adjusting entries for the year.

a. The Mynard Co. acquired an $18,000, 12% note on October 1, 1997. On December 31, 1997, Interest Receivable had a balance of $540. How much cash interest did the Mynard Co. collect on this note during 1997, and through what date had interest been received?
b. The Arthur Corporation borrowed $14,250 on August 30, 1997. The note is due in six months, and the total interest paid when the note is due will be $855. What is the interest rate on the note?
c. On January 1, 1993, the Jackson Corporation bought a machine for $80,000. It has a 12-year useful life. On December 31, 1997, after the adjusting entry to record depreciation, the book value of the machine is $50,000. What is its estimated salvage value?
d. On January 1, 1994, the Edwards Company purchased a new machine for $92,000 with a $7,000 salvage value. The machine has an estimated useful life of 10 years. What is the book value on December 31, 1997, after the adjusting entry to record depreciation is made?
e. The Waco Pat Company purchased a building for $1,400,000. The building has a $200,000 salvage value and an estimated useful life of 30 years. On December 31, 1997, after the entry to record depreciation expense, the building's current book value is $1,300,000. When was the building purchased?

P4-7
General Ledger System
LO 3

Holly Togs has decided to implement a computer-based general ledger system. Automated and manual journal entries will be input to the general ledger system. The system will access a chart of accounts file and will maintain a general ledger system. In addition, the system will print a posting summary report each time the system is run. The flow within this system was illustrated in Exhibit 4-23.

REQUIRED:

1. Identify the specific data items that should be included for each journal entry in the automated journal entry file.
2. Identify the specific data items that should be included for each account in the general ledger file.
3. Design a posting summary report. Your report should include an appropriate heading and column headings.

P4-8
Summary Review Problem
Review

The McMillan Company was organized on January 2, 1995. During the year the following events occurred:

a. Ten thousand shares of capital stock were issued in exchange for $120,000.
b. A $75,000 bank loan was obtained on February 1 at 12% interest. The principal and interest are due in one year.
c. On April 1, the firm purchased for $7,200 cash a comprehensive two-year insurance policy.
d. During the first half of the year, inventory costing $210,000 was purchased on account.
e. The firm signed a lease on April 30 to rent office space. Because the firm is new, the lessor required a full year's rent of $48,000, to be paid immediately.
f. Sales during the first half of the year were $280,000, of which $210,000 were on account and the remainder were for cash.
g. Cost of goods sold for the first half of the year amounted to $170,000.
h. Payments on inventory purchases in item (d) were $172,000.
i. Cash collections on accounts were $150,000.
j. Additional inventory purchases on account were $250,000.
k. Supplies totaling $6,800 were purchased for cash.

l. Various pieces of store furniture and fixtures were purchased for $140,000. A 20% down payment was made, and the remainder was obtained through a 12% note payable issued on May 1.
m. Sales for the second half of the year were $350,000, of which $260,000 were on account and $90,000 were for cash.
n. Cost of goods sold for the second half of the year was $205,000.
o. Cash collections on account amounted to $205,000.
p. Payments on account for inventory purchases (items (d) and (j) amounted to $248,000.
q. The following expenses were paid in cash:

Salaries	$84,000
Legal and accounting	55,400
Advertising	25,000
Delivery	5,000
Repairs	4,000
Utilities	2,100

r. The firm declared and paid dividends of $4,000.

Additional information:

a. Interest on the bank loan and the note payable must be accrued.
b. The expired portion of prepaid insurance must be written off.
c. The expired portion of prepaid rent must be written off.
d. Supplies totaling $3,900 were used during the year.
e. The store furniture and fixtures have a ten-year life with a $5,000 salvage value. (To simplify, record a full year's depreciation on the store furniture and fixtures.)
f. Salaries of $3,600 must be accrued at year-end.
g. A December utility bill of $800 was received in January. This amount has not been included in the utility expense listed on the unadjusted trial balance. Use Accounts Payable to record the transaction.
h. The tax rate is 30% of income before taxes.

The firm's chart of accounts is below.

Cash	101
Accounts receivable	102
Inventory	103
Supplies	105
Prepaid insurance	106
Prepaid rent	107
Store furniture and fixtures	110
Accumulated depreciation—store furniture and fixtures	111
Accounts payable	201
Bank loan payable	202
Taxes payable	203
Note payable	205
Specialist fees payable	209
Salaries payable	210
Interest payable	212
Capital stock	310
Retained earnings	311
Sales	400

(continued)

Cost of goods sold	501
Salaries expense	502
Legal and accounting expense	503
Advertising expense	504
Delivery expense	506
Repairs expense	507
Utility expense	508
Depreciation expense	509
Insurance expense	510
Rent expense	511
Supplies expense	512
Interest expense	513
Taxes expense	520
Income summary	1000

REQUIRED:

1. Make the summary journal entries for the year, and post them to the ledger accounts. As a posting reference, use the number of the account and page 1 of the general journal.
2. Prepare an unadjusted trial balance.
3. Make the adjusting journal entries and post them to the ledger accounts.
4. Prepare an adjusted trial balance.
5. Prepare an income statement and statement of retained earnings for the year ended December 31, 1995.
6. Prepare the closing entries and post them to ledger accounts.
7. Prepare a post-closing trial balance.
8. Prepare a balance sheet as of December 31, 1995.

DISCUSSION AND INTERPRETATION PROBLEMS

D4-1 Understanding Financial Statements

The consolidated statement of earnings (in thousands) for Nordstrom, Inc. and Subsidiaries is as follows:

(dollars in thousands except per share amounts)	*Year ended January 31, 1991*	*% of Sales*	*Year ended January 31, 1990*	*% of Sales*	*Year ended January 31, 1989*	*% of Sales*
Net sales	$2,893,904	100.0	$2,671,114	100.0	$2,327,946	100.0
Costs and expenses:						
Cost of sales and related buying and occupancy costs	2,000,250	69.1	1,829,383	68.5	1,563,832	67.2
Selling, general and administrative	747,770	25.8	669,159	25.1	582,973	25.0
Interest, net	52,228	1.8	49,121	1.8	39,977	1.7
Service charge income and other, net	(84,660)	(2.9)	(55,958)	(2.1)	(57,268)	(2.4)
Total costs and expenses	2,715,588	93.8	2,491,705	93.3	2,129,514	91.5
Earnings before income taxes	178,316	6.2	179,409	6.7	198,432	8.5
Income taxes	62,500	2.2	64,500	2.4	75,100	3.2
Net earnings	$ 115,816	4.0	$ 114,909	4.3	$ 123,332	5.3
Net earnings per share	$ 1.42		$ 1.41		$ 1.51	
Cash dividends paid per share	$ .30		$ .28		$ .22	

You have also gathered the following balance sheet data (in thousands):

	January 31,	
	1991	*1990*
Cash	$ 24,662	$ 33,051
Stockholders' equity	826,410	733,250

In addition, the company issued $1,842 (in thousands) worth of capital stock during the year.

REQUIRED:

1. Make the summary closing entries that Nordstrom would have made.
2. What amount of dividends did the company declare during the year ended December 31, 1991?
3. What are the relationships, if any, between the increase in retained earnings and the decrease in cash during the year ended December 31, 1991?

D4-2
Financial Decision Case

Bill Gilroy is considering buying an apartment house for $500,000. Bill will make a 20% down payment and will finance the remainder through a 10%, 30-year mortgage. Monthly payments including principal and interest will be $3,510. Bill put together the following projected income statement for the first year. He expects this statement to reflect the operations of the apartment house for the next two years, except that interest expense will decrease slightly.

Revenues		
Rents		$55,000
Expenses		
Interest	$33,000	
Depreciation	16,667	
Repairs and maintenance	6,000	
Insurance	2,400	
		58,067
Net loss		$ (3,067)

Bill is concerned that he will be unable to generate enough cash flow from the building to pay the necessary cash outflows. He gives you the following additional information and asks you to prepare a statement of cash flows for the first year:

a. All rents will be paid in cash at the beginning of each month. No prepayments or deposits are required.
b. The building has a 30-year life and no salvage value.
c. The insurance expense of $2,400 represents one-half the cost of the two-year comprehensive insurance policy he purchased.
d. Finally, in preparing your statement, do not consider the 20% down payment as part of the cash outflows.

In addition to your statement of cash flows, write a brief memo to Bill explaining the differences in the two statements.

D4-3
Research Assignment

The scenario at the beginning of this chapter briefly discussed the differences between the work of a bookkeeper and that of an accountant. Using the reference materials in your school's library and/or other materials, answer the following questions:

a. How many CPAs are there in the United States? If possible, find out how many CPAs there are in your state.
b. What are the average national entry-level salaries for CPAs in public practice and for bookkeepers? If possible, determine these amounts for the state in which you live.
c. Describe in your own words the work of a bookkeeper and that of a CPA. If you found a salary difference between the two in item b, explain why you think this difference occurs.

D4-4
Ethical Issues

Sarah Winston is the accountant for Technobusiness, a high-end computer store for sophisticated users. The company is owned by the Knox family. The company has a $500,000 line of credit from Westwood National Bank. As part of the loan agreement, the company is to provide the bank with quarterly financial statements prepared by the company's internal accountant.

Sarah, who has been working for Technobusiness for a number of years, is in charge of preparing the firm's financial statements which are distributed to the family and to the bank. Sarah is in the midst of preparing the company's quarterly financial statements for March 31, 1995, the end of its first quarter. Sarah has been extremely busy and has not had time to analyze the accounts for the purpose of making adjusting entries. Because the bank insists on receiving the financial statements as soon as possible after the last day of the quarter, Sarah decided to shortcut the adjustment process by going back to her December 31, 1994 worksheet, taking the amounts of the year-end adjusting entries, and dividing them by four. She would then use these amounts for the amount of adjustments for the first quarter of 1995. For example, depreciation expense for the year ended December 31, 1994 amounted to $32,000, so she made an entry of $8,000 (1/4 of $32,000) for depreciation expense for the quarter ended March 31, 1995. She figured that this process would result in adjustments similar to those she would make if she did a complete analysis, and it would certainly save her considerable time. Anyway, she knew she had three additional quarters to correct any errors. In addition, she knew that Technobusiness had been consistently profitable and was not going to default on the bank loan. Thus, she saw little risk in using her shortcut.

REQUIRED:

1. Do you think Sarah's shortcut will have a material effect on Technobusiness's financial statements? Why or why not?
2. Do you think her rationale that the company had little chance of defaulting on the loan was a sufficient reason for her actions?
3. If you were in Sarah's situation, what would you do?

CHAPTER 5
FINANCIAL STATEMENTS: THE OUTPUT OF THE SYSTEM

LEARNING OBJECTIVES

After studying this chapter, you should be able to:

1. Describe how financial reporting standards are set in the United States.
2. Describe the important accounting concepts and conventions including the objectives of financial reporting.
3. Define the main elements of a classified balance sheet and prepare one.
4. Explain the uses and limitations of a classified balance sheet.
5. Define the main elements of a classified income statement and prepare one.
6. Explain the uses and limitations of a classified income statement.
7. Prepare a retained earnings statement and a statement of stockholders' equity, and discuss their uses and limitations.
8. Explain the uses and limitations of the statement of cash flows.
9. Discuss the uses of other financial data in the annual report.
10. Describe the relationship between a financial reporting system and the general ledger system.
11. State the four possible categories that may be found on a corporate income statement and prepare a simple corporate income statement (Appendix).

Scenario

Jeannie Bowman just graduated from a small liberal arts college in California, and was thrilled when she received 1,000 shares of AMR Corporation stock as a graduation present from her grandparents. AMR Corporation is the parent company of American Airlines, the largest airline in the United States. Jeannie, who was going to enter an MBA program in the fall, was anxious to find out more about AMR and its financial condition and future prospects.

"Jeannie, what you should do is write to AMR and ask for their latest annual report," suggested Bob Page, one of her classmates. "I own stock in UAL, the parent company of United Airlines, and have a copy of their annual report. Once you receive the one from AMR we can compare and contrast the two companies and decide whether or not we should keep the stock we own. Besides, we can study the report and get a head start on the accounting course we have to take in the fall."

A couple of weeks later Jeannie received a copy of AMR's latest annual report and was overwhelmed by the amount of information it contained. Among other items, the report included:

- Management's discussion and analysis of the company's performance, as well as that of the entire airline industry.
- The company's financial statements.
- Notes to the financial statements.
- Report of the independent auditors.

Jeannie was particularly struck by the extent of the explanatory notes that accompanied the statements. "Bob, this is hard to believe but there are about twice as many pages of notes to the financial statements as the financial statements themselves. There are about two pages alone of notes relating to AMR's debt and about a page of notes relating to retirement benefits to its employees."

"One thing I'm really having a difficult time understanding is what the income statement has to do with the statement of cash flows. According to the income statement, AMR lost over $240 million during the year! Yet their cash flow statement shows that over $744 million in cash was provided by operating activities during the same period. I don't understand how the firm can have a net loss and yet have positive cash flows from operations."

Bob was curious about the auditors' report in both AMR's and UAL's annual report. Bob knew that every public company had to have an annual audit, but he had no idea what that meant. Bob was especially surprised to read that auditing standards require that the auditors plan and perform an audit to obtain reasonable assurance about whether the financial statements are free of material misstatement and that the audit was performed only on a test basis. "I thought an audit was a complete review of a firm's financial statements in which all transactions were examined," he told Jeannie. "Do you think we can rely on the auditors' report on the fairness of AMR's and UAL's financial statements? What do you think the phrase 'financial statements fairly present' really means?"

Jeannie Bowman and Bob Page are just two examples of the many present and potential investors and creditors who rely on the published financial statements of public firms to make investment and credit decisions. A public firm's annual report and the financial statements contained therein provide users with a great deal of financial information. Understanding and being able to make decisions based on these financial statements is essential to becoming a well informed investor.

As illustrated in the opening scenario, the published financial statements of a public company are contained in the firm's annual report which is distributed to all shareholders. This chapter introduces you to the financial statements of such companies and the financial reporting system that generates the financial statements. It also explains how accounting standards are set in the United States and details some of the more important objectives and concepts that are the basis for financial statements. The financial statements of Albertson's, a large market chain in the West, South, and Midwest is used to illustrate these various standards, concepts and practices. In addition, this chapter discusses other aspects of an annual report and how information contained in that report can be used to analyze a company's financial position and performance. Although you are only beginning your study of accounting, after studying this chapter you will be able to understand and analyze the financial information contained in the statements of such major companies as Albertson's and AMR.

ACCOUNTING STANDARD SETTING

Objective 1
Describe how financial reporting standards are set in the United States.

Chapter 1 briefly introduced you to how accounting standards and generally accepted accounting principles (GAAP) are set in the United States. The first part of this chapter provides more detail on this process. It is important to recognize that the process that will be described is unique to the United States. Each country has a somewhat different process ranging from pure governmental regulation to private-sector standard setting such as exists in the United States.

As noted in Chapter 1, the development of GAAP is a complex process involving a mixture of theory, governmental regulation, and conventions derived from actual practice. It is impossible to specify one source of GAAP or one book that codifies all of the accounting principles. However, the major groups involved in the standard-setting process include the American Institute of Certified Public Accountants (AICPA), the Financial Accounting Standards Board (FASB), the Securities and Exchange Commission (SEC), the American Accounting Association (AAA), and the Governmental Accounting Standards Board (GASB).

The American Institute of Certified Public Accountants

The AICPA was organized around the beginning of the century and is the major professional organization of CPAs. Over its more than 80-year history, the AICPA formed several committees to develop accounting standards. The two most important were the Committee on Accounting Procedures (CAP) and the Accounting Principles Board (APB).

The CAP was formed in the 1930's, and until the 1950's it issued a number of Accounting Research Bulletins (ARBs) that recommended the use of certain accounting procedures and practices. By the 1950's, the AICPA became convinced that its efforts in the standard-setting process had to be expanded. In 1959, it set up the APB to develop accounting principles and methods. Before going out of existence in 1973, the APB formally issued 31 Opinions, each carrying the authority of the AICPA. The burden of justifying a departure from the Board's Opinions has to be assumed by those adopting other practices.

Although the APB went out of existence in 1973, the AICPA continues to play an active role in the accounting standard-setting process. Several AICPA committees provide input to the FASB and set accounting guidelines for unique financial reporting problems facing the profession, as well as emerging issues. Auditing guidelines and standards continue to be set by the AICPA.

Financial Accounting Standards Board

The APB was criticized because of its part-time nature and the board's perceived lack of independence from the accounting profession for which it was setting standards. In response to this criticism, the Financial Accounting Standards Board (FASB) was created in 1973 as an organization independent of the AICPA. The primary purpose of the FASB is to develop accounting standards. The Opinions issued by the APB, however, are still in force today unless they have been superseded by the Statements issued by the FASB.

The FASB consists of seven full-time members who are independent of other responsibilities. Among its members are CPAs and other individuals in private industry and academia. The FASB has a full-time accounting research and administrative staff and also appoints outside task forces to study various accounting issues. The FASB issues Statements and Concepts Statements relating to broader issues. Through the Spring of 1993 it issues 111 Statements and 6 Concepts Statements. The statements issued by the FASB and the earlier opinions issued by the APB are a major portion of generally accepted accounting principles, especially as they relate to specific methods of accounting for certain events.

Securities and Exchange Commission

The Securities and Exchange Commission (SEC) was established by Congress during the Great Depression that followed the stock market crash of 1929. The securities laws of 1933 and 1934 that founded the SEC gave it power to establish accounting principles governing the form and content of financial statements of companies issuing securities for sale to the public. Because most large U.S. corporations are publicly-held, they are required to satisfy SEC accounting standards.

Its power to set accounting standards for publicly-held corporations gives the SEC considerable impact. However, the SEC has explicitly recognized the FASB as the primary standard setter for all business entities. For many years, therefore, the SEC set principles for publicly-held companies that reflected the existing standards developed by the private sector of the accounting profession, the APB and the FASB. More recently, however, the SEC has sometimes moved in its own direction. For example, it issued several technical pronouncements that were at variance with those of the public accounting profession. In these cases, the accounting profession has usually had to conform its rules to those of the SEC. Although relatively rare, controversies such as these show that accounting rules are sometimes as much the result of political factors as of good accounting theory.

American Accounting Association

American Accounting Association (AAA)

The **American Accounting Association (AAA)** is a professional association of accountants, principally academics and practicing accountants, who are concerned with accounting education and research. Members of the AAA contribute to the development of accounting concepts and standards through research studies which are distributed by a series of research monographs and articles in academic journals. Members of the AAA also participate in various task forces and standard setting bodies.

Governmental Accounting Standards Board

In 1984, the Financial Accounting Foundation (the group that selects FASB members, funds their activities, and provides general oversight of the Board) created the Governmental Accounting Standards Board (GASB). The purpose of the GASB is to establish and improve financial accounting standards for state and local governments. In most respects, the GASB is structured like the FASB. Although this book is primarily concerned with the standards issued by the FASB, standards issued by the GASB are important in the study of governmental accounting.

Accounting Standards: A Multidimensional Process

In summary, generally accepted accounting principles include concepts, opinions, standards, and regulations from various sources. The SEC plays an important role in setting these principles, as do the private standard setters in the accounting profession. As noted, it is impossible to find these principles collected in a single book or codified in state or federal law. Accounting principles are not set in this way in all countries, however. For example, in many European countries, such as France and Germany, the government is the primary standard setter, so accounting rules tend to be more uniform.

The next section of this chapter details some of the more important accounting concepts and conventions.

ACCOUNTING CONCEPTS AND CONVENTIONS

Objective 2
Describe the important accounting concepts and conventions including the objectives of financial reporting.

The basic financial statements prepared by accountants were introduced in Chapter 1. Some of the concepts and assumptions that underlie the basic financial statements were discussed in the previous chapters as well. This section provides a more comprehensive introduction to the concepts upon which financial statements are prepared.

Objectives of Financial Reporting

The Financial Accounting Standards Board (FASB) has spent considerable time and energy in developing objectives of financial reporting. The purpose of these objectives and related concepts is to help users better understand the content and limitations of financial statements. The FASB identified three main objectives of financial reporting in Concepts Statement 1. These objectives are:

1. Financial reporting should provide information that is useful to present and potential investors and creditors and other users in making rational invest-

ment, credit, and similar decisions. The information should be comprehensible to those who have a reasonable understanding of business and economic activities and are willing to study the information with reasonable diligence.
2. Financial reporting should provide information to help present and potential investors and creditors and other users in assessing the amounts, timing, and uncertainty of prospective cash receipts from dividends or interest and the proceeds from the sale, redemption, or maturity of securities or loans. Since investors' and creditors' cash flows are related to enterprise cash flows, financial reporting should provide information to help investors, creditors, and others assess the amounts, timing, and uncertainty of prospective net cash inflows to the related enterprise.
3. Financial reporting should provide information about the economic resources of an enterprise, the claims to those resources (obligations of the enterprises to transfer resources to other entities and owners' equity), and the effects of transactions, events, and circumstances that change resources and claims to those resources.[1]

The FASB considers present and potential investors and creditors to be the primary users of financial statements, and it notes that these users need information concerning the possibility of receiving cash flows from investments or loans. This data can best be provided by giving investors and creditors information about the enterprise's resources, claims to those resources, and changes in them. However, the FASB is quite clear in noting that business and economic activities are complex and that financial statement users must be willing to study the information carefully. Thus communicating financial information about the complex economic activities of a firm such as AMR is a process which requires study on the part of the user and decision maker.

Important Concepts, Conventions, and Principles

Financial statements in the United States rest on a set of agreed upon accounting concepts and conventions.[2] Exhibit 5-1 summarizes 13 of the more important accounting concepts and conventions grouping them into three categories: basic assumptions about the accounting environment, qualitative characteristics of accounting information, and the generally accepted accounting conventions that result from the above. You have already been introduced to the two basic assumptions about the accounting environment—the business entity assumption and the going concern. Now we will turn to the qualitative characteristics.

Qualitative Characteristics of Financial Information. According to the FASB, to be useful in decision making, accounting information must possess certain qualitative characteristics, including quantifiability, relevance, and reliability. Concepts Statement No. 2, *Qualitative Characteristics of Accounting Information*, discusses these characteristics, and is the basis for much of the discussion that follows.

Quantifiability. Financial statements represent only the effects of economic events which can be represented in numerical (primarily monetary) terms. This

1. Financial Accounting Standards Board, Concepts Statement No. 1, *Objectives of Financial Reporting of Business Enterprises* (Stamford, Conn.: FASB, November 1978), Pars. 34, 37 and 40.
2. This book will use the terms *concept* and *convention* to apply to general, fundamental ideas on which financial reporting in the United States is based. The term *principle* will be used to refer to specific accounting methods, in the sense of generally accepted accounting principles.

Exhibit 5-1
Accounting Concepts and Conventions

Basic Assumptions About the Accounting Environment	
Business Entity	Business entities are separate economic units that control resources and obligations and must have separate and distinct records.
Going Concern	There is an assumption that a particular business enterprise will continue in existence for a period of time long enough to carry out its objectives and commitments.
Qualitative Characteristics of Accounting Information	
Quantifiability	Money is the basic measuring unit. This means that in the United States, items included in the accounting system must be quantifiable in dollars.
Relevance	Accounting information is relevant if it is capable of making a difference in a decision.
Reliability	Accounting information is reliable if it measures without bias what it is supposed to measure. Verifiability is a prime ingredient of reliability.
Comparability and Consistency	Accounting information is comparable if it enables users to identify similarities and differences between two sets of economic events. Consistency refers to using the same accounting principles in different periods.
Conservatism	Uncertainties in accounting are resolved by choosing from the alternatives the one that produces the lowest asset valuation or the least amount of income.
Materiality	Accounting information is material if the judgment of a reasonable user would have been changed or influenced by the omission or misstatement of the information.
Full Disclosure	All information useful to an informed decision maker should be disclosed.
Generally Accepted Accounting Conventions	
Historical Cost	Historical cost is the primary valuation method used in financial statements. Assets are recorded at their acquisition cost and are usually not adjusted for increases in value until a sale has occurred.
Time Period	Although a business enterprise is assumed to have an indefinite life, measurement of financial condition and operations must be made at relatively short intervals, such as quarterly or yearly.
Matching	Under the matching concept, expenses must be offset against the revenues earned in the period. Thus expenses of the period are matched against the revenues of the same period, and the result is net income or loss for the period.
Revenue Recognition	Revenue is usually recognized for accounting purposes when goods are delivered or services performed. In some cases, revenue is recognized before or after the delivery of goods or the performance of services.

quantifiability

characteristic is known as **quantifiability.** An event that cannot be expressed in numerical terms is not represented on the financial statements. Clearly, a firm is affected by a number of events that cannot be quantified in a reasonable manner. Although this information can be very important to decision makers, it is not part of the information that goes into the preparation of the dollar amounts shown on the face of the financial statements. To illustrate, the backlog of aircraft orders and options as well as changes in those orders and options is essential information to those interested in assessing the future prospects of Boeing or McDonnell Douglas, but until the planes are delivered these orders and options cannot be represented as sales. However, information is often presented in the notes to the firm's financial statements.

Relevance and Reliability. According to the FASB, *relevance* and *reliability* are the two primary qualities that make accounting information useful.

relevance

Relevance is a characteristic of accounting information that is capable of making a difference in a decision by helping users to form predictions about the outcome of past, present, and future events or to confirm or correct prior expectations.[3] That is, information is relevant if it has predictive and/or feedback value to users. This means the information helps users predict the future or evaluate past decisions. Further, timeliness is an important ingredient of relevance. Information loses its relevance if it is not given to users when it is capable of influencing their decision.

reliable

Information is **reliable** to the extent that it measures what it should measure. From an accounting perspective, information is reliable if users can depend on it to represent the economic conditions or events that it purports to represent. For example, if receivables are shown on the balance sheet at $500,000, this figure will be reliable only if the real collectibility of these receivables closely approximates $500,000. We use the word *approximate* because informed users of accounting information know that estimates and approximations rather than exact measures must often be made.

verifiability

Verifiability is an important ingredient of reliability. Similar to objectivity, **verifiability** means that several individuals or measures would reach similar conclusions. For example, $500,000 balance in Accounts Receivable is verifiable if supporting documentation shows that the actual amount of cash likely to be realized from the receivables is, in fact, $500,000. Verifiability is important because external users do not have access to a firm's accounting records and must rely on published financial statements as well as other public data in making their decisions. Verifiablility increases users' confidence in accounting information.

In their attempt to provide useful information, accountants are often forced to make a trade-off between relevance and reliability. In many cases, the more relevant the information is, the less reliable it becomes. The controversy surrounding the use of certain current cost and market value data is an example of a debate that involves this trade-off. Many feel that current cost data are more relevant than historical cost data for use in decision making. For example, if you were to measure your net worth and owned a plot of land, its current cost might be more relevant to you than its historical cost would be. However, current cost data is less reliable. You may have several individuals appraise the land and receive a different appraisal value from each of them. There might be no measurement consensus. Accountants are often confronted with this trade-off; as with

3. Financial Accounting Standards Board, Concepts Statement No. 2, *Qualitative Characteristics of Accounting Information* (Stamford, Conn.: FASB, May 1980), Summary.

other issues in accounting, there is no single solution—the accountant's judgment is required.

Comparability and Consistency. *Comparability* and *consistency* are important factors in evaluating the usefulness of accounting information. Accounting information has **comparability** if it allows users to identify similarities and differences between two sets of economic events. When accounting information is comparable, it can be used to evaluate the financial position and performance of one firm over time or in comparison with other firms at the same time. However, comparability does not imply that accounting procedures or methods should be the same for all firms. This would disguise real differences that exist in the economic circumstance reported.

comparability

Consistency is related to comparability and is also an important quality of accounting information. **Consistency** means that a firm uses the same accounting procedures and policies from one period to the next. It presumes that once an accounting principle has been adopted, it will be used when accounting for similar events. For example, once a firm selects a certain method of determining the cost of the inventory that it has sold, it should not change the method in the next period and then switch back to the original method in the following period. However, as the FASB notes, such consistency should not inhibit necessary changes in accounting principles and practices. If such a change is made, the full disclosure principle requires that the effect of this change on net income be fully noted.

consistency

Conservatism. Conservatism, which may qualify as more a convention than as a qualitative characteristic of accounting information, has been a pervasive factor in U.S. accounting for over 50 years. Generally, **conservatism** means prudence in financial reporting because of the uncertainty surrounding business and economic activities. According to Statement 4 of the Accounting Principles Board:

conservatism

Frequently, assets and liabilities are measured in a context of significant uncertainties. Historically, managers, investors, and accountants have generally preferred that possible errors in measurement be in the direction of understatement rather than overstatement of net income and net assets. This has led to the convention of conservatism. . . .[4]

This convention developed in the early stages of financial reporting when bankers and lenders were the main users of financial reports, and when the balance sheet was viewed as the most important financial statement. Assets provide a greater margin of safety to a banker as security for loans when they are understated. The tendency to recognize losses as soon as they become evident, while not recognizing gains until they are assured, is an example of conservative accounting that bankers have traditionally desired.

In Concepts Statement 2, the FASB clearly stated: "Conservatism in financial reporting should no longer connote deliberate, consistent understatement of net assets and profits."[5] The board correctly noted that understatement in one period leads to overstatement in another period. To demonstrate how this works, assume that an enterprise starts operating on January 2, 1993 and ceased operating three years later on December 31, 1995. At the end of the three-year period,

4. American Institute of Certified Public Accountants, Accounting Principles Board, Statement No. 4, *Basic Concepts and Accounting Principles Underlying Financial Statements of Business Enterprises* (New York: AICPA, 1970), par. 171.

5. FASB Concepts Statement 2, par. 93.

it can be determined with certainty that the firm earned a net income of $300,000. However, annual income in each one of these years cannot be known with certainty. Accountants must therefore make estimates and allocations in order to determine the amount of income earned and expense incurred each year. If income in years 1 and 2 is deliberately understated by a total of $50,000, income in year 3 must be overstated by $50,000 if total income over the three-year period is to equal $300,000.

Nonetheless, conservatism is still a reasonable reaction to the uncertainties inherent in business and economic events. For example, if two estimates of the amount to be collected on an account receivable are equally likely, the less optimistic estimate should be used. If the two estimates are not equally likely and the more optimistic one is more likely, however, it would be an incorrect application of conservatism to use the less optimistic one.

materiality

Materiality. In an accounting context, **materiality** refers to the relative importance or significance of an item to an informed decision maker. An item or event is material if it is probable that the judgment of a reasonable person, relying on that information, would have been changed or influenced by its omission or misstatement. If a particular item or transaction is not considered material, then it does not make any difference whether it is accounted for in the theoretically correct manner. For example, if a firm purchases a wastepaper basket for $2.50, this item theoretically should be considered an asset and its cost allocated over its lifetime. However, because of the immaterial nature of the amount, a firm would most likely consider the entire $2.50 an expense of the current period. Clearly, this decision would not affect the decisions of informed users of financial statements.

Many decisions regarding materiality are less clear-cut than the above example and call for the careful application of the accountant's judgment. The application of materiality often depends on the size of the particular item in relation to the overall size of the firm. Obviously, what is material to Smith's Shoe Store is not material to General Motors. Because of the difficulty in applying the materiality concept, a rule of thumb is often used. For example, an accountant may decide that an item is material if it equals or exceeds 5% of net income or 10% of total assets. Although such yardsticks are helpful, they do not replace the accountant's judgment.

full disclosure

Full Disclosure. For accounting information to be useful, all relevant information must be disclosed to users. This characteristic is known as **full disclosure.** Furthermore, this information should be disclosed in a manner that is understandable by informed users. As we have noted, some information is properly disclosed in the body of the financial statements while other information is disclosed in the notes to the financial statements. Notes are integral parts of the financial statements and are used to provide quantitative information in more detail as well as other important information such as the particular accounting policies used by the firm.

Generally Accepted Accounting Conventions

Exhibit 5-1 lists and describes four important generally accepted accounting conventions. The historical cost convention was discussed in Chapter 1, while the time period assumption, the revenue recognition and matching conventions were discussed in Chapter 3.

Accounting Concepts and General Purpose Financial Statements: A Summary

The assumptions, qualitative characteristics, and accounting conventions ensure that financial information is useful to the variety of groups who are likely to use it for decision making purposes. Users of financial information include stockholders, creditors, labor unions, regulatory agencies, attorneys, educators, and internal management. Each of these groups uses financial statements for overlapping but somewhat different purposes. Because it would be costly to prepare special-purpose financial statements for each user group, general-purpose financial statements are prepared aimed to serve the needs of a wide range of users.

For financial statements to meet these needs, they must be presented in a manner that allows investors and creditors to evaluate the financial strength and profitability of business enterprises. Therefore the information on these financial statements is often divided into categories that allow for meaningful interfirm and interperiod comparison. Such statements are called **classified financial statements.** Albertson's published financial statements will be used to illustrate classified financial statements.

classified financial statements

CLASSIFIED BALANCE SHEETS

Objective 3
Define the main elements of a classified balance sheet and prepare one.

The purpose of the balance sheet is to present the financial position of a company at a specific date. The balance sheet helps financial statement users answer the following types of questions:

1. What is the company's overall financial strength?
2. How liquid is the company?
3. Will the company be able to meet its short-term obligations?
4. What proportion of the company's assets has been contributed by creditors and investors, respectively?
5. How does the company's financial position compare with that of others in the same industry?

The decisions on what subcategories are listed under the major categories of assets, liabilities, and stockholders' equity are made by management. While for a specific firm and within a specific industry, such as the airline industry, there often are some unique accounts and classifications. The financial statements of U.S. companies overall tend to have a great deal of similarity. Thus, the statements presented in this chapter are typical of those found in major U.S. corporations in the retailing and manufacturing industries.

The classifications used and the order of the particular elements within the balance sheet for a French, Dutch, or other non-U.S. company, would be considerably different. This diversity occurs because generally accepted accounting principles are the result of the economic and political systems within particular countries.

Albertson's is a large retail grocery chain located in several states in the U.S. We will use Albertson's financial statements in this chapter and in subsequent chapters to illustrate financial reporting. When examining Albertson's balance sheets (Exhibit 5-2), notice that the company's fiscal year ends on a different date for each of the three years presented. Albertson's uses a 52-53 week fiscal year, which allows a firm to end its fiscal year on the same day of the week every year.

Exhibit 5-2

Albertson's, Inc.
Consolidated Balance Sheets
(in thousands)

ASSETS	*January 30, 1992*	*January 31, 1991*	*February 1, 1990*
CURRENT ASSETS			
Cash and cash equivalents	$ 34,404	$ 23,433	$ 43,708
Accounts and notes receivable	55,835	52,274	44,103
Inventories	613,233	562,713	544,676
Prepaid expenses	10,602	11,591	10,536
Deferred income tax benefits	37,212	27,380	25,082
TOTAL CURRENT ASSETS	$ 751,286	$ 677,391	$ 668,105
OTHER ASSETS	72,283	67,665	47,872
LAND, BUILDINGS, AND EQUIPMENT			
Land	289,526	259,897	215,407
Buildings	721,280	637,225	546,644
Fixtures and equipment	835,592	763,645	696,573
Leasehold improvements	180,034	158,054	142,872
Assets under capital lease	139,773	140,623	143,725
	$2,166,205	$1,959,444	$1,745,221
Less accumulated depreciation and amortization	773,527	690,990	598,509
	$1,392,678	$1,268,454	$1,146,712
TOTAL ASSETS	$2,216,247	$2,013,510	$1,862,689

LIABILITIES AND STOCKHOLDERS' EQUITY	*January 30, 1992*	*January 31, 1991*	*February 1, 1990*
CURRENT LIABILITIES			
Accounts payable	$ 400,417	$ 391,845	$ 396,198
Notes payable	30,000	10,000	0
Salaries and related liabilities	80,719	70,967	68,122
Taxes other than income taxes	37,807	30,743	26,698
Income taxes	9,589	9,443	2,768
Self-insurance	47,238	40,460	32,591
Unearned income	16,429	3,955	1,033
Other current liabilities	20,826	18,247	16,443
Current maturities of long-term debt	3,588	4,481	6,008
Current obligations under capital leases	5,634	5,426	5,122
TOTAL CURRENT LIABILITIES	$ 652,247	$ 585,567	$ 554,983
LONG-TERM DEBT	52,510	56,056	111,503
OBLIGATIONS UNDER CAPITAL LEASES	99,159	103,039	106,949
OTHER LONG-TERM LIABILITIES AND DEFERRED CREDITS			
Deferred compensation	24,755	22,013	18,807
Deferred income taxes	9,219	12,299	15,303
Deferred rents payable	66,575	62,021	53,333
Self-insurance	80,075	71,963	57,486
Unearned income	22,791	3,598	1,060
Other	9,464	9,072	13,773
	$ 212,879	$ 180,966	$ 159,762

(continued)

Exhibit 5-2
(continued)

LIABILITIES AND STOCKHOLDERS' EQUITY	*January 30, 1992*	*January 31, 1991*	*February 1, 1990*
STOCKHOLDERS' EQUITY			
Common stock	132,131	133,820	66,960
Capital in excess of par value	718	2,131	22,346
Retained earnings	1,066,603	951,931	840,186
TOTAL STOCKHOLDERS' EQUITY	$1,199,452	$1,087,882	$ 929,492
TOTAL LIABILITIES AND STOCKHOLDERS' EQUITY	$2,216,247	$2,013,510	$1,862,689

Albertson's fiscal year always ends on the Thursday nearest to the end of January. This means that sometimes its year ends in the last week of January and other times in the first week of February. (Thus, in some years the accounting period has 52 weeks while in others there are 53 weeks.) Retailing firms commonly use this type of fiscal year-end, with Saturday being the most popular choice for the day. This method simplifies the accounting and closing process.

consolidated statement

Albertson's balance sheet, as well as its other financial statements, is a **consolidated statement.** Albertson's owns a number of other companies, called *subsidiaries,* and because of the entity concept, the balance sheet of Albertson's and its subsidiaries are consolidated into one statement. This enables the users of the statement to assess the financial position of Albertson's based on all of the assets under its control.

Published balance sheets of publicly-held companies are comparative and present data for at least two years. Albertson's presents three years of comparative data.

Finally, Albertson's financial statements are expressed in thousands of dollars. For example, cash and cash equivalents are shown at $34,404 with the understanding this amount has been rounded to the nearest thousand dollars. This is an example of the materiality concept in practice. Listing the accounts at their actual amount will not make a material difference to a financial statement user evaluating a company the size of Albertson's. However, a smaller store might prepare statements that show the exact amount of the items.

Assets

Most balance sheets contain up to five categories in the assets section: (1) current assets; (2) long-term investments; (3) property, plant, and equipment; (4) intangible assets; and (5) other assets. Not all of these categories are found on all balance sheets, and particular firms often use slightly different classifications and labels.

current assets

Current Assets. The Accounting Principles Board defined **current assets** as:

. . . cash and other assets that are reasonably expected to be realized in cash or sold or consumed during the normal operating cycle of a business or within one year if the operating cycle is shorter than one year.[6]

6. APB Statement 4, par. 198.

operating cycle

The **operating cycle** of a business is the time it takes a firm to go from cash back to cash. An enterprise uses its cash or incurs payables to purchase or manufacture merchandise for resale. The inventory is then sold, and the enterprise receives cash or a receivable. The operating cycle is completed when the receivables from credit sales are collected and the payables are paid. Exhibit 5-3 illustrates the flows involved in a typical operating cycle. Notice the similarities between transaction processing cycles and the typical operating cycle.

Most firms have an operating cycle of less than one year. However, because some firms have operating cycles that extend for several years, assets that are used up or turned into cash during that longer cycle are considered current. Examples of companies with operating cycles longer than one year are construction companies, tobacco growers, distillers, and cattle breeders. Some firms have several operating cycles of different lengths. For example, a bank might have a short operating cycle for checking accounts and a long operating cycle for notes and mortgages. As a result, the current/noncurrent categories often are not used on bank balance sheets.

Current assets include cash, short-term investments, accounts receivable, inventories, supplies, and various prepaid items. Only in rare situations is cash not included as a current asset. An example is cash maintained in a foreign country whose currency regulations prohibit its transfer to the United States. Investments can be classified as current or noncurrent. In some cases, management will invest idle cash in the capital stock of other companies. If such investments are on a temporary basis and if the securities are readily marketable, they are classified as a current asset. If the investment does not meet these criteria, it is classified as a noncurrent asset in the long-term investment section of the balance sheet.

Trade accounts receivable and other loans or notes receivable due within one year of the operating cycle are classified as current. Because some accounts receivable will not be collected, a contra account called Allowance for Doubtful

Exhibit 5-3
The Business Operating Cycle

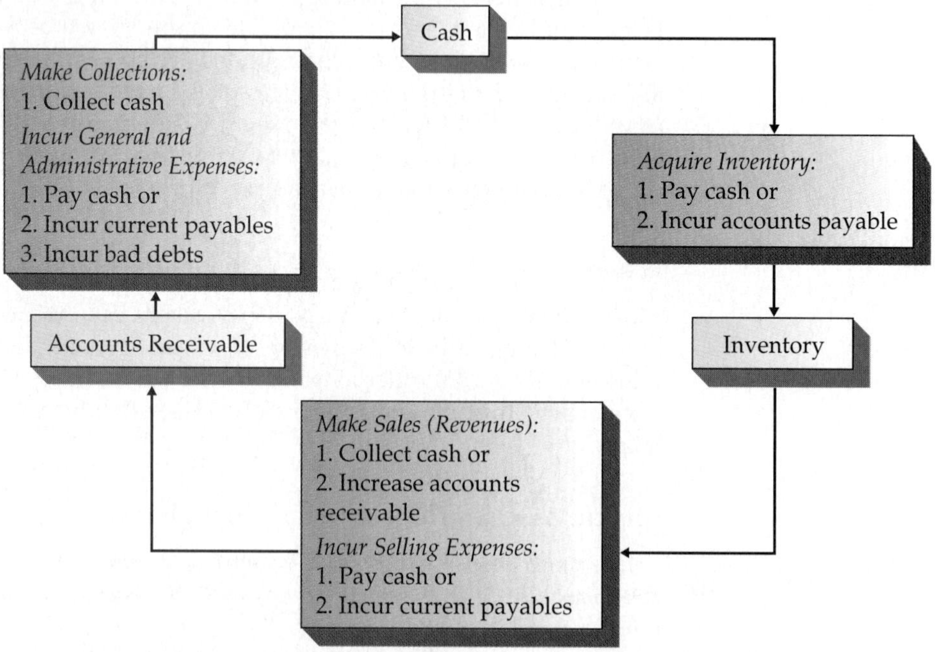

Source: Loren D. Nikolai and John D. Bazley, *Intermediate Accounting*. Copyright 1992 by South-Western Publishing Company.

contra account

Accounts is established. A **contra account** is an account that wholly or partially offsets another account. The balance in this account represents management's estimate of the uncollectible accounts. On the balance sheet, the total in this account is deducted from the total in Accounts Receivable. As a result, the net amount in Accounts Receivable represents the total estimated to be collectible, or the net realizable value of the receivables (a term used to describe the net amount expected to be collectible). The techniques used to estimate and record the Allowance for Doubtful Accounts will be described in Chapter 7.

Inventories, supplies, and prepaid expenses are current assets because they will be sold or used up during the following year or operating cycle. In some situations, prepaid expenses may benefit several years or operating cycles. Because these amounts are usually not material, however, common practice is to show the entire amount as a current asset. If these long-term prepaids are material, the noncurrent portion will be listed under Other Assets, often labeled deferred charges.

When you examine Albertson's balance sheet in Exhibit 5-2 you see that current assets are listed in order of their liquidity. That is, cash is shown first, followed by accounts receivable and then inventories, prepaids and other current assets. Cash and receivables are referred to as monetary assets which are assets that are either cash or rights to receive specific amounts of cash. On the other hand, nonmonetary assets do not represent claims to specific amounts of cash, and are assets whose costs represent future benefits that will become expenses as they are used up by the firm. On a balance sheet nonmonetary assets are listed after monetary current assets. In the Albertson's case deferred income tax benefits, which result from unique standards related to accounting for income taxes is shown as a current asset. This complex topic is introduced in Chapter 8.

long-term investments

Long-Term Investments. **Long-term investments** include cash not available for current use and holdings in securities (stocks and bonds) not classified as current. Property, plant, and equipment not used in production but held for resale or future use are often listed in this category. Other assets listed under long-term investments include special cash accounts called sinking funds, which are established to purchase property, plant, and equipment or to repay bonds and other long-term debts. Albertson's does not have this category on its balance sheet.

Property, Plant, and Equipment. Assets classified under property, plant, and equipment represent the firm's productive capacity. These assets are purchased by the firm because of their ability to generate future revenues for a very long time. In effect, property, plant, and equipment, as well as similar assets, represent bundles of service potentials that the firm gradually uses up during future operations. This occurs because of wear and tear, obsolescence, and other factors. Excluding land, which does not lose its future benefits, the matching convention (see Exhibit 5-1) requires that a portion of these assets be systematically allocated against the revenues generated by the use of these assets. As noted previously **depreciation** is the name given to this allocation process.

depreciation

The annual amount of depreciation expense is accumulated in a separate account called, Accumulated Depreciation, which is a contra account similar to the Allowance for Doubtful Accounts. Using the accumulated depreciation account rather than the actual asset account to total the depreciation to date allows the accounting system to maintain the original historical cost of the asset in one account and to accumulate the depreciation to date in the accumulated depreciation account.

Albertson's titles this category Land, Buildings, and Equipment. The total historical cost of these assets at January 30, 1992 is $2,166,205,000 while the accumulated depreciation to date is $773,527,000 leaving a net cost of $1,392,678,000. This net cost is the **net book value** or simply *book value* of the assets. Although the specific order in which the assets are listed in this category varies, land is usually shown first.

net book value

The land, buildings, and equipment section of Albertson's balance sheet is typical of those found in the balance sheets of many U.S. companies in that it also includes Leasehold Improvements and Assets Under Capital Leases. Leasehold improvements are improvements such as air conditioning, partitioning, and other construction made by the individual or firm that is leasing (the lessee) a particular piece of property. At the end of the lease these improvements revert to the owner of the property; they are not the property of lessee.

Albertson's also includes in this category Assets Under Capital Lease. These are stores that Albertson's has leased under long-term agreements. Generally accepted accounting principles require that these leases be treated as if the stores had been purchased outright. Chapter 12 will discuss this asset in more detail.

intangible assets

Intangible Assets. **Intangible assets** are assets that have no physical or tangible characteristics, as do buildings or equipment. They are agreements, contracts, or rights that provide economic benefits to the firm, the use of a certain production process, trade name, or similar item. Typical assets included in this category are patents, trademarks, copyrights, franchises, and goodwill.

goodwill

From an accounting perspective, **goodwill** refers to the excess cost of a group of assets over the fair value of the assets individually. That is, the cost of the entire bundle of assets is more valuable than the cost of the individual assets. This is due to the extra earning power that has resulted from someone combining those assets into a working whole. *Goodwill cannot be recorded unless a firm is purchased by another.* If such a purchase takes place, and the purchaser pays more than the fair market value for the net assets acquired, the difference is considered goodwill. Only in this way can the amount of goodwill be verified. Because all intangible assets eventually lose their economic benefits, their costs are written off over the shorter of their useful or economic life. This process, called amortization, will be explored further in Chapter 10.

Other Assets. Other Assets is a catchall category that many firms use for assets that do not fit well elsewhere. Examples are long-term receivables, if not listed under the investment category, and long-term prepayments such as property insurance paid several years in advance. Although this category usually appears last on the balance sheet, it is the second category on Albertson's balance sheet. This is another indication that there is more than one balance sheet format in use.

Liabilities

Liabilities represent the economic obligations of the firm. For balance sheet purposes, they are usually divided into two categories, current liabilities and long-term liabilities or debt.

current liabilities

Current Liabilities. **Current liabilities** are those that will either be paid or will require the use of current assets within one year or one operating cycle, if the operating cycle exceeds one year. Typical current liabilities are short-term notes and loans payable, accounts payable, taxes payable, wages, other accrued expenses, and earned income or advances from customers. Some liabilities, such as mortgages, are payable in equal monthly installments over a specified number of years. The portion of these liabilities that is payable within 12 months from the balance sheet date is called **current portion of long-term debt** and is classified as a current liability. The remaining portion is classified as a noncurrent liability. In Exhibit 5-2, for example, two such items, the current maturities of long-term debt and current obligations under capital leases, are shown in the current liabilities section.

current portion of long-term debt

Note that Albertson's has a liability called "self-insurance" listed in the current liabilities section of its balance sheet. The company has decided not to purchase insurance for property loss, workers' compensation, and general liability costs. Rather, it accumulates in this account the dollar amount of claims already filed as well as estimates for future claims incurred but not reported. Because of the increasing costs of insurance many firms have chosen to self insure in this way.

Long-Term Liabilities. Liabilities that do not meet the criteria to be considered current are classified as noncurrent or long-term. Included in this category are bonds payable, mortgages payable, leases, and long-term bank loans payable. Remember that the portion of these liabilities that is due within the next 12 months or a longer operating cycle is classified as current.

Albertson's has decided to establish three separate categories of long-term liabilities on its balance sheet: long-term debt, obligations under capital lease, and other long-term liabilities and deferred credits. One approach that many companies use is to group these three accounts under one category just called *long-term debt.*

Included in Albertson's third category, other long-term liabilities and deferred credits, are three deferred credit accounts: Deferred Compensation, Deferred Income Taxes, and Deferred Rents Payable. Deferred Compensation and Deferred Rents Payable represent compensation and rents that will be paid sometime in the future.

deferred income taxes

Deferred income taxes are taxes that Albertson's has incurred based on the current year's accounting income that may not be payable to the government until a future period. Deferred income taxes are complex; the topic is discussed briefly in Chapter 8.

Stockholders' Equity

Included in the Stockholders' Equity category are the following accounts: common stock (or the more general term, capital stock), capital in excess of par value, and retained earnings. The total of the common stock and the capital in excess of par value represents the stockholders' permanent investment in the corporation.

The total permanent investment by stockholders at January 30, 1992 equals \$132,849,000 (\$132,131,000 in common stock and \$718,000 in capital in excess of par value). The fact that this investment is divided between the Common Stock account and the Capital in Excess of Par Value account is not significant. Most issues of common stock are assigned a par value by the corporation's Board of Directors. The reasons for assigning a par value and dividing the permanent investment between these two accounts will be explained in Chapter 13.

As noted in Chapter 1, retained earnings represent the accumulated earnings of the business less any distributions to stockholders. At January 30, 1992, Albertson's balance in its retained earnings account is $1,066,603,000. The changes that affect this account during the year are described in the statement of changes in stockholders' equity presented later in the chapter.

THE USES AND LIMITATIONS OF CLASSIFIED BALANCE SHEETS

Objective 4
Explain the uses and limitations of a classified balance sheet.

This discussion of classified balance sheets began with a list of questions that present and potential investors and creditors can answer from the information provided. These questions usually center on measuring a company's overall financial strength. This can be accomplished through financial statement analysis, using ratios to highlight important relationships. Some significant ratios and other analytic data will be considered next.

Measuring Liquidity

As noted, financial statement users are interested in a firm's liquidity. That is, they would like to know whether a firm has enough current assets to pay its current liabilities and/or to respond to changes in the business environment. Two measures, working capital and the current ratio, are commonly used to make this assessment.

working capital

Working Capital. **Working capital,** or net working capital, is defined as current assets minus current liabilities. Thus, working capital represents the amount of current assets that the firm has available to respond to its business needs after repaying all of its current liabilities. Firms need enough working capital to continue operating on a day-to-day basis. Even profitable firms can face financial difficulties if they are unable to maintain a significant amount of working capital. Consequently, a firm's creditors often require it to maintain a certain level of working capital. For example, Albertson's is required by certain of its creditors to maintain working capital of not less than $30,000,000.

Albertson's working capital, as shown in Exhibit 5-4, is $99,039,000 and $91,824,000, at January 30, 1992 (1991 year-end) and January 31, 1991 (1990 year-end), respectively.[7]

Exhibit 5-4
Determination of Working Capital and the Current Ratio

(in thousands)

Working Capital	*Current Ratio*
Current Assets less Current Liabilities	$\frac{\text{Current Assets}}{\text{Current Liabilities}}$
1991: $751,286 − $652,247 = $99,039	$\frac{\$751,286}{\$652,247} = 1.15$
1990: $677,391 − $585,567 = $91,824	$\frac{\$677,391}{\$585,567} = 1.16$

7. Because Albertson's uses a fiscal year ending in late January or early February, the year ended January 30, 1992 is referred to as year-end 1991 and the year ended January 31, 1991 is referred to as year-end 1990.

Two important questions come to mind: How much working capital is sufficient, and how does Albertson's working capital compare to that of other retail grocery chains? The answer to the first question depends on the company's particular needs and the characteristics of the industry within which the firm operates. One way to answer this question is to compare the amount of working capital of a particular firm with that of other firms of similar size in the industry or with an industry average. In addition, the financial working capital over several years should be compared and analyzed.

Answering the second question is more difficult. Interfirm comparisons are tentative because the firm's absolute size affects the amount of its working capital. For example, because Albertson's is thousands of times larger than a local company with one or two stores, one would expect Albertson's to have more working capital. But whether Albertson's is in better financial shape than this local company cannot be answered by just comparing the dollar amount of the working capital of the two companies.

current ratio

Current Ratio. One solution to this problem is to calculate a ratio called the *current ratio.* The **current ratio** is determined by dividing the total current assets by the total current liabilities. It allows meaningful comparisons among firms of different sizes, because all dollar amounts are standardized by the ratio. As shown in Exhibit 5-4, the 1991 and 1990 current ratios for Albertson's are 1.15 and 1.16, respectively.

Evaluating these data accurately rests on several considerations. For example, firms in some industries traditionally have higher current ratios than do firms in other industries. Thus a firm's specific ratio should be compared with its industry average. For example, the average current ratio for firms in the retail grocery industry is 1.2. Thus, Albertson's current ratio appears to be about average.[8] Most financial analysts would probably agree that for many industries a ratio of 2.0 is sufficiently high for most firms.

The particular makeup of the current assets is also important. Approximately 12% of Albertson's current assets (cash and accounts receivable) at January 30, 1992 can quickly be turned into cash (the figure is 11% for year-end 1990). This is not unusual for a retail grocery store such as Albertson's due to the large amount of inventory that it must maintain.

Long-Term Measures of Financial Strength

Investors and creditors are also interested in a firm's long-term strength and financial viability. The amount of debt in relation to total equity or total assets is an indication of this strength. Two ratios, debt-to-equity and debt-to-total-assets, are standard measures of a firm's long-term strength.

debt-to-equity ratio

Debt-to-Equity Ratio. The **debt-to-equity ratio** is calculated by the following formula:

$$\frac{\text{Total Liabilities}}{\text{Total Stockholders' Equity}}$$

8. Industry averages taken from *Industry Norms and Key Business Ratios, Desktop Edition, 1991-2,* Dun & Bradstreet Information Services, p. 153.

This ratio measures the relative risk assumed by creditors and owners. The higher this ratio, the more difficult it will be for a firm to raise additional capital by increasing long-term debt.

Albertson's debt-to-equity ratios for year-end 1991 and 1990 are 84.8% and 85.1%, respectively, as calculated in Exhibit 5-5. These ratios indicate that Albertson's is a financially strong company that will be able to command large amounts of external financing from creditors. These figures are below the industry average of 219%, which implies that Albertson's is in better financial condition than other firms in the industry.

debt-to-total-assets ratio

Debt-to-Total-Assets Ratio. The **debt-to-total-assets ratio** is determined by applying the following formula:

$$\frac{\text{Total Liabilities}}{\text{Total Assets}}$$

This ratio measures the amount of assets provided by the creditors versus the amount provided by the stockholders. As you may recall, assets must be provided either by creditors or by stockholders and profitable operations. The relative percentage of assets contributed by each group is measured by this ratio. A ratio higher than the industry average indicates that the creditors have provided a larger share of the firm's assets than is common in the industry. When this is the case, a banker or other creditor may be unwilling to extend additional credit.

The debt-to-total-assets ratios for Albertson's are also shown in Exhibit 5-5. As this calculation indicates, the ratios for years ended 1991 and 1990 are 45.9% and 46.0%, respectively. This means that roughly 46% of the assets at year-end 1991 and 1990 were contributed by Albertson's creditors.

Another way to look at these relationships is to consider the inverse of the debt-to-total-assets ratio, which is the ratio of stockholders equity to total assets. This ratio is calculated as follows:

$$\frac{\text{Total Stockholders' Equity}}{\text{Total Assets}}$$

Exhibit 5-5
Determination of the Debt-to-Equity Ratio and the Debt-to-Total-Assets Ratio

(in thousands)

	Debt-to-Equity Ratio	*Debt-to-Total-Assets Ratio*
	$\frac{\text{Total Liabilities*}}{\text{Total Stockholders' Equity}}$	$\frac{\text{Total Liabilities*}}{\text{Total Assets}}$
1991:	$\frac{\$1,016,795}{\$1,199,452} = 84.8\%$	$\frac{\$1,016,795}{\$2,216,247} = 45.9\%$
1990:	$\frac{\$925,628}{\$1,087,882} = 85.1\%$	$\frac{\$925,628}{\$2,013,510} = 46.0\%$

*Albertson's total liabilities is the sum of the Total Current Liabilities, Long-Term Debt, Obligations Under Capital Leases, and Other Long-Term Liabilities and Deferred Credits on its balance sheet.

As this ratio has the same denominator as the ratio of debt-to-total-assets, they are the inverse of one another. Thus, for year-end 1991 and 1990 respectively, this ratio is 54.1% (100% − 45.9%) and 54% (100% − 46%).

Taken together, these ratios indicate Albertson's is a financially strong company that has been able to finance its growth through operations and with only a reasonable amount of debt. In the discussion of its results for 1991 the management of Albertson's notes:

The company's excellent operating results enhanced its financial position and ability to continue its 1991 planned expansion program without additional long-term financing.

Limitations of the Balance Sheet

This chapter has pointed out some of the ways that a balance sheet helps financial statement users evaluate financial position and strength. However, a number of problems inherent in the accounting model limit the usefulness of balance sheets. These problems include the way in which accountants define assets, the use of historical cost, the need for arbitrary cost allocations, and the use of different methods of accounting.

Limited Definition of Assets. In Chapter 1, Assets were defined as economic resources, controlled by an enterprise, that have future benefits. Transactions must be quantifiable in monetary terms and have benefits that are measurable and verifiable to be included in the accounting system. A number of items that one might consider assets, such as good management and research and development efforts, do not meet these criteria and are not considered assets. Accordingly, not all of the real economic assets that a firm owns or controls are listed on the balance sheet.

Use of Historical Cost. Net assets on a firm's balance sheet are recorded at their historical cost or net book value (historical cost less accumulated depreciation deducted to date). Remember that accountants do not record increases in value or market value until an external transaction occurs. Except in the case of a newly formed company, the balance sheet generally does not indicate the current or market value of the company's net assets. Therefore, investors or creditors cannot use the balance sheet to determine the current value of the company's net assets.

Arbitrary Cost Allocation. Investors and creditors need information about an enterprise on a periodic and timely basis. The matching convention ensures that the costs of assets that benefit several periods are allocated to those periods. This requires a number of allocations, such as depreciation, that are inherently estimates. To the extent that these required estimates are arbitrary management decisions, the balance sheet is less useful to investors and creditors.

Use of Different Accounting Methods. Another limitation of the balance sheet, as well as of the other financial statements, is that alternative generally accepted accounting principles are available under current standards. For example, as will become clear in later chapters, firms can use different depreciation methods. Management can choose among alternatives and often does. This makes it difficult to compare and contrast the financial positions of various firms.

CLASSIFIED INCOME STATEMENTS

Objective 5
Define the main elements of a classified income statement and prepare one.

The purpose of the income statement is to provide financial statement users with information concerning the profitability of an enterprise for a particular period of time. This statement lists all of the revenues, expenses, gains, and losses that the enterprise earned or incurred during the accounting period. Gains and losses result from the sale of assets or the settlement of liabilities that are not related to sales of its goods and services. The difference between the total of revenues plus gains and the total of expenses plus losses is either net income or net loss. The income statement has become very important because, as Concepts Statement 1 notes, "the primary focus of financial reporting is information about . . . earnings and its components."[9]

By analyzing the income statement, the investor or creditor can answer such questions as these:

1. Did the company earn a profit this year, and if so, how does it compare with its profits from other years?
2. What is the company's gross margin on sales, and is it large enough to cover other operating expenses?
3. What are the various components of revenues and expenses, and how do they compare with those of prior years?
4. Did the firm generate enough revenues from operations to pay the current interest charges?
5. How profitable is the firm compared with others in its industry?

Income Statement Format and Categories

As with the balance sheet, management has some discretion over the exact format of the income statement. Published income statements are rather condensed whereas the income statements prepared for management use are quite detailed. The consolidated income statements of Albertson's for the years ended January 30, 1992, January 31, 1990, and February 1, 1990 are shown in Exhibit 5-6. Keep in mind that these income statements are typical of those issued by most U.S. firms but that a foreign firm may use a different format.

The income statement for Albertson's reproduced in Exhibit 5-6 has several major categories: gross profit on sales, operating and administrative expenses, operating profit, other income and expenses, income before taxes, net income, and net earnings.

gross profit on sales

Gross Profit on Sales. **Gross profit on sales,** sometimes just referred to as gross profit or gross margin, is sales less cost of goods sold. The gross margin figure is significant in evaluating a company's ability to earn enough profit on its sales to cover its operating expenses.

operating expenses

Operating and Administrative Expenses. **Operating expenses** are the costs incurred to conduct normal business operations. Operating expenses generally include selling expenses, such as sales commissions and advertising, and general and administrative expenses, such as office salaries, rent, utilities, and insurance.

9. FASB Concepts Statement 1, par. 43.

Exhibit 5-6

Albertson's, Inc.
Consolidated Earnings
(in thousands except per share data)

	52 Weeks January 30, 1992	*52 Weeks January 31, 1991*	*52 Weeks February 1, 1990*
Sales	$8,680,467	$8,218,562	$7,422,663
Cost of sales	6,598,950	6,293,881	5,722,036
Gross profit	$2,081,517	$1,924,681	$1,700,627
Operating and administrative expenses	1,667,355	1,549,061	1,381,017
Operating profit	$ 414,162	$ 375,620	$ 319,610
Other (expenses) income			
Interest, net	(23,106)	(24,812)	(18,898)
Other, net	15,338	15,201	9,064
Earnings before income taxes	$ 406,394	$ 366,009	$ 309,776
Income taxes	148,600	132,235	113,225
NET EARNINGS	$ 257,794	$ 233,774	$ 196,551
EARNINGS PER SHARE	$1.94	$1.75	$1.47
Average number of shares outstanding	133,169	133,777	134,136

Many published financial statements condense this data, reporting only one total for all operating expenses. In the Albertson's income statement, this total is labeled operating and administrative expenses.

operating profit

Operating Profit. **Operating profit** (or income from operations) is the next category on the income statement. It is the difference between the gross profit on sales and the total of the operating expenses. If the firm's total operating expenses exceed its gross margin on sales, the category will be labeled *operating loss* or *loss from operations.*

other expenses and income

Other Expenses and Income. A firm often earns income from sources other than sales and incurs expenses other than from operations. These are listed under a category called **other expenses and income.** Other income items include rent revenue, investment revenue from dividends and interest, and gains from sales of property, plant, and equipment. Other expenses include losses from sales of plant and equipment and interest expense. Accountants consider interest to be a financing charge and not an operating expense.

Albertson's has netted its interest income and expense and only reported one figure, interest expense, net. They have done the same with their category for other income. This is a typical presentation.

Earnings Before Income Taxes and Net Earnings. Earnings (sometimes referred to as Income) before taxes is determined by adding or subtracting other income and expenses from operating profit. The income tax expense for the period is then deducted from that amount, and net earnings (sometimes referred to as net income) is determined. Again, because of the significance of income taxes, they are shown separately as the last item before net earnings.

earnings per share (EPS)

Other Data. Income statements of publicly-held corporations may include such categories as discontinued operations, extraordinary items, and the effects of changes in accounting methods. These are unusual items that, under generally accepted accounting principles, must be shown separately as discussed in the appendix to this chapter. **Earnings per share (EPS)** data are also required to be disclosed on the income statement. On Albertson's income statement, the only one of these items shown is earnings per share. Although this can be complicated to calculate for a company as complex as Albertson's, it is basically determined by dividing net income by the average number of common shares outstanding during the year. Many financial analysts use EPS data to compare earnings among firms.

USES AND LIMITATIONS OF CLASSIFIED INCOME STATEMENTS

Objective 6
Explain the uses and limitations of a classified income statement.

This section began with a list of questions investors and creditors could use the income statement to answer. These questions center on measuring and evaluating a firm's profitability.

Measuring Profitability

One way to measure and evaluate a firm's profitability is to compute percentages that compare particular income statement items, such as gross profit and net income, to sales. Two such percentages are the *gross profit percentage* and the *profit margin percentage.* These ratios for Albertson's are calculated in Exhibit 5-7.

gross profit percentage

Gross Profit Percentage. The **gross profit percentage** is determined by dividing gross profit by sales. This ratio provides information concerning the percentage of cost of goods sold to sales and gross profit on sales. Albertson's gross margin percentages for year-end 1991 and 1990 are 24.0% and 23.4%, respectively. This means that for every dollar of 1991 sales Albertson's gross margin or gross profit was 24.0 cents. Conversely, the cost of goods sold percentages for year-end 1991 and 1990 are 76.0% (100% − 24.0%) and 76.6% (100% − 23.4%), respectively. Thus, for every dollar of 1991 sales, 76.0 cents was needed to cover the cost of goods sold. As with all ratios, individual percentages should be evaluated in terms of industry norms. For example, the average gross profit percentage for the retail grocery industry is 20.9%.

profit margin percentage

Profit Margin Percentage. The **profit margin percentage** relates net income to total sales. It is calculated by dividing net income by sales. Albertson's profit

Exhibit 5-7
Determination of Gross Profit Percentage and Profit Margin Percentage

(in thousands)

	Gross Profit Percentage	*Profit Margin Percentage*
	$\frac{\text{Gross Profit on Sales}}{\text{Sales}}$	$\frac{\text{Net Income}}{\text{Sales}}$
1991:	$\frac{\$2,081,517}{\$8,680,467} = 24.0\%$	$\frac{\$257,794}{\$8,680,467} = 2.97\%$
1990:	$\frac{\$1,924,681}{\$8,218,562} = 23.4\%$	$\frac{\$233,774}{\$8,218,562} = 2.84\%$

Exhibit 5-8
Determination of Return on Assets and Return on Stockholders' Equity

(in thousands)

	Return on Assets		*Return on Stockholders' Equity*	
	Net Income / Average Total Assets		Net Income / Average Stockholders' Equity	
1991:	\$257,794 / (\$2,216,247 + \$2,013,510) ÷ 2	= 12.2%*	\$257,794 / (\$1,199,452 + \$1,087,882) ÷ 2	= 22.5%*
1990:	\$233,774 / (\$2,013,510 + \$1,862,689) ÷ 2	= 12.1%*	\$233,774 / (\$1,087,882 + \$929,492) ÷ 2	= 23.2%*

*These ratios are slightly different from those shown in the annual report. This is due to rounding differences.

margin percentages for year-end 1991 and 1990 are 2.97% and 2.84%, respectively (See Exhibit 5-7). This means that for every dollar of sales in these two years, Albertson's ended up with less than 3 cents in net earnings. Retail firms such as Albertson's tend to be high-volume, low profit-margin businesses.

Return on Investment. A number of ratios can be used by investors and creditors to determine how effectively management is operating a business and the return that is accruing to the various equity holders on their investment. Two such common ratios are return on assets and return on stockholders' equity. These ratios are computed in Exhibit 5-8.

return on assets

Return on Assets. In its simplest form, the ratio **return on assets** is determined by dividing net income by average total assets.[10] Note that in ratios that use an income statement figure in the numerator and a balance sheet figure in the denominator, the denominator should be an average. This is because revenue and expense items are for a period of time, and it is most appropriate to relate these items to average assets for that period.

The return on assets ratio is important because it measures how efficiently a firm is using its assets or resources to produce profits. Albertson's return on asset ratios for year-end 1991 and 1990 are 12.2% and 12.1%, respectively compared to an industry average of only 1.7%.

return on stockholders' equity

Return on Stockholders' Equity. The ratio **return on stockholders' equity** measures the return that stockholders are receiving on their investment. It is calculated by dividing net income by average stockholders' equity. This ratio calculated in Exhibit 5-8, is 22.5% for year-end 1991 and 23.2% for year-end 1990. Again, evaluation of these ratios depends on industry norms and firm trends. The average in the retail grocery industry for large firms is about 5.0%.

Limitations of the Income Statement

Clearly, the income statement is extremely useful for evaluating and measuring a firm's profitability. As with all financial statements, however, there are limitations to its usefulness. Because the income statement is linked to the bal-

10. More complex ways to calculate this ratio are explored in chapter 14. However, the method used in this chapter conveys the essential meaning of the ratio.

ance sheet, some of the criticisms regarding the balance sheet also apply to the income statement. As stated earlier, these include the use of historical costs, the problems associated with cost allocation, and the use of different accounting methods.

RETAINED EARNINGS STATEMENT AND STATEMENT OF STOCKHOLDERS' EQUITY

Objective 7
Prepare a retained earnings statement and a statement of stockholders' equity, and discuss their uses and limitations.

statement of stockholders' equity

As previously noted, the retained earnings statement discloses the items that have caused a change in retained earnings. This fairly simple statement shows the effect of net income or loss and dividends on retained earnings.

The statement is adequate only when companies do not have significant changes in other stockholders' equity accounts. Large, publicly-held firms are likely to enter into various transactions, such as issuing additional common stock or converting bonds into common stock, that affect a variety of stockholders' accounts. These firms prepare a more extensive statement called a **statement of stockholders' equity.** This statement, which is reproduced in Exhibit 5-9 for Albertson's, details the changes in all the stockholders' equity accounts.

Exhibit 5-9

Albertson's, Inc.
Consolidated Stockholders' Equity
(in thousands)

	Common Stock $1.00 Par Value	*Capital in Excess of Par Value*	*Retained Earnings*	*Total*
Balance at February 2, 1989	$ 66,929	$36,317	$ 697,250	$ 800,496
Exercise of stock options	521	6,369		6,890
Tax benefits related to stock options		3,956		3,956
Cash dividends, $.40 per share			(53,615)	(53,615)
Stock purchases	(490)	(24,296)		(24,786)
Net earnings			196,551	196,551
Balance at February 1, 1990	$ 66,960	$22,346	$ 840,186	$ 929,492
Exercise of stock options	503	3,544		4,047
Tax benefits related to stock options		4,265		4,265
Cash dividends, $.48 per share			(64,215)	(64,215)
Stock purchases	(530)	(12,582)	(6,369)	(19,481)
Two-for-one stock split	66,887	(15,442)	(51,445)	
Net earnings			233,774	233,774
Balance at January 31, 1991	$133,820	$ 2,131	$ 951,931	$1,087,882
Exercise of stock options	395	3,097		3,492
Tax benefits related to stock options		4,536		4,536
Cash dividends, $.56 per share			(74,446)	(74,446)
Stock purchases	(2,084)	(9,046)	(68,676)	(79,806)
Net earnings			257,794	257,794
Balance at January 30, 1992	$132,131	$ 718	$1,066,603	$1,199,452

STATEMENT OF CASH FLOWS

Objective 8
Explain the uses and limitations of the statement of cash flows.

The statement of cash flows is the fourth required financial statement. The purpose of this statement is to provide relevant information about the cash receipts and disbursements of an enterprise during a period. It is useful in answering the following questions:

1. What are the sources of the firm's cash?
2. What proportion of the firm's cash is generated internally or from operations?
3. What other financing and/or investing activities took place during the year?
4. Why was the firm profitable, although there was only a slight increase in cash?

The statement of cash flows for Albertson's is shown in Exhibit 5-10. Chapter 14 explains the actual preparation of this statement; the purpose here is to introduce you to its usefulness.

The statement of cash flows has three major categories; cash flows from operating activities, cash flows from investing activities, and cash flows from financing activities. Operating activities are primarily those related to sales of the firm's goods and services. The statement of cash flows for Albertson's shows that operating activities for year-end 1991 resulted in a positive cash flow of $408,020,000 which is substantially more than the net income for the year. This difference occurs because the income statement measures income as defined by generally accepted accounting principles whereas the statement of cash flows measures only cash inflows and outflows. The two measures usually do not coincide. The cash flow statement in Exhibit 5-10 details the reconciliation between net earnings and cash provided by operating activities. Chapter 14 will explain this reconciliation in depth; at this point in your studies it is important only to understand that net income and cash provided from operations are different concepts.

Cash flows from investing activities result primarily from lending cash to others and collecting cash from repayment of loans, purchasing and selling securities, and purchasing and selling property, plant, and equipment. Albertson's investing activities include cash paid for various capital expenditures such as the purchase of land, buildings, and equipment, and cash received from the disposal of land, buildings, and equipment.

Financing activities relate to obtaining financing from owners and creditors and, where appropriate, repaying such financing. In Albertson's case, cash was used in various financing activities, such as the repayment of long-term debt and the payment of cash dividends. As a result of all these activities—operating, investing, and financing—Albertson's cash and cash equivalents (marketable securities purchased for temporary investments) increased by $10,971,000 in 1991.

OTHER ELEMENTS OF ANNUAL REPORTS OF PUBLICLY-HELD COMPANIES

Objective 9
Discuss the uses of other financial data in the annual report.

Publicly-held companies are required to provide stockholders with an annual report of their activities. Included in this annual report are the firm's financial statements including explanatory notes, the auditors' report, management's statement for responsibility of financial reporting, management's discussion and analysis of results of operations and financial condition, and a variety of other information. The following section will briefly cover the notes to the financial

Exhibit 5-10

Albertson's, Inc.
Consolidated Cash Flows
(in thousands)

	52 Weeks *January 30, 1992*	52 Weeks *January 31, 1991*	52 Weeks *February 1, 1990*
Cash Flows from Operating Activities:			
Net earnings	$257,794	$233,774	$196,551
Adjustments to reconcile net earnings to net cash provided by operating activities:			
Depreciation and amortization	132,813	122,185	105,920
Net deferred income tax benefits	(12,912)	(5,302)	6,040
Changes in operating assets and liabilities:			
Receivables and prepaid expenses	(2,572)	(9,226)	(2,427)
Inventories	(50,520)	(18,037)	(112,354)
Refundable income taxes			5,748
Accounts payable	8,572	(4,352)	45,642
Other current liabilities	19,541	15,369	12,511
Self-insurance	14,890	22,346	19,500
Unearned income	31,667	5,459	1,825
Other long-term liabilities	8,747	8,785	12,904
Net cash provided by operating activities	$408,020	$371,001	$291,860
Cash Flows from Investing Activities:			
Increase in other assets	(4,618)	(19,793)	(8,543)
Capital expenditures excluding noncash items	(268,500)	(254,858)	(296,147)
Proceeds from disposals of land, buildings, and equipment	12,696	11,387	5,010
Net cash used in investing activities	($260,422)	($263,264)	($299,680)
Cash Flows from Financing Activities:			
Net proceeds from line of credit borrowings	20,000	10,000	
Proceeds from long-term borrowings			50,000
Payment on long-term borrowings	(10,403)	(62,628)	(12,558)
Proceeds from stock options exercised	8,028	8,312	10,846
Cash dividends	(74,446)	(64,215)	(53,615)
Stock purchases	(79,806)	(19,481)	(24,786)
Net cash used in financing activities	($136,627)	($128,012)	($ 30,113)
Net Increase (Decrease) in Cash and Cash Equivalents	10,971	(20,275)	(37,933)
Cash and Cash Equivalents at Beginning of Year	23,433	43,708	81,641
Cash and Cash Equivalents at End of Year	$ 34,404	$ 23,433	$ 43,708

statements, the auditors' report, and management's statement of financial responsibility.

Notes to The Financial Statements

It would be impossible to include all important information in the body of the financial statements. Yet the full-disclosure principle requires that a firm's financial statements provide users with all relevant information about the various transactions of the firm. As a result, financial statements must be accompanied by notes, which are narrative explanations of the important aspects of various items. Albertson's has notes that range from an explanation of its significant accounting policies to a discussion of significant events subsequent to January 30, 1992. Albertson's complete financial statements, including all notes, are reproduced in Appendix A.

Auditors' Report

Public companies are required by U.S. securities laws to engage CPAs to conduct an annual audit. Though this requirement applies only to publicly held companies owner-managers of private companies may want an audit for several reasons, including the need to provide information to bankers and other creditors. In all cases, the general purpose of an audit is to assure users that the financial statements prepared by the firm's management are in conformity with generally accepted accounting principles (GAAP).

auditor's report

The **auditors' report** for Albertson's is reproduced in Exhibit 5-11. As the first paragraph in the auditor's report clearly indicates, financial statements are the responsibility of management. The auditors' responsibility, as noted in the first and third paragraphs, is to express an opinion on whether or not the financial statements are presented fairly in conformity with generally accepted accounting principles. Albertson's received what is called an unqualified or clean opinion by the auditors as indicated by the statement that the financial statements are fairly presented in accordance with GAAP. The second or middle paragraph indicates the procedures that auditors follow in arriving at their opinion. You should note

Exhibit 5-11

Independent Auditors' Report

The Board of Directors and Stockholders of Albertson's, Inc.:

We have audited the accompanying consolidated balance sheets of Albertson's, Inc. and subsidiaries as of January 30, 1992, January 31, 1991, and February 1, 1990, and the related consolidated statements of earnings, stockholders' equity and cash flows for the years then ended. These financial statements are the responsibility of the Company's management. Our responsibility is to express an opinion on these financial statements based on our audits.

We conducted our audits in accordance with generally accepted auditing standards. Those standards require that we plan and perform the audit to obtain reasonable assurance about whether the financial statements are free of material misstatement. An audit includes examining, on a test basis, evidence supporting the amounts and disclosures in the financial statements. An audit also includes assessing the accounting principles used and significant estimates made by management, as well as evaluating the overall financial statement presentation. We believe that our audits provide a reasonable basis for our opinion.

In our opinion, the consolidated financial statements referred to above present fairly, in all material respects, the financial position of Albertson's, Inc. and subsidiaries at January 30, 1992, January 31, 1991, and February 1, 1990, and the results of their operations and their cash flows for the years then ended in conformity with generally accepted accounting principles.

Deloitte & Touche

Boise, Idaho—March 18, 1992

that the auditors do not examine every transaction, but examine on a test basis evidence supporting the amounts and disclosures in the financial statements.

Management also explicitly recognizes its responsibility for financial reporting in a statement in the annual report placed immediately before the auditors' report. Such a statement for Albertson's is shown in Exhibit 5-12.

Other Aspects of the Annual Report

All public companies issue annual reports to their stockholders and other interested users. These reports contain the firm's audited financial statements and related notes, including management's discussion and analysis of operations, the president's letter, summaries of significant financial statistics, and other data.

Exhibit 5-12
Statement of Managements' Responsibility—Albertson's

Responsibility for Financial Reporting

The Management of Albertson's, Inc. is responsible for the preparation and integrity of the consolidated financial statements of the Company. The accompanying consolidated financial statements have been prepared by the Management of the Company, in accordance with generally accepted accounting principles, using Management's best estimates and judgment where necessary. Financial information appearing throughout this Annual Report is consistent with that in the consolidated financial statements.

To help fulfill its responsibility, Management maintains a system of internal controls designed to provide reasonable assurance that assets are safeguarded against loss or unauthorized use and that transactions are executed in accordance with Management's authorizations and are reflected accurately in the Company's records. The concept of reasonable assurance is based on the recognition that the cost of maintaining a system of internal accounting controls should not exceed benefits expected to be derived from the system. The Company believes that its long-standing emphasis on the highest standards of conduct and ethics, set forth in comprehensive written policies, serves to reinforce its system of internal controls.

Deloitte & Touche, independent auditors, audited the consolidated financial statements in accordance with generally accepted auditing standards to independently assess the fair presentation of the Company's financial position, results of operations and cash flows.

The Audit Committee of the Board of Directors, comprised entirely of outside directors, oversees the fulfillment by Management of its responsibilities over financial controls and the preparation of financial statements. The Committee meets with internal and external auditors at least three times per year to review audit plans and audit results. This provides internal and external auditors direct access to the Board of Directors.

Management recognizes its responsibility to conduct Albertson's business in accordance with high ethical standards. This responsibility is reflected in key policy statements that, among other things, address potentially conflicting outside business interests of Company employees and specify proper conduct of business activities. Ongoing communications and review programs are designed to help ensure compliance with these policies.

Chairman of the Board and
Chief Executive Officer

Senior Vice President, Finance and
Chief Financial Officer

THE FINANCIAL REPORTING SYSTEM

Objective 10
Describe the relationship between a financial reporting system and the general ledger system.

financial reporting system

Accounting exists to provide useful financial information to decision makers. In the previous chapter, you learned how to use journal entries to record transactions, and how to classify and summarize transactions through the posting process. Preparing and posting journal entries, however, is not the purpose of accounting. Those techniques are only tools or procedures that are used to meet the accounting information system's objective of providing useful information to decision makers. A **financial reporting system** is a manual or computer-based system that uses accounting data that has been collected and summarized in ledgers to produce financial reports and financial statements. Most large organizations use computer-based financial reporting systems. The relationship between a computer-based general ledger system and the financial reporting system is summarized in Exhibit 5-13.

The financial reporting system receives inputs from two different files, the general ledger file and the chart of accounts file. The financial reporting system uses the data contained in the general ledger (which is output by the general ledger system) to produce the financial statements that are the subject of this chapter. The chart of accounts file is also input into the financial reporting system. The chart of accounts file contains information about where the various general ledger accounts are placed on the different financial statements.

Computer-based accounting systems are used extensively because they provide two significant advantages over manual systems. Computers can process information much more rapidly than individuals can. For example, an airline that manages ticket sales with a computer-based transaction processing system

Exhibit 5-13
Systems Flowchart—General Ledger and Financial Reporting Systems

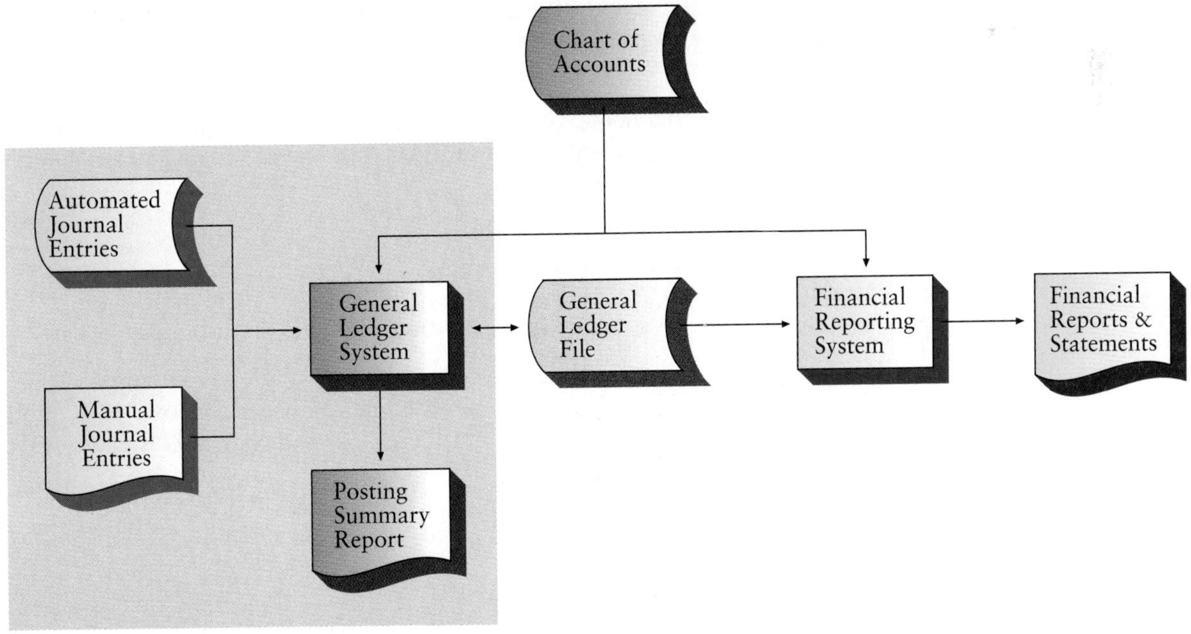

records about 1,500 transactions per second, twenty-four hours a day.[11] This advantage is important because of the large volume of data that is processed by most organizations. In fact, modern organizations could not operate without computers. Can you imagine an airline processing 1,500 transactions per second without a computer system?

Computers, in addition to processing data very quickly, are also very consistent. A computer system that has been correctly programmed will consistently process data correctly. On the other hand, a system that has been incorrectly programmed will consistently process data incorrectly. Unfortunately, it is impossible to program a computer to perform a task that you don't know how to do.

The financial reporting concepts that you learned in this chapter are used in both manual and computer-based financial reporting systems. In fact, most accounting concepts are technologically independent. This means that the underlying concepts are relevant in both manual and computerized information processing environments.

APPENDIX: CORPORATE INCOME STATEMENTS

Objective 11
State the four possible categories that may be found on a corporate income statement and prepare a simple corporate income statement.

A corporation or even a large private enterprise usually derives income and incurs expenses from many sources. Since the mid-1960s, the accounting profession has felt that net income should be a comprehensive figure. That is, comprehensive net income should include "all changes in equity during a period except those resulting from investments by owners and distribution to owners [dividends]."[12]

The notion of comprehensive income does, however, present a problem for users of the income statement. One of the primary purposes of this statement is to help users predict future income patterns. Yet when a firm derives income from various types of transactions, it is difficult to separate recurring from nonrecurring transactions, so the predictive ability of the income statement may be decreased. As the FASB noted:

Characteristics of various sources of comprehensive income may differ significantly from one another, indicating a need for information about various components of comprehensive income.[13]

In order to meet this need, generally accepted accounting principles require that the four major components of income be segregated on the income statement. These four components are:

1. Income from continuing operations
2. Discontinued operations
3. Extraordinary items
4. Cumulative effect of changes in accounting methods or principles

A related component is earnings per share for each of the above items.

An income statement that includes all these components is shown in Exhibit 5A-1. In reviewing this income statement, keep in mind that is is unlikely that

11. Peter G. W. Keen, *Shaping the Future*, Cambridge, MA: Harvard Business School Press, 1991, p. 5.
12. Financial Accounting Standards Board, Concepts Statement No. 6, *Elements of Financial Statements* (Stamford, Conn.: FASB, December 1985), par. 76.
13. Ibid., par. 61.

an enterprise would have income from all these sources in any one year; they are presented for illustrative purposes only. If all these categories do in fact exist, however, they must be listed in the manner and order shown in Exhibit 5A-1. The numbers 1–4 are presented for reference purposes only.

Exhibit 5A-1

The Logit Computer Corporation
Comparative Income Statement
For the Years Ended December 31
(in millions)

	1995	*1994*
Net sales	$6,000	$5,700
Cost of goods sold	3,900	3,648
Gross margin	$2,100	$2,052
Selling and general and administrative expenses	1,260	1,230
Operating income	$ 840	$ 822
Other income		
Gain on sale of building	15	0
Interest income	5	2
	$ 860	$ 824
Other expenses		
Interest expense	10	6
1. Income from continuing operations, before taxes	$ 850	$ 818
Provision for income taxes	340	327
Income from continuing operations	$ 510	$ 491
2. Discontinued operations		
Loss from operations of discontinued segment, net of tax savings of $18 in 1995 and $14 in 1994	(27)	(21)
Gain on disposal of business segment, net of applicable taxes of $24	36	0
Income before extraordinary items and cumulative effect of accounting change	$ 519	$ 470
3. Extraordinary item—Gain on expropriation of subsidiary, net of applicable taxes of $40	0	60
4. Cumulative effect of change in accounting method for depreciation, net of taxes of $20	30	0
Net income	$ 549	$ 530
Earnings per share		
Income from continuing operations	$ 2.04	$ 1.96
Discontinued operations	.04	(.08)
Income before extraordinary items and cumulative effect of accounting change	$ 2.08	$ 1.88
Extraordinary gains	0	.24
Cumulative effect of accounting change	.12	0
Net income	$ 2.20	$ 2.12

Income from Continuing Operations

income from continuing operations

Income from continuing operations includes all of the recurring and usual transactions that the firm enters into as it produces its goods and services. Thus, such items as sales, cost of goods sold, operating expenses, and other income and expense items are included in income from continuing operations. For 1995 and 1994, income from continuing operations from the Logit Computer Corporation is $510 million and $491 million, respectively, as shown in Exhibit 5A-1. The significance of these amounts is that as decision makers use the income statement to make predictions about the future, these items indicate how profitable the corporation has been and how profitable it might be on a recurring and continuing basis.

intraperiod income tax allocation

interperiod income tax allocation

It is important to note that the total income tax expense is divided among the four components of the income statement. This is called **intraperiod income tax allocation.** It means that the total income tax expense for the period is related to the proper component that caused the income. Conversely, **interperiod income tax allocation,** discussed in Chapter 8, refers to the allocation of income taxes among different accounting periods. Intraperiod income tax allocation is necessary in order to maintain an appropriate relationship between income tax expense and income from continuing operations, discontinued operations, extraordinary items, and cumulative effects of accounting changes.

To illustrate, the total income tax expense, assuming a 40% tax rate for simplicity, for 1995 for Logit is $366 million, computed as in Exhibit 5A-2. Instead of showing just one figure for taxes, $366 million, this amount is allocated to the various components of net income. Thus, the reader of the income statement knows how each item affected the firm's total tax expense and what the income tax expense can be expected to be in the future on a recurring basis.

At first glance, it may seem strange that a loss is reduced by a tax savings. For example, as noted in Exhibit 5A-1, the firm suffered a loss on discontinued operations of $45 ($27 + $18) million in 1995. Because a loss reduces income, income tax is lower. Thus, in this example, total taxes are reduced by $18 million because of this loss, and this tax savings is netted against the before-tax loss of $4.5 million to arrive at the net loss of $27 million. By convention, discontinued operations, extraordinary items, and cumulative effects of accounting changes are

Exhibit 5A-2

The Logit Computer Corporation
Income Tax Expense for 1995
(in millions)

	Before-Tax Amount	*Tax—40% (Tax Savings)*
Income from continuing operations before taxes	$850	$340
Discontinued operations		
Loss from operations	(45)	(18)
Gain on sale	60	24
Cumulative effect of accounting change	50	20
	$915	$366

Net income ($915 − $366) = $549

shown net of their tax effects, whereas income from continuing operations is shown both before and after taxes.

Discontinued Operations

The Accounting Principles Board, in Opinion No. 30, stated that results from discontinued operations and the gain or loss from the disposal of the discontinued segment should be shown separately from income from continuing operations. These figures should be disclosed immediately below income from continuing operations.

segment

According to professional pronouncements, a **segment** of a business is a "component of an entity whose activities represent a separate major line of business or class of customer."[14] A segment may be a subsidiary, a division, or a department, as long as its activities can be clearly distinguished from other assets both physically and operationally for financial reporting purposes. A few years ago, for example, CBS discontinued its cable division, which had produced certain cable programming. This represents a discontinued operations. If CBS sold one of its corporate-owned television stations, however, this would not be considered a discontinued operation because CBS still owns several other stations and has several hundred affiliates.

Extraordinary Items

extraordinary items

Extraordinary items are gains and losses that result from transactions that are both unusual in nature and infrequent in occurrence. Because these transactions are unusual and infrequent, they need to be separated from continuing operations so that investors can better use the income statement to predict future income.

Criteria for Determining Extraordinary Items. The criteria for determining whether an item is extraordinary have caused much controversy. Prior to the issuance of Opinion No. 30 in 1973, the management of a firm had considerable discretion in determining whether an item was extraordinary. Thus, several items were considered extraordinary when, under current accounting principles, they would be included in income from continuing operations. For example, there was considerable controversy over Penn Central's decision in 1969 to consider the sale of certain real estate as an ordinary gain rather than an extraordinary gain. Many observers felt that this classification was made in order to conceal operating losses during the year.[15] In order to limit the number and type of extraordinary items, current accounting pronouncements restrict them to those transactions that are both unusual and infrequent.

An unusual event or transaction is one that is highly abnormal or is clearly only incidentally related to the enterprise's ordinary and typical activities, taking into account the environment in which the entity operates. For an event to be infrequent in occurrence, it should be of a type that would not reasonably be expected to recur in the foreseeable future, again taking into account the environment in which the entity operates.

14. American Institute of Certified Public Accountants, Accounting Principles Board, Opinion No. 30, *Reporting the Results of Operations* (New York: AICPA, 1973), par. 13.
15. Abraham Briloff, *Unaccountable Accounting* (New York: Harper & Row, 1972), p. 194.

Although an event or transaction must meet both of these criteria to be extraordinary, considerable judgment is still needed. For example, in order to determine a business's ordinary and typical activities, the specific characteristics of the entity, such as its scope of operations and line of business, should be considered. The entity's environment includes such factors as the characteristics of the industry in which the entity operates, its geographical location, and the extent of governmental regulations. Thus, an item may be unusual and/or infrequent for one enterprise but not for another, because of the differences in their environments.

To demonstrate the judgment required in this area, suppose that a Florida citrus grower's crop of oranges is destroyed by frost. Is this an extraordinary item? No, frost damage in Florida is normally experienced every three to four years; given the environment in which the entity operates, the infrequency-of-occurrence criterion has not been met.[16] If it were a California grower, on the other hand, would this answer be different? Most likely yes, because damage from frost is unusual and infrequent in California, so any loss would be extraordinary.

Examples of Extraordinary Items. Because of the judgment involved in determining extraordinary items, both the APB and the FASB have stated that certain items or transactions definitely are and definitely are not extraordinary items. The more important ones are listed in Exhibit 5A-3. Some of the items that are not considered extraordinary in the exhibit are classified that way because they are unusual or infrequent but not both. In these cases, the item should be

Exhibit 5A-3
*Illustration of Extraordinary Items**

Considered Extraordinary	*Not Considered Extraordinary*
1. Destruction by an earthquake of one of the oil refineries owned by a large, multinational oil company.	1. Write-downs or write-offs of receivables, equipment, or similar items.
2. Destruction of a large portion of a tobacco manufacturer's crops by a hailstorm in an area in which severe damage from hailstorms is rare.	2. Gains and losses from a disposal of a segment.
3. Expropriation of assets by a foreign government.	3. Gains and losses from the sale or abandonment of property, plant, or equipment.
4. Gains or losses due to a prohibition under a newly created law.	4. Effects of strikes against the firm and/or competitors and major suppliers.
5. Gains and losses on early extinguishment of debt.†	5. Changes in accounting estimates and methods.

†FASB Statement 4 requires these gains and losses, if material, to be treated as extraordinary, regardless of the criteria set forth by Opinion 30.

*Sources:
1. APB Opinion No. 30, *Reporting the Results of Operations* (New York: AICPA, 1973).
2. Accounting Interpretations of APB Opinion No. 30, *Reporting the Results of Operations* (New York: AICPA, 1973).

16. American Institute of Certified Public Accountants, Accounting Principles Board, Accounting Interpretations of APB Opinion No. 30, *Reporting the Results of Operations* (New York: AICPA, 1973).

recorded as a separate component of income from continuing operations. However, these accounting pronouncements have not entirely quieted the arguments surrounding the proper classification of certain nonoperating items.

The income statement in Exhibit 5A-1 shows how both extraordinary items and transactions that do not meet both criteria are disclosed. The extraordinary item in this example is a gain from expropriation of a subsidiary. The gain occurred because the firm received compensation in excess of the book value of its subsidiary. The 1994 gain of $60 million is shown net of tax. Thus the actual gain of $100 million is reduced by the related taxes of $40 million. It is disclosed on the income statement immediately after discontinued operations, if any. If there were no discontinued operations, extraordinary items would follow income from operations. The gain on the sale of the building, which does not meet both criteria, is shown before taxes in the continuing operations section of the income statement.

Types of Accounting Changes

change in accounting method

change in accounting estimate

Over a period of time, a firm is likely to make two different types of accounting changes: a change in accounting method and a change in accounting estimate. A **change in accounting method** results when a firm changes from one generally accepted accounting principle or method to another generally accepted one. A **change in accounting estimate** occurs when a firm changes a particular estimate, such as an asset's depreciable life, as a result of new information that was not available when the original estimate was made.

Change in Method or Principle

As previously noted, management can sometimes choose among acceptable accounting methods. As you will see throughout this book, there are different methods of determining bad debts, cost of goods sold, and depreciation expense. Once a particular method is chosen, accountants feel that it should be consistently used unless a change to a different method is preferable, or unless revision of a particular accounting standard mandates the change. When there is a change in accounting method, current accounting rules generally require that the cumulative effect of the change be included in income of the current period.[17] The cumulative effect is the amount required to adjust the asset or liability to what it would have been had the new accounting method always been used. This amount, which is either a gain or a loss, is shown on the income statement, net of taxes, immediately before net income.

In the example in Exhibit 5A-1, there is a gain resulting from the cumulative effect of a change in depreciation method. The total gain is $50 million but is shown at $30 million, or net of the tax effect of $20 million. Full disclosure requires that the effect of this change be reported in the notes to the financial statements as well as in the auditor's report.

Change in Estimate

In order to make the allocations required under the matching convention, accountants must make estimates. Examples of some of these estimates are ser-

17. American Institute of Certified Public Accountants, Accounting Principles Board, Opinion No. 20, *Accounting Changes* (New York: AICPA, 1971). There are several exceptions to this general rule, for example, certain changes in inventory methods.

vice lives for depreciable assets, uncollectible receivables, residual values, and warranty costs. Because an estimate is inherently uncertain, new information may require a change in the original estimate. This is quite common in accounting and does not require a cumulative catch-up. A change in estimate affects only the current period in which the change is made and the future period.

To demonstrate, assume that an enterprise purchases equipment which is depreciated over a life of ten years. At the beginning of 1995, year 3 of the asset's life, the firm decides to decrease the equipment life from ten years to eight, thus writing the asset off over a shorter period of time. This change in estimate is handled by now spreading the remaining cost over its remaining life of six years. The depreciation expense in 1995 and for each of the next five years is based on its new life. There is no cumulative effect of a change in accounting method on the income statement.

SUMMARY OF LEARNING OBJECTIVES

1. Describe how financial reporting standards are set in the United States. The development of accounting concepts and standards is a complex process involving government and the accounting profession. The Securities and Exchange Commission has the legal authority from Congress to determine accounting standards, but has basically accepted the standards determined by the accounting profession, sometimes modifying them or calling for different types of information. The Financial Accounting Standards Board is the organization created to develop the concepts and standards that constitute generally accepted accounting principles (GAAP).

2. Describe the important accounting concepts and conventions including the objectives of financial reporting. Accounting concepts and conventions, such as the entity assumption, and the historical cost convention provide and underlying theory which guides the development of accounting principles. These concepts and conventions affect the ways that transactions are selected, recorded, and summarized within an accounting system.

3. Define the main elements of a classified balance sheet and prepare one. Given accounting norms and conventions, the actual format of the balance sheet is at the discretion of a firm's management. However, most balance sheets of U.S. firms include at least some of these major categories: Current Assets; Long-term Investments; Property, Plant, and Equipment; Intangible Assets; Other Assets; Current Liabilities; Long-term Liabilities; and Stockholders' Equity.

4. Explain the uses and limitations of a classified balance sheet. Investors and creditors can use a balance sheet to analyze a firm's financial position, liquidity, and strength. This can be accomplished by considering such items and ratios as working capital, the current ratio, the debt-to-equity ratio, and the total-debt-to-assets ratio. However, there are limitations to the usefulness of the balance sheet because of the way in which assets are defined, the use of historical costs, the use of different accounting methods, and the need for cost allocation.

5. Define the main elements of a classified income statement and prepare one. As with balance sheets, the usefulness of income statements can be increased by classifying items that appear on the statement. The degree of detail depends on whether the statement is prepared for external or internal use.

6. Explain the uses and limitations of a classified income statement. Classified income statements are useful to investors and creditors in evaluating a firm's profitability and the returns that accrue to each equity group. Percentages and ratios such as the gross profit percentage, the profit margin percentage, the return on total assets, and the return on stockholders' equity are useful in this evaluation. However, as with the balance sheet, there are limitations to the usefulness of the income statement. These include the use of historical costs, cost allocations, and the existence of alternative generally accepted accounting principles.

7. Prepare a retained earnings statement and a statement of stockholders' equity, and discuss their uses and limitations. The retained earnings statement details the factors that caused changes in the retained earnings account. The statement of stockholders' equity details the changes in all of the stockholders' equity accounts. In recent years, large firms have begun to prepare the statement of changes in stockholders' equity rather than the retained earnings statement. This is because firms are entering into more complex transactions that can best be disclosed in this statement.

8. Explain the uses and limitations of the statement of cash flows. In order to gain a full understanding of a company, an investor or creditor must look beyond the balance sheet, the income statement, and the statement of changes in stockholders' equity. The statement of cash flows is useful in gaining an understanding of how a firm obtains and uses its cash.

9. Discuss the uses of other financial data in the annual report. The full disclosure principle requires that all of the relevant information pertaining to a firm's economic activities be disclosed. Such items as footnotes, summaries of financial statistics, and the auditors' report are found in published annual reports and provide essential information to users.

10. Describe the relationship between a financial reporting system and the general ledger system. The output from the general ledger system, the general ledger file, is input into the financial reporting system. Financial reports and statements are prepared by the financial reporting system for use by owners, managers, and other interested parties.

11. State the four possible categories that may be found on a corporate income statement and prepare a simple corporate income statement (Appendix). Large businesses generally earn income and incur expenses from a variety of sources. Because users of financial statements want to use the income statement to make predictions about future income flows, the various income sources must be segregated. There may be up to four separate categories on the income statement: (1) income from continuing operations, (2) discontinuing operations, (3) extraordinary items, and (4) cumulative effect of a change in accounting principles. Intraperiod income allocation requires that the income tax expense that relates to each of the categories be allocated to it.

KEY TERMS

American Accounting Association (AAA) 195
Auditors' report 219
Change in accounting estimate 227
Change in accounting method 227
Classified financial statements 201
Comparability 199
Conservatism 199
Consistency 199
Consolidated statements 203
Contra account 205
Current assets 203
Current liabilities 206
Current portion of long-term debt 207
Current ratio 209
Debt-to-equity ratio 209
Debt-to-total-assets ratio 210
Deferred income taxes 207
Depreciation 205
Earnings per share (EPS) 214
Extraordinary items 225
Financial reporting system 221
Full disclosure 200
Goodwill 206
Gross profit (margin) on sales 212
Gross profit percentage 214
Income from continuing operations 224
Intangible assets 206
Interperiod income tax allocation 224
Intraperiod income tax allocation 224
Long-term investments 205
Materiality 200
Net book value 206
Operating cycle 204
Operating expenses 212
Operating profit 213
Other expenses and income 213
Profit margin percentage 214
Quantifiability 198
Relevance 198
Reliability 198
Return on assets 215
Return on stockholders' equity 215
Segment 225
Statement of stockholders' equity 216
Verifiability 198
Working capital 208

REVIEW PROBLEMS

1
Classified Balance Sheet

The accounts of the Artesian Company are shown below (in alphabetical order):

Artesian Company
List of Accounts
December 31, 1995

Accounts payable	$10,000	Cash	$ 8,000
Accounts receivable	12,500	Common stock	30,000
Accumulated depreciation—plant and equipment	20,000	Current maturities of long-term debt	12,000
Bonds payable	50,000	Inventories	18,000
Bond sinking fund	15,000	Investments, long-term	5,000

(continued)

Land	$ 40,000	Prepaid insurance	$ 2,000
Marketable securities for temporary purposes	4,500	Plant and equipment	100,000
Mortgage payable less current portion	20,000	Retained earnings	?
Patents, net of amortization	5,000	Salaries payable	5,000
		Taxes payable	3,000

REQUIRED: Prepare in good form a classified balance sheet at December 31, 1995 for the Artesian Company.

Solution

Artesian Company
Balance Sheet
December 31, 1995

Assets			*Liabilities and Stockholders' Equity*	
Current assets			Current liabilities	
Cash		$ 8,000	Current maturities of long-term debt	$ 12,000
Marketable securities		4,500	Accounts payable	10,000
Accounts receivable		12,500	Salaries payable	5,000
Inventories		18,000	Taxes payable	3,000
Prepaid insurance		2,000	Total current liabilities	$ 30,000
Total current assets		$ 45,000	Long-term liabilities	
Investments			Bonds payable	$ 50,000
Long-term investments		$ 5,000	Mortgage payable	20,000
Bond sinking fund		15,000	Total long-term liabilities	$ 70,000
Total long-term investments		$ 20,000	Total liabilities	$100,000
Property, plant, and equipment				
Land		$ 40,000	Stockholders' equity	
Plant and equipment	$100,000		Common stock	$ 30,000
Less: Accumulated depreciation	20,000	80,000	Retained earnings	60,000
Total property, plant and equipment		$120,000	Total stockholders' equity	$ 90,000
Intangible assets				
Patents, net of amortization		$ 5,000		
Total assets		$190,000	Total liabilities and stockholders' equity	$190,000

Points to consider:

1. The marketable securities are considered a current asset because they are marketable and held temporarily.
2. Intangible assets such as patents are usually shown net of amortization, whereas for plant and equipment both the historical costs and the accumulated depreciation are disclosed.
3. A bond sinking fund is a collection of cash and other assets held for the eventual payoff of the bonds. It is considered an investment.

4. Current maturities of long-term debt must be classified as a current liability.
5. The order within the current liabilities section is not particularly significant.
6. In this example, retained earnings must be calculated. It is the amount needed to make the equities equal the assets, or $190,000 − $130,000 = $60,000.

2
Classified Income Statement

The revenue expense and related accounts of the Artesian Company are listed below (in alphabetical order).

Artesian Company
Revenues and Expenses and All Related Accounts
For the Year Ended December 31, 1995

Advertising expense*	$ 3,500	Repairs and maintenance	$ 1,000
Commissions*	4,500	Retained earnings,	
Cost of goods sold	167,000	January 1, 1995	39,500
Depreciation and amortization	10,000	Sales	250,500
Dividends declared and paid	?	Salespersons' salaries*	12,000
Insurance expense	3,000	Income tax rate	40%
Interest expense	2,000		

*Indicates selling expenses. Other expenses besides cost of goods sold, interest, and taxes should be classified as general and administrative.

REQUIRED:

1. Prepare in good form an income statement for the year ended December 31, 1995 that would be typical of that published by a public corporation. Where appropriate, condense expenses into the categories, (1) selling and (2) general and administrative.
2. Prepare in good form a statement of retained earnings for the year ended December 31, 1995. (The amount of dividends must be determined).

Solution 1
Income Statement

Artesian Company
Income Statement
For the Year Ended December 31, 1995

Sales		$250,500
Cost of goods sold		(167,000)
Gross profit		$ 83,500
Operating expenses		
Selling	$20,000	
General and administrative	14,000	
Total operating expenses		(34,000)
Income from operations		$ 49,500
Interest expense		(2,000)
Income before taxes		$ 47,500
Income taxes—40%		(19,000)
Net income		$ 28,500

2
Statement of Retained Earnings

Artesian Company
Statement of Retained Earnings
For the Year Ended December 31, 1995

Retained earnings, January 1, 1995	$39,500
Add: Net income	28,500
	$68,000
Less: Dividends[a]	(8,000)
Retained earnings, December 31, 1995	$60,000

[a]The dividends figure must be calculated. Because beginning and ending retained earnings are given and net income is determined above, dividends can be calculated as follows:

$39,500	Retained earnings, 1/1/95
28,500	(See income statement)
$68,000	
− 60,000	Retained earnings, 12/31/95
$ 8,000	Dividends

3
Analysis

Using the data in parts 1 and 2, calculate the following ratios for the Artesian Company:

a. Working capital
b. Current ratio
c. Debt-to-equity ratio
d. Debt-to-total-assets
e. Gross profit percentage
f. Profit margin percentage
g. Return on assets
h. Return on stockholders' equity

Solution

a. Working Capital = Current Assets − Current Liabilities
$15,000 = $45,000 − $30,000

b. Current Ratio = $\frac{\text{Current Assets}}{\text{Current Liabilities}}$ $\frac{\$45{,}000}{\$30{,}000} = 1.5$

c. Debt-to-Equity Ratio = $\frac{\text{Total Liabilities}}{\text{Total Stockholders' Equity}}$ $\frac{\$100{,}000}{\$\ 90{,}000} = 1.11$

d. Debt-to-Total Assets Ratio = $\frac{\text{Total Liabilities}}{\text{Total Assets}}$ $\frac{\$100{,}000}{\$190{,}000} = .526$

e. Gross Profit Percentage = $\frac{\text{Gross Profit}}{\text{Sales}}$ $\frac{\$\ 83{,}500}{\$250{,}500} = .333$

f. Profit Margin Percentage = $\frac{\text{Net Income}}{\text{Sales}}$ $\frac{\$\ 28{,}500}{\$250{,}500} = .114$

g. Return on Assets = $\frac{\text{Net Income}}{\text{Average Total Assets}}$ $\frac{\$\ 28{,}500}{\$190{,}000^{a}} = .15$

h. Return on Stockholders' Equity = $\frac{\text{Net Income}}{\text{Average Total Stockholders' Equity}}$ $\frac{\$\ 28{,}500}{\$90{,}000^{a}} = .317$

[a]Only year end balance available.

QUESTIONS

1. Describe in your own words the way in which accounting standards are set in the United States. How do you think that accounting standards would be set in a country with a socialistic government?
2. Describe the role and function of each of the following groups:
   a. Securities and Exchange Commissions
   b. Financial Accounting Standards Board
   c. American Accounting Association
   d. Governmental Accounting Standards Board
3. In this chapter, the text states that accountants are often confronted with a trade-off between relevance and reliability. Discuss this trade-off in terms of the use of historical cost rather than current cost.
4. Define reliability. How does the concept of verifiability affect reliability?
5. What do accountants mean by conservatism? Why do you think that this characteristic of financial information has been part of accounting for so long? Are there situations in which it is possible to be too conservative? When?
6. Because of a change in general economic conditions, a firm decides to switch from one generally accepted accounting method to another. What principle is being violated, and what principle would require that the change be noted in the financial statements?
7. What are the primary purposes and uses of a balance sheet? How does it enable a user to analyze a company?
8. What are the important limitations of a balance sheet, and what are their causes?
9. Describe the differences between a calendar year, a fiscal year, and a 52-53 week year.
10. What is the operating cycle of a business? Describe the operating cycles of the following businesses:
    a. Distillery
    b. Savings and loan company
    c. Gas station
    d. Construction company
    e. Book publisher
11. Assume a firm made the following two investments:
    a. One thousand shares of General Motors stock
    b. One hundred fifty thousand shares (a 15% ownership interest) in DLX Motors

    How would each of the above investments likely be classified on a balance sheet? Why?
12. What does the debt-to-equity ratio measure?
13. What are the purposes of the income statement, and what information does it provide to users?
14. What are the limitations of the income statement, and what are some of their causes?
15. In recent years, many large firms have decided to prepare statements of stockholders' equity rather than retained earnings statements. What is the reason for this change?
16. What is the full-disclosure principle, and what is its relationship to financial statement footnotes?
17. What are the notes to the financial statements? Describe several types of information contained in the notes.
18. What are the purposes of an audit of financial statements conducted by CPAs? What information is contained in the auditors' report? What is management's responsibility in relation to the data contained in the financial statements?
19. Describe the relationship between a computer-based general ledger system and a computer-based financial reporting system.

EXERCISES

E5-1
Review of Financial Accounting Concepts
LO 2

For each of the following independent situations, describe the accounting assumptions, characteristics, or conventions that have been violated. There may be more than one answer for each situation. The concepts involved have been discussed in this chapter and in previous chapters.

a. Hilary Wong is the sole proprietor of Wong Jewelry Imports. During March, the following items were recorded as expenses on the firm's books:

Rent on office	$500
Employees' wages	700
Supplies for personal use	100
Advertising	250
Pleasure travel	800

b. The Weiss Corporation spent $200,000 on employee training during the current year. This amount was listed in the intangible assets section of the balance sheet, labeled Investment in Employees.
c. Over the past few years, the president of the Federal Company has purchased a number of paintings to decorate her office. Recently one of the artists died, and his paintings have increased in value over 200%. The president has therefore instructed the accounting department to increase the recorded cost of the paintings to reflect this change.
d. Carol Inman, the accountant for the Borsting Company, was preparing the firm's financial statements. During her analysis she noticed that the firm had five acres of land in the heart of downtown that it had purchased a couple of years ago for $700,000. Because of a rather severe economic recession that began last year, the market value of real estate has fallen. A similar plot of land recently sold for $600,000, and Carol decided to reduce the cost of the land on the Borsting Company's books to $600,000.

E5-2
Accounting Conventions and Principles
LO 2

For each of the following independent situations, state the accounting convention, characteristic, or assumption that is involved. There may be more than one answer for each situation. The concepts involved have been discussed in this chapter and in previous chapters.

a. Earth Airlines has suffered huge losses in recent years and may not be able to continue to operate. The firm's public accountants feel that this information should be disclosed in their opinion.
b. The following footnote was taken from an annual report of General Motors:

There are various claims and pending actions against the Corporation and its subsidiaries with respect to commercial matters, including warranties and product liability, governmental regulations including environmental and safety matters, civil rights, patent matters, taxes and other matters arising out of the conduct of the business. Certain of these actions purport to be class actions, seeking damages in very large amounts. The amounts of liability on these claims and actions at December 31, 1982, were not determinable but, in the opinion of the management, the ultimate liability resulting will not materially affect the consolidated financial position or results of operations of the Corporation and its consolidated subsidiaries.

c. The Crazy Accounting Supply Co. is not a publicly-held company but is owned by ten investors. The company's president, who is also one of the owners, has decided not to prepare financial statements this year because the company suffered huge losses.
d. A fancy staple machine costing $126 was recorded in the office equipment account and will be depreciated over ten years.

E5-3
Classification of Balance Sheet Accounts
LO 3

Below are the classifications commonly found on classified balance sheets. In the space next to each of the numbered items, write the letter that best indicates to which classification it belongs.

a. Current assets
b. Long-term investments
c. Property, plant, and equipment
d. Intangible assets
e. Other assets
f. Current liabilities
g. Long-term liabilities
h. Stockholders' equity
i. Not a balance sheet item

_____ 1. Trucks used in business
_____ 2. Copyright owned by firm
_____ 3. Accounts payable
_____ 4. Prepaid insurance
_____ 5. Supplies on hand
_____ 6. Supplies used during the year
_____ 7. Bonds payable
_____ 8. Land held for future use
_____ 9. Land
_____ 10. Accounts receivable

_____ 11. Retained earnings	_____ 15. Rent expense
_____ 12. Accumulated depreciation—truck	_____ 16. Capital stock
_____ 13. Current maturities of long-term debt	_____ 17. Marketable securities
_____ 14. Inventory	_____ 18. Note receivable, due in five years
	_____ 19. Leasehold improvements
	_____ 20. Sales made on account

E5-4
Preparation of a Classified Balance Sheet
LO 3

From the accounts listed below prepare a classified balance sheet for the Nigel Corporation as of December 31, 1995:

Accounts payable	$ 15,600
Accounts receivable	20,500
Accumulated depreciation—building	20,000
Accumulated depreciation—equipment	2,500
Building	100,000
Cash	16,000
Cash in restricted investment fund	5,000
Common stock	100,000
Equipment	40,000
Inventory	20,000
Long-term investments	5,000
Interest payable	3,500
Land	50,000
Long-term note payable	30,000
Marketable securities	2,500
Retained earnings	77,000
Short-term note payable	10,400

E5-5
Balance Sheet Analysis
LO 4

The balance sheet for the Morita Corporation is as follows:

Morita Corporation
Balance Sheet
December 31, 1995

Assets		*Liabilities and Stockholders' Equity*	
Current assets		Current liabilities	
Cash	$ 16,000	Accounts payable	$ 21,000
Accounts receivable	28,000	Salaries payable	9,000
Total current assets	$ 44,000	Total current liabilities	$ 30,000
Long-term investments	45,000	Long-term liabilities	
Property, plant and equipment, net	82,000	Note payable—Due 1/97	28,000
		Total liabilities	$ 58,000
		Stockholders' equity	
		Common stock	$100,000
		Retained earnings	13,000
		Total stockholders' equity	$113,000
Total assets	$171,000	Total liabilities and stockholders' equity	$171,000

REQUIRED:

1. Calculate the following:
   a. Working capital
   b. Current ratio
   c. Debt-to-equity ratio
   d. Debt-to-total-assets ratio
2. If you were considering making a $20,000, two-year loan to the firm, how would you assess its financial strength and stability? Would you make the loan?

E5-6
Effect of Transactions on Balance Sheet Ratios
LO 4

The condensed balance sheet of the Ramon Company appears below:

The Ramon Company
Condensed Balance Sheet
December 31, 1995

Current assets	$ 80,000	Current liabilities	$ 64,000
Long-term investments	25,000	Long-term liabilities	75,000
Property, plant, and equipment, net	100,000	Stockholders' equity	81,000
Other assets	15,000		
Total assets	$220,000	Total liabilities and stockholders' equity	$220,000

REQUIRED:

1. Calculate the following:
   a. Working capital
   b. Current ratio
   c. Debt-to-equity ratio
   d. Debt-to-total-assets ratio
2. Determine the effect on each of these ratios assuming the following independent events:
   a. The company pays a current liability of $11,000.
   b. The company borrows $15,000 on a six-month note.
   c. The company borrows $25,000 on a two-year note.
   d. The company pays a cash dividend of $5,000.

E5-7
Classification of Income Statement Accounts
LO 5

Below are classifications commonly found on an income statement. In the space next to each of the numbered items, write the letter that best indicates to which classification it belongs.

a. Revenues
b. Cost of goods sold
c. Selling expenses
d. General and administrative expenses
e. Other revenue and expense
f. Not an income statement item

_____ 1. Sales
_____ 2. Taxes payable
_____ 3. Supplies on hand
_____ 4. Gain on sale of land
_____ 5. Dividends paid
_____ 6. Interest payable
_____ 7. Depreciation expense—administrative office equipment
_____ 8. Sales commissions paid
_____ 9. Depreciation expense—delivery trucks

_____ 10. President's salary
_____ 11. Office rent
_____ 12. Delivery expenses
_____ 13. Interest expense
_____ 14. Advertising expense
_____ 15. Prepaid insurance

E5-8
Preparation of an Income Statement
LO 5

Given the following information, prepare an income statement for the Iyengar Corporation for the year ended December 31, 1995.

Rent expense	$12,000
Taxes expense	2,250
Sales	75,000
Selling expense	6,000
Cost of goods sold	42,000
General and administrative expense	2,500

E5-9
Income Statement Analysis
LO 6

You have obtained the following data for the Cardinal Company:

Sales	$200,000
Gross profit ratio	40%
Profit margin ratio	5%
Income tax rate	20%

REQUIRED:

1. Based on the above data determine the following:
   a. Cost of goods sold
   b. Net income
   c. Income taxes
   d. Operating expenses (assume that there are no "other expenses and revenues")
2. Prepare a condensed income statement (assume a December 31, 1995 year-end).

E5-10
Income Statement and Balance Sheet Analysis
LO 4, 6

Answer each of the following independent questions:

a. The Ching Toy Company had net income for the year ended December 31, 1995 of $25,000. Its total beginning assets were $1,000,000, and its total ending assets were $1,500,000. Its total stockholders' equity at January 1, 1995, was $500,000; at December 31, 1995 it was $700,000. Calculate the return on total assets and the return on owners' equity.
b. On January 1, 1995, McGinn's Bookstore had current assets of $672,000 and current liabilities of $531,000. By the end of the year, its current assets had increased to $790,000 and its current liabilities to $685,000. Determine the increase or decrease in working capital that occurred during the year. Did the current ratio change? If so, by how much?
c. The total liabilities and stockholders' equity of the Simmonds Corporation is $500,000. Its current assets equal 20% of total assets and the current ratio is 1.25. Further, the ratio of stockholders' equity to total liabilities is 4 to 1. Determine the amount of (1) current liabilities, (2) working capital, (3) the debt-to-equity ratio, and (4) the debt-to-total-assets ratio.

E5-11
Financial Statement Analysis
LO 4, 6

You have obtained the following data for the Marigold Company for the year ended December 31, 1995. (Some income statement items are missing.)

Cost of goods sold	$410,000
General and administrative expenses	55,000
Interest expense	5,000
Net income	66,000
Sales	650,000
Tax rate	20%

Answer each of the following questions:

a. What is the gross profit on sales?
b. What is the amount of income from operations?
c. What is the amount of selling expenses?
d. What is the gross profit percentage?
e. If the return on total assets is 2.5%, what were the average total assets during 1995?
f. If the return on stockholders' equity is 5%, what was the amount of average stockholders' equity during 1995?
g. What is the profit margin percentage?

E5-12
Statement of Cash Flows
LO 8

State whether each of the following activities should be classified as an operating activity, an investing activity, or a financing activity. Also indicate whether the transaction would result in an increase or decrease in cash.

a. The firm issued capital stock for $1 million.
b. A plant was sold for $500,000.
c. Cash dividends of $50,000 were paid.
d. A net loss of $250,000 was reported for the year.
e. A new accounts receivable billing system was installed at a cost of $200,000.
f. The firm exchanged some capital stock for a plot of land in Silicon Valley, where it was going to build a new plant.
g. A long-term note payable was paid off.

E5-13
Notes to the Financial Statements and Other Data
LO 9

Answer each of the following questions:

a. The following notice appears at the bottom of the published financial statements of public companies:

   The accompanying notes to the financial statements are an integral part of the statements.

   What does that notice mean and what accounting principle or concept is involved?
b. Refer to the Auditors' Report for Albertson's on page 219. Explain in your own words the meaning of each of the three paragraphs. If you were a stockholder of Albertson's do you feel that you could rely on this opinion in making investment decisions concerning the company? Why? Why not?

E5-14
Chart of Accounts File
LO 10

The chart of accounts file is used by the general ledger system and by the financial reporting system. Information in the chart of accounts file is used by the general ledger system to validate the accounts used in journal entries. Information in the file is used by the financial reporting system to format the financial statements. Identify the data items in the file that are used by the general ledger system and by the financial reporting system.

E5-15
Albertson's Financial Statements
LO 4, 6

Using the data from Albertson's financial statements for the year ended January 30, 1992 (Exhibits 5-4, 5-5, 5-7, and 5-8), calculate the following items:

a. Working capital
b. Current ratio
c. Debt-to-equity ratio
d. Debt-to-total-assets ratio
e. Gross profit percentage
f. Profit margin percentage
g. Return on assets (total assets at February 1, 1990 were $1,862,689,000)
h. Return on stockholders' equity (total stockholders' equity at February 1, 1990 was $929,492,000).

How do these ratios compare with those for 1991 and 1992?

E5-16
Albertson's Financial Statements
LO 4, 5 & 6

Refer to the notes and other related data from Albertson's financial statements reproduced in Appendix A to answer the following questions:

a. What does the company consider to be cash equivalents?
b. How does the company compute earnings per share?
c. Accounts and Notes Receivable amounted to $55,835,000 at January 30, 1992. What is the breakdown between the different items?
d. At January 30, 1992 how many shares of common stock was the company authorized to issue?
e. What was the amount of dividends per share for the year ended January 30, 1992? How much were the dividends per quarter for year-end 1991? Year-end 1990?
f. What stock exchanges is Albertson's traded on and what is its symbol?

E5-17
Corporate Income Statements (Appendix)
LO 11

The controller of Moreno Technical Systems gave you the following information for the year ended December 31, 1994:

Sales	$4,000,000	Loss on disposal of discontinued operations	$40,000
Cost of goods sold	2,800,000	Extraordinary loss from earthquake damage	70,000
Selling expenses	500,000	Tax rate on all items	30%
General and administrative expenses	200,000		
Income from discontinued operations	100,000		

Prepare in good form the income statement for the year ended December 31, 1994.

E5-18
Extraordinary Items (Appendix)
LO 11

During a very eventful year, the following happened to the Bacuall Corporation:

a. The first hurricane in 100 years occurred in the area where the corporation's headquarters was located, and its headquarters building was completely destroyed.
b. The company recorded a loss on the abandonment of some equipment formerly used in the business.
c. A customer that owed Bacuall $20,000 declared bankruptcy. Since Bacuall knows that it will never collect the loan, it has decided to write off the loan receivable and consider the $20,000 a loss.
d. One of the company's major employee unions went on strike, and the firm was shut down for several weeks. Management estimates that profits of $500,000 were lost.

REQUIRED: Which of the above items should be classified as extraordinary, and why?

PROBLEMS

P5-1
Review of Financial Accounting Concepts
LO 2

For each of the following independent situations, state which accounting concept, if any, has been violated. If more than one concept has been violated, so state. If you feel the item has been appropriately handled, so state. Be sure to explain your answers.

a. Recently, Cardulucci's Fine Restaurant hired one of the country's outstanding chefs. Based on the anticipated increased earnings, the firm increased its assets by $100,000.
b. The accountant for Watts Equipment analyzed the firm's accounts receivables and determined that they should be recorded at $1 million, his best estimate of their ultimate collectibility. However, his boss, Watts' treasurer, decided it was better to be safe and sure and set the amount at $850,000 just in case the economy got worse.
c. The Ecological High Tech Company began operations early in 1994. Because of high start-up costs, the firm suffered a large loss during 1994. However, the company's prospects appear to be very good for 1995 and beyond. In order not to discourage the firm's stockholders, the president of Ecological High Tech decided not to issue financial statements until 1995 or until the firm can show a profit.
d. Natural Foods, Inc., is a large producer of natural foods. During the last half of 1994, the firm undertook a large advertising campaign in an attempt to increase its market share. Because the firm believes that the expenditures for advertising will reap benefits in increased sales for several years, it has decided to consider the costs an asset and to write them off over a five-year period.
e. The Colossus Oil Co. has always had difficulty taking an actual physical count of its inventory because its inventory is spread across the entire world. As a result, the chief financial officer decided to estimate this year's inventory by increasing the amount of last year's by 10% to cover estimated price increases.

P5-2
Preparation of a Classified Balance Sheet
LO 3

The account balances of the Vera Video Games Company follow (in alphabetical order):

Vera Video Games Company
Account Balances
December 31, 1995

Accounts payable	$20,000
Accounts receivable	30,000
Accumulated depreciation—plant and equipment	25,000
Bonds payable	25,000
Cash	17,000
Common stock	50,000
Copyright	10,000
Current maturities of long-term debt	14,000
Inventories	60,000
Investments, long-term	5,000
Marketable securities, held for temporary investment	10,000
Mortgage payable, less current portion	20,000
Plant and equipment	70,000
Prepaid insurance	5,000
Retained earnings	?
Salaries payable	5,000
Supplies on hand	1,000
Taxes payable	8,000
Unearned commissions	10,000

REQUIRED: Prepare in good form a classified balance sheet at December 31, 1995.

P5-3
Preparation of an Income Statement
LO 5

The revenue, expense, and related accounts of the Weiss Company for the year ended June 30, 1995 are as follows:

Advertising expense*	$ 2,500
Beginning retained earnings	42,750
Cost of goods sold	25,000
Delivery expense*	6,850
Depreciation expense	10,000
Insurance expense	1,000
Interest expense	200
Repairs and maintenance expense	2,500
Sales	75,000
Salaries Expense*	5,000
Supplies expense	750
Tax rate	30%

*Indicates selling expenses. Other expenses besides interest are general and administrative. Included in the salaries expense of $5,000 is $1,000 of dividends paid to the owner, E. Weiss.

REQUIRED:

1. Prepare in good form an income statement similar to that which would be prepared by a public corporation.
2. Prepare in good form a retained earnings statement.
3. Assuming that the firm has issued capital stock in the amount of $75,000, what is the total stockholders' equity at June 30, 1995?

P5-4
Ratio Analysis
LO 3, 5

The following financial data is taken from the records of the Compeq Company:

The Compeq Company
Comparative Balance Sheet
December 31

Assets	*1995*	*1994*
Cash	$ 30,000	$ 21,000
Accounts receivable	4,000	7,000
Inventory	240,000	215,000
Property, plant, and equipment, net	40,000	40,000
Total assets	$314,000	$283,000

Liabilities and Stockholders' Equity		
Current liabilities	$ 45,000	$ 33,000
Noncurrent liabilities	109,000	100,000
Stockholders' equity	160,000	150,000
Total liabilities and stockholders' equity	$314,000	$283,000

The Compeq Company
Comparative Income Statement
For the Year Ended December 31

	1995	1994
Sales	$500,000	$430,000
Cost of goods sold	220,000	180,000
Gross profit on sales	$280,000	$250,000
Operating expense	190,000	165,000
Net income	$ 90,000	$ 85,000

REQUIRED:

1. Compute the following ratios for 1994 and 1995:
   a. Working capital
   b. Current ratio
   c. Debt-to-equity
   d. Debt-to-total-assets
   e. Gross profit percentage
   f. Profit margin percentage
   g. Return on total assets (December 31, 1993 total assets, $251,000)
   h. Return on stockholders' equity (December 31, 1993 stockholders' equity, $140,000)
2. Have the firm's performance and financial position improved from 1994 to 1995? Explain.

P5-5 Preparation of Financial Statements and Analysis (Alternative to P5-6)

LO 3, 4, 5 & 6

The following accounts have been taken from the December 31, 1995 records of the Porter Press Corporation. They are not listed in any particular order.

Notes receivable—due in 6 months	$ 5,000
Accumulated depreciation—building	14,000
Common stock	10,000
Sales	600,000
Salaries expense	45,000
Cash	25,000
Accounts payable	38,000
Long-term debt	39,000
Land	12,000
Building	50,000
Taxes expense	10,000
Rent expense	12,000
Gain on sale of land	5,000
Accounts receivable	6,000
Prepaid assets	2,000
Accrued salaries and other payables	8,000
Interest payable	5,000
Depreciation expense	18,000
Machinery and equipment	20,000
Patents, net	6,000
Additional paid in capital	2,000
Retained earnings	13,000
Repairs and maintenance expense	6,000
Inventory	30,000
Interest expense	20,000
Cost of goods sold	450,000

(continued)

Accumulated depreciation—machinery and equipment	7,000
Supplies expense	9,000
Long-term investments	15,000

REQUIRED:

1. Assume that all expenses other than interest are split into one-third selling and two-thirds general and administrative. Prepare in good form the following statements:
   a. An income statement for the year ended December 31, 1995 similar to the one illustrated in the text (Exhibit 5-6).
   b. A balance sheet as of December 31, 1995.
2. Based on the above data, calculate:
   a. Working capital
   b. Current ratio
   c. Debt-to-equity ratio
   d. Debt-to-total-assets ratio
   e. Gross profit percentage
   f. Profit margin percentage
   g. Return on total assets (use-end-of-year figures only in denominator)
   h. Return on Stockholders' equity (use-end-of year figures only in denominator)

P5-6
Preparation of Financial Statements and Analysis (Alternative to P5-5)
LO 3, 4, 5 & 6

The following accounts have been taken from the records of the Scully Corporation at June 30, 1995:

Land	$ 70,000	Capital stock	$ 75,000
Buildings, net	100,000	Accounts receivable	30,000
Salary expense	27,000	Cost of goods sold	145,000
Utilities expense	6,000	Cash	20,000
Equipment	20,000	Notes payable—	
Accounts payable	41,000	October 1, 1996	30,000
Sales	275,000	Rent expense	18,000
Inventory	58,000	Dividends declared and paid	5,000
Retained earnings—July 1,		Income taxes expense	35,000
1994	117,000	Interest expense	4,000

Classify all expenses other than cost of goods sold, interest, and taxes as operating expenses.

REQUIRED:

1. Prepare in good form the following statements:
   a. An income statement for the year ended June 30, 1995 similar to the one illustrated in the text (Exhibit 5-6).
   b. A statement of retained earnings for the year ended June 30, 1995.
   c. A balance sheet as of June 30, 1995.
2. Based on the above data, calculate:
   a. Working capital
   b. Current ratio
   c. Debt-to-equity ratio
   d. Debt-to-total-assets ratio
   e. Gross profit percentage
   f. Profit margin percentage
   g. Return on total assets (use year-end figures only in denominator)
   h. Return on stockholders' equity (use year-end figures only in denominator)

3. Why do you think that the balance in the retained earnings account at June 30, 1995 is so large compared to the balance in the capital stock account?

P5-7
Balance Sheet Analysis
LO 4

Below is a partial list of the accounts for the Diamond Company.

Accounts payable	$ 28,000
Accounts receivable	45,000
Interest payable	12,000
Cash	30,000
Current portion of long-term debt	30,000
Inventories	60,000
Investment, long-term	20,000
Long-term debt	30,000
Notes receivable, due in 12 months	5,000
Retained earnings	45,000
Sales	400,000

REQUIRED: Referring to these figures where appropriate, answer the questions which follow.

1. What is the amount of working capital?
2. What is the current ratio?
3. For this question only, assume that the company has a current ratio of 3:1. If the company purchased $5,000 of inventory on account, what effect (that is, increase, decrease, or no effect) would this transaction have on:
   a. Working capital?
   b. Current ratio?
4. Again for this question, assume that the company has a current ratio of 3:1. If the company purchased some equipment for $10,000 cash, what effect would this transaction have on:
   a. Working capital?
   b. Current ratio?
5. Assume the same current ratio as in item 4 and the same purchase, but now assume that the equipment was purchased on account, with the payable due in two years. For simplicity, assume that there is no interest on the notes. What effect would this transaction have on:
   a. Working capital?
   b. Current ratio?

P5-8
Analysis of Financial Statements
LO 3, 5

The financial statements for the R.J.P. Company are below. (All accounts are listed.)

R.J.P. Company
Balance Sheet
December 31, 1995

Assets		*Liabilities and Stockholders' Equity*	
Cash	$25,000	Accounts payable	$ d
Accounts receivable	a		
		Total liabilities	e
Total current assets	$45,000	Stockholders' equity	f
Property, plant and equipment	b		
		Total liabilities and	
Total assets	$ c	stockholders' equity	$ g

R.J.P. Company Income Statement For the Year Ended December 31, 1995		
Revenues		
Sales		$h
Expenses		
Cost of goods sold	$35,000	
Selling	20,000	
General and administrative	6,000	
Interest	900	
City taxes	1,100	
Total expenses		i
Net income		$j

In addition, you have gathered the following data:

Working capital	$7,500
Current ratio	1.2
Debt-to-equity ratio	1.25
Gross profit percentage	50%
Profit margin percentage	10%

REQUIRED: Complete the financial statements of R.J.P. Company by determining the amount of items (a) through (j). It is not necessary to determine the missing figures in order.

P5-9
The Statement of Cash Flows
LO 8

Following is a condensed version of the statement of cash flows for year-end 1990 and 1989 for Checkpoint Systems, Inc., an actual company which is a leading supplier of electronic signatures and electronic identifiers used by department and other retail stores.

Checkpoint Systems, Inc.
Condensed Statement of Cash Flows
For the Years Ended December 31
(in thousands)

	1990	*1989*
Cash inflow from operating activities:		
Net earnings	$ 6,932	$ 5,603
Adjustments to reconcile net income to cash provided by operating activities	1,142	(3,714)
Net cash provided by operating activities	$ 8,074	$ 1,889
Cash inflow (outflow) from investing activities:		
Acquisition of property, plant, and equipment	(10,022)	(6,406)
Proceeds of investment securities	12	500
Other investing activities	(445)	70
Net cash used by investing activities	($10,455)	$(5,836)
Cash inflow (outflow) from financing activities:		
Proceeds from stock options	1,779	1,430
Payments of short-term debt	(900)	(600)
Net cash provided by financing activities	$ 879	$ 830

(continued)

	1990	1989
Net decrease in cash and cash equivalents	$ (1,502)	$(3,117)
Cash and cash equivalents:		
Beginning of year	2,992	6,109
End of year	$ 1,490	$ 2,992

REQUIRED: Based on this statement, answer the questions that follow:

1. What other financial statement shows the figures reported for net earnings on the statement of cash flows?
2. What other financial statement shows the figures for cash and cash equivalents reported on the statement of cash flows?
3. Explain in your own words why it is possible for cash provided by operations to be greater than the net earnings for the same year.
4. During both 1989 and 1990 Checkpoint Systems, Inc., showed a significant decrease in its cash balance. Is this a bad sign? Explain your answer. Do you feel that you need additional information to adequately answer? If so, what additional information do you need?

P5-10
Manual and Computer-Based Financial Reporting Systems
LO 10

Manual and computer-based financial reporting systems exhibit significant similarities and differences.

REQUIRED:

1. Compare and contrast each of the following characteristics of manual and computer-based financial reporting systems:
   a. Objectives
   b. Inputs
   c. Processes
   d. Outputs
2. Identify and discuss the potential advantages of computer-based financial reporting systems that would cause an enterprise to convert from a manual system to a computer-based system.

P5-11
Income Statement Construction (Appendix)
LO 11

During the current year, 1994, the Fullerton Manufacturing Company sold its carpet manufacturing division because of consistently poor performance. In addition, you obtained the following information about the events that affected the firm during 1994:

	Continuing Operations	*Discontinued Operations*
Sales	$4,500,000	$1,800,000
Expenses		
Cost of goods sold	3,000,000	1,500,000
Operating expenses	500,000	500,000
Loss on disposal of discontinued operations		(300,000)
Gain on expropriation of assets by foreign country	300,000	
Gain on sale of building	100,000	
Cumulative effect (gain) of change of depreciation method	50,000	

All of the above items are shown prior to any tax effect. Assume that a tax rate of 30% applies to all items.

REQUIRED: Prepare an income statement in good form for the year ended December 31, 1994.

DISCUSSION AND INTERPRETATION PROBLEMS

D5-1 Understanding Financial Statements

The following financial statements were taken from the annual report of Safeway Stores, Inc., a large U.S. market chain. Safeway Stores was the object of a leveraged buyout in 1986, but since that time has issued shares of stock to the public.

Safeway, Inc. and Subsidiaries
Consolidated Balance Sheets
(in millions, except per share amounts)

	Year-end	
	1990	*1989*
Assets		
Current assets:		
Cash and equivalents	$ 150.6	$ 123.2
Receivables	141.1	141.3
Merchandise inventories, net of LIFO reserve of $56.8 and $41.7, respectively	1,208.1	1,167.7
Prepaid expenses and other	70.6	56.2
Income taxes receivable	12.2	—
Total current assets	1,582.6	1,488.4
Property:		
Land	288.7	240.8
Buildings	624.3	537.1
Leasehold improvements	769.1	717.2
Fixtures and equipment	1,273.3	1,060.1
Property under capital leases	331.9	341.2
	3,287.3	2,896.4
Less accumulated depreciation and amortization	992.0	742.8
Total property, net	2,295.3	2,153.6
Goodwill, net of amortization of $54.9 and $44.5, respectively	$ 379.6	$ 390.0
Prepaid pension costs	304.6	303.7
Other assets	177.0	202.3
Total assets	$4,739.1	$4,538.0
Liabilities and Stockholders' Deficit		
Current liabilities:		
Current maturities of notes and debentures	$ 58.1	$ 398.0
Current obligations under capital leases	21.0	21.7
Accounts payable	843.1	776.9
Accrued salaries and wages	173.5	173.4
Other accrued liabilities	284.0	259.1
Income taxes payable	—	74.2
Total current liabilities	1,379.7	1,703.3
Long-term debt:		
Notes and debentures	2,761.4	2,427.3
Obligations under capital leases	243.1	271.6
Total long-term debt	3,004.5	2,698.9
Deferred income taxes	328.6	319.3
Accrued claims and other liabilities	209.7	205.4
Total liabilities	4,922.5	4,926.9

(continued)

	Year-end 1990	Year-end 1989
Commitments and contingencies		
Stockholders' deficit:		
Common stock: par value $.01 per share; 300 shares authorized; 79.3 and 67.7 shares outstanding, respectively	0.8	0.7
Additional paid-in capital	258.5	138.4
Subscriptions receivable	(0.3)	(0.6)
Cumulative translation adjustments	60.9	63.0
Accumulated deficit	(503.3)	(590.4)
Total stockholders' deficit	(183.4)	(388.9)
Total liabilities and stockholders' deficit	$4,739.1	$4,538.0

Safeway, Inc. and Subsidiaries
Consolidated Statements of Income
(in millions, except per share amounts)

	1990	1989	1988
Sales	$ 14,873.6	$ 14,324.6	$ 13,612.4
Cost of goods sold	(10,897.0)	(10,635.1)	(10,176.6)
Gross profit	3,976.6	3,689.5	3,435.8
Operating and administrative expenses	(3,441.3)	(3,227.1)	(3,110.2)
Gain on divestiture of assets	—	—	73.3
Operating profit	535.3	462.4	398.9
Interest expense	$ (384.1)	$ (382.8)	$ (401.2)
Other income, net	43.5	14.4	67.6
Income before income taxes	194.7	94.0	65.3
Income tax expense	(107.6)	(91.5)	(34.1)
Net income	87.1	2.5	31.2
Dividends on redeemable preferred stock	—	—	(3.6)
Net income to common stockholders	$ 87.1	$ 2.5	$ 27.6
Income per common share and common share equivalents:			
Primary	$ 0.91	$ 0.05	$ 0.38
Fully diluted	$ 0.91	$ 0.03	$ 0.38
Weighted average common shares and common share equivalents:			
Primary	96.0	79.6	78.7
Fully diluted	96.0	89.4	78.7

REQUIRED:

1. Why do you think that cash and cash equivalents are shown together as one item on the balance sheet?
2. Explain the difference between accounts payable and other accrued liabilities.
3. Compute the following data for year-end 1990 and 1989:
   a. Working capital
   b. Current ratio
   c. Debt-to-total-assets ratio
   d. Gross profit percentage

e. Profit margin percentage
f. Return on total assets

4. Would you say that the firm's financial performance and position improved from 1989 to 1990? Explain.
5. Compare the ratios and the financial position and performance with those of Albertson's.

D5-2
Financial Decision Case

Rebecca Webb is head of the loan department at Wilshire National Bank. She has been approached by two firms in the retail toy business. Each firm is requesting a nine-month term loan in order to purchase inventory for the holiday season. She must make her recommendations to the loan committee and has gathered the following data in order to make her analysis.

The Fun Toy Company was organized in early 1994. The first year of operations was fairly successful, as the firm earned net income of $45,000. Total sales for the year were $600,000, and total assets at year-end December 31, 1994, were $350,000. A condensed balance sheet at September 30, 1995 follows. The firm is requesting a $100,000 loan.

Assets	
Cash	$ 60,000
Accounts receivable	65,000
Inventory	125,000
Prepaids	5,000
Furniture and fixtures, net	155,000
Total assets	$410,000

Liabilities and Stockholders' Equity	
Accounts payable	$ 70,000
Note payable, due 10/5/95	100,000
Stockholders' equity	240,000
Total liabilities and stockholders' equity	$410,000

The Toy Store, the other firm, has been in business for many years. The firm's net income is $100,000 on total sales of $2,000,000. Total assets at year-end December 31, 1995 follow. The firm is seeking a $200,000 loan.

Assets	
Cash	$ 60,000
Accounts receivable	100,000
Inventory	400,000
Supplies	10,000
Prepaids	5,000
Property, plant, and equipment	825,000
Total assets	$1,400,000

Liabilities and Stockholders' Equity	
Accounts payable	$ 350,000
Current bank loan payable	150,000
Long-term debt	400,000
Stockholders' equity	500,000
Total liabilities and stockholders' equity	$1,400,000

REQUIRED:

1. Calculate the ratios that you think will help Rebecca Webb in her analysis.
2. Based on these ratios and your further analyses, what should Rebecca Webb recommend to the loan committee regarding each firm's request? Explain your reasoning.

D5-3 Research Assignment

Obtain from your library an annual report of a French, Dutch, German, or English company. Write a brief report comparing and contrasting the financial statements in that annual report with those in this chapter.

D5-4 Research Assignment

Obtain the latest information concerning Albertson's from your library. This could be the latest annual report (1993 or beyond), the latest quarterly reports and/or an article from the financial press (The Wall Street Journal or business publication) concerning Albertson's. Answer the following questions:

a. Have there been any significant events involving Albertson's since the information given in this chapter? If so, explain.
b. Using the information you obtained, calculate each of the ratios discussed in the chapter and compare them to the year-end 1991 data. Comment on any significant trends.
c. At what price is Albertson's stock currently trading? How does this compare with the stock prices contained in the 1991 annual report reproduced in Appendix A?

D5-5 Ethical Issues

Helen Gernon is the chief financial officer (CFO) of Trident Systems, Inc. a major defense contractor. Helen is preparing for the year-end meeting of the firm's executive committee which includes herself, the chief executive officer and chair of the board of directors, Jon Goodman, the chief information officer, Ces Jackson; and the treasurer, Ravi Kumar. The committee is meeting in early December to plan the firm's final financial moves prior to the end of its calendar year.

Helen is quite concerned because she knows she will be asked what the firm can do to meet the restrictions in their loan agreements. These restrictions call for a current ratio of 2:1 and working capital totaling $5 million at year-end. Failure to meet these restrictions will put the firm into default and impair their ability to bid for new government contracts. The effect on the financial viability of the firm could be serious.

Helen has come up with several options. She knows that if she can pay about $1 million of outstanding payables, the firm's current ratio, which is about 1:75 to 1 will rise to 2:1. This payment would not change the firm's total working capital, which currently meets the restrictions in the loan agreement. However, Trident currently does not have the cash to make this payment. Therefore, Helen is going to propose to the executive committee that they offer a 5% discount to one of their major customers, Inforteck, Inc., if they will make a $1 million payment on their $1.5 million receivable due January 15 of the next year.

Finally, Helen is aware that the firm has a $500,000 note payable due January 31 of the coming year. This note is classified as a current liability. Helen is negotiating with the First Security Bank, the holder of the note, to postpone payment until January 31 of the following year. Although negotiations have been quite difficult, Helen is confident a deal can be made sometime within the next 30 days. She, therefore, is going to suggest to the executive committee that the note be reclassified as long-term.

REQUIRED: Answer each of the following questions:

1. Some individuals refer to such actions as contemplated by Helen as "window dressing." Do you think that it is ethical for the firm to consider such actions? Why? Why not? Is Helen within the scope of her proper job duties by suggesting such actions? What would you do in her situation?
2. Describe how each of the actions contemplated by Helen will improve the firm's current ratio and/or working capital. For each action state whether or not you think it is ethical.

CHAPTER 6
MANAGEMENT CONTROLS, FRAUDULENT FINANCIAL REPORTING, AND ACCOUNTING INFORMATION SYSTEMS

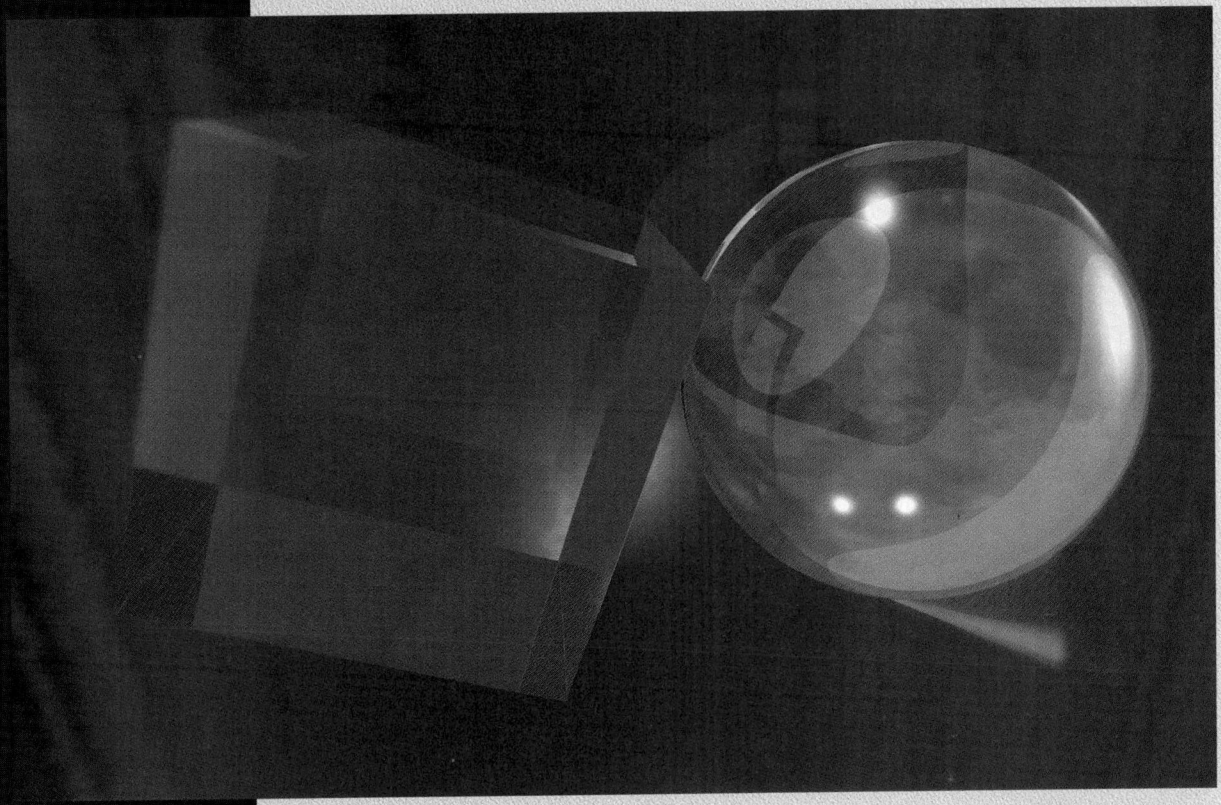

LEARNING OBJECTIVES

After studying this chapter, you should be able to:

1. Define fraudulent and questionable financial reporting and give examples.
2. Explain the financial reporting system for a public company.
3. Describe the internal control framework and explain the elements of an internal control structure.
4. Describe the types of internal controls that are used in computer-based accounting systems and provide examples.

Scenario

Auditor's Downfall Shows a Man Caught in a Trap of His Own Making

Miami—Jose L. Gomez, a former managing partner of the Grant Thornton accounting firm, surrenders today to begin a 12-year prison term.

The 38-year-old Mr. Gomez pleaded guilty last year to charges, in two federal courts and an Ohio state court, involving his role in the fraud at E.S.M. Government Securities Inc., the once-obscure Fort Lauderdale, Florida, firm that collapsed two years ago today and triggered one of the biggest financial scandals of the decade. As E.S.M.'s auditor, Mr. Gomez knowingly approved the firm's false financial statements for five years, thus allowing the massive fraud to continue. He must serve at least four years.

In these days when white-collar crime is rocking Wall Street, Mr. Gomez's story is a particularly telling one. In some regards, he was almost a cliche: an ambitious young man who rose too far too fast and wound up in the worst sort of trouble. He says he crossed the line into criminality without even realizing it.

When Mr. Gomez's activities came to light, many people were stunned, for he had seemed the model of success. He was one of the youngest people ever to be made partner at his Chicago-based firm, which then was called Alexander Grant & Co. He was active in community affairs.

But he was also a fraud. Investors initially lost some $320 million in the scheme Mr. Gomez helped perpetuate, and the scandal was even blamed for a brief decline in the dollar on international markets.

In a recent interview, Mr. Gomez talked of his rise and fall. He says he never intended to do anything wrong. But in August 1979, just days after being told of his promotion to partner at Grant, two officers of E.S.M. told him of a crude accounting ruse that was hiding millions of dollars in losses; they had to bring Mr. Gomez in on the scheme to keep it from unraveling.

Mr. Gomez says he had missed the ruse in two previous annual audits, signing off on bogus financial statements showing E.S.M. to be in robust condition. He says one of the E.S.M. officers used that error to draw him into the fraud.

GOMEZ: He must have said it four or five times: "How's it going to look. It's going to look terrible for you, and you just got promoted to partner. Just give us a chance. It just takes time. We're not going to have those losses."

WSJ (*Wall Street Journal*): Do you think he was trying to intimidate you?

GOMEZ: No question about it. And it worked. I was 31 years old. I felt I had a terrific career path in front of me and a lot of ambition. . . . And I agreed just to think about it. And a day or two later, I felt I already had gone too far. I also didn't want to face it. I didn't want to face walking in (to his superiors at Alexander Grant) and saying this is what happened.

In Chicago, Burt K. Fischer, executive partner of Grant Thornton, says Mr. Gomez's fears about his blunder were misplaced. "I can't think of a partner who made an honest mistake who has been hung out to dry," he says. The firm also contends that Mr. Gomez learned of the fraud before 1979.

Mr. Gomez says he decided to go along with the scheme at E.S.M., convinced that the firm's managers could make up the losses.

GOMEZ: I really wanted to believe they could do it. So I just made up my mind, OK, I'm going to let them do it. At this point in time I was looking at maybe $10 million (in losses) as being the problem, in a business that you can make $10 million very easily. I never evaluated at that point, or later either, a criminal side to what I was doing. If I had, it might have been a deterrent.

WSJ: What did you think of it as?

GOMEZ: It was a professional decision, a judgment decision that I was making that I felt would eventually work itself out. I had a terrific argument with myself. It just came out that way. If I had sought some counsel from someone that I had some respect for, if I even talked to my wife. . . .

WSJ: Did you go home and tell your wife?

GOMEZ: No. It's interesting. We've been married 17 years now. And it's the only item I never discussed with her or shared with her in any way.

E.S.M.'s losses continued to mount, and Mr. Gomez continued to approve phony financial statements.

GOMEZ: When I looked at this thing again in 1980 . . . the accumulated deficit is close to $100 million, and now it's a really big number no matter how you look at it. And I was trapped, I just totally felt that I'd lost control of it.

In late 1980, E.S.M. officers began arranging loans for Mr. Gomez, who was having personal financial problems. The loans which weren't repaid, totaled $200,000.

GOMEZ: I don't know how all these things relate to my own inability to handle my personal finances. For an accountant, it's tough to fathom—but not only would there not be a budget, there would be spending without thinking of such things as monthly payments. I had been spending on credit cards and borrowing from banks to pay the credit cards for some time. I was also looking to put a pool in my house. There were a lot of little things added together. No discipline whatsoever.

WSJ: Did you view the E.S.M. loans as a quid pro quo?

GOMEZ: No. I never—and it's hard for people to accept this—I never related my actions to the money. I didn't do it for moeny. I did it because I didn't want to have to face up that I had made a mistake, that I had missed it originally.

WSJ: Did you have to do special things to prevent your staff from coming upon the accounting fraud?

GOMEZ: I never did.

WSJ: Did you hold your breath during audits, thinking somebody would spot it?

GOMEZ: I often wondered what I would do if somebody walked in and said, "Look what I've found." But it never happened. I gave them (his team of auditors) the same baloney answer that I had been given back in '78. It never dawned on them that it just didn't make sense.

WSJ: Was this the only government-securities dealer your staff was auditing?

(continued)

GOMEZ: Yes. They had nothing else to look at, to draw a basis on. And that was a weakness.

WSJ: What do you think the flaws were in the structure of the review process that allowed this thing to go on?

GOMEZ: It's very easy for other professionals to look down their noses at this and say, "My God, this was so obvious." But I think the ones who are really honest are going to look at this and say, "My God, that could have happened here."

In 1977, it became apparent to me that those being promoted early were the business producers. Not necessarily that they were weak technically, but they were the ones that were able to produce new clients, who had extensive contacts. The salesmen. It became apparent to me . . . that my promotion depended on my becoming more productive. That's when I began turning more sales-oriented.

I think I would have been able to be more objective about my client relationships if I weren't so concerned about selling. And E.S.M. was a very strong selling point for me. (The E.S.M. account) had produced other clients, and I looked at them as being a productive vehicle.

WSJ: So you think you would have caught the fraud if it weren't for the sales pressure?

GOMEZ: If I had not had the sales pressure, I would perhaps have caught it before it happened.

He also thinks, in hindsight, that he was too inexperienced to be heading an audit—which he was doing at age 31 even before he was named partner in 1979.

GOMEZ: It's interesting for me to say this now, because if you had asked me then, I would have said, "No, you're crazy; I know more than these guys." I used to hate the term, "There's no substitute for experience," and now I realize how wise it was.

Grant Thornton's Mr. Fischer acknowledges that there has been a greater emphasis on marketing in the auditing field since the 1960s. "But it's not in lieu of the auditing function," he says. "It's in addition to auditing, which is our bread and butter. With respect to Mr. Gomez's contention that he was too young to have so much responsibility, Mr. Fischer says: "I don't buy it. That's no excuse. I was promoted to partner at a younger age than he was, and I didn't steal."

In March 1985, E.S.M. collapsed. Mr. Gomez retained a lawyer, who told him he faced serious criminal liability. Mr. Gomez says he fell into "deep depression, and I am not a depressed individual." He was jolted out of it by the suicide in July of Stephan W. Arky, a 42-year-old Miami lawyer who had represented E.S.M. before its collapse. Fearing that his own depression could lead to a similar end, Mr. Gomez began cooperating with the authorities. He was the first E.S.M. figure to do so.

WSJ: Do you know how much time you've spent in terms of testifying and giving information?

GOMEZ: About 300 hours. I kept a log.

WSJ: Has that been a cathartic thing?

GOMEZ: Oh sure. It's had a tremendous therapeutic effect. And while I have many regrets about everything that happened in the past, I have no regrets about what I've done since then. I think ultimately it's been the best thing because it will allow me and my family to function without this big burden on us.

WSJ: How old are your children?

GOMEZ: Thirteen and 11.

WSJ: Can they understand it?

GOMEZ: They understand that there was something that happened to a company. They understand that Daddy was in a position to do something and he didn't do it right. And they understand that he's faced up to it and he's got to pay for it. And they also I hope understand that in their own life they're going to have to face things when they happen and they can't just try to get by. I've tried to use this as a lesson for them.

WSJ: How about preparing for prison?

GOMEZ: I don't know. I'm in limbo. I'd like to be able to find out what can I do, what can I bring. I'd like to be able to know whether I can have access to a typewriter or a mini-computer. You have to do something with your day. I imagine you can't just lie around doing nothing. I'd like to at least be able to maintain my technical profession by reading and working on things. Who knows?

The opening scenario for this chapter is an actual case, reported in a *Wall Street Journal* interview with Jose Gomez, a former partner in the large international accounting firm of Grant Thornton. The interview describes his involvement with a widely publicized case of fraudulent financial reporting at E.S.M. Government Securities. This case, unfortunately, is just one example of several recent instances of the intentional misstatement of financial information. Other companies, such as ZZZZ Best, Penn Square Bank, Drysdale Government Securities, BCCI, and Lincoln Savings and Loan, have been implicated in similar frauds involving the loss of millions and even billions of dollars by the companies themselves, their stockholders, their employees, the U.S. taxpayer, and even international investors.

expectation gap

Cases of this sort have brought public and congressional attention to the financial reporting process. In the public mind, there has arisen what has been termed an **expectation gap**—the difference between "what the public and financial statement users believe accountants and auditors are responsible for and what accountants and auditors themselves believe they're responsible for."[1] The public and financial statement users believe that auditors should:

a. Assume more responsibility for the detection and reporting of fraud and illegal acts.

1. Dan M. Guy and Jerry D. Sullivan, "The Expectation Gap Auditing Standards," *Journal of Accountancy*, (April, 1988), p. 36.

b. Improve audit effectiveness—that is, improve detection of material misstatements.
c. Communicate to users of financial statements more useful information about the nature and results of the audit process—including early warnings about the possibility of business failure.
d. Communicate more clearly with audit committees and others interested in or responsible for reliable financial reporting.[2]

This chapter provides an overview of the issues surrounding fraudulent financial reporting and discusses the accounting profession's responses. These responses include a revised and expanded AICPA code of professional conduct (discussed in Chapter 1), the development of new auditing standards (referred to as the expectation gap standards), a new and expanded audit report, and the development of an integrated internal control framework. This chapter also discusses the specific elements of a good internal control system and how these elements are incorporated into a computer-based accounting system.

INSTANCES OF FRAUDULENT FINANCIAL REPORTING

Objective 1
Define fraudulent and questionable financial reporting and give examples.

fraudulent financial reporting

The Treadway Commission defines **fraudulent financial reporting** as:

intentional or reckless conduct, whether act or omission, that results in materially misleading financial statements. Fraudulent financial reporting can involve many factors and take many forms. It may entail gross and deliberate distortions of corporate records, such as inventory count tags, or falsified transactions, such as fictitious sales or orders. It may entail the misapplication of accounting principles. Company employees at any level may be involved, from top to middle management to lower-level personnel.[3]

In the E.S.M. Government Securities scandal described in this chapter's scenario, losses by investors and others totaled over $320 million. "The SEC charged that E.S.M. had engaged in a pattern of fraud from its inception in 1976, hiding losses totaling $196.5 million in an affiliated dummy company, while its customers were led to believe that it was a healthy company because of its audited accounts."[4] In another well-known example of alleged fraudulent financial reporting, the president of ZZZZ Best Company was found guilty of recording major sales that never took place. He also went to great lengths to create false records and bogus transactions to enhance the value of the firm's stock.

The cost to individual customers and the U.S. taxpayer for the Lincoln Savings and Loan fraud, along with other alleged frauds in the savings and loan industry, will be in the billions of dollars. The actions of Charles Keating, past head of Lincoln Savings, which led to his conviction on criminal and civil charges sent shock waves through the accounting profession, the U.S. Congress, and directly to the U.S. taxpayer. One of the major accounting firms settled with the U.S. government for over $400 million for its alleged negligence in the Lincoln and other cases. The Lincoln fraud and the large settlement certainly focused the U.S. taxpayer's attention on the role of the auditor and the audit opinion.

These cases all involved fraud by top executives, and in each case, the firm's auditors failed, either intentionally or unintentionally, to report any wrongdo-

2. Ibid.
3. Report of the National Commission on Fraudulent Financial Reporting (October 1987), p. 2.
4. Ahmed Belakoui, *The Coming Crises in Accounting,* Quorum Books, New York, 1989, p. 96.

ings. That is, the auditors gave the firm a clean (or unqualified) opinion prior to the ultimate disclosure of the fraud. Other cases are less dramatic and involve lower levels of management. Examples of fraudulent and questionable reporting practices are discussed in the following sections.

Fraudulent and Questionable Financial Reporting Practices

In a 1987 study, Kenneth Merchant notes that "most fraudulent reporting practices overstate assets or understate liabilities, usually with positive effects on current period income."[5] Exhibit 6-1, reproduced from his study, provides specific examples of fraudulent financial reporting techniques.

Questionable Financial Reporting

questionable reporting practices

As Merchant points out, the expectation gap in the mind of the public is a response not only to actions that are clearly fraudulent, like those in Exhibit 6-1, but also to **questionable reporting practices**—those involving "legal but deceptive—perhaps unethical or at least questionable—reporting practices."[6] He goes on to give the following examples of accounting practices which are not fraudulent in a legal sense but many would consider deceptive, unethical, or immoral:

- Choosing the most "liberal" accounting policy allowable under generally accepted accounting principles ("pushing GAAP to the limit"). Extreme forms of this practice involve opinion shopping: When the firm's external auditors do not find a given accounting procedure acceptable, the firm attempts to find an auditor who does.
- Changing accounting policies to boost income, not because they provide more meaningful information.
- Failing to establish a reserve for a recognized inventory obsolescence (that is, not writing off inventory that no longer has value) and justifying the omission by explaining that the amount was "immaterial."
- Timing the amounts of significant write-offs or write-downs of assets. This often involves writing down assets in the fourth quarter of years in which the firm is having a bad year (that is, a "big bath" is taken) or postponing write-downs until periods when they can be covered by good performance.
- Changing judgments about reserves (estimates of future losses) depending on what the corporation "can afford." That is, being conservative in periods of good performance and less conservative in periods of poor performance.[7]

In a later survey of corporate general managers and finance, control, and audit managers, Merchant and William Bruns found little consensus on which types of acts or behaviors are considered unethical or inappropriate. This was especially true in areas in which managers have the ability to manage short-term earnings. For example, Merchant and Bruns asked corporate managers to respond to the ethics of the following hypothetical earnings-management practice:

In September, a general manager realized that his division would need a strong performance in the last quarter of the year to reach the budget targets. He decided to implement a sales program offering liberal payment terms to pull some sales that would normally

5. Kenneth A. Merchant, *Fraudulent and Questionable Financial Reporting: A Corporate Perspective* (Financial Executives Research Foundation, Morristown, New Jersey, 1987), p. 4.
6. Ibid.
7. Ibid., p. 6.

Exhibit 6-1

Type of Fraud	Examples
Manipulating, falsifying, or altering records or documents	Changing dates on supplier invoices so that expenses are not recorded until the following accounting period
	Changing dates on shipping documents in order to book sales (and recognize profits) before the time of the actual shipment
	Changing invoice amounts to understate the amount of expense booked in the accounting records
	Creating false inventory count sheets
Suppressing or omitting the effects of completed transactions from records or documents	Failing to record supplier invoices at year end
Recording transactions without substance	Creating fictitious customer orders
Misapplying accounting policies	Capitalizing start-up and tooling costs and other items that should be expensed according to generally accepted accounting principles
	Recognizing revenue and profits on sales for which a significant risk of return still existed
	Purposely booking inadequate reserves to show a predetermined amount of earnings
	Recording prepayments as expenses of current period
Failing to disclose significant information	Concealing an impairment in the value of certain assets
	Concealing pending litigation
	Not reporting a change in accounting policy

Kenneth Merchant, *Fraudulent and Questionable Financial Reporting: A Corporate Perspective,* Financial Executives Research Foundation, Morristown, New Jersey, 1987, p. 5. Reprinted with permission.

occur next year into the current year. Customers accepting delivery in the fourth quarter would not have to pay the invoice for 120 days.[8]

Opinions on the acceptability of this practice were divided as follows:[9]

Ethical	43%
Questionable	44
Unethical	13

8. William J. Bruns and Kenneth A. Merchant, "The Dangerous Morality of Managing Earnings," *Management Accounting,* August 1990, p. 22.
9. Bruns and Merchant, p. 23.

Fraudulent Financial Reporting and the Accounting Profession

The examples do not imply that all managers engage in fraudulent or questionable reporting practices, or that the accounting profession is an unethical one. Indeed, a survey by Louis Harris found that CPAs are ranked as the most highly respected of all professionals, and the profession earned top marks for ethics and honesty.[10]

At the same time, however, the combination of business failures, greater incidence of fraudulent financial reporting, and questions of unethical behavior has increased scrutiny of the accounting profession. The Government Accounting Office has charged the accounting profession with poor-quality audits of many savings and loan institutions that have gone bankrupt. The revelation that a CPA such as Jose Gomez participated with management in the fraudulent financial reporting of a firm has caused many to question the ethical standards of the accounting profession. Lack of confidence in the profession can have far-reaching consequences for our economic system. This was clearly spelled out by Joe Conner, former head of Price Waterhouse, when he stated:

Confidence in business and confidence in the accounting profession are inseparable. The profession's primary role is to help sustain confidence in our business and economic system by ensuring the integrity of financial information. When the public's faith in our effectiveness in carrying out that role wanes, so does faith in the system itself.[11]

The leadership of the accounting profession is responding to the need for greater confidence and ensurance of integrity. Various professional groups such as the AICPA and the AAA have sponsored and funded the National Commission on Fraudulent Financial Reporting, known as the Treadway Commission (after its Chairman, James S. Treadway, Jr.), as well as a follow-up study aimed at developing an internal control framework. In response to these actions and other pressures, the AICPA has revised some of its auditing standards and issued new ones, referred to as *expectation gap standards,* which have expanded the role of the auditor in evaluating internal control and fraud detection. Congress also has addressed some of these concerns in various hearings investigating the role of the auditor in fraud detection, oversight procedures by the SEC, and other matters related to the audit process and fraudulent financial reporting. Finally, all those interested in financial reporting have been quick to call for increased teaching of ethics in business schools. These initiatives should lead to a closing of the expectation gap.

THE FINANCIAL REPORTING SYSTEM FOR PUBLIC COMPANIES

Objective 2
Explain the financial reporting system for a public company.

One of the first tasks of the Treadway Commission was to develop an overview of the financial reporting system for public companies. This financial reporting system is outlined in Exhibit 6-2. The three major components shown are public companies, independent public accountants, and oversight bodies such as the SEC. As the report of the Commission emphasizes, "the company and its management are the key players in the financial reporting system; they bear the primary responsibility for the preparation and content of the financial

10. Laurel English, "Ethics: Shades of Gray Cloud a Black and White Issue," *Outlook,* Summer 1991, p. 11.
11. Ralph Walters, "Operation Highroad: A Plan to Restore Confidence and Balance," *Ethics in the Accounting Profession* (May 1986), p. 69.

Exhibit 6-2
Financial Reporting System

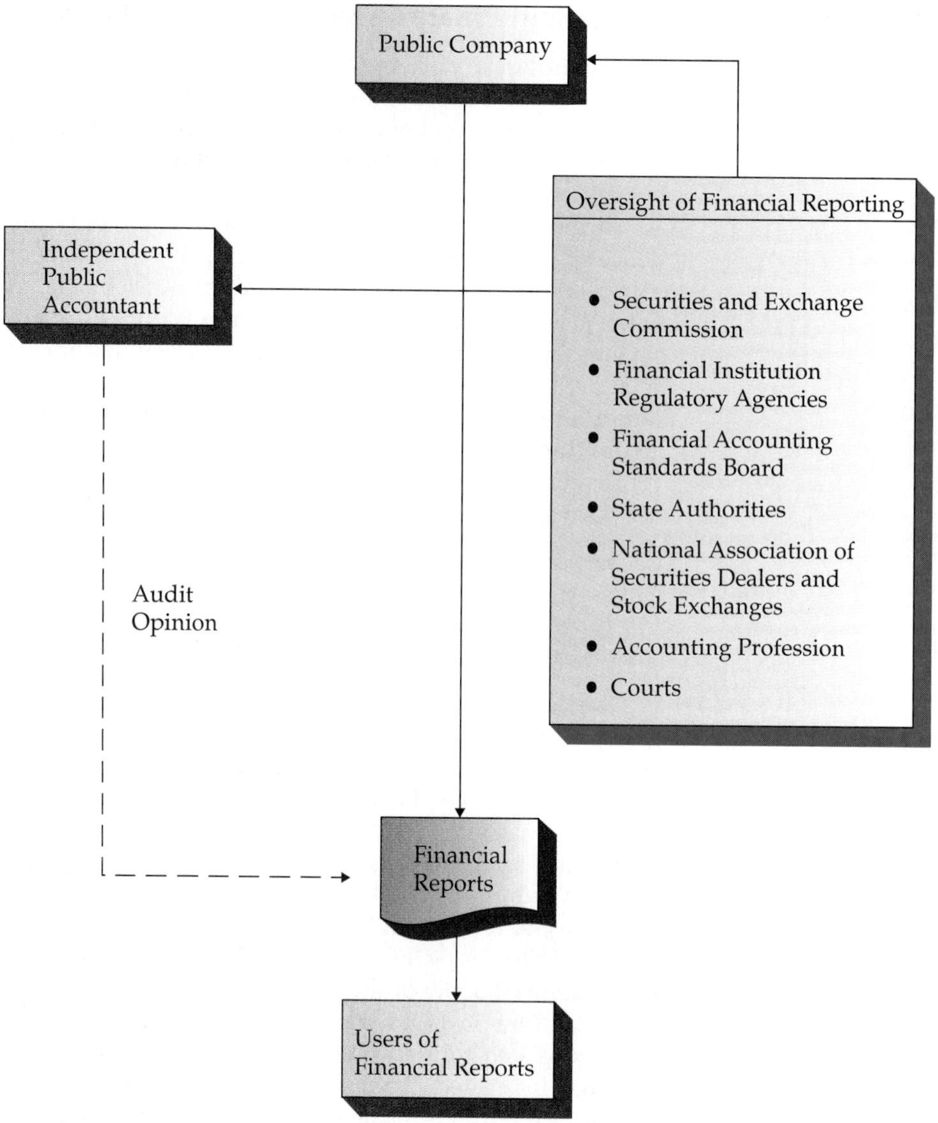

Source: Report of the National Commission on Fraudulent Financial Reporting, © 1987, American Institute of Certified Public Accountants, Inc. Reprinted with permission.

statements."[12] The CPA, through the audit opinion, reports on the fairness of the financial statements, and the several oversight bodies affect financial reporting through standard setting and monitoring of compliance.

Exhibit 6-3 details the public company box in Exhibit 6-2 by listing the individuals and areas within a public company that play roles in the financial reporting system. A key area is, of course, the accounting department which is responsible for the actual preparation of the firm's financial statements. The controller and the chief financial officer, who report to the chief executive officer, oversee the accounting department. Both the legal and the internal audit departments

12. Report of the National Commission on Fraudulent Financial Reporting (October 1987), p. 17.

Exhibit 6-3
The Public Company

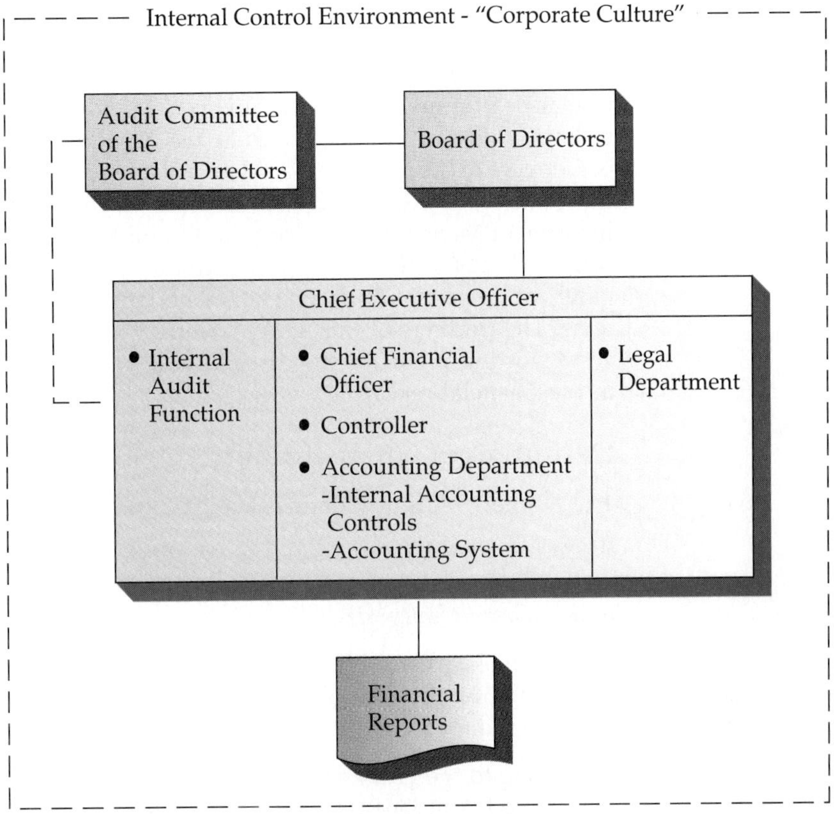

Source: Report of the National Commission on Fraudulent Financial Reporting, © 1987, American Institute of Certified Public Accountants, Inc. Reprinted with permission.

play important supporting roles. The legal department, or the office of the general counsel, reviews financial statements and annual report disclosures for compliance with various state and federal securities laws. The internal audit department oversees the firm's compliance with its own internal controls. Finally, the board of directors, through its audit committee, is ultimately responsible to shareholders for the content of financial reports, as well as management's overall performance.

THE IMPORTANCE OF INTERNAL CONTROL AND THE INTERNAL CONTROL FRAMEWORK

Objective 3
Describe the internal control framework and explain the elements of an internal control structure.

Instituting a strong system of internal control has long been recognized as an effective means of reducing the incidence of fraudulent financial reporting, as well as reducing errors in the published financial statements. One of the primary oversight functions of management is to ensure that such a system is in place and functioning as designed. However, no system of internal control, no matter how well designed, can be foolproof. It can only provide reasonable assurance that management's objectives are being met. Such breakdowns as human failures, errors in judgment, and deliberate circumvention by management can occur.

Although one of the first steps in an audit is a thorough evaluation of the firm's internal control system and structure, there are widely differing views as to what constitutes an effective internal control system. Thus, one of the recommendations of the Treadway Commission was a call for the many professional accounting organizations to develop a common definition of internal control and to make recommendations on how best to judge the effectiveness of internal controls. A study of internal controls has been undertaken by the accounting firm of Coopers & Lybrand. This study was funded by the American Institute of CPAs, the American Accounting Association, the Institute of Internal Auditors, the Institute of Management Accountants, and the Financial Executives Institute. The primary focus of this study is to provide an internal control framework that preparers and users of financial statements can use in assessing internal control systems. The findings of this study (referred to as the Framework Study) provide a good starting point for the discussion of internal controls and their importance in the financial reporting system.

Definition of Internal Control

internal control

The Framework Study defines **internal control** as:

A process effected by an entity's board of directors, management, and other personnel designed to provide reasonable assurance regarding the achievement of specific objectives in the following categories:

- Effectiveness and efficiency of operations.
- Reliability of financial reporting.
- Compliance with applicable laws and regulations.[13]

According to the Framework Study, internal control consists of the five following interrelated components:

1. *Control environment*—The core of any business is its people—their individual attributes, including integrity, ethical values, and competence-and the environment in which they operate. They are the engine that drives the entity and the foundation on which everything rests.
2. *Risk assessment*—The entity must be aware of and deal with the risks it faces. It must set objectives, integrated with the sales, production, marketing, financial and other activities so that the organization is operating in concert. It must also establish mechanisms to identify, analyze, and manage the related risks.
3. *Control activities*—Control policies and procedures must be established and executed to help ensure that the actions identified by management as necessary to address risks to achievement of the entity's objectives are effectively carried out.
4. *Information and communication*—Surrounding these activities are information and communication systems. These enable the entity's people to capture and exchange the information needed to conduct, manage and control its operations.
5. *Monitoring*—The entire process must be monitored, and modifications made as necessary. In this way, the system can react dynamically, changing as conditions warrant.[14]

13. Coopers & Lybrand, "Internal Control—Integrated Framework, Executive Summary," (Committee of Sponsoring Organizations, AICPA, Harborside, Jersey City, 1992), p. 1.
14. Coopers & Lybrand, "Internal Control—Integrated Framework, Framework," (Committee of Sponsoring Organizations, AICPA, Harborside, Jersey City, 1992), pp. 12 and 14.

Exhibit 6-4 contains a graphic representation of the way in which these components are interrelated.

According to the study, this definition is based on certain concepts:

- Internal control is a process. It is a means to an end, not an end itself.
- Internal control is effected by people. It is not merely policy manuals and forms, but people at every level of the organization.

Exhibit 6-4
Internal Control Model

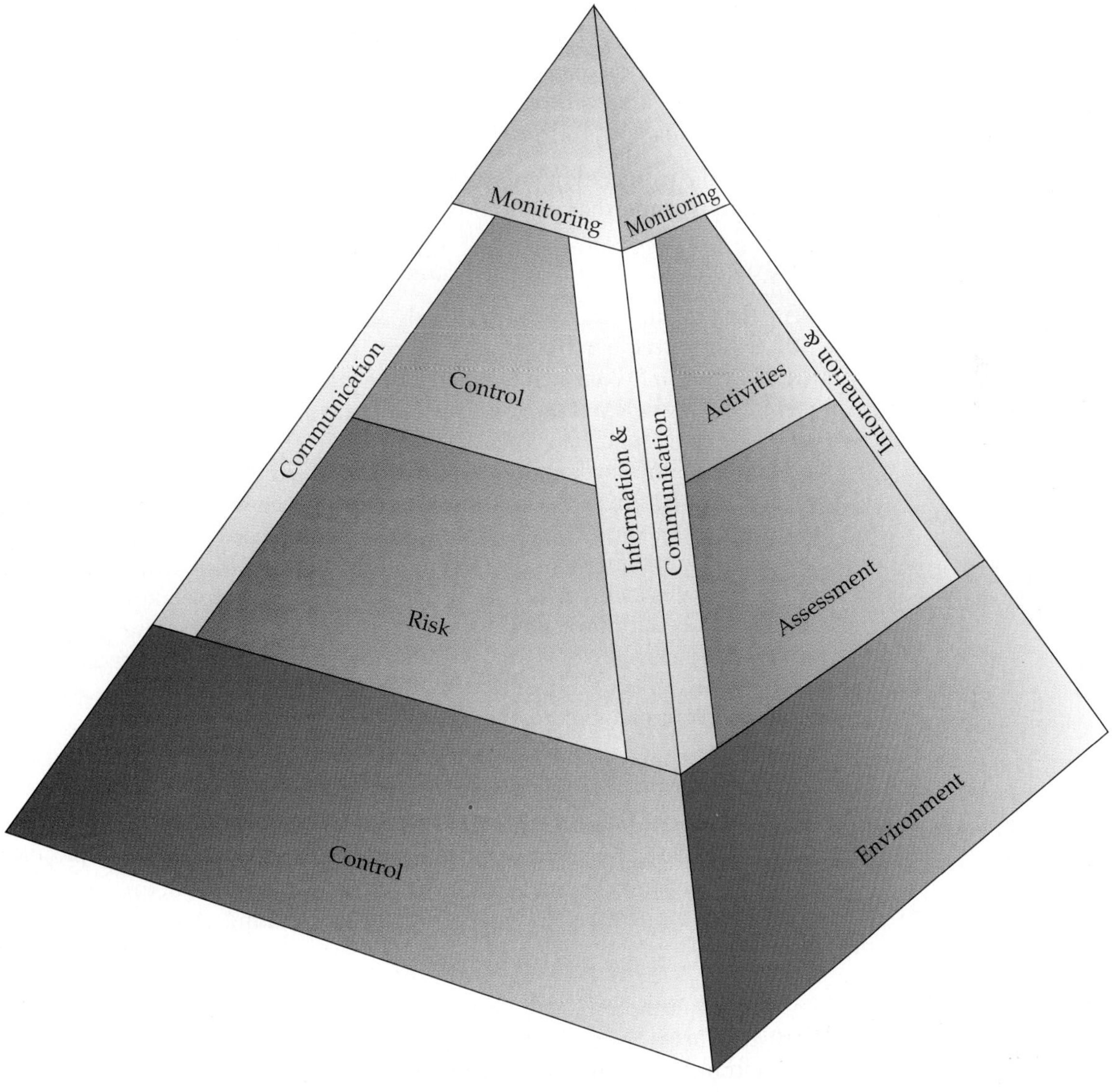

The *control environment* provides an atmosphere in which people conduct their activities and carry out their control responsibilities. It serves as the foundation for the other components. Within this environment, management *assesses risks* to the achievement of specified objectives. *Control activities* are implemented to help ensure that management directives to address the risks are carried out. Meanwhile, relevant *information* is captured and *communicated* throughout the organization. The entire process is *monitored* and modified as conditions warrant.

Source: Coopers & Lybrand "Internal Control—Integrated Framework," © 1992, American Institute of Certified Public Accountants, Inc. Reprinted with permission.

- Internal control can be expected to provide only reasonable assurance, not absolute assurance, to an entity's management and board.
- Internal control is geared to the achievement of objectives in one or more separate but overlapping categories.[15]

What Internal Controls Can and Cannot Do

Before discussing internal control structures in detail, it is important to understand what a good internal control system can accomplish and what it cannot accomplish. According to the Framework Study:

Internal control can help an entity achieve its performance and profitability targets, and prevent loss of resources. It can help ensure reliable financial reporting. And it can help ensure that the enterprise complies with laws and regulations, avoiding damage to its reputation and other consequences. In sum, it can help an entity get to where it wants to go, and avoid pitfalls and surprises along the way.[16]

However, the expectation gap referred to earlier in this chapter has led some individuals to assume that internal controls can ensure an entity's success and survival and can ensure the reliability of financial reporting and compliance with laws and regulations. Again, as the framework study notes:

- Even effective internal control can only *help* an entity achieve success or survival. It can provide management information about the entity's progress, or lack of it, toward their achievement. But internal control cannot change an inherently poor management into a good one. Internal control cannot ensure success or even survival.
- An internal control system, no matter how well conceived and operated, can provide only reasonable—not absolute—assurance to management and the board regarding the achievement of an entity's objectives. Internal controls are limited by the fact that judgments in decision-making can be faulty, and that breakdowns can occur because of a simple error or mistake. Additionally, controls can be circumvented by the collusion of two or more people, and management has the ability to override the system. Further, internal control systems must reflect the fact that there are resource constraints that benefits of the controls must exceed their cost.[17]

Elements of an Internal Control Structure

internal control structure

An entity's **internal control structure** consists of "the policies and procedures established to provide reasonable assurance that specific entity objectives will be achieved."[18] According to the AICPA, an entity's control structure consists of three elements: the control environment, the accounting system, and control procedures.

control environment

The Control Environment. The **control environment** is the organizational climate and structure within which the accounting and control systems operate. The control environment is the product of several different factors which affect the

15. Ibid., p. 12.
16. Framework Study, Executive Summary, p. 3.
17. Adapted from the Framework Study, Executive Summary, p. 4.
18. "Consideration of the Internal Control Structure in a Financial Statement Audit," *Statement on Auditing Standards No. 55,* AICPA (April 1988), par. 6.

establishment and operational effectiveness of specific control policies and procedures. Some of the factors noted in the AICPA's latest statement on internal control are:

- Management's philosophy and operating style.
- The entity's organizational structure.
- The functioning of the board of directors and its committees, particularly the audit committee.
- Methods of assigning authority and responsibility.
- Management's control methods for monitoring and following up on performance, including internal auditing.
- Personnel policies and practices.
- Various external influences that affect an entity's operations and practices, such as examinations by bank regulatory agencies.[19]

Management's Role in Preventing Fraudulent Financial Reporting. As shown in Exhibit 6-3, the internal control environment, or "corporate culture," is a major factor in contributing to the overall integrity of the financial reporting process. The Treadway Commission felt that companies and their managements play a key role in reducing the potential for fraudulent financial reporting. Management is responsible for establishing the appropriate tone, the overall control environment in which financial reporting occurs. On a more detailed level, management should "maximize the effectiveness of the functions within the company that are critical to the integrity of financial reporting, the accounting function, the internal audit function, and the audit committee of the Board of Directors."[20] Thus management must develop an internal control system—a crucial element in preventing fraudulent financial reporting as well as unintentional misstatements. Again, while many in the organization have a role in internal controls, management has a key responsibility. As clearly noted in the framework study, "The chief executive officer is ultimately responsible and should assume "ownership" of the system. More than any individual, the chief executive sets the "tone at the top" that affects integrity and ethics and other factors of a positive control environment."[21]

Management's Responsibility for the Financial Statements. A company's management is responsible for the preparation and integrity of the firm's financial statements. This responsibility is clearly spelled out in the first paragraph of a standard audit opinion: "The financial statements are the responsibility of XXX's management." Many public companies also prepare a statement describing in more detail their responsibility for financial reporting. About 25% of all public companies (and 60% of Fortune 500 companies) prepare such a statement in their annual report to shareholders.[22] These statements vary widely in their scope and discussion. The statement of management's responsibility from Albertson's year-end 1992 annual report is reproduced in Appendix A.

The authors of the Framework Study believe that all public companies should be required to include such a statement in their annual reports to shareholders

19. Ibid., par. 9.
20. Ibid.
21. Ibid., p. 4.
22. Coopers & Lybrand, "Internal Control—Integrated Framework, Reporting to External Parties," (Committee of Sponsoring Organizations, AICPA, Harborside, Jersey City, 1992), p. 1.

and that this statement should specifically address management's evaluation of the firm's internal controls. According to the Framework Study, this report should include the following items:

- The category of controls being addressed (controls over the preparation of the entity's published financial reports).
- A statement about the inherent limitations of any internal control system.
- A statement about the existence of mechanisms for system monitoring and responding to identified control deficiencies.
- A time frame of reference for reporting—that is, identification of the criteria against which the internal control system is measured.
- A conclusion on the effectiveness of the internal control system. If one or more material weaknesses exist, precluding a statement that the system is effective, a description of the material weaknesses should be included.
- The date on which (or the period for which) the conclusion is made.
- The names of the report signers.[23]

Exhibit 6-5 illustrates the type of report that the Framework Study recommends.

As noted, the board of directors is ultimately responsible to shareholders for management's performance and actions. Both the Treadway Commission and the Framework Study recommend that the board of directors establish an audit com-

Exhibit 6-5

SAMPLE REPORT

XYZ Company maintains a system of internal control over financial reporting, which is designed to provide reasonable assurance to the company's management and board of directors regarding the preparation of reliable published financial statements. The system contains self-monitoring mechanisms, and actions taken to correct deficiencies as they are identified. Even an effective internal control system, no matter how well designed, has inherent limitations—including the possibility of the circumvention or overriding of control—and therefore can provide only reasonable assurance with respect to financial statement preparation. Further, because of changes in conditions, internal control system effectiveness may vary over time.

The company assessed its internal control system as of December 31, 19XX in relation to the criteria for effective internal control over financial reporting described in "Internal Control—Integrated Framework" issued by the Committee of Sponsoring Organizations of the Treadway Commission. Based on this assessment, the company believes that, as of December 31, 19XX, the system of internal control over financial reporting met those criteria.

____________________ ____________________
Date Signature (CEO)

____
Signature (CFO/Chief Accounting Officer)

Source: Coopers & Lybrand, "Internal Control—Integrated Framework, Reporting to External Parties," (Committee of Sponsoring Organizations, AICPA, Harborside, Jersey City, 1992), p. 15.

23. Ibid., p. 14.

mittee to provide oversight in regard to the preparation and integrity of the firm's financial statements. As stated in the Treadway Commission report:

The audit committee of the board of directors plays a critical role in the integrity of the company's financial reporting. The Commission recommends that all public companies be required to have audit committees composed entirely of independent directors. To be effective, audit committees should exercise vigilant and informed oversight of the financial reporting process, including the company's internal controls. The board of directors should set forth the committee's duties and responsibilities in a written charter. Among other things, the audit committee should review management's evaluation of the independence of the public accountant and management's plans for engaging the company's independent public accountant to perform management advisory services.[24]

A key feature of the audit committee is that it consists of outside directors, that is, directors who are not part of the management of the company.

Many public companies, but not all, have established audit committees. For example, in their statement of responsibility for financial reporting reproduced in Appendix A, Albertson's management states:

The Audit Committee of the Board of Directors, comprised entirely of outside directors, oversees the fulfillment by Management of its responsibilities over financial controls and the preparation of financial statements. The Committee meets with internal and external auditors at least three times per year to review audit plans and audit results. This provides internal and external auditors direct access to the Board of Directors.

A slightly different version of the same statement is found in the report of management responsibilities in a recent annual report of McDonnell Douglas:

The Board of Directors has appointed four of its non-employee members as an Audit Committee. This Committee meets periodically with management and the internal and independent auditors. Both internal and independent auditors have unrestricted access to the Audit Committee to discuss the results of their examinations and the adequacy of internal controls.

accounting system

The Accounting System. The **accounting system** consists of the methods and records established by management to identify, assemble, analyze, classify, record, and report an entity's transactions and to maintain accountability for the firm's assets and liabilities. According to the AICPA, an effective accounting system attempts to establish methods and accounting records that will accomplish the following functions:

- Identify and record all valid transactions.
- Describe on a timely basis the transactions in sufficient detail to permit proper classification of transactions for financial reporting.
- Measure the value of transactions in a manner that permits recording their proper monetary value in the financial statements.
- Determine the time period in which transactions occurred to permit recording of transactions in the proper accounting period.
- Present properly the transactions and related disclosures in the financial statements.[25]

24. Treadway Commission, p. 12.
25. "Consideration of the Internal Control Structure in a Financial Statement Audit," *Statement on Auditing Standards 55,* AICPA (April 1988), par. 10.

control procedures

operations controls

financial reporting controls

compliance controls

Control Procedures. **Control procedures** are the transaction processing steps established by management to provide reasonable assurance that the firm's objective will be met. Control procedures are often grouped into three categories: *operations controls, financial reporting controls,* and *compliance controls.* **Operations controls** provide reasonable assurance that business activities such as purchases, sales, and production are performed in accordance with management's authorizations. **Financial reporting controls** provide reasonable assurance that financial records and reports are reliable. **Compliance controls** provide reasonable assurance that an enterprise complies with local, state, and federal regulations.

Note that all three types of control provide a reasonable assurance, not absolute assurance, that proper control is maintained. The concept of reasonable assurance, which is explicitly noted in the definition of internal control (see page 262), is important and implies a cost-benefit trade-off. Thus, the cost of implementing and using a control procedure should not exceed the value of the benefits derived from control compliance. For example, management could implement a control requiring specific approval each time a journal entry is prepared. Such a control procedure might reduce the frequency of journal entry errors. However, it would also result in a significant increase in the time needed to prepare journal entries and, probably the hiring of additional employees to keep up with the work flow. Thus, this control is not cost effective and should not be implemented. Alternative control procedures should be implemented in this case to provide reasonable assurance that only valid and authorized journal entries are prepared.

According to the AICPA, control procedures include:

- Proper authorization of transactions and activities.
- Segregation of duties to reduce the opportunities for any person to be in a position to both perpetrate and conceal errors or irregularities in the normal course of his or her duties—different people should be in charge of authorizing transactions, recording transactions, and maintaining custody of assets.
- Design and use of adequate documents and records to help ensure the proper recording of transactions and events, such as monitoring the use of prenumbered shipping documents.
- Adequate safeguards over access to and use of assets and records, such as secured facilities and authorization for access to computer programs and data files.
- Independent checks on performance and proper valuation of recorded amounts, such as clerical checks, reconciliations, comparison of assets with recorded accountability, computer-programmed controls, management review of reports that summarize the detail of account balances, and user review of computer-generated reports.[26]

Although control procedures should be tailored to a firm's specific needs, features common to all effective systems include separation of duties, clear lines of authority, maintenance of formal policies and procedures, physical control over assets and records, adequate documents and checks, and the hiring and development of competent, trustworthy personnel. Probably the critical component of good internal control is separation of duties. This means that each of the following duties is handled by a different individual or group within the organization:

26. Ibid., par. 11.

- authorizing economic activities
- custody of assets
- accountability for those assets.

To illustrate this concept, the person who receives cash collections from customers who are paying their accounts (the cashier) should not be the same person who maintains the accounts receivable records. Entrusting the same employee with both tasks would give a dishonest person the opportunity to steal the funds and conceal the action by authorizing a bad-debt write-off to that account.

Legislative Influences on Internal Control

The topic of internal and management controls was not a high legislative priority until the Watergate incident of the 1970s. The investigation that followed Watergate brought to light the fact that several U.S. corporations had made illegal or questionable payments to U.S. politicians and foreign officials. This, in turn, brought to the public's attention the issue of American business ethics in general, and corporate internal control issues in particular. This led to action by Congress and several proposals by the Securities and Exchange Commission.

Foreign Corrupt Practices Act

Foreign Corrupt Practices Act. One of the first legislative results of the congressional concern over the questionable activities of U.S. corporations was the passage of the **Foreign Corrupt Practices Act** in 1977. Although the prohibition of bribes to foreign officials is the main focus of the act, it also has two accounting provisions relating to publicly held corporations. Under this act, publicly traded companies must:

1. Keep reasonably detailed records which accurately reflect company financial activities.
2. Devise and maintain a system of internal accounting controls sufficient, among other things, to provide reasonable assurance that transactions are properly authorized, recorded, and accounted for.

In the view of the act's backers, a strong internal control system should be a strong deterrent to illegal payments and bribes.

Other Activities by the SEC and Congress. In response to the concern over illegal payments and fraudulent and questionable financial reporting, the SEC proposed mandatory management reports on an entity's internal control. Although this proposal was eventually withdrawn after much criticism from the accounting profession, it did signal the SEC's interest in management reporting on internal controls.

Various congressional oversight committees have and continue to consider the issue of fraudulent and questionable financial reporting, and have proposed several bills to reduce the incidence of these activities. Most recently, a bill relating to banks, known as the Federal Deposit Insurance Corporation Improvement Act, has become law. This law requires the management of banks to assess and report on the effectiveness of internal controls.

Although this bill is limited to one specific industry, it does indicate Congress' strong interest in fraudulent financial reporting and internal controls. This interest, including the issuance of additional proposals, is bound to continue. Such proposals will continue to put pressure on the accounting profession to police itself or face additional regulation from Congress and/or the SEC.

INTERNAL CONTROL AND COMPUTER-BASED ACCOUNTING SYSTEMS

Objective 4
Describe the types of internal controls that are used in computer-based accounting systems and provide examples.

So far this chapter has discussed the general attributes of a good internal control system, especially as outlined in the framework study and the pronouncements of the AICPA. This part of the chapter discusses the application of these concepts to computer-based accounting systems.

The need for an effective control structure does not change when an enterprise implements a computer-based accounting system. However, the type of control procedures depend on whether the system is manual or computer-based. For example, the segregation of certain duties or functions is one of the most common control procedures in a manual accounting system. However, most accounting functions are concentrated within the computer when a computer-based accounting system is used. Consequently, it becomes impossible to increase control over the system by segregating accounting functions, and the development of other control procedures becomes necessary.

Control Categories

As noted previously, controls may be categorized in different ways. The two broad categories of controls in a computer environment are general controls and application controls. **General controls,** such as hardware and system security controls, are pervasive or global controls that affect all system users and application systems. **Application controls** are controls that have been tailored to reduce specific risks in a given information system. For example, application controls are designed to ensure the reliability of a general ledger system. General and applications controls can be further classified by their control objective. For example, controls can be designed to either *prevent* or *detect* errors and irregularities. In this context, an **error** is an unintentional misstatement of financial information. For example, an error exists when an accountant mistakenly posts a transaction to the wrong general ledger account. On the other hand, an **irregularity** is the intentional misstatement of financial information. For example, the preparation of an unauthorized journal entry to hide the theft of an asset is an irregularity.

general controls

application controls

error

irregularity

Controls that are designed to prevent errors and irregularities are called **preventive controls,** and provide the first line of defense around a system. The use of a double entry accounting system is a preventive control because it provides a reasonable assurance that the accounting equation is always in balance. When possible, such preventative controls are the preferred type of controls.

preventive controls

Controls that are designed to detect errors and irregularities after they have occurred are **detective controls.** A trial balance is a detective control. The trial balance does not prevent errors and irregularities; however, when not in balance it may indicate that debits do not equal credits in the general ledger and that an error or irregularity exists. Whenever a detective control indicates the existence of a problem an investigation is made and corrective action is taken. However, if you have ever corrected a general ledger after the trial balance indicated a problem you know that error correction can be more difficult and time consuming than error detection.

detective controls

Controls that facilitate the correction process are called **corrective controls.** Posting references in the general ledger and general journal and transaction descriptions in the general journal are examples of corrective controls. For example, it is possible to use posting references and transaction descriptions to work backwards from a posted transaction in the general ledger to the source docu-

corrective controls

Exhibit 6-6
Control Categories

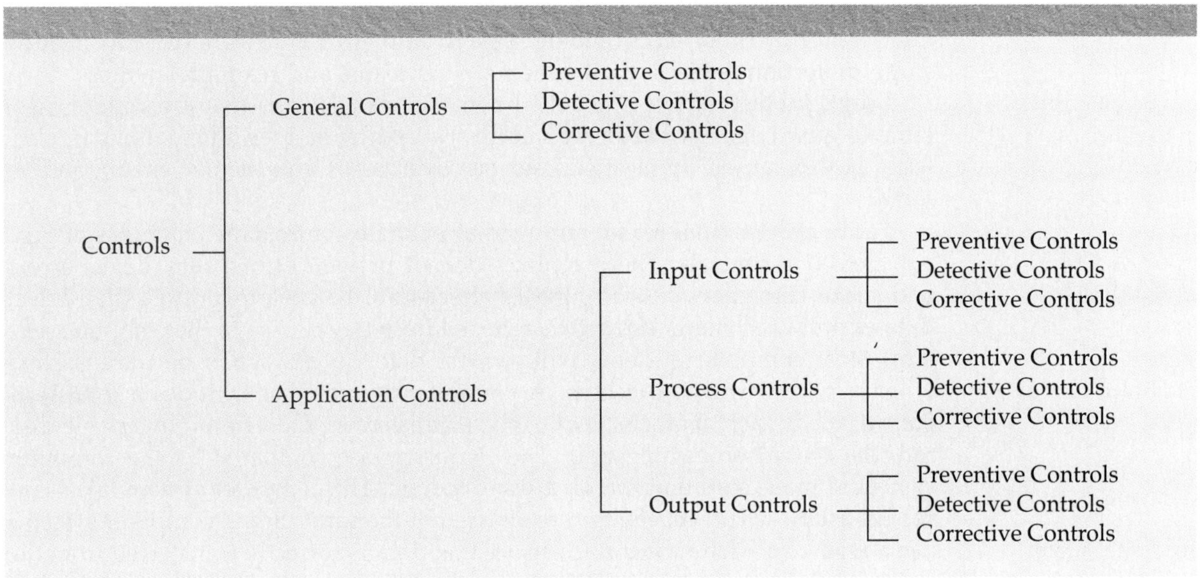

ments that provide the original evidence of the transaction. The information on the source documents may help correct the error or irregularity. Detective and corrective controls are usually used together so that errors and irregularities can be both easily detected and corrected.

input controls
process controls
output controls

Application controls are further classified into input, process, and output controls. **Input controls** either prevent, or detect and facilitate the correction of erroneous input. **Process controls** either prevent or detect and facilitate the correction of errors during processing. **Output controls** either prevent or detect and facilitate the correction of erroneous output. Exhibit 6-6 illustrates the interrelationship between the different control categories in a computer-based environment.

In the following paragraphs we will first discuss general controls and then turn our attention back to application controls.

General Controls

As noted, general controls affect all system users and all application systems. Exhibit 6-7 lists the different types of general controls and their objectives. Some of these controls are embedded within the computer system while others are part of an enterprise's organizational structure or are developed as policies and procedures.

Exhibit 6-7
General Controls

Control Type	*Control Objective*
Hardware controls	Detection
System security controls	Prevention
Systems development procedures	Prevention
Integrity controls	Correction
Segregation of MIS functions	Prevention

hardware controls

Hardware Controls. Most hardware controls are developed and implemented by computer manufacturers. **Hardware controls** are general controls that operate whenever computer hardware is used. These controls are designed to prevent and detect errors caused by hardware malfunctions, power fluctuations, and interference by other electronic devices. Examples of hardware controls include surge protection devices, parity checks, dual reads, and read-after-writes.

surge protectors

Surge protectors are preventive controls installed on many computer systems to guard against hardware failures caused by sudden fluctuations in electrical power caused by electrical storms, overuse of a particular circuit, and so forth.

parity checks

dual-read control

read-after-write control

Parity checks, dual reads, and read-after-write controls are examples of general detective controls. These controls do not prevent errors, they detect errors and make correction possible. **Parity checks** are hardware controls that detect data errors when characters are transferred from any device to the computer system. Most computer systems will request that the characters be retransferred when a parity error is detected. A computer system that includes a **dual-read control** reads each character twice when transferring data from a magnetic disk into the central processing unit. The characters are compared by the computer system to make sure that the read was accurate. The computer system takes corrective action whenever the two reads are not the same. Some computer systems use a **read-after-write control** to ensure that data is correctly transferred from the computer to a magnetic disk. This control reads data after it is written to a disk and compares the data that was written with the data that should have been written to detect write errors.

system security controls

password protection

System Security Controls. **System security controls** are controls that prevent unauthorized access to or destruction of system resources. *Password protection* and *physical security controls* are examples of common system security controls. **Password protection** is a general control that restricts access to computer systems to authorized system users. Individuals must have a valid password to gain access to many computer systems. Individuals with invalid passwords are prevented from accessing the computer system, and moreover, the unsuccessful attempt to access the system may be reported to the systems manager so that additional action can be taken.

physical security controls

Physical security controls are general controls that prevent unauthorized access to or destruction of a computer facility. Most organizations restrict access to computer facilities to a limited group of individuals to reduce the risk of hardware misuse. Typically only computer operators, maintenance personnel, and data librarians are able to access the computer facility. The installation of a fire detection and suppression system in a computer center is another example of a system security control designed to prevent the destruction of system resources.

systems development procedures

Systems Development Procedures. **Systems development procedures** are general controls that ensure that application systems are properly designed and installed. Standard systems development procedures include documentation standards, testing standards, and review and approval procedures. These controls minimize errors and irregularities in application systems by requiring that the systems be well designed, documented, tested, reviewed, and approved before the systems are implemented. Assume, for example, that program changes are not reviewed and authorized prior to implementation. A programmer, in this situation, might make an unauthorized change to a payroll program that would cause his or her payroll check to be printed twice each pay period. This unauthorized change might go undetected in a large organization. The combination of access controls, restricting access to application programs, and review and approval procedures could prevent this irregularity.

integrity controls

Integrity Controls. **Integrity controls** are corrective controls that minimize losses due to data and system destruction. The two most common integrity controls are back-up procedures and disaster plans. Back-up procedures minimize loss due to program and data destruction. Effective back-up procedures require that copies of programs and files be periodically created and stored in a safe location. These copies can be retrieved and used if the original files are destroyed. Common practice is to maintain two copies of each program and file and to store them in different locations. Imagine, for example, how the authors of this text book would have felt if the only disk-based copy of the manuscript had been destroyed just before the text was to be printed. Several copies of each chapter were created and stored in different locations as the book was being written to minimize the risk of loss.

A disaster plan minimizes losses due to the destruction of computer hardware. Disaster plans range from the procedures to purchase replacement computers with the proceeds of insurance policies to the establishment of fully equipped back-up computer centers. All enterprises that rely on computer-based systems should develop disaster plans.

Segregation of MIS Functions. It is impossible to segregate most accounting functions in a computer-based environment because the functions are concentrated in the computer system. However, it is still possible and important to segregate incompatible functions within the management information systems (MIS) department. Effective segregation of MIS functions is a preventive control. Critical functions that should be segregated include data origination, data entry, computer operations, computer file library maintenance, output distribution, systems design, and programming. An individual who is able to perform two or more of these functions is able to misuse system resources. For example, a computer file librarian who is able to operate the computer system could gain access to a payroll master file and make unauthorized changes to employee pay rates. A data entry operator who was able to originate transaction data could create a fictitious company and then prepare fraudulent accounts payable input that resulted in the payment of nonexistent liabilities to the fictitious company.

Application Controls

Application controls are designed to minimize specific risks in application systems such as the preparation and submission of invalid or unauthorized input, data entry errors, file processing errors, and the loss or misplacement of output. As noted, input, process, and output controls are three different categories of application controls that are designed to prevent and detect errors and irregularities. Exhibit 6-8 illustrates the different application controls discussed next.

Input Controls. The objective of input controls is to provide reasonable assurance that all valid, and only valid, data are input for processing. Input controls will either allow a transaction to be input for processing or will reject a transaction and keep it from being processed. Well-designed input controls minimize errors that result when valid transactions are rejected or when invalid transactions are input for processing.

Exhibit 6-8
Application Controls

Control Type	*Control Objective*
Input	
Review and approval	Preventive
Edits	Detective
Direct data entry	Preventive
Processing	
Edits	Detective
File labels	Preventive
Recovery and restart procedures	Corrective
Output	
Control log	Detective
Distribution list	Preventive

transaction review and authorization controls

Three common input controls are *transaction review and authorization, data edits,* and *direct data entry procedures.* **Transaction review and authorization controls** are controls that prevent the submission of data that contains errors or that is unauthorized. To illustrate, in some systems, accountants transfer information contained on business documents such as invoices and time cards onto journal entry forms. The journal entry forms summarize the relevant transaction data contained on the business documents. The journal entry forms are reviewed and approved by an accounting supervisor before the forms are submitted to data processing for input into an accounting system. As part of this control, unapproved journal entries should be rejected by data processing. This procedure provides a reasonable assurance that only valid and authorized transactions are submitted for processing.

edits

Approved transactions are input into an information system by data entry clerks. A well-designed accounting system contains an edit program that validates transaction or journal entry data while it is being input. **Edits** are detective controls that identify and reject input that appears to be erroneous. One of the most common edits in an accounting system is an account lookup. This edit is used to ensure that all general ledger account numbers included in journal entries are valid. Every time a general ledger account number is input the edit program looks the number up in the chart of accounts to make sure that it is valid. Journal entries with invalid account numbers are rejected.

journal entry balance edit

A **journal entry balance edit** compares the sum of the debits in a journal entry with the sum of the credits to ensure that every journal entry balances. A journal entry is rejected whenever a transaction's debits are not equal to its credits.

limit test

range test

Limit tests and *range tests* are common edits in transaction processing systems. A **limit test** is a control that rejects transactions which include amounts that are either less than or greater than a predetermined limit. For example, a payroll system should reject time cards that report that the hours worked by an employee are less than zero. A **range test** is a control that rejects transactions which include an amount that does not fall within an allowable range. For example, a company may decide that an employee will never work more than 60 hours or less than zero hours in a week. The appropriate range test would reject time cards that reported negative hours worked and time cards that reported more than 60 hours worked per week. All of these edits are designed to detect input errors so that the invalid data can be corrected and reentered.

direct data entry procedures

Direct data entry procedures are procedures and devices that allow input to be entered directly from source documents, with minimal human intervention. These procedures prevent errors by removing people, as much as possible, from the data input process. Grocery store checkout counters that include bar code scanners are examples of direct data entry terminals. The terminal reads the information that is encoded on the bar code and then inputs the data directly into the grocery store's transaction processing system. Errors are reduced because grocery clerks do not key-enter sales transaction data when the bar code scanner is used.

Input controls are designed to meet the specific processing requirements of a transaction processing system. Unfortunately, input controls provide a reasonable rather than an absolute assurance that all input is valid. Consequently, input errors do occur and, thus, process and output controls are also necessary.

Process Controls. Process controls are controls that provide reasonable assurance that the results of computer processing are valid. Several problems may occur which result in invalid processing and incorrect output. Obviously, invalid input will result in invalid output. However, other problems may occur as well. For example, a computer operator may inadvertently mount the wrong version of a master file on a disk drive, or a power failure may interrupt processing. Although it happens infrequently, a computer may even make a computational error. Common process controls designed to prevent or detect these, and other processing errors include *edits, file labels,* and *recovery and restart procedures.*

The same types of edits that were used to validate input can also be used to validate the results of computer processing. Thus edits, depending on where they are used, are either input controls or output controls.

file labels

All physical computer files should contain both external and internal labels. **File labels** are controls that physically and logically identify computer files. They are preventive controls because they prevent errors that result from incorrect file accesses. For example, imagine how much time you would expend trying to find the specific diskette that contained a file that you needed if you had a box of ten diskettes that had no identifying labels. Now imagine a computer-file library with thousands of disks and magnetic tapes that were not labeled, and you had to find a specific disk. It would be harder than trying to find a specific book in your university library if none of the books had call numbers on their covers. An external label provides human-readable file identification. An internal label provides computer program-readable file identification. File librarians, computer operators, and computer programs can all verify that the appropriate file has been accessed when appropriate file labels are used.

recovery and restart procedures

Occasionally computer systems fail while an application system is running. The system failure results in abnormal program termination. This can happen on any size computer system. **Recovery and restart procedures** are corrective controls that facilitate the resumption of processing after abnormal program termination. Imagine that you are typing a term paper on a computer and that your roommate trips over the power cord, unplugging the computer. If your word processor had recovery and restart procedures you would be able to plug the computer back in and start typing where you left off before the interruption.

Output Controls. Output controls are controls that provide reasonable assurance that output is complete and properly distributed. Assume that Adam Zweig worked in a medium-sized firm that employed 527 people. A computer operator loaded blank payroll checks into a printer before starting the payroll system. Unfortunately, the operator had placed only 526 blank checks in the printer and did not notice that Adam's check was never printed. This error could present a real problem to Adam when he does not get paid. Most transaction processing systems print output control logs so that computer operators can check off each report as it is printed and thus verify that all reports and documents which should be printed are actually printed.

Systems should also print distribution lists. The distribution list identifies each printed report and document and identifies the individual(s) that is supposed to receive the output. This list provides reasonable assurance that output is distributed only to authorized individuals.

Summary of Application Controls. Controls are an essential part of all accounting systems, both manual and computer-based. The need for controls results from the risk of errors and irregularities in an accounting system. Errors and irregularities, if not controlled, can result in erroneous or fraudulent financial reporting.

Exhibit 6-8 (page 274) summarized the various application controls. However, this list of controls is not exhaustive. Remember that application controls are tailored to the specific requirements and risks within an application system. Thus different controls are used in different situations. As part of their role as system designers, accountants identify the risks that an accounting system may be subject to and then design appropriate controls to reduce those risks. Auditors assess the adequacy of controls in accounting systems as part of every audit. However, it is important to remember that internal controls, whether in a manual system and or computerized system, can only provide reasonable assurance, not guarantees, regarding the effectiveness and efficiency of operations, the reliability of financial reporting, and the compliance with applicable laws and regulations.

SUMMARY OF LEARNING OBJECTIVES

1. Define fraudulent and questionable financial reporting and give examples. Fraudulent financial reporting has been defined as the intentional or reckless conduct, whether act or omission, that results in materially misleading financial statements. Questionable financial reporting practices involve legal but deceptive methods to improve financial statements or other financial data. Unfortunately, there are ample examples of both types of practices. This has led to an expectation gap between what the public perceives auditors should do and what they do in fact.

2. Explain the financial reporting system for a public company. Independent public accountants and oversight bodies such as the SEC play an important role in the financial reporting system for a public company. The financial reporting structure of a public company includes the accounting department, the controller and the chief financial officer, the legal department, and the internal audit function.

3. Describe the internal control framework and explain the elements of an internal control structure. Internal control is the process by which an entity's board of directors, management, and other personnel obtain reasonable assurance as to achievement of specified objectives. A firm's internal control structure consists of three elements: the control environment, the accounting system, and control procedures. Management plays the key role in establishing the overall control environment. Management has the ultimate responsibility for the preparation of financial statements. This responsibility is explicitly noted in the auditors' opinion and in the more detailed statement of management responsibilities prepared by many public companies. The board of directors oversees this process, usually through its audit committee. This committee, consisting of directors who are not part of the company's management, has responsibility for selecting the firm's auditors.

4. Describe the types of internal controls that are used in computer-based accounting systems and provide examples. Controls, in computer-based accounting systems, can be classified as either general controls or application controls. General controls are pervasive controls that operate on all system users and application systems. Application controls are tailored to reduce specific risks in a transaction processing system. Application control categories include input controls, processing controls, and output controls. Both general and application controls include preventive, detective, and corrective controls.

KEY TERMS

REVIEW PROBLEM

A
Ethical Situations

Review each of the following situations and decide whether or not the individual involved acted ethically. If necessary refer to a particular professional code of ethics that was described in the text.

1. Ali Bangor is the audit partner on the FastGrowth Company audit. The company, whose stock is traded on a regional exchange has had a very successful year and will report record earnings. Earnings are due to be realized in two weeks. Ali is aware of this fact, and has told her spouse to purchase the stock before the earnings release.
2. Robert Givens is financial officer for a local college bookstore. As such he is in charge of textbook purchases. He has been approached by a publisher's representative whose text is being used in one of the college's classes. The representative told Robert that he would provide the bookstore with two dozen free textbooks that could be used for sale to students if Robert would only order new textbooks and not stock any used books. Robert thought this was a good deal for the store and accepted the offer.
3. Brent Abrahmson is the President of Microfax Export Company, a small publicly traded company. Brent has been trying to break into the market of Enox, a small country in the Eastern hemisphere. He has been unsuccessful to date. He has been approached by the import official of Enox and told that if he (the import official) received a substantial gift, entry into Enox's market would be assured. Brent asked several of his colleagues who were already doing business in Enox and was told that this is typical and accepted behavior. On this basis Brent decided to go ahead and make the gifts.

Solutions

1. Ali acted unethically and violated the AICPA Code of Professional Conduct as well as Securities Law relating to insider trading. Insider trading refers to security's transactions by those who have inside knowledge of the financial or operating affairs of the company. She should not reveal confidential information relating to the company she is auditing. Further, if her spouse purchased the stock she would violate the independence rules of the AICPA as she would be deemed to also be an owner.
2. Robert Givens probably acted unethically in this situation. Although he did not receive any direct benefit from the arrangement with the publisher's representative, he denied students access to used books. Thus, the bookstore most likely benefitted at the expense of those purchasing the textbooks. The publisher's representative definitely acted unethically by proposing such an arrangement and carrying through with it.
3. Brent acted unethically and violated the Foreign Corrupt Practices Act which makes bribes to foreign officials unlawful.

B
Internal Control

Answer the following two multiple-choice questions.

1. An internal control system should follow certain basic principles to achieve the objectives of internal control. One of these principles is the segregation of functions or duties. Which one of the following examples does **not** violate the principle of segregation of functions:
   a. The treasurer has the authority to sign checks, but gives her signature block to the assistant treasurer to run in the check-signing machine.
   b. The warehouse clerk, who has custodial responsibility over inventory in the warehouse, may authorize the disposal of any damaged goods.
   c. The sales manager has the responsibility to approve credit and to authorize the removal of an accounts receivable from the books because of a bad debt.
   d. The department time clerk is given the authority to mail undistributed payroll checks to absent employees.
2. In a well-designed internal control system where the cashier receives checks from customers who are making payments on their accounts, from the mailroom, the cashier should **not**:
   a. endorse the checks.
   b. prepare the bank deposit slip.
   c. deposit the checks daily at the bank.
   d. prepare the list of checks received.
   e. make the entries in the company's books to record the receipt of the customers' checks.

Solutions

1. Item (d) is the only one that does not violate the concept of separation of duties or functions. In each of the others there is possibility for theft. In case (a) the assistant treasurer could write checks without the knowledge and approval of the treasurer. In case (b) the warehouse clerk could steal the merchandise and indicate in the records that it was damaged goods and had no value. In case (c) the sales manager could authorize both the sale of goods and the bad debt. Thus a customer might receive goods on account and never pay the bill.
2. In this case the cashier could also endorse the checks, prepare a bank deposit slip and make the deposit (items a–c) without violating internal control principles. The cashier, however, should not also make a list of checks received (d) or make the entries in the company's records (e), as he or she could steal the money, not record its actual receipt, and indicate a bad debt for that account. With one person doing both functions there would be no way to determine whether this action did or did not take place.

C Computer-Based Controls

Review each of the following situations and identify the best type of control that could be used to prevent or detect and correct the problem in the future.

a. Bill Smith saw a diskette labeled "Customer Master File" sitting on a desk one day while visiting an acquaintance at MedTek Services. Bill stole the disk, made several copies of it, and then sold the copies to MedTek's competitors.
b. A group of students gained unauthorized access to a large computer system through a computer terminal in their classroom. They destroyed several important computer files and ran up a large bill for the computer time that they used.
c. A data entry clerk was interrupted while entering a series of journal entries. As a result, the trial balance is out of balance because only the debit portion of a journal entry was entered into the general ledger system.
d. An accountant transposed a general ledger account number on a journal entry form. As a result, the credit portion of the journal entry was posted to a nonexistent account and the trial balance was out of balance.
e. Upscale Industries had just printed 10,000 of its 12,000 year-end W-2 forms when a power failure caused the payroll system to terminate abnormally. The computer operator had to print all of the W-2 forms a second time when power was restored.

Solution

a. Access controls. Access to computer and, in this case, to computer files should be restricted to authorized individuals.
b. Password controls. Only authorized users should be able to gain access to a computer system.
c. Input edit—journal entry balance edit. The system should include an edit to reject all transactions where debits do not equal credits.
d. Input edit—account lookup. The system should include an edit to reject all transactions with invalid account numbers.
e. Processing control—recovery and restart procedures. With recovery and restart procedures the computer operator would only have needed to print the final 2,000 W-2 forms when power was restored.

QUESTIONS

Note to student: Many of the following questions, exercises, and problems present ethical situations. As a result, there is no one correct answer. They require judgment on your part, and it is quite likely (and perfectly acceptable) that you will reach different conclusions from those of your fellow students. What is important is that you think carefully about each situation and support your response with sound reasoning.

1. What is the "expectation gap"? How did it arise?
2. Define questionable financial reporting and compare it to fraudulent financial reporting.
3. What steps has the accounting profession taken to close the expectation gap?
4. The Tennessee Company is in the final month of a very successful year. However, the outlook for next year is uncertain because the firm does a great deal of business in countries that are currently undergoing major political changes. To reduce this year's income and increase next year's, the controller, Jan Williams, has decided to write off large amounts of what she feels are accounts receivable that are overdue for collection. Do you consider this a case of questionable or fraudulent financial reporting practices?
5. Define internal control. What is its role in the preparation of reliable financial statements?
6. List and briefly describe the components of an internal control structure.
7. An entity's control system has three elements: the control environment, the accounting system, and control procedures. Describe and give examples of each of these elements.
8. What is an audit committee and what are its most important functions?

9. What is management's responsibility in the financial reporting process? How does management disclose to external users its responsibility in this process?
10. Why are internal controls necessary when a computer-based accounting system is used?
11. What are the differences between general controls and application controls?
12. What are the different categories of application controls?

EXERCISES

E6-1 Questionable or Fraudulent Financial Reporting
LO 2

The president of the Daniels Corporation was concerned about the amount of net profits the firm would show for the year. He decided to forego his annual bonus of $80,000 (considered to be a material amount) in order to keep the firm's profits as high as possible. Do you think that this is a case of questionable or fraudulent financial reporting? Would your answer differ if at the same time the president took out a loan from the company equal to the amount of the foregone bonus? Why or why not?

E6-2 Questionable or Fraudulent Financial Reporting
LO 2

The Pena Company was having a very poor year and was expecting to incur a huge net loss. The vice-president and controller was reviewing the firm's inventory record, and decided to write off $500,000 of obsolete inventory that was recorded on the books. The inventory probably should have been written off in prior years, but the firm never quite got around to it. Is this a case of questionable or fraudulent financial reporting? Why or why not?

E6-3 Questionable or Fraudulent Financial Reporting
LO 3

The chief financial officer (CFO) of the Bronson Corporation was reviewing the company's financial records in anticipation of the year-end audit. The CFO was concerned that the firm was not going to meet its revenue goals for the year, and decided to start a bonus plan for the regional sales staffs. According to the plan, the sales force would receive a 2% bonus on any sales booked in the month of December. Is this a case of questionable or fraudulent financial reporting? Why or why not?

E6-4 Questionable or Fraudulent Financial Reporting
LO 1

The treasurer of the Drabeck Company worried all year about the deteriorating financial performance of the company. According to loan agreements with lenders, the firm had to maintain certain levels of financial statement ratios and achieve a certain profit level for the year. Failure to meet these terms would put the firm into default. The treasurer decided that immediate action was necessary, and negotiated the following agreement with one of the firm's best customers:

The customer would purchase $750,000 of merchandise before the end of December. The customer would then return the items purchased over the months of January and February so that by the end of February all the sales would have been returned.

The treasurer then recorded these transactions as sales in December, thereby ensuring that the firm's financial position and performance met the agreed-upon constraints. Is this a case of fraudulent or questionable financial reporting? Why or why not?

E6-5 Ethical Choices
LO 1

The following three situations were taken from an Ethics Test in the *Harvard Business Review*.[27] Evaluate the practices described in these scenarios as they apply to a major $100-million division of a billion-dollar public company. Use the following scale to indicate how you judge their acceptability.

1. Ethical practice.
2. Questionable practice. I would not say anything to the manager, but it makes me feel uncomfortable.

27. William Bruns and Kenneth Merchant, "Ethics Test for Everyday Managers," *Harvard Business Review*, March-April 1989, p. 220-221.

3. Minor infraction. The manager should be warned not to do it again.
4. Serious infraction. The manager should be severely reprimanded.
5. Totally unethical. The manager should be fired.
   A. The division's headquarters building was scheduled to be painted in 1995. But since profit performance was way ahead of budget in 1994, the division general manager decided to have the work done in 1994. The painting cost is $150,000.
   B. The division general manager ordered his employees to defer all discretionary expenditures (e.g., travel, advertising, hiring, maintenance) into the next accounting period, so that his division could make its budgeted profit targets. Expected amount of deferrals; $150,000.
   C. In November, 1995, the division was straining to meet budget. The division general manager called the engagement partner of a consulting firm that was doing some work for the division and asked that the firm not send an invoice until next year. The partner agreed. Estimated work done but not invoiced, $500,000. Would your answer differ if the amount of work done was $30,000?

E6-6
Internal Control Concepts
LO 3

Answer the following two multiple choice questions. Explain the reasons for your answers.

a. Which of the following is *not* an element of an entity's internal control structure:
   1. Control risk
   2. Control procedures
   3. The accounting system
   4. The control environment
b. Which of the following statements about internal control structure is correct?
   1. A properly maintained internal control structure reasonably assures that collusion among employees cannot occur.
   2. The establishment and maintenance of the internal control structure is an important responsibility of the internal auditor.
   3. An exceptionally strong internal control structure is enough to satisfy the auditor that the financial statements "fairly present."
   4. The cost/benefit relationship is a primary criterion that should be considered in designing an internal control structure.

(AICPA adapted)

E6-7
Responsibility for Financial Statements
LO 3

Answer each of the following two questions:

a. Both the management of a company and the firm's outside auditors have a role in the preparation of the firm's financial statements. Does management or the auditor have ultimate responsibility for the financial statements? How is that responsibility disclosed?
b. The CFO of the Hansen Company asked the Chairperson of the board of directors to be placed on the board's audit committee. The chairperson is unsure whether this is a good idea or not. What would you recommend? Why?

E6-8
Internal Control
LO 3

Answer each of the following two multiple choice questions. Explain your answer.

a. When considering internal control, an auditor should be aware of the concept of reasonable assurance, which recognizes that:
   1. Segregation of incompatible functions is necessary to ascertain that internal control is effective.
   2. Employment of competent personnel provides assurance that the objectives of internal control will be achieved.
   3. Establishment and maintenance of an internal control structure is an important responsibility of the management and *not* the auditor.
   4. Cost of internal control should *not* exceed the benefits expected to be derived from internal control.

b. Proper segregation of functional responsibilities in an effective structure of internal control calls for separation of functions of:
   1. Authorization, execution, and payment.
   2. Authorization, recording, and custody.
   3. Custody, execution, and reporting.
   4. Authorization, payment, and recording.

(AICPA adapted)

E6-9
Internal Control
LO 3

Answer each of the following two multiple choice questions. Explain your answer.

a. Internal controls are *not* designed to provide reasonable assurance that:
   1. Transactions are executed in accordance with management's authorization.
   2. Irregularities will be eliminated.
   3. Access to assets is permitted only in accordance with management's authorization.
   4. The recorded accountability for assets is compared with the existing assets at reasonable intervals.
b. Which of the following is a provision of the Foreign Corrupt Practices Act?
   1. It is a criminal offense for an auditor to fail to detect and report a bribe to be paid by an American business entity to a foreign official for purpose of obtaining business.
   2. The auditor's detection of illegal acts committed by officials of the auditor's publicly held client in conjunction with foreign officials should be reported to the Securities and Exchange Commission.
   3. If the auditor of a publicly held company concludes that the effects on the financial statements of a bribe given to a foreign official are *not* susceptible of reasonable estimation, the auditor's report should be modified.
   4. Every publicly held company must devise, document, and maintain an internal control structure sufficient to provide assurance that internal control objectives are met.

(AICPA adapted)

E6-10
Computer System Controls
LO 4

Identify the best control that could prevent, or detect and correct, each of the following problems.

a. A fire destroyed a manufacturing firm's data processing center. The fire started when a computer operator threw his cigarette in the wastebasket in the computer room.
b. An escorted visitor leaned against the emergency power shutoff switch in the computer center causing the computer systems to crash.
c. A group of high school students gained unauthorized access to the computer center at a major research facility. The students found the computer center's 800 telephone number on a computer bulletin board and then wrote a computer program that tried all possible passwords. The 745,891 password that the program tried was accepted by the system.
d. A programmer, who was concerned about pending layoffs, made an unauthorized change to the payroll system. The change erased the payroll master file one year after the programmer's job was eliminated.
e. The distribution center for a national retail firm was unable to process restock orders from retail outlets for three weeks after the computer center was destroyed by a flash flood.

E6-11
Computer Controls
LO 4

Identify the best control to prevent, or detect and correct, each of the following problems that occurred with an application system.

a. An accounting clerk prepared a fraudulent journal entry and submitted it to data processing for input. The journal entry, which was used to cover the theft of a substantial amount of inventory, was processed with a group of valid journal entries.
b. An insurance policy application was processed for an individual who, according to the completed application, was born in 2052.

c. The general ledger system displayed a message to the computer operator asking that the current general ledger master file disk be mounted on drive A. The operator mistakenly mounted last year's year-end general ledger rather than the current file. As a result, all of the financial statements were wrong and a month's worth of data had to be reprocessed.
d. A computer operator placed all of the day's output on a table outside the computer center with a sign that said "Here it is . . . find your output." Someone walked by and stole all of the accounts payable checks that had been printed that day.

E6-12
Albertson's Financial Statements
LO 2

Review the portions of Albertson's annual report that are in Appendix A. Does Albertson's management make any statement concerning its ethical practices? If so, where is the statement, and what does it say? Do you think that such disclosures are adequate? Why or why not?

PROBLEMS

P6-1
Ethical Situations
LO 2

Micro Dynamics, a developer of database software packages, is a publicly-held company whose stock is traded over the counter. The company recently received an enforcement release proceeding through an SEC administrative law judge that cited the company for inadequate internal controls. In response, Micro Dynamics has agreed to establish an internal audit function and strengthen its audit committee.

In addition to hiring a manager to establish and run an internal audit department, Micro Dynamics has changed the composition of the audit committee to include all outside directors. An initial planning meeting has been held to discuss the roles of the various participants in the internal control and financial reporting process. Participants at the meeting included the company president, the chief financial officer, a member of the audit committee, a partner from Micro Dynamics' external audit firm, and the newly appointed manager of the internal audit department. Comments by the various meeting participants are presented below.

President: "We want to ensure that Micro Dynamics complies with the SEC's enforcement release, and that we don't find ourselves in this position again. The internal audit department should help to strengthen our internal control system by correcting the problems. I would like your thoughts on the proper reporting relationship for the manager of the internal audit department."

Chief Financial Officer: "I think the manager of the internal audit department should report to me, since much of the department's work relates to financial issues. The audit committee should have oversight responsibilities only."

Audit committee member: "I believe we should think through our roles more carefully. The Treadway Commission has recommended that the audit committee play a more important role in the financial reporting process; the duties of today's Audit Committee have expanded beyond rubber-stamp approval. We need to have greater assurance that controls are in place and are being followed."

External audit partner: "We need a close working relationship among all of our roles. The internal audit department can play a significant role in monitoring the control systems on a continuing basis and should have strong ties to your external audit firm."

Internal audit department manager: "The internal audit department should be more involved in operational auditing [an audit to improve operations by suggesting more efficient and effective procedures], but also should play a significant monitoring role in the financial reporting area."

(IMA adapted)

REQUIRED:

1. Describe the role of each of the following in the establishment, maintenance, and evaluation of Micro Dynamics' system of internal control.
   a. Management
   b. Audit committee
   c. External auditor
   d. Internal audit department
2. Describe the responsibilities that Micro Dynamic's audit committee has in the financial reporting process.
3. Discuss the characteristics of an audit committee in terms of the following.
   a. Composition, size, and terms of membership.
   b. Relationship with management, the external auditor, and the internal auditor.

P6-2
Ethical Situation
LO 4

Kazunas Industries is a manufacturer of auto parts with 70% of its sales to the large domestic auto companies and 30% to auto parts retailers. Kazunas' sales to retailers are increasing at a 20% annual rate, largely due to the increasing average age of U.S. automobiles. However, sales to domestic auto companies are decreasing because many of the parts are not compatible with new auto technology.

Domestic auto companies currently are decreasing the number of their suppliers as they seek better inventory management and quality control, and Kazunas Industries is a prime candidate for deletion. Also, the sales to retailers have a built-in decline as old-technology automobiles reach the end of their life cycles.

Kazunas has decided to build new production facilities and has applied for a $20 million loan from Commerce Bank to finance the modernization. Loan conditions were agreed to in a meeting between Peter Lisko, Kazunas's vice-president of finance, and David Pearson, a loan officer for the bank. The loan conditions limit Kazunas' cash dividend payments to 50% of net income and provide for Commerce Bank's approval of several types of transactions should the current ratio fall below 1.5 to 1. The terms of the agreement were approved by Commerce Bank's loan committee, and Kazunas Industries received the cash on August 15, 1992.

Joan Miraldi, Kazunas' controller, received instructions from Peter Lisko concerning the preparation of financial statements for the year ended May 31, 1993. After reviewing the preliminary statements Lisko instructed Miraldi to capitalize some ordinary repairs and to charge some unrelated maintenance labor cost to the installation of new equipment. (The effect of these transactions will be to decrease current expenses and thus increase net income.) Lisko also directed Miraldi not to record a May 30 purchase and to omit it from the inventory.

Miraldi met with Lisko to tell him that she believes these actions are contrary to proper accounting practice and may materially misstate the financial statements (that is, make the financial statements materially incorrect). Lisko told Miraldi that he did not think these actions violated generally accepted accounting principles and that these principles were just guidelines anyway. He explained the loan conditions to her and said, "The loan conditions were sweeteners suggested by the bank's loan officer to get the loan application by the bank's loan committee. We are bound by the loan conditions but not by generally accepted accounting principles. Therefore, I want you to do as I told you so that these loan conditions are met!"

(IMA adapted)

REQUIRED:

1. Discuss the ethical considerations that Joan Miraldi should recognize in this situation.
2. Identify possible courses of action that are available to Joan Miraldi in this situation.
3. Recommend the course of action you would follow, explaining the reasons for recommending this course of action, and discussing the consequences, if any, of this course of action.

P6-3
Ethical Situation
LO 1

The Curry Company has been a manufacturer of office machines for over 40 years. Curry was both innovative and aggressive during the era of mechanical office machines, and by the first half of its corporate life it had a 35% share of its market. However, the company was slow to develop electronic office machines.

Curry's market share was reduced by one-half when its competitors introduced electronic machines. This resulted in excess capacity in both of its plants and a shortage of capacity at many of its competitors'.

Curry reacted to this situation by retooling both plants. The main plant has been reorganized as the Cojeen Division and now produces a line of simple, low-cost, high-quality electronic office machines. The other plant has been reorganized as the Belding Division and produces the consoles, racks, tables, and trays used with office computers and word processors. The Belding Division derives 80% of its sales from a former competitor. Top management at Curry, in addition to reorganizing the company, became extremely cost-conscious and implemented a freeze on base salaries as part of its cost-reduction programs.

Ken Bender, Belding Division controller, has become aware that Susan Stans, the Belding sales manager, has routinely claimed what appeared to be excessive and unsubstantiated travel expenses. The expense claims are regularly approved by Bob Porter, Belding Division manager. Concerned about the possible consequences to the division, Bender asked Porter about this situation.

Porter, in the privacy of his office, told Bender, "In the two years that Sue Stans has been the sales manager we have not lost a single important customer. She knows our customers' business and has worked closely with them so they will remain customers. I can't authorize a salary increase because of the freeze, so I told her the company wouldn't look too closely at her expense accounts for a while."

Porter also asked Bender to help Ron Warren, the production manager, "by making whatever entries are needed to increase the gross margin percentage." This would increase Warren's bonus, which is based in part upon gross margin percentage. Porter added, "If these key people are not given monetary increases in some way they may leave us, something I want to avoid at all costs."

(IMA adapted)

REQUIRED:

1. Ken Bender has already approached Bob Porter regarding the padded expense accounts of Susan Stans.
   a. Identify other alternative courses of action Bender should consider taking.
   b. Select the course of action you think Bender should take and explain why you selected this course of action.
2. Explain why Ken Bender should refuse the division manager's request to manipulate the gross margin percentage.
3. Assume Bob Porter insists on manipulating the gross margin percentage in order to help Ron Warren.
   a. Identify the alternative courses of action that Ken Bender should consider taking.
   b. Select the course of action you think Bender should take and explain why you selected this course of action.

P6-4
Internal Control
LO 3

William Stolen works in the accounting department of Computech, a retail minicomputer store. He is in charge of the purchasing function as well as accounts payable. Many of the computers purchased by Computech are delivered by the manufacturer directly to Computech's clients without first being delivered to the Computech store.

Stolen decided to divert the firm's computers to his own use in the hope of opening his own store. In order to do this, Stolen did the following: He first prepared fake purchase orders under Computech's name for computers and peripheral equipment. He had the suppliers deliver the merchandise to a little store he rented called Specialty Computer Sales. When the order arrived at Specialty, Stolen entered them in the proper manner on Computech's books.

When the invoices were due, Stolen prepared the checks and sent them to the treasurer for signature. Based on a purchase order and vendor's invoice, the checks were signed and mailed to the vendor.

REQUIRED:

1. Discuss the weaknesses in internal control, if any, in the system just described.
2. What suggestions would you make?

P6-5
Internal Control
LO 3

The Lovable Egg Society operates a small museum in Minneapolis. Members of the Society are allowed to enter the museum free of charge. Nonmembers pay a $2 entrance fee, which is collected by two clerks stationed at the museum entrance.

At the end of each day, one of the clerks takes the proceeds to the museum treasurer. The treasurer then counts the cash in the presence of the clerk and puts the cash in the safe. On Friday of each week, the clerk takes the cash to the bank and receives a signed deposit slip from the bank clerk, which serves as the basis for the weekly entry to the company's accounting records.

REQUIRED:

1. Identify the weaknesses in the internal control system.
2. What recommendations would you make?

P6-6
Computer Controls
LO 4

The flow of transactions through Trent Distributors order entry system is illustrated in the following system flowchart.

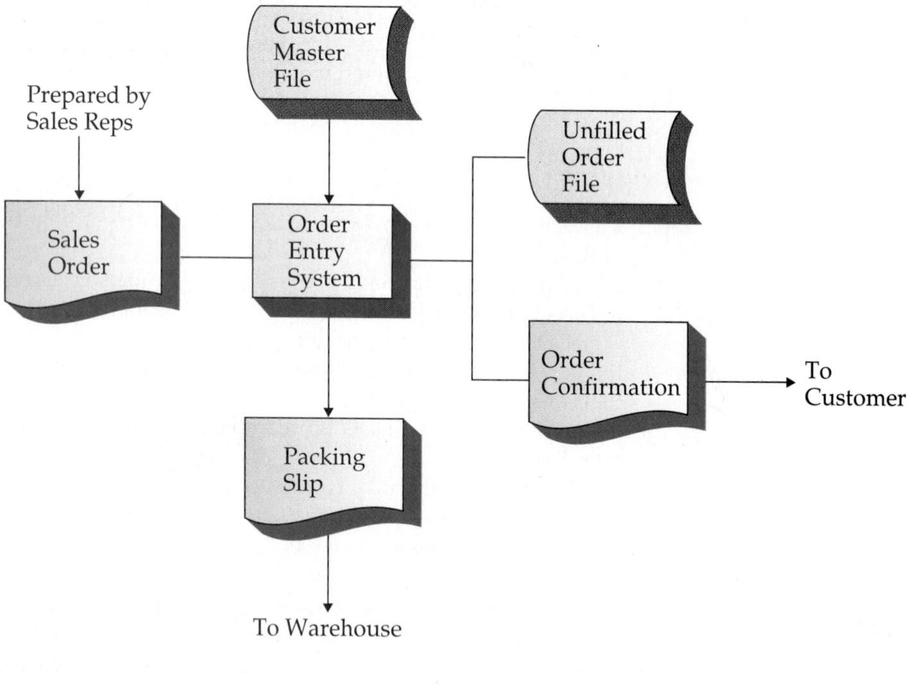

REQUIRED:

1. List the possible errors that could occur in the processing cycle.
2. For each possible error, list at least one control procedure that could be used to prevent or detect and correct the error.

P6-7
Application Controls
LO 4

Max's Janitorial is a home-based business. Max hires college students to clean local businesses. All of the cleaning supplies and equipment are stored in Max's garage. Student's pick up the supplies and equipment that they need to clean their assigned businesses every night. Max uses a computer-based inventory control system to keep track of the supplies and the jobs for which they are used.

The employees log onto the computer system by typing their first names. The system asks them to list the supplies that they are taking and the job on which they will be used. This information is used to update the supplies inventory and to bill customers for the supplies used to clean their offices. Max has noticed that he seems to be losing a little more money each month on supplies. He doesn't seem to be billing his customers enough for the supplies used. This is surprising because the total amount billed to customers for supplies used has been increasing each month.

REQUIRED:

1. Identify the potential internal control weakness in Max's inventory system.
2. Identify the potential cause of the increase in supplies billings and the increasing loss on supplies billed.
3. Identify specific control procedures that Max should use to prevent the problems and weakness that you have identified.

P6-8
Computer Controls
LO 4

Cimmaron Distributors is an autoparts firms that owns 23 retail stores in the Mid-West. The firm's purchasing and warehouse operations are located in Perkins, Oklahoma. Buyers prepare and send purchase orders to manufacturing firms to order the goods that are stocked in the warehouse. Warehouse clerks open shipments from manufacturers, inspect the goods, and enter receipt information on a computer terminal located in the warehouse.

The following data are input into a computer terminal each time goods are received:

Purchase order number
Item number
Quantity received
Quality code
Receipt date

The quality code indicates whether the goods received meet Cimmaron's quality standard (code = "OK") or whether the goods are substandard (code = "XX").

REQUIRED: For each data item entered, identify the edits that you would expect to find in a well-designed receiving data entry program.

DISCUSSION AND INTERPRETATION PROBLEMS

D6-1
Understanding Financial Statements

The following statement was taken from a recent annual report of Toys "R" Us:

Report of Management

Responsibility for the integrity and objectivity of the financial information presented in this Annual Report rests with Toys "R" Us management. The accompanying financial statements have been prepared from accounting records which management believes fairly and accurately reflect the operations and financial position of the Company. Management has established a system of internal controls to provide reasonable assurance that assets are maintained and accounted for in accordance with its policies and that transactions are recorded accurately on the Company's books and records.

The Company's comprehensive internal audit program provides for constant evaluation of the adequacy of and adherence to management's established policies and procedures. The Company has distributed to key employees its policies for conducting business affairs in a lawful and ethical manner.

The financial statements of the Company have been audited by Deloitte & Touche, independent auditors. Their accompanying report is based on an audit conducted in accordance with generally accepted auditing standards, including a review of internal accounting controls and financial reporting matters.

Charles Lazarus Chairman of the Board and Chief Executive Officer	Michael Goldstein Vice Chairman—Chief Financial and Administrative Officer

REQUIRED: Review the Toys "R" Us Management Report. Compare and contrast this report to the report suggested by the Framework Study detailed in the chapter. How does it compare?

D6-2 Understanding Financial Statements

The following statement of corporate social responsibility was taken from a recent annual report of Reebok International Ltd.

The main focus of **The Reebok Foundation** is to promote individual freedom and social change, and to challenge others to help solve society's common problems. The Foundation's traditional approach has been to provide grants to qualified non-profit organizations that offer services to meet educational, welfare, cultural and civic needs.

Active involvement with the nation's minority communities was increased during 1990, as The Reebok Foundation took steps to help introduce organizations like the Eastern Massachusetts Chapter of The National Urban League and the Jackie Robinson Foundation, to Boston area corporations. This helping-people-to-help-themselves philosophy is characteristic of The Foundation's hands-on approach to corporate philanthropy.

In addition, during the past year, the Company increased its involvement with the nation's minority communities via expanded advertising schedules in minority-owned media, the placing of deposits in minority banks, the increased use of minority professional services, as well as a renewed effort to increase the Company's minority hiring.

Reebok's social responsibility also embraces the fundamental principles of freedom of expression and **human rights** worldwide.

The Third Annual Reebok Human Rights Award Ceremony substantially furthered the Company's human rights agenda, as more than 1,700 people jammed a Boston hotel in December to hear a host of international entertainers present Reebok awards to human rights activists from around the world.

The concept of the Friends of the Reebok Human Rights Award was also established last year and, for the future, will see human rights activists from the fields of entertainment, sports, academia and business, for starters, carry out human rights consciousness-raising activities on behalf of the Reebok award program.

As time and resources allow, Reebok's human rights activities will continue to expand as a clear and unique statement of how one company chooses to make a difference!

Source: 1990 Annual Report of Reebok International Ltd., Stoughton, MA.

The company does not include a report of management responsibility in its annual report.

REQUIRED:

1. Reebok International Ltd. is one of the few companies to include such a statement in its annual report. Do you think that such a statement should be required of all publicly held companies? Why or why not?

2. Do you think that such a social responsibility statement should take the place of a statement on management responsibility like the one suggested by the Framework Study? Why or why not?

D6-3
Financial Decision Case

The Metro Gold Store is owned by two partners, Ed Roebuck and Sharon Sears. Their primary business is the purchase and resale of gold bars and gold coins. Each day a large number of cash receipts and disbursements are made. All transactions are conducted by check. The company has grown in recent years, and the firm has been able to obtain a $200,000 line of credit from the bank.

Controlling the daily cash balance is an important aspect of their business. Ed is primarily in charge of this aspect. At the end of each day, he calls the bank and finds out what the current balance is in their account. He then adds the amount of the day's deposits, and this gives him the amount of cash available to use. He then writes checks for that amount, and in some cases, in excess of that amount. He feels comfortable writing checks in excess of the amount available, because he knows that it will take a few days before those checks are paid.

As the firm's business has expanded, the available cash balance has continued to decrease, and they have been forced to use most of their line of credit. They are both happy with the increase in their sales as the price of gold has increased, but they are concerned about their cash position.

REQUIRED:

1. Comment on the procedures that Ed uses to control the firm's cash. Explain to him why he may not be getting an accurate cash figure.
2. What circumstances could cause their cash problems as their sales continue to rise?
3. Describe several procedures the firm could institute to gain better control over the daily cash balance.

D6-4
Research Assignment

The text made reference to several well-publicized cases of fraudulent financial reporting. From your library obtain two articles describing the events from one of the following cases:

a. E.S.M Government Securities
b. BCCI
c. ZZZZ Best

REQUIRED: Briefly describe the fraudulent reporting that took place and how the case was resolved (one page). Attach copies of the articles that you obtained.

D6-5
Research Assignment—Computer Controls

Visit the computer center at your college or university and identify the general controls that have been implemented.

REQUIRED: Write a brief report summarizing the potential risks at your school's computer center and the controls that have been designed to reduce those risks.

COMPREHENSIVE CASES

C6-1 A Review of the Annual Report of Nordstrom Inc.[1]

The following questions relate to the financial statements of Nordstrom, Inc., for the year ended January 31, 1992. (See pages 290–293 for selected financial information.) Answer each of them to the fullest extent possible.

1. What is the date on the balance sheet?
2. What does "consolidated" mean?
3. How much is shown for total assets for Nordstrom at January 31, 1992? How much is shown for current assets?
4. What is the total amount shown for noncurrent assets?
5. What does "net" mean in the account titled "Property, buildings, and equipment, net"?
6. Are all Nordstrom's assets listed on the balance sheet? If not, what do you think is missing?
7. How much is shown for total liabilities at January 31, 1992?
8. Do you think that all of Nordstrom's liabilities are shown on the balance sheet? If not, what do you think is missing?
9. How much is total stockholders' equity at January 31, 1992? How much represents retained earnings?
10. Is the date on the income statement the same as the date on the balance sheet? Why or why not?
11. How much is the sales revenue for the fiscal year ended January 31, 1992? Is this the same as cash collection from customers? Explain.
12. What is the total for costs and expenses for the fiscal year ended January 31, 1992? Can you determine how much is related to advertising? Explain.
13. How much was Nordstrom's net income for the fiscal year ended January 31, 1992? How does that amount compare with the net incomes for the prior two years?
14. What was the total amount paid in dividends during the fiscal year ended January 31, 1992? How does this amount compare with the total dividends paid in each of the two prior years? Are dividends an expense? Explain.
15. Describe the purposes of the statement of cash flows. Did cash and cash equivalents increase or decrease during each of the three years presented?
16. For the year ended January 31, 1992, the net cash inflow from operations was $153,987,000. Why is that not equal to the net earnings for the same period?
17. How much cash was paid to acquire new property, buildings, and equipment during the fiscal year ended January 31, 1992?

Nordstrom, Inc. and Subsidiaries
Consolidated Statements of Earnings
(dollars in thousands except per share amounts)

	Year ended January 31, 1992	*% of Sales*	*Year ended January 31, 1991*	*% of Sales*	*Year ended January 31, 1990*	*% of Sales*
Net sales	$3,179,820	100.0	$2,893,904	100.0	$2,671,114	100.0
Costs and expenses:						
Cost of sales and related buying and occupancy expenses	2,169,437	68.2	2,000,250	69.1	1,829,383	68.5

(continued)

1. This case was adapted from one prepared by Professor Mark Defond of the School of Accounting at the University of Southern California, and is used with his permission.

	Year ended January 31, 1992	*% of Sales*	*Year ended January 31, 1991*	*% of Sales*	*Year ended January 31, 1990*	*% of Sales*
Selling, general and administrative	831,505	26.2	747,770	25.8	669,159	25.1
Interest, net	49,106	1.5	52,228	1.8	49,121	1.8
Service charge income and other, net	(87,443)	(2.7)	(84,660)	(2.9)	(55,958)	(2.1)
Total costs and expenses	2,962,605	93.2	2,715,588	93.8	2,491,705	93.3
Earnings before income taxes	217,215	6.8	178,316	6.2	179,409	6.7
Income taxes	81,400	2.5	62,500	2.2	64,500	2.4
Net earnings	$ 135,815	4.3	$ 115,816	4.0	$ 114,909	4.3
Net earnings per share	$ 1.66		$ 1.42		$ 1.41	
Cash dividends paid per share	$ .31		$ .30		$ .28	

Nordstrom, Inc. and Subsidiaries
Consolidated Balance Sheets
(dollars in thousands)

	January 31, 1992	*1991*
Assets		
Current assets:		
Cash and equivalents	$ 14,651	$ 24,662
Accounts receivable, net	608,227	575,508
Merchandise inventories	506,632	448,344
Prepaid expenses	48,128	41,865
Total current assets	1,177,638	1,090,379
Property, buildings and equipment, net	856,404	806,191
Other assets	7,833	6,019
Total assets	$2,041,875	$1,902,589
Liabilities and Shareholders' Equity		
Current liabilities:		
Notes payable	$ 134,735	$ 149,506
Accounts payable	216,432	204,266
Accrued salaries, wages and taxes	145,792	128,697
Accrued expenses	31,741	34,668
Accrued income taxes	16,402	24,268
Current portion of long-term liabilities	8,801	10,430
Total current liabilities	553,903	551,835
Long-term debt	482,275	457,718
Obligations under capitalized leases	19,924	21,024
Deferred income taxes	46,542	45,602
Contingent liabilities		
Shareholders' equity	939,231	826,410
Total liabilities and shareholders' equity	$2,041,875	$1,902,589

Nordstrom, Inc. and Subsidiaries
Consolidated Statements of Stockholders' Equity
(dollars in thousands except per share amounts)

	Year Ended January 31,		
	1992	*1991*	*1990*
Common stock			
Authorized 250,000,000 shares, issued and outstanding 81,844,227, 81,737,910 and 81,584,710 shares			
Balance at beginning of year	$150,699	$148,857	$147,629
Issuance of common stock	2,356	1,842	1,228
Balance at end of year	153,055	150,699	148,857
Retained Earnings			
Balance at beginning of year	675,711	584,393	492,312
Net earnings	135,815	115,816	114,909
Cash dividends paid ($.31, $.30 and $.28 per share)	(25,350)	(24,498)	(22,828)
Balance at end of year	786,176	675,711	584,393
Total shareholders' equity	$939,231	$826,410	$733,250

Nordstrom, Inc. and Subsidiaries
Consolidated Statements of Cash Flows
(dollars in thousands)

	Year Ended January 31,		
	1992	*1991*	*1990*
Operating Activities			
Net earnings	$135,815	$115,816	$114,909
Adjustments to reconcile net earnings to net cash provided by operating activities:			
Depreciation and amortization	96,034	85,615	70,873
Change in:			
Accounts receivable, net	(32,719)	(39,234)	(54,694)
Merchandise inventories	(58,288)	(28,368)	(16,181)
Prepaid expenses	(6,263)	(20,018)	(9,294)
Accounts payable	12,166	8,928	4,583
Accrued salaries, wages and taxes	17,095	6,090	28,238
Accrued expenses	(2,927)	5,588	2,628
Income tax liabilities	(6,926)	13,710	(18,907)
Net cash provided by operating activities	153,987	148,127	122,155
Investing Activities			
Additions to property, buildings and equipment, net	(145,761)	(199,407)	(168,462)
Other investments, net	(1,393)	(1,277)	(237)
Net cash used in investing activities	(147,154)	(200,684)	(168,699)
Financing Activities			
(Decrease) increase in notes payable	(14,771)	46,933	6,670
Proceeds from issuance of long-term debt	107,475	100,000	100,000
Debt issue costs	(907)	(869)	(729)

(continued)

	Year Ended January 31,		
	1992	1991	1990
Proceeds from issuance of common stock	2,356	1,842	1,228
Principal payments on long-term debt and obligations under capitalized leases	(85,647)	(79,240)	(20,804)
Cash dividends paid	(25,350)	(24,498)	(22,828)
Net cash (used in) provided by financing activities	(16,844)	44,168	63,537
Net (decrease) increase in cash and cash equivalents	(10,011)	(8,389)	16,993
Cash and cash equivalents at beginning of year	24,662	33,051	16,058
Cash and cash equivalents at end of year	$ 14,651	$ 24,662	$ 33,051

C6-2 Review of Accounting Transactions

On January 2, 1995, John Naperski started his own CPA firm. During the year the following summary events occurred:

1. Naperski invested $170,000 cash, in exchange for capital stock, in order to start his practice.
2. Two years' rent of $19,200 was paid in advance on January 3, 1995.
3. Office supplies of $8,200 were purchased for cash.
4. Office furniture and fixtures were purchased for $25,000 cash.
5. Office equipment of $5,000 was purchased on account.
6. Marketable securities for short-term investment were purchased for $95,000 cash.
7. Fees earned during the first half of the year were $42,000, of which $22,000 was on credit and the remainder was for cash.
8. A $5,000 advance for services yet to be performed was received in cash.
9. Utilities expense for the first half of the year amounted to $750 and was paid in cash.
10. Salaries of $19,200 were paid in cash during the first half of the year.
11. On July 1, the firm purchased a comprehensive three-year insurance policy for $6,000 cash.
12. Supplies costing $3,400 were purchased on account.
13. The firm accepted a $15,000 note receivable from a client for services rendered on August 1, 1995. The note has an interest rate of 10% and is due in a year.
14. On November 1, the firm paid $3,000 cash in advance for a three-year subscription to a professional journal.
15. The firm paid the full amount due for office equipment purchased in item 5.
16. The firm returned $1,500 of the supplies purchased in item 12 because they were defective. Its account was credited, and the remaining balance was paid in full.
17. Supplies costing $2,500 were purchased on account.
18. Fees earned during the second half of the year amounted to $63,000, of which 85% was on credit and the remainder was received in cash.
19. One-half of the marketable securities were sold for $49,000 cash.
20. The following expenses were paid in cash during the second half of the year:

Salaries	$13,900
Utilities	950
Legal	1,500

21. Cash collections on accounts receivable were $34,000.
22. Land was purchased for $25,000 cash.
23. Naperski withdrew $12,000 cash as a dividend.

Additional information:

a. Interest on the note receivable must be accrued.
b. The necessary amount of prepaid insurance must be written off.
c. The necessary amount of prepaid subscriptions must be written off.
d. Prepaid rent must be written off.
e. Supplies on hand at December 31, 1995, amounted to $3,700.
f. The office furniture and fixtures have a seven-year life and a $4,000 salvage value.
g. The office equipment has a five-year life and no salvage value.
h. Salaries of $1,300 were earned but unpaid at year-end.
i. Fees of $2,000 were earned at year-end, for which the receivable and the revenue have not yet been recorded.
j. The tax rate is 30% on income before taxes.

The firm's chart of accounts is as follows:

Cash	101
Marketable securities	102
Accounts receivable	103
Note receivable	104
Interest receivable	105
Supplies	106
Prepaid rent	107
Prepaid insurance	108
Prepaid subscriptions	109
Land	110
Office furniture and fixtures	120
Accumulated depreciation—office furniture and fixtures	130
Office equipment	140
Accumulated depreciation—office equipment	150
Accounts payable	201
Unearned accounting fees	202
Salaries payable	203
Taxes payable	204
Capital stock	300
Retained earnings	310
Accounting fees earned	400
Supplies expense	500
Salaries expense	501
Legal expense	502
Utility expense	503
Subscription expense	504
Insurance expense	505
Rent expense	506
Depreciation expense	507
Taxes expense	510
Gain on sale of marketable securities	600
Interest revenue	610
Income summary	1000

REQUIRED: Depending on your instructor's directions, use either T accounts or a three-column running balance ledger account in completing the following work. If required by your instructor, item (3) can be prepared on a worksheet.

1. Make the summary journal entries for the year, and post them to the ledger accounts. As a posting reference, use the number of the account and page 1 of the general journal.

2. Prepare an unadjusted trial balance.
3. In order to complete the accounting cycle:
   a. Prepare the adjusting entries and post them to the ledger accounts.
   b. Prepare an adjusted trial balance.
4. Prepare an income statement, a retained earnings statement, and a statement of cash flows for the year ended December 31, 1995.
5. Prepare closing entries and post them to the ledger accounts.
6. Prepare a post-closing trial balance.
7. Prepare a classified balance sheet as of December 31, 1995.

C6-3
Interpreting Financial Statements

The financial statements of Walgreen Co. and selected footnotes are reproduced below. Based on these financial statements and data, answer the following questions:

1. The income statement shows a category called selling, occupancy, and administration. Describe in your own words the nature of these expenses.
2. What is the amount of accounts receivable prior to any deduction for doubtful accounts at August 31, 1991 and 1990? What kind of account is allowance for doubtful accounts?
3. What is the amount of the accumulated depreciation and amortization at August 31, 1991 and 1990?
4. Did the company's cash and cash equivalents increase or decrease from 1990 to 1991? What are the primary reasons for this increase or decrease?
5. What depreciation method does Walgreen employ? What is the amount of depreciation and amortization expense for the years ended August 31, 1991 and 1990?
6. What was the per share amount of dividends issued in fiscal 1991 and 1990? What was the total amount of dividends issued in each of these years? What was the amount of dividends paid during fiscal years 1991 and 1990? Why do you think that the amount of dividends declared does not equal the amount of dividends paid?
7. On the face of the balance sheet only one amount is shown for the following items:
   Other Non-Current Assets
   Accrued Expenses and Other Liabilities
   Other Non-Current Liabilities
   However, in the footnotes, these items are described in more detail. What principles or concepts are involved in Walgreen's decision to disclose the information in this manner?

Supplementary Financial Information

The Consolidated Statements of Earnings include advertising costs of $78,700,000 in 1991, $76,042,000 in 1990 and $77,952,000 in 1989.

Included in the Consolidated Balance Sheets captions are the following assets and liabilities (in thousands):

	1991	*1990*
Other Non-Current Assets:		
Cash surrender value of life insurance	$ 37,605	$24,923
Other	314	4,446
	$ 37,919	$ 29,369
Accrued Expenses and Other Liabilities:		
Accrued salaries	$ 78,966	$ 73,508
Taxes other than income taxes	39,941	33,985
Insurance	45,982	37,788
Accrued rent	38,626	34,236
Other	93,869	81,936
	$297,384	$261,453

(continued)

	1991	*1990*
Other Non-Current Liabilities:		
Deferred compensation	$ 17,965	$ 14,882
Obligations under capital leases	13,166	16,060
	$ 31,131	$ 30,942

8. Who are the firm's auditors? What type of audit opinion did Walgreen receive?
9. Calculate the following ratios or financial statistics at August 31, 1991 and 1990, or for the years ended August 31, 1991 and 1990, if appropriate.
   a. Net working capital
   b. Current ratio
   c. Debt-to-equity ratio
   d. Total-debt-to-total-assets ratio
   e. Gross profit percentage
   f. Profit margin percentage
   g. Return on total assets

Walgreen Co. and Subsidiaries
Consolidated Balance Sheets
At August 31, 1991 and 1990

(dollars in thousands)

Assets	*1991*	*1990*
Current Assets		
Cash and cash equivalents	$ 72,011	$ 207,925
Marketable securities, at cost which approximates market	63,126	5,941
Accounts receivable, net of allowances for doubtful accounts of $11,783 in 1991 and $6,262 in 1990	132,407	97,608
Inventories	911,995	827,997
Other current assets	67,884	47,574
Total current assets	1,247,423	1,187,045
Non-Current Assets		
Property and Equipment, at cost, less accumulated depreciation and amortization	809,295	697,170
Other Non-Current Assets	37,919	29,369
Total Assets	$2,094,637	$1,913,584
Liabilities and Shareholders' Equity		
Current liabilities:		
Trade accounts payable	$ 365,540	$ 348,526
Accrued expenses and other liabilities	297,384	261,453
Income taxes	16,696	19,070
Current maturities of long-term debt	4,177	3,240
Total Current Liabilities	683,797	632,289
Long-Term Obligations		
Long-Term Debt, net of current maturities:		
General company obligations	118,925	122,675
Real estate obligations	4,035	24,065
	122,960	146,740
Deferred Income Taxes	175,592	156,364
Other Non-Current Liabilities	31,131	30,942

(continued)

Liabilities and Shareholders' Equity	*1991*	*1990*
Shareholders' equity		
Preferred stock, $.50 par value; authorized 4,000,000 shares; none issued	—	—
Common stock, $.625 par value; authorized 400,000,000 shares; issued and outstanding 123,070,536 in 1991 and 123,047,872 in 1990, at stated value	76,919	76,905
Retained earnings	1,004,238	870,344
	1,081,157	947,249
Total Liabilities and Shareholders' Equity	$2,094,637	$1,913,584

The accompanying statement of major accounting policies is an integral part of these statements.

10. Compare and contrast the company's performance from 1990 to 1991.
11. Obtain from your library average ratios for retail drug stores and compare the ratios you calculted for Walgreen in items 9 and 10 with the average ratios that you obtained.
12. Obtain from your library a recent article about Walgreen and the analysis of Walgreen by an investment service such as *Moody's Investors Service* or *Standard & Poor's Industrial Surveys*. Given the information you obtained in items 9 through 12, how well is Walgreen doing? Explain your answer.

Walgreen Co. and Subsidiaries
Consolidated Statements of Cash Flows
For the Years Ended August 31, 1991, 1990, and 1989

(dollars in thousands)

Fiscal Year	*1991*	*1990*	*1989*
Cash Flows from Operating Activities			
Net earnings	$194,965	$174,577	$154,242
Adjustments to reconcile net earnings to net cash provided by operating activities—			
Depreciation and amortization	84,346	70,375	63,752
LIFO inventory provision	40,288	38,781	38,793
Deferred income taxes	19,228	23,287	17,131
Loss on disposition of assets	4,118	—	6,114
Other	(685)	1,423	294
Changes in current assets and liabilities:			
Inventories at FIFO	(124,286)	(138,234)	(115,271)
Trade accounts payable	17,014	48,970	44,007
Accrued expenses and other liabilities	30,857	26,177	27,354
Income taxes	(18,343)	(9,315)	(34,790)
Accounts receivable, net	(30,799)	(4,243)	(13,249)
Other current assets	(4,341)	7,339	(4,956)
Net cash provided by operating activities	212,362	239,137	183,421
Cash (Used for) Provided by Investing Activities			
Additions to property and equipment	(202,452)	(191,697)	(121,322)
Investment in marketable securities	(57,185)	(995)	(1,930)
Proceeds from disposition of property and equipment	3,847	3,111	9,059
Investment in corporate-owned life insurance	(8,914)	(8,983)	(8,983)
Other	132	111	92
Net cash used for investing activities	(264,572)	(198,543)	(123,084)

(continued)

Fiscal Year	*1991*	*1990*	*1989*
Cash Used for Financing Activities			
Cash dividends paid	(54,770)	(47,369)	(40,603)
Payments of long-term obligations	(24,460)	(4,452)	(4,198)
Cost of employee stock purchase and option plans	(4,474)	(1,533)	(1,663)
Net cash used for financing activities	(83,704)	(53,354)	(46,464)
Changes in Cash and Cash Equivalents			
Net (decrease) increase in cash and cash equivalents	(135,914)	(12,670)	13,873
Cash and cash equivalents at beginning of year	207,925	220,595	206,722
Cash and cash equivalents at end of year	$ 72,011	$207,925	$220,595

The accompanying statement of major accounting policies is an integral part of these statements.

Walgreen Co. and Subsidiaries
Consolidated Statements of Earnings and Retained Earnings
For the Years Ended August 31, 1991, 1990, and 1989
(dollars in thousands except per share data)

Earnings	*1991*	*1990*	*1989*
Net Sales	$6,733,044	$6,047,494	$5,380,133
Costs and Deductions			
Cost of Sales	4,829,186	4,356,392	3,848,546
Selling, occupancy and administration	1,582,725	1,406,922	1,278,116
	6,411,911	5,763,314	5,126,662
Other Expense (Income)			
Interest expense	18,157	18,813	18,841
Interest income	(13,086)	(15,556)	(15,323)
Loss on disposition of assets	4,118	—	6,114
	9,189	3,257	9,632
Earnings			
Earnings before income tax provision	311,944	280,923	243,839
Income tax provision	116,979	106,346	89,597
Net earnings	$ 194,965	$ 174,577	$ 154,242
Net Earnings per Common Share	$ 1.58	$ 1.41	$ 1.25

Retained Earnings	*1991*	*1990*	*1989*
Balance, beginning of year	$ 870,344	$ 746,505	$ 635,752
Net earnings	194,965	174,577	154,242
Cash dividends declared: $.46 per share in 1991, $.40 in 1990 and $.34 in 1989	(56,618)	(49,216)	(41,834)
Employee stock purchase and option plans	(4,453)	(1,522)	(1,655)
Balance, end of year	$1,004,238	$ 870,344	$ 746,505

The accompanying statement of major accounting policies is an integral part of these statements.

Walgreen Co. and Subsidiaries
Statement of Major Accounting Policies

Principles of Consolidation

The consolidated statements include the accounts of the Company and all majority-owned subsidiaries. All significant intercompany transactions have been eliminated. Certain amounts in the 1990 and 1989 Consolidated Financial Statements have been reclassified to be consistent with the 1991 presentation.

Pre-Opening Expenses

Non-capital expenditures incurred prior to the opening of a new or remodeled store are charged against earnings when they are incurred.

Cash and Cash Equivalents

Cash and cash equivalents include cash on hand and all highly liquid investments with an original maturity of three months or less. All other temporary investments are classified as marketable securities.

Inventories

Inventories are valued on a last-in, first-out (LIFO) cost basis. At August 31, 1991 and 1990, inventories would have been greater by $325,431,000 and $285,143,000 respectively, if they had been valued on a lower of first-in, first-out (FIFO) cost or market basis. Cost of sales is primarily computed on an estimated basis and adjusted based on physical inventories which are taken at all locations at least annually.

Property and Equipment

Depreciation is provided on a straight-line basis over the estimated useful lives of owned assets. Leasehold improvements and leased properties under capital leases are amortized over the estimated physical life of the property or over the term of the lease, whichever is shorter. Major repairs which extend the useful life of an asset are charged to the property and equipment accounts. Routine maintenance and repairs are charged against earnings. The composite method of depreciation is used for equipment; therefore, gains and losses on retirement or other disposition of such assets are included in earnings only when an operating location is closed or completely remodeled. Fully depreciated property and equipment are removed from the cost and related accumulated depreciation and amortization accounts.

Property and equipment consists of (in thousands):

	1991	*1990*
Land and land improvement	$ 23,696	$ 16,720
Buildings and building improvements	350,120	307,169
Equipment	711,369	607,015
Strategic Inventory Management System	41,971	31,744
Capital lease properties	27,426	30,384
	1,154,582	993,032
Less accumulated depreciation and amortization	345,287	295,862
	$ 809,295	$697,170

In fiscal 1987, the Company commenced development of the Strategic Inventory Management System. All direct costs associated with the development of this system are being capitalized and will be amortized over a five-year period as phases of the project are implemented. Amortization of these costs began in 1989 and were $2,876,000, $804,000 and $200,000 in 1991, 1990 and 1989, respectively.

Income Taxes

The Company provides federal and state income taxes on items included in the Consolidated Statements of Earnings regardless of the period when such taxes are payable. Deferred income taxes result from timing differences in the recognition of income and expense for tax and financial reporting purposes. These timing differences principally result from additional tax deductions available due to the use of accelerated methods of depreciation.

Adoption of Financial Accounting Standards Board Statement No. 96 "Accounting for Income Taxes" is required by fiscal 1993. The Statement requires the adjustment of deferred and current income tax liabilities to reflect current tax rates rather than tax rates in effect at the time the liabilities arose. The Company may elect to restate previously issued financial statements to reflect the cumulative effect of the change in the year of adoption. Recently, the Financial Accounting Standards Board issued proposals modifying Statement 96. The Company will await the outcome of the proposed changes before deciding when and what will have to be adopted; however, based on a preliminary review, a favorable impact on financial position is expected.

Walgreen Co. and Subsidiaries
Report of Independent Public Accountants

To the Board of Directors and Shareholders of Walgreen Co.:

We have audited the accompanying consolidated balance sheets of Walgreen Co. (an Illinois corporation) and Subsidiaries as of August 31, 1991 and 1990, and the related consolidated statements of earnings, retained earnings and cash flows for each of the three years in the period ended August 31, 1991. These financial statements are the responsibility of the Company's management. Our responsibility is to express an opinion on these financial statements based on our audits.

We conducted our audits in accordance with generally accepted auditing standards. Those standards require that we plan and perform the audit to obtain reasonable assurance about whether the financial statements are free of material misstatement. An audit includes examining, on a test basis, evidence supporting the amounts and disclosures in the financial statements. An audit also includes assessing the accounting principles used and significant estimates made by management, as well as evaluating the overall financial statement presentation. We believe that our audits provide a reasonable basis for our opinion.

In our opinion, the financial statements referred to above present fairly, in all material respects, the financial position of Walgreen Co. and Subsidiaries as of August 31, 1991 and 1990, and the results of their operations and their cash flows for each of the three years in the period ended August 31, 1991, in conformity with generally accepted accounting principles.

Arthur Andersen & Co.

Chicago, Illinois
October 4, 1991

Walgreen Co. and Subsidiaries
Management's Report

The primary responsibility for the integrity and objectivity of the consolidated financial statements and related financial data rests with the management of Walgreen Co. The financial statements were prepared in conformity with generally accepted accounting principles appropriate in the circumstances and included amounts that were based on management's most prudent judgments and estimates relating to matters not concluded by fiscal year-end. Management believes that all material uncertainties have been either appropriately accounted for or disclosed. All other financial information included in this annual report is consistent with the financial statements.

The firm of Arthur Anderson & Co., independent public accountants, was engaged to render a professional opinion on Walgreen Co.'s consolidated financial statements. Their report contains an opinion based on their audit, which was made in accordance with generally accepted auditing standards and procedures, which they believed were sufficient to provide reasonable assurance that the consolidated financial statements, considered in their entirety, are not misleading and do not contain material errors.

Three outside members of the Board of Directors comprise the Company's Audit Committee, which meets at least quarterly and is responsible for reviewing and monitoring the Company's financial and accounting practices. In order to insure and maintain complete independence, Arthur Anderson & Co. and the Company's General Auditor have access to meet alone with the Audit Committee, which also meets with Company management to discuss financial matters, auditing and internal accounting controls.

The Company's systems are designed to provide an effective system of internal accounting controls to obtain reasonable assurance at reasonable cost that assets are safeguarded from material loss or unauthorized use, and transactions are executed in accordance with management's authorization and properly recorded. To this end, management maintains an internal control environment which is shaped by established operating policies and procedures, an appropriate division of responsibility at all organizational levels, and a corporate ethics policy which is monitored annually. The Company also has an Internal Control Evaluation Committee, comprised mostly of senior management from the Accounting and Auditing Departments, which oversees the evaluation of internal controls on a Company-wide basis. Management believes it has appropriately responded to the internal auditors' and independent public accountants' recommendations concerning the Company's internal control system.

C. R. Walgreen III
Chairman of the Board
and Chief Executive Officer

R. H. Clausen
Controller
and Chief Accounting Officer

C. D. Hunter
Vice Chairman
and Chief Financial Officer

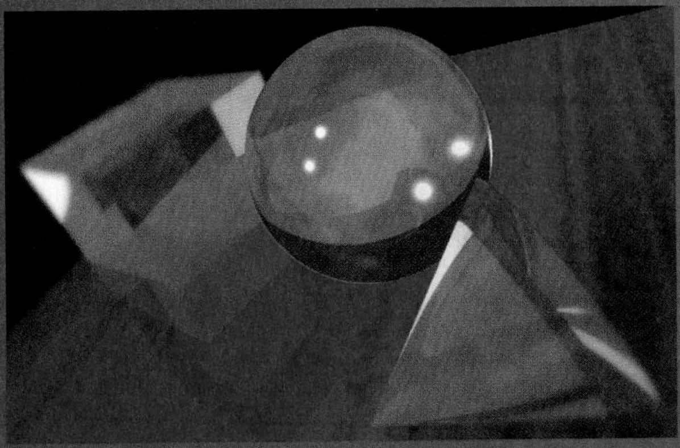

PART 2

OPERATING ACTIVITIES

Business activities include those related to operating, investing, and financing. For example, the operating cycle of a business includes the use of cash to purchase inventories for resale. These inventories are sold for receivables, which are converted back to cash to purchase more inventories. This continuous cycle generally is repeated several times a year. Investing activities are longer-term cycles involving the use of cash to purchase machinery, equipment, buildings, and similar assets to support the operations of the firm. As these assets contribute to operations they help generate additional cash flows which are used in future operations. Often, at the end of their useful life, these assets are sold for cash. Finally, financing activities such as borrowing and issuing debt and equity securities also provide cash for the purchase of machinery, equipment, inventory, and other important assets. Thus these three key categories of business activities are interrelated.

As discussed in previous chapters, the statement of cash flows is organized along the categories of operating, investing, and financing activities. This classification scheme is a useful way to discuss many accounting issues, and is the basis for the next three parts of this book. First, accounting issues that arise from operating activities, such as the generation of revenues and incurrence of expenses related to those revenues, are discussed. These topics are discussed in the three chapters that make up Part 2:

Chapter 7: The Revenue Cycle: Sales, Receivables, and Cash
Chapter 8: Expense/Payable Generation, Recognition, and Measurement
Chapter 9: Inventory Valuation

Part 3 presents issues related to investing activities, including the purchase and disposal of (1) property, plant, and equipment and (2) investments in debt and equity securities. Part 4 covers issues related to financing activities, including the issuance and retirement of (1) debt securities and (2) equity securities.

CHAPTER 7
THE REVENUE CYCLE: SALES, RECEIVABLES, AND CASH

LEARNING OBJECTIVES

After studying this chapter, you should be able to:

1. Explain how transactions are processed through the revenue cycle.
2. State the recognition and measurement issues involved in accounting for sales transactions.
3. Explain the nature of uncollectible accounts and the allowance method of accounting for uncollectible accounts.
4. Evaluate management controls over receivables.
5. Explain the classification of cash and receivables on the balance sheet.
6. List other types of revenues generated from operations.
7. Explain the revenue cycle computer system.

Scenario

It is budget planning time at the Symtoptic Medical Technology Corporation, and the weekly meeting of major corporate officers is about to begin. Present are (1) Paula Domont, the chief financial officer, (2) Leslie Vargus, the vice-president of sales, (3) Michael Moore, the chief executive officer, and (4) Calvin Freed, the head of Symtoptic's credit office.

Symtoptic is a major manufacturer and supplier of medical technology products to hospitals and clinics. The firm's sales have grown about 20% a year for the past five years and now approach $150 million. In reviewing the outlook for the current year, the CFO, Paula Domont, is quite concerned about the lingering economic recession and fears that with increased costs and decreased sales the upcoming year will see a 12–15% decline in the firm's net income, the first decline in the firm's history. The purpose of the current meeting is to see how best to respond to this gloomy economic outlook.

PAULA DOMONT: It is clear that next year is going to be tough. Industry estimates project a 15–20% decline in the purchase of medical technology products. Further, we are facing ever-increasing costs of research and development, production, and marketing that are necessary to keep pace with the competition. We need to consider steps to increase our sales.

LESLIE VARGUS: We are going to have to loosen our credit terms to increase our sales. Hospitals and clinics are being hit very hard by the recession and are having definite cash flow problems. I think we should take two immediate steps. First, let's give better credit terms by lengthening the time period for payment. Second, we should reconsider our tight credit-granting policy and allow more hospitals and clinics to purchase on credit. I recognize that there is a risk here, but we are losing sales to the competition by not providing some of our customers with credit.

CALVIN FREED: As head of the credit department, I am very much against such changes. I have done a survey, and we currently have one of the lowest bad-debt rates in the industry. I see no reason to institute new policies that may raise this rate. My department has worked very hard to keep this rate at less than 0.5% of total credit sales. Why throw money away on bad customers?

LESLIE VARGUS: I understand your concerns, Calvin, but the competition is killing us. We are losing sales every day. I know that some of these customers are not good credit risks, but clearly many of them will meet their debts. Besides, we have high gross profit margins and can handle some bad debts. Remember, if we don't make the sale, we won't collect a dime!

MICHAEL MOORE: It seems to me that you both might be correct. Although a bad-debt rate of less than 0.5% might look good, we are clearly losing sales to customers who have a reasonable probability of meeting their obligations. However, obviously we can't sell to everyone. I am going to ask Paula to do an in-depth analysis of our customers and develop a credit policy that meets our objectives of increasing sales while at the same time limiting bad debts to a reasonable amount. It just seems to me that 0.5% is probably too low.

The scenario which opened this chapter illustrates that the selection of a target amount of acceptable bad debts is more than an accounting decision, it is a business decision. As is often the case, decisions related to accounting issues have far reaching implications for businesses. Consequently, accountants must understand the effects of their decisions and actions on decision makers. This chapter examines procedures and choices related to accounting for revenue cycle transactions such as sales, accounts receivable, collections on accounts receivable, and bad debts.

THE REVENUE CYCLE

Objective 1
Explain how transactions are processed through the revenue cycle.

Most operating activities which generate revenue are processed by the revenue cycle, which is highlighted on the transaction cycle diagram illustrated in Exhibit 7-1. Sales represent the main revenue generation activity of merchandising and manufacturing firms and are the primary transaction processed by the revenue cycle. Merchandising firms such as Albertson's, Sears, and L. L. Bean purchase finished goods for resale to the public. Manufacturing firms such as Kellogg, IBM, Toyota, and Phillips produce finished goods for sale to merchandisers or dealerships while, perhaps, selling a limited quantity directly to the public.

To illustrate the various application systems in the revenue cycle for merchandising firms, recall that customer orders are first processed through the order

Exhibit 7-1
Transaction Cycles—Merchandising Firm

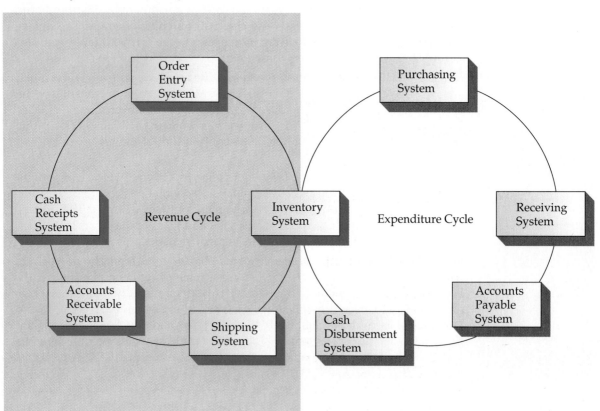

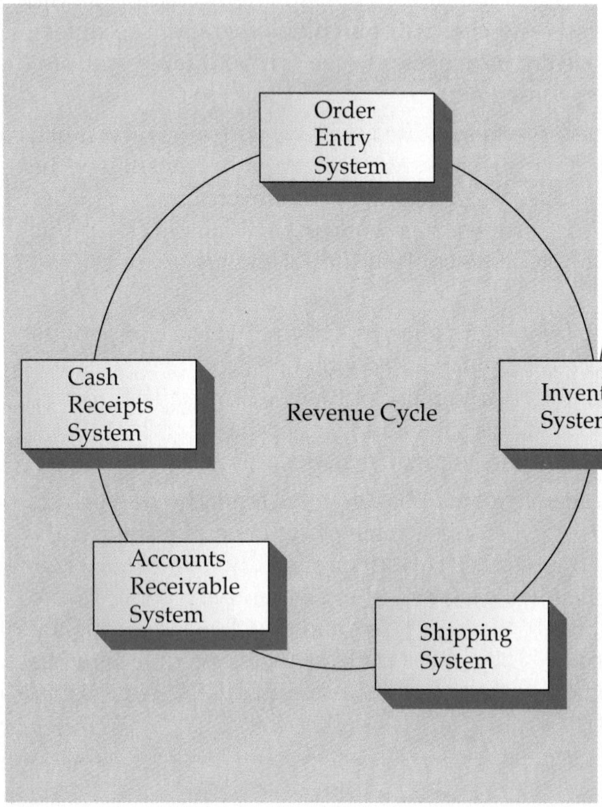

entry system. After the order has been processed, the shipping system insures that goods are withdrawn from the firm's inventory and then shipped to the customer. After the goods have been shipped, the accounts receivable system insures that the correct customer is billed on a timely basis. Finally, the customer's payment is received and processed by the cash receipts system.

Firms such as legal, accounting, and consulting firms, derive their revenues by providing services. Manufacturing firms earn revenue by selling the products that they manufacture. The transactions in service and manufacturing firms are processed by application systems similar to those found in merchandising firms.

This chapter introduces the accounting concepts that are used to process transactions through the revenue cycle. The application systems that process revenue transactions will be discussed in more detail after accounting concepts have been presented.

RECOGNITION AND MEASUREMENT OF SALES TRANSACTIONS

Objective 2
State the recognition and measurement issues involved in accounting for sales transactions.

Merchandising firms are likely to make both cash and credit sales, while manufacturing firms are more likely to make only credit sales. Revenue from sales is the dollar price of goods sold by the firm. When the sale is for cash, the amount of revenue recognized is the amount of the actual cash received (the agreed-upon sales price less any trade or quantity discounts) not including any sales taxes collected for a taxing authority. If the sale is made on credit and an account receivable arises, the amount of revenue recognized is based on the net realizable value of the receivable. The **net realizable value** of the receivable initially is the agreed-upon sales price prior to sales taxes less any trade or quantity discounts and sales discounts. Adjustments might later be made for sales returns and allowances and uncollectible accounts or bad debts.

net realizable value

Trade and Quantity Discounts and Sales Taxes

Sales are recorded at the agreed-upon sales price, and no accounting recognition is given to any trade or quantity discounts that may be allowed. Merchandising firms often allow such reductions from list or catalog prices. **Trade discounts** are price reductions offered to a certain class of buyers. For example, a furniture store may allow certain trade discounts to professional decorators but charge the general public the full retail price. **Quantity discounts** are reductions from the list price based on quantity purchases. For example, the price of pens may be $20 per dozen, but a purchase of 30 dozen may entitle the purchaser to a 10% quantity discount, thus dropping the price to $18 a dozen. Both trade and quantity discounts are adjustments to the sales price, and generally accepted accounting principles require that transactions be recorded at the agreed-upon price, net of these discounts.

trade discounts

quantity discounts

Most states and many counties and cities impose sales or excise taxes. These taxes usually are imposed on the consumer, with the retailer collecting and remitting them to the taxing authority. Upon collection the retailer recognizes a liability for the amount of the tax and does not include it in total sales revenues.

To illustrate these points, assume that Professor Bert Steece purchases a computer with a list price of $1,800 from the USC bookstore. As a faculty member Professor Steece is entitled to a trade discount of 10% on the list price. The computer is subject to a 7.5% sales tax that must be collected by the bookstore and later remitted to the California State Board of Equalization. Assuming that this is a cash sale, it would be recorded as follows:

Cash	1,741.50	
Sales		1,620.00
Sales Taxes Payable		121.50
To record cash sale computed as follows:		

List price	$1,800.00
Less: 10% trade discount	180.00
Net price	$1,620.00
Sales tax @ 7.5%	121.50
Cash collected	$1,741.50

When sales taxes are remitted to the taxing authority, the account Sales Taxes Payable is debited and the Cash account is credited.

Both trade and quantity discounts are adjustments to the sales price and may result from either cash or credit sales. Although financial reporting rules do not require explicit recognition of trade or quantity discounts, management may want to keep records of these discounts to monitor their quantity and effectiveness. This can be important in certain retail areas, such as automobile dealerships, in which discounts from the list price are common and salespeople are paid on a commission basis. The indiscriminate use of discounts may be in the salesperson's short-run best interest but not in the long-run best interest of the firm. By establishing a separate discount account (offset against the sales account when external financial statements are prepared), discounts can be monitored and potential problems controlled.

Sales taxes apply only to retail sales; they do not apply to goods sold by a manufacturer to a merchandiser for resale. For example, sales by Compaq, a computer manufacturer, to a computer retailer are not subject to sales taxes. The taxes are levied when the retailer sells the computer to a customer. However, other types of excise taxes and/or luxury taxes may be levied at different stages of production and/or sale.

Sales Discounts

sales discounts

Sales discounts arise only when sales are made on credit, and usually apply only to sales made by a manufacturer to a merchandiser. **Sales discounts** are cash reductions offered to customers who purchase merchandise on account and pay for the goods within a specific time period. The discount is a means of encouraging prompt payment within the normal billing cycle, which is the interval of time between bills. For example, a meat packer may allow the supermarkets it supplies to take a discount for prompt payment. In effect, the seller is willing to accept less cash than the agreed-upon sales price if the customer will pay within a specified period of time. The seller benefits because prompt payment decreases both the probability of bad debts and the need for short-term financing. Prompt conversion of receivables into cash is essential to maintaining liquidity.

The type and amount of the sales discount depend on the credit terms set by the seller. Exhibit 7-2 lists the most common types of sales discounts and credit

Exhibit 7-2
Common Credit Terms

Type of Credit Term	*Explanation*
2/10, n/30	A 2% discount is allowed if payment is made within 10 days of the invoice date. The full price is due within 30 days of the invoice date.
1/5, n/45	A 1% discount is allowed if payment is made within 5 days of the invoice date. The full price is due within 45 days of the invoice date.
5 EOM	The full invoice price is due within 5 days after the end of the month of the sale.
n/30	The entire invoice price is due within 30 days of the invoice date.

terms. As noted, sales discounts, such as those listed, are offered primarily to wholesale customers to encourage payment within the normal 30-day billing cycle. They are made available to retail customers only infrequently. Retail customers, as well as merchandisers, generally face interest charges if they delay payment beyond the normal billing cycle.

The purchaser generally should take a sales discount when it is offered. The following example points out the potential benefits to the purchaser. Assume that a customer made a $1,500 purchase on account and that the terms of the sale are 2/10, n/30. In this situation the customer has two choices: pay $1,470 on day 10 or $1,500 on day 30. The two logical payment dates are day 10 and day 30. There is no additional benefit to paying before day 10, and if the discount is not taken there is no incentive to pay before day 30. A customer who chooses not to take the discount has the use of the additional $30 for 20 days. This represents an annual interest rate of 36.7% for the use of the money as shown in Exhibit 7-3. The customer must decide if having use of the $30 for those additional 20 days is worth such a high annual interest cost.

Obviously, the lower the allowable discount, the lower the effective annual interest rate. If the terms were 1/10, n/30, the annual rate would be 18.2%. However, because most firms can borrow funds at less than 36.7% or, in many cases, at less than 18.2%, they would benefit by taking the discount even if they had to borrow funds from other creditors to do so.

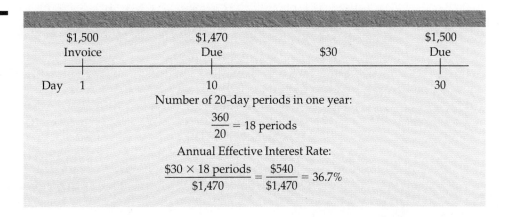

Exhibit 7-3
Effective Interest Rate on Sales Discounts

	$1,500 Invoice	$1,470 Due	$30	$1,500 Due
Day	1	10		30

Number of 20-day periods in one year:

$$\frac{360}{20} = 18 \text{ periods}$$

Annual Effective Interest Rate:

$$\frac{\$30 \times 18 \text{ periods}}{\$1,470} = \frac{\$540}{\$1,470} = 36.7\%$$

Some firms have stopped using cash discounts and instead levy an interest charge of 1% to 1½% per month on accounts that are outstanding over 30 days. This service or finance charge, if and when accrued, should be credited to interest income.

Unlike trade or quantity discounts, sales discounts are given explicit accounting recognition. There are two popular methods used to record sales discounts, the *gross method* and the *net method*. The journal entries for both alternatives, based on a $100 sale on account with stated terms of 2/10, n/30, are shown in Exhibit 7-4. These methods are described in more detail next to help you visualize how revenue from the sale in both cases is recorded ultimately at the expected amount of cash to be received.

gross method of accounting for sales discounts

Gross Method. The **gross method of accounting for sales discounts** records the sale and receivable at the gross amount before any discount. If the customer takes the discount, the account entitled Sales Discounts must be debited. In the example shown in Exhibit 7-4, a $2 debit is made to that account, Cash is debited for $98, and Accounts Receivable is credited for $100. Remember, Accounts Receivable was originally debited for the full invoice price of $100 and so must be credited for $100 to clear the customer's account. Sales Discounts is a contra-sales account, which means that it is a deduction from gross sales to arrive at the net sales figure shown on the income statement. If the customer fails to take the discount, the entry to record the eventual payment is straightforward. Cash is debited for $100, and Accounts Receivable is credited for $100, the full invoice price paid.

net method of accounting for sales discounts

Net Method. As the journal entries in Exhibit 7-4 illustrate, the **net method of accounting for sales discounts** records the receivable and sale after deducting the allowable discount. The net method of accounting for sales discounts is based on the assumption that the customer will take the discount. As noted before, this is a reasonable assumption. The receivable is recorded at its net realizable value—the expected cash receipt at the time of the sale. Likewise, the sale is recorded at the lowest cash price that the seller is willing to accept. If payment is made within the discount period, Cash and Accounts Receivable respectively, are debited and credited for the amount at which the receivable was recorded originally. In this example, the amount is $98.

Exhibit 7-4
Illustration of Accounting for Sales Discounts

Journal Entires to Record Sales Discounts
$100 Sale—Stated Terms 2/10, n/30

Transaction	*Gross Method*			*Net Method*		
1. Sale of $100 of merchandise on account	Accounts Receivable	100		Accounts Receivable	98	
	Sales		100	Sales		98
2a. Customer pays within discount period	Cash	98		Cash	98	
	Sales Discounts	2		Accounts Receivable		98
	Accounts Receivable		100	Cash	100	
2b. Customer does not pay within discount period	Cash	100		Sales Discounts Not Taken		2
	Accounts Receivable		100	Accounts Receivable		98

10,000 200

The full invoice price must be paid if the customer does not make the payment in the discount period. The difference between this full invoice price and the net amount at which the receivable was recorded is credited to an account called Sales Discounts Not Taken. This is a revenue account and generally is listed with other items under the caption Other Revenues and Expenses in the income statement because of its similarity to interest revenue.

Comparison of the Two Methods. The gross method is commonly used because most manual and computer-based accounts receivable systems have been designed to record invoices at the billed price. However, there are no technical reasons why those systems can not be designed as net method systems. Moreover, there are conceptual problems with the gross method. It is based on the assumption that the customer will not take the discount. To the extent that customers eventually do take the discount, both accounts receivable and sales are overstated at the time the sale is recorded. In this regard, the net method is preferable because accounts receivable are recorded at their net realizable value at the time of sale.

Furthermore, the gross method highlights the discounts taken, whereas management may be more interested in identifying those customers who fail to take the discount. Because it generally benefits the purchaser to take the discount, failure to take a discount may indicate potential credit problems with that customer. That is, those customers who do not pay within the discount period may be experiencing cash flow problems.

Credit Card Sales

Credit cards are a common part of business worldwide. All sizes and types of merchandisers are likely to accept one or more of the many common credit cards. Even large retail chains such as J.C. Penney and Sears accept credit cards in addition to their own charge cards. Further, in the last couple of years the ability to charge grocery purchases at large retail market chains such as Albertson's has become common place. These worldwide credit cards are accepted by retailers because they stimulate business, cash is often received sooner than are payments on accounts carried by the business, and it can be cheaper to accept a credit card than to carry individual accounts. In effect, the risk of bad debts is shifted to the credit card company.

Credit card companies charge for their services and for this assumption of risk. The amount of this charge is based on a number of factors, such as the volume of the retailer's gross charge sales and the type of product or service sold. For example, most credit cards charge between 2% and 5% of the sales price to process a credit card sale. This charge is deducted from the total cash receipts credited to the retailer's account when the sale is processed. The retailer considers this charge an expense of doing business; thus, the sale is shown at the agreed-upon price before the credit card service charge.

Sales Returns and Allowances

sales returns

sales allowances

Sales returns and allowances are a fact of everyday life for the retailer or merchandiser. **Sales returns** occur when a customer returns an item for a cash refund or a credit on account. It is called a credit because, from the retailer's point of view, it reduces accounts receivable or cash. **Sales allowances** are a reduction in the actual sales price, and the customer keeps the merchandise. A retailer might offer

credit memorandum

a sales allowance because the particular item did not meet customer expectations or had other defects. A **credit memorandum** is prepared to document the sales return or allowance transaction. This document identifies the customer, the goods that were returned or for which an allowance has been granted, and the transaction amount.

In most situations, one account, Sales Returns and Allowances, is used to record both of these types of transactions. Although it would be possible to debit these returns and allowances directly to the sales account, doing so would not provide as much control as does the use of a separate sales returns and allowances account, which enables a firm to monitor the dollar amount of this adjustment activity.

To demonstrate the use of a sales returns and allowances account, assume that the Chang Company purchased $10,000 of goods from the Graf Company on account. The Chang Company determined that these goods were defective and returned them for a credit. Based on the information contained on an approved credit memorandum, an accountant at the Graf Company made the following entry to record the transaction:

Sales Returns and Allowances	10,000	
Accounts Receivable		10,000
To record return of defective merchandise.		

If the sale had been made for cash and a cash refund granted, the credit would be made to the Cash account rather than to Accounts Receivable.

The method just described assumes that sales returns and allowances are recorded in the period in which the item is returned or the allowance granted, regardless of whether the sale took place in that or the preceding period. Because of the matching requirement, sales returns and allowances should be recorded in the period of the sale. This requires making an estimate of sales returns and allowances when financial statements are prepared. For most companies, however, sales returns and allowances are not material; over time there usually is little variation in the amounts, so such an estimate is rarely made. If a firm (such as a mail-order house or catalog firm like Lands' End) does have material sales returns and allowances, the matching rule requires that such an estimate be made at the time of sale.

MEASUREMENT AND VALUATION OF ACCOUNTS RECEIVABLE

Objective 3
Explain the nature of uncollectible accounts and the allowance method of accounting for uncollectible accounts.

This section will focus on the measurement and valuation of accounts receivable that arise from credit sales. Such issues as accounting for subsequent cash collections and uncollectible accounts are discussed.

Uncollectible Accounts

uncollectible accounts

Uncollectible accounts are receivables that the firm is unable to collect in full from the customer. They arise because firms decide to make sales to individuals from whom the collection of the entire amount of the sale is questionable. The ability of a firm to collect its credit sales depends on (1) how strict the firm is in its granting of credit in the first place, (2) the particular credit policies of the firm, such as the use of sales discounts or interest charges on uncollected accounts, and (3) general economic conditions. A firm obviously has more control over the first two factors than over the third.

In large firms, the credit department is responsible for granting credit as well as for subsequently collecting accounts. In smaller firms, these responsibilities often rest with the owner-manager. In deciding initially whether to grant credit or to extend credit limits, the firm must obtain information about customers, such as their financial condition and past credit history. This information can be obtained through credit applications and the services of credit-rating bureaus.

The opening scenario to this chapter centered on a discussion of a firm's credit-granting policy. As suggested by the credit manager in that scenario, a firm could adopt a very conservative policy and extend credit only to customers with excellent credit ratings. Leslie Vargus, the firm's VP of sales, makes the point strongly that although such a policy virtually eliminates bad debts or uncollectible accounts, the firm can lose sales and profits by not extending credit to individuals or firms who have less than perfect credit histories but who might pay their accounts in full. These are difficult decisions which require much judgment.

In theory, a firm should extend credit to all customers from whom the cash ultimately collected will (through either partial or full payment on account) exceed the total of the cost of goods sold plus other incremental selling and general and administrative expenses. A firm that follows such a credit policy will still incur some bad debts or uncollectible accounts. As long as these uncollectible accounts do not exceed the incremental profits from sales to customers in this credit class, however, the firm will be better off.

Accounting for Uncollectible Accounts

The primary accounting issue regarding accounting for uncollectible accounts is matching the bad debts with the sales of the period that gave rise to the bad debts. That is, the bad-debt expense should be recognized in the period in which the sale took place and the receivable was generated, not in the period in which management determined that the customer was unable or unwilling to pay. The accounting problem arises because it may be the following year before management discovers that the amount due for a sale made in the current year will not be collectible. When waiting to record the bad-debt expense until it is known with certainty could result in recognizing the expense in the year following the sale, the matching convention would be violated.

allowance method

uncollectible accounts expense

In order to provide the best matching, the allowance method is used. Under the **allowance method,** the *uncollectible accounts expense* for the period is matched against the sales for that period. The **uncollectible accounts expense** is the amount of current period sales that are not expected to be collected. This method requires that the uncollectible accounts expense be estimated in the period of the sale. An estimate is required because of course it is impossible to know with certainty which outstanding accounts at the end of the year will become uncollectible during the next year. However, it is known that some accounts will become uncollectible. This estimate usually is recorded through an adjusting journal entry at year-end. Although estimates are uncertain, accountants feel that the benefits of applying the matching convention outweigh the uncertainties associated with estimates.

Recording Uncollectible Accounts Expense

To demonstrate the application of the allowance method, the necessary journal entries will be discussed first, and then the different methods used to make the required estimates will be examined.

Assume that during 1994, Delta Company's first year in business, sales totaled $1 million. All sales were made on credit, and cash collections on account totaled $750,000. After analyzing the ending balance of $250,000 in Accounts Receivable, management estimated that $12,500 of these accounts ultimately would become uncollectible.

Recording Original Estimate. The summary journal entries required to record the sales, the cash collections, and the $12,500 in uncollectible accounts are as follows:

Summary entries for the year:		
Accounts Receivable	1,000,000	
Sales		1,000,000
To record sales during the year.		
Cash	750,000	
Accounts Receivable		750,000
To record cash collected on account during the year.		
December 31, 1994—Adjusting entry:		
Uncollectible Accounts Expense	12,500	
Allowance for Uncollectible Accounts		12,500
To record estimated uncollectible accounts.		

The first two entries are familiar. The adjusting entry on December 31, 1994, which records the estimated uncollectible accounts, however, needs to be explained.

The debit part of the adjusting entry is made to the Uncollectible Accounts Expense account. Another title for this account is Bad Debt Expense. This account generally is shown as a selling expense on the income statement and is closed to the income summary account, though some firms show this item as a deduction from gross sales in arriving at net sales. The credit part of the entry is to an account called Allowance for Uncollectible Accounts, a contra asset. This account, rather than Accounts Receivable, is credited because the firm is only making an estimate of uncollectible accounts and does not know which particular accounts will ultimately prove uncollectible. If a firm knows that a particular account is, in fact, uncollectible, it should already have been written off.

The Allowance for Uncollectible Accounts account is a contra-asset account with a credit balance. Other titles for this account include Allowance for Doubtful Accounts and Allowance for Bad Debts. In preparing a balance sheet, the allowance account is netted against Accounts Receivable. This net amount of accounts receivable represents management's estimate of the net realizable value of the receivables. Exhibit 7-5 shows the current asset section of the Delta Company's balance sheet at December 31, 1994, after the adjusting entry has been made. Because this is the first year of the firm's operations, the balance in the allowance account equals the amount of the journal entry. In future years this may not be the case.

To extend this illustration, assume that the following events occur in 1995:

1. On April 14, Corona Company, one of Delta's customers, informs Delta that it is entering bankruptcy proceedings. Because Delta's management feels that it is unlikely that it will be able to collect anything from the $6,000 balance in Corona's account, it decides to write off the entire balance.
2. On November 29, Delta receives $400 from the bankruptcy court as the final settlement of Corona's account.

Exhibit 7-5

Delta Company Partial Balance Sheet December 31, 1994		
Current Assets		
Cash		$ 15,000
Temporary investments		5,000
Accounts receivable	$250,000	
Less: Allowance for uncollectible accounts	12,500	
		237,500
Inventory		180,000
Prepaids		2,500
Total current assets		$440,000

Recording Actual Write-Off. Based on these data, Delta makes the following entry on April 14, 1995, to write off the $6,000 account:

Apr. 14, 1995: Allowance for Uncollectible Accounts	6,000	
Accounts Receivable—Corona		6,000
To write off balance in Corona Company's account receivable.		

As this entry shows, the debit part of the entry is to the allowance account. Note that the entry does not include the uncollectible accounts expense account because it is assumed that the $6,000 is included in the $12,500 debit to expense as part of the December 31, 1994, adjusting entry. The credit part is to Accounts Receivable—Corona. This part of the entry must be posted to both the general ledger accounts receivable and to Corona's account in the accounts receivable subsidiary ledger.

After the $6,000 entry to write off the specific account, the net amount of accounts receivable (Accounts Receivable less Allowance for Uncollectible Accounts) remains the same, as illustrated in Exhibit 7-6. The entry on April 14, 1995, decreases the allowance account and the accounts receivable account by the same $6,000 required to write off the account but has no effect on the net realizable value of the receivable. Once a particular account is determined to be bad, the balance that pertains to that account is taken out of both the allowance account and the accounts receivable account, and there is no effect on net receivables. The decrease in the net occurred earlier, when for matching purposes the estimate was recorded at December 31, 1994.

Exhibit 7-6
Comparison of Net Receivables

	Balances	
	Before Write-Off of Accounts	*After Write-Off of Accounts*
Accounts receivable	$250,000	$244,000
Less: Allowance for uncollectible accounts	12,500	6,500
Net accounts receivable	$237,500	$237,500

Recording Subsequent Collection of Accounts Previously Written Off. In some cases a customer whose account has been written off will pay part or all of the account later. For example, in the Corona case, Delta's management decided it was prudent to write off the entire balance when Corona entered bankruptcy proceedings, because in Delta's opinion the outcome of such proceedings is uncertain. In November 1995, when Delta received $400 as its full settlement, it had to make the following two entries:

Nov. 29, 1995:	Accounts Receivable—Corona	400	
	Allowance for Uncollectible Accounts		400
	To reinstate $400 of Corona's account receivable.		
	Cash	400	
	Accounts Receivable		400
	To record receipt of $400 cash.		

The first entry reinstates Corona's account receivable in the amount collected, $400. This entry is a reversal of the entry to write off the receivable and reinstates the account receivable. The second entry is the normal cash receipts entry to record a collection from a customer. These two entries should not be combined, for the following reasons. First, there may be a lag between the notification of the intention to pay and the actual receipt of the cash. Second, the two entries create a complete record in Corona's subsidiary accounts receivable account of the actual bad debt. A combined entry would not accomplish this. Finally, an entry that debits the cash account and credits an allowance account cannot arise from normal external transactions. For internal control purposes, therefore, unusual entries should be explained and combining entries should be avoided.

The previous examples demonstrate the entries made to write off an account declared uncollectible and reinstate an account that had previously been written off. During the year, similar entries are made to record other accounts declared uncollectible. At December 31, 1995, the Delta Company again would make an estimate of its uncollectible accounts at December 31, 1995, and make the necessary adjusting entry to Uncollectible Accounts Expense and the Allowance for Uncollectible Accounts.

Estimating Uncollectible Accounts Expense

Two approaches to estimating the allowance for uncollectible accounts are frequently used: *the percentage-of-net-sales method* and *the aging method*. Both methods are based on the accountant's ability to estimate future uncollectible accounts that result from current year's sales.

percentage-of-net-sales method

Percentage-of-Net-Sales Method. The **percentage-of-net-sales method** is a method of determining the amount of uncollectible accounts expense by analyzing the relationship between net credit sales and uncollectible accounts expense of prior years. (Net sales is equal to gross sales less any sales discounts and any sales returns and allowances.) This method is often called the *income statement approach* because the accountant attempts to measure the uncollectible accounts expense account as accurately as possible using income statement information. The balance in Allowance for Uncollectible Accounts is the result of the entry needed to record the estimated expense for the period.

Exhibit 7-7

Account	*Balance 12/31/94 (Before Adjustments)*
Credit sales—net	$1,000,000
Accounts receivable	200,000
Allowance for uncollectible accounts—Credit balance	2,000

To demonstrate the percentage-of-net-sales method, assume that at the end of 1994, prior to making any adjusting entries, you have gathered the Porter Company data shown in Exhibit 7-7. This exhibit assumes that all accounts determined to be uncollectible during the period have already been written off against Accounts Receivable and the allowance account. The management of the Porter Company has analyzed the relationship of the losses from uncollectible accounts and net credit sales for the past five years (1989–1993) and determined that uncollectible accounts expense will be approximately 2% of credit sales based on the analysis in Exhibit 7-8. Based on this data, the debit to Uncollectible Accounts Expense is 2% of net credit sales of $1 million or $20,000. The correct adjusting entry at December 31, 1994, to record this estimate is:

Dec. 31, 1994: Uncollectible Accounts Expense	20,000	
Allowance for Uncollectible Accounts		20,000
To record uncollectible accounts expense based on 2% of net sales.		

After this entry is posted, the relevant T accounts appear as follows:

Allowance for Uncollectible Accounts

Debit	Credit	
	12/31/94 Bal.	2,000
	12/31/94 Adj.	20,000
	12/31/94 Adj. Bal.	22,000

Uncollectible Accounts Expense

Debit		Credit
12/31/94 Adj.	20,000	

Exhibit 7-8

Year	*Net Credit Sales*	*Losses Resulting From Uncollectible Accounts*
1989	$ 650,000	$12,000
1990	680,000	15,000
1991	780,000	14,820
1992	850,000	17,850
1993	940,000	18,330
	$3,900,000	$78,000

Average percentage: $78,000/$3,900,000 = 2%

The balance in the uncollectible accounts expense account represents 2% of net credit sales. The balance in this account will always be a function of a predetermined percentage of credit sales if the percentage-of-net-sales method is used. The balance in Allowance for Uncollectible Accounts is $22,000—$2,000 from prior years' sales that have not been written off as uncollectible and $20,000 for 1994 sales. At the end of any particular year, the credit balance in this account will fluctuate, and only by coincidence will it equal the balance in Uncollectible Accounts Expense. At December 31, 1994, the accounts receivable would be shown as follows in the current assets section of the balance sheet:

Accounts Receivable	$200,000
Less: Allowance for Uncollectible Accounts	22,000
Accounts Receivable, net	$178,000

Each year the Porter Company would analyze its accounts receivable, calculate the percentage of net sales that it expects to be uncollectible, and make the series of entries shown above.

aging method

Aging Method. The **aging method** is a method of estimating the balance in the account Allowance for Uncollectible Accounts by analyzing the age of each accounts receivable account. The accountant attempts to estimate what percentage of outstanding receivables at year-end will ultimately not be collected; this amount becomes the desired ending balance in Allowance for Uncollectible Accounts. An entry to this account is then made to adjust the previous balance to the new, desired balance. The offsetting part of this entry is to the account Uncollectible Accounts Expense. The aging method is often called the *balance sheet approach* because the accountant attempts to measure, as accurately as possible, the net realizable value of Accounts Receivable at the balance sheet date.

The method used to estimate the desired year-end balance in the allowance account is called the aging of accounts receivable, an analysis of the individual customer balances based on the length of time they have been outstanding. Categories such as current, 31–60 days, 61–90 days, and over 90 days often are used. On the assumption that the longer an account is outstanding the less likely it is to be collected, an increasing percentage is applied to each of these categories. The total of these figures represents the desired balance in Allowance for Uncollectible Accounts.

To demonstrate the application of the aging method, we will use the data for the Porter Company from Exhibit 7-7. At the end of 1994, Porter's balance in Accounts Receivable was $200,000. In the aging schedule presented in Exhibit 7–9 it is assumed for simplicity that the entire $200,000 is owed by only five customers.

Based on the data in Exhibit 7-9, the Porter Company makes the following adjusting entry at December 31, 1994, to record the uncollectible accounts expense:

Dec. 31, 1994:	Uncollectible Accounts Expense	17,700	
	Allowance for Uncollectible Accounts		17,700
	To record uncollectible accounts expense based on the aging method.		

Exhibit 7-9
Aging of Accounts Receivable

Porter Company
Aging of Accounts Receivable
December 31, 1994

			Age of Receivables		
Customer	*Total*	*Current*	*31–60 Days*	*61–90 Days*	*Over 90 Days*
A.B. Dick	$ 30,000	$ 10,000	$15,000	$ 5,000	$
T.V. Marsh	65,000	45,000	15,000	5,000	
J. Ong	45,000	30,000	5,000	5,000	5,000
L. Tse	10,000	9,000			1,000
M.S. Worth	50,000	40,000	5,000	5,000	
	$200,000	$134,000	$40,000	$20,000	$6,000
Percentage estimated to be uncollectible		5%	10%	30%	50%
Desired balance in Allowance account	$ 19,700	$ 6,700	$ 4,000	$ 6,000	$3,000
Current credit balance	(2,000)				
Required entry	$ 17,700				

After this entry is posted, the relevant T accounts appear as follows:

Allowance for Uncollectible Accounts

Debit	Credit	
	12/31/94 Bal.	2,000
	12/31/94 Adj.	17,700
	12/31/94 Adj. Bal.	19,700

Uncollectible Accounts Expense

Debit		Credit
12/31/94 Adj.	17,700	

A number of points need to be made about this example. First, the amount of the journal entry is the amount needed to bring the allowance account to the desired balance of $19,700. Because the allowance account had a $2,000 credit balance prior to adjustment, the required entry is for $17,700, or the difference between $19,700 and $2,000. In some situations, the allowance account may have a debit balance before the adjustment. This may occur if during the year more accounts were written off than had been estimated for in the prior year. In this situation, the debit balance should be *added* to the desired credit balance in the allowance account to determine the correct amount of the entry. For example, if the Porter Company's allowance account had a $300 debit balance before the entry to record the uncollectible accounts expense was made, the allowance account would require a credit entry of $20,000 in order to establish the necessary ending balance of $19,700.

The second issue is how the accountant determines what percentages to apply to each age category. Generally, the percentages are based on past experience adjusted for current economic and credit conditions; they should be evaluated on a regular basis and adjusted when necessary.

Finally, in some cases the aging of the accounts receivable will indicate that a particular account has no possibility of collection. If this occurs, this account should be written off by debiting the allowance account and crediting accounts receivable before determining the desired ending balance in the allowance account. In effect, this particular customer account is eliminated from the aging process, as it is already considered uncollectible.

At December 31, 1994, the accounts receivable would be shown as follows in the current assets section of the balance sheet:

Accounts Receivable	$200,000
Less: Allowance for uncollectible accounts	19,700
Accounts Receivable, net	$180,300

Each year the Porter Company would age its accounts receivable, determine the proper balance that should be in the allowance account, and make the series of entries shown above.

Comparison of the Two Methods. Both the percentage-of-net-sales method and the aging method follow generally accepted accounting principles because both attempt to match revenues and expenses in the proper accounting period. The percentage-of-net-sales method determines the amount of uncollectible accounts expense for a period, and the aging method determines the net realizable balance of accounts receivable for the balance sheet. Therefore, these methods probably will show different balances in both the expense and the contra-asset accounts. This is illustrated in Exhibit 7-10 by using the data from the 1994 Porter Company example.

These differences illustrate that in applying generally accepted accounting principles management has a choice of methods, and these choices affect the firm's financial statements. However, once a method of estimating bad debts is chosen, it should be consistently followed to enhance the comparability of the firm's financial statements.

Both the aging method and the percentage-of-net-sales method are found in practice. The percentage-of-net-sales method is easier to apply, but the aging method forces management to analyze the status of accounts receivable and credit policies annually. Some firms use the percentage-of-net-sales method to prepare monthly and quarterly statements, and the aging method to make the final adjustment at year-end.

Exhibit 7-10
Comparison of Allowance Methods

	Balance—12/31/94	
Method	*Allowance for Uncollectible Accounts*	*Uncollectible Accounts Expense*
Percentage-of-net-sales	$22,000	$20,000
Aging	19,700	17,700

Difference Between Estimates and Actual Experience

Regardless of which method is used, the actual accounts written off seldom equal the estimates made in the prior year. Estimates are inherent in accounting, because the accountant attempts to match revenues and expenses. Most individuals feel that the benefits of this proper matching outweigh the disadvantages of using estimates. Furthermore, for stable companies, the amount of receivables and uncollectible accounts tends to be steady from year to year.

As this section has shown, reasonable errors in estimates are adjusted in current and future years; the accountant does not retroactively change a prior year's statement. However, if estimates are materially and consistently incorrect, management should reevaluate the method used to make the estimate.

A Note on Loan Losses of Financial Institutions

In this chapter we have been discussing bad debts arising from credit sales of merchandising firms. For illustration purposes, the amounts involved tended to be small. However, bad debts and nonperforming loans (in which collections are lagging or are in default) have become a serious problem in many industries. Nowhere is this more serious than with financial institutions (banks and savings and loans).

In recent years these financial institutions have been hit very hard by bad loans. In the early 1980s these loan write-offs resulted from nonperforming loans to foreign countries. By the early 1990s nonperforming real estate loans had caused huge losses that threatened the solvency of the nation's banking system. To illustrate, Wells Fargo, the nation's tenth-largest bank, allocated $700 million to cover possible loan losses during the fourth quarter of 1991. (The article reproduced in Exhibit 7-11 describes this loss in more detail.) Wells Fargo is just one of many banks that experienced such large losses. These losses continued into 1992 and 1993.

MANAGEMENT CONTROL AND ANALYSIS OF RECEIVABLES

Objective 4
Evaluate management controls over receivables.

Management control and analysis of receivables are important parts of the overall cash management system. Chapter 6 discussed some important management control issues. An additional point regarding the proper authorization of receivables to be written off as uncollectible must be emphasized. Only the controller or an individual who does not have day-to-day operational control over receivables or cash should authorize a write-off or a sales return. Written authorization should be attached to the customer's subsidiary ledger or file. These controls will ensure that an employee is not able to steal a cash payment on account and conceal the theft by recording the transaction in a customer's account as a bad debt or a sales return.

Other control procedures include monitoring the age and size of the accounts receivable balance and the use of a cash budget to forecast collections of receivables. The ability to convert receivables into cash quickly is important in maintaining the firm's liquidity. A regular aging of accounts receivable and a review of credit policies can help ensure that the collections of receivables do not lag. Projecting when and how much cash will be collected from receivables is also important input for managers. Knowing the timing and quantity of cash collections allows managers to engage in more effective planning and control.

Exhibit 7-11

WELLS FARGO PREDICTS HUGE LOSS IN FOURTH QUARTER

Wells Fargo & Co., the nation's 10th-largest banking company, said Thursday that it expects to lose as much as $240 million in the fourth quarter, largely because of California's worsening commercial real estate market.

The San Francisco-based bank also said that to conserve capital it is slashing in half the dividend it pays shareholders. It will also allocate about $700 million for possible losses on loans, many of them related to real estate.

Although Thursday's disclosure—which had been anxiously awaited in the industry—is a clear reminder of California's deep economic woes, it was not the cataclysmic event some doomsayers had predicted.

As a result, many investors, fearing an even bigger loss, reacted by bidding Wells Fargo's stock up $3.25 to $60.50. Stock prices for other California banks jumped as well.

"What it says is that California is not Texas . . . yet," said Stephen Berman, a banking analyst with County Natwest Securities.

More than any other California bank, Wells Fargo is viewed as a bellwether. Its operations are concentrated in California, and it has the most exposure to the state's real estate market. In addition, it is widely viewed as the banking industry's best real estate lender, and until now had remained relatively unscathed by the real estate downturn.

Thursday's announcement came as regulators with the Office of the Comptroller of the Currency are wrapping up a special review of Wells Fargo's real estate portfolio. The regulatory examination had been the subject of extraordinary rumor and speculation, with bank analysts widely split over the company's condition.

Although the results were worse than a number of bank analysts had predicted, many expressed relief that the loss was not reminiscent of the disastrous losses that pummeled New England and Texas banks in recent years.

"I think the main thing you are seeing in the market is relief at knowing what it is and that it isn't higher than it is," said Lisa Todaro, senior banking analyst at SNL Securities in Charlottesville, Va.

Wells Fargo Chief Financial Officer Rodney L. Jacobs said investors responded favorably after witnessing what he described as "a clear test of the strength of the franchise." Even with the fourth-quarter results, Jacobs noted, Wells Fargo will still post a small profit for 1991. Wells Fargo earned $252 million in the first nine months of 1991, down from $555 million a year earlier.

Even still, some bank analysts cautioned that it is too early to sound an "all-clear" signal that Wells Fargo's problems are over.

That a quarterly bank loss exceeding $200 million can be considered good news says a lot about the anxiety nationwide over California's anemic economy, its overbuilt commercial real estate market and the health of loans made by the state's largest banks.

In its brief announcement, Wells Fargo said it is boosting the total amount allocated for possible loan losses to $1.65 billion. That accompanies a net $200-million charge-off for bad loans, an action that occurs when a bank writes off loans it no longer expects borrowers to repay.

In a statement, Chief Executive Carl E. Reichardt said that increasing the funds covering loan losses is prudent because Wells Fargo is "operating in a difficult environment full of pessimism and anxiety about the economy in general and real estate in particular."

Wells said its estimated net loss for the quarter will be from $4.20 to $4.60 a share, or $220 million to $240 million. The bank also slashed its quarterly dividend to 50 cents a share from $1.

Regulators have been pressuring a number of major banks to take steps to conserve capital, but Jacobs said the decision to slash the dividend, as well as boost the reserves, was recommended by Wells Fargo's management to its directors.

Should Wells Fargo weather the next few quarters successfully and California's economy slows its decline, analysts believe that the bank will be poised for an aggressive expansion. Reichardt, the bank's acquisition-minded leader, has made no secret in the past that he is interested in a possible merger with Los Angeles-based First Interstate Bancorp.

But most banking analysts are skeptical that anything meaningful will happen for a while. Wells would first have to be assured that its own problems are behind it, that all of First Interstate's problems have been identified and that the economy will improve.

Short-sellers, who bet that stocks will fall in price, have been targeting Wells Fargo for three years. Some were undaunted by

(continued)

Exhibit 7-11 *continued*

Thursday's results. Michael Murphy, whose Overpriced Stock Service has in the past gone so far as to predict the bank's failure, said he interprets the results as an indication that Wells Fargo won the latest hard-fought round with regulators.

But other analysts said they doubt that the battle was as intense as has been rumored.

Source: "Wells Fargo Predicts Huge Loss in Fourth Quarter," by James Bates, *Los Angeles Times*, December 13, 1991, part 4, p. 1.

Receivable Analysis: Turnover and Collection Period

receivable turnover

To help management monitor receivables, the *receivable turnover* and the *average collection period* (in days) are often calculated. The **receivable turnover** is computed by dividing credit sales by the average accounts receivable for the period. For example, a firm with annual credit sales of \$2.5 million and average accounts receivable of \$500,000 has a receivable turnover of 5 times, calculated as follows.

$$\text{Receivable turnover} = \frac{\text{Credit sales}}{\text{Average accounts receivable}}$$

$$5 \text{ times} = \frac{\$2{,}500{,}000}{\$500{,}000}$$

average collection period

The **average collection period** is a statistic that shows, on average, how long an account is outstanding. The turnover figure can be converted easily into the average number of days that the receivables are outstanding, by dividing 365 days by the turnover. In this case, receivables are outstanding an average of 73 days (365 days/5). Within the constraints of the firm's credit policies, management is interested in reducing the turnover period and thus quickly turning receivables into cash. If sales are made on a 2/10, n/30 basis, the turnover should be close to 12 times in a year, and the average age of receivables should be less than 30 days. The company in the preceding illustration (5 times and 73 days) has a severe collection problem.

If a company is in need of immediate cash, it can use its receivables to generate such cash. Accounts receivable can be assigned, pledged, or factored. Essentially, in all these situations the company that owns the receivable either sells it to a bank or other lender or borrows against it to obtain immediate cash. The ability to raise cash in this manner is especially important to small and medium-size businesses, which often are strapped for cash. The cost of receivables financing can be quite high, and obviously depends on the firm's having receivables which are collectible. The actual accounting for the assigning, pledging, or factoring of accounts receivable is a topic covered in intermediate accounting texts.

Budgeting Cash Collections

Knowledge of cash flows is critical to a business. Often a business is successful in producing and selling a product but fails because of timing problems associated with cash inflows and outflows. By knowing when cash deficiencies and surpluses are likely to occur, a firm's management can plan to borrow cash when needed and repay the loans during periods of excess cash. The principal source of cash inflow is from current cash and credit sales and from the collection of cash from past sales made on credit. Because a significant proportion of sales is usually on account, a major task of an organization is to determine the pattern of collection for its accounts receivable. The collection pattern for receivables is a function of such factors as industry, firm size, and the firm's credit policy.

To illustrate how cash receipts are budgeted, assume that at the beginning of October 1994, the Timmins Company, a small manufacturer of electronic components, is preparing a cash budget for the first quarter of 1995 (January, February, and March). The controller of the Timmins Company has developed the following data:

a. Past experience reveals that 20% of sales are for cash and the remaining 80% are on credit.
b. An aging schedule reveals the following pattern which is considered typical:

30% of credit sales are collected in the month of sale
50% of credit sales are collected in the month following sale
18% of credit sales are collected in the second month following sale
2% of credit sales are never collected

c. In October, Timmins Co. developed the following sales forecast for the next five months:

November	$100,000
December	200,000
January	100,000
February	50,000
March	150,000

Given the above information, a budgeted schedule of cash collections for the months of January, February, and March is presented in Exhibit 7-12.

As Exhibit 7-12 indicates, total cash collections for January amounted to $138,400. This amount includes:

1. Cash sales equal to 20% of January forecast sales or $20,000 (0.20 × $100,000)
2. Cash collections from January forecast credit sales are $24,000. Of the $100,000 of sales forecast for January 20% are for cash (see item 1 above). Of the remaining $80,000 in credit sales the aging indicates that 30% will be collected in January so that 0.30 × $80,000 = $24,000.
3. Cash collections from the prior month (December) are $80,000. December forecast sales were $200,000 of which 80% or $160,000 ($200,000 × 0.80) were on credit. The aging of the accounts receivable indicates that 50% of these credit sales will be collected in January which is the month following the sale. Therefore, December sales collected in January are $80,000 or 0.50 × $160,000.
4. Cash collections from sales of two months prior (November) are $14,400. November forecast sales were $100,000 of which 80% or $80,000 ($100,000 × 0.80) were on credit. The aging of accounts receivable indicates that 18% of these credit sales will be collected in January which is two months following

Exhibit 7-12
Schedule of Cash Collections

	January	*February*	*March*
Cash sales[a]	$ 20,000	$10,000	$ 30,000
Credit sales:			
First month[b] (January)	24,000	12,000	36,000
Prior month[c] (December)	80,000	40,000	20,000
Two months ago[d] (November)	14,400	28,800	14,400
Total cash collections	$138,400	$90,800	$100,400

[a]20% of current month sales
[b]30% of current month *credit* sales: 0.30 × (0.80 × $100,000); 0.30 × (0.80 × $50,000); 0.30 × (0.80 × $150,000)
[c]50% of *prior* month *credit* sales: 0.50 × (0.80 × $200,000); 0.50 × (0.80 × $100,000); 0.50 × (0.80 × $50,000)
[d]18% of *credit* sales from *two* months ago: 0.18 × (0.80 × $100,000); 0.18 × (0.80 × $200,000); 0.18 × (0.80 × $100,000)

the month of the sale. Therefore, November sales collected in January are $14,400 or 0.18 × $80,000.

Cash collections for February and March are determined in the same manner.

The management of the Timmins Company would then compare these estimated cash inflows to their estimated cash expenditures as determined from their cash expenditure budget (this budget is introduced in Chapter 8). This comparison is then used to determine whether the firm is in need of short term cash financing. Cash budgeting will be explained in greater detail in Chapter 24.

CLASSIFICATION OF CASH AND RECEIVABLES

Objective 5
Explain the classification of cash and receivables on the balance sheet.

Cash arises from cash sales and the ultimate collection of accounts receivable and, in most cases, is included in the current asset section of the balance sheet. In certain situations, however, cash may be excluded from the current asset section. These situations occur when restrictions on the use of cash make it unavailable for current use. For example, a firm may set aside cash in a special fund to repay bonds or for the future purchase of a building. Such funds are called *sinking funds* and are shown in the long-term section of the balance sheet. Another situation is cash on deposit in banks in foreign countries where regulations prohibit its being returned to the United States or used in current operations in that country. Finally, there are times when a company overdraws its bank account and has a cash overdraft. (Cash overdrafts are not shown as a negative item in the current asset section, but as a liability in the current liability section of the balance sheet.)

Accounts receivable that arise from ordinary sales usually are collected within 30 days and are classified as current assets. Other receivables that might arise from loans to outsiders, employees, or stockholders should be listed separately from accounts receivable. If the receivable is due within a year of the operating cycle, it should be classified as current. If the receivable arises from a loan to a stockholder or employee and there is no definite due date, it should be considered noncurrent and included in either the long-term investment or other asset section of the balance sheet.

OTHER OPERATING REVENUES

Objective 6
List other types of revenues generated from operations.

A firm is likely to enter into various transactions which give rise to other types of revenues, including interest, dividends, and gains and losses on the sale of operating or fixed assets. The FASB feels that cash flows from interest and dividend revenues represent cash flows from operating activities. However, the notes and loans receivable, and/or the investments in debt and equity securities that give rise to these revenues, are considered investing activities. Depending on the magnitude of these items, they often are shown separately on a firm's income statement as "other items" but included in income from continuing operations.

Firms are also likely to sell some of their fixed assets, such as their equipment, land, and buildings. These items are often classified as separate nonoperating items on the income statement and included in the broad category of income from continuing operations.

REVENUE CYCLE APPLICATION SYSTEMS

Objective 7
Explain the revenue cycle computer system.

manual input symbol
on-page connector symbol

Transaction processing within the revenue cycle was discussed at the beginning of this chapter. The actual systems within the revenue cycle, and their interrelationships, are shown in a systems flowchart in Exhibit 7-13. Two new systems flowchart symbols are introduced in this exhibit, the *manual input symbol* and the *on-page connector symbol*. The **manual input symbol** is used to show where data is input into a computer system from a standard keyboard. The **on-page connector symbol** is used to connect two flowchart symbols when a connector line can not be easily used. It just represents a connection symbol without a line.

The systems flowchart in Exhibit 7-13 provides a more detailed picture of the processes used to record transactions in a computer-based accounting system than that provided by a transaction cycle diagram illustrated in Exhibit 7-1. That is, Exhibit 7-13 is a blowup of the computer process shown in the revenue cycle diagram in Exhibit 7-1. The systems flowchart identifies major input and outputs to the systems and the computer files that are used to process transactions. The systems flowchart also identifies the specific applications systems (that is, the order entry system, the cash receipts system, the accounts receivable system, the shipping system, and the inventory system) that are used to process revenue-cycle transactions. Notice that the inventory system, although it is included in the transaction cycle diagram in Exhibit 7-1, is not included in the systems flowchart in Exhibit 7-13. The inventory master file provides the interface between revenue cycle systems and the inventory system. However, several of the systems in Exhibit 7-13 access or change data contained in the inventory master file.

Order Entry System

Customer purchase orders are entered into the computerized order entry system as they are received. The order entry system reads data contained on two master files, the customer master file and the inventory master file. Information on the customer master file is used to preform a credit check. Data on the inventory master file is checked to verify that sufficient quantities of the ordered goods are on hand to fill the order. Accepted orders are written to the unfilled order file.

Exhibit 7-13
Revenue Cycle Systems Flowchart

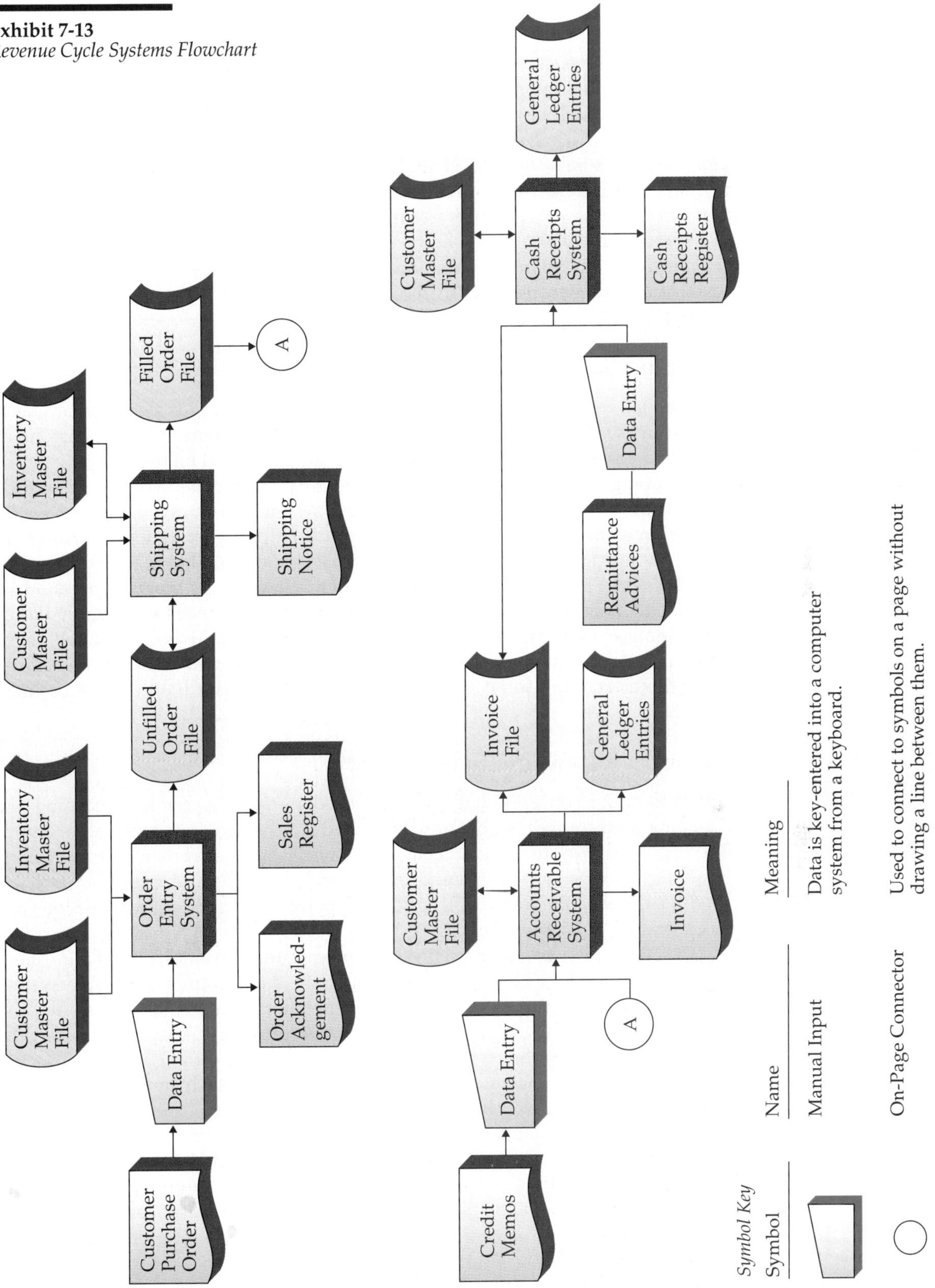

This file contains all of the information needed for subsequent processing of the accepted orders. The order entry system prints an order acknowledgement which is mailed to the customer. The order acknowledgement is a business document that confirms that an order has been accepted and informs the customer that the ordered goods will be shipped.

register

The order entry system also prints an order register. A **register** is a list of all of the transactions processed by a system. Registers are important corrective control reports because they provide detailed information about every transaction that was processed. The *order register* then is a detailed list of every order that was processed by the order entry system. The order register can be used to answer questions about when an order was processed, how the order was processed, and can also be used to reconstruct order files if they are destroyed or corrupted.

Shipping System

The unfilled order file is input into the shipping system. This system again reads data from the customer master file. In this case, the system reads the customer's name and address from the file so that they can be printed on the shipping notice. The shipping system also accesses the inventory master file. Note that a bidirectional connector is used to tie the shipping system to the inventory master file. The bidirectional connector implies that the shipping system is *updating* the inventory master file. An **update** is a file operation that changes the contents of a master file. The shipping system updates or changes the quantity on hand for various items in inventory because goods have been withdrawn from inventory for shipment to a customer. Inventory quantities would be overstated if the inventory update did not occur. The shipping system also updates the unfilled order file by moving filled orders from the unfilled order file to the filled order file.

update

Accounts Receivable System

The accounting concepts that are introduced in this chapter for recording and adjusting accounts receivable are performed by the accounts receivable system. The order entry system and the shipping system process business transactions. However, they do not generate journal entries, they capture information that is used by the accounts receivable system in performing accounting functions and in generating journal entries.

The filled order file, along with credit memos for sales returns and allowances and the write-offs of bad debts, are input into the accounts receivable system. The accounts receivable system reads the customer's name and address from the customer master file so that the invoice can be printed. The accounts receivable system also updates the customer master file by adding the current transaction amount to the customer's account balance. The updated balance is the amount that the customer currently owes on account. Thus, the customer master file is the computer-based accounts receivable subsidiary ledger.

Invoice detail is written to the invoice file. This file contains invoice-level rather than account-level information and consequently is more detailed than the customer master file. The accounts receivable system also generates journal entries to record all of the accounts receivable transactions that have been processed.

Cash Receipts System

remittance advice

The objective of the cash receipts system is to properly record all cash receipt transactions. Processing begins when *remittance advices* are entered into the system. A **remittance advice** is a business document returned by a customer that identifies their account number and the amount being paid on their account. In most cases the remittance advice is printed with the invoice and is detached by the customer when they pay the invoice. The part of the monthly statement that you return to a credit card company with your payment is a remittance advice. Remittance advices are preventive control documents. That is, they prevent the transposition or incorrect recording of customer account numbers because the numbers are already preprinted on the document.

The cash receipts system prints a cash receipts register every day after the day's cash transactions have been processed. This register lists every cash receipts transaction processed by the system. The remittance advices and the register together provide a detective control over the payments received. Detective controls are controls that help protect against errors. For example, notice that in the flowchart (Exhibit 7-13) that the remittance advices, and not the cash receipts, are input into the cash receipts system. Totals on the cash receipts register, which came from the remittance advices, are compared with the amount of the bank deposit. A difference between the register total and the total deposit indicates an error or an irregularity.

The accounts receivable system generates general ledger journal entries and also updates the customer master file (subsidiary ledger) and the invoice file to record the amounts paid on accounts and invoices. The balance in the accounts receivable account in the general ledger should always be the same as the totals in the customer master file and the invoice register. Differences indicate processing errors which require management attention.

Types of Computer Files

master file

The accounts receivable system makes use of two different types of files, *master files* and *transaction files.* A **master file** is a file that contains relatively permanent information about an entity. The customer master file contains permanent information about customers, for example, customer names and addresses, and account balances. The inventory master file contains permanent information about inventory items like item numbers, descriptions, selling price, and quantity on hand.

transaction file

A **transaction file** on the other hand contains information that is used to update a master file. For example, information in the unfilled order file was used to update the inventory master file, while information in the filled order file was used to update the customer master file. Journal entries in the general ledger entries file are used to update the general ledger master file. Registers duplicate and can be used to list much of the information contained in transaction files. Consequently, registers are primarily used as controls.

Summary

The primary focus of this text is on accounting concepts and principles. However, accounting exists within the firm's information system and provides a service function. Consequently, it is also important to understand where accounting information fits into a firm's transaction processing cycles and where the information that accountants and managers use comes from. The accounts receivable system and the cash receipts system are *accounting systems* within the revenue cycle. The order entry system and the shipping system are *transaction processing systems.* These transaction processing systems provide interfaces between the accounting function and other business functions within the organization such as receiving orders and shipping goods.

SUMMARY OF LEARNING OBJECTIVES

1. Explain how transactions are processed through the revenue cycle. Customer orders are processed by the order entry system. Information about accepted orders are input into the shipping system which updates the inventory master file and provides the accounts receivable system with the information that is needed to bill customers. These two transaction processing systems provide an interface between the accounting function and marketing. The accounts receivable system bills customers, updates the customer master file (accounts receivable subsidiary ledger) and the invoice file, and generates accounts receivable journal entries. Customer payments are processed by the cash receipts system. The cash receipts system also updates the customer master file, invoice file, and generates cash receipts journal entries.

2. State the recognition and measurement issues involved in accounting for sales transactions. Merchandising firms are likely to make both cash and credit sales, while manufacturing firms are more likely to make only credit sales. When the sale is for cash, the amount of revenue recognized is the amount of the actual cash received (the agreed-upon sales price less any trade or quantity discount) not including any sales taxes collected for a taxing authority. If the sale is made on credit and an account receivable results, the amount of revenue recognized is based on the net realizable value of the receivable.

Trade and quantity discounts are adjustments to arrive at an agreed-upon sales price, and no accounting recognition is given. Sales discounts, on the other hand, are recognized in the accounting. They may be recorded using either the net or the gross method, although the net method is conceptually preferable. Separate accounts are maintained for sales taxes payable, credit card fees, and sales returns and allowances.

3. Explain the nature of uncollectible accounts and the allowance method of accounting for uncollectible accounts. Uncollectible accounts are a fact of life in business. The allowance method attempts to match the uncollectible accounts against the sale in the period the sale takes place. This is accomplished by estimating uncollectible accounts in the period of sale.

Both the percentage-of-net-sales method and the aging method are acceptable to estimate uncollectible accounts. The percentage-of-net-sales method is often called the income statement approach because it attempts to estimate the amount of uncollectible accounts expense, whereas the aging method is often called the balance sheet approach because it attempts to estimate the net realizable value of the accounts receivable.

4. Evaluate management controls over receivables. To help management monitor receivables, two statistics: the receivable turnover and the average collection period in days are often calculated. The receivable turnover is computed by dividing credit sales by the average accounts receivable for the period. The turnover figure is converted into the average number of days that the receivables are outstanding by dividing 365 days by the turnover.

5. Explain the classification of cash and receivables on the balance sheet. Except in rare circumstances cash is considered a current asset. These circumstances occur when the cash is not available for use by the firm. Different types of receivables should be classified separately. Accounts receivable are not combined with loans to employees, stockholders, or others.

6. List other types of revenues generated from operations. Other economic events generate revenues from operations. These include revenues from interest and dividends. Gains on sales of fixed assets are usually considered nonoperating items, but are included on the income statement in the overall category of income from continuing operations.

7. Explain the revenue cycle computer system. The various systems within the overall revenue cycle system include the order entry system, the shipping system, the accounts receivable system, and the cash receipts system. The accounts receivable and cash receipts system are accounting systems while the order entry and shipping systems are transaction processing systems.

KEY TERMS

REVIEW PROBLEM

Uncollectible Accounts

During your review of the financial statements of the SBC Company, you have gathered the following data relating to receivables as of December 31, 1995 (prior to any adjusting entries):

Net sales, all on credit	$5,000,000
Accounts receivable balance	800,000
Allowance for uncollectible account—debit balance	5,000

REQUIRED:

1. Assuming the firm estimates that 1 1/2% of all credit sales will become uncollectible:
   a. Make the required adjusting entry at 12/31/95 under each of the two methods, percentage-of-net-sales and aging.
   b. What are the balances in (1) Uncollectible Accounts Expense and (2) Allowance for Uncollectible Accounts after the 12/31/95 adjusting entry?
2. Assume that an aging of accounts receivable at 12/31/95 reveals the following:

Age	*Total*	*Estimated Percentage Uncollectible*
Current	$450,000	5%
31–60 days	150,000	10%
61–90 days	75,000	15%
91–120 days	100,000	20%
Over 120 days	25,000	50%
	$800,000	

a. Make the required adjusting entry at 12/31/95.
b. What are the balances in (1) Uncollectible Accounts Expense and (2) Allowance for Uncollectible Accounts after the 12/31/95 adjusting entry?

Solution 1 Percentage-of-Net-Sales Method

a. Estimate of uncollectible accounts expense:

$5,000,000 × .015 = $75,000

Adjusting entry, 12/31/95		
Uncollectible Accounts Expense	75,000	
Allowance for Uncollectible Accounts		75,000

b. Balance in accounts

Uncollectible Accounts Expense		Allowance for Uncollectible Accounts	
		12/31/95 5,000	
Adj. 75,000			Adj. 75,000
12/31/95 Bal. 75,000			12/31/95 Bal. 70,000

2 Aging Method

a. Estimate of uncollectible accounts expense:

Age	*Total*	*Estimated Percentage Uncollectible*	*Total*
Current	$450,000	5%	$22,500
31–60 days	150,000	10%	15,000
61–90 days	75,000	15%	11,250
91–120 days	100,000	20%	20,000
Over 120 days	25,000	50%	12,500
	$800,000		

Required balance	$81,250
Unadjusted balance—debit	5,000
Amount of adjusting entry	$86,250

Adjusting entry—12/31/95		
Uncollectible Accounts Expense	86,250	
Allowance for Uncollectible Accounts		86,250

b. Balance in accounts

Uncollectible Accounts Expense		Allowance for Uncollectible Accounts	
		12/31/95 5,000	
Adj. 86,250			Adj. 86,250
12/31/95 Bal. 86,250			12/31/95 Bal. 81,250

QUESTIONS

1. List and describe three types of operating activities in which firms engage.
2. What are the characteristics of merchandising firms? How do they differ from manufacturing firms?
3. What amount of revenue should be recognized on a cash sale? On a credit sale?
4. Define (a) trade discounts, (b) sales discounts, and (c) quantity discounts.
5. Describe the differences between the gross method and the net method of recording sales discounts. What are the basic assumptions of each method?
6. What are the theoretical problems with the gross method of recording sales discounts? How does the net method overcome these problems?
7. What factors affect a firm's ability to collect its credit sales?
8. The controller of the Switch and Save Stores is proud of herself because she has eliminated all bad debts by giving credit to only a small number of very creditworthy customers. Do you think that this a good policy? Why or why not?
9. Briefly describe the allowance method of accounting for uncollectible receivables. Why is this method preferable to just recording the bad-debt expense

when it becomes clear that a customer has defaulted on his or her account?

10. What accounting procedure should a firm use to reinstate a receivable that has previously been written off as uncollectible?
11. In estimating the amount of future uncollectible accounts, a business may use the balance sheet approach or the income statement approach. Briefly describe these two approaches.
12. In what situations would there be a debit balance in Allowance for Uncollectible Accounts?
13. Explain and describe the receivable turnover and average collection period statistics. During an economic recession, how would you expect these statistics to change for a typical department store?
14. How can companies use accounts receivables to generate cash?
15. Describe a situation in which cash would not be listed as a current asset.
16. Describe the difference between a master file and a transaction file.
17. Explain how registers provide internal control in a computer-based accounting system.
18. Explain why the inventory system appears in the transaction processing cycle diagram for a merchandising firm, but not in the systems flowchart for the revenue cycle.

EXERCISES

E7-1 Accounting for Trade and Quantity Discounts

LO 2

Gar's Paint and Decorating Shop offers both trade and quantity discounts. Quantity discounts are given as follows:

Quantity Purchased	*% Discount*
1–9 cans	0
10–19 cans	5
More than 20 cans	8

Professional painters also receive an additional 5% discount on the list price per gallon before any quantity discounts. Finally, cash buyers receive an additional 2% off the total price. The retail price of each can of paint is $14.

REQUIRED: Make the entry to record the sale for each of the following two situations:

1. Joe Kelly, a professional painter, purchases 35 cans of paint. The purchase is made on account.
2. Al Companies, a do-it-yourself painter, purchases 12 cans of paint. He pays cash.

E7-2 Recording Sales Discounts

LO 2

The following transactions were selected from the records of McCasky and Daughters Retailers:

a. January 2: Sold merchandise to the Vox Corporation for $8,000 cash.
b. January 12: Sold merchandise on account to the Chief Company for $6,500. Terms 3/10, n/30.
c. January 15: Sold merchandise on account to the Foothill Company for $10,000. Terms 2/10, n/30.
d. January 21: Received payment from Foothill Company net of the discount.
e. January 30: Received payment from the Chief Company.

REQUIRED: Prepare the necessary entries to record these sales, assuming that McCasky and Daughters Retailers uses (a) the gross method and then (b) the net method of recording sales discounts.

E7-3
Recording Sales Discounts and Sales Returns
LO 2

The Stanga Corporation sells supplies to various pet grooming stores. During March, the following transactions occurred. The gross method of recording sales discounts was used:

a. March 2: Supplies with a price of $9,500 sold on account to Williams' Pets. Terms 2/10, n/30.
b. March 4: Sale of merchandise for $4,800 cash.
c. March 6: Williams' Pets returned $1,500 of supplies and received a credit.
d. March 10: Williams' Pets paid the amount owed to Stanga.
e. March 15: Sale of $14,000 of merchandise to the Ramsey Pet Hotel. Terms 2/10, n/30.
f. March 17: Sale of $6,800 of merchandise to Ron's Groomers. Because this is a new customer, terms are 5 EOM.
g. March 20: Payment received from the Ramsey Pet Hotel.
h. March 31: Payment received from Ron's Groomers.

REQUIRED: Record the above transactions on the books of the Stanga Corporation.

E7-4
Sales Taxes
LO 2

During March, the Ancient Book Sellers had taxable sales of $15,000. The state sales tax is 7% and all sales were for cash.

REQUIRED: Make the entries to record the sales for the month.

E7-5
Uncollectible Accounts Journal Entries
LO 3

During your examination of the Danos Co. you discovered the following series of journal entries:

1994			
a.	Uncollectible Accounts Expense	2,500	
	Allowance for Uncollectible Accounts		2,500
b.	Allowance for Uncollectible Accounts	250	
	Accounts Receivable		250
c.	Accounts Receivable	100	
	Allowance for Uncollectible Accounts		100
d.	Cash	100	
	Accounts Receivable		100

REQUIRED: Describe the events that caused these entries. What effect did each of these transactions have on net income, gross accounts receivable, allowance for uncollectible accounts, and net accounts receivable?

E7-6
Recording Sales and Uncollectible Accounts
LO 2, 3

During 1994, its first year of operations, Baker's Department Store had total sales of $1,200,000, of which 70% were on credit. During the year, $850,000 was collected on credit sales. Management uses the allowance method and estimates that $24,750 of accounts receivable will be uncollectible.

REQUIRED: Prepare the journal entries to record:

1. Sales during the year.
2. Cash collected on account.
3. The establishment of the account Allowance for Uncollectible Accounts.

E7-7
Recording Sales and Uncollectible Accounts
LO 2, 3

On March 15, 1994, the Sonat Company purchased on account from the Stallon Manufacturing Company merchandise costing $55,000. On December 31, 1994, the accounts receivable of the Stallon Manufacturing Company showed a balance of $950,000, including $40,000 owed to it by the Sonat Company. Stallon's management estimates that 3.5% of all accounts receivable will be uncollectible. At December 31, 1994, there is no balance in either Uncollectible Accounts Expense or Allowance for Uncollectible Accounts. On February 4, 1995, the Sonat Company enters into bankruptcy proceedings. The Stallon Manufacturing Company feels that only 10% of Sonat's outstanding receivable balance will ever be collected. On November 12, 1995, Stallon receives $4,000 from Sonat in payment of the receivable. No other funds will be received on this account.

REQUIRED: Prepare the necessary journal entries on Stallon's books for the following dates:

1. March 15, 1994
2. December 31, 1994
3. February 4, 1995
4. November 12, 1995

E7-8
Accounting for Uncollectible Accounts
LO 3

The following data was taken from the unadjusted trial balance of the Burnside Company:

	Debit	*Credit*
Accounts receivable	$340,000	
Allowance for uncollectible accounts		$ 2,800
Total sales—45% for cash		700,000

Actual uncollectible accounts written off during the year amounted to $3,200.

REQUIRED: If the firm uses the allowance method to record uncollectible accounts, compute uncollectible accounts expense under each of the following assumptions:

1. Two percent of total sales.
2. Three percent of credit sales.
3. Allowance for Uncollectible Accounts is increased to 6% of the ending receivable balance.

E7-9
Uncollectible Accounts Percentage-of-Sales Method
LO 3

The following information has been taken from the records of the Kataki Company prior to any adjusting entries on December 31, 1994:

Account	*Balance—12/31/94*
Credit sales	$4,200,000
Sales returns and allowance	24,000
Accounts receivable	640,000
Allowance for uncollectible accounts—debit balance	1,200

Management uses the percentages of net credit sales to estimate uncollectible accounts. Actual credit sales and uncollectibles for the five previous years have been as follows:

Year	*Net Credit Sales*	*Uncollectible Accounts*
1989	$ 650,000	$ 22,750
1990	780,000	39,000
1991	1,400,000	58,800
1992	2,750,000	115,500
1993	3,750,000	183,800

REQUIRED: Using the above information, prepare the adjusting entry to record the uncollectible accounts expense for 1994. What is the balance in Allowance for Uncollectible Accounts after the adjusting entry?

E7-10
Uncollectible Accounts Aging Method
LO 3

On December 31, 1994, the balance in Accounts Receivable of the Kwon Company is $217,820. The company sells highly specialized products to a small number of customers. The following aging schedule was prepared by the company's bookkeeper:

			Age of Accounts Receivable		
Customer	*Totals*	*Current*	*31–60 Days*	*61–90 Days*	*Over 90 Days*
M. A. Duncan	$ 30,500	$ 500	$12,000	$18,000	$ 0
C. Q. Jackson	52,700	3,100	24,000	15,000	10,600
P. C. Dimitri	65,950	0	33,450	0	32,500
S. A. Savett	68,670	60,000	0	8,670	0
Totals	$217,820	$63,600	$69,450	$41,670	$43,100

Based on past experience, management makes the following estimate of uncollectible accounts:

Age	%
Current	5
31–60 days	10
61–90 days	35
Over 90 days	40

Prior to any adjustment, Allowance for Uncollectible Accounts has a debit balance of $3,000. Prepare the necessary journal entry to record the uncollectible accounts expense at December 31, 1994.

E7-11
Determining Journal Entries
LO 3

After examining the records of the Columbo Mystery Store you determined the following end-of-year amounts:

	1995	*1994*
Credit sales	$120,000	$105,000
Accounts receivable	30,500	26,000
Allowance for uncollectible accounts	1,200	900
Bad debts written off and then recovered	300	100

Your examination of the records of the Columbo Mystery Store indicates that they are using the percentage-of-net-sales method to estimate bad debts and a percentage rate of 4%.

REQUIRED:

1. Determine the amount of accounts receivable that were actually written off during 1995.
2. Prepare summary journal entries to record the activity in Accounts Receivable and Allowance for Uncollectible Accounts during 1995.

E7-12
Bad Debts and Financial Statement Analysis

The Levitt Company sells housewares to hardware stores. The company is reviewing its records *prior to any adjustments for uncollectible accounts.* Prior to these adjustments its net income for the year amounted to just over $1 million. At year-end, also prior to any adjustments, Accounts Receivable totaled $300,000 and Allowance for Uncollectible Accounts had a balance of $22,400. After conducting its review, the company decided to make two

(Review of Material in Previous Chapters)
LO 3

entries regarding uncollectible accounts: (a) write off accounts of $21,000 determined to be uncollectible and (b) record this year's estimate of $24,000 in uncollectible accounts.

REQUIRED: Assuming that the firm has a positive net working capital ratio, determine the effect of each entry on the firm's (a) net working capital ratio, (b) gross profit percentage, (c) profit margin percentage, and (d) return on total assets.

E7-13
Receivables Management
LO 4

K & J Electronics had total credit sales of $1,940,000 during 1994. The beginning balance in Accounts Receivable was $340,000, and the ending balance in the account was $630,000.

REQUIRED: Compute the receivable turnover rates and the average number of days that the receivables were outstanding. Explain what these figures mean. What advice can you give to management to improve these figures?

E7-14
Receivables Management
LO 4

The president of the Abrahamson Corporation has been analyzing their accounts receivable and is concerned about the length of time it is taking to collect them. She determines that during the past 12 months the average days outstanding has been 34.76. Assuming that during the same period the average accounts receivable balance has been $80,000, determine the amount of credit sales for the period.

E7-15
Cash Receipts Budget
LO 5

Hillerman's Department Store has found from past experience that 20% of its sales are for cash. The remaining 80% use credit. An aging schedule for accounts receivable reveals the following pattern.

10% of credit sales are paid in the month of sale
70% of credit sales are paid in the month following sale
17% of credit sales are paid in the second month following sale
3% of credit sales are never collected

Credit sales which have not been paid until the second month following sale are considered "overdue" and are subject to a 2% late charge.

Hillerman's Department Store has developed the following sales forecast:

May	$ 76,000
June	85,000
July	68,000
August	80,000
September	100,000

REQUIRED: Prepare a schedule of cash receipts for August and September.

E7-16
Cash Receipts Budget
LO 5

CeCe's Gift Shop in Sedona, Arizona, sells a variety of t-shirts (screen printed with desert themes) and objets d'art. CeCe accepts cash, check, VISA, Mastercard, and American Express. These methods of payment have the following characteristics:

a. Cash: Payment is immediate, no fee is charged.
b. Check: Payment is immediate, the bank charges $.25 per check, 1% of check revenue is from "bad" checks and CeCe cannot collect.
c. VISA/Mastercard: CeCe accumulates these credit card receipts throughout the month and submits them in one bundle for payment on the last day of the month. The money is credited to her account by the 5th day of the following month. A 1½% fee is charged by the credit card company.

d. American Express: CeCe accumulates these receipts throughout the month and mails them to AmEx for payment on the last day of the month. AmEx credits her account by the 6th day of the following month. A 3½% fee is charged by American Express.

During a typical month, CeCe has sales of $20,000, broken down as follows:

American Express	20%
VISA/Mastercard	50%
Check	5% (checks average $37.50 each)
Cash	25%

REQUIRED: If CeCe estimates sales of $20,000 in April and $30,000 in May (May sales are higher due to the Memorial Day weekend), what are her planned net cash receipts for May?

E7-17
Master Files and Transaction Files
LO 7

Information contained in the unfilled order file is used by the shipping system to update the inventory master file.

REQUIRED:

1. Describe the information that you would expect to find in the unfilled order file.
2. Describe the effect that the information in the unfilled order file would have on item quantities in the inventory master file when it is updated.
3. Identify other transactions that should affect item quantities in the inventory master file, describe the effect (increase or decrease), and identify the transaction cycle where the transaction would originate.

E7-18
Albertson's Financial Statements
LO 3

The following information was taken from footnotes of a recent financial statement of Albertson's:

	January 30, 1992	*January 31, 1991*	*February 1 1990*
Trade accounts receivable	$54,832	$50,732	$43,828
Trade notes receivable	1,658	2,280	757
Less allowance for doubtful accounts	(655)	(738)	(482)
	$55,835	$52,274	$44,103

Sales for the period ending January 31, 1992 amounted to $8,680,467,000. Assuming that 10% of these were on credit, and that $450,000 of accounts receivable were written off as uncollectible during 1991, (1) determine the amount of uncollectible accounts expense for 1991, and (2) the amount of cash collected on receivables during 1991.

PROBLEMS

P7-1
Accounting for Sales Discounts
LO 2

During the month of November, Hubble Ltd. made the following sales on account:

a. Nov. 12: $50,000 of merchandise to the Lock Co. Terms 2/10, n/30.
b. Nov. 21: $80,000 of merchandise to the Glazer Corporation. Terms 2/10, n/30.
c. Nov. 29: $25,000 of merchandise to the Palmrose Supply Co. Terms 2/10, n/30.

On December 5 Hubble received the entire $50,000 from Lock. On December 20 Hubble received a partial $50,000 payment from Glazer. The remaining amount was received from Glazer on December 31. No payments were received on the sale to Palmrose.

REQUIRED:

1. Assuming that Hubble Ltd. uses the gross method of recording sales discounts, make the entries to record the sales and subsequent cash collections.
2. Assuming that Hubble Ltd. uses the net method of recording sales discounts, make the entries to record the sales and subsequent cash collections.
3. Assuming that the balance in Accounts Receivable at November 1 was $14,000, determine the balance in this account at December 31 under both methods.

P7-2
Accounting for Sales Transactions (Alternative to P7-3)
LO 2

The following accounts were listed on the post-closing trial balance of the Keating Company at December 31, 1994:

Accounts receivable	$500,000
Allowance for uncollectible accounts	34,000

During 1995 the following transactions occurred:

a. The firm sold merchandise for cash for $50,000. Sales taxes of 8% are levied on these sales.
b. Sold merchandise on credit to the Al Bruckner Company for $110,000. Terms are 2/10, n/30. No sales taxes are levied on these sales.
c. Sold merchandise on credit to the Barcomb Corporation for $75,000 less a 10% trade discount. Terms are 1/10, n/30. No sales taxes are levied.
d. The Al Bruckner Company paid the entire invoice within the discount period.
e. The firm determined that $24,000 of accounts that had been considered uncollectible should be written off.
f. The Barcomb Corporation returned defective merchandise worth $5,000 (price before the discount) to the Keating Company. Their account was credited for the proper amount.
g. The Keating Company was surprised to receive a check for $2,500 from the Donnelly Company. The Donnelly Company's account totaling $6,000 was written off in item (e). The $2,500 is from the bankruptcy court and is in full settlement of the firm's account.
h. The Barcomb Corporation paid the remaining full amount of their account. No discount was taken.
i. The firm estimates its uncollectible account expense to be 4% of total credit sales.
j. The Keating Company paid the appropriate amount of sales taxes.

The company uses the gross method of recording sales discounts.

REQUIRED:

1. Make the required journal entries for the above transactions.
2. Determine the balance in the following accounts:
   a. Accounts Receivable
   b. Allowance for Uncollectible Accounts
   c. Uncollectible Accounts Expense

P7-3
Accounting for Sales Transactions (Alternative to P7-2)
LO 2

The following accounts were listed on the post-closing trial balance of the Polanski Partnership at December 31, 1994:

Accounts receivable	$350,000
Allowance for uncollectible accounts	16,000

During 1995 the following transactions occurred:

a. The firm sold merchandise for cash for $67,000. Sales taxes of 7% are levied on these sales.
b. Sold merchandise on credit to Barttov, Inc., for $71,000. Terms are 2/10, n/30. Sales taxes of 7% are levied on these sales.
c. Sold merchandise on credit to the Cook Company for $45,000 less a 5% trade discount. Terms are 2/10, n/30. No sales taxes are levied.
d. Barttov, Inc., was very unhappy with $10,000 of the merchandise it received in transaction (b). It returned the merchandise within the discount period and its account was credited.
e. Barttov, Inc., then paid the remainder of its bill within the discount period.
f. The firm determined that $19,000 of accounts that had been considered uncollectible should be written off.
g. The Polanski Partnership was surprised to receive a check for $500 from the Knox Company. The Knox Company's account totaling $6,000 was written off in item (f). The $500 is from the bankruptcy court and is in full settlement of the firm's account.
h. The Cook Company paid the full amount of their account. No discount was taken.
i. The Polanski Partnership estimates its uncollectible account expense to be 5% of the current balance in Accounts Receivable.
j. The Polanski Partnership paid the amount of sales taxes due.

The company uses the net method of recording sales discounts.

REQUIRED:

1. Make the required journal entries for the above transactions.
2. Determine the balance in the following accounts:
   a. Accounts Receivable
   b. Allowance for Uncollectible Accounts
   c. Uncollectible Accounts Expense

P7-4 Uncollectible Accounts Expense (Alternative to P7-5)

LO 3

The Europe Company has been experiencing a high rate of bad debts in the past few years. On December 31, 1994, before the company made any year-end adjustments, the balance in Europe Company's accounts receivable account was $1 million and Allowance for Uncollectible Accounts had a debit balance of $4,000. Allowance for Uncollectible Accounts will be adjusted using the aging method and applying the following schedule:

Days Account Is Outstanding	*Amount*	*Probability of Default*
Current	$ 540,000	0.05
31–60 days	310,000	0.10
61–90 days	90,000	0.20
91–120 days	35,000	0.30
Over 120 days	25,000	0.70
	$1,000,000	

REQUIRED:

1. Make the journal entry or entries to record the required adjustment.
2. What is the appropriate balance for Allowance for Uncollectible Accounts on December 31, 1994?
3. Show how Accounts Receivable would be presented on the balance sheet prepared on December 31, 1994.
4. What is the dollar effect of the year-end uncollectible accounts expense adjustment on income for 1994?

P7-10 Controls in Computer-Based Revenue Cycle Application Systems
LO 7

Auditors use system flowcharts to help them analyze internal control risks. Refer to Exhibit 7-13 and complete the following internal control worksheet by identifying potential control risks in the revenue cycle and the controls that you would expect to find to reduce the control risk.

Control Objective	*Control Risk*	*Expected Control*
Transactions are authorized	Process an unauthorized purchase order	Review and approval of purchase orders prior to input

DISCUSSION AND INTERPRETATION PROBLEMS

D7-1 Understanding Financial Statements

The current assets section of the HI-tec, Inc., balance sheet is reproduced below:

HI-tec, Inc. and Subsidiaries
Consolidated Balance Sheets
(in millions)

Assets	*December 31, 1994*	*1993*
Current Assets:		
Cash and short-term investments	$ 445	$ 35
Accounts and other receivables	64	73
Merchandise inventories	1,390	1,275
Prepaid expenses	28	21
Total Current Assets	$1,927	$1,404

Net sales for 1994, assumed to be all on account, totaled $5,500,000,000. The accounts and other receivables are shown net of an allowance for doubtful accounts of $1,280,000 in 1994 and $1,760,000 in 1993. In 1994, the company determined that $2,200,000 of receivables previously allowed for were uncollectible and decided to write them off.

REQUIRED:

1. How much cash did the company collect from its accounts and other receivables during the year ended December 31, 1994?
2. Determine the amount of uncollectible accounts expense for the year ended December 31, 1994.

D7-2 Understanding Financial Statements

The following note is taken from a recent annual report of Security Pacific National Bank, a large California-based bank:

Security Pacific Corporation
Notes to Consolidated Financial Statements

The following is a summary of activity in the reserve for credit losses:

(dollars in millions)	*1991*	*1990*	*1989*
Balance, January 1	$1,448.1	$1,162.3	$1,135.8
Provision charged to expense	2,617.9	1,165.9	547.8
Other[1]	(74.0)	32.9	9.8
Subtotal	3,992.0	2,361.1	1,693.4

(continued)

(dollars in millions)	*1991*	*1990*	*1989*
Charge-offs	(1,586.4)	(1,010.6)	(658.2)
Recoveries	113.0	97.6	127.1
Net credit losses	(1,473.4)	(913.0)	(531.1)
Balance, December 31	$2,518.6	$1,448.1	$1,162.3

[1]Includes the effect of acquisitions, dispositions and foreign currency translation adjustments.

The following is a summary of non-performing loans and leases and related interest forgone:

(dollars in millions)	*December 31, 1991*	*December 31, 1990*	*December 31, 1989*
Non-accrual loans and leases	$2,740	$2,057	$1,631
Restructured loans and leases	13	13	12
Total	$2,753	$2,070	$1,643

	1991	*1990*	*1989*
Domestic:			
Contractual interest due	$241.4	$178.9	$161.8
Interest recognized	(17.4)	(12.2)	(24.4)
Net interest forgone	224.0	166.7	137.4
International:			
Contractual interest due	80.9	80.3	53.0
Interest recognized	(4.5)	(11.5)	(21.3)
Net interest forgone	76.4	68.8	31.7
Total net interest forgone	$300.4	$235.5	$169.1

REQUIRED:

1. What is the amount of receivables written off as uncollectible in 1991 and 1990, respectively?
2. How much did the reserve for credit losses (another name for allowance for doubtful accounts) increase from 1990 to 1991 and from 1989 to 1990?
3. What was the amount of bad-debt expense for 1991? Given the events of 1991 does that amount appear to be reasonable? Why or why not?
4. Make the entries Security Pacific National Bank would have made in 1991 to record the accounts written off during 1991 and the provision for credit losses at the end of 1991.

D7-3
Financial Decision Case

The Muppett Computer Store sells computers and software to individuals and to businesses. Because of the high price of the goods it sells, Muppett has always had a very stringent credit policy and will sell on credit only to customers with a AAA credit rating. However, the president of the company has begun to notice that many of the firm's competitors have begun to advertise that they welcome credit sales. As a result, the president is concerned that the firm's profits are suffering by its insistence on such a tough credit policy. She gives you the following data and asks your advice as to whether the firm's credit policies should be relaxed.

Current sales are running about $10 million a year, of which only 10% are currently made on credit. The firm's gross profit on sales is 30% or, correspondingly, the cost of goods sold equals 70% of sales. Current uncollectible accounts amount to only 1% of credit sales. The firm has analyzed its potential customers and feels that there are three additional classes of credit customers to which it could extend credit. If it does, the firm expects to increase sales and to incur the following amount of uncollectibles and additional selling expenses for each of the three classes:

Class Rating	*Additional Sales*	*Percent Uncollectible*	*Additional Expenses*
A	$100,000	5	$10,000
B	60,000	10	11,000
C	90,000	20	13,000

REQUIRED:

1. Advise the president as to whether the firm's credit policies should be revised and, if so, to what extent. Include a discussion of what effect there will be on profits if sales are made to the additional customers.
2. What else should the president take into consideration before making a final decision on extending credit to these potential customers?

D7-4 Financial Decision Case

The Metro Gold Store is owned by two partners, Ed Roebuck and Sharon Sears. Their primary business is the purchase and resale of gold bars and gold chains. Each day a large number of cash receipts and disbursements are made. All transactions are conducted by check. The company has grown in recent years, and the firm has been able to obtain a $200,000 line of credit from the bank.

Controlling the daily cash balance is an important aspect of their business. Ed is primarily in charge of this aspect. At the end of each day, he calls the bank and finds out what the current balance is in their account. He then adds the amount of the day's deposits, and this gives him the amount of cash available to use. He then writes checks for that amount, and in some cases in excess of that amount. He feels comfortable writing checks in excess of the amount available, because he knows that it will take a few days before those checks are paid.

As the firm's business has expanded, the available cash balance has continued to decrease, and they have been forced to use most of their line of credit. They are both happy in the increase in sales as the price of gold has increased, but they are concerned with their cash position.

REQUIRED:

1. Comment on the procedures that Ed uses to control the firm's cash. Explain to him why he may not be getting an accurate cash figure.
2. What circumstances could cause their cash problems as their sales continue to rise?
3. Describe several procedures the firm could institute to gain better control over the daily cash balance.

D7-5 Research Assignment

As discussed in the chapter, many banks and other financial institutions suffered large loan losses in the first part of the 1990's. Citibank and Bank of America were two such banks. Using the resources of your library obtain the financial statements of either bank for 1991 and 1992 (or later if available). Based on this information answer the following questions:

a. What does management say about the provision for loan losses from 1990 through 1992? What does management attribute the change in the loan loss reserve to?
b. What is the actual provision for 1990? 1991? and 1992?
c. Describe the general economic conditions facing financial institutions in the early 1990's. How did these conditions effect Citicorp and/or Bank of America?

D7-6 Ethical Considerations

Jerry Dunphy is the sales manager for the XCAL radio station. He is charged with selling advertising for the radios various programs. He receives a salary plus a bonus of 10% of all advertising revenues that he sells.

The station has strict credit policies and only sells advertising to companies that are in a strong financial position. Jerry is aware of this policy, but has often expressed his disagreement with it as he feels that he loses sales and thus commission. He is currently negotiating a large advertising package with a local supermarket chain. The chain has been experiencing financial difficulties lately, and Jerry is concerned that XCAL may not accept their advertising.

Jerry knows that XCAL only does a quick review of advertiser's financial statements and often relies on the salespeople to vouch for the advertiser's financial strength. Jerry has met with the supermarket's chief financial officer and has helped her prepare the application for credit. He knows the tricks of the trade and helps make the application look as good as possible. Jerry figures that the XCAL needs the advertising and that he could certainly use the commission. Anyway, it is not his job to collect the fees; his job is only to sell advertising.

REQUIRED:

1. Do you think that the bonus plan provided to Jerry is in XCAL's best interest? How might you change the plan, if at all?
2. Do you think that Jerry acted ethically by helping the supermarket's chief financial officer prepare the credit application. Why or why not?

CHAPTER 8
THE EXPENDITURE CYCLE: PURCHASES AND PAYABLES

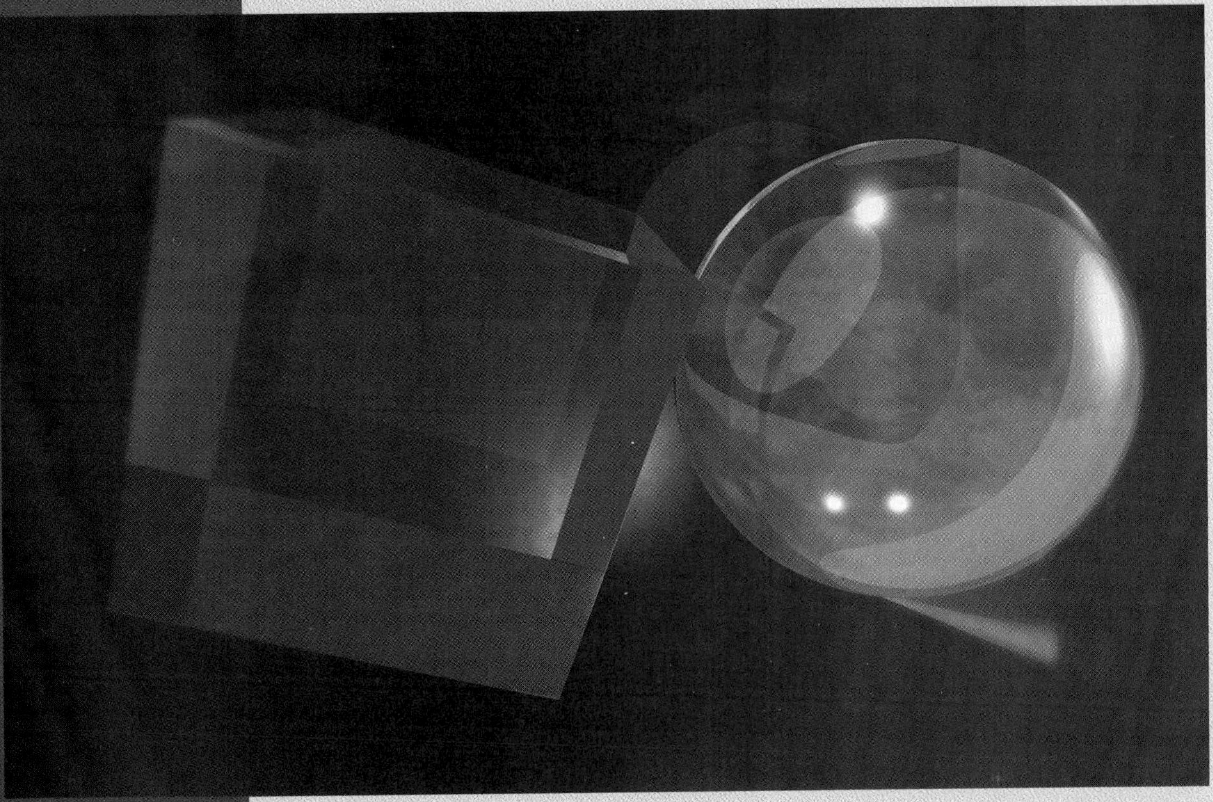

LEARNING OBJECTIVES

After studying this chapter, you should be able to:

1. Define liabilities and state the criteria used to recognize, measure, and value them.
2. Explain the accounting concepts related to (a) existing liabilities with known amounts, and (b) contingent liabilities.
3. Explain the accounting issues related to payables arising from operations.
4. Explain the special issues involved in recording inventory transactions.
5. State how liabilities are presented on a typical balance sheet.
6. Describe the accounting systems used to process expenditure cycle transactions.

Scenario

The executive vice-president for administration at South Central University, Lois Hutton, was meeting with the university's auditors. They were discussing how to account for the university's guarantee of certain student tuition loans.

South Central is a large private university with a total student population of about 24,000, of which 17,000 are undergraduates. The university provides a financial aid package to all freshmen who enter the school. Depending upon the circumstances, this aid takes the form of outright scholarships and/or a combination of scholarships and student loans. Currently, about $60 million in loans to South Central students are outstanding.

Some of these student loans are through state and federal agencies and some are through banks. The university has guaranteed payment of the student loans held by banks. Past experience has indicated that the university will be called upon to make good a small percentage of these loans.

Lois Hutton feels that these student loan guarantees should be disclosed in the notes to the financial statements. She argues that the amounts South Central ultimately might have to pay are difficult to estimate and that the university will probably not have to make any significant payments. The university's auditors, however, feel that past experience could be used to estimate any loan losses that the university might experience and that this amount should be accrued as a liability.

Lois decides to do a little homework and see what current accounting standards say about these types of guarantees. Her investigation of the issue leads her to Statement of Financial Accounting Standards No. 5, *Accounting for Contingencies.* This statement says that a contingency such as a loan guarantee should be accrued as a liability if (a) it is *probable* that the person or firm guaranteeing the loan will have to make the loan payment and (b) the amount can be *reasonably estimated.* Her interpretation of this standard is that, although some small loan payments will have to be made, the amounts are very difficult to estimate, and they are immaterial in nature. Thus, she feels that note disclosure is all that is required.

Further, she asked her assistant to review the annual reports of other universities to see how they handled this issue. He found that although practice varied, most universities just provided note disclosure. This is the position Lois decided to take with the auditors.

This chapter discusses those operating activities of the firm which relate to the purchase of its goods and services, payment to suppliers for these goods and services and other operating activities such as employee compensation costs, the incurrence of taxes and interest, and the subsequent payment of these taxes and interest. Most of these transactions are processed by the expenditure cycle which is highlighted in Exhibit 8-1. The payroll system is shown as part of the expenditure cycle because labor is purchased through this system. As the firm enters into these activities it normally incurs liabilities such as accounts payable and

Exhibit 8-1
The Expenditure Cycle

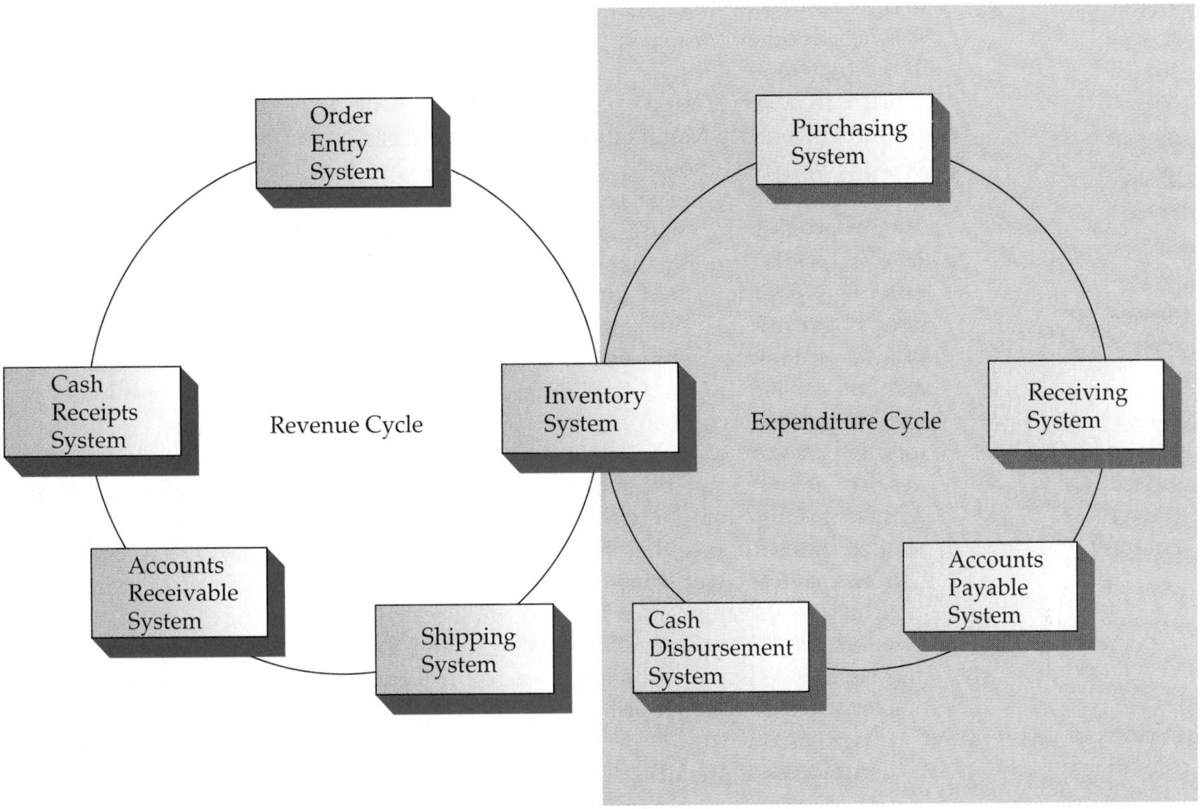

taxes payable. These liabilities are liquidated when subsequent cash payments are made.

The first part of this chapter deals with accounting concepts related to the recognition, measurement, and valuation of liabilities incurred in the operating cycle. The second part of the chapter discusses the accounting issues related to liabilities arising from operations, while the third part takes a closer look at special accounting issues related to the purchase of inventories for resale. The final part of the chapter explores the computer-based processing of expenditure cycle transactions.

LIABILITY RECOGNITION, MEASUREMENT, AND VALUATION

Objective 1
Define liabilities and state the criteria used to recognize, measure, and value them.

Liabilities represent the economic obligations of the enterprise. In recent years, as many firms have struggled to maintain an adequate level of liquidity, issues involving the determination, measurement, and recognition of liabilities have become increasingly important. This part of the chapter will discuss the accounting concepts and procedures related to those current liabilities generated from the firm's operating cycle.

Definition and Recognition of Liabilities

The FASB defines liabilities as "probable future sacrifices of economic benefits arising from present obligations of a particular entity to transfer assets or provide services to other entities in the future as a result of past transactions or events."[1] To recognize a liability a firm need not know the actual recipient of the assets that are to be transferred or for whom the services are to be performed. For example, when General Motors guarantees or warrants an automobile, a liability must be recorded, even though at the time of sale GM does not know which particular customer's automobile may require repair.

For a liability to exist, an event or transaction must already have occurred. In effect, only present (not future) obligations are liabilities. For example, the exchange of promises of future performance between two firms or individuals does not result in the recognition of a liability or the related asset. The signing of a labor contract between a firm and an individual does not cause the firm to recognize a liability; rather, the liability is recognized when the employee performs services for which compensation has not yet been received. In the automobile warranty case the liability occurs at the time of sale, because at that time the firm obligates itself to make certain repairs. Thus, the event has occurred, and a present obligation is incurred.

monetary liabilities

nonmonetary liabilities

Liabilities can be either *monetary* or *nonmonetary*. **Monetary liabilities** are obligations that are payable in a fixed sum of money. Examples of monetary liabilities are accounts payable, notes payable, and accruals such as wages and interest payable. **Nonmonetary liabilities** are obligations to provide fixed amounts of goods and services. They include items such as revenues received in advance of a sale or performance of a service.

Classification of Liabilities on the Balance Sheet

In preparing a balance sheet, liabilities are classified as either current or long-term. Current liabilities are obligations satisfied through the use of existing resources that are classified as current assets or through the creation of new current liabilities. Current liabilities include such accounts as accounts payable, short-term notes payable, current maturities of long-term debt (the principal portion of a long-term liability due within the next 12 months), taxes payable, and other accrued payables. All but short-term notes and current maturities of long-term debt relate to the firm's operating cycle. (Short-term debt instruments such as notes and loans payable result from the firm's financing activities.)

Long-term liabilities, discussed in subsequent chapters, are those liabilities that will not be satisfied within one year or within the operating cycle (if longer than one year). Examples of long-term liability accounts included in this category are mortgages payable, bonds payable, and lease obligations all resulting from financing activities. However, any amounts currently due on these long-term liabilities are classified as current.

Measurement and Valuation of Current Liabilities

Like assets, liabilities originally are measured and recorded according to the historical cost principle. That is, when incurred, the liability is measured and recorded at the current market value of the asset or service received. Because

1. Financial Accounting Standards Board, Concepts Statement No. 6, *Elements of Financial Statements* (Stamford, Conn.: FASB, December 1985), par. 35.

current liabilities are payable within a relatively short period of time, they are recorded at their face value, which is the amount of cash needed to discharge the principal of the liability. No recognition is given to the fact that the *present value* of these future cash outlays is less. **Present value** is the concept that the value of money is affected by time. Essentially, this means that cash received or paid in the future is worth less than the same amount of cash received or paid today. For example, one dollar today (a present value) is worth more than one dollar received one year from now (a future value). This is because cash on hand today can be invested and thus can grow to a greater future amount. Therefore, the value of the liability at the time it is incurred actually is less than the cash required to be paid in the future.

present value

In connection with current liabilities, the difference between value today and future cash outlay is not material because of the short time span between the time the liability is incurred and the time it is paid. Thus, current liabilities are shown at the amount of the future principal payment. However, present-value concepts are applied to long-term liabilities, liabilities with no stated interest, and liabilities with a stated interest rate materially different from the market rate for similar transactions. These cases will be explored in a later chapter.

TYPES OF CURRENT LIABILITIES

Objective 2
Explain the accounting concepts related to (a) existing liabilities with known amounts, and (b) contingent liabilities.

Liabilities often are divided into two major types: (1) those that exist and whose amounts usually are known, and (2) *contingent liabilities* which depend on some future event. Examples of these types of liabilities resulting from the operating activities of the firm are discussed next. In general, most of these liabilities are also classified as current.

Existing Liabilities With Known Amounts

It is easy to determine the existence of many liabilities, as well as the amount of such liabilities. Included in this category are accounts payable, wages payable and other employee benefit costs and liabilities, interest payable, current maturities of long-term debt, and dividends payable. The accounting issues related to these liabilities are: (a) determining their existence and amount and (b) ensuring that they are recorded in the proper accounting period. For example, if the cost of an item is included in the ending inventory but a corresponding payable and/or purchase is not recorded, there will be an understatement of both cost of goods sold and total liabilities. The actual accounting issues related to these liabilities are discussed later in the chapter.

Contingent Liabilities

contingent liabilities

Contingent liabilities are potential future liabilities whose existence is contingent upon some future event. In effect, a contingent liability is the result of an existing condition or situation whose final resolution depends on some future event. Generally, the amount of these liabilities must be estimated; the actual amount cannot be determined until the event that confirms the liability occurs. Furthermore, in many cases the actual person or company to whom payments will be made is not known until the future event occurs.

Examples of contingent liabilities include product warranties and guarantees, pending or threatened litigation, and the guarantee of others' indebtedness. The scenario at the beginning of this chapter described a contingent liability, the student loans guaranteed by South Central University. In all these situations, an event has occurred that may give rise to a liability depending on some future event. For example, when General Motors sells a car, it gives the purchaser a 60,000-mile or six-year guarantee against defects. Thus, an event—the sale of a car—has taken place. However, the actual amount of the liability and the person to whom it will be paid depend on some future action—the customer's bringing the car in for repair.

Contingent Liabilities That Are Accrued. Under generally accepted accounting principles, contingent liabilities are recorded as actual liabilities only if the potential liability is probable and its amount can be reasonably estimated.[2] An automobile guarantee and other product warranties are examples of contingent liabilities that usually are recorded on a company's books. Past experience indicating that a certain percentage of products will be defective can also be used to make a reasonable estimate of the amount of the future expenditure required by a particular warranty. The matching convention requires the expense to be recorded in the period of the sale, not when the repair is made. As of December 31, 1991, General Motors had an $8.2 billion liability recorded for warranty claims and other customer and dealer allowances.

To illustrate, assume that the Micro Printing Company manufactures and sells high-speed laser printers for personal computers. The retail price per unit is $1,200, and each printer is guaranteed for three years; that is, the firm will repair the unit free of charge during this period. During the 1994 calendar year, the firm sold 2,000 printers. Past experience indicates that Micro Printing will incur an average of $40 in repair expense for each of the printers sold. Finally, during 1994, the company actually incurred $35,000 of warranty expenditures related to these printers. The following summary journal entries were made by Micro Printing Company in 1994 to reflect these events:

Cash or Accounts Receivable	2,400,000	
Sales		2,400,000
To record sales for the year. $2,400,000 = 2,000 units × $1,200		
Product Guarantee Expense	80,000	
Estimated Liability for Product Guarantees		80,000
To record estimated liability for product guarantees. $80,000 = 2,000 units × $40		
Estimated Liability for Product Guarantees	35,000	
Cash, Supplies, Accrued Wages, etc.		35,000
To record actual expenditures incurred for product guarantees during the year.		

For each accounting period, the entries are repeated. As the firm makes sales, an estimated liability is accrued. Then, as the guarantee expenditures are made by the firm, the liability is debited, and the appropriate accounts are credited.

Other contingent liabilities that may be accrued if it is probable that the liability exists and the amount of the liability can be reasonably estimated. Examples include, among others, the threat of expropriation of assets, possible claims and assessments, and premium offers.

2. Financial Accounting Standards Board, Statement No. 5, *Accounting for Contingencies* (Stamford, Conn.: FASB, March 1975).

Contingent Liabilities That Are Not Accrued. Contingent liabilities that are not probable and/or whose amounts cannot be reasonably estimated are not accrued on the company's books. Instead, they are usually disclosed in the notes to the financial statements. These types of contingencies commonly include pending litigation and certain guarantees of indebtedness. For example, a company might guarantee the collectibility of a receivable that it has sold to a bank or borrowed against at the bank. This type of guarantee, if material, is disclosed in the notes to the financial statements. The following example, taken from a recent annual report of Ford, shows how such contingent liabilities are disclosed.

Various legal actions, governmental investigations and proceedings and claims are pending or may be instituted or asserted in the future against the company and its subsidiaries, including those arising out of alleged defects in the company's products, governmental regulations relating to safety, emissions and fuel economy, financial services, intellectual property rights, product warranties and environmental matters. Certain of the pending legal actions are, or purport to be, class actions. Some of the foregoing matters involve or may involve compensatory, punitive, or antitrust or other treble damage claims in very large amounts, or demands for recall campaigns, environmental cleanup programs, sanctions, or other relief which, if granted, would require very large expenditures.

Litigation is subject to many uncertainties, the outcome of individual litigated matters is not predictable with assurance, and it is reasonably possible that some of the foregoing matters could be decided unfavorably to the company or the subsidiary involved. Although the amount of liability at December 31, 1991, with respect to these matters cannot be ascertained, the company believes that any resulting liability should not materially affect the consolidated financial position of the company and its consolidated subsidiaries at December 31, 1991.[3]

In effect, the same event may either be accrued as a liability or just disclosed depending upon the specific circumstances. For example, claims, assessments, and pending litigation usually are reported through footnote disclosure. However, if it is probable that the specific claim, assessment, or litigation is going to result in a liability and the amount of the liability can be estimated, it should be accrued. Finally, unspecified or general business risks should not be accrued or disclosed in the notes. For example, the risk of loss due to a poor year because of a recession is a general risk faced by the entire economic community and should not be accrued or disclosed.

ACCOUNTING ISSUES RELATED TO PAYABLES ARISING FROM OPERATIONS

Objective 3
Explain the accounting issues related to payables arising from operations.

Operating activities which give rise to expenses and corresponding liabilities include the purchase of inventories for resale, purchase of employee services (including fringe and retirement benefits), other accrued liabilities related to operations, and the incurrence of income taxes. These items are explored in detail next.

Purchase of Inventories for Resale

inventories

The purchase of *inventory* for resale represents a major activity of a merchandising firm. **Inventories** are items held for resale to customers in the normal course

3. Ford Motor Company, Annual Report 1991, Note 16.

of business or items that are to be consumed in producing or manufacturing goods or rendering services. For merchandising and manufacturing companies, inventories often are the single largest current asset. For example, at February 1, 1992, the inventories of Toys "R" Us, a large chain of retail toy stores, totaled over $1.3 billion, representing 72% of current assets and over 30% of total assets.

Accounting information for inventory purchases must be designed to allow management to maintain the proper level of inventories and to ensure that ending inventories and cost of goods sold are properly recorded and costed. This section will cover the nature of inventories, the recording of inventory purchases, and the related issues of purchase discounts and purchase returns and allowances. The final section of this chapter will detail the expenditure cycle application systems. The next chapter will deal with how a firm determines the cost of its ending inventory and the cost of those items sold during the period.

Issues Involved in Recording Inventory Purchases

It is important that inventory purchases be recorded at the time title passes from the seller to the buyer and that inventory purchases be recorded in accordance with the historical cost principle. In this regard, historical cost includes the cash-equivalent price of the item plus all costs incurred by the purchasing company for freight and handling to deliver the merchandise to a location for its use or sale. (These delivery charges, called *freight-in* are explained later in the chapter.) Specific items that affect the historical cost of inventory purchases include purchase discounts, purchase returns and allowances, and freight charges.

purchase discounts

Recording Purchase Discounts.[4] Accounting for **purchase discounts** is similar to accounting for sales discounts. The two methods, gross and net, are briefly illustrated in the journal entries shown in Exhibit 8-2. The example is based on a $100 purchase with terms of 2/10, n/30, and parallels the seller's side of the transaction as presented in Exhibit 7-2 on page 309.

gross method of recording purchase discounts

The Gross Method. The **gross method of recording purchase discounts** records the purchase of merchandise inventory and the payable at the gross amount before any discount. Purchase Discounts will be credited for the amount of the discount, if it is taken by a firm. This account eventually is transferred to Cost of Goods Sold through an adjusting entry at the end of the period. The result is to reduce cost of goods sold by the amount of the discounts taken.

The entry to record the payment is straightforward when a business fails to take the discount. Accounts Payable is debited, and Cash is credited for $100, the full invoice price. Like the gross method of recording sales discounts, the gross method of recording purchase discounts is very common. However, it is vulnerable to the same criticisms made against recording sales at the gross amount when discounts are offered.

net method of recording purchase discounts

The Net Method. As Exhibit 8-2 indicates, the **net method of recording purchase discounts** records the purchase of merchandise and the accounts payable net of the allowable discount. If the payment is made within the discount period, Accounts Payable should be debited and Cash credited for the amount at which the payable was originally recorded. If the firm does not pay within the discount period, then the full invoice price is paid. The difference between the

4. The explanation in this part of the chapter assumes the use of the perpetual inventory system. This has been the system that has been used thus far in this book. The periodic inventory system will be explained in detail later in this chapter.

Exhibit 8-2

Journal Entries to Record Purchase Discounts (Perpetual Inventory System)
$100 Purchase—Stated Terms 2/10, n/30

Transaction	*Gross Method*			*Net Method*		
1. Purchase of $100 of merchandise on account	Merchandise Inventory Accounts Payable	100	 100	Merchandise Inventory Accounts Payable	98	 98
2a. Firm pays within discount period	Accounts Payable Purchase Discounts Cash	100	 2 98	Accounts Payable Cash	98	 98
2b. Firm *does not* pay within discount period	Accounts Payable Cash	100	 100	Accounts Payable Purchase Discount Lost Cash	98 2	 100

amount at which Accounts Payable is debited and Cash is credited is debited to an account titled Purchase Discounts Lost. This new account is treated as a financial cost or interest expense. The argument for treating discounts lost as interest expense is based on the fact that the firm consciously chose not to pay within the allowable discount period, thus causing an additional cost. This additional cost represents a cost for the use of money and, therefore, is considered interest.

As in the case of sales discounts, the net method is preferable. Accounts payable are recorded at their expected cash payment at the time of purchase. Furthermore, the use of the Purchase Discounts Lost account highlights the total cost of not paying within the discount period. As noted in Chapter 7 this can be a significant amount, and it is generally in the firm's best interest to pay within the discount period.

Recording Purchase Returns and Allowances. The accounting treatment for *purchase returns and allowances* is similar to that for sales returns and allowances, except that it involves the accounts Purchases Returns and Allowances and Accounts Payable. **Purchase returns and allowances** are transactions which result when goods are returned to vendors or when vendors offer price reductions on goods which have been purchased. To illustrate, assume that the Russell Company purchased ten television sets for resale at a total cost of $2,800. The periodic inventory system is used, and the payable is recorded at the gross or invoice price. If one television costing $280 is found defective and is returned, the Russell Company will make the following entry:

purchase returns and allowances

Accounts Payable	280	
Purchase Returns and Allowances		280
Return of defective merchandise.		

The purchase returns and allowances account is a contra-purchase account and its balance is offset against total purchases in computing cost of goods sold. The ultimate effect is to reduce cost of goods sold. Although the Merchandise Inventory account could be directly credited for any returns and allowances, the use of the Purchases Returns and Allowances account gives management more control over these items.

freight-in
transportation-in

freight-out

Recording Freight Charges. The cost of freight for goods purchased for resale is referred to as **freight-in,** or **transportation-in.** In some circumstances the seller pays the freight, and in other circumstances the purchaser does. Freight charges paid by the purchaser are debited to Freight-in and are an addition to the cost of merchandise purchased and, ultimately, to cost of goods sold. This is in accordance with the historical cost principle and ensures that the purchases carry their full cost. Freight charges paid by the seller are referred to as **freight-out.** They are considered a selling expense and as such are not included in the computation of cost of goods sold.

Freight-in is added to the cost of goods sold. Other expenses that could be considered additional inventory costs and ultimately part of the cost of goods sold include such items as the expenses of the merchandise-receiving department, warehousing, insurance cost, and other costs of carrying inventory. Clearly, these costs are incurred because of the inventory and logically could be allocated to the cost of inventory and the cost of goods sold. Because of the difficulty of allocating these items, however, accountants consider them to be period expenses and include them in either selling or general and administrative expenses. Only items that are directly related to the receipt of the inventory, such as freight-in, are included in its inventory cost.

Employee Compensation

Employee compensation is one of the largest operating costs incurred by most firms. Total employee compensation far exceeds the amounts immediately paid in cash for services rendered. In addition to these immediate costs, firms incur payroll taxes, employee benefits such as health and life insurance, vacation pay, and retirement and pension costs. These costs are substantial, in many cases equaling or exceeding 30% or more of an employees' base salary. Accounting for some of these items, such as retirement and pension costs, is quite complex and is briefly introduced in this chapter because of the significant amounts involved.

Payroll Systems. Payroll processing is performed in most organizations by a payroll system. In fact, payroll systems were among the first computer-based accounting applications developed. Exhibit 8-3 depicts a computer-based payroll system. Employee time sheets or time cards are the primary input into the payroll system. A time sheet documents the time worked by an employee in a pay period. The time sheet may also identify the different jobs that the employee worked on and the time spent on each job. The payroll system accesses the employee master file to retrieve pay rate and deduction information for each employee, calculates each employees' pay and outputs the payroll checks, a payroll register, payroll tax and deduction reports, and the necessary payroll general journal entries. The payroll system also updates the employee master file with current pay period information so that the necessary quarterly and year-end reports can be prepared. This section describes the accounting processes that are performed by the payroll system as it computes employee pay and processes payroll tax liabilities.

Payroll Tax Liabilities. Certain federal and state taxes are incurred by the employee and the employer as employees earn wages. These taxes include federal and state withholding taxes, social security taxes, and unemployment taxes. The employer must account for these taxes and file appropriate tax returns on a quarterly or yearly basis.

Exhibit 8-3
Payroll System Flowchart

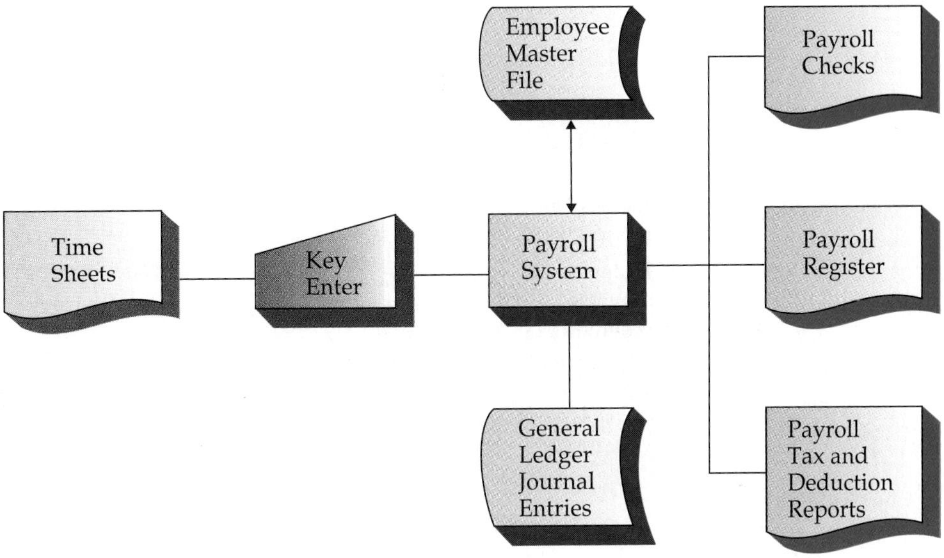

FICA (Federal Insurance Contributions Act) taxes

FICA (Federal Insurance Contributions Act) taxes usually are referred to as *social security taxes.* These taxes are a combination of Old Age Survivors and Disability Insurance (OASDI) and Medicare Insurance. FICA taxes are levied on both the employer and the employee. These taxes are a certain percentage of the employee's wages, with the percentage rate and base pay changing from year to year. Each year the Social Security system recomputes the actual tax and the amount of wages to which it applies based upon the funding needs of the system and changes in the cost of living. For our purposes, we will assume a tax rate of 8% for both employer and employee on the first $60,000 per year of the employee's wages. (In 1992, the actual rate was 6.2% on the first $55,500 of wages earned and an additional 1.45% of the first $130,200 earned for medicare taxes, for a total of 7.65%.)

In addition to their share of social security taxes, employers must pay federal and state unemployment insurance taxes. Federal unemployment taxes (FUTA) are currently 6.2% of the employee's first $7,000 of wages. However, employers can receive a maximum credit of 5.4% against these federal taxes for state unemployment taxes incurred, thereby lowering their federal unemployment taxes to 0.8%. The actual amounts and limits of state unemployment taxes vary from state to state. The tax in most states also differs from firm to firm, depending on the unemployment claims made by the former employees of the specific firm.

The federal government, many states, and even some cities have adopted pay-as-you-go requirements for the collection of individual income taxes. This requires the employer to withhold income taxes from employees' paychecks and to remit these taxes to the appropriate federal and state governments.

To demonstrate these points, assume that the monthly payroll of the Walters Liabilities Company is $60,000. Further, assume that the entire payroll is subject to FICA taxes of 8% for both the employee and the employer, but only $40,000 of the wages is subject to state unemployment taxes of 5.4% (SUI) and federal unemployment taxes (FUTA) of 0.8%. Finally, federal income taxes of $9,800, state income taxes of $3,500, and union dues of $600 are withheld. The entries to record the payroll and payroll taxes are as follows:

Wages Expense	60,000	
Federal Withholding Income Taxes Payable		9,800
State Withholding Income Taxes Payable		3,500
Union Dues Withheld		600
FICA Taxes Payable		4,800
Cash		41,300
To record wages for the month.		
FICA taxes = $4,800, or $60,000 × .08		
Payroll Taxes Expense	7,280	
FICA Taxes Payable		4,800
State Unemployment Taxes Payable		2,160
Federal Unemployment Taxes Payable		320
To record employer's share of payroll taxes.		
FICA = $4,800, or $60,000 × .08		
SUI = $2,160, or $40,000 × .054		
FUTA = $320, or $40,000 × .008		

Notice that FICA Taxes Payable was credited twice for the same amount. The first entry reflects the employees' share and the second the employer's contribution.

The timing of the actual payment of these taxes to the appropriate government agency depends on the size of the firm's payroll. Payments may be required on a weekly or monthly basis. Generally, the payroll tax returns are filed on a quarterly basis. The entry to record the payment of the liabilities shown in the two prior entries is as follows:

FICA Taxes Payable (2 × $4,800)	9,600	
Federal Withholding Income Taxes Payable	9,800	
State Withholding Income Taxes Payable	3,500	
Union Dues Withheld	600	
State Unemployment Taxes Payable	2,160	
Federal Unemployment Taxes Payable	320	
Cash		25,980
To record payment of various payroll taxes and union dues withheld.		

compensated absences

Compensated Absences. **Compensated absences** are absences for which the employee will continue to be paid. These absences include such benefits as vacation and sick pay. Under current accounting practices, a firm should accrue the liability for these benefits as they are earned. For example, many employees receive a two-week paid vacation every year. As the employee works throughout the year, he or she earns a portion of that vacation, so an estimated liability should be accrued for that amount. To illustrate, assume that during the current quarter, a firm estimates that its employees have earned 20 vacation days at an average salary of $200 per day. Thus, the firm should accrue a $4,000 ($200 × 20 days) liability as follows:

Vacation Pay Expense	4,000	
Accrued Vacation Pay		4,000
To record an estimated liability of $4,000 for vacation pay.		

Accrued Vacation Pay, a liability account, is debited and Cash is credited when the employees take their vacation and are paid.

The economic environment of the 1990s has seen many companies "downsizing" or "rightsizing." Companies have been offering inducements to current employees to leave or accept early retirement in an effort to combat rising costs. Large U.S. companies such as IBM and General Motors have offered such programs to over 40,000 employees. Many service firms, such as large accounting and law firms, have also offered inducements to a significant number of their partners to encourage early retirement. These inducements often include a full year's pay. Current accounting pronouncements require that the costs associated with these special termination programs be recognized when they are offered, assuming that the conditions for contingent liability recognition are met. That is, if it is probable that the employees will accept the offer, and if the amount can be reasonably estimated. The current cost of these programs can be quite substantial, running into millions of dollars for some companies.

pension

post-retirement health care costs

Pension and Post-Retirement Health Care Costs. Pension and post-retirement health benefits now represent an every-increasing cost to firms of all sizes and types. A **pension** is an agreement in which an employer promises to make certain payments to employees after they retire. The amount of the payment usually is based on the employees' years of service and wages earned. **Post-retirement health care costs** are the insurance costs that the employer agrees to pay for health and similar insurance on behalf of the employee. Again, these costs can be quite substantial. The most significant point to remember about these costs is that they are a current cost of employee compensation for services rendered. The employee earns these benefits today, even though the actual benefit may not be realized until some future date. Thus, the expense of these programs must be recognized in the current period when the related employees' salary is recognized, not deferred until the employee actually takes advantage of them.

Pension Costs. As noted, a pension is really a deferred compensation plan. In effect, employees work for an employer over a period of years, and some of the pay for this service is received after retirement. Most pension plans require the employer and the employee to make payments to an established plan while the employee is working. At retirement, the employee receives his or her pension, the amount depending on the contributions made to the plan, the estimated life expectancy of the employee, and other factors.

Although actual accounting for pension plans is extremely complicated and controversial, the concepts behind the accounting procedures and methods are understandable. Basically, the employer recognizes a current expense for the value today of the pension benefits earned by the firm's employees for their work during the current period. When current pension funding is less than the current pension expense, the firm must recognize a pension liability. Conversely, a prepaid asset is recognized when current pension funding exceeds the current pension expense. Sometimes the amount of the employer's total pension obligation exceeds the fair value of the pension plan's assets. If this occurs, an additional liability, along with a related intangible asset, must be recognized on the firm's financial statements.

As noted, the actual accounting procedures and calculations involved in the determination of current pension expense and pension liability are very complicated and are covered in more advanced textbooks. The amounts involved, however, are large, and can have a material effect on the financial statements of a particular firm. For example, the following pension provision data were obtained from the 1991 annual reports of these companies:

Company	*Pension Expense*
Boeing	$315 million
Sears, Roebuck and Co.	90 million
Pacific Enterprises	48 million

Post-Retirement Benefits. In addition to pension benefits, employers often offer employees other benefits after their retirement. These benefits can include the employer's contributions to health care plans, life insurance premiums, and other assistance plans. Until recently, most firms did not set up formal plans to accumulate assets to cover these costs, and, as a result, accounting recognition of these expenses was delayed until the employers had made cash payments on behalf of the employees.

The potential liabilities for these future payments can be quite significant for many firms. Thus, the FASB recently changed the accounting standards for these other post-retirement benefits. Now the FASB requires that firms currently recognize the expense and liability associated with the post-retirement benefits that are earned in the current period and will be paid when the employee retires. The actual accounting is complex but similar to that required for pensions.

By late 1991 many firms had begun to implement the new FASB accounting standard for post-retirement benefits. For many of these firms, the effect on their financial statements, was indeed quite substantial, as the following illustrates:

Acknowledging that it faces monumental expenses over the next 20 years for retiree health-care benefits, the General Motors Corporation said yesterday that it was taking a $20.8 billion after-tax charge against 1992 earnings. The accounting adjustment means that G.M. will post a net loss of about $23.5 billion for 1992, far exceeding the American corporate record loss of $4.97 billion that IBM set just last week.

The $20.8 billion write-off is a "catch-up" to recognize the total cumulative retiree health-care expenses for working and retired workers, as if the accounting standard had been in effect during the employee's working years. G.M. said it would take a separate $1.4 billion charge to reflect the actuarial increases incurred by workers and retirees in 1992 for future health-care liabilities.[5]

Other Liabilities Related to Operations

Other transactions that give rise to liabilities related to operations include interest, local, state, and federal taxes, and advances from customers.

Interest Expense and Interest Payable. The FASB considers interest expense to be an operating item. However, for the most part, the notes and loans that give rise to this interest expense is considered a financing activity or transaction. Interest expense is considered an operating item because it is a determinant of net income.

Accounting for interest expense was introduced in Chapter 4 when adjusting entries were discussed. These concepts are elaborated upon in Chapter 12 when accounting for long-term debt is discussed.

5. New York Times (February 2, 1993), p. C3.

Local, State, and Federal Taxes. Firms and individuals are subject to a variety of local, state, and federal taxes. Many local and state jurisdictions impose sales taxes on retail sales. The federal government also imposes excise taxes and luxury taxes on the sale of certain items. These taxes usually are imposed on the retail purchaser with the selling firm collecting these taxes for the taxing authority as explained in Chapter 7.

Accounting for taxes on corporate income is a difficult and controversial accounting problem. We have included a short introduction to this important, but complex topic starting at the bottom of this page.

Advances from Customers. A firm may receive cash in advance of performing some service or providing some goods. These advance payments are called

unearned revenues

unearned revenues. Because the firm has an obligation to perform the service or provide the goods, this advance payment is a liability. Unearned revenues include such items as subscriptions or dues received in advance, prepaid rent, and deposits. These nonmonetary liabilities generally are classified as current, because the goods or services usually are delivered or performed within one year or within the operating cycle (if longer than one year). If this is not the case, they should be classified as noncurrent liabilities.

To illustrate, assume that the Sensor Company has negotiated a contract to sell 50,000 board feet of lumber to Armstrong's Lumber Yard for $220,000. Sensor demands an immediate $40,000 advance payment; actual delivery will take place in one month. The Sensor Company would make the following entry to record the receipt of the advance payment or deposit:

Cash	40,000	
Advances from Customers		40,000
To record receipt of advance payment.		

When the lumber is delivered one month later, Sensor would make the following entry:

Accounts Receivable	180,000	
Advances from Customers	40,000	
Sales		220,000
To record sale of lumber.		

Accounting for Corporate Income Taxes

Throughout this book we will point out various differences between generally accepted accounting principles (GAAP) and the provisions of the Internal Revenue Code (IRC). These differences result from the differing objectives of GAAP and the IRC. The objectives of GAAP are aimed at providing investors and other users of financial statements with reliable and relevant financial information. The objectives of the tax law contained in the IRC include social equity, ease of administration, political considerations, and ensuring that individuals and corporations are taxed when they have the ability to pay (that is, when they have received the cash from the transaction).

There are many cases when the management of a firm will use one accounting method for financial statement purposes and another method for tax purposes. One of the most common examples is the use of straight-line depreciation for financial reporting purposes and the use of an accelerated or quicker depreciation method for tax purposes. A prudent management will select those accounting methods allowed by the IRC that will minimize the firm's taxable income, thus reducing its cash outflow for taxes. On the other hand, the same management may select a different set of accounting principles for financial reporting purposes.

Sources of Differences Between Accounting Income and Taxable Income. Differences between accounting income and taxable income can be classified into *permanent and temporary differences.* **Permanent differences** enter into the determination of accounting income but never into the determination of taxable income. They are, in effect, statutory differences between GAAP and the IRC. An example of a permanent difference is interest on state and local bonds. Although interest on these items represents revenue from an accounting perspective, it is not included in taxable income in either the year received or the year earned. Congress provided that the interest on these obligations would be nontaxable in order to make it easier for states and local governments to raise revenues. Because these differences indeed are permanent, they do not cause accounting complications.

permanent differences

Temporary differences are the other reason that accounting income in any year may be different from taxable income. **Temporary differences** result from the fact that some transactions affect taxable income in a different period from when they affect pretax accounting income. (**Pretax accounting income** is a term used to describe income based on generally accepted accounting principles before income tax expense is deducted.) Over the life of a particular transaction, the amount of income or expense for accounting and tax purposes is the same, but it is different within the various periods.

temporary differences

pretax accounting income

There are several temporary differences between taxable income and accounting income. Some of the more important ones are summarized in Exhibit 8-4. You should remember two points: (1) temporary differences affect two or more periods: the period in which the difference originates and the later periods when it turns around or reverses; (2) over the life of a single transaction, the amount of accounting and taxable income or expense related to that transaction will be the same. It is just a question of *when* temporary differences affect accounting and taxable income.

As noted, the use of different depreciation methods for tax and accounting purposes is probably the most common example of a timing difference. That is, the tax laws are written so that a firm can deduct a greater amount of depreciation in the earlier years of an asset's life and consequently less in later years than if the straight-line method had been used. These depreciation methods that allow a greater amount of depreciation in the earlier years of an asset's life are

Exhibit 8-4
Summary of Selected Temporary Differences

Transaction	*Accounting Method*	*Tax Method*
Rent received in advance	Recognized when earned	Recognized when cash received
Installment sales	Recognized at point of sale	Installment basis; income recognized as cash collected
Construction contracts	Percentage-of-completion	Completed contract
Inventories	FIFO	Average cost
Depreciation	Straight-line	Accelerated

accelerated depreciation methods

referred to as **accelerated depreciation methods.** The actual total depreciation which is based on the asset's cost is the same regardless of which method is used; it is just allocated differently between years. Discussion of different depreciation methods will be continued in Chapter 10, when various depreciation methods are covered in more detail.

Rent received in advance (unearned rent) is a good example of a timing difference for illustration purposes. Assume that PDP Partnership decides to lease some excess office space in its building. On December 19, 1993 PDP rents this space to Astrophysics and receives two years' rent of $18,000 immediately upon signing the lease. The space will be occupied for two years by Astrophysics beginning on January 1, 1994. For tax purposes PDP must recognize all $18,000 of the rent in 1993, the year it was received. For financial accounting purposes, however, the $18,000 rent would be recognized over a two-year period, $9,000 in 1994 and $9,000 in 1995. It is important to note that by the end of 1995 the transaction evens out. That is, the amount of rent recognized for tax purposes and the amount recognized for accounting purposes is the same, or $18,000 in this case.

The Need for Interperiod Income Tax Allocation. The temporary difference just discussed illustrates that certain transactions affect accounting and taxable income in different periods. In order to deal with this problem, accountants follow a procedure called *interperiod income tax allocation.* **Interperiod income tax allocation** is the recording of the tax effects of temporary differences as assets and liabilities which are then reported on the balance sheet. These tax effects reconcile the differences between pretax accounting income and taxable income. Thus the total tax liability for a period is the tax liability based on taxable income plus or minus the tax effect of the temporary difference.

interperiod income tax allocation

Corporate Tax Rates. Corporate tax rates, like individual tax rates are subject to changes made by Congress. The last major change was in 1986, when the Tax Reform Act of 1986 was enacted into law. As of the time this book was published corporate tax rates were as follows:[6]

Income Tax Rate	*Corporate Income Subject To This Rate*
15%	First $50,000 of taxable income
25	Next $25,000 of taxable income
34	Next $25,000 of taxable income
39	Next $235,000 of taxable income
34	All remaining taxable income

The variations in the tax rate are meant to ensure that all income up to $335,000 will be taxed at a flat rate of 34% (assuming the corporation's taxable income is above that amount), and that the tax rate on income above $335,000 will be limited to 34%. In most of our examples we will use a tax rate of 30% or 40% for simplicity.

Example. Interperiod income tax allocation procedures are very complex and controversial. After many false starts, the FASB issued Statement No. 109 revising

6. In February, 1993, President Clinton proposed that certain corporate and individual tax rates be increased to help decrease the federal budget deficit. At press time, the outcome of his proposals are uncertain.

the accounting procedures related to interperiod income tax allocation.[7] In order to give you the flavor of the issues involved, a simplified example is presented. Assume that the Price Corporation uses the same accounting principles for financial reporting purposes as it does for tax purposes, except for depreciation expense. Because of the current tax laws the Price Corporation is able to deduct more in depreciation expense for tax purposes than it records as an expense in determining pretax income for financial reporting purposes. This represents a $10,000 temporary difference. Further, the firm earned interest on state bonds, which is not taxable and thus represents a permanent difference. For simplicity, a tax rate of 30% is assumed.

As a result of these timing and permanent differences Price Corporation determines that its income tax expense for the period to be $58,500 and its income taxes payable to be $55,500. The $3,000 difference ($58,500 − $55,500 or 30% of $10,000 temporary difference) represents the deferred income tax liability. The journal entry to record taxes expense for 1994, the first year of the asset's life, is:

Dec. 31, 1994: Income Tax Expense	58,500	
Income Taxes Payable		55,500
Deferred Income Taxes		3,000
To record income taxes payable for 1994.		

In this simple example, the only temporary difference is due to the two different depreciation amounts. In reality, these computations are much more complex and involve detailed analysis on the part of the firm's accountants and auditors.

The Controversy Surrounding Accounting for Income Taxes. Accounting for income taxes has always generated much controversy in the accounting profession. In December 1987, the FASB issued Statement No. 96, *Accounting for Income Taxes,* which replaced the long-standing Accounting Principles Board Opinion related to taxes. This statement added significant complexities to accounting for taxes and did not meet with much enthusiasm from financial statement preparers. In fact, its effective date was delayed several times; finally the FASB decided to reconsider the entire matter. In February 1992 the FASB issued Statement No. 109, which addressed some of the issues that concerned financial statement preparers. The basic theory behind the statement has remained the same as in Statement No. 96, but some of the complex calculations have been simplified.

Much of the past controversy surrounding accounting for income taxes centered around the increasing size of the deferred tax liability account. Research studies have shown that prior to the issuance of Statement No. 96 and No. 109, deferred tax liabilities increased over the years; for many firms, they represent a large item in the liability section of the balance sheet. The primary reason for this is the current use of accelerated or quick depreciation methods for tax purposes. A company with a relatively stable or growing investment in depreciable assets that uses straight-line depreciation to determine pretax accounting income but uses an accelerated depreciation method in determining taxable income is likely to have an increasing credit balance in its deferred income tax account. This is because the continued investment in higher-priced assets indefinitely postpones

7. Financial Accounting Standards Board, Statement No. 109, *Accounting for Income Taxes* (Norwalk, CT: FASB, February, 1992).

the total reversal of the temporary difference, even though differences due to individual assets completely reverse. That is, as the effect of the accelerated depreciation method reverses on assets purchased in earlier years, it is offset by the effect of higher-priced assets purchased in the current year.

This raises the issue of how to treat the deferred tax account in analyzing financial statements. If, in fact, there is substantial evidence that the balance in the deferred tax liability account will not be reduced by future tax payments, should this account be classified as a liability? Many analysts feel that in such cases this account should be considered part of stockholders' equity or at least not be considered a liability in computing debt-to-equity ratios. The way in which this account is treated can have a substantial impact on the meaning of the resulting ratios.

Statement No. 96, as revised by Statement No. 109, changed the manner in which the deferred tax account is calculated. This, in conjunction with the lowering of maximum corporate tax rates from 46% to 34%, probably will cause a reduction in the deferred income taxes account, with a corresponding increase in income.

SPECIAL ISSUES INVOLVED IN RECORDING INVENTORY TRANSACTIONS

Objective 4
Explain the special issues involved in recording inventory transactions.

The second part of this chapter discussed measurement and valuation issues related to recording inventory transactions. In this part of the chapter you will explore two additional issues: (1) accounting information systems that have been developed to account for and record inventory transactions, and (2) taking a physical inventory.

Alternative Inventory Systems

Two different accounting information systems have been developed to deal with accounting for inventories: *perpetual* and *periodic.*

perpetual inventory system

Perpetual Inventory System. The **perpetual inventory system** keeps a running balance of inventory on hand and in some cases the cost of goods sold to date. Therefore, management is always aware of inventory levels and is able to make timely purchases to maintain desired levels. Up to this point we have been using the perpetual inventory system in our examples.

The use of perpetual inventory systems has been enhanced in recent years through the use of electronic point-of-sale devices and computers. Even with such sophisticated equipment, however, perpetual records often are kept only in units; the costs of ending inventories and goods sold are determined by an end-of-period count using what is called the *periodic method.* For example, optical scanners in markets and other retail stores keep track of inventory quantities, but at the end of the accounting period, an inventory count is made to compute the cost of the ending inventory and the cost of goods sold during the period.

Accounting for Perpetual Inventories. The accounting for perpetual inventories is shown in the following example. Assume that a firm started the year with a beginning inventory of pens that cost $10,000. During the first quarter, the following transactions occurred:

Date	Amount of Sale	Cost of Inventory Sold	Cost of Inventory Purchased
1. 1/20	$12,000	$ 8,000	
2. 1/28			$25,000
3. 2/10	30,000	24,000	
4. 3/28			10,000

These illustrations will assume that all sales are for cash and purchases are made on account. The appropriate journal entries and the resulting T accounts using the perpetual system are presented below:

Transaction	*Journal Entries—Perpetual System*		
1/20 sale for $12,000 with a cost of $8,000	Cash	12,000	
	Sales		12,000
	Cost of Goods Sold	8,000	
	Merchandise Inventory		8,000
1/28 purchase of inventory costing $25,000	Merchandise Inventory	25,000	
	Accounts Payable		25,000
2/10 sale for $30,000 with a cost of $24,000	Cash	30,000	
	Sales		30,000
	Cost of Goods Sold	24,000	
	Merchandise Inventory		24,000
3/28 purchase of inventory costing $10,000	Merchandise Inventory	10,000	
	Accounts Payable		10,000

Merchandise Inventory

1/1 Bal.	10,000	1/20	8,000
1/28	25,000	2/10	24,000
3/28	10,000		
3/30 Bal.	13,000		

Cost of Goods Sold

1/20	8,000		
2/10	24,000		
3/30 Bal.	32,000		

Under the perpetual system, when inventory is purchased the merchandise inventory account is debited. As the inventory is sold, the merchandise inventory account is credited, and the cost of goods sold account is debited for the cost of the inventory sold. (This is the same series of entries we have used in previous inventory examples in the first seven chapters of the book.)

One of the features of the perpetual system is to provide the firm with up to date information concerning its inventory levels. The system design reflects this goal. As the series of journal entries illustrated above shows, the balance in the merchandise inventory account at a particular time should reflect the actual cost of the goods on hand at that time. In the example, the ending balance in the merchandise inventory account is $13,000, which should represent the actual cost of inventory on hand.

The word *should* is used because the balance in the merchandise inventory account will not always equal the cost of the items remaining in the inventory. This is due to clerical errors, spoilage, theft, and other problems. An actual inventory count should be made at specified intervals—usually once a year. The balance in the merchandise inventory account is then adjusted to the actual ending inventory as determined by the physical count.

Although the perpetual inventory system provides management with a great deal of information, it is costly and often time-consuming to maintain unless the firm has completely computerized its inventory control system. Many firms, therefore, use a periodic inventory system.

periodic inventory system

Periodic Inventory Systems. A **periodic inventory system** does not keep continuous track of inventories and cost of goods sold. Instead, these items are determined only periodically, usually at the end of each quarter, each year, or other accounting period. Although this system may be easier to use for record-keeping purposes, it results in a significant loss of information for managerial decision making. Frequently however, the sheer volume of transactions in some merchandising businesses makes it impossible to use anything but a periodic system for purposes of inventory costing, especially when a manual accounting system is used.

Accounting For Periodic Inventories. The journal entries necessary to record inventories under the periodic system are shown in Exhibit 8-5. For comparison purposes the journal entries necessary to record the inventories under the perpetual method are also shown. The original data on which these entries are based are also reproduced in that exhibit. When the periodic system is used, no entry is made to record the cost of the inventory sold for a particular sale. Furthermore, as the journal entries show, inventory purchases are not debited to the merchandise inventory account. Rather, they are accumulated in a separate account called Purchases. As a result, there are no entries during the period to the asset account, Merchandise Inventory. Therefore, before any adjusting entries, the balance in the merchandise inventory account will reflect the amount of inventory at the beginning of the period year, as indicated in the following T accounts.

Purchases

1/28	25,000	
3/28	10,000	
3/30 Bal.	35,000	

Merchandise Inventory

1/1 Bal.	10,000	

Exhibit 8-5
Comparative Journal Entries for Merchandise Purchases

Transaction	*Journal Entries—Periodic System*			*Journal Entries—Perpetual System*		
1/20 sale for $12,000 with a cost of $8,000	Cash	12,000		Cash	12,000	
	Sales		12,000	Sales		12,000
	No entry to record cost of goods sold.			Cost of Goods Sold	8,000	
				Merchandise Inventory		8,000
1/28 purchase for $25,000	Purchases	25,000		Merchandise Inventory	25,000	
	Accounts Payable		25,000	Accounts Payable		25,000
2/10 sale for $30,000 with a cost of $24,000	Cash	30,000		Cash	30,000	
	Sales		30,000	Sales		30,000
	No entry to record cost of goods sold.			Cost of Goods Sold	24,000	
				Merchandise Inventory		24,000
3/28 purchase for $10,000	Purchases	10,000		Merchandise Inventory	10,000	
	Accounts Payable		10,000	Accounts Payable		10,000

Exhibit 8-6

Journal Entries to Record Purchase Discounts
$100 Purchase—Stated Terms 2/10, n/30

Transaction	*Gross Method*			*Net Method*		
1. Purchase of $100 of merchandise on account	Purchases	100		Purchases	98	
	Accounts Payable		100	Accounts Payable		98
2a. Firm pays within discount period	Accounts Payable	100		Accounts Payable	98	
	Purchase Discounts		2	Cash		98
	Cash		98			
2b. Firm *does not* pay within discount period	Accounts Payable	100		Accounts Payable	98	
	Cash		100	Purchase Discount Lost	2	
				Cash		100

Purchase Discounts with the Periodic System. As with the perpetual inventory system, purchase discounts can be recorded either gross or net when the periodic inventory system is used. Exhibit 8-6 compares the gross and net methods under the periodic inventory system. The entries are identical to those used with the perpetual inventory system except that Purchases rather than Merchandise Inventory is debited for the appropriate amounts.

Determining Cost of Goods Sold and Ending Inventory. Before financial statements can be prepared under the periodic system, the cost of goods sold during the period as well as the ending inventory must be calculated. This is done by taking a **physical inventory,** or counting the end-of-period inventory, to determine the quantity and the cost of the ending inventory and then applying the following formula (the data are from the current example):

physical inventory

	Beginning inventory	$10,000
Plus +	Inventory purchases	35,000
Equals =	Goods available for sale	$45,000
Less −	Ending inventory	13,000
Equals =	Cost of goods sold	$32,000

In effect, the total of the beginning inventory and the purchases during the period represents the total of all goods that the firm has available for sale. If the ending inventory is subtracted from this total, the remaining balance represents the cost of the items sold.

Determining the cost of the ending inventory and the resulting cost of goods sold is extremely important in determining the periodic income and financial position of the firm. The next chapter examines the alternative accounting methods that have been developed to do this. At this point, it is assumed that these amounts have been determined, and the journal entries to record these figures are illustrated here.

Adjusting and Closing Entries Under the Periodic System. Once the ending inventory and cost of goods sold have been determined, the accounts must be adjusted to reflect the ending inventory balance and the cost of goods sold. There are several ways to do this; the following adjusting and closing entries are recommended.[8]

Adjusting and Closing Entries at End of Accounting Period

Adjusting Entry:		
Merchandise Inventory (ending)	13,000	
Cost of Goods Sold*	32,000	
Purchases		35,000
Merchandise Inventory (beginning)		10,000
To adjust inventory to ending balance and create Cost of Goods Sold account.		
Closing Entry:		
Income Summary	32,000	
Cost of Goods Sold		32,000
To close Cost of Goods Sold account.		

*As calculated on page 368.

The adjusting entry is based on the formula to calculate cost of goods sold. That is, the two credits, purchases and merchandise inventory (beginning), are added together and represent goods available for sale. The debit, merchandise inventory (ending), is subtracted from that total to determine the balancing debit to cost of goods sold. (For convenience, merchandise inventory is labeled *beginning* and *ending*; however, there is only one ledger account, Merchandise Inventory.) Note that the result of this adjusting entry is to adjust the merchandise inventory account to its proper ending balance, to zero out the purchases account, and to create a cost of goods sold account. The entry to close cost of goods sold to Income Summary or Retained Earnings is like all entries to close expense accounts explained in Chapter 4.

After the adjusting and closing entries have been posted, the T accounts appear as follows:

Merchandise Inventory

1/1 Bal.	10,000	Adj. Entry	10,000
Adj. Entry	13,000		
3/30 Bal.	13,000		

Purchases

1/23	25,000	Adj. Entry	35,000
3/28	10,000		
	0		

Cost of Goods Sold

Adj. Entry	32,000	Cl. Entry	32,000
	0		

Income Summary

Cl. Entry	32,000		

8. An alternative method to record the ending inventory and to determine cost of goods sold is by means of the following closing entry:

Merchandise Inventory (ending)	13,000	
Income Summary	32,000	
Purchases		35,000
Merchandise Inventory (beginning)		10,000

Although this method requires one less entry, cost of goods sold is not specifically determined. However, since this account is necessary in order to prepare the income statement, the adjusting and closing procedure shown in the body of the text is preferred.

Taking a Physical Inventory

Taking a physical inventory is an important part of maintaining control over merchandising operations. When a perpetual inventory system is used, the physical inventory verifies that the firm does, in fact, have the inventory that its records show it has. When a periodic inventory system is used, a physical inventory is needed to determine cost of goods sold. The two steps in taking a physical inventory are the item count and the determination of the inventory's cost. This section will consider the issues pertaining to the item count; the issues pertaining to determining the cost of the ending inventory will be studied in the next chapter.

In taking a physical inventory, special care must be taken to ensure that all items of inventory to which the firm has legal title are counted. In addition, care must be taken to ensure that items that have been sold but are still physically present are not counted in the seller's year-end inventory. In this regard, items that require special analysis are *goods in transit, goods on consignment, and goods in public warehouses.*

goods in transit

Goods in Transit. **Goods in transit** are goods that have been purchased but have not yet been received by the purchaser. These goods can be easily overlooked when counting the ending inventory because they are not physically located at either the seller's or the purchaser's warehouse. In accounting for goods in transit, the main question is whether a sale has taken place, resulting in the passage of title to the buyer. If this is the case, the seller records a sale and a receivable or cash and does not include the item in the ending inventory. The purchaser records the payable or the payment of cash and the purchase and includes the item in the ending inventory. Conversely, if title has not passed, no sale or purchase has taken place, so the inventory is included in the seller's ending inventory.

goods on consignment

Goods on Consignment. **Goods on consignment** are goods held by a firm for resale, but title remains with the manufacturer of the product. In effect, the merchandiser has agreed to display the goods but, for a variety of reasons, is not willing to purchase them. When and if the retail firm sells the consigned goods, it receives a commission. Until the sale takes place, however, the title to the goods remains with the manufacturer. The manufacturer of the items is willing to accept such an agreement in order to get new or unusual goods into the hands of retailers for possible sale. Retailers agree to this arrangement because they do not have to accept the risks of ownership and will still receive a commission if the goods are sold.

goods in public warehouses

Goods in Public Warehouses. **Goods in public warehouses** are goods which a firm may own, but which are stored in a public warehouse, rather than a warehouse that the firm owns. Merchandising firms often store goods in public warehouses. If the firm has title to the goods in the warehouses, they must be included in the ending inventory. Failure to count these items will understate the ending inventory, net assets, and profits for the period.

Sales, Purchases, and Cost of Goods Sold Summarized

At this point, let's summarize the various components of net sales and cost of goods sold by reviewing the partial income statement is shown in Exhibit 8-7. For purposes of this illustration, this income statement details each account and

Exhibit 8-7

Celica Software Sales Partial Income Statement For the Year Ended December 31, 1994			
Gross sales			$199,300
Less: Sales returns and allowances		$ 800	
Sales discounts		3,500	
			4,300
Net sales			$195,000
Cost of goods sold			
Beginning inventory		$ 18,000	
Purchases	$146,500		
Less: Purchase returns and allowances	(2,000)		
Purchase discounts	(4,000)		
Net purchases		140,500	
Add: Freight-in		3,000	
Cost of goods available for sale		$161,500	
Less: Ending inventory		25,000	
Cost of goods sold			136,500
Gross margin on sales			$ 58,500

how it affects net sales and cost of goods sold. Most published financial statements are not as detailed and usually only contain amounts for net sales and cost of goods sold.

BALANCE SHEET PRESENTATION OF LIABILITIES

Objective 5
State how liabilities are presented on a typical balance sheet.

This chapter has discussed issues related to liability generation, recognition, and measurement. The final part of the chapter shows how current liabilities are disclosed on the balance sheet. The liability section of the balance sheet is divided into a current and long-term section. The current liability section of Warner-Lambert's balance sheet shown in Exhibit 8-8 is typical of those found in the

Exhibit 8-8

Warner-Lambert Company and Subsidiaries
Consolidated Balance Sheets

(in millions of dollars)	*December 31, 1991*	*December 31, 1990*
Notes payable—banks and other	$ 113.7	$ 222.6
Current portion of long-term debt	14.7	7.7
Accounts payable, trade	336.6	327.0
Accrued compensation	98.9	77.6
Other current liabilities	511.4	339.3
Federal, state, and foreign income taxes	174.6	126.5
Total current liabilities	$1,249.9	$1,100.7

balance sheets of most U.S. companies. The particular order in which current liabilities are presented on the balance sheet is a management decision. Notes and loans usually are listed first, then accounts payable, and finally accrued liabilities and taxes. The long-term liabilities section follows the current section. Balance sheet presentation of long-term liabilities is discussed and illustrated in Chapter 12.

EXPENDITURE CYCLE APPLICATION SYSTEMS

Objective 6
Describe the accounting systems used to process expenditure cycle transactions.

Four of the application systems found in the expenditure cycle are depicted in the systems flowchart in Exhibit 8-9. The first two application systems in the expenditure cycle, the purchasing and receiving systems, are transaction processing systems that do not generate journal entries. The other two systems, accounts payable and cash disbursements, are accounting systems that use information from the transaction processing systems to generate journal entries.

The Purchasing System

purchasing system

reorder point

The purpose of the **purchasing system** is to maintain adequate inventory stock levels by generating purchase orders when the quantity-on-hand plus the quantity-on-order is less than the *reorder point.* The **reorder point** is the stock level at which additional units of an inventory item should be purchased to meet expected demand. The purchasing system updates the quantity-on-order in the inventory master file when an order is placed. The purchasing system also prints purchase orders and an order register that lists every purchase order printed. No liability is incurred when a purchase order is printed so the purchasing system does not generate any journal entries to record the purchase of inventory. However, the system does send data to an open purchase order file. This file is used by the receiving system to ensure that received goods were actually ordered.

The Receiving System

receiving system

Clerks in the receiving department count and inspect goods that have been received from vendors. They often use a computer terminal to enter information about the goods received into the receiving system. The purpose of the **receiving system** is to control and record information about goods as they are received from vendors, and to compare the items received with those ordered. This control prevents the acceptance of goods which were not ordered and provides a reasonable assurance that only ordered goods are accepted by the firm. The receiving system transfers data from the open purchase order file to the closed purchase order file and prints a receipt register. The receipt register lists the purchase orders that have been closed and the items that have been received. The receiving system does not update the inventory master file or generate purchase journal entries because it lacks sufficient data to do so. Both quantity and cost information are needed to record a purchase in the general ledger and in the inventory master file. Receiving clerks enter quantity received data into the receiving system; however, they typically do not have access to cost data. The cost data is contained on the vendor's invoice, which is processed by the accounts payable system.

Exhibit 8-9
Expenditure Cycle Application Systems

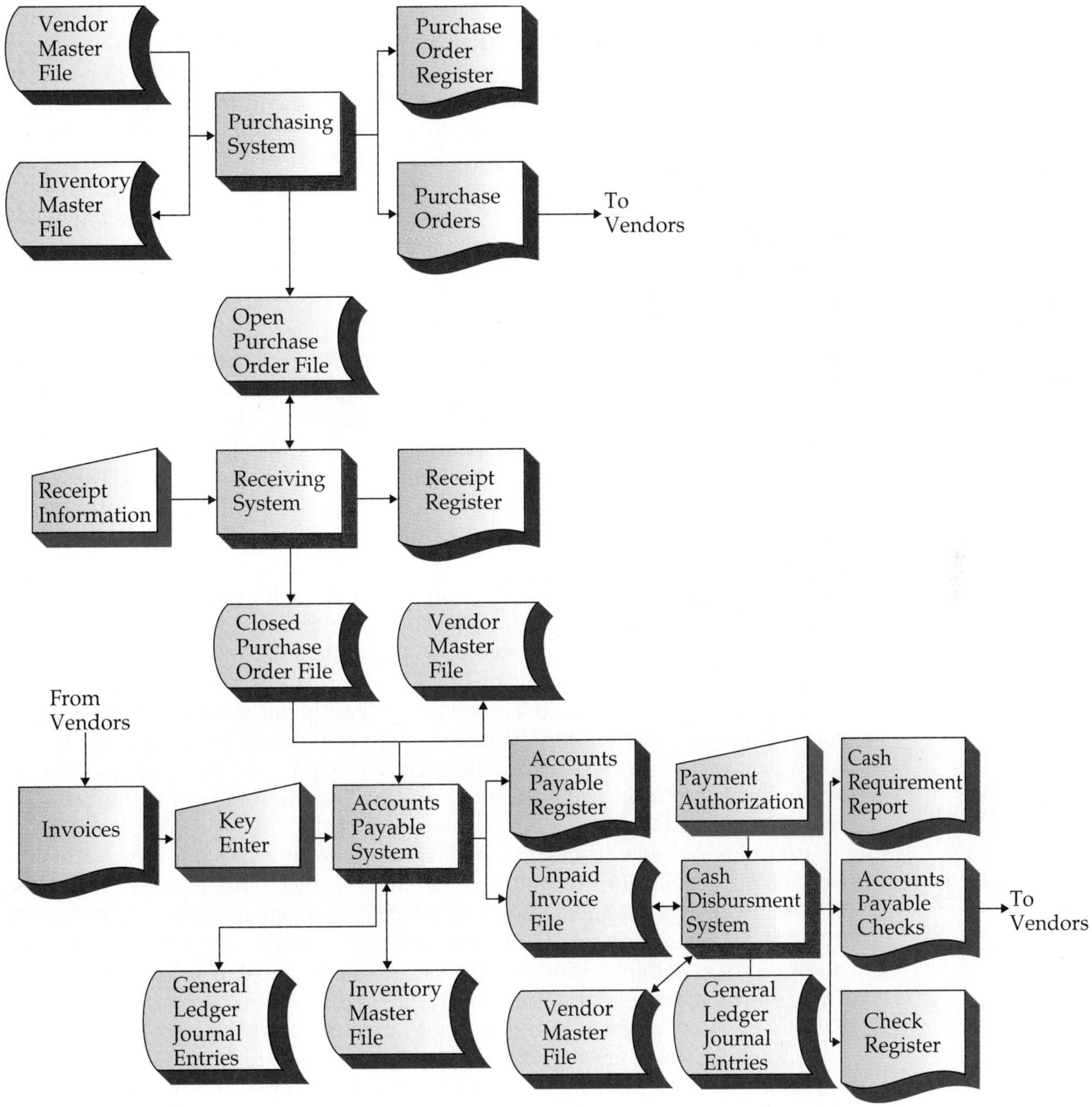

The Accounts Payable System

accounts payable system

The purpose of the **accounts payable system** is to keep track of liability transactions. The accounts payable system records a liability for the purchase of inventory after an invoice has been received and input into the system, *and* after the system has compared the invoice with the information in the closed purchase order file. This important control is designed to provide reasonable assurance that only valid liabilities, those incurred for goods that have actually been received, are processed.

Because both the quantities of items received and the costs of those items are now available, the accounts payable system is able to record the purchase liability and update the inventory master file. Summary journal entries to general ledger control accounts are written to the general ledger journal entry file. In addition, the subsidiary ledger, the vendor master file, is updated to reflect the amounts owed specific vendors. Invoice data (invoice number, vendor number, invoice date and terms, and invoice amount for example) are also written to the unpaid invoice file which is used by the cash disbursements system when it pays the liabilities that have been recorded. The accounts payable register is a detailed listing of the information that is written to the unpaid invoice file.

The Cash Disbursements System

The major purpose of the cash disbursements system is to manage and account for cash payment transactions. This system also provides the information needed to prepare a *budgeted* schedule of cash disbursements. The cash disbursements system analyzes invoices in the unpaid invoice file and selects those that should be paid each day to maximize the benefits offered by payment terms. For example, if payment terms of 2/10, net 30 were offered on an invoice then the cash disbursements system would select that invoice for payment on the last day that the discount could be taken.

A cash requirements report is printed after the relevant invoices have been selected for payment. The cash requirements report lists each invoice that has been selected for payment, its corresponding balance, and the total amount of cash that will be required if all of the selected invoices are paid. An accounts payable manager reviews this list and selects any invoices for which payment is not authorized. For example, payment is often withheld on an invoice that is being disputed with the vendor. The required review and approval of the cash requirements report is a preventive control by preventing the unauthorized disbursement of cash.

check register

Accounts payable checks are printed, along with a check register, after the payments authorizations have been entered. The **check register** lists each check, by number, the payee name, the check amount, and the invoices that were paid by each check. Cash disbursement journal entries are also generated at this time, as are entries to the vendor master file (accounts payable subsidiary ledger). These entries reduce the recorded liabilities to reflect payments made on account. Paid invoices are deleted from the unpaid invoice file at this time as well.

Knowledge of cash outlays is critical for effective cash planning. The cash requirements report is a useful planning tool, but it only lists the required cash outlays for a particular point in time. Managers also need to know the expected cash outlays for longer periods of time. Most organizations prepare a schedule of cash disbursements that covers longer periods of time, for example, for a quarter or even a full year. This cash disbursements schedule lists all expected (budgeted) cash outlays for the period of interest.

For example, suppose that a merchandising firm purchases a variety of goods. All purchases are made on account and occur evenly throughout a month. Terms are 2/10, n/30. Payments are made on the 10th (for purchases made during the first ten days of the month), the 20th (for purchases made during the second ten days of the month), and the 30th (for purchases made during the third

Exhibit 8-10
Schedule of Cash Disbursements

	April	May	June	Total
Purchases*	$49,000	$ 98,000	$147,000	$294,000
Rent	5,000	5,000	5,000	15,000
Property taxes	—	—	10,000	10,000
	$54,000	$103,000	$162,000	$319,000

*0.98 × $50,000; 0.98 × $100,000; 0.98 × $150,000

ten days). Thus, the firm always takes the 2% discount. Purchases are arranged so that none is made on the 31st of any month. The *forecast* purchases for the second quarter of the year are given below:

April	$ 50,000
May	100,000
June	150,000

In addition to the purchases, the company pays monthly rent of $5,000 and property taxes of $10,000 (due and payable at the end of each quarter). A cash disbursements schedule for the second quarter is illustrated in Exhibit 8-10. This schedule is an important component of a cash budget, which is discussed in detail in Chapter 24.

SUMMARY OF LEARNING OBJECTIVES

1. Define liabilities and state the criteria used to recognize, measure, and value them. Liabilities are probable future sacrifices of economic benefits arising from present obligations to transfer assets or provide services. Liabilities, like assets, are classified as either current or noncurrent. Current liabilities are generally valued on the balance sheet at their face value, while long-term liabilities are shown at their present value.

2. Explain the accounting concepts related to (a) existing liabilities with known amounts and (b) contingent liabilities. Generally, it is easy to determine the existence of many liabilities, as well as the amount of such liabilities. Included in this category are such accounts as Accounts Payable, Wages Payable and other employee benefit costs and liabilities, Interest Payable, Current Maturities of Long-Term Debt, and Dividends Payable.

Contingent liabilities are potential future liabilities whose existence is contingent upon some future event. A contingent liability is the result of an existing condition or situation whose final resolution depends on some future event. The appropriate accounting treatment depends on whether the future event is probable and/or the amount of the liability can be reasonably estimated. Contingent liabilities are accrued if the potential liability is probable and the amount can be reasonably estimated. Examples of such liabilities usually include warranties and premiums. Contingent liabilities that do not meet both of these criteria are usually reported through footnote disclosure. Examples of these types of contingent liabilities include claims and assessments against a firm.

3. Explain the accounting issues related to payables arising from operations. Operating activities that give rise to expenses and corresponding liabilities include the purchase of inventories for resale, the purchase of employee services including fringe and retirement benefits, other accrued liabilities related to operations, and the incurrence of income taxes.

Inventory Purchases. The accounting for purchases of inventories for resale parallels the accounting for sales. Accounting recognition is not given to trade or quantity discounts, but is given to purchase discounts. Either the net or the gross method can be used to account for purchase discounts. Because freight-in is directly related to merchandise purchases, it ultimately becomes part of cost of goods sold and inventory.

Employee Costs. Employee costs include not only the actual cash payment for services but also fringe benefits, including compensated absences, pension costs, and post-retirement benefits.

Corporate Income Taxes. Because of differing objectives, there are significant differences between taxable income as defined by the IRC and pretax accounting income as defined by GAAP. Management often takes advantage of these differences to report taxable income that is lower than pretax accounting income. Temporary differences make interperiod income tax allocation necessary. The total tax liability for the period is based on taxable income plus or minus the effect of temporary differences.

4. Explain the special issues involved in recording inventory transactions. Both perpetual and periodic inventory systems are used to record inventory transactions. The perpetual system records and provides management with a continuous record of inventories on hand and cost of goods sold. The record keeping involved is quite complex and without electronic point-of-sale devices or other computer systems, can be costly to maintain. The periodic system records only the cost of purchases. The entries for each system are shown in Exhibit 8-5.

If the periodic system is used, an adjusting entry must be made at the end of the accounting period to determine the cost of goods sold and the ending balance in the merchandise inventory account. The form of the entry, based on the formula to compute cost of goods sold is:

Merchandise Inventory (ending)	XXX	
Cost of Goods Sold	XXX	
Purchases		XXX
Merchandise Inventory (beginning)		XXX

Issues involved in taking a physical inventory include ensuring that the cost includes all items to which the firm has title. All goods to which the firm has title, even those in transit or in public warehouses or on consignment must be included in ending inventories.

5. State how liabilities are presented on a typical balance sheet. Liabilities are classified as either current or long-term. Sometimes deferred taxes payable are included within the long-term debt section. Other times they are shown as a separate item.

6. Describe the accounting systems used to process expenditure cycle transactions. Five computer-based accounting systems are typically required to process expenditure cycle transactions. These systems are: purchasing, receiving, accounts payable, cash disbursements, and payroll. The first four systems are used to process transactions for the purchase of goods and services. The payroll system is used to purchase and pay for employees' labor.

KEY TERMS

Accelerated depreciation methods *363*
Accounts payable system *373*
Check register *374*
Compensated absences *358*
Contingent liabilities *351*
FICA (Federal Insurance Contributions Act) or *social security taxes* *357*
Freight-in *356*
Freight-out *356*
Goods in public warehouses *370*
Goods in transit *370*
Goods on consignment *370*
Gross method of recording purchase discounts *354*
Interperiod income tax allocation *363*
Inventories *353*
Monetary liabilities *350*
Net method of recording purchase discounts *354*
Nonmonetary liabilities *350*
Pension *359*
Periodic inventory system *367*
Permanent differences *362*
Perpetual inventory system *365*
Physical inventory *368*
Post-retirement health care costs *359*
Present value *351*
Pretax accounting income *362*
Purchase discounts *354*
Purchase returns and allowances *355*
Purchasing system *372*
Receiving system *372*
Reorder point *372*
Temporary differences *362*
Transportation-in *356*
Unearned revenue *361*

REVIEW PROBLEMS

A. During the month of October, Tiny Tots, Inc. (the seller), entered into the following transactions with Little Kids (the purchaser).

a. October 2: Tiny Tots, Inc., sold merchandise to Little Kids on account. The sale totaled $10,000 and the terms were 2/10, n/30.

b. October 8: Little Kids returned $1,000 of merchandise because it was defective.
c. October 9: Tiny Tots, Inc., made an additional sale of $5,000 on account to Little Kids, terms 2/10, n/30.
d. October 10: Tiny Tots, Inc., received the required payment for the October 2 sale.
e. October 25: Tiny Tots, Inc., received full payment on the October 9 purchase from Little Kids.

REQUIRED: Make all the required entries on the books of both Tiny Tots, Inc., and Little Kids, assuming that:

1. Each company uses the gross method of recording sales and purchases.
2. Each company uses the net method of recording sales and purchases.

Assume Little Kids uses the periodic inventory system.

Solution 1
Gross method

	Tiny Tots, Inc. (Seller)			*Little Kids (Buyer)*		
October 2	$10,000 sale on account, terms 2/10, n/30					
	Accounts Receivable	10,000		Purchases	10,000	
	Sales		10,000	Accounts Payable		10,000
October 8	Return of $1,000 of defective merchandise					
	Sales Returns and Allowances	1,000		Accounts Payable	1,000	
	Accounts Receivable		1,000	Purchase Returns and Allowances		1,000
October 9	$5,000 sale on account, terms 2/10, n/30					
	Accounts Receivable	5,000		Purchases	5,000	
	Sales		5,000	Accounts Payable		5,000
October 10	Receipt of payment on October 2 sale					
	Cash	8,820*		Accounts Payable	9,000	
	Sales Discounts	180		Purchase Discounts		180
	Accounts Receivable		9,000	Cash		8,820*
October 25	Receipt of payment on October 9 sale					
	Cash	5,000		Accounts Payable	5,000	
	Accounts Receivable		5,000	Cash		5,000

*$8,820 = .98 × $9,000

2
Net method

	Tiny Tots, Inc. (Seller)			*Little Kids (Buyer)*		
October 2	$10,000 sale on account, terms 2/10, n/30					
	Accounts Receivable	9,800[a]		Purchases	9,800[a]	
	Sales		9,800	Accounts Payable		9,800
October 8	Return of $1,000 of defective merchandise					
	Sales Returns and Allowances	980[b]		Accounts Payable	980[b]	
	Accounts Receivable		980	Purchase Returns and Allowances		980
October 9	$5,000 sale on account, terms 2/10, n/30					
	Accounts Receivable	4,900[c]		Purchases	4,900[c]	
	Sales		4,900	Accounts Payable		4,900
October 10	Receipt of payment on October 2 sale					
	Cash	8,820		Accounts Payable	8,820	
	Accounts Receivable		8,820	Cash		8,820

(continued)

	Tiny Tots, Inc. (Seller)			*Little Kids (Buyer)*		
October 25	Receipt of payment on October 9 sale					
	Cash	5,000		Accounts Payable	4,900	
	Accounts Receivable		4,900	Purchase Discounts Lost	100	
	Sales Discounts Not Taken		100	Cash		5,000

[a]$9,800 = .98 × $10,000
[b]$980 = .98 × $1,000
[c]$4,900 = .98 × $5,000

B. Sun Microwave manufactures and sells microwave ovens to the public. The retail price of each unit is $300, and Sun Microwave warrants each oven for 24 months. During 1995 the firm sold 2,000 units and incurred actual warranty costs of $57,000. Past experience indicates that Sun Microwave will incur warranty costs of $33 per unit.

REQUIRED: Make the summary journal entries during 1995 to record the above events. Assume that all sales are for cash.

Solution

Cash	600,000	
Sales		600,000
To record sales for the year: $300 × 2,000 = $600,000		
Product Guarantee Expense	66,000	
Estimated Liability for Product Guarantee		66,000
To record estimated liability for product guarantees: $33 × 2,000 = $66,000		
Estimated Liability for Product Guarantee	57,000	
Cash, Supplies, Accrued Wages, etc.		57,000
To record actual guarantee expenditures incurred during the year.		

QUESTIONS

1. Distinguish between the following types of liabilities and give examples of each:
   a. Monetary and nonmonetary
   b. Current and noncurrent
2. What are the characteristics of liabilities that are known to exist and whose amounts are usually known? Provide three examples of such liabilities.
3. What are contingent liabilities? How do they differ, if at all, from other types of liabilities?
4. Give an example of a contingent liability that is accrued and one that is just disclosed in the financial statements. Explain what criteria are used in deciding whether to accrue a liability.
5. In December 1994, there was an accident at the No-Nuke Nuclear Power Plant. As a result, personal injury suits totaling $10 million have been filed against the company. Although it appears that the company will lose several of the lawsuits, there is no way to make a reasonable determination of the final amount of the loss. In preparing its December 31, 1994, financial statements, how do you think these facts should be disclosed? Would your answer be different if the accident had taken place in early January 1995, but before the firm's December 31, 1994 financial statements were prepared?
6. What are purchase discounts? Is it to the buyer's advantage to take any purchase discounts that are offered? Why or why not?
7. In examining the unadjusted trial balance of Jacob's Ladders, a large store specializing in puzzles, you notice an account entitled Purchase Discounts, with a credit balance of $1,457. Does Jacob's Ladders use the gross or the net method of recording purchase discounts? Explain your answer.
8. What is the effect of purchase returns and allowances in computing cost of goods sold?

9. List the most common payroll taxes incurred by employers and those incurred by employees.
10. What is a compensated absence? Give three examples.
11. What are pensions and post-retirement health care costs? What are the main accounting issues involved with these benefits?
12. What are temporary differences, and how do they relate to accounting for income taxes?
13. There are several instances when the management of a firm can use one accounting method to determine pretax accounting income and a different method to compute taxable income. Give three examples.
14. Discuss the primary controversy surrounding interperiod income tax allocation.
15. Compare and contrast the perpetual and periodic inventory methods. Should a firm's choice of methods affect the amount included in cost of goods sold and inventory on the year-end financial statements? Why or why not?
16. Under the periodic system, how is cost of goods sold determined?
17. What are goods in transit, and what problems can occur with them in determining the ending inventory?
18. What is meant by goods on consignment? If the Mada Store is holding goods on consignment should the cost of these goods be included in the cost of Mada's ending inventory? Why or why not?
19. What information systems are found within the expenditure cycle? What is the objective of each system?
20. Which systems in the expenditure cycle generate general ledger journal entries? Why or why not?

EXERCISES

E8-1 Accounting for Contingencies

LO 2

The Healtex Corporation manufactures and sells artificial heart valves. The company is currently being sued by Genetex for patent infringement. Genetex has filed a suit in the U.S. federal courts alleging that Healtex has infringed on its patent and is asking for $12 million in damages. Healtex's attorneys have reviewed the lawsuit and feel that it has no merit. Further, they feel that even if Genetex should win the suit the damages would be difficult to estimate and would not amount to much.

REQUIRED:

1. Healtex is now preparing its year-end 1994 financial statements. How should the lawsuit be handled in the financial statements? Explain your answer.
2. Now assume that it is 1995 and Genetex has won the lawsuit against Healtex. The patent judge awarded Genetex $10 million in damages. Healtex has appealed the judgment, but the court of appeals has declined to hear the case. Healtex now plans to appeal to the Supreme Court, although the Supreme Court very rarely hears patent suits. Given this information, how should Healtex handle the lawsuit in its year-end 1995 financial statements? Explain your answer.

E8-2 Accounting for Warranties

LO 2

The Akowa Corporation manufactures and sells executive cellular telephones. Each telephone sells for $300 and is warranted for two years against all defects. During the year, the firm sold 60,000 telephones. Past experience indicates that 10% of the telephones will need some type of repair during the warranty period. In the past, the firm has incurred expenditures of $12 on each telephone needing repair due to manufacturing defects. At the beginning of the year, the Estimated Liability for Warranties account had a credit balance of $1,800. Actual expenditures for warranties amounted to $46,000 during the year.

REQUIRED: Prepare the journal entries to record the transactions regarding the warranties. What is the balance in the Estimated Liability for Warranties account at the end of the year, and where is the account shown on the financial statements?

E8-3 Accounting for Contingencies

LO 2

The opening scenario to this chapter raised the issue of how a university should account for student loan guarantees. Review the scenario and take a position on the proper accounting treatment for the student loan guarantees.

E8-4
Accounting for Purchase Discounts
LO 3

Jan's Fabric Shoppe entered into the following transactions during May:

a. May 2: Purchased $7,000 of fabric on account. Terms 1/10, n/30.
b. May 10: Purchased $9,500 of fabric on account. Terms 2/10, n/30.
c. May 10: Returned $600 of goods purchased on May 2 because they were defective. The company's account was credited.
d. May 11: Made the required payment on the May 2 purchase.
e. May 20: Received a $250 freight bill on the May 10 purchase, payable at the end of the month.
f. May 30: Made the required payment on the May 10 purchase. Also paid the related freight bill received on May 20.

The company uses the periodic inventory system.

REQUIRED: Make the necessary entries, assuming that the company used the gross method and then the net method of recording purchase discounts.

E8-5
Accounting for Purchases
LO 4

On December 28, 1994, the Hungary Tiger Company entered into the following transactions:

a. Merchandise costing $20,000 was purchased from Gatwick Corporation, terms 1/10, n/30. The goods arrived on January 3, 1995. All required payments were made on January 4, 1995.
b. Merchandise costing $18,000 was purchased from London Industries, 5 EOM with transportation costs of $500 to be paid by Hungary Tiger. The goods arrived on January 4, 1995. All required payments were made on January 5, 1995.

REQUIRED: Assuming that the Hungary Tiger Company uses the periodic inventory system and records purchases using the net method, prepare the necessary journal entries for these transactions.

E8-6
Analysis
LO 3

Given the following information, compute the beginning inventory:

Purchases returns and allowances	$ 7,200
Transportation-in	2,400
Purchases	134,500
Cost of goods sold	112,700
Ending inventory	38,575
Sales returns	6,250
Freight-out	1,300

E8-7
Payroll Taxes
LO 3

The payroll expense for the Ziggy Corporation for the week ending April 18, 1994, is $12,000. The entire payroll is subject to FICA taxes of 7.5%, but only 80% is subject to state unemployment taxes of 2.7% and federal unemployment taxes of 0.8%. Federal income taxes of $2,100, state income taxes of $750, and $300 payable to the pension fund were all withheld.

REQUIRED: Prepare the necessary journal entries to record the payroll and the payroll taxes.

E8-8
Compensated Absences
LO 3

The Marcus Company policy regarding paid vacations is as follows: Each employee is awarded 15 days paid vacation after working for the company one full year. After reviewing payroll records, the controller estimates that 60% of the individuals employed during November will qualify for vacation pay. Total payroll for November is $120,000.

REQUIRED: Compute the amount of estimated vacation pay liability for November and make the required entry to record the liability.

E8-9
Pension, Post-Retirement Health Care Benefits, and Other Fringe Benefits
LO 3

The president of Moretax is confused about the accounting treatment for pension and other post-retirement benefits. Please answer the questions which follow:

a. I don't understand why we must record pension expense in the current period for our employees. After all, they will not collect the pension until after they retire.
b. I feel the same way about post-retirement health care benefits. We don't pay these until our employees retire.
c. As the economy has slowed, we are planning to lay off about 50 employees. We are going to offer them a year's pay, which will amount to about $40,000 per employee, to be paid over the next 12 months. How do we handle the accounting for this in the current year?

E8-10
Accounting for Income Taxes
LO 3

The McNee Company pretax accounting income for the year ended December 31, 1994 is $150,000. In doing your year-end analysis, you determined the following:

a. The firm paid life insurance premiums totaling $20,000 on its officers. These life insurance premiums are included in general and administrative expenses but are a permanent difference and are not deductible for tax purposes.
b. The firm uses straight-line depreciation for accounting purposes and an accelerated depreciation method for tax purposes. Depreciation expense of $30,000, which exceeds tax depreciation by $12,000, is included in pretax accounting income.

REQUIRED:

1. Determine the amount of taxable income for 1994.
2. Assuming a tax rate of 30%, make the entry to record the taxes for the year.

E8-11
Accounting for Income Taxes and Financial Statement Analysis
LO 3

You have gathered the following data for the Technical Phone Company:

	Year Ended	
	1994	*1993*
Deferred taxes (credit balance)	$ 50,000	$ 35,000
Total liabilities	200,000	180,000
Stockholders' equity	100,000	80,000

REQUIRED:

1. Compute the debt-to-equity ratio and the debt-to-total-assets ratio, based on the following assumptions:
   a. Deferred taxes are considered a liability and have already been included in the total liability figure presented above.
   b. Deferred taxes are considered part of stockholders' equity.
   c. Deferred taxes are ignored in the computation of the ratios.
2. Comment on the significance of item 1. Assume that the industry averages for the ratios are:
   a. Debt-to-equity = 1.5 to 1
   b. Debt-to-total-assets = .55 to 1

E8-12
The Periodic Versus the Perpetual System of Accounting
LO 4

The Bee Company began business during the current year. The following events occurred during its first month of operation:

a. January 2: Merchandise costing $7,000 was purchased for cash.
b. January 10: Merchandise costing $10,000 was purchased on account. Terms n/30.
c. January 15: Sales for the first half of January totaled $16,500. Of this amount, $9,500 was for cash and the remaining on account. The cost of goods sold was $12,000.
d. January 20: Merchandise costing $16,000 was purchased on account. Terms n/30.

e. January 31: Sales for the last half of January were $24,000. Of this amount, $18,000 was for cash and the remaining on account. The cost of goods sold was $16,500.

REQUIRED: Prepare the necessary entries to record these transactions, assuming that the firm uses (a) the periodic system and then (b) the perpetual system. (Ignore adjusting and closing entries.)

E8-13
Determining Cost of Goods Sold
LO 4

Given the following information, determine the missing amounts:

	Case 1	*Case 2*	*Case 3*
Sales	$25,000	$18,050	$?
Beginning inventory	8,000	8,000	10,000
Purchases	15,000	?	23,000
Purchase returns and allowances	1,500	2,000	?
Goods available for sale	?	17,000	28,500
Ending inventory	4,000	?	2,150
Cost of goods sold	?	11,500	?
Gross profit on sales	?	?	7,500

E8-14
Determining the Cost of the Ending Inventory
LO 4

The Gild Antique Shop asks your help in determining the cost of its ending inventory at December 31. It has counted all the items in its store and determined their cost to be $112,475. In addition, the shop gives you the following information:

a. Goods costing $26,000 were held by others on consignment.
b. Goods costing $55,000 were in transit from England. Legal title passed to Gild Antique when the goods were placed on the container vessel for shipment.
c. Gild Antique Shop held items costing $65,000 on consignment for others. These items were included in the ending inventory count.
d. Goods costing $11,000 were in transit from Spain. Gild will not receive title to the goods until they reach Gild's warehouse.

REQUIRED: What is the cost of their ending inventory?

E8-15
Periodic System—Adjusting and Closing Entries
LO 4

The following accounts were taken from the trial balance of the Mori Company on December 31:

Sales	$500,000
Beginning inventory	40,000
Freight-in	4,000
Ending inventory	42,000
Sales discounts	5,000
Purchases	331,000
Purchase returns and allowances	2,400
Sales returns and allowances	15,000
Purchase discounts	7,400

REQUIRED:

1. Prepare an income statement in good form through gross profit on sales.
2. Prepare the necessary adjusting and closing entries related to the above information.

E8-16
Perpetual Inventory—Recording Transactions
LO 4

The Conners Company is a small distributor of radiators for specialty automobiles. The firm carries only three different models and uses the perpetual inventory system. At the beginning of March, the firm had 100 radiators, Model 467, that it purchased for $27 per radiator. During March, the following cash purchases and sales took place in regard to this model:

a. March 8: Purchased 40 radiators at $40 each.
b. March 15: Sold 80 radiators for $60 each. (Assume that the radiators are sold in the order that they are purchased. Thus all radiators in the beginning inventory are sold before those purchased on March 8, and so forth.)
c. March 20: Purchased 50 radiators at $35 each.
d. March 22: Returned two of the radiators purchased on March 20 because they were defective.
e. March 30: Sold 30 radiators for $60 each.

REQUIRED: Make the necessary journal entries to reflect the purchases and sales during March.

E8-17
Cash Disbursements Schedule
LO 6

The controller of Gardner Company is gathering data to prepare a cash disbursements schedule for April 1995. He plans to develop the schedule from the following information:

a. Sales for the first six months of the year are given below. (The first three months are actual sales and the last three months are estimated sales.)

	Sales		*Sales*
January	$230,000	April	$565,000
February	300,000	May	600,000
March	500,000	June	567,000

b. The company sells all that it produces each month. The cost of raw materials (used in production) equals 20% of each sales dollar. The company requires a monthly ending inventory equal to the coming month's production requirements. Of raw material purchases, 50% is paid for in the month of purchase, and the remaining 50% is paid for in the following month.
c. Wages total $50,000 each month and are paid in the month they occur.
d. Budgeted monthly operating expenses total $168,000, of which $22,000 is depreciation and $3,000 is expiration of prepaid insurance (the annual premium of $36,000 is paid on January 1).
e. Dividends of $65,000, declared on March 31, will be paid on April 15.
f. Old equipment will be sold for $13,000 on April 3.
g. On April 10, new equipment will be purchased for $80,000.

REQUIRED: Prepare a cash disbursements schedule for April.

E8-18
Purchasing and Receiving System Controls
LO 6

Buildmart, a builders supply store, orders inventory from a variety of vendors. A copy of each purchase order is sent to the receiving department. A clerk records the quantity of goods received on the receiving copy of the purchase order. The copy of the purchase order, with quantities received noted on it, is sent to the accounting department where the necessary journal entries are prepared. The goods are moved from the receiving dock to the warehouse after the updated copy of the purchase order is sent to accounting.

REQUIRED:

1. What errors or irregularities may occur as a result of these procedures?
2. What controls should be implemented to correct each potential problem?

E8-19
Expenditure Cycle Transactions and Systems
LO 6

Match each of the following expenditure cycle transactions with the application system that would be used to process the transaction.

Transaction	*Application Systems*
Credit purchase	Purchasing
Payment on account	Receiving
Receipt of goods	Accounts payable
Return of goods	Cash Disbursements
Employee labor	Payroll
Purchase order preparation	

E8-20
Albertson's Financial Statements
LO 3

Refer to Albertson's financial statements in Appendix A and answer the following questions:

a. Briefly describe the employee benefit and pension plans Albertson's contributes to.
b. What is the amount of the net periodic pension cost for years ended January 1992 and 1991?
c. Has the firm adopted FASB Statement No. 106 relating to accounting for post-retirement benefits? What does management report in the financial statements, including footnotes, in regard to post-retirement benefits?
d. How does the company report contingent liabilities related to legal proceedings? Does their accounting appear to be reasonable? Why or why not?

PROBLEMS

P8-1
Analysis of Payables and Receivables
LO 2

When the accountant for the Papaya Company prepared the partial balance sheet at October 31, 1994, he failed to make the required monthly adjusting entries. Company policies require that these entries be made monthly.

During your analysis, you have obtained the following additional information:

a. The $200,000 accounts payable general ledger balance includes an account with a debit balance of $3,975 which resulted when the Papaya Company returned some defective goods. Papaya has asked the vendor to refund its money.
b. The interest payable relates to a $60,000 note that was signed six months ago.
c. When the firm records its sales, applicable sales taxes are included in the sales account. At the end of each month, an adjusting entry is made to reverse out the amount of the sales taxes and to set up a payable account. During October, sales were $212,000, including sales taxes of 6%.

Papaya Company
Partial Balance Sheet
October 31, 1994

Current assets		
Accounts receivable	$243,875	
Less allowance for uncollectible accounts	1,250	
		$242,625
Notes receivable		32,700
Current liabilities		
Accounts payable		$200,000
Interest payable		2,500
Notes payable		60,000

REQUIRED:

1. Make the necessary adjusting entries at October 31, 1994.
2. Prepare a revised partial balance sheet as of October 31, 1994.

P8-2
Accounting for Current Liabilities
LO 2

Super O Discount Stores entered into the following transactions during the current fiscal year:

a. On March 1, the store purchased a delivery truck for $18,000. A 20% downpayment was made, and the firm signed a 12%, one-year note for the balance. Both principal and interest are due at the maturity date.
b. The firm purchased inventory for $60,000 on account (use the periodic method).
c. The store purchased some additional office equipment for $15,000, subject to credit terms of 2/10, n/30. (Use the gross method of recording discount.)
d. $1,400 of the inventory purchased in (b) above arrived damaged and was returned to the manufacturer. Super O's account was credited.
e. The office equipment purchased in (c) above was paid for within the discount period.
f. Sales for the year amounted to $160,000, of which 40% were on account and the remainder were for cash. State and local sales taxes amounted to 7%.
g. The department store rents part of its space to Tasty Croissants. The agreement calls for Tasty to pay a year's rent in advance. Tasty began business on October 1 and made the $9,600 required payment to Super O on that date.
h. Super O's payroll for the year amounted to $38,000, all of which was paid in cash. Applicable payroll taxes and related items were as follows: federal and state income taxes withheld, $2,900 and $800, respectively; FICA taxes, 7.5% for both employee and employer on entire payroll; state unemployment taxes of 2.7% on $24,000 of the payroll; and federal unemployment taxes of 0.8% on $24,000 of the payroll.
i. Sales and payroll taxes were fully paid before year-end.

REQUIRED:

1. Make the necessary journal entries to record the above transactions.
2. Make any necessary adjusting entries at February 28 other than depreciation.

P8-3
Recording Purchases and Sales Transactions (Alternative to P8-4)
LO 3

The Lion Company uses the periodic inventory system. Assume that the company uses the gross method of recording discounts. The following transactions relating to sales and purchases occurred during the month of October:

a. October 3: Purchased merchandise on account, $10,000, from Tiger Company. Terms 2/10, n/30.
b. October 4: Sold merchandise to Chitah Company for $3,400 cash.
c. October 6: Sold merchandise to Zoo Company on account, $5,800, 5 EOM. Freight charges to be paid by Zoo Company.
d. October 8: Made required payment to Tiger Company on October 3 purchase.
e. October 10: Purchased merchandise for $6,200 from Zebra Company. Terms 2/10, n/30.
f. October 15: Sold merchandise to Hippo, Inc., on account, $5,000, 1/10, n/30.
g. October 17: Permitted Hippo, Inc., to return for credit $700 of merchandise purchased on October 15.
h. October 24: Received required cash due from Hippo, Inc., for October 15 sale.
i. October 25: Made required payment to Zebra Company on October 10 purchase.

REQUIRED: Prepare the necessary journal entries for the above transactions.

P8-4 Recording Purchases and Sales Transactions (Alternative to P8-3)

LO 3

The American Company uses the periodic inventory system and the gross method of recording sales and purchase discounts. The following transactions relating to sales and purchases occurred during March:

a. March 3: Purchased merchandise on account for $12,000 from the Washington Company. Terms 2/10, n/30.
b. March 4: Sold merchandise to the Jefferson Company on account for $3,500. Terms 1/10, n/30.
c. March 5: Sold merchandise to the Adams Company on account for $5,500. Terms 7 EOM, Freight charges to be paid by the Adams Company.
d. March 8: Made the required payment to the Washington Company for the March 3 purchase.
e. March 12: Purchased merchandise on account for $9,000 from the Lincoln Company. Terms 2/10, n/30.
f. March 13: Received payment from the Jefferson Company, net of the discount.
g. March 16: Sold merchandise to the Grant Company on account for $7,000. Terms 1/10, n/30.
h. March 21: Received required payment from the Adams Company for March 5 sale.
i. March 31: Made payment to the Lincoln Company for the March 12 purchase.

REQUIRED: Prepare the necessary journal entries for the above transactions.

P8-5 Cash Disbursements Schedule

LO 6

Hillerman's Department Store purchases a wide variety of merchandise. Purchases are made evenly throughout the month and all are on account. On the first of every month, Hillerman's accounts payable clerk pays for all of the previous month's purchases. Terms are 2/10, n/30.

The forecast purchases for the months of May through September are as follows:

May	$40,000	August	$60,000
June	50,000	September	64,000
July	30,000		

REQUIRED:

1. Prepare a cash disbursements schedule for the months of August and September.
2. Now suppose that the store manager wants to see what difference it would make to have the accounts payable clerk pay for any purchases that have been made three times per month, on the first, the 11th, and the 21st. Prepare a cash disbursements schedule for the months of July and August, assuming this new schedule.
3. Suppose that Hillerman's accounts payable clerk does not have time to make payments on two extra days per month, and a temporary employee is hired on the 11th and 21st of the month at $22 per hour, for four hours each of those two days. Is this a good decision? Explain your answer.

P8-6 Gross and Net Methods of Recording Discounts

LO 3

The Turner Company, which uses the periodic inventory system, entered into the following transactions during April:

a. April 2: Purchased inventory items from the Jennings Company for $5,400. Terms 2/10, n/30.
b. April 6: Sold merchandise on account to the Rather Company for $25,000. Terms 1/10, n/30.
c. April 9: Paid freight charges of $75 in cash on items purchased on April 2.
d. April 10: Made the required payment to the Jennings Company on the April 2 purchase.
e. April 13: $1,500 worth of the merchandise sold on April 6 was returned because of defects. Accounts Receivable was credited.

f. April 15: Received required payment from the Rather Company.
g. April 20: Purchased $8,000 of merchandise from the Koppel Company. Terms 2/10, n/30.
h. April 23: Sold various items of merchandise to Walters, Inc., for $9,800. Terms 1/10, n/30.
i. April 29: Made the required payment to the Koppel Company.

REQUIRED:

1. Make the necessary journal entries, assuming that the firm uses the gross method of recording purchase and sales discounts.
2. Prepare the cost of goods sold section of the income statement, assuming that the beginning inventory is $6,800 and the ending inventory is $4,700.
3. Make the necessary journal entries, assuming that the firm uses the net method of recording purchase and sales discounts.
4. Prepare the cost of goods sold section of the income statement using the data from item (2) but assuming that the net method is used.
5. Compare and contrast the two income statements prepared in items (2) and (4).

P8-7
Income Statement of a Merchandising Company
LO 4

The following information was taken from the records of the Newton Company at year-end:

	Year 1	*Year 2*
Gross sales	$235,000	$238,430
Sales returns and allowances	5,000	?
Net sales	?	231,080
Beginning inventory	36,050	?
Purchases	101,530	?
Purchase returns and allowances	3,250	4,535
Ending inventory	?	7,254
Cost of goods sold	?	?
Gross profit on sales (45%)	?	?
Operating expenses	33,570	27,280
Income tax expense (30%)	?	?
Net income	?	53,694

REQUIRED: Supply the missing information. Show all computations, rounding them to the nearest dollar.

P8-8
Computing Income Statement Amounts
LO 4

Complete the following table by filling in the missing dollar amounts for the income statement of the Blue Monday Corporation. Each case is independent, and all amounts are in dollars.

Blue Monday Corporation
Income Statement

Case	*Sales Revenue*	*Beginning Inventory*	*Purchases*	*Goods Available for Sale*	*Ending Inventory*	*Cost of Goods Sold*	*Gross Profit on Sales*	*Operating Expenses*	*Income (Loss)*
1	2,100	250	1,600	?	420	?	?	300	?
2	2,400	350	?	?	300	1,900	?	240	?
3	2,400	300	1,800	?	?	?	?	250	100
4	3,000	?	2,500	?	200	?	250	?	(100)
5	1,800	?	1,100	?	400	?	?	300	110

P8-9
Product Warranty
LO 3

The Wolfer Company manufactures and sells high-quality stereo equipment. It has a special line of speakers that sell for $1,400 apiece. The parts on the speaker are guaranteed for three years. During the first year, all labor for repairs is performed free of charge. During the next two years of the guarantee, there is a set labor charge of $55 per repair. During 1994, the firm sold 750 of these speakers. Past experience indicates that 20% of these units will need repair within the guarantee period, average replacement parts will cost $92, and labor costs will be $54. During the year, the firm incurred $6,200 in labor costs and $7,000 in replacement costs. Also during the year, the firm collected $3,600 in revenue from labor performed on guarantee work. At the end of 1994, before any adjustments were made, the account Estimated Liability for Guarantee Work had a *debit* balance of $1,500.

REQUIRED:

1. How is it possible for the account Estimated Liability for Guarantee Work to have a debit balance prior to the adjusting entry at the end of the year? What was the actual balance in the account at the beginning of 1994?
2. Prepare the summary journal entries to record the above events related to guarantees. Assume that all sales are made on credit.
3. Determine the balance in the Estimated Liability for Guarantee Work account at the end of 1994 after all adjusting entries have been made.

P8-10
Payroll Taxes and Compensated Absences
LO 3

The Bubble Laundry Company had four employees on its payroll for the fourth quarter of 1994. The unemployment compensation rate at the state level is 2.7%; the federal rate is 0.8%. The maximum unemployment wage is $8,000 for both federal and state unemployment taxes. Current FICA taxes are 7.5% of the first $55,000 of the current year's wages. Each employee is entitled to two weeks' compensated vacation pay yearly. The pay is based on the average salary for the year assuming a 50-week year. Each quarter, the firm accrues 25% of that amount as an estimated liability.

During your review of Bubble Laundry's records, you have obtained the following information:

Name	*Earnings to 9/30/94*	*Earnings 4th Quarter 1994*
J. Korman	$ 45,920	$11,490
O. Jones	26,480	7,990
T. Glasson	16,230	2,780
R. Sato	42,500	15,000
Totals	$131,130	$37,260

REQUIRED:

1. For each employee, determine the correct amount of payroll taxes for the fourth quarter.
2. Assume that the federal income tax withheld and state income tax withheld equaled $6,800 and $3,300, respectively, for the quarter. Make the journal entries to record the payroll and related expenses for the fourth quarter.
3. Determine the amount of vacation pay each employee is entitled to. Make the journal entry to record the estimated liability for the fourth quarter.

P8-11
Expenditure Cycle Files
LO 6

Several different files are required in computer-based expenditure cycle systems to process transactions.

REQUIRED:

1. List the different files used by expenditure cycle application systems.
2. State, for each file, whether the file is a master file or a transaction file.

3. Identify, for each transaction file, the master file that will be updated by data in the transaction file.

DISCUSSION AND INTERPRETATION PROBLEMS

D8-1 Understanding Financial Statements

The following data were taken from a recent annual report of the Circle K Corporation, one of the largest operators of convenience stores in the United States.

Circle K Corporation (in thousands)	
Sales	$3,686,314
Inventories, beginning	239,916
Inventories, ending	175,308
Cost of goods sold	2,796,559

REQUIRED:

1. Determine the amount of gross profit on sales for the year and the amount of net purchases made during the year.
2. Do you think the Circle K Corporation uses the perpetual or the periodic system in accounting for inventories in its stores? Explain your reasoning.
3. Do you think the firm allows its customers to take a sales discount? Why or why not?

D8-2 Understanding Financial Statements

The following information was taken from the 1991 annual report of the Boeing Company:

Note 6: Federal Taxes on Income
The Company adopted the provisions of Statement of Financial Accounting Standards No. 96 in 1989. The effect of the change in accounting was an increase to 1989 earnings of $298 or $.86 per share.

The provision for federal taxes on income consisted of the following:

Year Ended December 31,	*1991*	*1990*	*1989*
Taxes paid or currently payable	$542	$705	$512
Change in deferred taxes	109	(107)	(247)
Amortization of investment credit	(14)	(11)	(18)
	$637	$587	$247

The provisions for federal taxes on income, exclusive of the 1989 accounting change, are less than those which result from application of the statutory corporate tax rate due to the following:

	1991	*1990*	*1989*
Statutory tax rate	34.0%	34.0%	34.0%
Amortization of investment credit	(0.6)	(0.6)	(2.0)
Foreign Sales Corporation tax benefit	(3.2)	(4.9)	(4.8)
Research benefit	(1.8)		(0.7)
Other	0.5	1.3	0.3
Effective tax rate	28.9%	29.8%	26.8%

The 1991 research benefit listed above relates to benefits earned in prior years. Deferred taxes that appear on the Consolidated Statements of Financial Position result from temporary differences, principally due to inventory valuation methods required for tax purposes, depreciation of property, plant and equipment, and recognition of employee benefit plan costs.

The change in deferred taxes, exclusive of the 1989 accounting change, principally resulted from the following:

Year Ended December 31,	*1991*	*1990*	*1989*
Long-term contract method and related inventory costs	$ 99	$(108)	$(250)
Aircraft financing	21	12	15
Domestic International Sales Corporation	(11)	(11)	(11)
Other			(1)
	$109	$(107)	$(247)

Income taxes have been settled with the Internal Revenue Service for all years through 1978. It is the Company's position that adequate provision has been made for all amounts due for the years 1979 through 1991. Federal income tax payments were $993, $563, and $403 in 1991, 1990, and 1989, respectively.

REQUIRED:

1. What was the total amount of tax expense for 1991?
2. How much did the deferred tax liability change during 1991? What caused the changes in the deferred tax account?
3. What is the statutory tax rate imposed on the Boeing Company? What was their effective tax rate, and why is it different?
4. Did Boeing adopt FASB Statement No. 96? If so, when, and what was the effect on their financial statements? What does Boeing say are the principal temporary differences that affect its deferred taxes?
5. What was the amount of taxes paid or currently payable for the year ended 1991?

D8-3
Financial Decision Case

David Schwartz recently decided to open a new-car dealership. The dealership will sell expensive imported cars and offer both engine and body repairs. David plans to organize the business into two divisions: One will sell the cars, and the other will provide the repair services. David has asked your advice concerning two matters:

a. Davis is in the process of setting up inventory systems for both divisions. The inventory of the car division will be made up of no more than 40 to 50 new cars at any one time. The repair division inventory will be made up of more than 3,000 different parts, in varying quantities, which must be inventoried and controlled. David is concerned about maintaining adequate quantities of fast moving parts, about 30% of the parts in inventory.
b. David will offer repair services on credit. He is trying to decide whether to carry his own receivable accounts such as VISA, MasterCard or Discover. He estimates that his annual repair service revenues will be $300,000 per year. If he uses bank cards, he figures that about 80% of the revenue will result from credit card sales. The bank card companies will charge David's firm a 5% fee. Because of some fraud, all but 0.5% of total charges, less the fee, will be remitted to the firm. If David decides to have the firm carry its own accounts, he estimates that 70% of the revenues will be charged on these accounts. If he carries his own accounts, David will have to hire a part-time bookkeeper at $8,000 per year. Finally, he estimates that about 3% of the charges will never be collected.

REQUIRED: Write David a memo outlining (1) his options concerning inventory systems (periodic versus perpetual) and (2) a quantitative and qualitative analysis of whether he should carry his own accounts or use a bank card. Assume that he will not do both.

D8-4
Research Assignment

General Motors announced in mid-December 1991 that it was going to reduce its work force by over 70,000 employees and close up to 21 plants. This decision will have a significant effect on the firm's financial statements. Using the resources of your library, obtain the General Motors' financial statements for 1991 and 1992 and report on what disclosures GM made relative to this "downsizing" and how its financial statements were affected.

D8-5
Research Assignment

The scenario at the beginning of this chapter raised the issue of accounting for student loan guarantees. If you are currently attending a private university obtain that university's annual report or other available information and determine how it accounts for student loan guarantees. If you are attending a public university, choose a private university in your immediate area and determine the same information.

D8-6
Ethical Issues

Anita Jones owns and runs a small computer printer retail store. Last year annual sales amounted to $425,000, and Anita expects a growth rate of about 10% a year for the next few years. Annual profits have been running about $50,000 and will probably grow slightly as sales grow. However, severe price competition may keep profits depressed in the coming year.

As the firm's accountant you are in the midst of preparing its annual financial statements. These statements will also be used by the bank as a basis for renewing its line of credit. The firm has always used a perpetual inventory system to keep track of inventory and cost of goods sold. At the end of each year a physical inventory is also taken to ensure that all items have been properly accounted for. In reviewing the December 31, 1994, inventory you noticed that it totaled about $5,000 less than indicated in the perpetual inventory records. When you brought this to the attention of Anita Jones, she told you not to worry. She said that during the year she had taken about 5 printers from the store for use in her own home (for both business and personal) and to give to other family members. She indicated that they would be returned to the store early in 1995 and would be sold at that time at discounted prices. Anita did not feel it was necessary to make any records of these withdrawals since the printers would be returned to the store and sold. She instructed you to just use the ending inventory figure as determined by the perpetual inventory system.

REQUIRED:

1. Determine the effect on the firm's net income by including $5,000 of costs for items in the ending inventory that were not actually there. (*Hint:* Use the cost of goods sold formula on page 368, and assume that the $5,000 is the only difference.)
2. As the store's accountant, what do you think you should do in this situation?

CHAPTER 9
INVENTORY VALUATION

LEARNING OBJECTIVES

After studying this chapter, you should be able to:

1. Explain the relationship between inventories and income determination.
2. Determine the cost of ending inventories.
3. Apply the four methods of attaching costs to the ending inventory.
4. Explain the factors that management considers in selecting among generally accepted accounting principles.
5. Apply the lower-of-cost-or-market rule as it relates to inventories.
6. Use inventory data in decision making.
7. Explain how the choice of a generally accepted accounting principle may affect the design of an accounting system.

Scenario

Bill Keene is a sophomore at his local university and is just beginning his first accounting class. He is a history major, but is taking accounting to "test the waters" to see if he wants to major in accounting or some other area of business.

Bill also works part-time at Molded Plastics, Inc., a local wholesale furniture company. The company purchases manufactured molded plastic chairs for offices and outdoor patios and sells them to various retailers. The chairs, identical except for color, come in two basic models, those for outdoor use and those for indoor use.

When the company took its year-end inventory, Bill helped count the chairs remaining on hand. The indoor and outdoor models were segregated by type in the large warehouse. At the end of the day, the inventory count was completed. There were 1,210 outdoor chairs and 765 indoor chairs in the year-end inventory.

After the counting was finished, Bill asked the controller, Ellen Glazerman, how the actual cost of the ending inventory was calculated. Ellen said, "Bill, this is a more difficult problem than it may seem. Although we know the number of each type of chair, we need to determine their cost." Bill replied, "This seems like an easy problem. Can't we just check the invoice price of each chair that remains and get a total? I know that the chairs are identical, but aren't they tagged for identification?" Ellen replied, "Yes, we could identify each individual chair, but that would take a lot of time; besides, that method of costing the ending inventory is not used by most firms." She went on to explain that Molded Plastics, Inc., uses a method called LIFO (last-in, first-out). "Under LIFO we assume that the last chairs we purchased from the manufacturer were the first chairs we sold. We use this cost flow assumption regardless of the actual order in which the chairs were sold. By using this method we don't have to specifically identify each chair."

Bill was quite confused. Why would a firm not use an obvious method of identifying the cost of each particular chair? To make an assumption that the last chairs the firm purchased from the manufacturer were the first chairs the firm sold didn't make any sense to him at all. Ellen explained that using a method such as LIFO actually simplifies the process and gives a good approximation of the cost of the chairs that have been sold.

She told him that, in addition to LIFO, there are other acceptable inventory methods; two frequently used methods are FIFO (first-in, first-out) and average cost. FIFO makes the opposite assumption of LIFO. That is, it assumes the first goods purchased from the manufacturer were the first goods sold. Average cost assumes that the cost of each unit sold is made up of an average of all units purchased and not yet sold up to that point. These methods are just as acceptable as LIFO. Ellen told Bill, "I know that this doesn't make much sense now, but come back after you have finished your accounting class and we can talk further. I think that you will see the logic of it all!"

Chapter 8 discussed accounting issues related to the purchase of inventories, including the use of the periodic and perpetual inventory systems. In Chapter 8, however, the discussion of inventory treatment centered on inventories that are

raw materials inventory

work in process inventory

finished goods inventory

purchased for *resale*. Thus, we were concerned with inventories held by merchandising firms. Manufacturing firms also hold inventories. In fact, there are three types of inventories that can be carried by manufacturing firms: *raw materials inventory, work in process inventory* and *finished goods inventory*. **Raw materials inventory** are stores of materials (usually purchased from outside suppliers) that are eventually converted into a final product. An auto manufacturer, for example, may have stocks of steel that is used to produce cars. The steel is not purchased for resale—at least not in its current state. Rather it must be converted to a final product.[1] **Work in process inventory** are stores of partially finished goods. At the end of a period, a manufacturer may have a significant amount of materials in production that are only partially converted. **Finished goods inventory** are stores of fully completed goods ready for sale to customers (often merchandising firms).

This chapter will focus on how accountants determine both the cost of ending finished goods inventories and the cost of the goods sold during the period for both merchandising and manufacturing firms. Since determination of the cost of ending raw materials inventory parallels that of the finished goods inventory, we also learn how to cost out the inventory. Determining the cost of ending work in process inventory, however, is more complicated, and is deferred to later chapters. (Chapters 16 and 17 provide detailed descriptions of how ending work in process inventory is costed.) In addition, inventories will be used to illustrate how management chooses among alternative accounting methods and how accounting choices affect the design of accounting systems.

INVENTORIES AND INCOME DETERMINATION

Objective 1
Explain the relationship between inventories and income determination.

Inventories are nonmonetary assets. As noted in Chapter 4, one of the major accounting issues regarding nonmonetary assets is determining the cost of the current benefits used or consumed (the expense of the period) and the cost of the future benefits (the cost of the assets at the end of the period). This process helps ensure that the costs of these assets are matched against the revenues they produce. For inventories, this requires that the cost of all goods available for sale be allocated between the items sold and the items remaining in ending inventory. The AICPA has stated:

A major objective of accounting for inventories is the proper determination of income through the process of matching appropriate costs against revenues.[2]

Exhibit 9-1 illustrates this allocation process. As the exhibit indicates, the cost of inventories at the end of the period is determined and subtracted from the cost of goods available for sale to derive the cost of goods sold. (Notice that this format applies to goods that are purchased for resale or manufactured.) The accounting methods and procedures accountants use to make this allocation are the main focus of this chapter.

1. This conversion activity requires the use of other manufacturing resources such as labor and machinery. The costs of these other manufacturing resources—along with the cost of the raw materials used—determine the cost of producing a unit of product (e.g. a car). In this chapter, we assume that this cost is known. In Chapters 15–19 we examine how manufacturing costs are actually assigned to products.

2. American Institute of Certified Public Accountants, Committee on Accounting Procedure, Accounting Research Bulletin No. 43, *Restatement and Revision of Accounting Research Bulletins* (New York: AICPA, 1961), Chapter 4, Statement 2.

Exhibit 9-1
Inventory Cost Allocation

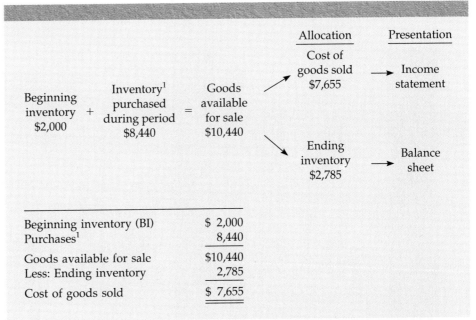

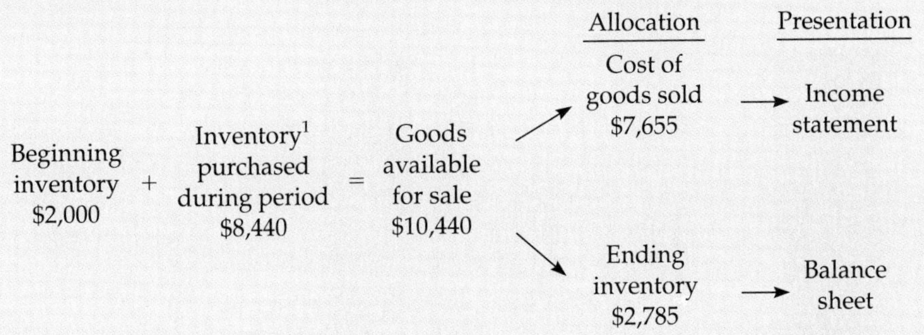

Beginning inventory (BI)	$ 2,000
Purchases[1]	8,440
Goods available for sale	$10,440
Less: Ending inventory	2,785
Cost of goods sold	$ 7,655

[1]For manufacturing firms, purchases would be replaced with the cost of goods manufactured. In this case, the beginning and ending inventory refers to inventory of finished goods. It should be mentioned that the changes in raw materials inventory and work in process inventory affect the computation of the cost of goods manufactured. However, in this chapter we will assume that the cost of goods manufactured is known. Chapter 15 describes the actual computation of this figure.

Measuring Ending Inventories and Income

The allocation of the cost of goods available for sale between the ending inventories and the goods sold affects both the balance sheet and the income statement. Ending inventories are usually a significant current asset, and an improper allocation of costs to the ending inventory can cause a serious error in current assets, total assets, working capital, and the current ratio. The cost of goods sold is often the largest expense item on the income statement. For some firms, this figure can reach 75% to 80% of total sales. A measurement error in cost of goods sold affects the gross profit amount, the gross profit percentage, and the net income. Furthermore, a measurement error in determining the ending inventory has a two-period effect, because the ending inventory for one period becomes the beginning inventory for the next period.

The effects of inventory on the determination of income can be demonstrated by analyzing the effect of an inventory measurement error. To illustrate, the data in Column 1 of Exhibit 9-2 shows the current amount of ending inventory as well as all other items. As the statements show, the gross profits for Years 1 and 2 are $25,000 and $20,000, respectively. The total gross profit for the two-year period is $45,000.

Effect of an Ending Inventory Measurement Error

Case A in Column 2 shows the effect of a $5,000 overstatement of ending inventory in Year 1. Assume that this error is the result of miscounting the items in the ending inventory. Keep in mind that this is the only error in the example; all other items are correct. The effect of this error in Year 1 is to understate the cost

Exhibit 9-2
Effect of Inventory Errors

Column 1			*Column 2 (Case A)*			*Column 3 (Case B)*		
Year 1			*Year 1 (EI overstated by $5,000)*			*Year 1 (EI understated by $5,000)*		
Sales		$110,000	Sales		$110,000	Sales		$110,000
Cost of goods sold			Cost of goods sold			Cost of goods sold		
Beginning inventory	$ 10,000		Beginning inventory	$ 10,000		Beginning inventory	$ 10,000	
Purchases	90,000		Purchases	90,000		Purchases	90,000	
Goods available for sale	$100,000		Goods available for sale	$100,000		Goods available for sale	$100,000	
Less			Less			Less		
Ending inventory (EI)	15,000		Ending inventory (EI)	20,000		Ending inventory (EI)	10,000	
Cost of goods sold		85,000	Cost of goods sold		80,000	Cost of goods sold		90,000
Gross profit		$ 25,000	Gross profit		$ 30,000[1]	Gross profit		$ 20,000[2]
Year 2			*Year 2 (BI overstated by $5,000)*			*Year 2 (BI understated by $5,000)*		
Sales		$135,000	Sales		$135,000	Sales		$135,000
Cost of goods sold			Cost of goods sold			Cost of goods sold		
Beginning inventory (BI)	$ 15,000		Beginning inventory (BI)	$ 20,000		Beginning inventory (BI)	$ 10,000	
Purchases	120,000		Purchases	120,000		Purchases	120,000	
Goods available for sale	$135,000		Goods available for sale	$140,000		Goods available for sale	$130,000	
Less			Less			Less		
Ending inventory	20,000		Ending inventory	20,000		Ending inventory	20,000	
Cost of goods sold		115,000	Cost of goods sold		120,000	Cost of goods sold		110,000
Gross profit		$ 20,000	Gross profit		$ 15,000[3]	Gross profit		$ 25,000[4]
Total for 2 years		$ 45,000	Total for 2 years		$ 45,000	Total for 2 years		$ 45,000

Relationships Between Inventories and Gross Profits
[1]*Overstating the ending inventory overstates the gross profit.*
[2]*Understating the ending inventory understates the gross profit.*
[3]*Overstating the beginning inventory understates the gross profit.*
[4]*Understating the beginning inventory overstates the gross profit.*

of goods sold by $5,000, from $85,000 to $80,000. Thus, there is a corresponding overstatement of the gross profit, from $25,000 to $30,000. Generally, everything else being equal, the higher the overstatement of ending inventory is, the higher the overstatement of the gross profit.

In Year 2, the ending inventory from Year 1 becomes the beginning inventory. As a result, the beginning inventory in Year 2 is overstated by $5,000, from $15,000 to $20,000. Therefore goods available for sale and cost of goods sold are overstated by $5,000, and gross profit is understated by $5,000. Again, everything else being equal, the higher the overstatement of the beginning inventory is, the more understated the gross profit will be.

Comparing Columns 1 and 2, you can see that over a two-year period, the gross profit in both cases is $45,000. In effect, the one overstatement of $5,000 in the ending inventory of Year 1 and the beginning inventory of Year 2 cancel each other out, so that Year 2's ending inventory and retained earnings, both balance sheet accounts, are correctly stated. However, there are important differences within each period. In Year 1, ending inventory and gross profit are overstated, and in Year 2, beginning inventory is overstated and gross profit is understated. Thus, although inventory errors can be self-correcting, there are serious allocation errors between the accounting periods that affect gross profit and income trends.

Case B in Column 3 illustrates the effect of a $5,000 understatement of the ending inventory in Year 1. Again, keep in mind that this is assumed to be the only error; all other items are correct. The effect of this error in Year 1 is to overstate the cost of goods sold by $5,000, from $85,000 to $90,000, and to understate the gross profit by the same $5,000. Generally, all else being equal, understating the ending inventory will cause the gross profit to be understated.

The ending inventory from Year 1 becomes the beginning inventory of Year 2. As a result, the cost of goods sold is understated by $5,000, from $115,000 to $110,000, and there is a corresponding $5,000 overstatement in the gross profit, from $20,000 to $25,000. Again, everything else being equal, an understatement in the beginning inventory will cause an overstatement in the gross profit.

Comparing Columns 1, 2, and 3, you can see that over a two-year period, the total gross profit in all three columns is $45,000. This emphasizes that a single inventory error is self-canceling over a consecutive two-year period, but that serious allocation errors occur each year.

DETERMINING THE COST OF ENDING INVENTORIES

Objective 2
Determine the cost of ending inventories.

Accountants must first determine the actual quantity of items on hand at the end of the period and then attach a cost to these items to calculate the total cost of ending inventories. This is usually done by taking a physical inventory, most often at year-end. A physical inventory is required at least once a year, regardless of whether a firm uses the perpetual or the periodic inventory system. After the quantity of items is determined, a particular cost flow pattern is assumed and costs are attached to each item in the inventory. The total of the costs times the quantity equals the cost of the ending inventory.

Ending Inventory Quantities

Determining the actual quantity of items in the ending inventory usually requires a physical count. This count can take more than a day and often requires that the firm halt its operations. For example, imagine the effort to count the ending inventory of a large department store. Or consider the problems involved in determining the ending inventory of completed automobiles, autos currently being manufactured, and all the parts and supplies for a company such as General Motors. For this reason, some firms use estimation and statistical sampling procedures to determine the quantity of their ending inventories.

Costs Included in the Ending Inventory

Inventories should be recorded at cost according to generally accepted accounting principles. In the AICPA definition, cost as applied to inventories means "the sum of the applicable expenditures and charges directly or indirectly incurred in bringing an article to its existing condition and location."[3] For the retailer or a manufacturer buying raw materials needed for production, this means that acquisition costs include the purchase price less any cash discounts, plus any freight charges, insurance in transit, and sales taxes that are incurred to get the product ready for sale. Costs such as freight charges and insurance are usually small, however, and the cost of trying to allocate them to individual items outweighs the benefit. Thus, most firms will use the net invoice price when attaching a cost to an individual item in the ending inventory. These other costs are collected and ultimately become part of the cost of goods sold. For the manufacturer, the cost of a unit of finished goods should include raw materials cost plus all costs needed to convert the raw materials to a finished good.

After determining the quantity of the ending inventory and deciding what to include in the acquisition or manufacturing cost, a decision still must be made as to what cost to attach to the particular items on hand. In other words, how does the accountant determine the acquisition or manufacturing cost or price paid for each item on hand when the items have been purchased (manufactured) at different times at different costs?

METHODS OF ATTACHING COSTS TO THE ENDING INVENTORY

Objective 3
Apply the four methods of attaching costs to the ending inventory.

As Bill Keene remarked in the opening scenario, at first glance it would seem easy to determine the acquisition cost of each item that is sold or that is in ending inventory. However, imagine a firm like Molded Plastics that sells identical products that were purchased at different prices and at different times throughout the year. Or imagine a large department store that sells a variety of products in different sizes and styles, again purchased at different prices and times. Even with a well-designed computer-based inventory system, the costs involved in attempting to determine the exact acquisition price of each item remaining at the end of the year would probably outweigh the benefits of such a system.

It is easy to determine the costs of ending inventory and items that have been sold when all of the items were purchased at the same price or manufactured at the same cost. However, because prices do not remain stable, accountants have developed alternative methods to attach costs to inventory items. These methods use an assumed cost flow rather than the actual physical flow. That is, an assumption is made that costs flow in one of four different patterns regardless of how the goods physically move into and out of the firm. These cost flow

3. Ibid., Statement 3.

assumptions are (1) first-in, first-out (FIFO), (2) last-in, first-out (LIFO), (3) average cost, and, in some limited situations, (4) specific identification.

first-in, first-out (FIFO)

First-in, first-out (FIFO) is an inventory valuation method that assumes that the costs attached to the first goods sold are the costs of the first goods purchased or produced. In effect, the items are assumed to be sold in the order that they were purchased (manufactured): thus the cost of the ending inventory is calculated from the cost of the most recent purchases (goods manufactured). **Last-in, first-out (LIFO)** makes the opposite assumption about the flow of costs. The *LIFO* method assumes that the costs attached to the last purchases or goods manufactured are assumed to be the cost of the first items sold. In effect, items are assumed to be sold in the opposite order from that in which they were purchased (manufactured). Thus, the cost of the ending inventory, under the LIFO method, is calculated from the cost of the earliest purchases (goods manufactured).

last-in, first-out (LIFO)

average cost

The **average cost** method attaches an average cost to both the cost of goods sold and the ending inventory. The average is determined by dividing the total cost of goods available for sale by the number of units available for sale. Finally, the **specific-identification method** determines the actual acquisition cost of each individual item in the ending inventory. Management is free to choose any one of these cost flow patterns, regardless of the physical flow of goods.

specific-identification method

Applying Different Cost Flow Assumptions—Periodic System

The data for the Cerf Company, a merchandising firm, shown in Exhibit 9-3 will be used to demonstrate the computations required to apply four different cost methods using a periodic inventory system. For manufacturing firms, if you replace units purchased with units manufactured, and acquisition cost with manufacturing cost, then the example illustrates how the four methods apply to the finished goods inventory. Furthermore, if you think of units purchased as units

Exhibit 9-3
Inventory Data for Illustrations

Cerf Company
Data for Cost Flow Illustration
Year Ended December 31, 1995

	Units	*Acquisition Cost*	*Total Cost*
Beginning inventory (January 1, 1995)	500	$4.00	$ 2,000
Purchases during year			
January 24	200	4.10	820
March 18	400	4.20	1,680
May 5	300	4.50	1,350
July 31	350	4.50	1,575
September 27	400	4.60	1,840
November 29	250	4.70	1,175
Goods available for sale	2,400		$10,440
Less: Items in ending inventory	600		
Items sold	1,800		
Total dollar value of sales 1,800 units @ $6 per unit	$10,800		

of raw materials and items sold as items of material issued to production, then the example shows how the four methods apply to raw material inventories. For raw materials, keep in mind that there would be no cost of goods sold associated. The only interest is determining the cost of ending inventory based on the four different cost flow assumptions. The basic message is that the four cost flow methods can be applied to different kinds of inventory. Note the following about this example:

1. The example is deliberately simplified, with only six purchases made during the year. However, the procedures shown for this example hold for more complex purchasing patterns.
2. The example uses a periodic inventory system, which for cost flow purposes does not require keeping track of the dates on which sales are made. Each of the four inventory costing methods can be used with the perpetual inventory system. With a perpetual system, dates for both sales and purchases are important. Because of the need to keep track of these dates, the calculations are more complex than with a periodic system. The concepts, however, are the same for both periodic and perpetual systems.
3. Each of these four methods is an acceptable alternative under generally accepted accounting principles.

First-in, first-out (FIFO). Recall that under the FIFO method, the costs attached to the first goods sold are assumed to be the costs of the first goods purchased, and the cost of the ending inventories consists of the costs of the latest goods purchased. The illustration in Exhibit 9-4 shows these cost flows. FIFO refers to a means of determining the cost of goods sold during the period. However, when applying the FIFO method, the cost of the ending inventory generally is determined first and the cost of the goods sold is then derived.

Using the data in Exhibit 9-3, the cost of the ending inventory under FIFO is $2,785, and the cost of goods sold is $7,655. These figures are shown in Exhibit 9-4. As this exhibit indicates, the 600 units in the ending inventory consist of (1) the 250 units purchased on November 29 and (2) 350 of the 400 units purchased on September 27. The 50 items remaining from the September 27 purchase, as well as the units from prior purchases and the beginning inventory, are assumed to have been sold. We could calculate the cost of goods sold directly, but this approach is rarely used because firms sell many more goods than they have on hand at the end of the year so it is easier to count and cost what is on hand.

The 1996 beginning inventory is the same as the 1995 ending inventory of $2,785, because the inventory at the beginning of the first day of the year is the same as the inventory at the end of the day on the last day of the previous year. This inventory consists of two distinct layers of 250 and 350 units, respectively, each purchased at different prices. However, it usually is not necessary to maintain these beginning inventory layers. The inventory can be brought forward as 600 units at a cost of $2,785. Under the FIFO method, these two layers can be merged because these goods will be assumed to be the first ones sold in the next year. When they become part of the goods sold, the cost becomes part of a large pool in which the identity of the layers is not important.

Most goods physically move on a FIFO basis. However, it is not necessary to match the cost flow assumption with the actual physical flow of goods through a firm. For example, think of a large barrel of nails in a hardware store. As additional nails are added to the barrel, they are placed on top of the older nails; when the nails are sold, the top nails (most recently purchased) are sold first. In this situation, the nails move in a last-in, first-out pattern. Nonetheless, the man-

Exhibit 9-4
FIFO Calculation Illustrated

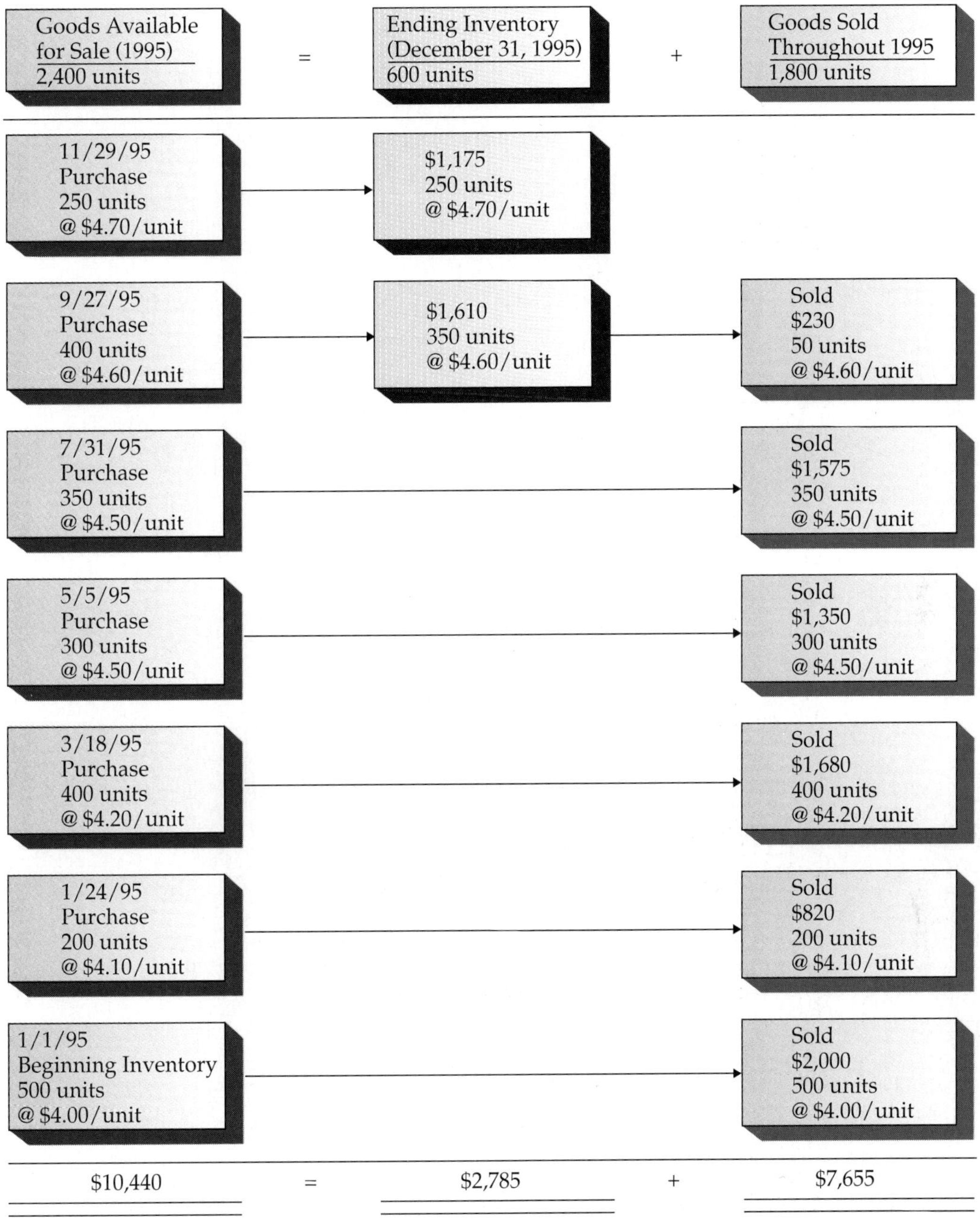

agement of the hardware store is free to choose the FIFO method of pricing its inventories.

Last-in, first-out (LIFO). Under the LIFO method of costing inventories, the cost attached to the last goods purchased is assumed to be the cost of the first goods sold. Therefore, the cost of the ending inventory is from the earliest purchases. The illustration in Exhibit 9-5 shows these cost flows.

Exhibit 9-5
LIFO Calculations Illustrated

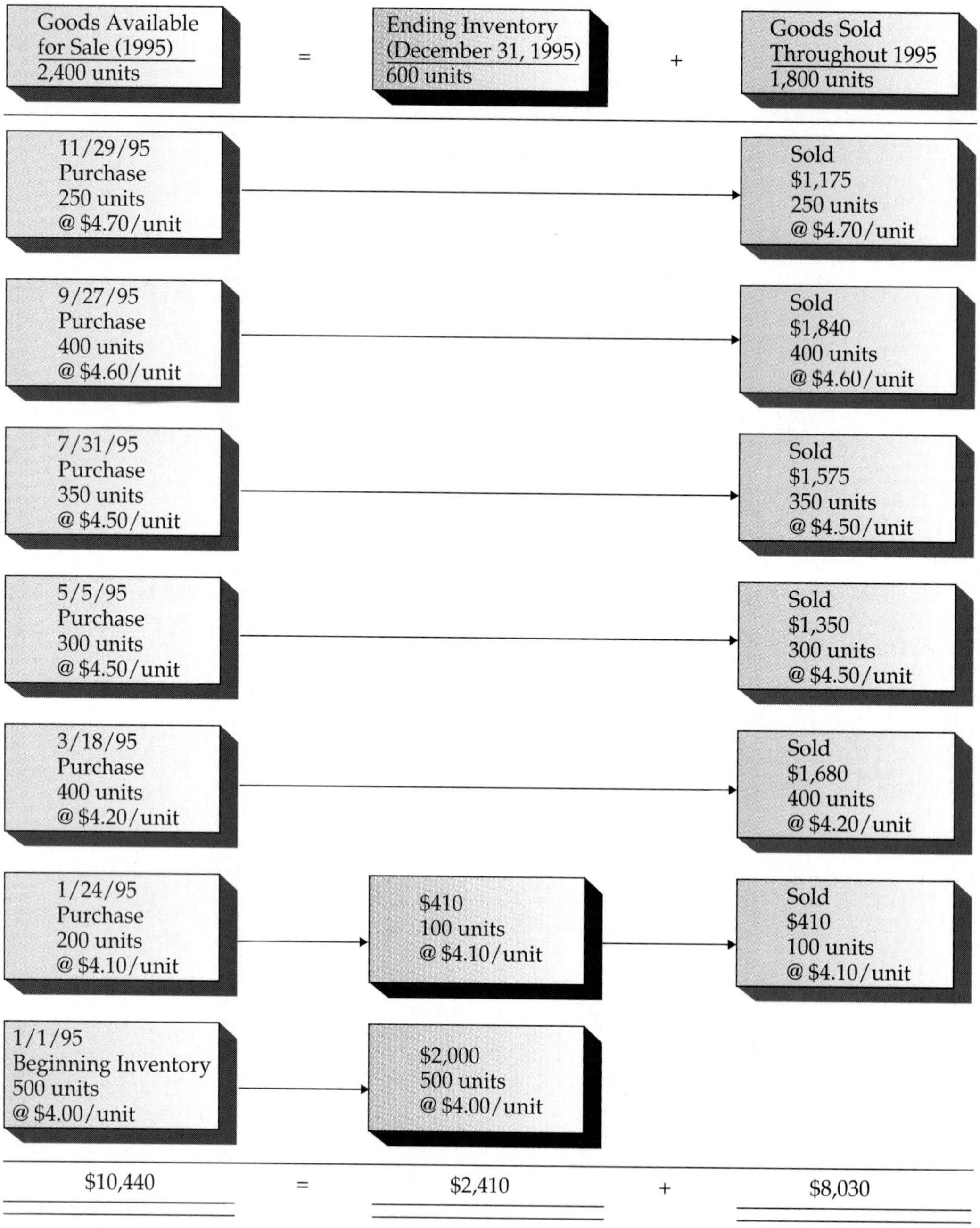

Using data from Exhibit 9-3, the cost of the ending inventory under LIFO is $2,410, and the cost of goods sold is $8,030. As Exhibit 9-5 indicates, the 600 units in the ending inventory are assumed to be (1) 500 units from the beginning inventory and (2) 100 units from the January 24 purchase.

When the LIFO method is used, it is important to maintain separate layers of costs of ending inventory. Therefore, in the illustration, the beginning inventory for the following period, 1996, is carried forward in two layers comprising 500 units at $4.00 and 100 units at $4.10. If next year's ending inventory falls below 600 units, the 100 units represented by the January 24 purchase would be included in cost of goods sold before the 500 units represented by the earlier layer. That is, inventory is decreased in reverse of the order in which it was added originally; because the layer comprising 100 units at $4.10 was added after the layer comprising 500 units at $4.00, under the LIFO method it is considered to be sold first.

To illustrate, assume that during 1996 the Cerf Company sold 5,000 units, but only purchased 4,960. This means that during 1996, the number of units in the inventory decreased by 40 and thus, the ending inventory at December 31, 1995 is only 560 (600 units in the beginning inventory less the 40-unit decrease during 1996). The ending inventory at December 31, 1996 is $2,246, calculated as follows:

Beginning inventory—500 units @ $4.00 =	$2,000
Inventory from Jan. 24, 1995 purchase—60 units @ $4.10 =	246
	$2,246

Average Cost. Under the average-cost method, a weighted average cost per unit is calculated by dividing the total cost of the goods available for sale for the year by the total number of units available for sale during the year.[4] For the Cerf Company, this calculation for 1995 is as follows:

$$\frac{\text{Cost of goods available for sale}}{\text{Units available for sale}} = \frac{\$10,440}{2,400} = \$4.35 \text{ average cost per unit}$$

This $4.35 cost per unit is applied to both the ending inventory and the goods available for sale as follows:

Ending inventory = 600 units × $4.35 =	$ 2,610
Cost of goods sold = 1,800 units × $4.35 =	7,830
	$10,440

In the next year, 1996, the beginning inventory consists of 600 units at an average cost of $2,610. At the end of 1996 a new average will be calculated.

Specific Identification. It is practical to determine the specific acquisition cost of the items remaining in the ending inventory in some situations. These situations are most common in firms whose products have high unit costs, are easily differentiated, and are sold in relatively low volumes. For example, an automobile dealer uses auto serial numbers to record the exact cost of every car sold and every car remaining in inventory. Other examples of such firms are furniture companies, antique stores, and coin and stamp dealers. Depending on the product, costs, and benefits, other firms might want to maintain such records.

4. If raw materials inventory costing were being done, you would replace Cost of goods available for sale with Materials available for use and Units available for sale with Units (or Materials) available for use.

Exhibit 9-6
Specific Identification Calculations Illustrated

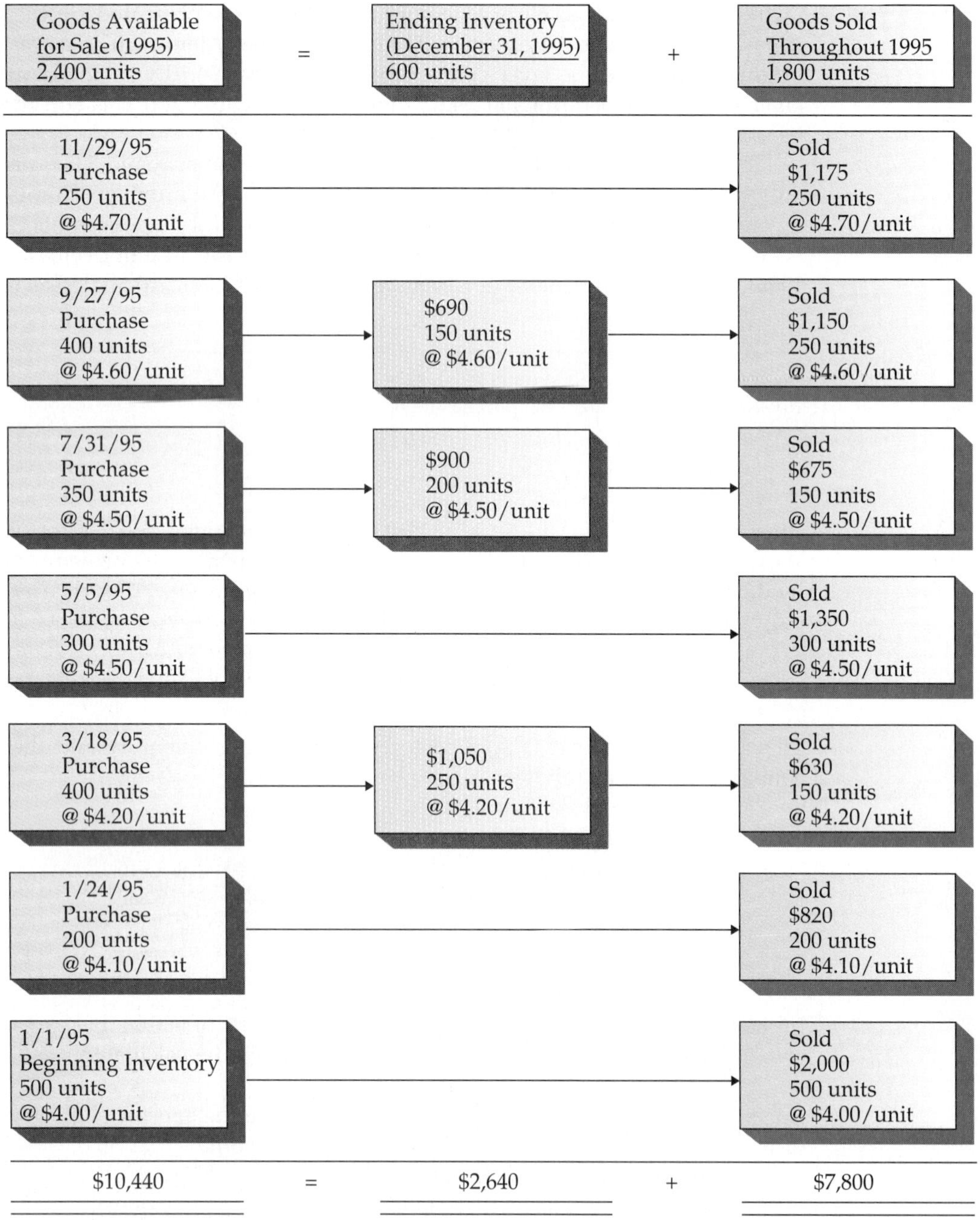

To illustrate this method, assume that the Cerf Company is able to determine that the 600 items in the ending inventory are from the specific purchases listed in Exhibit 9-6. The cost of the ending inventory is computed to be $2,640 and the cost of goods sold to be $7,800.

In addition to the practical problems of keeping track of the costs of the specific items in the inventory, there are theoretical problems involved in using the specific-identification method. For example, assume that a firm produces only one product and that all units of the product are identical, or *fungible*. Wheat and other commodities are examples of fungible goods. Buyers of such products don't care which specific item or lot they buy because they are all the same. Consequently, the firm's management is free to sell the specific lot(s) it desires. That is, the buyer of 10 ounces of gold does not care which lot the gold comes from, as long as all the gold is of the same quality. Thus, the firm's management can sell the gold from any lot it chooses. Management is able to manipulate income by selling lots with certain acquisition costs. To demonstrate this point, assume that the management of the Cerf Company wants to maximize its income for the current year. In this situation, the firm sells those goods with the lowest acquisition costs (that is, the items purchased at $4.00 and $4.10). Next year, if management decides to minimize reported income, it will sell those products with the highest acquisition cost. Therefore, management has more ability to manipulate the firm's income.

Comparing the Methods

Exhibit 9-7 compares the effects of the FIFO, average cost, and LIFO cost flow assumptions on ending inventory, cost of goods sold, and gross profit for the Cerf Company.[5] In this illustration, the highest gross profit and ending inventory cost, and lowest cost of goods sold result when FIFO is used. The lowest gross profit and ending inventory cost, and highest cost of goods sold result when LIFO is used. Average cost falls between these two extremes. This is because the acquisition price of the inventory consistently rose during the year, from $4.10 to $4.70. This example was deliberately constructed to reflect rising prices, which are more common than falling prices in today's economy. However, in some sectors of the economy, such as electronics, prices have been falling. In that situation, the effects of LIFO and FIFO would be just the opposite of the rising-price situation. That is, in a period of falling prices, LIFO would produce the highest gross profit and the highest ending inventory cost.

Rising Prices and FIFO. In a period of rising prices, FIFO produces the highest gross profit and the highest ending inventory. The high gross profit is produced because the earliest and thus the lowest costs are allocated to cost of goods sold. Thus, FIFO cost of goods sold is the lowest of the three inventory costing methods, and FIFO gross profit is correspondingly the highest of the three methods. Ending inventory reflects the highest cost under FIFO because the latest, highest costs are allocated to ending inventory. These results are logical, given the relationship between ending inventories and gross profit.

Many accountants approve of using FIFO because ending inventories are recorded at costs that approximate their current acquisition or replacement cost. Thus, inventories are realistically valued on the firm's balance sheet. On the other hand, accountants criticize FIFO because it matches the earliest cost against current sales and results in the highest gross profit. Some accountants argue that these profits are overstated because, in order to stay in business, a going concern must replace its inventory at current acquisition prices or replacement costs. These overstated profits, often referred to as **inventory profits** (or **holding gains**), are realized when current revenue is matched with low historical inventory costs that do not approximate the current replacement cost of inventory.

inventory profits
holding gains

5. Specific identification has not been included in this comparison because, as mentioned, the physical flow of goods is subject to discretion and manipulation. Thus, there is no predictable pattern.

Exhibit 9-7
Cost Flow Assumptions Compared

Cerf Company			
	Periodic		
	FIFO	*Average Cost*	*LIFO*
Sales	$10,800	$10,800	$10,800
Cost of goods sold	7,655	7,830	8,030
Gross margin	$ 3,145	$ 2,970	$ 2,770
Ending inventory	$ 2,785	$ 2,610	$ 2,410

To illustrate the concept of inventory profits, assume that a firm enters into the following transactions:

- January 2: Purchases one unit of inventory at $60.
- December 15: Purchases a second unit of inventory at $85.
- December 31: Sells one unit at $100. Current replacement cost of inventory, $85.

On a FIFO basis, the firm reports a gross profit of $40 ($100 – $60). The firm will not have $40 available to cover operating expenses, however, because it must replace the inventory at a cost of at least $85. Thus, in reality, the firm has only $15 ($100 – $85) available to cover its operating expenses. The $25 difference between the $85 replacement cost and the $60 historical cost is the inventory profit or holding gain. These inventory profits are not available to cover operating costs because they must be used to replace inventory at higher prices. Exhibit 9-8 illustrates the concept of inventory profits or holding gains.

Rising Prices and LIFO. In a period of rising prices, LIFO results in the lowest gross profit and the lowest ending inventory. The low gross profit results when the latest and highest costs are allocated to cost of goods sold. Thus, cost of goods sold is the highest of the three inventory costing methods, and gross profit is the lowest. Also, under LIFO, the ending inventory is recorded at the lowest cost of the three methods, because the earliest and lowest prices are allocated to it. In fact, if a company had switched to LIFO 20 years ago, the original LIFO layers, if unsold, would be costed at 20-year-old prices.

LIFO has the opposite effect from FIFO on the balance sheet and income statement. Consequently, LIFO is criticized because the inventory cost on the balance sheet often is unrealistically low. Therefore, working capital, the current ratio, and current assets tend to be understated. This possible effect can be significant, as illustrated by the following excerpt from a recent annual report of Albertson's:

Inventories

Approximately 96% of the Company's inventories are valued using the last-in, first-out (LIFO) method. If the first-in, first-out (FIFO) method had been used, inventories would have been $172,470,000, $160,877,000 and $137,804,000 higher at the end of 1991, 1990 and 1989. Net earnings would have been higher by $7,354,000 ($.06 per share) in 1991, $14,477,000 ($.11 per share) in 1990 and $14,660,000 ($.11 per share) in 1989. The replacement cost of inventories valued at LIFO approximates FIFO cost.

This disclosure is typical of that made by companies which use LIFO and provides users with information concerning the effect of LIFO.

Exhibit 9-8
Inventory Profits or Holding Gains

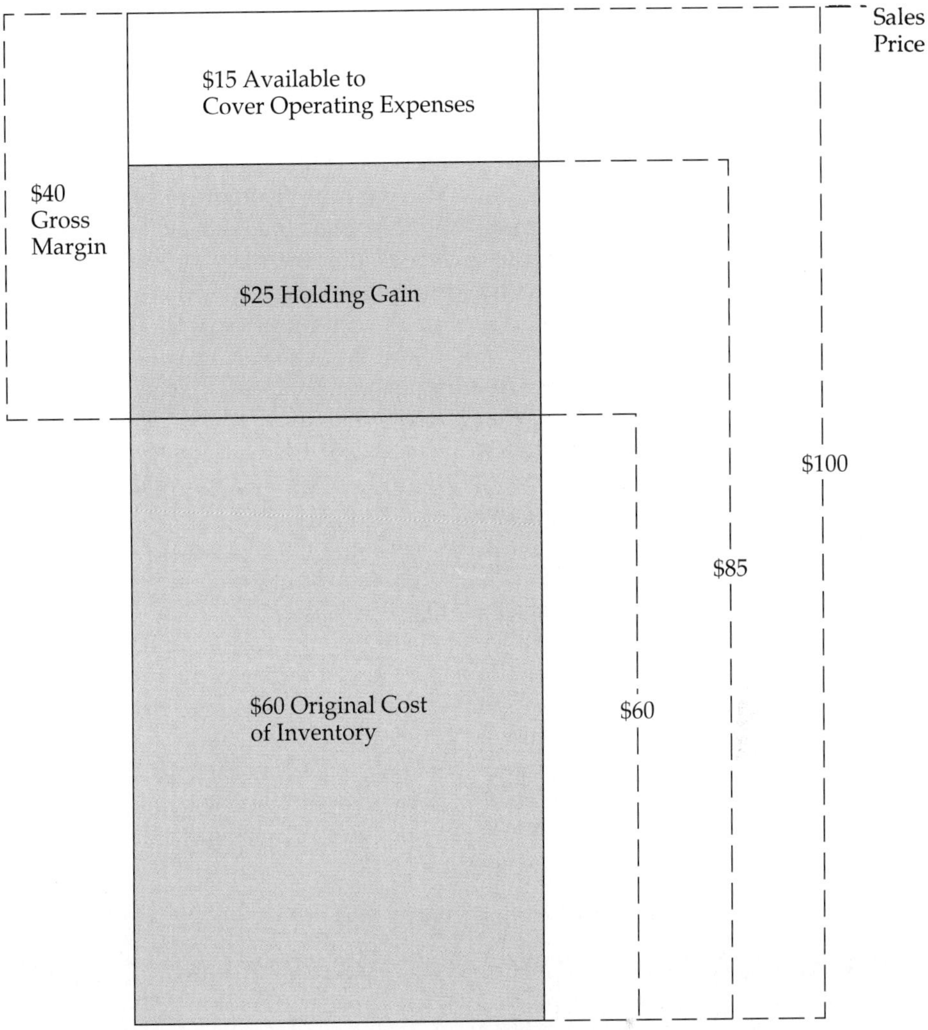

The screened portion represents the amount needed (as of the balance sheet date) to replace the inventory item that was sold. The holding gain is part of that amount.

Many accountants argue, however, that LIFO provides a more realistic income figure because it eliminates a substantial portion of inventory profit. In the three transactions listed on page 406, you will see that on a LIFO basis the firm's gross profit is $15, because the December 15 purchase is matched against the $100 sale. In this case, the acquisition price of the inventory did not change between the last purchase on December 15 and its sale on December 31, so all of the inventory profits are eliminated. In reality, LIFO will not eliminate all inventory profits but will substantially reduce them.

In summary, in a period of rising prices, FIFO and LIFO have opposite effects on the balance sheet and income statement. LIFO usually provides a realistic income statement at the expense of the balance sheet. Conversely, FIFO provides a realistic balance sheet at the expense of the income statement. In a period of falling prices, the reverse is true. In either case, average cost will fall between FIFO and LIFO.

How Current Cost Can Alleviate the Problem

current cost

Using current costs can alleviate the need for a cost flow assumption and can help solve the problem of choosing between a realistic income statement and a realistic balance sheet. In general, **current cost** is the cost of currently acquiring an item. Cost of goods sold is recorded at the current cost of the item at the time of its resale. Thus, the gross profit figure, which is the difference between sales and the current cost of goods sold, represents income available to the firm to cover operating expenses after maintaining its ability to purchase new inventory. Returning to the example on page 406, the gross profit figure on the basis of current cost is $15, or the selling price of $100 less the cost of the December 15 purchase which is the approximate current cost of the inventory item. On the balance sheet, ending inventory is recorded at the current cost at the statement date; in our example $85. The difference between the current cost of the ending inventory and its historical cost is considered a holding gain which is yet to be realized. Thus, the figures on the income statement and balance sheet represent realistic amounts.

Current-cost accounting is not a generally accepted accounting principle for primary financial statements. Many accountants feel that the information is difficult to obtain and does not meet the reliability criterion. Because of the perceived relevance of these data to present and potential investors and creditors, however, the FASB encourages certain companies to disclose selected current-cost data on a supplemental basis. In regard to inventories, FASB Statement No. 33, as amended by Statement No. 89, suggests that firms disclose income from continuing operations on a current-cost basis and the current-cost amounts of inventory and property, plant, and equipment at the end of the year. Not many firms, however, choose to make these disclosures. Current-cost accounting is examined in more advanced accounting courses.

CHOOSING AMONG GENERALLY ACCEPTED ACCOUNTING PRINCIPLES

Objective 4
Explain the factors that management considers in selecting among generally accepted accounting principles.

The choice a firm's management has in selecting among alternative inventory cost flow assumptions is representative of the choice management has, in general, in selecting among acceptable accounting principles. For example, there are several acceptable depreciation methods (to be discussed in Chapter 10), different methods of estimating uncollectible accounts (discussed in Chapter 7), and two ways of accounting for construction contracts (briefly discussed in Chapter 3). The choice involves not only financial reporting considerations but also tax considerations. As noted in the previous chapter, in many instances management can choose one method for tax purposes and another for financial reporting purposes.

After selecting an accounting method, management can change methods in future years, even though the comparability characteristic of accounting information requires that accounting methods and principles be applied consistently across accounting periods. When a change in accounting principles is made, the auditor's report must be modified to indicate the nature of the change and the fact that the financial statements are not consistent with those of preceding years. For tax purposes, most accounting changes require the approval of the IRS commissioner and cannot be made at will.

Motivation for Selecting Certain Accounting Methods

The motivation of management often is straightforward when selecting accounting methods or principles for tax purposes: to postpone or reduce current tax payments. By doing so, cash flows to the firm are increased and thus stockholders' wealth is increased. The selection of accounting principles for external financial reporting is considerably more complex. Not all managements have the same motivation. Considerations such as increasing the "bottom line" (net income), enhancing management's own compensation, and providing reliable financial reports all play a part. The management of a public company may have different pressures and motivations from those of the owner-manager of a private company.

The motivations in selecting accounting principles for tax purposes may conflict with those in selecting accounting principles for financial reporting purposes, because often management wishes to reduce taxable income while at the same time increasing reported accounting income. In many cases, this is not a problem—management can select one principle for tax purposes and another for financial reporting purposes. When deciding whether to use FIFO or LIFO, however, this is not the case.

Selecting FIFO or LIFO. The Internal Revenue Code contains a provision called the *LIFO conformity rule,* which requires a company to use LIFO for financial reporting purposes if LIFO is used for tax purposes. This is one of the few situations in which the choice of accounting principles for tax and financial reporting purposes cannot be made independently. This conformity rule applies only to LIFO. That is, a firm can use FIFO for external financial reporting purposes and average cost for tax purposes. This rule was inserted in the Code by Congress to keep businesses from reporting low earnings to the government while reporting high earnings (using FIFO) to stockholders and other financial statement users.

Given the tax effects of LIFO, this conformity rule has important implications. To demonstrate, assume the following facts for the Golden Bear Company at year-end 1995:

Sales	$1,700,000
Cost of goods sold—FIFO	800,000
Cost of goods sold—LIFO	1,100,000
All other operating expenses	100,000
Tax rate	25%

The summary income statements based on both FIFO and LIFO are shown in Exhibit 9-9. If the firm uses the LIFO method, its income before taxes will be reduced by $300,000, the difference between the FIFO and the LIFO inventories. Thus, taxes using the LIFO method are only $125,000, versus $200,000 using the FIFO method. This represents a cash savings of $75,000, or 25% of the $300,000 difference between FIFO and LIFO inventories.

Given the conformity rule and the tax effects of LIFO, what inventory cost method should management select? In a period of rising prices, because LIFO reduces the current period's taxable income and taxes, thus increasing cash flows

Exhibit 9-9
FIFO vs. LIFO: Example of Impact on Income

Golden Bear Company Summary Income Statement Year-End 1995		
	FIFO	*LIFO*
Sales	$1,700,000	$1,700,000
Cost of goods sold	800,000	1,100,000
Gross profit on sales	$ 900,000	$ 600,000
Operating expenses	100,000	100,000
Income before taxes	$ 800,000	$ 500,000
Taxes—25%	200,000	125,000
Net income	$ 600,000	$ 375,000

to the firm, many accountants argue that LIFO should be selected, even at the expense of lower reported earnings. The argument is made that increased cash flows enhance stockholders' wealth, even though reported earnings are lower. Furthermore, many financial analysts have begun to evaluate a firm's *quality of earnings*. The **quality of earnings** is a qualitative measure of the extent to which reported earnings are the result of economic events rather than of accounting principles. Quality of earnings attempts to measure the degree to which earnings might have been manipulated by management. For example, in a period of rising prices, if a firm chooses FIFO and other accounting principles that tend to increase reported earnings, analysts may consider the quality of such earnings to be lower than that of earnings determined by more conservative accounting principles. Indeed, accounting research has generally indicated that the stock market is not fooled by reported earnings and recognizes the value of the increased cash flows available to LIFO firms versus those available to FIFO firms.

quality of earnings

This discussion is not meant to imply that all firms should use LIFO or should switch to LIFO. As will be seen later, there are practical reasons why using LIFO is not advantageous for all firms. In fact, the 1992 AICPA survey shows that approximately 60% of the 600 firms sampled used LIFO.[6]

Although a large number of firms use LIFO, some have changed from LIFO to FIFO. Chrysler Corporation's 1970 change from LIFO to FIFO is an example. Estimates indicate that this change cost Chrysler $75 million in future taxes. Why did Chrysler make a change that might increase its taxes by $75 million? The effect of this change was to decrease the current year's losses and to increase the current ratio and retained earnings. To a management concerned with short-term goals of decreasing losses and meeting loan agreements related to maintaining a current ratio and debt-to-equity ratio, such a change may seem worthwhile, even at the expense of short- and long-run cash flows. Although this example is from the 1970s, it does indicate the many variables that enter into management's selection of a particular accounting method.

LIFO versus FIFO—A Summary. In summary, the selection of accounting principles for both financial reporting and tax purposes is an important management decision. In the LIFO-versus-FIFO case, it is even more important because of the

6. AICPA, *Accounting Trends and Techniques*, 46th ed. (New York: AICPA, 1992), p. 142.

LIFO conformity rule, whereby management is forced to consider the utility of increased cash flows versus the effect LIFO will have on the balance sheet and income statement.

Most important, the LIFO-versus-FIFO case illustrates the conflicting demands that management must consider in its choice of accounting principles and methods. As long as different accounting methods are permitted, the question of which method to use will continue to be debated.

Issues Related to LIFO. A number of issues and problems related to LIFO can decrease its advantages. Some of the more important ones are the effects of falling prices, the possibility of LIFO liquidation, management of purchasing behavior, and inventory turnover. Finally, the international dimensions of this issue will be explored briefly.

Falling Prices. LIFO-based earnings and income taxes are higher when prices decrease. This is because the latest and, in this case, the lowest prices are allocated to cost of goods sold. In some industries, prices are volatile and thus unpredictable. In particular, this is the case with commodities such as oil and sugar. In 1974, for example, a number of sugar companies changed to LIFO as sugar prices rose at a rapid pace. By switching to LIFO, these companies reduced their taxable income and their resulting tax payments. A year later, however, sugar prices declined. With LIFO in place, the sugar companies now reported an increase in earnings and faced tax payments higher than they would have been with FIFO.

LIFO liquidation

LIFO Liquidation. The possibility of *LIFO liquidation* is a major concern to LIFO users. As noted, at least a portion of the inventories costed under LIFO are priced at the firm's early purchase prices, which might go all the way back to the date when LIFO was adopted. **LIFO liquidation** is the sale of prior year inventory layers, and occurs when a firm sells more units than it purchases in any one year. Thus, LIFO layers that have been built up in the past are liquidated—that is, included in the current period's cost of goods sold. In effect, a firm may be selling units that have 1950 or 1960 costs attached to them. The result is a lower cost of goods sold, higher gross profit, and higher taxes. Although firms can often plan ahead to prevent LIFO liquidation by making sufficient purchases near year-end, events sometimes occur that are beyond management's control. For example, a supplier's strike or an unanticipated demand can cause unplanned LIFO liquidation. The effect of a LIFO liquidation is illustrated by the following excerpt of a note taken from a recent financial statement of Corning, Inc:

Inventories

Inventories are valued at the lower of cost or market. The LIFO (last-in, first-out) method of determining cost is used for a substantial portion of inventories for which LIFO costing would be appropriate. Minor inventories, supplies and the inventories of subsidiaries operating in hyperinflationary economics are valued using the FIFO (first-in, first-out) method.

In 1990, 1989, and 1988, certain inventory quantities were reduced, resulting in liquidations of LIFO inventory quantities carried at lower costs prevailing in prior years. The effect was to increase net income by $5.9 million ($0.06 per share), $3.4 million ($0.04 per share), and $6.1 million ($0.07 per share) in 1990, 1989 and 1988, respectively.[7]

7. From a note to the Corning Incorporated 1990 Annual Report.

Purchasing Behavior. The use of LIFO, especially in connection with the periodic inventory method, offers management a certain degree of flexibility to manipulate profits. From management's perspective, this is not a problem, but critics of LIFO point to this as a disadvantage. In any event, by timing purchases at year-end, management is able to determine what costs will be allocated to cost of goods. Remember that under LIFO the cost of a purchase made at year-end will be included in cost of goods sold. A purchase at the beginning of the next year, however, could end up in next year's ending inventory as a new LIFO layer if the units purchased during this year exceed the units sold.

inventory turnover

Inventory Turnover. Inventory turnover, or the rate at which a company sells its inventory, can affect the differential between FIFO and LIFO. The advantage of LIFO over FIFO is not as great when a company has a high turnover rate because FIFO-based cost of goods will approximate a LIFO-based or current-cost cost of goods sold. Thus, inventory profits usually found in connection with FIFO would be substantially decreased.

LIFO—The International Dimension. The LIFO inventory method has been used in the United States since the late 1930's. Although LIFO is relatively new in other countries throughout the world, in recent years it has increased in popularity. Despite this increase in popularity, the International Accounting Standards Committee (IASC) issued an exposure draft on inventories that prohibited the use of LIFO. This exposure draft caused quite a debate among standard-setters in countries throughout the world. Finally, the IASC bowed to this pressure and, in its recently issued revised standard on inventories, allows the use of LIFO as an "allowed alternative." According to this standard:

- Specific identification is used to assign costs to inventory items that are not ordinarily interchangeable and goods or services produced and segregated for specific projects. (This, in effect, severely limits the use of specific identification.)
- The costs of other inventory items are assigned using either weighted average or FIFO cost formulas.
- As an allowed alternative, the LIFO formula may be used.[8]

INVENTORY VALUATION—LOWER OF COST OR MARKET

Objective 5
Apply the lower-of-cost-or-market rule as it relates to inventories.

lower of cost or market (LCM)

Earlier sections of this chapter explained how to determine the cost of ending inventory. As noted, under generally accepted accounting principles, the presumption is that inventories will be recorded at cost. If, however, the utility (usefulness) of the goods in inventory is not as great as their cost, the goods must be written down to the **lower of cost or market (LCM).** Although this is a departure from the historical cost convention, accountants feel that losses should be recorded as soon as they become evident. Thus, in this case, the concept of conservatism takes precedence over the historical cost convention. Approximately 90% of the 600 companies surveyed by the AICPA reported their inventory at the lower of cost or market.[9]

Theory of Lower of Cost or Market

market

In applying the lower-of-cost-or-market rule, cost is determined by one of the cost methods; **market,** in this case, generally means replacement cost, or the cost to purchase a similar item. The use of lower of cost or market is based on the

8. International Accounting Standard 2, *Inventories,* Revised 1992, pars. 19-24.
9. AICPA, *Accounting Trends and Techniques,* 46th ed. (New York: AICPA, 1992), p. 127.

theory that if replacement cost decreases during the current period, the present sales price will ultimately decrease. Because accountants feel that all losses should be recognized when they occur, this loss should be recognized in the period that it occurs—that is, when the price declines—not in a later period, when the item is eventually sold.

To illustrate the theory behind the lower-of-cost-or-market rule, assume the following facts:

1. During year 1, the Shanken Company purchases one item of inventory for $80. The normal selling price is $100, which represents a gross profit percentage of 20%.
2. The item is held during the entire year. However, the replacement cost (market) falls 10%, from $80 to $72. No other transactions take place during the year.
3. During year 2, the item is sold for $90.

The analysis in Exhibit 9-10 shows the effect on reported earnings over a two-year period, both with and without the application of the lower-of-cost-or-market rule. This example assumes that when the replacement cost dropped 10%, or $8 from $80 to $72, there was a corresponding decrease of 10%, or $10 from $100 to $90, in the item's selling price.

Case 1 shows the effect of applying the lower-of-cost-or-market rule. In Year 1, there is a reported loss of $8 due to the decline in the replacement cost. In Year 2, when the actual sale takes place, there is an $18 gross profit on sales. This $18 gross profit represents a 20% gross profit percentage, the normal gross profit percentage that the Shanken company earns. The result of applying the lower-of-cost-or-market rule is to force the company to take a loss in Year 1, the year of the price decline, but it allows the company to earn its normal gross profit percentage in future years. Over the two-year period, the combined income is $10.

Case 2 shows the effect of not applying the lower-of-cost-or-market rule. There is no income or loss in Year 1; the entire effect is felt in Year 2, when the sale takes place. In Year 2, the gross profit falls to $10, and the gross profit percentage falls to 11%. Over a two-year period, combined income is $10, the same

Exhibit 9-10
Illustration of Lower of Cost or Market

Shanken Company
Case 1: With the Application of Lower of Cost or Market

Year 1		*Year 2*		*Total*
Sales	$0	Sales	$90	$90
Loss on write-down of inventory	8[a]	Cost of goods sold	72	80
Gross profit	($8)	Gross profit	$18	$10

Case 2: Without the Application of Lower of Cost or Market

Year 1		*Year 2*		*Total*
Sales	$0	Sales	$90	$90
Loss on write-down of inventory	0	Cost of goods sold	80	80
Gross profit	$0	Gross profit	$10	$10

[a]This inventory write-down would be accomplished by the following journal entry:

Loss on Decline in Market Value of Inventory	8	
Inventory		8

as in Case 1. Thus the application of lower of cost or market changes the allocation of income within the two-year period but does not change the combined income.

This illustration is based on the assumption that a decrease in the replacement cost of an item will result in a corresponding decrease in its sales price. In reality, however, a decrease in replacement cost does not always lead to a decrease in its selling price. For example, assume that although the replacement cost of the inventory item held by the Shanken Company drops 10%, there is little or no change in the sales price. To apply lower of cost or market in this situation would understate income in Year 1 and overstate income in Year 2; thus it would be an improper application of conservatism. Lower of cost or market must be applied with caution.

Application of Lower of Cost or Market

The application of lower of cost or market is a two-step process. In the first step, market, defined as replacement cost, is determined. This can usually be done by examining vendors' invoices at the end of the year. In the second step, market or replacement cost is compared with cost, and if necessary, the inventory is reduced to the lower amount. Under generally accepted accounting principles, this comparison can be made on (1) an item-by-item basis, (2) a group-of-items basis, or (3) the inventory as a whole.

The LCM comparison on all three bases is shown in Exhibit 9-11. When an item-by-item basis is used, individual comparisons of cost to market for each item must be made. This results in an LCM value of $24,000. On a group basis, the inventory is divided into a luxury group and a standard group, and the comparison then is made for the total of each group. For example, in the luxury

Exhibit 9-11
Lower of Cost or Market (LCM) Computations

		Per Unit		*Total*		*LCM*		
	Quantity	*Cost*	*Market*	*Cost*	*Market*	*Item-by-Item*	*Group*	*Total Inventory*
Luxury group								
Item A	100	$50	$40	$ 5,000	$ 4,000	$ 4,000		
Item B	250	70	72	$17,500	$18,000	17,500		
Total luxury group				$22,500	$22,000		$22,000	
Standard group								
Item C	50	$25	$20	$ 1,250	$ 1,000	1,000		
Item D	100	15	18	1,500	1,800	1,500		
Total standard group				$ 2,750	$ 2,800		2,750	
Total inventory				$25,250	$24,800			$24,800
Inventory value—item by item						$24,000		
Inventory value—group basis							$24,750	
Inventory value—total								$24,800

group, the cost of $22,500 is compared with the market of $22,000, so the LCM of the group is determined to be $22,000. The same comparison is then made for the standard group, and its LCM is $2,750. This results in a total LCM value of $24,750. On a total inventory basis, the cost and the market of the entire inventory are compared, resulting in an LCM value of $24,800.

Comparing all three methods, it is clear that the item-by-item method is the most conservative; that is, it results in the lowest inventory value. This is because increases in the value of one item cannot offset decreases in other items, as is the case under the group and total inventory methods.

Lower of Cost or Market and Income Taxes

The Internal Revenue Code contains rules pertaining to the use of lower of cost or market for federal tax purposes. Two of these provisions differentiate the use of lower of cost or market for tax purposes from financial reporting purposes. First, for tax purposes, only FIFO (not LIFO) can be used in conjunction with lower of cost or market. For generally accepted accounting purposes, however, LIFO combined with lower of cost or market is a valid method. Second, for tax purposes, lower of cost or market can be applied only on an item-by-item basis. The group and total inventory method cannot be used.

USING INVENTORY DATA FOR DECISION MAKING

Objective 6
Use inventory data in decision making.

gross profit percentage

Because inventories have a substantial effect on both the balance sheet and the income statement, they offer important data to investors and managers in evaluating a firm's financial performance and position. Two ratios often are used in this evaluation—the *gross profit percentage* and the *inventory turnover.* As noted, the **gross profit percentage** is gross profit on sales divided by sales.

Inventory turnover indicates how quickly a firm is able to sell its inventory. In effect, the more quickly the inventory turns over, the less cash the firm has tied up in inventory and the less need there is for inventory financing. Furthermore, the quicker the turnover is, the less chance there is for obsolescence or spoilage. With too quick a turnover, however, certain items may not be available to meet consumer demand, and sales may be lost as a result. The optimal inventory turnover, therefore, depends on the firm's characteristics and policies. Manufacturing firms, however, that have adopted *Just-in-Time (JIT) manufacturing and purchasing* have decided that they want to have insignificant raw materials and finished goods inventories. The JIT approach is to have materials delivered just in time for production needs, and goods produced just in time for customers to buy them. Thus, a firm with a JIT approach would want very low inventories and, a very high turnover ratio. Chapters 19 and 23 explore the JIT inventory management model in greater detail.

The inventory turnover is computed by dividing cost of goods sold by average inventory. The average inventory generally is determined by taking the average of the beginning and ending inventories. If a firm had a cost of goods sold of $1.2 million and average inventories of $100,000, the inventory would turn over 12 times during the year, calculated as follows:

$$\frac{\text{Cost of goods sold}}{\text{Average inventory}} = \frac{\$1{,}200{,}000}{\$\ 100{,}000} = 12 \text{ times}$$

If the inventory turnover is divided into 365 days, the result will be the average number of days that the inventory is on hand. In this case, the average time is about 30 days (365/12), or one month.

When evaluating inventory data and ratios, remember that they are sensitive to the cost flow assumption adopted. For example, when prices are rising, inventory turnover under LIFO is apt to be higher than under FIFO. This is because under LIFO, cost of goods sold (the numerator) is higher, and average inventories (the denominator) are lower. The result is higher turnover. Thus, accounting data must be used carefully when evaluating a firm or comparing several firms.

THE DESIGN OF ACCOUNTING SYSTEMS FOR INVENTORIES

Objective 7
Explain how the choice of a generally accepted accounting principle may effect the design of an accounting system.

Management must chose the most appropriate accounting methods from the set of generally accepted accounting principles and use those methods for financial reporting. Often, as illustrated above with inventory, management may choose between several different generally accepted accounting principles. The choice may affect the reported financial position and net income of the firm. The selection of an accounting principle or method may also have a significant effect on the design of the accounting information system.

Accounting information systems must be able to process the data that are required by the application of accounting methods selected by management. For example, different processes and data are required to support the specific identification method and the LIFO inventory costing method. The specific identification method requires data about the specific inventory items that are sold. This data may include an item number, description, and purchase cost. Inventory cost is computed by summing the costs of the specific items that remain in inventory. Data about the specific inventory items sold, however, are not required when the LIFO method is used. The LIFO method, does require information about the different inventory purchases or inventory layers. For example, data about the number of items purchased, purchase dates, and item unit costs are required for each inventory layer and every inventory item in that layer when the LIFO method is used.

Because different accounting methods have different data requirements, the choice of an accounting principle or method often affects the design of the specific computer files used by accounting information systems. The design of these files is discussed next.

Computer File Design

The design of a computer-based file involves the identification of the data to be included in the file and the selection of the most appropriate file structure. As noted, data identification requires an understanding of the data requirements imposed by the choice of an accounting method. File selection requires an understanding of the ways that the data will be accessed and used. These steps are discussed in the following paragraphs.

data elements
fields

Data Element Identification. The first step in file design is to identify or list the *data elements* that are required for the correct application of a specific accounting method or principle. **Data elements,** which are sometimes referred to as **fields,** are individual information attributes which help define an entity or a "thing." For example, an inventory item is an entity. Attributes which help define the entity "inventory item" include: item number, item description, item cost,

key data element

quantity on hand, reorder point, and selling price. One of these attributes is selected as the **key data element,** a data element that can be used to uniquely identify an entity. Quantity on hand and even item description are not good key data elements because two or more inventory items may have the same quantity on hand or description. Item number is a good key data element because each inventory item should have a unique number.

data record

The attributes which define an entity are combined together to form a *data record.* A **data record** is a set of related data elements or fields that define a single entity. Your college or university maintains a student information system. This information system contains a data record for each of the students enrolled at the school. In fact, there is a data record in the student information system that contains information (data elements or fields) about you. This data record most likely includes your student number, student name, address, phone number, major, and cumulative GPA. All of these data records are combined together to form a student information *file.* A **file** is a group of records with the same data-element format.

file

To illustrate these concepts let us return to The White-Water Boat Company which Kim Colby started and has now been operating for several months. She has decided to develop and install a computer-based inventory control system. Kim prepared a list of data elements, based on the use of the LIFO method, which she thought would be needed by the inventory control system. She then sat down with her CPA, Bob Tegeder, to review the list. Bob and Kim considered the information requirements imposed by the choice of the LIFO method for inventory valuation, and developed the record layouts shown in Exhibit 9-12. The item number is the key data element in the inventory record because it is the only data element that will always uniquely identify an individual inventory item.

The second record shown in Exhibit 9-12, the inventory purchase record, maintains the inventory layer information that is needed for LIFO costing. Thus, an inventory layer is also an entity which can be defined by data elements. The item number alone is not sufficient to uniquely identify an inventory layer because an inventory item may have more than one corresponding inventory purchase record. Purchase order number alone will not uniquely identify an inventory layer because many different items may be purchased on the same pur-

Exhibit 9-12
Inventory System Record Layouts

Inventory Record
- Item number (key data element)
- Item description
- Quantity on hand
- Quantity on order
- Reorder point
- Reorder quantity
- Year-to-date quantity sold
- Selling price

Inventory Purchase Record
- Item number (key data element)
- Purchase order number (key data element)
- Purchase date
- Quantity purchased
- Unit price

chase order. However, item number and purchase order number together uniquely identify each layer in inventory.

File Structure Selection. The second step in file design is to select the most appropriate file structure. Three traditional file structures are used in accounting information systems: *sequential, direct access, and indexed sequential.* A **sequential file** is a file that stores records in key data element sequence, and is most appropriate when a significant portion of the records in a file will be processed every time the file is accessed. As examples, the records in a sequential inventory master file would be physically recorded in the file in item number sequence, and the student records in a sequential student information file would be recorded in student number sequence. The sequential file structure is the most appropriate file structure for an inventory master file if every record in the file was read each time the file was used. This is especially the case when the inventory master file is only used to prepare a report that listed all items in inventory and their respective costs and quantities. One of the major disadvantages of sequential files is that the records must always be read sequentially. This means that, to access the 289th record on a file, a system must read the first 288 records even if they contain data that is not currently needed.

sequential file

direct access file

A **direct access file** is a file that stores records in a way that permits immediate access to a specific record. Unlike the records in a sequential file, which must be read in sequence, any record in a direct access file can be read and processed without reading the preceding records. The direct access file structure is most appropriate in those situations where one, or a very few, records must be processed each time the file is accessed. Airline reservation systems have traditionally employed direct access files because a passenger is usually interested in a specific flight and not in all of the flights that an airline may offer. The direct access structure lets a reservation clerk quickly access information about specific flights without having to read the entire file.

indexed sequential file

The **indexed sequential file** structure combines the attributes of sequential and direct access file structures. This text book is an example of an indexed sequential file. You are able to read the text in your book sequentially (sequential access); however, you are also able to access specific data through the index. The index refers you directly to a specific page (direct access).

The data records in an indexed sequential file are stored in a sequential file, as well as a separate index file. The index file contains all of the key data elements and their corresponding records' locations in the sequential file. Index sequential files are appropriate in those situations where it is necessary to access a significant portion of the data in a file some of the time, and one or a few records other times. For example, all of the data in an inventory master file may be accessed each time inventory status reports are prepared, but specific records are accessed by the order entry system each time an order is processed. In this situation, the indexed sequential file structure would be appropriate.

To continue with The White-Water Boat Company, Kim decided that she wants the inventory system to print several different reports: a reorder report that lists items that have reached the reorder point, a stock status report that lists every item in inventory, and a stock movement report that lists year-to-date sales for each item in inventory. She also explained that she needs to be able to verify the quantity on hand of specific inventory items when processing customer phone orders. In this case, an indexed sequential file is the most appropriate as, at appropriate times, Kim needs to access all the information in the inventory file while at other times she needs to access data about a specific inventory item. As we will see in Chapter 10, it is also possible to use a data base management system to gather the inventory data Kim needs to manage White-Water's inventory.

As just illustrated, the design of an accounting system is affected not only by accounting method choice decisions, but also by business functions. The information that Kim needs to maintain in her inventory files was determined by the inventory valuation method that she had selected, while the selection of the most appropriate traditional file structure was determined by Kim's need to use the inventory information in different ways at different times. Thus, accounting system designers must be sensitive to the effects of accounting method choices and business functions when they design and implement information systems.

SUMMARY OF LEARNING OBJECTIVES

1. *Explain the relationship between inventories and income determination.* Inventories are nonmonetary assets; the major accounting issue is allocating the cost of goods available for sale between the ending inventory and the cost of goods sold. The process of matching these costs against revenues helps ensure the proper determination of income. The measurement of ending inventories affects two accounting periods because the ending inventory for the first year becomes the beginning inventory for the second year. Although a single measurement error is self-canceling, it causes an improper allocation of income between the two accounting periods.

2. *Determine the cost of ending inventories.* The cost of ending inventory is determined by multiplying the quantity on hand by the acquisition cost of the items. The quantity on hand is determined by taking a physical inventory. Cost is the price paid to get the item ready for sale. When items are purchased at different prices, the accountant must use a cost flow assumption to assign acquisition costs to the ending inventory.

3. *Apply the four methods of attaching costs to the ending inventory.* There are four generally accepted accounting methods of determining the cost of inventory quantities: (1) FIFO, (2) LIFO, (3) average cost, and (4) specific identification. FIFO assumes that the costs attached to the first goods sold are the costs of the first goods purchased. The cost of the ending inventory is that of the most recent purchase. LIFO makes the opposite assumption: the costs of the latest purchase are assumed to be the cost of the first item sold. Thus, the cost of the ending inventory is that of the earliest purchases. Average cost attaches a weighted average cost per unit—determined by dividing the total cost of the goods available for sale by the total number of units available for sale—to both the cost of goods sold and the ending inventory. Specific identification determines the actual acquisition cost of each separately identifiable item in the ending inventory. Because of practical problems, this method is not often used. In a period of changing prices, the selection of a particular cost flow assumption may have a dramatic effect on a firm's balance sheet and income statement.

4. *Explain the factors that management considers in selecting among generally acceptable accounting principles.* Management has a choice in selecting among generally accepted accounting principles for financial reporting purposes. The LIFO conformity rule, however, requires management to use LIFO for financial reporting purposes if it is adopted for tax purposes. As a result, in periods of rising costs, management is often confronted with choosing between increased cash flows caused by lower tax payments with LIFO, and higher reported profits with FIFO.

5. *Apply the lower-of-cost-or-market rule as it relates to inventories.* Generally accepted accounting principles assume that inventories should be valued at cost, unless the replacement cost of the items falls below cost. In applying the lower-of-cost-or-market rule, market (or replacement cost) is compared with cost; if necessary, the inventory is written down to the lower of the two. This comparison can be made on an item-by-item basis, a group basis, or a total inventory basis for financial reporting purposes. For tax purposes, only an item-by-item basis can be used. The lower-of-cost-or-market rule is an excellent example of the conservatism convention in accounting.

6. *Use inventory data in decision making.* Because inventories and cost of goods sold are substantial components of the balance sheet and the income statement, they provide important data for evaluating a firm's financial position and profitability. In this respect, two common ratios used are the gross profit percentage and the inventory turnover. However, because these ratios are very sensitive to the cost flow assumption adopted, they must be used with caution.

7. *Explain how the choice of a generally accepted accounting principle may affect the design of an accounting system.* Accountants must select and implement one of several different generally accepted accounting principles to account for a class of transactions in many situations. The different methods usually require different data. Consequently, an accounting system designed to support one accounting method may not work for different accounting methods. For example, an inventory system designed to support the specific identification method could not be used to perform LIFO or FIFO inventory valuation. As a result, accountants must be sensitive to the effects of their choices and decisions on the design of accounting information systems.

KEY TERMS

Average cost 399
Current cost 408
Data elements 416
Data record 417
Direct access file 418
Fields 416
File 417
Finished goods inventory 394
First-in, first-out (FIFO) 399
Gross profit percentage 415
Holding gain 405
Indexed sequential file 418
Inventory profits 405
Inventory turnover 412
Key data element 417
Last-in, first-out (LIFO) 399
LIFO liquidation 411
Lower of cost or market (LCM) 412
Market 412
Quality of earnings 410
Raw materials inventory 394
Sequential file 418
Specific-identification method 399
Work in process inventory 394

REVIEW PROBLEMS

A. Cost Flow Assumption. The following data relate to the beginning inventory and purchases of the Valenzuela Company:

	Purchases		*Sale*	*Balance*
Date	*Units*	*Cost*	*Units*	*Units*
Beginning inventory	200	$ 9.75		200
January 3	50	10.00		250
January 10	100	10.50		350
January 15			175	175
January 20	225	10.80		400
January 31			150	250

REQUIRED: Assuming that the Valenzuela Co. uses a periodic inventory system, calculate the ending inventory and cost of goods sold as of January 31, based on the following methods.

1. FIFO
2. LIFO
3. Average cost

Solutions

Total goods available for sale are calculated as follows:

	Units	*Acquisition Cost*	*Total Cost*
Beginning balance	200	$ 9.75	$1,950
Purchases			
January 3	50	10.00	500
January 10	100	10.50	1,050
January 20	225	10.80	2,430
	575		$5,930
Sales	325		
Ending inventory	250		

1 FIFO

Goods available for sale		$5,930.00
Ending inventory—FIFO		
225 × $10.80 =	$2,430.00	
25 × $10.50 =	262.50	
Ending inventory		2,692.50
Cost of goods sold		$3,237.50

2 LIFO

Goods available for sale		$5,930.00
Ending inventory—LIFO		
200 × $ 9.75 =	$1,950.00	
50 × $10.00 =	500.00	
Ending inventory		2,450.00
Cost of goods sold		$3,480.00

3 Average Cost

$$\frac{\text{Goods available for sale}}{\text{Units available for sale}} = \frac{\$5{,}930.00}{575} = \$10.31^{a} \text{ Unit}$$

Ending inventory	250 @ $10.31 =	$2,577.50
Cost of goods sold	325 @ $10.31 =	3,352.50[b]
Goods available for sale		$5,930.00

[a]Rounded
[b]Rounded so that ending inventory and cost of goods sold equal goods available for sale.

B. Lower of Cost or Market. The Duffy Company uses the lower-of-cost-or-market convention in valuing its inventory. The company has divided its products into two groups, with two types within each group. The following schedule presents the relevant data as of December 31.

	Group 1		*Group 2*	
	Type A	*Type B*	*Type C*	*Type D*
Number of units	50	100	100	200
Selling price per unit	$30	$40	$35	$20
Replacement cost per unit—12/31	20	28	26	16
Cost per unit	19	29	27	15

REQUIRED: Determine at what amount the ending inventory should be shown, assuming that the firm applies the lower-of-cost-or-market rule on

1. An item-by-item basis.
2. A group basis.
3. A total inventory basis.

Solution

Group 1				
Type A	Cost = 50 × $19 =	$ 950	Market = 50 × $20 =	$1,000
Type B	Cost = 100 × $29 =	2,900	Market = 100 × $28 =	2,800
Total Group 1		$3,850		$3,800
Group 2				
Type C	Cost = 100 × $27 =	$2,700	Market = 100 × $26 =	$2,600
Type D	Cost = 200 × $15 =	3,000	Market = 200 × $16 =	3,200
Total Group 2		$5,700		$5,800
Total inventory		$9,550		$9,600

1 Item-by-item $9,350 = $950 + $2,800 + $2,600 + $3,000

2 Group basis $9,500 = $3,800 + $5,700

3 Total inventory $9,550

QUESTIONS

1. Assume that the ending inventory in Year 1 is overstated by $1,000 and that all other items in the cost of goods sold computation are correct. What is the impact on:
   a. the beginning inventory in Year 2?
   b. gross margins for Years 1 and 2?
   c. retained earnings balance at the end of Year 2?
2. One of your fellow students stated, "Determining the quantity of items in the ending inventory is easy—you just count the number of items in the storeroom." Do you agree? Why or why not?
3. Both merchandising and manufacturing firms buy inventories from outside suppliers. How do these inventories differ?
4. What are work in process inventories? Are these inventories found in retail firms? Why or why not?
5. Both manufacturing and merchandising firms have finished goods inventory. However, the way in which they obtain the inventory differs. Explain.
6. What costs should be included in ending (a) finished goods inventory, and (b) raw materials inventory? In practice, how are these costs handled by most firms?
7. Explain the four cost flow assumptions that are considered generally accepted accounting principles.
8. Safeway Stores uses the LIFO method of determining the cost of its inventories. Another large grocery chain uses the FIFO method. In a period of rising prices, how does this affect each firm's (a) total assets and (b) net income?
9. Why do some accountants feel that the specific-identification method is not appropriate in most circumstances?
10. The Quick Chip Company is in an industry in which material prices have been declining. If the firm wants to report the highest gross margin and ending inventory and lowest cost of goods sold, which inventory cost method should it use?
11. For a number of years, the Jackson Co. has been using the FIFO method of costing its inventories. During the past few years, the prices of its inventory have been steadily rising. The controller is concerned that the firm's reported gross margin may not reflect its economic ability to repurchase future inventories for resale. Do you agree or disagree with the controller? Why?
12. Describe the concept of inventory profits. Why do they occur?
13. How do the regulations contained in the Internal Revenue Code affect management's choice of inventory methods for financial reporting purposes?
14. What are some of the factors that management considers when selecting an inventory costing method?
15. What is LIFO liquidation, and what are its potential effects on net income?

16. It is December 28, and the president of Olka Company is reviewing the financial position of the firm. The Olka Company uses the LIFO method of inventory costing. The firm has had a very good year; the president is concerned about the firm's tax position and is looking for ways to reduce its taxes. The cost of the products the firm sells has been steadily rising during the year, and the president is considering making a large purchase of merchandise for resale prior to year-end. What would you advise the president in this regard? Would your advice be different if the firm used the FIFO method of inventory costing?
17. What is the accounting concept behind the lower-of-cost-or-market rule? Should lower of cost or market be applied in all circumstances?
18. The Regal Company began business at the beginning of the current year. The firm has decided to use the FIFO method of inventory costing. If LIFO inventory costing had been used, the cost of the ending inventory would have been higher. Can you determine the direction that the cost of the purchases moved in during the year? If so, in what direction did they move?
19. How does the choice of an inventory method affect the design of accounting information systems?

EXERCISES

E9-1
Inventory Errors, Manufacturing Firm
LO 1

During 1995, the Edward Corporation had sales of $950,000 and cost of goods manufactured of $670,000. Finished goods inventories on January 1, 1995 amounted to $335,000 and inventories at December 31, 1995 were $290,000.

REQUIRED:

1. Compute cost of goods sold and gross profit for 1995.
2. Now assume that an error was made in determining the ending finished goods inventory in 1993, and as a result the inventory was overstated by $48,000. What is the effect of this error on the gross profit for 1994 and 1995? What is the effect on the balance in the Retained Earnings account at the end of 1995?

E9-2
Inventory Errors
LO 1

Shown below are condensed income statements for the TG Company, a retail firm, for two consecutive years:

	Year 1	*Year 2*
Sales	$900,000	$880,000
Cost of goods sold	590,000	632,000
Gross profit on sales	$310,000	$248,000
Operating expenses	170,000	148,000
Net income	$140,000	$100,000

At the beginning of the third year, the new controller of the TG Company found that there had been two inventory errors in Year 1. She determined that the beginning inventory had been overstated by $5,000 and the ending inventory had been understated by $6,700. At the end of Year 2, the Retained Earnings account had a balance of $320,000.

REQUIRED:

1. Determine the correct amount of net income for Years 1 and 2.
2. Compute the correct balance in the Retained Earnings account at the end of Year 2.

E9-3 Comparison of Inventory Costing Methods, Manufacturing Firm

LO 3

The Robinson Football Equipment Company manufactures a variety of football equipment. The equipment is produced in batches. The following data is provided regarding one of its products, football helmets:

Date	*Quantity*	*Cost per Unit*
Beginning	50 units	$130
2/28 batch	110	125
6/24 batch	90	122
10/4 batch	80	120

The ending finished goods inventory consisted of 85 units.

REQUIRED:

1. Determine the cost of the
   a. goods available for sale,
   b. ending inventory, and
   c. goods sold, under the FIFO, LIFO, and average-cost inventory methods.
2. Explain the relationship between the cost of goods sold figure under each of the methods. That is, which is higher and lower and what are the reasons for this relationship?

E9-4 Determining the Cost of Ending Inventories

LO 3

The Ojeda Company uses the periodic inventory system. During March, the following sales and purchases of inventories were made:

	Number of Units	*Cost per Unit*	*Total Cost*
March 1 inventory	100	$13.20	$1,320
March 3 sale	80		
March 15 purchase	260	15.00	3,900
March 20 sale	135		
March 29 purchase	160	16.00	2,560
March 30 sale	120		

REQUIRED: Determine the ending inventory and cost of goods sold for the Ojeda Company under the following cost flow assumptions:

1. FIFO
2. LIFO
3. Average cost

E9-5 Determining the Cost of Ending Raw Materials Inventory

LO 3

The following data were taken from the records of the Imdieke Co. regarding the purchases of gold, a raw material used in the production of watches and chains:

April 1: Beginning inventory 300 units @ $10.00 per unit
April 4: Purchase 900 units @ $10.20 per unit
April 10: Purchase 800 units @ $10.25 per unit
April 18: Purchase 700 units @ $10.25 per unit
April 30: Purchase 600 units @ $10.40 per unit

At the end of the month, there were 1,100 units remaining in the ending inventory.

REQUIRED: Determine the cost of the ending inventory and the cost of the raw material used in production under each of the following cost flow assumptions:

1. FIFO
2. LIFO
3. Average cost

E9-6
Specific-Identification Method
LO 3

Smith's Specialty Desk Company uses the specific-identification method of inventory costing. You obtained the following records for the year:

Quantity Purchased	*Purchase Price per Unit*	*Units on Hand at End of Year*
10	$120.00	3
15	130.00	2
12	124.50	5
20	122.00	0
15	128.00	6

REQUIRED:

1. Determine the cost of the ending inventory using the specific-identification method.
2. Assume that all the desks are substantially identical and that their selling price is $200 each. Determine the gross profit from the sales. How would your answer differ if the entire inventory of 16 units was from the items purchased at $122 per unit? What does this suggest about some of the conceptual problems with the specific-identification method?

E9-7
Inventory Costing Methods—Two-Period Analysis
LO 3

The Strawberry Company began business on January 1, 1994. During 1994 and 1995, the firm made the following purchases:

1994:	
January 2	75 units @ $2.00
February 5	50 units @ $2.10
April 14	125 units @ $2.20
July 14	100 units @ $2.20
September 28	80 units @ $2.25
November 29	70 units @ $2.30
1995:	
January 14	100 units @ $2.35
March 25	600 units @ $2.40
August 19	400 units @ $2.38
December 4	60 units @ $2.36

During 1994 and 1995, the firm sold 360 units and 1,200 units, respectively.

REQUIRED: Determine the amount of cost of goods sold and the ending inventories for 1994 and 1995 under both the FIFO and LIFO methods.

E9-8
Effects of Different Inventory Cost Methods
LO 3

The president of Pete's Pickles is confused about the effects of different inventory cost methods on income. The firm has been in business since the beginning of 1993, and the president gives you the following inventory data for 1993 through 1995:

Date	*LIFO Cost*	*FIFO Cost*	*Average Cost*
12/31/93	$8,000	$8,400	$6,200
12/31/94	6,800	7,100	7,025
12/31/95	7,300	7,200	7,040

REQUIRED:

1. Which inventory method will show the highest net income in each of the years?
2. Which inventory method will show the lowest net income in each of the years?

E9-9
Inventory Turnover
LO 6

The following information was taken from the records of the Hoffman Company:

Beginning inventory—1/1/95	$ 76,000
Net purchases	235,000
Ending inventory—12/31/95	58,000

REQUIRED:

1. Determine the inventory turnover and the average number of days that the inventory is on hand.
2. Suppose Hoffman Company is a manufacturing firm, and the inventory is raw materials. Discuss the effect of just-in-time purchasing on the inventory turnover ratio and the average number of days on hand.

E9-10
LIFO Liquidation
LO 4

The president of the Red Baron Corporation is concerned about the company's potential tax situation for the current year. The company has been on the LIFO method of inventory cost for many years. The president gives you the following data, which reflects inventory sales and purchases through December 15 of the current year:

Beginning inventory	1,000 units @ $5.00 per unit
Sales during the year	50,800 units @ $50.00 per unit
Purchases during the year	50,000 units @ $35.00 per unit
Current replacement cost per unit	$40.00 per unit

The company has the opportunity to purchase an additional 2,000 units at the current replacement cost prior to year-end.

Assuming that the tax rate is 40%, advise the president whether another purchase should be made before year-end. (*Hint*: Calculate cost of goods sold with and without an additional purchase. Assume that all expenses other than taxes remain the same.)

E9-11
Inventory Profits
LO 4

The president and the chief financial officer of the Walsea Company are discussing the concept of holding gains. The president has been arguing that the firm's financial statements are not showing "economic reality." He states, "We purchased most of our inventory during the first part of the year when prices were fairly stable. During the past six months the cost to replace our inventory has increased over 25%, and yet our gross profit does not reflect this increase in costs." The chief financial officer explains that the firm uses FIFO and some of that gross profit is really a holding gain.

REQUIRED:

1. Explain to the president what a holding gain is. Develop a numerical example.
2. Given the circumstances described, should the president of the Walsea Company be concerned about a holding gain? Why or why not?
3. The president has heard something about the benefits of using current cost and asks you to explain how using current cost might solve the holding gain problem.

E9-12
Inventory Costing Methods
LO 4

Following are four statements concerning inventory costing methods. Discuss the accuracy of each statement.

a. If inventory quantities are to be maintained, part of the earnings must be invested (plowed back) in inventories when FIFO is used during a period of rising prices.
b. LIFO tends to smooth out the net income pattern since it matches current cost of goods sold with current revenue, when inventories remain at constant quantities.
c. When a firm using the LIFO method fails to maintain its usual inventory position (reduces stock on hand below customary levels) there may be a matching of old costs with current revenue.
d. The use of FIFO permits some control by management over the amount of net income for a period through controlled purchases, which is not true with LIFO.

(IMA adapted)

E9-13
Inventory Methods and Taxes
LO 3, 4

You have obtained the following information for the Rodriguez Company:

Sales	$950,000
Operating expenses	235,500
Interest expense	26,000
Tax rate	30%

This is the first year of the company's operations. Its accounting records are currently based on the FIFO method. Under FIFO, the cost of goods sold is $555,000, and the ending inventory is $50,000. However, to lower its taxes, the company's controller is considering using either LIFO or the average-cost method. The controller has determined that ending inventories would be $30,000 under LIFO and $42,000 under the average-cost method.

REQUIRED:

1. Determine cost of goods sold under LIFO and under average cost.
2. Compute income before taxes, tax expense, and net income under the three inventory methods.
3. Compare and contrast the effects of the three methods. What constraints does management face in choosing inventory methods?

E9-14
Inventory Methods and Ratio Analysis
LO 6

The Alto Teck Company has always used the FIFO method of computing inventory cost. As of December 31, 1995, you have been given the following data by the company's president:

Average inventories during 1995	$ 8,000,000
Cost of ending inventory at year-end 1995	8,500,000
Cost of goods sold for the year ended 1995	54,000,000
Current assets at year-end 1995	15,000,000
Current liabilities at year-end 1995	9,000,000
Net income for the year ended 1995	10,000,000

While giving serious thought to converting to the LIFO cost flow assumption, the president determined that if LIFO had been used during 1995, ending inventories would have decreased by $1,000,000 and average inventories by $500,000.

REQUIRED:

1. The president is concerned that switching to LIFO will have a negative effect on several ratios. Calculate the following amounts and ratios using both the FIFO and the LIFO data:
   a. Working capital
   b. The current ratio
   c. Profit margin ratio
   d. Inventory turnover
2. Which ratios are affected and why?
3. If you were a banker evaluating this company for a loan, what would you think of the possible change to LIFO?

E9-15
Lower of Cost or Market
LO 5

The following information pertains to the ending inventory of the Gorby Corporation:

Item	*Cost per Unit*	*Replacement Cost per Unit*
A	$60	$78
B	85	79
C	75	67
D	35	29
E	45	46

The firm values its inventory using lower of cost or market on an item-by-item basis.

REQUIRED:

1. At what value should the ending inventory be shown on the balance sheet?
2. Can you think of a situation when it would not be appropriate to use lower of cost or market?

E9-16
Inventory Methods and Files
LO 7

The following data has been extracted from an inventory master file:

Inventory Item Record			
Item Number	A-4893		
Description	3-ring binder		
Quantity on hand	15		
Quantity on order	60		
Reorder point	50		
Reorder quantity	60		
Suggested vendor	890342		
Inventory Layer Records			
Item Number	A-4893	A-4893	A-4893
Date	04-01-94	06-15-94	12-28-94
Quantity purchased	60	60	60
Unit Price	$1.87	$1.89	$1.91

REQUIRED:

1. Compute the FIFO cost of ending inventory.
2. Compute the LIFO cost of ending inventory.
3. Compute the weighted average cost of ending inventory.

E9-17
Traditional File Structure Selection
LO 7

Select the most appropriate traditional file structure (sequential, indexed sequential, or direct access) for each of the following files.

a. An employee master file is used once each month when payroll is computed. All of the records in the file are accessed because a paycheck is printed for each employee.
b. A motel chain has computerized its reservation system. The system maintains a reservation file that is accessed each time a potential customer requests a room reservation.
c. The student master file at a major university is used to print class schedules and student bills at the beginning of each term. In addition, the file is accessed each time a student adds or drops a class and when payments on student accounts are made.

E9-18
Albertson's Financial Statements
LO 3, 6

Refer to the Albertson's financial statements in Appendix A. Based on that information, answer the following questions.

a. What method does the company use to determine the cost of its ending inventories?
b. Calculate the amount of net working capital and the current ratio for the years ended 1992 and 1991.
c. Determine the gross profit ratio and inventory turnover for the years ended 1992 and 1991.
d. Were there any significant changes from one year to the next in the ratios calculated in (c) above?
e. If the company used FIFO, would there be any change in the above ratios?

PROBLEMS

P9-1
Inventory Errors
LO 1

The Taktech Company uses the periodic inventory system. The accountant for the company prepared the following condensed income statements for the years ended June 30, 1993 and 1994:

	1993	*1994*
Net sales	$700,000	$950,000
Cost of goods sold		
Beginning inventory	$ 80,000	$110,000
Purchases, net	580,000	770,000
Goods available for sale	$660,000	$880,000
Less: Ending inventory	110,000	150,000
Cost of goods sold	$550,000	$730,000
Gross profit on sales	$150,000	$220,000
Operating expenses	70,000	100,000
Net income	$ 80,000	$120,000

During 1995, the accountant found that several errors had been made in determining the amount of ending inventories in the prior two years:
In 1993:

a. On June 30, the company had several personal computers being held on consignment by some retailers that were not included in Taktech's ending inventory. These computers had a cost of $8,400.

b. A sale was made in late June; the customer did not take delivery of the equipment until sometime in July. As a result, ending inventory was overstated by $3,900, and sales were understated by $5,400.

In 1994:

c. A purchase was made on June 25; the merchandise did not arrive until July. The purchase had been recorded properly in the purchases journal, but the item was not included in the ending inventory. The merchandise had a cost of $13,400.
d. Some equipment that was being held on consignment for others was included in Taktech's ending inventory. As a result, ending inventory was overstated by $4,100.

REQUIRED:

1. Prepare a correct set of income statements for the years ended June 30, 1993 and 1994.
2. Assume that the firm had net assets of $365,000 and $377,000, respectively, prior to any corrections for the preceding items. Determine the correct amount of net assets after you have made the necessary corrections.

P9-2
Inventory Errors and Review Items to Be Included in Inventory
LO 1

The Wedstein Corporation is a manufacturer and wholesaler of office furniture. The company manufactures desks, credenzas, and various types of cabinets and bookcases. The company does not manufacture any chairs, but purchases them from several suppliers and markets them under the Wedstein label.

Wedstein sells its office furniture to office supply houses throughout the country. However, Wedstein's top-of-the-line wood furniture is sold through specialty office equipment stores on a consignment basis.

Wedstein uses a fiscal year that ends on May 31. The year-end physical inventory of goods already manufactured and held for resale has been completed and costed at $3.5 million. The company includes any appropriate freight costs as part of the cost of the inventory. The merchandise involved in the following six transactions has **not been included** in the year-end inventory of $3.5 million as of May 31.

a. Transaction 1: A purchase of executive chairs from one of Wedstein's regular suppliers was shipped on May 29. The purchase price of the order was $150,000 and its resale value to Wedstein was $200,000 (that is, Wedstein expects to sell the chairs for $200,000). The shipping charges of $1,400 were prepaid by the supplier. The shipment had not been received by the close of business on May 31, but Wedstein took legal title on the date the chairs were shipped.
b. Transaction 2: On May 23 a purchase of secretarial chairs was shipped from the supplier FOB destination. (This means that title to the goods does not transfer until the goods arrive at the destination point.) The purchase arrived at Wedstein's warehouse on May 30, but Wedstein had not yet received the invoice from the supplier. The purchase price of the order was $175,000, while its resale value to Wedstein was $225,000. The shipment charges of $1,800 were prepaid by the supplier.
c. Transaction 3: A purchase of executive and secretarial chairs was received on May 10 and remains in the receiving area of the warehouse. These chairs were purchased for use in Wedstein's new executive office building, which was not yet completed. The chairs cost Wedstein $50,000 and would have a wholesale value of $75,000 if they were sold to retailers. The invoice of $51,000, including freight, has been paid.
d. Transaction 4: A special order of executive desks, credenzas, and bookcases was completed and segregated in the warehouse. The order was to be shipped to Nissen Enterprises the first week in June. The special order had a cost of $225,000 and has already been invoiced to the purchaser for $325,000. The freight charges, estimated at $2,500, were to be prepaid by Wedstein and billed later.

e. Transaction 5: An order of office furniture was loaded and shipped to Desk Mart, Inc., on May 31. The sales order had a cost to Wedstein of $250,000. The order was actually invoiced by Wedstein on June 4 for $308,000, which included freight charges of $3,000.
f. Transaction 6: Wedstein's furniture being held on consignment by retailers had a cost of $750,000. Wedstein has paid $8,000 in freight charges to ship the furniture to those holding it on consignment. The sales value of the furniture is $1.2 million. Those holding the furniture will receive a 10% commission upon the sale of the furniture. The seller remits the sales price of the furniture less the commissions to Wedstein when the furniture is sold.

REQUIRED: For each of the six transactions described above:

1. Explain whether or not the merchandise should be included in Wedstein's year-end inventory.
2. Calculate the dollar value to be added to the year-end inventory cost for the merchandise which should be included in the inventory.

(IMA adapted)

P9-3
Inventory Determination
LO 3

The Edwards-Downey Company uses the periodic inventory system and prepares financial statements every December 31. One of the items produced is basketball and baseball jerseys. The jerseys are produced in batches—usually three times per year. You have gathered the following data regarding the finished goods inventory of jerseys:

	Number of Units	*Unit Cost*	*Total Cost*
1994			
Beginning inventory	0		
Units produced:			
January	500	$2.00	$1,000
April	400	2.10	840
July	400	2.25	900
Total for year	1,300		
Less items sold	850		
Ending inventory	450		
1995			
Beginning inventory	450		
Units produced:			
February	450	3.00	1,350
June	800	3.10	2,480
November	200	3.20	640
Total for year	1,900		
Less items sold	1,550		
Ending inventory	350		

REQUIRED: Determine the cost of the ending inventory and the cost of goods sold for each year, assuming the use of each of the following inventory methods:

1. FIFO
2. LIFO
3. Average cost

P9-4
Inventory Determination (Raw Materials Inventory)
LO 3

Ekbog, Inc., produces herbal teas. One of the ingredients used is ginseng root. During 1994 and 1995, the firm made the following inventory purchases of ginseng root (quantity measured in pounds):

	1994		
	Quantity	*Price*	*Total*
Beginning inventory	200	$ 5.00	$1,000
Purchases: 2/20	300	9.00	2,700
5/20	200	9.50	1,900
8/15	300	9.25	2,775
11/15	400	9.20	3,680
Ending inventory	450	?	?
	1995		
Beginning inventory	450	?	?
Purchases: 3/15	600	$ 9.50	$5,700
6/15	200	10.00	2,000
9/15	200	10.50	2,100
12/15	300	10.20	3,060
Ending inventory	400	?	?

REQUIRED: Determine the cost of the ending raw materials inventory of ginseng and the cost of ginseng used in production for 1994 and 1995 under each of the following methods.

1. FIFO
2. LIFO
3. Average cost

P9-5
Inventory Methods and Income Taxes
LO 3, 4

The chief financial officer of the Vitkoski Company gave you the following data for the year ended December 31, 1995:

Sales	$1,000,000
Inventory, January 1, 1995	100,000
Inventory, December 31, 1995	150,000
Inventory turnover	5 times
Other operating expenses	70,000
Average tax rate	30%

The company currently uses the FIFO method of costing its inventory but is considering changing to the LIFO method. The chief financial officer has estimated the cost of goods sold on a LIFO basis would be 130% of the FIFO cost of goods sold. The chief financial officer has asked you to prepare an analysis comparing the effects of FIFO and LIFO.

REQUIRED:

1. Prepare comparative income statements for the year ended December 31, 1995. Use the following form:

	FIFO	*LIFO*
Sales	1,000,000	1,000,000
Cost of goods sold	- 625,000	- 812,500
Gross profit on sales	375000	187500
Operating expenses	- 70,000	- 70000
Income before taxes	305,000	117,500
Taxes	91500	35,250
Net income	213500	82250

2. Explain the reasons for the differences in the two statements.
3. From your analysis, can you determine whether prices paid for the inventory have fallen or risen during the year? Explain your reasoning. prices went up

P9-6
Effects of Changing from FIFO to LIFO
LO 4

The management of the Trezevant Company has asked its accounting department to describe the effect upon the company's financial position and its financial statements of accounting for inventories on the LIFO basis rather than the FIFO basis during 1994 and 1995. The accounting department is to assume that the change to LIFO would have been effective January 1, 1994, and that the initial LIFO base would have been the inventory cost on December 31, 1993. Presented below are the company's financial statements and other data for 1993, 1994 and 1995 when the FIFO method was in fact employed:

Balance Sheets

Accounts	*12/31/93*	*12/31/94*	*12/31/95*
Cash	$ 67,700	$121,300	$176,050
Accounts receivable	40,000	54,000	61,750
Inventory	69,000	75,000	84,000
Other assets	114,000	114,000	114,000
Total assets	$290,700	$364,300	$435,800
Accounts payable	$ 23,000	$ 30,000	$ 36,400
Other liabilities	40,000	40,000	40,000
Common stock	140,000	140,000	140,000
Retained earnings	87,700	154,300	219,400
Total equities	$290,700	$364,300	$435,800

Income Statements

Accounts	*12/31/94*	*12/31/95*
Sales	$540,000	$617,500
Less: Cost of goods sold	$294,000	$355,000
Other expenses	135,000	154,000
	$429,000	$509,000
Net income before taxes	$111,000	$108,500
Income taxes (40%)	44,400	43,400
Net income	$ 66,600	$ 65,100

Other Data:

a. Inventory on hand at 12/31/93 consisted of 30,000 units with a cost of $2.30 each.
b. Sales (all sales sold at the same unit price in a given year):
   1994—120,000 units @ $4.40 each
   1995—130,000 units @ $4.75 each
c. Purchases (all units purchased at the same price in a given year):
   1994—120,000 units @ $2.50 each
   1995—130,000 units @ $2.80 each
d. Income taxes at the effective rate of 40% are paid on December 31 each year.

REQUIRED: Name the account(s) presented in the financial statements that will have different amounts for 1995 if LIFO rather than FIFO has been used and state the new amounts for each account that has been named.

(IMA adapted)

P9-7 Lower of Cost or Market

LO 5

The Rimbau Company sells home and office telephones. It has divided its product into a basic and a luxury group and has two telephones in each group. The firm uses the lower-of-cost-or-market rule in determining the value of its ending inventory. Data pertaining to the December 31 inventory is presented below.

	Luxury Group		*Basic Group*	
	Type 1	*Type 2*	*Type 3*	*Type 4*
Number of units	60	150	120	250
Selling price per unit	$60	$80	$75	$40
Replacement cost	40	56	52	32
Purchase cost	38	58	54	30

REQUIRED: Determine the value of the December 31 ending inventory, applying the lower-of-cost-or-market rule under each of the following independent assumptions:

24,420 1. applied individually to each item.
24,780 2. applied to each group of products.
24,960 3. applied to the inventory as a whole.

P9-8 Accounting Systems

LO 7

Bill's Auto has decided to computerize its inventory control system. The inventory control system is used to maintain information on new cars, used cars, and parts and supplies used by the service department.

REQUIRED:

1. Which inventory method would you recommend for accounting for new and used automobiles?
2. Which inventory method would you recommend for accounting for parts and supplies?
3. Which file structure(s) should be used for the inventory file(s)?
4. Design the record layout for automobiles.
5. Design the record layout for parts and supplies.
6. Explain how the choice of an inventory accounting method affects the design of the inventory file(s).

DISCUSSION AND INTERPRETATION PROBLEMS

D9-1 Understanding Financial Statements

Presented on pages 291–292 as part of Comprehensive Case C6-1 are the asset section and the income statement of Nordstrom, Inc., and subsidiaries. In addition, the inventory note is reproduced below.

Merchandise Inventories: *Merchandise inventories are stated at the lower of cost (first-in, first-out basis) or market, using the retail method.*

REQUIRED:

1. State the gross profit percentage, the profit margin percentage, and the inventory turnover for year-ends 1992 and 1991.
2. State the current ratio for year-ends 1992 and 1991.
3. Obtain similar information for year-ends 1992 and 1991 from either Carter, Hawley, Hale, Dayton Hudson, or a similar-size department store and compare this information to that obtained from Nordstrom. Compare and contrast your results.

D9-2 Financial Decision Case

In mid-December, the Diamond Gold Company is reviewing its financial and tax position prior to year-end. The price of gold has been falling, and the company is considering making an additional purchase of 5,000 ounces of gold prior to year-end. The company uses the LIFO method of costing its inventory. The following data reflect inventory purchases and sales through mid-December:

	Ounces of Gold	*Cost per Ounce*	*Total Cost*
Beginning inventory	6,000	$200	$1,200,000
Purchases during year			
First	10,000	400	4,000,000
Second	8,000	380	3,040,000
Third	12,000	350	4,200,000

During the year, the company sold 34,000 ounces of gold and does not expect to make any additional sales prior to year-end. The company has been offered 5,000 ounces of gold at $340 per ounce. Although this price appears attractive, the company feels that the price of gold will continue to decline and finally stabilize at $300 per ounce at the beginning of the next year.

REQUIRED:

1. Determine cost of goods sold, assuming that the purchase (a) is not made; (b) is made.
2. Assume that the 34,000 ounces of gold were sold at $450 per ounce and that all expenses other than taxes amounted to $1 million. Determine net income, assuming that the purchase (a) is not made; (b) is made.
3. Determine the difference in cash flow to the firm if the purchase is made in December at $340 per ounce or in January at $300 per ounce.
4. What course of action would you suggest the firm take?

D9-3 Financial Decision Case

Ron Hansen, president of Carter, Inc., recently read an article claiming that at least 100 of the country's 500 largest companies were either adopting or considering adopting the LIFO method of costing inventories. The article stated that the firms were switching to LIFO to (1) neutralize the effects of inflation in their financial statements, (2) eliminate inventory profits, and (3) reduce income taxes. Hansen wondered if the switch would benefit his company.

Carter Inc., currently uses the FIFO method in its periodic inventory system. The company has a high inventory turnover rate, and inventories represent a significant portion of the assets.

In discussing this trend toward adoption of the LIFO inventory method with business friends, he has been told that the LIFO system is more costly to operate and will provide little benefit to companies with a high inventory turnover. Hansen wants to use the inventory method that is best for his company in the long run and not select a method just because it is a current fad.

REQUIRED:

1. Explain to Mr. Hansen what "inventory profits" are and how the LIFO method of inventory costing could reduce them.
2. Explain to Mr. Hansen the conditions that must exist for Carter Inc., to receive tax benefits from a switch to the LIFO method.

D9-4 Research Assignment

As discussed in this chapter, LIFO has become increasingly popular in the United States. Using your library and/or other resources answer the following questions:

a. When was LIFO first introduced in the United States for financial reporting purposes? For tax purposes?
b. Based on the latest *Accounting Trends and Techniques*, what percentage of the companies surveyed are now using LIFO? Has this percentage changed from that in the last three years?
c. Investigate the financial reporting practices of the following countries and state whether and in what manner LIFO is used for financial reporting and tax purposes:
   1. Great Britain
   2. Germany
   3. France
   4. Japan
   5. Canada
   6. Singapore

D9-5 Ethical Issues

Pietro Armondo is the chief financial officer of Agricultural Commodities, Inc., a privately-held company owned by the Armondo family. The company purchases and stores a variety of agricultural commodities such as wheat, soya beans, and corn. These products are then sold to a variety of different customers in the U.S. and abroad. Customers include large agricultural combines, individual farmers, and grain elevator operators.

In reviewing the current year's operations through mid-December, 1994, Pietro estimates that it has been a rather slow year. The U.S. economy and the economies of Europe and the new independent countries of the Eastern bloc have been quite sluggish. Sales and net income are down over 40% and the company estimates its first net loss. Pietro is concerned about this because of existing loan agreements with several banks.

Agricultural Commodities accounts for inventories using LIFO. In reviewing the pattern of purchases and sales throughout the year Pietro notices that the firm purchased about the same number of units of commodities as it sold. Any sales that take place in December would cause a liquidation in the LIFO inventory with extremely high gross profits from these sales. (Early inventory costs are very low compared to current replacement costs.) In fact, the firm has a chance to turn a net loss into net income with substantial sales between now and the end of 1994. The problem is that the last two weeks of December are traditionally very slow in the agricultural commodity business, and chances of making substantial sales are quite small.

Pietro has been discussing this problem with one the firm's major customers, Northern Iowa Grain Suppliers. After some bargaining, Northern Iowa agrees to make a major purchase of soya beans and corn at going market prices. This purchase will take place on December 29, and all the grain will be delivered to Northern Iowa by December 31. As part of the agreement, Agricultural Commodities will repurchase all the grain on January 5, 1995, at current market price plus 12%. Agricultural Commodities will also pay the transportation charges to and from Northern Iowa.

REQUIRED:

1. Describe the advantages and disadvantages of this agreement to Agricultural Commodities and Northern Iowa.
2. In your opinion, has an accrual sale taken place? Why or why not?
3. Do you think that such sales—repurchase agreements—are ethical? Why or why not?
4. Would your answer to (3) change if Agricultural Commodities were a public rather than a private company?

COMPREHENSIVE CASES

C9-1 Recording Sales, Inventory, and Other Transactions

Lakeshore is a large retailer of school supplies. Although most of its sales are made to teachers and other individuals in the education business, Lakeshore does make some wholesale sales to school supplies stores in the local area.

Lakeshore's policy is to take all discounts offered on purchases and thus uses the *net method* to record purchase discounts. Because Lakeshore assumes that most of its wholesale customers will not take any sales discounts offered, however, it uses the *gross method* to record sales discounts. Finally, Lakeshore uses the periodic inventory system to record and keep track of inventory purchases.

The trial balance at January 2, 1995, is presented below, followed by transactions for the first quarter of 1995.

Lakeshore School Supplies
Unadjusted Trail Balance
January 2, 1995

Accounts	*Debit*	*Credit*
Cash	$ 7,500	
Accounts receivable	14,300	
Allowance for uncollectible accounts		$ 900
Inventory	18,000	
Supplies	2,500	
Land	50,000	
Building	100,000	
Accumulated depreciation—building		15,000
Store equipment	40,000	
Accumulated depreciation—store equipment		10,000
Accounts payable		9,000
Mortgages payable		70,000
Capital stock		100,000
Retained earnings		27,400
Totals	$232,300	$232,300

Transactions for the first quarter of 1995:

Jan. 5: Sold $20,000 of merchandise on account to Altadena School Supply. No sales discount allowed and the sale is not subject to sales taxes.

Jan. 7: Purchased supplies for cash, $2,200.

Jan. 12: Purchased $12,000 of merchandise from Puente Manufacturing Company. Terms are 2/10, n/30.

Jan. 13: Received cash from Altadena School Supply.

Jan. 14: Sold $20,000 of merchandise on account to City Unified School District. Terms of sale 2/10, n/30, and sale not subject to sales taxes.

Jan. 19: Paid total due to Puente Manufacturing Company.

Jan. 20: Made cash purchase of merchandise for $8,000.

Jan. 30: Sold $17,400 of merchandise for cash. Sale subject to sales tax of 7%.

Jan. 30: Purchased $15,000 of merchandise on account from Buckley Supplies. Terms of the purchase are 1/10, n/30.

Feb. 1: Merchandise totaling $3,000 was returned by the purchaser of the merchandise sold for cash on Jan. 30. A cash refund was made.

Feb. 2: Received $17,000 from sale to City Unified School District sale on January 14.
Feb. 8: Sold $8,000 of merchandise on credit to Keeting Books and Supplies. Terms of the sale are 2/10, n/30, and the sale is not subject to sales taxes.
Feb. 9: Paid in full the amount owed to Buckley Supplies from January 30 purchase.
Feb. 12: Purchased $10,000 of merchandise for cash.
Feb. 13: Received total amount owed by Keeting on February 8 sale.
Feb. 14: Made cash sales of $5,000, all subject to 7% sales tax.
Feb. 15: Lakeshore returned $4,000 of merchandise purchased for cash on February 12, as the items were defective. Received a cash refund.
Feb. 21: Sold a parcel of land for $19,000. The land had an original cost of $14,500, and was sold for cash.
Feb. 28: Purchased $13,000 of merchandise from Buck Chalk and Board Company on account. Terms of the purchase are 2/10, n/30.
March 1: Sold merchandise on account to Gardena School Supplies for $15,000. Terms of the sale are 2/10, n/30.
March 4: Made a cash purchase of merchandise for $4,000.
March 9: Received partial payment of $10,000 from sale on March 1 to Gardena School Supplies.
March 10: Paid full amount due to Buck Chalk and Board on February 28 purchase.
March 12: Made sale on account to D.C. Districts for $10,000. No discount allowed and sale not subject to sales tax.
March 15: Received remainder due from March 1 sale to Gardena School Supplies.
March 19: Purchased merchandise on account from Little Kids Manufacturing for $11,000. Terms of the purchase are 1/10, n/30.
March 20: Invested $10,000 of excess cash in a long-term investment.
March 25: Made cash sales of $8,000, all subject to 7% sales tax.
March 31: Operating expenses of $4,400 for the quarter, excluding salaries, were paid in cash.
March 31: Sales taxes owed were paid in full.
March 31: Salaries of $5,000 were accrued. FICA taxes of 7.5% and state unemployment taxes of 2.4% are due on the entire payroll. In addition, federal taxes of $500, state taxes of $230, and FICA taxes of 7.5% were withheld.
March 31: Accounts receivable of $810 were deemed to be uncollectible and were written off.
March 31: Dividends of $1,200 were declared and paid in cash.

REQUIRED:

1. Make all the required journal entries. Open T accounts with the January 2, 1995, balances and post the journal entries to these T accounts.
2. Prepare an unadjusted trial balance as of March 31, 1995.
3. Your analysis of the accounts indicated that adjusting journal entries for the following need to be made (worksheet optional):
   a. Supplies of $3,000 remained on hand at March 31.
   b. Depreciation expense of $3,500 ($2,500 on the building and $1,000 on the store equipment) must be recorded.
   c. Uncollectible accounts expense of 3% of credit sales must be recorded.
   d. A calculation of the ending inventory indicated that its LIFO cost is $19,400.
   e. Interest on the mortgage note must be accrued. The note carries an interest rate of 12% and no interest has been accrued for 1995.
   f. The income tax rate is 20%. Assume that pretax accounting income is equal to taxable income.
4. Post the adjusting journal entries to the T accounts. Prepare an adjusted trial balance.
5. Prepare an income statement and a statement of retained earnings for the quarter ending March 31, 1995.
6. Prepare closing entries and post them to the T accounts.
7. Prepare a balance sheet at March 31, 1995.

C9-2 Effect of Differences in Accounting Methods—Recording and Analysis

The Fastrack Corporation is a wholesaler of ultra high speed hard disk drives. The company purchases finished disk drives from a U.S. manufacturer and sells them directly to computer manufacturers and retail computer stores. Since all disk drives are sold for resale, no sales taxes are imposed on Fastrack. The firm fully guarantees its products for one year. Fastrack will cover the cost of all defects.

Fastrack was organized in mid-1994. At that time the firm moved into its present headquarters, which it rents for $25,000 a year included in operating expenses. A trial balance at January 2, 1995, follows:

The Fastrack Corporation
Trial Balance
January 2, 1995

Accounts	*Debit*	*Credit*
Cash	$ 23,000	
Accounts receivable	31,000	
Allowance for uncollectible accounts		$ 2,400
Inventory	47,500	
Prepaid assets	2,400	
Furniture and equipment	100,000	
Accumulated depreciation—Furniture and equipment		10,000
Accounts payable		30,000
Estimated liability for product guarantees		4,200
Notes payable		25,000
Income taxes payable		
Capital stock		100,000
Retained earnings		32,300
Totals	$203,900	$203,900

During 1995 the following summary transactions occurred:

a. Sales for the year were as follows:
   Jan. 20: 1,000 units @ $70 per unit for cash.
   March 28: 2,500 units @ $70 per unit on account.
   June 20: 2,200 units @ $72 per unit for cash.
   Sept. 7: 5,000 units @ $73 per unit on account.
   Nov. 29: 7,200 units @ $75 per unit on account.
b. Purchases during the year were as follows:
   Feb. 14: 4,000 units @ $42.50 per unit for cash.
   May 8: 3,800 units @ $43 per unit on account.
   July 7: 2,500 units at $43 per unit on account.
   Oct. 10: 5,700 units @ $43.50 per unit for cash.
   Dec. 19: 1,000 units @ $45 per unit on account.
c. Operating expenses, including rent paid in cash during the year, amounted to $375,000. (All expenses other than interest are included in the category Operating Expenses.)
d. Cash collected on accounts receivable during the year amounted to $1,000,000.
e. Cash paid on accounts payable during the year amounted to $300,000.
f. Fastrack incurred expenses of $16,000 to repair products it had guaranteed. Cash was credited for the entire amount.
g. The firm invested its excess cash of $95,000 in Iowa state bonds. These bonds are not subject to federal income tax, and thus are a permanent difference for interperiod income tax purposes.
h. Fastrack received $5,000 in interest on the Iowa state bonds.
i. The firm decided to write off $3,000 of its accounts receivable as uncollectible.

At year-end Fastrack's accountant analyzed the firm's account and provided you with the following information:

a. Accounting policies:
   1. The firm records inventory transactions under the periodic system and uses FIFO to cost its inventory. The beginning inventory at January 2, 1994, was made up of 2,100 units with the following costs:
      1,000 units @ $20 per unit (acquired first)
      1,100 units @ $25 per unit.
      These units were purchased from the previous owner at substantial discounts.
   2. The firm neither gives sales discounts to its customers nor is allowed purchase discounts by the manufacturer.
   3. The firm's furniture and equipment was purchased last year, and during 1994 one-half of a year's depreciation on the straight-line method was taken. A five-year life is used for financial reporting purposes. (This equals a 10% rate in the first year, as only half of a year's depreciation is taken.)
   4. Fastrack estimates the amount of guarantee expense that it incurs for current sales. Based on the firm's experience during 1994, 10% of all units sold will be returned because of defects, with an estimated cost of $8 per unit for repairs.
   5. Fastrack uses the allowance method to estimate its bad debts. An aging of its accounts receivable revealed the following:

	Total	*Current*	*31–60 Days*	*61–90 Days*	*91–120 Days*	*Over 120 Days*
Amount	$108,000	$58,000	$26,000	$12,000	$8,000	$4,000
% Uncollectible		0.05	0.1	0.15	0.3	0.5

b. Other items:
   1. Prepaid assets in the amount of $1,000 were used up during 1995.
   2. The note payable carries an interest rate of 10% and an entire year's interest must be accrued.
   3. The income tax rate is 30%.

REQUIRED:

1. Prepare summary journal entries for the year.
2. Prepare T accounts and post these entries to the T accounts. Prepare an unadjusted trial balance.
3. Make the necessary adjusting entries. (*Hint:* Review the above information and be sure to make all the adjusting entries required, including the one to record income taxes.) Post those entries to the T accounts. Prepare an adjusted trial balance.
4. Prepare an income statement and a statement of retained earnings for the year ended December 31, 1995.
5. Make the appropriate closing entries.
6. Prepare a balance sheet at December 31, 1995.
7. Prepare the following ratios and other statistics for 1995:
   a. Working capital
   b. Current ratio
   c. Gross profit percentage
   d. Profit margin percentage
   e. Return on assets
   f. Accounts receivable turnover
   g. Inventory turnover
8. Repeat steps (3) through (7), this time assuming that Fastrack uses LIFO. Compare and contrast your answer with that obtained for FIFO.

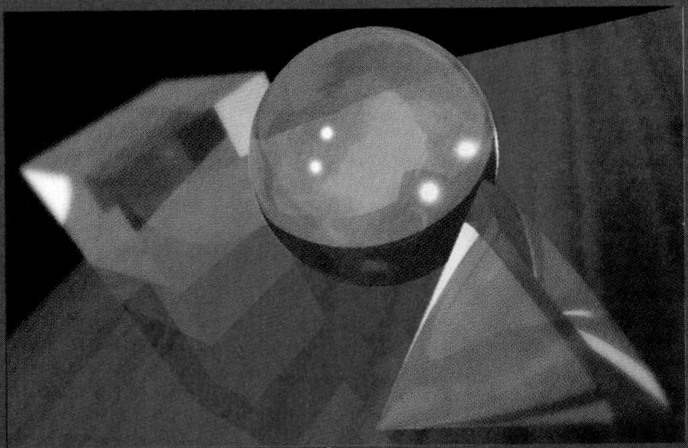

PART 3

INVESTING ACTIVITIES

Investing activities include (1) the acquisition and sale of operating assets such as property, plant, and equipment, and (2) the acquisition and sale of debt and equity securities of other firms, and (3) the lending of money and the collection of these loans. A firm purchases these assets in the expectation that they will be used in operations to generate revenues in the form of future cash flows or will provide a cash return in excess of their cost.

Cash inflows from investing activities include receipts from the sale of property, plant, and equipment, receipts from the sale of investments in the debt or equity securities of other firms, that are not cash equivalents, and collection of loans made to others. On the other hand, cash outflows from investing activities include payments to acquire property, plant, and equipment, purchase of investments in the debt or equity securities of other firms, and loans made to others. The chart below summarizes these activities and shows the chapter in which they are discussed:

Receipts	Payments
From the sale of operating and intangible assets (Chapter 10)	To purchase operating and intangible assets (Chapter 10)
From sale of debt or equity securities (Chapter 11)	To purchase debt or equity securities (Chapter 11)
From the collection of principal on loans to another entity (Chapter 12)	To make loans to another entity (Chapter 12)

The two chapters that make up this part of the book introduce you to the accounting issues related to investing activities of the firm. However, discussion of these activities begins after management has already made the critical decisions — whether or not to purchase the asset and how to finance the purchase. In many cases, these purchase and financing decisions drive the appropriate accounting treatment. Because of this, a brief introduction to how these investing decisions are made follows. Further, since present value techniques are important in investing and financing decisions, a module on present value follows this introduction. Studying this module will assist you in understanding the various topics discussed in the remainder of this book.

PRESENT VALUE MODULE

Perhaps you have heard advertisements stating that if you invest $2,000 a year in an Individual Retirement Account (IRA) or other retirement fund beginning at age 30, you will have accumulated over $500,000 by the time you retire at age 65. As the advertisements point out, you will receive substantially more than the $70,000 ($2,000 × 35 years) you have invested because of the interest your investment will earn. This highlights the importance of interest and how quickly it accumulates over a period of time. The focus of this module is on the time value of money and how this concept is used in personal and business financial decisions.

All investment or capital budgeting decisions involve giving up a certain amount of money today in the hope of receiving a greater amount at some future time. In order to determine whether you have made a wise investment, you must consider the time value of money. For example, assume that you are given the following investment opportunity: A real estate developer offers to sell you a vacant lot today for $100,000 and guarantees to repurchase it ten years from now for a minimum of $175,000. Does that sound like a good investment? Although it is tempting to say yes, because you would be making a profit of $75,000, you must also consider the time value of money. The $175,000 you will receive in ten years is not really comparable to the $100,000 you have to give up today. Money you will receive in the future will not be as valuable as money you receive today, because money received today can be invested and, as a result, will increase in amount. In the example, if you did not make the investment but instead put the $100,000 in a savings account that earned 8% interest per year, you would have accumulated over $215,800 at the end of ten years. The best way to analyze investment opportunities such as this one is to determine the rate of return they offer. In this example, if you invested $100,000 today and received $175,000 in ten years, you would have earned a rate of return of about 5.76%. You can compare this rate of return with those of other investments of similar risk and logically decide which one presents the best opportunity. In order to make this and similar analyses, you must understand five concepts:

1. Simple versus compound interest
2. Future value of a single amount
3. Present value of a single amount
4. Future value of an annuity
5. Present value of an annuity

SIMPLE VERSUS COMPOUND INTEREST

Interest is payment for the use of money for a specified period of time. Interest can be calculated on either a simple or a compound basis. The distinction between the two is important because it affects the amount of interest earned or incurred.

Simple Interest

simple interest

With **simple interest,** the interest payment is computed on only the amount of the principal for one or more periods. That is, if the original principal of the note is not changed, the interest payment will remain the same for each period. Most of the examples in this book so far have assumed simple interest. For example, if you invested $10,000 at 12% interest for three years, your yearly interest income would be $1,200 ($10,000 × 0.12).[1] The total interest earned over the three years would be $3,600, and you would eventually receive $13,600 ($10,000 + $3,600).

Compound Interest

compound interest

With **compound interest,** interest is computed on the principal of the note plus any interest that has accrued to date. That is, when compound interest is applied, the accrued interest of that period is added to the principal to determine the amount on which future interest is to be computed. Thus, by compounding, interest is earned or incurred not only on the principal but also on the interest left on deposit.

To demonstrate the concept of compound interest, assume that the interest in the previous example now will be compounded annually rather than on a simple basis. As Exhibit M-1 shows, during year 1 interest income is $1,200, or 12% of $10,000. Because the interest is compounded, it is added to the principal to determine the accumulated amount of $11,200 at the end of the year. Interest in year 2 is $1,344.00, or 12% of $11,200, and the accumulated amount at the end of year

1. Interest rates fluctuate based upon a number of economic factors. For example, in the mid-1980s it was possible to earn 12% on certain fixed investments. By 1992 these rates of return had fallen to less than 6%. In this module, interest rates are chosen not for their current economic reality but for their ease of use in calculations and explanations.

Exhibit M-1
Interest Compounded Annually

Year	Principal Amount Beginning of Year	Annual Interest Income, 12%	Accumulated at End of Year
1	$10,000.00	$1,200.00	$11,200.00
2	11,200.00	1,344.00	12,544.00
3	12,544.00	1,505.28	14,049.28

2 is now $12,544.00. The interest and the accumulated amount at the end of year 3 are calculated in the same manner. Your total interest income is $4,049.28 rather than the $3,600 you earned with simple interest.

Interest Compounded More Often Than Annually. Interest can be compounded as often as desired. The more often interest is compounded, the more quickly it will increase. For example, many financial institutions compound interest daily. This means that interest is calculated on the beginning balance of your account each day. This interest is added to the accumulated amount to determine the base for the next day's interest calculation. Clearly, this is more advantageous than interest that is compounded yearly.

When calculating interest compounded more frequently than once a year, it is quite easy to make the necessary adjustments. For example, if interest is compounded quarterly, there are four interest periods in each year. The interest rate, which is stated in annual terms, must be reduced accordingly. Thus, instead of using an interest rate of 12% in the example, the interest rate would be 3% (12%/4 quarters) each quarter. As a general rule, the annual interest rate is divided by the number of compounding periods to determine the proper interest rate each period.

If interest is compounded quarterly in the previous $10,000, 12% example, it will equal $4,257.60, and the total amount of the investment will grow to $14,257.60. This is shown in Exhibit M-2. In this straightforward example, the total interest increases by $208.32, from $4,049.28 to $4,257.60, when interest is compounded quarterly instead of annually.

Exhibit M-2
Interest Compounded Quarterly

Period	Principal Amount at Beginning of Period	Amount of Interest Each Period at 3%	Accumulated Amount at End of Period
1	$10,000.00	$300.00	$10,300.00
2	10,300.00	309.00	10,609.00
3	10,609.00	318.27	10,927.27
4	10,927.27	327.82	11,255.09
5	11,255.09	337.65	11,592.74
6	11,592.74	347.78	11,940.52
7	11,940.52	358.22	12,298.74
8	12,298.74	368.96	12,667.70
9	12,667.70	380.03	13,047.73
10	13,047.73	391.43	13,439.16
11	13,439.16	403.17	13,842.33
12	13,842.33	415.27	14,257.60

FUTURE VALUE OF A SINGLE AMOUNT

future value of a single amount

The previous example was an attempt to determine what the future amount of \$10,000 invested at 12% for three years would be, given a certain compounding pattern. This is an example of determining the **future value of a single amount.** Future value means the amount to which the investment will grow by a future date if interest is compounded. Single amount means that a lump sum was invested at the beginning of year 1 and was left intact for all three years. Thus there were no additional investments or withdrawals. These future value or compound interest calculations are important in many personal and business financial decisions. For example, an individual may be interested in determining how much an investment of \$50,000 will amount to in five years if interest is compounded semiannually versus quarterly, or what rate of return compounded annually must be earned on a \$10,000 investment if \$18,000 is needed in seven years. All of these situations relate to determining the future value of a single amount.

One way to solve problems of this type is to construct tables similar to the one in Exhibit M-2. However, this method is time-consuming and not very flexible. Mathematical formulas also can be used. For example, the tables used in Exhibits M-1 and M-2 and in Appendix B to determine the accumulated amount of a single deposit at different compounded rates are based on the following formula:

$$\text{Accumulated amount} = p(1 + i)^n$$

where

$$p = \text{principal amount}$$
$$i = \text{interest rate}$$
$$n = \text{number of compounding periods}$$

That is, in the example of the \$10,000 compounded annually for three years at 12%, the \$14,049.28 can be determined by the following calculation:

$$\$14,049.28 = \$10,000(1 + 0.12)^3$$

One of the simplest methods is to use tables that give the future value of \$1 at different interest rates and for different periods. Essentially, these tables interpret the mathematical formula just presented for various interest rates and compounding periods for a principal amount of \$1. Once the amount of \$1 is known, it is easy to determine the amount for any principal amount by multiplying the future amount for \$1 by the required principal amount. Most hand calculators also have function keys that can be used to solve these types of problems.

To illustrate, Exhibit M-3, an excerpt from the future value of a single amount table (see Table 1 in Appendix B at the end of the book), shows the future value of \$1 for ten interest periods for interest rates ranging from 2% to 14%. Suppose that you want to determine the future value of \$10,000 at the end of three years if interest is compounded annually at 12% (the previous example). In order to solve this, look down the 12% column in the table until you come to the third interest period. The factor from the table is 1.40493, which means that \$1 invested today at 12% will accumulate to \$1.405 at the end of three years. Because you are interested in \$10,000 rather than \$1, just multiply the factor of 1.40493 by \$10,000 to determine the future value of the \$10,000 principal amount. The

Exhibit M-3
Future Value of a Single Amount

(n) Periods	2%	4%	6%	8%	10%	12%	14%	(n) Periods
1	1.02000	1.04000	1.06000	1.08000	1.10000	1.12000	1.14000	1
2	1.04040	1.08160	1.12360	1.16640	1.21000	1.25440	1.29960	2
3	1.06121	1.12486	1.19102	1.25971	1.33100	1.40493	1.48154	3
4	1.08243	1.16986	1.26248	1.36049	1.46410	1.57352	1.68896	4
5	1.10408	1.21665	1.33823	1.46933	1.61051	1.76234	1.92541	5
6	1.12616	1.26532	1.41852	1.58687	1.77156	1.97382	2.19497	6
7	1.14869	1.31593	1.50363	1.71382	1.94872	2.21068	2.50227	7
8	1.17166	1.36857	1.59385	1.85093	2.14359	2.47596	2.85259	8
9	1.19509	1.42331	1.68948	1.99900	2.35795	2.77308	3.25195	9
10	1.21899	1.48024	1.79085	2.15892	2.59374	3.10585	3.70722	10

amount is $14,049.30, which, except for a slight rounding error, is the same as was determined from Exhibit M-1.

The use of the future value table can be generalized by using the following formula:

Accumulated amount = Factor (from the table) × Principal

$14,049.30 = 1.40493 × $10,000

This formula can be used to solve a variety of related problems. For example, as noted above, you may be interested in determining what rate of interest must be earned on a $10,000 investment if you want to accumulate $18,000 by the end of seven years. Or you may want to know the number of years an amount must be invested in order to grow to a certain amount. In all these cases, you have two of the three items in the formula and you can solve for the third.

Interest Compounded More Often Than Annually

As previously stated, interest usually is compounded more often than annually. In such situations, simply adjust the number of interest periods and the interest rate. If you want to know what $10,000 will accumulate to by the end of three years if interest is compounded quarterly at an annual rate of 12%, just look down the 3% column until you reach 12 periods (see Table 1 in Appendix B). The factor is 1.42576 and (employing the general formula) the accumulated amount is $14,257.60, determined as follows:

Accumulated amount = Factor × Principal

$14,257.60 = 1.42576 × $10,000

Determination of the Number of Periods or the Interest Rate

There are many situations in which the unknown variable is the number of interest periods that the dollars must remain invested or the rate of return (interest rate) that must be earned. For example, assume that you invest $5,000 today in a financial institution that will pay interest at 10% compounded annually. You need to accumulate \$8,857.80 for a certain project. How many years does the investment have to remain in the savings and loan association? Using the general formula, the answer is six years, determined as follows:

$$\text{Accumulated amount} = \text{Factor} \times \text{Principal}$$

$$\text{Factor} = \frac{\text{Accumulated amount}}{\text{Principal}}$$

$$1.77156 = \frac{\$8{,}857.80}{\$5{,}000.00}$$

Looking down the 10% column in Table 1 of Appendix B, the factor of 1.77156 appears at the sixth-period row. Because the interest is compounded annually, the sixth period is interpreted as six years. This example was constructed so that the factor equals a round number of periods. If it does not, interpolation is necessary. The examples, exercises, and problems in this book will not require interpolation.

You can use the same method to determine the required interest rate. For example, assume that you invest \$10,000 for eight years. What rate of return or interest rate compounded annually must you earn if you want to accumulate \$28,525.90? Using the general formula, the answer is 14%, determined as follows:

$$\text{Accumulated amount} = \text{Factor} \times \text{Principal}$$

$$\text{Factor} = \frac{\text{Accumulated amount}}{\text{Principal}}$$

$$2.85259 = \frac{\$28{,}525.90}{\$10{,}000.00}$$

Looking across the eight-period row, you find the factor of 2.85259 at the 14% column.

PRESENT VALUE OF A SINGLE AMOUNT

In many business and personal situations, you are interested in determining the value today of receiving a fixed single amount at some time in the future. For example, assume that you want to know the value today of receiving \$15,000 at the end of five years if a rate of return of 12% is earned. Another way of asking this question is, what is the amount that would have to be invested today at 12% (compounded annually) if you wanted to receive \$15,000 at the end of five years? This is a problem of determining the **present value of a single amount,** because you are interested in knowing the present value, or the value today, of receiving a set sum in the future.

present value of a single amount

Intuitively, it is clear that the present value will be less than the future value. For example, if you had the choice of receiving \$12,000 today or in two years, you would take the \$12,000 today. This is because you can invest the \$12,000 so that it will accumulate to more than \$12,000 by the end of two years. Another way of looking at this is to say that because of the time value of money, you would take an amount less than \$12,000 if you could receive it today, instead of \$12,000 in two years. The amount you would be willing to accept depends on the interest rate or the rate of return you receive.

In present value problems, the interest rate often is called the *discount rate.* This is because a future value is being discounted back to the present. Present value problems are sometimes called *discounted* present value problems.

One way to solve present value problems is to use the general formula previously developed for future value problems. For example, returning to the previous example, assume that at the end of five years, you wish to have $15,000. If you can earn 12% compounded annually, how much do you have to invest today? Using the general formula for Table 1 in Appendix B, the answer is $8,511.41, determined as follows:

$$\text{Accumulated amount} = \text{Factor} \times \text{Principal}$$

$$\text{Principal} = \frac{\text{Accumulated amount}}{\text{Factor}}$$

$$\$8{,}511.41 = \frac{\$15{,}000}{1.76234}$$

This is equivalent to saying that at a 12% interest rate, compounded annually, it does not matter whether you receive $8,511.41 today or $15,000 at the end of five years. Thus, if someone offered you an investment at a cost of $8,000 that would return $15,000 at the end of five years, you would take it if the minimum rate of return were 12%. This is because at 12% the $15,000 is actually worth $8,511.41 today. Therefore, your smaller investment of $8,000, for the same amount of $15,000 in five years, would earn more than the 12% interest.

Present Value Tables

Rather than using future value tables and making the necessary adjustments to the general formula, you can use present value tables. As is the case with future value tables, present value tables are based on the mathematical formula used to determine present values. Because of the relationship between future and present values, the present value table is the inverse of the future value table. Exhibit M-4 presents an excerpt from the present value tables (Table 3 found in Appendix B). The table works the same way the future value table does, except that the general formula is

$$\text{Present value} = \text{Factor} \times \text{Accumulated amount}$$

For example, if you want to use the table to determine the present value of $15,000 to be received at the end of five years, compounded annually at 12%, simply look down the 12% column and multiply that factor by $15,000. Thus the answer is $8,511.45,[2] determined as follows:

$$\text{Present value} = \text{Factor} \times \text{Accumulated amount}$$

$$\$8{,}511.45 = .56743 \times \$15{,}000$$

Other Present Value Situations

As in the future value case, you can use the general formula to solve other variations, as long as you know two of the three variables. For example, assume that you want to know what interest rate compounded semiannually you must earn

2. The difference between the $8,511.41 calculated above and the $8,511.45 is due to rounding and is not material.

Exhibit M-4
Present Value of a Single Amount

(n) Periods	2%	4%	6%	8%	10%	12%	14%	(n) Periods
1	.98039	.96154	.94340	.92593	.90909	.89286	0.87719	1
2	.96117	.92456	.89000	.85734	.82645	.79719	0.76947	2
3	.94232	.88900	.83962	.79383	.75132	.71178	0.67497	3
4	.92385	.85480	.79209	.73503	.68301	.63552	0.59208	4
5	.90573	.82193	.74726	.68058	.62092	.56743	0.51937	5
6	.88797	.79031	.70496	.63017	.56447	.50663	0.45559	6
7	.87056	.75992	.66506	.58349	.51316	.45235	0.39964	7
8	.85349	.73069	.62741	.54027	.46651	.40388	0.35056	8
9	.83676	.70259	.59190	.50025	.42410	.36061	0.30751	9
10	.82035	.67556	.55839	.46319	.38554	.32197	0.26974	10

if you want to accumulate \$10,000 by the end of three years, with an investment of \$7,903.10 today. The answer is 4% semiannually, or 8% annually, determined as follows:

$$\text{Present value} = \text{Factor} \times \text{Accumulated amount}$$

$$\text{Factor} = \frac{\text{Present Value}}{\text{Accumulated Amount}}$$

$$.79031 = \frac{\$\ 7{,}903.10}{\$10{,}000.00}$$

Looking across the sixth-period row in Exhibit M-4, you come to .79031 in the 4% column. Because interest is compounded semiannually, the annual rate is 8%.

The Distinction Between Future Value and Present Value

In beginning to work with time value of money problems, you should be careful to distinguish between present value and future value problems. One way to do this is to use time lines to analyze the situation. For example, the time line relating to the example in which you determined the future value of \$10,000 compounded annually at 12% for three years is as follows:

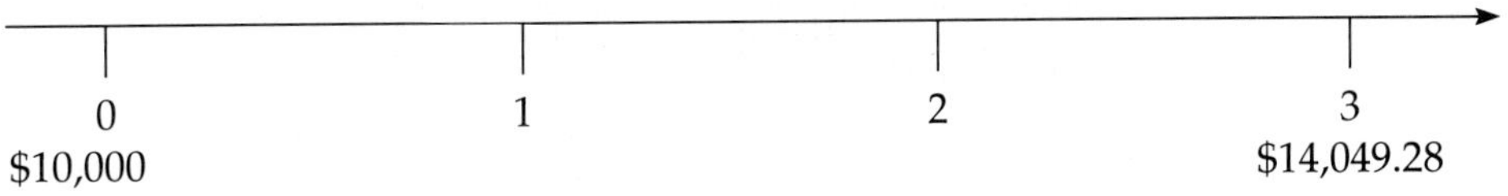

But the time line relating to the present value of \$15,000 discounted back at 12% annually for five years is:

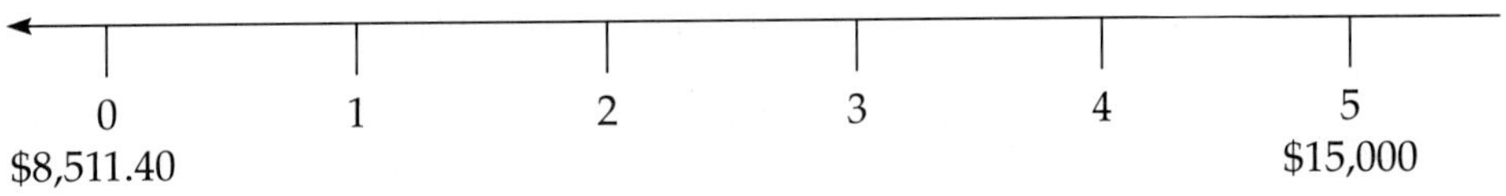

FUTURE VALUE OF AN ANNUITY

annuity

An **annuity** is a series of equal payments made at specified intervals. Interest is compounded on each of these payments. Annuities often are called *rents* because they are like the payment of monthly rentals. Annuity payments can be made at the beginning or the end of the specified intervals. A payment made at the beginning of the period is called an *annuity due;* a payment made at the end of the period is called an *ordinary annuity.* The examples in this book use ordinary annuities, so it always will be assumed that the payment takes place at the end of the period.

Annuities are encountered frequently in business and accounting situations. For example, a lease payment or a mortgage represents an annuity. Life insurance contracts involving a series of equal payments at equal times are another example of an annuity. In some cases, it is appropriate to calculate the future value of the annuity; in other cases, it is appropriate to calculate the present value of the annuity.

Understanding the Future Value of an Annuity

future value of an annuity

The **future value of an annuity** is the sum of all the periodic payments plus the interest that has accumulated on them. To demonstrate how to calculate the future value of an annuity, assume that you deposit \$1 at the end of each of the next four years in a savings account that pays 10% interest, compounded annually. Exhibit M-5 shows how these \$1 payments will accumulate to \$4.6410 at the end of the fourth period, or year in this case. The future value of each dollar is determined by compounding interest at 10% for the appropriate number of periods. For example, the \$1 deposited at the end of the first period earns interest for three periods. It earns interest for only three periods because it was deposited at the end of the first period and earns interest until the end of the fourth. Using the factors from Table 1 in Appendix B, the future value of this first \$1.00 single payment is \$1.3310, determined as follows:

$$\text{Future value} = \text{Factor} \times \text{Principal}$$

$$\$1.3310 = 1.3310 \times \$1.00$$

The second payment earns interest for two periods and accumulates to \$1.2100, and the third payment earns interest for only one period and accumulates to \$1.10. The final payment, made at the end of the fourth year, does not earn any interest, because the future value of the annuity is being determined at the end of the fourth period. The total of all payments compounded for the appropriate number of interest periods equals \$4.6410 the future value of this ordinary annuity.

Fortunately, you do not have to construct a table like the one in Exhibit M-5 in order to determine the future value of an annuity. You can use tables that present the factors necessary to calculate the future value of an annuity of \$1, given different periods and interest rates. Table 2 in Appendix B is such a table. It is constructed by simply summing the appropriate factors from the compound interest table. For example, the factor for the future value of a \$1.00 annuity at the end of four years at 10% compounded annually is \$4.6410. This is the same amount determined when the calculation was performed independently by summing the individual factors.

Exhibit M-5
Future Value of an Annuity

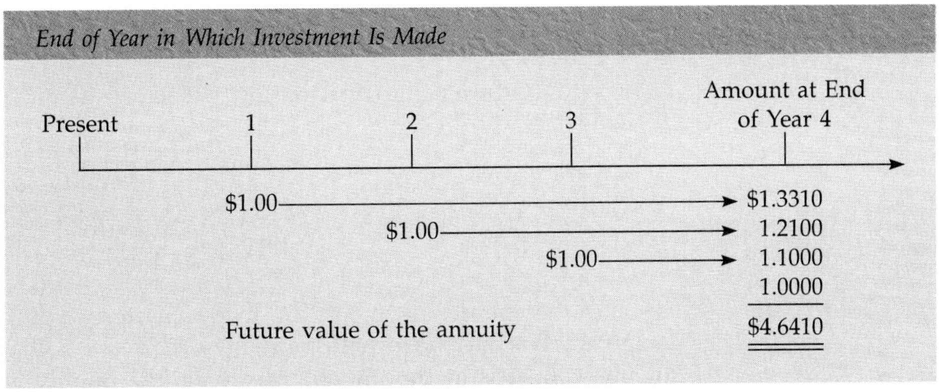

Solving Problems Involving the Future Value of an Annuity

By using the general formula below, you can solve a variety of problems involving the future value of an annuity:

$$\text{Future value of an annuity} = \text{Factor} \times \text{Annuity payment}$$

As long as you know two of the three variables, you can solve for the third. Thus, you can solve for the future value of the annuity, the annuity payment, the interest rate, or the number of periods.

Determining Future Value. Assume that you deposit in a savings and loan association $4,000 per year at the end of each of the next eight years. How much will you accumulate if you earn 10% compounded annually? The future value of this annuity is $45,743.56, determined as follows:

$$\text{Future value of an annuity} = \text{Factor} \times \text{Annuity payment}$$

$$\$45{,}743.56 = 11.43589 \times \$4{,}000$$

Determining the Annuity Payment. Assume that by the end of 15 years, you need to have accumulated $100,000 to send your daughter to college. If you can earn 12% at your financial institution, how much must you deposit at the end of each of the next 15 years in order to accumulate this amount? The annual payment is $2,682.42, as determined in the following:

$$\text{Future value of an annuity} = \text{Factor} \times \text{Annuity payment}$$

$$\text{Annuity payment} = \frac{\text{Future value of an annuity}}{\text{Factor}}$$

$$\$2{,}682.42 = \frac{\$100{,}000}{37.27972}$$

Determining the Interest Rate. In some cases you may want to determine the interest rate that must be earned on an annuity in order to accumulate a predetermined amount. For example, assume that you invest $500 per quarter for ten years and want to have $30,200.99 by the end of the tenth year. What interest rate is required? You need to earn 2% quarterly, or 8% annually, determined as follows:

$$\text{Future value of an annuity} = \text{Factor} \times \text{Annuity payment}$$

$$\text{Factor} = \frac{\text{Future value of an annuity}}{\text{Annuity payment}}$$

$$60.40198 = \frac{\$30{,}200.99}{\$500}$$

Because the annuity payments are made quarterly, you must look at Table 2 in Appendix B across the fortieth-period (10 years × 4) row until you find the factor. In this case it is at the 2% column. Thus the interest rate is 2% quarterly, or 8% annually.

In some situations, the interest rate is known, but the number of periods is missing. These problems can be solved by using the same technique you used to determine the interest rate. When the factor is determined, you must be sure to look down the appropriate interest column to find the factor on the annuity table.

PRESENT VALUE OF AN ANNUITY

present value of an annuity

The value today of a series of equal payments or receipts to be made or received on specified future dates is called the **present value of an annuity.** As in the case of the future value of an annuity, the receipts or payments are made in the future. Present value is the value today, and future value relates to accumulated future value. Furthermore, the present value of a series of payments or receipts will be less than the total of the same payments or receipts, because cash received in the future is not as valuable as cash received today. On the other hand, the future value of an annuity will be greater than the sum of the individual payments or receipts, because interest is accumulated on the payments. It is important to distinguish between the future value and the present value of an annuity. Again, time lines are helpful in this respect.

Mortgages and certain notes payable in equal installments are examples of present value of an annuity problems. For example, assume that a bank lends you $60,000 today, to be repaid in equal monthly installments over 30 years. The bank is interested in knowing what series of monthly payments, when discounted back at the agreed-upon interest rate, is equal to the present value today of the amount of the loan, or $60,000.

Determining the Present Value of an Annuity

Assume that you want to determine the value today of receiving $1 at the end of each of the next four years. The appropriate interest or discount rate is 12%. To solve this, construct a table that determines the present values of each of the receipts, as shown in Exhibit M-6. The exhibit shows that the present value of receiving the four $1.00 payments is $3.03735 when discounted at 12%. Each of the individual dollars was discounted by using the factors in the present value of a single amount table in Exhibit M-4. For example, the present value of the dollar received at the end of year 4, when discounted back four years, is $0.63552. It must be discounted back four years because the present, or today, is the beginning of year 1. The dollar received at the end of year 3 must be discounted back three periods; the dollar received at the end of year 2 must be discounted back two periods; and so forth.

Exhibit M-6
Present Value of an Annuity

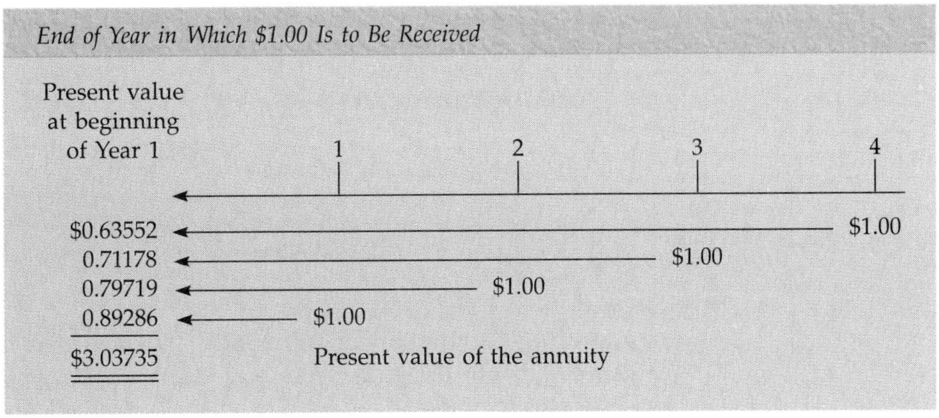

As with the calculation of the future value of an annuity, you can use prepared tables. Table 4 in Appendix B is such a table. It is constructed by summing the individual present values of $1 at set interest rates and periods. Thus the factor for the present value of four $1.00 payments to be received at the end of each of the next four years, when discounted back at 12%, is 3.03735, the value that was determined independently.

Problems Involving the Present Value of an Annuity

Problems involving the present value of an annuity can be solved by using the following general formula:

Present value of an annuity = Factor × Amount of the annuity

As long as you know two of the three variables, you can solve for the third. Thus, you can determine the present value of the annuity, the interest rate, the number of periods, or the amount of the annuity.

Determining the Present Value. To demonstrate how to calculate the present value of an annuity, assume that you are offered an investment that pays $2,000 a year at the end of each of the next ten years. How much would you pay for it if you want to earn a rate of return of 8%? This is a present value problem, because you would pay the value today of this stream of payments discounted back at 8%. This amount is $13,420.16, determined as follows:

Present value of an annuity = Factor × Amount of the annuity
$13,420.16 = 6.71008 × $2,000

Another way to interpret this problem is to say that if you want to earn 8%, it makes no difference whether you keep $13,420.16 today or receive $2,000 a year for ten years.

Determining the Annuity Payment. A common variation of present value problems requires computing the annuity payment. In many cases, these are loan or mortgage problems. For example, assume that you purchase a house for $100,000 and make a 20% down payment. You will borrow the rest of the money from the bank at 10% interest. To make the problem easier, assume that you will make a payment at the end of each of the next 30 years. (Most mortgages require monthly payments.) How much will your yearly payments be?

In this case, you are going to borrow \$80,000 (\$100,000 × 80%). The yearly payment would be \$8,486.34, determined as follows:

$$\text{Present value of an annuity} = \text{Factor} \times \text{Amount of the annuity}$$

$$\text{Amount of the annuity} = \frac{\text{Present value of an annuity}}{\text{Factor}}$$

$$\$8{,}486.34 = \frac{\$80{,}000}{9.42691}$$

Determining the Number of Payments. Assume that the Black Lighting Co. purchased a new printing press for \$100,000. The quarterly payments are \$4,326.24 and the interest rate is 12% annually, or 3% a quarter. How many payments will be required to pay off the loan? In this case, 40 payments are required, determined as follows:

$$\text{Present value of an annuity} = \text{Factor} \times \text{Amount of the annuity}$$

$$\text{Factor} = \frac{\text{Present value of an annuity}}{\text{Amount of the annuity}}$$

$$23.11477 = \frac{\$100{,}000}{\$4{,}326.24}$$

Looking down the 3% column in Table 4 in Appendix B, you find the factor 23.11477 at the fortieth-period row. Thus 40 quarterly payments are needed to pay off the loan.

Solving Combination Problems. Many accounting applications related to the time value of money involve both single amounts and annuities. For example, say that you are considering purchasing an apartment house. After much analysis, you determine that you will receive net yearly cash flows of \$10,000 from rental revenue, less rental expenses, from the apartment. To make the analysis easier, assume that the cash flows are generated at the end of each year. These cash flows will continue for 20 years, at which time you estimate that you can sell the apartment building for \$250,000. How much should you pay for the building, assuming that you want to earn a rate of return of 10%?

This problem involves an annuity the yearly net cash flows of \$10,000 and a single amount the \$250,000 to be received once at the end of the twentieth year. As a rational person, the maximum that you would be willing to pay is the value today of these two cash flows discounted at 10%. That value is \$122,296, as determined below:

Present value of the annuity of \$10,000 a year for 20 years \$10,000 × 8.51356 (Table 4)	\$ 85,136
Present value of the single amount of \$250,000 to be received at the end of year 20 \$250,000 × 0.14864 (Table 3)	37,160
Total purchase price	\$122,296

ACCOUNTING APPLICATIONS OF THE TIME VALUE OF MONEY

The concepts related to the time value of money, especially present value, have many applications in financial and managerial accounting. For example, from a theoretical perspective, assets and liabilities should be valued at the present value of the future cash inflows expected from the asset or of the cash outflows from the liability. Accountants rarely use this method to value assets, however, because of the difficulty of estimating future cash flows and discount rates.

However, present value often is used to value long-term liabilities at their origination date, because the cash flows for liabilities such as mortgages and bonds are known with certainty. For example, a bond has a stated interest rate and a set principal amount. As Chapter 12 will show, bonds are recorded at the present value of these cash outflows, based on the yield interest rate at the time of their issuance.

KEY TERMS

Annuity 452
Compound interest 445
Future value of an annuity 452
Future value of a single amount 447
Present value of an annuity 454
Present value of a single amount 449
Simple interest 445

REVIEW PROBLEM

Solve each of the following time value of money problems.

1. Determine the future value of:
   a. a single payment of $15,000 at 8%, compounded semiannually, for ten years.
   b. ten annual payments of $2,000 at 12%.
2. Determine the present value of:
   a. six semiannual payments of $1,000 at 10%, compounded semiannually.
   b. a single payment of $12,000 discounted at 12% annually, received at the end of five years.
3. You have decided you would like to take a trip around the world at the end of ten years. You expect that the trip will cost $150,000. If you can earn 10% annually, how much would you have to invest at the end of each of the next ten years to accumulate the $150,000?

Solution 1

a. Future value of single amount $15,000, 8% compounded semiannually for ten years (4% × 20 periods)

Principal × Factor = Accumulated amount
$15,000 × 2.19112 = $32,866.80

b. Future value of an ordinary annuity ten payments, 12% interest

Annuity payment × Factor = Future value of annuity
$2,000 × 17.54874 = $35,097.48

2

a. Present value of six semiannual payments discounted at 5% each period

Annuity payment × Factor = Present value of annuity
$1,000 × 5.07569 = $5,075.69

b. Present value of single payment of $12,000 discounted at 12% for five years

Future value × Factor = Present value
$12,000 × .56743 = $6,809.16

3 Annual payment required to accumulate $150,000 by the end of ten years at 10% interest (future value of an annuity)

$$\text{Annuity payment} = \frac{\text{Future value of annuity}}{\text{Factor}}$$

$$\$9{,}411.81 = \frac{\$150{,}000}{15.93743}$$

QUESTIONS

1. Explain the difference between simple and compound interest. If all were equal, would you rather earn simple or compound interest?
2. Describe the differences among the following:
   a. Future value of a single amount
   b. Future value of an annuity
   c. Present value of a single amount
   d. Present value of an annuity
3. You are considering purchasing a car that will be financed through a bank loan. The bank loan will be for $7,000 at 12% for four years. Payments are to be made monthly. You are attempting to determine the amount of the monthly payments. Describe how you would solve this problem. It is not necessary to make the actual calculations.
4. Assume that you are determining the future value of an annuity. If the interest you can earn falls from 14% to 10%, what will happen to the future value of the annuity?
5. Your firm is considering establishing a fund that will be used in ten years to retire a large amount of long-term debt. You need to accumulate $5 million. You are contemplating making annual payments in a fund that will earn 7% and you want to know how much you must contribute to the fund. Describe how you would solve this problem. It is not necessary to make the actual calculations.
6. Assume that you are trying to determine the present value of an annuity. If the discount rate increases from 10% to 12%, what effect will this have on the present value of the annuity?

EXERCISES

Note: Because recognizing the type of problem you are being asked to solve is an important part of the learning process, the descriptions of the exercises and problems have been deliberately omitted.

E1 Determine the future value of $10,000 deposited in a savings and loan association for five years at 12% interest under each of the following compounding assumptions:

a. Annual compounding
b. Semiannual compounding
c. Quarterly compounding

E2 Assume that you invested $10,000 today at 10% interest, compounded annually. Several years from now, you had accumulated $25,937. For how many years did your investment compound?

E3 At the end of ten years, you will receive $25,000. If the interest rate is 10%, what is the present value of this amount, assuming that the interest is compounded:

a. annually?
b. semiannually?
c. quarterly?

E4 If you have a $2,000 investment that will accumulate to $3,077.25 at the end of five years, what rate of interest did you earn, compounded annually?

E5 You are approached with the following investment opportunity: If you invest $7,000 today, you will receive a guaranteed payment of $13,000 at the end of six years. If you desire a 14% rate of return for this type of investment, would you make the investment? Why or why not?

E6 Mr. Fumble is considering the following two investment alternatives:

a. $10,000 in a savings account earning interest at 10% compounded semiannually for four years.
b. $10,000 in a thrift account earning 11% simple interest for four years.
   Which one should he make?

E7 If $500 is invested at the end of each of the next four years at 8% interest, compounded annually, what will it accumulate to at the end of the seventh year?

E8 At the end of ten years, you are planning to take a cruise around the world on the QE2 that will cost $81,215. You are planning to save for this cruise by making yearly deposits in a savings and loan association. If you can earn 12% interest compounded annually and the payments are made at year-end, how much must each yearly deposit be?

E9 You wish to accumulate $226,204 by the end of ten years by making $3,000 quarterly deposits in your interest-earning money market account. What interest rate do you have to earn on a quarterly basis? All payments are made at quarter-end.

E10 What is the present value of receiving $10,000 at the end of each of the next 12 years at an interest rate of 8%, compounded annually?

E11 Charlie Kaplan is considering making a $95,076 investment that will provide a guaranteed return of $12,500 at the end of each of the next 15 years. What interest rate, compounded annually, will Charlie earn on this investment?

E12 Lisa West is considering whether to borrow $6,000. Under the proposed terms of the loan, she will have to repay the loan in 36 equal monthly payments, including interest at 2% per month on the unpaid principal. What will the amount of Lisa's monthly payments be?

E13 You are deciding whether to undertake the following investment: You must make an initial payment of $2,500 and then an additional $100 per quarter at the end of each of the next

40 quarters. If the investment earns 10%, compounded quarterly, how much will it be worth at the end of ten years?

E14 The Walbanger Corporation is planning a major plant expansion in eight years and wants to start accumulating the funds today in a special interest-earning account. The firm estimates that it will need \$2.5 million to finance the expansion. The company decides to invest 20% of the funds today and the rest on a quarterly basis for the next eight years. If the firm can earn 8%, compounded quarterly, what will be the amount of its quarterly deposits into the special fund? All payments are made at quarter-end.

E15 You have been offered the following investment opportunity: You will receive \$100,000 at the end of 15 years. In addition, you will receive semiannual payments of 4% of the \$100,000 until the \$100,000 is paid. If you want to earn 10% compounded semiannually, what is the maximum that you would pay for this investment?

E16 A local used-car dealer is advertising interest-free 48-month loans. After shopping around for comparable cars, you notice that his prices are higher than those of other dealers. Why do you think this is so?

PROBLEMS

PM-1 Paul Kupcheck's dog died recently. Paul, who loved his dog very much, had the foresight to take out an insurance policy on the dog's life. After the dog died, the insurance company offered Paul the following options:

a. Taking \$100,000 immediately.
b. Taking \$30,000 immediately and then receiving annual payments of \$11,067, to be made at the end of each of the next ten years.
c. Taking \$20,000 immediately and then receiving quarterly payments of \$5,196, to be made at the end of each quarter for the next five years.
d. Taking \$30,000 immediately, \$30,000 at the end of year 3, \$30,000 at the end of year 6, and another \$30,000 at the end of year 9.

REQUIRED: Assuming an interest rate of 10% per annum, which option should Paul take, and why?

PM-2 Bill Smith, an instructor of accounting, opens a tax-deferred retirement account with the university. He plans to deposit \$5,000 a year in that account, which will pay interest of 10%, compounded annually. He will make his first deposit at the end of the year and 19 additional deposits at the end of each of the following 19 years. (A total of 20 deposits will be made.)

REQUIRED:

1. How much cash will Bill Smith have accumulated in the account when he retires at the end of 20 years?
2. How much of the amount calculated above will be interest? Principal?
3. Bill plans to withdraw the funds in ten equal installments immediately after the end of the 20th year or at the beginning of the 21st year. Assuming an interest rate of 10%, how much will he be able to withdraw each year?

CHAPTER 10
INVESTMENTS IN OPERATING AND INTANGIBLE ASSETS

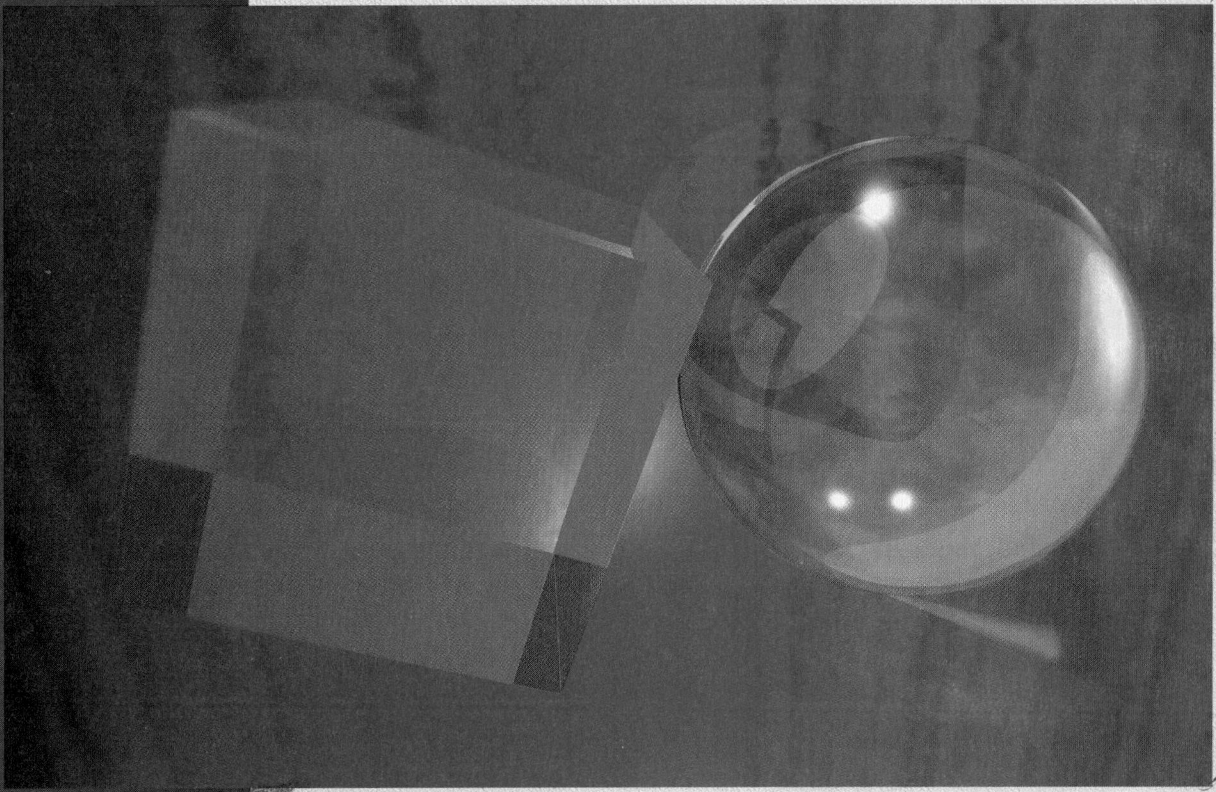

LEARNING OBJECTIVES

After studying this chapter, you should be able to:

1. Describe the nature and purpose of capital budgeting.
2. Explain accounting concepts and issues of noncurrent, nonmonetary assets.
3. Discuss the importance of differentiating between capital and revenue expenditures.
4. Measure and record the acquisition cost of property, plant, and equipment.
5. Explain the accounting concept of depreciation.
6. Compute depreciation expense using the methods acceptable for financial reporting purposes and for income tax purposes.
7. Identify depreciation problems relating to partial-year depreciation, revision of depreciation rates, and the effect of inflation.
8. Account for subsequent expenditures related to plant and equipment.
9. Account for disposal of assets.
10. Describe the components of an accounting system for operating assets.
11. Describe accounting concepts for intangible assets and their amortization.
12. Explain the accounting issues related to impairment of operating assets and understand that differences exist among countries in accounting for operating assets.

Scenario

Jane Goodman is the founder and president of a small high-tech start-up company called Energy Resources, Inc. Energy Resources has developed a new method of extracting methane gas from garbage and other waste materials using a technology that is more cost efficient than existing technologies.

The past three years have been spent developing the technology and testing the production method. Production is about to begin, and a number of large utilities in the state are quite interested in purchasing the methane gas from Energy Resources.

The production process is extremely capital intensive; to date Energy Resources has invested in over $20 million of equipment. Additional investments will be necessary as production increases, and Energy Resources will be forced to find additional sources of capital, including possibly going public.

Jane Goodman has called her financial advisors together to discuss the future of the company and how to best position it for future expansion and capital needs. Present at the meeting are her chief financial officer, Eric Levale; her treasurer, Bruce Synder; and one of the venture capitalists who has supplied start-up funds for the company, Emily Elias.

JANE GOODMAN: I continue to be concerned about our ability to show net income over the next few years. We have already signed up enough customers to generate sufficient revenues as soon as we start production. Yet, the heavy depreciation expense we are incurring because of our large plant and equipment investment will force us into a loss position. I think this will hurt our future ability to raise capital and even make it difficult to go public within the next few years.

ERIC LEVALE: Jane, you need to understand that we have decided to use accelerated depreciation methods for both financial reporting purposes and tax purposes. The result is that we can expect quite large depreciation charges for the next four to six years.

JANE GOODMAN: I understand that we are allowed to choose a different depreciation method for tax purposes than for financial reporting purposes. Why don't we switch to straight-line for financial reporting purposes? Won't that spread out our depreciation more evenly and at least help us smooth earnings?

BRUCE SYNDER: We could do that, Jane, but there are some conceptual reasons for using accelerated depreciation methods for financial reporting. The equipment we use is very technologically advanced, but it is subject to rapid obsolescence because new equipment is continually evolving. Our equipment loses most of its economic benefits in the early years; thus, we should take larger write-offs in those years.

JANE GOODMAN: Bruce, why do we have to be concerned about conceptual niceties? Can't we pick any of the several depreciation methods that are considered generally accepted? Let's pick the one that serves our current and future goals best.

BRUCE SYNDER: That's right Jane, but . . .

EMILY ELIAS: Look, this argument is not getting us anywhere. The most important issue is cash flow, not net income. When we want to go public, potential investors will be looking at cash flows, present and future, not some contrived number called net income.

BRUCE LEVALE: We have an obligation to prepare financial statements that present fairly our position and results of operations. We need to be concerned about how net income is determined.

EMILY ELIAS: I know that, Bruce, but cash flow is still the larger issue. Depreciation is not a cash expense and will not drain cash resources. In fact, to the extent that depreciation reduces taxes, it is really a source of cash. As long as the company is taking the maximum amount of depreciation for tax purposes and fully discloses what method it uses for financial reporting purposes, our potential investors will be comfortable.

After the meeting adjourned, Jane still felt uneasy about the entire depreciation issue. On one hand, she appreciates the chief financial officer's and treasurer's concern about accounting concepts, but the reality of the situation is that she as president has a number of conflicting choices to consider. She is certainly glad to have the freedom to choose among different accounting principles, but wonders about the efficiency of a system that allows so much choice and use of judgment.

In this chapter, the accounting concepts and procedures related to a firm's investment in property, plant, and equipment and intangible assets are explained. As the scenario indicated, accountants and other business executives must consider many different factors when selecting the most appropriate method to account for depreciation of plant and equipment. For example, the scenario briefly discussed the effect of depreciation on net income and cash flow. This chapter includes a discussion of depreciation and amortization concepts and the accounting for the disposition of these assets. Property, plant, and equipment and intangible assets, often referred to as *operating assets,* are part of a broader category of noncurrent, nonmonetary assets which includes those assets that do not represent specific claims to cash. **Operating assets** are the assets used to conduct business operations. The first part of this chapter presents an overview of capital budgeting, which is a significant part of management investment decisions.

operating assets

CAPITAL BUDGETING

Objective 1
Describe the nature and purpose of capital budgeting.

capital budgeting

Decisions relating to the acquisition of operating assets often are referred to as *capital budgeting decisions.* **Capital budgeting** is the process of planning, setting goals and priorities, arranging financing, and identifying criteria for making long-term investments. These decisions involve the outlay of a significant amount of cash and other resources that a firm must put at risk for a considerable period of time. These types of decisions take a great deal of managerial thought and time, and are closely linked to the financing decisions discussed in Part 4 of this book. While capital budgeting is a topic discussed in detail in Chapter 22, its close relationship to the accounting for investing activities makes it important for you to have a brief introduction to this topic.

Capital budgeting decisions involve choosing among competing investment alternatives. Even the largest firms have limited resources and must decide how best to invest them. For example, American Airlines must decide if and when to purchase new aircraft and must decide which competing aircraft, such as the MD-11, the Airbus 320, or the Boeing 747, to purchase. Further, as part of this decision, firms must decide how best to finance these purchases. That is, should they make an outright cash purchase, borrow the funds through a variety of different financing instruments such as leases or notes, and/or use the proceeds from the issuance of equity securities? In the American Airlines example, should the company purchase the planes outright with cash generated from operations, lease from the manufacturer or an aircraft leasing company, or perhaps even use the proceeds from a capital stock issue?

Capital budgeting decisions such as the purchase of operating assets or the purchase of another firm or part of another firm are basically cash flow decisions. The firm gives up a certain amount of cash flows today (the purchase price) and in the future (operating outlays) in the expectation of receiving a greater amount of cash flows in the future as the asset generates revenues and/or produces cost savings. To continue with the American Airlines example, American purchases airplanes because they generate cash flows in the form of ticket sales. Offset against these revenues are cash outflows associated with flying and maintaining the planes. Each type of plane American may be thinking about purchasing has different costs as well as different passenger capacities and different operating and maintenance costs. American's management would have to evaluate the comparative cash inflows and outflows associated with the different types of planes, and then consider its alternatives. This analysis, while not the only factor in the purchase decision, would play an important role.

Several models have been developed to help managers make capital budgeting decisions. These models and examples of their applications are discussed in Chapter 22.

NONCURRENT, NONMONETARY ASSETS

Objective 2
Explain the accounting concepts and issues related to noncurrent, nonmonetary assets.

tangible assets
natural resources
intangible assets

Noncurrent, nonmonetary assets often are categorized as either *tangible* or *intangible*. **Tangible assets** are assets that have physical substance and capabilities and include property, plant, and equipment and other similar productive assets. **Natural resources,** considered tangible assets, are physical substances that, when taken from the ground, produce revenues for a firm. Oil, natural gas, coal, iron ore, uranium, and timber are all examples of natural resources. **Intangible assets** are assets that have no physical substance; rather, they give the enterprise the right of ownership or use. Patents, copyrights, leaseholds, trademarks, and franchises are examples of intangible assets.

All noncurrent, nonmonetary assets have the following common characteristics:

1. They represent future economic services acquired for use in the business and usually are not held for resale.
2. The future services will benefit a firm for several accounting periods.
3. Except for land, the cost of consumed services is systematically allocated to the periods in which revenues are earned.

Future Services Not Held for Resale

Property, plant, and equipment, as well as other noncurrent, nonmonetary assets, are acquired by an enterprise because of their ability to generate future revenues and ultimately, cash flows. In effect, these assets are viewed as future service potentials that are consumed in the merchandising or production cycle. For example, accountants are not concerned with the physical properties of a computer-driven lathe but rather with its ability to produce a product that will provide future benefits.

Assets not currently being used in the merchandising or production process are not included in the property, plant, and equipment category. For example, a warehouse that is no longer being used or land held for speculation is not classified under the category of property, plant, and equipment. Rather, these assets are included in the long-term investment category on the balance sheet. Similarly, land that a real estate firm holds for resale is shown in the inventory section of the balance sheet.

Long-Term Nature of the Assets

The economic or service life of a noncurrent, nonmonetary asset is the period of time that a firm expects to receive benefits from the asset, which, in turn, depends on economic and legal factors. For example, a building generally has an economic life of at least 20 to 30 years; a delivery truck might have a life of 5 years or 100,000 miles. Intangible assets have a legal life as well as an economic life. In the U.S., a patent has a legal life as long as 17 years, but its economic life may be shorter. Generally, any such assets that have a life longer than one year are included in the noncurrent section of the balance sheet.[1]

Allocation of Benefits to Accounting Periods

The matching convention requires that the cost of expired benefits be matched with the revenues they produce. Accountants do this for all nonmonetary assets (other than land), whether classified as current or noncurrent. For example, when prepaid assets such as insurance are written off as their benefits expire, the asset is reduced and an expense is recorded. Further, as noted in Chapter 9, various cost flow assumptions are used to allocate the cost of goods available for sale to ending inventory and cost of goods sold. This chapter will consider how the cost of noncurrent, nonmonetary assets, such as property, plant, and equipment, are systematically allocated to accounting periods. Land is not depreciable because its benefits are considered to last indefinitely.

Listed below are the major categories of noncurrent, nonmonetary assets and the expenses associated with the cost allocation process:

Asset Category	*Expense*
Tangible assets	
Land	None
Plant, buildings, equipment, and other similar assets	Depreciation
Natural resources (e.g., oil and gas)	Depletion
Intangible assets	Amortization

1. Long-term prepaid expenses represent an exception to this. In Chapter 5, it was noted that prepaid expenses that benefit several years are still classified as current. Since these items are not material the financial statements are not distorted.

Major Accounting Issues Associated With Operating Assets

The major accounting issues related to operating assets include:

1. Distinguishing between capital and revenue expenditures.
2. Measuring and recording acquisition cost.
3. Measuring the costs of using the assets, including depreciation, depletion, and amortization expense and subsequent expenditures.
4. Accounting for the disposal of such assets.

The following sections of this chapter are concerned with these issues as they relate to property, plant, and equipment and intangible assets.

CAPITAL VERSUS REVENUE EXPENDITURES

Objective 3
Discuss the importance of differentiating between capital and revenue expenditures.

expenditure
capital expenditure
revenue expenditure

Throughout this book, the term **expenditure** has been used to refer to a payment of an asset or the incurrence of a liability in exchange for another asset or a service rendered. That is, the expenditure is made in cash or on credit and results in the firm's receiving another asset, such as a delivery truck, or using a service, such as the repair of a delivery truck. When an expenditure results in the acquisition of an operating asset, it is called a **capital expenditure.** Thus, when used in this sense, the term *capitalize* means to consider an expenditure an asset. When the expenditure results in the purchase of goods or services whose benefits are consumed in the current period, the expenditure is called a **revenue expenditure.** Revenue expenditures are current expenses such as ordinary repairs, maintenance, fuel, and other items required to keep the asset in normal working condition.

Exhibit 10-1 illustrates the difference between capital and revenue expenditures. This distinction is important in determining periodic net income, because capital expenditures affect several future accounting periods, whereas revenue expenditures affect only the current period. If an error is made and a capital expenditure, such as the purchase of equipment, is recorded as a revenue expenditure, the net income of both the current period and future periods will be misstated. The current period's income will be understated because the entire expenditure was expensed when only a portion of it, the current year's depreciation, should have been. Future periods' income will be overstated because no depreciation expense is recorded in those years. Over the useful life of the asset the error is self-correcting, but the interim incomes are misstated.

How do firms differentiate between capital expenditures and revenue expenditures? Clearly, the purchase of a delivery truck is a capital expenditure, whereas an engine tune-up is a revenue expenditure, but what about the purchase of a wastepaper basket or the major rebuilding of an engine? A firm's management develops guidelines or formal policies to handle these items so that consistent accounting policies are followed from year to year. Materiality plays a large role in the design of such policies; therefore most firms establish some minimum dollar limit for capital expenditures. The minimum can range from one hundred dollars for small companies to several thousand dollars for large companies.

This problem is further complicated because the same item sometimes can be considered a capital expenditure and at other times a revenue expenditure. For example, the labor cost to install a new machine is considered a capital expen-

Exhibit 10-1
Capital Versus Revenue Expenditure

Category	*Classification*	*Financial Statement Impact*	
Capital Expenditure	Asset	Balance Sheet —Current Period	Income Statement —Current and Future Periods
Revenue Expenditure	Expense	Income Statement —Current Period	

diture and part of the acquisition cost of the machine because the expenditure is necessary to get the machine ready for use. On the other hand, the labor cost after installation is a revenue expenditure because it is a normal and recurring cost. Thus, both the purpose and the nature of the expenditure must be considered when deciding whether an item is a capital or revenue expenditure.

MEASURING AND RECORDING THE ACQUISITION COST OF PROPERTY, PLANT, AND EQUIPMENT

Objective 4
Measure and record the acquisition cost of property, plant, and equipment.

According to the FASB, "the historical cost of acquiring an asset includes the costs necessarily incurred to bring it to the condition and location necessary for its intended use."[2] For property, plant, and equipment, this means that all the reasonable and necessary costs required to get the asset in place and ready for use are included in the acquisition cost. For example, the acquisition cost of equipment includes any transportation charges, insurance in transit, installation, testing costs, and normal repairs needed before putting the asset into service. However, the acquisition cost does not include unexpected costs, such as the cost of repairing damage incurred in transportation, purchase discounts lost, or, in most cases, interest costs. These costs, as well as normal repairs and maintenance expenses incurred in subsequent periods, are considered period expenses when incurred.

Each type of asset within the property, plant, and equipment category has special conventions regarding which items should be included in the acquisition cost. For example, when land is purchased, the various incidental costs that must be included in acquisition cost include real estate commissions, title fees, legal fees, delinquent property taxes, and the costs to drain, grade, and clear. Nevertheless, in many cases judgment must be used to determine which items should be capitalized.

Cash Acquisitions

Determination of the acquisition price is straightforward when property, plant, and equipment are purchased for cash. The acquisition price is the cash price paid plus all other costs necessary to get the asset ready to use. To illustrate, assume the Miller Company purchases an electronic molding unit from the Arnold Company. The price of the molding unit is $15,000, and the terms of sale are 2/10, n/30. Sales tax is 6%, freight charges are $850, and installation costs are $150. The total acquisition cost of the equipment is $16,600, computed as follows:

2. Financial Accounting Standards Board, Statement No. 34, *Capitalization of Interest Cost* (Stamford, Conn.: FASB, October 1979), par. 6.

Purchase price		$15,000
Less: 2% discount		(300)
Net price		$14,700
Add: Sales tax (6% of $15,000)	$900	
Freight charges	850	
Installation charges	150	1,900
Total acquisition cost		$16,600

Even if the discount is not taken, the $300 should not be included in the cost of the equipment; instead it should be considered interest expense.

Other Methods of Acquiring Property, Plant, and Equipment

A firm can acquire property, plant, and equipment in a variety of ways other than by a direct cash purchase. These include basket purchases, noncash exchanges, donations, self-construction, and leases. The determination of cost for these types of acquisitions is more difficult than for a straightforward cash purchase and thus warrants special attention.

Basket or Group Purchases. Whether or not the purchase is for cash, property, plant, and equipment often are purchased together in one lump sum. For example, when an existing building is purchased, the land on which that building is situated usually is purchased as well. The agreed-upon purchase price represents the total cost of both the building and the land, and the total purchase price may be more or less than the fair market values of the building and the land individually. As a result, the total purchase price must be allocated between the individual assets. This is especially important because the building is subject to depreciation, whereas the land is not. The allocation often is based on appraisals or real estate tax records.

To illustrate, assume that the H. Janees Company purchases an existing office building and site land. The total purchase price is $1 million. An independent appraiser determines that the building and land have fair market values of $900,000 and $300,000, respectively. The $1 million purchase price is allocated as follows:

	Appraised Value	*Relative Percentage of Total Appraised Value*[a]	*Purchase Price*	*Allocation of Cost*
Building	$ 900,000	75%	× $1,000,000 =	$ 750,000
Land	300,000	25	× 1,000,000 =	250,000
Total	$1,200,000	100%		$1,000,000

[a]$900,000/$1,200,000 = 75%; $300,000/$1,200,000 = 25%.

As this example illustrates, acquisition cost is the basis for recording assets, even though their individual appraised values may be higher.

Noncash Exchanges. In some situations, property, plant, or equipment is purchased through noncash transactions. For example, a firm may purchase land

and, in exchange, issue the firm's stock to the seller. In such transactions, the application of the cost method requires that the acquisition price of the asset be equal to any cash given plus the fair market value of any noncash consideration. However, if it is difficult or impossible to determine with reasonable accuracy the fair market value of the noncash consideration, the market value of the particular asset that is purchased should be used.

To illustrate, assume that the Orange Company, a large public company, purchases site land in downtown Los Angeles on which to build its corporate office. In exchange for the land, the Orange Company issues 10,000 shares of its capital stock to the seller. At the time of the transaction, Orange Company's stock is selling on a national exchange for $78 per share. To record this transaction, the Orange Company makes the following entry:

Land	780,000	
Capital Stock		780,000
To record purchase of land in exchange for capital stock. ($78 × 10,000 shares = $780,000)		

If the stock of the Orange Company is not traded on an exchange and it is otherwise difficult to determine its fair market value, the land should be recorded at its fair market value.

Donations. There are circumstances in which an enterprise may acquire its property, plant, or equipment through donation. For example, a city, county, or state may try to entice a large corporation to locate within its boundaries by donating site land for plant construction. In these rare situations, if the historical cost convention were strictly followed, accountants would assign a zero cost to the land. Because this would be clearly misleading, accountants record the donated asset at its fair market value at the time it is received. The credit portion of the entry is to a stockholders' equity account, Donated Capital.

self-constructed assets

Self-Constructed Assets. In some circumstances a building or a piece of equipment is constructed by the enterprise itself. The acquisition costs of **self-constructed assets** include materials and labor used directly in the construction process, as well as a portion of overhead. Overhead costs include supervisory labor, utilities, and depreciation on the factory building. In addition, as explained next, interest costs incurred during construction and related to the financing of the construction are part of the acquisition cost.

Capitalization of Interest. Interest is the time cost of money and generally is considered an expense in the period incurred. Thus, when property, plant, or equipment is purchased through the issuance of a note, the interest related to that note is expensed when incurred. However, in 1979, the FASB issued Statement No. 34 which required that in limited circumstances interest be capitalized, thus including it in the acquisition cost of certain noncurrent, nonmonetary assets.[3] In particular, Statement No. 34 requires that when an enterprise constructs its own assets, or has another entity construct an asset for it, and there is an extended period to get it ready for use, interest incurred in the construction should be capitalized as part of the acquisition cost of the asset. The following note from a recent report of Toys "R" Us illustrates a typical disclosure relating to capitalized interest:

3. Ibid.

Capitalized Interest

Interest on borrowed funds is capitalized during construction of property and is amortized by charges to earnings over the depreciable lives of the related assets. Interest of $12,237,000, $9,437,000, and $8,482,000 was capitalized during 1991, 1990, and 1989 respectively.[4]

The complex rules relating to capitalized interest are discussed more fully in intermediate accounting texts.

Leasing Operating Assets. In the last two decades leasing has been a popular method of acquiring and financing operating assets. For example, airlines such as American, Delta, and United often lease many of their airplanes. Leasing operating assets is, in many cases, similar to financing a purchase through a bank loan. Only a small downpayment is required followed by monthly payments extending several years.

The accounting concepts and methods relating to leases can be quite complicated. Briefly, if the lease is in substance a purchase, the asset acquired is recorded in the property, plant, and equipment section of the balance sheet. The resulting lease liability is shown as a liability (current for payments within the next twelve months and noncurrent for the remaining payments) on the balance sheet. The asset is then depreciated according to the methods discussed in the next part of this chapter.

THE ACCOUNTING CONCEPT OF DEPRECIATION

Objective 5
Explain the accounting concept of depreciation.

Depreciation probably is the most misunderstood and yet one of the most important of all accounting concepts that you will study. Perhaps the best way to understand the nature of depreciation is to explore what depreciation is and what it is not.

The Nature of Depreciation

depreciation

depletion

amortization

Operating assets are purchased because they represent future benefits. All of these assets, with the exception of land, eventually give up these benefits as the firm uses them to produce revenues. **Depreciation,** as discussed earlier in the text, is the process of allocating the cost of operating assets, such as plant and equipment, to the periods in which the enterprise receives benefits from these assets. **Depletion,** on the other hand, is the allocation of the cost of natural resources to the periods in which the enterprise receives the benefits from these assets. **Amortization** is the process of allocating the cost of intangible assets to the proper accounting periods. The concept of depreciation will be analyzed next, but the concepts and the analysis apply to depletion and amortization as well.

Depreciation Is an Allocation Process. From an accounting perspective, depreciation is an allocation process. That is, the cost of the asset is allocated to the periods in which the enterprise receives benefits from the asset. Although determining this expense rests on subjective estimates such as useful life and salvage

4. Toys "R" Us, Inc. and Subsidiaries, Notes to Consolidated Financial Statements, Year Ended February 1, 1992.

value, accountants believe that the benefits to financial statement users of recognizing depreciation expense outweigh the subjectivity of these estimates.

Depreciation Is Not a Valuation Concept. A common misconception is that depreciation represents a decrease in the value of an asset.[5] Accounting records do not attempt to show the current value of an asset, and depreciation is not used to value plant or equipment. For example, because of market conditions, the value of a building may increase substantially over a specific period of time. Nevertheless, accountants continue to depreciate the building because they know that eventually the building will give up its benefits to the firm, and the matching concept requires that as these benefits expire, they should be offset against the revenues they help produce. Also, the going concern principle assumes the productive assets are not purchased for resale but will be consumed in the operations of the business. Thus, depreciation is used to allocate the cost of an asset over its estimated useful life, regardless of current market value.

Depreciation Is Not a Direct Source of Cash. Another common misconception regarding depreciation is that it is a source of cash. Depreciation is a noncash expense because it does not require a cash payment at the time the expense is recorded. This is no different from the write-off of prepaid insurance. The cash outlay takes place when the payment for the related asset is made. As a result, depreciation does not result in a direct cash outflow or inflow, nor does the balance in the accumulated depreciation account represent cash. The balance in this account represents only the total of the expired costs of the particular asset and is recorded as a debit to Depreciation Expense and a credit to Accumulated Depreciation. Neither cash nor any other current asset or current liability account is involved. Unless a company purposely sets aside cash by taking it out of its regular cash account and putting it into a special fund, there is no guarantee that the firm will have the funds to replace its plant and equipment.

There is one way, however, in which depreciation is an indirect source of cash to a firm. Depreciation is a noncash expense that reduces taxable income. The lower the firm's income is, the lower the cash outflows for tax payments will be. Thus, the higher the depreciation expense for tax purposes, the more cash the firm will be able to retain through lower tax payments. Only in this way does depreciation affect cash flow. The effect of depreciation on income taxes was briefly introduced in Chapter 8, and will be explained in more detail later in this chapter.

What Causes Depreciation?

There are two factors that cause a tangible asset to give up its economic benefits: deterioration and obsolescence.

Physical Deterioration. Tangible assets deteriorate because of use, the passage of time, and exposure to the elements such as weather and other climatic factors. Clearly, a good maintenance policy can keep a firm's tangible assets in good repair and performing according to expectations. For example, a well-maintained airplane can last over 20 years. Even the best-maintained asset, however, will

5. From an economic viewpoint, this may be the case. From an accounting perspective, however, depreciation is strictly an allocation concept.

eventually wear out and need to be replaced. Thus, depreciation is recorded for all tangible assets other than land. In addition, depreciation is recorded for those items that are temporarily not in use. As time passes, physical deterioration takes place to a certain extent, regardless of use.

obsolescence

Obsolescence. **Obsolescence** is the process of becoming outdated, outmoded, or inadequate. Certain high-tech equipment, such as computers and other electronic devices, are subject to rapid obsolescence. Although these assets continue to perform, new technology makes them outdated in a relatively short period of time. Some assets, although technologically sound, become obsolete because they are no longer able to produce at the increased levels required as a result of expanded growth and sales.

Physical deterioration and obsolescence are factors that cause depreciation. It is not necessary to distinguish between them in determining depreciation. They are related primarily to determining the economic, or useful, life of assets and no attempt is made to separate the two factors in that determination.

METHODS OF COMPUTING DEPRECIATION

Objective 6
Compute depreciation expense using the methods acceptable for financial reporting purposes and for income tax purposes.

As is the case with determining the cost of ending inventory, there are acceptable alternative methods of computing periodic depreciation. The primary guideline is that the method be rational and systematic. The four most common depreciation methods are straight-line, units-of-production, and two accelerated methods, declining-balance and sum-of-the-years- digits. Management is free to choose any of these methods and can depreciate one class of assets using one method and another class of assets using a different method.

Factors in Computing Depreciation

Regardless of which depreciation method is used, certain factors in addition to the acquisition cost of the asset must be considered: (1) its residual or salvage value, (2) its depreciable cost, and (3) its estimated useful or economic life.

Residual or Salvage Value. The residual or salvage value is management's best estimate of what an asset will be worth at the time of its disposal—that is, the amount that the firm expects to receive or recover from the asset, less any cost to dispose of it. In many cases, a firm will assume that the cost of asset disposal is about equal to what it will recover and thus gives the asset a zero residual value. The residual value is obviously an estimate and often is based on management's past experience. Note that assets are not depreciated below their salvage value.

depreciable cost

Depreciable Cost. **Depreciable cost** is determined by subtracting an asset's estimated residual value from its acquisition cost. The starting point for most depreciation methods is the asset's depreciable cost. Often this amount is referred to as the asset's *depreciable base.*

estimated useful or economic life

Estimated Useful or Economic Life. The asset's **estimated useful or economic life** is a measure of the service potential that the current user may expect from the asset. Thus, when a used asset is purchased, it is assigned a life based on its use to the new owner, regardless of the life assigned to it by the former owner.

It can be in years, percentage rates, or units produced such as expected miles. For example, a delivery truck may have an estimated five-year life. A five-year life represents a 20% per-year depreciation rate (1/5 = 20%). In the case of a delivery truck, it may be appropriate to express its estimated life in terms of expected miles, such as 150,000 miles. All of these methods of expressing useful or economic lives are used for various assets.

Of the factors that affect the depreciation computation, the useful life of an asset is, perhaps, the most difficult to estimate. Information such as past experience, the asset's physical condition, the firm's maintenance policy, and the state of technology are all used to determine the estimate.

Methods of Computing Depreciation

The following data will be used to demonstrate the previous concepts, as well as the various depreciation methods:

Equipment purchase date	January 2, 1995
Acquisition cost	$40,000
Estimated residual value	$4,000
Depreciable cost	$36,000
Estimated useful life	5 years

straight-line depreciation

Straight-Line Depreciation Method. The **straight-line depreciation** method is the simplest of the various depreciation methods. Under this method, yearly depreciation is calculated by dividing an asset's depreciable cost by its estimated useful life. For example, using the above data, yearly straight-line depreciation is $7,200, calculated as follows:

$$\frac{\text{Cost} - \text{Salvage value}}{\text{Useful life}} = \frac{\$40{,}000 - \$4{,}000}{5} = \$7{,}200$$

When the straight-line method is used, the depreciable cost of the asset is spread evenly over its life; in this case at a uniform rate of 20% (1/5 = 20%). Therefore depreciation expense is the same each year, and by the end of the fifth year, the asset's book value has been reduced to its estimated residual value of $4,000. Even if the equipment is still being used after the fifth year, it is left at its book value of $4,000. These points are summarized in the depreciation schedule shown in Exhibit 10-2.

This example assumes that an entire year's depreciation is taken in the year of acquisition. A firm purchases assets at different times during the year, how-

Exhibit 10-2
Straight-Line Depreciation Schedule

Year	*Acquisition Cost*	*Yearly Depreciation*	*Accumulated Depreciation*	*Book Value*
1995	$40,000	$7,200	$ 7,200	$32,800
1996	40,000	7,200	14,400	25,600
1997	40,000	7,200	21,600	18,400
1998	40,000	7,200	28,800	11,200
1999	40,000	7,200	36,000	4,000

ever, and a full year's depreciation need not be taken on a midyear purchase. Furthermore, depreciation often is calculated monthly or quarterly for the preparation of interim financial statements. To illustrate the calculation of partial-year depreciation, assume that in the previous example the asset was purchased on April 1 rather than on January 2. In this case, only nine months of depreciation expense, or $5,400 ($7,200 × 9/12) is recorded on December 31, 1995.

Straight-line depreciation is widely used because of its simplicity and the fact that it allocates an equal amount of expense to each period of the asset's life. From a conceptual perspective, straight-line depreciation is most appropriate for an asset whose benefits diminish on a fairly uniform basis. Nevertheless, management can choose straight-line depreciation regardless of the pattern in which the asset's benefits are consumed.

units-of-production depreciation

Units-of-Production Depreciation Method. The cost of some assets can be more easily allocated according to their estimated production or output, rather than their estimated useful life. The **units-of-production depreciation** method assumes that the primary depreciation factor is use rather than the passage of time. Therefore, it is appropriate for assets such as delivery trucks and other equipment incurring substantial variations in use. To illustrate, assume it is estimated that the equipment described above will produce 120,000 units over its useful life. In this case, depreciation per unit is $0.30, determined as follows:

$$\frac{\text{Cost} - \text{Salvage value}}{\text{Estimated total production in units}} = \frac{\$40{,}000 - \$4{,}000}{120{,}000\ \text{units}} = \$0.30/\text{unit}$$

This cost per unit is applied to the actual units produced during each year. Exhibit 10-3 presents the asset's units-of-production depreciation schedule. It has been assumed that the 120,000 units produced by the equipment are spread over five years. However, when the units-of-production method is used, the life in years is of no consequence.

The units-of-production method requires that the production base, or output measure, be appropriate to the particular asset. For example, miles driven or flown might be most appropriate for a delivery truck or airplane, whereas units produced is most appropriate for a lathe or other equipment. The units-of-production method meets the criterion of being rational and systematic and provides a good matching of expenses and revenues for assets for which use is an important factor in depreciation. For static assets such as buildings, however, the units-of-production method is inappropriate.

Exhibit 10-3
Units-of-Production Depreciation Schedule

Year	*Acquisition Cost*	*Units Produced*	*Yearly Depreciation*	*Accumulated Depreciation*	*Book Value*
1995	$40,000	22,000	$6,600	$ 6,600	$33,400
1996	40,000	24,000	7,200	13,800	26,200
1997	40,000	18,000	5,400	19,200	20,800
1998	40,000	26,000	7,800	27,000	13,000
1999	40,000	30,000	9,000	36,000	4,000
		120,000			

accelerated depreciation methods

Accelerated Depreciation Methods. **Accelerated depreciation methods** allocate a greater portion of an asset's cost to the early years of its useful life and consequently less to later years. These methods are based on the assumption that some assets produce greater benefits or revenues in their earlier years, and thus a greater portion of their cost should be allocated to those years. The two most common accelerated methods are declining-balance and sum-of-the-years-digits.

declining-balance depreciation

Declining-Balance Depreciation Method. Under the **declining-balance depreciation** method, yearly depreciation is calculated by applying a fixed percentage rate to an asset's remaining book value at the beginning of each year. Because twice the straight-line rate generally is used, this method often is referred to as *double-declining-balance depreciation.*

In the example, the equipment has a five-year life. This results in an annual straight-line percentage rate of 20% (1/5 = 20%). The double-declining-balance rate is 40% (2 × 20%). Note that this rate is applied to the asset's remaining book value (cost less depreciation to date) at the beginning of each year and *not* to the depreciable cost (cost less salvage value). Salvage value is considered only in the last year of the asset's life, when that year's depreciation cannot be greater than the asset's book value at the beginning of the year minus its residual value. These points are illustrated in the depreciation schedule shown in Exhibit 10-4.

Partial-year depreciation can be calculated by using the declining-balance method. For example, if the equipment in the previous illustration is purchased on October 1 rather than on January 2, depreciation for the period between October 1 and December 31 is $4,000 ($16,000 × 3/12). In the second year, depreciation is calculated in the regular manner by multiplying the remaining book value of $36,000 ($40,000 − $4,000) by 40%.

The previous example assumed a depreciation rate equal to twice the straight-line rate. However, many firms use a rate equal to one and one-half times the straight-line rate; this is called *150% declining-balance depreciation*. It is calculated in the same manner as is double-declining-balance depreciation, except that the rate is 150% of the straight-line rate.

sum-of-the-years-digits

Sum-of-the-Years-Digits Depreciation Method. The **sum-of-the-years-digits** depreciation method is another variation of accelerated depreciation. Under this method, the asset's depreciable base (again, cost less salvage value) is multiplied by a declining rate. This rate is a fraction. The numerator is the number of years remaining in the asset's life at the beginning of the year, and the denominator is the sum of the digits of the asset's useful life. To demonstrate how this fraction is computed, assume that an asset has a five-year life. In the

Exhibit 10-4
Double-Declining Balance Depreciation Schedule

		Yearly Depreciation			
Year	*Cost*	*Computation (Beginning BV × Rate)*	*Expense*	*Accumulated Depreciation*	*Book Value (BV)*
1995	$40,000	$40,000 × .40	$16,000	$16,000	$24,000
1996	40,000	24,000 × .40	9,600	25,600	14,400
1997	40,000	14,400 × .40	5,760	31,360	8,640
1998	40,000	8,640 × .40	3,456	34,816	5,184
1999	40,000	*	1,184	36,000	4,000

*Depreciation expense in 1999 is the amount required to reduce the equipment's book value to its residual value of $4,000 ($5,184 − $4,000 = $1,184).

Exhibit 10-5
Sum-of-the-Years-Digits Depreciation Schedule

		Depreciation Calculation						
Year	Cost	Depreciable Cost (Does not change)	×	Fraction (declines)	=	Expense	Accumulated Depreciation	Book Value
1995	$40,000	$36,000	×	5/15	=	$12,000	$12,000	$28,000
1996	40,000	36,000	×	4/15	=	9,600	21,600	18,400
1997	40,000	36,000	×	3/15	=	7,200	28,800	11,200
1998	40,000	36,000	×	2/15	=	4,800	33,600	6,400
1999	40,000	36,000	×	1/15	=	2,400	36,000	4,000

first year, the rate is a fraction with a numerator of 5, the number of years remaining at the beginning of the year. The denominator is 15, or 1 + 2 + 3 + 4 + 5.[6] In the second year, the fraction is 4/15, and so forth. The depreciation schedule using the sum-of-the-years-digits method for the equipment appears in Exhibit 10-5.

As with the double-declining-balance method, the sum-of-the-years-digits method allocates more depreciation in early years and less in later years. Unlike the double-declining-balance method, however, the sum-of-the-years-digits method is calculated by applying a declining rate to a constant base; the asset's depreciable cost.

Partial-year depreciation can also be calculated under the sum-of-the-years-digits method. Under this method for partial-year depreciation, an overlap from each prior year must be included in the current year's calculation. For example, assume that the equipment is purchased on October 1 of the current year. In this case, the equipment is in use for only three months during the year, and the sum-of-the-years-digits depreciation is $3,000, calculated as follows:

$$\$3{,}000 = 3/12 \times \$12{,}000, \text{ or } 3/12 \times (\$36{,}000 \times 5/15)$$

In the second year, the depreciation expense of $11,400 must be calculated in two steps, as follows:

$$\begin{aligned} 9/12 \times (\$36{,}000 \times 5/15) &= \$\ 9{,}000 \text{ (overlap from year 1)} \\ 3/12 \times (\$36{,}000 \times 4/15) &= \underline{\ \ 2{,}400} \\ &\ \ \ \underline{\underline{\$11{,}400}} \end{aligned}$$

In the third year, the depreciation expense will again require two steps, as will every year to follow:

$$\begin{aligned} 9/12 \times (\$36{,}000 \times 4/15) &= \$7{,}200 \text{ (overlap from year 2)} \\ 3/12 \times (\$36{,}000 \times 3/15) &= \underline{\ \ 1{,}800} \\ &\ \ \ \underline{\underline{\$9{,}000}} \end{aligned}$$

6. The denominator of the fraction can easily be computed from the following formula:

$$N\frac{(N+1)}{(2)}$$

Where N equals the asset's life. In the above illustration, the denominator is calculated as follows:

$$5\frac{(5+1)}{(2)} = 5(3) = 15$$

If the asset's life is 10 years, the denominator is 55, calculated as follows:

$$10\frac{(10+1)}{(2)} = 10(5.5) = 55$$

Thus, depreciation expense for the remaining two years is calculated in a similar manner.

Both declining-balance and sum-of-the-years-digits are examples of accelerated depreciation. From a conceptual perspective, these methods are most appropriate for assets that give up a greater portion of their benefits in their early years. Therefore, most of the cost of these assets should be allocated to these same early years. High-tech products are examples of assets in which the decline of benefits is likely to follow such a pattern. Accelerated depreciation is also appropriate for assets that have a greater amount of repair expense in later years. This results in a reasonably constant expense related to the asset, because depreciation expense declines as repair expense increases.

Regardless of these conceptual arguments, the management of a firm can choose either accelerated-depreciation method for any depreciable asset. The only guideline is that the depreciation method be systematic and rational; as noted, all of the depreciation methods discussed so far meet this requirement. Furthermore, management can choose straight-line depreciation for financial reporting purposes and a form of accelerated depreciation for tax purposes. This allows a firm to report higher income for financial statement purposes and lower income for tax return purposes.

Comparison of Depreciation Methods

Exhibit 10-6 compares the four depreciation methods graphically, and Exhibit 10-7 compares them in tabular fashion. One of the most important points to note is that in all cases, total depreciation expense over all five years is $36,000. As a consequence, the balance in the accumulated depreciation account at the end of the fifth year is also $36,000 in all four cases. These exhibits show that each of the various ways to allocate the depreciable cost of $36,000 results in a different expense pattern within the five-year period. These differences are significant and can have a great effect on earnings for each year. For example, in the first year,

Exhibit 10-6
Graphical Comparison of Depreciation Methods

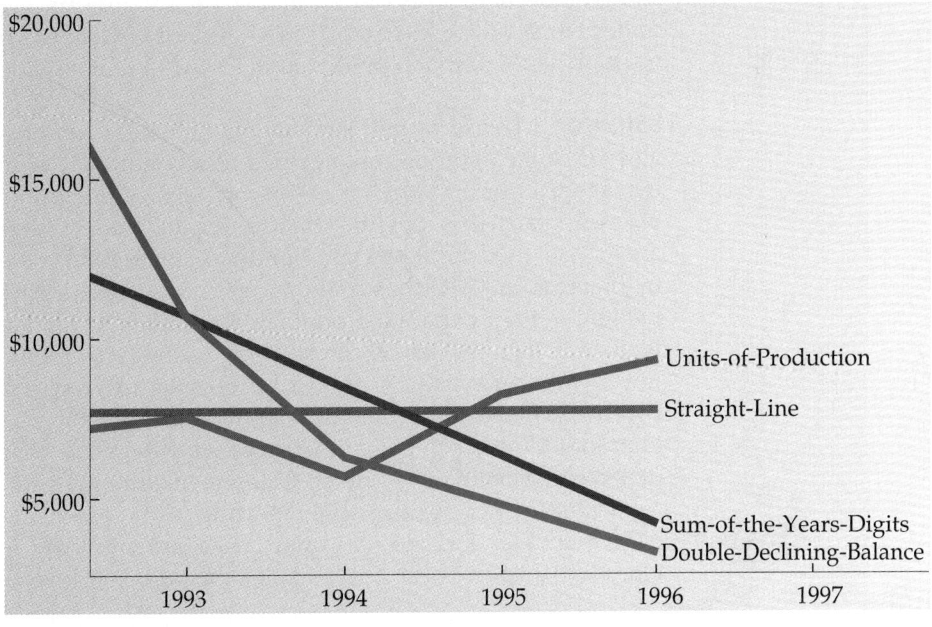

Exhibit 10-7
Comparison of Four Depreciation Methods

	Depreciation Expense			
Year	*Straight-line*	*Units-of-production*	*Double-declining-balance*	*Sum-of-the-years-digits*
1995	$ 7,200	$ 6,600	$16,000	$12,000
1996	7,200	7,200	9,600	9,600
1997	7,200	5,400	5,760	7,200
1998	7,200	7,800	3,456	4,800
1999	7,200	9,000	1,184	2,400
Total	$36,000	$36,000	$36,000	$36,000

	Accumulated Depreciation			
Year	*Straight-line*	*Units-of-production*	*Double-declining-balance*	*Sum-of-the-years-digits*
1995	$ 7,200	$ 6,600	$16,000	$12,000
1996	14,400	13,800	25,600	21,600
1997	21,600	19,200	31,360	28,800
1998	28,800	27,000	34,816	33,600
1999	36,000	36,000	36,000	36,000

double-declining depreciation is $16,000, and depreciation under the units-of-production method is only $6,600. These differences tend to lessen in the middle years of the asset's life and then to increase again in the last years of the asset's life. In the last years, however, the differences reverse. That is, at that time, straight-line and units-of-production depreciation is greater than depreciation under either of the accelerated methods. Of course, the pattern under the units-of-production method could vary under different situations.

Selecting a Depreciation Method for Financial Reporting Purposes. Because all four of the depreciation methods are generally accepted accounting methods, management has the option of selecting any of them for financial reporting purposes. In fact, it is possible to use one method to depreciate equipment and another method to depreciate buildings. Though all of these methods are used in practice, an AICPA survey of 600 companies shows that the straight-line method is by far the most popular. Theoretically, the best depreciation method is the one that allocates the cost of the individual asset to the years of its useful life in the same pattern as the benefits or revenues that the asset produces. Because different assets have different revenue patterns, all of the methods are appropriate in specific circumstances. However, the theoretical soundness of a depreciation method is not an absolute requirement for its use. In choosing a particular method for financial reporting purposes, management usually is more concerned with practical motives, such as simplicity and financial statement effects. To a large extent, this explains the popularity of straight-line depreciation.

Exhibit 10-8
Toys "R" Us Footnote Disclosures

Property and Equipment
Property and equipment are recorded at cost. Depreciation and amortization are provided using the straight-line method over the estimated useful lives of the assets or, where applicable, the terms of the respective leases, whichever is shorter.

(in thousands)	*Useful Life (in years)*	*February 1, 1992*	*February 2, 1991*
Land		$ 599,886	$ 479,802
Buildings	20-50	1,164,323	961,892
Furniture and equipment	5-20	695,820	581,971
Leaseholds and leasehold improvements	12½-50	419,457	364,065
Construction in progress		83,032	66,334
Leased property under capital leases		21,172	21,172
		$2,983,690	$2,475,236
Less accumulated depreciation and amortization		425,603	333,895
		$2,558,087	$2,141,341

It is easy to compute and results in a constant expense spread over the asset's useful life.

Because the choice of depreciation methods can have a significant effect on a firm's financial statements, current accounting rules require that a firm disclose how it depreciates its assets. This disclosure usually is made in the footnote to the financial statements that summarizes the firm's accounting policies. Such a footnote from the Toys "R" Us financial statements reads in part as shown in Exhibit 10-8.

Selecting a Depreciation Method for Tax Purposes. Since 1981, Congress has made several significant changes in the depreciation rules for tax purposes. The changes were made in the name of tax reform and tax simplification, but in some ways they have served to confuse the tax rules related to depreciation. One result is that assets placed in service at various times during the 1980s will be depreciated under different tax rules.

Under the tax laws put into place by the Tax Reform Act of 1986, depreciable business property other than real estate is assigned to one of six classes. These classes, called *recovery periods,* prescribe the length of time over which various assets can be written off or depreciated. Current recovery periods range from three to twenty years. Primary types of assets included in each are:

- The *three-year class* includes small tools.
- In the *five-year class* are light trucks, automobiles, computer equipment, typewriters, calculators, and copiers. Also included: assets used in research and development, oil and gas drilling, construction, and the manufacture of certain products, such as chemical and electronic components.
- Assets in the *seven-year class* include office furniture and fixtures and most other machinery and equipment.

- There are also *ten-*, *fifteen-*, and *twenty-year classes*, but only a small number of assets—including land improvements, such as drainage pipes—fall into these categories.[7]

The Tax Reform Act of 1986 developed the Modified Accelerated Cost Recovery System (MACRS) of depreciation. Under this system, assets in the three-, five-, and seven-year classes can be depreciated using the double-declining-balance method. Assets in the other classes must be depreciated using the 150% declining-balance method. The tax rules for depreciation also involve a rule called the *half-year convention:* for tax purposes, property is depreciated for half the taxable year in which it is placed in service, regardless of when use actually begins. Finally, the salvage or residual value of the asset can be ignored for tax purposes. In the tax code, computations are simplified by the use of percentage depreciation rates that accomplish the tax depreciation methods just described.

To illustrate, assume that a piece of equipment costing $100,000 is purchased and placed into service in 1995. For tax purposes, the asset is placed in the five-year class. Straight-line depreciation with the half-year convention is used for financial reporting purposes for all depreciable assets. However, MACRS depreciation is used for tax purposes. Depreciation expense for the asset's life for both tax and financial reporting purposes is calculated in Exhibit 10-9.

As indicated in Exhibit 10-9, the depreciation for tax purposes provides substantial tax benefits in the asset's first years. Under the tax method, total depreciation expense for the first three years equals $71,200, as compared to $50,000 for financial reporting purposes. Higher depreciation expense for tax purposes means lower taxable income and thus lower tax payments. In later years, these benefits reverse—depreciation for financial reporting purposes exceeds that for tax purposes. However, the fact that tax payments are deferred until later years benefits the firm, since it is able to invest and earn a return on the cash saved through lower taxes in the early years.

OTHER PROBLEMS RELATED TO DEPRECIATION

Objective 7
Identify depreciation problems relating to partial-year depreciation, revision of depreciation rates, and the effect of inflation.

In order to explain depreciation concepts, the examples and illustrations so far have been purposely simplified. Actual businesses confront a number of practical problems related to depreciation, including partial-year's depreciation, revision of depreciation patterns, and the effect of inflation on depreciation.

Depreciation for a Partial Year

The section explaining how depreciation is calculated under the four depreciation methods included an explanation of how partial-year depreciation is computed to the nearest full month.[8] Because depreciation is inherently an estimate, many firms do not feel that it is necessary to calculate partial-year depreciation so precisely. Two common conventions are used most often. Under one convention, depreciation expense is calculated for the entire year if the asset is purchased in the first half of the year. If the asset is purchased in the last half of the year, no

7. *The Price Waterhouse Personal Tax Adviser* (New York: Simon & Schuster, 1990). Reprinted with permission of Price Waterhouse and Simon & Schuster.

8. In working the exercises and problems at the end of the chapter, unless otherwise stated, you should compute partial-year depreciation based on the nearest full month since the purchase or up to the full month closest to the time of disposal.

Exhibit 10-9
Comparison of Depreciation for Tax and Financial Reporting Purposes

	Tax Reporting Double-declining-balance Depreciation (MACRS)		Financial Reporting Straight-line Depreciation	
Year	Computation[a]	Expense	Computation[a]	Expense
1993	$100,000 × 20%[b]	$ 20,000	$100,000/5 years × 1/2	$ 10,000
1994	$100,000 × 32%	32,000	$100,000/5 years	20,000
1995	$100,000 × 19.2%	19,200	$100,000/5 years	20,000
1996	$100,000 × 11.52%	11,520	$100,000/5 years	20,000
1997	$100,000 × 11.52%	11,520	$100,000/5 years	20,000
1998	$100,000 × 5.76%	5,760	$100,000/5 years × 1/2	10,000
	Total depreciation	$100,000		$100,000

[a]Assumes an asset cost of $100,000 and an estimated useful life of five years.
[b]These are the MACRS percentage rates for an asset with a five-year life.

depreciation is taken. Under another convention, six months of depreciation is taken in the year of purchase and six months in the year of retirement or disposal, regardless of the date of actual purchase or disposal. As noted previously, this is referred to as the *half-year convention,* and is built into the IRS tax depreciation tables for assets other than real estate.

Revision of Depreciation Patterns

Factors such as useful economic life and residual value are estimates made at the time the asset is purchased. Later events may require that these original estimates be revised. For example, improved maintenance techniques may increase the life of an airplane an additional five years beyond the estimate made at the time it was purchased. Failure to revise these estimates for the new information will cause a mismatching of revenue and expense.

A change in estimate is not an error correction. As noted, new events or new information may require a revision of the original estimates. Because of this, changes in depreciation estimates, such as a revision in useful life, are handled by spreading the remaining undepreciated base (undepreciated cost or book value less estimated residual value) of the asset over the years of the new remaining useful life. That is, there is no correction of prior years' financial statements; only current year's and future years' depreciation are affected. This treatment is required by the accounting profession in APB Opinion No. 20.

To illustrate, assume that on January 2, 1994, the Pen and Ink Company purchases a piece of equipment for $12,000 with a $2,000 residual value. The firm estimates that the equipment will have a useful life of ten years and elects to use straight-line depreciation. At the beginning of the asset's fourth year of life, January 2, 1997, management decides that ten more years, instead of seven, still remain in the life of the asset. Further, it is estimated that the asset's residual value will be $1,000 at the end of its new remaining useful life. The first step in determining the revised depreciation pattern is to calculate the asset's undepreciated cost, or book value, at the beginning of the fourth year, January 2, 1997. From that value, $9,000 in this case, the new estimated residual value of $1,000 is subtracted. The resulting amount is the remaining depreciable base, which is then spread over the new remaining life. This is done as follows:

Asset's historical cost:	$12,000
Asset's depreciable cost as of 1/2/94:	
$12,000 − $2,000 = $10,000	
Yearly depreciation: $10,000/10 years = $1,000	
Accumulated depreciation as of 1/2/97: $1,000 × 3 =	(3,000)
Book value as of January 2, 1997	$ 9,000
Remaining depreciable base	
($9,000 − $1,000 residual value)	$ 8,000
Remaining life based on new estimate	10 years
Yearly depreciation for 1997 and afterwards:	
$8,000/10 years =	$800

A change in the estimated lives of the depreciable assets of a firm can have a significant effect on the firm's earnings in current and future periods. For example, in 1987 General Motors increased the lives of its tools, dies, and other equipment used to manufacture automobiles. This change is estimated to reduce GM's pretax expenses by $1.5 billion a year. This is only one example of a company changing the lives of its assets.

A change in depreciation method used for financial accounting purposes is another event that will revise the future depreciation pattern. Under current accounting rules, a change in method, such as a change from sum-of-the-years-digits to straight-line depreciation, requires a catch-up adjustment that affects the current period's income. This catch-up adjustment is classified as a separate item on the income statement labeled as a cumulative effect of an accounting change.

To illustrate, assume that on January 2, 1994, a firm purchased a piece of equipment at a cost of $100,000. The equipment has a useful life of ten years with no residual value. In 1994 and 1995, the firm used double-declining balance depreciation, but at the beginning of 1996, the third year of the asset's life, the firm switched to straight-line. The difference of $16,000 between what the depreciation was for the first two years with double-declining balance and what it would have been with straight-line is a cumulative effect of an accounting change, as calculated in Exhibit 10-10.

The cumulative effect of $16,000 can be calculated either by comparing the difference in the total depreciation expense for the two years or by comparing the asset's net book value under each of the depreciation methods. Both of these methods are shown in Exhibit 10-10. Finally, the $16,000 gain, net of any tax effect, is shown on the income statement on a separate line below income or loss from operations as the cumulative effect of the change. The depreciation expense for 1996 calculated using the straight-line method is $10,000.

Arbitrary Allocation

Financial statements are based on many estimates as costs are allocated to accounting periods. Depreciation expense, no matter how it is calculated, is an example of an allocation that is based on estimates. Even though some of the methods, such as double-declining-balance and sum-of-the-years-digits, appear quite scientific, they are based on estimated lives and salvage values. In analyzing financial statements with ratios and other techniques, it is important to keep in mind that these estimates do limit the usefulness of the financial information. Without making such estimates, however, it would be impossible to prepare periodic financial statements.

Exhibit 10-10

Difference in Depreciation

	Double-declining-balance	Straight-line	Difference
Year 1, 1994	\$20,000[a]	\$10,000[c]	\$10,000
Year 2, 1995	16,000[b]	10,000	6,000
	\$36,000	\$20,000	\$16,000

Difference in Book Value

	Double-declining-balance	Straight-line	Cumulative Effect of Accounting Change
Historical cost	\$100,000	\$100,000	\$ 0
Accumulated depreciation	36,000[d]	20,000[d]	16,000
Book value	\$ 64,000	\$ 80,000	\$16,000

[a]\$100,000 × .20 = \$20,000
[b](\$100,000 − \$20,000) × .20 = \$16,000
[c]\$100,000 × .10 = \$10,000
[d]From previous schedule.

Inflation and Depreciation

Historical cost is the primary basis for recording assets; periodic depreciation is based on the historical cost of such assets. Many people feel that when price levels rise in the economy, historical-cost depreciation overstates profits and does not provide a reasonable picture of a firm's financial position.

To illustrate, assume that a firm purchases a piece of equipment for \$2 million in 1987. Straight-line depreciation is used throughout the asset's ten-year life. In 1997, the firm purchases a similar asset as a replacement. The cost of the new machine is \$4 million. In this situation, many accountants feel that the \$2 million of depreciation is not adequate and that depreciation expense should have totaled the \$4 million replacement cost, the expenditure the firm must ultimately make to maintain its productive capacity. Using this replacement cost method would mean that depreciation expense increases as the asset's current cost increases.

Because of the difficulty in obtaining objective data on current costs, it is not the primary method used in recording assets; rather, the historical cost of the assets is maintained in the records. Because of the conceptual importance of current cost data, however, the FASB urges public companies to make supplemental disclosure of certain current cost data. With respect to productive assets, large firms are urged to disclose the current cost of their property, plant, and equipment and the related depreciation expense based on current costs. As noted previously, not many companies provide these supplemental disclosures. In countries where inflation is a chronic economic problem, however, it is often required to disclose inflation-adjusted data.

ACCOUNTING FOR SUBSEQUENT EXPENDITURES

Objective 8
Account for subsequent expenditures related to plant and equipment.

Subsequent expenditures made on property, plant, and equipment can be in the form of either capital or revenue expenditures. As noted, the distinction between the two is often hazy and depends on the accounting policies developed by management. However, the distinction is important because it affects the determination of current and future periods' income.

Revenue Expenditures

repair or maintenance

Revenue expenditures are expenditures whose benefits are used up or consumed in the current period. In terms of plant and equipment, revenue expenditures usually are called *repairs and maintenance.* Technically, a **repair or maintenance** is an expenditure that maintains the asset's expected level of service or output, neither extending its useful life nor increasing the quantity or quality of its output. These expenditures are accounted for in the current period by debiting Repairs and Maintenance or a similar expense account.

Capital Expenditures Subsequent to Purchase

additions
betterments
extraordinary repairs

Capital expenditures are those that benefit several accounting periods. In terms of plant and equipment, capital expenditures made in periods subsequent to putting an asset in service are considered additions, betterments, or extraordinary repairs. **Additions** are enlargements, such as the addition of a new wing to an existing plant. **Betterments** are improvements to existing assets, such as the installation of a computer-controlled temperature-monitoring system in a department store. **Extraordinary repairs** are a major reconditioning or overhaul of existing assets, such as a major overhaul or installation of a new engine. Regardless of how these expenditures are described, they either extend the asset's useful life or increase the quantity or quality of its output. Accounting for these expenditures often is accomplished by debiting the asset's accumulated depreciation account or, in the case of an addition, debiting the asset account itself. In either case, Cash or an appropriate liability account is credited. The asset's book value is increased by the amount of the capital expenditure, and subsequent depreciation expense is revised.

DISPOSAL OF OPERATING ASSETS

Objective 9
Account for disposal of assets.

Disposal of operating assets can occur through retirement of discarded assets, sales, involuntary conversions, or trade-ins. No matter how the disposal is accomplished, the accounting procedures are quite similar. Depreciation must be recorded up to the date of disposal and, where appropriate, a gain or loss must be recorded on the disposal. These concepts are explained by demonstrating the accounting for the sale and trade-in of operating assets.

Sale of Operating Assets

In some cases, operating assets are sold, rather than retired for no value. An asset can be sold during its useful life when it has a book value greater than its residual value, or at the end of its life when it is fully depreciated. In either situation, a gain or loss will usually result. A gain occurs if the cash or other assets received (referred to as *consideration*) are greater than the book value at the time of sale.

Exhibit 10-11
Sale of Delivery Truck

Case 1: Sale Price $7,000

Cash	7,000	
Accumulated Depreciation	30,000	
Delivery Truck		35,000
Gain on Disposal of Asset		2,000
To record $2,000 gain on disposal of asset:		
Cash Received	$7,000	
Book Value of Delivery Truck	5,000	
Gain	$2,000	

Case 2: Sale Price $4,000

Cash	4,000	
Accumulated Depreciation	30,000	
Loss on Disposal of Asset	1,000	
Delivery Truck		35,000
To record a $1,000 loss on disposal of asset:		
Cash Received	$4,000	
Book Value of Delivery Truck	5,000	
Loss	($1,000)	

Conversely, a loss occurs if the consideration received is less than the book value at the time of sale.

To illustrate, assume that a delivery truck with a historical cost of $35,000 and accumulated depreciation to date of $30,000 (book value of $5,000) is sold for cash, in case 1 for $7,000 and in case 2 for $4,000. The journal entries are shown in Exhibit 10-11. As the journal entries show, both the cost of the asset and the amount of related accumulated depreciation are removed from the books. For simplicity, these examples assume that depreciation has been recorded up to the date of the disposal of the delivery truck. However, because depreciation normally is recorded as an adjusting entry at a date (quarter or year-end) other than the sale date, an entry is required to record the depreciation expense from the date of the previous depreciation entry to the date of the sale.

Trade-in of Operating Assets

Depreciable assets, such as automobiles, computers, and copy machines, are often traded in for similar new assets. In most cases, the trade-in allowance on the asset may be considerably different from its book value. If the trade-in allowance is higher than the book value, a gain will be realized on the trade-in. However, care must be exercised when using a trade-in allowance to measure a gain or loss. Dealers such as automobile companies often set an unrealistically high list price in order to offer an inflated trade-in allowance. This is done to make the transaction appear more attractive to the buyer.

The accounting procedures that govern trade-ins are quite complex, but for present purposes they can be stated as follows:

1. Realized gains on the trade-in of assets for similar assets usually are not recognized as accounting gains. The cost basis of the new asset is the book value of the old, plus the additional cash or other consideration paid.
2. Realized losses on the trade-in of similar assets are always recognized.[9]

Both of these situations will be described next.

Gain Realized But Not Recognized. Realized refers to an actual economic gain, while recognized refers to the fact that the gain is recorded as such in the accounting records. To illustrate the accounting procedures when a gain on a trade-in is realized but not recognized, assume that the Jackson Company trades in a delivery truck for a new one. At the time of the trade-in, the old delivery truck has a historical cost of $40,000 and accumulated depreciation to date of $30,000 (book value equals $10,000). The new truck has a list price of $65,000 and the dealer gives the Jackson Company a trade-in allowance for the old truck of $14,000, which is assumed to be equal to its fair market value at that time. Thus, a cash payment of $51,000 ($65,000 − $14,000) is made for the difference. Since the asset was traded in for a similar one, the realized gain of $4,000 (trade-in allowance of $14,000 less book value of $10,000) is not recognized in the accounting records, and the cost basis of the new truck is $61,000, computed as follows:

Book Value of Old Truck	$10,000
Cash Paid	51,000
Cash Basis of New Truck	$61,000

The entry to record this trade-in is:

Delivery Truck, New	61,000	
Accumulated Depreciation	30,000	
Delivery Truck, Old		40,000
Cash		51,000
To record trade-in of old delivery truck and purchase of new delivery truck.		

Though it may seem strange that a realized gain is not recognized in the accounting records, the view of the Accounting Principles Board (APB) is that revenue should not be recognized merely because one productive asset is exchanged or substituted for a similar one. According to the APB, revenue flows from the production and sale of the goods and services made possible by the new asset, not from the exchange of one asset for another.[10] In effect, the realized gain of $4,000 is just postponed. It ultimately is realized through lower depreciation charges in future years, which are based on a cost of $61,000 rather than the list price of $65,000. Furthermore, because the new asset has a lower book value than it would have if the realized gain of $4,000 had been recognized, a larger gain or a smaller loss will be recognized if and when it is finally disposed of in a non-trade-in manner.

9. American Institute of Certified Public Accountants, Accounting Principles Board, Opinion No. 29, *Accounting for Nonmonetary Transactions* (New York: AICPA, 1973), par. 22.
10. Ibid., par. 16.

Loss Realized and Recognized. Because of the conservatism concept in accounting, any realized loss on a trade-in must be recognized in the accounting records. For example, assume the same facts as in the previous example, but now the dealer offers a trade-in allowance of only $8,000, which is assumed to be equal to the asset's fair market value. As a result, a loss of $2,000 ($10,000 book value less $8,000 trade-in allowance) is both realized and recognized. Because the trade-in allowance is only $8,000, a cash payment of $57,000 must also be made by the Jackson Company. Finally, the new asset cannot be recorded at a value higher than the fair market value of $65,000. Failure to record the loss would inflate the cost of the new asset above its present fair value. The appropriate entry is:

Delivery Truck, New	65,000	
Accumulated Depreciation	30,000	
Loss on Disposal	2,000	
Delivery Truck, Old		40,000
Cash		57,000
To record $2,000 loss on trade-in and purchase of new delivery truck.		

ACCOUNTING INFORMATION SYSTEMS FOR OPERATING ASSETS

Objective 10
Describe the components of an accounting system for operating assets.

The accounting functions you have just studied are usually performed by a fixed or operating-asset accounting system. The system may be manual or it may be computer based. The objectives of the system are the same in either case; to provide reasonable assurance that: (1) control over operating assets is adequate, (2) proper authorization is obtained for all operating asset transactions, and (3) operating asset records, including depreciation, are accurate. Operating asset accounting systems usually process a very limited number of high dollar volume transactions. Because of the high dollar amounts of the transactions, proper control is critical.

Operating Asset Controls

Several techniques are used to maintain control over operating assets. Physical security is often used as a preventive control—only authorized employees are able to gain access to these assets. For example, manufacturing firms often store small, expensive tools in a locked storeroom; employees must check the tools out when needed.

Complete inventory records provide detective and corrective controls. The inventory records should identify the location of each operating asset and, when appropriate, the individual responsible for the asset. Every operating asset should have an asset tag which provides the cross reference to the inventory record. Operating asset accountants or accounting clerks periodically take a physical inventory and verify that the operating assets are in the proper location and that they are in the custody of the appropriate individual. This control does not prevent the misuse, misplacement, or theft of operating assets. It does however, identify missing assets and assets that have been relocated.

Adequate insurance coverage is another important control. Insurance can not prevent the loss or destruction of an asset. However, adequate coverage can prevent the economic loss associated with the physical loss of the asset. Accountants and auditors periodically review the adequacy of insurance coverage.

Authorization controls are also used to control operating asset transactions. Because the acquisition of an operating asset may represent a substantial expenditure, high-level approvals are often required before an operating asset is purchased. Firms may also require competitive bids from potential vendors to identify the best source for the asset. Approval is also required before assets are retired. Auditors review the minutes of board of director meetings to find documentation of purchase and retirement approvals for major operating assets. The accounting system must provide reasonable assurance that transactions, once authorized, are properly recorded in the operating asset records.

Operating Asset Records and Systems

Operating-asset records may be maintained on asset ledger cards by small firms that use a manual operating-asset accounting system, or by a computer-based operating asset accounting system in larger organizations. The type of information, and the accounting processes, are the same in either case. Exhibit 10-12 illustrates the basic components of a computer-based operating-asset accounting system.

Exhibit 10-12
Operating-Asset Accounting System Flowchart

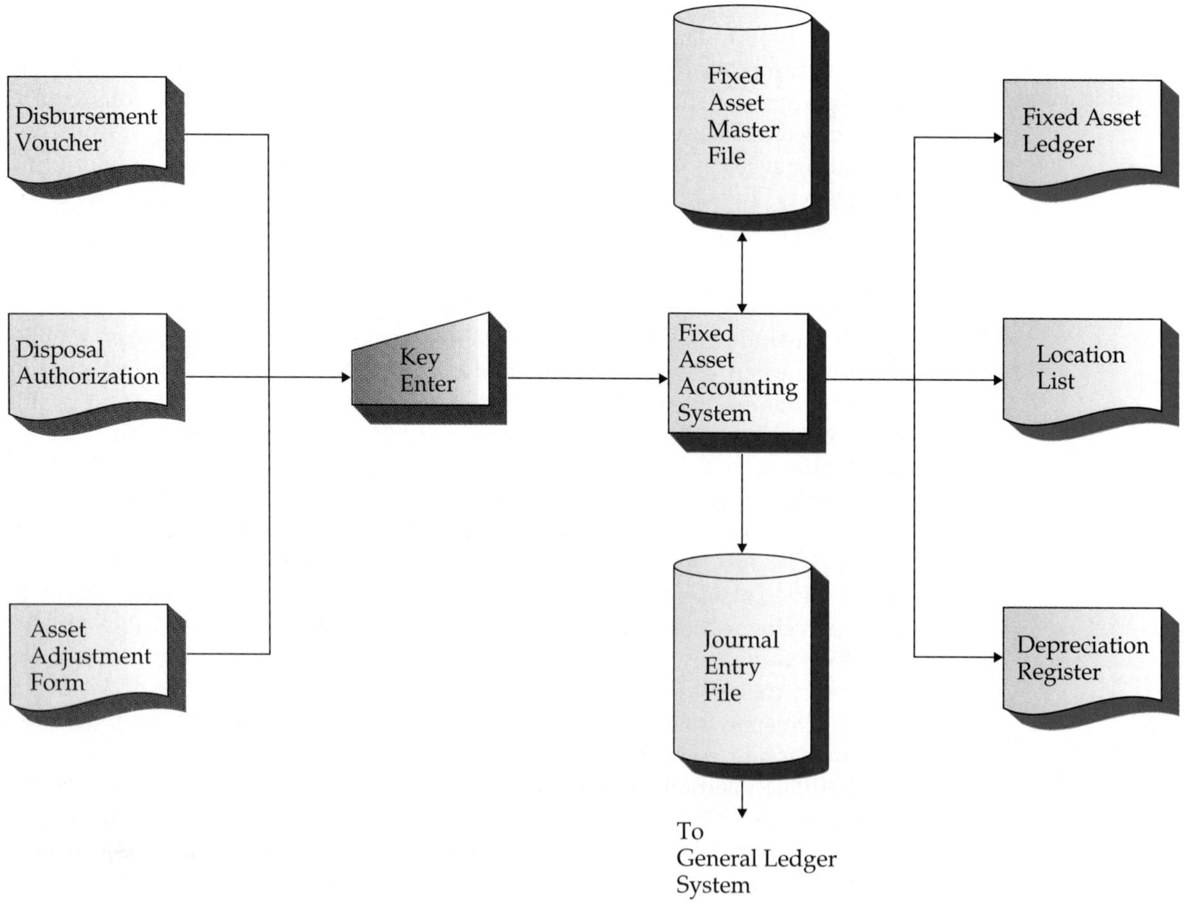

The three major sources of input into this system are disbursement vouchers, disposal authorizations, and asset adjustment forms. The disbursement voucher contains the information that is needed to record the initial acquisition of an asset. This information includes: the asset tag number, asset description, cost, date placed in service, depreciation method, expected life, and expected salvage value. The disposal authorization provides evidence of managements' approval for the disposal of an asset, indicates the date and method of disposal, and proceeds received from disposal. The asset adjustment form is used to document changes in depreciation assumptions, for example, a change in life or salvage value; and to document additional capital expenditures associated with an asset.

The operating-asset accounting system updates the operating-asset master file (using the data provided on the input forms), prints several different reports, and generates the necessary general ledger journal entries. In addition, the system periodically computes depreciation for all operating assets and generates the depreciation journal entries. The most common reports printed by an operating-asset accounting system are the operating asset ledger, a location list, and a depreciation register. The **operating-asset ledger** is a report that lists each operating asset and its corresponding acquisition date, cost, book value, salvage value, depreciation method, and life. The **location list** identifies each asset and its corresponding custodian and location. This report is normally printed in location sequence and is used when the physical asset inventory is taken. The **depreciation register** lists the current deprecation expense as computed for each operating asset. This report contains the same information that is included in the general ledger journal entries that are generated by the operating-asset accounting system.

operating-asset ledger

location list

depreciation register

The previous chapter discussed the various methods of organizing data using traditional files structures. Operating-asset master files can be organized as sequential files or as index-sequential files. However, a new data organization tool, the data base management system, is replacing traditional file structures in almost all accounting applications. A **data base management system** is a program that accesses data for other application programs and users, and manages the physical storage of the data. Data base management systems make it possible for diverse users and application programs to access the same set data and thus eliminate the need for each user and application to maintain their own traditional files. One of the most powerful and common data base forms is the **relational data base.** A relational data base organizes data into tables and provides users and application programs with access to the necessary rows and columns of data. Each row in a relational table represents a unique entity, for example, a specific operating asset. Each column in the table represents a specific attribute of the entity being represented. For example, some of the columns in an operating-asset relational data base would include the asset identification number, asset description, and asset cost. Exhibit 10-13 illustrates a relational operating-asset data base. The relational database provides users and application programs with a great deal of data access flexibility. For example, the location list could be prepared by accessing the asset number, asset description, custodian and location columns in the data base for all of the rows. Other columns would be accessed to produce the operating-asset ledger.

data base management system

relational data base

Data base management systems, in addition to facilitating data access also provide enhanced security over the data stored in the data base. This feature is very important in accounting systems because it increases the level of control within the system.

Exhibit 10-13
Relational Operating-Asset Data Base

Asset No.	Description	Acquisition Date	Cost	Salvage Value	Life	Depr. Method	Accum. Depr.	Custodian	Location
1234	Truck	011594	19450	2000	5	SYD	5817	Smith	A-23
1342	Microcomputer	042894	3400	0	7	DDB	971	Jones	C-34

INTANGIBLE ASSETS

Objective 11
Describe the accounting concepts related to intangible assets and their amortization.

Intangible assets are noncurrent, nonmonetary assets that have no physical properties. They generate revenues because of the right of ownership or use. Generally, however, there is more uncertainty about the benefits from intangible assets than from tangible assets. In addition, intangible assets are differentiated from nonphysical assets, such as accounts receivable or prepayments, because intangible assets are long-term in nature and contribute to the production or operating cycle of a business.

specifically identifiable intangible assets

Intangible assets generally are divided into two categories: those that are specifically identifiable and those that are not. **Specifically identifiable intangible assets** are those intangibles whose costs can be easily identified as part of the cost of the asset and whose benefits generally have a determinable life. Examples include patents, trademarks, franchises, and leaseholds. Conversely, intangibles that are not specifically identifiable represent some right or benefit that has an indeterminate life and whose cost is inherent in a continuing business. The primary example of such an intangible is goodwill. Exhibit 10-14 contains a list of the most common intangible assets.

Accounting Problems Related to Intangible Assets

The accounting treatment of intangible assets parallels the accounting treatment of tangible noncurrent assets. Thus, it is necessary to (1) measure and capitalize their acquisition cost; (2) amortize their cost over the shorter of their legal life, if any, or their economic life (in no case can the amortization period exceed 40 years); and (3) account for any gain or loss of their disposition.

Determining Acquisition Cost. Intangible assets originally are recorded at cost. As with tangible assets, cost includes all the expenditures necessary to get the intangible asset ready for its intended use. Included in the acquisition cost are the purchase price and any legal fees. If an intangible asset such as a trademark or goodwill is acquired without a cost, it is not shown on the balance sheet. Subsequent valuation of intangibles is a net book value (that is, at cost less accumulated amortization to date).

Operating Expenses and Intangible Assets. Because intangible assets are characterized by a lack of physical qualities, it is difficult to determine the value of their future benefits and the life of those benefits. As a consequence, it is difficult to separate expenditures that are essentially operating expenses from those that give rise to intangible assets. For example, advertising and promotion campaigns

Exhibit 10-14
Common Intangible Assets

Type of Intangible Asset	*Description*
Specifically Identifiable	
Patent	An exclusive right to use, manufacture, process, or sell a product granted by the U.S. Patent Office. Patents have a legal life of 17 years, but their economic life may be shorter.
Copyright	The exclusive right of the creator or heirs to reproduce and/or sell an artistic or published work. Granted by the U.S. government for a period of 50 years after the death of the creator. Amortized over the shorter of its economic or legal life.
Trademark and Trade Names	A symbol or name that allows the holder to use it to identify or name a specific product or service. A legal registration system allows for an indefinite number of 20-year renewals.
Organization Cost	Costs incurred in the creation of a corporation, including legal fees, registration fees, and fees to underwriters.
Franchise	An exclusive right to use a formula, design, technique, or territory.
Not Specifically Identifiable	
Goodwill	Present value of expected excess earnings of a business above average industry earnings. Recorded only when a business is purchased at a price above the market value of the individual net assets of the business.

and training programs provide future benefits to the firm. If this were not the case, firms would not spend the millions of dollars on these programs that they do. However, it is extremely difficult to measure the amount and life of the benefits generated by such programs. Therefore, expenditures for these and similar items are written off as an expense in the period incurred. When recurring expenditures are made for these items in approximately equal amounts, the effect on periodic income is not much different than if they were capitalized and then amortized over their estimated life.

research and development costs

Research and Development Costs. Research and development costs are expenditures incurred in discovering, planning, designing, and implementing a new product or process. Accounting for these costs has presented the accounting profession with significant problems. Clearly, they provide the firm with some future benefits. The billions of dollars spent by firms such as IBM result in successful new products but also in products that either never reach the marketplace or achieve no success there. Thus, it is difficult to measure the ultimate benefits that accrue from research and development expenditures that are made in 1995 but that may not result in a product until 1998. Furthermore, in today's highly competitive world economy, it is almost impossible to measure how long any of the benefits produced by research and development expenditures will last. The failure of IBM's PC Jr. in the mid-1980s is a good example of this. Because of these problems and the diversity of accounting practices that were used to record such expenditures, the FASB now requires that all research and development costs be expensed in the period incurred.

Amortization of Intangible Assets. For accounting purposes, intangible assets do not have an indefinite life, so their cost must be systematically written off to expense over their useful life.[11] This generally is done by debiting Amortization Expense account and crediting the Intangible Asset account directly. By convention, an Accumulated Amortization account is not used, although there is no reason why it could not be.

Estimating the useful life of intangible assets is quite difficult. Some assets, such as patents, have legal lives, whereas others, such as trademarks, have indefinite lives. If a legal life exists, the intangible asset should be amortized over its useful economic life or legal life, whichever is shorter. The APB decided that if an intangible asset has a legal life of over 40 years or has an indeterminate economic life, the period of amortization should not exceed 40 years.[12] In practice, straight-line amortization is used, although any systematic rational method can be used.[13]

Gains and Losses on Disposition. When intangible assets are sold or otherwise disposed of, a gain or a loss equal to the difference between the amount received for the asset (if any) and its book value is recorded. If there has been a substantial or permanent decline in the value of an intangible asset still on hand, the unamortized cost should be reduced or written off as an expense of the current period.

Accounting for Intangible Assets

Exhibit 10-14 listed some of the more common intangible assets. The following section will outline the accounting for two of the more significant intangible assets, patents and goodwill.

patent

Patents. A **patent** is an exclusive right to use, manufacture, process, or sell a product; it is granted by the U.S. Patent Office. Patents can be purchased from the inventor or holder or they can be generated internally. When a patent is purchased from the inventor, its capitalized cost includes its acquisition cost and other incidental costs, such as legal fees. The legal costs of successfully defending a patent also are capitalized as part of its cost.

If a patent results from successful research and development efforts, its cost is only the legal or other fees necessary to patent the invention, product, or process. This is because all the research and development costs expended to develop the patent, including those in the year the patent is obtained, must be written off to expense in the period the expenditure occurs.

A patent has a legal life of 17 years. In many cases, however, its useful economic life is less than 17 years. As a result, patents should be amortized over their remaining legal life or economic life, whichever is shorter. For example, assume that a patent with a remaining legal life of ten years is purchased from its inventor for $240,000. At purchase, the patent is estimated to have a remaining economic life of eight years. In this case, the patent should be amortized over

11. In previous years, some accountants argued that some intangibles had an indefinite life. This view was rejected by both the AICPA and the FASB.

12. American Institute of Certified Public Accountants, Accounting Principles Board, Opinion No. 17, *Intangible Assets* (New York: AICPA, 1970), par. 29.

13. Under the current Internal Revenue Code regulations, goodwill or other intangible assets that the IRS considers to resemble goodwill cannot be amortized for tax purposes. Therefore amortization of those intangibles does not reduce taxable income.

eight years. Assuming the straight-line method, the following journal entry would be made each year.

Amortization Expense	30,000	
Patent		30,000
To amortize the patent at $30,000 per year ($240,000 over 8 years).		

goodwill

Goodwill. Goodwill has a specific meaning in accounting. **Goodwill** represents the value today of the excess earnings of a particular enterprise. Excess earnings represent earnings above what is normal in that industry. Excess earnings result when a firm is able to earn a rate of return on its recorded net assets above the industry average rate of return. Such excess earnings are the result of a number of factors, including superior management, well-trained employees, good location, monopoly, and manufacturing efficiencies. Unlike the other intangible assets, goodwill is not specifically identifiable and is not separable from the firm. Thus goodwill can be recorded only when purchased. The existence of internally generated goodwill is verified only when a firm is purchased by another party; at that time, the goodwill (if any) is paid for and recorded.

To illustrate the concept of goodwill, assume that a group of investors purchases an electronic components manufacturing business. At the time of the purchase, the fair market value of the firm's net assets totals $1 million, consisting of the following:

Inventory	$ 400,000
Property, plant, and equipment, net	900,000
Other assets	200,000
Total assets acquired	$1,500,000
Total liabilities assumed	500,000
Net assets acquired	$1,000,000

The agreed-upon purchase price is $1,250,000, implying goodwill of $250,000—the purchase price of $1,250,000 less the identifiable net assets acquired of $1 million. The entry to record the purchase is as follows:

Inventory	400,000	
Property, Plant, and Equipment	900,000	
Other Assets	200,000	
Goodwill	250,000	
Liabilities		500,000
Cash		1,250,000

As this journal entry shows, the purchase price is first allocated to the identifiable net assets based on their fair market value. Any remaining portion is considered goodwill and is recorded by a debit to the Goodwill account. Subsequently, goodwill is amortized over a period not exceeding 40 years.

Goodwill arises when one firm purchases another and pays a price that exceeds the market value of the assets acquired. During the late 1980s, merger mania reached a high, with many firms being acquired by others. Examples include the purchase of many U.S. companies by non-U.S. multinationals, such as the purchase of Pillsbury by Grand Metropolitan, an English multinational. At that time, English firms were able to offset goodwill directly against their shareholders' equity, and many individuals argued that this accounting treatment gave Grand Metropolitan an unfair advantage over U.S. companies also bidding for Pillsbury. Firms following U.S. GAAP have to write goodwill off against current earnings over a 40 year period. This very important issue is discussed in more detail in the next chapter when accounting for mergers and acquisitions is introduced.

OTHER DIMENSIONS OF ACCOUNTING FOR INVESTMENTS IN OPERATING ASSETS

Objective 12
Explain the accounting issues related to impairment of operating assets and understand that differences exist among countries in accounting for operating assets.

This chapter has provided an extensive overview of the important accounting issues related to accounting for investments in operating assets. Two areas deserve additional attention: asset impairments and the international dimensions of accounting for these assets.

Impairment of Operating Assets

Accounting for the impairment of long-lived assets and identifiable intangibles is an important issue now being debated by the profession. In this context, impairment means a decrease in value of these assets below their carrying value or net book value. The proper accounting for such decreases in value has not been settled, and the FASB is currently studying this issue.[14]

Under current accounting standards, assets are shown in the financial statements at historical costs. In some circumstances, decreases in the value of these assets are recognized in the financial statements. For example, inventories generally are valued on the balance sheet at the lower of cost or market. However, this usually has not been the case for decreases in values of operational assets, and in many cases no recognition is given to these decreases.

Accounting for the impairment of operating assets became quite controversial in the 1980s as many firms experienced economic downturns and decided to write down their assets. These write-downs are quite significant, as noted by a study by the Institute of Management Accountants, which indicated that over $30 billion in post-tax dollars were written off by firms between 1980 and 1985.[15]

As the economic recession took hold in 1990 and 1991, these write-offs picked up again as companies renewed their "downsizing." This led the FASB to consider the entire issue of impairments of long-lived assets.

The FASB has identified a number of issues that need to be resolved. For example, how should impairment be measured, how should assets be grouped for measurement purposes, and how should the impairment be shown in the financial statements? The ultimate resolution of these issues could have a significant effect on financial statements of many U.S. and non-U.S. companies.

International Dimensions of Accounting for Operating Assets

The accounting for operating assets varies considerably in the international environment. Some of the differences can result in financial statements that are not very comparable across countries. The following is a brief overview indicating a few of these differences.

14. In December, 1990, the FASB issued a Discussion Memorandum, "Accounting for the Impairment of Long-lived Assets and Identifiable Intangibles." This is the beginning of a process that will possibly lead to an Exposure and a final Statement of Financial Accounting Standards relating to these issues.
15. Dov Fried, Michael Schiff, and Ashwinpaul Sondhi, "Impairments and Writeoffs of Long Lived Assets" (Montvale, NJ.: IMA), 1989, pg. 3.

Carrying Value of Operating Assets. As fully described in this chapter, operating assets in the U.S. are reported at their carrying, or book value (cost less depreciation to date). No adjustments are made for increases in market values, and, as noted, adjustments for impairments are uncertain. Canada, Japan, and Germany follow similar accounting standards. Other countries, however, allow both upward and downward revaluation of operating assets. Revaluation to current cost is common in the Netherlands; while also allowed in the United Kingdom it is less commonly practiced there. Clearly, the amount at which these assets are carried will affect the amount of annual depreciation.

International accounting standards developed by the International Accounting Standards Committee (IASC) also allow for the upward and downward evaluation of property, operating assets, and equipment. An upward evaluation generally is made to stockholders' equity, while a downward evaluation is charged to income unless it can be offset against a previous upward evaluation.

Differences in Research and Development Costs and Goodwill. The accounting for research and development costs and goodwill also varies around the world. These differences are illustrated in Exhibit 10-15, which summarizes the accounting treatment for these items in the U.S., the United Kingdom (U.K.), Germany, and Japan.[16]

Interestingly, the standard write-off of goodwill over 40 years is not a common procedure in many countries. Many countries and the IASC recommend a maximum write-off period of 20 years or less.

These examples illustrate some of the important differences between U.S. accounting principles and practices and those followed in other countries. These

Exhibit 10-15
Accounting for Goodwill and R & D in Selected Countries

Country	*Accounting Treatment of Goodwill*
U.S.	Goodwill is capitalized and amortized by charges to earnings over not more than 40 years.
U.K.	The current preferred treatment is to write off goodwill immediately against certain reserves.
Germany	Goodwill is either capitalized or written off to reserves (if capitalized, it is amortized by charges to earnings over at least four years or systematically over the estimated period benefitted).
Japan	Immediate write-off of goodwill against earnings is encouraged; if capitalized, it is amortized over five years or less.

Country	*Accounting Treatment of R & D*
U.S.	Expenditures are charged to earnings.
U.K.	Development expenditures may be capitalized in special circumstances.
Germany	Expenditures are charged to earnings.
Japan	Expenditures may be capitalized and amortized over five years.

Source: *1991 International Accounting Summaries*, Coopers & Lybrand (New York: John Wiley & Sons, 1991). Copyright © 1991 by John Wiley & Sons. Reprinted by permission of John Wiley & Sons, Inc.

16. Adopted from *1991 International Accounting Summaries*, Coopers & Lybrand, (John Wiley & Sons, New York, NY) 1991 pg. X.

differences certainly have implications for users as they attempt to compare and contrast the performance of companies reporting under different accounting principles. Some feel that differences in accounting between the U.S. and other countries for such items as goodwill even affect the competitiveness of U.S. firms.

SUMMARY OF LEARNING OBJECTIVES

1. Describe the nature and purpose of capital budgeting. Capital budgeting is the process of allocating resources among competing investment alternatives. It involves planning, setting goals and priorities, arranging financing, and identifying criteria for selecting investments. Capital budgeting decisions, such as the purchase of operating assets, are basically cash flow decisions and often involve significant long-term resource commitments.

2. Explain the accounting concepts and issues related to noncurrent, nonmonetary assets. Noncurrent, nonmonetary assets include both tangible and intangible assets. Tangible assets include property, operating assets, and equipment and natural resources. Intangible assets have no physical substance and include such assets as patents, franchises, and goodwill. All noncurrent, nonmonetary assets:

a. Represent future economic services.
b. Affect several accounting periods.
c. Are systematically allocated over the periods in which the benefits are received (except for land).

3. Discuss the importance of differentiating between capital and revenue expenditures. When a firm makes an expenditure that results in the acquisition of an asset, it is called a *capital expenditure.* When the expenditure results in a service whose benefits are consumed in the current period, it is called a *revenue expenditure.* The distinction between capital and revenue expenditures is important when determining periodic net income, because capital expenditures affect several periods, whereas revenue expenditures affect only the current period's income.

4. Measure and record the acquisition cost of property, plant, and equipment. The historical cost of operating assets includes all the costs necessary to get the assets to their location and in condition to be used. Included are such costs as transportation charges, insurance in transit, installation, and testing costs. When the purchase is made for cash, the acquisition cost is the net cash price. When a noncash acquisition is made, the acquisition cost is equal to the cash given plus the fair market value of the noncash consideration given. If it is difficult or impossible to obtain the fair market value of the noncash consideration given, the transaction should be recorded at the fair market value of the asset received.

5. Explain the accounting concept of depreciation. Depreciation is the process of allocating the cost of operating assets and equipment to the period in which the enterprise receives the benefits from the assets. Depreciation is not a valuation concept, nor is it a direct source of cash. Rather, it is caused by such factors as physical deterioration and obsolescence.

6. Compute depreciation expense using methods acceptable for financial reporting purposes and for income tax purposes. There are several alternative methods of computing depreciation, all of which meet the criteria of being systematic and rational. The four most common methods are straight-line and units-of-production, and two accelerated methods, declining-balance and sum-of-the-years-digits. Management is free to choose any of these methods for financial reporting purposes. For tax purposes, depreciation is calculated under the IRS recovery tables.

7. Identify depreciation problems relating to partial-year depreciation, revision of depreciation rates, and the effect of inflation. There are several other problems related to accounting for depreciation: depreciation for partial years, revision of depreciation rates, and the effects of inflation. Because depreciation is an estimate, firms often use conventions to calculate partial year's depreciation. For example, many firms take six months depreciation in the year of purchase and six months in the year of disposal regardless of the exact time during the year the asset was placed into service.

Many estimates, including service life and salvage value, are used in the original depreciation calculation. Firms often change these estimates, and these changes affect the current and future years. In some situations, the firm will change the actual method of depreciation. This represents a change in method that usually is handled through a cumulative effect change.

Finally, historical cost is the primary method of recording assets. As such, periodic depreciation is based on this cost, and when the price levels rise in the economy many individuals feel that historical cost depreciation does not provide an accurate picture of the firm's financial position. They advocate depreciation based on current or replacement cost.

8. Account for subsequent expenditures related to plant and equipment. Expenditures made on operating assets and equipment consist of either revenue expenditures or capital expenditures. Revenue expenditures are generally for repairs and maintenance that maintain the asset's expected level of service. They neither extend the asset's useful life nor increase the quantity or quality of its output. Capital expenditures after acquisition benefit several accounting periods; they may be additions, betterments, or extraordinary repairs.

9. Account for disposal of assets. Disposal of operating assets occurs through retirements, sales, or trade-ins. In most cases, a firm will realize a gain or loss on disposal. The gain or loss is measured by the difference between the book value of the disposed asset and the consideration (if any) received for it. However, when the operating asset is traded in for a similar one, a gain is not recognized, though a loss is always recognized. The following table summarizes these concepts:

Method of Disposal	*Is the Gain/Loss to Be Recognized for Accounting Purposes?*
Sale of asset at realized gain	Yes
Sale of asset at realized loss	Yes
Trade-in of asset for similar asset at realized gain	No
Trade-in of asset for similar asset at realized loss	Yes

10. Describe the components of an accounting system for operating assets. The components of an operating-asset accounting system include control policies and procedures, the procedures or computer programs designed to process transactions, and the operating-asset records. Control policies and procedures are developed to provide reasonable assurance that all (and only) valid operating-asset transactions are submitted for processing. Operating-asset procedures and computer programs update the operating-asset records, compute depreciation, and generate the necessary general ledger journal entries.

11. Describe the accounting concepts related to intangible assets and their amortization. Intangible assets have no physical properties. They generate revenue for the firm because they give it the right of ownership or use. Intangible assets include patents, trademarks, franchises, leaseholds, and goodwill. Intangible assets have a definite life and must be amortized over the shorter of their legal life or economic life. In no case, however, can the amortization period exceed 40 years.

12. Explain the accounting issues related to impairment of operating assets and recognize that differences exist among countries in accounting for operating assets. The main issues regarding accounting for impairment of operating assets are: how should the impairment be measured; how should assets be grouped for measurement purposes; and how should the impairment be shown in the financial statements? Countries often differ on generally accepted methods of accounting. With regard to operating assets, three areas of difference are: the carrying value, research and development costs, and goodwill.

KEY TERMS

Accelerated depreciation methods 475
Additions 484
Amortization 470
Betterments 484
Capital budgeting 463
Capital expenditure 466
Data base management system 489
Declining-balance depreciation 475
Depletion 470
Depreciable cost (base) 472
Depreciation 470
Depreciation register 489
Estimated (useful) economic life 472
Expenditure 466
Extraordinary repairs 484
Goodwill 493
Intangible assets 464
Location list 489
Natural resources 464
Operating assets 463
Operating-asset ledger 489
Obsolescence 472
Patent 492
Relational data base 489
Repair or maintenance 484
Research and development costs 491
Revenue expenditure 466
Self-constructed assets 469
Specifically identifiable intangible assets 490
Straight-line depreciation 473
Sum-of-the-years-digits 475
Tangible assets 464
Units-of-production depreciation 474

REVIEW PROBLEMS

A Acquisition Cost of Assets

During 1995, the C. Price Company had the following asset transactions:

a. January 15: Purchase of land and building in which to conduct business. The entire cost was $5,000,000, cash. The assets were appraised at the following individual values:

Land	$1,500,000
Buildings	4,500,000

b. April 14: Store equipment with a list price of $10,000 was purchased on account. The terms were 2/10, n/30. Other costs incurred for cash were:

Shipping	$500
Insurance in transit	50
Installation	100
Repair for damage in transit	200

REQUIRED: Make all the required journal entries. It is not necessary to make the December 31, 1995 depreciation entries for the operating assets still on hand.

Solution

January 15	Land	1,250,000	
	Buildings	3,750,000	
	Cash		5,000,000
	To record purchase of land and buildings, allocated as follows:		

Account	*Fair Market Value*	*%*	*Total Purchase Price*		*Allocation of Total Purchase Price*
Land	$1,500,000	25% ×	$5,000,000	=	$1,250,000
Buildings	4,500,000	75% ×	$5,000,000	=	3,750,000
	$6,000,000				$5,000,000

April 14	Store Equipment	10,450[a]	
	Repair	200	
	Accounts Payable		9,800
	Cash		850
	To record purchase of store equipment on account.		

[a]$10,450 = ($10,000 × .98) + $500 + $50 + $100

B Depreciation Methods

Commute Air, a small commuter airline, purchased an airplane for $6 million. The president of the company is trying to decide how to depreciate the plane.

REQUIRED: Calculate the annual depreciation for each of the next three years under each of the following methods:

1. Straight-line
2. Units-of-production
3. Double-declining-balance
4. Sum-of-the-years-digits

In each case, the asset has a ten-year life, or a 110 million-mile life. Miles flown are as follows:

Year	*Miles Flown*
1	8,800,000
2	10,000,000
3	15,000,000

The plane has an estimated residual value of $500,000.

Solution

	Year 1	Year 2	Year 3
Straight-line[a]	$ 550,000	$550,000	$550,000
Units-of-production[b]	440,000	500,000	750,000
Double-declining-balance[c]	1,200,000	960,000	768,000
Sum-of-the-years-digits[d]	1,000,000	900,000	800,000

[a] $\frac{\$6,000,000 - \$500,000}{10 \text{ years}} = \$550,000$ per year

[b] $\frac{\$6,000,000 - \$500,000}{110,000,000 \text{ miles}} = \$.05$ per mile

[c] Year 1 $6,000,000 × .20[1] = $1,200,000
Year 2 ($6,000,000 − $1,200,000) × .20 = 960,000
Year 3 ($4,800,000 − $960,000) × .20 = 768,000

[d] Year 1 ($6,000,000 − $500,000) × 10/55 = $1,000,000
Year 2 ($6,000,000 − $500,000) × 9/55 = 900,000
Year 3 ($6,000,000 − $500,000) × 8/55 = 800,000

[1] Straight-line rate = 10%; twice the straight-line rate = 20%. Salvage value is not considered until the last year.

$$\frac{N(N+1)}{2} = \frac{10(11)}{2} = 55$$

QUESTIONS

1. List and describe the characteristics that many noncurrent, nonmonetary assets have in common.
2. Explain the meaning of *capital expenditure.* How does it differ from a revenue expenditure? From an accounting perspective, describe the consequences of recording a capital expenditure as a revenue expenditure.
3. Explain the accountant's concept of depreciation. Why do accountants insist on depreciating a building whose fair market value is increasing?
4. What is meant by each of the following terms, and how are they estimated?
   a. Residual or salvage value
   b. Economic or useful life
   c. Depreciable cost
5. How is depreciation determined for tax purposes? How does this method compare with depreciation methods used for financial reporting purposes? Why do you think the Internal Revenue Code departs from generally accepted accounting principles in this regard?
6. Why would a company change its original estimate of an asset's useful life? How is this change accounted for?
7. Many individuals argue that in a period of inflation, historical-cost depreciation overstates earnings. What do they mean, and how can this problem be overcome?
8. Define the following terms:
   a. Additions
   b. Betterments
   c. Extraordinary repairs
   d. Revenue expenditures.
9. Why is a gain not recognized when an asset is traded in for a similar one? What is the ultimate effect of not recognizing the gain on the firm's financial statements over the life of the new asset?
10. Describe the objectives of an operating-asset accounting system and explain why intangible assets may not be accounted for by the operating-asset accounting system.
11. Explain why an operating-asset master file might be structured as a sequential file or as an indexed sequential file but not as a direct access file.
12. Explain why data base management systems are replacing traditional file structures in accounting information systems.
13. Briefly define and describe intangible assets. How do these assets offer future benefits to a firm?
14. What are research and development costs? Under current accounting principles, how are these costs accounted for? Do you agree with this treatment? Why or why not?
15. What is meant by asset impairment? Describe current accounting standards relating to impairments of operating assets.
16. Describe three methods firms can use to help them make capital budgeting decisions.

EXERCISES

E10-1 Revenue Versus Capital Expenditures
LO 2

Identify each of the following items as a revenue or capital expenditure. If you cannot make a clear distinction, state why not.

a. Immediately after the purchase of a new warehouse and before its use, it was painted at a cost of $50,000.
b. Immediately after the purchase of a used delivery truck, new tires were purchased at a cost of $200.
c. Purchased a wastepaper basket for the office at a cost of $7.
d. Installed air conditioning in an office building that had been owned for several years. The cost of the air conditioning was $24,000.
e. Purchased land for possible future use as a site for a new building. Paid a guard $200 per week to protect the site.
f. Acme Freight Corporation decided to overhaul one of its trucks instead of purchasing a new one. Total overhaul cost is $3,500, including a new drive train.

E10-2 Determining Acquisition Cost
LO 3

For each of the following independent situations, determine the appropriate acquisition cost:

a. Coral, Inc. purchased a tract of land for $424,750 as a potential building site. To acquire the land, the firm paid a $42,000 commission to a real estate agent. Additional costs of $18,000 were incurred to clear the land.
b. On August 15, the Nigerian Export Company purchased a tract of land for $975,000. Additional expenses incurred by the company were a $45,000 commission paid to a real estate agent, $79,500 clearing fees, and $90,000 in delinquent property taxes. This property was adjacent to the Nigerian Export Company's present warehouse, and two months later the company incurred expenses of $60,000 for paving and $4,500 for fencing to turn the land into a parking lot.
c. New office equipment was purchased by the Davenport Corporation. The equipment had a list price of $105,000. Terms of purchase were 2/10, n/30. State taxes were 7%. Davenport incurred the following additional costs in connection with the purchase:

Transportation	$3,600
Installation	4,000
Removal of old equipment	2,500
Testing of new equipment	900
Repair of damage incurred in transit	240

REQUIRED: Determine the acquisition cost of the new equipment assuming that (1) payment was made within the discount period and (2) payment was not made within the discount period.

E10-3 Lump-Sum Purchase
LO 3

On November 15, the Hutch Company acquired four pieces of machinery for a lump sum of $925,000. The company then paid $40,600 to have the machines installed. Based on an outside appraisal the individual values of the machines were:

Machine 1	$ 312,400
Machine 2	426,000
Machine 3	568,000
Machine 4	113,600
Total	$1,420,000

REQUIRED: Determine the acquisition cost of each machine.

E10-4
Exchange of Assets for Stock
LO 3

On October 15, Bloes, Inc., a private company, purchased a used machine from the Finwick Company. The machine had a book value of $87,000 on Finwick's books and a fair market value of $102,000. In return for the machine, Bloes, Inc. gave the Finwick Company $9,000 and 1,000 shares of its capital stock. Because Bloes, Inc. is a private company, it is almost impossible to determine the fair market value of the stock.

Prepare the journal entry to record this transaction on the books of Bloes, Inc. Would your answer be different if Bloes, Inc. were a public company and its stock were trading at $79 per share? Why or why not?

E10-5
Depreciation Concepts
LO 4

You overhear the following conversation about depreciation among five of your friends:
SUMI—As generally used in accounting, depreciation applies to all items of property, plant, and equipment.
HELENE—No, depreciation does not apply to land. Depreciation is, however, used to value operating assets.
JAY—You are both wrong. Depreciation records only the decline in value of nonmonetary assets other than land. Accountants do not record increases in value.
MICHELLE—No, depreciation is essentially an allocation concept used to match revenues and expenses. And it does not apply to land.
ERNESTO—All of you are wrong. Depreciation has nothing to do with cost or value. It is used solely to generate cash for the firm.

REQUIRED: Evaluate each of their comments.

E10-6
Calculating Depreciation
LO 5

The Brett Aviation Corporation at the beginning of the current year purchased a 12-passenger commuter plane for $4.5 million. The plane has an estimated salvage value of $750,000.

REQUIRED:

1. The airplane has a useful life of eight years and the firm uses straight-line depreciation. Calculate the annual depreciation for the first four years of the asset's life.
2. Now assume that the firm believes that the plane will fly 2 million miles and that it has decided to use the units-of-production method of calculating depreciation. Calculate the depreciation for each of the first four years, assuming the plane flew the following miles:

Year 1	300,000
Year 2	250,000
Year 3	275,000
Year 4	240,000

E10-7
Calculating Depreciation
LO 5

Equipment with a useful life of five years was purchased by Lectrom, Inc. on January 2, 1995 for $48,000. Salvage value is estimated to be $2,000.

REQUIRED: Compute annual depreciation expense relating to this equipment for the next five years, using the following methods:

1. Straight-line
2. Double-declining balance
3. Sum-of-the-years-digits

E10-8
Analysis of Depreciation Calculations
LO 5

Answer each of the following independent questions:

a. At the beginning of 1994, the Lombardi Company purchased a heavy-duty power generator for $240,000. The firm estimates that the generator will have a $30,000 salvage value at the end of its useful life. The firm uses sum-of-the-years-digits depreciation, which was as follows for years 1994 and 1995:

Year	*Annual Depreciation*
1994	$70,000
1995	56,000

What would be the depreciation for 1996, assuming that the straight-line basis had been used since the purchase of the equipment in 1994?

b. U-Do-It Self Storage bought a warehouse for $23 million. It estimated that this building will have a useful life of 35 years and a salvage value of $2 million. On the firm's December 31, 1992 financial statements, the warehouse's book value was $20.6 million. Assuming that the firm uses straight-line depreciation, when was the warehouse purchased?

c. On January 2, 1996, Ecology Cosmetics bought a machine that liquefies certain chemicals. The firm estimates that the machine will have a useful life of 12 years and a salvage value of $1,800. On December 31, 2001, the machine will have a book value of $22,300 based on straight-line depreciation. If the firm had used double-declining-balance depreciation rather than straight-line, what would be the depreciation expense for the years ended December 31, 1996, and December 31, 1997?

E10-9
Partial Year's Depreciation
LO 6

On March 1, 1994, Radar Enterprises purchased a machine for $190,000. The machine has a useful life of eight years and a salvage value of $10,000. The policy of Radar Enterprises is to calculate depreciation expense from the beginning of the month the asset was purchased.

REQUIRED: Calculate depreciation expense of 1994 and 1995, assuming that the firm uses (1) sum-of-the-years-digits depreciation and (2) double-declining-balance depreciation.

E10-10
Comparing Depreciation for Accounting and Tax Purposes
LO 5

In April of the current year, the West Valley Company purchased for $100,000 a new light truck for making deliveries. For financial reporting purposes, the asset was given a five-year life with a $5,000 residual value and will be depreciated using the straight-line method. The firm's policy is to take six months' depreciation in the year of purchase. Thus, one-half year's depreciation is taken in Year 1 and one-half year's depreciation in Year 6. For tax purposes, the truck falls into the five-year life class. Depreciation for tax purposes is based on the following percentages:

Year 1: 20%	Year 2: 32%
Year 3: 19.2%	Year 4: 11.52%
Year 5: 11.52%	Year 6: 5.76%

REQUIRED:

1. Prepare a five-year schedule comparing annual depreciation expense for financial reporting purposes and for tax purposes.
2. Assume that the firm's income before taxes and depreciation for both financial reporting purposes and tax purposes over the five years of the asset's life is as follows: Year 1, $240,000; Year 2, $290,000; Year 3, $260,000; Year 4, $310,000; Year 5, $325,000; and

Year 6, $305,000. In addition, the firm's tax rate is 30%. For each year, determine the firm's net income for financial reporting purposes and the firm's taxable income.
3. Explain the benefit the firm received, if any, from using depreciation for tax purposes.

E10-11
Revision of Depreciation Estimates
LO 6

At the beginning of 1993, the Hubble-Bates Corporation purchased a piece of heavy equipment for $750,000. The firm estimates that the asset will have a $60,000 residual value at the end of its 15-year life. The firm uses straight-line depreciation. At the beginning of 1996, the firm decides the machine has a remaining life of only ten years.

REQUIRED: Calculate depreciation for 1996, given the new estimate of the asset's economic life.

E10-12
Change in Depreciation Methods
LO 6

Air North is a small commuter airline. At the beginning of the current year, 1995, it made the following accounting changes:

a. The firm decided to change the method of depreciation on one of its new airplanes. The plane was purchased at the beginning of 1992 at a price of $3 million. The plane has a useful life of ten years and no salvage value. The firm had been using double-declining-balance depreciation, but has decided to change to straight-line.
b. The firm decided to change the remaining life of one of its older aircraft. The plane was purchased at the beginning of 1991 at a cost of $1.5 million. At that time, the firm estimated that the aircraft would have a useful life of 20 years and no salvage value. However, at the beginning of 1995, the firm estimated that the aircraft would have a remaining useful life of only ten years, but would now have a salvage value of $10,000. Straight-line depreciation has always been used on this particular aircraft.

REQUIRED: Assuming that these are the only depreciable assets, determine the amount of depreciation expense for 1995 and the cumulative effect of the change in accounting method. Ignore income taxes.

E10-13
Revenue Versus Capital Expenditures
LO 7

The following expenditures were made by the R & G Corporation. For each item, indicate whether the expenditure is a capital expenditure, a revenue expenditure, or neither. State if you cannot make a clear-cut decision, and explain why.

a. Paid $500 for a small machine..
b. Paid $600 for ordinary repairs to a large machine.
c. Paid premiums of $760 for insurance for the firm's officers.
d. Paid $1,500 for a patent.
e. Paid $10 for an electric pencil sharpener.
f. Paid $1,750 to overhaul a large delivery truck.
g. Removed a wall during installation of a new computer, $500.

E10-14
Extraordinary Repairs
LO 7

Hollis Answering Service began operations on January 2, 1991. At that time, the firm purchased switchboard equipment for $45,000 cash. The equipment had an estimated useful life of ten years and a salvage value of $2,000. The company uses straight-line depreciation. During 1994, ordinary repairs totaling $500 were made and paid in cash. At the beginning of 1995, an employee spilled coffee on the equipment. As a result, a major overhaul of the equipment was made. The equipment was upgraded at the same time. The total cost was $12,000, which was paid in cash. These expenditures will increase the total useful life of the equipment from 10 years to 15.

REQUIRED:

1. Prepare the entries required to record the $500 expenditure in 1994 and the depreciation expense in 1994.
2. Prepare the entries required to record the $12,000 expenditures in 1995 and the depreciation expense in 1995.

E10-15
Retirement of Plant Assets
LO 8

On March 31, 1995, Shirt Tails, Inc. retired a machine used in manufacturing designer jeans. The machine was acquired on May 1, 1992. Straight-line depreciation was used. The asset had an estimated salvage value of $200 and a five-year life. On December 31, 1995, the balance in the Accumulated Depreciation account was $3,200. The machine was scrapped without Shirt Tails receiving any consideration.

REQUIRED:

1. Make the entry to record the depreciation expense for the period January through March 1995. Depreciation is calculated from the date of acquisition. (*Hint:* You must first determine the acquisition cost of the machine.)
2. Make the entry to record the retirement of the asset on March 31, 1995.

E10-16
Sale of Plant Assets
LO 8

On September 30, 1995, Schneider's Maintenance Service sold one of its vans. The acquisition cost of the van was $19,500. It had an estimated useful life of five years and a salvage value of $1,500. Straight-line depreciation was used. The balance in the Accumulated Depreciation account on December 31, 1994 was $9,900.

REQUIRED:

1. Calculate the gain or loss on the sale assuming that the asset is sold for either (a) $14,200 or (b) $8,300. In both cases the sale is for cash.
2. Make the necessary journal entries to record the transaction for each of the cases in item 1.
3. Now assume that the van was scrapped without any consideration. Make the journal entry to record the retirement.

E10-17
Asset Sale
LO 8

On December 31, 1995, the records of the Benson Company showed the following information with regard to one of the company's delivery trucks:

Delivery truck	$21,500
Accumulated depreciation—12/31/95	14,250

Depreciation is based on a four-year useful life, a $2,500 salvage value, and straight-line depreciation. On February 1, 1996, the truck is sold for $7,900 cash.

REQUIRED:

1. How old was the truck on January 1, 1996? Show your computations.
2. Prepare the necessary journal entries to record the sale of the truck.
3. Prepare the necessary journal entries to record the sale, now assuming a cash sale price of $6,500.

E10-18
Asset Trade-in
LO 8

On July 1, 1995, Drake Co. traded a machine used in the production of bottle caps for a newer model. Drake received a trade-in allowance of $14,500 on the new machine, which had a list price of $88,000. The old machine was purchased seven years and three months earlier at a price of $62,000. It had an estimated useful life of ten years and a salvage value of $2,000. Straight-line depreciation was used.

REQUIRED:

1. How much cash did Drake have to pay for the new machine?
2. Make the necessary journal entry to record the acquisition of the new machine.

E10-19
Operating Asset Controls
LO 9

The Internal Auditors at CONALEP identified a number of problems in the recent audit of the operating asset account. You have been given the responsibility of developing new operating asset controls to ensure that the same problems do not recur. The problems uncovered by the auditors included:

a. The Research and Development Division had expended its capital budget for the year. Nevertheless, it acquired an expensive piece of laboratory equipment, a capital asset, by recording the purchase of the individual equipment components and charging the purchases to the Repair and Maintenance account.
b. A manager purchased a cabin in the Rocky Mountains and processed the purchase as the acquisition of a branch office headquarters building.
c. Several employees took their laptop computers, which had been purchased by CONALEP, with them when they resigned from the firm.
d. The purchase, by CONALEP, of a small truck was never recorded.

REQUIRED: Describe one control that could be used to prevent or detect and correct each of the problems above.

E10-20
Intangible Assets
LO 10

Imagination, Inc. has the following intangible assets on December 31, 1995, which is the end of the firm's year:

a. A patent was purchased on January 2, 1995 for cash of $8,195. This patent had been registered with the U.S. Patent Office on January 2, 1989 and is to be amortized over its remaining legal life.
b. On January 2, 1994, the company purchased a copyright for cash of $13,800. The remaining legal life is 20 years; however, management estimates that the copyright would have no value at the end of 15 years.
c. On July 1, 1995, the company received a patent on a product developed by the firm. Expenses of $22,500 were incurred in the development of the product. Legal fees and costs associated with obtaining the patent amounted to $8,270. The company will amortize the patent over its legal life beginning on July 1, 1995.
d. On January 2, 1995, Imagination, Inc. hired a public relations firm to develop a trademark. The fees to the firm amounted to $25,000. Legal fees associated with the trademark amounted to $5,000. Assume a 20-year life.

REQUIRED: Determine the amortization expense for 1995 and the book value of each of the intangible assets that should be shown on the December 31, 1995 balance sheet.

E10-21
Determining Goodwill
LO 10

The Mann Corporation is negotiating the purchase of the Horace Company. After auditing the Horace Company's books, the accountant for the Mann Corporation gathered the following information:

Accounts	*Book Value*	*Fair Market Value*
Current assets	$100,000	$150,000
Property, plant, and equipment	500,000	600,000
Other assets	40,000	5,000
Current liabilities	80,000	80,000
Long-term debt	200,000	240,000
Stockholders' equity	360,000	435,000

After considerable negotiation, the Mann Corporation agreed to purchase the Horace Company for $500,000 cash. As part of the agreement, the Mann Corporation will acquire all of the Horace Company's assets as well as assume all of its liabilities.

REQUIRED:

1. Determine the amount of goodwill that the Mann Corporation should record as a result of this purchase.
2. Make the necessary journal entries on the books of the Mann Corporation to record the acquisition of the Horace Company.

E10-22
Asset Impairment
LO 12

The Weight Management Corporation provides diet services and exercise programs for its clients. Several years ago the firm purchased $200,000 of exercise equipment to be used in its various weight control centers. Recently, new equipment has come onto the market which has depressed the market for the equipment purchased by Weight Management. Further, the firm is considering closing several centers and expects to have excess exercise equipment. Management estimates that it will cost about $500,000 to close a center and move the equipment to a center that will stay open. Management also estimates that the value of the exercise equipment has decreased from a carrying value of $125,000 to approximately $60,000.

REQUIRED:

1. Explain the concept of asset impairment. Do any of the assets of Weight Management meet this definition?
2. Describe current accounting standards related to the impairment of long-lived assets in the U.S.
3. How should Weight Management account for the costs of the store closings and the decrease in the value of the exercise equipment?

E10-23
International Dimensions
LO 12

Briefly describe the accounting for goodwill in the United Kingdom as compared to that in the U.S. Assume that a U.S. firm acquired another firm by purchase and recorded $1 million of goodwill. How would the goodwill be accounted for? Now assume that a multinational firm in the U.K. purchased this same company. How would the U.K. account for the goodwill? How will the future financial statements of each company be affected by the purchase?

E10-24
Albertson's Financial Statements
LO 1, 3

Using the information contained in the annual report of Albertson's found in Appendix A, answer the following questions:

a. A company like Albertson's is likely to open and close several stores during a given year, as well as to remodel stores. How does Albertson's account for store opening and closing costs? How does Albertson's account for major remodeling and improvement costs?
b. During 1991 Albertson's continued to invest in new stores. What was the total amount of capital expenditures the firm made during 1991? How did Albertson's expect to fund these capital expenditures?
c. During 1992 Albertson's expects to continue to invest in capital expansion. What is the dollar amount of anticipated capital expenditures for that year, and how does the company plan to finance that program?

PROBLEMS

P10-1
Concepts Related to Accounting for Property, Plant, and Equipment
LO 1

Property, plant, and equipment generally represent a material portion of the total assets of most companies. Accounting for acquisition and usage of such assets is, therefore, an important part of the financial reporting process.

REQUIRED:

1. Distinguish between revenue and capital expenditures and explain why this distinction is important.

2. Briefly define depreciation as the term is used in accounting.
3. Identify the factors that are relevant in determining annual depreciation and explain whether these factors are determined objectively or are based on judgment.
4. Explain why depreciation is added back to net income in determining cash flows from operations on the statement of cash flows.

P10-2
Acquisition of Nonmonetary Assets
LO 2

The following transactions were made during 1995 by Dawson Enterprises, a manufacturer of novelty T-shirts:

a. A tract of land was acquired for $320,000. In addition, commissions of $28,000 were paid to real estate agents, and a special assessment for late taxes of $7,500 was also incurred. The taxes and fees were paid in cash. A 15% down payment was made, and a 20-year mortgage was used to finance the project.
b. A small building and tract of land were purchased for a lump sum of $550,000 cash. The property was appraised for tax purposes near the end of 1994 as follows: building, $230,000 and land, $270,000. The building has an estimated useful life of 20 years and a salvage value of $25,000. The company will be using double-declining-balance depreciation and will take a full year's depreciation in the year of purchase.
c. A machine is acquired in exchange for 40,000 shares of Dawson Enterprises' capital stock. The stock had a closing market value of $21 per share on a national stock exchange on the date the machine was acquired. The machine has an estimated useful life of five years and no salvage value. The company decided to use straight-line depreciation, and a full year's depreciation was taken in 1995.
d. The city of Hidden Hills donated a parcel of land to Dawson Enterprises on the condition that the firm build a new factory. Hidden Hills acquired the land several years ago at a cost of $150,000. At the time the land was donated to the firm, it had a current market value of $220,000.

REQUIRED:

1. Prepare the necessary journal entries to record the above acquisitions.
2. Make the required adjusting entries for depreciation expense for 1995. Make a separate entry for each depreciable asset.

P10-3
Calculating Depreciation
LO 5

Washington, Inc. purchased an automated conveyer belt on April 1, 1993 at a cost of $340,000. The machine had an estimated useful life of ten years and a $10,000 salvage value. Washington, Inc. estimates that the machine will be able to handle 1.65 million units before it must be scrapped. Actual output in the first three years was: 1993—350,000 units; 1994—470,000 units; and 1995—450,000 units.

REQUIRED: Determine the annual depreciation expense and book value of the conveyer belt under each of the following methods at the end of the first three years of the asset's life. Assume that the firm takes a full year's depreciation in the year of purchase.

1. Straight-line
2. Units-of-production
3. Sum-of-the-years-digits
4. Double-declining-balance

P10-4
Depreciation Calculations and Adjusting Entries
LO 5

Lindsey and Sons Ltd. is an automobile parts importer. You have obtained the following data relative to the firm's depreciable assets:

	Building	*Furniture*	*Equipment*	*Trucks*
Date acquired	7/1/90	1/2/93	7/6/95	10/3/95
Cost	$250,000	$16,500	$8,000	$16,000
Salvage value	$10,000	$0	$800	$1,000
Useful life	30 years	10 years	8 years	5 years
Method of depreciation	Straight-line	Sum-of-the-years-digits	Double-declining-balance	Sum-of-the-years-digits

The policy of Lindsey and Sons is to calculate depreciation expense from the beginning of the month in which the asset is purchased.

REQUIRED:

1. For each asset group, determine the balance in the Accumulated Depreciation account as of January 1, 1996.
2. Make the adjusting entries to record depreciation expense for the year ended December 31, 1996. Make a separate entry for each asset group.

P10-5
Revision of Depreciation Rates
LO 6

Strawberry's Sports Manufacturing Co. owns a special machine that makes baseballs. The machine was purchased at the beginning of 1993 for a price of $425,000. The machine is being depreciated on the straight-line basis. It has an estimated life of 15 years and a salvage value of $20,000. At the beginning of 1995, new information was obtained that made the firm increase the estimated life of the asset to 20 years. At the same time, salvage value was reduced from $20,000 to $5,000.

REQUIRED:

1. Compute the amount of depreciation expense that should be recorded in 1994 and the book value of the machine on December 31, 1994.
2. Compute the amount of depreciation expense for 1995. Show all computations and round to the nearest dollar, if necessary.

P10-6
Selecting Depreciation Methods
LO 5 & 6

You are the controller of the J. C. Ray Company. The firm has just purchased a specialized piece of equipment for $300,000. The equipment has a salvage value of $12,000 and an estimated useful life of eight years. In order to choose the most beneficial depreciation method, you have been asked to determine the following data:

a. At what point in the equipment's life does sum-of-the-years-digits depreciation exceed double-declining-balance depreciation?
b. At what point in the equipment's life does straight-line depreciation exceed both sum-of-the-years-digits and double-declining-balance depreciation?
c. If the equipment falls into the five-year class under tax depreciation, what would annual depreciation be for the next six years? (Only one-half year's depreciation is taken in the first year of the asset's life, and thus one-half year's depreciation is taken in Year 6.) See page 481 for percentage depreciation rates.
d. Assuming the firm desires to smooth earnings for financial reporting purposes and to increase cash flows by decreasing tax payments, which method or methods should the firm choose?

P10-7
Analyzing Depreciation Calculations
LO 5

Answer each of the following independent questions:

a. On July 1, 1992, Kickson Co. acquired equipment with an estimated useful life of eight years and a residual value of $5,000. On December 31, 1994, the Accumulated Depreciation account for this equipment amounted to $37,500, including the depreciation expense for 1994. If the firm only took six months' depreciation in 1992, determine the acquisition cost of the equipment. The firm uses straight-line depreciation.

b. On January 2, 1993, Pinky Co. purchased a building with an estimated useful life of 20 years and a residual value of $20,000. Depreciation expense for the year ended December 31, 1995 was $16,200. The firm uses double-declining-balance depreciation. Determine the acquisition cost of the building.

c. On January 2, 1994, the Bingo Company acquired a machine with a cost of $300,000. The firm estimated that the machine would have a life of seven years. The policy of Bingo is to use straight-line depreciation. On December 31, 1996, the book value of the machine was $180,000. Determine the residual value of the machine.

P10-8
Depreciation and Financial Statement Analysis
LO 5

The President of Laslow Products is reviewing the firm's financial position, and is concerned about how things are going. This is the firm's second year of operations, and while they have shown a small profit each year, the president worries that his primary financial backers, a group of small banks and investors, might not be satisfied with the firm's performance. The firm's condensed balance sheet follows:

Laslow Products
Balance Sheet
December 31, 1995

Assets			
Current assets			$120,000
Property and equipment			
Land		$ 60,000	
Equipment	$250,000		
Less: Accumulated depreciation	93,750		
		156,250	
			216,250
Total assets			$336,250
Liabilities and Stockholders' Equity			
Current liabilities			$ 92,500
Long-term debt			40,000
Stockholders' equity			
Capital stock		$100,000	
Retained earnings		103,750	
			203,750
Total liabilities and stockholders' equity			$336,250

The President indicates that during the previous year, 1994, the firm's net income was $54,230, and that during the two years the firm has been in existence, no dividends were issued. Finally, he can't remember what depreciation method the firm uses, but he knows all the firm's equipment was acquired at once. The equipment has a salvage value of $25,000 with an eight-year life, and two full years of depreciation has been taken.

REQUIRED:

1. Help the president by determining the depreciation method the firm uses and the amount of depreciation expense for the current year.
2. Determine the amount of net income for the year ended December 31, 1995.
3. Calculate the following ratios:
   a. Current ratio
   b. Total debt to equity

c. Profit margin percentage
d. Debt-to-equity ratio

4. Now the president wants you to recalculate net income using a different depreciation method, one that would result in higher net incomes for each of the prior two years. Determine what net income would have been if the depreciation on the equipment had always been calculated using this method.
5. Now determine the following ratios using the new depreciation method for year-end 1995:
   a. Current ratio
   b. Total debt to equity
   c. Profit margin percentage
   d. Debt-to-equity ratio
6. Compare and contrast the ratios you calculated under each of the two different methods.

P10-9
Purchase and Depreciation of Equipment
LO 2, 5 & 6

During your examination of the records of the Current Deterrent Company, you obtained the following information concerning the purchase of a new piece of equipment:

Acquisition date	4/1/94
Purchase price	$260,000
Terms	2/10, n/30
Installation costs	$ 7,500
Freight costs	$ 500
Repairs required for damage while in transit	$ 200
Normal repairs and maintenance, 12/1/95	$ 1,000
Estimated useful life	10 years
Salvage value	$ 0
Depreciation method	straight-line

REQUIRED:

1. Determine the acquisition cost of the equipment.
2. Assuming that depreciation is calculated from the month of purchase, determine the depreciation expense for 1994 and 1995.
3. Now assume that on January 2, 1996, the firm performs a complete rebuilding of the machine for $40,000. Because of this the firm believes that the asset's life will be extended an additional ten years from the beginning of 1996. Determine the correct amount of depreciation expense of 1996.

P10-10
Disposal of Plant Assets
LO 8

The Corona Company purchased a metal crusher for $225,000 on January 2, 1992. The asset has a five-year useful life and a salvage value of $15,000. The firm uses sum-of-the-years-digits depreciation.

REQUIRED: Make the entry to record the disposition of the asset under each of the following independent situations. Assume that depreciation has been recorded to the date of sale. (You do not have to make the depreciation entry unless so instructed.)

1. The asset is retired without consideration at the end of its useful life.
2. The asset is sold for cash at the end of its useful life for $11,500.
3. The asset is sold for cash on March 31, 1995, for (a) $106,000 and (b) $60,000. Depreciation for the period January 1, 1995, to March 31, 1995, must be recorded.
4. The asset is traded in for a similar one on January 2, 1996. A trade-in allowance of (a) $75,000 and (b) $45,000 is received. In both Cases (a) and(b), assume that the trade-in

allowance represents the fair market value of the asset given up at that time. The list price of the new machine is $120,000.

P10-11
Purchase and Disposal of Equipment
LO 2, 5 & 8

On January 2, 1992, the Pawlaski Cal Corporation purchased for cash a piece of high-tech equipment. The equipment, which cost $200,000, had a five-year life and a $20,000 salvage value. Straight-line depreciation is used. Installation costs were $10,000. At the beginning of 1994, the firm decided to upgrade the equipment and spent $50,000 in the process. The asset's Accumulated Depreciation account was debited for this amount. As a result, the asset was considered to have a life of six years from the beginning of 1994. In addition, the salvage value was increased by $5,000. However, at the end of 1995, a new machine came on the market that made the old equipment obsolete. As a result, Pawlaski Cal traded its old piece of equipment for a new one. The trade-in was made on December 31, 1995, but prior to any adjusting entries. The list price of the new equipment was $180,000, and Pawlaski Cal received a $40,000 trade-in allowance on the old equipment. The trade-in allowance was equal to the asset's fair market value at that time.

REQUIRED:

1. Record the purchase of the equipment on January 2, 1992.
2. Record depreciation expense for 1992 and 1993.
3. Record the relevant entries for 1994, including the depreciation expense.
4. Record all the relevant entries for 1995, including the depreciation expense.

P10-12
Operating Asset Accounting Systems
LO 9

Your consulting firm has been hired to design and implement an operating-asset accounting system for IPN Enterprises. The client firm has several different operating asset classifications: buildings, vehicles, office equipment, and production equipment. Each asset is assigned to a specific department and location.

REQUIRED:

1. Design an operating-asset register report. Your design should include appropriate page and column headings and identify the necessary subtotals and grand totals.
2. Design the input screen that would be used by accountants to enter information about a new operating asset into the system. Your design should include a screen title, data entry prompts, and spaces for information input.

P10-13
Patents
LO 10

Think, Inc. manufactures state-of-the-art electronic products. Its products are manufactured under two patents.

The first patent, No. 106-235, was developed by the firm. During 1994 and 1995, the firm incurred research and development costs of $600,000 and $200,000, respectively. In addition, in 1995, the firm incurred $100,000 of legal and other related costs to have its work patented. Management estimates that the patent will have a ten-year economic life, although the legal life is 17 years.

The second patent, No. 203-589, was purchased at the beginning of 1993 from its inventor for $120,000. The firm decided to amortize it over 15 years. During 1994, the firm was sued for patent infringement in connection with this patent. Think, Inc. was successful in defending the suit. Legal costs were $56,000. As a result of this suit, management decided that beginning in 1995, the remaining useful life of the patent should be reduced to ten years.

REQUIRED:

1. Make all the entries for 1994 and 1995 relative to each patent. Make a separate set of entries for each patent. Assume that the firm's year-end is December 31 and that adjusting entries are made yearly at this time.
2. At what amount should each patent be shown on the firms's December 31, 1995 balance sheet?

DISCUSSION AND INTERPRETATION PROBLEMS

D10-1 Understanding Financial Statements[17]

Boeing is the largest aerospace corporation in the United States as well as the nation's largest exporter of manufactured goods. Boeing is so large that the net cash expended on property, plant, and equipment during 1990 exceeded the gross national products of many countries. Refer to the information provided below from Boeing's annual report to answer the following questions:

a. What depreciation method does Boeing use for financial reporting purposes and why do you think they choose this particular method?
b. The bar chart reproduced below shows the pattern of net expenditures on property, plant, and equipment (PP&E) over the last five years. Why do you think that they had such a sharp increase?

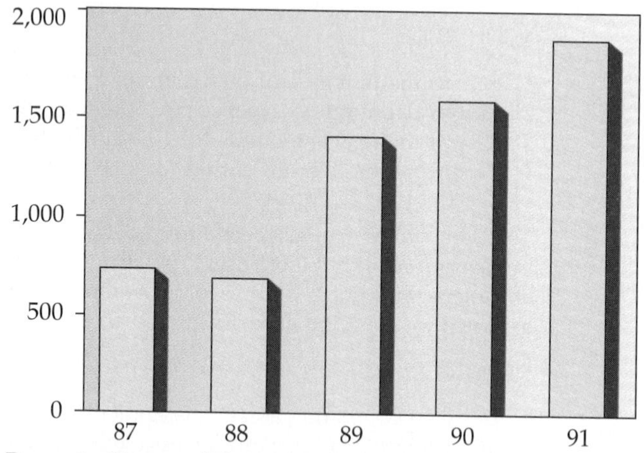

Property, Plant and Equipment: Net Additions**
Dollars in millions

-Depreciation
** Exclusive of acquisitions - UTL in 1990, ARGOSystems in 1987.

c. Note 5 indicates that $22 million in interest was capitalized. What does this mean? Why was it done?
d. The cash flow statement discloses the net additions to property, plant, and equipment during 1990 (i.e., the total cash paid out for new PP&E less the total cash received for sales of PP&E). You have learned that the cost of the PP&E sold was $208 million.
   1. How much were the purchases of PP&E during 1990?
   2. Make the journal entry that must have been made to record the sales of PP&E. (*Hint:* Make sure also to analyze the Accumulated Depreciation account.)

Capital Assets

Property, plant, and equipment, and aircraft and related aircraft equipment on operating leases are recorded at cost and depreciated over useful lives, principally by accelerated methods. Interest costs are capitalized with respect to plant and equipment additions.

17. This case was prepared by Professor Mark Defond of the School of Accounting at the University of Southern California.

Note 5
Property, Plant, and Equipment (in millions of dollars)

Property, plant, and equipment at December 31 consisted of the following:

	1991	*1990*
Land	$ 415	$ 380
Buildings	3,487	3,148
Machinery and equipment	5,533	4,816
Construction in progress	1,165	647
	$10,600	$8,991

Interest capitalized amounted to $44, $22, and $18 in 1991, 1990, and 1989, respectively.

D10-2 Financial Decision Case

The Oldham Corporation is in the paper products industry. The industry is very capital intensive, and it has been following the standard industry policy of calculating depreciation on the straight-line basis. The company is contemplating the purchase of a large milling machine that will cost $3 million. The machine will probably have a useful life of ten years, at which time the machine's salvage value will be negligible. However, the machine is most productive in its first five years. After that, increasing repairs and maintenance requirements will increase the machine's downtime and decrease its efficiency. Past experience indicates that repairs and maintenance will be $40,000 during its first year and increase at a rate of 10% per year.

REQUIRED: The president is contemplating the use of different depreciation methods and asks you, his financial adviser, the following questions:

1. I have read in a business magazine that for this type of asset an accelerated depreciation method such as double-declining balance is conceptually the most appropriate method. Why is this so? If you disagree, please let me know.
2. Most firms in the industry use straight-line depreciation. Prepare a comparative schedule for me showing the annual expense related to this machine if (a) straight-line or (b) double-declining-balance depreciation is used. Include both depreciation and repairs and maintenance expense in your schedule. (Round to whole dollars where appropriate.)
3. I am concerned that if I use double-declining balance depreciation, the earnings of the company, especially in the early years, will not look good in comparison with those of firms using straight-line depreciation. Because I am interested in selling the company in the near future, how will a potential buyer view our earnings, in comparison with those of other companies in the industry?
4. Our present machine is fully depreciated, and although not as productive as the new one would be, is still working. I understand that there would be some tax benefits to buying the new machine. Explain to me how depreciation is calculated for tax purposes and what the potential tax benefits are. (Assume that the equipment falls into a five-year-life class.)

D10-3 Research Assignment

In the text, mention was made of the FASB's project on asset impairment. Obtain a copy of the Discussion Memorandum (DM) published by the FASB and answer the following questions:

a. The FASB identified 7 issues of concern. List and explain these issues.
b. The DM provided an overview of accounting for asset impairment in several countries. Based on this information, briefly describe how asset impairments are accounted for:
   1. By the International Accounting Standards Committee.

2. In the following countries:
   a. United Kingdom
   b. Japan
   c. Mexico

D10-4
Research Assignment

In the text, the diversity of methods used in different countries to account for intangibles was described. Using information obtained from your library and other sources briefly describe how research and development costs are accounted for in:

a. Canada
b. France
c. The Netherlands
d. Australia

D10-5
Ethical Issues

Louie Madino is the division controller for the farming equipment manufacturing subsidiary of Plowshares, Inc., a large diversified agricultural concern. Louie has been lobbying his immediate boss, Sandra Vitkoski, to allow him to purchase some new automated equipment. Louie feels that the new equipment will increase the profitability of the division and thus increase his bonus, which is equal to 15% of the division profits before taxes.

Sandra has asked Louie to put together a formal proposal with estimated costs and benefits of the purchase. Louie asks his staff to prepare the proposal. He has made it clear to them that he wants this equipment and they should come forth with a proposal that will be received favorably by Sandra. He will personally review any proposal before it goes to Sandra. Louie recognizes that many of these capital budgeting decisions are based on estimating a number of variables, many of which are difficult to prove or disprove. He is also aware that the company does little, if any, follow-up comparison of actual results versus estimated cost savings realized from purchases. Louie has had a great deal of experience with these matters, and really trusts his gut feeling. He is sure that the equipment will provide benefits to the firm, and that notwithstanding any quantitative analysis, Plowshares should make the purchase. He is convinced that everyone will win on the purchase.

REQUIRED:

1. Comment on Louie's mandate to make the proposal work. Is he acting in the best interest of Plowshares? Why or why not?
2. Plowshares does not appear to have any follow-up procedures to review capital budgeting decisions. What type of procedures would you recommend in this case?
3. If you were Sandra Vitkoski, what procedures might you institute to make sure that subsidiary managers such as Louie provide you with accurate information upon which to make decisions?

CHAPTER 11
INVESTMENTS IN EQUITY SECURITIES

LEARNING OBJECTIVES

After studying this chapter, you should be able to:

1. Discuss the nature of publicly-held corporations and the role of security exchanges.
2. Discuss the nature of debt and equity securities.
3. Account for debt and equity securities when the investor has no influence or control over the investee.
4. Account for ownership interests between 20% and 50%.
5. Account for ownership interests above 50%.
6. Discuss the major international issues related to accounting for investments in debt and equity securities.
7. Discuss the major systems and control issues related to accounting for investments in debt and equity securities.

Scenario

Angela Lim has been a stockholder in American Telephone & Telegraph (AT&T) for a number of years. She began purchasing the stock when she was a student in college and has continued to make small but steady stock purchases over the past twenty years. As a result, she currently owns over 5,000 shares of AT&T common stock and expects to continue her purchases over the foreseeable future.

Angela has seen quite a bit of change at AT&T. Perhaps the greatest change faced by AT&T was the divestiture order which required the breakup of AT&T and the creation of the regional Bell companies. As the result of this divestiture, the information technology explosion, and worldwide competition, AT&T began to consider acquiring certain companies to strengthen its position in information technology. In early 1991 AT&T made a bid for NCR, one of the nation's large computer and business machine companies. After quite a battle between AT&T and NCR management, AT&T finally took control of NCR in a $7.5 million merger.

As a stockholder and interested individual Angela received and studied a great deal of information concerning the merger. Angela was particularly interested in an article which appeared in the *Wall Street Journal* describing the proposed terms of the merger. She was fascinated by the discussion of how, according to accountants, "American Telephone & Telegraph could save hundreds of millions of dollars in reported profits with the flick of a pen by changing its hostile $6.12 billion cash offer for NCR Corp. into a friendly stock swap."[1]

As Angela read the article she learned that there are two different methods of accounting for such mergers and that the resulting financial statements are substantially different. In the AT&T case, one method would result in a charge for goodwill amortization of over $400 million a year for up to 40 years, while the other method would result in no such charge.

Angela asked her accountant, Ben Inman, to explain how such a difference could occur. He told her that the merger could be accounted for by using either the "purchase" or the "pooling of interests" method. He explained that a firm's management does not have free choice in deciding what method to use; accounting standards for mergers and acquisitions depend upon how the particular merger or acquisition is structured. What is important is to structure the transaction in such a way as to achieve the accounting results desired. Ben pointed out that this was, in fact, what AT&T was contemplating in structuring its takeover of NCR so that it could be considered a pooling of interests.

Although Angela did not fully understand the accounting issues involved, it seemed to her that AT&T's management was acting prudently in structuring the merger this way. She was particularly pleased to learn that structuring it as a pooling of interests would probably save her some immediate tax dollars since the tax effects of the transaction would probably be delayed until such time as she decides to sell her stock in AT&T.

1. *The Wall Street Journal,* March 22, 1991, p. A5.

A decision to invest in another business is a complex business decision. Accountants help top management make this decision by providing financial information and by structuring the investment to meet management's objectives. This chapter explores investment-related accounting issues such as those faced by AT&T managers when they decided to merge with NCR.

INVESTMENTS

Objective 1
Discuss the nature of publicly-held corporations and the role of security exchanges.

The securities of business firms are purchased by many groups and individuals, including corporations, mutual funds, bank trust departments, and individual investors. Individuals or other entities may invest in the securities of other firms for several reasons. The investment may be made to invest idle cash in the hope of realizing a gain or in order to have significant influence or control over another corporation. In recent years, many companies have taken over others, through either friendly merger or hostile takeover. General Electric's purchase of RCA and Mitsushita's purchase of MCA are examples of friendly takeovers. Texaco's purchase of Getty Oil and AT&T's takeover of NCR are examples of what can happen during a hostile takeover attempt.

equity securities

debt securities

Equity and debt securities are the two major types of securities purchased by investors.[2] **Equity securities** are any securities, such as common and preferred stock, that represent an ownership interest in an enterprise. Equity securities also include rights and options to purchase or dispose of capital stock. **Debt securities** are any securities that represent a creditor relationship with a firm or government agency. Examples of debt securities include U.S. Treasury securities, U.S. government agency securities, municipal securities, corporate bonds, and commercial paper. Acquiring and disposing of equity and debt securities represent major investing activities (or in some cases operating activities) of a firm. This chapter focuses on accounting for both short-term and long-term investments in equity and certain debt securities. Some of the more complex issues in accounting for debt securities that are held to maturity are closely related to the accounting for the issuance of those securities and thus are discussed in Chapter 12, Long-Term Debt Financing.

Most investors purchase the securities of publicly-held corporations whose stock is traded on national and regional exchanges. National exchanges include the New York Stock Exchange, the American Stock Exchange, and the national over-the-counter market (NASDQ). The stocks of the largest publicly-held corporations are listed on the New York Stock Exchange, and the stocks of smaller corporations are listed on the American Stock Exchange or regional exchanges such as the Pacific Stock Exchange. The stocks of some corporations are not listed on these large organized exchanges, but rather on the over-the-counter market. The over-the-counter market is maintained by numerous brokerage firms buying and selling securities for their customers. Corporations whose stocks are traded on this market are generally smaller corporations or ones that have recently issued stock for the first time (often referred to as *going public*).

2. In recent years a number of different types of securities have been developed. Often, these securities are hybrids between debt and equity and have been given unusual names, such as "zebras." They are part of a broader range of items referred to as *financial instruments*.

A publicly-held corporation must comply with regulations of both the Securities and Exchange Commission (SEC) and the exchange on which its stock is listed. For example, these companies must file an annual report, called a *10-K*, with the SEC. In effect, this report is an expanded version of the financial data contained in the annual report to shareholders. The 10-K form must contain the corporation's financial statements, which have been audited by a certified public accounting firm. These same corporations must also file condensed quarterly reports, called *10-Qs*. Stock exchanges also have certain filing requirements. For example, the listing agreement between the New York Stock Exchange and member companies provides for the timely disclosure of earnings statements, dividend notices, and other financial information that might reasonably be expected to have a material effect on the market for a firm's securities.

THE NATURE OF DEBT AND EQUITY SECURITIES

Objective 2
Discuss the nature of debt and equity securities.

Accounting for investments in debt and equity securities depends upon: (1) the nature of the securities (debt versus equity); (2) management's intention to sell the securities or hold them to maturity; and (3) the degree of influence or control the investment gives the company making the investment (the investor) in the company in which it invested (the investee). Exhibit 11-1 summarizes how these variables relate to current accounting standards.

No significant influence or control exists when the investor is unable to have an important impact on either the financing or operating policies of the investee. Under current accounting standards, it is presumed that all levels of investment in debt securities, equity ownership of less than 20% of the voting stock, or any amount of the investee's nonvoting stock will not result in significant influence or control. In some rare cases, however, this presumption can be overcome. The correct accounting practices for these types of investments then depend upon whether debt or equity securities are involved, the marketability of these investments, and management's intention as to whether the investments will or will not be sold.

Significant influence exists when an investor can influence, but cannot control, the operating and financing policies of the investee. In many situations, this influence is evidenced by the investor's having a seat on the board of directors of the investee company, other participation in the policy-making process, material intercompany transactions, interchange of management personnel, or technological interdependencies. Current accounting standards presume that significant influence, but not control, exists when the investor holds at least 20%, but not more than 50%, of the voting stock of another company. In this situation, an investor can influence the investee's operating policies but cannot control them, because the investor does not have majority control.

Finally, a controlling interest exists when an investor is able to determine both the financial and operating policies of another company. Control is presumed when the investor owns more than 50% of the voting stock of another company.

The following section introduces you to the accounting concepts and standards related to investments in which no significant influence or control exists. The accounting standards for situations involving influence or control are discussed in subsequent parts of this chapter.

Exhibit 11-1

Amount of Influence or Control	*Percentage Owned*	*Accounting*
1. No significant influence or control:		
a. All debt securities	up to 100%	
• Held-to-Maturity		Amortized cost
• Trading		Fair value—unrealized holding gains or losses in current period's income
• Available-for-Sale		Fair value—unrealized holding gains or losses in stockholders' equity
b. Equity securities	Less than 20%	
• Trading		Fair value—unrealized holding gains or losses in current period's income
• Available-for-Sale		Fair value—unrealized holding gains or losses in current period's income
2. Significant Influence or Control	20% to 50%	Equity method—no fair value
3. Controlling Interest	More than 50%	Consolidated financial statements

Source: Four related pronouncements govern accounting for long-term investments: American Institute of Certified Public Accountants, Accounting Principles Board, Opinions No. 16, *Business Combinations* (New York: AICPA, 1970), and No. 18, *The Equity Method of Accounting for Investments in Common Stock*, (New York: AICPA, 1971); Financial Accounting Standards Board, Statement No. 94, *Consolidation of All Majority-Owned Subsidiaries* (Stamford, Conn: FASB, October 1987); and Financial Accounting Standards Board, Statement No. 115, *Accounting for Certain Investments in Debt and Equity Securities* (Norwalk, Conn: FASB, May 1993).

DEBT AND EQUITY SECURITIES—NO INFLUENCE OR CONTROL

Objective 3
Account for debt and equity securities when the investor has no influence or control over the investee.

As noted in Exhibit 11-1, no significant influence or control exists when a firm invests in debt securities of another company or equity securities that represent less than 20% of the voting stock or any amount of nonvoting stock. Investments at this level are primarily made to earn interest or dividend revenue and/or to earn gains while holding these securities. The accounting for these debt and equity securities has increased in complexity over the last few years as corporations have issued a variety of new securities. Many of the securities, with strange names like "zebras," blur the traditional distinction between debt and equity. In addition, the highly publicized failures of many financial institutions increased public attention to these issues. As a result, many individuals feel that the traditional accounting model based on the conservative doctrine of lower-of-cost-or-market valuation is no longer realistic and does not provide users of financial statements with relevant information.

The FASB came under extreme pressure from a variety of groups, including the Securities and Exchange Commission, the General Accounting Office, the accounting profession, and even members of Congress, to make substantive changes in accounting standards and practices related to certain investments in debt and equity securities. In May 1993, after much debate, the FASB issued Statement No. 115, *Accounting for Certain Investments in Debt and Equity Securities.* This statement, by requiring fair value accounting for many debt and equity securities, has made fundamental changes in the accounting practices for these securities. The discussion in this section is based upon the requirements of this new standard.[3]

Accounting for Certain Equity Securities and Debt Securities

FASB Statement No. 115 applies to all investments in debt securities and to investments in equity securities that have a readily determinable fair market value. According to Statement No. 115, an equity security has a readily determinable fair market value if:

- The sales price is currently available on a securities exchange such as the New York or American Stock Exchange, the national over-the-counter market, or other similar exchanges.
- When traded on a foreign exchange, the exchange has the breadth and scope of trading comparable to a U.S. market.
- The fair market value of an investment in a mutual fund is determined and published for current transactions.[4]

FASB Statement No. 115 does not apply to equity securities accounted for by the equity method of accounting (20%–50% ownership) and investments in consolidated subsidiaries (over 50% ownership). Both of these situations are discussed in later sections of this chapter.

According to the provisions of this statement, debt and equity securities with a readily determinable fair market value must be classified into one of the following three categories:

held-to-maturity securities

1. **Held-to-maturity securities:** Debt securities that management intends to hold to maturity. In order to classify a debt security in this category, management must not only have the positive intent to hold them to maturity but must also have the ability to do so. Equity securities are not included in this category, as they do not have a maturity date.

trading securities

2. **Trading securities:** Debt and equity securities that are purchased and held primarily for sale in the near term. Securities in this category are purchased and held principally for the purpose of selling them in the near future and thus are held for a short period of time. Management purchases these securities with the intent of generating short-term trading profits.

available-for-sale securities

3. **Available-for-sale securities:** These are debt and equity securities that are not classified as either held-to-maturity or trading.

Management must make the appropriate classification when the particular security is purchased. However, management should reassess this classification at the

3. This statement is effective for fiscal years beginning after December 31, 1993.
4. Financial Accounting Standards Board, Statement No. 115, *Accounting for Certain Investments in Debt and Equity Securities* (Norwalk, Conn: FASB, May 1993), par. 3a.

end of each reporting period. Certain procedures beyond the scope of an introductory textbook are required when debt or equity securities are transferred between categories. The correct accounting for each of these categories of debt and equity securities is described in Exhibit 11-2 and explained below.

Held-to-Maturity Securities. This category includes debt securities that management has the ability to hold to maturity and intends to do so. Because the accounting practice for investments in held-to-maturity securities parallels the accounting for the issuance of these securities, the actual accounting procedures are fully explained in the next chapter. However, to contrast the accounting for held-to-maturity securities with the other categories of securities, a brief explanation is provided below.

As noted in Exhibit 11-2, held-to-maturity securities are reported on the balance sheet at amortized cost. Interest income, including the amortization of premiums and discounts (discussed in detail in the next chapter), are included in current-period earnings. Because these debt securities will be held to maturity, no accounting recognition is given to unrealized holding gains and losses unless there is a permanent impairment (loss) in value.

As an example, on January 2, 1994, a firm purchases 100 $1,000, 6% (interest of 3% is paid semiannually every January 2 and July 2 until maturity), 30-year bonds and intends to hold them until they mature in 2024. The bonds were purchased at par or the face value for $100,000 (100 bonds × $1,000 each). The entry to record this purchase is:

Investment in Held-to-Maturity Debt Securities	100,000	
Cash		100,000
To record purchase of 100 $1,000, 6%, 30-year bonds.		

Exhibit 11-2
Accounting for Debt and Certain Equity Securities—No Influence or Control

Category	*Accounting Treatment*
Held-to-maturity Debt securities only that are expected to be held to maturity.	Reported at amortized cost. Interest income recognized in current earnings. No recognition of unrealized gains or losses.
Trading securities Debt and equity securities purchased and held for sale in the near term.	Reported at fair value. Interest and dividend income recognized in current earnings. Unrealized gains and losses recognized in current earnings.
Available-for-sale. Debt and equity securities purchased and not classified as trading or held-to-maturity.	Reported at fair value. Interest and dividend income recognized in current earnings. Unrealized gains and losses not included in current earnings, but shown as a separate item in stockholders' equity.

Every six months the firm receives interest of $3,000 (3% × $100,000). The entry to record this interest on July 2, 1994 is:

Cash	3,000	
Interest Revenue		3,000
To record semiannual interest payment of $3,000.		

The January 2 interest receipt is handled a little differently because of the necessity to make an interest receivable accrual at the December 31 year-end. The entries at December 31, 1994 and January 2, 1995 are:

Dec. 31, 1994	Interest Receivable	3,000	
	Interest Revenue		3,000
	To record interest receivable for six months.		
Jan. 2, 1995	Cash	3,000	
	Interest Receivable		3,000
	To record receipt of interest receivable.		

Most debt securities, like equity securities, trade on national exchanges. However, because the bonds in our example are assumed to be held to maturity, no recognition is given to increases or decreases in market values. The only time an adjustment would be necessary is when there is a permanent price decline. This might occur if the firm issuing the bonds entered bankruptcy proceedings. This would most likely cause a permanent decline in the market value of the bonds, and the investing firm would be required to write down the cost basis of the bonds to their new fair market value. The amount of this write-down is then included in the investing firm's current earnings for the period.

Trading Securities. The most significant changes in accounting standards made by FASB Statement No. 115 relate to securities classified as trading securities. These are either debt or equity securities whose market prices are readily determinable and are purchased and held for sale in the near term. In effect, management purchases these securities in the hope of realizing a short-term trading profit. As summarized in Exhibit 11-2, these securities are first recorded at cost and then adjusted to fair value at the balance sheet date. Dividends and interest are recorded in the current period's income as earned. Any unrecognized holding gains and losses that result from the adjustment to fair value are also reflected in current period earnings on the income statement.

To illustrate the accounting for trading securities, assume that during its first year of operations, the Haskell Corporation made the following purchases of equity securities which it classified as trading securities (although debt and equity trading securities are accounted for similarly, for ease of illustration, this example only includes equity securities):

Security	*Number of Shares*	*Price per Share**	*Total Cost*
Kahn, Inc.—Common	100	$ 75	$ 7,500
Webb Construction—Preferred	100	200	20,000
Stern-Price Piano—Common	50	60	3,000
			$30,500

*Includes all brokerage commissions.

Haskell Corporation made the following entry to record this transaction:

Investment in Trading Securities	30,500	
Cash		30,500
To record purchase of trading securities.		

Accounting for Subsequent Events. Investors purchase trading securities in the hope of realizing a return on their investment. This return is in the form of dividends and interest received while the equity and debt securities are held and a gain (or loss) when the securities are sold. Because the securities in our example are classified as trading, both dividends received and unrealized holding gains and losses are included in current period's income.

To demonstrate, assume that the Haskell Corporation still owns all 100 shares of Kahn, Inc. On December 1, Kahn, Inc., declares a $.75 per share dividend payable on December 20. Haskell makes the following entry on December 20:

Dec. 20 Cash	75	
Dividend Revenue		75
To record dividend received of $75. ($.75 × 100 shares)		

As noted, investors intend to sell trading securities in the near future, hopefully at a price above the original purchase price. The market price of these securities reacts to general economic conditions as well as to specific events that affect the firm. Thus the market price of the investor's stock or bonds may rise or fall during a particular accounting period. The investor may choose to sell the securities and realize a gain or loss on the completed transaction or hold them and incur an unrealized holding gain or loss. One of the issues confronting the accounting profession was how to account for these unrealized holding gains and losses. This issue was finally resolved when the FASB issued Statement No. 115 requiring that these trading securities be reported at fair value on the balance sheet and that unrealized holding gains and losses be included in current period's income. The FASB adopted this position based upon the following reasoning:

For securities that are actively managed (trading securities), the Board believes that financial reporting is improved when earnings reflect the economic consequences of the events of the reporting enterprise (such as changes in fair value) as well as the transactions (such as purchases and sales of securities) that occur. Including changes in fair value in the determination of earnings results in more relevant financial information to current shareholders . . .[5]

To illustrate the steps necessary to adjust trading securities to fair value, we will continue the Haskell example. Because Haskell prepares financial statements once a year as of December 31, it must revalue its trading securities as of that date. The cost and market values of the trading securities at December 31, 1994 are shown in Exhibit 11-3. Notice that the total fair value of the securities as of December 31, 1994 is $33,500, or $3,000 above the recorded cost of $30,500. Thus

5. Statement No. 115, par. 92.

Exhibit 11-3

Haskell Corporation
Trading Securities
December 31, 1994

Security	*Cost*	*Fair Value Dec. 31, 1994*	*Unrealized Gain or (Loss)*
Kahn, Inc.—Common	$ 7,500	$10,000	$2,500
Webb Construction—Preferred	20,000	21,400	1,400
Stern-Price Piano—Common	3,000	2,100	(900)
Totals	$30,500	$33,500	$3,000

Haskell must make the following adjusting entry at December 31, 1994 to record this $3,000 unrealized holding gain:

Dec. 31, 1994	Investment in Trading Securities	3,000	
	Unrealized Holding Gain or Loss on Trading Securities		3,000
	To record unrealized holding gain on trading securities.		

It is important to understand that the debit increases the reported amount of the securities in the Investment in Trading Securities account to fair value or $33,500. Because trading securities are expected to be sold in the near future, they are classified as a current asset on the balance sheet. The credit to the Unrealized Holding Gain appears on the income statement and increases current period's earnings. Depending upon the materiality of the amount, it will most likely be included in the Other income and expense category.

Events During 1995. To continue the example, assume that two events occurred in 1995 involving trading securities: (1) on April 14, 1995, Haskell sold 50 shares of Kahn, Inc., at $88 per share, and (2) an adjustment was made at December 31, 1995 to value the securities at fair value. The entry to record the 50 shares of Kahn, Inc., is:

April 14, 1995	Cash	4,400	
	Loss on Sale of Trading Securities	600	
	Investment in Trading Securities		5,000
	To record sale of 50 shares of Kahn, Inc.		

Fair value of Kahn, Inc., at 12/31/94:	
50 shares at $100 per share	$5,000
Sale price of Kahn, Inc.:	
50 shares at $88 per share	4,400
Loss on sale	$ 600

Notice that a loss of $600 is recorded, which is the difference between the reported $5,000 fair value of Kahn, Inc., at December 31, 1994 and the sales price of $4,400 on April 14, 1995. This realized loss is reported in income for the year ending December 31, 1995.

The fair values of the remaining trading securities at December 31, 1994 and December 31, 1995 are shown in Exhibit 11-4. At the end of 1995 the total fair value of the trading securities is only $26,400, compared to a fair value at December 31, 1994 of $28,500. Thus Haskell has suffered an unrealized holding loss of $2,100 during 1995. This unrealized holding loss is recorded in a December 31, 1995 adjusting entry as follows:

Dec. 31, 1995		
Unrealized Holding Gain or Loss on Trading Securities	2,100	
Investment in Trading Securities		2,100
To record unrealized holding loss on trading securities.		

As a result of this adjusting entry, the trading securities are reported on Haskell's December 31, 1995 balance sheet at their fair value of $26,400, and an unrealized holding loss of $2,100 is shown on the income statement along with the realized loss of $600 that resulted from the April 14, 1995 sale. The T account for Investment in Trading Securities as of December 31, 1995 is shown below.

Investment in Trading Securities

1994 Purchase	30,500		
12/31/94 Unrealized Gain	3,000		
12/31/94 Balance	33,500	4/14/95 Sale	5,000
		12/31/95 Unrealized Loss	2,100
12/31/95 Balance	26,400		

Exhibit 11-4

Haskell Corporation
Trading Securities
December 31, 1994 and 1995

Security	*Fair Value Dec. 31, 1994*	*Fair Value Dec. 31, 1995*	*Unrealized Gain or (Loss)*
Kahn, Inc.—Common	$ 5,000	$ 3,600	($1,400)
Webb Construction—Preferred	21,400	21,000	(400)
Stern-Price Piano—Common	2,100	1,800	(300)
Totals	$28,500	$26,400	($2,100)

Available-for-Sale Securities. Available-for-sale securities are either current or noncurrent debt or equity securities that are not classified as either trading or held-to-maturity securities. If management's intention is to hold these securities beyond one year or the firm's operating cycle, they would be classified as a noncurrent asset; otherwise they would be considered current. The primary difference in the accounting for these securities versus trading securities is that any unrealized holding gains and losses resulting from revaluing these securities to fair value at the balance sheet date is reported as a separate item in stockholders' equity until realized. That is, the unrealized holding gain or loss is not a component of current period's income as is the case for trading securities. The FASB took this approach because it was concerned about reporting fluctuations in the fair value of these types of securities in reported earnings.

Available-for-Sale Securities Example. To illustrate the accounting procedures mandated in FASB No. 115 for available-for-sale securities, assume that on July 1, 1994, the Popper Company purchased 100 shares of Bailey, Inc., at $40 per share (total cost $4,000) and 100 shares of Essence, Inc., at $60 per share (total cost $6,000 per share). These securities are properly classified as available-for-sale. The Popper Company made the following journal entry at July 1, 1994:

July 1, 1994	Investment in Available-for-Sale Securities	10,000	
	Cash		10,000
	To record purchase of available-for-sale securities.		

As is the case for trading securities, dividends or interest are recorded as income when they are earned. Furthermore, at each balance sheet date, the securities are valued at their fair value. However, in this situation any unrealized holding gain or loss is considered a component of stockholders' equity and not included in current period's income.

To continue with this illustration, assume that on December 31, 1994 Bailey, Inc., stock was valued at $34 per share and Essence, Inc., at $62 per share. The comparative costs and fair values are shown in Exhibit 11-5. Because fair value of the securities is only $9,600, versus their recorded amount of $10,000, an unrealized holding loss of $400 must be recorded as follows:

Dec. 31, 1994	Unrealized Holding Gain or Loss on Available-for-Sale Securities	400	
	Investment in Available-for-Sale Securities		400
	To record unrealized holding loss on available-for-sale securities.		

This journal entry reduces the recorded cost of the available-for-sale securities to their fair value. As stated, the Unrealized Holding Gain or Loss on Available-for-Sale Securities account is not an income statement account; it is a separate component of stockholders' equity. In this case the account has a debit balance.

Exhibit 11-5

Popper Company
Available-for-Sale Securities
December 31, 1994

Security	Total Cost	Fair Value Dec. 31, 1994	Unrealized Holding Gains (Losses)
Bailey, Inc.	$ 4,000	$3,400	($600)
Essence, Inc.	6,000	6,200	200
Totals	$10,000	$9,600	($400)

To continue with this example, assume that next year at December 31, 1995, the fair value of the available-for-sale securities is $10,600. Thus, an unrealized holding gain occurred in the amount of $1,000 ($10,600 – $9,600, the fair value at 12/31/94) during 1995. This assumes that no other transactions affecting this account occurred. The following journal entry would be made at December 31, 1995:

		Debit	Credit
Dec. 31, 1995	Investment in Available-for-Sale Securities	1,000	
	Unrealized Holding Gain or Loss on Available-for-Sale Securities		1,000
	To record unrealized holding gain on available-for-sale securities.		

After this journal entry is posted, the Investment in Available-for-Sale Securities account would now be shown at $10,600 (see T account below), the fair value of the securities, and the Unrealized Holding Gain or Loss on Available-for-Sale Securities account would have a credit balance of $600. This is last year's debit balance of $400 plus the $1,000 unrealized holding gain that occurred this year.

Investment in Available-for-Sale Securities

7/1/94 Purchase	10,000	12/31/94 Unrealized Loss	400
12/31/94 Balance	9,600		
12/31/95 Unrealized Gain	1,000		
12/31/95 Balance	10,600		

FASB Statement No. 115 Required Disclosures

As of the writing of this text, there have not been any actual examples of FASB Statement No. 115 disclosures; the statement becomes effective after December 15, 1993. Exhibit 11-6, however, does list the financial statement disclosures required by FASB Statement No. 115.

Exhibit 11-6[6]
FASB Statement No. 115 Required Disclosures

Balance Sheet

Balances

For securities classified as available-for-sale or held-to-maturity, disclosure (as of each balance sheet date and for each major security type) is made of:

- Aggregate fair value
- Gross unrealized holding gains
- Gross unrealized holding losses
- Amortized cost basis

Maturities

As of the date of the most recent financial statment presented, information must be disclosed about contractual maturities:

- Within one year
- After 1 year through 5 years
- After 5 years through 10 years
- Over 10 years

Income Statement

For each period that an income statment is presented, the following disclosures are made:

- Proceeds from sale of available-for-sale securities and the gross realized gains and losses.
- The cost basis (specific identification, average cost, etc.) used in computing realized gains and losses.
- Gross gains and losses included in earnings resulting from transfers from available-for-sale to trading.
- The change during the period in net unrealized holding gain or loss on available-for-sale securities included in stockholders' equity.
- The change during the period in net unrealized holding gain or loss on trading securities included in income.
- For any held-to-maturity securities sold (or transferred to another category), the security's amortized cost, the resulting realized gain or unrealized gain or loss and the circumstances leading to the decision to sell or transfer.

Evaluation of FASB Statement No. 115

FASB Statement No. 115 represents a major shift away from the historical cost model. The economic environment of the late 1980s and early 1990s caused many financial statement users to question the relevance of historical costs when fair values were readily available. Under the then leadership of Chairman Richard Breeden, the Securities and Exchange Commission was particularly adamant in its push towards fair value accounting for financial instruments. After much debate, FASB Statement No. 115 was adopted in May 1993.

The accounting standards outlined in Statement No. 115 are a reasonable approach to recognizing fair values in certain debt and equity securities. However, this statement does not address all the related issues. For example, firms often incur liabilities in the purchase of these debt and equity securities. How-

6. Adapted from James T. Parks, "FASB 115: It's Back to the Future for Market Value Accounting," *Journal of Accountancy*, September 1993, p. 56.

ever, there are no provisions in Statement No. 115 to revalue these related liabilities to fair value. In the future, we can expect additional fair value disclosures and requirements.

OWNERSHIP INTEREST BETWEEN 20% AND 50%

Objective 4
Account for ownership interests between 20% and 50%.

Significant influence but not control is presumed to exist when an investor holds an interest in the investee of at least 20% but not more than 50%. In this situation, the investor can influence the investee's operating and financial policies but cannot completely control them. For example, the investor may control one or two seats on the investee's board of directors, gained through the exercise of a large block of stock, but the investor is unable to control the investee completely as there are other significant investors.

When this relationship exists between the investor and the investee, dividends paid to the investor by the investee are no longer a proper measure of income received. This is because the investor is able to influence the investee's dividend policy. Thus, an investor may pressure an investee to pay dividends in an amount that has little to do with the investee's profitability. For example, if the investee is forced to issue a large dividend that otherwise would not be issued, the cost method of accounting is not appropriate and the equity method should be used.

The Equity Method of Accounting for Investments

equity method

The primary differences between the equity and the cost/fair value method of accounting for investments are the way in which income from the investment is recognized and the fact that fair value is not applied when the equity method is used. Under the **equity method** of accounting, the investment is first recorded at its acquisition cost. Subsequently, the investment account is adjusted to reflect the proportionate increase or decrease in the investee's stockholders' equity that results from the investee's net income or loss for the period. That is, as the investee earns net income, its stockholders' equity increases; the investor then recognizes its proportionate share of the increase as investment income. If the investee suffers a loss, the investor will recognize a proportionate share of the loss.

Under the equity method of accounting, dividends declared are not considered income but rather a reduction in the investment account. This is because a cash dividend reduces the net assets (stockholders' equity) of the investee, so the investor records a proportionate decrease in its investment account. In effect, dividends received represent a conversion of the investment into cash. Thus, under the equity method, investors recognize revenue as the investee earns it rather than at the time dividends are declared or received.

Illustration of the Equity Method. Assume that at the beginning of the year, the Jackson Corporation purchased for $300,000 a 30% interest in Wildcat Ventures. At the time of purchase, Wildcat Ventures' net assets totaled $1 million, so the $300,000 purchase exactly equaled a 30% interest in Wildcat's net assets.[7] Dur-

7. In reality, the purchase price rarely equals the book value of the investee's net assets. This assumption has been made in order to simplify the illustration. Adjustments can be made if the purchase price is more or less than the book value.

ing the year, Wildcat Ventures reported net income of $70,000 and declared cash dividends of $25,000. Jackson Corporation would make the following entries to reflect these events:

At time of acquisition:		
Investment in Wildcat Ventures	300,000	
Cash		300,000
To record 30% interest in Wildcat Ventures.		
At Jackson's year-end:		
Investment in Wildcat Ventures	21,000	
Investment Income		21,000
To record increase in investment from 30% share of net income earned by Wildcat, $70,000 × 30% = $21,000.		
Cash	7,500	
Investment in Wildcat Ventures		7,500
To record decrease in investment due to receipt of dividends, $25,000 × 30% = $7,500.		

Note that after these events, Wildcat Ventures' net assets or stockholders' equity is $1,045,000, or the book value of $1 million at acquisition plus the net income of $70,000 less the dividends of $25,000. The balance in the investment account is now $313,500, or the original investment of $300,000 plus Jackson's share of the net income, $21,000 less its share of the dividend, $7,500. Thus, the balance in the investment account equals 30% of the net assets of Wildcat Ventures ($1,045,000 × 30% = $313,500). The equity method ensures that the balance in the investment in the investee account equals the investor's proportionate share of the net assets purchased. These points are illustrated in the following T accounts:

Wildcat's Books
Stockholders' Equity, Wildcat Ventures

		Beg. Bal.	1,000,000
Dividends	25,000	Net income	70,000
			1,045,000

Jackson's Books
Investment in Wildcat Ventures

Beg. Bal.	300,000	Dividends	7,500
Net income	21,000		
	313,500		

To summarize, the equity method of accounting for long-term investments ensures that the investor reflects in its statements, during the period it was earned, the income or loss of the company in which it invested. The lower-of-cost-or-market method is not applied, so no adjustments are made for declines (if any) in the investment's market value. Finally, the disclosure requirements outlined in FASB Statement No. 107 do not apply to investments of 20% or more.

OWNERSHIP INTEREST ABOVE 50%—ACCOUNTING FOR MERGERS AND ACQUISITIONS

Objective 5
Account for ownership interests above 50%.

parent company
subsidiary

Often, a corporation owns more than 50% of the stock of another corporation. The corporation that owns the majority of stock is called the **parent company,** and the corporation that is wholly or partially owned is called a **subsidiary.** One parent often owns several subsidiaries. The degree of ownership interest in these subsidiaries may vary between 50 and 100%.

Once a corporation owns more than 50% of the stock of another company, the parent corporation can elect the board of directors of the subsidiary and can control its operating and financial policies. In effect, the parent and subsidiary or subsidiaries represent one economic unit, and the entity assumption requires that it be reported as such.

The parent company and the subsidiary or subsidiaries are separate legal entities, so they each maintain separate records and prepare separate financial statements for internal purposes and, under some circumstances, for external purposes. On the parent's books, the investment in the subsidiary is accounted for by the equity method of accounting. Since the parent and subsidiary represent one economic unit, the parent company prepares consolidated financial statements to be distributed to external users. These consolidated balance sheets, income statements, and statements of cash flows show the financial position, operating results, and cash flows of the entire economic unit.

In some cases, the subsidiary will also publish separate financial statements. This usually happens when the subsidiary is located in a different country from the parent company. For example, assume that one of Xerox's subsidiaries is a French company located in France. Most likely, that subsidiary will publish its separate financial statements for dissemination in France that comply with French GAAP. The consolidated entity obviously will also prepare consolidated financial statements according to U.S. GAAP for dissemination in the U.S. and worldwide.

Consolidated Financial Statements

consolidated financial statements

Consolidated financial statements are financial statements of a parent company and its subsidiaries presented as if the firms were a single economic entity. Consolidated financial statements should not be confused with combined financial statements. Although the assets, liabilities, revenues, and expenses of all the entities are combined to provide a single set of financial statements, certain eliminations and adjustments are made. These eliminations are necessary to ensure that only arm's-length transactions between independent parties are reflected in the consolidated statements; transactions between related parties are not counted. For example, a parent and subsidiary may make intercompany sales and/or loans and borrowings. Viewed independently, the transactions represent sales and expenses or assets and liabilities on the books of the respective entities. When consolidated statements are prepared, these intercompany transactions must be eliminated.

When to Prepare Consolidated Financial Statements. If one company owns more than 50% of the voting stock of another company, consolidated financial statements must be prepared unless control of the subsidiary is temporary or does not rest with the majority owner.[8] Prior to 1987, many firms did not consolidate their financing subsidiaries. For example, General Motors did not consolidate GMAC, its huge financing subsidiary (GMAC is the subsidiary that provides auto loans for customers of General Motors), nor did General Electric consolidate its financing subsidiary, General Electric Financial Services, Inc. (GEFS). These were shown on the respective balance sheet as a one-line item, investments in unconsolidated subsidiaries, accounted for by the equity method. In effect, only one number represented General Motor's equity in GMAC or General Electric's equity in GEFS on the balance sheet, but that one number represented the net of billions of dollars of assets and liabilities of GMAC or GEFS.

The FASB, as well as users of financial statements, were concerned that not allowing companies to consolidate majority-owned financing subsidiaries made it difficult to determine the true financial picture of the consolidated company. Huge liabilities of these subsidiaries were not fully disclosed. This phenomenon, called *off-balance-sheet financing*, was and continues to be a major problem in financial reporting. In late 1987, the FASB decided to act; it issued Statement No. 94, which except for two minor exceptions, requires the consolidation of all majority-owned subsidiaries. The FASB stated:

The Board believes that the objectives of financial reporting are better met if significant amounts of assets, liabilities, revenues, and expenses are not omitted from balance sheets. That omission is an important factor in what is often criticized as "off-balance-sheet financing." By requiring consolidation of all subsidiaries, Statement 94 is a major step in resolving the problem of off-balance-sheet financing.[9]

Preparing Consolidated Financial Statements—An Introduction

Accounting procedures for consolidation are quite complex and depend on the exact nature in which the transaction is structured; they occupy many chapters in advanced accounting texts. The purpose here is to introduce you to the basics so that you will be able to interpret and understand consolidated financial statements. First to be considered is consolidation of a 100% owned subsidiary acquired through a cash purchase at book value. A more complex situation will be treated later.

Consolidation of a 100% Owned Subsidiary at Date of Acquisition. To illustrate the preparation of consolidated financial statements, assume that on January 2, 1995, Scientific Instruments purchased 100% of the common stock of Technical Tools, Inc. The purchase price was $100,000, which represented the book value of Technical Tool's net assets at that time. Before the purchase, Scientific Instruments had made a $25,000, non-interest-bearing loan to Technical Tools. The individual balance sheets of the two companies immediately after the purchase are shown in Exhibit 11-7.

8. Financial Accounting Standards Board, Statement No. 94, *Consolidation of All Majority-Owned Subsidiaries* (Stamford, Conn.: FASB, October 1987).

9. Financial Accounting Standards Board, Status Report No. 190 (Stamford, Conn.: FASB, October 30, 1987), p. 1.

Exhibit 11-7

Scientific Instruments and Technical Tools Balance Sheets January 2, 1995		
Accounts	*Scientific Instruments*	*Technical Tools*
Cash	$ 20,000	$ 18,000
Notes receivable from Technical Tools	25,000	—
Accounts receivable, net	60,000	22,000
Investment in Technical Tools	100,000	—
Other assets	165,000	140,000
Total assets	$370,000	$180,000
Notes payable to Scientific Instruments	—	$ 25,000
Accounts payable	$ 10,000	5,000
Other liabilities	60,000	50,000
Common stock	175,000	55,000
Retained earnings	125,000	45,000
Total liabilities and stockholders' equity	$370,000	$180,000

A *worksheet* is a common tool used by accountants to gather information needed for various purposes including consolidation. The worksheet used to prepare consolidated financial statements for Scientific Instruments immediately after the acquisition of Technical Tools is shown in Exhibit 11-8. Remember that

Exhibit 11-8

Consolidated Balance Sheet Worksheet January 2, 1995—Acquisition Date					
			Intercompany Eliminations		
Accounts	*Scientific Instruments*	*Technical Tools*	*Debit*	*Credit*	*Consolidated Balance Sheet*
Cash	$ 20,000	$ 18,000			$ 38,000
Notes receivable from Technical Tools	25,000	—		$ 25,000[a]	
Accounts receivable, net	60,000	22,000			82,000
Investment in Technical Tools	100,000	—		100,000[b]	
Other assets	165,000	140,000			305,000
Total assets	$370,000	$180,000			$425,000
Notes payable to Scientific Instruments	—	$ 25,000	$ 25,000[a]		—
Accounts payable	$ 10,000	5,000			$ 15,000
Other liabilities	60,000	50,000			110,000
Common stock	175,000	55,000	55,000[b]		175,000
Retained earnings	125,000	45,000	45,000[b]		125,000
Total liabilities and stockholders' equity	$370,000	$180,000	$125,000	$125,000	$425,000

[a]To eliminate intercompany debt.
[b]To eliminate investment in Technical Tools against stockholders' equity of Technical Tools.

each firm maintains separate books and records. Thus, a worksheet is needed to prepare a consolidated balance sheet. However, the elimination entries on the worksheet are not made in the individual accounting records of the parent or subsidiary; they are made for consolidation purposes only.

As noted, certain elimination entries must be made before a consolidated balance sheet is prepared. Typical intercompany eliminations pertain to intercompany stock ownership, intercompany debt, and intercompany revenue and expenses. Since this example involves constructing a consolidated balance sheet at the date of acquisition, only entries to eliminate the investment and intercompany debt are required. Eliminations of revenue and expense accounts are more complex matters, required after the consolidated entity begins to operate. These entries are discussed in advanced textbooks.

Elimination of Intercompany Stock Ownership. The entry to eliminate the Investment in Technical Tools account is necessary in order to keep from double-counting the amount of the investment. Before the consolidation, the $100,000 investment in Technical Tools was shown in the investment account. However, the purpose of the consolidated balance sheet is to combine the individual accounts of the parent and subsidiary. Thus, the $100,000 investment account must be eliminated so that the individual assets and liabilities of Technical Tools that net to $100,000 can be added to the respective accounts of Scientific Instruments to form the consolidated balance sheet. Another way to view this is that the consolidated financial statements represent the two companies joined as one. It would not make sense for the consolidated firm to show an investment in itself as an asset on the consolidated balance sheet.

The elimination of the investment account is made against the stockholders' equity accounts of Technical Tools. Essentially, there are no external stockholders of Technical Tools. All the stock is owned internally by the consolidated entity. Ownership of a company's own stock does not give rise to either an asset or stockholders' equity. Thus the purpose of the entry is to eliminate the investment account that Scientific Instruments shows on its books against the stockholders' equity accounts of Technical Tools.

Elimination of Intercompany Debt. Before Scientific Instruments purchased Technical Tools, it lent the firm $25,000. Scientific Instruments thus recorded a note receivable, and Technical Tools recorded a note payable. From a consolidated entity point of view, this transaction results only in the transfer of cash from one part of the entity to another and does not give rise to a receivable or a payable. Thus, in preparing a consolidated balance sheet, an entry must be made to eliminate the notes receivable and payable.

Preparation of a Consolidated Balance Sheet. After the two elimination entries are posted to the worksheet, the remaining assets and liabilities and stockholders' equity accounts are combined to prepare the consolidated balance sheet columns in the worksheet shown in Exhibit 11-8. The actual consolidated balance sheet is presented in Exhibit 11-9.

Purchase Above or Below Book Value. To simplify the discussion, it was assumed that the purchase price has been equal to the book value of the net assets acquired. Usually this will not be the case. The price an investor is willing to pay for a business depends on several factors, such as general economic conditions, market prices, estimates of future anticipated earnings, and the relative bargaining position of the buyer and seller. The book value of a subsidiary's net

Exhibit 11-9

Scientific Instruments, Inc.
Consolidated Balance Sheet
January 2, 1995

Assets		*Liabilities & Stockholders' Equity*		
Cash	$ 38,000	Liabilities		
Accounts receivable	82,000	Accounts payable		$ 15,000
Other assets	305,000	Other liabilities		110,000
		Stockholders' equity		
		Common stock	$175,000	
		Retained earnings	125,000	300,000
		Total liabilities		
Total assets	$425,000	and stockholders' equity		$425,000

assets therefore bears little relationship to what a buyer may be willing to pay for them. For example, a parent will pay more for a business if it feels that the potential subsidiary's assets are undervalued, that there is a potential for future excess earnings, or perhaps that the subsidiary owns a valuable patent needed by the parent. On the other hand, the parent may pay less than the book value for a potential subsidiary's net assets if these assets are overvalued, the firm is in a declining industry, or it has suffered losses in the past.

The Accounting Principles Board has developed a number of guidelines to be used when the purchase price differs from the book value of the net assets acquired.[10] Briefly, the purchase method which basically assumes the outright purchase for cash of one company by another follows the principles normally found under historical cost accounting in regard to the purchase of assets. Thus, when the purchase price exceeds the book value of the net assets acquired, the purchase price is first allocated to the identifiable assets acquired and liabilities assumed, based on their respective fair market values. Any excess cost of the acquired company over the amounts assigned to the identifiable assets, less liabilities assumed, should be recorded as goodwill. In effect, the acquired net assets of the acquired company are recorded at their fair market value, and any excess cost is considered goodwill. This is based on the assumption that the reason the parent is willing to pay more for a subsidiary than the fair market value of its identifiable net assets is the existence of goodwill.

In some circumstances, the parent will purchase the subsidiary at a price below the book value of the subsidiary's net assets. This implies that some assets are recorded at amounts above their current values. In this situation, the assets of the company are written down to their fair market value. Negative goodwill is rarely recorded.

To demonstrate the preparation of a consolidated balance sheet when the parent pays more than the book value of the subsidiary's net assets, assume that on December 31, 1995, the Peter Corporation purchased 100% of the Mary Company

10. Opinion 16. The actual procedures depend upon how the transaction is structured and the resulting accounting method. As discussed later, either the purchase or the pooling of interests method is used.

for $140,000. The book value of Mary Company's net assets (common stock plus retained earnings) on the date of acquisition (see Exhibit 11-10) is $130,000. The Peter Corporation paid $10,000 in excess of the book value of Mary's net assets. The parent company evaluated the fair market value of the Mary Company's net assets and decided to increase the property, plant, and equipment by $7,500. The remaining $2,500 was allocated to goodwill.

The consolidated worksheet is shown in Exhibit 11-11. The following worksheet entry is made to write off the investment account against the stockholders'

Exhibit 11-10

Mary Company
Balance Sheet
December 31, 1995

Assets		*Equities*	
Cash	$ 10,000	Current liabilities	$ 20,000
Accounts receivable, net	15,000	Long-term debt	15,000
Inventory	40,000	Common stock	75,000
Property, plant, & equipment, net	100,000	Retained earnings	55,000
Total assets	$165,000	Total liabilities and stockholders' equity	$165,000

Exhibit 11-11

Consolidated Balance Sheet Worksheet
December 31, 1995—Acquisition Date

Accounts	*Peter Corporation*	*Mary Company*	*Eliminations* *Debit*	*Eliminations* *Credit*	*Consolidated Balance Sheet*
Cash	$ 24,000	$ 10,000			$ 34,000
Accounts receivable	36,000	15,000		$ 6,000[a]	45,000
Inventory	80,000	40,000			120,000
Investment in Mary Company	140,000	0		140,000[b]	0
Property, plant, and equipment, net	200,000	100,000	$ 7,500[b]		307,500
Goodwill	0	0	2,500[b]		2,500
Total assets	$480,000	$165,000			$509,000
Current liabilities	$ 60,000	$ 20,000	6,000[a]		$ 74,000
Long-term debt	100,000	15,000			115,000
Common stock	100,000	75,000	75,000[b]		100,000
Paid-in capital	50,000	0			50,000
Retained earnings	170,000	55,000	55,000[b]		170,000
Total liabilities and stockholders' equity	$480,000	$165,000	$146,000	$146,000	$509,000

[a]To eliminate intercompany debt of $6,000.
[b]To eliminate investment account and to increase property, plant, and equipment to fair market value and to record goodwill.

equity accounts of the Mary Company, to increase the property, plant, and equipment account to fair market value, and to record goodwill:

Property, Plant, and Equipment	7,500	
Goodwill	2,500	
Common Stock	75,000	
Retained Earnings	55,000	
Investment in Mary Company		140,000

Goodwill must be amortized over a maximum of 40 years, whereas the plant and equipment will be depreciated over their remaining useful lives. The allocation between goodwill and other assets will affect future periods' income. The other entry is made to eliminate intercompany receivables and payables.

In this example, the amount of goodwill is relatively insignificant. However, this is not always the case. In actual situations, the amount of goodwill is likely to be very significant. To illustrate, when Philip Morris purchased Kraft Foods for $12.9 billion, $11.6 billion (over 90% of the purchase price) was considered goodwill.

Consolidated Income and Other Financial Statements. To this point, the illustration has involved only the preparation of consolidated balance sheets at the date of acquisition. Subsequent to the date of acquisition, consolidated income statements, statements of retained earnings, and statements of cash flows are also prepared, as well as balance sheets. Essentially, a consolidated income statement is prepared by combining the revenues and expenses of the parent and subsidiary companies after eliminating intercompany revenues and expense transactions such as sales, cost of goods sold, and interest revenue and expense. Because of their complex nature, the preparation of consolidated income statements is not illustrated here.

Alternative Methods of Accounting For Consolidations—Purchase Versus Pooling of Interests

There are various ways in which a parent may acquire a controlling interest in a subsidiary. For example, the investor may acquire it by paying cash, by issuing stock for stock, or through a combination of stock and cash. How the investment is made and other circumstances surrounding the investment or business combination determine the correct accounting method of consolidation. Either the *purchase method* or the *pooling of interests method* must be used. Each will produce significantly different consolidated statements.

In all of the examples to this point, it has been assumed that the purchase method of accounting has been used. This method must be used when the acquisition is made for cash and/or if the parent company issues debt or equity securities to the previous shareholders of the subsidiary. The **purchase method** assumes that the company's shareholders have sold out their interest to the parent company. Therefore, accounting principles applied to any purchase of assets are followed, and the acquired assets are recorded at their fair market value. Any goodwill resulting from the excess of the purchase price over the fair market value of the identifiable net assets is amortized over a maximum of 40 years.

purchase method

In some situations, the acquisition is structured in a different manner. Substantially all of the subsidiary's stock may be acquired in exchange for the parent's common stock. If this occurs and if certain other restrictive requirements are met, the acquisition must be considered a pooling of interests rather than a purchase. Essentially, a **pooling of interests method** assumes that the subsidiary's stockholders are now stockholders of the parent company and that a mutual pooling of interests rather than an outright purchase has taken place.

pooling of interests method

If a pooling of interests has in fact taken place, then there has not been a sale of the subsidiary's net assets. The subsidiary's net assets are therefore not revalued to their fair market value as they are when the purchase method is used. Thus, when a consolidated balance sheet is prepared under the pooling of interests method, the book value of the parent's assets and liabilities is combined with the corresponding book value of the subsidiary's assets and liabilities. As a result, no goodwill is recognized, and there is no subsequent goodwill amortization.

Another difference between the purchase and the pooling of interests methods of consolidating financial statements exists in the timing of income consolidation. Under the purchase method, only the subsidiary's earnings after the acquisition date are combined with the parent's earnings. Thus, if a purchase took place on October 1, only the subsidiary's earnings from that date to the year-end would be consolidated with the parent's earnings for the entire year.

Under the pooling of interests method, on the other hand, in the year of acquisition, the subsidiary's earnings for the entire year would be combined with the parent's earnings, regardless of the date of the acquisition. Thus, even if an acquisition took place on October 1, the subsidiary's earnings for the entire year would be consolidated with the parent's earnings when preparing a consolidated income statement for the year ending December 31. This is based on the idea that the two companies have merely combined their resources and operations.

These are significant factors and help to explain why the pooling method of accounting is popular with the managements of many companies. If the pooling of interests method is used when the purchase price exceeds the value of the acquired assets:

- The consolidated net assets will be recorded at lower amounts than if the purchase method is used.
- In the year of acquisition, earnings can be consolidated for the entire year.

The result is that ratios such as return on investment and earnings per share will be better when the pooling of interests method is used than when the purchase method is used. Exhibit 11-12 summarizes the major differences between these two methods of accounting for acquisitions.

Because of the dramatic effect that the pooling of interests method can have on consolidated statements, as well as its abuse during the 1960s, the Accounting Principles Board set certain conditions that must be met if the pooling of interests method is to be used. A transaction may only be structured as an exchange of the parent's stock for substantially all of the subsidiary's stock (pooling of interest) if all of the 12 requirements are met. If any of the 12 requirements are not met, the purchase method must be used. In effect, the purchase and pooling of interests methods are not alternatives for the same acquisition, and the correct accounting treatment depends on the nature of the transaction.

As discussed in the opening scenario, the takeover of NCR by AT&T is a good example of the issues that management confronts in structuring a merger to

Exhibit 11-12

	Method of Consolidation	*Recording of Net Assets*	*Subsidiary's Earnings*
Purchase Method	Acquisition of more than 50% of a subsidiary's voting stock for cash and/or other assets, debt, or securities.	Subsidiary's assets are revalued to fair market value. Excess of cost over fair market value, if any, is considered goodwill. Goodwill amortized over a maximum of 40 years.	In year of acquisition, earnings of subsidiary are combined with those of the parent from date of acquisition.
Pooling of Interests Method	Acquisition of substantially all (90% or more) of the subsidiary's voting stock for voting stock of parent.	Subsidiary's net assets are shown on consolidated balance sheet at book value. As a result, no goodwill is recognized. Retained earnings of subsidiary are carried over.	In year of acquisition, earnings of subsidiary are combined with those of the parent for the entire year.

ensure the results that it wants. In 1991 AT&T made a bid for NCR and eventually prevailed at a $7.5 billion price. During the bidding, AT&T's management was considering how best to structure the transaction to have it meet the requirement as a pooling of interests. The merger was ultimately structured as a pooling of interests, with the result that AT&T avoided recording and ultimately amortizing $4.5–$5 billion of goodwill.

To demonstrate the pooling of interests method, return to the Peter Corporation's acquisition of 100% of the Mary Company for a total price of $140,000. (See Exhibit 11-10.) Now assume that instead of making the acquisition for cash, the Peter Corporation issues 10,000 shares of its common stock, which currently has a fair market value of $14 per share, for all of the shares of the Mary Company. Under the pooling of interests method, the investment in Mary Company is recorded at the book value of the net assets acquired—$130,000—not at the fair market value of the stock exchanged—$140,000—as it would be if the purchase method were used. Assuming a $6 par value for the Peter Corporation stock, the journal entry to record this acquisition under the pooling of interests method is:

Investment in Mary Company	130,000	
Common stock (10,000 shares × $6 par)		60,000*
Paid-In Capital		15,000
Retained earnings		55,000
To record investment in Mary Company under the pooling-of-interests method.		

*The sum of the common stock and paid-in capital recorded by the parent must equal the subsidiary's total capital stock; in this case the total is $75,000.

Notice that under the theory of a pooling of interest, the Mary Company's retained earnings was carried over in total to the parent's books since it is assumed that the two companies have always been one. The worksheet to consolidate these companies under the pooling of interests method is shown in Exhibit 11-13. The investment elimination entry is as follows:

Common stock	50,000	
Paid-in capital	25,000	
Retained earnings	55,000	
Investment in Mary Company		130,000
To eliminate investment account against the subsidiary's equity account.		

In this worksheet entry, the investment account is eliminated against Mary Company's equity accounts. Because all the net assets of the Mary Company are carried over at their net book value, no revaluation of assets is made, nor is goodwill recorded.

In contrast, as illustrated earlier, under the purchase method, the investment account is recorded at $140,000, which is the fair value of the shares exchanged. The $10,000 paid in excess of the book value of the net assets required is allocated $7,500 to the property, plant, and equipment and $2,500 to goodwill. After the elimination entry, the stockholders' equity (including retained earnings) of the subsidiary is completely eliminated, and consolidated retained earnings is equal

Exhibit 11-13

Consolidated Balance Sheet Worksheet—Pooling of Interests
December 31, 1995—Acquisition Date

Accounts	*Peter Corporation*	*Mary Company*	*Eliminations* Debit	*Eliminations* Credit	*Consolidated Balance Sheet*
Cash	$164,000	$ 10,000			$174,000
Accounts receivable	36,000	15,000		$ 6,000[a]	45,000
Inventory	80,000	40,000			120,000
Investment in Mary Company	130,000	0		130,000[b]	0
Property, plant, and equipment, net	200,000	100,000			300,000
Total assets	$610,000	$165,000			$639,000
Current liabilities	$ 60,000	$ 20,000	$ 6,000[a]		$ 74,000
Long-term debt	100,000	15,000			115,000
Common stock	160,000	75,000	75,000[b]		160,000
Paid-in capital	65,000	0			65,000
Retained earnings	225,000	55,000	55,000[b]		225,000
Total liabilities and stockholders' equity	$610,000	$165,000	$136,000	$136,000	$639,000

[a]To eliminate intercompany debt.
[b]To eliminate investment account.

to the parent's retained earnings of $170,000. The consolidated balance sheet under the pooling of interests method, compared with the purchase method, is shown in Exhibit 11-14.

INTERNATIONAL ASPECTS OF ACCOUNTING FOR DEBT AND EQUITY INVESTMENTS

Objective 6
Discuss the major international issues related to accounting for investments in debt and equity securities.

The use of the equity method to account for investments in companies in which the investor has significant influence and control as well as the preparation and dissemination of consolidated financial statements has been standard accounting practice in the U.S. for many years. Until recently, however, these accounting methods were not used as consistently throughout the rest of the world.

Currently, IASC accounting standards, accounting standards spelled out in the European Community Company Law, and the accounting standards of most countries now require the use of the equity method of accounting for long-term investments. Further, international accounting standards as well as those of most countries now require the preparation of consolidated statements. However, significant differences still exist. For example, there are various interpretations on control and differing views of whether or not dissimilar companies should be consolidated. As noted, current U.S. standards now require all subsidiaries meeting control requirements to be consolidated regardless of the nature of their business. Other countries allow the exclusion of certain subsidiaries from consolidation if the nature if their business is dissimilar from that of the consolidated group.

Exhibit 11-14

Peter Corporation
Consolidated Balance Sheets
December 31, 1995

Assets	*Purchase*	*Pooling of Interests*
Cash	$ 34,000	$174,000
Accounts receivable	45,000	45,000
Inventory	120,000	120,000
Property, plant, and equipment, net	307,500	300,000
Goodwill	2,500	
Total	$509,000	$639,000
Liabilities and Stockholders' Equity		
Current liabilities	$ 74,000	$ 74,000
Long-term debt	115,000	115,000
Common stock	100,000	160,000
Paid-in capital	50,000	65,000
Retained earnings	170,000	225,000
Total	$509,000	$639,000

Chapter 10 briefly discussed differences in accounting for goodwill across countries. Given the number of international mergers and acquisitions which have taken place in the last decade, this is an extremely important issue. As discussed in Chapter 10, many influential people feel that U.S. accounting standards for goodwill put U.S. companies at a competitive disadvantage vis-à-vis their English counterparts.

SYSTEMS AND CONTROL ISSUES RELATED TO DEBT AND EQUITY INVESTMENTS

Objective 7
Discuss the major systems and control issues related to accounting for investments in debt and equity securities.

The system designed to account for investments, like all manual and computer-based accounting systems, should provide reasonable assurance that all authorized investment transactions are properly recorded. Investment transactions, like capital asset transactions, are less frequent than revenue and expense transactions, but individually the transactions are more material. Consequently, control over investment transactions is very important.

This chapter discussed the accounting for three different events in the life of an investment: investment acquisition, recognition of investment revenue, and the disposal of an investment. Investment acquisition and disposal transactions normally require top management approval. Hence, management approval is the primary control over accounting for these events. Accountants typically do not need top management approval to record investment revenue transactions. These transactions are similar to other revenue transactions and are evidenced by externally generated business documents. Control over these transactions is normally provided by transaction review and authorization prior to transaction input. In addition to accounting for investment transactions, accountants must prepare investment reports and analyses and consolidated financial statements which show the effects of major investments.

Some organizations have developed complex computer programs to prepare consolidated financial statements. These programs use detailed accounting data from the parent company and its subsidiaries to identify intercompany transactions which should be eliminated. General ledger account balances, after intercompany transactions have been eliminated, are used to prepare consolidated financial statements. The elimination entries do not effect the account balances in the general ledgers of the separate companies, only the amounts reported on the consolidated financial statements.

Consolidated financial statements are accurate only if all intercompany transactions are correctly identified and eliminated. The use of consolidation software increases control over the consolidation process because the software is able to scan all transactions to identify the few intercompany transactions which may have taken place. Most accountants would not be able to manually scan every transaction in a general ledger to identify the few intercompany transactions that require elimination. This repetitive task is ideally suited for computerization. Consolidation systems reduce the amount of mechanical work that accountants must do so that they can concentrate on more difficult and critical account analysis and decision-making tasks.

SUMMARY OF LEARNING OBJECTIVES

1. Discuss the nature of publicly-held corporations and the role of security exchanges. Publicly-held corporations are those whose securities are owned by outside investors and whose stocks and/or bonds are listed on a national or regional stock exchange. These exchanges, which include the New York Stock Exchange, the American Stock Exchange, and the over-the-counter market conduct the buying and selling of securities. Publicly-held corporations are required to file certain reports with the Securities and Exchange Commission and various exchanges.

2. Discuss the nature of debt and equity securities. Accounting for investments in debt and equity securities depends upon: (1) the nature of the security (debt versus equity); (2) management's intention as to whether the securities are purchased for sale in the near term, in the future, or whether they will be held to maturity; (3) the degree of control the investment gives the company making the investment (the investor) in the company in which it invested (the investee). Exhibit 11-1 summarizes how these variables relate to current accounting standards.

3. Account for equity and debt securities when the investor has no influence or control over the investee. No influence or control exists when a firm invests in debt securities of another company or equity securities that represent less than 20% of the voting stock or any amount of nonvoting stock. Investments at this level are primarily made to earn interest or dividend revenue and/or to earn gains while holding these securities.

FASB Statement No. 115, issued in May 1993, applies to all investments in debt securities and in equity securities that have a readily determinable fair market value. According to this statement, debt and equity securities with a readily determinable fair market value must be classified into one of the following three categories:

1. Held-to-maturity
2. Trading
3. Available-for-sale

Exhibit 11-2 summarizes the correct accounting treatment for each of the categories.

4. Account for ownership interest between 20% and 50%. Significant influence but not control is presumed to exist when an investor owns between 20% and 50% of an investee's stock. Because the investor can influence the operating policies of the investee, the cost or fair value method of accounting is not appropriate; rather, the equity method is used. Under the equity method, the investor records as income the proportionate share of the investee's income. Dividends declared serve to decrease the investment account. Thus, the investment account is carried at an amount equal to the investor's proportionate share of the purchased net assets of the investee.

5. Account for ownership interest above 50%. Complete control exists when the investor owns more than 50% of the investee's stock. In these situations, consolidated financial statements should be prepared. The preparation of these statements requires using certain elimination entries. These entries eliminate the investment account against the subsidiary's stockholders' equity as well as all intercompany transactions.

a. Acquisitions must be accounted for by using either the purchase or the pooling of interests method. These methods are not alternatives for the same acquisition; rather, the use of a particular one depends on how the acquisition is structured.
b. When the purchase method is used, all assets and liabilities are revalued to their fair market values, and any remaining excess cost is considered goodwill. When the pooling of interests method is used, all of the assets and liabilities of the subsidiary are combined with the parent's assets and liabilities at their net book value. Furthermore, under a pooling of interests, in the year of acquisition the subsidiary's earnings for the entire year are combined with the parent's earnings.

6. Discuss the major international issues related to accounting for investments in debt and equity securities. Use of the equity method as well as the preparation and dissemination of consolidated financial statements has been a common practice in the U.S. for a long time. Only within the last two decades have these accounting treatments become common worldwide. There are still differences, however, in what subsidiaries are consolidated; not all countries consolidate both similar and dissimilar subsidiaries as is now the practice in the U.S. Also, the recognition and handling of goodwill varies greatly throughout the world.

7. Discuss the major systems and control issues related to accounting for investments in debt and equity securities. Investment accounting systems should provide a reasonable assurance that all authorized and valid transactions are recorded. Review and approval controls are the primary controls over investment transactions. Control over the preparation of consolidated financial statements can be improved through the use of consolidation software which identifies all intercompany transactions before preparing consolidated financial statements.

KEY TERMS

Available-for-sale securities 520
Consolidated financial statements 531
Debt securities 517
Equity method 529
Equity securities 517
Held-to-maturity securities 520
Parent company 531
Pooling of interests method 538
Purchase method 537
Subsidiary 531
Trading securities 520

REVIEW PROBLEMS

A. At the beginning of the current year, West Coast Silicon held the following portfolio of equity securities classified as trading securities:

Security	*Number of Shares*	*Total Cost*	*Fair Value*
Allied, Inc.	50	$ 4,000	$ 4,600
Gora Company	100	2,500	2,300
Leaky Oil and Gas	200	6,000	5,400
		$12,500	$12,300

During the current year, West Coast Silicon entered into the following transactions:

a. Sold 100 shares of Leaky Oil and Gas for $2,800 net of commissions.
b. Purchased 100 shares of EG&P for $40 per share, including commissions.
c. Current fair values at the end of the year are:

Stock	*Total Fair Value*
Allied, Inc.	$ 4,400
Gora Company	2,200
Leaky Oil and Gas	2,000
EG&P	4,100
	$12,700

REQUIRED:

1. Prepare all the necessary journal entries for the year.
2. How would the marketable securities be shown on the balance sheet?
3. Assume that all securities were held throughout the next year and that at the end of the year their fair values totaled $14,000. (All securities remain classified as trading securities. The shares are expected to be sold soon.) Make the required entry at year-end.

Solution
1. Journal Entries

Cash	2,800	
Gain on Sale of Trading Securities		100
Investment in Trading Securities		2,700
To record sale of 100 shares of Leaky Oil and Gas.		

Sales price	$2,800
Fair value at beginning of year (½ of $5,400)	2,700
Gain on sale	$ 100

Investment in Trading Securities	4,000	
Cash		4,000
To record purchase of 100 shares of EG&P at $40 per share.		
Unrealized Holding Gain or Loss on Trading Securities	900	
Investment in Trading Securities		900
To record decrease in fair value of securities at the end of the first year.		

Fair value of securities at beginning of year	$12,300
Fair value of Leaky Oil and Gas shares sold	(2,700)
	$ 9,600
Purchase cost of EG&P shares purchased	4,000
Balance in Investment in Trading Securities account	$13,600
Fair value at end of current year	12,700
Unrealized holding loss at year end	$ 900

2. Balance Sheet Presentation

Investment in Trading Securities	$12,700

3. Year-end Entry

Investment in Trading Securities	1,300	
Unrealized Holding Gain or Loss on Trading Securities		1,300
To record unrealized holding gain on trading securities.		

Fair value at end of second year	$14,000
Fair value at beginning of second year	12,700
Unrealized holding gain	$ 1,300

B. Several years ago, the Anger Company purchased a 25% interest in the Zebra Corp. The purchase price was $50,000, which represented a 25% interest in the book value of Zebra's net assets at that time. At the beginning of the current year, the book value of Zebra's net assets was $350,000. During the current year, Zebra reported the following:

Net income	$75,000
Dividends paid	40,000

REQUIRED:

1. Make the appropriate entries on Anger's books to reflect these events during the current year.
2. What is the balance in the investment in Zebra account at the end of the year?

Solution

1. Journal Entries

Investment in Zebra	18,750	
Investment Revenue		18,750
To record investment revenue. ($75,000 × 25% = $18,750)		
Cash	10,000	
Investment in Zebra		10,000
To record receipt of dividend. ($40,000 × 25% = $10,000)		

2.

Zebra's net book value at beginning of year		$350,000
Anger's interest		.25
Anger's interest in Zebra's beginning of the year net book value		$ 87,500
Current year's transactions		
Income	$18,750	
Dividend received	(10,000)	8,750
Balance in the Investment account		$ 96,250

QUESTIONS

1. Define and give three examples each of debt and equity securities.
2. What are the variables that affect the accounting for debt securities?
3. Recently, many users of financial statements have argued that certain debt and equity securities should be valued at fair value. What is the basis of their argument? Do you agree or disagree? Why?
4. How do accountants determine whether or not an equity security has a readily determinable fair value?
5. What are the classifications that apply to debt securities and equity securities with a readily determin-

able fair market value? Describe the accounting treatment required in each category.

6. The Smith Corporation owns trading securities with a cost of $5,200 and a fair value of $3,600 at the end of the current year. This is the first year the securities have been owned. At what amount should the securities be shown on the year-end balance sheet? How is the firm's income statement for the period affected?
7. Now assume that the securities described in Question 6 are classified as available-for-sale. How are the firm's balance sheet and income statement affected?
8. According to FASB Statement No. 115, securities classified as held-to-maturity should be accounted for using the amortized cost method. What types of securities are included in this category? Explain the accounting procedures required by the amortized cost method.
9. According to FASB Statement No. 115, what is the correct accounting practice when the value of debt or equity securities is permanently impaired?
10. Briefly describe the equity method of accounting, why it is used, and when it is used.
11. Explain why dividends received are not considered revenue when the equity method of accounting for long-term investments is applied.
12. Under what circumstances should consolidated statements be prepared? How do these consolidated statements differ from just combining the financial statements of two companies?
13. List and describe at least three different elimination entries. Why must these entries be made?
14. Often when one company purchases another, the purchase is made at a price above the net book value of the assets acquired. Describe the accounting procedures to handle this when the purchase method of accounting is used.
15. Compare and contrast the purchase method of accounting for acquisitions with the pooling of interests method. If you were the manager of a company that was about to acquire another company, what factors would you consider in deciding which method to use?
16. Accounting for goodwill is often used as an example of how differing international accounting standards can have an economic impact. Describe the reason(s) why this argument is made. Do you think it is valid? Why or why not?
17. The Xron Corporation is a multinational firm with subsidiaries throughout the world. One such subsidiary is in the U.K. Are that subsidiary's financial statements consolidated with those of the other Xron subsidiaries in preparing U.S. GAAP financial statements? Under what circumstances, if any, would that subsidiary's financial statements be published separately?
18. What are the primary types of controls used with investment transactions?
19. How does the use of consolidation software increase control over the consolidation process?

EXERCISES

E11-1
Cash Equivalents and Equity Securities
LO 2

The Balsam-Coldwell Corporation held the following investments at year-end:

a. 2,000 shares of Ford Motor Corporation common stock purchased at $45.00 per share with a current market value of $49.50 per share. These shares will be sold in the near term.
b. $10,000 of the commercial paper of TRW paying an interest rate of 7.4%. The commercial paper matures in 45 days.
c. $50,000 of U.S. 3-month treasury bills.
d. 5,000 shares of Exxon Corporation common stock purchased about a year and a half ago at $35.75 per share. Year-end market value is $31.25 per share. These shares are available for sale but will not be sold within the next 12 months.
e. 10,000 shares of Rolo, Inc., a small, privately-held corporation owned by the brother of the president of Balsam-Coldwell. The shares were purchased several years ago at $10.00 per share. Current market value cannot be determined.

REQUIRED:

1. How should each of these items be classified on the year-end balance sheet of Balsam-Coldwell?

2. At what amount should each of these items be listed on the year-end balance sheet of Balsam-Coldwell? Explain your logic.
3. What effect do these transactions have on the firm's income for the year?

E11-2
Accounting for Equity Securities
LO 3

On February 2, 1994, the Suzar Company purchased 100 shares of Pops Brewery at $56 per share, plus brokerage commissions of $4 per share. During 1994 and 1995, the following events occurred regarding this investment:

a. December 15, 1994: Pops Brewery declares and pays a $2.20 per-share dividend.
b. December 31, 1994: The market price of Pops Brewery's stock is $52 per share at year-end.
c. December 1, 1995: Pops Brewery declares and pays a dividend of $2.00 per share.
d. December 31, 1995: The market price of Pops Brewery's stock is $55 per share at year-end.

REQUIRED: Assuming the shares are considered trading securities and this is the only investment that the Suzar Company made during 1994 and 1995, record the entries to reflect these events. How would the investment be disclosed on the December 31, 1995, balance sheet?

E11-3
Accounting for Equity Securities
LO 3

The following items were taken from the December 31, 1994 balance sheet of the Simmonds Company:

Simmonds Company
Partial Balance Sheet
December 31, 1994

Current assets	
Cash	$ 50,000
Accounts receivable, less allowance for uncollectible accounts of $6,000	120,000
Investment in Akro Corporation at fair value	25,000

The investment in Akro Corporation consisted of 1,000 shares of Akro common stock purchased on November 29, 1994.

REQUIRED:

1. Can the purchase price per share of the Akro Corporation common stock be determined from the data given?
2. What was the market price per share of the Akro Corporation common stock on December 31, 1994?
3. On April 1, 1995, the Simmonds Company sold 500 shares of Akro at $28 per share. Make the journal entry necessary to record this sale.
4. Simmonds held the remaining 500 shares of Akro throughout the remaining year. At December 31, 1995, Akro was selling at $26.50 per share. Make the necessary entry, if any, to value the securities at December 31, 1995.

E11-4
Application of Fair Value
LO 3

During 1994, the Ambrosia Corp. made several purchases of equity securities. No securities were owned prior to 1994. None of these purchases represented an interest of 20% or more. The cost and market value of these securities are as follows:

		Market Value—December 31,		
Securities	*Cost*	*1994*	*1995*	*1996*
BPOE Inc.	$ 1,500	$ 1,200	$ 1,100	$ 1,600
Laird, Inc.	5,600	5,700	5,600	5,500
Showboat Co.	4,900	4,400	4,300	4,600
Total	$12,000	$11,300	$11,000	$11,700

REQUIRED:

1. Make the adjusting entries at December 31 of each year to reflect these changes in market values, assuming the securities are considered trading.
2. How should the account Investment in Marketable Equity Securities be disclosed on the December 31, 1996 balance sheet?
3. Make the adjusting entries at December 31 of each year assuming these securities are considered available-for-sale. Contrast your answer to that in Requirement 1.

E11-5
Accounting for Debt Securities
LO 3

On January 2, 1994, the Thesaurus Co. purchased 10 $1,000, 12% bonds of Webster Corporation. The bonds were purchased for $9,850 plus $300 of brokerage commissions and accrued interest. The bonds pay interest every January 2 and July 1. On July 1, 1995, after receipt of the semiannual interest payment, the firm sold all the bonds at $10,410 less $400 brokerage commissions.

REQUIRED:

1. Make the required journal entries on January 2, 1994, December 31, 1994 (the firm's year-end), January 2, 1995, and July 1, 1995, to record these bond transactions.
2. If the price of the bonds had declined below their cost at December 31, 1994, would the Thesaurus Co. have to make an entry to reflect this fact?

E11-6
Accounting for Current and Long-Term Equity Investments
LO 3 & 4

At the end of 1993, the CIJI Ware Corporation owned two equity investments that it classified as trading securities. The relevant cost and market data at December 31, 1993, are as follows:

Security	*Cost*	*Market*
Lockness, Inc.	$10,400	$10,100
Scottish Co.	7,400	7,500

During 1994, CIJI Ware Corporation sold all of its holdings in Lockness for $10,250 after commissions. In addition, the firm purchased 500 shares of English Inc. on November 1, 1994, at a price of $29 per share including commissions. The firm considers this to be an available-for-sale investment.

At December 31, 1994, Scottish Co. had a market value of $7,000, and English Inc. had a market value of $14,200.

REQUIRED:

1. Prepare the journal entries to record the transactions that took place during 1994.
2. How much income or loss would the CIJI Ware Corporation report during 1994 regarding these stock transactions? How would this income or loss be classified?
3. Determine the December 31, 1994, balances in the balance sheet accounts regarding these stock investments.

E11-7 Accounting for Investments and Financial Statement Analysis

LO 3 & 4

A condensed balance sheet for the Rockhard Corporation follows:

Current assets	$175,000
Other assets	220,000
Current liabilities	145,000
Long-term liabilities	115,000
Stockholders' equity	135,000

Net income for the current year amounted to $32,450 on total sales of $220,000.

Included in current assets are 5,000 shares of Quad, Inc., that Rockhard purchased at $10 per share. These shares had a year-end market value of $6 per share. Rockhard considered these shares to be trading securities and accounted for them correctly under GAAP.

REQUIRED:

1. Calculate the following statistics and ratios:
   a. Current ratio
   b. Net working capital
   c. Total debt to equity
   d. Long-term debt to equity
   e. Profit margin ratio
2. Now assume that Rockhard's accountant had made an error and that these securities should have been classified as available-for-sale. Now calculate the following ratios:
   a. Current ratio
   b. Net working capital
   c. Total debt to equity
   d. Long-term debt to equity
   e. Profit margin ratio
3. Comment on the differences in the ratios that you calculated under each assumption and the reasons for these differences.

E11-8 Cost and Equity Method of Accounting for Long-Term Investments

LO 4

At the beginning of 1994, the El Paso Corp. purchased two long-term investments. The first purchase was a 30% interest (30,000 shares) in the common stock of Houston Inc. for $1.5 million. The second purchase was a 15% interest (15,000 shares) in the common stock of Lubbock Inc. for $495,000. Although market values for Lubbock are readily determinable, the firm does not intend to sell these securities in the near future. The following data are available regarding these companies:

Company	Reported Income	Dividends Declared and Paid	Market Price per Share, 12/31/94
Houston	$ 500,000	$100,000	$45
Lubbock	1,000,000	300,000	35

REQUIRED:

1. Which of these investments should be accounted for by the fair value or equity method? Why?
2. As a result of these two investments, what should be the income reported by El Paso for the year ended December 31, 1994?
3. As a result of these two investments, what should be the balance in the investments account for El Paso at December 31, 1994?

E11-9
Equity Method of Accounting
LO 4

At the beginning of the current year, the Bond Company purchased for $400,000 as a long-term investment common stock representing a 30% interest in the Spy Corporation. This represented a 30% interest in the book value of Spy Corporation's net assets. During the year, Spy declared and issued dividends totaling $90,000. Spy reported net income of $140,000 during the current year.

REQUIRED:

1. Make the required journal entries on the Bond Company's books to record these events.
2. What is the balance in the investment in Spy Corporation account at the end of the current year?

E11-10
Accounting for Long-Term Investments
LO 4

For several years, Altadena Corporation has held a 40% interest in the Pasadena Co. At the time of purchase, Pasadena's net assets were $2 million and Altadena paid $700,000 for its interest. At the end of 1992, Altadena reported a balance of $1.8 million in its investment in Pasadena account.

During 1994, Pasadena reported a loss of $170,000. Because management considered this loss to be temporary, Pasadena declared dividends of $28,000.

REQUIRED:

1. Does Altadena use the cost or the equity method of accounting for its investment in Pasadena? Explain your answer.
2. Make the appropriate journal entries on the books of Altadena to record the events that occurred during 1994.
3. As a result of these transactions, what is the December 31, 1994 balance in the investment in Altadena account?

E11-11
Elimination Entries—Date of Acquisition
LO 5

During the year, First Air purchased 100% of the common stock of Royal Hotels for $900,000 in cash. At the time of the purchase, the book value of Royal Hotels' net assets was $900,000, consisting of common stock of $400,000 and retained earnings of $500,000. Also at the time of acquisition, First Air had an accounts receivable on its books in the amount of $55,000 from Royal Hotels. Royal Hotels had a corresponding accounts payable.

REQUIRED: Prepare the elimination entries that would be made on the worksheet required for the preparation of a consolidated balance sheet.

E11-12
Elimination Entries
LO 5

During June 1994, Oniix Inc. purchased 100% of the common stock of Praim for $750,000 cash and a note of $132,000. At the time of the purchase, Praim's stockholders' equity accounts were common stock of $500,000 and retained earnings of $194,000. Included in Oniix's accounts payable at the time of acquisition was a $5,000 liability to Praim. A corresponding receivable was on Praim's books. Any excess of cost and book value should be assigned to goodwill.

REQUIRED:

1. Prepare the journal entry to record Oniix's purchase of Praim.
2. Prepare the elimination entry that would appear on a worksheet necessary to prepare a consolidated balance sheet at the date of acquisition.
3. How much goodwill was generated by this purchase? How will Oniix have to account for this goodwill in future years?

E11-13
Accounting for Consolidations and Goodwill
LO 5

On April 1, 1994, the Pual Co. purchased 100% of the common stock of Santos Inc. for $175,000 cash. Immediately after the purchase, the balance sheet of each company appeared as follows:

Assets	*Pual Co.*	*Santos Inc.*
Cash and receivables	$ 50,000	$ 20,000
Inventory	80,000	35,000
Investment in Santos	175,000	—
Property, plant and equipment, net	240,000	200,000
Total assets	$545,000	$255,000
Accounts payable	$ 60,000	$ 15,000
Long-term debt	80,000	85,000
Common stock	200,000	60,000
Retained earnings	205,000	95,000
Total equities	$545,000	$255,000

After evaluating the assets of Santos, Pual decided that the fair market value of the inventory was $40,000 and that the fair market value of the property, plant, and equipment was $210,000. The remaining cost of the acquisition over the assets acquired should be considered goodwill.

REQUIRED:

1. Prepare the entry to record the acquisition of Santos by Pual.
2. Prepare the elimination entry that would be made on the worksheet required to prepare a consolidated balance sheet at the date of acquisition.
3. After consolidation, what will be the amount of the total assets of the consolidated entity?
4. After consolidation, what will be the amount of the total stockholders' equity of the consolidated entity?

E11-14
Consolidation Worksheet
LO 5

On November 1, 1994, the Rosenberg Rose Co. purchased 100% of the stock of the Seedy Seed Co. for $200,000 cash. Immediately after the purchase, the condensed balance sheets of the two companies were as follows:

	Rosenberg Rose	*Seedy Seed*
Receivable from Seedy	$ 10,000	$ 0
Other assets	800,000	250,000
Investment in Seedy	200,000	0
Total assets	$1,010,000	$250,000
Payable to Rosenberg	$ 0	$ 10,000
Other liabilities	300,000	100,000
Common stock	400,000	100,000
Retained earnings	310,000	40,000
Total equities	$1,010,000	$250,000

After a detailed analysis, Rosenberg has decided that the fair market value of Seedy's assets approximates their book value, and so any excess of the cost of the investment over the book value of the acquired net assets should be considered goodwill.

REQUIRED: Prepare a worksheet consolidating the two companies as of the date of acquisition.

E11-15
Purchase Versus Pooling
LO 5

On March 1, 1995, Northstar Tech purchased 100% of Tahoe Limited by exchanging 10,000 shares of its common stock for all of Tahoe's common stock. Tahoe's common stock has a balance of $100,000. At the acquisition date, Northstar's common stock was selling at $21 per share. At the time of the purchase, the book value and fair market value of Tahoe's net assets appeared as follows:

	Book Value	*Fair Market Value*
Monetary assets	$ 50,000	$ 50,000
Inventory	75,000	85,000
Property, plant, and equipment, net	150,000	175,000
Total assets	$275,000	$310,000
Total liabilities	$100,000	$100,000

Tahoe's net income during the year amounted to $150,000, earned as follows:

January 2, 1995, to February 28, 1995	$ 40,000
March 1, 1995, to December 31, 1995	110,000

REQUIRED:

1. Assuming that the purchase method of accounting is used, make the required entries and answer the following questions:
   a. Make the entry to record the acquisition.
   b. Make the elimination entry that would be made on the date of acquisition.

c. At what dollar amount would Tahoe's net assets be consolidated with Northstar's assets?
d. How much income would Northstar report on its consolidated income statement from Tahoe's operations?

2. Make the required entries and answer the preceding questions, assuming that the pooling of interests method of accounting is used.

E11-16
International Accounting for Goodwill
LO 6

The Istaben Corporation purchased the European Corporation for $20 million. At the time of purchase the book value of European's net assets was $12 million. The acquisition was accounted for under the purchase method of accounting, and Istaben determined that the book value of the net assets it acquired was equal to their fair market value.

REQUIRED:

1. Assume that Istaben is a U.S. multinational following U.S. GAAP. How would the resulting goodwill, if any, be accounted for?
2. Now assume that Istaben is a multinational in the United Kingdom following U.K. GAAP. How would the resulting goodwill, if any, be accounted for? (*Hint:* Review the material in Chapter 10.)
3. Now assume that Istaben decides to follow GAAP as prescribed by the International Accounting Standards Committee. How would the resulting goodwill, if any, be accounted for? (*Hint*: Review the material in Chapter 10.)
4. Compare and contrast your answers to the above and explain the effect of the accounting for goodwill on the future financial statements in each case.

E11-17
Accounting Information Systems
LO 7

Identify the one best control that should be implemented to prevent the recurrence of each of the following problems.

a. Brokerage statements, showing interest and dividends earned on marketable securities, were received prior to year-end but the necessary journal entry was not made until the next year.
b. An employee stole stock certificates, that were held as marketable securities, from the file cabinet where they were stored and sold them. The employee gained over $37,000 in the transaction.
c. An accountant, who thought he had received a hot investment tip, withdrew $2,000,000 from his company's bank account and invested the money, for the company, in the stock market. The tip was bad and the firm lost over $1,000,000 on the investment.
d. The treasurer of a large company sold investment securities for a substantial gain. He prepared documents showing that the sale was made at a loss and kept the difference between the actual sales proceeds and the reported amount.

E11-18
Albertson's Financial Statements
LO 2 & 5

Based on the Albertson's financial statements in Appendix A, answer the following questions:

a. How does Albertson's disclose its short-term investments?
b. Does Albertson's consolidate all of its subsidiaries? How did you arrive at your conclusion?

PROBLEMS

P11-1
Accounting for Debt and Equity Securities
LO 3

At the beginning of 1994, the Rose Corporation held the following current marketable equity securities:

Security	*Number of Shares*	*Total Cost*	*Total Market*
MG, Inc.	1,000	$35,000	$30,000
Drof Co.	500	10,000	12,000

During 1994, the following transactions took place:

a. March 1: Purchased 200 shares of Joellen Inc., at $45 per share including commissions.
b. March 31: Received dividends of $1.50 per share on MG, Inc. stock.
c. May 2: Sold all of its shares in Drof Co. for $22 per share.
d. September 1: Sold 500 shares of MG, Inc., for $29 per share.
e. September 30: Received cash dividends of $1.50 per share on MG, Inc., stock.
f. December 1: Purchased 10 $1,000, 12% bonds of United Inc. for $9,800.
g. December 31: Accrued interest for one month on the United Inc. bonds.
h. December 31: You have obtained the following market values as of December 31, 1994:

Joellen Inc.	$ 46 per share
MG, Inc.	34 per share
United Inc. bonds	970 per $1,000 bond

All securities are considered trading securities.

REQUIRED:

1. Prepare the journal entries to record the above transactions regarding the marketable securities.
2. Show how the securities would be disclosed on the December 31, 1994, balance sheet.

P11-2
Accounting for Debt and Equity Securities
LO 3

At the beginning of 1994, the Modem Corporation held the following current marketable equity securities:

Security	*Number of Shares*	*Total Cost*	*Total Market*
Tele Inc.	2,000	$80,000	$74,000
Byte Co.	800	16,000	29,000

During 1994, the following transactions took place:

a. February 1: Purchased 300 shares of Alexis Inc. at $60 per share including commissions.
b. March 31: Received dividends of $1 per share of Tele Inc. stock.
c. April 14: Sold 400 of the shares in Byte Co. for $22 per share.
d. August 14: Sold 1,000 shares of Tele Inc. for $39 per share.
e. September 30: Received cash dividends of $1 per share on Tele Inc. stock.

f. November 1: Purchased 20 $1,000, 10% bonds of Americo, Inc., for $20,400.
g. December 31: The company accrues two months' interest on the Americo, Inc. bonds.
h. December 31: You have obtained the following market values as of December 31, 1994:

Alexis Inc.	$ 61 per share
Tele Inc.	38 per share
Byte Co.	23 per share
Americo bonds	100 per unit

All securities are considered available-for-sale.

REQUIRED:

1. Prepare the journal entries to record the above transactions related to the marketable securities.
2. Show how the securities would be disclosed on the December 31, 1994 balance sheet.
3. Describe how the income statement accounts relative to these transactions would be shown on the income statement.

P11-3
Valuation of Equity Securities
LO 3

Included in the information contained in the footnotes to the financial statements of Grenada Corporation at December 31, 1994 and 1995 is the following information related to investments in equity securities:

	1995	*1994*
Equity securities, at cost	$160,000	$75,000
Gross unrealized gains	14,300	5,100
Gross unrealized losses	(17,200)	(2,300)
Equity securities, at market	$157,100	$77,800

During 1995, the firm sold securities with a fair value of $30,000 for $38,500.

REQUIRED: Based on this information, answer the following questions:

1. At what amount should the equity securities be shown on the balance sheet for 1995 and 1994?
2. What are the amounts of the unrealized holding gains and/or losses, if any, for 1995 and 1994 that should be disclosed, and where should these amounts be disclosed?
3. What is the amount of realized gain or loss for 1995 that should be disclosed, and where should this amount be disclosed?
4. What is the fair value of the securities purchased by the Grenada Corporation during 1995?

P11-4
Investment in Equity Securities
LO 3

During 1994 and 1995, the Crafty Tool Corporation entered into the following transactions related to equity investments. All investments represent less than a 20% interest in the related companies. All securities classified as available-for-sale are considered long-term investments. Prior to 1994, Crafty Tool had no equity investments.

1994:

a. January 29: Purchased 200 shares of Fast Industries (considered a trading security) for $60 per share.
b. March 24: Purchased 300 shares of Celeste (considered an available-for-sale security) at $45 per share.
c. September 30: Received a $2 per-share cash dividend on Fast Industries' stock.
d. October 13: Purchased 2,000 shares of Cool Pen (considered a trading security) for $20 per share.
e. December 31: The market value per share of stocks was:

Fast Industries	$63
Celeste	35
Cool Pen	19

1995:

a. February 12: Purchased an additional 100 shares of Fast Industries at $65 per share.
b. May 29: Sold 200 shares of Celeste for $34 per share.
c. September 30: Received a $2 per-share dividend on Fast Industries stock.
d. December 31: The market value of the stocks held at December 31, 1995, was as follows:

Fast Industries	$66.00 per share
Celeste	32.00 per share
Cool Pen	19.25 per share

REQUIRED:

1. Make the appropriate journal entries for 1994 and 1995.
2. Prepare the appropriate sections of Crafty's balance sheet at December 31, 1994 and 1995 and its income statements for those year-ends.

P11-5
Equity Method of Accounting
LO 4

At the beginning of 1994, Eastbound Inc. purchased a 40% interest (representing 50,000 shares) in Earth Co. for $1,250,000 cash. Earth had a good year during 1994 and reported net income of $300,000. In addition, on June 30, 1994, Earth declared and issued cash dividends totaling $1.50 per share. At year-end, the price of Earth's stock was $22 per share.

During 1995, business increased significantly, and Earth reported a net income of $480,000 for the year. The firm declared and paid dividends of $2.00 per share. Because of the firm's strong performance, the price per share of its stock at year-end increased to $30.

REQUIRED:

1. Make the journal entries to record these transactions during 1994 and 1995.
2. How much income would Eastbound report from this investment during 1994 and 1995?
3. Prepare the long-term investment section of Eastbound's balance sheet at December 31, 1994 and 1995.
4. If this investment was accounted for under the cost method of accounting for long-term investment, how much income would Eastbound report from this investment during 1994 and 1995?

P11-6
Accounting For Long-Term Investments
LO 3 & 4

The Epcal Company has supplied you with the following information regarding three investments, which were made during 1993:

a. On January 2, 1993, Epcal purchased for cash 40% of the 500,000 shares of the common stock of the Newport Company for $2,400,000, that was equal to 40% of the carrying value of the net assets of Newport. Newport's net income for the year ended December 31, 1993 was $850,000, and Newport paid dividends of $1.25 per share. The market value of Newport's common stock was $12.50 per share on December 31, 1994.
b. On July 1, 1994, Epcal also purchased for cash 15,000 shares representing 5% of the common stock of the Tokial Company for $450,000. Tokial's net income for the six months ended December 31, 1994, was $450,000 and for the year ended December 31, 1994 was $700,000. Tokial paid dividends of $.50 per share each quarter during 1994. The market value of Tokial's common stock (classified as available-for-sale) was $32 per share on January 1, 1994, and $34 per share on December 31, 1994.
c. Epcal purchased $12,000 of the commercial paper of LTD on November 1, 1994. The commercial paper has an interest rate of 6% and pays interest at maturity, three months after the purchase date.

REQUIRED:

1. As a result of these investments, what should be the balance in the accounts related to investments of the Epcal Company at December 31, 1994. Be sure to show your computations.
2. As a result of these investments, what should be the income reported by Epcal for the year ended December 31, 1994? Be sure to show your computations.

P11-7
Cost Versus Equity Method of Accounting
LO 3 & 4

During 1994, the Carolina Company made the following two investments.

a. January 2: Carolina purchased for cash and notes 30% of the 1 million shares of common stock of the Micronet Computer Co. The purchase was made for $2.5 million cash and notes of $1 million. Micronet Computer Co.'s net income for the year ended December 31, 1994 was $700,000. In addition, Micronet Computer paid total dividends of $2.00 per share. At December 31, 1994, the market price of Micronet Computer's stock was $10.50 per share.
b. April 1: Carolina purchased 50,000 shares of Chow, Inc., for $600,000 cash. This purchase represented a 10% interest in Chow. Chow's net loss during 1994 was $100,000, and Chow paid dividends of $.10 the last day of each quarter during 1994. At December 31, 1994, the market price of Chow's stock (classified as available-for-sale) was $5 per share. However, Carolina considers this to be a temporary price decline.

These are the only two long-term investments made by the Carolina Company.

REQUIRED:

1. Make the journal entries to record these investments.
2. At the end of 1994, what is the balance in the investment account of the Carolina Company?
3. What should be the income reported by the Carolina Company related to these two investments during 1994?

P11-8
Consolidation Worksheet and Balance Sheet
LO 5

On June 1, 1994, the Upbeat Corporation purchased a 100% interest in the Deadbeat Co. for $250,000 cash. At the date of acquisition, the condensed balance sheets of each company are as follows:

Assets	*Upbeat Corporation*	*Deadbeat Company*
Cash	$ 60,000	$ 15,000
Accounts receivable	107,000	24,000
Inventory	300,000	126,000
Investment in Deadbeat	250,000	0
Property, plant, and equipment, net	525,000	180,000
Total assets	$1,242,000	$345,000
Equities		
Current liabilities	$ 220,000	$ 95,000
Long-term debt	150,000	0
Common stock	600,000	100,000
Retained earnings	272,000	150,000
Total equities	$1,242,000	$345,000

Included in the accounts receivable and current liabilities is intercompany debt amounting to $8,000.

REQUIRED:

1. Prepare a worksheet to consolidate Upbeat and Deadbeat.
2. Prepare a consolidated balance sheet at the date of acquisition.

P11-9
Purchase Versus Pooling of Interests
LO 5

The Minneapolis Company intends to merge with the St. Paul Corporation by exchanging 10,000 shares of its common stock for 100% of the shares of the St. Paul Corporation. At the time of the merger, the Minneapolis Company's common stock was selling for $18 per share. Presented below are the condensed balance sheets of the two firms immediately prior to the acquisition.

Assets	*Minneapolis Company*	*St. Paul Corporation*
Current assets	$100,000	$ 45,000
Property, plant, and equipment, net	250,000	150,000
Total assets	$350,000	$195,000
Current liabilities	$ 40,000	$ 30,000
Long-term debt	140,000	45,000
Common stock	115,000	75,000
Retained earnings	55,000	45,000
Total equities	$350,000	$195,000

REQUIRED:

1. Prepare journal entries to record the acquisition of St. Paul by Minneapolis, assuming that (a) the pooling of interests method is used; (b) the purchase method is used.
2. Prepare a worksheet as of the date of acquisition, assuming that (a) the pooling of interests method is used; (b) the purchase method is used. (Apply the excess cost over the book value of net assets acquired to goodwill.)

3. Prepare a consolidated balance sheet at the date of acquisition for the two different methods. Compare and contrast the two balance sheets.

P11-10
Accounting Systems for Investments
LO 7

Northwest Water Products has been investing excess cash in marketable securities for several years and has a very active portfolio. Management has decided to develop an investment accounting system rather than to hire an additional employee to account for all of the investment transactions.

REQUIRED:

1. Design an input form to be used to capture all of the information needed to record investment transactions. The form will be used for investment, investment revenue, and investment sale transactions.
2. Design the contents of the investment master file record that will be used by the computer system to keep track of each investment.
3. Design the contents of an investment analysis report that will be used by management to evaluate the profitability of each investment in the portfolio.

DISCUSSION AND INTERPRETATION PROBLEMS

D11-1
Understanding Financial Statements

The following note appeared in the financial statements of the Pennzoil Company:

	1987	*1986*
Current assets (in thousands)		
Cash	$ 22,186	$ 21,371
Temporary cash investments	164,103	126,287
Marketable equity securities	159,127	242,482

Notes to Consolidated Financial Statements

Note 1 (in part): Summary of Significant Accounting Policies—Marketable Equity Securities

At December 31, 1987, the current and noncurrent portfolios of marketable equity securities are each carried at the lower of aggregate cost or market value (as detailed below). Current marketable equity securities are comprised of a managed portfolio of common and preferred stocks.

	December 31, 1987		
	Cost	*Market*	*Gross and Net Unrealized (Loss)*
Current	$183,863,000	$159,127,000	$(24,736,000)
Noncurrent	29,644,000	22,921,000	(6,723,000)

At December 31, 1986, the current and noncurrent marketable equity securities portfolios totaled $242,482,000 and $31,441,000, respectively, and were carried at cost, which approximated market. At December 31, 1985, a valuation allowance for unrealized losses on noncurrent marketable equity securities of $4,679,000 was charged to shareholders' equity.

The following sales of marketable equity securities occurred during the periods indicated below. The cost of the securities sold was based on the average cost of all the shares of each security held at the time of sale. There was no resulting material effect from the sale of marketable equity securities in 1986.

	Net Realized Gain (Loss)
1987	$(21,813,000)
1985	13,546,000

REQUIRED:

1. For the years ended 1987 and 1986, are the marketable equity securities carried at cost or market?
2. During 1987, the company had a net realized loss on the sale of the marketable equity securities. On what financial statement is the loss shown?
3. During 1987, the company had gross and net unrealized losses on marketable current equity securities of $24,736,000. On what financial statement is this loss shown?
4. Assume that the company did not purchase any additional marketable current equity securities during 1987, and that all securities sold during 1987 were current. For how much were the securities sold?

D11-2
Financial Decision Case

The Space Parts Company has been in business for several years. In the last couple of years, growth in the industry has slowed down and the company is facing its first net loss. In order to increase its future prospects, the company is considering purchasing 100% of a competing company called High Tech Parts.

The president of Space Parts asks your advice concerning the contemplated purchase of High Tech Parts. He tells you that it is now December 1, and it appears that Space Parts will have a loss of $300,000 for the year ended December 31, 1994. On the other hand, High Tech has had a successful year, with estimated profits through November of $500,000. Profits for December are estimated to be another $75,000. Further, the president of Space Parts feels that the net assets of High Tech are substantially undervalued. The purchase price will be substantially above net book value of High Tech's net assets and probably above the fair value of the net assets.

The president of Space Parts had heard about purchase and pooling of interests accounting, but he is confused about the difference between them. He asks your advice on the following points:

a. In structuring the contemplated purchase of High Tech, do I have a choice between using purchase accounting and pooling of interests accounting?
b. I am considering either purchasing High Tech entirely with cash or exchanging common stock of Space Parts for all the common stock of High Tech. What effect does this have, if any, on whether I can use the purchase or the pooling of interests method of accounting? Compare other possible effects on Space Parts' financial statements of using the two different methods.
c. Prepare a schedule for me that compares the effect on Space Parts' current period's income of using the pooling of interests method versus the purchase method.

REQUIRED: Answer the president's questions.

D11-3
Financial Decision Case

Jacob Fitzwater is the president and chief executive officer (CEO) of a small electronics company called Fitzwater's Transistors. The company is privately held and has never had its financial statements audited until this year. As a condition for obtaining a line of credit granted from a bank, the firm is now required to have an annual audit of its financial statements.

Fitzwater's Transistors has been very successful over the past few years and has accumulated a large amount of cash. Jacob Fitzwater recognizes that these excess funds should be invested in financial instruments that earn interest and have a possibility for common growth. He has instructed the firm's treasurer to purchase a variety of instruments with differing maturities.

The treasurer suggests to Fitzwater that the firm's intentions as to how long these instruments will be held actually affects the accounting for them. He goes on to note that in some cases, the firm might have to recognize a loss on the income statement for unrealized losses, and in other cases no loss would have to be realized. The treasurer states that the actual classification of these items is an important issue. Jacob Fitzwater finds this somewhat strange and asks the following questions:

a. Does the classification of an investment in a security affect its accounting? If it does, why can't I just decide how to classify the investment?
b. Explain to me in which situations I might have to recognize an unrealized loss. After all, I want to avoid this as the bank may look unfavorably on any losses.
c. I remember taking a finance class where the instructor said the entire classification issue was not important—that classification doesn't matter as long as users know the real market value of the securities. Can't we just disclose the market values and forget accounting for them?

REQUIRED: Answer Jacob Fitzwater's questions.

D11-4
Research Assignment

In late 1991 the FASB issued a discussion memorandum (DM) which analyzed the issues related to consolidation policies and procedures. Obtain a copy of this discussion memorandum from your library and/or other sources and answer the following questions:

a. Consolidation of financial statements has been common practice in the U.S. for many years. Why did the FASB decide to add this topic to its agenda?
b. The DM discusses seven issues related to consolidation policies and procedures. Briefly describe the first two of these issues.
c. Describe current consolidation policies in New Zealand and Canada. In what ways do they differ from those in the U.S.?

D11-5
Research Assignment

Using the resources in your library and/or other sources, obtain the financial statements, 1991 or later, of the following companies:

a. General Motors
b. Coca-Cola
c. Wendy's International
d. Time Warner

REQUIRED:

1. Determine the dollar amount of long-term investments shown on the balance sheet of each of these companies.
2. Calculate the percentage of total assets these dollar amounts equal.
3. Report how these items are valued on the balance sheet and briefly describe the disclosures made in the footnotes relative to long-term investments.

D11-6
Ethical Issues

The Common Corporation has just acquired 100% of the stock of Taylor Publications, a large, diversified magazine publisher. Taylor Publications had been very successful, and Common paid $1.5 billion for the firm.

Magazine publishers do not have many tangible assets. Probably the most significant asset is the subscription list, whose value does not appear on Taylor's balance sheet. The chief financial officer (CFO) of Common, Joe Crandall, determined that at least $800 million of the $1.5 billion should be allocated to goodwill, his estimate of the value of the subscription list purchased by Common. The president of the company was not at all happy with this allocation. He recognized that creating so much goodwill would be an earnings drag on the company. Further, since goodwill amortization is not deductible for tax purposes, Common would not receive any benefit from such a high allocation to goodwill. On the other hand, increasing the allocation of the cost to tangible assets would result in higher depreciation charges and a better tax break. For these reasons, the president ordered Joe to revise his allocation of the purchase price and report back to him.

Joe was uncomfortable with this order and hired an expert to appraise the assets of Taylor Publications. The expert basically agreed with Joe's allocation scheme, and Joe went back to the president with the same suggested allocation. The President felt it did not meet the future considerations of the company. Further, he felt that these allocations were only estimates, and that his estimate was just as good as the others. He went ahead and allocated the $1.5 billion as follows—$1.2 million to tangible net assets and $300 million to goodwill.

REQUIRED:

1. Comment on the president's insistence that Joe Crandall review his initial allocation of the purchase price.
2. Comment on Joe's hiring of an expert to review his estimates. Do you think that he was acting properly in his capacity as CFO?
3. Comment on the president's decision to make the allocation the way he did. Is this according to GAAP? Is he acting ethically? Explain your answer.

COMPREHENSIVE CASES

C11-1 Recording Transactions Related to Investing Activities

As the associate accounting manager for EKBOG Enterprises, one of your primary responsibilities is to record journal entries related to the firm's investing activities. At the beginning of 1995 the property, plant, and equipment section of the EKBOG's balance appeared as follows:

Property, plant, and equipment	
Land	$1,000,000
Building	2,500,000
Furniture and equipment	750,000
	$4,250,000
Less: Accumulated depreciation	733,594
Total property, plant, and equipment	$3,516,406

Footnote disclosure:
The firm acquired all property, plant, and equipment in a single purchase on January 2, 1992, the day the firm was organized. Buildings are depreciated on a 25-year life using the straight-line method with no residual value. Furniture and equipment are depreciated on an eight-year life using the double-declining-balance method. Depreciation has been calculated since the day the assets were placed in service, January 2, 1992.

As of January 2, 1995, EKBOG did not have any short- or long-term investments or intangible assets.

During 1995 the following transactions took place:

Jan. 2: The firm purchased five acres of land in Hidden Hills to use as a future plant location. EKBOG issued 50,000 shares of its publicly-traded common stock par value $10 in exchange for the land. The market price on January 2, 1995, was $21 per share. A recent appraisal indicated the land had a fair market value of $1,112,000. The stock is widely traded.

Feb. 1: EKBOG invested some idle cash by purchasing 5,000 shares of LTS, a publicly-traded company, at $46 per share, and 10,000 of Endoplast, a publicly-traded company, at $12 per share. These are both considered short-term investments.

March 1: The firm's board of directors approved a management plan to begin the development of a new wonder drug called Genosis. As a first step, EKBOG purchased 40% (or 200,000 shares) of the shares of Tilokmed, a genetics splicing company, for $500,000 cash.

March 1: EKBOG purchased new laboratory equipment costing $500,000. A 20% downpayment was made and the remainder financed through a $400,000 12% note with principal payments of $20,000 and interest on the outstanding balance due for each of the next 20 quarters. Payments are due June 1, September 1, December 1, and March 1.

EKBOG gave the laboratory equipment a five-year life and will use sum-of-the-years-digits depreciation with six months in the year of purchase and six months in the year of sale. The equipment has a residual value of $50,000. A new account entitled Laboratory Equipment will be established for this purchase.

May 15: EKBOG sold some of the furniture and equipment it purchased on January 2, 1992. The furniture and equipment, which had an original cost of $80,000, was sold for $21,000 cash. No depreciation has been recorded in 1995, and the firm's policy is to take six months in the year of sale regardless of the exact date the asset was sold.

June 1: The first quarterly interest and principal payment was made on the note dated March 1.

July 1: Continuing with its development of Genosis, EKBOG purchased a patent from a start-up company relating to a process called introfusion needed to bind genes in an artificial environment. The patent was purchased for $200,000 cash. The patent had a remaining legal life of 15 years. However, EKBOG estimates that its useful life is only five years. Straight-line amortization is used and should be recorded from the date of purchase.

Sept. 1: The second quarterly interest and principal payment was made on the note dated March 1.

Nov. 15: On the advice of its investment counselor, EKBOG sold its 5,000 shares in LTS for $56 per share after commissions. EKBOG also purchased 8,000 shares of International Alliance at $61 per share as a short-term investment.

Dec. 1: EKBOG received a $1.25 per share dividend from Tilokmed. EKBOG also received a $1.00 per share dividend from its investment in Endoplast.

Dec. 1: The third quarterly interest and principal payment was made on the note dated March 1.

Dec. 15: Internal documents indicated that the firm spent $100,000 cash on research and development related to the ongoing development of Genosis.

Adjusting entries must be made to record:

a. depreciation
b. amortization
c. interest on the note payable

In addition, you have gathered the following data:

a. Market value per share of International Alliance—$48
b. Market value per share of Endoplast—$12.50
c. Market value per share of Tilokmed—$4
d. Tilokmed earnings for 1994 amounted to $1,850,000.

REQUIRED:

1. Make the required journal entires for 1995.
2. Prepare the property, plant, and equipment section of EKBOG's balance sheet at December 31, 1995. In addition, show how other accounts affected by the above transactions would be shown on EKBOG's financial statements.

C11-2 Understanding Financial Statements

Comsat Corp. is an international communications company carrying voice, video, data, information, news, and entertainment around the globe by both fixed and mobile media. Its December 31, 1991, balance sheet listed property, plant, and equipment at $1,171,594,000 and investments at $31,256,000. Footnote information pertaining to the property, plant, and equipment, as well as partial footnote information relating to the investments, is reproduced below and on page 566.

Excerpts from the Comsat Corp. notes to consolidated financial statements for each of the three years in the period ended December 31, 1991 (in thousands of dollars):

3. Property and Equipment
Property and equipment include the corporation's share of INTELSAT, Inmarsat, and MARISAT property and equipment, as well as wholly-owned assets.

	1991	1990	1989
Property and equipment at cost			
Satellites	$1,004,344	$ 794,920	$ 608,670
Support equipment	407,789	347,592	408,049
Buildings and improvements	86,879	85,346	87,846
Land	4,108	4,182	4,401
Total	1,503,120	1,232,040	1,108,966
Less accumulated depreciation	647,013	563,207	531,430
Net property and equipment in service	856,107	668,833	577,536
Property and equipment under construction			
INTELSAT satellites	221,729	208,127	283,798
Inmarsat satellites	49,869	74,823	130,255
Other	43,889	72,783	40,199
Total	$1,171,594	$1,024,566	$1,031,788

Depreciation is calculated using the straight-line method over the estimated service lives of the assets. The service life for satellites and support equipment is 5 to 12 years and the service life for buildings and improvements is 6 to 40 years.

Costs of satellites which are lost at launch or that fail in orbit are carried, less any insurance proceeds, in the property accounts, and the remaining net amounts are depreciated over the estimated service life for satellites of the same series. A launch vehicle failure occurred during the second INTELSAT VI satellite launch in March 1990. The corporation's share of this satellite and launch is valued at approximately $69,000.

4. Investments

In November 1989, the corporation acquired a 62.5% interest in a limited partnership (the Partnership) which acquired the Denver Nuggets, a franchise of the National Basketball Association. The corporation has subsequently acquired additional interest in the Partnership, bringing its ownership to 65.3% as of December 31, 1991. In addition to owning limited partnership interests, the corporation is also one of the two general partners. The other general partner is the managing general partner and is responsible for owner's oversight of the franchise.

The corporation loaned $25,000 to the Partnership in October 1989 and a total of $1,500 during March and April 1990. The loans plus accrued interest were repaid in April 1990. The corporation made additional capital contributions to the Partnership of $2,491 in 1991 and $3,125 in 1990.

The corporation's share of the Partnership's losses for the three-year period ending 1991 was $6,603, $6,140, and $530. The Partnership had assets of approximately $63,600 and liabilities of $51,700 at December 31, 1991.

The Partnership has a $28,112 note payable and $4,380 outstanding under a $5,000 revolving credit facility as of December 31, 1991. These facilities are non-recourse to the corporation, and are backed by the Partnership's assets as well as by letters of credit totaling $9,362 issued by the corporation.

On Command Video: In 1991, the corporation paid $13,655 for a 47% interest in On Command Video Corporation (OCV), a California-based company that develops and markets a proprietary video entertainment system to hotels. The corporation plans to provide administrative and programming support to OCV, and to market OCV systems.

REQUIRED:

1. Why are Property and Equipment Under Construction listed as assets in this section even though the assets have not been placed in service?

2. What is your opinion of the accounting treatment Comsat employs for satellites that are lost at launch or fail in orbit? Do they meet the accountant's usual definition of an asset? Why or why not?
3. What method of accounting should Comsat use to account for its investment in the Denver Nuggets? Under this method, how does Comsat account for its share of the loss totaling $6,603,000?
4. What method of accounting should Comsat use to account for its interest in On Command Video?

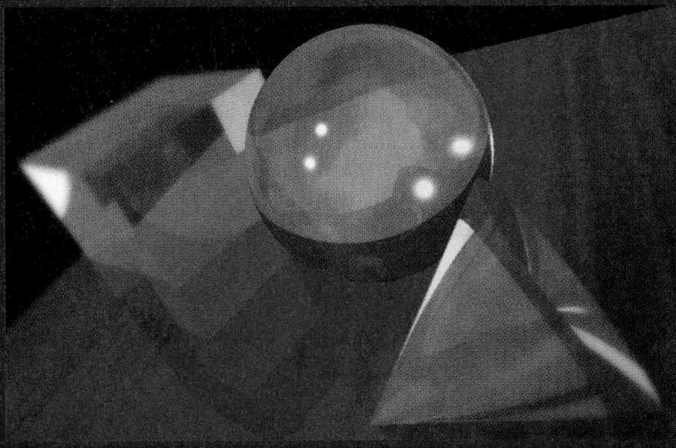

PART 4

FINANCING ACTIVITIES

Part 4 discusses accounting issues related to a firm's financing decisions, which include (1) obtaining resources from creditors through issuance of debt securities, (2) repaying borrowings, (3) obtaining resources from owners through issuance of equity securities, and (4) providing a return to owners through issuance of dividends. Cash inflows from financing activities include issuance of notes, bonds, and mortgages, other short- or long-term borrowings, and common and preferred stock. Cash outflows from financing activities include repayment of borrowings, payments of cash dividends, and purchase of treasury stock.

These activities are discussed as summarized below:

Receipts	*Payments*
From the issuance or sale of bonds (Chapter 12)	To repay bond debt (Chapter 12)
From the issuance of equity securities (Chapter 13)	To distribute earnings as dividends to shareholders (Chapter 13)

While accounting for bond investment, discussed in Chapter 12, is an investing activity, not a financing activity, the related accounting concepts are best understood after accounting for bond issuance is first introduced.

The discussion in Chapters 12 and 13 assumes that there are clear distinctions between debt securities and equity securities. However, the development of innovative financial instruments has blurred this distinction. This blurring has complicated the accounting for debt and equity instruments. Clearing up the confusion is currently a major project of the FASB.

When deciding how best to raise capital, corporate management often considers issuing debt and/or equity securities. The required accounting treatment of a particular security may influence management's decision on what amounts of debt and equity to issue. This important and complicated decision is one in which accountants play a key role.

CHAPTER 12
LONG-TERM DEBT FINANCING

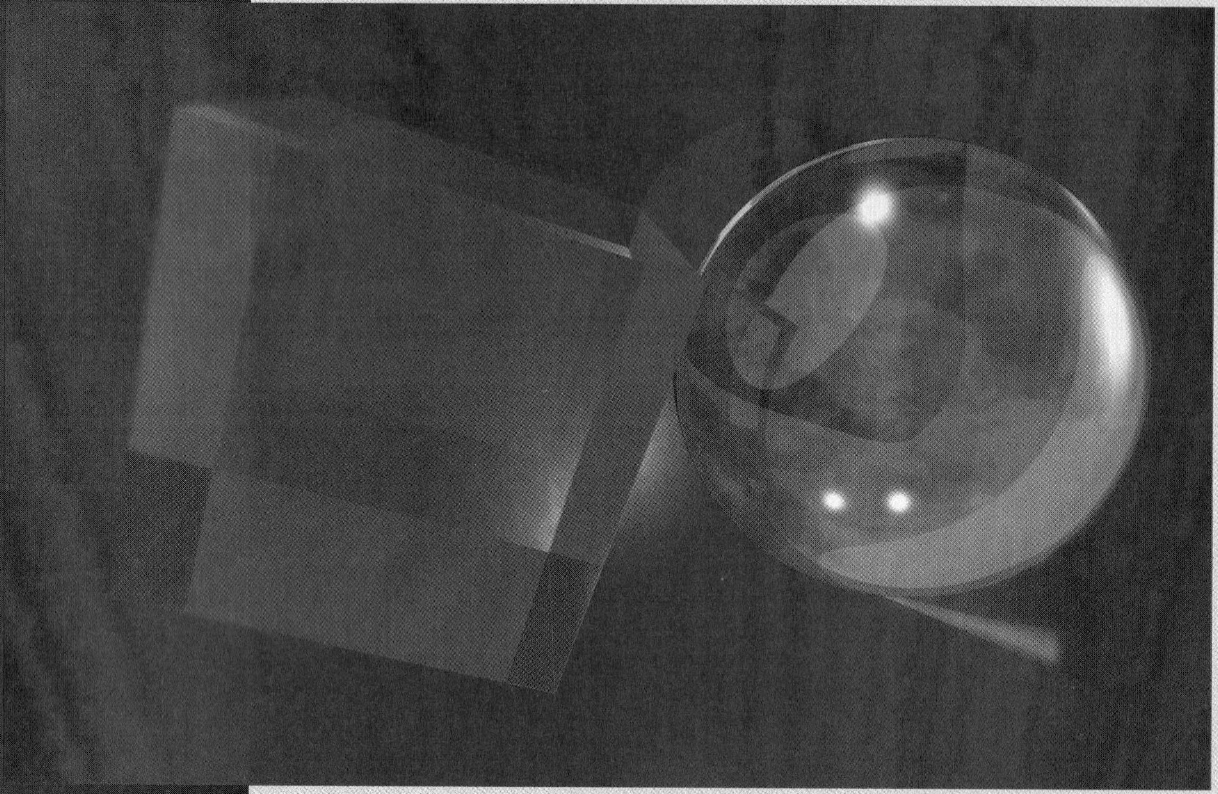

LEARNING OBJECTIVES

After studying this chapter, you should be able to:

1. Explain the nature and features of bonds.
2. Account for bonds by issuers.
3. Account for bonds purchased by investors.
4. Account for other forms of long-term debt including mortgages and leases.
5. Explain the balance sheet and note disclosure requirements for long-term debt.
6. Understand how long-term debt information can be used in decision making.
7. Explain how decision support systems are used by accountants to analyze data in complex decision situations.

Scenario

Alicen Wong is the president and founder of Electrox, a manufacturer of laser video disks. After completing an MBA degree with an option in entrepreneurship, Alicen worked for a high-tech company in Silicon Valley. Several years later she decided to start her own firm. In 1990, after obtaining the backing of a venture capital firm, Alicen founded Electrox.

The company was successful from the very beginning and, by going public, in late 1991 raised about $50 million. Since that time, sales and profits have continued to grow. In early 1993 Electrox signed a multimillion dollar contract with a large Korean manufacturing firm to produce laser video disks for its new line of consumer electronics.

Alicen recognized that the company was going to need additional financing to continue its growth and to meet the production schedule that it agreed to under the terms of the contract with the Korean firm. She decided to discuss the issue with Electrox's treasurer, Jon Goodman.

ALICEN: When I studied accounting in my MBA curriculum, I learned about sources of financing, especially the difference between issuing debt and equity. During that time, issuing debt generally meant issuing long-term bonds or notes with stated interest rates for a fixed period of time. However, I have been reading with great interest about firms that have issued new and innovative types of bonds. Can you fill me in?

JON: You are right, Alicen. In the past few years many types of financial instruments have been developed, some of which blur the distinction between debt and equity. You are probably aware of zero-coupon bonds. These are bonds which are sold at a deep discount, that is, at an amount well below their face or maturity value. For example, a $1,000 face value bond might be issued at $450. Instead of receiving interest, the holder pays only $450 and then receives the $1,000 at maturity. These types of bonds are attractive to smaller investors who might not have the funds to purchase bonds at their face value. These bonds are also popular with issuing companies because no cash interest payments must be made until maturity.

ALICEN: I have heard about these types of bonds. Perhaps we could create some type of financial instrument that includes profit sharing based on how well we do on the contract with the Korean company.

JON: It is interesting that you mention such an instrument. I read in a newspaper that Walt Disney Co. was going to issue some bonds called *ZEBRAs*.[1] These bonds were to pay interest of only 4%, but also provide holders the promise of a 20% return if certain Disney shows were put into syndication.

ALICEN: What an interesting idea. How did the market react?

JON: Actually, the bonds were never issued. Investors were concerned that several of Disney's best shows were not included in the deal. Further, the issue was scheduled for late 1991, just as interest rates were falling. Disney felt that even a 4% interest rate was probably higher than necessary and pulled the issue back.

1. *Los Angeles Times*, December 24, 1991, p. D1.

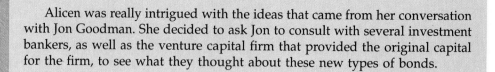

Alicen was really intrigued with the ideas that came from her conversation with Jon Goodman. She decided to ask Jon to consult with several investment bankers, as well as the venture capital firm that provided the original capital for the firm, to see what they thought about these new types of bonds.

Long-term liabilities are a primary source of capital for an enterprise. Included in the long-term liability section of a typical balance sheet are accounts such as Bonds Payable, Mortgages Payable, Long-Term Notes Payable, and Lease Obligations. Because bonds are a common form of long-term corporate debt, they will be used to explain the key accounting procedures for long-term liabilities. Accounting for long-term investments in bonds, which is similar to accounting for bond liabilities, is also discussed in this chapter. Finally, you are briefly introduced to two other common forms of long-term debt, mortgages and leases.

NATURE AND FEATURES OF BONDS

Objective 1
Explain the nature and features of bonds.

bond

A **bond** is a written agreement between a borrower and a lender in which the borrower agrees to repay a stated sum on a future date and, in most cases, to make periodic interest payments at specified dates. Bonds can be issued by local, state, or federal governments and not-for-profit institutions, such as universities. This section, however, will concentrate on bonds issued by corporations to public investors.

Features of Bonds[2]

If you purchase a bond, you receive a bond certificate that spells out the terms of agreement between the issuer and the investor. These terms include the denomination of the bond, the maturity date, the stated rate of interest, the interest payment terms, and any other agreements made between the borrower and lender.

denomination

Denomination of the Bond. Individual bonds usually have a **denomination** of $1,000, although bonds are also issued in $5,000 and $10,000 denominations. The denomination, or *principal,* of a bond is often referred to as its *face value, maturity value,* or *par value;* it is always on this amount that the required interest payment is calculated.

A total bond issue usually contains several hundreds or thousands of individual bonds. For example, a $10 million bond issue might be made up of 10,000 individual $1,000 bonds. Investors can purchase as many of these individual bonds as they wish. After bonds are issued by a large publicly-held company, they are traded, in the U. S., on the New York Bond Exchange. This

2. The features described in this section, and indeed the entire discussion of bonds in this chapter, assume unless otherwise stated, a typical $1,000 bond which pays interest every six months. In recent years, a number of creative financial instruments have been issued, some of which have many, but not all, of the features of the typical bond. Keep in mind that there are now many types and forms of bonds.

enables investors to sell and purchase bonds after their initial issue, just as they do with shares of stock.

maturity date

term bonds

serial bonds

Maturity Date. The date that the principal of the bond is to be repaid is called the **maturity date.** Bonds usually mature in from 5 years to more than 30 years from their date of issue. Bonds whose entire principal is due at a single date are called **term bonds,** and bonds that are payable on various dates are called **serial bonds.**

stated interest rate

market interest rate

Stated Interest Rate and Interest Payment Dates. Most bonds have a **stated interest rate,** which is part of the bond agreement. This rate is often referred to as the *nominal interest rate* and is specified on the bond at the time it is issued. This rate does not change over the life of the bond. The stated rate of interest is fixed by the firm's management in conjunction with its financial advisers. They attempt to set the rate as close as they can to the **market interest rate** that exists at the time the bond is issued. The market rate is the interest rate that the money market establishes through hundreds of individual transactions; it depends on such factors as prevailing interest rates in the economy and the perceived risk of the company.

Most bonds pay interest semiannually, or every six months. However, the stated interest rate is an annual rate based on the face value of the bond. For example, a $1,000, 12% bond that pays interest on January 2 and July 1 will pay interest of $60 ($1,000 × .12 × 6/12) on each of these dates until it matures. In effect, the bond in this example pays 6% interest every six months.

zero-coupon bonds

In recent years **zero-coupon bonds** have become very popular. These are bonds which do not pay interest periodically. Instead they are issued at a discount, the amount of which represents interest to be earned over the life of the bond. For example, a $1,000 bond which matures in 10 years and has a stated interest rate of 8% may be issued at $463, which is the present value of receiving $1,000 in 10 years at 8% interest. At the end of year 10 the bond will pay the holder its maturity value of $1,000. The difference of $537 is the interest which has been earned over the bond's 10-year life.

Zero-coupon bonds are very popular with federal, state, and local governments as they do not require periodic interest payments. They are also popular with small investors, who can purchase the bond with a much smaller cash outlay than they can a bond paying periodic interest.

bond indentures

Other Agreements. Bondholders, unlike shareholders, do not vote for corporate management or otherwise participate in corporate affairs. Therefore, bondholders often insist on written covenants as part of the bond agreement. These agreements, often referred to as **bond indentures,** can take a variety of forms. They usually include restrictions as to dividends, working capital, and the issuance of additional long-term debt. The purpose of these agreements is to ensure that the borrower will maintain a strong enough financial position to meet the interest and principal payments.

Types of Bonds

There are several different types of bonds, including term, serial, secured, unsecured, convertible, and callable bonds.

Term Versus Serial Bonds. Most corporate bonds are term bonds. Thus, a given batch of bonds all issued on the same date, will mature on the same date. In contrast, a batch of serial bonds will mature at specific intervals. Serial bonds are often issued by state or local municipalities. To illustrate, assume that the city of Atlanta issues $5 million of serial bonds whose terms require that $500,000 of the bonds are to be repaid every five years beginning five years after the date of issue. Thus, for the first five years, $5 million of bonds will be outstanding; for the second five years, $4.5 million will be outstanding, and so on. From both the investors' and the issuer's point of view, serial bonds help ensure that the issuer will be able to repay the entire principal.

unsecured bonds

Secured Versus Unsecured Bonds. **Unsecured bonds,** called *debentures,* are issued without any security to back them. Investors purchase them based on the creditworthiness of the company. Some bonds are secured by the borrower's collateral or specified assets. Bonds secured in this way are often referred to as *mortgage bonds.*

convertible bonds

Convertible Bonds. **Convertible bonds** may at some future, specified date, be exchanged for, or converted into, the firm's common stock; thus they enable the bondholder eventually to obtain an equity interest in the firm. This conversion feature allows the firm to issue the bond at a lower interest rate. Convertible bonds are usually *callable,* which means that the borrower, or issuer, is able to call or redeem the bonds prior to their maturity. Thus, the bondholder is forced either to convert the bonds or to have them paid off before their maturity date.

Bond Prices

Traditionally, bond prices are quoted in terms of 100. A price of 100 means that the bond is quoted at 100% of its face value. This is often referred to as *selling at par.* If a bond is quoted at 104, this means that its price is $1,040, or $1,000 × 104%. Any time the bond's price is above 100, the bond is selling *at a premium.* Conversely, if the bond is quoted at 97 1/2, its price is $975, or $1,000 × 97.5%. Any time the bond's price is below 100, the bond is selling *at a discount.*

Bond Exchanges. The bonds of public corporations are traded on various bond exchanges which are similar to stock exchanges. Exhibit 12-1 presents a portion of the New York Bond Exchange listings from the *Wall Street Journal.* The list for AT&T, highlighted in the exhibit, is reproduced below.

Bond	*Cur Yld*	*Vol*	*Close*	*Net Chg*
ATT 7 ⅛ 02	6.7	284	105 ⅝	+⅛

As can be seen from the exhibit, there are several issues of AT&T bonds. The issue highlighted has a stated interest rate of 7 1/8 and is due in 2002. Its current yield is 6.7, which means that if the bonds were purchased at their closing price of 105 5/8, the investor would earn a 6.7% rate of return to maturity. To illustrate, the bond pays interest of 7.125% (or 7 1/8%) on the stated value of $1,000, or $71.25 per bond. If the bond sells for 105.625 (105 5/8%) or $1,056.25 ($1,000 × 1.05625), the return is 6.7% ($71.25/$1,056.25). During the day, 284 bonds were

Exhibit 12-1

Corporation Bonds Volume, $42,730,000									
Bonds	*Cur Yld*	*Vol*	*Close*	*Net Chg.*	*Bonds*	*Cur Yld*	*Vol*	*Close*	*Net Chg.*
AMR 9s16	8.8	126	102⅝ +	1¼	ATT4⅜99	4.7	45	93 −	¼
AMR zr06	...	100	45½ +	⅛	ATT 6s00	6.0	307	100⅛	...
AMR 8.10s98	7.8	8	104½ +	½	ATT 5⅛01	5.5	138	93½ −	⅛
Advst 9s08	cv	15	97½ −	1½	ATT 7⅛cld	...	10	$101\frac{19}{32}$	...
AetnLf 8⅛07	7.9	243	103¼ +	¼	ATT 8⅝cld	...	33	$105\frac{25}{32}$	...
AirbF 6¾01	cv	57	99	...	ATT 8⅝31	7.6	39	113¾ +	⅜
AlskAr 6⅞14	cv	32	85½ −	½	ATT 7⅛02	6.7	284	105⅝ +	⅛
AlskAr zr06	...	208	36⅜ +	¼	ATT 8⅛22	7.5	253	107⅞	...
AlldC zr98	...	7	73⅞ +	1	ATT 8⅛24	7.5	78	108½ +	½
AlldC zr96	...	3	87⅜ −	⅛	ATT 4½96	4.5	1	100 −	¼
AlldC zr2000	...	3	62¼ +	⅞	Amoco 6s98	5.9	19	101½ −	1
AlldC zr97	...	15	77½ +	1¼	Amoco 7⅞96	7.8	60	101½ −	¾
AlldC zr99	...	30	68½ +	2⅞	AmocoCda 7⅜13	5.9	20	125½	...
AlldC zr01	...	10	57⅝	...	Apache 7½00	cv	33	140⅛ −	⅞
AlegCp 6½14	cv	12	99 +	½	Arml 8.7s95	8.7	21	100	...
Allwst 7¼14	cv	18	95 +	¼	Arml 9.2s00	9.2	5	100 +	¼
AmBrnd 8½03	7.7	10	111 +	3⅛	Arml 8½01	8.9	25	95¾ −	¼
AmBrnd 7½99	7.2	50	103½ +	½	ARich 8⅝00	8.3	64	103½	...
AmBrnd 7⅞23	7.7	3	102½ +	1¼	ARich 7¾03	7.5	5	102⅞ +	⅜
AmStor01	cv	31	113¼ +	¼	ARch 9⅛11	7.7	5	118 +	2
ATT 5½97	5.5	95	100⅛ −	⅛	AubrnHl 15⅜20f	...	188	140½	...

Source: *The Wall Street Journal,* April 19, 1993, p. C16.

traded, and the closing price per bond was 105 5/8% × $1,000 (or $1,056.25). The closing price represented an increase of 1/8% from the previous day's closing price.

Determination of Bond Prices. Bond prices at the issue date and during subsequent trading are the result of the interaction among the stated interest rate, the prevailing market rate, the length of time to maturity, and the perceived risk of the investment. When a bond is issued, the company will receive the full face amount of the bond only if the stated rate of interest equals the market rate at the time of issue. That is, when $100,000, 12%, 10-year bonds are issued, the company will receive $100,000 only if the prevailing market rate is 12% for bonds of that duration and perceived risk. If the prevailing market rate is above 12%, say 14%, the bond will be issued at a discount, and the firm will receive less than $100,000. Conversely, if the market rate of interest for such bonds is below 12%, say 10%, the bonds will be issued at a premium, and the firm will receive more than $100,000 at the time of issue. The amount of the discount or the premium is the difference between the face value of the bond and the amount for which the bond was actually issued. You should keep in mind that the issuing company is obligated to repay the full face amount of the bond, regardless of whether the bond is issued at a discount or at a premium. Furthermore, all interest payments are based on the face value.

To demonstrate further this relationship between interest rates and bond prices, assume that you are considering investing in a $1,000, five-year, 10% bond that pays 6% interest semiannually. Therefore, you will receive $60 every six months ($1,000 × 6%). Because this stated interest will not change, you will receive this $60 every six months for five years, regardless of what happens to future interest rates. However, assume that you have an alternative $1,000, five-year investment that represents the same risk as the bond investment. The alternative investment pays 14%, or 7% every six months. Clearly, the second alternative is more valuable, because it pays a semiannual interest of $70, versus $60 for the first investment. If you wanted to purchase the first investment, one way to equalize the difference between the two investments would be to pay less than $1,000 for the first investment. By paying less than $1,000 and still receiving $60 every six months, your rate of return would increase. In effect, as a rational economic person, you would pay for the first investment only an amount that would provide a return of 14%. Such an amount would be less than $1,000, in this case $929.

This is exactly what happens with bonds. Bonds having a stated rate less than the prevailing market rate for investments of similar risk will attract investors only if they are issued at a discount. In effect, the price of the bonds will be bid down until they yield a rate of return equal to the prevailing market rate of return for investments of similar risk. Conversely, if the stated rate is higher than the market rate, the demand for these bonds will cause their price to be bid up, and they will be issued at a premium. The actual rate at which the bond is issued is referred to as the **yield rate,** or *effective rate.*

yield rate

To illustrate this concept, the following example will show how the price of a bond can be computed. Assume that $100,000, five-year, 12% bonds are issued to yield 14%. Given these data, the prevailing market interest rate, the stated interest rate, and the maturity date, the bond price can be calculated using present value techniques.[3] When bonds are issued, the borrower agrees to make two different types of payments: an annuity made up of the future cash interest payments and a single future amount constituting the bond's maturity value. Rational investors would not pay any more than the present value of these two future cash flows, discounted at the market rate of interest or desired yield.

These concepts are shown graphically in Exhibit 12-2, while the issue price of $92,976 is calculated in Exhibit 12-3. As these exhibits indicate, the issue price is composed of the present value of the maturity payment of $100,000 discounted at 7% for ten periods and the present value of semiannual cash interest payments of $6,000 ($100,000 × .06), also discounted at 7%. Ten periods are used because the five-year bonds pay interest semiannually. The discount rate is the semiannual yield, or an effective rate of 7%. You should remember that the $6,000 annuity, which is the cash interest payment, is calculated on the actual semiannual stated rate of 6%.

3. For a review of present value concepts and techniques, see the present value module preceding Chapter 10.

Exhibit 12-2

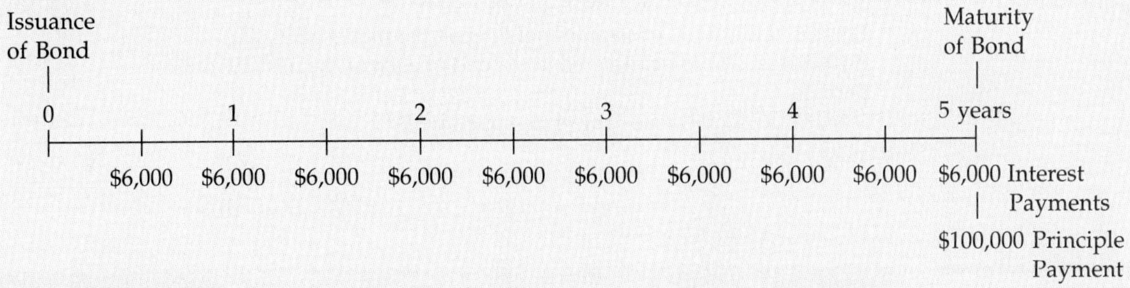

Present Value (PV)

$50,835 = $100,000 × PV of $1 factor for 10 periods at 7%

42,141 = $6,000 × PV of an annuity factor for 10 periods at 7%

$92,976 = 14% (7% semiannual) yield rate

Exhibit 12-3
Determination of Bond Price ($100,000, five-year, 12% bonds issued to yield 14%)

Present value of $100,000 to be received at end of ten periods at 7% semiannually	
$100,000 × .50835 (See Table 3 in Appendix B)	$ 50,835
Present value at 7% of semiannual interest payments of $6,000 ($100,000 × .06) to be received at the end of each of the next 10 interest periods	
$6,000 × 7.02358 (see Table 4 in Appendix B)	+ 42,141
Total issue price	$ 92,976
Amount of discount	
Face value of bonds	$100,000
Total issue price	− 92,976
Amount of discount	$ 7,024

If the bonds were issued at par (that is, to yield 12%), the issue price would be $100,000, as calculated in Exhibit 12-4. Borrowers and investors need not make these calculations because various bond tables are available that determine the correct prices at different yield rates and maturity dates. The same relationships hold after the bonds are issued and are trading in the marketplace. Remember that the stated rate is specified on the bond and does not change over its life. However, market rates of interest constantly change as economic conditions change. Taken as a whole, when there is a general rise in interest rates, the bond market declines, and when interest rates decline, bond prices tend to rise. Exhibit 12-5 illustrates these relationships. Because of the historical cost convention, however, subsequent price changes in the bonds are not reflected in the accounting records of the issuer or the investor.

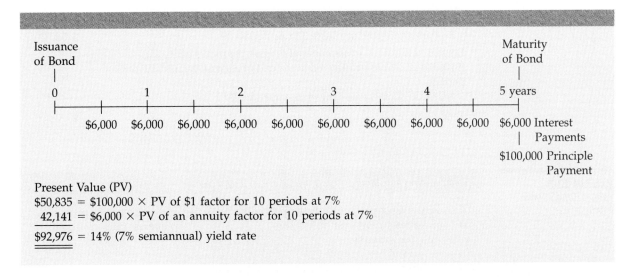

Determination of Interest Rates on Individual Bond Issues. Obviously, interest rates play an important role in determining bond prices. As previously noted,

Exhibit 12-4
Determination of Bond Price ($100,000, five-year, 12% bonds issued to yield 12%)

Present value of $100,000 to be received at end of 10 periods at 6% semiannually	
$100,000 × .55839 (see Table 3 in Appendix B)	$ 55,839
Present value at 6% of semiannual interest payments of $6,000 ($100,000 × .06) to be received at the end of each of the next 10 interest periods	
$6,000 × 7.36009 (see Table 4 in Appendix B)	+ 44,161
Total issue price	$100,000

Exhibit 12-5
Why a Bond's Price Changes

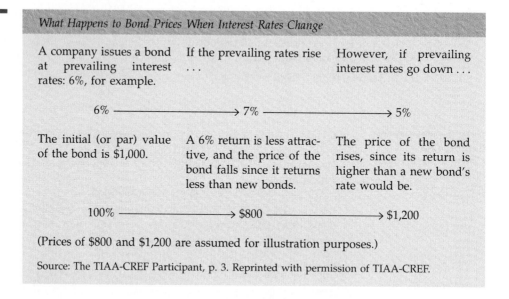

What Happens to Bond Prices When Interest Rates Change

A company issues a bond at prevailing interest rates: 6%, for example.	If the prevailing rates rise . . .	However, if prevailing interest rates go down . . .
6% →	7% →	5%
The initial (or par) value of the bond is $1,000.	A 6% return is less attractive, and the price of the bond falls since it returns less than new bonds.	The price of the bond rises, since its return is higher than a new bond's rate would be.
100% →	$800 →	$1,200

(Prices of $800 and $1,200 are assumed for illustration purposes.)

Source: The TIAA-CREF Participant, p. 3. Reprinted with permission of TIAA-CREF.

the stated interest rate is set by management and in some cases by the underwriters. Underwriters help the issuing company market the bond. They often agree to purchase the entire bond issue at a certain price and then assume the risks involved in selling the bonds to institutions and/or private investors. Management and the underwriters attempt to set the stated or face interest rate as close as possible to the prevailing market rate. The stated rate must be decided on far enough in advance of the actual issue date to allow regulatory bodies such as the Securities and Exchange Commission to approve the issue and then to allow the firm to have the bond certificate printed. There is a consequent lag time between the time the decision must be made on the stated interest rate and the time the bonds are actually issued. A number of economic and financial events during the interim period may cause changes in the rates, so bonds are often issued at a discount or a premium.

The determination of market interest rates is as difficult to understand as the rates are to predict. They are affected by the federal government's economic policies, the Federal Reserve Board, investors' expectations about inflation, the risk of the particular investment, and various other factors. In recent years, these rates have been very volatile, reaching new highs and by early 1992 new lows. For example, the cost of borrowing through traditional debt instruments, such as bonds, rose sharply in the early 1980s, and the number of new bond issues at that time dropped correspondingly. However, the lower interest rates of the early 1990s resulted in an increase in the number of new bond issues during that period.

Determination of Bond Risk and Future Price Changes. The entire bond market is affected by changes in interest rates. Individually, however, bonds are also subject to price changes due to perceived changes in their individual risk. For example, if a company is experiencing financial difficulty, this might be reflected through a decrease in the price of the bond as investors demand a higher rate of return through increased interest rates. To illustrate, in the mid-1980s firms issued what came to be called *junk bonds,* bonds that carry a high rate of interest due to their high risk. Because of the high stated interest rates, these bonds became popular investments with savings and loans and insurance companies. However, as the companies which issued these bonds began to experience financial difficulties, the price of these junk bonds decreased dramatically, leading to the bankruptcy of several insurance companies, such as Executive Life Insurance Company of California.

One way in which a bond's risk can be measured is through bond ratings. Financial advisory services such as Standard and Poor's and Moody's rate the bonds of major corporations, states, and cities. The higher the rating, the less risky the bond will be in the opinion of the rating service. Thus, firms with high ratings can issue bonds with a lower stated interest rate than firms with lower ratings.

ACCOUNTING FOR BONDS BY ISSUERS

Objective 2
Account for bonds by issuers.

Accounting for the issuance of bonds and accounting for the purchase of bonds closely parallel each other. The accounting concepts and procedures involved will first be discussed in detail from the issuer's, or borrower's, point of view and then from the investor's point of view.

The decision to issue bonds represents a major financial commitment by an enterprise. Approval must be obtained from its board of directors, from regulatory agencies, and often from its stockholders. The bond issue can be made through underwriters or issued directly to the public and to private institutions without the aid of underwriters. Regardless of the method used to issue the bonds or whether the bonds are issued at par, at a discount, or at a premium, the accounting issues are similar.

Bonds Issued at Par or Face Value

Bonds will be issued at par or face value if the stated interest rate equals the prevailing rate for similar investments at the issue date. Because bonds can be issued on an interest date or between interest dates, both cases will be discussed.

Bonds Issued at Par on an Interest Date. If bonds are issued at par or face value on an interest date, the entry is straightforward. Cash is debited for proceeds received and Bonds Payable is credited for the face value of the bond issue. For example, assume that on January 2, 1994, the Valenzuela Corporation issues \$100,000, five-year term bonds with a stated interest rate of 12%. The bonds pay interest every January 2 and July 1. The bonds were issued to yield 12%, thus the company received the full $100,000. The entry to record this bond issue is as follows:

Jan. 2, 1994	Cash	100,000	
	Bonds Payable		100,000
	To record the issuance of $100,000, 5-year, 12% bonds at face value.		

The Valenzuela Corporation is required to make semiannual interest payments of $6,000, or $100,000 × 6%. The entry on July 1, 1994, is:

July 1, 1994	Interest Expense	6,000	
	Cash		6,000
	To record payments of semiannual interest of $6,000.		

The next interest payment is due on January 2, 1995. The corporation's year-end is December 31, and the firm must make an adjusting entry to record interest expense for the six-month period July 1 to December 31. This adjusting entry and the entry to record the subsequent payment are:

Dec. 31, 1994	Interest Expense	6,000	
	Interest Payable		6,000
	To record interest accrual for 6 months on $100,000, 5-year, 12% bonds.		
Jan. 2, 1995	Interest Payable	6,000	
	Cash		6,000
	To record payment of 6 months' accrued interest.		

In this case, the interest accrual is for the entire six-month period, because the last interest payment was on July 1. If the year-end were other than December 31, the interest accrual would be for less than six months.

Bonds Issued at Par Between Interest Dates. Bonds are often issued between interest dates. When this occurs, the investors pay the issuing corporation for the interest that has accrued since the last interest date. This payment is made because the investors will receive the entire six months' interest on the next interest payment date, regardless of how long they have held the bonds. This procedure has definite record-keeping advantages for the issuer, whether or not the bonds are registered. If the bonds are registered, the corporation does not have to maintain records of when each particular bond was purchased or to compute individual partial interest payments. Interest on unregistered or coupon bonds is paid by authorized banks upon presentation of the coupon. Banks, however, will not honor a partial coupon. These problems are alleviated by the fact that the accrued interest is collected from the investors when the bonds are sold, freeing the corporation from having to make any partial payments of interest at the first interest payment date.

For example, now assume that the Valenzuela Corporation issues $100,000, five-year, 12% bonds on March 1, 1994. The bonds, dated January 2, 1994, pay interest semiannually, on January 2 and July 1. In this situation, the investor must pay the Valenzuela Corporation for two months of accrued interest (from January 2, when the bonds were dated, to February 28, when the bonds were issued), or $2,000 ($100,000 × .06 × 2/6). The entry to record this transactions is:

Mar. 1, 1994	Cash	102,000	
	Interest Payable		2,000
	Bonds Payable		100,000
	To record issuance of $100,000, 5-year, 12% bonds on March 1 plus accrued interest of $2,000.		

Several points should be emphasized about this entry. Bonds Payable is always credited for the face value of the issue, so the accrued interest element must be accounted for separately. This is done by crediting Interest Payable for the two months of accrued interest, or $2,000. Interest Payable is credited because these funds are owed when the next interest payment is made on July 1. The following entry is recorded:

July 1, 1994	Interest Expense	4,000	
	Interest Payable	2,000	
	Cash		6,000
	To record interest payment for 6 months' interest.		

In this entry, Cash is credited for $6,000, Interest Payable is debited for $2,000, and Interest Expense is debited for $4,000. This entry results in a zero balance in the interest payable account and a $4,000 balance in the interest expense account. This $4,000 balance represents the actual interest expense that the Valenzuela Corporation incurred from March 1, 1994, to July 1, 1994 ($100,000 × .06 × 4/6). These relationships are illustrated in the diagram below and in relevant T accounts.

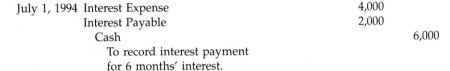

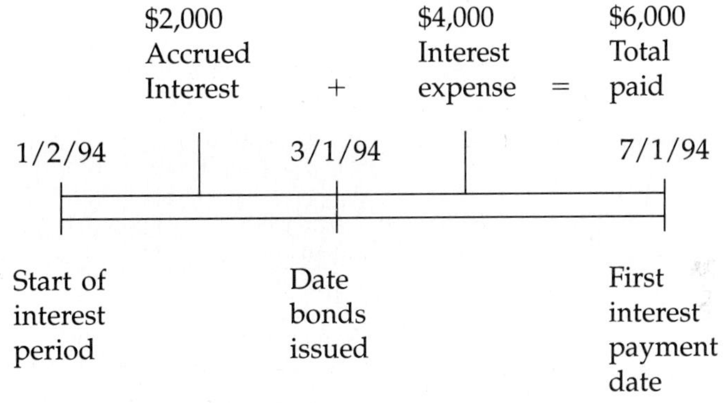

Interest Payable

7/1	2,000	3/1	2,000
			0

Interest Expense

7/1	4,000	
	4,000	

Bonds Issued at Other Than Face Value

As previously noted, bonds are often issued above or below their face value. If the prevailing market interest rate is above the stated rate, the bonds will be issued at a discount. Conversely, if the prevailing interest rate is below the stated rate, the bonds will be issued at a premium.

Recording Bonds Issued at a Discount. To illustrate the issuance of bonds at a discount, assume that on January 2, 1994, the Valenzuela Corporation issues

$100,000, five-year, 12% term bonds. Interest of 6% is payable semiannually, on January 2 and July 1. The bonds were issued when the prevailing market interest rate for such investments was 14%. Thus, the bonds were issued at a discount to yield 14%. This rate is called the **effective interest rate.** Based on this effective rate, the bonds would be issued at a price of 92.976, or $92,976. The calculation of this issue price was illustrated in Exhibit 12-3 (page 577).

effective interest rate

The journal entry to record the issuance of Valenzuela bonds at an effective interest rate of 14% is:

Jan. 2, 1994	Cash	92,976	
	Discount on Bonds Payable	7,024	
	Bonds Payable		100,000
	To record issuance of $100,000, 5-year, 12% bonds at $92,976.		

As this entry illustrates, Cash is debited for the proceeds received, and Bonds Payable is credited for the face value of the bonds. The difference of $7,024 is debited to an account called Discount on Bonds Payable.

The discount account is a contra-liability account, that is, it is deducted from the bonds payable account on the balance sheet in order to arrive at the bonds' net carrying value. To illustrate, a balance sheet prepared on January 2, 1994, immediately after the bonds were issued, would include the long-term liabilities section shown in Exhibit 12-6.

Nature of the Discount Account. It is important to understand the nature of the bond discount account. In effect, the discount should be thought of as additional interest expense that is recognized over the life of the bond. Remember that the bond was issued at a discount because the stated interest rate was below the market rate. As Exhibit 12-7 shows, the bondholders are receiving only $6,000

Exhibit 12-6

Valenzuela Corporation
Partial Balance Sheet
January 2, 1994

Long-term liabilities	
Bonds payable, 12% due 1/2/99	$100,000
Less: Discount on bonds payable	7,024
	$ 92,976

Exhibit 12-7

0 1 2 3 4 5 years

Interest desired	$7,000	$7,000	$7,000	$7,000	$7,000	$7,000	$7,000	$7,000	$7,000	$7,000
Interest earned	6,000	6,000	6,000	6,000	6,000	6,000	6,000	6,000	6,000	6,000
Interest deficit	$1,000	$1,000	$1,000	$1,000	$1,000	$1,000	$1,000	$1,000	$1,000	$1,000

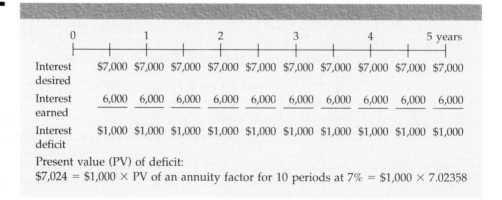

Present value (PV) of deficit:
$7,024 = $1,000 × PV of an annuity factor for 10 periods at 7% = $1,000 × 7.02358

every six months, whereas comparable investments yielding 14% are paying \$7,000 every six months (\$100,000 × .07). The discount of \$7,024 represents the present value of the \$1,000 that the bondholders are not receiving over each of the next ten interest periods (five years' interest paid semiannually). Essentially, the company incurs that additional interest of \$7,024 at the time of issuance by receiving \$92,976 rather than \$100,000. Because of the matching concept, this cost of \$7,024 cannot be expensed when the bonds are issued but must be written off over the life of the bond.

As a result of issuing the bonds at a discount, the total interest expense incurred by the Valenzuela Corporation over the five-year life of the bond is \$67,024, calculated as follows:

Interest expense paid in cash to bondholders	
Face value of bonds	\$100,000
Semiannual stated interest rate	.06
Semiannual interest	\$ 6,000
Number of interest periods	× 10
Total cash interest	\$ 60,000
Discount on issuance	7,024
Total interest expense incurred	\$ 67,024

Another way to view this is to look at the difference between the cash that the company will eventually repay the bondholders versus what it received at the time of issuance. This calculation is:

Total cash repaid to bondholders	
Principal	\$100,000
Cash interest (see prior calculation)	60,000
Total cash paid	\$160,000
Total cash received at issuance	92,976
Total interest expense incurred	\$ 67,024

Discount Amortization—Straight-Line Method. The discount of \$7,024 must be written off, or amortized, over the life of the bond. There are two methods used to do this: the straight-line method and the effective-interest method. The effective-interest method is conceptually preferable, and accounting pronouncements require its use unless there is no material difference from the periodic amortization computed by the straight-line method.[4] However, the straight-line method is easy to compute and understand, so it is examined first in order to aid in your understanding of the concepts. The effective-interest method will be discussed later in the chapter.

The *straight-line method* allocates the discount evenly over the remaining life of the bond. Thus, there is a constant interest charge each period. An entry is

4. "Interest on Receivables and Payables," Accounting Principles Board Opinion No. 21 (New York: AICPA, 1971), par. 15.

made on every interest date, and if necessary, an adjusting journal entry is made at the end of each period to record the discount amortization.

To demonstrate the application of the straight-line method, let's return to the Valenzuela Corporation example introduced on page 579. In this case, the discount of $7,024 will be amortized over ten interest periods at a rate of $702 (rounded) per interest period ($7,024/10). The total interest expense for each period is $6,702, consisting of the $6,000 cash interest and the $702 amortized discount. The rounding error of $4 is accounted for on the final interest payment date. Another way to calculate the $6,702 is to divide the total interest cost, $67,024, into the ten interest periods of the bond's life. The journal entry at July 1, 1994, and each interest payment date thereafter is:

July 1, 1994	Interest Expense	6,702	
	Discount on Bonds Payable		702
	Cash		6,000
	To record cash interest payment and amortization of discount on the straight-line method.		

As the bonds approach maturity, their carrying value increases, and the result of this and subsequent entries is to reflect this increase. This is because the discount account, which is offset against bonds payable in arriving at the bonds' carrying value, is decreased each time a credit entry is made to that account. To illustrate, the relevant T account and a partial balance sheet as of July 1, 1994, are presented in Exhibit 12-8. In each interest period, the bond's carrying value will be increased by $702. Thus, by the time the bond matures, the balance in the discount on bonds payable account will be zero, and the bond's carrying value will be $100,000. Exhibit 12-9 presents an amortization schedule for this bond on the straight-line method. Thus, when the company repays the principal, it makes the following entry:

Jan. 2, 1999	Bonds Payable	100,000	
	Cash		100,000
	To record the repayment of $100,000, 5-year, 12% bonds.		

Exhibit 12-8

Bonds Payable

Debit	Credit
	1/2/94 100,000

Interest Expense

Debit	Credit
7/1/94 6,702	

Discount on Bonds Payable

Debit	Credit
1/2/94 7,024	7/1/94 702
7/1/94 Bal. 6,322	

Valenzuela Corporation
Partial Balance Sheet
July 1, 1994

Long-term liabilities	
Bonds payable, 12% due 1/2/99	$100,000
Less: Discount on bonds payable	6,322
	$ 93,678

Exhibit 12-9
Discount Amortization—Straight-Line

Date	Cash Interest (1)	Discount Amortization (2)	Total Interest Expense (3)	Carrying Value of Bonds (4)
1/2/94				$ 92,976
7/1/94	$6,000	$702	$6,702	93,678
1/2/95	6,000	702	6,702	94,380
7/1/95	6,000	702	6,702	95,082
1/2/96	6,000	702	6,702	95,784
7/1/96	6,000	702	6,702	96,486
1/2/97	6,000	702	6,702	97,188
7/1/97	6,000	702	6,702	97,890
1/2/98	6,000	702	6,702	98,592
7/1/98	6,000	702	6,702	99,294
1/2/99	6,000	706	6,706	100,000

(1) $6,000 = $100,000 × .06

(2) $\$\ 702 = \dfrac{\$7{,}024}{10 \text{ periods}} = \$702.40$ rounded to $702

(3) $6,702 = $6,000 + $702

(4) Carrying value at beginning of period plus discount amortization for period ($93,678 = $92,976 + $702). Last year's interest expense rounded to make carrying value $100,000.

Recording Bonds Issued at a Premium. To show how to account for bonds issued at a premium, let us now assume that on January 2, 1994, the Valenzuela Corporation issues $100,000, five-year, 12% term bonds. Interest is payable semiannually, on January 2 and July 1. In this case, however, the bonds are issued when the prevailing market interest rate for such investments is 10%. Therefore, the bonds are issued at a premium to yield 10% and are sold at a price of 107.721, or $107,221. Exhibit 12-10 shows how the issue price of $107,721 is determined. The calculations are similar to those for the discount example in Exhibit 12-3, except that the cash flows are discounted at a semiannual yield rate of 5%. The entry to record this bond issue is:

Jan. 2, 1994	Cash	107,721	
	Premium on Bonds Payable		7,721
	Bonds Payable		100,000
	To record issuance of $100,000, 5-year, 12% bonds at $107,721.		

This entry is similar to the one to record bonds issued at a discount, except that a premium account is involved. Cash is debited for the entire proceeds, and Bonds Payable is credited for the bond's face amount. The difference in this case is a credit to Premium on Bonds Payable of $7,721.

adjunct account

The premium account is called an **adjunct account** because it is added to the Bonds Payable account in determining the bonds' carrying value. To illustrate, the Valenzuela balance sheet prepared on January 2, 1994, immediately after the bonds were issued, would include the long-term liabilities section shown in Exhibit 12-11.

Nature of the Premium Account. In effect, the premium should be thought of as a reduction in interest expense that is amortized over the life of the bonds. The bonds were issued at a premium because the stated interest rate was higher

Exhibit 12-10
Determination of Bond Price ($100,000, five-year, 12% bonds issued to yield 10%)

Present value of $100,000 to be received at end of 10 periods at 5% semiannually	
$100,000 × .61391 (see Table 3 in Appendix B)	$ 61,391
Present value at 5% of semiannual interest payments of $6,000 ($100,000 × .06) to be received at the end of each of the next 10 interest dates	
$6,000 × 7.72173 (see Table 4 in Appendix B)	+ 46,330
Total issue price	$107,721
Amount of premium	
Total issue price	$107,721
Face value of bonds	− 100,000
Amount of premium	$ 7,721

Exhibit 12-11

Valenzuela Corporation
Partial Balance Sheet
January 2, 1994

Long-term liabilities	
Bonds payable, 12% due 1/2/94	$100,000
Plus: Premium on bonds payable	7,721
	$107,721

than the prevailing market rate. The bondholders are receiving $6,000 ($100,000 × .06) every six months when comparable investments were yielding only 10% and paying $5,000 ($100,000 × .05) every six months. The premium of $7,721 represents the present value of that extra $1,000 that the bondholders will receive in each of the next ten interest periods. Because the bond is an attractive investment, its price is bid up to $107,721, and the premium of $7,721 is considered a reduction of interest expense. Although the borrower receives all of the funds at the time of the issue, the matching convention requires that the premium be recognized over the life of the bond.

After issuing the bonds at premium, the total interest expense incurred by the Valenzuela Corporation over the five-year life of the bonds is $52,279, calculated as follows:

Interest expense paid in cash to bondholders	
Face value of bonds	$100,000
Semiannual interest rate	.06
Semiannual interest	$ 6,000
Number of interest periods	× 10
Total cash interest	$ 60,000
Premium upon issuance	(7,721)
Total interest expense	$ 52,279

Again, another way to view this is to consider what the company will ultimately repay the bondholders versus what it received at the time of issuance. This calculation is:

Total cash repaid to bondholders	
Principal	$100,000
Cash interest	60,000
Total cash paid	$160,000
Total cash received at issuance	107,721
Total interest expense incurred	$ 52,279

Premium Amortization—Straight-Line Method. The premium of $7,721 is amortized by using either the straight-line method or the effective-interest method. Again, the straight-line method will be discussed first. The effective-interest method of amortization will be discussed for both the discount and the premium examples.

Under the straight-line method, the premium of $7,721 is amortized over ten interest periods at a rate of $772 ($7,721/10) per period. Thus, the total interest expense for each period is $5,228, consisting of the $6,000 cash interest less the premium amortization of $772. Another way to calculate the $5,228 is to divide the total interest cost of $52,279, as just calculated, into the ten interest periods of the bond's life. Exhibit 12-12 presents an amortization schedule for this bond issue, on a straight-line basis.

Exhibit 12-12
Premium Amortization—Straight-Line

Date	*Cash Interest Payment (1)*	*Premium Amortization (2)*	*Total Interest Expense (3)*	*Carrying Value of Bond (4)*
1/2/94				$107,721
7/1/94	$6,000	$772	$5,228	106,949
1/2/95	6,000	772	5,228	106,177
7/1/95	6,000	772	5,228	105,405
1/2/96	6,000	772	5,228	104,633
7/1/96	6,000	772	5,228	103,861
1/2/97	6,000	772	5,228	103,089
7/1/97	6,000	772	5,228	102,317
1/2/98	6,000	772	5,228	101,545
7/1/98	6,000	772	5,228	100,773
1/2/99	6,000	773	5,230	100,000

(1) $6,000 = $100,000 × .06

(2) $\$\ 772 = \dfrac{\$7{,}721}{10 \text{ interest periods}} = \$772.10$ rounded to $772

(3) $5,228 = $6,000 − $772

(4) Carrying value = carrying value at beginning of period, less premium amortized during period ($106,949 = $107,721 − $772). 1/2/99 rounded up to equal $100,000.

The journal entry at July 1, 1994, and each interest payment date thereafter, is:

July 1, 1994	Interest Expense	5,228	
	Premium on Bonds Payable	772	
	Cash		6,000
	To record cash interest payment and amortization of the premium on the straight-line method.		

The effect of this and subsequent entries is to decrease the carrying value of the bonds as the premium account is reduced each period. By the time the bonds reach maturity, their carrying value will have been reduced to their face value of $100,000. The relevant T accounts and partial balance sheet as of July 1, 1994 are presented in Exhibit 12-13.

Applying the Effective-Interest Method. Although the straight-line method is simple to use, it does not produce the accurate amortization of the discount or premium. It makes the unrealistic assumption that the interest cost for each period is the same, even though the carrying value of the liability is changing. For example, under the straight-line method, interest expense is the same each period, so as the carrying value of the bond increases or decreases, the actual interest rate correspondingly decreases or increases.

Returning to our example, the Valenzuela bonds issued at a discount (see Exhibit 12-9) had a carrying value of $92,976 at the date of their issue. The interest expense based on straight-line amortization for the periods between January 2, 1994, and July 1, 1994, is $6,702. This results in an interest rate of 7.2%, ($6,702/$92,976). In the next period, the interest expense for the period remains at $6,702, but as shown in Exhibit 12-8, the bond's carrying value has increased to $93,678. The interest rate is now 7.15% ($6,702/$93,678). Over the life of the bond, this interest rate continues to decrease until January 2, 1999, when it reaches 6.75%, ($6,706/$99,294).

Exhibit 12-13

Premium on Bonds Payable

7/1/94	772	1/2/94	7,721
		7/1/94 Bal.	6,949

Bonds Payable

		1/2/94	100,000

Interest Expense

7/1/94	5,228		

Valenzuela Corporation
Partial Balance Sheet
July 1, 1994

Long-term liabilities	
Bonds payable	$100,000
Premium on bonds payable	6,949
	$106,949

With a premium example, the same conceptual problem occurs, except that the percentage rate increases as the carrying value of the bond decreases from $107,721 to $100,000, since the semiannual interest expense remains constant at $5,228.

effective-interest method

Under the **effective-interest method,** a constant interest rate equal to the effective rate of interest at the time of issue is used to calculate periodic interest expense. Thus, the interest rate for determining interest expense does not change over the term of the bond; rather, the amount of the interest expense changes as the carrying value of the bond changes. Furthermore, when the effective-interest method is used, the carrying value of the bonds will always equal the present value of the future cash outflow at that amortization date. Illustrations of the effective-interest method for both the discount and the premium cases follow.

Discount Amortization—Effective-Interest Method. Recall that the $100,000, five-year, 12% bonds issued to yield 14% were sold at a price of $92,976, or at a discount of $7,024. Exhibit 12-14 shows how this discount is amortized over the life of the bond using the effective-interest method. The effective periodic bond interest expense is calculated by multiplying the bond's carrying value at the beginning of the period by the semiannual yield rate determined at the time the bond was issued. In this case, the interest expense of $6,508 in column 2 at July 1, 1994, is equal to $92,976 multiplied by 7%. The difference between the required cash interest payment of $6,000 in column 3 ($100,000 × 6%) and the effective-interest expense of $6,508 is the required discount amortization of $508. Finally, the unamortized discount of $6,516 at July 1, 1994, in column 5 is

Exhibit 12-14
Discount Amortization Table—Effective-Interest Method

		Debit	*Credit*			
Date	*Carrying Value at Beginning of the Period (1)*	*Effective Bond Interest Expense, 7% of Carrying Value from Col. 1 (2)*	*Cash Interest Paid, 6% of $100,000 (3)*	*Discount Amortization Col. 2 − Col. 3 (4)*	*Unamortized Discount Balance at End of the Period—Previous Balance Less Col. 4 (5)*	*Carrying Value of Bond at End of the Period Col. 1 + Col. 4 (6)*
1/2/94					$7,024	$ 92,976
7/1/94	$92,976	$ 6,508[a]	$ 6,000	$ 508	6,516	93,484
1/2/95	93,484	6,544	6,000	544	5,972	94,028
7/1/95	94,028	6,582	6,000	582	5,390	94,610
1/2/96	94,610	6,623	6,000	623	4,767	95,233
7/1/96	95,233	6,666	6,000	666	4,101	95,899
1/2/97	95,899	6,713	6,000	713	3,388	96,612
7/1/97	96,612	6,763	6,000	763	2,625	97,375
1/2/98	97,375	6,816	6,000	816	1,809	98,191
7/1/98	98,191	6,873	6,000	873	936	99,064
1/2/99	99,064	6,936[b]	6,000	936	—	100,000
		$67,024	$60,000	$7,024		

[a]Rounded to whole dollars.
[b] Rounded to balance.

equal to the original discount of $7,024, less the amortized discount of $508. The carrying value of the bond in column 6 is increased by $508, from $92,976 to $93,484. Alternatively, the bond's carrying value on July 1, 1994, is equal to $100,000 less the unamortized discount of $6,516.

The information for the journal entry to record the semiannual interest expense can be drawn directly from the amortization schedule. The entry on July 1, 1994, is:

July 1, 1994	Interest Expense	6,508	
	Discount on Bonds Payable		508
	Cash		6,000
	To record semiannual interest expense based on the effective-interest method.		

Exhibit 12-15 compares the two different methods of discount amortization for the first three interest periods and for the total over all ten periods. Under the straight-line method, the interest expense for each period is $6,702. Under the effective-interest method, the semiannual interest expense is $6,508 in the first period and increases thereafter as the carrying value of the bond increases. With the effective-interest method, as with the straight-line method, the total interest expense over all ten periods is $67,024. The important point is that there is no difference in the total interest expense but only in the allocation within the five-year period of time.

Premium Amortization—Effective-Interest Method. Exhibit 12-10 showed that the $100,000, five-year, 12% bonds issued to yield 10% were issued at a price of $107,721, or at a premium of $7,721. The schedule in Exhibit 12-16 shows how the premium is amortized under the effective-interest method. This schedule is set up in the same manner as the discount amortization schedule in Exhibit 12-14, except that the premium amortization reduces the cash interest expense every period. For each period, the interest expense in column 2 is the semiannual yield rate at the time of issue, 5%, multiplied by the carrying value of the bonds at the beginning of the period. The difference between this amount and the cash interest in column 3 is the premium amortization in column 4. The carrying value of the bond at the end of the period in column 6 is reduced by the premium amortization for the period.

Exhibit 12-15

	Interest Expense	
Date	*Straight-line*	*Effective-interest*
July 1, 1994	$ 6,702	$ 6,508
January 2, 1995	6,702	6,544
July 1, 1994	6,702	6,582
"	"	"
"	"	"
"	"	"
January 2, 1999	6,702	6,936
Total for all 10 interest periods	$67,024	$67,024

Exhibit 12-16
Premium Amortization Table—Effective-Interest Method

Date	Carrying Value at Beginning of the Period (1)	Debit: Effective Bond Interest Expense, 5% of Carrying Value from Col. 1 (2)	Credit: Cash Interest Paid, 6% of $100,000 (3)	Discount: Premium Amortization Col. 2 − Col. 3 (4)	Unamortized Premium Balance at End of the Period—Previous Balance Less Col. 4 (5)	Carrying Value of Bond at End of the Period Col. 1 − Col. 4 (6)
1/2/94					$7,721	$107,721
7/1/94	$107,722	$ 5,386[a]	$ 6,000	$ 614	7,107	107,107
1/2/95	107,108	5,355	6,000	645	6,462	106,462
7/1/95	106,463	5,323	6,000	677	5,785	105,785
1/2/96	105,786	5,289	6,000	711	5,074	105,074
7/1/96	105,075	5,254	6,000	746	4,328	104,328
1/2/97	104,329	5,216	6,000	784	3,544	103,544
7/1/97	103,545	5,177	6,000	823	2,721	102,721
1/2/98	102,722	5,136	6,000	864	1,857	101,857
7/1/98	101,858	5,093	6,000	907	950	100,950
1/2/99	100,951	5,050[b]	6,000	950	—	100,000
		$52,279	$60,000	$7,721		

[a]Rounded to whole dollars.
[b]Rounded to balance.

The journal entry to record the semiannual interest expense can be drawn directly from this schedule. The entry on July 1, 1994, is:

July 1, 1994	Interest Expense	5,386	
	Premium on Bonds Payable	614	
	Cash		6,000
	To record semiannual interest expense based on the effective-interest method.		

As with the discount example, the total interest expense over the life of the bond under the straight-line and the effective-interest methods is the same. However, it is allocated differently among periods. In both the discount and the premium examples, the difference between the straight-line and the effective-interest amortization methods is not significant, but for large bond issues, the difference between these two methods can become material. If this is the case, generally accepted accounting principles require that the effective-interest amortization be used.

Other Considerations in Accounting for Bonds Payable

Besides the basic concepts and procedures related to the issuance and subsequent accounting for bonds payable, you should be familiar with other issues concerning bonds.

Bonds Issued at a Premium or Discount Between Interest Dates. Bonds are often sold between interest dates at either a discount or a premium. When this occurs, the face value, the discount or premium, and the accrued interest must be accounted for separately. These calculations are rather complex and are the topic of more advanced textbooks.

Year-End Accruals of Interest Expense. It is likely that the issuing firm's year-end will not coincide with an interest payment date. A previous example on page 580 showed the proper accounting procedures to handle this situation when bonds are issued at par; it is more complex to handle premiums or discounts related to year-end accruals.

Bond Issue Costs. When a corporation issues bonds, various expenses are incurred, such as printing and engraving costs and legal and accounting fees. Furthermore, many bonds are marketed through investment bankers, who receive a commission for underwriting the bond issue. These costs reduce the cash proceeds that the issuer would otherwise receive. Current accounting principles require that these costs be accumulated in a noncurrent asset account titled Bond Issue Costs and be amortized over the life of the bond on a straight-line basis.

Accounting for the Retirement of Bonds

Bonds can be retired in different ways, including repayment at maturity, early extinguishment of the debt before maturity, and conversion into capital stock.

Retirement of Bonds at Maturity and Bond Sinking Funds. When bonds are repaid at maturity, the journal entry is straightforward: Bonds Payable is debited and Cash is credited. There are no problems with discounts or premiums, since they have been amortized to zero at the time of the last interest payment.

Some bond agreements require that the issuing corporation create and maintain a sinking fund to ensure the repayment of the principal. A **sinking fund** is a collection of cash (or perhaps other assets such as marketable securities) that is set aside to be used only for a specified purpose. This fund is generally under the control of a trustee or agent who is independent of the enterprise that established the fund. The monies are invested by the trustee and eventually used to pay the interest and repay the principal of the bond. The amount of periodic payments to the fund is based on the expected return that the trustee can earn on the assets in the fund.

sinking fund

The sinking fund is an asset account shown under the investment section on the balance sheet of the issuing corporation. The accounting procedure regarding interest expense recognition and other aspects of bonds is not affected by the existence of a bond sinking fund.

early extinguishment of debt

Early Extinguishment of Debt. **Early extinguishment of debt** occurs whenever a firm's long-term debt is retired before maturity. Management can accomplish this extinguishment by repurchasing the bonds on the market. Other bonds are callable and give the issuing corporation the right to buy back the bonds before maturity at a specified price. This price is usually set above the par or face value of the bond because the bondholder will be forgoing future interest income. The amount above par is often referred to as a *call premium*. When a firm extinguishes its debt prior to maturity, there will be a gain or a loss. The gain or loss is the difference between the reacquisition price and the carrying value of the bonds. Under current accounting principles, this gain or loss is considered *extraordinary* and must be shown as a separate item on the income statement.[5]

To illustrate the accounting for the early extinguishment of debt, assume that the $100,000, five-year, 12% term bonds that were issued at a discount of $7,024 by the Valenzuela Corporation were called on July 1, 1996. The bonds were reacquired at a price of 104. The firm uses the straight-line method of amortization. The entries to record (1) the payment of interest and the amortization of the discount and (2) the retirement of the bonds are as follows. (See Exhibit 12-9 for the necessary data.)

July 1, 1996	Interest Expense	6,702	
	Discount on Bonds Payable		702
	Cash		6,000
	To record semiannual interest payment and discount amortization.		
July 1, 1996	Bonds Payable	100,000	
	Extraordinary Loss on Early Extinguishment of Debt	7,514	
	Discount on Bonds Payable		3,514
	Cash		104,000
	To record early retirement of bonds at 104.		

Reacquisition price ($100,000 × 1.04)	$104,000
Less: Carrying value on July 1, 1996	96,486
Loss on reacquisition	$ 7,514

The first entry records the interest payment and the discount amortization from January 2, 1996 to July 1, 1996. The second entry records the actual extinguishment of the debt. The unamortized balance in Discount on Bonds Payable must be written off (See Exhibit 12-9 for the amount). There is a loss in this case because the reacquisition price exceeds the carrying value of the bonds.

ACCOUNTING FOR BONDS BY INVESTORS

Objective 3
Account for bonds purchased by investors.

Accounting for the purchase of bonds is similar to accounting for the issuance of bonds, except that the investor records an asset, Investment in Bonds, rather than a liability, Bonds Payable. The accounting standards followed by bond investors depend upon whether the bonds are considered to be: (1) Held-to-maturity; (2) Trading securities; or (3) Available-for-sale. Held-to-maturity securities are classified as long-term until the year prior to their maturity. Available-for-sale debt securities can either be classified as long-term or current depending upon whether or not management's intention is to sell these securities within the operating cycle or twelve months. Trading debt securities are classified as

5. "Reporting Gains and Losses from Extinguishment of Debt," Statement of Financial Accounting Standards No. 4 (Stamford, Conn.: FASB, 1975). For an item to be considered extraordinary, it must meet certain criteria. If it meets these criteria, the item is disclosed separately on the income statement. Extraordinary items were discussed in the Appendix to Chapter 5 on pages 222–228.

current. These categories were explained in detail in Chapter 11. The accounting procedures followed by investors for long-term debt securities were also briefly introduced in that chapter. A more detailed example is provided next.

Accounting for Held-to-Maturity Bonds

The acquisition cost of bonds includes their purchase price, brokerage commissions, and any other costs related to the purchase. Bonds may be purchased at their face value, at a discount or a premium, and at or between interest dates. In practice, Investment in Bonds is debited at cost, including all acquisition costs but excluding the accrued interest element.[6] A separate account is not maintained for the premium or discount. This practice varies from the accounting procedures used by the issuer. However, the investor seldom purchases an entire bond issue, and the amount of the discount or premium generally is not material. The remaining portion of this chapter will not use a separate discount or premium accounting in accounting for debt investments.

Accounting at Acquisition. As explained earlier, if bonds are purchased between interest dates, the investor must pay the issuer or the previous bondholder for any interest accrued since the last interest date. Then the purchaser will collect the full six months' interest amount on the next interest date. To illustrate these procedures, assume that the Zano Corporation purchased 12, $1,000, five-year, 10% bonds on March 1, 1994. The bonds are dated January 1, 1994, and pay interest semiannually on January 2 and July 1. The total face value of the bonds is $12,000, but the bonds were purchased at 98 or for $11,760 plus accrued interest. The firm purchased these bonds with the intention of holding them to maturity, and therefore they are classified as held-to-maturity. The entry to record this investment is as follows:

Mar. 1, 1994	Investment in Held-to-Maturity Bonds	11,760	
	Interest Receivable	200	
	Cash		11,960
	To record purchase of $12,000 bonds at 98 plus accrued interest of $200.		

Acquisition cost: ($12,000 × .98)	=	$11,760
Interest receivable: ($12,000 × .05 × 2/6)	=	200
Cash payment required		$11,960

Investment in Held-to-Maturity Bonds is recorded at $11,760, net of the discount of $240 ($12,000 − $11,760). The $11,760 also represents the carrying value of the bonds at their purchase date. Interest Receivable is debited for the two months' interest that has accrued since the last payment date on January 2. The receivable is debited because the investor will receive all six months' interest on July 1, 1994.

6. The accounting for the acquisition of bonds is not affected by whether the bonds are classified as held-to-maturity, available-for-sale, or trading. Only the accounting at subsequent reporting dates is affected.

Amortizing the Discount or Premium. As noted, the effective-interest method should be used unless there is no material difference between that method and the straight-line method. For ease of illustration, the straight-line method will be used in this part of the chapter. Regardless of which method is used, a discount is amortized by debiting the investment account, and a premium is amortized by crediting the investment account. This procedure ensures that after the discount or premium is fully amortized, the investment account will reflect the bond's maturity value.

To demonstrate these concepts, let's continue with the Zano Corporation example. The first interest payment is on July 1, 1994, and the following entry would be made to record the receipt of the cash interest and the amortization of the discount:

July 1, 1994	Cash	600	
	Investment in Held-to-Maturity Bonds	17	
	Interest Receivable		200
	Interest Revenue		417
	To record semiannual interest payment and discount amortization.		

In this entry, Cash is debited for $600, which is the full six months' interest payment ($12,000 × .05). The investment account is debited for four months of discount amortization. The total discount of $240 is amortized over the remaining 58 months of the bond's life at the time of issue. This equals $4.14 ($240/58 months) per month, and four months' amortization from March 1, 1994, to July 1, 1994, is $16.56 ($4.14 × 4). This is rounded off to $17 in the journal entry. Interest Revenue is credited for $417 which consists of four months' cash interest plus $17 of the amortized discount. Recall that from the issuer's point of view, the discount amortization increases interest expense.

Thereafter, the Zano Corporation would make the following set of journal entries each year until the bonds mature. (The corporation has a December 31 year-end.)

Dec. 31	Interest Receivable	600	
	Investment in Held-to-Maturity Bonds	25	
	Interest Revenue		625
	To record accrual of 6 months' interest plus the amortization of 6 months' discount. ($4.14 × 6 = $24.84, rounded to $25)		
Jan. 1	Cash	600	
	Interest Receivable		600
	To record receipt of accrued interest receivable.		
July 1	Cash	600	
	Investment in Held-to-Maturity Bonds	25	
	Interest Revenue		625
	To record receipt of 6 months' interest and amortization of discount.		

Finally, because these bonds are classified as held-to-maturity, they are reported on the balance sheet at amortized cost (cost plus or minus the amortized discount or premium). No adjustment is made for unrealized gains or losses due to changes in fair value.

These examples illustrate the accounting procedures for discounts. Premiums are handled in a similar manner, except that the premium decreases interest revenue and is recorded by crediting the investment account.

Accounting at Maturity. When the bonds mature, the investor receives the total face value of the bonds regardless of whether they were originally purchased at a discount or premium. To illustrate, assume that the held-to-maturity bonds purchased by the Zano Corporation matured at the end of their five-year life on December 31, 1998. At that time Zano received the full face value of the bonds, or $12,000. The following journal entry would be made at that date:

Dec. 31, 1998	Cash	12,000	
	Investment in Held-to-Maturity Bonds		12,000
	To record maturity of five-year bonds.		

Accounting for Available-for-Sale Securities

As noted in Chapter 11, the debt and equity securities classified as available-for-sale or trading are reported at fair value rather than at amortized cost. The accounting procedures at acquisition and the amortization of the premium or discount are not affected by the classification of the debt securities.

Adjustment to Fair Value. To illustrate these procedures, we will return to the previous example where the Zano Corporation purchased 12, $1,000, five-year, 10% bonds. However, we will now assume that these bonds are properly classified as available-for-sale. The journal entry to record these bonds on March 31, 1994, the receipt of the cash interest and discount amortization on July 1, 1994, and the interest accrual and discount amortization at December 31, 1994 are shown on page 595. (At March 31, 1994, the debit will be to Investment in Available-for-Sale Bonds rather than Investment in Held-to-Maturity Bonds.) After these entries are posted, the Investment in Available-for-Sale Bonds T account is as follows:

Investment in Available-for-Sale Bonds

3/1/94	11,760	
7/1/94	17	
12/31/94	25	
12/31/94	11,802	

Assume now that at December 31, 1994, the fair value of the bonds is determined to be $12,400 versus their amortized cost of $11,802. Because the fair value of the bonds exceeds their amortized cost by $598 ($12,400 − $11,802), the Zano Corporation must recognize an unrealized holding gain of $598. Because these bonds are considered available-for-sale, the unrealized holding gain (or loss) is taken to stockholders' equity rather than to the income statement as is the case for trading debt securities. The following journal entry is made at December 31, 1994 to record this unrealized holding gain.

Dec. 31, 1994	Investment in Available-for-Sale Bonds	598	
	Unrealized Holding Gain or Loss on Available-for-Sale Bonds		598
	To record unrealized holding gain on available-for-sale bonds.		

Again, it is important to note that the Unrealized Holding Gain or Loss on Available-for-Sale Bonds is a stockholders' equity account. If the bonds had been considered trading securities, this account would be an income statement account.

Each year the Zano Corporation determines the year-end fair value of the bonds and compares it to the current balance in the account. The difference is then debited or credited to the Unrealized Holding Gain or Loss on Available-for-Sale Bonds account. This ensures that at each balance sheet date, the bonds are recorded at fair value.

Sale of Bonds Prior to Maturity. Investors often sell available-for-sale bonds prior to maturity. The sale is recorded by debiting Cash for the net proceeds received (sale price less commission and fees). If the bonds are sold between interest dates, the seller also receives the interest that has accrued since the last interest date. The investment account is credited for the reported amount of the bonds (their fair value at the last balance sheet date, plus or minus any discount or premium amortization from the last balance sheet to the date of sale).

To illustrate, assume that the Zano Corporation decides to sell its bonds in the previous example on October 31, 1995, for $11,900 plus accrued interest. As of the last interest date, July 1, 1995, the balance in the Investment in Available-for-Sale Bonds account is $12,425, as shown in the following T account:

Investment in Available-for-Sale Bonds

3/1/94	11,760	
7/1/94	17	
12/31/94	25	
12/31/94	598	
7/1/95	25	
7/1/95 Bal.	12,425	

The first step is to record the discount amortization for the three months from July 1 to October 1, 1995. This amounts to $12 ($4.14 x 3 = $12.42, rounded to $12) and is recorded as follows:

Oct. 1, 1995	Investment in Available-for-Sale Bonds	12	
	Interest Revenue		12
	To record discount amortization for 3 months.		

After this entry, the Investment account has a balance of $12,437 ($12,425 + $12). Because the firm sold the bonds for $11,900, it suffered a $537 loss, recorded as follows:

Oct. 1, 1995	Cash	12,200	
	Loss on Sale of Available-for-Sale Bonds	537	
	Investment in Available-for-Sale Bonds		12,437
	Interest Revenue		300
	To record sale of bonds and interest revenue for 3 months.		

The cash proceeds of $12,200 represent the sale price of $11,900 plus three months' accrued interest of $300 ($12,000 x 5% x 3/6) that the buyer is paying the Zano Corporation. There is a corresponding credit of $300 to Interest Revenue. This represents the cash portion of the interest revenue, and the $12 from the previous October 1, 1995, entry represents the amortized discount portion. Again, the loss of $537 is the difference between the carrying value of the bonds, $12,437, and the sale price of $11,900, excluding interest.

OTHER FORMS OF LONG-TERM DEBT

Objective 4
Account for other forms of long-term debt including mortgages and leases.

This chapter has been concerned primarily with accounting concepts and practices related to bonds, but there are other types of long-term debt, including mortgages payable and leases.

Mortgages Payable

mortgage

A **mortgage** is a promissory note secured by an asset whose title is pledged to the lender. Mortgages are generally payable in equal installments consisting of interest and principal. To demonstrate the accounting procedures, assume that on January 2, 1994, Clear Creek Associates purchases a small building for $1 million and makes a downpayment of $200,000. The mortgage is payable over 30 years at a rate of $8,229 monthly. The annual interest rate is 12%, and the first payment is due on February 1, 1994. The entry to record the purchase of the building is:

Jan. 2, 1994	Building	1,000,000	
	Mortgage Payable		800,000
	Cash		200,000
	To record purchase of building and issuance of 12%, 30-year mortgage.		

Subsequent entries are based on dividing the monthly payment of $8,229 between principal and interest. A mortgage amortization table can be used for this purpose, and such a table for the first 5 months of 1994 is shown in Exhibit 12-17. Each month, the total payment of $8,229 is divided into interest and principal. The interest is based on 1% (12%/12 months) of the note's carrying value at the beginning of the month. On February 1, the interest is $8,000 (or $800,000 × 1%), and the principal portion of the payment is thus $229 (or $8,229 − $8,000). In March, the interest is $7,998, or 1% of $799,771, and this pattern continues monthly. The journal entry for February 1994 is:

Feb. 1994	Interest Expense	8,000	
	Note Payable	229	
	Cash		8,229
	To record February mortgage payment of $8,229.		

Because most mortgages are payable in monthly installments, the principal payments for the next 12 months following the balance sheet date must be shown

Exhibit 12-17
Mortgage Amortization Table

Date	*Total Payment*	*1% Monthly Interest*	*Principal*	*Carrying Value of Mortgage*
January 1				$800,000
February 1	$8,229	$8,000	$229	799,771
March 1	8,229	7,998	231	799,540
April 1	8,229	7,995	234	799,306
May 1	8,229	7,993	236	799,070
June 1	8,229	7,991	238	798,832

in the current liability section as a current maturity of long-term debt. The remaining portion is, of course, classified as a long-term liability.

Leases

lease
lessor
lessee

A **lease** is a contractual agreement between the **lessor** (owner of the property) and the **lessee** (the user of the property), giving the lessee the right to use the lessor's property for a specific period of time in exchange for stipulated cash payments. As an alternative to full ownership, leases have become very popular in recent years, because the lessee does not have to assume full financial and operating risk for the leased property. All types of companies lease various kinds of property. For example, airlines currently lease a large percentage of their planes, and railroads lease much of their train equipment. Leasing is also very popular in the retail, hotel, and computer industries. In fact, leasing is one of the largest sources of corporate financing.

The accounting treatment of leases has long been a controversial subject. The basic controversy centers on the classification and accounting treatment for capital leases that are essentially equivalent to installment purchases.

operating leases
capital leases

Types of Leases. From the lessee's point of view, there are two types of leases: **operating leases** and **capital leases.** The distinction between them is important because a different accounting treatment is required for each; there are substantial effects on the balance sheet and income statement according to whether a lease is classified as a capital or an operating lease.

According to FASB Statement No. 13, "Accounting for Leases," a lease should be classified as a capital lease if the lease meets *one or more* of the following criteria:

1. The lease transfers ownership of the property to the lessee at the end of the lease term.
2. The lease contains a bargain purchase option (the asset can be purchased by the lessee at a price significantly lower than its then fair market value).
3. The lease term is 75 percent or more of the leased property's estimated economic life.
4. The present value of the minimum lease payment is 90 percent or more of the fair market value of the property to the lessor at the inception of the lease.[7]

Thus capital leases are accounted for essentially as purchases of equipment or other property. A lease rather than a bank loan is used to finance the purchase. Accounting for such leases requires that the asset and the liability be recorded on the lessee's books just as if a purchase had taken place.

A lease that does not meet any of the criteria just listed is considered an operating lease. With this type of lease, the lessor retains control and ownership of the property, which reverts back to the lessor at the end of the lease term. Accounting for an operating lease requires only that the lessee record an expense for the periodic lease payments as they are made. Keep in mind that these two types of leases are not alternatives for the same transaction. If the terms of the lease agreement meet any of the previously enumerated four criteria, the lease must be accounted for as a capital lease.

7. "Accounting for Leases," Statement of Financial Accounting Standards No. 13 (Stamford, Conn.: FASB, 1976), par. 7. Reprinted by permission.

Accounting for Leases. To demonstrate the proper accounting for leases, assume that on January 2, 1994, the Scully Corporation enters into a lease with the Porter Company in which the Scully Corporation agrees to lease a piece of equipment for five equal annual payments of $13,870. Each payment is made at year-end.[8] This data will be used to compare and contrast the accounting treatment for operating and capital leases. Note that this is for illustrative purposes only—in reality, the lease must be considered either a capital lease or an operating lease.

Accounting for Operating Leases. Assuming this agreement is an operating lease, the Scully Corporation does not make an entry on January 2, 1994, when the lease agreement is signed. At this point, the lease is considered just an agreement or contract that neither party has yet carried out. The Scully Corporation makes the following entry on December 31 of each of the next five years:

Equipment Lease Expense	13,870	
Cash		13,870
To record annual lease payment.		

The entire lease payment is shown as an expense. The equipment is still on the books of the lessor and is depreciated by the lessor. Over the five-year lease term, the Scully Corporation incurs total lease expenses of $69,350, or $13,870 × 5.

Accounting for Capital Leases. Under a capital lease, the Scully Corporation actually records the equipment as an asset and the required lease payments as a liability. The asset and liability are recorded at the present value of the required lease payments by using an appropriate interest rate (assume 12% for this lease). Subsequently, the Scully Corporation makes the yearly payments, which are divided between principal and interest, and also depreciates the equipment. In a corresponding manner, the lessor takes the leased equipment off their books and records a receivable at the present value of the lease payments.

The present value of the lease payments of $13,870, based on an interest rate of 12%, is $50,000.[9] Based on this data, the Scully Corporation makes the following entry on January 2, 1994, the inception of the lease:

Jan. 2, 1994	Leased Equipment under Capital Lease	50,000	
	Obligation under Capital lease		50,000
	To record capital lease with payment of $13,870 at 12%.		

The account Leased Equipment under Capital Lease is a noncurrent asset, generally shown under the property, plant, and equipment section. The account Obligation under Capital Lease is a liability, of which part is classified as current and part as long-term. At the end of each year, Scully Corporation makes a $13,870 annual payment. Exhibit 12-18 shows how these payments are divided between interest and principal. The interest each year is based on 12% of the balance of the lease obligation at the beginning of the year. In 1994, for example, interest is $6,000 (12% × $50,000) and in 1995, it is $5,056 (12% × $42,130). The

8. Most lease payments are made monthly. However, annual payments are assumed here for ease of illustration.

9. This is determined by discounting the annuity of $13,870 for five years at 12%. The factor from Table 4 in Appendix B is 3.60478; thus the present value is $50,000 or $13,870 × 3.60478.

Exhibit 12-18
Lease Payment Schedule

Date	Annual Lease Payment	12% Interest	Principal Portion	Balance of Lease Obligation
1/2/94				$50,000
12/31/94	$13,870	$ 6,000	$ 7,870	42,130
12/31/95	13,870	5,056	8,814	33,316
12/31/96	13,870	3,998	9,872	23,444
12/31/97	13,870	2,813	11,057	12,387
12/31/98	13,870	1,483	$12,387[a]	0
	$69,350	$19,350		

[a]Rounded to reduce lease obligation to zero.

difference between the annual lease payment and the interest portion is the principal portion. The entry to record the first payment is:

Dec. 31, 1994	Interest Expense	6,000	
	Obligation under Capital Lease	7,870	
	Cash		13,870
	To record first lease payment of $13,870.		

The Scully Corporation needs to make one additional entry each year to record depreciation expense on the leased equipment. The leased equipment is depreciated over its life of five years using straight-line depreciation and no salvage value. Thus the Scully Corporation makes the following adjusting entry at the end of each year:

Dec. 31	Depreciation Expense	10,000	
	Accumulated Depreciation-Leased Equipment		10,000
	To record annual depreciation expense of $10,000. ($50,000/5 years = $10,000)		

Operating Versus Capital Leases. Exhibit 12-19 shows the difference between accounting for this lease as an operating lease and as a capital lease. Over the entire five-year period, the total expense in both cases is $69,350, which represents the total outflows. However, each method results in a different expense pattern within the five-year period of time. In the first three years, the capital lease method results in a higher annual expense than does the operating lease method. This means that annual net income is lower in these years. This pattern then reverses in the last two years of the lease term.

These relationships lie at the heart of the controversy over the accounting for leases. Prior to the issuance of Statement 13, companies had a good deal of latitude in deciding whether a lease should be classified as an operating or a capital lease. Most companies felt that it was in their best interest to classify as many leases as possible as operating leases, and some obvious purchases that were being financed through leases were considered operating leases when they should have been considered capital leases.

If a lease is considered to be an operating lease, no liability is recorded on the balance sheet for the required lease payments. This means that the lessee's working capital position or current ratio is not affected by the lease agreement.

Exhibit 12-19
Operating and Capital Leases Compared

	Operating Lease	Capital Lease			
	Equipment Lease Expense (1)	Interest Expense (2)	Depreciation (3)	Total (Cols. 2 + 3) (4)	Difference Between Operating and Capital Lease Expense (Cols. 4 − 1) (5)
1994	$13,870	$ 6,000	$10,000	$16,000	$2,130
1995	13,870	5,056	10,000	15,056	1,186
1996	13,870	3,998	10,000	13,998	128
1997	13,870	2,813	10,000	12,813	(1,057)
1998	13,870	1,483	10,000	11,483	(2,387)
	$69,350	$19,350	$50,000	$69,350	$ 0

Remember that if a liability were recorded on a balance sheet, the next year's payment would have to be considered a current liability, whereas the entire balance in the account Leased Equipment under Capital Lease is considered a noncurrent asset. The fact that the lessee was in substance making an installment purchase but did not have to record the asset or liability on the balance sheet is referred to as **off-balance-sheet financing.** Off-balance-sheet financing also has a tendency to decrease a firm's debt-to-equity ratio and to increase its return on investment. Furthermore, the annual expense associated with an operating lease is less in the first few years of the lease term than that with a capital lease. Because of these facts and the fear that creditors might react adversely if leases were capitalized on the balance sheet, some managers had a definite bias to classify leases as operating leases.

off-balance-sheet-financing

The criteria set forth in Statement 13 corrected a number of obvious situations in which agreements that were in substance capital leases were being accounted for as operating leases. The four criteria in this Statement ensure that leases that are in fact installment purchases are recorded as capital leases. Thus the appropriate asset and liability, interest expense, and depreciation are recorded. In addition, current accounting rules require substantial footnote disclosure concerning lease terms and agreements.

DISCLOSURE OF LONG-TERM DEBT

Objective 5
Explain the balance sheet and note disclosure requirements for long-term debt.

Under generally accepted accounting principles companies must make substantive disclosures concerning their long-term debt and leasing arrangements. Most of the detailed disclosures are found in the notes to the financial statements. To illustrate, Exhibit 12-20 presents the liability and stockholders' equity section of the Warner-Lambert Company and its subsidiaries, as well as the appropriate footnote disclosures. The notes provide considerable detail concerning interest rates and other debt terms. Any significant restrictions placed on the company by lenders would also be disclosed

Exhibit 12-20

Warner-Lambert Company and Subsidiaries
Partial Consolidated Balance Sheets
(millions of dollars)

	December 31 1991	December 31 1990
Liabilities and Stockholders' Equity:		
Notes payable—banks and other	$ 113.7	$ 222.6
Current portion of long-term debt	14.7	7.7
Accounts payable, trade	336.6	327.0
Accrued compensation	98.9	77.6
Other current liabilities	511.4	339.3
Federal, state, and foreign income taxes	174.6	126.5
Total current liabilities	1,249.9	1,100.7
Long-term debt	447.9	306.8
Deferred income taxes	37.5	180.6
Other noncurrent liabilities	696.0	270.9
Total liabilities	2,431.3	1,859.0
Stockholders' equity:		
Preferred stock—none issued	—	—
Common stock—160,330,268 shares issued	160.3	160.3
Capital in excess of par value	92.6	71.0
Retained earnings	1,895.7	2,097.5
Cumulative translation adjustments	(128.9)	(87.7)
	2,019.7	2,241.1
Treasury stock, at cost:		
1991—25,736,008 shares; 1990—25,988,851 shares	(849.0)	(838.8)
Total stockholders' equity	1,170.7	1,402.3
Total liabilities and stockholders' equity	$3,602.0	$3,261.3

Note 7—Long-Term Debt

	December 31 1991	December 31 1990
7 1/2% notes due 1993	$100.0	$100.0
8 1/8% notes due 1996	100.0	100.0
8% notes due 1998	150.0	—
8 7/8% sinking fund debentures due 2000	15.3	15.3
Industrial revenue bonds due 2014	24.7	24.8
Other notes payable—including capitalized lease obligations	57.9	66.7
	$447.9	$306.8

In September 1991, Warner-Lambert issued $150 million of unsecured 8 percent notes due September 1, 1998. The notes were issued at par, and are not callable at Warner-Lambert's option prior to maturity.

The 8 7/8 percent sinking fund debentures are redeemable at the option of Warner-Lambert at diminishing premium rates. Sufficient open market purchases and sinking fund payments have been made to enable the company to satisfy sinking fund requirements completely through the maturity of these debentures.

(continued)

Exhibit 12-20
(continued)

The industrial revenue bonds due 2014 have a stated interest rate of 7.6 percent and an effective interest rate of 7.2 percent.

The aggregate annual maturities of long-term debt at December 31, 1991, payable in each of the years 1992 through 1996, are $14.7 million, $120.7 million, $9.2 million, $8.5 million, and $106.3 million, respectively.

Warner-Lambert has lines of credit arrangements with numerous banks with interest rates generally equal to the prime rate. At December 31, 1991, worldwide unused lines of credit amounted to $1.1 billion.

Total interest paid related to short-term borrowings and long-term debt was $53.7 million, $64.7 million, ad $55.5 million in 1991, 1990, and 1989, respectively.

Note 9—Leases:

Warner-Lambert rents various facilities and equipment under lease arrangements which are classified for financial statement purposes as either capital or operating leases.

Property, plant, and equipment included capitalized leases of $25.1 million, less accumulated depreciation of $17.4 million, at December 31, 1991, and $25.5 million, less accumulated depreciation of $14.5 million, at December 31, 1990. Long-term debt included $10.5 million and $12.1 million, respectively, at those dates relating to such leases.

Rental costs charged to income under all operating leases totaled $66.9 million in 1991, $61.7 million in 1990, and $53.6 million in 1989.

The future minimum rental commitments under noncancellable capital and operating leases at December 31, 1991, are summarized below:

(in millions)	*Capital*	*Operating*
1992	$ 2.8	$ 26.2
1993	1.8	19.1
1994	1.8	13.8
1995	1.6	11.8
1996	1.3	10.9
Remaining years	14.4	40.9
Total minimum lease payments	23.7	$122.7
Less amount representing interest	(11.5)	
Present value of minimum lease payments	$12.2	

in the footnotes. The partial balance sheet and footnotes do not reflect FASB statement No. 115.

The notes also provide information concerning capital and operating leases. Cash flow information such as the minimum lease payments due for the next five years and beyond are also disclosed.

USING LONG-TERM DEBT INFORMATION IN DECISION MAKING

Objective 6
Understand how long-term debt information can be used in decision making.

The amount and nature of long-term debt provides important information to management and external financial statement users about the financial health and stability of a company. Most companies have some amount of both short and long-term debt, and use that to their advantage.

leverage

Using debt to finance asset purchases is called **leverage.** Highly leveraged companies have a greater proportion of their assets financed through debt than companies that are less leveraged. Leverage can provide a positive return to stockholders as long as the after tax cost of borrowing is less than the returns the company can earn on the assets it owns. That is, if a firm can borrow at 8% after tax and earn a rate of return of 12% on the assets purchased with these funds, the stockholders of the company will benefit. However, leverage can be dangerous. If the interest rate on borrowed funds exceeds the rate of return the company can earn on such funds, the stockholders will suffer.

Ratio Analysis

Several ratios can be used to measure the amount of leverage used by a company, as well as the debt paying ability of the company. The *equity ratio* and the *debt ratio* are two of the most common ratios used in this regard. The financial statements of Warner-Lambert reproduced in Exhibit 12-20 will be used to illustrate the calculation and use of these and other ratios.

equity ratio

Equity and Debt Ratios. The **equity ratio,** a measure of leverage is calculated as follows:

$$\text{Equity ratio} = \frac{\text{Total stockholders' equity}}{\text{Total assets}}$$

This ratio relates the proportion of assets supplied by the stockholders to the proportion supplied by the creditors. The lower this ratio is, the higher degree of leverage. Because the total assets of a particular firm must be supplied by the stockholders and creditors, 100% minus the equity ratio produces the debt ratio. The **debt ratio** measures the amount of assets supplied by creditors. It can be calculated independently as follows:

debt ratio

$$\text{Debt ratio} = \frac{\text{Total liabilities}}{\text{Total assets}}$$

The equity and debt ratios for Warner-Lambert are calculated as-follows:

$$\text{Equity ratio} = \frac{\text{Total stockholders' equity}}{\text{Total assets}}$$

$$32.5\% = \frac{\$1{,}170.7}{\$3{,}602.0} \times 100$$

$$\text{Debt ratio} = \frac{\text{Total liabilities}}{\text{Total assets}}$$

$$67.5\% = \frac{\$2{,}431.3}{\$3{,}602.0} \times 100$$

In Warner-Lambert's case about two-thirds of the assets are provided by creditors and one-third by stockholders. To adequately evaluate these ratios they must be compared to other companies in the pharmaceutical and consumer health care field.

Debt-to-Equity Ratio. The debt to equity ratio, first discussed in Chapter 5, is another ratio that measures the balance of funds being provided by creditors and stockholders. To review, this ratio is calculated by dividing total liabilities by total stockholders' equity. Clearly, the higher the debt-to-equity ratio, the more debt the company has, and (all else being equal) the riskier it is. The debt-to-equity ratio for Warner-Lambert is calculated below:

$$\text{Debt-to-equity ratio} = \frac{\text{Total liabilities}}{\text{Total stockholders' equity}}$$

$$207.7\% = \frac{\$2{,}431.3}{\$1{,}170.7} \times 100$$

In this case, Warner-Lambert's debt is twice the amount of its equity.

This ratio, as calculated is somewhat misleading since it includes all liabilities. Another way to calculate this ratio is just to include short and long-term debt. This amount for Warner-Lambert is $576.3 million consisting of:

Notes payable—banks and other	$113.7
Current portion of long-term debt	14.7
Long-term debt	447.9
Total	$576.3

Using this figure the debt-to-equity ratio is 49.23%, calculated as follows:

$$\text{Debt-to-equity ratio} = \frac{\text{Total debt}}{\text{Total stockholders' equity}}$$

$$49.23\% = \frac{\$576.3}{\$1{,}170.7} \times 100$$

times interest earned

Times Interest Earned Ratio. Creditors like to have an indication of the ability of the company to meet the required interest payments. **Times interest earned** is the ratio of the income that is available for interest payments to the annual interest expense. The computation of times interest earned is as follows:

$$\text{Times interest earned} = \frac{\text{Income before interest and taxes (operating profit)}}{\text{Annual interest expense}}$$

To illustrate the computation of this ratio we will return to the Warner-Lambert example. For year-end 1991 Warner-Lambert's interest expense was $58.2 million and its income before taxes was $221.5 million. This results in times interest earned of 4.81.

$$4.81 = \frac{\$221.5 + \$58.2}{\$58.2}$$

In summary, long-term creditors provide substantial capital to many businesses. In evaluating credit decisions, these individuals are primarily concerned with the ability of the firm to meet its interest and principal payments. The ratios described in this section provide some indication of this ability.

DECISION SUPPORT SYSTEMS

Objective 7
Explain how decision support systems are used by accountants to analyze data in complex decision situations.

The decision to issue or purchase bonds can have a significant effect on a firm's financial position and its operating results. For example, the issuance of bonds increases total liabilities on a firm's balance sheet which, in turn, affects the firm's debt-to-equity ratio. Required bond interest payments result in an increase in interest expense on the income statement, and a corresponding reduction in net income. Moreover, cash is needed to make periodic interest payments and redeem the bonds at maturity. Interest rate fluctuations can effect the premium or discount with which a bond is issued or purchased, the bond's effective interest rate, and the interest expense recognized on the income statement. The potential effects of the issuance or purchase of bonds on a firm are carefully considered by financial managers before they enter into a transaction.

A variety of tools have evolved to help accountants and other financial managers assess the potential effects of debt and investment transactions. *Decision support systems* are one of the most powerful tools available to managers. A **decision support system (DSS)** is a flexible computer-based system that helps individuals analyze quantitative data in complex decision situations. A decision support system provides users with access to decision relevant data and with models that can be used to analyze the data.

decision support system (DSS)

A typical DSS includes what-if analysis and goal-seeking analysis. What-if analysis tries to determine the most likely effect of changes in one or more decision parameters on the decision outcome. Goal-seeking analysis attempts to make changes in decision parameters so that a desired outcome will be achieved. Data is manipulated by the decision maker when what-if analysis is performed and the model computes the expected outcome. When goal-seeking analysis is performed, the data is manipulated by the model after the user specifies the desired outcome. A user, when performing goal-seeking analysis, might identify several parameters that the model may manipulate, sales and advertising expense for example, and the desired net income. The model would manipulate sales and advertising to show how the desired net income could be achieved.

Spreadsheet packages are well suited for performing what-if analyses and can be used as simple DSS. For example, a spreadsheet-based income statement can be viewed as a DSS model. Certain values (data) can changed on the income statement (model) to see *what* would happen to net income *if* those changes were made. For example, an accountant might construct balance sheet and income statement models on a spreadsheet to see what would happen if bonds were sold at several different prices. The price changes, based on changes in the effective interest rate of the bonds, would cause changes in balance sheet and income statement amounts.

A DSS cannot and should not replace a decision maker. However, a DSS can help an accountant or a manager make more informed decisions. With a DSS an accountant is able to quickly analyze many different decision scenarios to select the most appropriate course of action. It is important however, for the accountant to understand the assumptions upon which the model is based, and the relationships between the different variables in the model. Only this way is the accountant able to judge the reasonableness of the information generated by the DSS.

SUMMARY OF LEARNING OBJECTIVES

1. Explain the nature and features of bonds payable. A bond is a written agreement between a borrower (issuer) and a lender (purchaser), in which the borrower agrees to repay a stated sum on a future date and to make periodic interest payments. Most bonds are in $1,000 denominations and pay interest semiannually. There are various types of bonds, including term, serial, secured, convertible, and callable bonds.

The issue price of bonds and subsequent trading prices depend on the relationship between the stated rate of interest and the prevailing market rates. For investments of similar risk, these two rates are often different. If the prevailing interest rate is above the stated interest, the bond will be issued or traded at a discount. Conversely, if the prevailing interest rate is below the stated rate, the bond will be issued or traded at a premium.

2. Account for bonds by issuers. Bonds will be issued at par, or face value, if the stated interest rate equals the prevailing market rate. In this situation, the journal entry to record the issuance of the bonds is straightforward and takes the following form:

Cash	xxxx	
Bonds Payable		xxxx

If the bond is issued between interest dates, the accrued interest element is accounted for separately by crediting Interest Payable.

Bonds are often issued at other than par or face value. Any discount or premium should be accounted for separately and should be thought of as an additional interest expense or a reduction of interest expense to be amortized over the life of the bond. The journal entries to record bond issues in these cases take the following form:

Discount		
Cash	xxx	
Discount on Bonds Payable	xxx	
Bonds Payable		xxx
Premium		
Cash	xxx	
Premium on Bonds Payable		xxx
Bonds payable		xxx

The straight-line and effective-interest methods are used to amortize the discount or premium. The straight-line method should be used only if there is no material difference between the two methods. The following table summarizes each:

Method	*Calculation/Interpretation*
Straight-line	Amortization is determined by dividing the discount or premium by the remaining life of bonds. The result is an equal amount of interest expense each period.
Effective-interest	Amortization is determined by multiplying the semiannual yield, or effective interest rate, by the bonds' carrying value at the beginning of the period. Thus, interest expense is a constant rate, although the amount changes with changes in carrying value.

If a discount or premium is issued between interest dates, the interest must be accounted for separately. Finally, any bond issue costs incurred by the issuing firm are generally accumulated in a deferred charge account and amortized on a straight-line basis over the bond's life.

When bonds mature, they are repaid by the firm. The journal entry is a debit to Bonds Payable and a credit to Cash. At maturity the premium or discount account should have been amortized to zero. If a bond is retired prior to its maturity, a gain or loss will usually result. This gain or loss is the difference between the reacquisition price and the carrying value of the bonds and is considered to be extraordinary.

3. Account for bonds purchased by investors. Accounting for bonds by the investor generally parallels accounting for bonds by the issuer. However, by convention, a separate account is not maintained for the discount or premium amount. The discount increases the investor's periodic interest revenue, and the premium reduces the investor's periodic interest revenue. Bonds classified as held-to-maturity are reported at amortized cost. Bonds classified as available-for-sale or trading are reported at fair value.

4. Account for other forms of long-term debt including mortgages and leases. Other forms of long-term debt include mortgages payable and leases. A mortgage is a promissory note secured by an asset whose title is pledged to the lender. Mortgages are generally payable in equal monthly installments divided between interest and principal.

Accounting for leases centers on whether the lease is classified as an operating lease or a capital lease. If a lease meets the criteria established by the FASB, it is a capital lease, and if not, it is an operating lease. Lease payments related to operating leases are expenses when paid. Capital leases are recorded at their present value on the lessee's books as both an asset and a liability.

5. Explain the balance sheet and note disclosure requirements for long-term debt. Under generally accepted accounting principles, companies must make substantive disclosures concerning their long-term debt. Most of these disclosures are found in the notes to the financial statements, and include a breakdown of particular notes and bonds and their interest rates.

6. Understand how long-term debt information can be used in decision making. The amount and nature of a company's long-term debt provide important information to management and external users. Using debt to finance asset purchases is called *leverage*. Companies with a high degree of leverage can provide excellent returns to shareholders only if the return earned on assets purchased is greater than the after-tax interest cost of the debt. The equity, debt, and debt-to-equity ratios are all indications of leverage. Times interest earned is a measure of the ability of the company to meet its interest obligations.

7. Explain how decision support systems are used by accountants to analyze data in complex decision situations. Decision support systems are computer-based systems that provide accountants with complex models that can be used to analyze business data. These models are used to perform what-if and goal-seeking analyses in complex decision situations such as bond issuance. Spreadsheet packages can be used to implement simple what-if DSS.

KEY TERMS

Adjunct account 585
Bond 572
Bond indentures 573
Capital leases 599
Convertible bonds 574
Debt ratio 605
Decision support system (DSS) 607
Denomination 572
Early extinguishment of debt 592
Effective-interest method 589
Effective interest rate 582
Equity ratio 605
Lease 599
Lessee 599
Lessor 599
Leverage 604
Market interest rate 573
Maturity date 573
Mortgage 598
Off-balance-sheet financing 602
Operating leases 599
Serial bonds 573
Sinking fund 592
Stated interest rate 573
Term bonds 573
Times interest earned 606
Unsecured bonds (*debentures*) 574
Yield rate 576
Zero-coupon bonds 573

REVIEW PROBLEM

On January 2, 1994, the Garvey Corporation issued $200,000, ten-year, 14% term bonds. The bonds were issued at a premium to yield 12%. The issue price was 111.4699, and the bonds pay interest every January 2 and July 1.

REQUIRED:

1. Make the entry to record the issue of the bonds on January 2, 1994.
2. Make the entry to record the first interest payment on July 1 and premium amortization, assuming that:
   a. straight-line amortization is used.
   b. effective-interest amortization is used.
3. If the Garvey Corporation has an August 31 year-end, make the appropriate entries at August 31, 1994, assuming that:
   a. straight-line amortization is used.
   b. effective-interest amortization is used.
4. The Garvey Corporation repurchased all bonds on January 2, 1997, at a price of 107. Assume that all interest payments and premium amortization for January 2, 1997, have been made and that the firm uses the straight-line method of amortization. Make the entry necessary for recording the repurchase of the bonds.
5. (Optional: present-value techniques) Using present-value techniques, prove that after the premium is amortized using the effective-interest method the carrying value of the bonds on July 1, 1994, is equal to the present value of the future cash outflows on that date.

Solution

1. Jan. 2, 1994	Cash	222,940	
	Premium on Bonds Payable		22,940
	Bonds Payable		200,000
	To record issuance of $200,000 bonds at a price of 111.4699.		

	$200,000
	× 1.114699
Issue price	$222,940
Face value	− 200,000
Premium	$ 22,940

2. July 1, 1994
   a. Straight-Line Method

Interest Expense	12,853	
Premium on Bonds Payable	1,147	
Cash		14,000

To record interest payment and premium amortization on a straight-line basis, calculated as follows:

Cash Interest	$200,000
×	.07
	$ 14,000

Premium Amortization

$$\frac{\$22{,}940}{20 \text{ interest periods}} = \$1{,}147 \text{ per period}$$

   b. Effective-Interest Method:

Interest Expense	13,376	
Premium on Bonds Payable	624	
Cash		14,000

To record interest payment and premium amortization on effective-interest basis, calculated as follows:

Carrying value 1/2/94	$222,940
Yield rate	.06
Effective interest	$ 13,376
Cash payment	14,000
Premium amortization	$ (624)
Carrying value 1/2/94	222,940
Carrying value 7/1/94	$222,316

3. 8/31/94 Year-end Accruals (2 months from 7/1/94 to 8/31/94)
   a. Straight-Line Method:

Interest Expense	4,285	
Premium on Bonds Payable	382	
Interest Payable		4,667

To record 2 months' interest accrual and premium amortization, calculated as follows:

Interest Payable = $200,000 × .07 × 2/6	= $4,667
Premium Amortization = $1,147 × 2/6	= (382)
Interest Expense	$4,285

b. Effective-Interest Method:

Interest Expense	4,446	
Premium on Bonds Payable	221	
Interest Payable		4,667

To record 2 months' interest accrual and premium amortization, calculated as follows:

Carrying value 7/1/94	$222,316 (see item 2b page 609)
Yield rate	.06
Effective interest	$ 13,339 (Rounded)
Two-months' adjustment	× 2/6
Interest expense	$ 4,446
Interest payable	4,667
Premium on bonds payable	$ 221

4. 1/2/97 Repurchase of Bonds:

Bonds Payable	200,000	
Premium on Bonds Payable	16,058	
Extraordinary Gain		2,058
Cash		214,000

To record repurchase of bonds at 107. The gain, which is extraordinary, is calculated as follows:

Face value	$200,000
Unamortized premium (see T-account, below)	16,058
Carrying value of bonds on 1/2/97	$216,058
Repurchase price	214,000
Gain	$ 2,058

Premium on Bonds Payable

7/1/94	1,147	1/2/94	22,940
1/2/95	1,147		
7/1/95	1,147		
1/2/96	1,147		
7/1/96	1,147		
1/2/97	1,147		
	6,882		
		1/2/97 Bal.	16,058

Note: This T-account ignores year-end accruals and records just the January 2 entries.

5. As of July 1, 1994, there are 19 interest periods remaining. The cash flows, discounted at 6% for 19 periods, equal $222,316, the carrying value of the bonds on that date. The calculations are:

Present value of $200,000 to be received at the end of 19 periods at 6% semiannually ($200,000 × .33051)	$ 66,102
Present value of $14,000 semiannual interest payments ($200,000 × .07) to be received at the end of each of the next 19 periods ($14,000 × 11.15812)	156,214
Total	$222,316

QUESTIONS

1. What is a term bond? Describe the common features of bonds.
2. Define the following terms regarding bonds:
   a. Face value
   b. Maturity value
   c. Maturity date
   d. Stated interest rate
   e. Market interest rate
3. Describe the following types of bonds:
   a. Serial bonds
   b. Term bonds
   c. Bearer bonds
   d. Debentures
   e. Convertible bonds
   f. Zero-coupon bonds
4. What are written covenants, and why are they included in certain bond agreements?
5. Several months ago, you purchased a $1,000, 8% bond of the Marlow Corporation at a price of 102. You recently looked in the paper and noticed that the latest price was 98.
   a. How much did you pay for the bond?
   b. How much interest will you receive every six months?
   c. If you sold the bond today, how much would you receive? (Assume all interest has been paid.)
6. What factors are considered in setting the stated rate of interest on a bond? How does this stated rate affect the bond's issue price?
7. One of your fellow students does not understand how a bond with a stated rate of interest of 10% set by management can be issued at a discount. Explain how this can happen.
8. Explain the relationship among the stated interest rate, the market interest rate, and the price at which the bond is issued.
9. Several years ago the Newburyport Corporation issued bonds with a stated interest rate of 12%, which approximated the market rate at the time. In recent years, however, interest rates in the economy have fallen to about 8%. What effect will this have on the current price of the bond? Why?
10. What are junk bonds and why were they issued? What risks are associated with junk bonds?
11. What is the proper method of presenting bonds payable and any related premium or discount on the balance sheet?
12. Recently, the Diome Corporation issued 100 $1,000, 8% bonds at 98. Were the bonds issued at a premium or a discount, and what is the amount of that premium or discount? How much cash did the firm receive from the issue? (Assume the bonds were issued on an interest date.)
13. The Jeffy Computer Corporation recently issued $100,000 of 10% bonds at 103. Interest is paid semiannually. The bonds were issued on an interest date.
    a. Were the bonds issued at a premium or a discount?
    b. How much cash did the company receive from the issue?
    c. What was the amount of interest expense in the first six-month period, assuming the firm uses the straight-line method of amortization and the bond will mature in ten years?
14. Describe the straight-line amortization method and the effective-interest amortization method. Which method is considered preferable?
15. What are bond issue costs, and how are they handled under current accounting practices?
16. What is a bond sinking fund, and what is its purpose?
17. Does an investor usually record any premiums or discounts related to the purchase of the bonds? Why or why not?
18. What is a mortgage, and how are mortgages classified on the balance sheet?
19. Define leases and describe the different types.
20. Why would a business wish to classify a lease as an operating lease rather than a capital lease?
21. What is leverage as it relates to the financial structure of the firm?
22. You are considering two very different companies as an investment possibility. One is highly leveraged; the other is only slightly leveraged. Assuming you

can only make one investment, which one will you choose?

23. What is the equity ratio? What is the debt ratio? How are they related to each other?
24. You have determined that the times interest earned statistic for the Bloor Corporation is 4.5. What does this mean and what does it tell you?
25. What is a decision support system?
26. What are the purposes of the two components of decision support systems?

EXERCISES

Note: Unless otherwise indicated, assume that all premiums and discount are amortized at each interest date and each time that adjusting entries are made.

E12-1
The Issuance of Bonds
LO 2

The Rugless Corporation issued $1 million of bonds on an interest date at a price of 108.

a. Determine the total cash the company received from the bond issue.
b. Did the bonds sell at par, at a discount, or at a premium?
c. Make the journal entry to record the issue of the bonds.

E12-2
Recording the Issuance of Bonds
LO 2

On January 2, 1994, the Alpha Beta Corporation issued $100,000 of ten-year term bonds with a stated rate of interest of 14%. The bonds pay interest semiannually on January 2 and July 1. At the time of the issue, the current market interest rate was also 14%.

REQUIRED: Prepare the necessary journal entries to record:

1. The issue of the bonds on January 2, 1994.
2. The interest payment on July 1, 1994.
3. The necessary adjusting entry on December 31, 1994 the firm's year-end.
4. The interest payment on January 2, 1995.

E12-3
Bonds Issued Between Interest Dates
LO 2

The Homestead Corporation issued $100,000 of 20-year, 9% term bonds on March 1, 1994. The bonds were issued at par and pay interest semiannually every January 2 and July 1.

REQUIRED: Prepare the necessary journal entries to record:

1. The issuance of the bonds on March 1, 1994.
2. The interest payment on July 1, 1994.
3. The adjusting entry on December 31, 1994, the firm's year-end.

E12-4
Issue of Bonds Not at Face Value
LO 2

On January 2, 1994, Vacation Cruises sold ten-year term bonds with a face value of $500,000. The bonds had a stated interest rate of 13%, payable semiannually on January 2 and July 1. The bonds were sold to yield 15% and were therefore issued at a price of $449,028.

REQUIRED:

1. Prepare the journal entry to record the issuance of the bonds.
2. Show how the bonds would be disclosed on the balance sheet immediately after their issue.
3. Make the entry to record the interest payment on July 1, 1994. Assume that straight-line amortization is used.
4. Show how the bonds would be disclosed on the balance sheet immediately after the interest payment on July 1, 1994.

E12-5
Issue of Bonds Not at Face Value
LO 2

El Cholos Restaurants, a franchiser of Mexican restaurants, issued $250,000 of 15-year 12% bonds on January 2, 1994. Interest is payable on January 1 and July 1. These bonds were issued to yield 10% and were sold at a price of $288,431.

REQUIRED:

1. Prepare the journal entry to record the issuance of the bonds.
2. Show how the bonds would be disclosed on the balance sheet immediately after their issue.
3. Assuming the firm uses the straight-line amortization method, make the required journal entry to record the interest payment on July 1, 1994.
4. Show how the bonds would be disclosed on the balance sheet on July 1, 1994, after the payment of the interest.

E12-6
Effective Interest Method of Amortization
LO 2

Using the data from (a) E12-4 and (b) E12-5, prepare the journal entries to record the payment of interest on July 1, 1994, and the interest accrual on December 31, 1994, assuming the two firms use the effective-interest method of amortization.

E12-7
Early Extinguishment of Bonds
LO 2

On January 2, 1990, South Central Airlines issued $500,000 of 20-year, 12% bonds at 102. The bonds pay interest every January 2 and July 1. On July 1, 1997, immediately after the interest payment, the bonds were called at a price of 105. The firm uses the straight-line method of amortization.

REQUIRED: Prepare the journal entries at:

1. January 2, 1990 the date of issue.
2. July 1, 1997 to record the interest payment and premium amortization.
3. July 1, 1997 to record the extinguishment of the bonds.

E12-8
Investment in Bonds
LO 3

On March 1, 1994, the Vargo Specialty Manufacturing Company purchased $15,000 of five-year, 12% bonds. The bonds were dated January 1, 1994. They pay interest semiannually on January 2 and July 1. The company purchased the bonds for $16,160. Straight-line amortization is used. The bonds are considered available-for-sale.

REQUIRED: Prepare the journal entries to:

1. Record the initial investment on March 1.
2. Record the receipt of the first interest collection on July 1.
3. Assume that the fair value of the bonds on December 31, 1994, is $15,800. Make the entry to record the necessary adjustments at December 31, 1995.

E12-9
Analysis Relating to Bond Amortization
LO 2

On January 2, 1993, the Old Time Brewer Co. issued $300,000 of 20-year, 12% bonds at a price of 86,667 that resulted in a 14% yield. The bonds pay interest semiannually on January 2 and July 1.

REQUIRED:

1. How much cash did the firm receive from the issue of the bonds?
2. Assuming the firm uses the straight-line method of amortizing any discount or premium:
   a. How much cash did the firm expend for interest from January 2, 1993, to January 2, 1994?
   b. How much interest expense did the firm incur from January 2, 1993, to January 2, 1994?
   c. How much interest expense did the firm incur because of the bond over its 20-year life?

3. Assuming that the firm uses the effective-interest method of amortizing any discount or premium:
   a. How much cash did the firm expend for interest from January 2, 1993, to January 2, 1994?
   b. How much interest expense did the firm incur from January 2, 1993, to January 2, 1994?
   c. How much interest expense did the firm incur because of the bond over its 20-year life?

E12-10
Determining the Price of a Bond
LO 2

(Requires present-value calculations.) On January 2, 1994, the Whodunit Corporation issued $250,000 of 15-year, 8% bonds to yield 10%. The bonds pay interest semiannually on January 2 and July 1.

REQUIRED:

1. Make the entry to record the issuance of the bonds on January 2, 1994.
2. Assuming that the firm uses the straight-line method of amortization, make the required entry at July 1, 1994.
3. Assuming that the firm uses the effective-interest method of amortization, make the required entry at July 1, 1994.

E12-11
Determining the Price of a Bond
LO 2

(Requires present-value calculations.) The Bendot Corporation issued $300,000 of eight-year, 12% bonds on July 1, 1994, to yield 10%. Interest is payable semiannually on July 1 and January 2.

REQUIRED:

1. Make the entry to record the issuance of these bonds on July 1, 1994.
2. Assuming the firm uses the straight-line amortization method, make the required entries at January 2, 1995. The firm's year-end is June 30.
3. Assuming the firm uses the effective-interest method of amortization, make the required entries at January 2, 1995.

E12-12
Determining the Discount
LO 2

(Requires present-value calculations.) The Vitkoski Corporation issued $100,000 of ten-year, 7% term bonds to yield 12% on January 2 of the current year. Interest is payable semiannually on July 1 and January 2.

REQUIRED: Using present-value techniques, directly determine the amount of the discount.

E12-13
Determining the Discount or Premium
LO 2

(Requires present-value calculations.) In a text example (page 576) a $1,000, five-year, 10% bond that pays interest of 6% semiannually, it was stated that if you wanted to purchase that investment to yield 7% semiannually you would pay $929.

REQUIRED: Prove this figure using present-value techniques.

E12-14
Accounting for Mortgages
LO 4

On January 1, 1994, the Caster Corp. purchased a building for $800,000. The firm made a 20% downpayment and took out a mortgage payable over 30 years, at a rate of $5,616.46 monthly. The first payment is due Febuary 1, 1994.

REQUIRED:

1. Make the entry to record the purchase of the equipment.
2. Make the entries to record the firt two mortgage payments on February 1 and March 1.

E12-15
Accounting for Leases
LO 4

On January 2, 1994, the Rainbow Company entered into a ten-year lease with IQ Computer Co. to lease one of their new computers. The Rainbow Company agreed to make ten equal annual payments of $10,619, beginning on December 31, 1994.

REQUIRED:

1. Assuming that the lease is properly recorded as an operating lease, prepare the necessary journal entry to record the first yearly payment.
2. Again, assuming that the lease is properly recorded as an operating lease, how much expense will the firm record on its books relative to this lease over its ten-year life?
3. Now assume that the lease is properly recorded as a capital lease with a present value of $60,000 based on a 12% interest rate. Make the entry to record the lease on January 2, 1994 and the first payment on December 12, 1994.
4. Again, assuming that the lease is properly recorded as a capital lease, how much expense will the firm record relative to the lease over its ten-year useful life with no salvage value?
5. Compare and contrast the effects on the firm's financial statements over the ten-year period if the lease is recorded as a capital lease rather than as an operating lease.

E12-16
Accounting for Capital Leases
LO 4

On January 2, 1993, the Powloski Company leased a small building from Sun Dance Properties, Inc. The Powloski Company agreed to make annual lease payments of $12,369 on December 31, 1993 and for the following nine years (a total of ten payments). Assume that the lease has a present value of $76,000 based on 10% interest rate. The Powloski Company estimates that the building will have an eight-year life and will use straight-line depreciation with no salvage value.

REQUIRED:

1. Prepare the necessary journal entries to record the lease for the Powloski Company on January 2, 1993 and the first payment on December 31, 1993. Include the entry for the recognition of the depreciation expense related to the lease.
2. How would the building and the related lease liability be shown on the December 31, 1993 balance sheet of the Powloski Company?

E12-17
Albertson's Financial Statements
LO 1 & 2

Review Albertson's financial statements reproduced in Appendix A. Based on these financial statements, answer the following questions:

a. What is the amount of long-term debt as of January 31, 1992, January 31, 1991, and February 1, 1990, respectively?
b. Briefly describe the type of long-term debt Albertson's has issued.
c. Does this debt carry any restrictions or covenants? If so, describe them. Is the company in compliance with these covenants?
d. What are the Albertson's long-term debt to equity and long-term debt to total assets ratios at January 31, 1992, January 31, 1991, and February 1, 1990?

E12-18
Decision Support Systems
LO 7

This chapter described how decision support systems could be used to help accountants analyze the effects of a proposed bond issue on a firm's financial statements.

REQUIRED:

1. List five other financial decisions where the use of decision support systems might be beneficial and explain.
2. List, for each decision, the data that would be used in the decision support system, and describe the nature of the decision model.

PROBLEMS

P12-1
Accounting for Bonds
LO 1 & 2

The Hemsted Corporation is considering issuing bonds and has asked your advice concerning several matters. The firm plans to issue $800,000 of 30-year, 10% bonds. Bond interest payments are on April 1 and October 1. The firm has a December 31 year-end.

REQUIRED:

1. If the bonds are issued on April 1 at a price of 91.977 to yield 11%, how much cash will the firm receive? Explain to the president of the corporation the difference in interest expense the firm will incur during the first year if the effective-interest method of amortization rather than the straight-line method is used. How will the firm's cash flow be affected in the first year?
2. If the bonds are issued on April 1 at a price of 109.201 to yield 9%, how much cash will the firm receive? Explain to the president the difference in interest expense the firm will incur during the first year if the effective-interest method rather than the straight-line method of amortization is used. How will the firm's cash flow be affected in the first year?
3. If the bonds are issued on June 1 at par, how much cash will the firm receive? Determine for the president the amount of interest expense the firm will incur relative to the bonds for the period between June 1 and April 1 of the following year. Ignore the 12/31 year-end.

P12-2
Bond Transactions—Straight-Line Amortization
LO 2

At the beginning of 1994, the long-term debt section of the China Export Corporation's balance sheet appeared as follows:

10% bonds payable	$200,000
Premium on bonds payable	3,600
	$203,600

The bonds were issued on January 2, 1982, and will mature in ten years from that date. The firm uses the straight-line method of amortization for bond issues. Interest on these bonds is payable semiannually on January 2 and July 1. During 1994 and 1995, the following transactions regarding bonds took place:

a. January 2, 1994: The interest payment on the 10% bonds was made. Assume that the company has a December 31 year-end and that all proper accruals were made at that time.
b. March 1, 1994: The firm issued $100,000 of ten-year, 8% bonds dated February 1 at 97. The bonds pay interest semiannually on February 1 and August 1 of every year.
c. July 1, 1994: The interest payment on the 10% bonds was made, and the premium was amortized.
d. August 1, 1994: The interest payment on the 8% bonds was made, and the discount was amortized.
e. December 31, 1994: The firm's year-end, and all interest accruals must be made.
f. January 2, 1995: The interest payment on the 10% bonds was made.
g. February 1, 1995: The interest payment on the 8% bonds was made, and the discount was amortized.
h. July 1, 1995: Immediately after the interest payment was made on the 10% bonds, they were called at a price of 104.

i. August 1, 1995: The interest payment on the 8% bonds was made, and the discount was amortized.
j. December 31, 1995: Year-end interest accruals must be made.

REQUIRED:

1. Make the necessary journal entries for 1994 and 1995.
2. Prepare the long-term debt section of the firm's balance sheet at December 31, 1994 and 1995.
3. Make the entry to record the last interest payment on the 8% bonds and their repayment at maturity.

P12-3
Accounting for Bond Issues and Bond Issue Costs
LO 2

Karim Corporation, a public company, had two bond issues during the fiscal year that ended November 30, 1994. At the close of the year, the company had not yet recorded either of the transactions listed below:

a. On July 1, 1994, the Karim Corporation issued, at a discount of $750,000, $20 million secured bonds with a maturity date of 2013. Interest is to be paid semiannually with the first payment due on December 31, 1994. The bonds were issued with a call provision allowing Karim to retire the bonds after November 30, 2003, at a stated price. There is no provision for a sinking fund. This public offering was coordinated by the company's investment banking firm, Brandler and Goodman, Inc., and the bond issue costs, to be paid from the proceeds, amounted to $1.2 million.
b. On September 1, 1994, Karim Corporation received from Municipal Life Insurance Co., a private insurance company, the proceeds of a $6 million bond issue at par to build a new corporate facility. Interest on the bonds is to be paid semiannually at a 10% stated interest rate, and the maturity date is August 31, 2008. There is a restrictive covenant in the formal agreement requiring Karim to maintain a specified debt-to-equity ratio. For the first five years, Karim will pay interest only, and the first payment is due on February 28, 1995. After five years, the company is required to make annual principal payments into a sinking fund.

The company uses the straight-line method for amortizing any bond discounts and bond issue costs, and calculates interest on a monthly basis.

REQUIRED: For each of the bond issues described above, prepare all the journal entries required to properly reflect these transactions on Karim Corporation's financial statements on November 30, 1994.

(IMA adapted)

P12-4
Bond Transactions—Effective-Interest Amortization
LO 2

The Manegold-Moore Corporation is about to undertake a major business expansion. On July 1, 1994, the firm issued $100,000 of 10% bonds to yield 11%. As a result the issue price was $94,025. The bonds mature on July 1, 2000, and pay interest semiannually on July 1 and January 2. The firm uses the effective-interest method of amortization. The long-term debt section of the firm's December 31, 1994, balance sheet appeared as follows:

Long-term debt	$100,000
10% bonds payable	5,804
Less: Unamortized discount	$ 94,196

During 1995 and 1996, the following events occurred regarding bonds:

a. January 2, 1995: The firm's year-end is December 31. The interest accrual made on that date for the 10% bonds was paid.

b. July 1, 1995: The semiannual interest payment on the 10% bonds was made, and the discount was amortized.
c. September 1, 1995: The firm issued $500,000 of 10% bonds to yield 10%. The bonds mature in ten years and pay interest every September 1 and March 1.
d. December 31, 1995: Year-end interest accruals and amortizations were made.
e. January 1, 1996: The interest payment on the $100,000 bonds was made.
f. March 1, 1996: The interest payment on the $500,000 bond was made.
g. July 1, 1996: The interest payment on the $100,000 bonds was made, and the proper amount of discount was amortized. Immediately thereafter, all of these bonds were called at a price of 101.
h. September 1, 1996: The interest payment on the $500,000 bond was made.
i. December 31, 1996: The proper interest accruals and amortizations were made at year-end.

REQUIRED:

1. Prepare the journal entries to record the above transactions.
2. Prepare the long-term debt section of the firm's balance sheet at December 31, 1995 and 1996.

P12-5 Effective-Interest Method Versus Straight-Line Method

LO 2

(Requires present-value calculations.) On January 2, 1994, The Gilbertson Company issued $1 million 15 year bonds with a stated interest rate of 7% to yield 10%. The bonds pay interest semiannually each January 2 and July 1.

REQUIRED:

1. Determine the amount of discount and premium that should be recorded when the bond is issued.
2. Determine the interest expense based on (a) straight-line amortization and (b) effective-interest amortization for the six months ended December 31, 1994.
3. Assuming that straight-line amortization is used, determine the actual interest rate based on the carrying value of the bonds at December 31, 1994, and July 1, 1995. Show your calculations.
4. Now assume that the effective-interest method is used. Determine the actual interest rate based on the carrying value of the bonds at December 31, 1994, and July 1, 1995. Show your calculations.
5. Compare the results you found in items (3) and (4). What do they say about the conceptual advantage of the effective-interest method of amortization?

P12-6 Interest Amortization Tables

LO 2

On January 2, 1995, the Peacock Corporation issued $350,000 of five-year bonds. The bonds have a stated rate of interest of 10% and were issued at 107.986 to yield 8%. Interest is payable *annually* on January 2 of each year.

REQUIRED: Prepare an amortization table for the bonds similar to those in Exhibits 12-12 and 12-16, assuming that (a) the straight-line method of premium amortization is used; (b) the effective-interest method of premium amortization is used. Use the following headings for your table:

a. Date
b. Carrying value of the bonds at the beginning of the period
c. Cash interest paid
d. Interest expense
e. Premium amortization
f. Unamortized premium at the end of the period
g. Carrying value of the bonds at the end of the period

P12-7
Investment in Bonds
LO 3

On May 1, 1993, the Price-Fisher Corporation issued $100,000 of five-year, 10% bonds dated January 2, 1993, at a price of 98. All of these bonds were purchased by Helen Chen. The bonds pay interest every July 1 and January 2. The bonds are considered trading bonds by Helen Chen.

REQUIRED:

1. Assuming that both Price-Fisher and Chen use the straight-line method of interest amortization, make the entries for these bonds for both Price-Fisher and Chen through January 2, 1995. Assume that both parties have a December 31 year-end. The bonds have a fair value of 101 at December 31, 1993, and 105 at December 31, 1994.
2. On July 1, 1995, after the interest payment, Price-Fisher calls one-half of the bonds at a price of 102. Make the entries to record this event on the books of both Price-Fisher and Chen.

P12-8
Determining Bond Prices
LO 2

(Requires present-value calculations.) The Zentos Corporation issued $500,000 of eight-year, 9% bonds to yield 10%. The bonds were issued on April 1, 1994, and pay interest every April 1 and October 1.

REQUIRED:

1. Compute the issue price, and determine the amount of any discount or premium.
2. Make the journal entry to record the issuance of the bonds.
3. Prepare an amortization table for the term of the bonds using the effective-interest method of amortization. Use a form similar to that used in Exhibit 12-14 or 12-16.
4. Using present-value techniques, independently determine the carrying value of the bonds on April 1, 1996, as shown in the amortization table.
5. Assume that the firm retired the bonds on April 1, 1996, at a price of 102. Make the entry to record the interest payment and the amortization on that date, and then the entry to record the retirement of the bonds.

P12-9
Mortgage and Lease Transactions
LO 4

During 1994, the West Corporation entered into the following transactions:

a. December 31: The firm purchased a building for $600,000. A $100,000 downpayment was made, and a 30-year mortgage was taken out for the remaining $500,000. Under the terms of the mortgage, payment of $71,408 are to be made annually for 30 years, beginning on December 31, 1994. The mortgage has a stated interest rate of 14%.
b. December 31: The firm signed a lease on a building that will be used to house its corporate offices. The terms of the lease call for 30 annual payments of $40,000 to be made at the end of each year, beginning on December 31, 1994. The lessor determined the annual lease payments in order to guarantee a return of 12%. The lease should be recorded as a capital lease.

REQUIRED: Make the required entries for 1994 and 1995. Assume that the firm has a December 31 year-end. (Ignore depreciation and amortization.)

DISCUSSION AND INTERPRETATION PROBLEMS

D12-1
Financial Decision Case

(Requires present-value calculations.) On January 2, 1985, the Lafler Corporation issued $600,000 of 20-year, 8% bonds to yield 10%. The bonds pay interest semiannually on January 2 and July 1. By January 2, 1995, interest rates in the economy had risen, and current market rates for investments of risk similar to that of the Lafler Corporation were 12%.

As a result, the current aggregate market value of the bonds on January 2, 1995 ($500,000) was below their carrying value. The president of the firm is considering repurchasing all these bonds in the open market at that price. To do that, however, the firm will have to issue new 30-year bonds with a stated rate of interest of 12%. Bonds with a face value of $500,000 would be issued at par. The president asks your advice on the feasibility of this proposed repurchase.

REQUIRED:

1. Determine the carrying value of the bonds on January 2, 1995. Assume that the firm uses the straight-line method of amortization.
2. Make the journal entry to issue the new bonds and retire the old bonds. Make two separate journal entries.
3. Is there a gain or a loss from the repurchase?
4. Present to the president the economic factors you think should be considered in this proposed repurchase.

D12-2 Research Assignment

Using your library or information from other sources, obtain financial information for six of the following eight corporations:

Westvaco	H&R Block
AMR	Walt Disney
Boeing	Sears
Safeway Stores	McDonald's

REQUIRED:

1. For each corporation listed above, determine or calculate for the last two years of information you obtained the:
   a. amount of long-term debt
   b. total-debt-to-equity ratio
   c. total-debt-to-total assets ratio
2. For each corporation find its credit rating from either Moody's or Standard & Poor's. Has that rating changed within the last two years? If so, explain.

D12-3 Ethical Issues

In a 1991 article *Forbes* commented on the difficulty of obtaining information concerning environmental liabilities incurred by U.S. corporations.[10] This article noted that there is little or no specific accounting guidance on recognizing and recording liabilities for potential environmental damages and suits. Many corporations provide some vague footnote reference to possible damages, but usually just note that they expect no material effect on their financial statements.

The article goes on to cite the specific case of Occidental Petroleum. According to the article, "Occidental Petroleum lumped $720 million of environmental charges into a $2.2 billion pretax 'big bath' (the concept of cleaning the financial statements by writing off many old costs when the corporation already faces huge losses) for restructuring costs.

REQUIRED:

1. Comment on the ethics involved in taking a "big bath" in general, and Occidental Petroleum's actions in particular.
2. What do current accounting standards say about recording such liabilities? (*Hint:* Review the material in Chapter 8 relating to contingent liabilities.)
3. Do you think that corporations have an ethical responsibility to disclose environmental damage they have caused but yet to be accused of? Explain your answer.

10. Reed Albeson, "Messy Accounting," *Forbes*, October 14, 1991, pp. 172–173.

CHAPTER 13
EQUITY FINANCING—CORPORATIONS

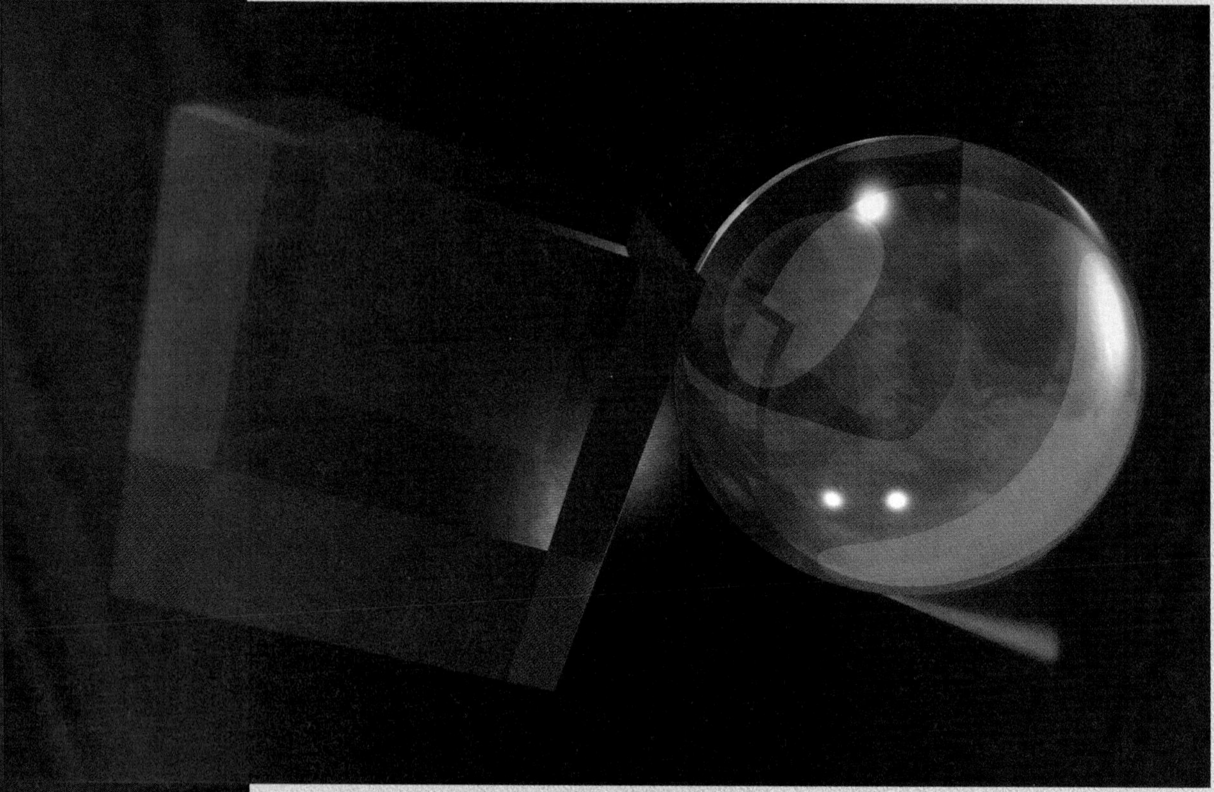

LEARNING OBJECTIVES

After studying this chapter, you should be able to:

1. List the characteristics of the corporate form of organization, including advantages and disadvantages.
2. Explain how corporations are formed and organized.
3. List the characteristics of capital stock: common and preferred.
4. Describe the components of stockholders' equity.
5. Discuss and apply the accounting concepts and procedures related to the issuance of capital stock.
6. Describe and record the different types of dividends issued by corporations.
7. Differentiate between stock splits and stock dividends.
8. Describe the effect of treasury stock transactions on financial accounting information.
9. Describe other transactions affecting retained earnings including prior period adjustments and appropriation of retained earnings.
10. Use stock information in making decisions.
11. Describe the types of procedures and techniques used to maintain control over debt and equity transactions and the associated accounting records.

Scenario

Ramon Martinez is a student at a local community college and is currently taking an introductory business course. One of his assignments for this course is to pick two large publicly-held companies and follow their stock prices during the semester. In addition, he is to read the business section of his local paper or a business newspaper such as the *Wall Street Journal* or *Investor's Daily* and find articles about the two companies whose stock he is following.

After some thought Ramon decided to follow General Motors (GM) and the Walt Disney Company. He figured that these were two rather different companies which have experienced diverse fortunes during the early 1990s. In early 1992 he began reading the stock page and kept a lookout for articles on GM and Disney.

Ramon was aware that GM, as well as the entire U. S. auto industry, was having a difficult time. The 1990–92 recession hit the auto industry particularly hard, with the "Big Three" U. S. auto companies experiencing huge losses. GM lost over $4 billion during 1991, and set in motion a plan to close dozens of plants and lay off thousands of workers over the coming years.

Yet, at the same time Ramon was reading about the huge losses suffered by GM, he was also reading that the company's board of directors had declared and issued its regular common stock dividend. He wondered how a company could declare and pay a dividend to its stockholders when it was experiencing such huge losses. It was Ramon's understanding that dividends represented a distribution of profits; clearly GM had not been profitable for the last couple of years and might not be profitable again for a few more years. He planned to ask his instructor to discuss what factors affect management's decision to declare cash dividends, and how a company like GM could declare a dividend in light of such a poor year.

The Walt Disney Company, on the other hand, had been enjoying several years of financial success. Even though attendance at some of its theme parks had suffered during the recession, the company's profits continued to grow. This profit growth was reflected in the stock price, which reached over $150 per share.

Ramon read with interest a recent article in his local newspaper stating that the board of directors of Disney had decided to declare a 4-for-1 common stock split, cutting the current price of the stock significantly to attract a broader range of investors. Ramon learned that when the stock price gets too high, it no longer becomes feasible for small investors to purchase it in round lots of 100 shares each, generally the most economical way to purchase stock.

Ramon checked the stock page and found out that Disney stock jumped $3.50 on the day of the announcement. He figured that investors must consider a stock split good news. He wanted to learn more about why a company declares a stock split and how it actually works. He decided he would add this to the growing list of questions he wanted to ask his instructor.

The corporation is the dominant form of organization in the United States. Although sole proprietorships and partnerships outnumber corporations, most major businesses, except for service-oriented businesses such as large accounting and law firms, are organized as corporations. The purpose of this chapter is to introduce you to corporate organizations, their formation, and related capital stock and dividend transactions.

CHARACTERISTICS OF A CORPORATION

Objective 1
List the characteristics of the corporate form of organization, including advantages and disadvantages.

A corporation is a separate legal entity created by the state, owned by one or more persons, and having rights, privileges, and obligations that are distinct from those of its owners. A corporation may sue or be sued and may be taxed, just as an individual may. However, it does not go out of existence with the death of an owner or a change in ownership.

Advantages of the Corporate Form of Organization

A corporation has certain characteristics that give it advantages over other forms of business organizations. These advantages, as discussed in Chapter 1, include limited liability for the shareholders, transferability of ownership, and ease of capital formation.

Limited liability refers to the fact that a corporation is responsible for its own obligations. Its creditors can look only to the assets of the corporation to satisfy their claims. The owners' total liability is generally limited to the amount they have invested in the corporation.

Ownership in a corporation is evidenced by possession of a share of stock, which usually can be transferred to another without any restrictions. Once the stock of a corporation is issued, the corporation is not affected by subsequent transfers of stock by individual shareholders, except that the names on its list of shareholders will change. Limited liability and transferability of ownership make it relatively easier for a corporation to raise capital than for a sole proprietorship or a partnership.

Disadvantages of the Corporate Form of Organization

Some of the characteristics that give the corporate form of organization its advantages may also result in some disadvantages. These disadvantages, which are especially relevant to smaller businesses, include double taxation, government regulation, and in some cases, the limited liability feature.

Double taxation is one of the major disadvantages of the corporate form. The earnings of a corporation are subject to taxes up to 35%. When corporate earnings are distributed to stockholders in the form of dividends, these dividends are not deductible by the corporation but are taxable to the recipient. In effect, corporate earnings are taxed twice, once at the corporate level and again at the individual shareholder level.

Corporations are chartered by a state and thus must comply with various state and federal regulations. For smaller companies, the cost of complying with these regulations may outweigh the other benefits of the corporate form of business organization. Although government regulation applies to all forms of business enterprise, it is generally not as great for sole proprietorships and partnerships.

For smaller companies, the limited liability feature of a corporation may be a disadvantage in raising capital. Because of this feature, creditors have claims against only the assets of a corporation; if a corporation defaults, the creditors have no recourse against the owners. As a result, smaller, closely-held corporations often find that loans from bankers and other creditors are limited to the amount of security offered by the corporation. In other cases, the shareholders may have to sign an agreement pledging their personal assets as security.

FORMATION AND ORGANIZATION OF A CORPORATION

Objective 2
Explain how corporations are formed and organized.

The procedures necessary to form a corporation and, subsequently, to conduct business are established by state law; as you might expect, the states differ somewhat in their laws and regulatory environments. For example, it has historically been easier to incorporate in some states (such as Delaware) than in other states (such as California). The following discussion is based on the general procedures found in most states.

Forming a Corporation

The first step in forming a corporation is for at least three individuals, generally the corporate president, vice-president, and secretary-treasurer, to file an application with the appropriate state official, often the secretary of state. Among the items included in the application are the articles of incorporation, which list:

1. The name and place of business of the corporation
2. The main purpose of the business
3. The names of the principal officers of the corporation
4. The names of the original stockholders
5. The type of stock to be issued; the number of authorized shares; their par value, if any; and their dividend and voting rights

Once the articles of incorporation have been approved by the appropriate state official, they are referred to as the *corporate charter.*

During the organization process, a corporation incurs certain costs, including state filing and incorporation fees, attorneys' fees, promotion fees, printing and engraving fees, and similar items. These costs all are necessary to get the corporation started. Because they are considered to have future benefit, they are capitalized and are referred to as **organization costs.** They are usually listed in the Other Assets section of the balance sheet.

organization costs

Stockholders

The stockholders are the owners of the corporation; this ownership is evidenced by stock certificates. A sample stock certificate from the Thomson Corporation is reproduced in Exhibit 13-1. A stock certificate is a legal document that shows the number, type, and par value (if any) of the shares issued by the corporation. Stock certificates are serially numbered and may include other data required by state laws.

In large corporations, the shareholders do not participate in the day-to-day operation of the business. They elect the board of directors and vote on important issues at the annual stockholders' meeting. The **board of directors** is charged with establishing broad corporate policies and appointing senior corporate man-

board of directors

Exhibit 13-1
A Share of Common Stock in The Thompson Corporation

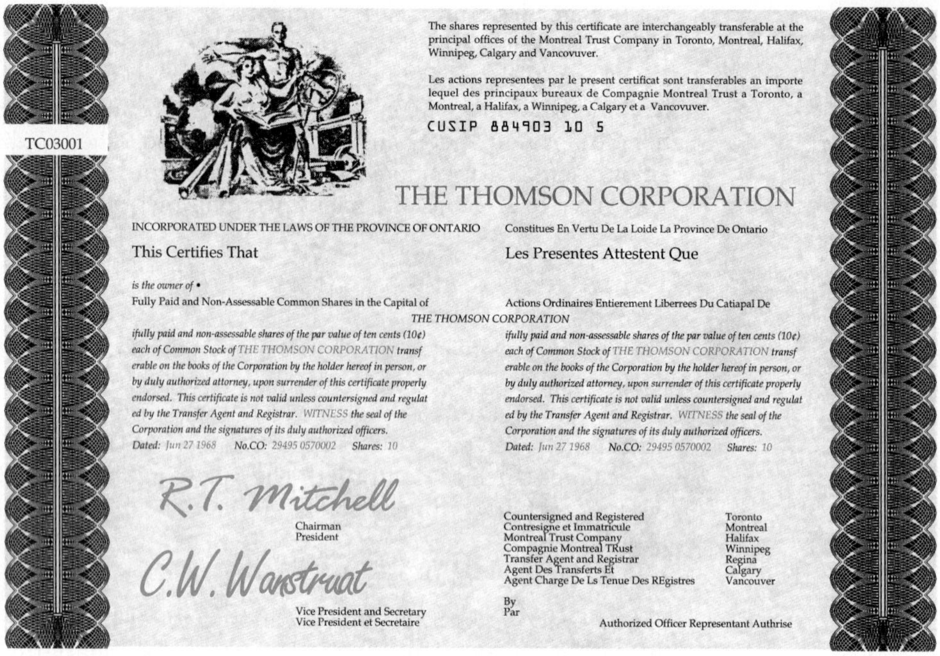

agement. However, depending upon the characteristics of the stock owned, stockholders do have certain rights, which include:

1. The right to attend all stockholders' meetings, to vote for the board of directors, and to vote on major corporate policies and decisions such as proposed mergers and consolidations. The number of votes is based on the number of shares owned. Stockholders who do not attend the meetings are able to vote through a proxy. A **proxy** gives another individual or individuals, usually the current management, the right to vote the shares in the manner the appointed individuals deem best.

proxy

2. The right to receive a proportionate share of all dividends declared by the board of directors.
3. The right to a proportionate share of remaining corporate assets upon the liquidation of the corporation. Remember that the stockholders' interest is a residual one and that they are entitled to the remaining assets only after all the claims of the creditors and, perhaps, other equity holders have been satisfied.
4. The preemptive right gives existing stockholders the right to purchase shares of a new stock issue in proportion to the shares already owned. This right ensures that the ownership of the current stockholders is not diluted by the issuance of additional shares. To illustrate, assume that Mark Wilson owns 5% of the outstanding shares of the Ironside Corporation. If the corporation decides to issue 100,000 new shares, Mark Wilson will have the right to purchase 5,000 (100,000 × .05) additional shares. Of course, Wilson does not have to purchase these shares. Stockholders often waive this right in order to facilitate mergers that require the issuance of additional shares.
5. The right to dispose of or transfer their shares if and when they desire. In some situations, this right of free transferability is limited. Such limitations, if and when they exist, are clearly noted on the stock certificate.

Board of Directors and Senior Management

The board of directors and the chairperson of the board are elected by the stockholders. The board usually consists of senior management and outside members. Outside members are individuals who are not otherwise employed by the company and thus are independent of senior management. In recent years, it has become commonplace for a majority of the board to be made up of such outside members. The board's primary function is to determine general corporate policies and to appoint senior management. The board is also charged with protecting the interests of stockholders and creditors.

The corporation's senior management is appointed by the board. Obviously, the primary function of senior management is to conduct the day-to-day operations of the company. The designations and functions of these individuals depend on the specific needs and organization of the company.

EQUITY SECURITIES

Objective 3
List the characteristics of capital stock: common and preferred.

Throughout this book, the terms *capital stock* and *stock* have been used to refer to the equity securities issued by a corporation. In reality, there are at least two major types of capital stock: common stock and preferred stock.

Common Stock

common stock

Common stock is a capital stock that must be issued by all corporations. Common stockholders have all the rights of stockholders previously listed. Generally, because common stock is the only type of stock with voting rights, common stockholders control the corporation. However, they have only a residual interest in its net assets. This means that in the event of a corporate liquidation, common shareholders will not receive any assets until the claims of the creditors and the preferred stockholders are satisfied.

Some states allow different classes of common stock. For example, a corporation may issue Class A and Class B common stock. Depending on state laws and the corporate charter, Class A stock may be voting, whereas Class B is not. However, it is relatively rare for large, publicly held corporations to issue two classes of common stock.

Preferred Stock

In addition to common stock, a corporation may issue a type of stock called *preferred stock.* Owning preferred stock is not necessarily better than owning common stock; the term *preferred* simply means that owners of this type of stock receive certain preferences over owners of common stock. **Preferred stock** generally has the following preferences and characteristics:

preferred stock

1. Preference as to dividends
2. Cumulative dividends
3. Preference over common stockholders upon liquidation
4. Callable shares
5. No voting rights

Preferred Dividends. Preferred stock has a preference in regard to dividends, which means that the preferred stockholders must receive all of the dividends to which they are entitled before any dividends can be declared and paid to the common stockholders. Unlike common stock, preferred stock usually has the amount of its dividends stated on the stock certificate. This is done in one of two ways. The actual dollar amount of the dividend may be stated on the stock certificate. For example, one issue of preferred stock for Wicke's is stated at $2.50 per share. This means that if a dividend is declared by the board of directors each stockholder will receive an annual dividend of $2.50 per share. In the second case, the dividend is stated as a percentage of par value. Par value is a stated amount printed on the stock certificate. For example, Sprint, another publicly-held corporation, has issued $100 par value, 9 3/4% preferred stock. This means that if and when dividends are declared, the preferred stockholder will receive an annual per-share dividend of $9.75, or 9.75% × $100. Because the amount of preferred dividends is stated, many individuals consider the stock more stable and less risky than common stock.

Cumulative Versus Noncumulative Dividends. As previously noted, a corporation does not have to issue a dividend. Only when the board of directors declares a dividend does it become an actual liability of the corporation. Many issues of preferred stock are cumulative. This means that preferred stockholders do not lose their claim to undeclared dividends. The right to receive these undeclared dividends accumulates over time and must be paid in full before common stockholders can receive any dividends. This is an attractive feature, so most preferred issues are cumulative. Conversely, if the stock is noncumulative, any dividends not declared in the current year will lapse, and preferred stockholders will lose their claim to such dividends.

To demonstrate, assume that the Place Publishing Corporation issued 10,000 shares of $3 cumulative preferred stock. At the beginning of 1993, all stated preferred dividends for prior years had been declared and paid. During 1993, profits were down, so Place decided to declare only $20,000 of preferred dividends. As a result, there was a shortfall of $10,000, calculated as follows:

Required dividend, $3 × 10,000 Shares	$30,000
Dividends declared	20,000
Dividends in arrears	$10,000

dividends in arrears

This shortfall is called **dividends in arrears.** Although this $10,000 is not a liability of the Place Publishing Corporation, if dividends are declared the next year (1994), the $10,000 dividends in arrears plus the 1994 preferred dividends of $30,000 must be paid before common stockholders will receive anything.

To continue the illustration, assume that in 1994, Place Publishing decided to declare total dividends of $75,000 to preferred and common stockholders. In this case, preferred stockholders would receive $40,000, and common stockholders would receive the residual of $35,000, calculated as follows:

Total dividends		$75,000
Preferred dividends		
Dividends in arrears	$10,000	
1994 current year's dividend	30,000	
Total to preferred stockholders		40,000
Total to common stockholders		$35,000

As previously noted, dividends in arrears are not liabilities of the corporation. However, full disclosure requires that any dividends in arrears be disclosed in the notes to the financial statements. For example, the following note was taken from an annual report of the Long Island Lighting Company:

Long Island Lighting Company*—December 31, 1991*
Preferred stock dividends are cumulative. At December 31, 1991, 1990, and 1989 there were no preferred stock dividends in arrears. On September 1, 1989, the Company resumed regular dividend payments on its preferred stock by paying all dividends, then in arrears, amounting to approximately $390 million.

Participating Versus Nonparticipating. In some situations, preferred stock has a participating feature. This means that in addition to the stated dividend, preferred stockholders can participate with common shareholders in additional dividends. This participation feature can range from limited to full. When full participation exists, the common shareholders receive dividends at the same rate as preferred, and any excess dividends are split on a proportionate basis between common and preferred shareholders.

Most preferred stock, however, is not participating; the preferred stockholder receives only the stated dividend rate, regardless of how profitable the company is. This is one of the major disadvantages of preferred stock. After the stated preferred dividend rate is paid, all of the benefits of above-average profitable years may accrue to the common stockholders through higher dividends. In effect, the stockholder who has purchased cumulative nonparticipating preferred stock trades off a possible higher return for less risk.

Preference on Liquidation. Normally, preferred stock has preference in the event of corporate liquidation. This means that after the creditors are satisfied, preferred shareholders must be fully satisfied before common stockholders can receive any assets. Further, dividends in arrears are included in this liquidation preference. Most preferred stock has an actual stated liquidation value per share that the shareholder will receive if liquidation occurs. Current accounting practices require that this liquidation value be disclosed in the stockholders' equity section of the balance sheet.

Other Features of Preferred Stock. In some situations, a corporation may issue **convertible preferred stock.** This enables preferred stockholders to convert their preferred stock for common stock at a stated rate and time. This conversion feature allows preferred stockholders to enjoy the stability of preferred dividends, and, if it becomes advantageous, to convert to common stock and benefit from increases in the price of the common shares. The issuing corporation also benefits from the conversion feature, because it can issue preferred stock with a lower stated dividend rate than it otherwise could have.

convertible preferred stock

Preferred stock can be redeemable or callable. Under certain conditions, **redeemable preferred stock** can be returned, for a stated price, to the issuing corporation by the owner of the stock (the investor). Some preferred stock has mandatory redemption requirements, by which the corporation can force redemption at a certain price and time.

redeemable preferred stock

Callable preferred stock gives the issuing corporation, at its option, the right to retire the stock at a specified price. The specified price (call price) is usually above the stated par value of the stock, and the difference between the call price and the par value is called the **call premium** To illustrate, $100 par value preferred stock with a call price of $108 has a call premium of $8. When the issuing

callable preferred stock

call premium

corporation calls the stock, the total price paid is the call price plus any dividends in arrears.

There are several reasons why a corporation may wish to issue callable, or redeemable, preferred stock. If the stock is also convertible, the call provision will allow the corporation to force conversion by threatening to call the stock. In addition, if interest and investment rates change in the economy, the call provision will give the corporation flexibility by allowing it to retire preferred stock with a high dividend rate and replace it with new stock at a lower rate. Finally, if the corporation has considerable amounts of excess cash, it may wish to retire its preferred stock and thus avoid paying future dividends on those shares.

COMPONENTS OF STOCKHOLDERS' EQUITY

Objective 4
Describe the components of stockholders' equity.

Stockholders' equity represents the stockholders' residual interest in the corporation's assets. Although terminology and form differ among firms, the shareholders' equity section of Westinghouse Electric Corporation consolidated balance sheet, presented in Exhibit 13-2, is typical of those found in most U.S. corporate balance sheets. Although not specifically designated as such in most published balance sheets, stockholders' equity consists of the following components: (1) contributed capital, including preferred and common stock and additional paid-in capital; (2) retained earnings; (3) treasury stock; and, in some situations, (4) certain debit items. You should keep in mind that the total of these categories represents owners' claims; they are subdivided only for legal and accounting purposes.

Contributed Capital

contributed capital

Contributed capital is the total capital contributed by all the stockholders as well as others. This capital comes from the original issue of common and preferred stock, subsequent issues of stock, and other sources such as donations to the corporation. Contributed capital has two components: the **legal (stated) capital** of the corporation and the **additional paid-in capital** The total contributed capital of Westinghouse, at December 31, 1992, is $1,924 million, consisting of the legal capital (the par value of the common stock and preferred stock) of $401 million and additional paid-in capital of $1,523 million.

legal (stated) capital
additional paid-in capital

Legal, or Stated, Capital. The definition of legal, or stated, capital depends on the laws of the state in which the corporation is chartered. Generally, it pertains to the number of shares of common and (if any) preferred stock listed at their total par values, stated values, or issue price if stock with no par value is issued. Thus, the legal capital of Westinghouse, is $401 million, consisting of the $393 million par value of common stock and $8 million of preferred stock. The definition and determination of legal capital have important legal implications. Many courts have ruled that if a corporation's legal capital is reduced through dividend payments or actions other than unprofitable operations, its creditors have a claim against the current stockholders to the extent of that reduction. As noted, the amount of legal capital is closely tied to the concept of par value, which will be explored next.

par value

Par Value. Par value is an accounting term that often is misunderstood. The **par value** of common or preferred stock is an amount designated in the articles of incorporation or by the board of directors and is printed on the stock certifi-

Exhibit 13-2

Westinghouse Electric Corporation Partial Consolidated Balance Sheet	1992	1991
Shareholders' equity (note 15):		
Preferred stock, $1.00 par value (25 million shares authorized):		
Series A preferred (no shares issued)	—	—
Series B conversion preferred (8 million shares issued)	8	—
Common stock, $1.00 par value (480 million shares authorized, 393 million shares issued)	393	393
Capital in excess of par value	1,523	1,039
Common stock held in treasury	(1,102)	(1,264)
Other	(498)	4
Retained earnings	2,020	3,582
Total shareholders' equity	2,344	3,754

cate. It does not represent the amount that the board feels the stock will sell for when issued or in the future. In fact, it does not represent real value at all.

Par value is a concept developed around 1900 to protect the creditors and investors of corporations. It was meant to provide an amount of assets that could not be distributed to shareholders unless there were no claims by creditors and/or investors that would be impaired by this distribution. However, the concept of par value has lost much of its significance today. The board of directors has the right to set the par value of stock at any amount it desires. Because it is unlawful in most states to issue stock below its par value, the board usually sets a relatively low par value, such as $1, $5, or $10. For example, the par value of both Westinghouse's common stock and preferred stock is $1 per share. From an accounting perspective, the main significance of par value is that it is often a basis on which the amount of the preferred stock dividends is derived.

no par stock

No Par Stock. Many states now allow corporations to issue no par stock. True **no par stock** has no stated value placed on it by the board of directors. In some situations, the board of directors will place a stated value on the no par stock. No par stock with a stated value is treated in the same way that par value stock is.

Shares Authorized and Issued. Under current accounting practices, the par value or stated value of a firm's capital stock and the number of shares authorized, issued, and outstanding must be disclosed in its financial statements. The number of shares authorized is stated in the articles of incorporation and is simply the number of shares that the corporation is allowed to issue. For example, Westinghouse is authorized to issue 480 million shares of common stock. The number of shares authorized in Westinghouse's articles of incorporation is clearly large enough to meet its present and future needs.

The shares issued represent the number of shares the corporation has actually issued to date. Westinghouse has issued 393 million $1 par value common shares at December 31, 1992 and December 31, 1991. Because of the common shares held in treasury at December 31, 1992, and 1991, not all of the issued shares were still outstanding. Outstanding shares are the difference between the shares issued and the shares held in treasury. Stock that is authorized but unissued (or issued and no longer outstanding) has no rights associated with it.

Additional Paid-in Capital. One of the primary sources of additional paid-in capital is the issue of stock in excess of the par or stated value. Other sources of additional paid-in capital include donated capital and the resale of treasury stock (stock repurchased by the corporation) above its cost. Westinghouse's additional paid-in capital, called capital in excess of par value, equals $1,523 million, and as noted, the total contributed capital equals $1,924 million, consisting of preferred stock, common stock and additional paid-in capital.

Donated capital is another source of additional paid-in capital. Several transactions can give rise to donated capital, including donated assets, stock returned to the corporation by stockholders, and forgiveness of corporate debt by a stockholder. The most common situation involving donated assets occurs when a city or municipality offers to a corporation, at no cost, land on which to locate its plant. Cities do this in the hope of improving local employment and increasing tax revenues. Such donated assets are recorded at their fair market value, by debiting the appropriate asset account and crediting the paid-in capital account, donated capital.

Retained Earnings

The second category in the stockholders' equity section is retained earnings. Retained earnings result from a business's profitable operations and represent part of the owners' residual claim. Dividends reduce retained earnings. These transactions are discussed later in this chapter.

Treasury Stock

The stockholders' equity section of the Westinghouse balance sheet (Exhibit 13-2), includes a listing for treasury stock, which represents the cost of Westinghouse's own stock that the company itself repurchased. As noted, at December 31, 1992, and 1991, the cost of the shares Westinghouse held in treasury were $1,102 million and $1,264 million, respectively. Treasury stock transactions are also discussed later in this chapter.

Debit Items in Stockholders' Equity

Under current accounting standards, a number of items other than treasury stock are treated as direct deductions to stockholders' equity. These include, among others, unrealized losses on long-term investments, and cumulative foreign currency translation adjustments. In Westinghouse's case, other debit items include foreign currency translation adjustments, and a pension liability adjustment. This breakdown of the other item in the stockholders's equity section was obtained from the notes to the financial statements.

ACCOUNTING FOR THE ISSUANCE OF STOCK

Objective 5
Discuss and apply the accounting concepts and procedures related to the issuance of capital stock.

When a corporation is formed, it must issue common stock. It may, in addition, issue preferred stock. Subsequently, if the corporation needs additional capital, it may decide to issue common stock, preferred stock, bonds, or other debt instruments. Large public corporations often issue stock through **underwriters**—brokerage firms, such as Merrill Lynch, or groups of firms that purchase the entire stock issue for a stated price. The underwriters assume the risks in

underwriters

marketing the stock to their clients. Some firms sell their stock directly to the public. Smaller firms that are going to issue only limited amounts of stock often do so through private solicitations and private placements. The decision on how to market a stock issue is an important management decision but does not affect the way in which the stock is recorded in the firm's books and records; it may, however, affect the total proceeds received on the issue.

Stock Issued for Cash

Large public corporations usually issue stock in exchange for cash. To illustrate the accounting entries, assume that on January 2, 1995, the Jackson Corporation decides to issue 5,000 of its 20,000 authorized shares of common stock and receives $25 per share. The following three independent cases will be considered:

1. The stock has a par value of $10 per share.
2. The stock is no par with no stated value.
3. The stock is no par but has a stated value of $5 per share.

Although common stock is used in these examples, the same concepts apply to preferred stock.

Exhibit 13-3 presents the appropriate journal entries for all three cases as well as the stockholders' equity section of the balance sheet immediately after the stock issue. In the first case, as in all of the cases, Cash is debited for the total proceeds received, $125,000 (5,000 × $25). When common stock has a par value,

Exhibit 13-3

Issue of 5,000 Shares of Stock at $25 per Share

Case 1 *$10 Par Value Stock*			*Case 2* *No Par, No Stated Value*			*Case 3* *No Par, $5 Stated Value*		
January 2, 1995			January 2, 1995			January 2, 1995		
Cash	125,000		Cash	125,000		Cash	125,000	
Common Stock		50,000	Common Stock		125,000	Common Stock		25,000
Paid-in Capital in Excess of Par		75,000				Paid-in Capital in Excess of Stated Value		100,000
To record issue of 5,000 shares of $10 par value stock at $25 per share.			To record issue of 5,000 shares of no par stock at $25 per share.			To record issue of 5,000 shares of no par, $5 stated value stock at $25 per share.		

The Jackson Corporation *Partial Balance Sheet* *January 2, 1995*		*The Jackson Corporation* *Partial Balance Sheet* *January 2, 1995*		*The Jackson Corporation* *Partial Balance Sheet* *January 2, 1995*	
Contributed capital		Contributed capital		Contributed capital	
Common stock, $10 par value, 20,000 shares authorized, 5,000 shares issued and outstanding	$ 50,000	Common stock, no par value, 20,000 shares authorized, 5,000 shares issued and outstanding	$125,000	Common stock, no par with $5 stated value, 20,000 shares authorized, 5,000 shares issued and outstanding	$ 25,000
Additional paid-in capital	75,000			Additional paid-in capital	100,000
Total stockholders' equity	$125,000	Total stockholders' equity	$125,000	Total stockholders' equity	$125,000

the common stock account is credited only for the par value of the total stock issued, or $50,000 (5,000 × $10), and Paid-in Capital From Issue of Common Stock in Excess of Par (often shortened to *Paid-in Capital in Excess of Par* or just *Additional Paid-in Capital*) is credited for the difference of $75,000 [(5,000 × ($25 − $10)].[1] The partial balance sheet pictured under Case 1 in Exhibit 13-3 shows that the corporation's contributed capital is divided into the legal capital of $50,000 (the par value of the stock) and the additional paid-in capital of $75,000. Total stockholders' equity, which does not include retained earnings (because in this example the corporation has just been organized), equals $125,000.

In Case 2, the stock is no par and has no stated value. Again, Cash is debited for the entire proceeds of $125,000. However, in this case, Common Stock is credited for the entire proceeds of $125,000 as well. There is no entry to an additional Paid-in Capital account. Since different stock issues are apt to be sold at different prices, there is no uniform value per share recorded for capital stock, as it is for par value stock. In this case, the corporation's legal capital is $125,000; the stockholders' equity is still $125,000.

In Case 3, the stock is no par but has a stated value of $5 per share. As before, Cash is debited for $125,000, but now Common Stock is credited for only $25,000 (5,000 × $5 = $25,000), or the stated value of the entire issue. Paid-in Capital in Excess of Stated Value is then credited for the difference of $100,000 [5,000 × ($25 − $5)]. Assuming that the stock's stated value remains the same, there will be a uniform amount per share recorded in the Common Stock account. Most states consider that the corporation's legal capital is the stock's total stated value—in this case $25,000. Total stockholders' equity, as with the other two cases, is $125,000.

There are a number of points to keep in mind when reviewing these examples. In all cases, total stockholders' equity remains the same. The difference occurs in the division of contributed capital between legal capital and other paid-in capital. Although the distinction between legal capital and contributed capital may have important legal ramifications, especially on liquidation, it has little accounting significance.

Stock Issued for Noncash Assets

In some circumstances, stock is issued for noncash assets or for services. For example, a corporation may receive land, buildings, or other assets in exchange for its stock. Attorneys and other promoters may accept stock in a corporation instead of cash in payment for their services. In either case, the transaction should be recorded in accordance with the historical cost principle. This means that the assets or services acquired should be recorded at the fair market value of the stock issued at the date of the transaction—that is, the consideration given. In transactions for which it is not feasible to determine the fair market value of the stock that has been issued, the fair market value of the assets or services received should be used.

To illustrate, assume that Rebecca Webb, the attorney for the Secco Corporation, agrees to take 1,000 shares of the corporation's $5 par value stock in

1. Corporations often maintain separate paid-in capital accounts for each type of transaction. For example, there is likely to be a separate paid-in capital account from the issue of common stock above par and a separate account for the issue of preferred stock above par. For simplicity, we will lump all these accounts in to one entitled, Paid-in Capital in Excess of Par.

exchange for the services she performed in organizing the corporation. Her normal fee for such work is $7,500. Because the corporation is owned by only a few individuals and is not traded on an exchange, its market value cannot be determined without extensive effort, so the value of the services performed will be used to value the transaction. The entry to record this transaction is:

Organization Costs	7,500	
Common Stock		5,000
Paid-in Capital in Excess of Par		2,500
To record issue of 1,000 shares of $5 par value stock in exchange for attorney's fees of $7,500.		

Organization Costs, an intangible asset account, is debited for the fair market value of the attorney's service, Common Stock is credited for the par value of the stock, and Paid-in Capital in Excess of Par is credited for the difference.

If stock is exchanged for noncash assets such as land or buildings, the entry would be similar. For example, now assume that at the same date the Secco Corporation issues 5,000 shares of its $100 par value preferred stock in exchange for land and a building. At the time of the transaction, the preferred stock has a fair market value of $120 per share, and so the total transaction is valued at $600,000 (5,000 × $120 = $600,000). The land and the building are valued at $200,000 and $400,000, respectively. The entry to record this transaction is:

Land	200,000	
Building	400,000	
Preferred Stock		500,000
Paid-in Capital in Excess of Par		100,000
To record issue of 5,000 shares of $100 par value preferred stock in exchange for land and building. Market value of preferred stock is $120 per share.		

If it is impossible to determine the fair market value of the stock, the fair market value of the land and building should be used to value the transactions. If the asset valuation figure cannot be reasonably determined, the board of directors would set a value for the transaction.

DIVIDENDS

Objective 6
Describe and record the different types of dividends issued by corporations.

Dividends, which represent a distribution to shareholders of assets that have been generated by profitable operations, can be in the form of cash, other assets, or, in some cases, the corporation's own stock.

Cash Dividends

Most investors purchase either common or preferred stock with the expectation of receiving cash dividends. The amount and regularity of cash dividends are two of the factors that affect the market price of a firm's stock. Many corporations, therefore, attempt to establish a regular quarterly dividend pattern that is maintained or slowly increased over a number of years. In especially profitable years, the corporation may issue a special year-end dividend in addition to the regular dividends. Such stable dividend policies increase the attractiveness of the firm's stock. The following, taken from a recent General Electric Company (GE) annual report, shows how one corporation implements this policy:

Dividends declared totaled $1.808 billion in 1991, or $2.08 per share. Even though substantial dividends were paid, the Company retained sufficient earnings to support capital expenditures to increase productive capability and to provide adequate financial resources for internal and external growth opportunities. The fourth-quarter 1991 increase of 8% in per-share dividends declared marked the 16th consecutive year of dividend growth. As shown in the chart on page 33, GE's 1991 and 1990 dividends per share were up 76% and 62% respectively, over 1986 while the S&P 500 dividends were up only 47% and 46%, respectively, from 1986 levels.

As this quotation indicates, management gives considerable thought to the amount and timing of dividends. In addition to the desire to maintain a stable dividend policy, other factors also affect the amount of cash dividends declared in any one year—for example, the amount of retained earnings or the firm's cash position and business needs.

From a theoretical and practical point of view, there must be a positive balance in retained earnings in order to issue a dividend. If there is a deficit (debit or negative balance) in retained earnings, any dividend would represent a return of invested capital and is therefore called a *liquidating dividend.* Even a corporation that incurs a loss in a given year can still issue a normal dividend (a dividend other than a liquidating one) as long as there is a credit (positive) balance in retained earnings. For example, even in the recession year of 1991 when many corporations racked up huge losses, they continued to issue dividends. General Motors (GM) which lost over $4 billion dollars in 1991, still declared and issued dividends totaling $1.60 per share of common stock.

Because there must be a positive balance in retained earnings before a normal dividend can be issued, the phrase "paying dividends out of retained earnings" developed. However, this is an inaccurate way to put it. Dividends are not paid out of retained earnings; as a distribution of assets, they are paid in cash or, in some circumstances, in other assets or even stock. Retained earnings are the increase in the firm's net assets due to profitable operations and represent the owners' claim against net assets, not just cash.

The maximum amount of dividends that can be issued in any one year is the total amount of retained earnings. However, distributing this whole amount is rarely, if ever, done. To repeat, a firm must have the necessary cash available to pay a cash dividend, and the amount of cash on hand is not directly related to retained earnings. Furthermore, as is evident from the statement in the GE annual report, a firm has other uses for its cash. Most mature and stable firms restrict their cash dividends to about 40% of their net earnings, but as noted in the GM example, some corporations declare a dividend even in a loss year.

Declaration of Dividends

All dividends must be declared by the board of directors before they become a liability of the corporation. Three dates are significant to the declaration and payment of dividends: the declaration date, the date of record, and the payment date.

declaration date

The **declaration date** is the date on which the board of directors declares the dividend. At that time, the dividend becomes a liability of the corporation and is recorded on its books. The declaration date is usually several weeks prior to the payment date. A typical dividend announcement may read as follows:

The Board of Directors on December 1 declared a $1.20 per share dividend payable on January 4 to common shareholders of record on December 21.

date of record

Only the stockholders as of the **date of record** are eligible for the dividend. Because of the time needed to compile the list of stockholders at any one date, the date of record usually is two to three weeks after the declaration date, but before the actual payment date.

payment date

The **payment date** is the date that the dividend is actually paid. It usually occurs within a few weeks after the declaration date.

Journal Entries to Record Cash Dividends. To demonstrate the journal entries required when a cash dividend is declared and paid, return to the above example in which the board of directors declared on December 1 a $1.20 per share dividend payable on January 4 to the common shareholders of record on December 21. Assuming there are 100,000 common shares outstanding, the total cash dividends will be $120,000.

Dec. 1 (Declaration Date):		
Retained Earnings	120,000	
Dividends Payable		120,000
To record declaration of $1.20 per share dividend on 100,000 shares of outstanding common stock. Dividend is payable on January 4 to shareholders of record on December 21.		
Dec. 21 (Date of Record):		
No Entry		
Jan. 4 (Payment Date):		
Dividends Payable	120,000	
Cash		120,000
To record payment of $1.20 per share dividend declared on December 1.		

When recording the declaration of a dividend, some firms debit an account titled Dividends Declared rather than debiting Retained Earnings. However, when this procedure is used an entry must be made to close Dividends Declared into Retained Earnings. An advantage of using a separate dividends declared account is that the retained earnings account remains constant throughout the period until closing.

Noncash Dividends

Occasionally, a firm will issue a dividend in which the payment is made with an asset other than cash. Noncash dividends, which are called *property dividends,* are more likely to occur in private corporations than in publicly-held ones. Under current accounting pronouncements, the property is revalued to its current market value as of the date of declaration, and a gain or loss is recognized on the revaluation of the asset.[2]

To illustrate, assume that the Ironside Corporation declared a property dividend on December 1, to be distributed on January 4. Marketable securities held by the firm that have a cost of $750,000 and a fair market value (FMV) of $1 million are to be distributed to the shareholders. The journal entries to reflect these transactions are:

2. American Institute of Certified Public Accountants, Accounting Principles Board, Opinion No. 29, *Accounting for Nonmonetary Transactions* (New York: AICPA, 1973), par. 18.

Dec. 1 (Date of Declaration):		
Investment in Marketable Securities	250,000	
Gain on revaluation of Marketable Securities		250,000
To record revaluation of marketable securities.		

FMV =	$1,000,000
Cost	750,000
Gain	$ 250,000

Retained Earnings	1,000,000	
Property Dividends Payable		1,000,000
To record declaration of property dividend payable on January 4.		
Jan 4 (Distribution of Property Dividend):		
Property Dividends Payable	1,000,000	
Investment in Marketable Securities		1,000,000
To record distribution of property dividend.		

STOCK DIVIDENDS AND STOCK SPLITS

Objective 7
Differentiate between stock splits and stock dividends.

Stock dividends and stock splits both result in the distribution of additional shares to existing stockholders. Because of their similarities, they will be discussed in turn.

Stock Dividends

stock dividend

Many corporations issue stock dividends instead of, or in addition to, cash dividends. A **stock dividend** is a distribution of the corporation's own stock to current shareholders on a proportional basis. That is, the current holders of stock receive additional shares of stock in proportion to their current holdings. For example, if a corporation in which you own 10,000 shares of common stock issues a 15% stock dividend, you will receive an additional 1,500 shares (15% × 10,000). Most stock dividends are given only to common stockholders.

When investors receive a stock dividend, the cost per share of their original shares is reduced accordingly. For example, assume that an individual owns 1,000 shares of South Gulf Oil Company. These shares were purchased at $60 per share, for a total cost of $60,000. Subsequently, South Gulf issues a 20% stock dividend, so the investor will receive an additional 200 shares (1,000 × .20). Therefore, the cost per share to the investor is reduced from the original $60 per share to $50 per share ($60,000/1,200 shares). Thus, no income is recognized on the stock dividends when they are received. The reduced cost per share may increase the gain or decrease the loss on subsequent sales of the stock.

Why Stock Dividends Are Issued. A corporation may issue a stock dividend rather than a cash dividend for a number of reasons. Clearly, a stock dividend conserves cash, thus allowing the firm to use its cash for growth and expansion. Corporations experiencing growth are generally more likely to issue a stock dividend than are stable, mature firms. In addition, stock dividends transfer a part of retained earnings to permanent capital. This is referred to as **capitalizing retained earnings**; it makes that part of retained earnings transferred to permanent capital unavailable for future cash dividends.

capitalizing retained earnings

Recording Stock Dividends. When a stock dividend is declared and issued, the corporation debits retained earnings for the total fair market value of the stock dividend. Assuming that the stock is issued immediately, the common stock account is credited for its par value, if any. Paid-in capital in excess of par is credited for the difference between the market value and the par value. If the stock has neither a par nor a stated value, common stock is credited for the entire market value.[3]

After these entries have been made, total stockholders' equity remains the same, because there has been no distribution of cash or other assets. The only difference is in the components of stockholders' equity: retained earnings is decreased, and contributed capital is increased. As noted, this is often referred to as capitalizing retained earnings, because a portion of retained earnings becomes part of the firm's permanent invested capital. In effect, after the stock dividend, each individual shareholder owns the same proportionate share of the corporation as he/she did before.

To demonstrate the journal entries to record stock dividends, assume that the stockholders' equity of the Korean Export Corporation immediately before the issue of a 10% stock dividend appears as shown in Exhibit 13-4.

On November 30, 1995, the corporation declares and issues a 10% stock dividend on its $5 par value common stock. At the time of the declaration, the stock is selling at $40 per share. As a result of the 10% dividend, a total of 6,000 shares (10% × 60,000) is issued. Based on this data, the following journal entry is made:

Nov. 30, 1994		
Retained Earnings	240,000	
Common Stock		30,000
Paid-in Capital in Excess of Par		210,000
To record declaration of 10% stock dividend; 6,000 shares distributed. FMV of stock at time of declaration is $40 per share.		

The stockholders' equity section of the Korean Export Corporation's balance sheet at November 30, immediately after the issuance of the stock dividend, appears as shown in Exhibit 13-5.

The most important thing to note in comparing the stockholders' equity section in both balance sheets is that the total is $3 million in both cases. The only difference is the total of the various accounts within stockholders' equity.

Exhibit 13-4

Korean Export Corporation
Stockholders' Equity
November 30, 1995—Before Stock Dividend

Common stock, $5 par value, 1,000,000 shares authorized, **60,000** shares issued and outstanding	$ 300,000
Paid-in capital in excess of par	800,000
Retained earnings	1,900,000
Total stockholders' equity	$3,000,000

3. In this example, it is assumed that the dividend was declared and issued at the same time. In reality, a period of time may elapse before the declared stock dividend is actually issued to the stockholders. Although this changes the required journal entries slightly, it does not change the effect of the dividend either when declared or issued.

Exhibit 13-5

Korean Export Corporation Stockholders' Equity November 30, 1995—After Stock Dividend	
Common stock, $5 par value, 1,000,000 shares authorized, **66,000** shares issued and outstanding	$ 330,000
Paid-in capital in excess of par	1,010,000
Retained earnings	1,660,000
Total stockholders' equity	$3,000,000

Large Versus Small Stock Dividends. Up to this point, the discussion has involved small stock dividends, which range up to 20% or 25%. Occasionally, a corporation will issue a large stock dividend, defined by the accounting profession as one in excess of 20% to 25%. Some stock dividends are as large as 100%; these have the effect of proportionately reducing the market price of the corporation's stock. Large stock dividends are recorded by debiting Retained Earnings and crediting Common Stock for the total par value of the stock issued by the stock dividend. The market value of the stock is ignored.

Stock Splits

stock split

A **stock split** occurs when a corporation increases the number of its common shares and proportionally decreases their par or stated value. The end result is a doubling, tripling, or quadrupling of the number of outstanding shares and a corresponding decrease in the market price per share of the stock. This price decrease is the main reason that a corporation decides to split its stock. When the market price per share is too high, the stock loses its attractiveness to many investors, because it is most economical to purchase stock in "round lots" of 100 shares. While shares of stock may be purchased (sold) in any quantity, most investors buy (sell) in multiples of 100 shares since brokerage fees on round lots make the per share cost lower than buying (selling) in partial lots. A stock price that is too high makes round-lot purchases impossible for some potential investors. For example, if a firm's stock is currently selling for $240, and the firm splits its stock 4 for 1, the price per share will fall to around $60. Thus, it takes only $6,000 rather than $24,000 to purchase 100 shares.

To illustrate, in February 1992 the Walt Disney Company announced a 4-for-1 stock split. According to the report in the *Los Angeles Times*:

Entertainment giant Walt Disney Co., whose stock surged to record levels this year, said Tuesday that its Board of Directors voted for a 4-for-1 stock split. Chairman Michael Eisner announced the plan at the company's annual meeting at Disney World. This news brought cheers from the 4,000 stockholders in attendance.

"The price of our shares has recently moved higher after having been well above the $100 figure for most of the past three years," Eisner said. "By taking this action, our board hopes to make Disney shares accessible to a broader segment of the investing public."

Disney's shares jumped $3.50 to $146.50 on the New York Stock Exchange. . . . Stock splits do not directly increase the value to a shareholder, but they are a bullish sign for Wall Street and share prices typically rise when a company announces a split.[4]

4. *Los Angeles Times*, February 19, 1992, Part D, p. 1.

Exhibit 13-6

Moreno Corporation Stockholders' Equity—Before Stock Split	
Common stock, $15 par value, 1,000,000 shares authorized, 50,000 shares issued and outstanding	$ 750,000
Additional paid-in capital	1,450,000
Retained earnings	1,800,000
Total stockholders' equity	$4,000,000

To demonstrate the accounting for stock splits, assume that the Moreno Corporation's stockholders' equity accounts are as shown in Exhibit 13-6. The corporation's stock is currently selling at $90 per share. The firm decides to issue a 3-for-1 stock split. As a result, the corporation reduces the par value of its stock from $15 to $5 and increases the number of shares issued and outstanding from 50,000 to 150,000. Although no journal entry is required, some firms will make a memorandum entry noting the stock split. Immediately after the stock split, the Moreno Corporation's stockholders' equity accounts are as shown in Exhibit 13-7. As you can see by comparing the corporation's stockholders' equity accounts before and after the stock split, there is no change in either total stockholders' equity or in the individual components. Only the par value and the number of issued and outstanding shares are different.

From the investor's viewpoint, each stockholder receives two additional shares for each share owned. In effect, the old shares are canceled, and shares with the new par value are issued. Because the price of the firm's stock is likely to fall to about $30, the total market value of each stockholder's investment immediately after the split will be about the same as it was before the split. Obviously, it is the hope of the corporation and its stockholders that the per share price of the stock will begin to increase.

Stock splits and large stock dividends are quite similar. They both serve to reduce the market price per share and increase the number of shares issued and outstanding. In each circumstance, total stockholders' equity remains the same, because there has been neither an increase nor a decrease in the entity's net assets. For example, a 2-for-1 stock split is similar to a 100% stock dividend. In both cases, the number of shares issued and outstanding doubles, and the market price per share should fall accordingly. However, if this event is a stock dividend, there will be no change in the stock's par or stated value, but there will be a decrease in the retained earnings account and an increase in the common stock account. If this event is a stock split, there is no change in either the retained earnings

Exhibit 13-7

Moreno Corporation Stockholders' Equity—After Stock Split	
Common stock, $5 par value, 3,000,000 shares authorized, 150,000 shares issued and outstanding	$ 750,000
Additional paid-in capital	1,450,000
Retained earnings	1,800,000
Total stockholders' equity	$4,000,000

account or the common stock account, just a decrease in par value and an increase in the number of issued and outstanding shares.

TREASURY STOCK AND RETIREMENT OF CAPITAL STOCK

Objective 8
Describe the effect of treasury stock transactions on financial accounting information.

treasury stock

Treasury stock is the corporation's own capital stock, either common or preferred, that has been issued and subsequently reacquired by the firm but not canceled. Such stock, held in the corporate treasury, loses its right to vote, receive dividends, or receive assets upon liquidation.

There are a number of valid business reasons why a firm may reacquire its own capital stock. For example, a firm may need to acquire additional shares (1) for employee stock option or bonus plans, (2) for mergers and acquisitions, (3) in order to support the price of its stock, (4) because the firm may believe the stock is a good investment, or (5) to stop a hostile takeover.

Accounting for Treasury Stock

Treasury stock is not considered an asset; it is a reduction in stockholders' equity. Nor can a firm record a profit or loss on the subsequent sale of treasury stock. Any difference between the reacquisition price and the selling price requires an adjustment to the equity accounts.

Recording the Purchase of Treasury Stock. To show how the purchase of treasury stock is recorded, assume that the stockholders' equity section of the Linefsky Corporation at September 30, 1994, is as shown in Exhibit 13-8. On October 1, the corporation repurchased 1,000 shares of its common stock at $24 per share. This transaction is recorded by debiting the stockholders' equity account, Treasury Stock, and crediting Cash for the cost of the purchase as follows:

Oct. 1, 1994	Treasury Stock	24,000	
	Cash		24,000
	To record purchase of 1,000 shares of treasury stock at $24 per share.		

Immediately after this purchase, the stockholders' equity section of the Linefsky Corporation appears as shown in Exhibit 13-9. As this partial balance sheet shows, treasury stock is not shown as an asset but as a negative item in stockholders' equity. The effect of the transaction is to reduce both assets and stockholders' equity by $24,000.

Exhibit 13-8

Linefsky Corporation
Stockholders' Equity
September 30, 1994

Common stock, $5 par value, 100,000 shares authorized, 10,000 shares issued and outstanding	$ 50,000
Paid-in capital in excess of par	150,000
Retained earnings	700,000
Total stockholders' equity	$900,000

Exhibit 13-9

Linefsky Corporation Stockholders' Equity October 1, 1994	
Common stock, $5 par value, 100,000 shares authorized, 10,000 shares issued, of which 9,000 are outstanding	$ 50,000
Paid-in capital in excess of par	150,000
Retained earnings	700,000
Less 1,000 shares of treasury stock at cost	(24,000)
Total stockholders' equity	$876,000

The corporation can sell its treasury stock any time that it desires. The subsequent resale can be either above or below its repurchase price. In no case, however, is net income for the current period affected.

Recording Subsequent Sales of Treasury Stock. Exhibit 13-10 shows the journal entries necessary to record the subsequent sale of treasury stock under two independent cases: (1) the resale price is greater than the original cost and (2) the resale price is less than the original cost. When treasury stock is sold at a price that is greater than its cost (Case 1), Cash is debited for the entire proceeds, Treasury Stock is credited for the original cost of the stock being sold, and Paid-In Capital from Sale of Treasury Stock Above Cost is credited for the difference. Remember the economic gain is recorded as part of contributed capital because tax and accounting rules do not allow a corporation to *increase* retained earnings by dealing in its own stock.

If treasury stock is resold at a price that is less than its original cost (Case 2), there will be an economic loss. This loss does not affect current period income, but reduces the credit balance in the paid-in capital account. Paid-in Capital in Excess of Par is debited for the remaining amount. Then, if necessary, Retained Earnings is debited. In the particular example illustrated in Case 2, Paid-in Capital from Sale of Treasury Stock Above Cost is debited for only $3,000, the balance

Exhibit 13-10

Journal Entries for Resale of Treasury Stock

Case 1: Sale of 500 shares of treasury stock at $30 per share originally purchased at $24 per share

Cash	15,000	
Treasury Stock		12,000
Paid-in Capital from Sale of Treasury Stock Above Cost		3,000

Case 2: Sale of 500 shares of treasury stock at $15 per share originally purchased at $24 per share

Cash	7,500	
Paid-in Capital from Sale of Treasury Stock Above Cost	3,000	
Paid-in Capital in Excess of Par from Issue of Common Stock	1,500	
Treasury Stock		12,000

in that account which resulted from the transaction in Case 1. The remaining $1,500 of the $4,500 economic loss is charged to Paid-in Capital in Excess of Par from Issue of Common Stock.

Retirement of Capital Stock

Occasionally, a corporation may repurchase its stock with the intent to retire it rather than to hold it in the treasury. Essentially, a corporation retires its stock for some of the same reasons that it purchases treasury stock. As with treasury stock transactions, income or loss for the current period is not affected, nor can retained earnings be increased when capital stock is retired.

OTHER ITEMS AFFECTING RETAINED EARNINGS

Objective 9
Describe other transactions affecting retained earnings including prior period adjustments and appropriation of retained earnings.

There are several other transactions into which a firm may enter that could affect retained earnings. These include prior period adjustments, appropriations of retained earnings, and foreign currency adjustments. The first two are briefly explained next.

Prior Period Adjustments

prior period adjustments

Under the all-inclusive concept of income, all items of profit and loss recognized during the period are included in net income for the period, with a few exceptions. These exceptions relate mainly to **prior period adjustments,** and they are accounted for by an adjustment to the beginning balance of retained earnings. There has been considerable controversy about what causes an event to qualify as a prior period adjustment. The correction of an error in the financial statements of a prior period is the primary event accountants consider to be a prior period adjustment.

Occasionally, a firm will discover a material error in a prior year's financial statements. Material errors are very rare, especially when a firm's financial statements are audited by a CPA firm. When they do occur and are discovered, however, the manner in which the error is corrected depends on whether the firm publishes single-year or comparative financial statements and on the year in which the error was made.

When single-year statements are published, the error is corrected by adjusting the beginning balance of Retained Earnings on the retained earnings statement. To demonstrate accounting for prior period adjustments in a single-year statement, assume that during the audit of its 1994 statements, the Mandrin Corporation discovered that depreciation on its building had been understated by $100,000 in 1994 (net of any tax effect). Because this is a material error, a prior period adjustment is required. The following journal entry is made in 1995 at year-end to correct this error:

Dec. 31, 1995	Retained Earnings	100,000	
	Accumulated Depreciation—Building		100,000
	To record error in 1994 through a prior period adjustment.		

The 1995 Statement of Retained Earnings would appear as shown in Exhibit 13-11. In addition, the prior period adjustment would be explained in the notes to the financial statement.

Exhibit 13-11

Mandrin Corporation Statement of Retained Earnings For the Year Ended December 31, 1995		
Retained earnings, January 1, 1995	$5,000,000	
Less: Prior period adjustment for error correction, net of tax	(100,000)	
Retained earnings, January 1, 1995 restated		$4,900,000
Net income for 1995		650,000
Less: Dividends		(150,000)
Retained earnings, December 31, 1995		$5,400,000

When comparative financial statements are presented, the procedure is different. If the error is in an earlier financial statement that is being presented for comparative purposes, that statement should be revised to correct the error. As a result, net income will be corrected, and after that corrected net income figure is reflected on the retained earnings statement, no further adjustment is required. If the error is in a year for which the financial statements are not being presented, the correction is made through a prior period adjustment to the earliest retained earnings balance presented.

Appropriation of Retained Earnings

appropriation of retained earnings

An **appropriation of retained earnings** occurs when the board of directors transfers a portion of the retained earnings account into a separate appropriated retained earnings account. The sole purpose of such a transfer is to indicate to stockholders and others that the balance in Appropriated Retained Earnings is not available for dividends. Thus, by appropriating retained earnings, the firm limits the amount of dividends it can declare.

The board may appropriate retained earnings in order to limit dividends voluntarily in the hope of conserving cash for projects such as the purchase of new buildings. In other cases, creditors may force the board to appropriate retained earnings and thus limit dividends. The creditors do so in the hope that the firm will not use its cash to pay dividends rather than make timely interest and principal payments.

In order to appropriate retained earnings, the firm debits Retained Earnings and credits Appropriated Retained Earnings. For example, if the Clayborn Corporation decides to appropriate retained earnings of $1 million for future plant expansion, out of a total of $7,435,000 in retained earnings, it will make the following entry:

Retained Earnings	1,000,000	
Appropriated Retained Earnings—Plant Expansion		1,000,000
To appropriate $1,000,000 of retained earnings for future plant expansion.		

Immediately after this entry, the Stockholders' Equity section of the Clayborn Corporation balance sheet appears as shown in Exhibit 13-12. If the appropriation is no longer needed or required, the Retained Earnings will be credited, and Appropriated Retained Earnings will be debited.

Exhibit 13-12

Clayborn Corporation Stockholders' Equity	
Common stock, no par, 1,000,000 shares issued, 500,000 shares issued and outstanding	$2,465,000
Retained earnings, unappropriated	6,435,000
Appropriated retained earnings, future plant expansion	1,000,000
Total stockholders' equity	$9,900,000

These entries point out the problem with the appropriation of retained earnings and some of the confusion surrounding it. If you review the entry to appropriate retained earnings, you will see that no cash is involved. Thus, retained earnings can be appropriated each year, but there is no guarantee that the cash will be there for its intended use. Although the amount of dividends is limited by appropriating retained earnings, cash can still be used for other purposes. The only way to ensure the availability of cash is to create a special cash fund and to set aside a certain amount each year. To the extent that users believe that appropriated retained earnings ensure that cash in that amount is available, it is a misleading concept.

Because of these issues, corporations seldom appropriate retained earnings. Instead, voluntary or required dividend restrictions are disclosed in the notes to the financial statements. For example, the following note was included in the 1991 annual report of AMR, Inc.

AMR Inc. Note Disclosure

The debt and credit facility agreements of American contain certain restrictive covenants, including a minimum net worth requirement and limitations on indebtedness and the declaration of dividends on shares of its capital stock. Such restrictions could affect AMR's ability to pay dividends. At December 31, 1991, under the most restrictive provisions of those agreements, approximately $1.7 billion of American's retained earnings was available for payment of cash dividends to AMR.

Certain of AMR's debt agreements contain restrictive covenants, including a limitation on the declaration of dividends on shares of capital stock. At December 31, 1991, under the terms of such agreements, all of AMR's retained earnings were available for payment of dividends.

USE OF STOCK INFORMATION

Objective 10
Use stock information in making decisions.

After the stock of a major corporation is issued, it trades on a national exchange, such as the New York or the American Stock Exchange, or possibly on a regional exchange. To evaluate a corporation, present and potential investors and creditors look at the market price of the stock and other indicators.

Market Value

The market value per share refers to the price at which a particular stock is currently trading. Clearly, this market price is most objective when there is a large market for the stock on a national exchange. In effect, the price is set by many individuals all acting independently as they buy and sell shares of stock. Such factors as general economic conditions, interest rates, the perceived risk of the company, expectations concerning future profits, and present and expected dividends contribute to the stock's current market price.

The Stock Page. The current market price of stocks traded on a major exchange is listed in major newspapers. A stock page (May 28, 1993) listing for Walt Disney is reproduced as follows:

High	*Low*	*Stock*	*Dividend*	*Yield*	*52-week P-E Ratio*	*Sales 100's*	*High*	*Low*	*Last*	*Change*
47 7/8	32 3/4	Disney	$.25	0.6	26	7,138	44 1/4	43 3/4	44	−3/8

The 52-week high and low columns show the highest and lowest price of the stock during the previous 52 weeks, including the current day. In this situation, Disney's high for the previous year was $47.875, and its low was $32.75. The dividend column shows the latest annual dividend, which, in Disney's case, is $0.25.

The yield column indicates the rate of return that a stockholder would receive if the stock were purchased at its latest price. In the Disney example, an annual dividend of $0.25 on an investment of $44.00 (last price) represents a yield of 0.6% (0.0057), calculated as follows:

$$\text{Yield} = \frac{\text{Annual dividend}}{\text{Current market price}}$$

$$0.57\% = \frac{\$.25}{\$44.00} \times 100$$

price-earnings (P-E) ratio

The **price-earnings (P-E) ratio** is a ratio used by many investors and analysts to compare stocks. The P-E ratio is calculated by means of the following formula:

$$\frac{\text{Current market price}}{\text{Earnings per share}}$$

earnings per share (EPS)

Earnings per share (EPS) shows the amount of current earnings available to common shareholders on a per share basis. Essentially, it is calculated by dividing the earnings available to common stockholders (net income less preferred dividends) by the average number of shares outstanding.[5] The P-E ratio uses these data to help investors compare firms having different market prices and earnings. For Disney, the P-E ratio of 29 is calculated as follows:

$$29 = \frac{\$44.00}{\$1.5172}$$

This means that Disney was selling at a multiple of 29, or 29 times its EPS. This can be used to compare alternative investments. For example, Paramount Communications, a somewhat similar company, has a PE ratio of 37, indicating that its stock sells at 37 times its EPS.

5. Financial statements may state primary earnings per share (PEPS) and fully diluted earnings per share (FDEPS). The calculation of these can be quite complex and the topic of an intermediate or advanced accounting course. For purposes of this text simple earnings per share (EPS) is sufficient.

The last five columns are relatively straightforward. The sales column, which is in 100s, indicates the total sales for the day. During the day being considered, 713,800 shares of Disney stock changed hands. The high and low columns show the highest and lowest price at which the stock traded during the day. The next column indicates the price of the last trade of the day, and the change column shows the net change from the prior day's last trade.

Book Value per Share

book value per share

Book value per share of common stock indicates the net assets represented by one share of common stock. Thus, book value is the equity that the owner of one share of common stock has in the net assets (assets minus liabilities), or stockholders' equity, of the corporation. It is the amount that each share would receive if the firm were liquidated and the firm received the amount shown on the balance sheet for the various assets less the liabilities. It is important to remember, however, that the term *value* in this sense does not mean market value or current value. Because the firm's net assets are recorded at historical cost less the write-offs to date, value is in terms of these historical costs, not in terms of market value or liquidation value. Thus, there is no particular reason that book value and market value per share should be related.

Book Value When Only Common Stock Is Outstanding. When a firm has only common stock outstanding, the book value per share is calculated as follows:

$$\text{Book value per share} = \frac{\text{Total stockholders' equity}}{\text{Number of common shares outstanding}}$$

To illustrate, let's return to Albertson's. (See Appendix A for the appropriate data.) The year-end 1991 book value per share of \$9.08 is calculated as follows:

$$\$9.08 = \frac{\$1{,}199{,}452{,}000}{132{,}130{,}528 \text{ shares}}$$

The denominator of 132,130,528 is from the capital stock note in the financial statements.

In comparison to the book value of \$9.08 price of Albertson's stock ranged between \$32.75 and \$51.275 during 1991.

Book Value When Both Common and Preferred Stock Are Outstanding. Book value refers to the common stockholders' interest in the firm's net assets. Thus, when preferred stock is outstanding, total stockholders' equity must be reduced by the preferred stockholders' claims to arrive at the common stockholders' equity. This is usually done by subtracting the liquidation or redemption value of the preferred stock and any dividends in arrears from the total stockholders' equity. Data from the Sears, Roebuck and Co. balance sheet at December 31, 1991 is reproduced in Exhibit 13-13, and will be used to demonstrate this procedure. Total stockholders' equity is \$14,188,200,000. The liquidation value of the preferred stock, \$325,000,000 (3,250 shares at \$100 liquidation value per share—not shown in Exhibit 13-13) must be subtracted to determine the common stockholders' equity of \$13,863,200,000. The firm had 344,100,000 common shares issued and outstanding at December 31, 1991.

The book value per share is \$36.56, calculated as follows:

$$\$40.29 = \frac{\$13{,}863{,}200{,}000}{344{,}100{,}000 \text{ shares}}$$

Exhibit 13-13

Sears, Roebuck and Co.
Excerpt from Consolidated Statement of Financial Position
(in millions)

	December 31 1991	December 31 1990
Commitments and contingent liabilities (notes 6, 10, 11, 13, 14)		
Shareholders' equity (note 14)		
Preferred shares ($1 par value, 325 shares outstanding in 1991)	$ 325.0	$ —
Common shares ($.75 par value, 344.1 and 343.1 shares outstanding)	289.5	289.1
Capital in excess of par value	2,153.4	2,137.9
Retained income	13,514.3	12,927.1
Treasury stock (at cost)	(1,746.4)	(1,765.8)
Deferred ESOP expense (note 6)	(739.4)	(777.7)
Unrealized net capital gains (losses) on marketable equity securities	365.5	(12.9)
Cumulative translation adjustments	26.3	26.1
Total shareholders' equity	$14,188.2	$12,823.8

At year-end 1991, Sear's common stock was selling at $37.875 (37 7/8) —somewhat less than its book value.

In these examples, the common stock of one company, Alberson's, was trading above its book value and the common stock of the other, Sear's, was trading below its book value. Market conditions, investor expectations, its financial condition and profitability, and other factors all affect the price of a firm's common stock. Thus, in some cases the market price may be below book value and in other cases above.

FINANCIAL CYCLE CONTROLS

Objective 11
Describe the types of procedures and techniques used to maintain control over debt and equity transactions and the associated accounting records.

financial cycle

The revenue and expenditure transaction cycles were introduced earlier in this book. Most business events in merchandising firms are processed by these two transaction cycles. However, as you have learned in the last two chapters, business events include more than acquiring goods and services (expenditure cycle transactions) and then selling those goods and services to customers (revenue cycle). Businesses also raise significant amounts of capital in the debt and equity markets and then invest the capital in productive resources. Capital acquisition and investment events are processed by the **financial cycle.**

Two types of business transactions are accounted for by the financial cycle: (1) capital acquisition transactions, and (2) capital investment transactions. The systems found within the financial cycle are the general ledger system (including journal entry), the financial reporting system, and the operating asset or property accounting system. The relationships between these systems are illustrated in Exhibit 13-14. The financial cycle, unlike the revenue and expenditure cycles, is not a true cycle but a collection of systems to account for the acquisition and use of capital resources.

Exhibit 13-14
Financial Cycle

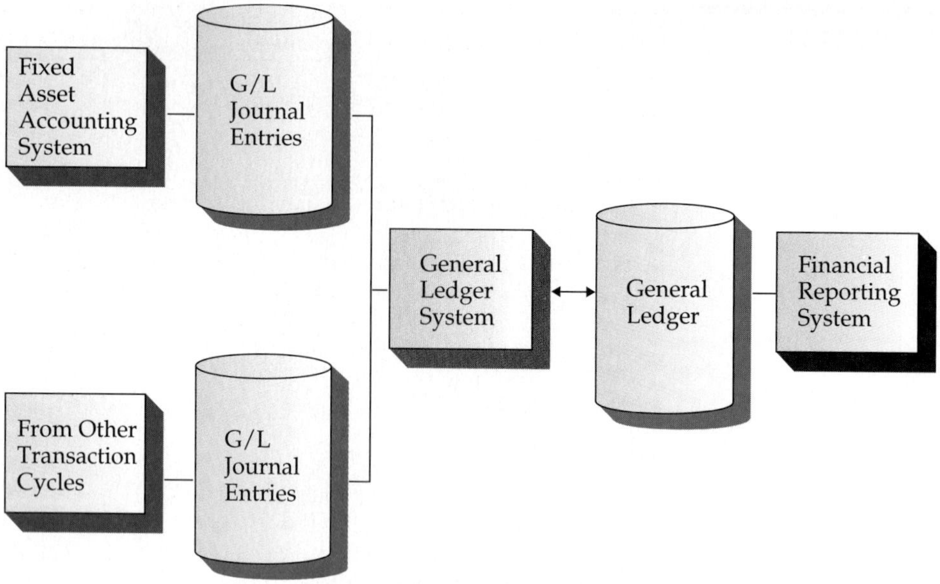

Capital is acquired through the issuance of long-term debt instruments, such as bonds, and through medium- to long-term bank loans, such as mortgages. As illustrated in this chapter, capital is also acquired by issuing stock. These capital-acquisition transactions occur less frequently than revenue and expenditure transactions, and are more material. Consequently, the journal entries for these transactions are normally entered manually into the general ledger system. Controls over these transactions are important because the transactions occur infrequently, they are large, and they are manually processed.

Controls

Authorization procedures and segregation of functions are the most common and most effective controls over debt and equity transactions.

Authorization Controls. Organizations should have formal procedures for the authorization of bank loans, bond issues, and stock transactions. Most frequently, approval by the board of directors is required before an organization can enter into a long-term bank loan, or issue bonds or stock. This approval must be noted in the minutes of the Board of Director's meeting. Approval of the chief financial officer or treasurer is usually required for less material short-term bank loans.

Segregation of Functions. Proper segregation of functions over debt and equity transactions is achieved in several ways. Transaction authorization is segregated from transaction recording. As noted above, transactions are authorized by the board of directors, or by the treasurer. The transactions are recorded by the controller's staff, thus segregating transaction authorization and transaction recording. Organizations often use other control techniques to further segregate functions for bond and stock issues.

independent trustee

An **independent trustee** is frequently used to provide additional control over bond transactions. The trustee, often a large bank, performs several important functions. The trustee maintains a record of all bondholders and updates the list when they sell their bonds to others. The trustee also maintains physical control over the bond certificates and cancels old certificates and issues new ones when bonds are traded. Finally, the bond issuer makes the interest payments to the trustee who, in turn, makes the interest payments to the individual bond holders. The trustee, by performing these functions, ensures that individual bond transactions are performed correctly and relieves the issuer of the responsibility of accounting for individual investor-level transactions.

independent registrar

transfer agent

Corporations use an *independent registrar* and a *transfer agent* to process stock transactions. Large banks also perform these functions. The **independent registrar** represents the stockholders and reviews all stock transactions to ensure that they have been approved by a company's board of directors. The registrar also monitors stock transactions to ensure that the number of shares issued never exceeds the number of shares authorized. The **transfer agent** maintains a record of all of the stockholders, updates the record when stock is traded, issues new shares of stock to new owners and cancels certificates when they are sold. In addition, the transfer agent receives dividend payments from the corporation and then makes the dividend payments to the individual stockholders. These functions, like those of the independent trustee, improve control by segregating some functions, and by providing an external review over transaction authorization and execution.

Document Controls. Bond and stock certificates are negotiable instruments. These documents, which evidence either a debt or equity interest in an organization, can be bought and sold in the market. Consequently, they, like cash, are susceptible to theft. Several control techniques are used to prevent the loss or theft of these documents. They should always be stored in a secure, locked location. Access to the unissued documents should be restricted and controlled. Finally, the documents, like unused checks, should be prenumbered and accounted for.

SUMMARY OF LEARNING OBJECTIVES

1. List the characteristics of the corporate form of organization, including advantages and disadvantages. Corporations are separate legal entities with a continuous life. Advantages of the corporate form include limited liability, transferability of ownership, and ease of capital formation. Disadvantages of the corporate form include double taxation, government regulation, and in some cases the limited liability feature.

2. Explain how corporations are formed and organized. Corporations are chartered by individual states and must comply with state and federal regulations. Control of a corporation lies ultimately with the common stockholders, who entrust this power to the board of directors. The board is responsible for setting broad corporate policies and appointing senior management.

3. List the characteristics of capital stock: common and preferred. Common and preferred stock are the two major types of capital stock. All corporations must issue common stock, and most common shareholders have the following rights:

a. The right to vote.
b. The right to a proportionate share of dividends when declared.
c. The right to a proportionate share of assets upon liquidation.
d. The preemptive right.

Preferred stockholders have certain preferences over common shareholders with respect to dividends and assets upon liquidation.

4. Describe the components of stockholders' equity. Stockholders' equity consists of contributed capital, retained earnings, treasury stock (if any), and, in some situations, certain debit items. Contributed capital is often divided into legal capital and additional paid-in capital. Legal capital is based on the par or stated value of the issued and outstanding shares. If true no par stock is issued, the legal capital will be the entire issue price of the stock. Sources of additional paid-in capital include the issue of capital stock in excess of par, sale of treasury stock above par, and donated capital.

5. Discuss and apply the accounting concepts and procedures related to the issuance of capital stock. If par value or no par stock with a stated value is issued, the capital stock account should be credited for the par or stated value. Additional Paid-in Capital in Excess of Par (or Stated Value) from the Sale of Capital Stock is credited for the difference between the issue price and the par or stated value. If true no par stock is issued, the capital stock account should be credited for the entire amount.

6. Describe and record the different types of dividends issued by corporations. Determining the amount and type of dividends a corporation will issue is a strategic decision made by management and the corporation's board of directors. Firms attempt to establish a stable dividend policy. Most firms issue cash dividends, but they can also declare and issue stock and property dividends.

7. Differentiate between stock splits and stock dividends. Stock splits are used by firms to decrease the price of their stock in order to make round-lot purchases more attractive to investors. Neither stock dividends nor stock splits change the firm's total assets or total stockholders' equity. Stock dividends do, however, change the balances in Retained Earnings and Common Stock and possibly Additional Paid-in Capital accounts.

8. Describe the effect of treasury stock transactions on financial accounting information. A firm may repurchase its own stock for a number of reasons. This stock is called *treasury stock.* These transactions neither result in an asset nor affect the current period's income. Any economic gain on the subsequent resale of treasury stock is credited to Additional Paid-in Capital account, and any economic loss is debited to Additional Paid-in Capital and/or Retained Earnings.

9. Describe other transactions affecting retained earnings including prior period adjustments and appropriation of retained earnings. Prior period adjustments and appropriation of retained earnings are two additional items that affect retained earnings. In recent years, the accounting profession has limited the items that qualify as prior period adjustments. Only error corrections and certain tax benefits qualify. Prior period adjustments are generally handled by adjusting the beginning balance of retained earnings on the statement of retained earnings.

The appropriation of retained earnings is either voluntary or required to restrict dividend payments. However, the balance in the appropriated earnings account does not imply that an equal amount of cash is available. Instead of appropriating retained earnings, many firms that have agreed to dividend and/or other restrictions just disclose these restrictions in the footnotes to the financial statements.

10. Use stock information in making decisions. Present and potential investors use stock information in their evaluation of a particular company. Included are such data as the stock's current market price, its price-earnings (P-E) ratio, and earnings per share (EPS). Book value per share is also used, but it does not provide data on market or liquidation values.

11. Describe the types of procedures and techniques used to maintain control over debt and equity transactions and the associated accounting records. Three broad techniques are used to control debt and equity transactions. Authorization controls are implemented over the issuance of bonds and stock. Accounting functions are segregated from transaction processing functions, often by having an outside party perform the processing functions. Finally, physical controls are implemented to protect critical business documents such as stock and bond certificates.

KEY TERMS

Additional paid-in capital *630*
Appropriation of retained earnings *645*
Board of directors *625*
Book value per share *648*
Call premium *629*
Callable preferred stock *629*
Capitalizing retained earnings *638*
Common stock *627*
Contributed capital *630*
Convertible preferred stock *629*
Date of record *637*
Declaration date *636*
Dividends in arrears *628*
Earnings per share (EPS) *647*
Financial cycle *649*
Independent registrar *651*
Independent trustee *650*
Legal (stated) capital *630*
No par stock *631*
Organization costs *625*
Par value *630*
Payment date *637*
Preferred stock *627*
Price-earnings (P-E) ratio *647*
Prior period adjustments *644*
Proxy *626*
Redeemable preferred stock *629*
Stock dividend *638*
Stock split *640*
Transfer agent *651*
Treasury stock *642*
Underwriters *633*

REVIEW PROBLEMS

A. The Square Pizza Corporation was organized in 1994 to manufacture and distribute square pizzas. The corporation was authorized to issue 5 million shares of $5 par value common stock and 1 million shares of $100, 6% par value preferred stock. The following transactions took place during 1994:

a. January 25: Issued 100,000 shares of common stock at $20 per share.
b. April 10: Issued 1,000 shares of common stock to the firm's attorneys in connection with the organization of the corporation. The fair market value of the attorneys' fees was $25,000.
c. July 1: Issued 10,000 shares of preferred stock at par.

REQUIRED:

1. Prepare the journal entries to record these events.
2. Assuming that net income for the year amounted to $500,000 and no dividends were declared, prepare the stockholders' equity section of the balance sheet at December 31, 1994.

Solution

1

Jan. 25	Cash	2,000,000	
	Common Stock (100,000 × $5)		500,000
	Paid-in Capital in Excess of Par		1,500,000
	To record issue of 100,000 shares of $5 par value common stock at $20 per share.		
April 10	Organization Costs	25,000	
	Common Stock (1,000 × $5)		5,000
	Paid-in Capital in Excess of Par		20,000
	To record issue of 1,000 shares of common stock in connection with organization costs.		
July 1	Cash	1,000,000	
	Preferred Stock		1,000,000
	To record issue of 10,000 shares of preferred stock at par.		

2

The Square Pizza Corporation
Partial Balance Sheet
December 31, 1994

Preferred stock, 6%, $100 par value, 1,000,000 shares authorized and 10,000 shares issued and outstanding	$1,000,000
Common stock, $5 par value, 5,000,000 shares authorized and 101,000 shares issued	505,000
Paid-in capital in excess of par from issue of common stock	1,520,000
Retained earnings	500,000
Total stockholders' equity	$3,525,000

B. Synder Football Equipment Corporation has 100,000 shares of $5 par value common stock outstanding. All stock was originally issued at $12 per share. During the current year, the company entered into the following transactions related to its common stock:

a. March 12: The company repurchased 10,000 shares of its common stock at a price of $22 per share.

b. May 19: The company resold 6,000 of these shares at $26 per share.
c. July 1: The company resold the remaining 4,000 shares held in treasury at $17 per share.
d. November 29: The firm retired 1,000 shares at a price of $15 per share.

REQUIRED: Prepare the journal entries to record these events.

Solution

March 12	Treasury Stock	220,000	
	Cash (10,000 × $22)		220,000
	To record purchase of 10,000 shares of stock at $22 per share.		
May 19	Cash (6,000 × $26)	156,000	
	Paid-in Capital from Sale of Treasury Stock Above Cost (6,000 × $4)		24,000
	Treasury Stock (6,000 × $22)		132,000
	To record sale of 6,000 shares of treasury stock at $26 per share.		
July 1	Cash (4,000 × $17)	68,000	
	Paid-in Capital from Sale of Treasury Stock Above Cost (4,000 × $5)	20,000	
	Treasury Stock (4,000 × $22)		88,000
	To record sale of 4,000 shares of treasury stock at $17 per share.		
Nov. 29	Common Stock (1,000 × $5)	5,000	
	Paid-in Capital in Excess of Par (1,000 × $7)	7,000	
	Retained Earnings ($1,000 × $3)	3,000	
	Cash (1,000 × $15)		15,000
	To record the retirement of 1,000 shares of stock at $15 per share.		

QUESTIONS

1. List and discuss the major characteristics of a corporation.
2. A famous business school professor recently stated that all businesses should be organized as corporations in order to take advantage of their special tax and legal treatment. Do you agree with this statement? Why or why not?
3. Shareholders have certain rights. Describe and discuss these rights and how they differ between common and preferred shareholders.
4. You recently purchased 100 shares of cumulative preferred stock, with a stated dividend of $2 per share. Because the current year's operations were barely profitable, the firm did not declare any dividends. How much in dividends will you be entitled to in the next year?
5. One of your friends invests only in stock with a par value above $10, because she feels this will guarantee that the price of the stock will not fall below this amount. Do you agree with her investment strategy? Why or why not?
6. Which of the following statements, if any, regarding par value is correct? Explain your answer.
   a. All stock must be issued at its par value.
   b. When stock has a par value, the total issue price is credited to the capital stock account.
   c. Par value differs from stated value because the par value is set by the board of directors and the stated value is set by the stock market.
   d. When stock has a par value, the capital stock account is credited for the par value, and the paid-in capital account is credited for the excess of the issue price over the par value.
7. In some circumstances, a corporation issues stock in exchange for services or other assets such as land and buildings. In these situations, what factors must the accountant consider in assigning a dollar value to the exchange?

8. What significance does each of the following dates have to the declaration and payment of cash dividends?
   a. Declaration date
   b. Date of record
   c. Payment date
9. What is a stock dividend? What are the benefits of stock dividends, if any, to the issuing corporation and the existing shareholders?
10. After a stock dividend is issued, what changes occur in total stockholders' equity and within individual components of stockholders' equity?
11. You overheard one of your friends say that stock dividends and stock splits are essentially the same. Do you agree or disagree? Why or why not?
12. The purchase of treasury stock is recorded by a debit to Treasury Stock and a credit to Cash. Treasury stock is shown as an asset on the balance sheet. Comment on these statements.
13. Why does a firm purchase its own stock? Once the purchase is made and the stock is resold, how is the economic gain or loss on the transaction, if any, recorded?
14. What items are considered prior period adjustments, and how are they accounted for?
15. Under what circumstances is a corporation likely to appropriate retained earnings?
16. Describe the yield on common stock and the P-E ratio and explain how they are used by investors.
17. Explain how the book value per share of common stock is calculated (a) when a corporation has only common shares outstanding and (b) when it has both common and preferred shares outstanding.
18. Discuss the meaning and usefulness of book value per share of common stock. Does it provide a good measure of the stock's current or market value?
19. Would you purchase stock in a company just because the price of the stock was below its book value? Why or why not?
20. What is the object of the financial cycle?
21. What systems are normally found in the financial cycle of a corporation?
22. Why would a corporation decide to use an independent registrar and a transfer agent?

EXERCISES

E13-1 Dividends on Preferred and Common Stock

LO 3

The El Tota Corporation has the following shares of stock outstanding:

Common stock, no par	100,000 shares
Preferred stock, cumulative, stated dividend $2	[illegible]000 shares = 40,000

The company had been very profitable until 1993, when its business and profits fell off. In 1993, for the first time in its history, the company was unable to pay all of its required dividends. The board of directors made the following funds available for dividends during 1993, 1994, and 1995:

1993	$32,000
1994	45,000
1995	55,000

REQUIRED: Determine the amount of dividends that the preferred and common shareholders will receive each year.

E13-2 Issuance of Stock

LO 5

The Software Corporation is authorized to issue 80,000 shares of common stock. During the current year, it decides to issue 25,000 shares. Make the required entry to record the issuance of the common stock under each of the following independent situations:

a. The shares have a $5 par value and were sold for $20 per share.
b. The shares are no par but have a stated value of $10. The total issue price was $850,000.

c. The shares are no par and have no stated value. They were issued at $25 per share.
d. The shares are no par and have no stated value. They were issued to an attorney in exchange for services rendered in connection with organizing the corporation. The attorney would normally charge $70,000 for these services. There is no reasonable way to determine the fair market value of the stock.

E13-3
Preparation of the Stockholders' Equity Section
LO 4, 5 & 6

The Baker Corporation was formed in early 1994. At that time, the corporation was authorized to issue 150,000 shares of $10 par value common stock and 70,000 shares of 5%, $100 par value cumulative preferred stock. At the time the corporation was formed, 30,000 shares of common stock were issued at $32 per share. Net income during 1994 amounted to $22,000.

At the beginning of 1995, the firm issued 15,000 shares of the preferred stock at par. Net income during 1995 amounted to $67,000. In addition to the preferred dividends, the firm declared common dividends of $8,000.

REQUIRED: Prepare the stockholders' equity section of the balance sheet as of December 31, 1995, the end of the firm's reporting year.

E13-4
Determining Missing Values
LO 5

The stockholders' equity section of the December 31, 1994, balance sheet of Microexpress appeared as follows:

Preferred stock, 6%, $75 par value, 200,000 shares authorized, 70,000 shares issued	$?
Common stock, $5 stated value, 500,000 shares authorized, ? issued and ? outstanding	500,000
Paid-in capital in excess of par	600,000
Retained earnings	1,000,000
Less: Common stock held in treasury at cost, 10,000 shares	(40,000)
Total stockholders' equity	$?

REQUIRED: Answer each of the following questions:

1. What is the total issue price of the preferred stock?
2. How many shares of common stock were issued?
3. How many shares of common stock are outstanding?
4. What was the total issue price of the common stock?
5. What is the total legal capital of the corporation?
6. What is the total contributed capital of the corporation?
7. What is the total stockholders' equity?
8. For how much per share was the treasury stock purchased?
9. What is the amount of the required preferred dividends?

E13-5
Stock Issued for Noncash Consideration
LO 5

On July 1, the Big Chill Corporation exchanged 2,600 shares of its $4 par value common stock for site land. A few months ago, the land was appraised by an independent appraiser for $100,000.

REQUIRED: Make the required journal entry to record this transaction, given the following two independent assumptions:

1. Big Chill Corporation's stock is currently trading on the New York Stock Exchange at $45 a share.
2. Big Chill Corporation is a privately-held corporation whose stock is owned by five family members. They estimate the stock has a fair market value of $53 per share.

E13-6 Cash Dividends
LO 6

Informatics has 150,000 shares of $7.50 par value common stock outstanding and 75,000 shares of 4%, $100 par value preferred stock outstanding. During December, the board of directors made the following dividend declarations:

On December 1, the board of directors declared that the preferred dividend would be paid on January 4 to preferred shareholders of record on December 25.

On December 10, the board of directors declared a $2.50 per share dividend payable on January 4 to common shareholders of record on December 25.

REQUIRED:

1. Make all the necessary entries related to the declaration and payment of the preferred dividends.
2. Make all the necessary entries related to the declaration and payment of the common dividends.

E13-7 Property Dividends
LO 6

The Klinger Company is a closely-held family corporation. On December 10, 1994, the board of directors decided to declare a property dividend. The dividend was to consist of a plot of land held by the corporation. The land was purchased several years ago at a cost of $240,000. Recently, the land was appraised at $450,000. On January 2, 1995, title to the land was transferred to the Klinger Family Trust.

REQUIRED: Make the entries to record the property dividend.

E13-8 Stock Dividends
LO 7

The Mister Mo Mart has 250,000 shares of $8 par value common stock outstanding. Although the company has been profitable, it has decided to issue stock dividends instead of cash dividends in order to conserve cash for future expansion. On December 10, when the common stock was selling at $31 per share, the board of directors declared a 10% stock dividend to be distributed immediately.

REQUIRED:

1. Make the entries to record the stock dividend.
2. Assume that you own 200 shares of Mister Mo stock that you purchased at $18 per share. How would the stock dividend affect your investment, and how would you account for it?
3. Independent of (1) and (2), now assume that Mister Mo declared a 30% stock dividend instead of the 10% dividend. Make the necessary entry to record the stock dividend.

E13-9 Stock Dividends and Stock Splits
LO 7

On December 31, 1994, the stockholders' equity section of the S. Bates Corporation appeared as follows:

S. Bates Corporation
Partial Balance Sheet
December 31, 1994

Stockholders' equity	
Common stock, $10 par value, 500,000 shares authorized, 300,000 shares issued and outstanding	$3,000,000
Paid-in capital in excess of par	1,500,000
Retained earnings	5,000,000
Total stockholders' equity	$9,500,000

REQUIRED:

1. Assume that on January 2, 1995, the board of directors declared and issued a 10% stock dividend. At that time, the stock was selling at $28 per share. Prepare the stockholders' equity section of the balance sheet after the declaration.
2. Now assume that instead of issuing a stock dividend, the board of directors declared a 2-for-1 stock split on January 2. Prepare the stockholders' equity section of the balance sheet after the stock split.

E13-10
Treasury Stock Transactions
LO 8

Make the appropriate journal entries to record the following treasury stock transactions:

a. January 5: The Truly Modern Corporation repurchases 700 shares of its $5 par value common stock at its current price of $32 per share.
b. April 15: The company resells 300 shares of the treasury stock at $41 per share.
c. November 29: The firm resells 200 additional treasury shares at $27 per share.
d. December 15: The firm sells the remaining 200 shares still held in the treasury at $20 per share.

E13-11
Prior Period Adjustments
LO 9

At the beginning of 1994, Newtonian Incorporated's retained earnings balance was $950,000. During the year, the firm's net income amounted to $132,000, and dividends of $30,000 were paid. During the preparation of the 1994 financial statements, it was discovered that a piece of equipment purchased at the beginning of 1993 at a cost of $80,000 had been entirely expensed in that year. Management feels the equipment has an eight-year life and should be depreciated on the straight-line basis with no salvage value.

REQUIRED:

1. Assuming that the current year's books have not been closed and that the reported income of $132,000 does not reflect the depreciation on the equipment, make the necessary entries to correct the error. Ignore taxes.
2. If single-year statements are published, prepare the retained earnings statement for 1994, based on the corrections made in (1).
3. If comparative 1994 and 1993 statements were prepared, explain how you would handle the error correction. Do not actually prepare new statements.

E13-12
Appropriation of Retained Earnings
LO 9

The Oops Chemical Corporation has been producing an insect spray for a number of years. Recently, it has been discovered that this spray is very dangerous, and the company has been sued by a number of individuals who contracted illnesses. On December 31, 1995, the board of directors decided to appropriate retained earnings in the amount of $50 million to cover future lawsuits. Just before the appropriation, the firm had 200,000 shares of no par, no stated value common stock outstanding that had been issued at an average price of $18 per share. In addition, total retained earnings at that time amounted to $140 million. Several years later, when all the lawsuits had been settled (the ultimate cost to the company was $67 million), the appropriation was removed by the board.

REQUIRED:

1. Make the entry to record the appropriation.
2. Prepare the stockholders' equity section of the balance sheet immediately after the appropriation.
3. Make the journal entry to record the removal of the appropriation.
4. Did the appropriation ensure that the firm had the cash to pay the lawsuits? What other method besides appropriation of retained earnings is available to handle situations such as these?

E13-13 Book Value per Share

LO 10

You have gathered the following data from the 1994 annual report of the STN Corporation:

Total common stockholders equity	$3,570,000
Net income from 1994	$1,780,000
Number of common shares outstanding	750,000
Dividends declared during 1994	$ 1.40 per share
Market price at end of 1994	$14.00 per share
EPS for 1994	$ 3.00

REQUIRED: Determine each of the following at the end of 1994:

1. Dividend yield
2. P-E ratio
3. Book value per share

E13-14 Book Value per Share—Preferred Stock Outstanding

LO 10

Stockholders' equity of the Logus Corporation as of December 31, 1994 is as follows:

Preferred stock, 7%, $100 par value, 30,000 shares authorized and issued (total liquidation value $3,200,000)	$3,000,000
Common stock, no par value, 50,000 shares authorized and issued	1,500,000
Donated capital	500,000
Retained earnings	4,500,000
Total stockholders' equity	$9,500,000

REQUIRED: Determine book value per common share, given the following two independent assumptions:

1. All preferred dividends are fully paid.
2. The preferred shares are cumulative, and the board of directors has decided to forgo all dividends this year.

E13-15 Equity Transaction Controls

LO 11

Identify, for each of the following situations, the one best control that should be implemented to ensure that the problem does not reoccur.

a. An employee accepted receipt of a box of newly printed stock certificates from the engraver. Each certificate represented 100 shares of stock. The employee removed one certificate from the box, completed the certificate in his wife's name, added her name to the stock register, and gave her the certificate as an anniversary present.
b. A clerk, who was assigned to fill out stock certificates, set the box of blank certificates on the floor next to his garbage can. He forgot the box because of repeated interruptions and meetings throughout the afternoon, and went home without replacing the unused certificates in the vault. The janitor assumed that the box of "old-looking" forms was garbage and threw it in the dumpster that evening while cleaning offices.
c. Accent, Inc., which has over 24,000 individual investors, must add an additional three employees this year just to keep up with stock ownership changes so that dividend checks can be properly disbursed. Management is concerned with this increasing cost which doesn't add any value to the firm's products.

E13-16
Albertson's Financial Statements
LO 10

Using the information contained in the Albertson's financial statements in Appendix A, answer the following questions:

a. What is the total legal capital of the corporation as of January 30, 1992?
b. What is the total contributed capital of the corporation as of January 30, 1992?
c. Determine the book value per share at January 30, 1992.
d. Earnings per share for the year ended January 30, 1992 were $1.94 and the common stock closed on that day at a price of $39.125 (39 1/8). Determine the P-E ratio.

PROBLEMS

P13-1
Preparation of Stockholders' Equity Section
LO 4

At the beginning of 1994, the Softlite Corporation was formed. The firm issued 60,000 of the 100,000 authorized shares of $3 par value common stock for $35 per share. In addition, the firm issued all 2,000 authorized shares of $100, 5% par value preferred. During the year the firm's net income amounted to $92,000. All dividends on the preferred shares were declared; no dividends on the common were declared. Finally, at the end of the year, the city of Westbridge donated a plot of land to the firm. The land was originally purchased by the city for $130,000 and had a fair market value of $76,000 at the time it was donated to Softlite.

REQUIRED: Prepare in good form the stockholders' equity section of Softlite's balance sheet at the end of 1994.

P13-2
Issuance of Stock
LO 5

In early 1994, Gerald Weinstein and several associates formed the Pico National Bank. The corporation was authorized to issue 500,000 shares of $100, 3% par value preferred stock and 1 million shares of $12 par value common stock. The following transactions occurred during 1994:

a. March 1: Sold 125,000 shares of common stock to a group of investors at $40 per share.
b. March 9: Issued 4,500 shares of the preferred stock to an individual in exchange for a building. The building was appraised at $655,000. It was impossible to determine the fair market value of the stock.
c. April 1: Issued 2,400 shares of common stock to the bank's attorney in exchange for services rendered in forming the corporation. The stock was currently selling at $50 per share. All parties agreed that this represented the value of the attorney's services.
d. December 1: Issued an additional 6,250 shares of preferred stock at $130 per share.
e. December 15: The bank had a very profitable year, so the board of directors decided to declare the stated dividend to the preferred shareholders as well as a $1.25 per share dividend to the common shareholders.
f. December 31: The dividends were paid in cash.

REQUIRED:

1. Make the journal entries to record these transactions.
2. Assuming that net income for the year amounted to $2.5 million, prepare the stockholders' equity section of the balance sheet at the end of December.

P13-3
Stock Transactions
LO 5, 6 & 8

Jackson Corporation was authorized to issue 900,000 shares of $100, 5% par value preferred stock and 1.5 million shares of no par $5 stated value common stock. The following transactions occurred during 1995:

a. January 2: 24,000 shares of common stock were sold to a group of investors at $24 per share.
b. January 15: 5,500 shares of preferred stock were issued to an individual in exchange for a plot of land to be held for future development. The land was appraised at $795,000. The preferred stock was not actively traded.

c. March 31: 2,500 shares of common stock were issued to an attorney in exchange for services rendered in forming the corporation. The stock was currently trading at $31 a share. All parties agreed that this represented the value of the attorney's services.
d. October 20: An additional 7,000 shares of common stock were issued at $45 per share.
e. October 31: 1,400 shares of common stock were repurchased at $35 per share. The shares are to be held in treasury.
f. November 15: An additional 1,000 shares of preferred stock were issued at $125 a share.
g. November 30: The firm resold 600 shares of the stock held in treasury at a price of $41 per share.
h. December 31: Preferred dividends were declared and paid in cash.

REQUIRED:

1. Make the journal entries to record these transactions.
2. Assuming that net income for the year amounted to $450,000, prepare the stockholders' equity section of the balance sheet at December 31, 1995.

P13-4
Preparation of the Stockholders' Equity Section
LO 5, 6 & 8

Adventure, Inc. was formed in early 1993. The following events occurred from 1993 through 1995:

1993

a. Issued 500,000 shares of 1,000,000 authorized of no par, no stated value common stock at $20 per share.
b. Issued 10,000 shares of 20,000 authorized of $100, 5% cumulative preferred stock at $105 per share.
c. The net loss for the year was $200,000. No dividends were declared.

1994

d. An additional 10,000 shares of common stock were issued at $15 per share.
e. Issued 5,000 shares of 10,000 authorized of $100, 8% preferred stock at par.
f. The net income for the year was $10,000. No dividends were declared.

1995

g. A plot of land was donated to the corporation by the city. The land was appraised at $100,000.
h. The firm repurchased 10,000 shares of its common stock at a price of $22 per share. The shares will be held in treasury.
i. Net income for the year amounted to $800,000. A $.10 per share dividend was paid on common stock. In addition, all required preferred dividends were declared and paid.

REQUIRED: Prepare in good form the stockholders' equity section of the balance sheet as of December 31, 1995.

P13-5
Determining Missing Figures
LO 4 & 10

Recently, California Valley Federal Savings and Loan converted from a depositor-owned savings and loan association to a publicly-held one. The stockholders' equity section of its 1995 balance sheet appears as follows (after conversion and with certain details omitted):

Stockholders' equity	
5% preferred stock, $100 par value, authorized 100,000 shares (liquidation value $110 per share)	$1,000,000
Common stock, no par value, stated value $5, authorized 1,000,000, issued 500,000	?
Paid-in capital in excess of stated value	4,000,000
Retained earnings	8,000,000

REQUIRED: Based on the above information, answer the following questions:

1. How many shares of preferred stock are outstanding?
2. At what price was the preferred stock issued?
3. What is the total of stockholders' equity?
4. What was the average issue price of the common stock?
5. What is the total contributed capital of the savings and loan association?
6. What is the total legal capital of the savings and loan association?
7. What is the book value per share of common stock?
8. What is the total dividend requirement on the preferred stock?
9. What is the total dividend requirement on the common stock?

P13-6 Stockholders' Equity Transactions

LO 5, 6 & 7

The stockholders' equity section of Federated Markets' balance sheet at December 31, 1994, is as follows:

Common stock, $10 stated value stock, authorized 1,000,000 shares, issued 75,000 shares	$ 750,000
Paid-in capital in excess of stated value	525,000
Paid-in capital from sale of treasury stock above cost	25,000
Retained earnings	900,000
Total stockholders' equity	$2,200,000

The following events occurred during 1995:

a. January 2: Sold 12,000 shares of unissued common stock for $22 per share.
b. January 20: Declared a cash dividend of $.30 per share, payable on February 20 to shareholders of record on February 10.
c. February 5: Exchanged 6,200 shares of authorized but unissued common stock for 600 acres of land. The stock had a fair market value of $25 per share.
d. February 20: Dividend declared on January 20 paid.
e. March 1: A 2-for-1 stock split was declared: per share market value $42.
f. July 1: Federated Markets purchased 1,800 shares of its own stock at the current market price of $38 per share.
g. July 18: A 10% stock dividend was declared and issued. Market value is currently $40 per share.
h. August 20: Sold 750 shares of treasury stock at $32 per share.
i. August 30: Declared a cash dividend of $0.35 per share, payable on September 10.

REQUIRED:

1. Make the appropriate journal entries to record these transactions. It may be useful to use T accounts as you proceed.
2. Prepare the stockholders' equity section of the balance sheet at December 31, 1995. Assume that net income during the year amounted to $430,000.

P13-7 Stock Splits and Stock Dividends

LO 7

Carl Bell purchased 1,000 shares of common stock of the Weather Corporation for a price of $50,000 several years ago. At the end of 1994, the stockholders' equity section of the balance sheet is as follows:

Weather Corporation
Partial Balance Sheet
December 31, 1994

Stockholders' equity	
Common stock $10 par value, 100,000 shares authorized, 90,000 shares outstanding	$ 900,000
Paid-in capital in excess of par	360,000
Retained earnings	950,000
Total stockholders' equity	$2,210,000

REQUIRED: For each of the following situations, make the appropriate journal entries or answer the required questions:

1. On June 30, 1995, the firm decided on a 2-for-1 stock split. At the time, the stock was trading at $34 per share.
   a. What entry should the firm make to record the stock split?
   b. What effect do you think the split will have on Carl's investment?
   c. What would happen if, several weeks after the split, Carl decided to sell some shares at $28 per share? How much gain or loss would he record per share?
2. On September 30, 1995, the firm declared a cash dividend of $.750 per share payable October 31.
   a. Make the entry required on the books of the Weather Corporation.
   b. After the cash dividend is declared, what is the balance of the retained earnings account, and what is the total stockholders' equity?
3. On December 31, 1995, the firm declared and distributed a 5% stock dividend. At the time of declaration, the stock was trading at $24 per share.
   a. Make the required entry on the books of the Weather Corporation.
   b. What effect does this dividend have on stockholders' equity and its various components?
   c. Assuming Carl Bell has never sold any shares of stock, what is his new basis per share after all of the above transactions?

P13-8 Stockholders' Equity—Comprehensive Problem

LO 5, 6, 7 & 8

The stockholders' equity section of the December 31, 1994 balance sheet of the Sandy Bean Corporation appeared as follows (certain details omitted):

Sandy Bean Corporation
Partial Balance Sheet
December 31, 1994

Preferred stock, 5%, $40 par value authorized 100,000 shares; __?__ issued	$2,400,000
Common stock, $5 par value, authorized 100,000 shares; __?__ issued, of which 1,000 are held in treasury	250,000
Paid-in capital in excess of par	750,000
Paid-in capital from sale of treasury stock	10,000
Donated capital	20,000
Retained earnings	560,000
Cost of treasury stock, common	22,000

REQUIRED: Answer each of the following questions:

1. How many shares of preferred stock were issued?
2. Was the preferred stock issued at par, above par, or below par?

3. How many shares of common stock were issued?
4. How many shares of common stock are outstanding?
5. What was the average issue price of the common stock?
6. Have the treasury stock transactions increased or decreased the firm's net assets, and by what amount?
7. How much did the treasury stock cost per share?
8. What is the total amount of dividends, both preferred and common, that the board of directors could legally declare? How would this amount be divided between preferred and common shareholders?
9. What is the total amount of the corporation's contributed capital?
10. What is the total amount of stockholders' equity?

P13-9
Stock Transaction Processing System
LO 11

GenePool, Inc., has used a transfer agent for several years to process its stock transactions. However, cost increases have caused management to rethink the assignment of these functions to an external agent. You have been asked to complete a high-level design of a stock transaction processing system to perform the same functions that are currently being performed by the transfer agent.

REQUIRED:

1. List the functions that the new stock transaction processing system must be able to perform.
2. Identify the types of input that would be used by the system and the reports that the system should generate.
3. Assume that one of the needed reports is a stockholder register that lists each stockholder, that individual's social security number, address, and number of shares held. Design the layout for this report.
4. What internal controls should be present in this system?
5. What potential problems will GenePool face if it decides to implement this system?

DISCUSSION AND INTERPRETATION PROBLEMS

D13-1
Understanding Financial Statements

The following stockholders' equity section was taken from the 1991 and 1990 comparative balance sheets of Lockheed Corporation:

(in millions)	*1991*	*1990*
Stockholders' equity		
Preferred stock		
Common stock, $1 par value, 100,000,000 shares authorized; 70,299,897 shares issued (70,155,154 in 1990)	$ 70	$ 70
Additional capital	712	707
Retained earnings	2,526	2,332
Treasury shares, at cost (7,536,496 shares in 1991, 6,957,096 shares in 1990)	(353)	(328)
Guarantee of ESOP obligations	(452)	(472)
Total stockholders' equity	$2,503	$2,309

In addition, you have gathered the following data:

	1991	*1990*
Cash dividends per share of common stock	$ 1.95	$ 1.80
EPS	4.86	5.30
Year-end market price	44.00	33.625

REQUIRED:

1. Calculate the dividend yield on the common stock at the end of 1991 and 1990.
2. Determine the P-E ratio at the end of both years.
3. Determine the book value per share of common for both years.
4. If the average number of common shares outstanding for 1991 and 1990 was 63.4 million and 63.2 million, respectively, determine the net income for each year.
5. Compare and contrast your answers for 1991 and 1990.
6. Describe the relationship, if any, between the book value and the market price per share.

D13-2 Understanding Financial Statements

Reproduced is a listing of the components of stockholders' equity for H&R Block, Inc., one of the world's largest preparers of tax returns, as of April 30, 1991.

	Common Stock		*Additional Paid-in Capital*	*Retained Earnings*	*Treasury Stock*	
	Shares	*Amount**			*Shares*	*Amount**
Balances at April 30, 1990	53,896,040	$ 539	$96,256	$443,912	(1,082,189)	$(37,359)
Net earnings for the year	—	—	—	140,108	—	—
Stock options exercised	—	—	(6,022)	—	1,059,883	36,589
Unrealized gain on translation	—	—	—	769	—	—
Decrease in provisions for net unrealized loss on noncurrent marketable equity securities	—	—	—	1,988	—	—
Acquisition of treasury shares	—	—	—	—	(630,300)	(24,231)
Effect of two-for-one stock split	53,896,040	539	—	(539)	(652,606)	—
Cash dividends paid: $.74 1/2 per share	—	—	—	(78,960)	—	—
Balances at April 30, 1991	107,792,080	$1,078	$90,234	$507,278	(1,305,212)	$(25,001)

*Dollar amounts are in thousands.

REQUIRED: Based on this information, answer the following questions or make the required journal entries.

1. Why do you think that H&R Block's fiscal year ends on April 30?
2. There was a 2-for-1 stock split. Determine how 652,606 additional treasury stock shares were issued because of the split.
3. Make the summary entries, if any, to record (a) the dividends paid, (b) the decrease in the provision for net unrealized loss on noncurrent marketable equity securities, (c) the stock split, and (d) the acquisition of treasury shares for the year ended April 31, 1991. The 2-for-1 stock split was accounted by H&R Block as a large stock split of 100%.

D13-3 Financial Decision Case

Abbey Smith is the founder and president of Microfoods, Inc., a manufacturer of lowfat packaged foods used primarily by hospitals. The company has been very successful and in 1992 went public with a $10 million stock offering. After the offering Abbey and her family still owned about 15% of the stock, with the remaining shares held by the public.

Using the proceeds from this offering, the company has continued to grow and prosper. The condensed financial information as of December 31, 1995, for the company follows:

Total assets	$24 million
Total debt (a)	7 million
Total stockholders' equity (b)	17 million

(a) Of the $7 million in debt, $4 million is long-term.
(b) Stockholders' equity consists of contributed capital (common stock and paid-in capital) of $11 million and retained earnings of $6 million.

Recently Abbey received inquiries from a large food processing company about a possible buyout. She indicated quite emphatically that she was not interested and turned the potential offer down flat. However, it appears that the food processing company may attempt a hostile takeover.

Abbey began discussing defensive actions with her investment advisers. They suggested that Microfoods undertake a large purchase of its own shares as a way of defending itself, but purchasing the 100,000 or more shares that the investment advisers suggested would cost the company at least $4 million. Abbey was unsure whether the company could afford to take on that kind of debt, yet she did not want to lose control of Microfoods.

REQUIRED:

1. What effect do you think the purchase would have on the market price of the stock?
2. How would the purchase of treasury stock help Abbey defend her company against a hostile takeover?
3. If Microfoods is able to fend off the hostile takeover, what effect will the large treasury stock purchase and bank financing have on the financial strength of the company? Consider calculating such ratios as the debt-to-equity and debt-to-total-assets ratios before and after the treasury stock purchase.
4. Can you think of any real-world examples that are similar to this case? If so, what companies were involved and what were the circumstances?

D13-4
Financial Decision Case

The Myers Corporation is a successful company owned solely by the members of the Myers family. The company manufactures and distributes animal care products. It has recently developed a new antiflea pill that will protect animals from fleas for up to one year. The formula is patented, and it appears that if the company can finance its manufacturing and distribution, the product will dominate that part of the animal care market.

The firm has been in existence for several years. There are currently 1,000 shares of $1 par value common stock outstanding, all of which are held by family members. The stockholders' equity section of the June 30, 1995, balance sheet is as follows:

Common stock, $1 par value, 1,000 shares authorized and issued	$ 1,000
Additional paid-in capital in excess of par	499,000
Retained earnings	3,450,000
Total stockholders' equity	$3,950,000

Although the company has been profitable, it needs additional cash in order to finance the production and distribution of the new product. Maintaining adequate cash has always been a problem for the firm. L. D. Myers, the current president of the company, tells you that the company is considering three alternatives to raise additional capital:

a. Borrowing $3 million in a five-year term loan from the bank at a 12% interest rate. Interest is due annually, the principal at the end of five years.
b. Issuing 30,000 shares of 8%, $100 par value cumulative preferred stock to a venture capitalist. Each share could be converted into five shares of common stock, beginning in five years.
c. Going public by issuing 50,000 shares of common stock at an estimated price of $6 per share. At their discretion, family members could purchase some of this stock at the $6 price.

Myers tells you that the family has two considerations. The first has to do with forced cash payments due to interest and/or dividends. He reminds you that maintaining adequate cash has always been a problem for the firm. He informs you that interest is deductible for tax purposes but dividend payments are not. The firm is currently in a 34% tax bracket. The second consideration has to do with family control. The company has always been family-owned, and Myers is concerned that the family may have to relinquish that control.

REQUIRED: Write a memo to Myers outlining the advantages and disadvantages of each proposal. Be sure to consider the issues the family has raised.

D13-5 Research Assignment

Obtain from your library the 1993 or later issue of *Accounting Trends and Techniques,* published by the AICPA. Based on the companies surveyed, report how many of the companies issued:

a. a large stock dividend — above 25%
b. a small stock dividend — 25% or less
c. a stock split

D13-6 Ethical Issues

Ian Flemming is the vice-president and controller of Globe Products, Inc., a manufacturer of computerized globe products. The company has been very successful and is in the process of going public. Ian Flemming is actively involved in the preparation of all the financial statements for the registration statement. He is working very closely on this project with Albert Brown, one of the senior staff accountants for the outside auditors working on the registration statement.

Ian is very pleased with how things are going. Initial discussions with the investment bankers indicate that the stock will come out at $22 per share, but that net income and cash flow projections could probably support a price of close to $30 per share. Both Ian and Albert are well aware of these facts, as they are both very close to the registration process.

Ian mentioned this stock pricing information to one of his jogging buddies, and suggested that he purchase the stock as soon as it hits the market. Albert also wanted to purchase some of the stock, but he knew that ethical rules prohibited him from doing so. Therefore, he told his best friend to make a purchase, and then he, Albert, would pay him for half of the stock.

REQUIRED:

1. Did Ian Flemming act ethically according to standards set forth by the FEI (Financial Executives Institute) and IMA (Institute of Management Accountants)? You might want to review the material in Chapter 1.
2. Did Albert Brown act ethically according to standards set forth by the AICPA? Again, you might want to review the material in Chapter 1.

COMPREHENSIVE CASES

C13-1 Recording Financial Transactions

(Requires present value calculations) Elaina Poskin and Haskal Votenka are two recent emigrés to the United States from Eastern Europe. In their home country they were both genetic research scientists. When they first came to the United States they worked for a large genetics engineering firm. Late in 1994 they decided to open their own genetics engineering firm called Microgenetics. The initial transactions took place in 1995. Selected transactions related to various financing transactions are described below.

Jan. 2, 1995: Poskin and Votenka each invested $100,000 and each received 5,000 shares of $4 par value common stock.

Jan. 15: Berliner and Associates, a venture capitalist firm, invested $150,000 in the firm in exchange for $100 par value, 6% preferred stock.

July 1: Microgenetics filed a registration statement with the SEC to issue bonds. The statement was effective immediately, and on July 1 the firm issued $300,000 of 7%, 15-year bonds to yield 8%. Interest is payable semiannually each July 1 and January 2.

Dec. 1: Microgenetics purchased a parcel of land and a building at a cost of $1.2 million in an industrial park to use as its research and development facility. The building's assigned cost was $1 million. Microgenetics made a 20% down payment and took out a 30-year, 10% fixed rate mortgage for the remainder. The mortgage is payable in 30 equal annual installments beginning November 30, 1996. (Annual payments rather than monthly payments are used for convenience.)

Dec. 31: Microgenetics reported an income of $120,000 for the year. The board of directors declares and pays the required preferred dividend payment.

Dec. 31: Interest on the bonds must be accrued including any discount or premium amortization. Microgenetics uses the effective-interest method of amortization. (Ignore the interest accrual on the mortgage.)

REQUIRED: Make the journal entries for 1995 and prepare the long-term debt and stockholders' equity section of Microgenetics' balance sheet as of December 31, 1995. Assume that these are the only transactions affecting these accounts.

Jan. 2, 1996: Microgenetics entered into a lease agreement with Scientific Instrumentation to lease a variety of high-precision equipment. The terms of the lease called for eight annual payments beginning December 31, 1996. (Annual payments are used for simplicity.) The lease carries an interest rate of 8%, and the cash equivalent price of the equipment is $125,000.

Jan. 2: Microgenetics made the required interest payments on its bonds.

March 1: Microgenetics repurchases as treasury stock 2,000 shares of common stock (1,000 shares each from Poskin and Votenka) at $26 per share.

July 1: Microgenetics made its semiannual interest payment on the bonds.

Aug. 15: Microgenetics sold 700 shares of the stock it held in treasury to the firm's attorney at a price of $32 per share.

Nov. 30: The first mortgage payment is made.

Dec. 31: The first lease payment is made.

Dec. 31: Microgenetics reported an income of $220,000 for the year. The board of directors declares and pays the required dividend on the remaining outstanding preferred stock.

Dec. 31: Microgenetics' board of directors declares and issues a 10% stock dividend to current common stockholders. Microgenetics' accountants determine that the fair market value of the common stock is $28 per share on this date.

Dec. 31: Interest on the bonds must be accrued, including any discount or premium amortization. Microgenetics uses the effective-interest method of amortization. (Ignore the interest accrual on the mortgage and the lease.)

REQUIRED: Make the journals for 1996 and prepare the long-term debt and stockholders' equity section of Microgenetics' balance sheet as of December 31, 1996. Assume that these are the only transactions affecting these accounts.

C13-2 Financing Decisions

Read the article taken from the May 3, 1992, edition of the *Los Angeles Times*, then answer the questions that follow.

REQUIRED:

1. From the information provided in the article, infer the price per share that GM hopes to issue the common stock for. Explain how you arrived at your answer.
2. Explain the following statement from the article:

   Look. GM is paying dividends of up to 9.125% on its exotic securities. Because dividends, unlike interest, aren't tax-deductible to GM, the 9.125% stock has the same after-tax cost as a 14% bond.

What tax rate is implied in this statement?

3. The next paragraph of the article states:

   GM paid this hideous price because the high-cost securities are considered equity rather than debt, and bond rating agencies abhor debt and love equity. Even though some of this so-called stock is very debt-like.

a. In what ways are these high-priced securities "very debt-like"? If they are very debt-like, why do accountants classify them as equity?
b. Why do bond agencies "abhor debt and love equity?"

GM's MIRACLE OF MIRACLES STOCK OFFERING

Will wonders never cease? General Motors actually seems to have gone back to basics. No, I'm not talking about GM's cars. I'm talking about its stock.

GM is in the process of trying to peddle more than $2 billion of new common stock to investors, a deal the company hopes to close by the end of the month. Selling common stock, a security that even those of us without degrees in higher mathematics can understand, is a welcome departure from GM's recent form. Since July, GM has raised $3.4 billion by selling three separate kinds of high-cost, high-confusion stock. As I've noted before, GM now offers more different lines of stock (eight) than it does models of cars (six).

Even Robert Stempel, GM's embattled chairman, seems happy to be peddling boring old GM common stock, whose current $1.60 annual dividend will cost GM less than 4% of what it gets for selling a new share, rather than costing 8% like Preference Equity Redemption Convertible stock or 6.5% like Series C preference stock convertible into shares of GM E stock.

"We think the one and two-thirds (GM-speak for GM common stock, which has a par value of one-and-two-thirds dollar) is something that people can understand," said Stempel, whom I cornered before he spoke at the Society of American Business Editors and Writers convention in Chicago last week. "The market is right," he continued, "the time is right to sell what most investors understand. What do most investors understand? The dividend on the one and two-thirds."

When I asked if this meant that people didn't understand GM's whoop-dee-do stocks, Stempel kept saying what he wanted to say regardless of what I asked, until I gave up. Oh, well. He didn't get to be chairman of GM by falling for trick questions.

Why do I welcome GM selling common stock? Because the company badly needs low-cost capital to cover its losses and bring out new products. Up to now, GM has been selling high-yielding securities in what amounts to an expensive gamble that the price of GM common and GM E stock would rise sharply. But when GM in effect is selling stock to raise money to help pay dividends on its preferred, preference and common shares, it's nuts to incur high dividend costs to finance stock market gambles.

Look. GM is paying dividends of up to 9.125% on its exotic securities. Because dividends, unlike interest, aren't tax-deductible to GM, the 9.125% stock has the same after-tax cost as a 14% bond.

GM paid this hideous price because the high-cost securities are considered equity rather than debt, and bond rating agencies abhor debt and love equity. Even though some of this so-called stock is very debt-like.

GM's preferred and preference stock dividends now cost the company more than $300 million a year, by my math, up from less than $50 million a year ago. Even for a company the size of GM, that's getting to be real money.

Selling common stock is a shrewd move in more ways than one. The stock market is at price levels that many people, including me, consider absurdly high, even if the long-awaited economic recovery has finally appeared. GM is making hay while the sun shines because rain may be just over the horizon.

GM, as almost everyone knows, plans to put $500 million of new common stock into its pension plans, freeing up $500 million of cash that it would otherwise contribute, and plans to sell at least 50 million new shares to investors. The new shares would produce $2.1 billion at current prices. Although the company won't talk, citing the pending stock sale, it wouldn't surprise me if GM hopes to sell more than 60 million shares, locking up all the capital it believes that it needs before the window of opportunity slams shut.

I don't know if GM stock is a good buy for you. I do know that it's a great sale for GM.

And I also know that access to the stock market has saved the company, at least for now. Counting the new stock, GM will have raised $6 billion or more by selling shares—a world indoor and outdoor record.

Normally, financial theoreticians rhapsodize about how stock markets let companies raise money, while almost everyone involved in the market knows that the market's main function is to let market professionals make a living, and to let the more venturesome among us indulge our gambling instincts.

This time, though, GM has actually used the stock market for the market's supposed purpose, rather than to finance takeovers or other nonsense. And GM is just selling instead of trying to bamboozle everybody with fancy securities. Maybe GM's newly assertive board of directors has told GM management to stop horsing around. Or maybe, it's just a Miracle on Wall Street.

Source: Allan Sloan, "GM's Miracle of Miracles Stock Offering," *Los Angeles Times,* May 3, 1992, p. D5. Reprinted with permission of Newsday.

PART 5

SPECIAL REPORTING ISSUES

Earlier chapters have focused on the use of accounting information and on the concepts and methods underlying the preparation of financial statements. This part turns to topics related to the interpretation of financial information, examining many of the analytical tools of financial statement users and, at the same time, addressing the limitations inherent in such analyses.

According to the FASB, financial reporting should, among other objectives, provide information to help present and potential investors and creditors and other users in assessing the amounts, timing, and uncertainty of prospective cash receipts from dividends or interest and the proceeds from the sale, redemption, or maturity of securities or loans. Since investors' and creditors' cash flows are related to enterprise cash flows, financial reporting should provide information to help investors, creditors, and others assess the amounts, timing, and uncertainty of prospective net cash inflows to the related enterprise.[1] Financial analysis and interpretation help users in their assessment. The chapter that follows provides you with these analytical tools. The first part of this chapter discusses the uses and concepts underlying the statement of cash flows, which provides users with extremely important information concerning present and future cash flows. The second part of this chapter summarizes the preparation, uses, and limitations of such analytical tools as ratio, vertical, horizontal, and trend analysis.

1. Financial Accounting Standards Board, Concepts Statement No. 1, Objectives of Financial Reporting by Business Enterprises (Norwalk, Conn.: FASB, November 1978), pars. 34, 37, and 40.

CHAPTER 14
THE STATEMENT OF CASH FLOWS AND FINANCIAL STATEMENT ANALYSIS

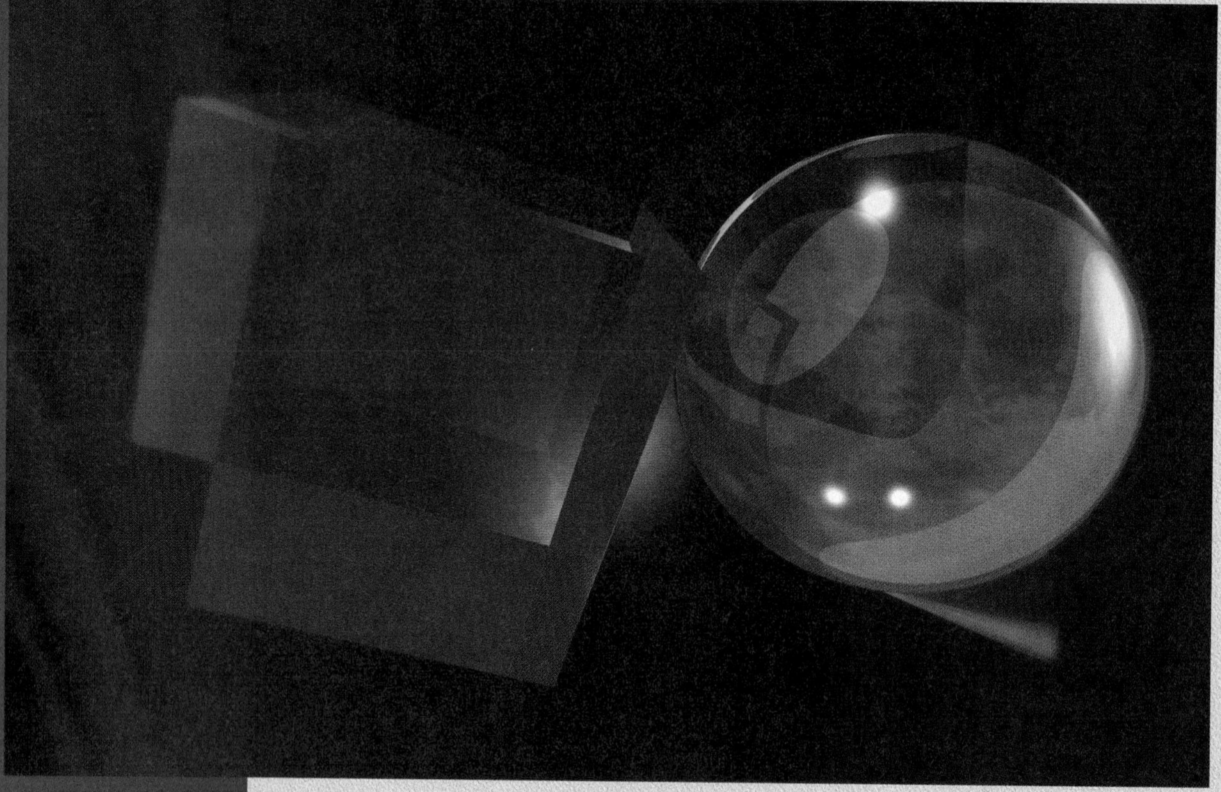

LEARNING OBJECTIVES

After studying this chapter, you should be able to:

1. Describe the statement of cash flows and give its purposes.
2. Differentiate among investing, financing, and operating activities.
3. Determine cash flows from operating activities using both the direct and the indirect methods.
4. Understand the basics of financial statement analysis and calculate common financial statement ratios.
5. Describe approaches to auditing financial statements generated by computer-based accounting information systems.

Scenario

Jacob Weisberg, a recent graduate of a large, well-known university, has been working since his graduation for a local and regional urban planning firm. After his first few months on the job Jacob realized that a large part of his work was evaluating the financial potential of various shopping centers and other real estate developments. At the urging of his employer, Jacob decided to enroll in a part-time MBA program at his local university.

One of the first courses Jacob took was introductory accounting. As a semester-long assignment Jacob was required to select and follow two companies in different industries. As part of this assignment Jacob was to perform a detailed analysis of these companies and compare their performance to industry norms and standards.

Jacob selected Paramount Communications, Inc., and Genetics Institute, Inc., for his project. Paramount is a global entertainment and publishing company, while Genetics Institute is involved with the discovery, development, and commercialization of innovative protein therapeutics to treat a variety of medical conditions. Paramount is a well-established, profitable company. On the other hand, Genetics Institute, a fairly young company, has never shown a profit due to extremely high research and development costs.

As Jacob began his analysis he quickly turned to the statement of cash flows prepared by both firms. In the real estate development business Jacob had been taught the amount of cash flows generated by a particular project was the most important figure. He had not really given much consideration to the accounting income generated by a particular project. However, in his accounting course a great deal of emphasis was given to income from operations and net income.

In his preliminary review of the financial statements of Paramount and Genetics Institute, one of the things that struck him quickly was the difference between reported net income and cash flows reported from operating activities. For example, Paramount's net income for the year ended December 31, 1991, amounted to $122.2 million, but it generated cash flows from operations of only $84.3 million. On the other hand, Genetics Institute's net loss for the year ended November 30, 1991, was over $10.7 million, but the firm generated over $14.8 million in cash flows from operations. As he compared these two companies Jacob was really surprised that in one case, Paramount, cash flows from operations were less than net income, while in the case of Genetics Institute, operations generated a positive cash flow even though the firm had a net loss for the period.

Jacob decided to review the statements of cash flows for both firms more thoroughly to see if he could get a better handle on these figures. He found that both cash flow statements had a category called "cash flows from operating activities" that provided a reconciliation of net income to cash flows from operating activities. One of the most significant items for Paramount was a $900 million increase in theatrical and television inventories, which used cash from operations but did not affect net income for the year. Other significant items included an increase in accounts receivable, which decreased cash flows from operations, and in depreciation, which decreased net income but had no effect on cash flows from operations.

A review of the Genetics Institute cash flow statement told a different story. The firm incurred a large net loss for the period but still generated cash flows from its operations. The two primary reasons were the depreciation and amortization expense of more than $11 million and an anticipated loss of over $11 million on a patent infringement suit. Both of these items decreased net income, but had no effect on cash flows from operations.

Jacob met with one of the students in his work group to discuss his results. They quickly realized that the two firms, Paramount and Genetics Institute, are so different that making meaningful comparisons is difficult, if not impossible. As a result, they decided to calculate a set of financial ratios and do some trend analysis to add to their analysis of cash flows. Jacob and his associate decided that the best approach would be to compare each company with others in its industry rather than only to each other. Although this analysis proved more fruitful, they were still concerned how to interpret their findings. What Jacob and his classmate are beginning to learn is that, in fact, financial reporting provides information which is comprehensible only to those who have a reasonable understanding of business and economic activities and are willing to study this information with reasonable diligence.

One of the primary objectives of financial reporting is to provide information of use to present and potential investors and creditors and others in making rational investment, credit, and similar decisions. The decisions made by these people require that they look at more than the bottom line or earnings per share. They must interpret the past performance of companies and assess their future prospects. This requires detailed financial and nonfinancial information that can be compared and contrasted among firms in the same or different industries and even among firms operating in different countries. Once this information is gathered, it must be analyzed and interpreted in a meaningful way. The first part of this chapter discusses the uses of the statement of cash flows, a primary financial statement very useful in interpreting a firm's operating and financial performance. The second part of the chapter summarizes the other tools of financial analysis and interpretation that have been presented throughout this book.

STATEMENT OF CASH FLOWS

Objective 1
Describe the statement of cash flows and give its purposes.

statement of cash flows

The **statement of cash flows** is a required financial statement, along with the balance sheet, income statement, and retained earnings statement or statement of changes in stockholders' equity. In recent years the statement of cash flows has taken on increasing importance to preparers and users of financial statements. This statement, which is the focus of this part of the chapter, provides information about an essential aspect of a business, its ability to generate cash flows.

The Purposes of the Statement of Cash Flows

The two primary purposes of the cash flow statement are to provide information about the firm's cash receipts and cash payments and information about the investing and financing activities of the firm. This statement is useful to present and potential investors and creditors because it helps them assess:

1. The firm's ability to generate future cash flows.
2. The firm's ability to meet its obligations and pay dividends and its needs for outside financing.
3. The reasons for the differences between income and cash receipts and payments.
4. Both the cash and noncash aspects of the firm's investing and financing activities.

Exhibit 14-1 shows a simplified cash flow statement. (An actual statement would show more detail under the category Cash flows from operating activities.) ETR Sound Systems was able to obtain cash from its operations, from investing activities such as the sale of equipment, and from various financing activities such as the issuance of common stock and bonds. On the other hand, ETR used cash to settle its long-term debt, pay dividends, and purchase a building. Looking at this statement as a whole, it appears that ETR is financing its expansion through the issuance of long-term debt and common stock. As these outside resources become less available in the future, ETR must begin to generate additional cash from operations.

The Meaning of Cash Flows

cash equivalents

The FASB feels that the cash flow statement should explain changes in both cash and cash equivalents. **Cash equivalents** are short-term, highly liquid investments such as treasury bills, commercial paper, and money market funds. These investments are readily convertible to known amounts of cash and are so near their maturity that there is little risk of change in values due to fluctuating interest rates. The purchase and sale of these investments are part of a firm's cash management activities and are included in the overall definition of cash. Thus changes in cash flows mean changes in both cash and cash equivalents.

Exhibit 14-1

ETR Sound Systems
Statement of Cash Flows
For the Year Ended December 31, 1995

Cash flows from operating activities		$ 16,500
Cash flows from investing activities		
Proceeds from sale of equipment	$ 20,000	
Purchase of building	(100,000)	
Net cash used in investing activities		(80,000)
Cash flows from financing activities		
Proceeds from issuing common stock	$ 50,000	
Proceeds from issuing bonds	80,000	
Payments to settle long-term debt	(40,000)	
Dividends paid	(6,000)	
Net cash provided by financing activities		84,000
Net increase in cash		$ 20,500

DIFFERENTIATING THE CAUSES OF CASH FLOWS

Objective 2
Differentiate among investing, financing, and operating activities.

The three major activities of a firm that cause cash flows are investing, financing, and operating activities. When a statement of cash flows is prepared, these activities should be clearly distinguished from one another.

Investing Activities

investing activities

Investing activities include cash inflows and outflows from (1) lending money and collecting on those loans, and (2) acquiring and selling securities and productive assets such as property, plant, and equipment. Cash inflows from investing activities thus include collections on loans made to others, certain receipts from the sale of investments in the debt or equity securities of other firms that are classified as held-to-maturity and available-for-sale securities, and receipts from the sale of property, plant, and equipment. Cash outflows from investing activities include loans made to others, investments in the debt or equity securities of other firms classified as held-to-maturity or available-for-sale securities, and cash payments to acquire property, plant, and equipment. (See Chapter 11 for a complete discussion of the criteria for the correct classification of debt and equity securities.)

Part 3 of this book is concerned with the accounting concepts and procedures related to investing activities. For example, Chapter 10 discussed the purchase and retirement of assets such as property, plant, and equipment, while Chapter 11 introduced you to the accounting for investments in other companies.

Financing Activities

financing activities

Major **financing activities** include obtaining resources from owners and providing them a return on their investment and obtaining resources from creditors and repaying those borrowings. Common examples of cash inflows from financing activities include the issuance of notes, bonds, mortgages, and other short- or long-term borrowings, and the issuance of common and preferred stock. Common examples of cash outflows from financing activities include repayment of these borrowings, the payment of cash dividends, and the purchase of treasury stock.

Part 4 of this book discussed the accounting concepts and issues related to how the firm obtains the financing necessary to conduct its activities. For example, Chapter 12 covered accounting for bonds and other long-term debt, while Chapter 13 covered the accounting for stockholders' equity. Other than operations, these are the primary sources of financing for a firm.

Operating Activities

operating activities

Operating activities include all transactions not considered either investing or financing. As such, they consist primarily of delivering or producing goods for sale and providing services. Cash flows from operating activities are really the cash effect of the transactions that enter into the determination of net income. Thus, cash inflows from operating activities primarily include cash receipts from the sale of goods or services. Cash inflows from operating activities also include the cash receipts from returns on loans and equity securities, such as interest and dividends received as well as the proceeds from sales and maturities of trading securities. Cash outflows from operating activities include cash payments to suppliers for the purchase of inventory, to employees for salaries, to governments for taxes, and to other suppliers for various expenses. Cash outflows from operating activities also include cash payments to lenders and other creditors for interest, as well as the purchase of trading securities.

The FASB had a difficult time determining how to classify interest and dividends paid or received. The Board finally declared that dividends paid to equity investors result from financing activity, and dividends received and interest paid and received result from operating activity. This distinction is based on the view that dividends are a distribution of income, whereas interest is a determinant of net income. Exhibit 14-2 summarizes these various cash inflows and outflows by type of activity.

Part 2 of this book covered the accounting concepts and practices related to a firm's operating activities. For example, Chapter 7 discussed accounting for revenue generation, while Chapter 8 discussed accounting for expense generation. It is through the generation of revenues and expenses that the firm generates cash flows from operations. A firm that is unable to generate positive cash flows from operations will be unable to continue in existence for any length of time.

Investing and Financing Activities Not Involving Cash Flows

noncash activity

Most investing and financing activities involve cash inflows and outflows. For example, a building is purchased with cash, or common stock is issued for cash. Occasionally, however, a firm enters into a **noncash activity**—an exchange of an asset or equity not involving cash. For instance, a firm may issue common stock in exchange for land or convert bonds into common stock. Because these transactions do not affect cash flows, they could be ignored in the preparation of the statement of cash flows. However, to do so would ignore important financing and investing activities. Therefore, the FASB requires that information about these noncash investing and financing activities be summarized in a separate schedule or disclosed in narrative form. These transactions should be clearly identified as not involving cash receipts or payments.

Albertson's Statement of Cash Flows

Albertson's statement of cash flows is reproduced in Exhibit 14-3. This statement shows the three cash flow categories highlighted above: (1) net cash provided by operating activities; (2) net cash used in investing activities; and (3) net cash used in financing activities. During the fiscal year ended January 30, 1992 Albertson's generated over $408 million dollars from its operating activities. This cash, as well as the amount of cash at the beginning of the year, was used to invest primarily in capital expenditures, and to pay long-term borrowings, pay cash dividends, and purchase treasury stock (financing activities). The net result was an increase in cash and cash equivalents of $10.9 million.

The picture portrayed in this statement is one of a healthy, growing company. Albertson's continues to generate significant amounts of cash flow from operations and uses that to expand its business through increasing the number of its stores. Further, each year, significant amounts of long-term borrowings are repaid.

Exhibit 14-2
Classification of Activities

Operating
- Payments
  - To suppliers for inventory
  - To employees for services
  - To governments for taxes
  - To other suppliers for other expenses
  - To creditors for interest
  - To purchase trading securities
- Receipts
  - From sale of goods or services
  - From dividends received
  - From interest received
  - From sale or maturity of trading securities

Investing
- Payments
  - To purchase property, plant, and equipment—includes capitalized interest
  - To acquire a business
  - To purchase debt or equity securities (other than cash equivalents) of other entities
  - To make loans to another entity
  - To purchase loans from another entity
  - To purchase held-to-maturity and available-for-sale securities
- Receipts
  - From sale of property, plant, and equipment
  - From sale of a business unit
  - From sale of debt or equity securities (other than cash equivalents)
  - From collection of principal on loans to another entity
  - From sale of loans made by the entity
  - From the sale or receipt of held-to-maturity and available-for-sale securities

Financing
- Payments
  - To shareholders as dividends
  - To repurchase own stock (treasury stock)
  - To repay amounts borrowed—includes amounts related to short-term debt, long-term debt, and capitalized lease obligations
- Receipts
  - From the sale of equity securities
  - From the issuance or sale of bonds, mortgages, notes and other short- or long-term borrowings

Sources: Adapted from Ernst & Young, *Financial Reporting Developments,* "Statement of Cash Flows, Understanding and Implementing FASB Statement No. 95," January 1988. Reprinted by permission of Ernst & Young. FASB Statement No. 115, "Accounting for Certain Investments in Debt and Equity Securities," May 1993.

DETERMINING CASH FLOWS FROM OPERATING ACTIVITIES

Objective 3
Determine cash flows from operating activities using both the direct and the indirect methods.

A statement of cash flows could be prepared by identifying only those transactions that resulted in a cash receipt or payment, plus noncash investing and financing activities. This would be rather tedious, because it would be necessary to review all the transactions the firm entered into during the period. Instead, the information contained in the balance sheet, the income statement, and the statement of changes in stockholders' equity can be utilized to prepare

Exhibit 14-3

Albertson's, Inc.
Consolidated Cash Flows
(in thousands)

	52 Weeks January 30, 1992	*52 Weeks January 31, 1991*	*52 Weeks February 1, 1990*
Cash Flows from Operating Activities:			
Net earnings	$257,794	$233,774	$196,551
Adjustments to reconcile net earnings to net cash provided by operating activities:			
Depreciation and amortization	132,813	122,185	105,920
Net deferred income tax benefits	(12,912)	(5,302)	6,040
Changes in operating assets and liabilities:			
Receivables and prepaid expenses	(2,572)	(9,226)	(2,427)
Inventories	(50,520)	(18,037)	(112,354)
Refundable income taxes			5,748
Accounts payable	8,572	(4,352)	45,642
Other current liabilities	19,541	15,369	12,511
Self-insurance	14,890	22,346	19,500
Unearned income	31,667	5,459	1,825
Other long-term liabilities	8,747	8,785	12,904
Net cash provided by operating activities	408,020	371,001	291,860
Cash Flows from Investing Activities:			
Increase in other assets	(4,618)	(19,793)	(8,543)
Capital expenditures excluding noncash items	(268,500)	(254,858)	(296,147)
Proceeds from disposals of land, buildings, and equipment	12,696	11,387	5,010
Net cash used in investing activities	(260,422)	(263,264)	(299,680)
Cash Flows from Financing Activities:			
Net proceeds from line of credit borrowings	20,000	10,000	
Proceeds from long-term borrowings			50,000
Payment on long-term borrowings	(10,403)	(62,628)	(12,558)
Proceeds from stock options exercised	8,028	8,312	10,846
Cash dividends	(74,446)	(64,215)	(53,615)
Stock purchases	(79,806)	(19,481)	(24,786)
Net cash used in financing activities	(136,627)	(128,012)	(30,113)
Net Increase (Decrease) in Cash and Cash Equivalents	10,971	(20,275)	(37,933)
Cash and Cash Equivalents at Beginning of Year	23,433	43,708	81,641
Cash and Cash Equivalents at End of Year	$ 34,404	$ 23,433	$ 43,708

the statement of cash flows. Thus the statement of cash flows usually is the last one prepared. A worksheet often is used to facilitate its preparation. The three steps involved in preparing the worksheet, and ultimately the statement, are determining cash flows from (1) operating activities, (2) investing activities, and (3) financing activities. The actual preparation of a statement of cash flows can be quite complex and is explained in detail in more advanced accounting textbooks. Because of the significance of the differences between operating income and cash flows from operating activities, we will concentrate on determining cash flows from operating activities and explaining how they are different from accrual based income from operations.

direct method

indirect method

The first step in preparing a cash flow statement is to determine cash flows from operating activities. There are two alternative methods of presenting operating activities: the direct method and the indirect method. The **direct method** involves reporting the major types of operating cash receipts and cash payments, such as receipts from the sale of goods and services and payments to suppliers for inventory. Cash flows from operating activities are the difference between the total of the operating receipts and the total of the operating payments. The **indirect method** involves presenting a reconciliation between net income and cash flows from operations. Essentially, the accrual-based income statement is reconciled to a cash-based statement.

Although the FASB prefers the direct method, it allows either method of presenting cash flows from operating activities. Regardless of which method is used, interest and income taxes paid must be disclosed. The sections that follow discuss both methods, with the emphasis on the direct method.

The Direct Method

As previously stated, the direct method involves reporting the major types of operating receipts and payments. The partial cash flow statement presented in Exhibit 14-4 shows, except for interest received and paid, taxes paid, and dividends received, the major categories of cash receipts and payments that the FASB suggests be disclosed.

A literal application of the direct method would require firms to keep their records on a cash rather than an accrual basis. The FASB expects firms to derive the necessary information by analyzing changes in appropriate balance sheet and income statement accounts. The best way to understand the required procedures is to work through the example that follows.

Exhibit 14-5 presents the December 31, 1994 and 1995, balance sheets for the East-West Corporation, and Exhibit 14-6 is the income statement for the year ended December 31, 1995. Since the statements are prepared according to generally accepted accounting principles, they are based on the accrual method. In order to simplify the example, the following assumptions are made:

1. All sales are on account.
2. All inventory purchases are made on account. The accounts payable account is used solely for this purpose.
3. All operating expenses except for prepaids used are first recorded in the accrued liabilities account.

Exhibit 14-4

East-West Corporation
Partial Statement of Cash Flows
For the Year Ended December 31, 1995

Cash flows from operating activities		
Cash received from customers		$488,500
Cash paid to suppliers and employees	$450,000	
Taxes paid	6,000	
Cash disbursed for operating activities		456,000
Net cash provided by operating activities		$ 32,500

Exhibit 14-5

East-West Corporation
Balance Sheets
December 31

Assets	*1995*	*1994*
Cash	$ 42,500	$ 10,000
Accounts receivable	36,500	22,000
Inventory	60,000	40,000
Prepaids	3,000	5,000
Property, plant, and equipment	62,000	70,000
Total assets	$204,000	$147,000
Liabilities and Stockholders' Equity	*1995*	*1994*
Accounts payable	$ 30,000	$ 35,000
Accrued liabilities	20,000	17,000
Taxes payable	2,000	3,000
Stockholders' equity	152,000	92,000
Total liabilities and stockholders' equity	$204,000	$147,000

Exhibit 14-6

East-West Corporation
Income Statement
For the Year Ended December 31, 1995

Revenues		
Sales		$503,000
Expenses		
Cost of goods sold	$340,000	
Depreciation	8,000	
Prepaids used	10,000	
Other operating expenses	80,000	
Taxes	5,000	
Total expenses		443,000
Net income		$ 60,000

4. Additions to prepaids are made in cash.
5. Income taxes are recorded in the income taxes payable account.
6. There have been no sales or additions to Property, Plant, and Equipment.
7. No interest has been paid or received. No dividends have been received.

In order to determine cash flows from operating activities, adjustments must be made to sales, cost of goods sold, and the various other operating expenses. This is best accomplished by analyzing the related balance sheet accounts.

Cash Inflows from Operations. Cash received from customers (or cash-basis sales) is the primary source of cash flows from operations. It represents cash collected from customers on account as well as cash sales during the period. In this example, there were no cash sales; all sales were made on credit. The relationship between accrual-basis and cash-basis sales can be illustrated by examining the following accounts receivable T account from the East-West Corporation:

Accounts Receivable			
1/1/95 Bal.	22,000		
Accrual Sales	503,000	Cash Collections	?
12/31/95 Bal.	36,500		

The beginning and ending balances in Accounts Receivable are known, from the data in the balance sheet. Accrual-basis sales cause increases in Accounts Receivable. Cash collections cause decreases or credits to Accounts Receivable. If the firm were on the cash basis, these cash collections would represent the revenues for the period. From these data, it can be determined that cash-basis sales, the missing figure, totaled $488,500 ($22,000 + $503,000 − $36,500).

From an analytical view, it is clear that the beginning balance of the accounts receivable account ($22,000) plus the accrual sales of $503,000 represent the maximum cash collections ($525,000) the firm could receive during the year. The fact that the ending balance in the accounts receivable account is $36,500 indicates that this is the amount of credit sales that remains uncollected at year-end. Thus, cash collections in this case are only $488,500. If the Accounts Receivable balance increases during the year, cash-basis sales will be less than accrual-basis sales by the amount of the increase. Similar reasoning indicates that if the Accounts Receivable balance decreases during the year, cash-basis sales will exceed accrual-basis sales by that amount. To see this, rework the previous example, only this time assume that the December 31, 1995, Accounts Receivable balance is only $15,000. You will see that in this situation, cash-basis sales are $510,000.

In general, the relationship between accrual-basis and cash-basis income arising from receivables is illustrated as follows:

Accrual-basis revenue + Decrease (− Increase) in receivables = Cash-basis revenue

Thus, in the accounts receivable example, cash-basis income (or cash received from customers) is $488,500, determined as follows:

Accrual-basis sales	$503,000
Less: Increase in accounts receivable during the period	(14,500)
Cash received from customers	$488,500

Cash Outflows from Operations. The two major categories of cash outflows from operations are cash paid to suppliers and employees and cash disbursed for taxes.

Cash Paid to Suppliers and Employees. Cash paid to suppliers and employees includes cash payments to suppliers for inventory purchases, to employees for wages, and to others for all other operating expenses. Taxes are shown as a separate item in determining cash flows from operations, and they are not included with cash paid to suppliers and employees.

Cash Paid to Suppliers. Accrual-based cost of goods sold is represented by inventory decreases during the year. For a cash flow statement, however, cost of goods is simply the cash paid for inventory during the year. If all inventory purchases are made on account through Accounts Payable, what must be determined is the decrease or debit to the accounts payable account. This represents the amount paid in cash for inventories during the period. Thus the relationship between accrual- and cash-based cost of goods sold involves both the inventory and accounts payable accounts.

The first step is to analyze the inventory account. From the balance sheet, the amount of the beginning and ending inventory is known, and the income statement shows the amount of cost of goods sold. Using these data, it can be determined in our example that the amount of inventory purchased during the year was $360,000, as follows:

Cost of goods sold	$340,000
Plus: Ending inventory	60,000
Cost of goods available for sale	$400,000
Less: Beginning inventory	(40,000)
Inventory purchases	$360,000

Since it was assumed that all inventory purchases are made on credit, the inventory purchases of $360,000 also represent an increase in Accounts Payable. Therefore, the cash purchases for inventory are determined to be $365,000, as follows:

Beginning balance in Accounts Payable	$ 35,000
Plus: Inventory purchases	360,000
Maximum that could be paid	$395,000
Less: Ending balance in Accounts Payable	(30,000)
Cash payments for purchases of inventories	$365,000

In effect, an increase in the inventory account indicates that the company purchased more goods during the year than it sold. In this case, the inventory account increased by $20,000, so inventory purchases were $20,000 greater than the cost of goods sold. The decrease of $5,000 in the accounts payable account indicates that $5,000 more goods were paid for during the year than were purchased. Thus, actual cash payments during the year were $365,000. The combination of the $20,000 inventory increase and the $5,000 accounts payable decrease is the amount by which the cash-basis expense exceeds the cost of goods sold on the accrual basis. These relationships are illustrated as follows:

Accrual cost of goods sold	+	Increases (− Decreases) in inventory	=	Net purchases during the year
Net purchases during the year	+	Decreases (− Increases) in accounts payable	=	Cash payments for purchases of inventories during the period

Cash Paid for Operating Expenses. Having determined cash paid to suppliers for inventory purchases, it is now necessary to determine cash paid to employees and others for various operating expenses. In the example, two accounts are involved—Prepaids and Accrued Liabilities.

Let's look at the prepaids account. Using the data in Exhibit 14-5, the prepaids T account appears as follows:

Prepaids

Debit		Credit	
1/1/95 Bal.	5,000		
Cash additions to prepaids	?	Prepaids used	10,000
12/31/95 Bal.	3,000		

As the credit to the prepaids indicates, it is clear that $10,000 worth of prepaids were used or expired during the year. Debits represent additions to the prepaids account through cash purchases; in this case, they amount to $8,000 ($3,000 + $10,000 − $5,000). Remember that it has been assumed that all additions to the prepaids account are made in cash. The $2,000 decrease in the balance of the prepaids account means that $2,000 more of prepaids expired than were purchased during the year, so accrual-based expenses are $2,000 more than cash-based expenses. In general, a decrease in the balance of any prepaid account means that accrual-basis expense will exceed cash-basis expense by that amount, and an increase in the balance of any prepaid account means that cash-basis expense will exceed accrual-basis expense by that amount.

The relationship between accrual-basis and cash-basis expenses arising from the expiration of various prepayments is as follows:

$$\text{Accrual-basis expenses} + \text{Increase } (-\text{ Decrease}) \text{ in related prepayments} = \text{Cash-basis expenses}$$

Thus, in the example, cash outflows for various prepayments included in operating expenses are $8,000, determined as follows:

Prepaid expense	$10,000
Less: Decrease in the prepaids account during the period	2,000
Cash outflows for prepaids	$ 8,000

Cash outflows for all other operating expenses, including salaries and wages and payments to suppliers other than those providing inventory, can be determined by analyzing the accrued liabilities account. Recall that all other operating expenses in the example were originally recorded in the accrued liabilities account. Based on the data in Exhibit 14-5, the accrued liabilities T account appears as follows:

Accrued Liabilities

Debit		Credit	
Cash payments of accrued expenses	?	1/1/95 Bal.	17,000
		Accrued expenses	80,000
		12/31/95 Bal.	20,000

The accrued liabilities account is analyzed in the same way as the accounts payable account. In the example, cash outflows for other operating expenses of $77,000 are determined as follows:

Other operating expenses	$80,000
Less: Increase in the accrued liabilities account during the period	3,000
Cash outflows for other operating expenses	$77,000

Combining the cash outflows for the three items just discussed gives the total of cash paid to suppliers and employees. This amount is $450,000, determined as follows:

Cash payments for purchases of merchandise	$365,000
Cash payments for prepaids	8,000
Cash payments for other operating expenses	77,000
Total cash paid to suppliers and employees	$450,000

It was not necessary to make any adjustment for depreciation expense. In the example, depreciation was disclosed as a separate item on the income statement and was not included with the operating expenses. If it were included in operating expenses, it would have to be subtracted from the total of the operating expenses to determine cash paid to suppliers and employees. Remember that depreciation expense is a noncash expense in that it does not affect cash flows at the time it is recorded.

Cash Paid for Taxes. The final category that is disclosed in determining cash flows from operations is cash paid for taxes. The amount of cash paid for taxes can be determined by analyzing the taxes payable account in the same manner as the accounts payable and the accrued liabilities accounts. That is, the general relationship is:

$$\text{Accrual-basis tax expense} + \text{Decrease } (-\text{ Increase}) \text{ in taxes payable} = \text{Cash outflow for taxes}$$

In the example, cash paid for taxes is $6,000, determined as follows:

Taxes expense	$5,000
Plus: Decrease in the taxes payable liability during period	1,000
Cash paid for taxes	$6,000

Cash Flows from Operating Activities—A Summary. All the information derived above can now be summarized to determine cash flows from operating activities using the direct method. The cash flow statement for the East-West Corporation (Exhibit 14-7) shows this disclosure. In this example, there were no other

Exhibit 14-7

East-West Corporation
Partial Statement of Cash Flows—Direct Method
For the Year Ended December 31, 1995

Cash flows from operating activities:		
Cash received from customers		$488,500
Cash paid to suppliers and employees	$450,000	
Taxes paid	6,000	
Cash disbursed for operating activities		456,000
Net cash provided by operating activities		$ 32,500

changes in the balance sheet accounts, so the $32,500 cash inflow from operating activities actually equals the cash inflow for the period.

The Indirect Method

The indirect method involves a reconciliation between net income and cash flows, or a change from accrual-basis to cash-basis income. This reconciliation involves both current and noncurrent balance sheet accounts, as well as income statement accounts.

The analysis required for current balance sheet accounts was explained when the direct method was presented. Exhibit 14-8 summarizes the relationships just discussed. Notice that when the balance in an asset account decreases during the year, cash-basis income is higher than accrual-basis income. When the balance in

Exhibit 14-8
Current Balance Sheet Accounts Reconciling Net Income to Cash Flows from Operating Activities

Account	*Balance During Year*	*Effect on Income or Expense Account*	*Cash-Basis Net Income in Relation to Accrual-Basis*
Accounts receivable	Decrease	Cash-basis sales exceed accrual-basis sales.	Higher
Other receivables (e.g., interest)	Decrease	Cash-basis income exceeds accrual-basis income.	Higher
Other nonmonetary assets (e.g., supplies, prepaids)	Decrease	Accrual-basis expense exceeds cash-basis expense.	Higher
Payables, including interest	Increase	Accrual-basis expense exceeds cash-basis expense.	Higher
Accounts receivable	Increase	Accrual-basis sales exceed cash-basis sales.	Lower
Other receivables (e.g., interest)	Increase	Accrual-basis income exceeds cash-basis income.	Lower
Other nonmonetary assets (e.g., supplies, prepaids)	Increase	Cash-basis expense exceeds accrual-basis expense.	Lower
Payables, including interest	Decrease	Cash-basis expense exceeds accrual-basis expense.	Lower

these same asset accounts increases, cash-basis income is lower than accrual-basis income. The opposite occurs when liability accounts are involved. Then increases in these liability accounts cause cash-basis income to exceed accrual-basis income and vice versa.

Exhibit 14-9 shows how the data developed in the previous discussion can now be used to reconcile East-West Corporation's net income to cash flows from operating activities. Notice that the amount of net cash flows from operating activities is the same as that shown in Exhibit 14-4 on page 680. The only difference is in the format of the disclosures. In Exhibit 14-4, taxes paid are disclosed separately as required by the FASB. If any interest had been paid, it would also be included in the disclosures. Finally, Exhibit 14-10 shows how the net increase of $35,500 in receivables, inventories, prepaids, and payables is determined. The depreciation adjustment is explained in the next section.

Other Adjustments Required to Determine Cash Flows from Operating Activities. In the East-West example, adjustments had to be made only for the balance sheet current accounts and depreciation. In order to prepare the statement of cash flows using the indirect method, other adjustments must often be made to net income to determine cash flows from operating activities. That is, adjustments to accrual-based net income must be made for items affecting non-current accounts such as depreciation, amortization, and bond discounts and premiums that affected net income but did not affect cash flows.

Exhibit 14-9

East-West Corporation
Partial Cash Flows Statement—Indirect Method
For the Year Ended December 31, 1995

Net cash flows from operating activities:	
Net income	$60,000
Noncash expenses and revenues included in income:	
Depreciation	8,000
Net increase in receivables, inventories, prepaids, and payables	(35,500)
Net cash provided by operating activities	$32,500

Exhibit 14-10

Account	*December 31, 1994*	*December 31, 1995*	*Increase (Decrease) in Income from Operations*
Accounts receivable	$22,000	$36,500	$14,500
Inventory	40,000	60,000	20,000
Prepaids	5,000	3,000	(2,000)
Accounts payable	35,000	30,000	5,000
Accrued liabilities	17,000	20,000	(3,000)
Taxes payable	3,000	2,000	1,000
Net increase			$35,500

Expenses That Do Not Reduce Cash. A number of expenses reduce net income but do not reduce cash. Included are such items as depreciation, amortization of intangible assets, and amortization of discounts on bonds payable. The accounts related to these expenses are noncurrent assets or liabilities and ultimately retained earnings; cash is not involved. The following two journal entries illustrate these points:

				Effect on	
Transaction	*Journal Entry*	*Debit*	*Credit*	*Net Income*	*Cash*
1. Depreciation	Depreciation Expense	10,000			
	Accumulated Depreciation		10,000	(10,000)	0
2. Amortization of bond discount	Interest Expense	2,500			
	Discount on Bonds Payable		2,500	(2,500)	0

Thus, to determine cash flows from operating activities, net income must be *increased* for all these expenses that reduced net income but did not reduce cash.

One additional point must be emphasized. Items that are added back to net income to determine cash from operations are not sources of cash. They are added back because they were deducted in calculating net income, which is used as the starting figure to determine cash flows from operating activities. Because depreciation is a very common example of this, many people consider depreciation as a source of cash. This is an incorrect interpretation; depreciation is just one of the expenses that have no effect on cash.

Income Items That Do Not Increase Cash. Occasionally, a firm will earn revenue or have an expense reduced by an item that does not increase cash. Perhaps the most common example is the amortization of a premium on a bond. The following entry decreases interest expense and thus increases income without affecting cash:

Premium on Bonds Payable	500	
Interest Expense		500

To determine cash flows from operations, these items must be subtracted from net income.

Nonoperating Gains and Losses. Cash flows from operating activities include only items generated from the operating activities of the firm. Gains and losses from nonoperating or financial changes, such as the sale or disposal of noncurrent assets or the early extinguishment of debt, are not included in income from operations. Rather, the proceeds from these transactions are included, in total, in the investing and/or the financing activities section of the statement of cash flows.

Assume that a firm sold a parcel of land for $120,000. The land had a historical cost of $100,000, so the $20,000 gain was included in the net income for the period. In preparing the statement of cash flows, the entire $120,000 is included under the category Cash flows from investing activities. As a result, the $20,000 gain must be deducted from net income in determining cash flows from operations. If this were not done, the $20,000 would be double-counted, because the full $120,000 is included in the investing activities section.

Similarly, nonoperating losses must be added back to net income in determining cash flows from operations. Again, assume that a firm sold land for \$100,000 cash, but now assume that the land had a historical cost of \$120,000. The \$100,000 cash is included in the investing activities section of the statement; the \$20,000 must be added back to net income. This assures that the \$20,000 loss is not double-counted and that cash flows from operating activities include only transactions resulting from the regular operating activities of the firm.

Exhibit 14-11 illustrates the typical items that must be added to or subtracted from net income in determining cash flows from operating activities when the indirect method is used.

Albertson's Net Cash Provided By Operating Activities

Refer to the cash flow from the operating activities section of Albertson's statement of cash flows in Exhibit 14-3, page 679. Under the subsection entitled *Changes in operating assets and liabilities,* all Albertson's current accounts other than cash are listed with the respective changes from year to year. To illustrate, consider the account inventories. During fiscal 1992 the inventory account increased by \$50,520. As Exhibit 14-10 shows, this increase in the inventory account means that cash basis expense (cost of goods sold) exceeds accrual basis expense and thus, accrual basis net income must be reduced to arrive at cash provided by operating activities. On the other hand, accounts payable increased during the year. As Exhibit 14-10 shows, this increase means that cash basis income is higher in relation to accrual basis income and thus the \$8.5 million increase must be added to accrual basis net income to arrive at cash provided by operating activities.

Investing and Financing Activities

After cash flows from operating activities are calculated, the next step in the preparation of a statement of cash flows is to determine cash flows from investing and financing activities. This is accomplished by analyzing the changes in the

Exhibit 14-11
Indirect Method

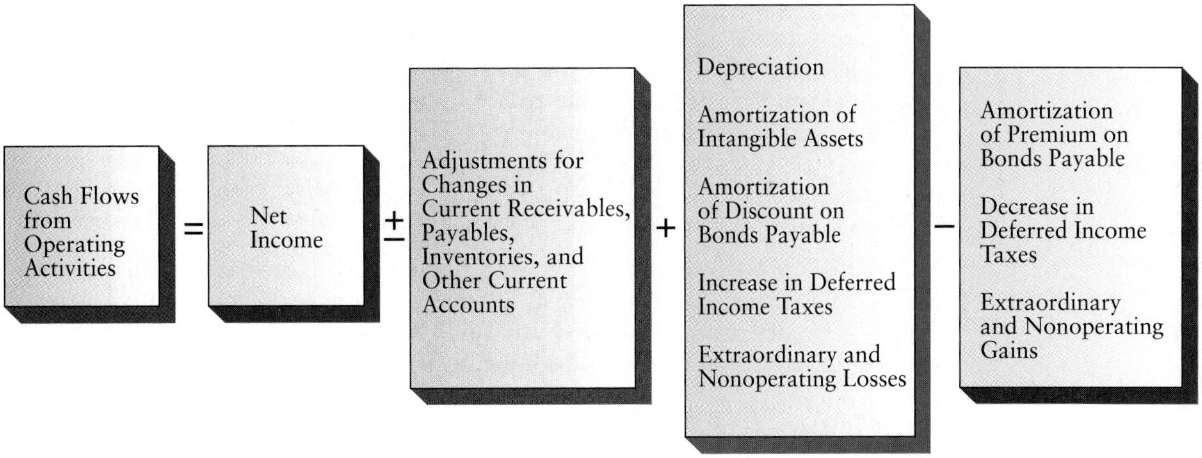

other balance sheet accounts not affecting cash flows from operations. These include most noncurrent assets, short- and long-term debt, and stockholders' equity accounts. This analysis, as well as the determination of cash flows from operating activities, is usually done by utilizing a worksheet. As noted, these worksheet procedures are beyond the scope of an introductory accounting text.

FINANCIAL STATEMENT ANALYSIS

Objective 4
Understand the basics of financial statement analysis and calculate common financial statement ratios.

financial statement analysis

Financial statement analysis is the set of techniques designed to provide relevant data to decision makers. It generally is based on a firm's published financial statements and other economic information about the firm and its industry. Major techniques involved in financial statement analysis include horizontal, vertical, and ratio analysis. In the following sections, we will illustrate horizontal and vertical analysis and conclude with a summary of the commonly used financial ratios that have been discussed in previous chapters.

Horizontal and Vertical Analysis

In trying to understand the current financial position of a firm and its future outlook, it is important to consider changes from year to year as well as trends over several years. One way to accomplish this is to use comparative financial statements and the five- or ten-year summary of data found in the firm's annual report to spot important or emerging trends.

horizontal analysis

Horizontal Analysis. **Horizontal analysis** focuses on the dollar and percentage changes that have occurred in certain accounts from year to year. Using percentage changes is better for comparative purposes than using actual dollar changes. For example, a $1 million increase in Microsoft's cash balance is likely to represent a much smaller percentage than a corresponding $1 million increase in Blockbuster Video's cash balance.

In order to calculate percentage changes, the following formula should be used:

$$\text{Percentage change} = \frac{\text{Amount of dollar change}}{\text{Base-year amount}} \times 100$$

The base year always is considered to be the first year in the comparison. For example, Albertson's total current assets were $677,391,000 at the end of fiscal year 1990 and $751,286,000 at the end of fiscal year 1991. This represents a dollar increase of $73,895,000 and a percentage increase of 10.91%, calculated as follows:

$$10.91\% = \frac{\$751{,}286{,}000 - \$677{,}391{,}000}{\$677{,}391{,}000} \times 100$$

Horizontal analysis can be used in conjunction with the balance sheet and the income statement. As an example, Exhibit 14-12 presents comparative balance sheets for Albertson's, and Exhibit 14-13 shows comparative statements of income. In both statements, both dollar and percentage changes are shown.

trend analysis

Trend Analysis. Horizontal analysis can be expanded easily to include more than a single change from one year to the next. This is called **trend analysis.** In

Exhibit 14-12

Albertson's, Inc.
Consolidated Balance Sheets
(in thousands)

Assets	*January 30, 1992*	*January 31, 1991*	*Dollar Change*	*Percentage Change*
Current Assets				
Cash and cash equivalents	$ 34,404	$ 23,433	$ 10,971	46.82%
Accounts and notes receivable	55,835	52,274	3,561	6.81
Inventories	613,233	562,713	50,520	8.98
Prepaid expenses	10,602	11,591	(989)	(8.53)
Deferred income tax benefits	37,212	27,380	9,832	35.91
Total current assets	751,286	677,391	73,895	10.91
Other Assets	72,283	67,665	4,618	6.82
Land, Buildings, and Equipment				
Land	289,526	259,897	29,629	11.40
Buildings	721,280	637,225	84,055	13.19
Fixtures and equipment	835,592	763,645	71,947	9.42
Leasehold improvements	180,034	158,054	21,980	13.91
Assets under capital lease	139,773	140,623	(850)	(.60)
	2,166,205	1,959,444	206,761	10.55
Less accumulated depreciation and amortization	773,527	690,990	82,537	11.94
	1,392,678	1,268,454	124,224	9.79
Total Assets	$2,216,247	$2,013,510	$202,737	10.07%

Liabilities and Stockholders' Equity	*January 30, 1992*	*January 31, 1991*	*Dollar Change*	*Percentage Change*
Current Liabilities				
Accounts payable	$ 400,417	$ 391,845	$ 8,572	2.19%
Notes payable	30,000	10,000	20,000	200.00
Salaries and related liabilities	80,719	70,967	9,752	13.74
Taxes other than income taxes	37,807	30,743	7,064	22.98
Income taxes	9,589	9,443	146	1.55
Self-insurance	47,238	40,460	6,778	16.75
Unearned income	16,129	3,955	12,474	315.40
Other current liabilities	20,826	18,247	2,579	14.13
Current maturities of long-term debt	3,588	4,481	(893)	(19.93)
Current obligations under capital leases	5,634	5,426	208	3.83
Total current liabilities	652,247	585,567	66,680	11.39
Long-Term Debt	52,510	56,056	(3,546)	(6.33)
Obligations Under Capital Lease	99,159	103,039	(3,880)	(3.77)
Other Long-Term Liabilities and Deferred Credits				
Deferred compensation	24,755	22,013	2,742	12.47
Deferred income taxes	9,219	12,299	(3,080)	(25.04)

(continued)

Liabilities and Stockholders' Equity	January 30, 1992	January 31, 1991	Dollar Change	Percentage Change
Deferred rents payable	66,575	62,021	4,554	7.34
Self-insurance	80,075	71,963	8,112	11.27
Unearned income	22,791	3,598	19,193	533.44
Other	9,464	9,072	392	4.32
	212,879	180,966	31,913	17.63
Stockholders' Equity				
Common stock	132,131	133,820	(1,689)	(1.26)
Capital in excess of par value	718	2,131	(1,413)	(66.31)
Retained earnings	1,066,603	951,931	114,672	12.05
	1,199,452	1,087,882	111,570	10.26
Total Liabilities and Stockholders' Equity	$2,216,247	$2,013,510	$202,737	10.07%

Exhibit 14-13

Albertson's, Inc.
Consolidated Statements of Income
(in thousands)

	52 Weeks January 30, 1992	52 Weeks January 31, 1991	Dollar Change	Percentage Change
Sales	$8,680,467	$8,218,562	$461,905	5.62%
Cost of sales	6,598,950	6,293,881	305,069	4.85
Gross profit	2,081,517	1,924,681	156,836	8.15
Operating and administrative expenses	1,667,355	1,549,061	118,294	7.64
Operating profit	414,162	375,620	38,542	10.26
Other (expenses) income:				
Interest expense, net	(23,106)	(24,812)	1,706	(6.88)
Other income, net	15,338	15,201	137	.90
Earnings before income taxes	406,394	366,009	40,385	11.03
Income taxes	148,600	132,235	16,365	12.38
Net earnings	$ 257,794	$ 233,774	$ 24,020	10.27%
Earnings per share	$1.94	$1.75		
Average number of shares outstanding	133,169	133,777		

many cases, it is important to look at changes over a period of time in order to evaluate emerging trends that are likely to have an impact on future years' performance. The five- or ten-year summary of selected financial data found in all annual reports is particularly useful in this regard.

When more than two years are involved, index numbers are used instead of percentage changes. Essentially, one year is selected as the base year and is set to 100%. All other years are represented as a percentage of the base year. An index number can be calculated by the following formula:

$$\text{Index number} = \frac{\text{Index-year dollar amount}}{\text{Base-year dollar amount}} \times 100$$

To illustrate, Albertson's sales in fiscal year 1987, the base year, were $5,869,423,000. Sales in fiscal year 1991, the index year, were $8,680,467,000. The index for 1991 was 147.89, calculated as follows:

$$147.89 = \frac{\$8{,}680{,}467{,}000}{\$5{,}869{,}423{,}000} \times 100$$

This means that Albertson's sales in 1991 were 147.89 or 1.48 times 1987 sales. Index numbers for other items are calculated in the same manner.

Index numbers are particularly useful in measuring real growth. In the Albertson's example, sales increased 1.48 times in 1991 over 1987. Does this represent a real growth in sales, the same number of unit sales but at higher prices, or a combination of both? One way to answer this question is to compare the index number for sales growth to the rate of inflation for the same period, measured by an index such as the Consumer Price Index for All Urban Consumers, or to a specific price index for the industry. If it is assumed that the index increased 1.20 times during the period, then Albertson's did experience some real growth in sales during the five-year period 1987 through 1991.

vertical analysis

Vertical Analysis. **Vertical analysis** is used to evaluate the relationships within a single financial statement. Essentially, the appropriate total figure in the financial statement is set to 100%, and other items are expressed as a percentage of that figure. For the balance sheet, this figure usually is total assets or the total of liabilities plus stockholders' equity. Net sales usually is the total figure used in the income statement. The financial statements that result from using these percentages often are referred to as **common-dollar statements.** Exhibits 14-14 and 14-15 present comparative common-dollar balance sheets and income statements for Albertson's.

common-dollar statements

Exhibit 14-14

Albertson's
Consolidated Common-Dollar Balance Sheets

Assets	*January 30, 1992*	*Percentage*	*January 31, 1991*	*Percentage*
Current Assets				
Cash and cash equivalents	$ 34,404	1.55%	$ 23,433	1.16%
Accounts and notes receivable	55,835	2.52	52,274	2.60
Inventories	613,233	27.67	562,713	27.95
Prepaid expenses	10,602	0.48	11,591	0.58
Deferred income tax benefits	37,212	1.68	27,380	1.36
Total current assets	751,286	33.90	677,391	33.64

(continued)

Assets	*January 30, 1992*	*Percentage*	*January 31, 1991*	*Percentage*
Other Assets	72,283	3.26	67,665	3.36
Land, Buildings, and Equipment				
Land	289,526	13.06	259,897	12.91
Buildings	721,280	32.55	637,225	31.65
Fixtures and equipment	835,592	37.70	763,645	37.93
Leasehold improvements	180,034	8.12	158,054	7.85
Assets under capital lease	139,773	6.31	140,623	6.98
	2,166,205	97.74	1,959,444	97.31
Less accumulated depreciation and amortization	773,527	34.90	690,990	34.32
	1,392,678	62.84	1,268,454	63.00
Total Assets	$2,216,247	100.00%	$2,013,510	100.00%

Liabilities and Stockholders' Equity	*January 30, 1992*	*Percentage*	*January 31, 1991*	*Percentage*
Current Liabilities				
Accounts payable	$ 400,417	18.07%	$ 391,845	19.46%
Notes payable	30,000	1.35	10,000	0.50
Salaries and related liabilities	80,719	3.64	70,967	3.52
Taxes other than income taxes	37,807	1.71	30,743	1.53
Income taxes	9,589	0.43	9,443	0.47
Self-insurance	47,238	2.13	40,460	2.01
Unearned income	16,429	0.74	3,955	0.20
Other current liabilities	20,826	0.94	18,247	0.91
Current maturities of long-term debt	3,588	0.16	4,481	0.22
Current obligations under capital leases	5,634	0.25	5,426	0.27
Total current liabilities	652,247	29.43	585,567	29.08
Long-Term Debt	52,510	2.37	56,056	2.78
Obligations Under Capital Lease	99,159	4.47	103,039	5.12
Other Long-Term Liabilities and Deferred Credits				
Deferred compensation	24,755	1.12	22,013	1.09
Deferred income taxes	9,219	0.42	12,299	0.61
Deferred rents payable	66,575	3.00	62,021	3.08
Self-insurance	80,075	3.61	71,963	3.57
Unearned income	22,791	1.03	3,598	0.18
Other	9,464	0.43	9,072	0.45
	212,879	9.61	180,966	8.99
Stockholders' Equity				
Common stock	132,131	5.96	133,820	6.65
Capital in excess of par value	718	0.03	2,131	0.11
Retained earnings	1,066,603	48.13	951,931	47.28
	1,199,452	54.12	1,087,882	54.03
Total Liabilities and Stockholders' Equity	$2,216,247	100.00%	$2,013,510	100.00%

Exhibit 14-15

Albertson's, Inc. Common-Dollar Income Statements				
	52 Weeks January 30, 1992	*Percentage*	*52 Weeks January 31, 1991*	*Percentage*
Sales	$8,680,467	100.00%	$8,218,562	100.00%
Cost of sales	6,598,950	76.02	6,293,881	76.58
Gross profit	2,081,517	23.98	1,924,681	23.42
Operating and administrative expenses	1,667,355	19.21	1,549,061	18.85
Operating profit	414,162	4.77	375,620	4.57
Other (expenses) income:				
Interest expense, net	(23,106)	(0.27)	(24,812)	(0.30)
Other income, net	15,338	0.18	15,201	0.18
Earnings before income taxes	406,394	4.68	366,009	4.45
Income taxes	148,600	1.71	132,235	1.61
Net earnings	$ 257,794	2.97%	$ 233,774	2.84%
Earnings per share	$1.94		$1.75	
Average number of shares outstanding	133,169		133,777	

Common-dollar statements are useful in comparing the financial statements of different companies. For example, comparing the dollar financial statements of Albertson's with those of a smaller retail grocery chain is difficult because of the difference in the magnitude of the numbers. When the financial statements are expressed in percentages, however, the differences in magnitude disappear, and comparison of the financial position and performance of two companies that are significantly different in size is facilitated.

Ratio Analysis

ratio analysis

Ratio analysis is a method of expressing relationships among various items in a company's financial statements. However, ratios are not substitutes for looking deeper into the financial position of the company. There is a danger that inexperienced financial statement analysts might use what is called *rule-of-thumb analysis* to make important decisions. However, there are few rules of thumb that are adequate in today's complex financial world. It is important to keep that caveat in mind when performing ratio analysis.

A number of ratios can be used in financial statement analysis. Throughout this text, important ratios have been introduced in appropriate chapters. These ratios are summarized in Exhibit 14-16 and illustrated in a review problem at the end of the chapter. Notice that the ratios are categorized in Exhibit 14-16 by the type of financial statement user who is likely to be most interested in the particular ratio. The three most common user groups in this regard are common and

Exhibit 14-16
Summary of Significant Ratios

Ratio	*Calculation*	*Measurement Significance*
Common and Preferred Stockholders		
Earnings per share	$\frac{\text{Net income less preferred dividend}}{\text{Average number of common shares outstanding}}$	Comparative figure of earnings on a per share basis
Price-earnings	$\frac{\text{Market price per common share}}{\text{Earnings per share}}$	Comparative measure of how the market values the firm's earnings
Dividend yield	$\frac{\text{Dividends per share}}{\text{Market price per share}} \times 100$	Dividend return to investors
Book value per share	$\frac{\text{Common stockholders' equity}}{\text{Number of common shares outstanding}}$	Investors' share of assets at historical cost
Return on total assets	$\frac{\text{Net income + interest expense}}{\text{Average total assets}} \times 100$	Profitability of firm and how efficiently assets are employed
Return on common stockholders' equity	$\frac{\text{Net income} - \text{preferred dividend}}{\text{Average common stockholders' equity}} \times 100$	Profitability of investment to owners
Equity ratio	$\frac{\text{Total stockholders' equity}}{\text{Total assets}} \times 100$	Proportion of assets supplied by creditors and by owners
Debt ratio	$\frac{\text{Total liabilities}}{\text{Total assets}} \times 100$	Same as previous ratio
Gross profit %	$\frac{\text{Gross profit}}{\text{Sales}} \times 100$	Percentage of gross profit (or gross margin) per dollar of revenue
Profit margin %	$\frac{\text{Net income}}{\text{Total revenues}} \times 100$	Percentage of net income per dollar of revenue
Long-Term Creditors		
Debt-to-equity	$\frac{\text{Total liabilities}}{\text{Total stockholders' equity}}$	Another measure of debt versus equity financing
Times interest earned	$\frac{\text{Income before interest and taxes}}{\text{Interest expense}}$	Ability of firm to meet interest payments
Short-Term Creditors		
Current ratio	$\frac{\text{Current assets}}{\text{Current liabilities}}$	Short-term liquidity of firm
Quick ratio	$\frac{\text{Monetary current assets}}{\text{Current liabilities}}$	Ability of firm to meet immediate debt
Inventory turnover	$\frac{\text{Cost of goods sold}}{\text{Average inventories}}$	Amount of inventory carried and how quickly it moves
Accounts receivable turnover	$\frac{\text{Net credit sales}}{\text{Average accounts receivable}}$	Amount of accounts receivable relative to sales and how quickly receivables are collected

preferred stockholders, short-term creditors, and long-term creditors. These categories are not hard and fast; various users are likely to study ratios in all three categories to make their decisions. The categories do, however, serve as a useful way to organize the various ratios.

AUDIT OF COMPUTER-GENERATED FINANCIAL STATEMENTS

Objective 5
Describe approaches to auditing financial statements generated by computer-based accounting information systems.

As you can no doubt see from this and other chapters, the preparation of financial statements can be very complex and time consuming. Consequently, many organizations often use computer-based accounting systems which rely on the financial reporting system to prepare the financial statements. Accountants provide necessary inputs to the financial reporting system and analyze and interpret the financial statements produced by the system. The accountants, in this role, are the *users* of the accounting information system.

Recall that accountants may assume the role as auditors of accounting information systems as well. The financial statements are examined by independent accountants or auditors who express an opinion on the fairness of the financial statements. This is the *auditor* role.

The nature of internal controls and accounting records change significantly when computer-based accounting systems are used to generate financial statements. Consequently, the use of a computer-based accounting information system has a significant effect on the way that an audit is conducted, but not on the objective of the audit.

Nature of Internal Controls and Accounting Records

Internal controls are used to provide a reasonable assurance that all and only valid transactions are processed and that the processing of transactions is complete and accurate. A variety of internal control procedures, such as transaction authorization and the segregation of incompatible functions, have been presented in previous chapters. Most internal control procedures, like these, are manual procedures. Many of these manual procedures are concentrated within the information system when a computer-based accounting system is used.

Transaction Authorization. Transactions, in a manual environment, are reviewed and approved by an accountant before the transactions are posted. In many advanced applications, transactions and the corresponding journal entries are completely processed by the computer system with no human intervention. For example, some companies have developed inter-company transaction systems. Using such a system a company's inventory control system may place an automated purchase order with a vendor's order entry system. When the goods are shipped, the vendor's billing system "mails" an electronic invoice to the company's accounts payable system. The entire transaction is electronic and without human intervention. Hence, there is no opportunity for the transaction control through review and authorization found in manual systems.

Segregation of Functions. Segregation of incompatible functions is affected in a similar manner. Functions, such as access to assets (the checkbook, for example) and the maintenance of the accounting records (for example, the cash account), can be divided between different individuals in a manual accounting system to increase control over both assets and the corresponding accounting records. The transaction processing functions are concentrated within the computer when an automated accounting system is used and there is less opportunity to segregate functions.

Potential for Errors and Irregularities. The potential for errors and irregularities in an automated accounting system may be greater when a computer-based accounting system is used. Individuals may be able to gain unauthorized access to assets and to accounting records with no visible trace. Decreased human involvement in transaction processing reduces the possibility that an error or an irregularity will be noticed and acted upon. Moreover, because a computer system is able to process such a tremendous volume of transactions in a short period of time, errors may multiply rapidly. For example, a payroll clerk may make a calculation error on an individual's payroll. However, that same error may not be repeated on every employee's payroll check. When a payroll program is incorrectly programmed the error may be repeated for every employee every pay period until the error is noticed and the program is modified.

Data Availability. Information about all transactions is easily available in the journals and the general ledger in a manual accounting system. Some computer-based accounting systems are designed so that detailed transaction information is maintained for a very short period of time, if at all. For example, some computer-based accounting systems delete all journal entry data as soon as the general ledger has been updated (posted). The general ledger, in addition, may only contain the current balance in the account, and not detailed information about each posting to the account.

Auditing Computer-Based Accounting Systems

The differences between manual and computer-based accounting systems increase the complexity of auditing financial statements generated by computer-based accounting systems. The most common approach to auditing computer-based accounting systems is to **audit through the system.**

audit through the system

When auditors audit through the system they gain an understanding of the controls within the system and the adequacy of system processes. An auditor may audit through a system by preparing a set of test transactions or test data. **Test data** are transactions that have been specifically designed to test a specific control or system process. The auditor, when preparing the test data, also determines what the system response should be if the system is working correctly. The test data are input into the computer system and the auditor compares the computer generated results with her or his expectations. If there are not material differences between the auditor's expectation and the system-generated output, then the auditor may safely conclude that the system is functioning properly and that the financial data are not misstated.

test data

Assume that an auditor is auditing salary and wage expenses on the income statement. The auditor would be interested in the controls and the adequacy of processing within the payroll system. If the payroll system is functioning correctly, then the risk of financial statement misstatement is reduced. The payroll system documentation states that the system will reject time card records that report more than 60 hours in any pay period (one week).

To test this control the auditor would create two test records. One record would include valid employee data and would report 60 work hours. The second test record would include valid employee data and would report 60.1 work hours. The auditor's expectation is that the first record will be accepted and processed and that the second record will reject because it exceeds the 60 hour limit. The auditor tests values on both sides of the limit to accurately establish it.

The auditor could have input a test record with 100 work hours. However, the auditor would not know that the 60 hour limit was working precisely as documented even if the 100 work hour record was rejected. The control could have been implemented at 75 hours rather than at 60 and the auditor would not know.

Auditing in a computerized environment increases the level of technical expertise that is demanded of auditors. Today most organizations that are audited use computer-based accounting systems. Consequently, it is important for all auditors and accountants to develop this technical expertise.

SUMMARY OF LEARNING OBJECTIVES

1. Describe the statement of cash flows and give its purposes. The statement of cash flows is one of the primary required financial statements. The two purposes of the statement are to provide information about the firm's cash receipts and cash payments and information about the investing and financing activities of the firm.

2. Differentiate among investing, financing, and operating activities. The three major activities of a firm that cause changes in cash flows are investing, financing, and operations. Investing activities include cash flows from lending money and collecting on the loans, and acquiring and selling productive assets and certain securities. Financing activities include obtaining resources from owners and creditors and repaying those borrowings. Operating activities include all transactions not considered either investing or financing.

3. Determine cash flows from operating activities using both the direct and the indirect methods. An important step in preparing a cash flow statement is to determine cash flows from operating activities. Either the direct or the indirect method can be used. Either method involves most of the steps for converting the income statement from the accrual to the cash basis. This requires making adjustments for those items that affected accrual-based operating income in one way but had a different effect on cash-based income. Exhibit 14-7 (page 686) summarizes these items.

4. Understand the basics of financial statement analysis and calculate common financial statement ratios. The most common types of financial statement analysis are horizontal, vertical, and ratio analysis. Horizontal and trend analysis are useful in understanding changes in a firm's financial position from year to year as well as changes over several years. Vertical analysis is used to evaluate the relationships within single financial statements. An appropriate total figure in the financial statements is set to 100%, and other items are expressed as a percentage of that figure.

Ratio analysis is a method of expressing relationships among various items on a set of financial statements. A number of ratios can be used by financial statement analysts. Groups with particular needs have developed their own ratios. These ratios are summarized in Exhibit 14-16.

5. Describe the approaches to auditing financial statements generated by computer-based accounting information systems. Most large organizations use computer-based accounting information systems. Consequently, their financial statements are usually computer generated. The automation of the accounting function changes audit methods and techniques, but not the objective of the audit. Internal controls, such as transaction authorization and the segregation of incompatible functions, and accounting records change when a computer-based system is used. Auditors, in these environments, usually audit through the computer system using a technique like the test data method to test controls and the adequacy of processes.

KEY TERMS

Audit through the system *698*
Cash equivalents *675*
Common-dollar statements *693*
Direct method *680*
Financial statement analysis *690*
Financing activities *676*
Horizontal analysis *690*
Indirect method *680*
Investing activities *676*
Noncash activity *677*
Operating activities *676*
Ratio analysis *695*
Statement of cash flows *674*
Test data *698*
Trend analysis *690*
Vertical analysis *693*

REVIEW PROBLEM

A. The data below were taken from comparative trial balances of the Alka Pro Swimwear Co.

In addition, you determined that the firm keeps its books on the accrual basis. Included in operating expenses are depreciation of $3,100 and amortization expense of $1,400.

	December 31,	
	1995	*1994*
Accounts receivable	$ 220,000	$245,000
Interest receivable	800	1,700
Inventories	420,000	405,000
Prepaid insurance	3,800	1,900
Accounts payable	365,000	345,000
Other accrued expenses payable	18,000	15,000
Net sales	1,200,000	
Interest revenue	6,500	
Cost of goods sold	800,000	
Insurance expense	4,800	
Accrued operating expenses	95,000	

REQUIRED: Determine the following information for the year ended December 31, 1995:

1. Cash-basis sales
2. Interest revenue collected during the year
3. Cash paid for insurance during the year
4. Cash paid for inventory purchases during the year
5. Cash paid for operating expenses during the year
6. Cash generated from operations

Solution

1. Cash-basis sales = Sales + Decrease in accounts receivable
   $1,200,000 + ($245,000 − $220,000) = $1,225,000
2. Interest revenue collected during the year = Interest revenue + Decrease in interest receivable
   $6,500 + ($1,700 − $800) = $7,400
3. Cash paid for insurance during the year = Insurance expense + Increase in prepaid insurance
   $4,800 + ($3,800 − $1,900) = $6,700
4. Cash paid for inventory purchases during the year = Cost of goods sold + Increase in inventory − Increase in accounts payable
   $800,000 + ($420,000 − $405,000) − ($365,000 − $345,000) = $795,000
5. Cash paid for operating expenses during the year = Accrued operating expenses − Increase in other accrued expenses payable − Depreciation expense − Amortization expense
   $95,000 − ($18,000 − $15,000) − $3,100 − $1,400 = $87,500
6. Cash generated from operations = Cash sales − Cash purchases + Interest revenue − Insurance expense − Operating expenses
   $1,225,000 − $795,000 + $7,400 − $6,700 − $87,500 = $343,200

B. Following are the financial statements for the Valda Valdes Corporation.

Valda Valdes Corporation
Balance Sheet
December 31

Assets	*1995*	*1994*
Current assets		
Cash	$ 26,000	$ 13,500
Accounts receivable, net	75,000	53,000
Inventory	86,000	67,000
Total	$187,000	$133,500
Property, plant, and equipment		
Land	$120,000	$120,000
Buildings, net	136,000	141,000
Equipment, net	15,200	14,600
Total property, plant, and equipment	$271,200	$275,600
Other assets	$ 25,800	$ 12,400
Total assets	$484,000	$421,500
Equities		
Current liabilities		
Accounts payable	$ 68,000	$ 70,000
Current maturities of long-term debt	3,000	3,000
Wages payable	1,200	1,000
Taxes payable	10,000	8,000
Interest payable	22,800	12,500
Total current liabilities	$105,000	$ 94,500
Long-term liabilities		
Mortgage payable, less current portion above	$150,000	$153,000
Stockholders' equity		
No par common stock, 10,000 shares outstanding	$100,000	$100,000
Retained earnings	129,000	74,000
Total stockholders' equity	$229,000	$174,000
Total liabilities and stockholders' equity	$484,000	$421,500

Valda Valdes Corporation
Income Statement
For the Year Ended December 31, 1995

Sales		$1,200,000
Cost of goods sold		768,000
Gross profit on sales		$ 432,000
Operating expenses		
Selling	$200,000	
General and administrative	100,000	300,000
Income before taxes		$ 132,000
Income taxes		57,000
Net income		$ 75,000

Additional data:

a. Dividends issued during the year amounted to $20,000.
b. Market price per share of common stock at year-end was $34.25.
c. Included in operating expenses is interest expense of $18,000.
d. Credit sales for the year amounted to $720,000.

REQUIRED: Calculate the following ratios for 1995:

1. Earnings per share (EPS)
2. Price-earnings (P-E) ratio
3. Dividend yield ratio
4. Book value per share
5. Return on total assets
6. Return on common stockholders' equity
7. Equity ratio
8. Debt ratio
9. Gross profit percentage
10. Profit margin percentage
11. Debt-to-equity ratio
12. Times interest earned
13. Current ratio
14. Quick ratio
15. Inventory turnover
16. Accounts receivable turnover

Solution:

1. $$\text{EPS} = \frac{\text{Net income less preferred dividends, if any}}{\text{Weighted average number of common shares outstanding}}$$

$$\$7.50 = \frac{\$75{,}000}{10{,}000}$$

2. $$\text{P-E ratio} = \frac{\text{Market price per common share}}{\text{Earnings per share}}$$

$$4.57 = \frac{\$34.25}{\$\ 7.50}$$

3. $$\text{Dividend yield} = \frac{\text{Dividends per share}}{\text{Market price per share}} \times 100$$

$$5.84\% = \frac{\$\ 2.00}{\$34.25} \times 100$$

$20,000 dividends ÷ 10,000 shares

4. $$\text{Book value per share} = \frac{\text{Total common stockholders' equity}}{\text{Number of common shares outstanding}}$$

$$\$22.90 = \frac{\$229{,}000}{10{,}000}$$

5. $$\text{Return on total assets} = \frac{\text{Net income plus interest expense}}{\text{Average total assets}} \times 100$$

$$20.54\% = \frac{\$75{,}000 + \$18{,}000}{(\$484{,}000 + \$421{,}500) \div 2} \times 100 = \frac{\$\ 93{,}000}{\$452{,}750} \times 100$$

6. $$\text{Return on common stockholders' equity} = \frac{\text{Net income less preferred dividends}}{\text{Average common stockholders' equity}} \times 100$$

$$37.22\% = \frac{\$75{,}000}{(\$229{,}000 + \$174{,}000) \div 2} \times 100 = \frac{\$\ 75{,}000}{\$201{,}500} \times 100$$

7. $\text{Equity ratio} = \dfrac{\text{Total stockholders' equity}}{\text{Total assets}} \times 100$

$$47.31\% = \frac{\$229{,}000}{\$484{,}000} \times 100$$

8. $\text{Debt ratio} = \dfrac{\text{Total liabilities}}{\text{Total assets}} \times 100$

$$52.69\% = \frac{\$105{,}000 + \$150{,}000}{\$484{,}000} \times 100 = \frac{\$255{,}000}{\$484{,}000} \times 100$$

9. $\text{Gross profit \%} = \dfrac{\text{Gross profit}}{\text{Sales}} \times 100$

$$36\% = \frac{\$432{,}000}{\$1{,}200{,}000} \times 100$$

10. $\text{Profit margin \%} = \dfrac{\text{Net income}}{\text{Sales}} \times 100$

$$6.25\% = \frac{\$75{,}000}{\$1{,}200{,}000} \times 100$$

11. $\text{Debt-to-equity ratio} = \dfrac{\text{Total liabilities}}{\text{Total stockholders' equity}}$

$$1.11 = \frac{\$255{,}000}{\$229{,}000}$$

12. $\text{Times interest earned} = \dfrac{\text{Income before interest and taxes}}{\text{Annual interest expense}}$

$$8.33 = \frac{\$132{,}000 + \$18{,}000}{\$18{,}000} = \frac{\$150{,}000}{\$\ 18{,}000}$$

13. $\text{Current ratio} = \dfrac{\text{Current assets}}{\text{Current liabilities}}$

$$1.78 = \frac{\$187{,}000}{\$105{,}000}$$

14. $\text{Quick ratio} = \dfrac{\text{Cash + marketable securities + receivables}}{\text{Current liabilities}}$

$$.96 = \frac{\$26{,}000 + \$75{,}000}{\$105{,}000} = \frac{\$101{,}000}{\$105{,}000}$$

15. $\text{Inventory turnover} = \dfrac{\text{Cost of goods sold}}{\text{Average inventory}}$

$$10.04 = \frac{\$768{,}000}{(\$86{,}000 + \$67{,}000) \div 2} = \frac{\$768{,}000}{\$\ 76{,}500}$$

16. $\text{Accounts receivable turnover} = \dfrac{\text{Credit sales}}{\text{Average accounts receivable}}$

$$11.25 = \frac{\$720{,}000}{(\$75{,}000 + \$53{,}000) \div 2} = \frac{\$720{,}000}{\$\ 64{,}000}$$

QUESTIONS

1. Describe the primary purposes of the statement of cash flows.
2. List the reasons why this statement is useful to present and potential investors and creditors.
3. What is meant by *cash equivalents*? Why is this definition important in preparing the statement of cash flows?
4. List and detail the three major activities of a firm that cause changes in cash flows.
5. Compare and contrast the direct and indirect methods of determining cash flows from operating activities.
6. One of your fellow students said that the more depreciation a firm has, the better off it is, because depreciation is a source of cash. How would you respond to this statement?
7. At the beginning of the year, the balance in the accounts receivable account was $220,000, and at the end of the year, the balance was $160,000. Accrual-basis sales were $270,000. What are cash-basis sales?
8. During the year, the balance in a prepaid asset account increased. Is the related cash-basis expense more or less than the related accrual-basis expense?
9. A number of transactions that affect net income also affect cash flows from operations. List four such transactions. Also list three transactions that affect net income but do not affect cash flows from operations.
10. What does the term *horizontal analysis* mean? How is it useful in financial statement analysis?
11. What does the term *trend analysis* mean? How is it used in financial statement analysis?
12. Sometimes financial statements are expressed in percentages referred to as *common-dollar statements*. What does this term mean, and why are these statements useful?
13. If you were a common shareholder, what ratios would you find most useful in evaluating the company?
14. Ratio analysis is the best way to evaluate the strengths and weaknesses of a firm. Do you agree or disagree with this statement? Why?
15. Describe the effects of the automation of the accounting function on internal controls.
16. Why is it important for an auditor to audit through the accounting system? Why not just audit the input and the output and ignore the computer system?

EXERCISES

E14-1 Types of Activities Affecting Cash Flows

LO 2

For each of the following transactions, state whether it would be classified as (1) an operating activity, (2) an investing activity, or (3) a financing activity.

a. Payment of federal income taxes
b. Dividend payments to shareholders
c. Retirement of short-term obligations
d. Loans made to another entity
e. Payments made to acquire a business
f. Salaries paid to employees
g. Interest paid to lenders

E14-2 Transactions Affecting the Cash Flow Statement

LO 2

Explain whether each of the following transactions would have no effect, would increase, or decrease cash flows and (if appropriate) by how much.

a. The firm issued 100,000 shares of $5 par value stock for $20 per share.
b. The firm obtained a $240,000 bank loan payable in ten equal installments over the next ten years.
c. Sales during the year amounted to $670,000, of which $340,000 was for cash and the remainder was on credit.

d. The firm sold a building with a book value of $1,000,000 for $900,000 cash.
e. Cash collections on account amounted to $160,000.
f. Dividends of $60,000 were declared; $48,000 was paid in the current year.

E14-3 Transactions Affecting Cash Flows

LO 2

Complete the following table by placing an X in the appropriate column to indicate whether the transaction increases cash, uses cash, or has no effect on cash.

	Effect on Cash		
Transaction	*Increase*	*Decrease*	*No Effect*
1. Amortization of intangible asset			
2. Conversion of bonds payable to common stock			
3. Sales on account			
4. Purchase of inventory on account			
5. Declaration of a dividend			
6. Payment of current accounts payable			
7. Collection of accounts receivable			
8. Amortization of premium on bonds payable			
9. Sale of building at a loss			

E14-4 Determining Cash Payments for Inventory Purchases

LO 3

You have determined the following information relative to Accounts Payable and Inventory:

	Accounts Payable	*Inventory*
Beginning balance	$ 230,000	$450,000
Ending balance	170,000	520,000
Cost of goods sold	1,900,000	

REQUIRED: Determine the amount of cash paid for inventory purchases.

E14-5 Determining Cash Flows from Operations

LO 3

Net income for the Stewart Company amounted to $255,000 for the current year-end. During the year, the following changes took place in these current accounts:

a. Accounts Receivable increased by $36,000.
b. Prepaid Insurance increased by $3,200.
c. Supplies decreased by $4,000.
d. Accounts Payable increased by $14,000.

Finally, depreciation for the year amounted to $7,000.

REQUIRED: Assuming that no other relevant changes took place, determine cash flows from operating activities.

E14-6 Understanding the Statement of Cash Flows
LO 1

You have obtained the following statement of cash flows for the Potsie Company:

The Potsie Company
Statement of Cash Flows
For the Year Ended December 31, 1995

Cash flows from operating activities		$165,000
Cash flows from investing activities		
Proceeds from sale of plant and equipment	$ 200,000	
Investment in KCA Company	(1,000,000)	
Net cash used by investing activities		(800,000)
Cash flows from financing activities		
Proceeds from issuing common stock	$ 500,000	
Proceeds from issuing long-term debt	800,000	
Payments to extinguish bonds	(400,000)	
Dividends paid	(200,000)	
Net cash provided by financing activities		700,000
Net increase in cash		$ 65,000

REQUIRED: Based on this statement, explain in detail the net increase in cash. How would you assess the company's prospects for the future?

E14-7 Discussion Exercise
LO 1

After much debate, the FASB decided in 1987 to issue Statement No. 95, which requires the preparation of statement of cash flows.

REQUIRED:

1. Explain the purposes of the statement of cash flows.
2. List and describe the two methods that are used to report cash flows from operations.
3. List and describe the three categories of activities that must be disclosed on the statement of cash flows.
4. How should noncash investing and financing activities be disclosed in the statement of cash flows? Provide an example of a noncash investing and financing transaction.

E14-8 Horizontal Analysis
LO 4

Presented below are condensed balance sheets of the Laguna Sea Corporation.

Laguna Sea Corporation
Comparative Balance Sheets
December 31

Assets	*1995*	*1994*
Current assets	$ 34,212	$ 40,250
Property, plant, and equipment, net	150,000	120,000
Total assets	$184,212	$160,250
Liabilities and Stockholders' Equity		
Current liabilities	$ 27,500	$ 25,000
Long-term liabilities	62,500	50,000
Stockholders' equity	94,212	85,250
Total liabilities and stockholders' equity	$184,212	$160,250

REQUIRED: Determine the dollar and percentage changes in the accounts from 1994 to 1995 and comment on the significance of these changes.

E14-9
Horizontal Analysis
LO 4

Comparative income statements of the Sizzel Company follow.

Sizzel Company
Comparative Income Statements
For the Years Ended December 31

	1995	*1994*
Sales	$1,365,000	$1,300,000
Cost of goods sold	914,550	845,000
Gross profit on sales	450,450	455,000
Operating expenses	210,000	200,000
Income before taxes	240,450	255,000
Taxes	96,180	102,000
Net income	$ 144,270	$ 153,000

REQUIRED: Determine the dollar and percentage changes in the accounts from 1994 to 1995 and comment on their significance.

E14-10
Trend Analysis
LO 4

The following data are taken from the ten-year summary of consolidated financial data of the Coca-Cola Company.

(in millions)	*1991*	*1990*	*1989*	*1988*	*1987*
Net operating revenues	$8.669	$7.212	$6.593	$6.154	$5.437
Operating income	1.145	984	990	937	825
Net income	934	678	622	553	494

REQUIRED:

1. Assume that 1987 is the base (index 100). Prepare a trend analysis for the Coca-Cola Company. (Round off to two decimal points where appropriate.)
2. Comment on the trends.

E14-11
Vertical Analysis
LO 4

Presented below are the comparative income statements of Silk Purse Publishers, Inc.

Silk Purse Publishers, Inc.
Consolidated Statements of Income
(in thousands of dollars except per share data)

	1995	*1994*	*1993*
Sales of products and services	$817,797	$676,949	$529,653
Operating expenses			
Cost of products and services sold	388,933	317,636	249,653
Selling, general and administrative	313,958	270,542	216,820
Total operating expenses	702,891	588,178	466,473
Operating income	114,906	88,771	63,180
Interest (expense), net	(11,003)	(5,234)	(3,259)

(continued)

	1995	1994	1993
Other income (expense), net	(108)	(913)	44
Total other (expense)	(11,111)	(6,147)	(3,215)
Income before income taxes	103,795	82,624	59,965
Income taxes	46,169	37,924	27,371
Income before extraordinary items	57,626	44,700	32,594
Extraordinary items, net of income taxes	1,900	700	—
Net income	$ 59,526	$ 45,400	$ 32,594
Earnings per common share			
Income before extraordinary items	$2.51	$2.04	$1.72
Extraordinary items	.08	.03	—
Net income	$2.59	$2.07	$1.72

REQUIRED:

1. Prepare a vertical analysis for 1995 and 1994. (Round off to two decimal points where appropriate.)
2. Comment on the significance of your findings.

E14-12
Vertical Analysis
LO 4

Presented below are comparative balance sheets of the King Smith Company.

King Smith Company
Comparative Balance Sheets
June 30

Assets	*1995*	*1994*
Current assets	$ 50,000	$ 57,000
Property, plant, and equipment, net	200,000	180,000
Total assets	$250,000	$237,000
Liabilities and Stockholders' Equity		
Current liabilities	$ 20,000	$ 25,000
Long-term debt	70,000	60,000
Stockholders' equity	160,000	152,000
Total liabilities and stockholders' equity	$250,000	$237,000

REQUIRED:

1. Prepare common-dollar balance sheets for both years. (Round off to two decimal points where appropriate.)
2. Comment on the significance of these figures and the changes that occurred.

E14-13
Ratio Analysis—Common and Preferred Shareholders
LO 4

You have obtained the following data relating to the Summerfield Corporation for the past two years:

	1995	*1994*
Earnings per share	$ 2.50	$ 2.40
Market price per share—year-end	20.00	18.00
Dividend per share	1.20	1.00
Net income	37,500	
Interest expense	1,700	
Total assets	500,000	480,000
Stockholders' equity (no preferred stock issued)	300,000	296,000

REQUIRED: Complete the following ratios for 1995 or at the end of 1995:

1. Price-earnings
2. Dividend yield
3. Return on total assets
4. Return on common stockholders' equity
5. Equity ratio
6. Debt ratio

E14-14
Ratio Analysis—Long-Term Creditors
LO 4

You have obtained the following data from the West Corporation:

	1995	*1994*
Total assets	$600,000	$550,000
Total liabilities	240,000	192,500
Interest expense	10,000	6,000
Taxes	15,000	12,000
Net income	60,000	49,500

REQUIRED:

1. Compute the following ratios for both years:
   a. Equity ratio
   b. Debt ratio
   c. Debt-to-equity ratio
   d. Times interest earned
2. Comment on the changes that have taken place from 1994 to 1995.

E14-15
Ratio Analysis—Short-Term Creditors and Liquidity Analysis
LO 4

Comparative balance sheets (unclassified) for the Peterson Company are shown below.

Peterson Company
Comparative Balance Sheets
December 31

Assets	*1995*	*1994*
Cash	$ 28,000	$ 25,000
Current marketable securities	10,000	8,000
Accounts receivable, net	45,000	47,000
Inventories, FIFO cost	82,000	73,000
Supplies	5,000	2,000
Property, plant, and equipment, net	95,000	93,000
Long-term investments and receivables	10,000	12,000
Total assets	$275,000	$260,000
Liabilities and Stockholders' Equity		
Accounts payable	$ 40,000	$ 45,000
Current maturities of long-term debt	20,000	17,000
Other accrued payables	12,000	15,000
Long-term debt, less current portion	80,000	100,000
Common stock, $5 par value	100,000	80,000
Retained earnings	23,000	3,000
Total liabilities and stockholders' equity	$275,000	$260,000

Additional data:

Sales for year, all on credit	$445,000
Cost of goods sold during year	$302,600

REQUIRED:

1. For both years, calculate the following ratios:
   a. Current ratio
   b. Quick ratio
   c. Receivables turnover and number of days receivables are outstanding (1995 only)
   d. Inventory turnover and number of days to turn inventory over (1995 only)
   e. Book value per share of common stock
2. Explain how the current ratio, the quick ratio, and the inventory turnover ratio would change if the firm had used the LIFO method of inventory costing and prices were rising during both years.

E14-16 Company Comparisons and Industry Averages

LO 4

You have obtained the following condensed income statements from the Alpha and Beta companies, both in the same industry. Data for the industry average are also provided.

	Alpha	*Beta*	*Industry Average*
Sales	$955,850	$136,550	100%
Cost of goods sold	573,510	71,066	53
Gross profit on sales	382,340	65,484	47
Operating expenses			
Selling	91,762	9,668	6
General and administrative	61,174	6,718	4
Total operating expenses	152,936	16,386	10
Income before taxes	229,404	49,098	37
Income taxes	97,094	10,315	9
Net income	$132,310	$ 38,783	28%

REQUIRED:

1. Prepare common-dollar financial statements for the two companies in columnar form. Add a column for the industry averages. Round to whole percentages.
2. Compare the performance of Alpha and Beta with the industry averages. Comment on any significant differences. What areas need improvement?

E14-17 Albertson's Financial Statements

LO 3

The cash flows statement from Albertson's is reproduced in Appendix A. Based on that statement, answer the following questions:

a. Was the statement prepared using the direct or the indirect method? Explain your reasoning.
b. What was the amount of dividend payments the company made during the year ended January 31, 1992?
c. The company's cash has been both increasing and decreasing over the three-year period covered by the statement. Explain the primary reasons for these changes each year.

E14-18 Financial Reporting Controls

LO 5

Bach Brothers, an upscale music and video store, has just implemented a computerized financial reporting system. The system accesses a disk-based general ledger and uses the general ledger data to generate a complete set of financial statements after a user identifies the reporting period for which the statements are to be prepared.

REQUIRED: What controls would you expect to find in the financial reporting system to ensure financial statement accuracy?

PROBLEMS

P14-1 Types of Changes in Cash

LO 1 & 2

Indicate which of the following are (a) operating changes, (b) investing changes, (c) financing changes, or (d) neither, by placing an X in the appropriate space.

Item	*Operating*	*Investing*	*Financing*	*Neither*
1. Net income for the year, $3,000				
2. Purchase of a new building through the issuance of a mortgage for the entire amount				
3. Issuance of dividends in the form of capital stock, $20,000				
4. Collection of accounts receivable, $12,000				
5. Purchase of merchandise on credit, $9,000				
6. Declaration of cash dividends, $12,000				
7. Issuance of additional common stock, $300,000				
8. Depreciation for year, $6,000				
9. Purchase of equipment for cash, $12,000				
10. Sale of bonds classified as held-to-maturity, $25,000				
11. Sale of merchandise on account, $35,000				
12. Deposit of cash in a savings account, $5,000				

P14-2 Determining Cash Flows from Operations

LO 3

The Laker Basketball Company reported net income of $500,000 for the year ended June 30, 1993. You have been able to gather the following information:

Unrealized loss on write-down of current marketable securities	$ 1,000
Depreciation expense	12,000
Bad debts expense	5,000
Loss on sale of land	20,000
Extraordinary gain on early extinguishment of debt	70,000
Purchase of long-term investment	55,000
Increase in balance of accounts receivable during year	8,000

There were no other changes in any current accounts.

REQUIRED: Prepare a schedule calculating cash flows from operations using the indirect method.

P14-3 Determining Cash Flows from Operations

LO 3

The following selected data were taken from the comparative trial balance of the Electric Horse Company:

	December 31, 1995	December 31, 1994
Accounts receivable	$450,000	$475,000
Rent receivable	4,200	4,000
Inventories	220,000	225,000
Property, plant, and equipment	600,000	500,000
Accumulated depreciation	105,000	100,000
Supplies	2,500	1,700
Accounts payable	265,000	270,000
Other accrued liabilities	54,000	51,000
Retained earnings	125,200	90,000

In addition, you learned that property, plant, and equipment with a historical cost of $20,000 were sold during the year for cash. Depreciation related to the assets sold was $5,000.

The Electric Horse Company
Income Statement
For the Year Ended December 31, 1995

Revenues		
Sales	$470,000	
Rental income	8,200	
Gain on sale of property, plant, and equipment	2,000	
Total revenues		$480,200
Expenses		
Cost of goods sold	$348,500	
Supplies used	4,700	
Other accrued expenses	77,000	
Depreciation expense	10,000	
Total expenses		440,200
Net income		$ 40,000

REQUIRED: Prepare a schedule determining cash generated from operations using the direct method.

P14-4
Trend Analysis
LO 4

The following information is taken from an annual report of the Colgate-Palmolive Company.

(in millions, except per share data)	*1991*	*1990*	*1989*	*1988*	*1987*
Net sales	$6,060.3	$5,691.3	$5,038.8	$4,734.3	$4,365.7
Income from continuing operations	124.9	321.0	280.0	152.7	145.7
Per common share:					
Operating income	$2.57	$2.28	$1.98	$1.11	$1.07
Dividends	1.02	.90	.78	.55	.695

REQUIRED:

1. Prepare a trend analysis for Colgate-Palmolive, assuming that 1987 is the base (index 100).
2. Comment on the results.

P14-5
Horizontal and Vertical Analysis
LO 4

The following statements were taken from the 1991 annual report of the Colgate-Palmolive Company.

Colgate-Palmolive Company
Consolidated Balance Sheet
(dollars in millions except per share amounts)

Assets	*1991*	*1990*
Current assets		
Cash and cash equivalents	$ 168.5	$ 166.4
Marketable securities	76.9	110.0
Receivables, net	744.2	665.7
Inventories	675.9	692.4
Other current assets	192.2	178.2
Total current assets	1,857.7	1,812.7
Property, plant, and equipment, net	1,394.9	1,362.4
Goodwill and other intangible assets, net	827.2	560.6
Other assets	430.8	422.2
	$4,510.6	$4,157.9

Liabilities and Shareholders' Equity		
Current liabilities		
Notes and loans payable	$ 137.1	$ 138.7
Current portion of long-term debt	69.3	135.3
Accounts payable	535.2	539.8
Accrued income taxes	6.9	32.5
Other accruals	513.2	450.4
Total current liabilities	1,261.7	1,296.7
Long-term debt	850.8	1,068.4
Deferred income taxes	211.1	261.9
Other liabilities	320.7	167.3
Shareholders' equity		
Preferred stock	421.3	422.7
Common stock, $1 par value (171,558,632 and 171,147,458 shares issued)	171.5	171.1
Additional paid-in capital	411.4	123.6
Retained earnings	1,928.6	1,960.8
Cumulative translation adjustments	(216.9)	(200.6)
	2,715.9	2,477.6
Unearned compensation	(401.9)	(407.5)
Treasury stock, at cost	(447.7)	(706.5)
Total shareholders' equity	1,866.3	1,363.6
	$4,510.6	$4,157.9

Colgate-Palmolive Company
Consolidated Statement of Income
(dollars in millions except per share amounts)

	1991	1990	1989
Net sales	$6,060.3	$5,691.3	$5,038.8
Cost of sales	3,296.3	3,121.0	2,843.0
Gross profit	2,764.0	2,570.3	2,195.8
Selling, general and administrative expenses	2,142.4	2,015.6	1,760.3
Provision for restructured operations	340.0	—	—
Other (income)	(1.0)	(2.3)	(26.8)
Interest expense, net of interest income of $33.4, $48.9 and $71.3, respectively	64.7	45.6	15.4
Income before income taxes	217.9	511.4	446.9
Provision for income taxes	93.0	190.4	166.9
Net income	$ 124.9	$ 321.0	$ 280.0
Earnings per common share, primary	$ .77	$ 2.28	$ 1.98
Earnings per common share, assuming full dilution	$ .75	$ 2.12	$ 1.90

REQUIRED:

1. Prepare a schedule showing dollar amount and percentage changes from 1990 to 1991 for the income statement and the balance sheet. (Round percentages to one decimal point.)
2. Prepare a common-dollar income statement and balance sheet for 1990 and 1991.
3. Comment on the above statements, including any significant changes or apparent trends.

P14-6
Ratio Analysis
LO 4

This problem asks you to use the data from the Colgate-Palmolive financial statements shown in P14-7 to calculate certain ratios.

REQUIRED:

1. Calculate for both years the following ratios:
   a. Book value per share of common stock. (Assume that the liquidation value of the preferred stock is the amount recorded on the financial statements.)
   b. Equity ratio
   c. Debt ratio
   d. Debt-to-equity ratio
   e. Times interest earned
   f. Current ratio
   g. Quick ratio
2. For 1991 only, calculate the following ratios:
   a. Return on total assets
   b. Return on common stockholders' equity
   c. Inventory turnover
   d. Receivables turnover. (Assume all sales are on credit.)

P14-7
Ratio Analysis and Accounting Principles
LO 4

The following data were obtained from the records of Congress Supply Store at the end of 1994:

Sales (80% on credit)	$2,000,000
Cost of goods sold (LIFO cost)	1,400,000
Average inventory (LIFO cost)	450,000
Average accounts receivable	400,000
Interest expense	30,000
Income taxes (30%)	102,000
Net income	238,000
Average total assets	1,780,000
Average total stockholders' equity	950,000

REQUIRED:

1. Determine the following ratios or statistics:
   a. Gross profit percentage
   b. Profit margin percentage
   c. Inventory turnover
   d. Debt-to-equity ratio. (Use average figures.)
   e. Return on total assets
   f. Return on total stockholders' equity
2. Now assume that the company is considering switching to the FIFO method of inventory accounting. The president of the firm tells you that if FIFO had been used, average inventories would have been $600,000 and cost of goods sold would have been $1.2 million. Recompute the above ratios and statistics and comment on the differences.

P14-8
Test Data Preparation
LO 5

An auditor is auditing financial statements generated by a computer-based accounting systems. Data on the financial statements related to property, plant, and equipment was generated by the Fixed Asset Accounting System.

REQUIRED:

1. What controls should the auditor expect to find within the Fixed Asset Accounting System?
2. What processes should the auditor be expected to test within the Fixed Asset Accounting System?
3. How could the auditor verify that the information related to fixed assets (current book value, accumulated depreciation, depreciation expense, acquisitions and disposals) which is presented on the financial statements is the same as that contained in the general ledger?

DISCUSSION AND INTERPRETATION PROBLEMS

D14-1
Understanding Financial Statements

The following stockholders' equity section was taken from the 1991 and 1990 comparative balance sheets of the Lockheed Corporation:

(dollars in millions)	*1991*	*1990*
Common stock, $1 par value, 100,000,000 authorized; 70,299,897 shares issued (70,155,154 in 1990)	$ 70	$ 70
Additional capital	712	707
Retained earnings	2,526	2,332
Treasury shares, at cost (7,536,496 shares in 1991; 6,957,096 shares in 1990)	(353)	(328)
Guarantee of ESOP obligations	(452)	(472)
Total stockholders' equity	$2,503	$2,309

In addition, you have determined the following information:

	1991	*1990*
Cash dividends per share	$ 1.95	$ 1.80
EPS	4.86	5.30
Year-end market price	44.00	33.625

REQUIRED:

1. Calculate the dividend yield on the common stock at the end of 1991 and 1990.
2. Determine the P-E ratio at the end of both years.
3. Determine the book value per share of common stock for both years.
4. Net income for 1991 was $308 million. Determine the return on stockholders' equity and the return on total assets for 1991. (Average total assets at 1991 equaled $6,738.5 million.)

D14-2 Financial Decision Case

The president of Denslowe Associates has become very concerned about the performance of his firm in the last couple of years. His controller reports that the firm has been profitable, but the president notices that the firm seems to be using cash at an alarming rate. The controller prepared the following statement of cash flows for the president.

Denslowe Associates
Statement of Cash Flows
For the Year Ended December 31, 1994

Cash flows from operating activities	
Net income	$ 100,000
Adjustments to reconcile net income to net cash used by operating activities	
Provision for depreciation and amortization	40,000
Gain on sale of plant	(90,000)
Changes in assets and liabilities	
(Increase) in receivables	(20,000)
(Increase) in inventory	(30,000)
(Decrease) in payables	(20,000)
Net cash used by operating activities	$ (20,000)
Cash flows from investing activities	
Proceeds from sale of plant	120,000
Addition to plant and equipment	(45,000)
Net cash provided by investing activities	$ 75,000
Cash flows used by financing activities	
Dividends paid	(35,000)
Repayment of notes payable	(80,000)
Net cash used by financing activities	$(115,000)
Decrease in cash	$ (60,000)

REQUIRED:

1. The president of Denslowe Associates has reviewed the above statement and has asked several questions. First, he would like you to explain in your own words what information this statement provides about the present and potential prospects of the company.

2. He is also concerned that the company has shown a profit for the year, yet is having trouble meeting its current debts. He would like you to help explain the reason for this.

D14-3 Financial Decision Case

George Carvers is the operations manager for the Macker Implement Division of GrowTyme Farm Equipment Corporation, which produces a variety of farm implements, including rotary plows and three-bottom plows. These tools are sold to a network of tractor and implement dealers throughout the midwestern states.

Macker has been in business for over 75 years, and its profits and return on assets employed have been acceptable to GrowTyme's management. However, because the facility and manufacturing equipment are approaching obsolescence, maintenance and renovation costs have created heavy cash drains on corporate resources. After analyzing the profitability of purchasing farm equipment products from an outside vendor, Brian Carroll, the chief financial officer of GrowTyme, has recommended phasing out Macker's manufacturing operation and selling the equipment through one of GrowTyme's other divisions.

The chairperson of the board of directors, a daughter of GrowTyme's founder, is dissatisfied with Carroll's recommendation. She believes that the division represents the original thrust of GrowTyme's business and is an integral part of the corporation. She also maintains that the division contributes to corporate profits and that better planning and cash budgeting would improve Macker's cash flow.

REQUIRED:

1. Explain the difference between net earnings and net cash flow.
2. In the past, the performance of the Macker Implement Division has been evaluated on the basis of net earnings. However, George Carvers would like to have the division's performance evaluated on the basis of cash flow. Discuss the advantages of using cash flow as a basis for evaluation.
3. In accordance with generally accepted accounting principles, cash flows from operating activities may be reported using the direct method or the indirect method. Explain why the direct method of reporting cash flows from operating activities might be more appropriate in this case for evaluating Macker Implement's cash flows.

(CMA Adapted)

D14-4 Research Assignment

Using the resources of your library, review current International Accounting Standards (IASC) relating to the statement of cash flows. Compare and contrast IASC requirements with those of FASB Statement No. 95.

D14-5 Research Assignment

Problems P14-4 and P14-5 provide 1991 data for the Colgate-Palmolive Company. Obtain the latest annual report from your library, 1992 or beyond, and calculate the following ratios:

a. Current
b. Quick
c. Accounts receivable turnover
d. Inventory turnover
e. Gross profit percentage
f. Operating income percentage
g. Net profit percentage

Comment on any significant changes that have occured since 1991.

D14-6 Research Assignment

Use an investment advisory service that is in your library (Moody's, Standard & Poor's, or a similar service) to gather information about Albertson's. Write a brief report on that service's evaluation of Albertson's. Compare that evaluation to the analysis of Albertson's in the chapter.

D14-7 Ethical Considerations

Eric Lassar is the CFO of the Endosystems Corporation. It is mid-December and the firm is getting ready for its year-end closing on December 31, 1994. Eric has prepared a draft of what the statement of cash flows may look like for the year ended December 31, 1994, and is concerned about how it looks. Although the firm is privately owned, it has a large credit line with a local bank and Eric is concerned that the cash flow statement will show operations used rather than generated cash flows. The firm will show a substantial profit for the year; nonetheless, the CFO wonders how the bank will interpret the negative cash flows from operations.

Eric has reviewed his receivables and payables and has decided to try to collect his receivables early while holding on to his payables. He has called all Endosystems customers and has offered them a 10% discount if they pay their receivables in full prior to December 31. He has decided to hold on to all payables until the first of the year.

REQUIRED:

1. Why do you think the firm would show a profit and yet use cash in it operations? Is this necessarily a bad sign for the future of the firm? Why or why not?
2. What do you think of Eric's plan to improve the firm's cash flows from operations? Is he doing anything contrary to generally accepted accounting principles or practices? Explain your view.

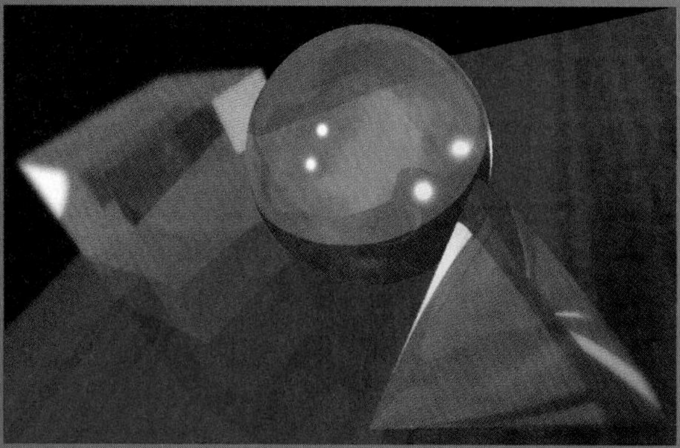

PART 6

FUNDAMENTAL CONCEPTS: PRODUCT COSTING AND COST MANAGEMENT

Part 6 introduces the fundamentals of product costing and cost management. Part 6 also begins a more extensive coverage of management accounting. Thus, some mention of how this important area differs from financial accounting is appropriate. Recall that the accounting information system within an organization has two major subsystems: a management accounting system and a financial accounting system. The principal distinction between the two systems is the targeted user. The management accounting system produces information for internal users, whereas the financial accounting system produces it for external users. Specifically, management accounting identifies, collects, measures, classifies, and reports information that is useful to managers in planning, controlling, and decision making. It should be emphasized, however, that both the management accounting information system and the financial accounting information system are part of the total accounting information system.

When comparing management accounting to financial accounting, some important differences emerge. Management accounting is not subject to the requirements of generally accepted accounting principles. The Securities and Exchange Commission (SEC) and the Financial Accounting Standards Board (FASB) set the accounting standards that must be followed for external financial reporting, but there is no official body that prescribes the format, content, and rules for preparing internal financial reports. Managers are free to choose whatever information they want, provided it can be justified on a cost-benefit basis. Also, management accounting emphasizes the use of accounting information for planning and decision making; because of this, management accounting focuses more on the future than does financial accounting. Financial accounting has a historical orientation—it records and reports what has happened.

As these differences suggest, management accounting is much broader than financial accounting. It includes aspects of managerial economics, industrial engineering, and management science, as well as numerous other areas. Because of its diversity and flexibility, management accounting offers tremendous opportunities for innovation and creativity, and your study of management accounting promises to be an interesting undertaking.

CHAPTER 15
COST CONCEPTS AND TERMINOLOGY

LEARNING OBJECTIVES

After studying this chapter, you should be able to:

1. Identify three different organizational categories and describe the role of cost information in each setting.
2. Define basic cost concepts.
3. Classify costs by function.
4. Prepare an absorption-costing income statement and explain how financial statements differ among manufacturing, service, and merchandising firms.
5. Explain the difference between variable and fixed cost behavior and prepare a variable-costing income statement.

Scenario

Matt Leonard and Ruth Brown were both alumni of the local university's MBA program, having graduated at the same time. Both viewed themselves as successful in their chosen careers. Matt was the administrator of the largest hospital in the community, and Ruth was a division manager of a company that produced medical products. The two met every Friday for lunch to discuss business (the hospital acquired a significant percentage of its supplies from Ruth's company) and exchange advice on the problems they faced in their respective organizations. This Friday Matt turned the discussion to a problem he was facing with a recently hired manager.

"Ruth, as you know, I have two assistant administrators. A month ago one of my assistants, Janice, resigned to become administrator of a small hospital in the southern part of the state. A pity, since she was by far the better of the two. Anyway, I hired an individual, Harold Capener, from a small MBA program as her replacement. This program did not have a specialization in hospital administration, but I discounted this because Harold had five years' experience as a surgical assistant in a large hospital and earned good grades in his graduate work. However, since hiring this guy, I've uncovered what seems to be a major deficiency in his training."

"What seems to be the problem?"

"Well, I called him into my office last Monday to review some of the projects and responsibilities that I planned to assign him. First, I requested that he supply me with a budget for the coming year. I indicated that he could use last year's budget as the basis for next year's, but I wanted him to work closely with our chief accountant to identify variable and fixed costs in the budget. I also indicated that we recently had a consultant identify the direct and indirect costs of all our surgical services as a preliminary step for evaluating the impact of the government's DRG reimbursement policies. I asked him to assess the profitability of each surgical service and to make recommendations for reducing direct and indirect surgical costs, where necessary, so that we could at least break even on each surgical service. Throughout this entire discussion I kept getting blank and puzzled looks. So before proceeding, I asked him if he had any questions or comments."

Ruth chuckled. "I'll bet I can guess his response—however, I'll let you confirm my suspicions."

"His response astonished me. He indicated that he did not know what I meant by variable or fixed costs. Nor did he understand the concept of direct and indirect surgical costs. Basically, he was totally unfamiliar with fundamental cost concepts. He also expressed surprise that he would be so strongly involved in budgeting and profitability analysis. He assumed that all of that was the responsibility of the accountants—not of managers. I spent the next 45 minutes explaining why managers must be able to work with financial information in order to direct an organization effectively. I think he now understands that every manager should be familiar with basic cost terminology and know how financial statements are prepared."

"I can certainly sympathize. I can't imagine having a marketing manager who doesn't understand the difference between fixed and variable manufacturing costs. Many of our bids depend on understanding that difference. How are you going to deal with Harold?"

"Well, he's bright and works hard. I think he'll eventually be a good assistant. But he does need some good training in the basic terminology, concepts, and uses of financial information. He has agreed to take an evening course in management accounting. I need somebody who has the basic financial training and who can become proficient in the use of financial information."

ORGANIZATIONAL FRAMEWORK

Objective 1
Identify three different organizational categories and describe the role of cost information in each setting.

As the dialogue above illustrates, managers of organizations must have the capability to use and understand financial information. To use financial information effectively, managers must have a basic knowledge of cost concepts and the associated terminology. Yet, is it necessary for a hospital administrator to use different cost information than, say, a manager of a manufacturing division? Must training in basic cost concepts be targeted for specific organizational types? These questions can be answered by examining the major types of organizations and seeing what differences exist among them.

In general, all organizations can be classified into one of three categories: (1) manufacturing, (2) merchandising, or (3) service. Manufacturing organizations produce goods by converting raw materials into a physical product through the use of labor and capital inputs such as plant, land, and machinery. Manufacturers include companies such as Panasonic, General Motors, IBM, and General Electric, producing goods such as televisions, automobiles, computers, and appliances. Manufacturing firms usually sell their goods to merchandising firms or to other manufacturing firms.

Merchandising firms buy goods already made (by manufacturers) and then sell them to consumers or other merchandising firms. They are not involved in manufacturing. Examples include firms such as Sears, WalMart, Radio Shack, and Ace Hardware. Merchandising firms selling directly to consumers are sometimes referred to as *retailers*. Merchandising firms selling to other merchandising firms are often referred to as *wholesalers*.

Service organizations provide a service to customers. Service organizations differ from both manufacturing and merchandising firms in two ways. First, they deal with intangible products (services) rather than tangible ones. Second, many service organizations are not profit making. Examples of profit-making service organizations are Price Waterhouse (an accounting firm), American Airlines, and Prudential (an insurance company). Examples of nonprofit service organizations include the IRS and the Veterans' Administration (government agencies), the Red Cross and United Way (charitable organizations), and some hospitals.

Each of these types of organization needs cost information. The type and quantity of cost information needed by managers, however, depends on the organization and the type of activities in which it engages. For example, manufacturing organizations are more complex and engage in more activities than either service or merchandising organizations; thus, managers in these firms need more cost information. While all profit-making organizations (and many nonprofit organizations) engage in marketing and administrative activities, only manufacturing firms are involved in production. Because of this, manufacturing firms have raw materials and work-in-process inventories not found in merchandising firms.[1] Similarly, they have work-in-process and finished-goods inventories not present in service organizations. As a result, manufacturing firms require a greater quantity and variety of cost information.

Although manufacturing organizations offer the richest array of cost concepts and applications, most of the management accounting practices are applicable to all organizational settings. Furthermore, given the increased importance of the service sector in our economy, it is vital to understand how management accounting practices can be used within service organizations. Thus, the examples, problems, and exercises described in this text are offered in a variety of organizational settings, with an emphasis on manufacturing and service organizations.

BASIC COST CONCEPTS

Objective 2
Define basic costs concepts.

Management accounting, like any discipline, has its own specialized vocabulary. Learning this vocabulary is essential to understanding the concepts and procedures discussed throughout this text. The main purpose of this chapter is to introduce the basic cost terminology used in management accounting.

cost

Before cost terminology can be discussed, the term *cost* itself must be defined. **Cost** is the cash or cash equivalent value sacrificed for goods and services that are expected to bring a current or future benefit to the organization. We say *cash equivalent* because noncash assets can be exchanged for the desired goods or services. For example, it may be possible to exchange land for some needed equipment.

expenses

loss

Costs are incurred to produce future benefits. In a profit-making firm, future benefits usually mean revenues. As costs are used up in the production of revenues, they are said to expire. Expired costs are called **expenses**. In each period, expenses are deducted from revenues in the income statement to determine the period's profit. A **loss** is a cost that expires without producing any revenue benefit. For example, some New York vendors purchased a large supply of "I Survived the New York Blackout" T-shirts after a major power failure. Now assume some of these T-shirts are still on hand one year after the blackout. These shirts are probably of little sales value and may literally be given away. Clearly, this produces little or no revenue, and the cost of the shirts would be shown as a loss on the income statement.

assets

opportunity cost

Many costs do not expire in a given period. These unexpired costs are classified as **assets** and appear on the balance sheet. Equipment and the addition to a factory building are examples of assets lasting more than one period. Note that the main difference between a cost being classified as an expense or an asset is timing. This distinction is important and will be referred to in the development of other cost concepts later in the text. An **opportunity cost** is the benefit given up or sacrificed when one alternative is chosen over another. For example, choosing to attend school instead of working has an opportunity cost equal to the wages foregone. Similarly, a firm may choose to invest $100,000 in inventory for a year instead of investing the capital in a productive investment that would yield a 12 percent rate of return. The opportunity cost of having the capital tied

1. Work-in-process inventories are inventories of partially completed goods.

up in inventory is $12,000 (0.12 × $100,000) and is part of the cost of carrying the inventory. While opportunity costs do not appear on the books or financial statements of an organization, they are often critical inputs for managerial decisions.[2] For example, the $12,000 opportunity cost of carrying inventory is equivalent to a cash outlay of $12,000. This cost is an important factor for a manager to consider when assessing different inventory policies.

differential cost

A **differential cost** is the amount by which a cost differs between two alternatives. Suppose, for example, that you are trying to decide whether to drive or fly to Padre Island over spring break. Upon investigation, you find that the cost of a round-trip plane ticket is $350. The cost of driving, including gasoline, is $200. The differential cost is computed as follows:

Flying option	$350
Driving option	200
Differential cost	$150

out-of-pocket cost
sunk cost

An **out-of-pocket cost** is a cost that involves a current cash outlay. Paying cash for office supplies is an example of an out-of-pocket cost. A **sunk cost** is a cost for which an outlay has already been made. It is a cost that has been paid and is irretrievable. Thus, sunk costs cannot be changed by any present or future decision. For example, depreciation is a sunk cost—it represents the assignment of a portion of a past cash outlay to a particular time period. Because sunk costs cannot be changed, they should have no bearing on the decision. Unfortunately, we attempt too often to consider these costs in our decisions. How often have you heard people say that they cannot afford to get rid of a car because they've sunk too much money into it (new carburetor, new tires, etc.)? Yet the outlays already made have no bearing on the decision because the funds spent in the past are irretrievable regardless of whether the car is kept or not. What they need to do is compare the future costs and benefits of keeping the car with the future costs and benefits of getting rid of it.

Often managers are given responsibility for certain cost items. They are held accountable for these items and are evaluated on their ability to ensure that expenditures for the items do not exceed some predetermined level. If managers are to be held accountable for certain costs, they must be able to control these costs. **Controllable costs** are those costs heavily influenced by a manager—in effect, costs a manager is authorized to incur. For example, a maintenance manager has the ability to authorize the use of supplies in repair work. The cost of these supplies is, therefore, a controllable cost for the maintenance manager. The maintenance manager, however, is not free to set his own salary. His salary is an example of a **noncontrollable cost**—a cost over which he has no significant influence. Although the maintenance manager may not have control over his salary, someone does. The plant manager, for example, may be the person who has this control. All costs are controllable at some level. Controllability, therefore, depends on the point of reference.

controllable costs

noncontrollable cost

direct costs
cost object

Direct costs are those costs that are traceable to a cost object. A **cost object** is any item or activity, such as products, departments, projects, and so on, to

2. Accountants focus on recording the costs of alternatives selected rather than the costs of rejected alternatives. Consequently, the formal accounting system does not record opportunity costs.

indirect costs

which costs are assigned. **Indirect costs** are those costs that are common to several cost objects and, accordingly, are not directly traceable to any one particular cost object. Assume, for example, that the cost object is an assembly department. The salary of the supervisor of this department is directly traceable to the department and, therefore, is a direct cost of the department. The salary of the plant custodian, however, is common to all departments in the plant. It is an indirect cost of the assembly department. Like controllable costs, traceability depends on the point of reference. While the salary of the supervisor is a direct cost of the assembly department, it is an indirect product cost if more than one product is assembled in that department.

As can be seen, there are many different types of costs. There are different costs for different purposes. For example, some costs are used for decision making (e.g., differential costs) and other costs are used for performance evaluation (e.g., controllable costs). There are also many different ways that costs can be classified. We have chosen to classify costs into two major categories: by function and by behavior. These cost categories correspond to two different ways of organizing costs for purposes of external and internal financial reporting. The functional classification, the traditional way of viewing costs, plays a key role in the external reporting activities of a firm. Classifying costs by behavior is extremely important for the planning and control activities that take place within a firm.

FUNCTIONAL CLASSIFICATION OF COSTS

Objective 3
Classify costs by function.

manufacturing costs
nonmanufacturing costs

In cost accounting, we try to organize costs in terms of the special purposes, or functions, they serve. In a manufacturing organization, costs are subdivided into two major functional categories: manufacturing and nonmanufacturing. **Manufacturing costs** are those costs associated with the production function in the plant or factory; **nonmanufacturing costs** are those costs associated with the functions of selling and administration. Manufacturing costs can be further subdivided into direct manufacturing costs and indirect manufacturing costs.

Direct Manufacturing Costs

direct manufacturing costs

Direct manufacturing costs are those manufacturing costs that are directly traceable to the product being manufactured. In a single-product firm, all manufacturing costs are traceable to the product. In a traditional, multiple-product firm, there are two types of direct manufacturing costs: the cost of raw materials and the cost of the labor needed to convert the raw materials into a finished product.

direct materials

Raw materials are those materials that actually become part of the product. Since they are directly traceable to the product, they are commonly referred to as **direct materials.** For example, steel in an automobile, wood in furniture, alcohol in cologne, denim in jeans, and plastic in a microcomputer would all be classified as direct materials.

direct labor

The cost of labor used to convert raw materials to a finished product is defined as the straight wages paid to those employees who actually combine materials and overhead into the product (straight wages exclude overtime). This labor cost, directly traceable to the product, is usually referred to as **direct labor.** Workers on an assembly line at Chrysler and in the mixing department at Nabisco are examples of direct laborers. Direct laborers do the work that converts the raw materials into finished goods and involves such activities as mixing, assembling, sewing, and packaging.

Indirect Manufacturing Costs

In a *traditional, multiple-product* manufacturing environment, direct materials and direct labor are the only manufacturing costs assumed to be directly traceable to products. All other costs associated with the manufacturing process are *indirect manufacturing costs;* these costs are common to all products. In other words, indirect manufacturing costs cannot be traced to any one product. Indirect costs are lumped into one category called **manufacturing overhead.** Manufacturing overhead is also known as *factory burden* or *indirect product costs*. For simplicity, we will usually refer to manufacturing overhead as *overhead*.

manufacturing overhead

The overhead cost category contains a wide variety of items. Many inputs other than direct labor and direct materials are needed to make a product. All factory-related indirect costs belong to the overhead category. Examples include depreciation on plant and equipment, maintenance, supplies (indirect materials), supervision, material handling and other indirect labor, utilities, property taxes, landscaping of factory grounds, and plant security. **Indirect materials** are generally those materials necessary for production that do not become part of the finished product. Lubricating oil for machinery used in production is an example of an indirect material. The oil is necessary to maintain the machinery but is not directly traceable to any one product.

indirect materials

Direct materials that form an insignificant part of the final product are usually lumped into the overhead category as a special kind of indirect material. This is justified on the basis of cost and convenience. The glue used in furniture or toys is an example.

indirect labor

Indirect labor is generally all factory labor other than those workers who actually transform the raw materials into a finished good. Examples include production-line supervisors, janitors, supply clerks, and maintenance workers.

The cost of overtime for direct laborers is usually assigned to indirect labor as well. The rationale is that typically no particular production run can be identified as the cause of the overtime. Accordingly, overtime cost is common to all production runs and is therefore an indirect manufacturing cost. Note that *only* the overtime cost itself is treated this way. If workers are paid an $8 regular rate and a $4 overtime premium, only the $4 overtime premium is assigned to overhead. The $8 regular rate is still regarded as a direct labor cost. In certain cases, however, overtime is associated with a particular production run; for example, a special order is taken when production is at 100 percent capacity. In these special cases, it is appropriate to treat overtime premiums as a direct labor cost.

In practice, many firms also treat the cost of direct labor fringe benefits as an overhead item. This practice can be justified only on the basis of convenience since the cost of fringe benefits for direct laborers technically should be a direct labor cost. Because fringe benefits represent a significant component of the total direct labor cost, the best approach for handling this item is to assign it to the direct labor cost category. With automation of the bookkeeping function, the argument of convenience is not convincing; therefore, direct labor fringe benefits generally should be treated as a direct labor cost.

Nonmanufacturing Costs

There are two categories of nonmanufacturing costs: selling costs and administrative costs. The level of these costs can be significant (often greater than 25 percent of sales revenue), and controlling them may bring greater cost savings to a manufacturing organization than the same control exercised in the area of production costs. Furthermore, the relative importance of selling and administrative costs is greater in merchandising firms because those firms do not engage in production. Service organizations, on the other hand, do produce an intangible product so the production function is present in this type of organization. The relative importance of selling and administrative costs depends on the nature of the service being produced. Physicians and dentists, for example, do very little marketing and thus have very low selling costs.

selling costs

Those costs necessary to market and distribute a product or service are marketing or **selling costs.** They are often referred to as *order-getting* and *order-filling* costs. Examples of selling costs include such items as salaries and commissions for sales personnel, advertising, warehousing, customer service, and shipping. The first two items are examples of order-getting costs; the last three are order-filling costs.

administrative costs

All costs associated with the general administration of the organization that cannot be reasonably assigned to either marketing or manufacturing are **administrative costs.** General administration has the responsibility of ensuring that the various activities of the organization are properly integrated so that the overall mission of the firm is realized. The president of the firm, for example, is concerned with the efficiency of *both* marketing and manufacturing as they carry out their respective roles. Proper integration of these two functions is essential to maximize the overall profits of a firm. Examples, then, of administrative costs are top executive salaries, legal fees, printing the annual report, general accounting, and research and development.

Related Cost Concepts

The manufacturing and nonmanufacturing classifications give rise to some related cost concepts. The functional delineation between nonmanufacturing and manufacturing costs is essentially the basis for the concepts of period costs and product costs—at least for purposes of external reporting. Combinations of different manufacturing costs also produce the concepts of conversion costs and prime costs.

period costs

Period Costs. Costs that are expensed in the period in which they are incurred are called **period costs.** Costs are incurred to produce future benefits (usually revenues) and as costs are used up, they expire and are matched against the revenues they generated.[3] Generally we can say that period costs benefit only the period in which they are incurred. This is not entirely accurate, of course. Some costs classified as period costs may actually benefit more than one period. For example, United Airlines advertises its flights to warm, sunny Florida in December. Some people will see these ads and immediately book a trip to Orlando. Others will let the idea sit quietly in the back of their minds until the following February and then buy tickets. One ad has led to sales in two different time periods. Thus, the extreme difficulty of matching advertising costs with benefitting periods justifies the expedient practice of expensing all of these costs immediately.

To illustrate the concept of period costs, we consider a sales supervisor. Her salary is incurred and expensed during the year because she is expected to pro-

3. The term *incurred* is not synonymous with *paid*. *Incurred* is used to imply an accrual basis of accounting instead of a cash basis. *Incurred* means that the firm has become liable for a payment, not that a payment has been made. Under an accrual basis of accounting, expired costs of the period are matched with revenues regardless of whether an actual cash payment has been made.

duce sales during the year. The next year the same cost is incurred with the expectation that sales will be produced in *that* year. The salary is period related and should be matched with the revenues produced during that period.

All selling and administrative costs are viewed as being period related. Thus, such costs as sales commissions, depreciation on delivery trucks and warehouses, salary of the pilot for the corporate jet, legal fees, and public relations are examples of period costs. They are deducted, in total, each and every period from the revenues of the period.

Product Costs. Some costs have the potential to produce revenues beyond the current period. The costs of manufacturing a product are incurred because benefits (revenues) will be realized upon sale of the product. But products produced currently can be placed in inventory and sold in some future period. When the product is sold, the potential benefits for which the costs were incurred are realized. Then, and only then, are the costs expensed. Consequently, costs to produce a product in a current period can appear as expenses in several different future periods.

Recall that the costs of direct materials, direct labor, and overhead are incurred to produce finished goods. These costs are product related, not period related. Until the finished goods are sold, these costs appear as assets (Inventory) on the balance sheet. Therefore, for external financial reporting, product costs are defined as manufacturing costs that are first inventoried and later expensed as the goods are sold.

The unit product cost is simply the cost of producing one unit of a product. For external financial reporting, **product costs** are defined as direct materials, direct labor, and overhead. Thus, the unit product cost is the amount of direct materials, direct labor, and overhead cost assigned to a single product. For example, in producing a can of soda, Coca-Cola might incur the following costs:

product costs

Direct materials (can, fructose, water, etc.)	$0.06
Direct labor	0.01
Overhead	0.08
Total unit cost	$0.15

The unit product cost just defined is driven by the requirements of external financial reporting. If a bottling company has 100,000 cans of soda on hand at the end of the year, it would be reported as a $15,000 asset ($0.15 × 100,000).

For managerial purposes, other definitions of product cost may, at times, be more suitable. For planning and decision making, managers may demand a different definition of product cost. For example, a manager may want to know the comprehensive cost of a new product—a unit cost that includes both manufacturing and nonmanufacturing costs—to have some idea of what selling price should be set to earn an acceptable return. In this case, a unit product cost might appear as follows:

Direct materials	$12
Direct labor	5
Overhead	14
Selling and administrative	6
Total unit cost	$37

The manager would then know that a proposed selling price of $36 per unit would be unacceptable. Unit selling and administrative costs must also be covered.

Other unit cost definitions based on cost behavior may also prove useful to managers. The key point to understand is that internal managerial needs should not be restricted by the formal external reporting requirements. Managerial product costing is designed to provide the information managers need and is not necessarily concerned with inventory valuation. This illustrates the maxim of "different costs for different purposes." It may also require "different systems for different purposes." One cost accounting system may be needed for inventory valuation (to satisfy external reporting requirements), another for managerial product costing, and a third for control.[4]

prime cost
conversion cost

Prime and Conversion Costs. Two other useful cost terms are *prime cost* and *conversion cost*. **Prime cost** is the sum of direct materials cost and direct labor cost. **Conversion cost** is the sum of direct labor cost and overhead cost. Conversion cost can be interpreted as the cost of converting raw materials into a final product.

FINANCIAL STATEMENTS AND THE FUNCTIONAL CLASSIFICATION

Objective 4
Prepare an absorption-costing income statement and explain how financial statements differ among manufacturing, service, and merchandising firms.

absorption-costing income

full-costing income

cost of goods sold

The functional classification is the cost classification required for *external* reporting. Regulatory bodies such as the Securities and Exchange Commission and the Financial Accounting Standards Board mandate the functional approach for financial statements prepared for external use.

The income statement based on a functional classification for a manufacturing firm is displayed in Exhibit 15-1. This income statement follows the traditional format taught in an introductory financial accounting course. Income computed by following a functional classification is frequently referred to as an **absorption-costing income** or **full-costing income** because *all* manufacturing costs are fully assigned to the product.

Under the absorption-costing approach, expenses are segregated according to function and then deducted from revenues to arrive at income before taxes. As can be seen in Exhibit 15-1, there are two major functional categories of expense: cost of goods sold and operating expenses. These categories correspond, respectively, to a firm's manufacturing and nonmanufacturing expenses. **Cost of goods sold** is the cost of direct materials, direct labor, and overhead attached to the units sold. To compute the cost of goods sold, it is first necessary to determine the cost of goods manufactured.

Cost of Goods Manufactured

cost of goods manufactured

The **cost of goods manufactured** represents the total cost of goods completed during the current period. The only costs assigned to goods completed are the manufacturing costs of direct materials, direct labor, and overhead. The details of this cost assignment are given in a supporting schedule, called the *statement of cost of goods manufactured*. An example of this supporting schedule for the income statement in Exhibit 15-1 is shown in Exhibit 15-2. Notice in Exhibit 15-2 that the total manufacturing costs added during the period are added to the

4. Robert S. Kaplan, "One Cost System Isn't Enough," *Harvard Business Review*, (January-February, 1988), pp. 61–66.

Exhibit 15-1

Income Statement. Functional Classification
For the Year Ended December 31, 1995

Sales		$4,000,000
Cost of goods sold:		
Beginning finished goods inventory	$ 500,000	
Add: Cost of goods manufactured	2,400,000	
Goods available for sale	$2,900,000	
Less: Ending finished goods inventory	(300,000)	2,600,000
Gross profit		$1,400,000
Less operating expenses:		
Selling expenses	$ 600,000	
Administrative expenses	300,000	(900,000)
Income before taxes		$ 500,000

manufacturing costs found in beginning work in process, yielding total manufacturing costs to account for. The costs found in ending work in process are then deducted from total manufacturing costs to arrive at the cost of goods manufactured. If the cost of goods manufactured is for a single product, then the average unit cost can be computed by dividing the cost of goods manufactured by the units produced. For example, assume that the statement in Exhibit 15-2 was prepared for the production of bottles of perfume and that 480,000 bottles were completed during the period. The average unit cost is $5 per bottle ($2,400,000/480,000).

work in process

Work in process consists of all partially completed units found in production at a given point in time. Beginning work in process consists of the partially completed units on hand at the beginning of a period. Ending work in process consists of those on hand at the period's end. In the statement of cost of goods manufactured, the cost of these partially completed units is reported as the cost of beginning work in process and the cost of ending work in process. The cost of beginning work in process represents the manufacturing costs carried over from the prior period; the cost of ending work in process represents the manufacturing costs that will be carried over to the next period. In both cases, additional manufacturing costs must be incurred to complete the units in work in process.

Cost Flows in a Manufacturing Organization

cost flows

Costs are accounted for from the point they are incurred to their recognition as expenses on the income statement. This process is referred to as **cost flows.** As will be shown, the cost flows of a manufacturing firm are more complex than those of a service firm or those of a merchandising firm.

The cost flow pattern of manufacturing firms is displayed in Exhibit 15-3. For a manufacturing firm, the selling and administrative costs are expensed immediately. However, the flow of product costs is more involved. In order to produce, the firm must purchase raw materials, acquire services of direct laborers, and incur overhead costs. As raw materials are purchased, the costs are initially assigned to an inventory account. When materials are placed in production, costs flow from the Raw Materials inventory account to the Work in Process inventory account. The cost of direct labor is assigned to the Work in Process account as it

Exhibit 15-2

Statement of Cost of Goods Manufactured
For the Year Ended December 31, 1995

Direct materials:		
Beginning inventory	$ 400,000	
Add: Purchases	900,000	
Materials available	$1,300,000	
Less: Ending inventory	(100,000)	
Direct materials used		$1,200,000
Direct labor		700,000
Manufacturing overhead:		
Indirect labor	$ 255,000	
Depreciation	345,000	
Rent	100,000	
Utilities	75,000	
Property taxes	25,000	
Maintenance	100,000	900,000
Total manufacturing costs added		$2,800,000
Add: Beginning work in process		400,000
Total manufacturing costs		$3,200,000
Less: Ending work in process		(800,000)
Cost of goods manufactured		$2,400,000

is incurred. Overhead costs are accumulated in a separate account and assigned periodically to the Work in Process account (the procedures for assigning overhead are discussed in a later chapter). When the goods being worked on are completed, the costs associated with these goods are transferred to the Finished Goods inventory account. Finally, when the goods are sold, the cost of the finished goods is transferred to the Cost of Goods Sold expense account.

Exhibit 15-3
Cost Flows: Manufacturing Firms

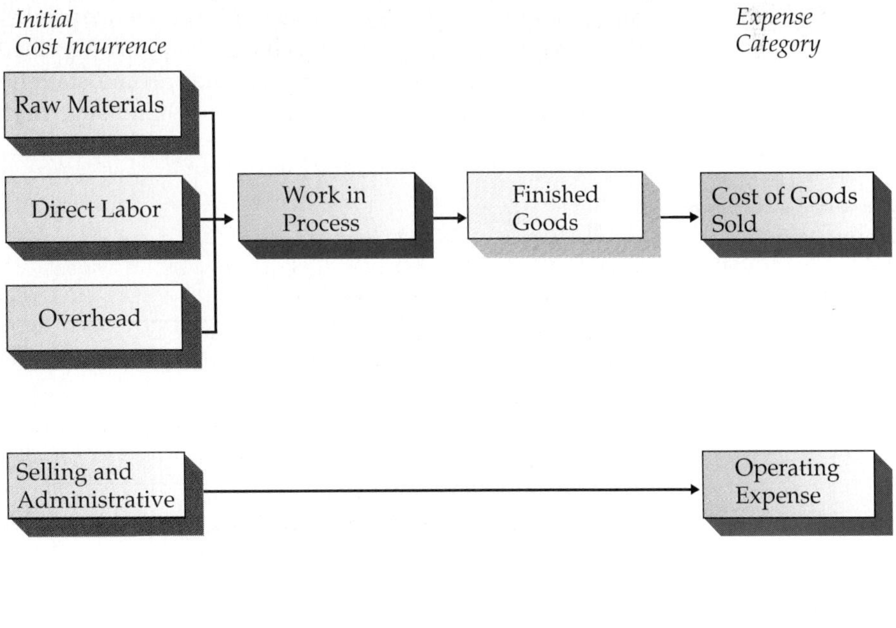

Exhibit 15-4
Income Statement for a Merchandising Firm

Sales		$5,000,000
Less cost of goods sold:		
Beginning inventory	$1,000,000	
Add: Purchases	3,000,000	
Goods available for sale	$4,000,000	
Less: Ending inventory	(850,000)	(3,150,000)
Gross profit		$1,850,000
Less operating expenses:		
Selling expenses	$ 500,000	
Administrative expenses	750,000	(1,250,000)
Income before taxes		$ 600,000

Comparison to Merchandising Organizations

An income statement for a merchandising firm is shown in Exhibit 15-4. Note that for a merchandising firm, the two major functional cost classifications still exist but correspond to *product costs* and *nonproduct costs.* The concept of cost of goods sold also differs. In a merchandising firm, cost of goods sold represents the acquisition cost of the goods, rather than the manufacturing cost. This acquisition cost is simply the amount paid for the goods being sold. This is more easily determined than is the cost of goods manufactured.

The cost flow pattern for a merchandising firm is shown in Exhibit 15-5. Operating costs, as incurred, are immediately expensed. Merchandise, however, is acquired, and the acquisition cost is first assigned to the Inventory account. Later, when the merchandise is sold, the costs flow, or are transferred, to an expense account.

When comparing the cost flows of manufacturing and merchandising firms, we find that a manufacturing firm possesses two additional categories of inventory: raw materials and work in process. Since a merchandising firm deals only with finished goods, these production-related inventories are not required. This difference manifests itself in two ways on the financial statements of the two entities. First, manufacturing firms have a supporting schedule for the cost of goods manufactured figure appearing on the income statement. The second manifestation affects the balance sheet. A merchandising firm will show only a Mer-

Exhibit 15-5
Cost Flows: Merchandising Firm

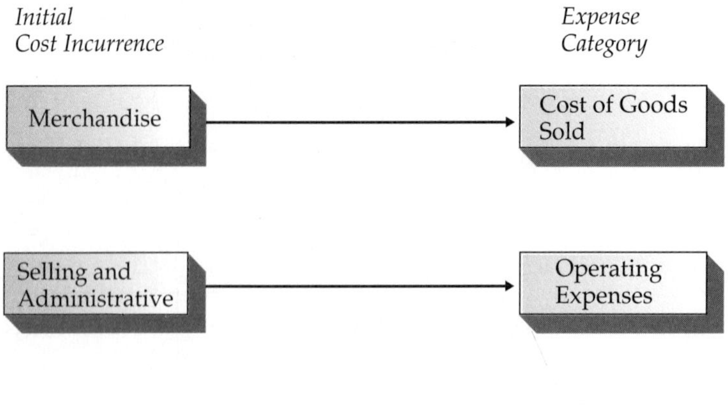

chandise inventory account in the asset section, whereas a manufacturing firm will show three inventory accounts: Raw Materials, Work in Process, and Finished Goods.

Comparison to Service Organizations

An income statement for a service organization is shown in Exhibit 15-6. For a service firm, the functional classifications correspond to service and nonservice categories. The cost of services sold is computed differently from the cost of goods sold in a manufacturing firm. For example, for a dentist, the cost of services would include raw materials (e.g., amalgam for fillings), overhead (e.g., depreciation on dental equipment, utilities, and rent), and direct labor (e.g., salary of a dental assistant). But unlike a manufacturing firm, the service firm has no finished goods inventories—it is not possible to inventory services. Thus, product costs for a service firm expire in the period incurred. In a direct comparison, cost of services sold would always correspond to cost of goods manufactured.

Since all product costs are effectively period costs in a service organization, no distinction is usually made between the service and nonservice categories when preparing the income statement. However, knowing the cost of services sold can provide valuable information for the managers or owners of service organizations. The need for many service organizations to accurately assign costs to services has become even more critical because of the deregulatory movement that has taken place over the past five to ten years. Additionally, if a service organization wants a loan, it is helpful to present an income statement in a format familiar to bankers.

In the past, regulated service organizations were allowed to set a price that covered costs and provided a specified rate of return. Deregulation has brought stiff competition, and managers in the affected industries (e.g., airlines and telecommunications) need to know the cost of each service being marketed to make pricing decisions and profitability assessments. According to some experts, deregulation in the service industry has unleashed an enormous demand for improved cost accounting.

Understanding how income statements differ across the three different kinds of organizations provides some insight into the cost flows that occur within them.

Exhibit 15-6
Income Statement for a Service Organization

Sales		$300,000
Less expenses:		
Cost of services sold:		
Direct materials	$ 50,000	
Direct labor	100,000	
Overhead	100,000	(250,000)
Gross profit		$ 50,000
Less operating expenses:		
Selling expenses	$ 4,000	
Administrative expenses	17,500	(21,500)
Income before taxes		$ 28,500

This, in turn, helps us to understand how cost accounting differs among the three types. Furthermore, studying the total cost flows for each of the three organizational categories provides a more comprehensive understanding of the cost accounting differences.

The cost flow pattern for a service firm is shown in Exhibit 15-7. Raw materials, those materials directly involved in providing the service and often referred to as *supplies*, are purchased and their cost flows into the Inventory account. As materials, direct labor, and overhead are used to provide the service, these costs are expensed immediately. The cost of materials flows from the Inventory account to the expense account Cost of Services Sold. As with service costs, the operating costs of selling and administration are expensed as they are incurred.

Comparing the manufacturing cost flows to the cost flows of service organizations reveals some significant differences. Service organizations use direct materials, direct labor, and overhead. However, service organizations cannot build inventories of services. Consequently, there are no work-in-process or finished goods inventories.

CLASSIFICATION BY COST BEHAVIOR

Objective 5
Explain the difference between variable and fixed cost behavior and prepare a variable-costing income statement.

cost driver

Cost behavior deals with how costs change with respect to changes in activity levels. To assess cost behavior, the activity and the changes in the activity level must be measured. The costs associated with an activity are those that are *caused* by the activity. Thus, in choosing a measure of activity-level changes, a measure must be chosen that is a *causal factor* for the activity's costs. A factor that causes (drives) activity costs is called a **cost driver.** For example, if work on the production line is the activity, then direct labor costs would be caused by the activity. Direct labor hours would then be a logical choice for a cost driver. Knowing how costs behave with respect to a relevant activity measure (cost driver) is essential for planning, control, decision making, and accurate product costing.

Exhibit 15-7
Cost Flows: Service Organization

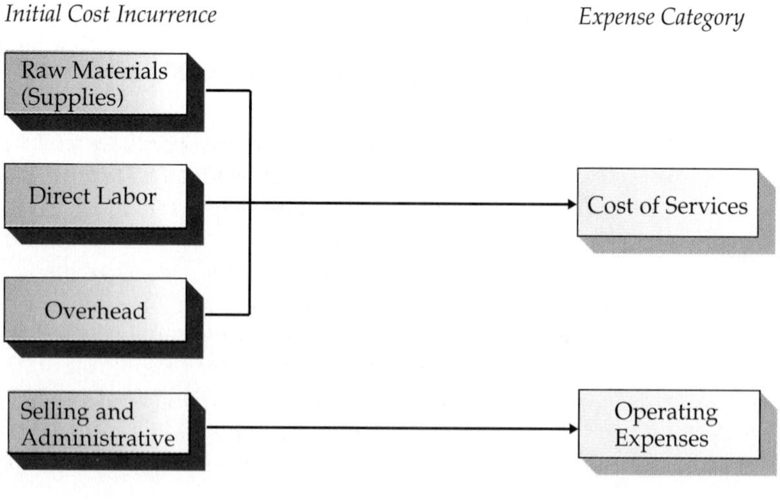

Assume that the cost driver is defined as the number of units produced. In general, economists assume that as the number of units produced increases, total costs will increase at a decreasing rate up to a certain point and then will increase at an increasing rate. Because of the difficulty in estimating the cost function, accountants usually approximate the underlying cost behavior by assuming a *linear relationship*. This means that total costs change at a constant rate.

Knowing how costs behave can be very important for product costing, planning, control, and decision making. Thus, identifying cost behavior is, perhaps, one of the most valuable contributions a management accountant can make to improve the overall management of an organization. Typically, three major categories of cost behavior are identified: fixed, variable, and mixed.

Fixed Costs

fixed costs

Fixed costs are costs that, *in total*, are constant within the relevant range as the level of the cost driver varies. To illustrate fixed cost behavior, consider a company that produces aluminum softball bats. Define the activity as producing bats and let the cost driver be the number of bats produced. The company operates one production line that can produce up to 5,000 bats per year. The production workers are supervised by a production-line manager who is paid $40,000 per year. The cost of supervision for several levels of production is given below.

Robin's Bats

	Number of Bats	
Supervision	*Produced*	*Unit Cost*
$40,000	1,000	$40.00
40,000	2,000	20.00
40,000	3,000	13.33
40,000	4,000	10.00
40,000	5,000	8.00

The first step in assessing cost behavior is defining a relevant cost driver (activity measure). In this case, the cost driver is the number of bats produced.

relevant range

The second step is defining what is meant by **relevant range,** the range over which the assumed fixed cost relationship is valid for the normal operations of a firm. Assume that the relevant range is 1,000 to 5,000 bats. Notice that the *total* cost of supervision remains constant within this range as more bats are produced. Robin's Bats pays $40,000 for supervision regardless of whether it produces 1,000, 2,000, or 5,000 bats.

Pay particular attention to the words *in total* in the definition of fixed costs. While the total cost of supervision remains unchanged as more bats are produced, the unit cost changes as the level of the cost driver changes. As the example in the table shows, the unit cost of supervision decreases from $40 to $8. Because of the behavior of per-unit fixed costs, it is easy to get the impression that fixed costs are affected by activity level changes when in reality they are not. Unit fixed costs can often be misleading and may adversely affect some decisions. It is often safer to work with total fixed costs.

Another note of caution is needed. As more bats are produced, a second production line may be needed. This requirement, in turn, may produce the need for an additional production-line manager. Assume that this is true to produce more than 5,000 bats. The cost of supervision would then double to $80,000 as production increased above the level of 5,000 bats.

Graphical Illustration of Fixed Costs

We can gain additional insight into the nature of fixed costs by portraying them graphically. Total fixed costs can be represented by the following simple linear equation:

$$\text{Total fixed costs} = \text{Dollar amount of fixed costs}$$
$$Y_f = F$$

$$\text{where } Y_f = \text{total fixed costs}$$
$$F = \text{Dollar amount of fixed costs}$$

In our example for Robin's Bats, supervision cost amounted to $40,000 for any level of output between 1,000 and 5,000 bats. Thus, supervision is a fixed cost, and the fixed cost equation in this case is:

$$\text{Total fixed costs} = \$40,000$$

To graph a simple linear equation, we need a horizontal axis to represent the cost driver (activity level) and a vertical axis to represent cost. For our example, production activity is measured in terms of units produced. The unit of measure for cost is dollars.

The graph representing fixed cost behavior is given in Exhibit 15-8. As can be seen, fixed cost behavior is described by a horizontal line. Notice that at zero bats produced, supervision cost is $40,000; at 1,000 bats produced, supervision is

Exhibit 15-8
Fixed Cost Behavior

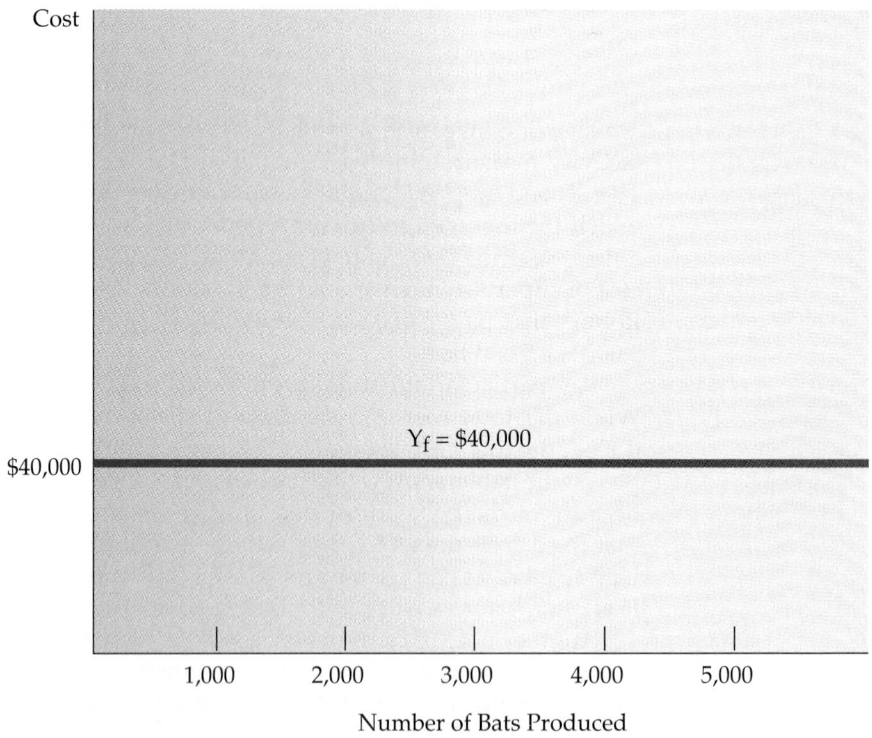

also $40,000. This line visually demonstrates that cost remains unchanged as the level of the cost driver varies.

Variable Costs

variable costs

Variable costs are defined as costs that, in total, vary in direct proportion to changes in a cost driver. To illustrate, let's expand the Robin's Bats example to include the cost of production-line workers. As with supervision, the activity is producing bats and the cost driver is number of bats. Each bat requires one-fourth hour of direct labor, and labor costs $12 per hour. Thus, the cost of production-line labor per bat is $3 (0.25 hour × $12 per hour). The cost of production-line labor for various levels of activity is given below:

Robin's Bats		
Cost of Direct Labor	*Number of Bats*	*Unit Cost*
$ 3,000	1,000	$3
6,000	2,000	3
9,000	3,000	3
12,000	4,000	3
15,000	5,000	3

As more bats are produced, the total cost of production-line labor increases in direct proportion. For example, as production doubles from 1,000 to 2,000 units, the *total* direct labor cost doubles from $3,000 to $6,000. Notice also that the unit cost of direct labor is constant.

Units of product, however, are not the only cost driver that can be used to describe the relationship. Direct labor hours can also be defined as the cost driver for direct labor cost. Why? Because direct labor hours also change in direct proportion to the number of units produced. The activity of producing bats can be measured in direct labor hours, using the fact that each bat requires one-fourth hour. The cost of direct labor for the Robin's Bats example, restated with direct labor hours as the cost driver, is displayed in Exhibit 15-9. As can be seen, the total variable costs predicted for each level of activity (measured by labor hours) are identical to the total variable costs predicted for each level of activity measured by units produced.

Exhibit 15-9
Unit-Based Cost Driver: Direct Labor Hours

Robin's Bats		
Cost of Direct Labor	*Direct Labor Hours*[a]	*Cost per Hour*
$ 3,000	250	$12
6,000	500	12
9,000	750	12
12,000	1,000	12
15,000	1,250	12

[a]1/4 × units produced (hours, therefore, correspond to different production levels).

Graphical Illustration of Variable Costs

Variable costs can also be represented by a linear equation. Here total variable costs depend on the level of cost driver. This relationship can be described by the equation below:

$$\text{Total variable costs} = \text{Variable cost per unit} \times \text{Number of units of cost driver}$$
$$Y_v = VX$$

$$\text{where } Y_v = \text{Total variable costs}$$
$$V = \text{Variable cost per unit}$$
$$X = \text{Number of units of cost driver}$$

In our example for Robin's Bats, the relationship that describes the cost of direct labor is:

$$\text{Total variable costs} = \$3 \times \text{Number of units produced}$$

or

$$Y_v = \$3X$$

Exhibit 15-10 graphically illustrates a variable cost. Variable cost behavior is represented as a straight line coming out of the origin. Notice that at zero units produced, total variable cost is zero. However, as units produced increase, the total variable cost also increases. Here it can be seen that total cost increases in direct proportion to increases in units of product (the cost driver); the rate of increase is measured by the slope of the line. At 1,000 bats produced, total direct labor cost is \$3,000 (or \$3 × 1,000 bats); at 2,000 bats produced, total direct labor cost is \$6,000.

Exhibit 15-10
Variable Cost Behavior

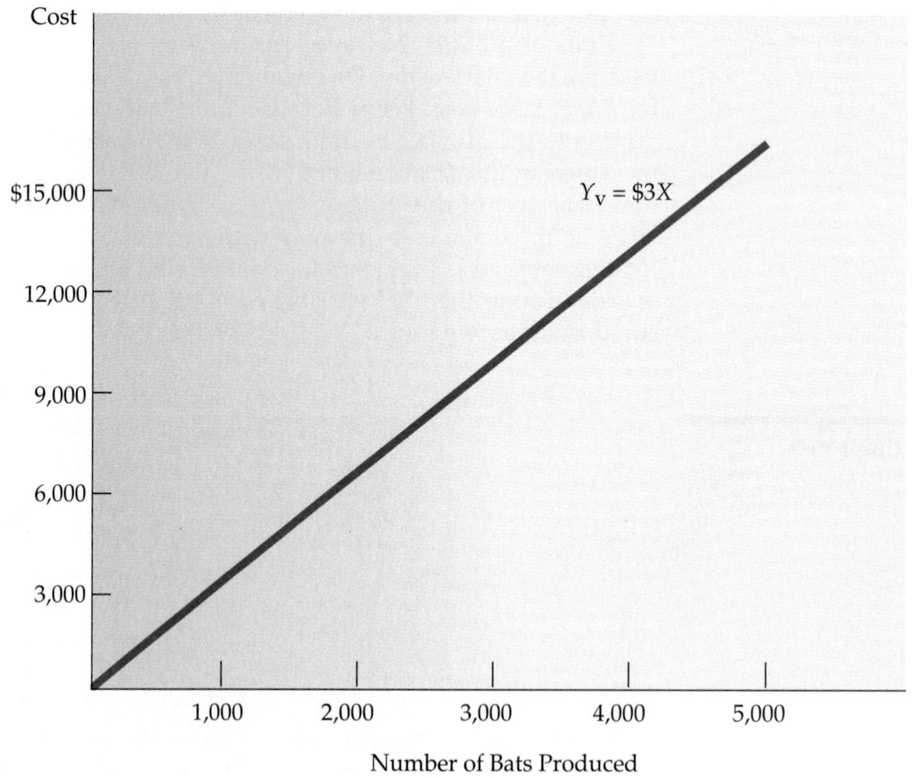

Mixed Costs

mixed costs

Mixed costs are costs that have both a fixed and a variable component. For example, a rental car often has a flat rate plus a charge per mile driven. Suppose the flat rate is $45 per day plus $0.20 per mile driven. If the car is rented for one day and driven 100 miles, the total rental is $65—the sum of the fixed charge of $45 plus the variable component of $20 ($0.20 × 100). Similarly, electricity is often billed at a flat rate per period plus a charge per kilowatt hour used. Assume that this is the case for the Robin's Bats example. Power is used to operate equipment used in the production of bats. The cost of power is $4,000 per year plus $0.50 per bat produced. The $0.50 charge per bat is based on the kilowatt hours used by each bat.

The linear equation for a mixed cost is given by:

$$\begin{aligned}\text{Total Cost} &= \text{Fixed Cost} + \text{Variable cost per unit} \times \text{Number of units}\\ &= \text{Fixed Cost} + \text{Total Variable Cost}\\ \text{or } Y &= F + VX\\ \text{where } Y &= \text{Total cost}\end{aligned}$$

For the Robin's Bats example, the total power cost is represented by the following equation:

$$\begin{aligned}\text{Total power cost} &= \$4{,}000 + \$0.50 \times \text{Number of units produced}\\ Y &= \$4{,}000 + \$0.50X\end{aligned}$$

Thus, for Robin's Bats, the following table shows the power cost associated with a variety of production levels:

Robin's Bats

Fixed Cost of Power	*Variable Cost of Power*	*Total Cost*	*Number of Bats*	*Power Cost Per Unit*
$4,000	$ 500	$4,500	1,000	$4.50
4,000	1,000	5,000	2,000	2.50
4,000	1,500	5,500	3,000	1.83
4,000	2,000	6,000	4,000	1.50
4,000	2,500	6,500	5,000	1.30

The graph of a mixed cost for the Robin's Bat example is given in Exhibit 15-11 (the graph assumes that the relevant range is 0 to 5,000 units). Mixed costs are represented by a line that intercepts the vertical axis (at $4,000 for this example). The intercept corresponds to the fixed cost component, and the slope of the line gives the variable cost per unit of cost driver (slope is $0.50 for the example portrayed).

Income Statement: Classification by Cost Behavior

Given an understanding of cost behavior, it is now possible to examine an income statement based on a cost behavioral classification. This type of income statement plays an important role in planning and control. It forms the basis for many of the conventional management accounting planning and control models.

An income statement based on a classification by cost behavior is displayed in Exhibit 15-12. Notice that the expenses are categorized by whether they are fixed or variable using units sold as the cost driver. Manufacturing and non-

Exhibit 15-11
Mixed Cost Behavior

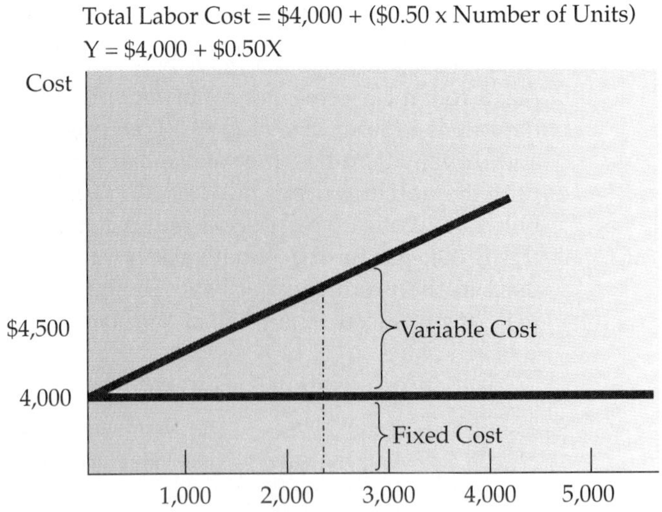

manufacturing costs both appear in the same category if they have the same kind of cost behavior. Cost behavior is the emphasis—not the function.

Even though the cost classification differs, the mechanics of computing income are very similar to the absorption-costing income described earlier. For example, *variable cost of goods sold* follows the same computational approach as cost of goods sold but uses *only* variable manufacturing costs. Thus, **variable cost of goods sold** is the total variable manufacturing costs attached to the units sold. Furthermore, variable cost of goods sold should be supported by a *variable cost of goods manufactured schedule*. This schedule again follows the same format used in computing cost of goods manufactured but it uses *only* variable manufacturing costs. Thus, **variable cost of goods manufactured** is the total variable manufacturing costs attached to the units produced. Variable manufacturing costs are direct materials, direct labor, and variable overhead. Examples of variable overhead items are power and supplies. Some overhead items are mixed costs and must be separated into their fixed and variable components. How this separation is done is the topic of a later chapter.

variable cost of goods sold

variable cost of goods manufactured

In computing income before taxes, total variable expenses are first deducted from sales revenue to determine the **contribution margin,** the amount available

contribution margin

Exhibit 15-12
Variable-Costing Income Statement: Classification by Cost Behavior

Sales		$10,000,000
Less variable expenses:		
Variable cost of goods sold	$5,750,000	
Variable selling expenses	700,000	
Variable administrative expenses	150,000	(6,600,000)
Contribution margin		$ 3,400,000
Less fixed expenses:		
Fixed overhead	$1,000,000	
Fixed selling expenses	650,000	
Fixed administrative expenses	400,000	(2,050,000)
Variable-costing income (before taxes)		$ 1,350,000

variable-costing income

to cover fixed costs and provide a profit. Deducting all fixed costs from the contribution margin yields **variable-costing income** (before taxes). This income statement often is referred to as a *variable-costing income statement.*

Variable-costing income is consistent with a product-costing approach that treats all fixed expenses, including fixed overhead, as period expenses. Under this product-costing approach, only variable manufacturing costs are viewed as product costs (variable selling and administrative expenses are still treated as period expenses). As already indicated, preparation of a variable cost of goods manufactured statement parallels that of the functional cost of goods manufactured statement using, however, only variable manufacturing expenses. Similarly, the average variable cost per unit can be computed by dividing the variable cost of goods manufactured by the units produced, assuming only one type of product.

The functional approach to income, on the other hand, is consistent with the traditional absorption product-costing approach that always views fixed overhead as a product cost. The two approaches can yield different income figures. Only absorption costing is permitted for external financial reporting purposes. More importantly, the two approaches provide different kinds of information. The variable-costing income statement provides information that facilitates planning, control, and decision making. For example, using the variable-costing income statement, a manager can assess the contribution each product line is making to cover the firm's fixed costs. If a product line is making a positive contribution, it may be a wise decision to keep the product line even though it cannot cover its *full* cost. Why? Because dropping a product line that is providing some coverage of fixed costs may actually reduce a firm's total profits. This insight is unavailable in the traditional income statement.

A comprehensive analysis of the differences between the traditional income statement and the contribution approach is covered in a later chapter. Important at this point is knowing how to prepare a variable-costing income statement and realizing that it has potential value for improving planning, control, and decision making.

Cost Behavior and Cost Systems

conventional (traditional) cost systems

activity-based cost (ABC) systems

Conventional (traditional) cost systems assume that all costs can be classified as fixed or variable with respect to changes in the *volume* of product produced. **Activity-based cost (ABC) systems,** on the other hand, assume that cost behavior is more complicated and requires additional cost drivers that are unrelated to the volume of product produced. For example, the costs of moving raw materials and partially finished goods from one point to another within a factory may be better described by the number of moves rather than the number of units produced. The net effect of an activity-based cost system is to increase the number of cost drivers that are used to describe cost behavior.

Both conventional and ABC approaches are found in practice. Conventional cost systems currently are much more widely used than ABC systems. The use of ABC systems, however, is increasing—particularly among organizations faced with increased product diversity, more product complexity, and intense competitive pressures. These organizations often adopt a just-in-time manufacturing approach (discussed in Chapters 19 and 23) and implement advanced manufacturing technology. For firms operating in this advanced manufacturing environment, the conventional cost systems may not work well. Better assessment of cost behavior and increased accuracy in product costing are both critical for the advanced manufacturing environment. The product-costing methods and the management accounting practices can differ significantly between the conventional and advanced manufacturing environments. Thus, in our study of management accounting, we will learn the methods and procedures for both conventional and advanced manufacturing environments.

SUMMARY OF LEARNING OBJECTIVES

1. Identify three different organizational settings and describe the role of cost information in each setting. The three organizational classifications are manufacturing, merchandising, and service. Manufacturing organizations produce goods by converting raw materials into a physical product through the use of labor and capital inputs. Merchandising firms buy goods made by manufacturers and sell them to consumers or other merchandising firms. Service organizations provide a service to customers. They deal with intangible products and many such organizations are not profit-making entities. Each type of organization requires cost information, although the type and quantity of information may differ.

2. Define basic cost concepts. Cost is the cash or cash equivalent value sacrificed for goods and services that are expected to bring a current or future benefit to the organization. There are a number of basic cost concepts that are useful for managers. These include such basic concepts as direct and indirect costs, controllable and noncontrollable costs, and sunk and out-of-pocket costs.

3. Classify costs by function. A functional classification of costs places costs into manufacturing and nonmanufacturing categories. Manufacturing costs are typically defined as the costs of direct materials, direct labor, and overhead. Nonmanufacturing costs are defined as the costs of general administration and selling. For external reporting purposes, product costs are costs that attach to the product and are inventoried; they are expensed only when the product is sold. Direct materials, direct labor, and overhead are all classified as product costs. Period costs are costs that are related to periods of time rather than units of output. Period costs are always expensed in the period incurred. Selling and administrative costs are always classified as period costs (for external reporting purposes). For managerial purposes, definitions of product cost may differ from that required by external reporting.

4. Prepare an absorption-costing income statement and explain how financial statements differ among manufacturing, service, and merchandising firms. If expenses are grouped according to function and then deducted from sales revenue, we have absorption-costing income statements. For manufacturing firms, the major functional expense classifications on the income statement are manufacturing and nonmanufacturing; for merchandising firms, the categories are product and nonproduct; for service firms, the categories are service and nonservice. For income determination in a manufacturing firm, the cost of goods manufactured must be calculated. No similar requirement exists for either a merchandising or service firm. For a service firm, the cost of services sold always corresponds to the cost of services produced. For a merchandising firm, the cost of goods acquired usually does not correspond to the cost of goods sold. The same is true for the cost of goods manufactured in a manufacturing firm.

5. Explain the difference between variable and fixed cost behavior and prepare a variable-costing income statement. Fixed costs are costs that, in total, are constant as the cost driver (activity level) changes. Variable costs do change, in total, with changes in the cost driver (activity level). Mixed costs have both a variable and a fixed component.

If costs are grouped according to unit-based cost behavior and then deducted from sales revenue, we have a variable-costing income statement. A variable-costing income statement cannot be used for external reporting, but it is an important managerial tool. Exhibit 15-12 shows how a variable-costing income statement is prepared.

KEY TERMS

Absorption-costing income *729*
Activity-based cost (ABC) system *741*
Administrative costs *727*
Assets *723*
Contribution margin *740*
Controllable costs *724*

REVIEW PROBLEM

Pop's Burger Heaven produces and sells quarter-pound hamburgers. Each burger sells for $1.50. During December, Pop's sold 10,000 burgers (the average amount sold each month). The restaurant employs cooks, servers, and one supervisor (the owner, John Peterson). All cooks and servers are part-time employees. Pop's maintains a pool of part-time employees so that the number of employees scheduled can be adjusted to the changes in demand. Demand varies on a weekly as well as a monthly basis.

A janitor is hired to clean the building on a weekly basis. The building is leased from a local real estate company. The building has no seating capabilities. All orders are filled on a drive-through basis.

The supervisor schedules work, opens the building, counts the cash, advertises, and is responsible for hiring and firing. The following costs were incurred during December:

Hamburger meat	$1,600
Lettuce	300
Tomatoes	250
Buns	300
Other ingredients	20
Cooks' wages	2,550
Servers' wages	2,032
Supervisor's salary	2,000
Utilities	500
Depreciation:	
Cooking equipment	200
Cash register	50
Advertising	100
Rent	800
Janitorial supplies	50
Janitor's wages	120

The only mixed cost is for utilities. The fixed component is $50.

REQUIRED:

1. Classify the costs for Pop's December operations in one of the following categories: direct materials, direct labor, overhead, and selling and administrative.

2. Prepare an absorption-costing income statement for the month of December.
3. Prepare a variable-costing income statement for December.

Solution:

1. Classification:
   a. *Direct materials*: Hamburger meat, lettuce, tomatoes, and buns
   b. *Direct labor*: Cooks' wages
   c. *Overhead*: Utilities, depreciation on the cooking equipment, rent, janitorial wages, janitorial supplies, and other ingredients
   d. *Selling and administrative*: Servers' wages, supervisor's salary, depreciation on the cash register, and advertising

Explanation of Classification:

Cooks are direct laborers because they make the hamburgers. "Other ingredients" are overhead because of cost and convenience, even though technically they are direct materials. Because the primary purpose of the building is production (cooking hamburgers), all of the rent and building-related costs are classified as indirect production costs. (An argument could be made that the building also supports the selling and administrative functions; consequently, a portion of the rent and building-related costs should be classified as selling and administrative costs.) Servers are responsible for taking and filling orders and are, therefore, classified as sales personnel. The cash register is used to support the sales function. The supervisor is responsible for overseeing the business as a whole and coordinating the sales and production functions. Thus, his salary is an administrative cost.

2. Sales ($1.50 × 10,000)		$15,000
Cost of goods sold:		
Direct materials	$2,450	
Direct labor	2,550	
Overhead	1,690	6,690
Gross profit		$ 8,310
Less operating expenses:		
Selling expenses	$2,182	
Administrative	2,000	(4,182)
Net income		$ 4,128

3. Sales ($1.50 × 10,000)		$15,000
Less variable expenses:		
Variable cost of goods sold:		
Direct labor	$2,550	
Direct materials	2,450	
Variable overhead:		
Other ingredients	20	
Utilities	450	
	$5,470	
Variable selling costs	2,032	(7,502)
Contribution margin		$ 7,498
Less fixed costs:		
Fixed overhead	$1,220	
Fixed selling	150	
Fixed administrative	2,000	(3,370)
Net income		$ 4,128

QUESTIONS

1. Why does the manufacturing organization offer a greater array of cost concepts and applications than either a mechandising or service organization?
2. Distinguish between the three types of organizations.
3. Does an organization incur a cost if it trades a building it owns for equipment? Explain.
4. What is a cost object?
5. What is a direct cost? An indirect cost?
6. What is a controllable cost?
7. What is a differential cost?
8. What is the difference between a direct manufacturing cost and an indirect manufacturing cost?
9. Explain why knowledge of cost behavior is useful information for a manager to have.
10. What is a cost driver?
11. What role does the relevant range play in the definition of a fixed cost?
12. On a per-unit basis, fixed costs are variable and variable costs are fixed. Do you agree? Explain your reasoning.
13. What is a conventional cost system? An ABC system? Which of the two is the most prevalent? Is this changing? Explain why.
14. Identify the three cost elements that determine the cost of making a product (for external reporting).
15. Product costs can be period costs, but period costs can never be product costs. Do you agree? Explain your reasoning.
16. Why are some direct materials classified as an overhead cost?
17. What is the difference between a loss and an expense?
18. What is the difference between a period cost and an expense?
19. How do the income statements of a merchandising firm and a manufacturing firm differ? How do the balance sheets differ?
20. How do the income statements of a service firm and a manufacturing firm differ? How do the balance sheets differ?
21. How does an absorption-costing income statement differ from a variable-costing income statement? Which of the two income statements must be used for external reporting? Which of the two statements has the most value for internal purposes?
22. Explain what is meant by cost flow. How do the cost flows of the three different organizational types differ?
23. Explain why the salary of a plant manager would be classified as an overhead cost, not as an administrative cost.
24. Explain why the overtime premium paid to direct laborers is treated as an overhead cost, not as a direct labor cost.
25. Explain the difference between an opportunity cost and an out-of-pocket cost.
26. Explain why depreciation is a sunk cost.
27. A cost that is not controllable at one level may be controllable at a higher level. Explain.
28. Explain why managerial product costing may produce a different unit cost than product costing for inventory (external reporting).

EXERCISES

E15-1
Cost Classification
LO 1, 2, 3

Harvey Johnson is a maintenance worker in a garden hose plant. Harvey's annual salary is $30,000. He maintains and repairs a special kind of machine located in each of the two production departments (Department 1—Assembly, where plastic tubing is cut into 75′ lengths and fitted with metal couplings; and Department 2—Packaging, where the hoses are coiled and wrapped). Helen Hunaker, who works for the same company as a sales representative, is responsible for creating and servicing customer accounts. Helen is paid $20,000 plus a 5% commission on new accounts.

REQUIRED:

1. Is Harvey's salary a manufacturing or nonmanufacturing cost? If manufacturing, is it direct or indirect labor? If nonmanufacturing, is it a selling or administrative cost?
2. Is Helen's salary a manufacturing or nonmanufacturing cost? If manufacturing, is it direct or indirect labor? If nonmanufacturing, is it a selling or administrative cost?
3. Is Harvey's salary a fixed, variable, or a mixed cost? Which is Helen's? Explain.

E15-2
Behavior of Overhead Costs; Service Company
LO 5

Harmony Funeral Home offers a full range of services. Based on past experience, Harmony has found that its total overhead costs can be represented by the following formula: Overhead = $100,000 + $25 × (number of funerals). During 1995, Harmony conducted 1,000 funerals.

REQUIRED:

1. What is the total overhead cost incurred by Harmony in 1995?
2. What is the total fixed overhead incurred by Harmony in 1995?
3. What is the total variable overhead incurred by Harmony in 1995?
4. What is the overhead cost per funeral?
5. What is the fixed overhead cost per funeral?
6. What is the variable overhead cost per funeral?
7. Recalculate requirements 4, 5, and 6 for the following levels of service activity: (a) 2,000 funerals, and (b) 500 funerals. Explain this outcome.

E15-3
Cost of Goods Manufactured and Sold
LO 4

Campwell, Inc., manufactures backpacks. At the beginning of August, the following information was supplied by their accountant:

Raw Materials inventory	$185,000
Work in Process inventory	120,000
Finished Goods inventory	102,000

During August, direct labor cost was $405,000, raw materials purchases were $800,000, and the total overhead cost was $1,050,750.

The inventories at the end of August were:

Raw Materials inventory	$168,000
Work in Process inventory	235,000
Finished Goods inventory	91,000

REQUIRED:

1. Prepare a cost of goods manufactured statement for August.
2. Prepare a cost of goods sold statement for August.

E15-4
Cost Classification
LO 5

Classify the costs below as variable, fixed, or mixed. Also identify the cost driver that allows you to define the cost behavior. (*Hint*: Cost behavior depends on the cost driver. For example, a receptionist's wages varies with the number of hours worked but is fixed with respect to units sold. Give some thought to the kind of activity associated with the cost drivers you choose.) Prepare your answer in the following format:

Cost	*Cost Behavior*	*Cost Driver*
Milk in ice cream	Variable	Units produced

a. Floppy disk drive in a microcomputer
b. Wages of a dental assistant
c. Advertising
d. Rental cars for sales personnel
e. Fuel for a commercial passenger jet
f. Depreciation on a warehouse

g. Cost of utilities in a factory
h. Surgical gauze used in a hospital
i. The cost of all factory indirect labor
j. Amalgam used by a dentist
k. Salary for a moving van driver
l. The cost of leasing a building for a supermarket
m. Salary of a receptionist in a doctor's office
n. Commissions paid to sales personnel
o. The cost of forms used to file insurance claims

E15-5 Preparation of Income Statements

LO 4, 5

Discon Corporation manufactures a popular doll called Teardrops. Last year 60,000 dolls were made and sold for $20 each. The actual unit cost for Teardrops is given below.

Direct materials	$ 2.00
Direct labor	0.50
Variable overhead	2.50
Fixed overhead	7.00
Total unit cost	$12.00

The only selling expenses were a commission of $2 per unit sold and advertising totaling $90,000. Administrative expenses, all fixed, equaled $40,000. There were no beginning and ending finished goods or work-in-process inventories.

REQUIRED:

1. Prepare an absorption-costing income statement.
2. Prepare a variable-costing income statement.

E15-6 Per Unit Costs

LO 3, 4

Refer to the data in Exercise 15-5. Calculate the following costs on a per-unit basis: prime cost, conversion cost, variable cost, full absorption cost, and variable manufacturing cost.

E15-7 Cost Classification

LO 3

Classify the following costs as product or period costs (for external reporting purposes). For those costs that are product costs, identify the costs as direct materials, direct labor, or overhead.

a. Legal fees paid by a corporation
b. Depreciation on the factory building
c. Property tax on work-in-process inventory
d. Salary of a factory storeroom clerk
e. Wages of a sewing machine operator in a clothes factory
f. Lubricating oil for sewing machines
g. Overtime wages paid to the sewing machine operators
h. Corporate-level research and development costs
i. Sugar in a candy bar
j. Insurance on a warehouse and its inventory
k. Salary of a janitor in a factory
l. Warranty costs
m. Depreciation on office equipment (at corporate headquarters)
n. Pencils and paper clips for a production manager
o. Property tax on plant and equipment

E15-8
Cost Classification
LO 3

Refer to Exercise 15-7 and revise each cost in such a way that it will change from product to period cost, or vice versa.

EXAMPLE: In (a.) above, legal fees paid by a corporation are period costs. To change them into their opposites, product costs, they will have to be linked specifically to manufacturing—perhaps legal fees paid to file a patent on a new manufacturing process.

E15-9
Cost of Goods Manufactured and Sold
LO 4

The following information comes from the accounting records of a manufacturing firm:

Direct labor cost	$13,000
Purchases of raw materials	8,000
Supplies used	675
Factory insurance	350
Commissions paid	2,000
Factory supervision	1,230
Advertising	782
Material handling	2,745
Beginning work-in-process inventory	12,500
Ending work-in-process inventory	14,250
Beginning raw materials inventory	4,000
Ending raw materials inventory	2,000
Beginning finished goods inventory	5,685
Ending finished goods inventory	3,250

REQUIRED:

1. Prepare a cost of goods manufactured statement.
2. Prepare a cost of goods sold statement.

E15-10
Prime and Conversion Costs
LO 3

During April, Grady Inc., incurred the following manufacturing costs:

a. Direct laborers worked a total of 600 hours, including 100 overtime hours. The regular wage rate is $10 per hour. Overtime hours are paid at $15 per hour ($10 straight-time wage and $5 overtime premium).
b. Beginning raw materials inventory was $8,550. Purchases of raw materials were $3,450. There was no ending raw materials inventory.
c. Depreciation on plant and equipment was $10,000.
d. Insurance was $600.
e. Indirect labor was $2,000.

REQUIRED:

1. Calculate the prime cost for March.
2. Calculate the conversion cost for March.

E15-11
Cost Assessment; Service Company
LO 3, 4

Harding Repair Inc. does all the repair work for a medium-sized manufacturer of televisions. The repair work is all associated with warranty claims. Sets are sent directly to Harding and after the work is completed, Harding bills the television manufacturer for cost plus 30%. In the month of March, purchases of materials (replacement parts) equaled $90,000, the beginning inventory of parts was $40,500, and the ending inventory of material was $15,250. Payments to repair technicians during the month totaled $63,000 (wages are paid monthly). Overhead incurred was $113,000.

REQUIRED:

1. What was the cost of materials used for repair work during the month of March?
2. What was prime cost for March?
3. What was conversion cost for March?
4. What was total repair cost for March? If this were a manufacturing firm, what would the corresponding cost be called?

E15-12
Cost of Goods Manufactured and Sold
LO 4

For each of the three companies (Lomax, Cardon, and Hindley) listed below, calculate the missing values.

	Lomax	*Cardon*	*Hindley*
Direct materials	$15,000	$ 41,014	$10,000
Direct labor	26,000	?	7,500
Overhead	17,500	50,000	20,700
Total manufacturing cost added	$?	$125,360	$?
Beginning work in process	—	?	5,112
Ending work in process	?	12,000	7,000
Cost of goods manufactured	$44,300	$?	$?
Beginning inventory, finished goods	30,000	51,500	16,000
Ending inventory, finished goods	26,400	36,000	?
Cost of goods sold	$?	$174,110	$50,000

E15-13
Cost Drivers
LO 5

Identify which of the following cost drivers explain changes in cost attributable to changes in the number of units produced.

a. Machine hours
b. Number of setups
c. Number of purchase orders
d. Kilowatt hours (machine-intensive production setting)
e. Number of material moves
f. Direct labor dollars
g. Direct material dollars
h. Number of inspection hours
i. Number of rework hours (rework hours are labor hours used to correct a defective or faulty product)

E15-14
Cost Behavior and Decision Making
LO 5

Redland Paper Products is a small company that specialized in the production of paper towels until several years ago. The company had generally prospered, but five years ago, the market for towels became very competitive and profits dropped sharply. The output of the one plant owned by the company was devoted exclusively to towels. Two years ago, a decision to add a product line was made. Management determined that existing idle capacity could easily be adapted to produce paper napkins. Moreover, the variable cost of producing a package of napkins was virtually identical to that of a package of towels. Since the fixed expenses would not change, the new product was forecast to increase profits significantly.

Two years after the addition of the new product line, profits had not improved—in fact, they had actually dropped. Upon investigation, the president of the company discovered that profits had not increased as expected because the so-called fixed cost pool had increased dramatically. The president interviewed the manager of each support department. Typical responses from three of those managers are given below.

Purchasing: The new line increased the number of purchase orders. We had to use more resources to handle this increased volume.

Accounting: There were more transactions to process than before. We had to increase our staff.

Setups: There are two styles of napkins—each requiring a different setup. The increased number of setups required us to increase our expenditures.

REQUIRED: Explain why the results of adding the new product line were not projected accurately.

PROBLEMS

P15-1 Cost Identification

LO 1, 2, 3, 5

Given below is a list of cost items described in the chapter and a list of brief descriptive settings where the items are described. Match the items with the settings. There may be more than one cost classification associated with each setting; however, select the setting that seems to fit the item best.

Cost terms:

a. Loss	g. Selling cost	m. Product cost
b. Sunk cost	h. Conversion cost	n. Direct materials cost
c. Opportunity cost	i. Variable cost	o. Overhead cost
d. Controllable cost	j. Fixed cost	p. Administrative cost
e. Differential cost	k. Prime cost	q. Mixed cost
f. Direct labor cost	l. Period cost	

Settings:

1. Marcus Armstrong, manager of Timmins Optical, estimated that the cost of plastic, wages of the technician producing the lenses, and overhead totaled $30 per pair of single-vision lenses.
2. Rachael Johnson, owner of Bright Travel Agency, is examining two different data-base software packages. Both packages offer essentially the same features, although one may have better documentation. The difference in cost between the two packages is $90.
3. Linda was having a hard time deciding whether to return to school or not. She was concerned about the good salary she would have to give up for the next four years.
4. Randy Harris is the finished goods warehouse manager for a medium-size manufacturing firm. He is paid a salary of $90,000 per year. As he studied the financial statement prepared by the local CPA firm, he wondered how his salary was treated.
5. Maria Sanchez was disgusted. Her entire inventory of silk blouses had been ruined by a leaky roof. The inventory wasn't insured, and all she could do was write off the cost of the inventory. Well, at least some tax savings might be realized.
6. Jamie Young is in charge of the legal department at company headquarters. Her salary is $95,000 per year. She reports to the chief executive officer.
7. All factory costs that are not classified as direct materials or direct labor.
8. Gary Sorenson was trying to reduce the cost of the material-handling activity. He discovered that material-handling costs increased in direct proportion to the number of moves made. Accordingly, he initiated a study to see whether manufacturing operations could be redesigned to reduce the number of moves.
9. Tom Wilson decided that the manager of the Cutting Department should be held responsible for the maintenance cost incurred. After all, he is the one who decides when and how frequently preventive maintenance is done.
10. The new product required machining, assembly, and painting. The design engineer requested the accounting department to estimate the labor cost of each of the three operations. The engineer supplied the estimated labor hours for each operation.
11. After obtaining the estimate of direct labor cost, the design engineer estimated the cost of the materials that would be used for the new product.

12. The design engineer totaled the costs of materials and direct labor for the new product.
13. The design engineer also estimated the cost of converting the raw materials into its final form.
14. In deciding whether to get rid of the Camaro, Bob reminded himself that it didn't really matter how much money he had spent on rebuilding the engine. The money was spent and gone! All that was important now was what it would cost him to continue owning the car.
15. The rental agreement on the company car called for a payment of $200 per month plus $0.20 per mile driven. There was no penalty for excess use. At the end of the agreement, however, ownership of the car reverted to the lessor.
16. The auditor pointed out that the depreciation on the corporate jet had been incorrectly assigned to Finished Goods inventory (the jet was used primarily to fly the CEO and other staff to various company sites). Accordingly, the depreciation charge was reallocated to the income statement.
17. The director of radiology argued that the cost of X ray film increased in direct proportion to the number of X rays taken—not the number of patients served.

P15-2
Cost Behavior; Service Company
LO 1, 5

HairPort Company offers a variety of hair treatment services. The marketing strategy of the company is fast service with high quality. The company operates all of its outlets in major shopping malls. To speed up its services, there are three outlets in each mall—where each outlet offers specialized hair treatment. One of the outlets offers shampooing and hair coloring. This outlet expects to service 5,000 clients for the coming year. The expected costs for servicing this number of clients are given below.

Direct materials	$25,000
Direct labor	40,000
Overhead:	
Supplies	3,000
Rent	15,000
Indirect labor	6,000
Power	1,000

Assume that all the individual cost items are either strictly fixed or strictly variable with respect to clients serviced.

REQUIRED:

1. Prepare a cost formula for the following costs:
   a. Direct materials
   b. Direct labor
   c. Variable overhead
   d. Fixed overhead
   e. Total costs
2. Assuming that 6,000 clients are serviced, use the cost formulas developed in Requirement 1 and compute the following:
   a. Total cost of direct materials
   b. Total cost of direct labor
   c. Total cost of variable overhead
   d. Total cost of fixed overhead
   e. Total manufacturing costs
3. What is the unit cost of shampooing and coloring if 5,000 clients are serviced as planned?
4. What is the unit cost if 6,000 clients are serviced? Why does the unit cost change from the one computed for 5,000 clients?

5. Explain how unit cost information may be helpful in choosing a price to charge for the service.

P15-3
Cost Classification
LO 3, 5

Classify each of the following items as (1) a direct or indirect product cost (or N/A if it is not a product cost), (2) a product or period cost, and (3) a fixed, variable, or mixed cost (assuming units of product as the cost driver).

a. Tacks in a large sofa
b. Salary of a plant security guard
c. Buttons on a shirt
d. Salary of a plant manager
e. Carpenters in a construction company
f. Salary of a warehouse clerk
g. Total overhead cost
h. Printing and postage for advertising circulars
i. Total selling costs
j. Sheetrock in a new home being built
k. Depreciation on the company's executive jet plane
l. Depletion on an existing oil well
m. Fees paid for an annual audit
n. The total cost of operating a power service center in a factory
o. Pipelines for transporting crude oil to a refinery
p. The cost of a market research study
q. Pipelines for transporting crude oil to customers

P15-4
Income Statement: Cost of Goods Manufactured
LO 4

W. W. Phillips Company produced 4,000 leather recliners during 1995. These recliners sell for $400 each. Phillips had 500 recliners in finished goods inventory at the beginning of the year. At the end of the year there were 700 recliners in finished goods inventory. Phillip's accounting records provide the following information:

Purchases of raw materials	$320,000
Raw materials inventory, January 1, 1995	46,800
Raw materials inventory, December 31, 1995	66,800
Direct labor	200,000
Indirect labor	40,000
Rent, factory building	42,000
Depreciation, factory equipment	60,000
Utilities, factory	11,956
Salary, sales supervisor	90,000
Commissions, salespersons	180,000
General administration	300,000
Work-in-process inventory, January 1, 1995	13,040
Work-in-process inventory, December 31, 1995	14,996
Finished goods inventory, January 1, 1995	80,000
Finished goods inventory, December 31, 1995	114,100

REQUIRED:

1. Prepare a cost of goods manufactured statement.
2. Compute the average cost of producing one unit of product in 1995.
3. Prepare an income statement on an absorption-costing basis.

P15-5
Cost of Goods Manufactured; Cost Identification; Contribution Margin; Solving for Unknowns
LO 3, 4, 5

Winn Company creates, produces, and markets games of strategy. Before any employee is hired, a puzzle of some sort must be solved successfully.

You are applying for a job as an entry-level accountant. The controller of the firm wishes to test your knowledge of basic cost terms and concepts, and, at the same time, evaluate your analytical skills. To do so, he gives you the following information for 1995:

a. Total fixed overhead, $190,000.
b. Per-unit variable manufacturing cost, $25. There are no other variable costs.
c. Total current variable manufacturing costs equal 125 percent of current conversion cost.
d. Units produced, 10,000.
e. Beginning work in process is one-half the cost of ending work in process.
f. There are no beginning or ending inventories for raw materials or finished goods.
g. Cost of goods sold is $400,000.
h. Variable overhead equals 133 percent of direct labor costs.

REQUIRED:

1. Prepare a statement of cost of goods manufactured for 1995.
2. If the selling price is $50 per unit, what is the gross margin? What is the total contribution margin?
3. If you were operating below capacity and someone offered to buy 1,000 units for a price of $29 per unit, what is the change in profits (incremental profits) assuming the order is accepted? (Assume that the 1,000 units will be produced using the extra capacity available.)

P15-6
Cost of Goods Manufactured; Cost Behavior; Unit Cost; Income Statements
LO 4, 5

Krispy Company produces a popular line of premium chocolate chip cookies. The following data are provided for the year ended July 31, 1995:

Units produced	50,000
Cost of goods sold	$140,800
Goods available for sale	$288,000
Cost of goods manufactured	$256,000
Beginning raw materials inventory	$ 34,000
Purchases, raw materials	$ 80,000
Direct labor	$ 56,000
Overhead	$100,000
Beginning work in process	—
Ending work in process	—

REQUIRED:

1. Prepare a statement of cost of goods manufactured. What is the full manufacturing cost per unit?
2. Assume that the total overhead can be described by the formula, Y = $40,000 + $1.20X, where X = units produced. Prepare a statement of the *variable* cost of goods manufactured. What is the variable manufacturing cost per unit?
3. During the year, 40,000 units were sold for a price of $8 per unit. Selling and administrative costs are fixed and total $70,000. Assume that the unit cost of finished goods in beginning inventory is the same as the current cost per completed unit (for both approaches). Prepare the following:
   a. An absorption-costing income statement
   b. A variable-costing income statement

P15-7
Cost of Goods Manufactured; Cost Behavior; Income Statements
LO 4, 5

Mallory Company produces a chemical used in the production of flares and fireworks. The chemical is packaged and sold in 25 lb. bags. For 1995, Mallory reported the following:

Inventories:	
Work in process, January 1	$ 50,000
Work in process, December 31	50,000
Finished goods, January 1 (48,000 bags)	480,000
Finished goods, December 31 (24,000 bags)	240,000
Raw materials, January 1	80,000
Raw materials, December 31	120,000
Costs:	
Direct materials used	$280,000
Direct labor	400,000
Plant depreciation	60,000
Salary, production supervisor	120,000
Indirect labor	80,000
Utilities, factory	24,000
Sales commissions	32,000
Salary, sales supervisor	80,000
Depreciation, factory equipment	20,000
Administrative costs (all fixed)	48,000
Indirect materials	16,000

Mallory produced 100,000 bags of chemical during 1995 and sold 124,000 at $30 per unit. Work-in-process and finished-goods inventories consisted of 80 percent variable costs. All costs listed above are strictly variable or strictly fixed. There are no mixed costs.

REQUIRED:

1. Prepare a statement of cost of goods manufactured. Calculate the average full manufacturing cost per unit produced.
2. Prepare a statement of the cost of goods manufactured using only variable manufacturing costs. Calculate the average variable manufacturing cost per unit.
3. Prepare an absorption-costing income statement.
4. Prepare a variable-costing income statement.

P15-8
Cost Behavior: Multiple Cost Drivers
LO 5

Anderson Company currently produces an electronic circuit board for stereo units. A manufacturing cost formula based on direct labor hours for this product is given below.

$$\text{Total manufacturing costs} = \$300{,}000 + \$15X$$

where X is direct labor hours. The plant is producing 10,000 units per year but has the capacity to produce 15,000. Market conditions probably will not permit any expansion of production for the stereo circuit board. The company, however, is planning to add a new product: a circuit board for small television sets. Existing equipment can be adapted to produce the product. Engineers estimate that the same direct labor hours will be used per unit. In fact, the same variable cost per direct labor hour will be incurred. The controller has argued that the fixed costs will remain at $300,000—after all, these costs should not change as production activity increases. Thus, the manufacturing cost formula will not change for the two-product setting.

Of the fixed costs, $100,000 represents depreciation, $100,000 is the cost of operating the purchasing department, and $100,000 is the cost of operating the engineering department. Currently, there is no unused capacity for either the purchasing department or the engineering department. Before making a final decision on the new product, a consultant was hired to assess the impact of the new product on the costs of the firm. The consultant developed the following cost formulas, using three different cost drivers:

Cost Formula	*Cost Driver*
Purchasing department cost = $40,000 + 30X_1$	X_1 = Number of purchase orders
Engineering department cost = $50,000 + 100X_2$	X_2 = Number of engineering orders
Remaining overhead cost = $100,000 + 15X_3$	X_3 = Direct labor hours

The consultant also provided the following estimates of activity for each product:

	Stereo Board	*Television Board*
Units of product	10,000	5,000
Direct labor hours	20,000	10,000
Purchase orders	2,000	2,000
Engineering orders	500	1,000

REQUIRED:

1. Calculate the total cost of producing the stereo circuit boards without the new product. Do you think this cost is accurate? Explain.
2. Using only the direct-labor-hour cost formula, calculate the total cost of producing both products.
3. Using the cost formulas developed by the consultant, calculate the total cost of producing both products. Explain why the two numbers differ. Which approach do you think provides the more accurate prediction? Why?
4. Using only the variable cost portion of the unit-based formula, calculate the variable cost per unit for each product. Now calculate the cost per unit for each product using only the variable elements from each of the consultant's formulas. Which method do you think provides the more accurate product costing? Explain.

P15-9
Cost Identification and Analysis
LO 3, 5

Melissa Scothern has decided to open a printing shop. She has secured a five-year contract to print a popular regional magazine. The contract calls for 5,000 copies each month.

Melissa has rented a building for $800 per month. Her printing equipment was purchased for $40,000 and has a life expectancy of eight years with no salvage value. Straight-line depreciation will be used.

Insurance costs for the building and equipment are $75 per month. Utilities are related directly to output and are expected to cost $250 for an output of 5,000 copies.

Materials to print the magazine will cost $0.50 per copy. Melissa will supervise the operation and will hire workers to run the presses as needed. She must pay $10 per hour. Each worker can produce 20 copies of the magazine per hour. Melissa will receive a salary of $1,200 per month.

A salesperson has been hired for $500 per month plus a 20 percent commission on all new sales. Advertising on the local radio station will cost $330 per month.

REQUIRED:

1. What is the full manufacturing cost per unit for the regional magazine?
2. How many workers will Melissa need to hire for the first month (assume 40 hours per week equals one worker; there are four weeks in a month)?
3. What is the variable manufacturing cost per unit?
4. What is the prime cost per unit? The conversion cost per unit?
5. In a single-product business, are there any indirect product costs? Explain.
6. If Melissa receives $1.80 per copy, how much will her income be for the first month of operations?

DISCUSSION AND INTERPRETATION PROBLEMS

D15-1
Cost Classification, Income Statements; Service Firm

Lindley Construction Company is a family-operated business, founded in 1937 by William Lindley. In the beginning, the company consisted of Lindley and two employees laying water pipeline as subcontractors. Currently, the company employs 20 to 25 people; it is directed by John Lindley, William's son.

Lindley Construction's main line of business is installing water and sewer lines. More than 90 percent of Lindley's work comes from contracts with city and state agencies. All of the company's work is located in the state of Idaho. The company's sales volume averages $1.5 million, and profits vary between 0 and 10 percent of sales.

Sales and profits have been somewhat below average for the past three years due to a recession and intense competition. Because of this competition, John Lindley is constantly reviewing the prices that other companies bid for jobs; when a bid is lost, he makes every attempt to analyze the reasons for the differences between his bid and that of his competitors. He uses this information to increase the competitiveness of future bids.

John has become convinced that Lindley's current accounting system is deficient. Currently, all expenses simply are deducted from revenues to arrive at net income. No effort is made to distinguish among the costs of laying pipe, obtaining contracts, and administering the company. Yet, all bids are based on the costs of laying pipe.

John also knows that knowledge of cost behavior is important. He is certain that the company could offer more competitive bids if he knew which costs were variable and which were fixed. For example, Lindley often has idle equipment (often, the company needs more equipment than is necessary so that it can bid on larger projects). If Lindley could bid enough to cover its variable costs and use the idle equipment, equipment operators could be more productively utilized and have more job stability. In fact, if the bid covered more than variable costs, profits would increase as well, since the fixed costs remain unchanged for increased activity.

With these thoughts in mind, John began a careful review of the income statement for the previous year shown below. First, he noted that jobs were priced on the basis of equipment hours, with an average price of $165 per equipment hour. However, when it came to classifying costs and identifying their behavior, he decided that he needed some help. One thing that puzzled him was how to classify his own salary of $57,000. About half of his time was spent in bidding and securing contracts, and the other half was spent in general administrative matters.

Lindley Construction
Income Statement 1995

Sales (9,100 equipment hours at $165)		$1,501,500
Less expenses:		
Utilities	$ 12,000	
Machine operators	109,000	
Rent (office building)	12,000	
CPA fees	20,000	
Other direct labor	122,850	
Administrative salaries	57,000	
Supervisor salaries	35,000	
Pipe	700,670	
Tires and fuel	209,300	
Depreciation on equipment	99,000	
Salaries of mechanics	25,000	
Advertising	7,500	
Total expenses		1,409,320
Net income		$ 92,180

REQUIRED:

1. Classify the costs as shown above as (1) costs of laying pipe (production costs); (2) costs of securing contracts (selling costs); or, (3) costs of general administration. For production costs, identify direct materials, direct labor, and overhead costs.
2. Using the functional classification developed in Requirement 1, prepare a functional income statement. What is the average cost per equipment hour for laying pipe?
3. Now classify the costs as fixed or variable (assuming a unit-based cost driver). Assume that any mixed cost is 50 percent fixed and 50 percent variable.
4. Prepare a variable-costing income statement. What is the variable cost per equipment hour? Suppose that John Lindley has idle equipment and has the opportunity to take a job at $135 per hour. Should he accept the job? Why or why not?

D15-2 Cost Information and Ethical Behavior; Service Organization

Jean Erickson, manager and owner of an advertising company in Charlotte, North Carolina, had arranged a meeting with Leroy Gee, the chief accountant of a large, local competitor. Jean and Leroy were lifelong friends. They had grown up together in a small town and attended the same university.

Leroy was a competent, successful accountant but currently was experiencing some personal financial difficulties. The problems were created by some investments that had turned sour, leaving Leroy with a $15,000 personal loan to pay off—just at the time that his oldest son was scheduled to enter college.

Jean, on the other hand, was struggling to establish a successful advertising business. She had recently acquired the rights to open a branch office of a large regional advertising firm headquartered in Atlanta, Georgia. During her first two years, she had managed to build a small, profitable practice; however, the chance to gain a significant foothold in the Charlotte advertising community hinged on the success of winning a bid to represent the state of North Carolina in a major campaign to attract new industry and tourism. The meeting Jean had scheduled with Leroy concerned the bid she planned to submit.

"Leroy, I'm at a critical point in my business venture. If I can win the bid for the state's advertising dollars, I'll be set. Winning the bid will bring $600,000 to $700,000 of revenues into the firm. On top of that, I estimate that the publicity will bring another $200,000 to $300,000 of new business."

"I understand," replied Leroy. "My boss is anxious to win that business as well. It would mean a huge increase in profits for my firm. It's a competitive business, though. As new as you are, I doubt that you'll have much chance of winning."

"You may be wrong. You're forgetting two very important considerations. First, I have the backing of all the resources and talent of a regional firm. Second, I have some political connections. Last year, I was hired to run the publicity side of the governor's campaign. He was impressed with my work and would like me to have this business. I am confident that the proposals I submit will be very competitive. My only concern is to submit a bid that beats your firm. If I come in with a lower bid and with good proposals, the governor can see to it that I get the work."

"Sounds promising. If you do win, however, there will be a lot of upset people. After all, they are going to claim that the business should have been given to local advertisers, not to some out-of-state firm. Given the size of your office, you'll have to get support from Atlanta. You could take a lot of heat."

"True. But I am the owner of the branch office. That fact alone should blunt most of the criticism. Who can argue that I'm not a local? Listen, with your help, I think I can win this bid. Furthermore, if I do win it, you can reap some direct benefits. With that kind of business, I can afford to hire an accountant, and I'll make it worthwhile for you to transfer jobs. I can offer you an up-front bonus of $15,000. On top of that, I'll increase your annual salary by 20 percent. That should solve most of your financial difficulties. After all, we have been friends since day one—and what are friends for?"

"Jean, my wife would be ecstatic if I were able to improve our financial position as quickly as this opportunity affords. I certainly hope that you win the bid. What kind of help can I provide?"

"Simple. To win, all I have to do is beat the bid of your firm. Before I submit my bid, I would like you to review it. With the financial skills you have, it should be easy for you to spot any excessive costs that I may have included. Or perhaps I included the wrong kind of costs. By cutting excessive costs and eliminating costs that may not be directly related to the project, my bid should be competitive enough to meet or beat your firm's bid."

REQUIRED:

1. What would you do if you were Leroy? Fully explain the reasons for your choice.
2. What is the likely outcome if Leroy agrees to review the bid? Is there much risk to Leroy personally if he reviews the bid? Should the degree of risk have any bearing on Leroy's decision?
3. Apply the code of ethics for management accountants to the proposal given Leroy. What standards would be violated if Leroy agrees to review the bid? Assume that Leroy is a member of the IMA and holds a CMA.

D15-3 Research Assignment

Using the resources in your library, obtain copies of financial statements for a manufacturing firm, a merchandising firm, and a service firm. Write a memo discussing the differences and similarities of the three statements.

D15-4 Research Assignment

Interview an accountant who works for a manufacturing firm (preferably one who works in cost accounting). Ask the following questions and prepare a written summary of the person's responses:

a. What product or products does your firm produce?
b. What costs are assigned to the product or products being produced?
c. For a particular product, what direct materials are used?
d. What percentage of total manufacturing costs is direct labor? materials? overhead?
e. How is overhead assigned to the products?
f. What are some examples of costs that vary with units produced? (Obtain at least five examples.)
g. What are some examples of costs that vary with other factors?
h. Does your accounting system separate fixed and variable costs? Why or why not?

CHAPTER 16
JOB ORDER COSTING

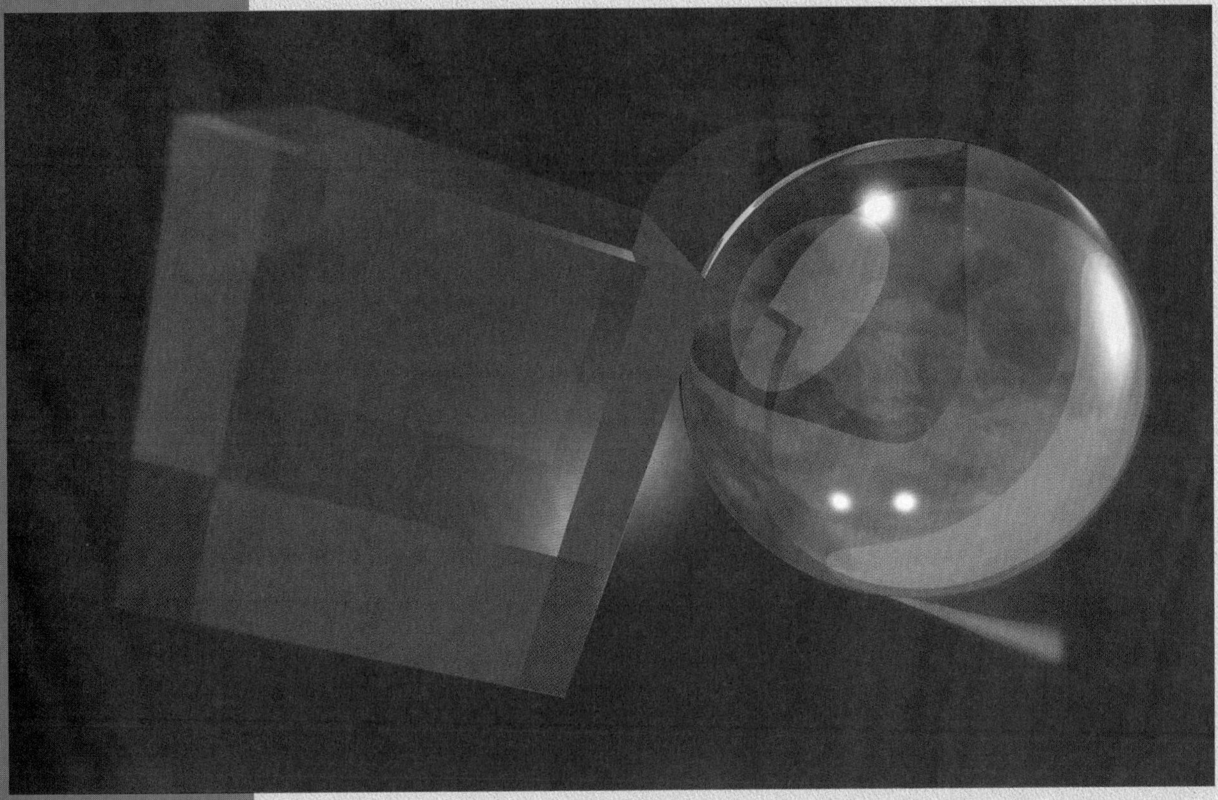

LEARNING OBJECTIVES

After studying this chapter, you should be able to:

1. Describe the approaches available to measure and assign costs to products and services.
2. Explain how a predetermined overhead rate is computed and how it is used to assign overhead to production.
3. Explain how manufacturing costs are assigned to individual jobs and how a unit is computed.
4. Describe the cost flows and prepare the journal entries associated with job-order costing.
5. Explain why departmental overhead rates may be preferred to a single, plant-wide overhead rate.

Scenario

The Applegate Construction Company was established in 1957. For more than thirty years, the company specialized in building subdivisions. The company could be described as a small but successful business with a good reputation for building quality homes. Recently, Walter Applegate, the founder and owner of the company, retired and his son, Jay Applegate, assumed control of the company.

Jay decided that the company needed to expand into custom-built homes and nonresidential construction. As he began to explore these possibilities, he encountered some problems with the company's current accounting system. Accordingly, he requested a meeting with his aunt, Bonnie Barlow, the financial manager. She was responsible for bookkeeping and payroll. A local CPA firm prepared quarterly financial reports and filed all the company's tax returns.

"Bonnie, as you know, I want to see our company become one of the largest in this region. To accomplish this objective, I am convinced that we need to expand our operations so that they include custom homes and some industrial buildings. I think we can gain business in both of these areas by capitalizing on our reputation for quality. However, I am afraid that as we enter these markets, we are going to have to change our accounting system. I'm going to need your help in making the changes."

"I'm not sure why you feel that we need to change our accounting procedures. They are simple, and they've worked well for thirty years."

"In the past, our company has built homes in subdivisions that are basically the same. We've had slight variations in design so that they aren't carbon copies, but each home has required essentially the same work and materials. The cost of each home has been computed by simply accumulating the actual costs incurred over the period of time it took to build all the homes and then dividing this total by the number of units constructed. This approach will not work when we enter the market for custom-built homes or industrial units."

"I think I see the problem. Custom-built homes, for example, may require different cement work, different carpentry work, and may use more expensive materials, like a jacuzzi instead of a regular bathtub. They may also differ significantly in size from our standard units. If we divide the total construction costs of a period by the number of units produced, we don't have a very accurate representation of what it's costing to build any individual home. Additionally, the cost of our standard units could be distorted. Industrial units would cause even worse problems. It sounds like we need a different method to accumulate our construction costs."

"I agree. We need some way of tracking the labor, materials, and overhead used by each job. I don't foresee much difficulty with labor or materials, but the measurement of overhead used by each job will be difficult. I am unclear as to how much overhead should be assigned to the different jobs. It seems unfair to omit property taxes from the cost of a home built in June simply because we pay them in November. Utilities also vary from month to month."

"Jay, it seems to me that we have two issues: how to measure our construction costs, especially overhead, and how we should assign those costs to the different jobs. I have a suggestion. Let me talk to our CPA and see what advice she can give us. I am sure that she can suggest a cost system that will address both of these issues."

Note: This scenario is based on the actual experiences of a mid-sized construction firm. The names of the company and people involved have been changed to preserve confidentiality.

TWO ISSUES: COST MEASUREMENT AND COST ASSIGNMENT

Objective 1
Describe the approaches available to measure and assign costs to products and services.

Conceptually, computing the unit manufacturing cost is simple. The unit cost is the total manufacturing cost associated with the units produced divided by the number of units produced. For example, if Applegate Construction builds 100 subdivision homes during the year and the total cost of materials, labor, and overhead for these homes is $6 million, then the cost of each home is $60,000 ($6 million/100 homes). Although the concept is simple, the practical reality of the computation can be somewhat more complex. As the dialogue between Jay and Bonnie reveals, the straightforward approach breaks down when there are products that differ from one another or when cost information for a product is needed before all of the actual costs associated with its production are known.

cost measurement

cost assignment

Total manufacturing costs must be *measured,* and then these costs must be *associated* with the units produced. **Cost measurement** consists of determining the dollar amounts of direct materials, direct labor, and overhead used in production. The dollar amounts may be the actual amounts expended for the manufacturing inputs, or they may be estimated amounts. Often, estimated amounts are used to ensure timeliness of cost information or to control costs. The process of associating the costs, once measured, with the units produced is called **cost assignment**.

Importance of Unit Costs

A cost accounting system has the purpose of measuring and assigning manufacturing costs so that the unit cost of a product can be determined. Unit cost is a critical piece of information for a manufacturer. Unit costs are essential for valuing inventory, determining income, and making a number of important decisions.

Disclosing the cost of inventories and determining income are financial reporting requirements that a firm faces at the end of each period. In order to report the cost of its inventories, a firm must know the number of units on hand and the unit cost. The cost of goods sold, used to determine income, also requires knowledge of the units sold and their unit cost.

Unit costs are also important for a wide variety of decisions. For example, bidding is a common requirement in the markets for custom homes and industrial buildings. It is virtually impossible to submit a meaningful bid without knowing the costs associated with the units to be produced. Product cost information is vital in a number of other areas as well. Decisions concerning product design and introduction of new products are affected by expected unit costs. Decisions to make or buy a product, accept or reject a special order, or keep or drop a product line require unit cost information.

Whether the unit cost information should include all manufacturing costs, as opposed to only variable or incremental costs, depends on the setting and the purpose for which the information is going to be used. For financial reporting, full or absorption unit cost information is required. If a firm is operating below its production capacity, however, incremental cost information may be much more useful in deciding whether to accept or reject a special order. Simply put, unit cost information needed for external reporting may not supply the information necessary for a number of internal decisions, especially those decisions that are short run in nature. Different costs are needed for different purposes.

It should be pointed out, however, that full cost information is useful for a number of important internal decisions as well as for financial reporting. In the long run, for any product to be viable, its price must cover its full cost. Decisions to introduce a new product, continue a current product, and analyze long-run prices are examples of important internal decisions that must rely on full unit cost information.

Production of Unit Cost Information

To produce unit cost information, both cost measurement and cost assignment are required. There are a number of different ways to measure and assign costs. This chapter introduces two measurement systems and two assignment systems and discusses one of each type in detail.

The two systems for assigning costs are *job-order costing* and *process costing*. The two measurement systems introduced are *actual costing* and *normal costing*. Combinations of measurement and assignment approaches define a cost accounting system. For example, actual costing measurement with job-order cost assignment creates an actual job-order cost system. Given the two measurement systems and the two assignment systems, a total of four cost accounting systems are possible, with each system presenting a different way to compute unit costs. The four possible systems are summarized in Exhibit 16-1.

Which system should be chosen depends on the type of cost data a manager needs for controlling and directing the activities of an organization. Of the four systems, the two systems using actual costing are rarely chosen because they generally fail to supply product cost information on a timely basis. Why actual costing fails will become apparent as it is examined.

Job-Order and Process Costing: Two Cost Assignment Systems

Manufacturing firms can be divided into two major industrial types based on different manufacturing processes: job-order manufacturing and process manufacturing. Two different cost assignment or accumulation systems have been

Exhibit 16-1
Four Possible Cost Accounting Systems

	Cost Measurement	
Cost Assignment	Job order—Actual	Job order—Normal
	Process—Actual	Process—Normal

developed, each corresponding to one of these systems. To understand the differences between these two cost assignment systems, we need to understand the differences in the two manufacturing processes.

Job-Order Manufacturing and Costing. Firms operating in job-order industries produce a wide variety of products or jobs that are usually quite distinct from each other. Customized or built-to-order products fit into this category. Examples of job-order processes include printing, construction, and furniture making. A job may be a single unit such as a house, or it may be a batch of units such as eight tables. Job-order systems may be used to produce goods for inventory that are subsequently sold in the general market. Often, however, a job is associated with a particular customer order.

job-order costing system

For job-order manufacturing systems, manufacturing costs are accumulated by *job*. This approach to assigning costs is called a **job-order costing system**. In a job-order firm, collecting costs by job provides vital information for management. Once a job is completed, the unit cost can be obtained by dividing the total manufacturing costs by the number of units produced.

For example, if the production costs for printing 100 wedding announcements total $300, the unit cost for this job is $3. Given the unit cost information, the manager of the printing firm can determine whether the prevailing market price provides a reasonable profit margin. If not, this may signal to the manager that the costs are out of line with other printing firms. He or she then can take action to reduce costs, if possible, or to emphasize other types of jobs for which the firm can earn a reasonable profit margin. In fact, the profit contributions of different printing jobs offered by the firm can be computed, and this information can be used to select the most profitable mix of printing services to offer.

Process Manufacturing and Costing. Firms in process industries mass-produce large quantities of similar or homogeneous products. Each product is essentially indistinguishable from its companion product. Examples of process manufacturers include food, cement, petroleum, and chemical firms. The important point here is that the cost of one product is identical to the cost of another. Therefore, service firms can also use a process costing approach. Discount stockbrokers, for example, incur much the same cost to execute a customer order for one stock as for another. Check clearing departments of banks incur a uniform cost to clear a check, no matter the size of the check or the name of the person to whom it is written.

Process firms accumulate production costs by *process* or by *department* for a *given period of time*. The output for the process for the same period of time is measured. Unit costs are computed by dividing the process costs for the given period by the output of the period. This approach to cost accumulation is known as a **process costing system**. Exhibit 16-2 summarizes and contrasts the characteristics of job-order and process costing.

process costing system

Actual Costing and Normal Costing: Two Cost Measurement Approaches

Cost measurement is concerned with determining the dollar amounts of manufacturing inputs used in production. There are three choices for measuring these amounts: (1) use the actual dollar amounts, (2) use estimated amounts, or (3) use actual and estimated amounts. This chapter (and Exhibit 16-1) describes the first

Exhibit 16-2
Comparison of Job-Order and Process Costing

Job-Order Costing	*Process Costing*
1. Wide variety of distinct products	1. Homogeneous products
2. Costs accumulated by job	2. Costs accumulated by process or department
3. Unit cost computed by dividing total job costs by units produced on that job	3. Unit cost computed by dividing process costs of the period by the units produced in the period

and third approaches—actual and normal costing. Chapter 25 describes the second approach, which is called standard costing.

actual cost system

Actual Costing. An **actual cost system** uses actual costs for direct materials, direct labor, and overhead. These actual costs are then used to determine the unit cost. In practice, strict actual cost systems are rarely used because they cannot provide accurate unit cost information on a timely basis. Interestingly, per-unit computation of the direct materials and direct labor costs is not the source of the difficulty. Direct materials and direct labor have a definite, identifiable relationship with units produced. The main problem with using actual costs for calculation of unit cost is with manufacturing overhead. Overhead items do not have the direct relationship that direct materials and direct labor do. For example, how much of the security guard's salary should be assigned to a unit of product? Because overhead items are indirectly related to the units produced, per-unit overhead costs must be calculated by averaging. Averaging requires totaling manufacturing overhead costs for a given period and then dividing this total by the number of units produced.

So that cost information can be produced in a timely manner if the time period chosen is relatively short (say, a month), averaging can yield per-unit overhead costs that fluctuate dramatically from month to month. This occurs for two major reasons. First, many overhead costs are not incurred uniformly throughout the year. Thus, they can differ significantly from one period to the next. Second, per-unit overhead costs fluctuate dramatically because of nonuniform production levels.

To illustrate, consider the following example. Assume a company produces a toy gun made of plastic. Each gun requires six ounces of plastic and fifteen minutes of direct labor. For the technology used, this input-output relationship is reasonably stable. Thus, the quantity of raw materials and the direct labor used for each toy gun are essentially the same regardless of how many toy guns are produced or when they are produced. The unit cost of these two inputs can be accurately computed.

If the cost of plastic in January is \$0.30 per ounce and the price of labor is \$6 per hour, then the cost of plastic per gun is \$1.80 (\$0.30 × 6 ounces), and the cost of direct labor per gun is \$1.50 (\$6 × 0.25 hours). The actual prime cost per gun, then, is \$1.80 + \$1.50, or \$3.30. If the prices of materials and labor are reasonably stable, the \$3.30 per-unit prime cost is the same regardless of how many guns are made or when they are produced during the year.

If actual overhead costs for the manufacturer were \$20,000 in April and 40,000 guns were produced, the per-unit overhead cost is \$20,000/40,000, or \$0.50 per gun. Unfortunately, this averaging approach has some severe limitations as shown in the following figures:

	April	*August*	*November*
Actual overhead	$20,000	$40,000	$ 40,000
Actual units produced	40,000	40,000	160,000
Per-unit overhead[1]	$0.50	$1.00	$0.25

[1]Actual overhead/Actual production

Notice that the overhead cost per unit is different for each of the three months. April and August have the same production but different monthly overhead costs. The difference in overhead cost could be attributable to higher utility costs due to increased cooling requirements in the month of August. Thus, the toy guns produced in August have a higher per-unit overhead cost ($1.00 rather than $0.50) just because they happened to be produced when cooling was required. The difference in the per-unit overhead cost is because overhead costs were incurred nonuniformly.

Nonuniform production is the second reason for variability in per-unit overhead costs, as August and November figures show. Both months have the same total monthly overhead costs but different output levels. November's output may be much larger because of anticipation of Christmas sales. Whatever the reason, the higher output in November creates a lower per-unit overhead cost ($0.25 compared to August's $1.00).

Notice that the varying per-unit overhead costs do not signal differences in value, or even in the underlying cost structure. A toy gun produced in April is identical to one produced in August or November. The higher utility costs in August may equal August utility costs of the previous year. The problem of fluctuating per-unit overhead costs can be avoided if the firm waits until the end of the year to assign the overhead costs. For example, if April, August, and November were the only months of operation for the toy gun manufacturer, the total overhead costs for the year are $100,000 ($20,000 + $40,000 + $40,000), and the total production is 240,000 guns (40,000 + 40,000 + 160,000). The per-unit overhead cost is $100,000/240,000, or $0.417. By waiting until the end of the year, the firm eliminates the problems of nonuniform overhead cost incurrence and nonuniform production. The result is the same overhead cost per unit for every unit produced.

Unfortunately, waiting until the end of the year to compute an overhead rate is unacceptable. A company needs unit cost information throughout the year. This information is needed on a timely basis both for interim financial statements and to help managers make decisions such as pricing. Most decisions requiring unit cost information cannot wait until the end of the year. Managers must react to day-to-day conditions occurring in the marketplace in order to maintain a sound competitive position.

Another possible solution is to approximate the end-of-the-year actual overhead rate at the *beginning* of the year and then use the predetermined rate throughout the year to obtain the needed unit cost information. The end-of-the-year actual rate can be approximated by estimating the overhead costs for the coming year and dividing these estimated costs by expected production. Suppose, for example, that the toy manufacturer estimates on January 1 that overhead costs for the year will be $90,000 and that expected production is 225,000 units. Using these estimated data, the predetermined overhead rate is $0.40 ($90,000/225,000). (You will learn shortly that there are a number of different ways to estimate production.)

normal costing systems

Normal Costing. Cost systems that measure overhead costs on a predetermined basis and use actual costs for direct materials and direct labor are called **normal costing systems**. The principal difficulty with normal costing is that the predetermined rate is likely to differ from the actual rate. Either actual overhead costs differ from the estimated costs or the actual level of production differs from the expected level, or both.

If the measurement error is small, however, the product cost resulting from normal costing will not differ significantly from the actual product cost determined after the fact. In the example above, the predetermined rate was $0.40, and the end-of-the-year actual rate was $0.417. Most would agree that this is not a significant difference.

Virtually all firms assign overhead to production on a predetermined basis. This fact seems to suggest that most firms successfully approximate the end-of-the-year overhead rate. Thus, the measurement problems associated with the use of actual overhead costs are solved by the use of estimated overhead costs. A job-order cost system that uses actual costs for materials and labor and estimated costs for overhead is called a *normal job-order cost system*. Similarly, in a process setting, the cost system is called a *normal process cost system*.

OVERHEAD APPLICATION: A NORMAL COSTING VIEW

Objective 2

Explain how a predetermined overhead rate is computed and how it is used to assign overhead to production.

In normal cost systems, overhead is assigned to production through the use of a predetermined overhead rate.

Predetermined Overhead Rates

predetermined overhead rate

The basic difference between actual costing and normal costing is the use of a predetermined overhead rate. A **predetermined overhead rate** is calculated using the following formula:

$$\text{Overhead rate} = \text{Budgeted overhead/Activity level}$$

Budgeted overhead is simply the estimated overhead costs for the coming year. The budgetary accountants of a firm are responsible for developing these estimates. The second input requires that the value for the activity level be specified. (Activity level is sometimes referred to as the *denominator activity level* since it appears in the denominator of the computation.) This second input has two steps: first, identify a measure of production activity; second, predict the level of this activity.

Because a predetermined overhead rate is calculated in advance, usually at the beginning of the year, it is impossible to use actual overhead or actual activity level for the year. On January 1, we do not know what actual levels will be; therefore, only estimated or budgeted amounts are used in calculating the predetermined overhead rate.

Measures of Production Activity

Production activity can be measured in many different ways. In assigning overhead costs, it is important to select an activity base that is correlated with overhead consumption. This will assure that individual products receive an accurate allocation of overhead costs. While there are many choices available, five common measures are:

1. Units produced
2. Direct labor hours
3. Direct labor dollars
4. Machine hours
5. Direct materials

The most obvious measure of production activity is output. If there is only one product, overhead costs are clearly incurred to produce that product. In a single-product setting, the overhead costs of the period are traceable directly to the period's output. Clearly, for this case, units produced satisfy the cause-and-effect criterion. Most firms, however, produce more than one product. Since different products typically consume different amounts of overhead, this allocation method is inaccurate. At Kraft, for example, one plant produces salad dressing, ketchup, and marshmallow creme—each in a range of sizes from personal application packs to 32-ounce jars. In a multiple-product setting, overhead costs are common to more than one product. Furthermore, different products may consume overhead at different rates.

For example, suppose a company produces fine wood furniture. One type of dining room table has very simple round legs. Another style of table has very elaborately turned and carved legs. Both types of table leg require the use of a lathe (a machine in which a piece of material is held and turned while being shaped by a tool); therefore, both types should share the cost of using this machine. Suppose that the cost of operating the lathe is \$20,000, and 10,000 units of each type of leg are produced. Using units produced, the overhead cost assigned to each product would be \$1 (\$20,000/20,000). But one product may spend sixty minutes on the lathe, the other only fifteen. Since one product spends four times as much time on the lathe as the other, many would argue that it should receive more of the machine's cost. Using the units produced method has not given a very accurate, meaningful, or fair assignment of overhead costs. How, then, should overhead be allocated?

Some believe that the allocation of overhead is essentially arbitrary. There is no single approach to allocating overhead that will satisfy all parties concerned. It could be argued that overhead should be allocated on an ability-to-bear basis with overhead assigned in proportion to revenues generated. Using this criterion, if the product spending less time on the lathe generates more revenues than the other product, more overhead would be allocated to it than to the other product.

The position taken in this text is that the allocation of overhead costs should follow, as nearly as possible, a cause-and-effect relationship. Efforts should be made to identify those factors that cause the consumption of overhead. Once identified, these causal factors or *cost drivers* should be used to assign overhead to products. It seems reasonable, for example, to argue that for products using the lathe, machine hours reflect differential machine time, and, consequently, reflect the consumption of machine cost. Units produced does not necessarily reflect machine time or consumption of the machine cost; therefore, it can be argued that machine hours is a better cost driver and should be used to assign this overhead cost.

In the table leg example shown in Exhibit 16-3, the simple leg uses fifteen minutes of machine time; the ornate leg uses one hour. The total machine hours consumed by the two products is 12,500 (2,500 + 10,000). The overhead cost assigned per machine hour (MHr) is $20,000/12,500, or $1.60 per MHr. Using this rate, the per-unit overhead assigned to the simple leg is $0.40 (0.25 machine hours × $1.60), and the per-unit overhead assigned to the ornate leg is $1.60 (1 machine hour × $1.60).

As the example illustrates, activity measures other than units of product are needed when a firm has multiple products. The last four measures listed earlier are all useful for multiple-product settings. Some may be more useful than others, depending on how well they correlate with the actual overhead consumption. As we will discuss later, it may even be appropriate to use multiple rates.

Activity-Level Choices

expected activity level

normal activity level

Although any reasonable level of activity could be chosen, the two leading candidates are expected activity and normal activity. **Expected activity level** is the production level the firm expects to attain for the coming year. **Normal activity level** is the average activity that a firm experiences in the long term (normal volume is computed over more than one year). Of the two choices, normal activity has the advantage of using the same activity level year after year. As a result, it produces less fluctuation from year to year in the assignment of per-unit overhead cost.

theoretical activity level

practical activity level

Other activity levels used for computing predetermined overhead rates are those corresponding to the theoretical and practical levels. **Theoretical activity level** is the absolute maximum production activity of a manufacturing firm. It is the output that can be realized if everything operates perfectly. **Practical activity level** is the maximum output that can be realized if everything operates efficiently. Efficient operation allows for some imperfections, such as normal breakdowns, some shortages, workers operating at less than peak capability, and so on. Normal and expected actual activities tend to reflect consumer demand while theoretical and practical activities reflect a firm's production capabilities. Exhibit 16-4 illustrates these four measures of activity.

Exhibit 16-3

Cost of operating lathe		$20,000
Total units produced		20,000
Total machine hours used		12,500
	Simple	*Ornate*
Number of legs	10,000	10,000
Time on lathe	0.25 MHrs	1 MHr
Operating cost assigned using units produced	$1	$1
Operating cost assigned using machine time	$0.40	$1.60

Exhibit 16-4
Measures of Activity Level

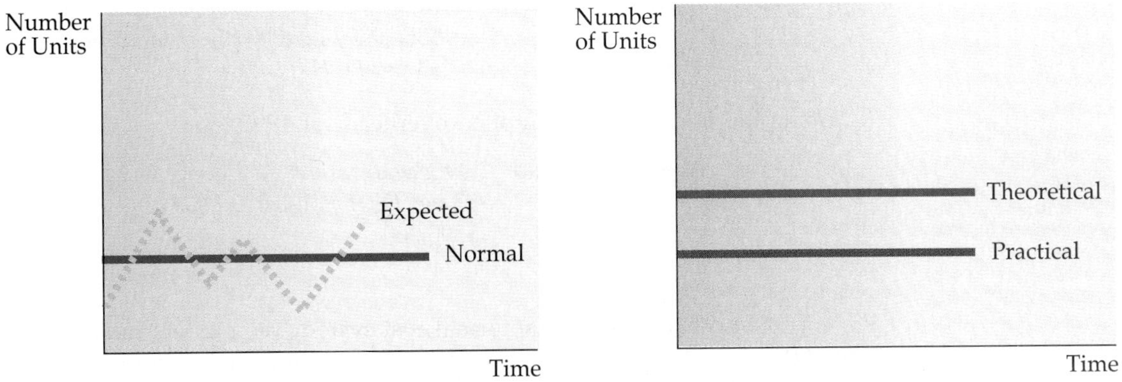

Consumer Demand–Oriented Measures of Activity Level

Productive Capability Measures of Activity Level

Given budgeted overhead, a measure of production activity, and a level of activity, a predetermined overhead rate can be computed and applied to production. Understanding exactly how overhead is applied is critical to understanding normal costing.

The Basic Concept of Overhead Application

applied overhead

Predetermined overhead rates are used to apply overhead costs to production as the actual production activity unfolds. The total overhead assigned to actual production at any point in time is called **applied overhead**. Applied overhead is computed using the following formula:

$$\text{Applied overhead} = \text{Overhead rate} \times \text{Actual production activity}$$

The measure of production activity used to determine the overhead rate must be the same as the measure of actual production activity. That is, if the predetermined overhead rate is calculated on the basis of direct labor hours, overhead must be applied on the basis of direct labor hours. Overhead can be applied on a daily, weekly, monthly, or any other basis as the need requires.

In attempting to understand the concept of applied overhead, there are two points that should be emphasized.

1. Applied overhead is the basis for computing per-unit overhead cost.
2. Applied overhead is rarely equal to a period's actual overhead.

These points are best illustrated with an example. Belring, Inc., produces two telephones: a cordless phone and a regular model. The company has the following estimated and actual data for 1995:

Budgeted overhead	$360,000
Normal activity (in direct labor hours)	120,000
Actual activity (in direct labor hours)	100,000
Actual overhead	$320,000

Now assume that the firm bases its predetermined overhead rate on normal activity measured in direct labor hours (*DLH*). Thus, for 1995:

Predetermined overhead rate = Budgeted overhead/Normal activity
= \$360,000/120,000 direct labor hours
= \$3 per *DLH*

Using the overhead rate, applied overhead for 1995 is:

Applied overhead = Overhead rate × Actual activity
= \$3 per *DLH* × 100,000 *DLH*
= \$300,000

Per-unit Overhead Cost. In a normal cost system, the predetermined overhead rate is the basis for per-unit overhead cost calculation. For example, assume that 40 percent of the actual direct labor hours worked were used to produce 80,000 units of the cordless phone, and the remaining 60 percent of direct labor time was used to produce 90,000 units of the regular model. Since the predetermined overhead rate is \$3 per *DLH*, the cordless phone would be assigned a total of \$120,000 of overhead (\$3 × 40,000), and the regular model would be assigned \$180,000 (\$3 × 60,000). The per-unit overhead cost of the cordless phone is \$120,000/80,000, or \$1.50, and for the regular model, \$180,000/90,000, or \$2.

	Cordless	*Regular*
Units produced	80,000	90,000
Direct labor hours	40,000	60,000
Overhead applied to production (\$3 × *DLH*)	\$120,000	\$180,000
Overhead per unit	\$1.50	\$2.00

Underapplied and Overapplied Overhead. Notice that the amount of overhead applied to production (\$300,000) differs from the actual overhead (\$320,000). Since the predetermined overhead rate is based on estimated data, applied overhead will rarely equal actual overhead. Since only \$300,000 was applied in our example, the firm has *underapplied* overhead by \$20,000. If applied overhead had been \$330,000, too much overhead would have been applied to production. The firm would have *overapplied* overhead by \$10,000. The difference between actual overhead and applied overhead is called an **overhead variance**. If the difference is positive (i.e., if actual overhead is greater than applied overhead) the variance is called **underapplied overhead**. If the difference is negative (i.e., if applied overhead is greater than actual overhead) the variance is called **overapplied overhead**.

overhead variance

underapplied overhead

overapplied overhead

Overhead variances occur because it is impossible to estimate perfectly future overhead costs and production activity. Their presence is virtually inevitable. A problem arises if the overhead variances are not corrected. In essence, the firm has traded off costing accuracy for convenience by applying overhead throughout the year. At year end, however, costs must be stated at actual—*not* estimated amounts. Accordingly, at the end of a reporting period, procedures must exist to deal with the overhead variances.

Disposition of Overhead Variances

From an actual costing perspective, the overhead variance represents an error in assigning overhead costs to production. At the end of the reporting period, something must be done with the overhead variance. Usually, the variance is disposed of in one of two ways.

1. All overhead variance is allocated to cost of goods sold.
2. The overhead variance is allocated among work in process, finished goods, and cost of goods sold.

Assigned to Cost of Goods Sold. The most common practice is to assign the entire overhead variance to cost of goods sold. This practice is justified on the basis of materiality, the same principle used to justify expensing the entire cost of a pencil sharpener in the period acquired rather than allocating (through depreciation) its cost over the life of the sharpener. Since the overhead variance is usually relatively small, the method of disposition is not a critical matter because all production costs should appear in cost of goods sold eventually. This method is reasonable if the variance is immaterial.

Thus, the overhead variance is added to the cost of goods sold if underapplied and subtracted from cost of goods sold if overapplied. For example, assume that Belring has an ending balance in its Cost of Goods Sold account equal to $500,000. The underapplied variance of $20,000 would be added to produce a new, adjusted balance of $520,000. (This makes sense—applied overhead was $300,000 while actual was $320,000. Thus, production costs were *under*stated by $20,000, and cost of goods sold must be increased to correct the problem.) If the variance had been overapplied, it would have been subtracted from cost of goods sold to produce a new balance of $480,000.

Allocation to Production Accounts. If the overhead variance is material, it should be allocated to the period's production. Conceptually, the overhead costs of a period belong to the production of the period. Overhead costs for a period should be associated with goods started but not completed (work in process), goods finished but not sold (finished goods), and goods finished and sold (cost of goods sold). Because a period's overhead costs may flow through these three different accounts, the overhead variance should be allocated to these accounts as well.

The recommended way to achieve this allocation is to prorate the overhead variance based on the ending *applied overhead balances* in each account. Although other ending balances could be used to allocate the variance (e.g., total manufacturing costs), the applied overhead balance best reflects the additional overhead that should be assigned to each account. Using applied overhead captures the original cause-and-effect relationships used to assign overhead. Using another balance, such as total manufacturing costs, may result in an unfair assignment of the additional overhead. For example, two products, identical on all dimensions except for the cost of raw material inputs, should receive the same overhead assignment. Yet, if total manufacturing costs were used to allocate an overhead variance, the product with the more expensive materials would receive a higher overhead assignment.

To illustrate the disposition of the overhead variance using the recommended approach, assume that Belring's accounts had the following applied overhead balances for the end of 1995:

Work in Process	$ 60,000
Finished Goods	90,000
Cost of Goods Sold	150,000
Total dollar balance	$300,000

Given the above data, the percentage allocation of any overhead variance to the three accounts in 1995 is:

Work in Process	20%	(60,000/300,000)
Finished Goods	30%	(90,000/300,000)
Cost of Goods Sold	50%	(150,000/300,000)

Recall that in 1995, Belring had an overhead variance that was $20,000 underapplied. Thus, Work in Process would receive 20 percent of $20,000 ($4,000), Finished Goods would receive 30 percent of $20,000 ($6,000), and Cost of Goods Sold would receive 50 percent of $20,000 ($10,000). Since underapplied means that too little overhead was assigned, these individual prorated amounts would be *added* to the ending account balances. Adding these amounts produces the following new adjusted balances of the three accounts:

	Unadjusted Balance	*Prorated Underapplied Overhead*	*Adjusted Balance*
Work in Process	$ 60,000	$ 4,000	$ 64,000
Finished Goods	90,000	6,000	96,000
Cost of Goods Sold	150,000	10,000	160,000

Of course, overapplied amounts would have been *subtracted* from the account balances because too much overhead was assigned to production.

We now have an understanding of how manufacturing costs are measured in a normal cost system. Considerable emphasis has been placed on describing how overhead costs are treated because this is the key to normal costing. Before we seriously examine any method for assigning costs, we first should know how these costs are to be measured. The way costs are measured affects the procedures followed in either job-order costing or process costing.

JOB-ORDER COSTING: GENERAL DESCRIPTION

Objective 3
Explain how manufacturing costs are assigned to individual jobs and how a unit cost is computed.

In illustrating job-order costing, we will assume a normal cost measurement approach. The actual costs of direct materials and direct labor are assigned to jobs along with a predetermined overhead rate. *How* these costs are actually assigned to the various jobs, however, is the central issue. In order to assign these costs, we must identify each job and the direct materials and direct labor associated with it. Additionally, some mechanism must exist to allocate overhead costs to each job.

job-order cost sheet

The document that identifies each job and accumulates its manufacturing costs is the **job-order cost sheet**. An example is shown in Exhibit 16-5. The cost accounting department creates such a cost sheet upon receipt of a production order. Orders are written up in response to a specific customer order or in conjunction with a production plan derived from a sales forecast. Each job-order cost sheet has a job-order number that identifies the new job.

work-in-process file

In a manual accounting system, the job-order cost sheet is a document. In today's world, however, most accounting systems are automated. The cost sheet usually corresponds to a record in a work-in-process master file. The collection of all job cost sheets define a **work-in-process file**. In a manual system, the file would be located in a filing cabinet, whereas in an automated system it is stored electronically on magnetic tape or disk. In either system, the file of job-order cost sheets serves as a subsidiary work-in-process ledger.

Both manual and automated systems require the same kind of data in order to accumulate costs and track the progress of a job. A job cost system must have the capability to identify the quantity of direct materials, direct labor, and overhead consumed by each job. In other words, documentation and procedures are needed to associate the manufacturing inputs used by a job with the job itself. This need is satisfied through the use of materials requisitions for direct material, time tickets for direct labor, and predetermined rates for overhead.

Exhibit 16-5
The Job-Order Cost Sheet

For	Benson Company	Job Order Number	16
		Date Ordered	April 2, 1995
Item Description	Valves	Date Completed	April 24, 1995
Quantity Completed	100	Date Shipped	April 25, 1995

Materials		Direct Labor				Overhead		
Requisition Number	Amount	Ticket Number	Hours	Rate	Amount	Hours	Rate	Amount
12	$300	68	8	$6	$ 48	8	$10	$ 80
18	450	72	10	$7	70	10	$10	100
	$750				$118			$180

Cost Summary

Direct Materials	$750
Direct Labor	$118
Overhead	$180
Total Cost	$1,048
Unit Cost	$10.48

Materials Requisitions

materials requisition form

The cost of direct materials is assigned to a job by the use of a source document known as a **materials requisition form**, illustrated in Exhibit 16-6. Notice that the form asks for the type, quantity, and unit price of the direct materials issued and, most importantly, for the number of the job. Using this form, the cost accounting department can enter the cost of direct materials onto the correct job-order cost sheet.

If the accounting system is automated, this posting may entail directly entering the data at a computer terminal, using the materials requisitions forms as source documents. A program enters the cost of direct materials onto the record for each job.

In addition to providing essential information for assigning direct materials costs to jobs, the materials requisition form may also have other data items, such as requisition number, date, and signature. These data items are useful for maintaining proper control over a firm's inventory of direct materials. The signature, for example, transfers responsibility for the materials from the storage area to the person receiving the materials, usually a production supervisor.

No attempt is made to trace the cost of other materials, such as supplies, lubricants, and so on, to a particular job. You will recall that these indirect materials are assigned to jobs through the predetermined overhead rate.

Job Time Tickets

time ticket

Direct labor also must be associated with each particular job. The means by which direct labor costs are assigned to individual jobs is the source document known as a **time ticket** (see Exhibit 16-7). When an employee works on a particular job, he or she fills out a time ticket that identifies his or her name, wage rate, hours worked, and job number. These time tickets are collected daily and

Exhibit 16-6
Materials Requisition Form

Material Requisition
Number 12

Date April 8, 1995
Department Grinding
Job Number 16

Description	Quantity	Cost/Unit	Total Cost
Casing	100	$3	$300

Authorized Signature Jim Lawson

Exhibit 16-7
Job Time Ticket

Job Time Ticket
Number 68

Employee Number 45

Name Ed Wilson

Date April 12, 1995

Start Time	Stop Time	Total Time	Hourly Rate	Amount	Job Number
8:00	10:00	2	$6	$12	16
10:00	11:00	1	6	6	17
11:00	12:00	1	6	6	16
1:00	6:00	5	6	30	16

Approved by Jim Lawson
Department Supervisor

transferred to the cost accounting department where the information is used to post the cost of direct labor to individual jobs. Again, in an automated system, posting involves entering the data onto the computer.

Time tickets are used only for direct laborers. Since indirect labor is common to all jobs, these costs belong to overhead and are allocated using the predetermined overhead rate.

Overhead Application

Jobs are assigned overhead costs with the predetermined overhead rate. Typically, direct labor hours is the measure used to calculate overhead. For example, assume a firm has estimated overhead costs for the coming year of $900,000 and expected activity is 90,000 direct labor hours. The predetermined rate is:

$$\$900,000/90,000 \text{ direct labor hours} = \$10 \text{ per direct labor hour}$$

Since the number of direct labor hours charged to a job is known from time tickets, the assignment of overhead costs to jobs is simple once the predetermined rate has been computed. For instance, Exhibit 16-7 reveals that Ed Wilson worked a total of eight hours on Job 16. From this time ticket, overhead totaling $80 ($10 $\times$ 8 hours) would be assigned to Job 16.

If an activity measure other than direct labor hours is used to assign overhead to jobs, then its actual value must also be collected and posted to the job cost sheets. For example, if machine hours is used to assign overhead, then a source document that will track the machine hours used by each job must be created. A machine time ticket could easily accommodate this need.

Unit Cost Calculation

Once a job is completed, its total manufacturing cost is computed by first totaling the costs of direct materials, direct labor, and overhead, and then summing these individual totals. The grand total is divided by the number of units produced to obtain the unit cost. (Exhibit 16-5 illustrates these computations.)

All completed job-order cost sheets of a firm can serve as a subsidiary ledger for the finished goods inventory. In a manual accounting system, the completed sheets would be transferred from the work-in-process files to the finished goods inventory file. In an automated accounting system, an updating run would delete the finished job from the work-in-process master file and add this record to the finished goods master file. In either case, adding the totals of all completed job-order cost sheets gives the cost of finished goods inventory at any point in time. As finished goods are sold and shipped, the cost records would be pulled (or deleted) from the finished goods inventory file. These records then form the basis for calculating a period's cost of goods sold.

JOB-ORDER COSTING: SPECIFIC COST FLOW DESCRIPTION

Objective 4
Describe the cost flows and prepare the journal entries associated with job-order costing.

Recall that cost flow is how we account for costs from the point at which they are incurred to the point at which they are recognized as an expense on the income statement. Of principal interest in a job-order system is the flow of manufacturing costs. Accordingly, we begin with a description of exactly how we account for the three manufacturing cost elements (direct materials, direct labor, and overhead).

A simplified job shop environment is used as the framework for this description. Better Works, a company recently formed by Stan Johnson, produces customized briefcases. Stan leased a small building and bought the necessary production equipment. For the first month of operation (January), Stan has finalized two orders: one for twenty engraved briefcases for a local firm and a second for ten orange and black briefcases for the coaches of a local college. Both orders must be delivered January 31 and will be sold for manufacturing cost plus 50 percent. Stan expects to average two orders per month for the first year of operation.

Stan created two job-order cost sheets and assigned a number to each job. Job 1 is the engraved briefcases, and Job 2 the orange and black briefcases.

Accounting for Materials

Since the company is beginning business, it has no beginning inventories. To produce the thirty briefcases in January and have a supply of materials on hand at the beginning of February, Stan purchases, on account, $2,500 of raw materials. This purchase is recorded as follows:

1. Raw Materials	2,500	
Accounts Payable		2,500

Raw Materials is an inventory account. It also is the controlling account for all raw materials. When materials are purchased, the cost of these materials "flows" into the raw materials account.

From January 2 to January 19, the production supervisor used three requisition forms to remove $1,000 of raw materials from the storeroom. From January 20 to January 31, two additional requisition forms for $500 of raw materials were used. The first three forms revealed that the raw materials were used for Job 1; the last two requisitions were for Job 2. Thus, for January, the cost sheet for Job 1 would have a total of $1,000 in direct materials posted, and the cost sheet for Job 2 would have a total of $500 in direct materials posted. In addition, the following entry would be made:

2. Work in Process	1,500	
Raw Materials		1,500

This second entry captures the notion of raw materials flowing from the storeroom to work in process. All such flows are summarized in the Work in Process account as well as being posted individually to the respective jobs. Work in Process is a controlling account, and the job cost sheets are the subsidiary accounts. Exhibit 16-8 summarizes the raw materials cost flows. Notice that the source document that drives the materials cost flows is the materials requisition form.

Accounting for Direct Labor Cost

Since two jobs were in progress during January, time tickets filled out by direct laborers must be sorted by each job. Once the sorting is completed, the hours worked and the wage rate of each employee are used to assign the direct labor cost to each job. For Job 1, the time tickets showed 120 hours at an average wage rate of $5 per hour, for a total direct labor cost of $600. For Job 2, the total was $250, based on 50 hours at an average hourly wage of $5. In addition to the postings to each job's cost sheet, the following summary entry would be made:

3. Work in Process	850	
Wages Payable		850

The summary of the labor cost flows is given in Exhibit 16-9. Notice that the direct labor costs assigned to the two jobs exactly equal the total assigned to Work in Process. Note also that the time tickets filled out by the individual laborers are the source of information for posting the labor cost flows. Remember that the labor cost flows reflect only direct labor cost. Indirect labor is assigned as part of overhead.

Accounting for Overhead

Under a normal costing approach, actual overhead costs are *never* assigned to jobs. Overhead is applied to each individual job using a predetermined overhead rate. Even with this system, however, actual overhead costs incurred must be

Exhibit 16-8
Summary of Materials Cost Flows

Purchase of Raw Materials → *Raw Materials*

Debit	Credit
1 2,500	2 1,500

Issue of Materials → *Work in Process*

Debit	Credit
2 1,500	

Subsidiary Accounts (Cost Sheets)

Job 1
Materials

Req. No.	Amount
1	$ 300
2	200
3	500
	$1,000

Job 2
Materials

Req. No.	Amount
4	$ 250
5	250
	$ 500

Source Documents: Material Requisition Forms

Exhibit 16-9
Summary of Direct Labor Cost Flows

Wages Payable		→ Labor Cost →	*Work in Process*	
	3 850		3 850	

WIP Subsidiary Accounts (Cost Sheets)

Job 1
Labor

Ticket	Hours	Rate	Amount
1	30	$5	$ 150
2	40	5	200
3	50	5	250
	120		$ 600

Job 2
Labor

Ticket	Hours	Rate	Amount
4	25	$5	$ 125
5	25	5	125
	50		$ 250

Source Documents: Time Tickets

accounted for. Thus, first we will describe how to account for applied overhead, and then we will discuss accounting for actual overhead.

Accounting for Overhead Application. Assume that Stan has estimated overhead costs for the year at $9,600. He also expects to use 4,800 direct labor hours. Accordingly, the predetermined overhead rate is:

$$\text{Overhead rate} = \$9{,}600/4{,}800 = \$2 \text{ per direct labor hour}$$

Overhead costs flow into Work in Process via the predetermined rate. Since direct labor hours are used to load overhead onto production, the time tickets serve as the source documents for assigning overhead to individual jobs and to the controlling Work in Process account.

For Job 1, with a total of 120 hours worked, the amount of overhead cost posted is $240 ($2 × 120). For Job 2, the overhead cost is $100 ($2 × 50). A summary entry reflects a total of $340 (i.e., all overhead applied to jobs worked on in January) in applied overhead.

4. Work in Process	340	
Overhead Control		340

The credit balance in the overhead control account equals the total applied overhead at a given point in time. In normal costing, only applied overhead ever enters the Work in Process account.

Accounting for Actual Overhead Costs. To illustrate how actual overhead costs are recorded, assume that Business Works incurred the following indirect costs for January:

Lease payment	$200
Utilities	50
Equipment depreciation	100
Indirect labor	65
Total overhead costs	$415

As indicated earlier, actual overhead costs never enter the Work in Process account. The usual procedure is to record actual overhead costs on the debit side of the Overhead Control account. For example, the actual overhead costs would be recorded as follows:

5. Overhead Control	415	
Lease Payable		200
Utilities Payable		50
Accumulated Depreciation		100
Wages Payable		65

Thus, the debit balance in the Overhead Control account gives the total actual overhead costs at a given point in time. Since actual overhead costs are on the debit side of this account and applied overhead costs are on the credit side, the balance in the Overhead Control account is the overhead variance at a given point in time. For Better Works at the end of January, the actual overhead of $415 and applied overhead of $340 produce underapplied overhead of $75 ($415 − $340).

The flow of overhead costs is summarized in Exhibit 16-10. To apply overhead to work in process, a company needs information from the time tickets and a predetermined overhead rate based on direct labor hours.

Exhibit 16-10
Summary of Overhead Cost Flows

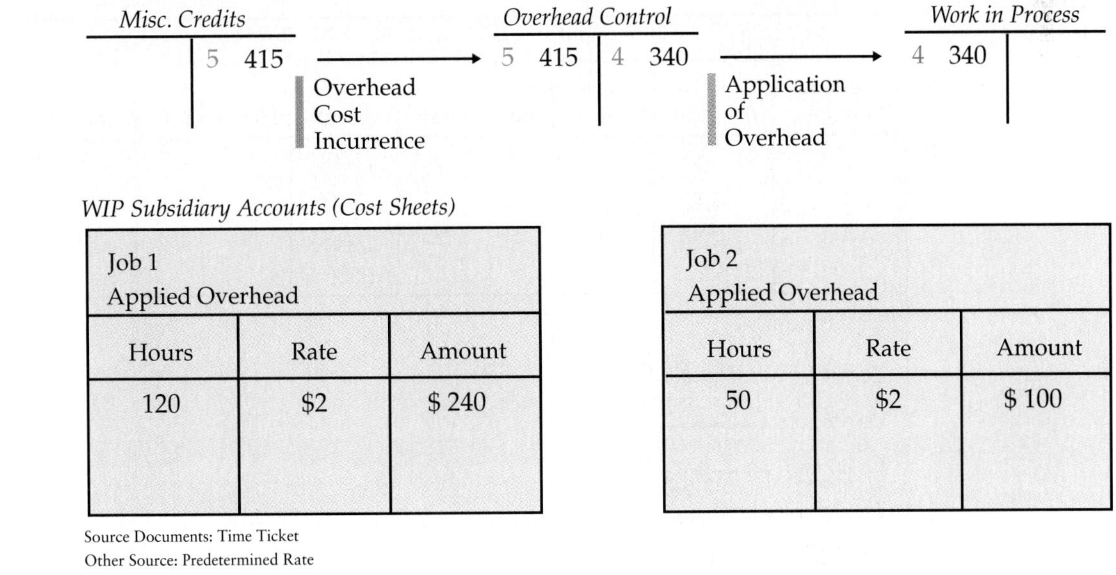

Accounting for Finished Goods

We have already seen what takes place when a job is completed. The columns for direct materials, direct labor, and applied overhead are totaled. These totals are then transferred to another section of the cost sheet where they are summed to yield the manufacturing cost of the job. This job cost sheet is then transferred to a finished goods file. Simultaneously, the costs of the completed job are transferred from the Work in Process account to the Finished Goods account.

For example, assume that Job 1 was completed in January with the completed cost sheet shown in Exhibit 16-11. Since Job 1 is completed, the total manufacturing costs of $1,840 must be transferred from the Work in Process account to the Finished Goods account. This transfer is described by the following entry.

6. Finished Goods	1,840	
Work in Process		1,840

A summary of the cost flows occurring when a job is finished is shown in Exhibit 16-12.

Completion of goods in a manufacturing process represents an important step in the flow of manufacturing costs. Because of the importance of this stage in a manufacturing operation, a schedule of the cost of goods manufactured is prepared periodically to summarize the cost flows of all production activity. This report is an important input for a firm's income statement and can be used to evaluate a firm's manufacturing effort. The cost of goods manufactured schedule

Exhibit 16-11
Completed Job-Order Cost Sheet

For	Johnson Company	Job Order Number	1
		Date Ordered	Jan. 1, 1995
Item Description	Engraved Briefcases	Date Completed	Jan. 29, 1995
Quantity Completed	20	Date Shipped	Jan. 31, 1995

Materials		Direct Labor				Overhead		
Requisition Number	Amount	Ticket Number	Hours	Rate	Amount	Hours	Rate	Amount
1	$ 300	1	30	$5	$150	30	$2	$ 60
2	200	2	40	$5	200	40	$2	80
3	500	3	50	$5	250	50	$2	100
	$1,000				$600			$240

Cost Summary

Direct Materials	$1,000
Direct Labor	$600
Overhead	$240
Total Cost	$1,840
Unit Cost	$92

Exhibit 16-12
Summary of Finished Goods Cost Flow

Work in Process		Finished Goods	
	6 1,840	6 1,840	

Transfer of → Finished Goods

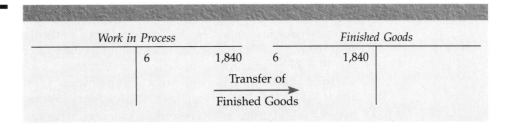

was first introduced in Chapter 15. However, in a normal cost system, the report is somewhat different than the actual cost report presented in that chapter.

The schedule of the cost of goods manufactured presented in Exhibit 16-13 summarizes the production activity of Better Works for January. The key difference between this report and the one appearing in Chapter 15 is the use of applied overhead to arrive at the cost of goods manufactured. Finished goods inventories are carried at normal cost rather than actual cost.

Notice that ending work in process is $850. Where did we obtain this figure? Of the two jobs, Job 1 was finished and transferred to finished goods. Job 2 is still in process, however, and the manufacturing costs assigned thus far are direct materials, $500; direct labor, $250; and overhead applied, $100. The total of these costs gives the cost of ending work in process.

Exhibit 16-13

Better Works Company
Schedule of Cost of Goods Manufactured
For the Month Ended January 31, 1995

Direct materials:		
Beginning raw materials inventory	$ 0	
Purchases of raw materials	2,500	
Total raw materials available	$2,500	
Ending raw materials	1,000	
Raw materials used		$1,500
Direct labor		850
Overhead:		
Lease	$ 200	
Utilities	50	
Depreciation	100	
Indirect labor	65	
	$ 415	
Less: Underapplied overhead	(75)	
Overhead applied		340
Current manufacturing costs		$2,690
Add: Beginning work in process		0
Total manufacturing costs		$2,690
Less: Ending work in process		(850)
Cost of goods manufactured		$1,840

Accounting for Cost of Goods Sold

In a job-order firm, units can be produced for a particular customer or they can be produced with the expectation of selling the units as market conditions warrant. If a job is produced especially for a customer (as with Job 1), when the job is shipped to the customer, the cost of the finished job becomes the cost of the goods sold. When Job 1 is shipped, the following entries would be made (recall that the selling price is 150 percent of manufacturing cost).

7. Cost of Goods Sold	1,840	
Finished Goods		1,840
8. Accounts Receivable	2,760	
Sales Revenue		2,760

In addition to these entries, a schedule of cost of goods sold usually is prepared at the end of each reporting period (e.g., monthly and quarterly). Exhibit 16-14 presents such a schedule for Better Works for January. Typically, the overhead variance is not material and, therefore, is closed to the Cost of Goods Sold account. Cost of goods sold *before* adjustment for an overhead variance is called **normal cost of goods sold**. After adjustment for the period's overhead variance takes place, the result is called the **adjusted cost of goods sold**. It is this latter figure that appears as an expense on the income statement.

normal cost of goods sold

adjusted cost of goods sold

However, closing the overhead variance to the Cost of Goods Sold account is not done until the end of the year. Variances are expected each month because of nonuniform production and nonuniform actual overhead costs. As the year unfolds, these monthly variances should, by and large, offset each other so that the year-end variance is small. Nonetheless, to illustrate how the year-end overhead variance would be treated, we will close out the overhead variance experienced by Better Works in January.

Closing the underapplied overhead to cost of goods sold requires the following entry:

9. Cost of Goods Sold	75	
Overhead Control		75

Notice that debiting Cost of Goods Sold is equivalent to adding the underapplied amount to the normal cost of goods sold figure. If the overhead variance had been overapplied, the entry would reverse and Cost of Goods Sold would be credited.

If Job 1 had not been ordered by a customer but had been produced with the expectation that the briefcases could be sold through a subsequent marketing

Exhibit 16-14
Statement of Cost of Goods Sold

Beginning finished goods inventory	$ 0
Cost of goods manufactured	1,840
Goods available for sale	$1,840
Less: Ending finished goods inventory	(0)
Normal cost of goods sold	$1,840
Add: Underapplied overhead	75
Adjusted cost of goods sold	$1,915

effort, then all 20 units may not be sold at the same time. Assume that on January 31, 15 briefcases were sold. In this case, the cost of goods sold figure is the unit cost times the number of units sold ($92 × 15, or $1,380). The unit cost figure is found on the cost sheet in Exhibit 16-11.

Closing out the overhead variance to Cost of Goods Sold completes the description of manufacturing cost flows. To facilitate a review of these important concepts, Exhibit 16-15 shows a complete summary of the manufacturing cost flows for Better Works. Notice that these entries summarize information from the underlying job-order cost sheets. Although the description in this exhibit is specific to the example, the pattern of cost flows shown would be found in any manufacturing firm that uses a normal job-order cost system.

Manufacturing cost flows, however, are not the only cost flows experienced by a firm. Nonmanufacturing costs are also incurred. A description of how we account for these costs follows.

Accounting for Nonmanufacturing Costs

Recall that costs associated with selling and general administrative activities are classified as nonmanufacturing costs. These costs are period costs and are *never* assigned to the product. They are not part of the manufacturing cost flows. They do not belong to the overhead category and are treated as a totally separate category.

Exhibit 16-15
Better Works Company Summary of Manufacturing Cost Flows

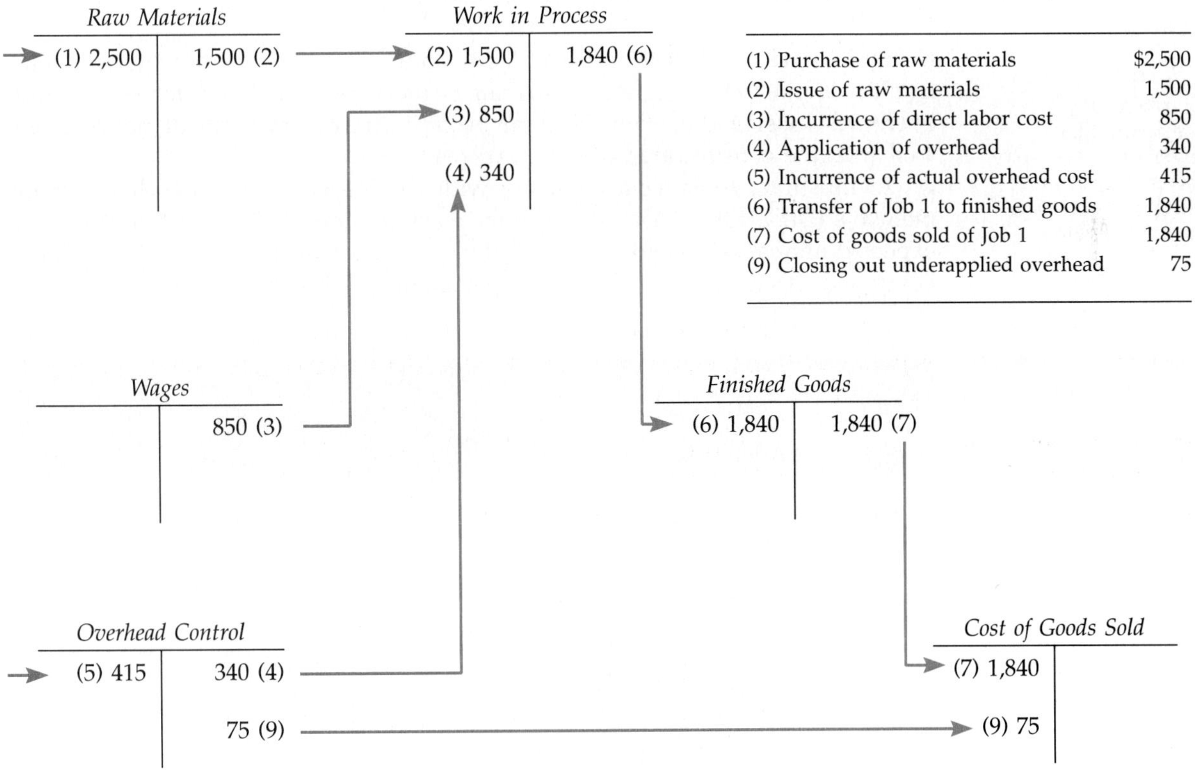

(1) Purchase of raw materials	$2,500
(2) Issue of raw materials	1,500
(3) Incurrence of direct labor cost	850
(4) Application of overhead	340
(5) Incurrence of actual overhead cost	415
(6) Transfer of Job 1 to finished goods	1,840
(7) Cost of goods sold of Job 1	1,840
(9) Closing out underapplied overhead	75

To illustrate how these costs are accounted for, assume Better Works had the following additional transactions in January:

Advertising circulars	$ 75
Sales commission	125
Office salaries	500
Depreciation, office equipment	50

The following compound entry could be used to record the above costs:

Selling Expense Control	200	
Administrative Expense Control	550	
Accounts Payable		75
Wages Payable		625
Accumulated Depreciation		50

Controlling accounts accumulate all of the selling and administrative expenses for a period. At the end of the period, all of these costs flow to the period's income statement. An income statement for Better Works is shown in Exhibit 16-16.

With the description of the accounting procedures for selling and administrative expenses completed, the basic essentials of a normal job-order costing system are also complete. This description has assumed that a single plant-wide overhead rate was being used. The use of a single overhead rate, however, can distort product costs.

SINGLE VERSUS MULTIPLE OVERHEAD RATES

Objective 5
Explain why departmental overhead rates may be preferred to a single, plant-wide overhead rate.

Using a single rate based on direct labor hours to assign overhead to jobs may result in unfair cost assignments (unfair in the sense that too much or too little overhead is assigned to a job). This can occur if direct labor hours do not correlate well with the consumption of overhead resources.

To illustrate, consider a company with two departments, one that is labor intensive (Department A) and the other machine intensive (Department B). The expected annual overhead costs and the expected annual usage of direct labor hours and machine hours for each department are shown in Exhibit 16-17.

Exhibit 16-16

Better Works Company
Income Statement
For the Month Ended January 31, 1995

Sales		$ 2,760
Less: Cost of goods sold		(1,915)
Gross margin		$ 845
Less selling and administrative expenses:		
Selling expense	$200	
Administrative expense	550	(750)
Net income		$ 95

Exhibit 16-17
Departmental Overhead Costs and Activity

	Department A	*Department B*	*Total*
Overhead costs	$60,000	$180,000	$240,000
Direct labor hours	15,000	5,000	20,000
Machine hours	5,000	15,000	20,000

Currently, the company uses a plant-wide overhead rate based on direct labor hours. Thus, the overhead rate used for product costing is $12 per direct labor hour [($60,000 + $180,000)/(15,000 + 5,000)].

Now consider two recently completed jobs, Job 23 and Job 24. Exhibit 16-18 provides production-related data concerning each job. The data reveal that Job 23 spent all of its time in Department A while Job 24 spent all of its time in Department B. Using the plant-wide overhead rate, Job 23 would receive a $6,000 overhead assignment ($12 × 500 direct labor hours) and Job 24 would receive a $12 overhead assignment ($12 × 1 direct labor hour). Thus, the total manufacturing cost of Job 23 is $11,000 ($5,000 + $6,000), yielding a unit cost of $11; the total manufacturing cost of Job 24 is $5,012 ($5,000 + $12), yielding a unit cost of $5.012. Clearly, something is wrong. Using a plant-wide rate, Job 23 received 500 times the overhead cost assignment that Job 24 received. Yet, as Exhibit 16-18 shows, Job 24 was produced in a department that is responsible for producing 75 percent of the plant's total overhead. Imagine the difficulties that this type of costing distortion can cause for a company. Some products would be overcosted while others would be undercosted, and the result could be incorrect pricing decisions that adversely affect the firm's competitive position.

The distortion in product costs is caused by the assumption that direct labor hours properly reflect the overhead consumed by the individual jobs. One cost driver for the firm as a whole does not seem to work. This type of problem can be resolved by using multiple overhead rates, where each rate uses a different cost driver. For this example, a satisfactory solution might be to develop an overhead rate for each department. In the case of the machine-intensive Department

Exhibit 16-18
Production Data for Jobs 23 and 24

	Job 23		
	Department A	*Department B*	*Total*
Prime costs	$5,000	$0	$5,000
Direct labor hours	500	0	500
Machine hours	1	0	1
Units produced	1,000	0	1,000

	Job 24		
	Department A	*Department B*	*Total*
Prime costs	0	$5,000	$5,000
Direct labor hours	0	1	1
Machine hours	0	500	500
Units produced	0	1,000	1,000

B, the rate could be based on machine hours instead of direct labor hours. It seems reasonable to believe that machine hours relate better to machine-related overhead than direct labor hours do and direct labor hours would be a good cost driver for a labor-intensive department. If so, more accurate product costing can be achieved by computing two departmental rates instead of one plant-wide rate.

Using data from Exhibit 16-17, the overhead rate for Department A is $4 per direct labor hour ($60,000/15,000), and the overhead rate for Department B is $12 per machine hour ($180,000/15,000). Using these rates, Job 23 would be assigned $2,000 of overhead ($4 × 500 direct labor hours) and Job 24 $6,000 of overhead ($12 × 500 machine hours). Job 24 now receives three times as much overhead cost as Job 23, which seems more sensible since Department B incurs three times as much overhead cost as Department A.

	Department A	*Department B*
Overhead cost	$60,000	$180,000
Cost driver	15,000 DLH	15,000 MHrs
Department overhead rate	$4/DLH	$12/MHr
Overhead applied to:		
Job 23	$2,000	—
Job 24	—	$6,000

While moving to departmental rates may provide sufficient product-costing accuracy for some firms, even more attention to how overhead is assigned may be necessary for other firms. This chapter has focused on cost drivers that are correlated with production volume (e.g., direct labor hours and machine hours). Greater product-costing accuracy may be possible through the use of nonvolume-related cost drivers. However, discussion of further refinements of overhead assignment is left to a later chapter.

SUMMARY OF LEARNING OBJECTIVES

1. Describe the approaches available to measure and assign costs to products and services. There are two approaches used to measure costs: an actual cost system and a normal cost system. An actual cost system requires the firm to determine the actual cost of direct materials, direct labor, and factory overhead in order to calculate unit cost. Normal cost is a mixture of actual costs for direct materials and labor and predetermined costs for overhead. Normal costing is preferred because it is capable of supplying unit cost information in a timely way. An actual cost system simply cannot supply the needed unit cost information on a timely basis. There are two assignment systems: job order costing and process costing. A job order system assigns costs to individual jobs and is used in those settings where products are custom produced. Unit costs are computed by dividing job costs by the units produced by the job. A process cost system assigns costs to processes and is used in those settings where homogeneous products are mass produced. Unit costs are computed by dividing the costs assigned to a process for a period by the output of the period.

2. Explain how a predetermined overhead rate is computed and how it is used to assign overhead to production. A predetermined overhead rate is computed by dividing the budgeted overhead for the period (typically a year) by the budgeted base for the period. Applying overhead to production is accomplished by multiplying the predetermined rate times the actual level of production activity. The base chosen to calculate the predetermined overhead rate and to apply overhead to production should bear a cause-and-effect relationship to overhead.

Any difference between the applied overhead and the actual overhead for a period is an overhead variance. If actual overhead is greater than applied, overhead is said to be underapplied. If actual overhead is less than applied, overhead is overapplied. If this overhead variance is not material, it usually is closed out to cost of goods sold. Otherwise, the variance is allocated among cost of goods sold, finished goods, and work in process.

3. ***Explain how manufacturing costs are assigned to individual jobs and how a unit cost is computed.*** In job-order costing, the key document or record for accumulating manufacturing costs is the job-order cost sheet. Materials requisition forms (for direct materials) and time tickets (for direct labor) are the source documents needed to assign prime costs to jobs. Overhead costs are assigned to jobs using a predetermined overhead rate. If the rate is labor-based, the overhead assigned to the job is the rate times the hours posted from the time tickets. Once the job is completed, the unit cost is computed by totaling the manufacturing costs and dividing the total by the number of units associated with the job.

4. ***Describe the cost flows and prepare the journal entries associated with job-order costing.*** In job-order costing, materials and direct labor are charged to the Work in Process account (Raw Materials and Payroll are credited, respectively). Overhead costs are assigned to Work in Process using a predetermined rate (Overhead Control is credited). The cost of completed units is credited to Work in Process and debited to Finished Goods. When goods are sold, the cost is debited to Cost of Goods Sold and credited to Finished Goods. Actual overhead costs are accumulated in the Overhead Control account on the debit side.

5. ***Explain why departmental overhead rates may be preferred to a single, plant-wide overhead rate.*** In order to achieve more accurate product costing, it may be necessary to use departmental overhead rates rather than a single, factory-wide rate. Departmental overhead rates provide more accurate costing by reflecting cause-and-effect relationships more accurately. By improving the accuracy of product costing, managers have better information to use in making pricing and product mix decisions.

KEY TERMS

Actual cost system 764
Adjusted cost of goods sold 782
Applied overhead 769
Cost assignment 761
Cost measurement 761
Expected activity level 768
Job-order costing system 763
Job-order cost sheet 773
Materials requisition form 774
Normal activity level 768
Normal costing system 766
Normal cost of goods sold 782
Overapplied overhead 770
Overhead variance 770
Practical activity level 768
Predetermined overhead rate 766
Process costing system 763
Theoretical activity level 768
Time ticket 774
Underapplied overhead 770
Work-in-process file 773

REVIEW PROBLEM

Timter Company uses a normal job-order costing system. The company has two departments through which most jobs pass. Selected budgeted and actual data for the past year follow:

	Department A	*Department B*
Budgeted overhead	$100,000	$500,000
Actual overhead	110,000	520,000
Expected activity (direct labor hours)	50,000	10,000
Expected machine hours	10,000	50,000
Actual direct labor hours	51,000	9,000
Actual machine hours	10,500	52,000

During the year, several jobs were completed. Data pertaining to one such job are as follows:

	Job 10
Direct materials	$20,000
Direct labor cost:	
Department A (5,000 hrs @ $6)	$30,000
Department B (1,000 hrs @ $6)	$ 6,000
Machine hours used:	
Department A	100
Department B	1,200
Units produced	10,000

Timter Company uses a plant-wide predetermined overhead rate to assign overhead (OH) to jobs. Direct labor hours (DLH) is used to compute the predetermined overhead rate.

REQUIRED:

1. Compute the predetermined overhead rate.
2. Using the predetermined rate, compute the per-unit manufacturing cost for Job 10.
3. Compute the overhead variance for the year and label it as over- or underapplied. Assuming that the variance is immaterial, provide the journal entry that will dispose of the variance at the end of the year.
4. Recalculate the unit manufacturing cost for Job 10 using departmental overhead rates. Use direct labor hours for Department A and machine hours for Department B. Explain why this approach provides a more accurate unit cost.

Solution

1. Predetermined overhead rate = $600,000/60,000 = $10 per DLH.
   Add the budgeted overhead for the two departments and divide by the total expected direct labor hours (DLH = 50,000 + 10,000).

2.

Direct materials	$ 20,000
Direct labor	36,000
Overhead ($10 × 6,000 DLH)	60,000
Total manufacturing cost	$116,000
Unit cost ($116,000/10,000)	$11.60

3. Applied overhead = Overhead rate × Total actual direct labor hours
   = $10 × (51,000 + 9,000)
   = $600,000
   Overhead variance = Total actual OH − Applied OH
   = $630,000 − $600,000
   = $30,000 underapplied

Cost of Goods Sold	30,000	
Overhead Control		30,000

4. Predetermined rate for Department A: $100,000/50,000 = $2 per DLH.
   Predetermined rate for Department B: $500,000/50,000 = $10 per machine hour.

Direct materials	$20,000
Direct labor	36,000
Overhead:	
Department A: $2 × 5,000	10,000
Department B: $10 × 1,200	12,000
Total manufacturing costs	$78,000
Unit cost ($78,000/10,000)	$7.80

Overhead assignment using departmental rates is more accurate because there is a higher correlation with the overhead assigned and the overhead consumed. Notice that Job 10 spends most of its time in department A, the least overhead intensive of the two departments. Departmental rates reflect this differential time and consumption better than plant-wide rates do.

QUESTIONS

1. What is cost measurement? cost accumulation? What is the difference between the two?
2. Explain why an actual overhead rate is rarely used for product costing.
3. Explain the differences between job-order costing and process costing.
4. What are some differences between a manual job-order cost system and an automated job-order cost system?
5. What is an overhead variance? Explain the difference between an underapplied and an overapplied overhead variance.
6. How are overhead variances disposed of at the end of the year? Which way of disposal is most common? Why?
7. What is the role of materials requisition forms in a job-order cost system? time tickets? predetermined overhead rates?
8. Explain why multiple overhead rates are often preferred to a plant-wide overhead rate.
9. Explain the role of cost drivers in assigning overhead costs to products.
10. Define the following terms: *expected actual activity*, *normal activity*, *practical activity*, and *theoretical activity*.
11. Why would some prefer normal activity to expected actual activity to compute a predetermined overhead rate?
12. When computing a predetermined overhead rate, why are units of output not commonly used as a measure of production activity?
13. Explain how overhead is assigned to production when a predetermined overhead rate is used.
14. What is the difference between applied overhead and budgeted overhead? Will they ever be the same? If so, explain how. What is the difference between applied overhead and actual overhead? Will these two ever be the same? When?
15. Wilson Company has a predetermined overhead rate of $5 per direct labor hour. The job-order cost sheet for Job 145 shows 1,000 direct labor hours costing $10,000 and materials requisitions totaling $7,500. Job 145 had 500 units completed and transferred to finished goods. What is the cost per unit for Job 145?
16. Why are the accounting requirements for job-order costing more demanding than those for process costing?
17. Explain the difference between normal cost of goods sold and adjusted cost of goods sold.

EXERCISES

E16-1 Predetermined Overhead Rate; Application of Overhead; Variances; Journal Entries

LO 2

Harris Company uses a normal job-order cost system. Budgeted overhead for the coming year is $600,000. Expected actual activity is 200,000 direct labor hours. During the year, Harris Company employees worked a total of 190,000 direct labor hours and actual overhead totaled $562,000.

REQUIRED:

1. Compute the predetermined overhead rate for Harris Company.
2. How much overhead will the company assign to the Work in Process account? Prepare the journal entry that corresponds to this assignment.
3. Compute the overhead variance and label the variance as under- or overapplied overhead. Assuming the variance is not material, write the journal entry that disposes of the variance at the end of the year.

E16-2
Predetermined Overhead Rate; Applied Overhead; Unit Cost
LO 1, 2

Bethel Industries uses a normal costing system. The following data are available for 1995:

Budgeted:	
Overhead	$675,000
Machine hours	25,000
Direct labor hours	75,000
Actual:	
Overhead	$681,000
Machine hours	25,050
Direct labor hours	75,700
Prime cost	$957,000
Number of units	400,000

Overhead is applied on the basis of direct labor hours.

REQUIRED:

1. What is the predetermined overhead rate?
2. What is the applied overhead for 1995?
3. Was overhead over- or underapplied and by how much?
4. What is the normal cost per unit produced?

E16-3
Predetermined Overhead Rate; Applied Overhead; Unit Cost
LO 1, 2

Using the information from E16-2, suppose Bethel Industries applied overhead to production on the basis of machine hours instead of direct labor hours.

REQUIRED:

1. What is the predetermined overhead rate?
2. What is the applied overhead for 1995?
3. Is overhead over- or underapplied and by how much?
4. What is the normal cost per unit produced?
5. How can Bethel decide whether to use direct labor hours or machine hours as the basis for applying factory overhead?

E16-4
Predetermined Overhead Rate; Application of Overhead
LO 2

Alpha Company and Beta, Inc., both use predetermined overhead rates to apply factory overhead to production. Alpha's is based on direct labor hours and Beta's is based on materials cost. Budgeted production and cost data for Alpha and Beta are as follows:

	Alpha	*Beta*
Manufacturing overhead	$240,000	$300,000
Units	10,000	20,000
Direct labor hours	6,000	7,500
Material cost	$150,000	$400,000

At the end of the year, Alpha Company had incurred overhead of $221,000 and produced 9,800 units using 6,100 direct labor hours and materials costing $147,000.

Beta, Inc., had incurred overhead of $316,500, and produced 20,500 units using 7,550 direct labor hours and materials costing $411,000.

REQUIRED:

1. Compute the predetermined overhead rates for Alpha and Beta.
2. Was overhead over- or underapplied for each company, and by how much?

E16-5
Journal Entries; Account Balances
LO 4

Kaycee, Inc., manufactures brown paper grocery bags. During the month of May, the following occurred:

a. Materials were purchased on account for $23,175.
b. Materials totaling $19,000 were requisitioned for use in production.
c. Direct labor payroll for the month was $17,850 with an average wage of $8.50 per hour.
d. Actual overhead of $15,500 was incurred and paid.
e. Factory overhead is charged to production at the rate of $7 per direct labor hour.
f. Completed units costing $36,085 were transferred to finished goods.
g. Bags costing $30,000 were sold on account for $36,000.

Beginning balances as of May 1 were:

Materials	$ 5,170
Work in Process	11,200
Finished Goods	2,630

REQUIRED:

1. Prepare the journal entries for the above events.
2. Calculate the ending balances of:
   a. Materials
   b. Work in Process
   c. Overhead Control
   d. Finished Goods

E16-6
Choice of Activity Levels; Pricing Concerns
LO 1, 2

Lomond Company is considering the use of expected actual activity for the assignment of overhead to jobs. John Simpson, Lomond's vice-president of marketing, is concerned about overhead assignment because different methods can affect the prices charged to customers. Lomond operates in an industry in which cost-plus pricing is heavily used. Firms must bid for jobs, and bids are usually expressed as full manufacturing cost plus a markup.

Simpson believes that Lomond's manufacturing costs are competitive with the rest of the firms in the industry. Since the costs of direct materials and direct labor are expected to be fairly stable over the next three years, any price changes are likely to come from changes in overhead costs. Simpson asked Beth Thompson, the controller, to estimate what the overhead rates would be for the coming three years, using expected actual activity. In response to this request, Beth prepared the following report:

	Year 1	*Year 2*	*Year 3*
Expected overhead	$341,250	$341,250	$341,250
Expected actual activity (DLH)	70,000	75,000	65,000
Predetermined overhead rate[1]	$4.875	$ 4.55	$5.25

[1]Expected overhead/Expected activity

Upon seeing the report, John Simpson vigorously objected to the method of overhead assignment. He argued that the company should continue to use the practical activity of 80,000 direct labor hours as it had done in the past.

REQUIRED:

1. Compute the overhead rates for each of the three years using practical activity. Why would John Simpson prefer using this measure for predetermined overhead rates? Can you think of any disadvantage that practical activity might have for this setting?

2. Suppose the controller suggests using normal activity to compute overhead rates. Recompute the overhead rates using normal activity for the next three years. Can you think of any advantage that normal activity might have over practical activity for this setting?

E16-7
Predetermined Overhead Rate; Overhead Variances; Journal Entries
LO 2

Rayburn Company uses a predetermined overhead rate to assign overhead to jobs. Because Rayburn's production is machine dominated, overhead is applied on the basis of machine hours. The expected overhead for the year was $2.5 million, and the practical level of activity is 50,000 machine hours.

During the year, Rayburn used 48,000 machine hours and incurred actual overhead costs of $2 million. Rayburn also had the following balances of applied overhead in its accounts:

Work in Process	$ 460,000
Cost of Goods Sold	1,440,000
Finished Goods	500,000

REQUIRED:

1. Compute a predetermined overhead rate for Rayburn.
2. Compute the overhead variance and label it as under- or overapplied.
3. Assume the overhead variance is immaterial. Prepare the journal entry to dispose of the variance at the end of the year.
4. Assume the variance computed in (2) is material. Prepare the journal entry that appropriately disposes of the overhead variance at the end of the year.

E16-8
Journal Entries; T-Accounts
LO 4

Porter Company uses job-order costing. During January, the following data were reported:

a. Materials purchased: direct materials, $82,000; indirect materials, $10,500.
b. Materials issued: direct materials, $72,500; indirect materials, $7,000.
c. Labor cost incurred: direct labor, $52,000; indirect labor, $15,750.
d. Other manufacturing costs incurred (all payables), $49,000.
e. Overhead is applied on the basis of 125 percent of direct labor cost.
f. Work finished and transferred to finished goods cost $160,000.
g. Finished goods costing $140,000 were sold on account for 150 percent of cost.

REQUIRED:

1. Prepare journal entries to record these transactions.
2. Prepare a T-account for Overhead Control. Post all relevant information to this account. What is the ending balance in this account? What does the ending balance represent?
3. Prepare a T-account for Work in Process. Assume a beginning balance of $10,000 and post all relevant information to this account. Did you assign any actual overhead costs to Work in Process? Why or why not?

E16-9
Applied Overhead; Cost of Goods Manufactured
LO 2

Shariff Company provided the following data for the year 1995:

Labor:	
Direct labor cost (25,000 hours)	$175,000
Indirect labor	35,000

(continued)

Materials:	
Direct materials:	
Inventory, January 1, 1995	$ 25,000
Purchases on account	200,000
Direct materials issued	190,000
Indirect materials issued	10,000
Other factory overhead costs:	
Depreciation	55,000
Maintenance	25,000
Miscellaneous	15,500
Work in process:	
Beginning inventory	110,000
Ending inventory	80,250

The company uses a predetermined overhead rate based on direct labor hours. The rate for 1995 was $5.20 per direct labor hour.

REQUIRED:

1. Compute the applied overhead for 1995. Is the overhead over- or underapplied? By how much?
2. Prepare a statement of cost of goods manufactured. Did you use actual or applied overhead when you prepared the statement of cost of goods manufactured? Explain.

E16-10
Overhead Assignment: Actual and Normal Activity Compared
LO 1

Reynolds Printing Company specializes in wedding announcements. Reynolds uses an actual job-order cost system. An actual overhead rate is calculated at the end of each month using actual direct labor hours and overhead for the month. Once the actual cost of a job is determined, the customer is billed at actual cost plus 50 percent.

During April, Mrs. Lucky, a good friend of owner Jane Reynolds, ordered three sets of wedding announcements to be delivered May 10, June 10, and July 10, respectively. Reynolds scheduled production for each order on May 7, June 7, and July 7, respectively. The orders were assigned job numbers 115, 116, and 117, respectively.

Reynolds assured Mrs. Lucky that she would attend each of her daughters' weddings. Out of sympathy and friendship, she also offered a lower price. Instead of cost plus 50 percent, she gave her a special price of cost plus 25 percent. Additionally, she agreed to wait until the final wedding to bill for the three jobs.

On August 15, Reynolds asked her accountant to bring the completed job-order cost sheets for Jobs 115, 116, and 117. She also gave instructions to lower the price as had been agreed upon. The cost sheets revealed the following information:

	Job 115	*Job 116*	*Job 117*
Cost of direct materials	$250.00	$250.00	$250.00
Cost of direct labor (5 hours)	25.00	25.00	25.00
Cost of overhead	200.00	400.00	400.00
Total cost	$475.00	$675.00	$675.00
Total price	$593.75	$843.75	$843.75
Number of announcements	500	500	500

Reynolds could not understand why the overhead costs assigned to Jobs 116 and 117 were so much higher than those for Job 115. She asked for an overhead cost summary sheet for the months of May, June, and July, which showed that actual overhead costs were

$20,000 each month. She also discovered that direct labor hours worked on all jobs were 500 hours in May and 250 hours each in June and July.

REQUIRED:

1. How do you think Mrs. Lucky will feel when she receives the bill for the three sets of wedding announcements?
2. Explain how the overhead costs were assigned to each job.
3. Assume that Reynolds's average activity is 500 hours per month and that the company usually experiences overhead costs of $240,000 each year. Can you recommend a better way to assign overhead costs to jobs? Recompute the cost of each job and its price given your method of overhead cost assignment. Which method do you think is best? Why?

E16-11
Departmental Overhead Rates
LO 5

Bryan Company uses a normal job-order cost system. Currently, a plant-wide overhead rate based on machine hours is used. Sam Perkins, the plant manager, has heard that departmental overhead rates can offer significantly better cost assignments than a plant-wide rate can offer. Bryan has the following data for its two departments for the coming year:

	Department A	*Department B*
Overhead costs (expected)	$50,000	$22,000
Normal activity (machine hours)	10,000	8,000

1. Compute a predetermined overhead rate for the plant as a whole based on machine hours.
2. Compute predetermined overhead rates for each department using machine hours.
3. Job 15 used 20 machine hours from Department A and 50 machine hours from Department B. Job 22 used 50 machine hours from Department A and 20 from Department B. Compute the overhead cost assigned to each job using the plant-wide rate computed in question 1. Repeat the computation using the departmental rates found in question 2. Which of the two approaches gives the fairer assignment? Why?
4. Repeat question 3 assuming the expected overhead cost for Department B is $40,000. For this company, would you recommend departmental rates over a plant-wide rate?

E16-12
Unit Cost; Journal Entries; Assignment Procedures
LO 3, 4

Hystle Furniture, Inc., received an order for ten specially designed sofas to be delivered by September 30. The order was assigned Job 237 and work began on September 1. During September, the following activity was associated with Job 237:

a. Purchased $2,000 worth of wood, $1,500 worth of fabric, and $200 worth of foam on account.
b. Issued $2,000 of wood, $1,500 of fabric, and $200 of foam.
c. Direct labor cost incurred: $1,360.
d. Overhead is assigned using a rate of 125 percent of direct labor cost.
e. Completed units are transferred to the warehouse.
f. Completed units are shipped to the customer. Selling price is 135 percent of cost.

REQUIRED:

1. Prepare the journal entries for the activity associated with Job 237.
2. What is the manufacturing cost per sofa?
3. Describe the procedures for identifying the materials issued to Job 237 and for identifying the cost of laborers who worked on the sofas.

PROBLEMS

P16-1
Predetermined Overhead Rates; Overhead Variances; Unit Costs
LO 2

Sanderson Company uses a predetermined overhead rate to apply overhead. Overhead is applied on the basis of direct labor hours in Department 1 and on the basis of machine hours in Department 2. At the beginning of 1995, the following estimates are provided for the coming year:

	Department 1	*Department 2*
Direct labor hours	100,000	20,000
Machine hours	10,000	30,000
Direct labor cost	$750,000	$160,000
Overhead cost	$250,000	$162,000

Actual results reported for all jobs during 1995 are as follows:

	Department 1	*Department 2*
Direct labor hours	98,000	21,000
Machine hours	11,000	32,000
Direct labor cost	$748,000	$168,000
Overhead cost	$247,500	$175,000

The accounting records of the company show the following data for Job 689:

	Department 1	*Department 2*
Direct labor hours	125	50
Machine hours	10	205
Direct materials cost	$1,580	$2,650
Direct labor cost	$ 937	$400

REQUIRED:

1. Compute the predetermined overhead rate for each department.
2. Compute the applied overhead for all jobs during 1995. What is the under- or over-applied overhead for each department? For the firm?
3. Prepare the journal entry that disposes of the overhead variance, assuming it is not material in amount.
4. Compute the total cost of Job 689. If there are 50 units in Job 689, what is the unit cost?

P16-2
Journal Entries; T-Accounts; Income Statement
LO 2, 4

Neptune, Inc., produces customized sailboats. The company uses a normal job-order costing system. At the beginning of the year, overhead was estimated at $420,000. Normal activity, measured in direct labor hours, is 12,000 hours. Overhead is applied on the basis of direct labor hours. Beginning balances in the accounts are reported as follows:

Work in Process	$25,000
Raw Materials	30,000
Finished Goods	24,000

During the year, the company experienced the following activity:

a. Raw materials purchased on account, $150,000.
b. Supplies purchased on account, $20,000.
c. Labor cost: $200,000. Of the total labor cost, 65 percent is direct labor, 10 percent is indirect labor, 20 percent is administrative, and 5 percent is sales.
d. Actual direct labor hours were 13,000.
e. Depreciation totaled $300,000; 70 percent was factory related, 20 percent administrative, and 10 percent sales.
f. Utilities, $15,000; 90 percent was factory related, 5 percent administrative, and 5 percent sales.
g. Other overhead, $155,000 (all payables).
h. Raw materials issued, $165,000; supplies issued, $50,000.
i. Job 179, the only unfinished job at the end of the year, had the following information on its job cost sheet:

Direct materials	$1,000
Direct labor cost	$ 900
Direct labor hours	90

j. Other selling expenses, $8,000. Other administrative expenses, $12,000.
k. Two jobs, Job 168 and Job 170, were not sold by the end of the year. The total cost of both jobs is $9,700.
l. Sales revenue for the year was $1.07 million.
m. Any over- or underapplied overhead is closed out to Cost of Goods Sold.

REQUIRED:

1. Using normal activity, compute a predetermined overhead rate.
2. Prepare journal entries for the year's activities.
3. Prepare T-accounts for Raw Materials, Overhead Control, Work in Process, Finished Goods, and Cost of Goods Sold. Post all relevant entries to these accounts.
4. Prepare an income statement for the year.

P16-3
Job Cost Sheets; Journal Entries; Inventories
LO 3, 4

On July 1, Jason Company had the following balances in its inventory accounts:

Raw Materials	$12,000
Work in Process	8,000
Finished Goods	20,000

Work in process is made up of two jobs with the following costs:

	Job 17	*Job 18*
Raw materials	$2,000	$1,410
Direct labor	1,500	1,200
Applied overhead	1,050	840

During July, Jason experienced the transactions listed below.

a. Materials purchased on account, $15,000.
b. Materials requisitioned: Job 17, $12,500; Job 18, $11,200.

c. Job tickets were collected and summarized: Job 17, 250 hours at $10 per hour; Job 18, 275 hours at $11 per hour.
d. Overhead is applied on the basis of direct labor cost.
e. Actual overhead was $4,000.
f. Job 18 was completed and transferred to the finished goods warehouse.
g. Job 18 was shipped, and the customer was billed for 160 percent of the cost.

REQUIRED:

1. Prepare job order cost sheets for Jobs 17 and 18. Post the beginning inventory data and then update the cost sheets for the July activity.
2. Prepare journal entries for the July transactions.
3. Prepare a schedule of inventories on July 31.

P16-4
Predetermined Overhead Rates; Applied Overhead; Disposition of Overhead Variances
LO 2, 5

Velma, Inc., uses a normal job-order cost system. The company has two departments, and predetermined overhead rates are computed for each department. Estimated cost and operating data are as follows for the year 1995:

	Department A	*Department B*
Estimated direct labor hours	50,000	10,000
Estimated machine hours	10,000	50,000
Estimated overhead	$200,000	$400,000

At the end of 1995, Velma reported the following actual cost and operating data:

	Department A	*Department B*
Direct labor hours	50,000	10,000
Machine hours	10,000	50,000
Overhead	$220,000	$440,000

The company also reported ending balances in the following accounts (prior to any closing entries):

	Total	*Applied Overhead*
Raw Materials	$ 40,000	—
Work in Process	100,000	$ 50,000
Finished Goods	300,000	200,000
Cost of Goods Sold	600,000	350,000

REQUIRED:

1. Assume that Department A uses direct labor hours and Department B uses machine hours to apply overhead. Compute a predetermined overhead rate for each department.
2. Compute the applied overhead for each department. Prepare the journal entry that assigns applied overhead to production.
3. Compute the under- or overapplied overhead for each department. What is the total overhead variance for the firm?
4. Prepare the journal entry to dispose of the under- or overapplied overhead under the assumption that (a) the overhead variance is immaterial and (b) the overhead variance is material.
5. How much will Velma's net income change if 4(b) is the method of disposing of the overhead rather than 4(a)?

P16-5
Journal Entries; T-Accounts; Cost of Goods Manufactured and Sold
LO 3, 4

During February, the following transactions were completed and reported by Bixby Products, Inc.:

a. Raw materials were purchased on account, $43,500.
b. Materials issued to production to fill job order requisitions, $35,000; supplies, $12,200.
c. Payroll for the month: direct labor, $60,000; indirect labor, $20,000; administrative, $18,000; sales, $9,000.
d. Depreciation on factory plant and equipment, $8,500.
e. Property tax (on factory) accrued during the month, $450.
f. Insurance (on factory) expired with a credit to the prepaid account, $6,200.
g. Factory utilities, $6,200.
h. Advertising, $5,000.
i. Depreciation on office equipment, $1,500; on sales vehicles, $650.
j. Legal fees for preparation of lease agreements, $750.
k. Overhead is charged to production at a rate of $6 per DLH. Records show 8,000 direct labor hours were worked during the month.
l. Cost of jobs completed during the month, $135,000.

The company also reported the following beginning balances in its inventory accounts:

Raw Materials	$ 5,000
Work in Process	30,000
Finished Goods	60,000

REQUIRED:

1. Prepare journal entries to record the transactions occurring in February.
2. Prepare T-accounts for Raw Materials, Overhead Control, Work in Process, and Finished Goods. Post all relevant entries to these accounts.
3. Prepare a statement of cost of goods manufactured.
4. If the overhead variance is all allocated to Cost of Goods Sold, by how much will Cost of Goods Sold decrease or increase?

P16-6
Journal Entries; T-Accounts; Disposition of Overhead; Income Statement
LO 3, 4

At the beginning of the year, Polson Manufacturing Company had the following balances in its inventory accounts:

Raw Materials	$70,000
Work in Process	20,000
Finished Goods	45,000

Polson applies overhead on the basis of 150 percent of direct labor cost. During the year, Polson experienced transactions as described below.

a. Direct materials purchased on account, $280,000.
b. Direct materials issued, $300,000.
c. Indirect materials issued, $82,000.
d. Labor costs:

Direct labor	$110,000
Indirect labor	60,000
Selling and administrative	70,000

e. Factory insurance expired, $5,000.
f. Advertising costs, $30,000.

g. Factory rent, $24,000.
h. Depreciation (office equipment), $10,000.
i. Miscellaneous factory costs, $7,850.
j. Utilities (70 percent factory, 30 percent office), $10,000.
k. Overhead was applied to production.
l. Sales totaled $983,000.

Ending balances in the inventory accounts were used to prorate the overhead variance.

Raw Materials	$50,000
Work in Process	30,000
Finished Goods	20,000
Cost of Goods Sold	?

REQUIRED:

1. Prepare journal entries for the above transactions.
2. Post the journal entries relating to manufacturing costs to the appropriate T-accounts.
3. Compute the under- or overapplied overhead variance. Give the journal entry that disposes of the variance by closing it out to Cost of Goods Sold. Give the journal entry required to close out the variance if it is prorated among the appropriate accounts.
4. Prepare an income statement assuming that the variance is closed to Cost of Goods Sold. Prepare another income statement based on prorating the variance. What is the difference in income figures? Would you judge the difference to be significant?

P16-7
Job-Order Costing: Housing Construction
LO 2, 3

Butter, Inc., is a privately held, family-founded corporation that builds single- and multiple-unit housing. Most projects Butter undertakes involve the construction of multiple units. Butter has adopted a job-order cost system for determining the cost of each unit. The costing system is fully computerized. Each project's costs are divided into the following five categories:

a. *General conditions*, including construction site utilities, project insurance permits and licenses, architect's fees, decorating, field office salaries, and clean-up costs
b. *Hard costs*, such as subcontractors, direct materials, and direct labor
c. *Finance costs*, including title and recording fees, inspection fees, and taxes and discounts on mortgages
d. *Land costs*, which refer to the purchase price of the construction site
e. *Marketing costs*, such as advertising, sales commissions, and appraisal fees

Recently, Butter purchased land for the purpose of developing 20 new single family houses. The cost of the land was $250,000. Lot sizes vary from 1/4 to 1/2 acre. The 20 lots occupy a total of eight acres.

General condition costs for the project totaled $120,000. This $120,000 is common to all 20 units that were constructed on the building site.

Job 3, the third house built in the project, occupied a 1/4-acre lot and had the following hard costs:

Materials	$ 8,000
Direct labor	6,000
Subcontractor	14,000

For Job 3, finance costs totaled $4,765 and marketing costs, $800. General condition costs are allocated on the basis of units produced. Each unit's selling price is determined by adding 40 percent to the total of all costs.

REQUIRED:

1. Identify all production costs that are directly traceable to Job 3. Are all remaining production costs equivalent to overhead found in a manufacturing firm? Are there nonproduction costs that are directly traceable to the housing unit? Which ones?
2. Develop a job-order cost sheet for Job 3. What is the cost of building this house? Did you include finance and marketing costs in computing the unit cost? Why or why not? How did you determine the cost of land for Job 3?
3. Which of the five cost categories corresponds to overhead? Do you agree with the way in which this cost is allocated to individual housing units? Can you suggest a different allocation method?
4. Calculate the selling price of Job 3. Calculate the profit made on the sale of this unit.

P16-8
Plant-wide Overhead Rate Versus Departmental Rates; Effects on Pricing Decisions
LO 5

Alden Peterson, marketing manager for Retlief Company, was puzzled by the outcome of two recent bids. The company's policy was to bid 150 percent of the full manufacturing cost. One job (labeled Job SS) had been turned down by a prospective customer who had indicated that the proposed price was $3 per unit higher than the winning bid. A second job (Job TT) had been accepted by a customer who was amazed that Retlief could offer such favorable terms. This customer revealed that Retlief's price was $43 per unit lower than the next lowest bid.

Alden has been informed that the company was more than competitive in terms of cost control. Accordingly, he began to suspect that the problem was related to cost assignment procedures. Upon investigating, Alden was told that the company uses a plant-wide overhead rate based on direct labor hours. The rate is computed at the beginning of the year using budgeted data. Selected budgeted data are given below.

	Department A	*Department B*	*Total*
Overhead	$500,000	$2,000,000	$2,500,000
Direct labor hours	200,000	50,000	250,000
Machine hours	20,000	120,000	140,000

Alden also discovered that the overhead costs in Department B were higher than those in Department A because B has more equipment, higher maintenance, higher power consumption, higher depreciation, and higher setup costs. In addition to the general procedures for assigning overhead costs, Alden was supplied with the following specific manufacturing data on Job SS and Job TT:

Job SS

	Department A	*Department B*	*Total*
Direct labor hours	5,000	1,000	6,000
Machine hours	200	500	700
Prime costs	$100,000	$20,000	$120,000
Units produced	14,400	14,400	14,400

Job TT

	Department A	*Department B*	*Total*
Direct labor hours	400	600	1,000
Machine hours	200	3,000	3,200
Prime costs	$ 10,000	$40,000	$50,000
Units produced	1,500	1,500	1,500

REQUIRED:

1. Using a plant-wide overhead rate based on direct labor hours, develop the bid prices for Job SS and Job TT. (Express the bid prices on a per-unit basis).

2. Using departmental overhead rates (use direct labor hours for Department A and machine hours for Department B), develop per-unit bid prices for Job SS and Job TT.
3. Compute the difference in gross profit that would have been earned had the company used departmental rates in its bids instead of the plant-wide rate.
4. Explain why the use of departmental rates in this case provides a more accurate product cost.

P16-9 Departmental Overhead Rates; Unit Cost

LO 5

Stoney End Recordings produces cassette tapes, records, and compact discs on a job-order basis for individuals and groups who want their music recorded. In some cases, customers want one or two copies for family and friends. In others, several hundred LPs or CDs are ordered to send to radio stations across the country in hopes of getting air time. In still other cases, several thousand records may be ordered by fledgling bands to leave with record stores on a consignment basis.

Stoney End uses a normal costing system with departmental overhead rates for the use of the recording studio (based on direct labor hours), the vinyl pressing department (based on machine hours), and the CD recording department (based on machine hours).

Budgeted amounts for 1995 were:

Overhead:	
Recording studio	$18,000
Vinyl pressing	$ 8,000
CD	$24,000
Direct labor hours:	
Recording studio	6,000
Vinyl pressing	4,000
CD	12,000
Machine hours:	
Recording studio	3,000
Vinyl pressing	1,600
CD	6,000
Average wage rates were:	
Recording studio	$12/DLH
Vinyl pressing	$ 6/DLH
CD	$25/DLH

In September, Billy Ryan and the Black Irish (a heavy metal rock band) ordered 300 LP records to distribute to radio stations and record company executives. Stoney End assigned this job the number 93-413. Job 93-413 used ten direct labor hours of recording studio time; and one direct labor hour, and five machine hours in the vinyl department. Direct materials (tape, vinyl, cardboard sleeves for the records, etc.) amounted to $372.

REQUIRED:

1. Calculate overhead rates for the recording, vinyl, and CD departments.
2. Determine the total cost of Job 93-413. What is the unit cost?

P16-10 Predetermined Overhead Rate; Departmental Overhead Rates; Job Cost

LO 2, 5

Anselmo's Kwik-Print provides a variety of photocopying and printing services. On June 5, 1995, Anselmo invested in some computer-aided photography equipment that enables customers to reproduce a picture or illustration, input it digitally into the computer, enter text into the computer, and then print out a four-color professional-quality brochure. Prior to the purchase of this equipment, Kwik-Print's overhead averaged $35,000 per year. After the installation of the new equipment, the total overhead increased to $85,000 per year. Kwik-Print has always costed jobs on the basis of actual materials and labor plus overhead assigned using a predetermined overhead rate based on direct labor hours. Budgeted direct labor hours for 1995 are 5,000, and the wage rate is $6 per hour.

REQUIRED:

1. What was the predetermined overhead rate prior to the purchase of the new equipment?
2. What was the predetermined overhead rate after the new equipment was purchased?
3. Suppose Jim Hargrove brought in several items he wanted photocopied. The job required 100 sheets of paper at $0.015 each, and 12 minutes of direct labor time. What was the cost of Jim's job on May 20, 1995? On June 20, 1995?
4. Suppose that Anselmo decides to calculate two overhead rates, one for the photocopying area based on direct labor hours as before, and one for the computer-aided printing area based on machine time. Estimated overhead applicable to the computer-aided printing area is $50,000; forecast usage of the equipment is 2,000 hours. What are the two overhead rates? Which overhead rate system is better—one rate or two?

DISCUSSION AND INTERPRETATION PROBLEMS

D16-1 Selection of Overhead Rates; Ethical Issues

Tonya Martin, CMA, and controller of the Parts Division of Gunderson, Inc., was meeting with Doug Adams, manager of the division. The topic of discussion was the assignment of overhead costs to jobs and their impact on the division's pricing decisions. Their conversation is presented below.

Tonya: "Doug, as you know, about 25 percent of our business is based on government contracts, with the other 75 percent based on jobs from private sources won through bidding. During the last several years, our private business has declined. We have been losing more bids than usual. After some careful investigation, I have concluded that we are overpricing some jobs because of improper assignment of overhead costs. Some jobs are also being underpriced. Unfortunately, the jobs being overpriced are coming from our higher-volume, labor-intensive products; thus, we are losing business."

Doug: "I think I understand. Jobs associated with our high-volume products are being assigned more overhead than they should be receiving. Then, when we add our standard 40 percent markup, we end up with a higher price than our competitors, who assign costs more accurately."

Tonya: "Exactly. We have two producing departments, one labor intensive and the other machine intensive. The labor-intensive department generates much less overhead than the machine-intensive department. Furthermore, virtually all of our high-volume jobs are labor intensive. We have been using a plant-wide rate based on direct labor hours to assign overhead to all jobs. As a result, the high-volume, labor-intensive jobs receive a greater share of the machine-intensive department's overhead than they deserve. This problem can be greatly alleviated by switching to departmental overhead rates. For example, an average high-volume job would be assigned $100,000 of overhead using a plant-wide rate and only $70,000 using departmental rates. The change would lower our bidding price on high-volume jobs by an average of $42,000 per job. By increasing the accuracy of our product costing, we can make better pricing decisions and win back much of our private-sector business."

Doug: "Sounds good. When can you implement the change in overhead rates?"

Tonya: "It won't take long. I can have the new system working within four to six weeks—certainly by the start of the new fiscal year."

Doug: "Hold it. I just thought of a possible complication. As I recall, most of our government contract work is done in the labor-intensive department. This new overhead assignment scheme will push down the cost on the government jobs, and we will lose revenues. They pay us full cost plus our standard markup. This business is not threatened by our current costing procedures, but we can't switch our rates for only the private business. Government auditors would question the lack of consistency in our costing procedures."

Tonya: "You do have a point. I thought of this issue also. According to my estimates, we will gain more revenues from the private sector than we will lose from our government contracts. Besides, the costs of our government jobs are distorted; in effect, we are overcharging the government."

Doug: "They don't know that and never will unless we switch our overhead assignment procedures. I think I have the solution. Officially, let's keep our plant-wide overhead rate. All of the official records will reflect this overhead costing approach for both our private and government business. Unofficially, I want you to develop a separate set of books that can be used to generate the information we need to prepare competitive bids for our private-sector business."

REQUIRED:

1. Do you believe that the solution proposed by Doug Adams is ethical? Explain.
2. Suppose that Tonya Martin decides that Adams's solution is not right. In your opinion, is Martin supported in this view by the standards of ethical conduct described in Chapter 1? Explain.
3. Suppose that, despite Martin's objections, Adams insists strongly on implementing the action. What should Tonya Martin do?

D16-2 Job-Order Costing: Dental Practice

Dr. Sherry Bird is employed by Dental Associates. Dental Associates recently installed a computerized job costing system to help monitor the cost of its services. Each patient is treated as a job and assigned a job number when he or she checks in with the receptionist. The receptionist-bookkeeper notes the time the patient enters the treatment area and when the patient leaves the area. The difference between the entry and exit times is the patient hours used and is the direct labor time assigned to the dental assistant (a dental assistant is constantly with the patient). Fifty percent of the patient hours is the direct labor time assigned to the dentist (the dentist typically splits her time between two patients).

The chart filled out by the dental assistant provides additional data that is entered into the computer. For example, the chart contains service codes that identify the nature of the treatment, such as whether the patient received a crown, a filling, or a root canal. The chart not only identifies the type of service but its level as well. For example, if a patient receives a filling, the dental assistant indicates (by a service-level code) whether the filling was one, two, three, or four surfaces. The service and service-level codes are used to determine the rate to be charged to the patient. The costs of providing different services and their levels also vary.

Costs assignable to a patient consist of materials, labor, and overhead. The type of materials used—and the quantity—are identified by the assistant and entered into the computer by the bookkeeper. Material prices are kept on file and accessed to provide the necessary cost information. Overhead is applied on the basis of patient hours. The rate used by Dental Associates is \$20 per patient hour. Direct labor cost is also computed using patient hours and the wage rates of the direct laborers. Dr. Bird is paid an average of \$36 per hour for her services. Dental assistants are paid an average of \$6 per hour. Given the treatment time, the software program calculates and assigns the labor cost for the dentist and her assistant; overhead cost is also assigned using the treatment time and the overhead rate.

The overhead rate does not include a charge for any X rays. The X ray department is separate from dental services; X rays are billed and costed separately. The cost of an X ray is \$3.50 per film; the patient is charged \$5 per film. If cleaning services are required, cleaning labor costs \$9 per patient hour.

Glen Johnson, a patient (Job 267), spent 30 minutes in the treatment area and had a two-surface filling. He received two Novocain shots and used three ampules of amalgam. The cost of the shots was \$1. The cost of the amalgam was \$3. Other direct materials used are insignificant in amount and are included in the overhead rate. The rate charged to the patient for a two-surface filling is \$45. One X ray was taken.

REQUIRED:

1. Prepare a job-cost sheet for Glen Johnson. What is the cost for providing a two-surface filling? What is the gross profit earned? Is the X ray a direct cost of the service? Why are the X rays costed separately from the overhead cost assignment?
2. Suppose that the patient time and associated patient charges are given for the following fillings:

	1 Surface	*2 Surface*	*3 Surface*	*4 Surface*
Time	20 minutes	30 minutes	40 minutes	50 minutes
Charge	$35	$45	$55	$65

Compute the cost for each filling and the gross profit for each type of filling. Assume that the cost of Novocain is $1 for all fillings. Ampules of amalgam start at two and increase by one for each additional surface. Assume also that only one X ray film is needed for all four cases. Does the increase in billing rate appear to be fair to the patient? Is it fair to the dental corporation?

D16-3 Research Assignment

Interview an accountant that works for a service organization that uses job order costing. For a small firm, you may need to talk to an owner/manager. Examples are a funeral home, insurance firm, repair shop, medical clinic, and dental clinic. Write a paper that describes the job-order cost system used by the firm. Some of the questions that the paper should address are:

a. What service or services does the firm offer?
b. What document or procedure do you use to collect the costs of the services performed for each customer?
c. How do you assign the cost of direct labor to each job?
d. How do you assign overhead to individual jobs?
e. How do you assign the cost of direct materials to each job?
f. How do you determine what to charge each customer?
g. How do you account for a completed job?

As you write the paper, state how the service firm you investigated adapted the job-order accounting procedures described in the chapter to its particular circumstances. Were the differences justified? If so, explain why. Also, offer any suggestions you might have for improving the approach that you observed.

CHAPTER 17
PROCESS COSTING

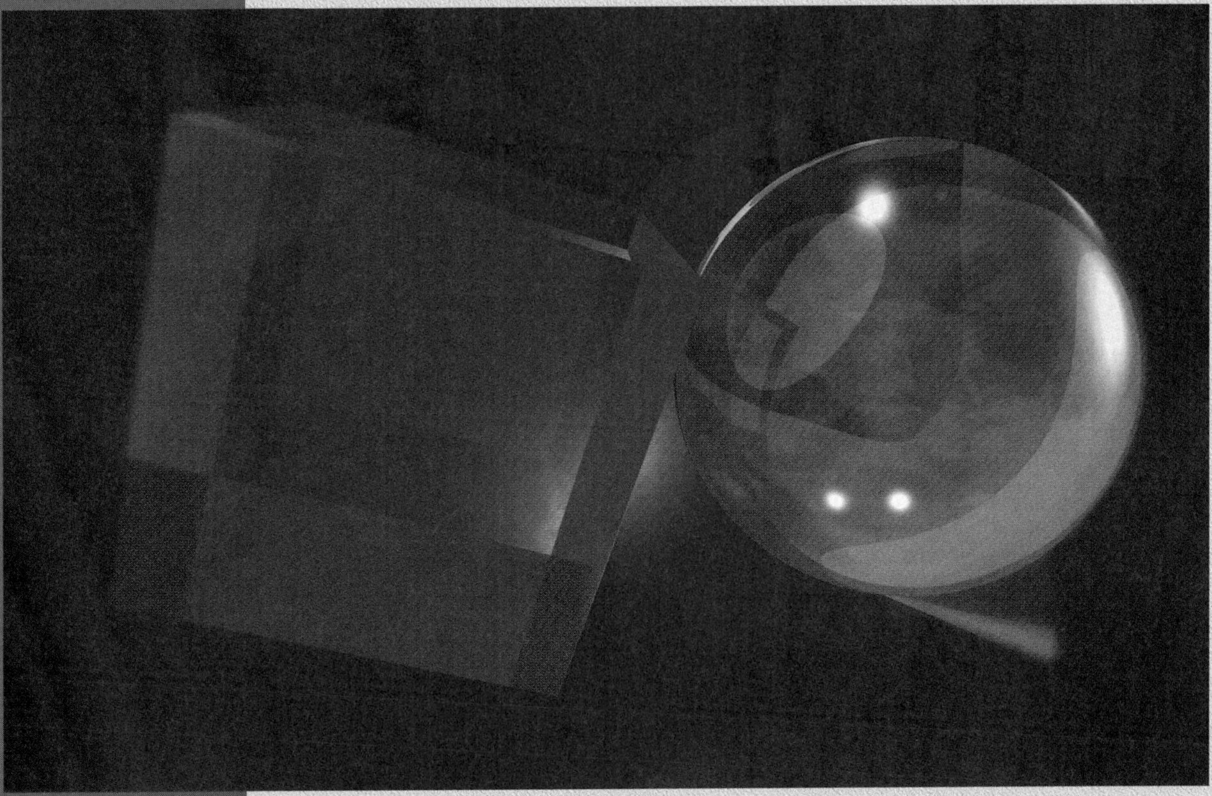

LEARNING OBJECTIVES

After studying this chapter, you should be able to:

1. Identify the settings for which process costing is appropriate.
2. Describe the basic characteristics of process manufacturing and process costing.
3. Prepare a production report using the weighted average method of accounting for process costs.
4. Explain how process costing is affected by nonuniform application of manufacturing inputs and the existence of multiple processing departments.

Scenario

Makenzie Gibson, owner of Healthblend Nutritional Supplements, was reviewing last year's income statement. The income reported to the IRS represented a 33 percent increase over the prior year. Makenzie was pleased with the success of the company she had founded ten years earlier. The idea for the company was the result of her recovery from some personal health problems. By working with some health-care professionals, Makenzie had learned to blend a number of different herbs into therapeutic formulas that had brought about an amazing recovery.

Convinced that the discoveries she had made should be shared with others, Makenzie began producing some of these same therapeutic formulas in the basement of her home. Now, ten years later, she is the owner of a multimillion-dollar business housed in a modern facility with more than 60 employees. The success of the business could be explained in part by two significant breakthroughs: (1) the creation of vitamin, herbal, and mineral lines that use capsules instead of tablets, and (2) the development of an improved process for the transportation and utilization of minerals.

Although pleased with the success of her business, Makenzie was convinced that she could not afford to be complacent. More than a month ago, the owner of a health food store had indicated to Makenzie that some other suppliers had dropped competing lines because they were no longer profitable. He asked Makenzie if all of her products were profitable or if she simply offered the full range as a marketing strategy. Makenzie had been forced to admit that she did not know whether all her products were profitable—in fact, she didn't even know how much it was costing to produce an individual product. All she knew was that she was earning significant profits in the aggregate.

After some reflection, she decided that knowing individual costs would be useful. Knowing product costs might have some bearing on production methods, prices, and the mix of products. With this objective in mind, she had called Jack Trench, a good friend and a partner in the local office of a large CPA firm. Jack had agreed to refer the problem to Judith Manesfield, manager of the firm's small business practice section. After several visits by some of Judith's staff, Makenzie received the following preliminary report:

Makenzie Gibson
Healthblend Nutritional Supplements
Tucson, Arizona

Dear Ms. Gibson:

As you are aware, your current accounting system does not collect the necessary data for costing out the various products that you produce. You are currently producing three major product lines: mineral, herb, and vitamin. Each product, regardless of the type, passes through three processes: picking, encapsulating, and bottling. In picking, the ingredients are measured, sifted, and blended together. In encapsulating, the powdered mix from the first process is put into two-sided capsules, then machines press the two sides together to produce the capsule. The capsules are then transferred to the bottling department where they are bottled, and the bottles are labeled and fitted with safety seals and lids.

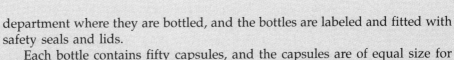

Each bottle contains fifty capsules, and the capsules are of equal size for all three product lines. We have also noticed that the cost of materials among the three product lines differs, but within a product line, the cost of materials for different products is not significantly different. The layout of the plant is structured so that all three product lines are produced simultaneously; thus, there are three different picking departments, one for each major product line.

Based on the nature of the manufacturing processes, our tentative recommendation is to accumulate costs of manufacturing by process for a given period of time and measure the output for that same period. By dividing the costs accumulated for the period by the output for the period, a good measure of what each individual product is costing can be obtained.

The cost system we are recommending will require the least amount of increase in your bookkeeping activities. If you have no objections, we will proceed with the development of the cost system. As part of this development, we will conduct several training seminars so that your financial staff can operate the system once it is implemented.

CHOICE OF A COST ACCUMULATION METHOD

Objective 1
Identify the settings for which process costing is appropriate.

Makenzie Gibson hired the consultant in order to determine the best method for costing out Healthblend's products. The consultant responded by first studying Healthblend's methods of production. The investigation revealed a large number of similar products passing through a set of identical processes. Since each product within a product line passing through the three processes would receive similar "doses" of materials, labor, and overhead, Judith Manesfield saw no need to accumulate costs by batches (a job-costing system). Instead, she recommended accumulating costs by *process*.

Process costing works well whenever relatively homogeneous products pass through a series of processes and receive similar amounts of manufacturing costs. Job-order costing, on the other hand, works well whenever products pass through a series of processes (similar or different) that deal out different amounts of manufacturing costs. Consider a pharmacy where every prescription filled requires a different drug, different direct labor time (to select the prescribed drug, count tablets or mix and fill a bottle with liquid), and different overhead (probably charged on the basis of direct labor, it would consist of costs of the building space, computer, utilities, and so on).

Let's consider the Healthblend example in more detail. From the consultant's letter, we know that there are three departments, or processes. In the picking department, direct labor selects the appropriate herbs, vitamins, minerals, and inert materials (typically some binder such as corn starch) for the product to be manufactured. Then the materials are measured and combined in a mixer to blend them thoroughly in the prescribed proportions. Only when the mix is complete is the resulting mixture sent to encapsulation. In encapsulation, the vitamin, mineral, or herb blend is loaded into a machine that fills one-half of a gelatin capsule. The filled half is matched to another half of the capsule and a safety seal is applied. This process is entirely mechanized. Overhead in this department consists of depreciation on machinery, maintenance of machinery, supervision, fringe benefits, light, and power. The final department is bottling. Filled capsules are transferred to this department, loaded into a hopper, and automatically counted into bottles. Filled bottles are mechanically capped, and direct labor then manually packs the correct number of bottles into boxes to ship to retail outlets.

Now let's look at Healthblend from an accounting perspective. Suppose that Healthblend has only one picking department through which all three major product lines pass. Since the product lines differ significantly in the cost of their material inputs, accumulating material costs by process no longer makes any sense. More accurate product costing can be achieved by accumulating materials costs by batch. In this case, labor and overhead could still be accumulated by process, but raw materials would be assigned to batches using the usual job-cost approach. Note, however, that even with this change, process costing could still be used for the encapsulating department and the bottling department. In these two departments, each product receives the same amount of material, labor, and overhead.

operation costing

This example illustrates that some manufacturing settings may need to use a blend of job and process costing. Using job-order procedures to assign material costs to products and a process approach to assign conversion costs is a blend known as **operation costing**. Other blends are possible as well. The example also shows that it is possible to use more than one form of costing within the same firm. This is the case if Healthblend uses operation costing for the picking department and process costing for the other two departments.

The fundamental point is that the cost accounting system should be designed to fit the nature of operations. Job-order and process costing systems fit pure job and pure process production environments. There are many settings, however, in which blends of the two costing systems may be suitable. By studying the pure forms of job-order and process costing, we can develop the ability to understand and use any hybrid form.

PROCESS MANUFACTURING AND PROCESS COSTING

Objective 2
Describe the basic characteristics of process manufacturing and process costing.

Units produced in a process firm typically pass through a series of manufacturing steps or processes. Each process is responsible for one or more operations that bring a product one step closer to completion. In each process, materials, labor, and overhead inputs may be needed (typically in equal doses). Upon completion of a particular process, the partially completed goods are transferred to another process. After passing through the final process, the goods are finished and transferred to the warehouse.

Processing Patterns

sequential processing

The processes used by Healthblend Nutritional Supplements are an example of **sequential processing**. In a sequential process, units pass from one process to another in a sequential pattern with each unit processed in the same series of steps. Exhibit 17-1 shows the sequential pattern of the manufacture of Healthblend's minerals, herbs, and vitamins.

parallel processing

Another processing pattern is **parallel processing**, in which two or more sequential processes are required to produce a finished good. Partially completed

Exhibit 17-1
Sequential Processing Illustrated

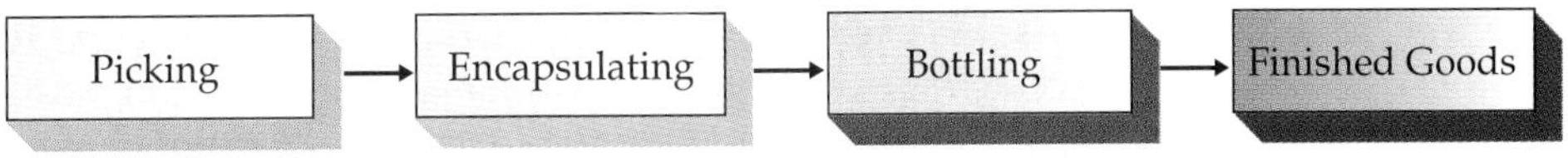

units (e.g., two subcomponents) can be worked on simultaneously in different processes and then brought together in a final process for completion. Consider, for example, the manufacture of a mass storage (hard disk) system for personal computers. In one series of processes, write heads and cartridge disk drives are produced, assembled, and tested. In a second series of processes, printed circuit boards are produced and tested. These two major subcomponents then come together for assembly in the final process. Exhibit 17-2 portrays this type of process pattern. Notice that processes one and two can occur independently of (or parallel to) processes three and four.

Other forms of parallel processes also exist. Exhibit 17-3 shows the production process at Hillendale Dairy. The dairy produces two products, milk and cheese, in a parallel process. Both products share a common original sequential process in which cows are milked and the milk is pasteurized. Then some of the pasteurized milk is transferred to the cheese department where rennin is added (to coagulate the milk), whey is drained off, and the cheese is aged and packaged. The remaining pasteurized milk is homogenized and bottled as whole milk.

Regardless of which processing pattern exists within a firm, all units produced share a common property. Since units are homogeneous and subjected to

Exhibit 17-2
Parallel Processing Illustrated

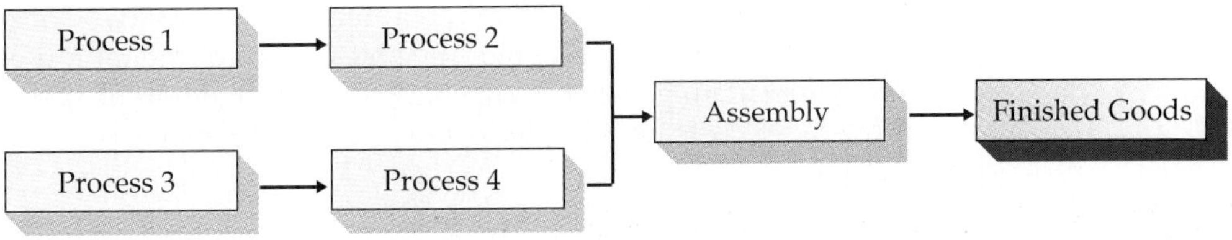

Process 1: Production and assembly of write-head and disk drive
Process 2: Testing of write-head and disk drive
Process 3: Production of circuit board
Process 4: Testing of circuit board

Exhibit 17-3
Alternative Form of Parallel Processing

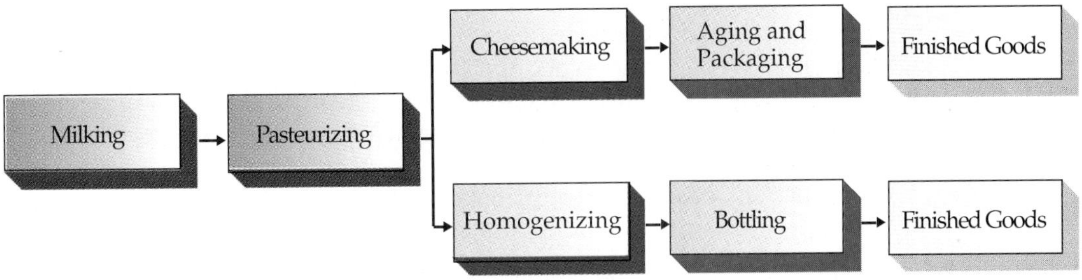

the same operations for a given process, each unit produced in a period should receive the same unit cost. Understanding how unit costs are computed requires an understanding of the manufacturing cost flows that take place in a process costing firm.

Process Costing: Cost Flows

The manufacturing cost flows for a process cost system are generally the same as those for a job-order system. As raw materials are purchased, the cost of these materials flows into a Raw Materials inventory account. Similarly, raw materials, direct labor, and applied overhead costs flow into a Work in Process account. When goods are ultimately completed, the cost of the completed goods is transferred from Work in Process to the Finished Goods account. Finally, as goods are sold, the cost of the finished goods is transferred to the Cost of Goods Sold account. The journal entries generally parallel those described in a job-order costing system (for a more detailed description of cost flows, see Chapter 16).

Although job-order and process cost flows are generally similar, some differences exist. In process costing, each processing department has its own Work in Process account. As goods are completed in a process, they are transferred to the next process. For example, if the cost of goods transferred from encapsulating to bottling is $10,000, the following journal entry would occur:

Work in Process—Bottling	10,000	
Work in Process—Encapsulating		10,000

transferred-in costs

The costs transferred from a prior process (here, encapsulating) to a subsequent process (bottling) are referred to as **transferred-in costs**. These transferred-in costs are (from the viewpoint of the subsequent process) a type of raw material cost. This is true because the subsequent process receives a partially completed unit that must be subjected to additional manufacturing activity, which includes more direct labor, more overhead, and, in some cases, additional raw materials. Thus, while encapsulating sees the capsules as a combination of raw materials, labor, and overhead costs, bottling sees only completed capsules—a raw material costing $10,000.

Cost Accumulation: The Production Report

production report

In process costing, costs are accumulated by department for a period of time. The **production report** is the document that summarizes the manufacturing activity that takes place in a process department for a given period of time. A production report contains all of the information necessary for it to function as a subsidiary Work in Process account. It is analogous to the job-order cost sheet in a job-costing system. The production report also serves as a source document for transferring costs from the Work in Process account of a prior department to the Work in Process account of a subsequent department. In the department that handles the final stage of processing, it serves as a source document for transferring costs from the Work in Process account to the Finished Goods account.

A production report provides information about the physical units processed in a department and also about the manufacturing costs associated with them. Thus, a production report is divided into a unit information section and a cost information section. The unit information section has two major subdivisions: (1) units to account for and (2) units accounted for. Similarly, the cost information section has two major subdivisions: (1) costs to account for and (2) costs accounted for. A production report traces the flow of units through a department, identifies the costs charged to the department, shows the computation of unit costs, and reveals the disposition of the department's costs for the reporting period.

Computing the unit cost for the work performed during a period is essential to producing a production report. This unit cost is needed both to compute the cost of goods transferred out of a department and to value ending work in process. In computing the unit cost, the output of the period must be defined. A major problem of process costing is making this definition.

Output Measurement: The Concept of Equivalent Units

To illustrate the output problem of process costing, assume that Department A had the following data for October:

Units, beginning work in process	—
Units completed	1,000
Units, ending work in process (25% complete)	600
Total manufacturing costs	$11,500

What is the output in October for this department? 1,000? 1,600? If we say 1,000 units, we ignore the effort expended on the units in ending work in process. Furthermore, the manufacturing costs incurred in October belong to both the units completed and to the partially completed units in ending work in process. On the other hand, if we say 1,600 units, we ignore the fact that the 600 units in ending work in process are only partially completed. Somehow output must be measured so that it reflects the effort expended on both completed and partially completed units.

equivalent units of output

The solution is to calculate equivalent units of output. **Equivalent units of output** are the complete units that could have been produced given the total amount of manufacturing effort expended for the period under consideration. Determining equivalent units of output for transferred-out units is easy; a unit would not be transferred out unless it were complete. Thus, every transferred-out unit is an equivalent unit. Units remaining in ending work-in-process inventory, however, are not complete. Thus, someone in production must "eyeball" ending work in process to estimate its degree of completion. In the example, the 600 units in ending work in process are 25 percent complete; this is equivalent to 150 fully completed units (600 × 25%). Therefore, the equivalent units for October would be the 1,000 completed units plus 150 equivalent units in ending work in process, a total of 1,150 units of output. Exhibit 17-4 illustrates the concept of equivalent units of production.

Knowing the output for a period and the manufacturing costs for the department for that period ($11,500 in this example), we can calculate a unit cost, which in this case is $10 ($11,500/1,150). The unit cost is used to assign a cost of $10,000 ($10 × 1,000) to the 1,000 units transferred out and a cost of $1,500 ($10 × 150) to the 600 units in ending work in process. This unit cost is $10 per *equivalent* unit. Thus, when valuing ending work in process, the $10 unit cost is multiplied by the equivalent units, not the actual number of partially completed units.

Exhibit 17-4
Equivalent Units of Production

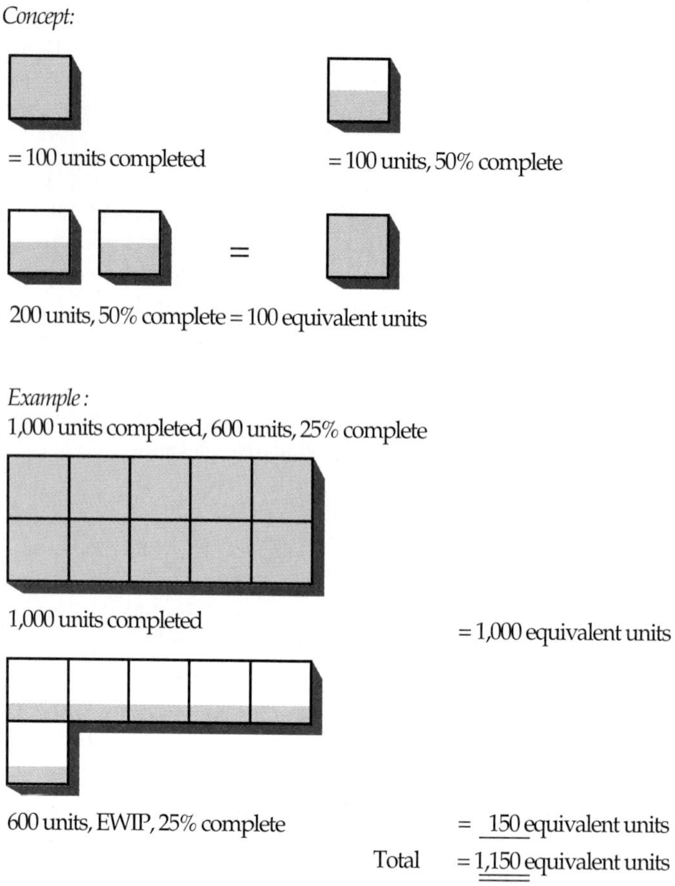

Exhibit 17-5 summarizes the basic characteristics of process costing. In reality, the details are more complicated than the basics just described. These complications are due to five factors.

1. The presence of beginning inventories
2. Different approaches to equivalent unit calculation
3. Nonuniform application of manufacturing costs (e.g., units half completed may not have half of the total manufacturing inputs needed)
4. Transferred-in goods from other processes
5. The need to gather cost and production information by department

Nonetheless, understanding these basics is essential to understanding the nature of process costing.

ACCOUNTING FOR PROCESS COSTS

Objective 3
Prepare a production report using the weighted average method of accounting for process costs.

The presence of ending work-in-process inventories requires us to adjust the denominator (number of units) used to compute unit cost. The presence of beginning work in process inventories also complicates the computation of the unit cost. Since many firms have partially completed units in process at the beginning of a period, there is a clear need to address the issue. The work done on these partially completed units represents prior-period work, and the costs

Exhibit 17-5
Basic Characteristics of Process Costing

1. Homogeneous units pass through a series of similar processes.
2. Each unit in each process receives a similar dose of manufacturing costs.
3. Manufacturing costs are accumulated by a process for a given period of time.
4. Manufacturing cost flows and the associated journal entries are generally similar to job-order costing.
5. The departmental production report is the key document for tracking manufacturing activity and costs.
6. Unit costs are computed by dividing the departmental costs of the period by the output of the period.
7. Output of a department is measured in equivalent units, not in units produced.

assigned to them are prior-period costs. In computing a *current period* unit cost for a department, two approaches have evolved for dealing with the prior-period output and prior-period costs found in beginning work in process: *the weighted average method* and the *first-in, first-out (FIFO) method*. Basically, the weighted average method combines beginning inventory costs with current-period costs to compute unit cost. In essence, the costs are pooled and only one average unit cost is computed and applied to both units transferred out and units remaining in ending inventory. The **FIFO costing method**, on the other hand, separates units in beginning inventory from those produced during the current period. It is assumed that units from beginning inventory are completed first, and transferred out with all of the prior-period costs as well as the current period costs necessary to complete those units. Then current period production is started and completed (and transferred out with only current costs) or left incomplete as ending work in process inventory (again, with current period costs). If product costs do not change from period to period, the FIFO and weighted average methods yield the same results. Of the two approaches, the weighted average method is the least complicated, and its study conveys all that is needed for an introduction to process costing; thus, further discussion of the FIFO method is reserved for a more advanced course.

FIFO costing method

Both the weighted average and FIFO approaches follow the same general pattern for costing out production. This general pattern is described by the following five steps:

1. Analysis of the flow of physical units
2. Calculation of equivalent units
3. Computation of unit cost
4. Valuation of inventories (goods transferred out and ending work in process)
5. Cost reconciliation

Knowing the physical units in beginning and ending work in process, their stage of completion, and the units completed and transferred out (Step 1) provides essential information for the computation of equivalent units (Step 2). This computation, in turn, is a prerequisite to computing unit cost (Step 3). Unit cost information and information from the equivalent unit schedule are both needed to value goods transferred out and goods in ending work in process (Step 4). Finally, the costs in beginning work in process and the costs incurred during the current period should equal the total costs assigned to goods transferred out and to goods in ending work in process (Step 5).

In the ensuing discussion, we will follow the five steps previously listed. Doing so gives some structure to the method of accounting for process costs and makes it easier to learn and remember.

Weighted Average Costing

weighted average costing method

The **weighted average costing method** picks up beginning inventory costs and the accompanying equivalent output and treats them as if they belong to the current period. Prior-period output and manufacturing costs found in beginning work in process are merged with the current-period output and manufacturing costs.

The merging of beginning inventory output and current period output is accomplished by the way in which equivalent units are calculated. Under the weighted average method, equivalent units of output are computed by adding units completed to equivalent units in ending work in process. Notice that the equivalent units in beginning work in process are included in the computation. Consequently, these units are counted as part of the current period's equivalent units of output.

The weighted average method merges prior-period costs with current-period costs by simply adding the manufacturing costs in beginning work in process to the manufacturing costs incurred during the current period. The total cost is treated as if it were the current period's total manufacturing cost.

To illustrate the weighted average method, consider the manufacturing operation of Healthblend Nutritional Supplements. Cost and production data for the picking department are as follows for July (assume that units are measured in gallons):

Production:	
Units in process, July 1, 30% complete	20,000
Units completed and transferred out	50,000
Units in process, July 31, 50% complete	10,000
Costs:	
Work in process, July 1	$ 1,170
Costs added during July	$ 9,830

Using the data for the picking department, Exhibit 17-6 illustrates the use of the weighted average method to allocate manufacturing costs to units transferred out and to units remaining in ending work in process. Notice that costs from beginning work in process (BWIP) are pooled with costs added to production during July. These total pooled costs ($11,000) are averaged and assigned to units transferred out and to units in ending work in process (EWIP). On the units side, we concentrate on the degree of completion of all units at the *end* of the period. We do not care about the percentage of completion of beginning work in process inventory. We only care about whether these units are complete or not by the end of July. Thus, equivalent units are computed by pooling manufacturing effort from June and July.

Let's take a closer look at the July production in Healthblend's picking department by focusing on the five steps of the weighted average method.

Step 1: Physical Flow Analysis. The purpose of Step 1 is to trace the physical units of production. Physical units are *not* equivalent units; they are units that may be in any stage of completion. We can see in Exhibit 17-6 that there are

Exhibit 17-6
Weighted Average Method

Costs:

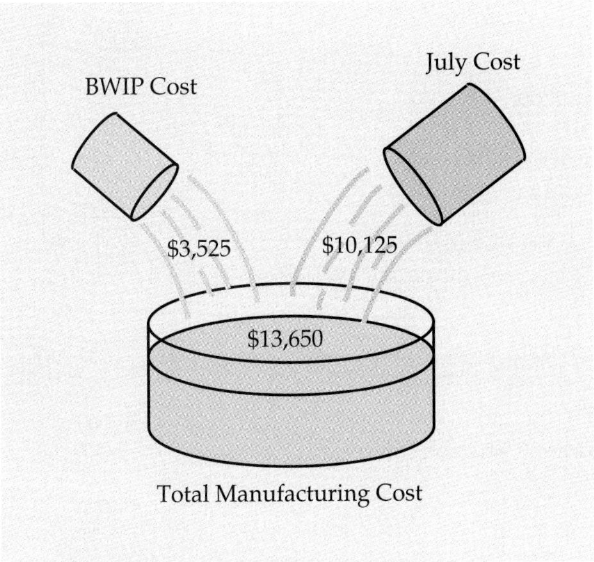

Output for July

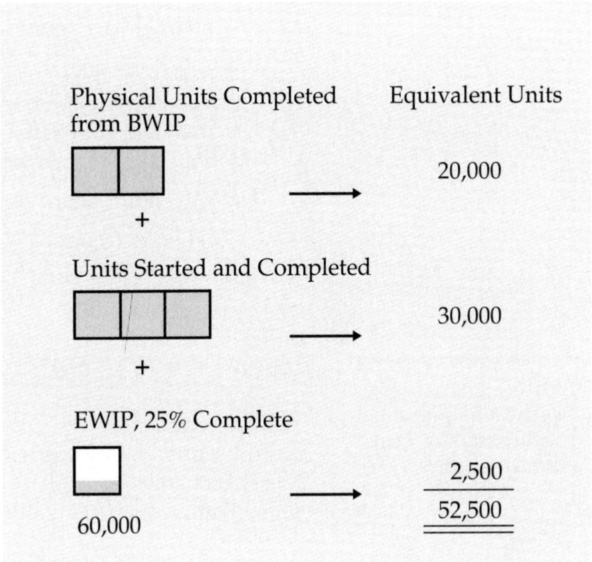

Cost Assignment

Cost/Unit = $13,650 ÷ 52,500 = $0.26

Transferred Out ($0.26 x 50,000)	=	$13,000
EWIP ($0.26 x 2,500)	=	650
Total Cost Assigned		$13,650

Key:

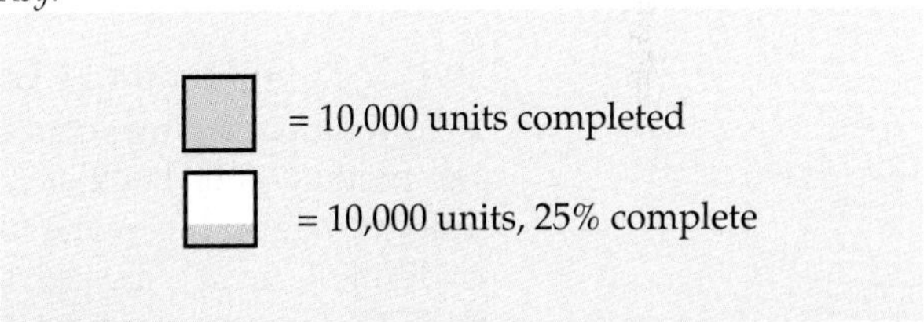

60,000 physical units. In this example, 20,000 are from beginning inventory. Another 40,000 were started in July. Finally, 10,000 remain in ending inventory, 50 percent complete. The analysis of physical flow of units is usually accomplished by preparing a **physical flow schedule** similar to the one shown in Exhibit 17-7. To construct the schedule from the information given in the example, two calculations are needed. First, units started and completed in this period are obtained by subtracting the units in beginning work in process from the total units completed. Next, the units started are obtained by adding the units started and completed to the units in ending work in process. Notice that the "total units to account for" must equal the "total units accounted for." The physical flow schedule in Exhibit 17-7 is important because it contains the information needed to calculate equivalent units (Step 2).

physical flow schedule

Step 2: Calculation of Equivalent Units. Given the information in the physical flow schedule, the weighted-average equivalent units for July can be calculated. This calculation is shown in Exhibit 17-8.

Notice that July's output is measured as 55,000 units. The 6,000 equivalent units (20,000 × 30%) found in beginning work in process are included in the 50,000 units completed. Thus, beginning inventory units are treated as if they were started and completed during the current period.

Exhibit 17-7
Physical Flow Schedule

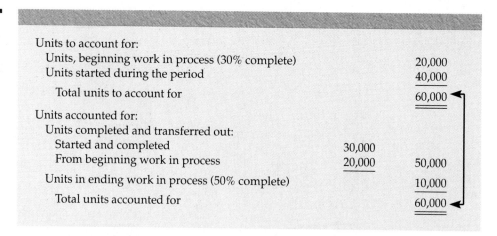

Units to account for:		
Units, beginning work in process (30% complete)		20,000
Units started during the period		40,000
Total units to account for		60,000
Units accounted for:		
Units completed and transferred out:		
Started and completed	30,000	
From beginning work in process	20,000	50,000
Units in ending work in process (50% complete)		10,000
Total units accounted for		60,000

Exhibit 17-8
Equivalent Units of Production: Weighted Average Method

Units completed	50,000
Add: Units, ending work in process × Fraction complete (10,000 units × 50%)	5,000
Equivalent units of output	55,000

Step 3: Computation of Unit Cost. In addition to the period's output, the period's manufacturing costs are needed to compute a unit cost. The weighted average method rolls back and includes the manufacturing costs associated with the units in beginning work in process. Thus, the total manufacturing cost for July is defined as $11,000 ($1,170 + $9,830). The manufacturing costs carried over from the prior period ($1,170) are treated as if they were current-period costs.

Given the manufacturing costs for July and the output for the month, the unit cost can be calculated and used to determine the cost of goods transferred out and the cost of ending work in process. For July, the weighted average method gives the following unit cost:

Unit cost = $11,000/55,000
= $0.20 per equivalent unit

Step 4: Valuation of Inventories. Using the unit cost of $0.20, the cost of goods transferred to the encapsulating department is $10,000 (50,000 units × $0.20 per unit), and the cost of ending work in process is $1,000 (5,000 equivalent units × $0.20 per unit). Notice that units completed (from Step 1), equivalent units in ending work in process (from Step 2), and the unit cost (from Step 3) were all needed to value both goods transferred out and ending work in process.

Step 5: Cost Reconciliation. The total manufacturing costs assigned to inventories are as follows:

Goods transferred out	$10,000
Goods in ending work in process	1,000
Total costs accounted for	$11,000

The manufacturing costs to account for are also $11,000.

Beginning work in process	$ 1,170
Incurred during the period	9,830
Total costs to account for	$11,000

cost reconciliation

Thus, the costs to account for are exactly assigned to inventories, and we have the necessary **cost reconciliation**. Remember—the total costs assigned to goods transferred out and to ending work in process *must agree* with the total of costs in beginning work in process and the manufacturing costs incurred during the current period.

Production Report

Steps 1 through 5 provide all of the information needed to prepare a production report for the picking department for July. This report is given in Exhibit 17-9.

Exhibit 17-9

Production Report
For July 1995
(Weighted Average Method)

Unit Information

Physical Flow:			
Units to account for:		Units accounted for:	
Units in beginning work in process	20,000	Units completed	50,000
Units started	40,000	Units, ending work in process	10,000
Total units to account for	60,000		60,000

Equivalent Units:	
Units completed	50,000
Units in ending work in process	5,000
Total equivalent units	55,000

Cost Information

Costs to account for:	
Beginning work in process	$ 1,170
Incurred during the period	9,830
Total costs to account for	$11,000
Cost per equivalent unit	$0.20

	Transferred Out	*Ending Work in Process*	*Total*
Costs accounted for:			
Goods transferred out ($0.20 × 50,000)	$10,000	—	$10,000
Goods in ending work in process ($0.20 × 5,000)	—	$1,000	1,000
Total costs accounted for	$10,000	$1,000	$11,000

Evaluation of the Weighted Average Method

The weighted average method combines the cost of beginning work in process with the production cost incurred for the current period. Thus, a weighted average unit cost is formed based on the contribution of beginning work in process and current-period production. If the unit cost in a process is relatively stable from one period to the next, this procedure has little effect on the calculation of a current-period unit cost.

The major benefit of the weighted average method is simplicity. By treating units in beginning work in process as belonging to the current period, all equivalent units belong to the same category when it comes to calculating unit costs. As a consequence, the requirements for computing unit cost are greatly simplified. The main disadvantage of this method is the sacrifice of accuracy in computing unit costs for current-period output and for units in beginning work in process. If the price of manufacturing inputs increases significantly from one period to the next, the unit cost of current output is understated, and the unit cost of beginning work-in-process units is overstated. If greater accuracy in computing unit costs is desired, a company should use the FIFO method to determine unit costs.

SOME COMPLICATIONS OF PROCESS COSTING

Objective 4
Explain how process costing is affected by nonuniform application of manufacturing inputs and the existence of multiple processing departments.

Accounting for production under process costing is complicated by nonuniform application of manufacturing inputs and the presence of multiple processing departments. How process costing methods address these complications will now be discussed.

Nonuniform Application of Manufacturing Inputs

Up to this point, we have assumed that work in process being 60 percent complete meant that 60 percent of materials, labor, and overhead needed to complete the process have been used and that another 40 percent are needed to finish the units. In other words, we have assumed that manufacturing inputs are applied uniformly as the manufacturing process unfolds.

Assuming uniform application of conversion costs (direct labor and overhead) is not unreasonable. Direct labor input is usually needed throughout the process, and overhead is normally assigned on the basis of direct labor hours. Direct materials, on the other hand, are not as likely to be applied uniformly. In many instances, materials are added at either the beginning or the end of the process.

For example, look at the differences in Healthblend's three departments. In the picking and encapsulating departments, all materials are added at the beginning of the process. However, in the bottling department, materials are added both at the beginning (filled capsules and bottles) and at the end (bottle caps and boxes).

Work in process in the picking department that is 50 percent complete with respect to conversion inputs would be 100 percent complete with respect to the material inputs. But work in process in bottling that is 50 percent complete with respect to conversion inputs would differ. It would be 100 percent complete with respect to bottles and transferred-in capsules, but 0 percent complete with respect to bottle caps and boxes.

Different percentage completion figures for manufacturing inputs at the same stage of completion pose a problem for the calculation of equivalent units. Fortunately, the solution is relatively simple. Equivalent unit calculations are done for *each* category of manufacturing input. Thus, there are equivalent units calculated for each category of materials and for conversion cost. The conversion cost category can be broken down into direct labor and overhead, if desired. If direct labor and overhead are applied uniformly, however, this serves no useful purpose.

To illustrate, assume the picking department of Healthblend has the following data for September:

Production:	
Units in process, September 1, 50% complete[1]	10,000
Units completed and transferred out	60,000
Units in process, September 30, 40% complete[1]	20,000
Costs:	
Work in process, September 1:	
Materials	$1,600
Conversion costs	200
Total	$1,800
Current costs:	
Materials	$12,000
Conversion costs	3,200
Total	$15,200

[1]With respect to conversion costs

Assuming that Healthblend uses the weighted average method for process costing, the effect of nonuniform application of manufacturing inputs is easily illustrated. Exhibit 17-10 illustrates Step 1, creating the physical flow schedule. As the exhibit reveals, the approach to accounting for the flow of physical units is not affected by the nonuniform application of manufacturing inputs because physical units may be in any stage of completion.

Exhibit 17-10
Physical Flow Schedule: Nonuniform Inputs

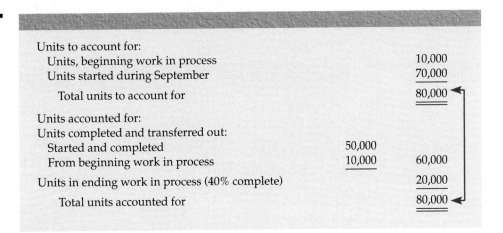

Units to account for:		
Units, beginning work in process		10,000
Units started during September		70,000
Total units to account for		80,000
Units accounted for:		
Units completed and transferred out:		
Started and completed	50,000	
From beginning work in process	10,000	60,000
Units in ending work in process (40% complete)		20,000
Total units accounted for		80,000

Nonuniform application of inputs, however, affects the computation of equivalent units (Step 2). Exhibit 17-11 illustrates this computation. Notice that two categories of input are used to calculate equivalent units. These categories of input are needed because manufacturing inputs are applied differently. Since all materials are added at the beginning of the process, there are 20,000 equivalent units of materials in ending work in process. However, since only 40 percent of the conversion costs have been applied, there are only 8,000 conversion equivalent units in ending work in process.

When different categories of equivalent units exist, a unit cost for each category must be computed. The cost per completed unit (Step 3) is the sum of these individual unit costs. The computations for the example are as follows:

$$\begin{aligned}
\text{Unit materials cost} &= (\$1{,}600 + \$12{,}000)/80{,}000 \\
&= \$0.17 \\
\text{Unit conversion cost} &= (\$200 + \$3{,}200)/68{,}000 \\
&= \$0.05 \\
\text{Total unit cost} &= \text{Unit materials cost} + \text{Unit conversion cost} \\
&= \$0.17 + \$0.05 \\
&= \$0.22 \text{ per completed unit}
\end{aligned}$$

Valuation of goods transferred out (Step 4) is accomplished by multiplying the unit cost by the goods completed.

$$\begin{aligned}
\text{Cost of goods transferred out} &= \$0.22 \times 60{,}000 \\
&= \$13{,}200
\end{aligned}$$

Costing out ending work in process is done by obtaining the cost of each manufacturing input and then adding these individual input costs. For the example, this requires adding the cost of the materials in ending work in process to the conversion costs in ending work in process.

The cost of materials is the unit material cost multiplied by the material equivalent units in ending work in process. Similarly, the conversion cost in ending work in process is the unit conversion cost times the conversion equivalent units. Thus, the cost of ending work in process is as follows:

Materials: $0.17 × 20,000	$3,400
Conversion: $0.05 × 8,000	400
Total cost	$3,800

Exhibit 17-11
Calculation of Equivalent Units: Nonuniform Application

	Materials	Conversion
Units completed	60,000	60,000
Add: Units, ending work in process × percentage complete:		
20,000 × 100%	20,000	—
20,000 × 40%	—	8,000
Equivalent units of output	80,000	68,000

Step 5, you will recall, reconciles the costs to ensure that the computations are correct.

Costs to account for:	
Beginning work in process	$ 1,800
Incurred during the period	15,200
Total to account for	$17,000
Costs accounted for:	
Goods transferred out	$13,200
Ending work in process	3,800
Total costs accounted for	$17,000

Using the information generated from the five steps, a production report can be prepared (see Exhibit 17-12). As the example has shown, applying manufacturing inputs at different stages of a process poses no serious problems. However, the effort required to compute the costs has increased.

Multiple Departments

In process manufacturing, some departments invariably receive partially completed goods from prior departments. These transferred-in goods are a type of raw material for the subsequent process—materials that are added at the beginning of the subsequent process. For example, consider a manufacturer of denim jeans. Department 1 is the cutting department where the denim fabric is cut out according to pattern. Department 2 is the assembly department. Here denim pieces are transferred in from cutting. Direct labor (using sewing machines and other overhead) sews thread, zippers, and rivets into the denim in the process of creating jeans. Thus, the assembly department has three categories of production cost: prior department cost (prepared denim pattern pieces transferred in from cutting), direct materials (thread, zippers, etc., added in assembly), and conversion cost (direct labor and overhead of the assembly department). The usual approach is to treat transferred-in goods as a separate material category when calculating equivalent units.

In dealing with transferred-in goods, two important points should be remembered. First, the cost of this material is the cost of the goods transferred out computed in the prior department. Second, the units started in the subsequent department correspond to the units transferred out from the prior department (assuming that there is a one-to-one relationship between the output measures of both departments).

For example, let's consider the month of September for Healthblend Company and restrict our attention to the transferred-in category. Assume that the encapsulating department had 15,000 units in beginning inventory (with transferred-in costs of $3,000) and completed 70,000 units during the month. Further, the picking department completed and transferred out 60,000 units at a cost of $13,200 in September. In constructing a physical flow schedule for the encapsulating department, its dependence on the picking department must be considered:

Units to account for:	
Units, beginning work in process	15,000
Units transferred in during September	60,000
Total units to account for	75,000
Units accounted for:	
Units completed and transferred out:	
Started and completed	55,000
From beginning work in process	15,000
Units in ending work in process	5,000
Total unit^ accounted for	75,000

Exhibit 17-12

Healthblend Company
Picking Department
Production Report For September 1995
(Weighted Average Method)

Unit Information

Units to account for:		Units accounted for:	
Units in beginning work in process	10,000	Units completed	60,000
		Units EWIP	20,000
Units started	70,000		
Total units to account for	80,000	Total units accounted for	80,000

Equivalent Units

	Materials	*Conversion Cost*
Units completed	60,000	60,000
Units in ending work in process	20,000	8,000
Total equivalent units	80,000	68,000

Cost Information

	Materials	*Conversion Cost*	*Total*
Costs to account for:			
Beginning work in process	$ 1,600	$ 200	$ 1,800
Incurred during the period	12,000	3,200	15,200
Total costs to account for	$13,600	$3,400	$17,000
Cost per equivalent unit	$0.17	$0.05	$0.22

	Transferred Out	*Ending Work in Process*	*Total*
Costs accounted for:			
Goods transferred out (60,000 × $0.22)	$13,200	—	$13,200
Ending work in process:			
Materials (20,000 × $0.17)	—	$3,400	3,400
Conversion (8,000 × $0.05)	—	400	400
Total costs accounted for	$13,200	$3,800	$17,000

Equivalent units for the transferred-in category are calculated as follows (ignoring other input categories):

Transferred in:	
Units completed	70,000
Add: Units in ending work in process × Fraction complete (5,000 × 100%)	5,000
Equivalent units of output	75,000

To compute the unit cost, we add the cost of the units transferred in from picking in September to the transferred-in costs in beginning work in process and divide by transferred-in equivalent units:

$$\text{Unit cost (transferred-in category)} = (\$13{,}200 + \$3{,}000)/75{,}000$$
$$= \$16{,}200/75{,}000$$
$$= \$0.216$$

The only additional complication introduced in the analysis for a subsequent department is the presence of the transferred-in category. As has just been shown, dealing with this category is similar to handling any other category. However, it must be remembered that the current cost of this special type of raw material is the cost of the units transferred in from the prior process and that the units transferred in are the units started.

SUMMARY OF LEARNING OBJECTIVES

1. Identify the settings for which process costing is appropriate. If a firm produces a homogeneous product that passes through a series of similar processes and receives similar amounts of manufacturing costs in each process, process costing is probably the appropriate method for assigning costs to production. In process costing, costs are accumulated by department, and a unit cost is calculated for the output of each department.

2. Describe the basic characteristics of process manufacturing and process costing. Cost flows under process costing are similar to those under job-order costing. Raw materials are purchased and debited to the Materials account. Direct materials used in production, direct labor, and overhead applied are charged to the Work in Process account. In a production process with several processes, there is a Work in Process account for each department or process. Goods completed in one department are transferred out to the next department where they are treated as a type of material. When units are complete in the final department or process, their cost is credited to Work in Process and debited to Finished Goods.

Equivalent units of production are the complete units that could have been produced given the total amount of manufacturing effort expended during the period being considered. That is, the number of physical units is multiplied by the percentage of completion to calculate equivalent units.

A production report summarizes the manufacturing activity occurring in a department for a given period. It discloses information concerning the physical flow of units, equivalent units, unit costs, and the disposition of the manufacturing costs associated with the period. It is analogous in its role to the job-order cost sheet. The physical flow of units within a production department consists of units to be accounted for and units accounted for. Units to be accounted for include units from beginning inventory and units started or transferred-in during the period. Units accounted for consists of units completed and transferred-out during the period and units on hand in ending inventory at the end of the period. Units to be accounted for must equal units accounted for.

3. Prepare a production report using the weighted average method of accounting for process costs. Under the weighted average method, equivalent units are treated as being produced during the current period. Thus, units completed and transferred out are counted as belonging to the current period. Furthermore, units remaining in ending inventory are multiplied by their percentage of completion and these equivalent units also count as part of the current period's output. Adding these two categories of units defines the output of the period. All costs—both in beginning inventory and those incurred currently—are also counted as belonging to the current period. The total of the current costs and the costs found in beginning work in process is divided by the output of the period to obtain a unit cost. This unit cost is used to value ending work in process and the goods transferred out. The cost of goods transferred out is equal to the number of units transferred out multiplied by the unit cost. The cost of ending work in process is equal to the unit cost multiplied by the number of equivalent units in ending inventory.

4. Explain how process costing is affected by nonuniform application of manufacturing inputs and the existence of multiple processing departments. When direct materials, direct labor, and overhead are not applied uniformly throughout the manufacturing process, equivalent units must be calculated for each category of input. The overall unit cost is the sum of the individual unit costs.

In a multiple-department setting, some departments receive partially completed goods from other departments. The production report for multiple-department setting is altered to reflect the presence of these transferred-in goods. Essentially, the transferred-in goods can be viewed as a raw material added at the beginning of the process. The cost of this raw material is simply the cost of the goods transferred out in the prior department. The transferred-in goods are accommodated by adding a transferred-in category to the equivalent unit schedule. Thus, we calculate equivalent units for three categories: transferred-in, materials (added), and conversion costs.

KEY TERMS

Cost reconciliation *817*
Equivalent units of output *811*
FIFO costing method *813*
Operation costing *808*
Parallel processing *808*
Physical flow schedule *815*
Production report *810*
Sequential processing *808*
Transferred-in costs *810*
Weighted average costing method *814*

REVIEW PROBLEM

Payson Company, which uses the weighted average method, produces a product that passes through two departments: mixing and cooking. In the mixing department, all materials are added at the beginning of the process. All other manufacturing inputs are added uniformly. The following information pertains to the mixing department for February:

a. Beginning work in process (BWIP), February 1: 100,000 pounds, 40 percent complete with respect to conversion costs. The costs assigned to this work are as follows:

Materials	$20,000
Labor	10,000
Overhead	30,000

b. Ending work in process (EWIP), February 28: 50,000 pounds, 60 percent complete with respect to conversion costs.

c. Units completed and transferred out: 370,000 pounds. The following costs were added during the month:

Materials	$211,000
Labor	100,000
Overhead	270,000

REQUIRED:

1. Prepare a physical flow schedule.
2. Prepare a schedule of equivalent units.
3. Compute the cost per equivalent unit.
4. Compute the cost of goods transferred out and the cost of ending work in process.
5. Prepare a cost reconciliation.

Solution:

1. Physical flow schedule:

Units to account for:		
Units, BWIP		100,000
Units started		320,000
Total units to account for		420,000
Units accounted for:		
Units completed and transferred out:		
Started and completed	270,000	
From BWIP	100,000	370,000
Units, EWIP		50,000
Total units accounted for		420,000

2. Schedule of equivalent units:

	Materials	*Conversion*
Units completed	370,000	370,000
Units EWIP × Fraction complete:		
Materials (50,000 × 100%)	50,000	—
Conversion (50,000 × 60%)	—	30,000
Equivalent units of output	420,000	400,000

3. Cost per equivalent unit:

Direct Materials unit cost = ($20,000 + $211,000)/420,000 = $0.550
Conversion unit cost = ($40,000 + $370,000)/400,000 = $1.025
Total unit cost = $1.575 per equivalent unit

4. Cost of goods transferred out and cost of ending work in process:

Cost of goods transferred out = $1.575 × 370,000
= $582,750
Cost of EWIP = ($0.55 × 50,000) + ($1.025 × 30,000)
= $58,250

5. Cost reconciliation:

Costs to account for:	
BWIP	$ 60,000
Costs added	581,000
Total to account for	$641,000
Costs accounted for:	
Goods transferred out	$582,750
EWIP	58,250
Total costs accounted for	$641,000

QUESTIONS

1. Distinguish between sequential processing and parallel processing.
2. Describe the differences between process costing and job-order costing.
3. What are equivalent units? Why are they needed in a process cost system?
4. Under the weighted average method, how are prior-period costs and output treated? How are they treated under the FIFO method?
5. Under what conditions will the weighted average and FIFO methods give essentially the same results?
6. How is the equivalent unit calculation affected when materials are added at the beginning or end of the process rather than uniformly throughout the process?
7. Explain why transferred-in costs are a special type of raw material for the receiving department.
8. What are the similarities and differences in the manufacturing cost flows for job-order firms and process firms?
9. What journal entry would be made as goods are transferred out from one department to another department? From the final department to the warehouse?
10. Describe the five steps in accounting for the manufacturing activity of a processing department and indicate how they interrelate.
11. What is a production report? What purpose does this report serve?
12. In assigning costs to goods transferred out, how do the weighted average and FIFO methods differ?
13. Describe the effect of automation on the process accounting system.

EXERCISES

E17-1
Weighted Average Method; Physical Flow; Equivalent Units
LO 2, 3, 4

Silverado Company manufactures a product that passes through two processes. The following information was obtained for the first department for May:

a. All materials are added at the beginning of the process.
b. Beginning work in process had 6,000 units, 33 percent complete with respect to conversion costs.
c. Ending work in process had 4,400 units, 25 percent complete with respect to conversion costs.
d. Started in process, 10,000 units.

REQUIRED:

1. Prepare a physical flow schedule.
2. Compute equivalent units.

E17-2
Weighted Average Method; Valuation of Goods Out and Ending Work in Process
LO 2, 3, 4

Wise Paper Products, Inc., manufactures products that pass through two or more processes. Wise uses the weighted average method to compute unit costs. During August, equivalent units were computed as follows:

	Materials	*Conversion Cost*
Units completed	4,000	4,000
Units, ending work in process		
× Fraction complete:		
2,000 × 0%	—	—
2,000 × 70%	—	1,400
Equivalent units of output	4,000	5,400

The unit cost was computed as follows:

Materials	$0.50
Conversion cost	0.25
Total	$0.75

REQUIRED:

1. Determine the cost of ending work in process and the cost of the goods transferred out.
2. If possible, prepare a physical flow schedule.

E17-3
Production Report; No Beginning Inventory
LO 2, 4

Bander Company manufactures an industrial solvent. Department 1 mixes the chemicals required for the solvent. The following data are for 1995:

Work in process, 1/1/95	—
Gallons started	75,000
Gallons transferred out	63,000
Raw materials cost	$75,000
Direct labor cost	$148,800
Overhead applied	$223,200

Materials are added at the beginning of the process. Ending inventory is 95 percent complete with respect to labor and overhead.

REQUIRED: Prepare a production report for Department 1 for 1995.

E17-4
Physical Flow; Equivalent Units; Unit Costs; Cost Assignment
LO 2, 3, 4

Banray, Inc., produces nonprescription sunglasses. The sunglasses are produced in two departments. The data for department 1 are as follows:

Beginning work in process	—
Units started	92,500
Raw materials cost	$92,500
Direct labor cost	$ 9,150
Overhead applied	$13,725
Units, ending work in process (100% materials; 80% conversion)	5,000

REQUIRED:

1. Prepare a physical flow schedule.
2. Calculate equivalent units of production for:
   a. Raw materials
   b. Conversion
3. Calculate unit costs for
   a. Raw materials
   b. Conversion
   c. Total manufacturing
4. What is the total cost of units transferred out? What is the cost assigned to units in ending inventory?

E17-5
Equivalent Units—Weighted Average Method
LO 3

The following are data for four independent process-costing departments.

	A	*B*	*C*	*D*
Beginning inventory	3,200	1,500	—	27,000
Percent completion	33	40	—	75
Units started	19,200	20,000	48,000	33,000
Ending inventory	4,000	—	9,000	8,000
Percent completion	25	—	30	20

REQUIRED: Compute the equivalent units of production for each of the above departments using the weighted average method.

E17-6
Weighted Average Method; Unit Cost; Value of Goods Transferred Out and Ending Work in Process
LO 3, 4

Mason Products, Inc., produces a chemical product that passes through three departments. For April, the following equivalent unit schedule was prepared for the first department:

	Materials	*Conversion Cost*
Units completed	5,000	5,000
Units, ending work in process		
× Fraction complete:		
6,000 × 100%	6,000	—
6,000 × 50%	—	3,000
Equivalent units of output	11,000	8,000

Costs assigned to beginning work in process: materials, $30,000; conversion, $5,000. Manufacturing costs incurred during April: materials, $25,000; conversion, $65,000. Mason uses the weighted average method.

REQUIRED:

1. Compute the unit cost for April.
2. Determine the cost of ending work in process and the cost of goods transferred out.

E17-7
Weighted Average Method; Equivalent Units, Unit Cost; Multiple Departments
LO 2, 3, 4

Kilian Company has a product that passes through three processes. During December, the first department transferred 10,000 units to the second department. The cost of the units transferred into the second department was $20,000. Materials are added uniformly in the second process.

The second department had the following physical flow schedule for December:

Units to account for:		
Units, beginning work in process	2,000	(40% complete)
Units started	?	
Total units to account for	?	
Units accounted for:		
Units, ending work in process	4,000	(50% complete)
Units completed	?	
Units accounted for	?	

Costs in beginning work in process for the second department were materials, $2,500; conversion costs, $3,000; transferred in, $4,000. Costs added during the month: materials, $16,000; conversion costs, $25,000; transferred in, $20,000.

REQUIRED:

1. Assuming the use of the weighted average method, prepare a schedule of equivalent units.
2. Compute the unit cost for the month.

E17-8
Weighted Average Method; Unit Costs; Inventory Valuation; Cost Reconciliation
LO 2, 3, 4

Brandy Company prepared the following schedule for the most recent month of operation:

	Beginning Work in Process	*Costs Added*	*Total*
Materials	$ 5,000	$15,000	$20,000
Conversion costs	10,000	30,000	40,000
Total	$15,000	$45,000	$60,000

The equivalent units produced are summarized in the following schedule:

	Materials	*Conversion Costs*
Units completed	3,000	3,000
Units, ending work in process		
× Fraction complete:		
2,000 × 100%	2,000	—
2,000 × 50%	—	1,000
Equivalent units of output	5,000	4,000

REQUIRED:

1. Calculate the unit costs for materials, conversion costs, and the total unit costs.
2. Compute the cost of ending work in process and the cost of goods transferred out.
3. Prepare a cost reconciliation.

E17-9
Journal Entries; Cost of Ending Inventories
LO 2

Eyrin Company has two processing departments: assembly and finishing. A predetermined overhead rate of $5 per *DLH* is used to assign overhead to production. The company experienced the following operating activity for September:

a. Raw materials issued to assembly, $12,000
b. Direct labor cost: assembly, 550 hours at $9.20 per hour; finishing, 400 hours at $8 per hour

c. Overhead applied to production
d. Goods transferred to finishing, $18,000
e. Goods transferred to finished goods warehouse, $20,500
f. Actual overhead incurred, $5,000

REQUIRED:

1. Prepare the required journal entries for the above transactions.
2. Assuming assembly and finishing have no beginning work-in-process inventories, determine the cost of each department's ending work-in-process inventories.

E17-10
Process Costing; Food Manufacturing
LO 2, 3

Wholesome Bread makes and supplies bread throughout the western United States. Six operations describe the production process.

a. Flour, milk, yeast, salt, butter, and so on are mixed in a large vat.
b. A conveyor belt transfers the dough to a machine that weighs it and shapes it into loaves.
c. The individual loaves are allowed to sit and rise.
d. The dough is moved to a 100-foot-long funnel oven. (The dough enters the oven on racks and spends twenty minutes moving slowly through the oven.)
e. The bread is removed from the oven, sucked from the pan by a vacuum, and allowed to cool.
f. The bread is sliced and wrapped.

During the week, 4,500 loaves of bread were produced. The total cost of materials (ingredients and wrapping material) was $675. The cost of direct labor and overhead totaled $1,575. There were no beginning or ending work-in-process inventories.

REQUIRED:

1. Compute the unit cost for the 4,500 loaves of bread produced during the week.
2. Would Wholesome Bread ever need to worry about using FIFO or weighted average? Why or why not? What implication does this have for the food industry in general?
3. Assume that Wholesome Bread also produces rolls and buns. Also assume that the only difference is that the machine is set to shape the dough differently. What adjustments would need to be made to cost out the three different bread products?

E7-11
Process Costing; Automated Operations
LO 1, 2

Sahara Soft Diapers has just opened a new plant for making its popular line of diapers. This plant is experimental in the sense that it has implemented a fully automated production process. Human hands never touch the diaper while it is in production. The production line operates as follows.

First, fluff pulp is shredded from large rolls (mechanically fed into a shredder). Next, diaper wrap is mechanically placed on a conveyor belt. The shredded pulp is sprayed onto the diaper wrap sheet as it passes underneath. As the wrap and pulp move along, another machine covers the pulp with a liner sheet. The three materials are held together by a construction adhesive. The next machine attaches a leg elastic along the sides (the product now has the appearance of a long sausage). A cutting machine then cuts the diapers into the proper length. The final machines attach the waist elastic, outer poly cover, and the release tapes. The diapers are placed in bags and then in boxes (four per box). The boxes move down the conveyor belt to a point where they are picked up by robots and cranes and carried to the finished goods storage area.

REQUIRED:

1. Describe how you would compute the unit cost of a box of diapers. Do you think that the computation of equivalent units will be needed? Explain. Also discuss the need for predetermined overhead rates.
2. Now assume that there are small, medium, and large diapers produced. Describe how you would compute unit costs for these three products.

E17-12
Weighted Average Method; Physical Flow; Equivalent Units; Unit Costs; Cost Assignment
LO 2, 3, 4

Funnifaces, Inc., manufactures various novelty noses. Each nose is shaped from a piece of rubber in the molding department. The noses are then transferred to the finishing department where they are painted and have elastic bands attached. In April, the molding department reported the following data:

a. In molding, all materials are added at the beginning of the process.
b. Beginning work in process consisted of 3,000 units, 20 percent complete with respect to direct labor and overhead. Cost in beginning inventory included direct materials, $450; and conversion costs, $138.
c. Costs added to production during the month were direct materials, $950; and conversion costs, $2,174.50.
d. At the end of the month, 9,000 units were transferred out to finishing; 1,000 units remained in ending work in process, 25 percent complete.

REQUIRED:

1. Prepare a physical flow schedule.
2. Calculate equivalent units of production for direct materials and conversion cost.
3. Compute unit cost.
4. Calculate the cost of goods transferred to finishing at the end of the month. Calculate the cost of ending inventory.

E17-13
Weighted Average Method; Equivalent Units; Cost per Unit; Cost of Ending Inventory; Cost of Completed Units
LO 2, 4

Canyon Walking Tours produces maps of the Grand Canyon that outline a variety of walking tours of the north and south rim areas. In June, Canyon Walking Tours incurred costs of $66 for materials (paper, ink, etc.) and $213 for direct labor and overhead. June production consisted of 200 completed maps and 130 maps that were 100 percent complete with respect to materials but only 10 percent complete with respect to conversion cost. There was no work-in-process inventory on June 1.

REQUIRED:

1. How many units were started and completed in June?
2. Compute the cost per equivalent unit for June.
3. Determine the cost of ending work-in-process inventory and the cost of the completed maps.

PROBLEMS

P17-1
Weighted Average Method; Single Department Analysis; One Cost Category
LO 2, 3

Littleton Company produces a product that passes through two processes: assembly and finishing. All manufacturing costs are added uniformly for both processes. The following information was obtained for the assembly department for the month of December:

a. Work in process, December 1, had 5,000 units (40 percent completed) and the following costs:

Direct materials	$4,000
Direct labor	6,000
Overhead	2,000

b. During the month of December, 10,000 units were completed and transferred to the finishing department, and the following costs were added to production:

Direct materials	$12,000
Direct labor	18,000
Overhead	6,000

c. On December 31, there were 2,500 partially completed units in process. These units were 80 percent complete.

REQUIRED: Prepare a production report for the assembly department for December using the weighted average method of costing. The report should disclose the physical flow of units, equivalent units, and unit costs and should track the disposition of manufacturing costs.

P17-2
Weighted Average Method; Single Department Analysis; Three Cost Categories
LO 2, 3, 4

Tristar Chemicals produces an industrial chemical that passes through two processes: blending and drying. The weighted average method is used to account for the costs of production. Two chemicals, A and B, are added at the beginning of the blending process and allowed to cook for 6 to 7 hours. After blending, the resulting product is sent to the drying department, where it is dried under heat lamps for 24 hours. The following information relates to the blending process for the month of August.

a. Work in process, August 1, 20,000 pounds, 60 percent complete with respect to conversion costs. Costs associated with partially completed units:

Material A	$1,000
Material B	5,000
Direct labor	500
Overhead	1,500

b. Work in process, August 31, 30,000 pounds, 70 percent complete with respect to conversion costs.
c. Units completed and transferred out: 500,000 pounds. Costs added during the month:

Material A	$ 25,500
Material B	127,500
Direct labor	12,750
Overhead	38,250

REQUIRED:

1. Prepare the following: (a) a physical flow schedule and (b) an equivalent unit schedule with cost categories for Material A, Material B, and conversion cost.
2. Calculate the unit cost for each cost category.
3. Compute the cost of ending work in process and the cost of goods transferred out.
4. Prepare a cost reconciliation.

P17-3
Weighted Average Method; Single Department Analysis; Two Cost Categories
LO 2, 3, 4

Lamdin, Inc., produces a product that goes through two departments, grinding and polishing. Materials are added at the beginning of the grinding operation; labor and overhead are added uniformly throughout the process. The grinding department had work in process at the beginning and end of 1995 as follows:

	Percentage of Completion	
	Materials	*Conversion Costs*
January 1, 1995, 2,500 units	100	60
December 31, 1995, 4,000 units	100	50

The company completed 42,500 units during the year and incurred the following manufacturing costs:

Direct materials	$158,000
Direct labor	98,750
Overhead	79,000

The inventory at the beginning of the year was carried at the following costs:

Direct materials	$9,750
Direct labor	6,125
Overhead	4,950

REQUIRED: Prepare a production report using the weighted average method.

P17-4
Weighted Average Method; Multiple Department Analysis; Transferred-in Goods
LO 3, 4

Blalack Company manufactures a product that passes through three departments. In department B, materials are added at the end of the process. Conversion costs are incurred uniformly throughout the process. During the month of October, department B received 30,000 units from department A. The transferred-in cost of the 30,000 units was $69,900.

Costs added by department B during October included the following:

Direct materials	$35,200
Direct labor	56,000
Overhead	25,600

On October 1, department B had 5,000 units in inventory that were 30 percent complete with respect to conversion costs. On October 31, 6,000 units were in inventory, one-third complete with respect to conversion costs. The costs associated with the 5,000 units in beginning inventory were as follows:

Transferred in	$11,650
Direct labor	8,750
Overhead	4,000

REQUIRED: Prepare a production report using the weighted average method. Use the five steps outlined in the chapter to produce the information required by the report.

P17-5
Weighted Average Method; Multiple Department Analysis; Transferred-in Goods
LO 3, 4

Hoth, Inc., manufactures a single product that passes through several processes. During the first quarter of 1995, the mixing department received 20,000 gallons of liquid from the cooking department (transferred in at $9,600). Upon receiving the liquid, the mixing department adds a powder and allows blending to take place for 30 minutes. The product is then passed on to the bottling department.

There were 4,000 gallons in process at the beginning of the quarter, 75 percent complete with respect to conversion costs. The costs attached to the beginning inventory were as follows:

Transferred in	$1,900
Powder	268
Conversion costs	600

Costs added by the mixing department during the first quarter were:

Powder	$1,400
Conversion costs	3,046

There were 3,500 gallons in ending inventory, 20 percent complete with respect to conversion costs.

REQUIRED: Prepare a production report using the weighted average method. Follow the five steps outlined in the chapter in preparing the report.

P17-6
Weighted Average Method; Journal Entries
LO 2, 3, 4

Kilgorn Company uses a process costing system. The company manufactures a product that is processed in two departments, A and B. In department A, materials are added at the beginning of the process; in department B, additional materials are added at the end of the process. In both departments, conversion costs are incurred uniformly throughout the process. As work is completed, it is transferred out. The following summarizes the production activity and costs for March:

	Department A	*Department B*
Beginning inventories:		
Physical units	10,000	8,000
Costs:		
Transferred in	—	$45,200
Direct materials	$ 22,000	—
Conversion costs	$13,800	$16,800
Current production:		
Units started	25,000	?
Units transferred out	30,000	35,000
Costs:		
Transferred in	—	?
Direct materials	$ 56,250	$ 39,550
Conversion costs	$103,500	$136,500
Percentage completion:		
Beginning inventory	40	50
Ending inventory	80	50

REQUIRED:

1. Using the weighted average method, prepare the following for department A:
   a. A physical flow schedule
   b. An equivalent units calculation
   c. Calculation of unit costs
   d. Cost of ending work in process and cost of goods transferred out
   e. A cost reconciliation
2. Prepare journal entries that show the flow of manufacturing costs for department A.
3. Repeat Requirements 1 and 2 for department B.

P17-7
Weighted Average Method; Two-Department Analysis
LO 3, 4

Healthway uses a process costing system to compute the unit costs of the minerals that it produces. It has three departments: picking, encapsulating, and bottling. In picking, the ingredients for the minerals are measured, sifted, and blended together. The mix is transferred out in gallon containers. The encapsulating department takes the powdered mix and places it in capsules. One gallon of powdered mix converts into 1,600 capsules. After the capsules are filled and polished, they are transferred to bottling where they are placed in bottles, which are then affixed with a safety seal and a lid and labeled. Each bottle receives 50 capsules.

During July, the following results are available for the first two departments:

	Picking	*Encapsulating*
Beginning inventories:		
Physical units	5 gallons	4,000
Costs:		
Materials	$120	$ 32
Labor	$128	$ 20
Overhead	$?	$?
Transferred in	$ —	$140
Current production:		
Transferred out	125 gallons	198,000
Ending inventory	6 gallons	6,000
Costs:		
Materials	$3,144	$1,584
Transferred in	$ —	$?
Labor	$4,096	$1,944
Overhead	$?	$?
Percentage of completion:		
Beginning inventory	40	50
Ending inventory	50	40

Overhead in both departments is applied as a percentage of direct labor costs. In the picking department, overhead is 200 percent of direct labor. In the encapsulating department, the overhead rate is 150 percent of direct labor.

REQUIRED:

1. Prepare a production report for the picking department using the weighted average method. Follow the five steps outlined in the chapter.
2. Prepare a production report for the encapsulating department using the weighted average method. Follow the five steps outlined in the chapter.

P17-8
Weighted Average Method; Multiple Department Analysis
LO 3, 4

Strathmore, Inc., manufactures educational toys using a weighted average process costing system. Plastic is molded into the appropriate shapes in the molding department. Molded components are transferred to the assembly department where the toys are assembled and additional materials (e.g., fasteners, decals) are applied. Completed toys are then transferred to the packaging department where each toy is boxed.

Strathmore showed the following data on toy production for February:

	Molding	*Assembly*	*Packaging*
Beginning inventory:			
Units	500	—	150
Prior department	—	—	$1,959
Direct materials	$2,500	—	$375
Conversion cost	$1,050	—	$225

(continued)

	Molding	Assembly	Packaging
Started or transferred in:			
Units	1,000	?	?
February costs:			
Prior department	—	$14,950	$11,754
Direct materials	$5,000	$487.60	$2,407.50
Conversion cost	$7,660	$1,166	$2,977.50
Ending inventory, units	200	400	—

Beginning and ending work in process for the three departments showed the following degree of completion:

	Molding	Assembly	Packaging
Degree of completion:			
BWIP, direct materials	100%	—	100%
BWIP, conversion costs	30	—	50
EWIP, direct materials	100	40%	—
EWIP, conversion costs	20	40	—

REQUIRED:

1. Prepare a physical flow schedule for February for the:
   a. Molding department
   b. Assembly department
   c. Packaging department
2. Compute equivalent units of production for direct materials and for conversion costs for the:
   a. Molding department
   b. Assembly department
   c. Packaging department
3. Complete the following unit cost chart:

	Molding	Assembly	Packaging
Unit prior department cost[1]			
Unit direct material cost			
Unit conversion cost			
Total Unit cost			

[1]Cost transferred in from prior department

4. Determine the cost of ending work in process and the cost of goods transferred out for each of the three departments.
5. Reconcile the costs for each department.

P17-9
Production Report
LO 2, 3, 4

Susan Manners, cost accountant for Lean Jeans, Inc., spent the weekend completing a production report for the inspection department for the month of December. Inspection is the final department in the production of fashion jeans. In that department, each pair of jeans is carefully inspected for quality workmanship. At the end of the inspection process, a slip of paper with "Inspected by #________" is slipped into a back pocket and the jeans are placed in a bin to be transferred to finished goods.

First thing Monday morning, Susan returned to work and found that someone had accidently spilled coffee on her report, partially obliterating some of the figures. Susan has only one hour to reconstruct her report.

Production Report for the Inspection Department
For the Month of December
(Weighted Average Method)

Unit Information

Units to account for:				
Beginning inventory	?			
Transferred in from assembly	4,000			
Total units to account for	4,700			
		Equivalent Units		
	Physical Flow	*Prior Department*	*Materials*	*Conversion Cost*
Units accounted for:				
Units completed	?	?	?	?
Units ending WIP	900	?	—	?
Total	4,700	?	3,800	4,250

Cost Information

	Prior Department	*Materials*	*Conversion Costs*	*Total*
Costs to account for:				
Beginning WIP	$11,900	?	$ 210	$12,110
Incurred in December	?	?	4,040	72,097
Total cost	$79,900	$57	$4,250	$84,207
Unit cost	$17.00	?	$1.00	?

	Transferred Out	*Ending WIP*	*Total*
Cost accounted for:			
Goods transferred out	?	—	?
Ending WIP:			
Prior department	—	?	?
Materials	—	—	—
Conversion cost	—	?	?
Total costs accounted for	$?	$15,750	$84,207

REQUIRED: Help Susan meet the deadline by filling in the appropriate number for each question mark.

DISCUSSION AND INTERPRETATION PROBLEMS

D17-1
Production Report; Ethical Behavior

Consider the following conversation between Gary Means, manager of a division that produces industrial machinery, and his controller, Donna Simpson, a CMA and CPA:

Gary: "Donna, we have a real problem. Our operating cash is too low, and we are in desperate need of a loan. As you know, our financial position is marginal, and we need to show as much income as possible—and our assets need bolstering as well."

Donna: "I understand the problem, but I don't see what can be done at this point. This is the last week of the fiscal year, and it looks like we'll report income just slightly above break even."

Gary: "I know all this. What we need is some creative accounting. I have an idea that might help us, and I wanted to see if you would go along with it. We have 200 partially finished machines in process, about 20 percent complete. That compares with the 1,000 units that we completed and sold during the year. When you computed the per-unit cost, you used 1,040 equivalent units, giving us a manufacturing cost of $1,500 per unit. That per-unit cost gives us cost of goods sold equal to $1.5 million and ending work in process worth $60,000. The presence of the work in process gives us a chance to improve our financial position. If we report the units in work in process as 80 percent complete, this will increase our equivalent units to 1,160. This, in turn, will decrease our unit cost to about $1,345 and cost of goods sold to $1.345 million. The value of our work in process will increase to $215,200. With those financial stats, the loan would be a cinch."

Donna: "Gary, I don't know. What you're suggesting is risky. It wouldn't take much auditing skill to catch this one."

Gary: "You don't have to worry about that. The auditors won't be here for at least six to eight more weeks. By that time, we can have those partially completed units completed and sold. I can bury the labor cost by having some of our more loyal workers work overtime for some bonuses. The overtime will never be reported. And, as you know, bonuses come out of the corporate budget and are assigned to overhead—next year's overhead. Donna, this will work. If we look good and get the loan to boot, corporate headquarters will treat us well. If we don't do this, we could lose our jobs."

REQUIRED:

1. Should Donna agree to Gary's proposal? Why or why not? To assist in deciding, review the standards of ethical conduct for management accountants described in Chapter 1. Do any apply?
2. Assume that Donna refuses to cooperate and Gary accepts this decision and drops the matter. Does Donna have any obligation to report the divisional manager's behavior to a superior? Explain.
3. Assume that Donna refuses to cooperate; however, Gary insists that the changes be made. Now what should Donna do? What would *you* do?
4. Suppose that Donna is 63 and that the prospects for employment elsewhere are bleak. Assume again that Gary insists that the changes should be made. Donna also knows that Gary's superior, the owner of the company, is his father-in-law. Under these circumstances, would your recommendations for Donna differ? If you were Donna, what would you do?

D17-2 Process Costing versus Alternative Costing Methods; Impact on Resource Allocation Decision

Golding Manufacturing, a division of Farnsworth Sporting, Inc., produces two different models of bows and eight models of knives. The bow-manufacturing process involves the production of two major subassemblies: the limbs and the handle. The limbs pass through four sequential processes before reaching final assembly: lay-up, molding, fabricating, and finishing. In the lay-up department, limbs are created by laminating layers of wood. In Molding, the limbs are heat treated, under pressure, to form a strong resilient limb. In the fabricating department, any protruding glue or other processing residue is removed. Finally, in finishing, the limbs are cleaned with acetone, dried, and sprayed with the final finishes.

The handles pass through two processes before reaching final assembly: pattern and finishing. In the pattern department, blocks of wood are fed into a machine that is set to shape the handles. Different patterns are possible, depending on the machine's setting. After coming out of the machine, the handles are cleaned and smoothed. They then pass to the finishing department where they are sprayed with the final finishes. In the final assembly department, the limbs and handles are assembled into different models using purchased parts such as pulley assemblies, weight adjustment bolts, side plates, and string.

Golding, since its inception, has been using process costing to assign product costs. A predetermined overhead rate is used based on direct labor dollars (80 percent of direct labor dollars). Recently, Golding has hired a new controller, Karen Jenkins. After reviewing the product costing procedures, Karen requested a meeting with the divisional manager, Aaron Suhr. The following is a transcript of their conversation:

Karen: "Aaron, I have some concerns about our cost accounting system. We make two different models of bows and are treating them as if they were the same product. Now I know that the only real difference between the models is the handle. The processing of the handles is the same, but the handles differ significantly in the amount and quality of wood used. Our current costing does not reflect this difference in material input."

Aaron: "Your predecessor is responsible. He believed that tracking the difference in material cost wasn't worth the effort. He simply didn't believe that it would make much difference in the unit cost of either model."

Karen: "Well, he may have been right, but I have my doubts. If there is a significant difference, it could affect our views of which model is the more important to the company. The additional bookkeeping isn't very stringent. All we have to worry about is the pattern department. The other departments fit what I view as a process costing pattern."

Aaron: "Why don't you look into it? If there is a significant difference, go ahead and adjust the costing system."

After the meeting, Karen decided to collect cost data on the two models: the Deluxe model and the Econo model. She decided to track the costs for one week. At the end of the week, she had collected the following data from the pattern department:

a. There were a total of 2,500 bows completed: 1,000 Deluxe models and 1,500 Econo models.
b. There was no beginning work in process; however, there were 300 units in ending work in process: 200 Deluxe and 100 Econo models. Both models were 80 percent complete with respect to conversion costs and 100 percent complete with respect to materials.
c. The pattern department experienced the following costs:

Direct materials	$114,000
Direct labor	45,667

d. On an experimental basis, the requisition forms for materials were modified to identify the dollar value of the materials used by the Econo and Deluxe models:

Econo model:	$30,000
Deluxe model:	84,000

REQUIRED:

1. Compute the unit cost for the handles produced by the pattern department assuming that process costing is totally appropriate.
2. Compute the unit cost of each handle using the separate cost information provided on materials.
3. Compare the unit costs computed in Questions 1 and 2. Is Karen justified in her belief that a pure process costing relationship is not appropriate? Describe the costing system that you would recommend.
4. In the past, the marketing manager has requested more money for advertising the Econo line. Aaron has repeatedly refused to grant any increase in this product's advertising budget because its per-unit profit (selling price less manufacturing cost) is so low. Given the results in Questions 1 through 3, was Aaron justified in his position?

D17-3 Research Assignment

Process costing may also apply to service firms. Possible examples include postal services, tax services (for profit), certain medical services (e.g., blood collection and testing), certain banking services (e.g., collection and processing of deposits), and tax collection (by government agencies). The key to identifying potential process costing applications (for service firms) is the repetitive performance of a service that is the same for every customer/user of the service.

REQUIRED: You must identify a service firm that has the potential for applying process costing. Arrange an interview to assess the firm's costing procedures. Write a paper that describes how this firm determines the cost of its repetitive service(s). Describe the differences between the firm's approach and the process costing model described in the chapter. Are the differences justified? Can you suggest any improvements in the firm's costing approach? In your assessment of the firm's cost system, include the following questions:

1. What service or services are offered by the firm?
2. Of the services offered, which ones are repetitive for each customer?
3. For the repetitive services, describe the different processes that are performed (e.g., sorting, transportation, etc.)?
4. How do you assign the costs of direct labor?
5. How do you assign the costs of direct materials?
6. How do you assign the costs of overhead?
7. What documents are used to account for the repetitive services?

CHAPTER 18
ALLOCATION: SERVICE CENTER COSTS AND OTHER CONCEPTS

LEARNING OBJECTIVES

After studying this chapter, you should be able to:

1. Describe the difference between service departments and producing departments.
2. Explain why service costs are allocated to producing departments.
3. Describe the basic guidelines for allocating service costs.
4. Use the direct and sequential methods to allocate service costs.

Scenario

Paula Barneck, the newly appointed director of the Lambert Medical Center (LMC), a large metropolitan hospital, was reviewing the financial report for the most recent quarter. The hospital had again shown a loss. For the past several years, it had been struggling financially. The financial problems had begun with the introduction of the federal government's new diagnostic-related group (DRG) reimbursement system. Under this system, the government mandated fixed fees for specific treatments or illnesses. The fixed fees were supposed to represent what the procedures should cost and differed from the traditional cost objective of the patient day of prior years. Although no formal assessment had been made, the general feeling of hospital management was that the DRG reimbursement was hurting LMC's financial state.

The increasing popularity of health maintenance organizations (HMOs) and physician provider organizations (PPOs) was also harming the hospital's financial well-being.[1] More and more of the hospital's potential patients were joining HMOs and PPOs, and, unfortunately, LMC was not capturing its fair share of the HMO and PPO business. HMOs and PPOs routinely asked for bids on hospital services and provided their business to the lowest bidder. In too many cases, LMC had not won that work.

Paula had accepted the position of hospital administrator knowing that she was expected to produce dramatic improvements in LMC's financial state. She was convinced that she needed more information about the hospital's product-costing methods. Only by having accurate cost information for the various procedures offered by the hospital could she evaluate the effects of DRG reimbursement and the hospital's bidding strategy.

Paula requested a meeting with Eric Rose, the hospital's controller. The following is their conversation:

Paula: "Eric, as you know, we recently lost a bid on some laboratory tests that would be performed on a regular basis for a local HMO. In fact, I was told by the director of the HMO that we had the highest bid of the three submitted. I know the identity of the other two hospitals that submitted bids, and I have a hard time believing that their costs for these tests are any lower than ours. Describe exactly how we determine the cost of these lab procedures."

Eric: "First, we classify all departments as either revenue-producing centers or service centers. Next, the costs of the service centers are allocated to the revenue-producing centers. Then, the costs directly traceable to the revenue-producing centers are added to the allocated costs to obtain the total cost of operating the revenue-producing center. This total cost is divided by the total revenues of the revenue-producing center to obtain a cost-to-charges ratio. Finally, the cost of a particular procedure is computed by multiplying the charge for that procedure by the cost-to-charges ratio."

1. In both HMOs and PPOs, users pay a fixed fee for access to medical services and must use the physicians, facilities, and services provided. In HMOs, physicians, who are employed full time, are usually located in a clinic owned by the HMO, and subscribers must use these physicians. In PPOs, the health provider contracts with a group of physicians in private practice. These physicians usually serve non-PPO patients as well as PPO patients. The PPO patient can select any physician from the list of physicians under contract with the particular PPO. The PPO approach usually offers a greater selection of physicians and tends to preserve the patient's traditional freedom of choice.

Paula: "Let me see if I understand. The costs of laundry, housekeeping, maintenance, and other service departments are allocated to all of the revenue-producing departments. Let's assume that the lab receives $100,000 as its share of these allocated costs. The $100,000 is then added to the direct costs—let's assume these are also $100,000—to obtain total operating costs of $200,000. If the laboratory earns revenues of $250,000, the cost-to-charges ratio is 0.80 ($200,000/$250,000). Finally, if I want to know the cost of a particular lab procedure, say a blood test for which we normally charge $20, all I do is multiply the cost-to-charges ratio of 0.8 by $20 to obtain the cost of $16. Am I right?"

Eric: "Absolutely. In that bid we lost, our bid was at cost, as computed using our cost-to-charges formula. Perhaps the other hospitals are bidding below their cost to capture the business."

Paula: "Eric, I don't agree. The cost-to-charges ratio is a traditional approach for costing hospital products, but I'm afraid that it is no longer useful. Given the new environment in which we're operating, we need more accurate product-costing information. We need accuracy to improve our bidding, to help us assess and deal with the new DRG reimbursement system, and to evaluate the mix of services we offer. The cost-to-charges ratio approach backs into the product cost. It is indirect and inaccurate. Some procedures require more labor, more materials, and more expensive equipment than others. The cost-to-charges approach doesn't reflect these potential differences."

Eric: "Well, I'm willing to change the cost accounting system so that it meets our needs. Do you have any suggestions?"

Paula: "Yes. I'm in favor of a more direct computation of product costs. Allocating service costs to the revenue-producing departments is only the first stage in product costing. We do need to allocate these service costs to the producing departments—but we need to be certain that we are allocating them in the right way. We also need to go a step farther and assign the costs accumulated in the revenue-producing departments to individual products. The costs directly traceable to each product should be identified and assigned directly to those products; indirect costs can be assigned through one or more overhead rates. The base for assigning the overhead costs should be associated with their incurrence. If at all possible, allocations should reflect the usage of services by the revenue-producing departments; moreover, the same criterion should govern the assignment of overhead costs to the products within the department."

Eric: "Sounds like an interesting challenge. With over 30,000 products, a job-order system would be too burdensome and costly. I think some system can be developed, however, that will do essentially what you want."

Paula: "Good. Listen, for our next meeting come prepared to brief me on why and how you allocate these service department costs to the revenue-producing departments. I think this is a critical step in accurate product costing. I also want to know how you propose to assign the costs accumulated in each revenue-producing department to that department's products."

Note: This scenario is based on the experiences of an actual hospital. The names have been changed to ensure confidentiality.

SERVICE DEPARTMENT COST ALLOCATION: FURTHER REFINEMENT OF OVERHEAD

Objective 1
Describe the difference between service departments and producing departments.

A modern hospital such as Lambert Medical Center or a manufacturing firm such as General Motors or Levi Straus is so complex that careful categorization and subdivision of cost is necessary to produce accurate product cost information. In Chapter 15, we looked at a variety of cost definitions and classifications. We saw that costs for a company could be divided into product and period costs. We further divided product cost into direct materials, direct labor, and factory overhead. In Chapter 16, overhead was assigned to units of production based on a predetermined rate. Sometimes that rate was a plant-wide rate; sometimes there were two or more departmental rates. Now, we are going to look further at the way factory overhead is assigned to products.

producing departments

service departments

The dialogue between Paula and Eric reveals the presence of two categories of department: producing departments and service departments. **Producing departments** are directly responsible for manufacturing or creating the products or services sold to customers. In a hospital, examples of producing departments are emergency, surgery, intensive care, obstetrics, and respiratory therapy. In a manufacturing setting, producing departments are those that work directly on the products being manufactured (e.g., grinding and assembly). **Service departments** provide essential support services for producing departments. These departments are indirectly connected with an organization's services or products. Examples include maintenance, grounds, laundry, housekeeping, and stores.

Once the departments have been identified, the overhead costs incurred by each department can be determined. In this way, all factory costs are assigned to a department. Cafeteria, for example, would have food costs, salaries of cooks and servers, depreciation on dishwashers and stoves, and supplies (napkins, plastic forks). Overhead directly associated with a producing department, such as assembly in a furniture-making plant, would include utilities measured in that department, supervisory salaries, and depreciation on equipment used in that department. Overhead that cannot be easily assigned to a producing or service department is assigned to a catchall department such as general factory. General factory might include depreciation on the factory building, rental of a Santa Claus suit for the factory Christmas party, the cost of restriping the parking lot, the plant manager's salary, and telephone service.

Exhibit 18-1 shows a factory that has been departmentalized into two producing departments (assembly and finishing) and four service departments (materials storeroom, cafeteria, maintenance, and general factory). Note that each factory overhead cost must be assigned to one, and only one, department.

The dialogue between Paula and Eric also reveals the need to assign service costs to producing departments. Although service departments do not work directly on the products or services that are sold, the costs of providing these support services are part of the total product costs and must be assigned to the products. This assignment of costs consists of a two-stage allocation: (1) allocation of service-department costs to producing departments and (2) assignment of these allocated costs to individual products. The second-stage allocation, achieved through the use of overhead rates, is necessary because there are multiple products being worked on in each producing department. If there were only one product within a producing department, all the service costs allocated to that department would belong to that product. Recall that a predetermined overhead rate is computed by taking total overhead for a department and dividing it by

Exhibit 18-1

Examples of Overhead Costs Assigned to Each Department

Producing Departments

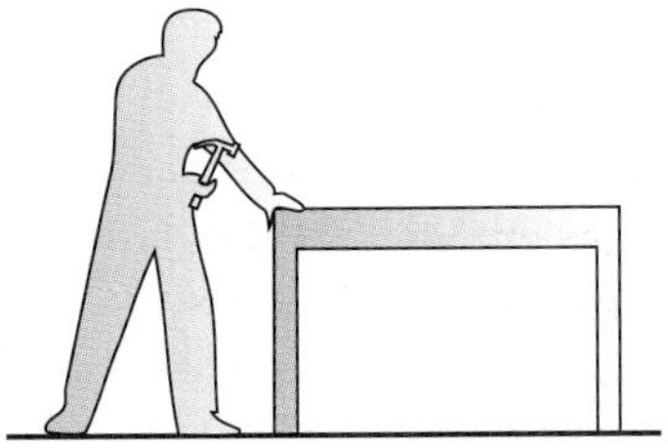

Assembly:
- Supervisory salaries
- Small tools
- Indirect materials
- Depreciation on machinery

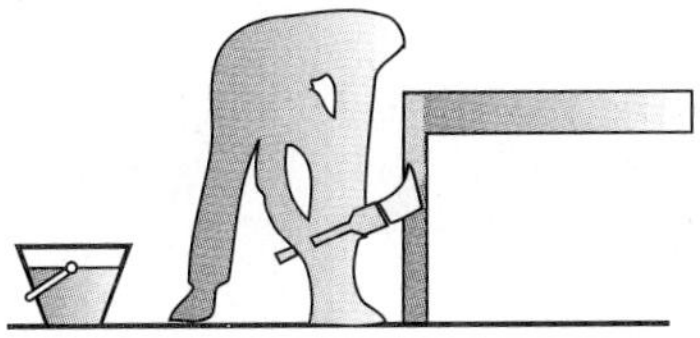

Finishing:
- Sandpaper
- Depreciation on sanders, buffers

Service Departments

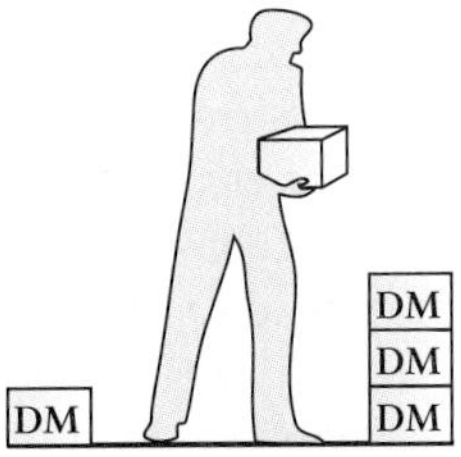

Materials Storeroom:
- Clerk's salary
- Depreciation on forklift

Cafeteria:
- Food
- Cooks' salaries
- Depreciation on stoves

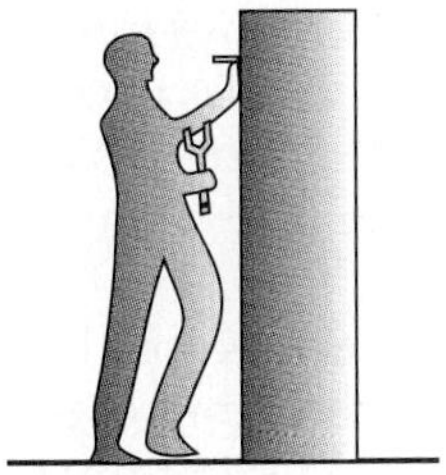

Maintenance:
- Janitorial labor
- Cleaning supplies
- Machine maintenance labor

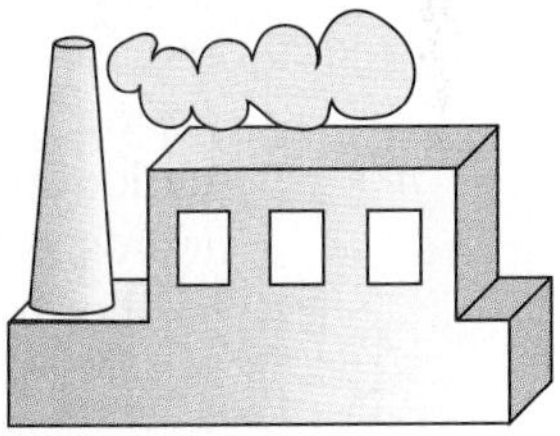

General Factory:
- Depreciation on building
- Security, utilities

an appropriate base. Now we see that a department's overhead consists of two parts: overhead directly associated with a producing department and overhead allocated to the producing department from the service departments. (A service department cannot have an overhead rate that assigns overhead costs to units produced because it does not make a salable product.) Both stages are important; however, since overhead rates have already been discussed extensively, the emphasis in this chapter is on the first-stage allocation.

OBJECTIVES OF ALLOCATION

Objective 2
Explain why service costs are allocated to producing departments.

A number of important objectives are associated with the allocation of service-department costs to producing departments and ultimately to specific products. The following major objectives have been identified by the IMA:[2]

1. To obtain a mutually agreeable price
2. To compute product-line profitability
3. To predict the economic effects of planning and control
4. To value inventory
5. To motivate managers

Of the five objectives, the first three are referred to in the introductory case. Paula, the hospital administrator, was seeking information about the costs of the individual services offered by the hospital. Only by knowing the costs of each service could meaningful bids be created. This is the pricing objective. If costs are not accurately allocated, the costs of some services could be overstated, resulting in bids that are too high and a loss of potential business. Alternatively, if the costs are understated, bids could be too low, producing losses on these services.

Knowing individual product costs also allows Paula to assess the profitability of those services being paid for on a DRG basis. This meets the profitability objective identified by the IMA. The current cost system apparently did not provide the information needed to assess the impact of DRG reimbursement. There was a definite belief that the new system was causing some financial damage, but how and where this was occurring was unknown. A major shortcoming of the old accounting system was its failure to accurately associate indirect costs with hospital services.

By assessing the profitability of various services, Paula is in a position to evaluate the mix of services offered by the hospital. From this evaluation, she may decide to drop some services, reallocate resources from one service to another, reprice certain services, or exercise greater cost control in some areas. These steps would meet the IMA's planning and control objective. The validity of any evaluation, however, depends to a great extent on the accuracy of the cost assignments made to individual products.

For a service organization such as a hospital, the IMA objective of inventory valuation is not relevant. For manufacturing organizations, however, this objective must be given special attention. Rules of financial reporting (GAAP) require that direct manufacturing costs and a fair share of indirect manufacturing costs be assigned to products. The procedure of allocating service costs and then assigning those costs to products is in keeping with this requirement. Inventories must be reported on a full costing basis.

Allocations can also be used to motivate managers. If the costs of service departments are not allocated to producing departments, managers may tend to overconsume these services. Consumption of a service may continue until the

2. *Statements of Management Accounting (Statement 4B),* "Allocation of Service and Administrative Costs" (Montvale, NJ: Institute of Management Accountants 1985).

marginal benefit of the service equals zero. In reality, of course, the marginal cost of a service is greater than zero. By allocating the costs and holding managers of producing departments responsible for the economic performance of their units, the organization ensures that managers will use a service until the marginal benefit of the service equals its marginal cost. Thus, allocation of service costs helps each producing department select the correct level of service consumption.

There are other behavioral benefits. Allocation of service-department costs to producing departments encourages managers of those departments to monitor the performance of service departments. Since the costs of the service departments affect the economic performance of their own departments, those managers have an incentive to control service costs through means other than simple usage of the service. For instance, the managers can compare the internal costs of the service with the costs of acquiring the service externally. If a service department is not as cost effective as an outside source, perhaps the company should not continue to supply the service internally. For example, many university libraries are moving toward the use of outside contractors for photocopying services. They have found that these contractors are more cost efficient and provide a higher level of service to library users than did the previous method of using professional librarians to make change, keep the copy machines supplied with paper, fix paper jams, etc. This possibility of comparison should result in a more efficient internal service department. Monitoring by managers of producing departments will also encourage managers of service departments to be more sensitive to the needs of the producing departments.

Clearly, there are good reasons for allocating service-department costs. The validity of these reasons, however, depends on the accuracy and fairness of the cost assignments made. Furthermore, it may not be possible to achieve all these objectives with a single allocation scheme; in many cases, multiple allocation schemes are needed.

COST ALLOCATION: SOME BASIC GUIDELINES

Objective 3
Describe the basic guidelines for allocating service costs.

Although it may not be possible to identify a single method of allocation that simultaneously satisfies all of these objectives, some basic guidelines should be followed when allocating service-department costs. These guidelines are essentially compatible with the five objectives.

1. As nearly as possible, cost drivers (causal factors) should be used as the basis for cost allocation.
2. Budgeted or expected costs, not actual costs, should be allocated.
3. Costs should be allocated by behavior; fixed costs and variable costs should be allocated separately.

Selection of Cost-Allocation Bases: Causal Factors

causal factors

Services exist to support activities within the producing departments. In effect, producing departments *cause* services; therefore, the costs of service departments are also caused by the activities of the producing departments. **Causal factors** are variables or activities within a producing department that provoke the incurrence of service costs. In choosing a basis for allocating service-department costs, every effort should be made to identify appropriate causal factors (cost drivers). Using causal factors results in product costs being more accurate; furthermore, if the causal factors are known, managers are more able to control the consumption of services.

To illustrate the types of cost drivers that can be used, consider the following three service departments: power, personnel, and materials handling. For power costs, a logical allocation base is kilowatt hours, which can be measured by separate meters for each department. If separate meters do not exist, perhaps machine hours used by each department would provide a good approximation of power usage. For personnel costs, both the number of employees and the labor turnover (e.g., number of new hires) are possible cost drivers. For materials handling, the number of material moves, the hours of material handling used, and the quantity of material moved are all possible cost drivers. When competing cost drivers exist, managers need to assess which provides the most convincing relationship.

Allocation: Budgeted Versus Actual Costs

Managers of service and producing departments usually are held accountable for the performance of their units. Their ability to control costs is an important factor in their performance evaluation. This ability is usually measured by comparing actual costs with planned or budgeted costs. If actual costs exceed budgeted costs, the department may be operating inefficiently, with the difference between the two costs the measure of that inefficiency. Similarly, if actual costs are less than budgeted costs, the unit may be operating efficiently.

A general principle of performance evaluation is that managers should not be held responsible for costs or activities over which they have no control. Since managers of producing departments have significant input regarding the level of service consumed, they should be held responsible for their share of service costs. This statement, however, has an important qualification: A department's evaluation should not be affected by the degree of efficiency achieved by another department.

This qualifying statement has an important implication for the allocation of service-department costs. *Actual* costs of a service department should not be allocated to producing departments because they include efficiencies or inefficiencies achieved by the service department. Managers of producing departments have no control over the degree of efficiency achieved by a service-department manager. By allocating *budgeted* costs instead of actual costs, no inefficiencies or efficiencies are transferred from one department to another.

Cost Behavior: Separate Allocation of Fixed and Variable Costs

For service departments, variable costs increase as the level of service increases. For example, the cost of fuel oil for a power department increases as the kilowatt hours produced increases. Fixed costs, on the other hand, do not vary with the level of service. For example, the salary of a supervisor of a service center does not change as service output changes. Because of this difference in behavior, the cause-and-effect relationship between the producing department and the service department also differs.

Allocation of Variable Costs. For variable costs, the cause-and-effect relationship is straightforward. Variable service costs increase in total as the quantity of service units increases. Thus, as a producing department uses more of a service, the costs of the service department increase. This suggests that the variable costs of a service department should be charged to producing departments on the basis of usage.

Whether budgeted usage or actual usage is used depends on the purpose of the allocation. For product costing, the allocation is done at the beginning of the year on the basis of budgeted usage so that a predetermined overhead rate can be computed. If the purpose is performance evaluation, however, the allocation is done at the end of the period and is based on actual usage. (Keep in mind the earlier caution about using actual *costs*. As you will see, the measure of actual usage is not the dollar cost of services but the number of service units a producing department consumes.) The use of cost information for performance evaluation is covered in more detail in the chapter on standard costing.

Both budgeted and actual usage allocations are achieved by following four steps:

1. *Determination of budgeted rate.* At the beginning of the year, the company determines what the variable cost per unit of service should be.
2. *Budgeting of usage.* Each producing department determines its expected or budgeted usage of the service for the year.
3. *Measurement of actual usage.* The actual units of service used by each producing department are measured.
4. *Allocation.* Variable service costs are allocated by multiplying the budgeted rate by the usage.
   a. For product costing, the formula is budgeted rate times budgeted usage.
   b. For performance evaluation, the allocation is found by multiplying budgeted rate by actual usage.

Consider, for example, the variable costs of a power department; these are the cost of fuel and supplies. At the beginning of the year, the manager of the power department, working with his supervisor and the accounting department, determined that the budgeted variable cost per kilowatt hour (kwh) would be \$0.04. The two producing departments, machining and assembly, estimated usage at 800,000 and 200,000 kwh, respectively. Given these data, the cost allocated to each department at the beginning of the year would be as follows:

Machining: \$0.04 × 800,000 = \$32,000
Assembly: \$0.04 × 200,000 = \$8,000

The power costs allocated to each department would be added to other overhead costs, including those directly traceable to each department plus other service-department allocations, to compute each department's predetermined overhead rate. This rate would be used throughout the year to assign overhead costs to products passing through the departments.

During the year, each producing department would also be responsible for measuring the amount of actual power usage. Suppose, for example, that by year's end the machining department had used 780,000 kwh and assembly had used 250,000 kwh. A second allocation is now made to measure the actual performance of each department against its budget. The actual power costs allocated to each department are as follows:

Machining: \$0.04 × 780,000 = \$31,200
Assembly: \$0.04 × 250,000 = \$10,000

Allocation of Fixed Costs. Fixed service costs can be considered capacity costs; they are incurred to provide the capacity necessary to deliver the service units required by the producing departments. When the service department was established, its delivery capability was created based on the long-term needs of the producing departments. Since the original service needs caused the creation of the service capacity, it seems reasonable to allocate fixed service costs based on those needs.

Either the practical or the normal activity of the producing departments provide reasonable measures of original service needs.[3] Thus, budgeted fixed service costs should be allocated in proportion to practical or normal capacity of the producing departments. Budgeted fixed costs are allocated in this way regardless of whether the purpose is product costing or performance evaluation.

The allocation of fixed costs follows a three-step procedure:

1. *Determination of budgeted fixed service costs.* The fixed service costs that should be incurred for a period need to be identified.
2. *Computation of the allocation ratio.* Using the practical or normal capacity of each producing department, it is necessary to compute an allocation ratio. The allocation ratio simply gives a producing department's percentage of total capacity of all producing departments.

   Allocation ratio = Producing department capacity/Total capacity

3. *Allocation.* The fixed service costs are allocated in proportion to each producing department's original service needs.

   Allocation = Allocation ratio × Budgeted fixed service costs

For example, assume that the budgeted fixed costs of the power department are $500,000 per year and that the practical capacities of the machining and assembly departments are 800,000 kwh and 200,000 kwh, respectively. The allocation ratio for the machining department is 0.80 (800,000/1,000,000), and the allocation ratio for the assembly department is 0.20 (200,000/1,000,000). Thus, the fixed service costs assigned to each department are as follows:

Machining: (0.8 × $500,000) = $400,000
Assembly: (0.2 × $500,000) = $100,000

Fixed Versus Variable Bases: A Note of Caution. Using normal or practical capacity to allocate fixed service costs provides a *fixed* base. As long as the capacities of the producing departments remain at the level originally anticipated, there is no reason to change the allocation ratios. Thus, each year the machining department receives 80 percent of the budgeted fixed power costs and the assembly department 20 percent no matter what their actual usage is. If the capacities of the departments change, the ratios should be recalculated.

In practice, some companies choose to allocate fixed costs in proportion to actual usage or expected actual usage. Since usage may vary from year to year, allocation of fixed costs would use a variable base. Variable bases, however, have a significant drawback: they allow the actions of one department to affect the amount of cost allocated to another department.

To see how this is so, assume that Department A and Department B each work on different products. Both departments are machine intensive, so the maintenance department exists to serve their needs. The budgeted fixed costs of

3. Practical capacity is the maximum capacity if the department operates efficiently. Normal capacity is the average capacity achieved over more than one fiscal period.

the maintenance department are allocated in proportion to the machine hours used by each producing department. The machine hours worked, the allocation ratios, the budgeted fixed costs, and the allocations for 1994 and 1995 are given in Exhibit 18-2. Notice that Department A's allocation of fixed costs increased by $16,200 from 1994 to 1995 even though the machine hours it used and the total budgeted fixed costs of the maintenance department remained unchanged. This increase is caused by a decrease in Department B's use of machine hours. Department A is being penalized because of B's drop in productive output. Imagine the feelings of the manager of Department A when he or she is told of this large increase in allocated fixed costs! The penalty occurs because a variable base is used to allocate fixed service costs; it can be avoided by using a fixed base.

METHODS OF ALLOCATING SERVICE DEPARTMENT COSTS TO PRODUCING DEPARTMENTS

Objective 4
Use the direct and sequential methods to allocate service costs.

direct method

So far, it has been assumed that service departments provide services only to producing departments. With this assumption, service costs can be allocated directly to the producing departments. This method of allocating service costs is known as the **direct method.**

For many companies, this assumption may not be realistic. When a company has multiple service departments, it is almost certain that they will interact. For example, personnel and cafeteria serve each other and other service departments as well as the producing departments.

Ignoring these interactions and allocating service costs directly to producing departments may produce unfair and inaccurate cost assignments. For example, power, although a service department, may use 30 percent of the services of the maintenance department. The maintenance costs caused by the power department belong to that department. By not assigning these costs to the power department, its costs are understated. Furthermore, a producing department that is a heavy user of power and an average or below-average user of maintenance may receive, under the direct method, a cost allocation that is also understated.

By considering service-department interactions, more accurate product costing is achieved. The result can be improved planning, control, and decision mak-

Exhibit 18-2
Variable Bases and the Allocation of Fixed Costs

	1994	1995
Machine hours worked:		
Department A	30,000	30,000
Department B	50,000	20,000
Total machine hours	80,000	50,000
Allocation ratio:		
Department A	0.375	0.60
Department B	0.625	0.40
Budgeted fixed costs	$72,000	$72,000
Allocation:		
Department A[a]	$27,000	$43,200
Department B[b]	$45,000	$28,800

[a]0.375 × $72,000; 0.60 × $72,000
[b]0.625 × $72,000; 0.40 × $72,000

ing. Two methods of allocation recognize interactions among service departments: the *sequential (or step) method* and the *reciprocal method.* These methods allocate service costs among some (or all) interacting service departments before allocating costs to the producing departments.

Using the direct method, service department cost is allocated to producing departments only. No cost from one service department is allocated to another service department. Thus, no service department interaction is recognized.

In the sequential method, service departments are usually ranked in accordance with direct costs. That is, the service department with the highest cost is ranked first, and so on. The costs of the highest-ranking service department are allocated first—to the producing departments and to lower-ranking service departments. Once the highest-ranking service-department's costs are allocated, the second highest-ranking service-department's costs are allocated—again, to lower-ranking service departments and producing departments. The costs of the lowest-ranked service department are allocated only to producing departments.

Under the reciprocal method the usage of one service department by another is calculated (using simultaneous equations), and then the new total of service department costs is allocated to the producing departments. This method fully accounts for service department interaction.

In the next two sections, the direct and sequential methods are described and illustrated. The reciprocal method is deferred to a more advanced course.

The Direct Method of Allocation

The direct method is the simplest and most straightforward method to allocate service-department costs. It allocates the costs directly to the producing departments. Variable service costs are allocated directly to producing departments in proportion to each department's usage of the service. Fixed costs are also allocated directly to the producing department, but in proportion to the producing department's normal or practical capacity.

To illustrate the direct method, consider the data in Exhibit 18-3. The data show the budgeted activity and budgeted costs of two service departments and two producing departments. (Note that the same data are used to illustrate the

Exhibit 18-3
Data for Illustrating Allocation Methods

	Service Departments		*Producing Departments*	
	Power	*Maintenance*	*Grinding*	*Assembly*
Direct costs:[1]	$250,000	$160,000	$100,000	$ 60,000
Normal activity:				
Kilowatt hours	—	200,000	600,000	200,000
Maintenance hours	1,000	—	4,500	4,500
Allocation ratios				
Direct method:				
Kilowatt hours	—	—	0.75	0.25
Maintenance hours	—	—	0.50	0.50
Sequential method:				
Kilowatt hours	—	0.20	0.60	0.20
Maintenance hours	—	—	0.50	0.50

[1]For a producing department, direct costs refer only to overhead costs that are directly traceable to the department.

sequential method; for the time being, ignore the allocation ratios at the bottom of Exhibit 18-3 that correspond to the sequential method.)

Assume that the causal factor for power costs is kilowatt hours, and the causal factor for maintenance costs is maintenance hours. These causal factors are used as the basis for allocation. In the direct method, only the kilowatt hours and the maintenance hours in the producing departments are used to compute the allocation ratios. The direct allocations based on the data given in Exhibit 18-3 are shown in Exhibit 18-4. (To simplify the illustration, no distinction is made between fixed and variable costs.)

The Sequential Method of Allocation

sequential (or step) method

The **sequential (or step) method** of allocation recognizes that interactions among the service departments occur. However, the sequential method does not fully recognize service-department interaction. Cost allocations are performed sequentially, following a predetermined ranking procedure. Usually, the sequence is defined by ranking the service departments in order of the service rendered, from the greatest to the least. Degree of service is usually measured by the direct costs of each service department; the department with the highest cost is seen as rendering the greatest service.

The costs of the service department rendering the greatest service are allocated first. They are distributed to all service departments below it in the sequence and to all producing departments. Then, the costs of the service department next in sequence are similarly allocated, and so on. In the sequential method, once a service department's costs are allocated, it never receives a subsequent allocation from another service department. In other words, costs of a service department are never allocated to service departments *above* it in the sequence. Also, note that the costs allocated from a service department are its direct costs *plus* any costs it receives in allocations from other service departments. The direct costs of a department, of course, are those that are directly traceable to the department.

To illustrate the sequential method, consider the data provided in Exhibit 18-3. Using cost as a measure of service, the service department rendering more service is power. Thus, its costs will be allocated first, followed by those for maintenance. The allocation ratios shown in Exhibit 18-3 will be used to execute the allocation. Note that the allocation ratios for the maintenance department ignore the usage by the power department since its costs cannot be allocated to a service department above it in the allocation sequence.

Exhibit 18-4
Direct Allocation Illustrated

	Service Departments		*Producing Departments*	
	Power	*Maintenance*	*Grinding*	*Assembly*
Direct costs	$ 250,000	$ 160,000	$100,000	$ 60,000
Power[1]	(250,000)	—	187,500	62,500
Maintenance[2]	—	(160,000)	80,000	80,000
	$ 0	$ 0	$367,500	$202,500

[1]Allocation of power based on ratios from Exhibit 18-3: 0.75 × $250,000; 0.25 × $250,000.
[2]Allocation of maintenance based on ratios from Exhibit 18-3: 0.50 × $160,000; 0.50 × $160,000.

The allocations obtained with the sequential method are shown in Exhibit 18-5. Notice that $50,000 of the power department's costs are allocated to the maintenance department. This reflects the fact that the maintenance department uses 20 percent of the power department's output. As a result, the cost of operating the maintenance department increases from $160,000 to $210,000. Also notice that when the costs of the maintenance department are allocated, no costs are allocated back to the power department, even though it uses 1,000 hours of the output of the maintenance department.

The sequential method is more accurate than the direct method because it recognizes some interactions among the service departments. It does not recognize all interactions; no maintenance costs were assigned to the power department even though it used 10 percent of the maintenance department's output. Use of the reciprocal method would correct this deficiency.

Departmental Overhead Rates and Product Costing

Upon allocating all service costs to producing departments, an overhead rate can be computed for each department. This rate assigns the service costs to the products of the department. It is computed by adding the allocated service costs to the overhead costs that are traceable directly to the producing department and dividing this total by some measure of activity, such as direct labor hours or machine hours.

For example, from Exhibit 18-5, the total overhead costs for the grinding department after allocation of service costs are $355,000. Assume that machine hours are the base for assigning overhead costs to products passing through the grinding department and the normal level of activity is 71,000 machine hours. The overhead rate for the grinding department is computed as follows:

Overhead rate = $355,000/71,000 machine hours
= $5 per machine hour

Similarly, assume that the assembly department uses direct labor hours to assign its overhead. With a normal level of activity of 107,500 direct labor hours, the overhead rate for the assembly department is as follows:

Overhead rate = $215,000/107,500 direct labor hours
= $2 per direct labor hour

Using these rates, the product's unit cost can be determined. To illustrate, suppose a product requires two machine hours of grinding per unit produced and one hour of assembly. The overhead cost assigned to one unit of this product

Exhibit 18-5
Sequential Allocation Illustrated

	Service Departments		*Producing Departments*	
	Power	*Maintenance*	*Grinding*	*Assembly*
Direct costs	$ 250,000	$ 160,000	$100,000	$ 60,000
Power[1]	(250,000)	50,000	150,000	50,000
Maintenance[2]	—	(210,000)	105,000	105,000
	$ 0	$ 0	$355,000	$215,000

[1]Allocation of power based on ratios from Exhibit 18-3: 0.2 × $250,000; 0.6 × $250,000; 0.2 × $250,000.
[2]Allocation of maintenance costs based on ratios from Exhibit 18-3: 0.50 × $210,000; 0.50 × $210,000.

would be \$12 [(2 × \$5) + (1 × \$2)]. If the same product uses \$15 of materials and \$6 of labor, its unit cost is \$33 (\$12 + \$15 + \$6).

One might wonder, however, just how accurate is this \$33 cost. Is this really what it costs to produce the product in question? Since materials and labor are traceable directly to products, the accuracy of product costs depends largely on the accuracy of the assignment of overhead costs. This, in turn, depends on the degree of correlation between the factors used to allocate service costs to departments and the factors used to allocate the department's overhead costs to the products. For example, if power costs are highly correlated with kilowatt hours and machine hours are highly correlated with a product's consumption of the grinding department's overhead costs, we can have some confidence that the \$5 overhead rate accurately assigns costs to individual products. However, if the allocation of service costs to the grinding department or the use of machine hours is faulty—or both—product costs will be distorted. The same reasoning can be applied to the assembly department. To ensure accurate product costs, great care should be used in identifying and using causal factors for both stages of overhead assignment. More will be said about this in a later chapter.

SUMMARY OF LEARNING OBJECTIVES

1. *Describe the difference between service departments and producing departments.* Producing departments create the product(s) that the firm is in business to manufacture and sell. Service departments provide support for the producing departments but do not themselves build components of product.

2. *Explain why service costs are allocated to producing departments.* Because service departments exist to support a variety of producing departments, the costs of the service departments are common to all producing departments and must be allocated to them to satisfy a number of important objectives. These objectives include inventory valuation, product-line profitability, pricing, and planning and control. Allocation can also be used to encourage favorable managerial behavior.

3. *Describe the basic guidelines for allocating service costs.* There are three basic guidelines: (1) Use of causal factors, (2) allocation of budgeted costs, and (3) allocation by cost behavior. Managers should attempt to identify those factors that cause service costs to be incurred because product costs can be more accurately determined. Furthermore, accurate identification of causal factors can help managers control costs. Budgeted, not actual costs, should be allocated so that the efficiencies or inefficiencies of the service departments themselves are not passed on to the producing departments. Because the causal factors can differ for fixed and variable costs, these types of cost should be allocated separately. Fixed costs should be allocated on the basis of the normal or practical activity of each producing department. Variable costs should be allocated on the basis of the department's usage of the service.

4. *Use the direct and sequential methods to allocate service costs.* Under the direct method, the percentage of usage of each service center by the producing departments is calculated. Then service-center costs are allocated to producing departments according to their percentage of usage. Under the sequential method, the service department rendering the greatest service is listed first and the department rendering the least service last. Costs of the first service center are allocated to lower-ranking service departments and to producing departments, based on percentage usage. The next highest-ranking service-department's costs (the sum of its direct costs plus those received from the first service department) are then allocated to lower-ranking service departments and to producing departments. The lowest-ranking service-department's costs are allocated only to producing departments.

KEY TERMS

Causal factors *847*
Direct method *851*
Producing departments *844*
Sequential (or step) method *853*
Service departments *844*

REVIEW PROBLEM

Clearfield Manufacturing produces machine parts on a job-order basis. Most business is obtained through bidding. Most firms competing with Clearfield bid full cost plus a 20 percent markup. Recently, with the expectation of gaining more sales, Clearfield reduced its markup from 25 percent to 20 percent. The company operates two service departments and two producing departments. The budgeted costs and the normal activity levels for each department are given below.

	Service Departments		*Producing Departments*	
	A	*B*	*C*	*D*
Overhead costs	$100,000	$200,000	$100,000	$50,000
Number of employees	8	7	30	30
Maintenance hours	2,000	200	6,400	1,600
Machine hours	—	—	10,000	1,000
Labor hours	—	—	1,000	10,000

The direct costs of Department A are allocated on the basis of employees, those of Department B on the basis of maintenance hours. Departmental overhead rates are used to assign costs to products. Department C uses machine hours, and Department D uses labor hours.

The firm is preparing to bid on a job (Job K) that requires three machine hours per unit produced in Department C and no time in Department D. The expected prime costs per unit are $67.

REQUIRED:

1. Allocate the service costs to the producing departments using the direct method.
2. What will the bid be for Job K if the direct method of allocation is used?
3. Allocate the service costs to the producing departments using the sequential method.
4. What will the bid be for Job K if the sequential method is used?

Solution:

1.

	Service Departments		*Producing Departments*	
	A	*B*	*C*	*D*
Direct costs	$100,000	$200,000	$100,000	$ 50,000
Department A	(100,000)	—	50,000	50,000
Department B	—	(200,000)	160,000	40,000
Total	$ 0	$ 0	$310,000	$140,000

2. Department C: Overhead rate = $310,000/10,000 = $31 per machine hour. Product cost and bid price are:

Overhead (3 × $31)	$ 93
Prime cost	67
Total unit cost	$160
Bid price ($160 × 1.2)	$192

3.

	Service Departments		*Producing Departments*	
	A	B	C	*D*
Direct costs	$100,000	$200,000	$100,000	$ 50,000
Department B	40,000	(200,000)	128,000	32,000
Department A	(140,000)	—	70,000	70,000
Total	$ 0	0	$298,000	$152,000

4. Department C: Overhead rate = $298,000/10,000 = $29.80 per machine hour. Product cost and bid price are:

Overhead (3 × $29.80)	$ 89.40
Prime cost	67.00
Total unit cost	$156.40
Bid price ($156.40 × 1.2)	$187.68

QUESTIONS

1. Describe the two-stage allocation process for assigning service costs to products in a traditional manufacturing environment.
2. Explain how allocating service costs can be helpful in pricing decisions.
3. Why must service costs be assigned to products for purposes of inventory valuation?
4. Explain how allocation of service costs is useful for planning and control.
5. Assume that a company has decided not to allocate any service costs to producing departments. Describe the likely behavior of the managers of the producing departments. Would this be good or bad? Explain why allocation would correct this type of behavior.
6. Explain how allocating service costs will encourage service departments to operate more efficiently.
7. Why is it important to identify and use causal factors to allocate service costs?
8. Identify some possible causal factors for the following service departments:
   a. Cafeteria
   b. Custodial services
   c. Laundry
   d. Receiving, shipping, and stores
   e. Maintenance
   f. Personnel
   g. Accounting
9. Explain why it is better to allocate budgeted service costs rather than actual service costs.
10. Why is it desirable to allocate variable costs and fixed costs separately?
11. Explain why either normal or practical capacity of the producing (or user) departments should be used to allocate the fixed costs of service departments.
12. Explain why variable bases should not be used to allocate fixed costs.
13. The personnel department has total variable costs of $20,000 and serves two producing departments, one with 100 employees and the other with 300. Using employees as the allocation base, allocate the costs of the personnel department to the producing departments using the direct method.
14. Explain the difference between the direct method and the sequential method.

EXERCISES

E18-1
Classifying Departments as Producing or Service
LO 1

Classify each of the following departments in a factory as a producing department or a service department.

a. Assembly
b. Payroll
c. Cafeteria
d. General factory
e. Maintenance
f. Machining
g. Inspection
h. Blending
i. Finishing
j. Personnel
k. Grounds
l. Data processing
m. Packaging
n. Cutting
o. Engineering

E18-2
Identifying Causal Factors
LO 3

For the following service departments, identify one or more causal factors that might be useful for service-department cost allocation purposes.

a. Supervision
b. Data processing
c. Quality control
d. Purchasing
e. Receiving
f. Shipping
g. Vending (stocking snack machines throughout the plant)
h. Grounds
i. Building depreciation
j. Power and light
k. Employee benefits
l. Housekeeping
m. Equipment repair
n. Heating and cooling

E18-3
Actual versus Budgeted Costs
LO 2, 3, 4

Bartlett Manufacturing Company evaluates managers of producing departments on their ability to control costs. In addition to the costs directly traceable to their departments, each production manager is held responsible for a share of the costs of a service center, the maintenance department. The total costs of the maintenance department are allocated on the basis of actual maintenance hours used. The total costs of maintenance and the actual hours used by each producing department are given below.

	1994	*1995*
Maintenance hours used:		
Department A	2,000	2,000
Department B	3,000	2,000
Total hours	5,000	4,000
Actual maintenance cost	$100,000	$100,000
Budgeted maintenance cost	$ 90,000[a]	$ 80,000[a]

[a]$10 per maintenance hour plus $40,000.

REQUIRED:

1. Allocate the maintenance cost to each producing department for 1994 and 1995 using the direct method with actual maintenance hours and actual maintenance costs.
2. Discuss the following statement: "The costs of maintenance increased by 25 percent for Department A and decreased by more than 16 percent for Department B. Thus, the manager of Department B is controlling maintenance costs better than the manager of Department A."
3. Can you think of a way to allocate maintenance costs so that a more reasonable and fairer assessment of cost control can be made? Explain.

E18-4
Fixed and Variable Cost Allocation
LO 2, 3, 4

Refer to the data in Exercise 18-3. When the capacity of the maintenance department was originally established, the normal usage expected for each department was 2,000 maintenance hours. This usage is also the amount of activity planned for the two departments in 1994 and 1995.

REQUIRED:

1. Allocate the costs of the maintenance department using the direct method assuming that the purpose is product costing.
2. Allocate the costs of the maintenance department using the direct method assuming that the purpose is to evaluate performance.

E18-5
Direct Method and Overhead Rates
LO 2, 4

Finlither Company manufactures men's and women's shoes, with each type of shoe produced in separate departments. Three service departments support the production departments: maintenance, building and grounds, and food services. Budgeted data on the five departments are as follows:

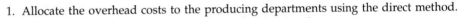

	Service Departments			*Producing Departments*	
	Maintenance	*Grounds*	*Food*	*Men's*	*Women's*
Overhead	$30,000	$70,000	$50,000	$20,000	$30,000
Number of employees	5	2	3	15	25
Square feet	2,000	—	3,000	5,000	10,000
Machine hours	—	—	—	2,000	3,000

The company does not break overhead into fixed and variable components.

REQUIRED:

1. Allocate the overhead costs to the producing departments using the direct method.
2. Using machine hours, compute departmental overhead rates.

E18-6
Sequential Method
LO 4

Refer to the data in Exercise 18-5. The company has decided to use the sequential method of allocation instead of the direct method.

REQUIRED:

1. Allocate the overhead costs to the producing departments using the sequential method.
2. Using machine hours, compute departmental overhead rates.

E18-7
Allocation; Fixed and Variable Costs
LO 2, 3

Thummer Temporary Employment Agency has two Texas offices, one in Dallas and the other in Austin. The owner of the agency purchased a minicomputer and established a computer service center located in Dallas. The Austin office was also hooked up with the computer via modem. The computer service center has budgeted fixed costs of $85,000 per year and a budgeted variable rate of $20 per hour of CPU time. The normal usage of the computer is 1,500 hours per year for the Dallas office and 1,200 hours per year for the Austin office. This corresponds to the expected usage for the coming year.

REQUIRED:

1. Determine the amount of computer service costs that should be assigned to each office.
2. Since the offices produce services, not tangible products, what purpose is served by allocating the budgeted costs? Should each office compute a predetermined overhead rate? If so, how would you use this rate?

E18-8
Allocation; Budgeted Fixed and Variable Costs
LO 2, 3

Refer to Exercise 18-7. Assume that during the year, the computer service center incurred actual fixed costs of $90,000 and actual variable costs of $62,350; it delivered 3,000 hours of CPU time, 1,600 hours to Muncie and 1,400 to Austin.

REQUIRED:

1. Determine the amount of the service center's costs that should be allocated to each office. Explain the purposes of this allocation.
2. Did the costs allocated differ from the costs incurred by the service center? If so, explain why.

E18-9
Fixed Cost Allocation; Variable Base
LO 2, 3

Restum Hotels are located throughout the Southwest. The central office's fixed administrative expenses are allocated to each hotel in proportion to the unit's revenues. In 1994, the total administrative expenses were $3.5 million. In 1995, this total increased to $4 million. The hotel chain had $100 million in revenues in 1994 and 1995. The hotel with the greatest proportion of revenues was located in Phoenix, Arizona. This hotel's revenues were $10 million in 1994 and $15 million in 1995.

REQUIRED:

1. Compute the amount of fixed administrative expenses allocated to the Phoenix hotel in 1994.
2. Compute the amount of fixed administrative expenses allocated to the Phoenix hotel in 1995.
3. Compare the 1994 and 1995 allocations for the Phoenix hotel. Explain why the allocation increased.
4. Assume that you are the manager of the Phoenix hotel and that your annual bonus is a function of net income, the computation of which includes the allocated fixed administrative expenses. How would you react to Restum's allocation method? Can you recommend a better method of allocation?

E18-10
Direct Method; Overhead Rates
LO 4

Carroll Publishing Company prints religious music. There are two producing departments (printing and binding) and two service departments (cafeteria and general factory). Budgeted data for the four departments are as follows:

	Service Departments		*Producing Departments*	
	Cafeteria	*General Factory*	*Printing*	*Binding*
Overhead before allocation	$20,000	$100,000	$40,000	$60,000
Employees	—	10	10	40
Square feet	2,000	—	1,500	4,500
Direct labor hours	10,000	32,000	20,000	80,000

Cafeteria costs are allocated on the basis of number of employees; general factory costs are allocated on the basis of square feet.

REQUIRED:

1. Allocate overhead costs to producing departments using the direct method.
2. Using direct labor hours, compute departmental overhead rates.

E18-11
Sequential Method; Overhead Rates
LO 4

Refer to the data in Exercise 18-10. Assume Carroll Publishing Company decides to use the sequential method.

REQUIRED:

1. Allocate overhead costs to producing departments using the sequential method.
2. Using direct labor hours, compute departmental overhead rates.

E18-12
Allocation; Fixed and Variable Costs
LO 2, 3

Walters Company is a medium-sized advertising firm on the west coast. Walters has three departments that specialize in advertising and public relations services for different markets: tangible goods, nonprofit organizations, and public relations. Previously, Walters had subcontracted out necessary printing and graphics work. However, recent technological advances in desktop publishing led to the formation of a new in-house graphics department that could produce brochures, booklets, posters, etc. The tangible goods and public relations departments immediately began to use the new graphics services. However, Carla Wilson, head of nonprofit organizations, was reluctant to switch her department from its traditional outside supplier. Top management strongly supported the new service department, and had encouraged all departments "to get on board" with graphics. Paul Murphy, the head of graphics, assured Carla Wilson that graphics could serve her departmental needs by spending an additional $2,000 above total 1994 costs. So during 1995, Carla switched her department's graphics work to the in-house department.

Data for the graphics department are as follows:

	1994	*1995*
Actual costs	$12,000	$14,000
Direct labor hours used by:		
Tangible goods	2,000	2,000
Public relations	2,000	2,000
Nonprofit organizations	—	1,000

Actual costs equaled budgeted costs in both 1994 and 1995. Graphics services are charged to user departments on the basis of actual cost per hour of graphics time used.

REQUIRED:

1. What was the graphics rate per hour charged in 1994? In 1995?
2. How much was the nonprofit organization department charged for graphics services in 1995? How do you think Carla Wilson reacted to the charges?
3. How can you reconcile the difference between the rate charged Carla Wilson during 1995 and the $2,000 incremental cost cited by Paul Murphy?

PROBLEMS

P18-1
Direct Method; Variable versus Fixed; Costing and Performance Evaluation
LO 2, 3, 4

AirBorne is a small airline operating out of Boise, Idaho. Its three flights travel to Reno, Salt Lake City, and Portland. The owner of the airline wants to assess the full cost of operating each flight. As part of this assessment, the costs of two service departments (baggage and maintenance) must be allocated to the three flights. The two service departments that support all three flights are located in Boise (any baggage or maintenance costs at the destination airports are traceable directly to the individual flights). Budgeted and actual data for 1994 are as follows for the service departments and the three flights:

	Service Departments		*Flights*		
	Maintenance	*Baggage*	*Salt Lake*	*Reno*	*Portland*
Budgeted data:					
Fixed overhead	$240,000	$150,000	$20,000	$18,000	$30,000
Variable overhead	$ 30,000	$ 64,000	$ 5,000	$10,000	$ 6,000
Number of passengers[1]	—	—	10,000	15,000	5,000
Hours of flight time[1]	—	—	2,000	4,000	2,000

[1]Normal activity levels

(continued)

	Service Departments		Flights		
	Maintenance	Baggage	Salt Lake	Reno	Portland
Actual data:					
Fixed overhead	$235,000	$156,000	$22,000	$17,000	$29,500
Variable overhead	$ 80,000	$ 33,000	$ 6,200	$11,000	$ 5,800
Number of passengers	—	—	8,000	16,000	6,000
Hours of flight time	—	—	1,800	4,200	2,500

REQUIRED:

1. Using the direct method, allocate the service costs to each flight assuming the objective is to determine the cost of operating each flight.
2. Using the direct method, allocate the service costs to each flight assuming the objective is to evaluate performance. Do any costs remain in the two service departments after the allocation? If so, how much? Explain.

P18-2
Comparison of Methods of Allocation
LO 4

Paulos Trucking is divided into two operating divisions: Perishable Foods (PF) and Household Goods (HG). The company allocates personnel and accounting costs to each operating division. Personnel costs are allocated on the basis of employees and accounting costs on the basis of the number of transactions processed. No effort is made to separate fixed and variable costs; however, only budgeted costs are allocated. Allocations for the coming year are based on the following data:

	Service Departments		Operating Divisions	
	Personnel	Accounting	PF	HG
Overhead costs	$100,000	$205,000	$80,000	$50,000
Number of employees	20	60	60	80
Transactions processed	2,000	200	3,000	5,000

REQUIRED:

1. Allocate the service costs using the direct method.
2. Allocate the service costs using the sequential method.

P18-3
Comparison of Methods of Allocation
LO 4

Kare Foods Company specializes in the production of frozen dinners. The first of the two operating departments cooks the food. The second is responsible for packaging and freezing the dinners. The dinners are sold by the case, each case containing 25 dinners.

Two service departments provide support for Kare's operating units: maintenance and power. Budgeted data for the coming quarter are given below. The company does not separate fixed and variable costs.

	Service Departments		Producing Departments	
	Maintenance	Power	Cooking	Packing and Freezing
Overhead costs	$340,000	$200,000	$ 75,000	$55,000
Machine hours	—	40,000	40,000	20,000
Kilowatt hours	20,000	—	100,000	80,000
Direct labor hours	—	—	5,000	30,000

The predetermined overhead rate for cooking is computed on the basis of machine hours; direct labor hours are used for packing and freezing. The prime costs for one case of standard dinners total $16. It takes two machine hours to produce a case of dinners in the cooking department and 0.5 direct labor hours to process a case of standard dinners in the packing and freezing department.

Recently, the Air Force has requested a bid on a three-year contract that would supply standard frozen dinners to Minuteman Missile officers and staff on duty in the field. The locations of the missile sites are remote, and the Air Force has decided that frozen dinners are the most economical means of supplying food to personnel on duty.

Kare Foods Company policy is to bid full manufacturing cost plus 20 percent. Assume that the lowest bid of other competitors is $48.80 per case.

REQUIRED:

1. Prepare bids for Kare Foods Company using each of the following allocation methods:
   a. Direct method
   b. Sequential method
2. Refer to Requirement 1. Did both of the methods produce winning bids? If not, explain why. Which method more accurately reflects the cost of producing the cases of dinners? Why?

P18-4
Predetermined Rates; Allocation for Performance Evaluation
LO 2, 3

Morsley Company operates three vehicle rental divisions: Budget, Luxury, and Trucks. The Budget Division specializes in renting compact and subcompact cars; the Luxury Division specializes in renting large luxury cars and vans; and the Truck Division rents pickups and small enclosed trucks for local moving.

Morsley has one service center, which is responsible for the service, maintenance, and cleanup of its fleet of vehicles. The costs of this service center are allocated to each operating unit on the basis of total miles driven. During the first quarter, the service center was expected to spend a total of $40,000. Of this total, $16,000 was viewed as being fixed. During the quarter, the service center incurred actual variable costs of $30,000 and actual fixed costs of $17,100. The normal and actual miles logged for each rental unit during the first quarter are as follows:

	Budget	*Luxury*	*Truck*
Normal activity	120,000	100,000	80,000
Actual activity	150,000	110,000	100,000

REQUIRED:

1. Compute the predetermined service cost per mile driven.
2. Compute the costs that would be allocated at the end of the quarter for purposes of performance evaluation.
3. Identify the costs of the service center that were not allocated to the three rental divisions. Why were these costs not allocated to the operating units?

P18-5
Sequential and Direct Methods
LO 3, 4

Lilly Candies has three producing departments, mixing, cooking, and packaging, and five service departments. The following is the basic information on all departments (bases represent practical annual levels):

	Number of Items Processed	*Number of Employees*	*Square Feet Occupied*	*Machine Hours*	*Labor Hours*
Cafeteria	300	5	5,000	—	—
Personnel	1,000	10	7,000	—	—
Custodial Services	200	7	2,000	—	—
Maintenance	2,500	15	16,000	—	—
Cost accounting	—	13	5,000	—	—
Mixing	2,800	20	40,000	4,000	30,000
Cooking	2,700	10	30,000	10,000	20,000
Packaging	3,000	20	20,000	6,000	50,000
Total	12,500	100	125,000	20,000	100,000

The budgeted overhead costs for the departments are as follows for the coming year:

	Fixed	*Variable*	*Total*
Cafeteria	$ 20,000	$ 40,000	$ 60,000
Personnel	70,000	20,000	90,000
Custodial services	80,000	—	80,000
Maintenance	100,000	100,000	200,000
Cost accounting	130,000	16,500	146,500
Mixing	120,000	20,000	140,000
Cooking	60,000	10,000	70,000
Packaging	25,000	40,000	65,000

REQUIRED:

1. Allocate the service costs to the producing departments using the direct method.
2. Compute a predetermined fixed overhead rate and a predetermined variable overhead rate. Assume that overhead is applied using direct labor hours for mixing and packaging and machine hours for cooking.
3. Allocate the service costs to the producing departments using the sequential method. (*Hint*: Allocate fixed costs in order of descending magnitude of direct fixed costs. Allocate variable costs in order of descending magnitude of direct variable costs.)
4. Compute predetermined fixed and variable overhead rates based on Requirement 3. Overhead is applied using direct labor hours for mixing and packaging and machine hours for cooking.
5. Assume that the prime costs for a batch of chocolate bars total $60,000. The batch requires 1,000 direct labor hours in mixing, 1,500 machine hours in cooking, and 5,000 direct labor hours in packaging. Assume that the selling price is equal to full manufacturing cost plus 30 percent. Compute the selling price of the batch assuming that costs are allocated using the direct method. Repeat using the sequential method. Comment on the implications of using different allocation methods, assuming that a markup of 30 percent is typical for the industry. Which allocation method do you think should be used?

P18-6
Direct Method; Sequential Method; Overhead Rates
LO 2, 4

Bright, Inc., has two producing departments and four service departments. It currently uses the direct method of service-department cost allocation. Data for the company are as follows:

	Producing Departments		*Service Departments*			
	PD1	*PD2*	*SD1*	*SD2*	*SD3*	*SD4*
Overhead	$183,000	$212,400	$30,000	$35,000	$40,000	$100,000
Square feet	2,000	2,000	400	5,000	600	—
Employees	15	45	—	12	20	3
Direct labor hours	30,000	90,000	—	24,000	20,000	6,000
Machine hours	10,000	20,000	—	—	—	—

Original Allocation Base:

SD1	Machine hours
SD2	Number of employees
SD3	Direct labor hours
SD4	Square feet

Cara James, controller of Bright, Inc., is considering changing to a more accurate method of service department cost allocation. She has discovered the following:

a. SD1 provides its services only to the producing departments.
b. SD2 provides services to both producing and service departments based on the number of employees.
c. SD3 provides 15 percent of its service to SD1 and the remainder to PD1 and PD2 based on direct labor hours.
d. SD4 provides services to all other departments based on square footage.

Cara has decided to rank the service departments in the following order for purposes of cost allocation: SD4, SD2, SD3, SD1.

REQUIRED:

1. Allocate service department costs using the direct method and the original allocation bases.
2. Allocate service department costs using the sequential method as outlined by Cara James.
3. Calculate overhead rates for PD1 (based on machine hours) and PD2 (based on direct labor hours) using total departmental overhead costs as determined by the:
   a. Direct method
   b. Sequential method

P18-7
Fixed and Variable Cost Allocation
LO 2, 3

Sonora Sam's is a chain of restaurants serving Sonora-style Mexican food in a family-type atmosphere. The chain has grown from one restaurant in 1989 to five restaurants located in Texas and New Mexico. In 1995, the owner of the company decided to set up an internal accounting department to centralize control of financial information. (Previously, local CPAs handled each restaurant's bookkeeping and financial reporting.) The accounting department was opened in January 1995 by renting space adjacent to corporate headquarters in Albuquerque, New Mexico. All restaurants have been supplied with personal computers and modems by which to transfer information to central accounting on a weekly basis.

The accounting department has budgeted fixed costs of $64,000 per year. Variable costs are budgeted at $18 per hour. Actual costs in 1995 equaled budgeted costs. Further information is as follows:

	Actual Revenues		*Actual Hours of Accounting Used in 1995*
	1994	*1995*	
El Paso	$337,500	$390,500	1,475
Albuquerque	450,000	456,000	400
Taos	360,000	375,000	938
Tucumcari	540,000	550,000	562
Amarillo	562,500	549,000	375

REQUIRED:

1. Suppose the total costs of the accounting department are allocated on the basis of 1995 sales revenue. How much will be allocated to each restaurant?
2. Suppose that Sonora Sam's views 1994 sales figures as a proxy for budgeted capacity of the restaurants. Thus, fixed accounting center costs are allocated on the basis of 1994 sales, and variable costs are allocated according to 1995 usage times the variable rate. How much accounting department cost will be allocated to each restaurant?
3. Comment on the two allocation schemes. Which is better? Explain.

P18-8 Service Department Cost Allocation; Plant-wide Overhead Rate versus Departmental Rates; Effects on Pricing Decisions
LO 2, 3, 4

Alden Peterson, marketing manager for Retlief Company, is puzzled by the outcome of two recent bids. The company's policy was to bid 150 percent of the full manufacturing cost. One job (labeled Job SS) had been turned down by a prospective customer, who had indicated that the proposed price was $3 per unit higher than the winning bid. A second job (Job TT) had been accepted by a customer, who was amazed that Retlief could offer such favorable terms. This customer revealed that Retlief's price was $43 per unit lower than the next lowest bid.

Alden knew that Retlief Company was more than competitive in terms of cost control. Accordingly, he suspected that the problem was related to cost assignment procedures. Upon investigating, Alden was told that the company used a plant-wide overhead rate based on direct labor hours. The rate was computed at the beginning of the year using budgeted data. Selected budgeted data follow:

	Department A	*Department B*	*Total*
Overhead	$500,000	$2,000,000	$2,500,000
Direct labor hours	200,000	50,000	250,000
Machine hours	20,000	120,000	140,000

The above information led to a plant-wide overhead rate of $10 per direct labor hour. In addition, the following specific manufacturing data on Job SS and Job TT were given.

Job SS

	Department A	*Department B*	*Total*
Direct labor hours	5,000	1,000	6,000
Machine hours	200	500	700
Prime costs	$100,000	$20,000	$120,000
Units produced	14,400	14,400	14,400

Job TT

	Department A	*Department B*	*Total*
Direct labor hours	400	600	1,000
Machine hours	200	3,000	3,200
Prime costs	$10,000	$40,000	$50,000
Units produced	1,500	1,500	1,500

This information led to the original bid prices of $18.75 per unit for Job SS and $60 per unit for Job TT.

Then Alden discovered that the overhead costs in Department B were higher than those of Department A because B has more equipment, higher maintenance, higher power consumption, higher depreciation, and higher setup costs. So he tried reworking the two bids by using departmental overhead rates. Department A's overhead rate was $2.50 per direct labor hour; Department B's overhead rate was $16.67 per machine hour. These rates resulted in unit prices of $14.67 for Job SS and $101.01 for Job TT.

Alden still was not satisfied, however. He did some reading on overhead allocation methods and learned that proper service-department cost allocation can lead to more accurate product costs. He decided to create four service departments and recalculate departmental overhead rates. Information on departmental costs and related items follows:

	Maintenance	*Power*	*Setups*	*General Factory*	*Dept. A*	*Dept. B*
Overhead	$500,000	$225,000	$150,000	$625,000	$200,000	$800,000
Maintenance hours	—	1,500	500	—	1,000	7,000
Kilowatt hours	4,500	—	500	15,000	10,000	50,000
Direct labor hours	10,000	12,000	6,000	8,000	200,000	50,000
Number of setups	—	—	—	—	40	160
Square feet	25,000	40,000	5,000	15,000	35,360	94,640

The following allocation bases (cost drivers) seemed reasonable:

Service Department	*Allocation Base*
Maintenance	Maintenance hours
Power	Kilowatt hours
Setups	Number of setups
General Factory	Square feet

REQUIRED

1. Using the direct method, verify the original departmental overhead rates.
2. Using the sequential method, allocate service department costs to the producing departments. Calculate departmental overhead rates using direct labor hours for Department A and machine hours for Department B. What would the bids for Job SS and Job TT have been if these overhead rates had been in effect?
3. Which method of overhead cost assignment would you recommend to Alden? Why?
4. Suppose that the best competing bid was $4.10 lower than the original bid price (based on a plant-wide rate). Does this affect your recommendation in Requirement 3? Explain.

DISCUSSION AND INTERPRETATION PROBLEMS

D18-1
Allocation; Pricing; Ethical Behavior

Emma Hanks, manager of a division that produces valves and castings on a special order basis, was excited about an order received from a new customer. The customer, a personal friend of Bob Johnson (Emma's supervisor), had placed an order for 10,000 valves. The customer agreed to pay full manufacturing cost plus 25 percent. The order was timely since business was sluggish, and Emma had some concerns about her division's ability to meet its targeted profits. Even with the order, the division would likely fall short in meeting the target by at least $50,000. After examining the cost sheet for the order, however, Emma thought she saw a way to increase the profitability of the job. Accordingly, she called Larry Smith, CMA, the controller of the division.

Emma: "Larry, this cost sheet for the new order reflects an allocation of maintenance costs to the grinding department based on maintenance hours used. Currently, 60 percent of our maintenance costs are allocated to grinding on that basis. Can you tell me what the allocation ratio would be if we used machine hours instead of maintenance hours?"

Larry: "Sure. Based on machine hours, the allocation ratio would increase from 60 percent to 80 percent."

Emma: "Excellent. Now tell me what would happen to the unit cost of this new job if we used machine hours to allocate maintenance costs."

Larry: "Hold on. That'll take a few minutes. . . . The cost would increase by $10 per unit."

Emma: "And with the 25 percent markup, the revenues on that job would jump by $12.50 per unit. That would increase the profitability of the division by $125,000. Larry, I want you to change the allocation base from maintenance hours worked to machine hours."

Larry: "Are you sure? After all, if you recall, we spent some time assessing the causal relationships, and we found that maintenance hours reflect the consumption of maintenance cost much better than machine hours. I'm not sure that would be a fair cost assignment. We've used this base for years now."

Emma: "Listen, Larry, allocations are arbitrary anyway. Changing the allocation base for this new job will increase its profitability and allow us to meet our targeted profit goals for the year. If we meet or beat those goals, we'll be more likely to get the capital we need to acquire some new equipment. Furthermore, by beating the targeted profit, we'll get our share of the bonus pool. Besides, this new customer has a prosperous business and can easily afford to pay somewhat more for this order."

REQUIRED:

1. Evaluate Emma's position. Do you agree with her reasoning? Explain. What should Emma do?
2. If you were the controller, what would you do? Do any of the standards for ethical conduct for management accountants apply to the controller (see Exhibit 1-3, p. 14)? Explain.
3. Suppose Larry refused to change the allocation scheme. Then, Emma issued the following ultimatum: "Either change the allocation or look for another job!" Then, Larry made an appointment with Bob Johnson and disclosed the entire affair. Suppose, however, Bob was not sympathetic. He advised Larry to do as Emma had requested, arguing that the request represented good business sense. What should Larry do?
4. Refer to Requirement 3. Larry decided that he cannot comply with the request to change the allocation scheme. Appeals to higher-level officials have been in vain. Angered, Larry submitted his resignation and called the new customer affected by the cost reassignment. In his phone conversation, Larry revealed Emma's plans to increase the job's costs in order to improve the division's profits. The new customer expressed her gratitude and promptly canceled her order for 10,000 valves. Evaluate Larry's actions. Should he have informed the customer about Emma's intent? Explain.

D18-2 Hospital Setting; Allocation Methods; Unit Cost Determination and Pricing Decisions

Reread the scenario at the beginning of the chapter. As Eric Rose mentally reviewed his meeting with Paula, he realized that the failure of bids could be attributable to inaccurate cost assignments. Because of this possibility, Eric decided to do some additional investigation to see whether the cost-to-charges ratio method of costing services was responsible.

Eric pulled the current year's budgeted data from his files. He found the data presented below. The number of departments and the budget have been reduced for purposes of simplification.

	Service Departments			*Revenue Departments*	
	Administrative	*Laundry*	*Janitorial*	*Laboratory*	*Nursing*
Overhead	$20,000	$75,000	$50,000	$43,000	$150,000
Square feet	1,000	1,200	500	5,000	20,000
Pounds of laundry	50	200	400	1,000	4,000
Employees	1	4	7	8	20

Service department costs are allocated using the direct method.

Eric decided to compute the costs of three different lab tests using the cost-to-charges ratio, and then, as Paula suggested, recompute them using a more direct method. By comparing the unit costs under each approach, he could evaluate the cost-estimating ability of the cost-to-charges ratio. The three tests selected for study were the blood count test (Test B), cholesterol test (Test C), and a chemical blood analysis (Test CB).

After careful observation of the three tests, Eric concluded that the consumption of the resources of the laboratory could be associated with the relative amount of time taken by each test. Based on the amount of time needed to perform each test, Eric developed relative value units (RVUs) and associated the consumption of materials and labor with these units. The RVUs for each test and the cost per RVU for materials and labor are given below.

Test	*RVUs*	*Material per RVU*	*Labor per RVU*
B	1	$2.00	$2.00
C	2	$2.50	$2.00
CB	3	$1.00	$2.00

Eric also concluded that the pool of overhead costs collected within the laboratory should be applied using RVUs. (He was convinced that RVU was a good cost driver for overhead.) The laboratory's expected RVUs for the year were 22,500. The laboratory usually performs an equal number of the three tests over a year. This year was no exception.

Eric also noted that the hospital usually priced its services so that revenues exceeded costs by a specified percentage. Based on the past total costs of the laboratory, this pricing strategy had led to the following fees for the three blood tests:

	Test B	*Test C*	*Test CB*
Fees charged	$5.00	$19.33	$22.00

REQUIRED:

1. Allocate the costs of the service departments to the two revenue-producing departments using the direct method.
2. Assume that the three blood tests are the only tests performed in the laboratory. Compute the cost-to-charges ratio (total costs of the laboratory divided by the laboratory's total revenues).
3. Using the cost-to-charges ratio computed in Requirement 2, estimate the cost per test for each blood test.
4. Compute the cost per test for each test using RVUs.
5. Which unit cost—the one using the cost-to-charges ratio or the one using RVUs—do you believe is the more accurate? Explain.
6. Assume that Lambert Medical Center has been requested by an HMO to bid on Test CB. Using a 5 percent markup, prepare the bid using the cost computed in Requirement 3. Repeat, using the cost prepared in Requirement 4. Suppose that anyone who bids $20 or less will win the bid. Discuss the implications that costing accuracy has on the hospital's problems with its bidding practices.

D18-3
Direct Method; Settlement of a Contract Dispute

A state government agency contracted with FlyRite Helicopters to provide helicopter services on a requirements contract. After six months, FlyRite discovered that the agency's original estimates of the number of flying hours needed were grossly overstated. FlyRite Helicopters is now making a claim against the state agency for defective specifications. The state has been advised by its legal advisors that its chances in court on this claim would not be strong, and, therefore, an out-of-court settlement is in order. As a result of the legal advice, the state agency has hired a local CPA firm to analyze the claim and prepare a recommendation for an equitable settlement.

The particulars on which the original bid was based are given below. The contract was for three different types of helicopters and had a duration of one year. Thus, the data below reflect the original annual expectations. Also, the costs and activity pertain only to the contract.

	Aircraft Type		
	Hughes 500D	*206B Jet Ranger*	*206L-1 Long Ranger*
Flying hours	1,200	1,600	900
Direct costs:			
Fixed:			
Insurance	$32,245	$28,200	$55,870
Lease payments	$31,000	$36,000	$90,000
Pilot salaries	$30,000	$30,000	$30,000
Variable:			
Fuel	$24,648	$30,336	$22,752
Minor servicing	$ 6,000	$ 8,000	$ 4,500
Lease	—	—	$72,000

In addition to the direct costs, the following indirect costs were expected:

	Fixed Costs	*Variable Costs*
Maintenance	$ 26,000	$246,667
Hangar rent	$ 18,000	—
General administrative	$110,000	—

Maintenance costs and general administrative costs are allocated to each helicopter on the basis of flying hours; hangar rent is allocated on the basis of the number of helicopters. The company has one of each type of aircraft.

During the first six months of the contract, the actual flying hours were as follows:

Type	*Flying Hours*
500D	299
206B	160
206L-1	204

The state agency's revised projection of total hours for the year is given below:

Type	*Flying Hours*
500D	450
206B	600
206L-1	800

REQUIRED:

1. Assume that FlyRite won the contract with a bid of cost plus 15 percent, where cost refers to cost per flying hour. Compute the original bid price per flying hour for each type of helicopter. Next, compute the original expected profit of the contract.
2. Compute the profit (or loss) earned by FlyRite for the first six months of activity. Assume that the planned costs were equal to the actual costs. Also assume that 50 percent of the fixed costs for the year have been incurred. Compute the profit that FlyRite should have earned during the first six months, assuming that 50 percent of the hours originally projected (for each aircraft type) had been flown.

3. Compute the profit (or loss) that the contract would provide FlyRite, assuming the original price per flying hour and using the state agency's revised projection of hours needed.
4. Assume that the state has agreed to pay what is necessary so that FlyRite receives the profit originally expected in the contract. This will be accomplished by revising the price paid per flying hour based on the revised estimates of flying hours. What is the new price per flying hour?

D18-4 Research Assignment

Contact the controller of a local hospital and arrange an interview. Ask the hospital controller the following questions and write up the responses:

a. How many service centers do you have in the hospital? Will you describe several for me?
b. How many different revenue-producing departments are there in the hospital? Will you describe several for me?
c. How do you assign service-center costs to revenue-producing departments?
d. How many different products are there in the hospital?
e. How do you assign the costs of the service centers to individual products?
f. How many different products are costed in your hospital?
g. How do you determine the cost of a particular product?

CHAPTER 19
PRODUCT COSTING AND COST MANAGEMENT: THE ADVANCED MANUFACTURING ENVIRONMENT

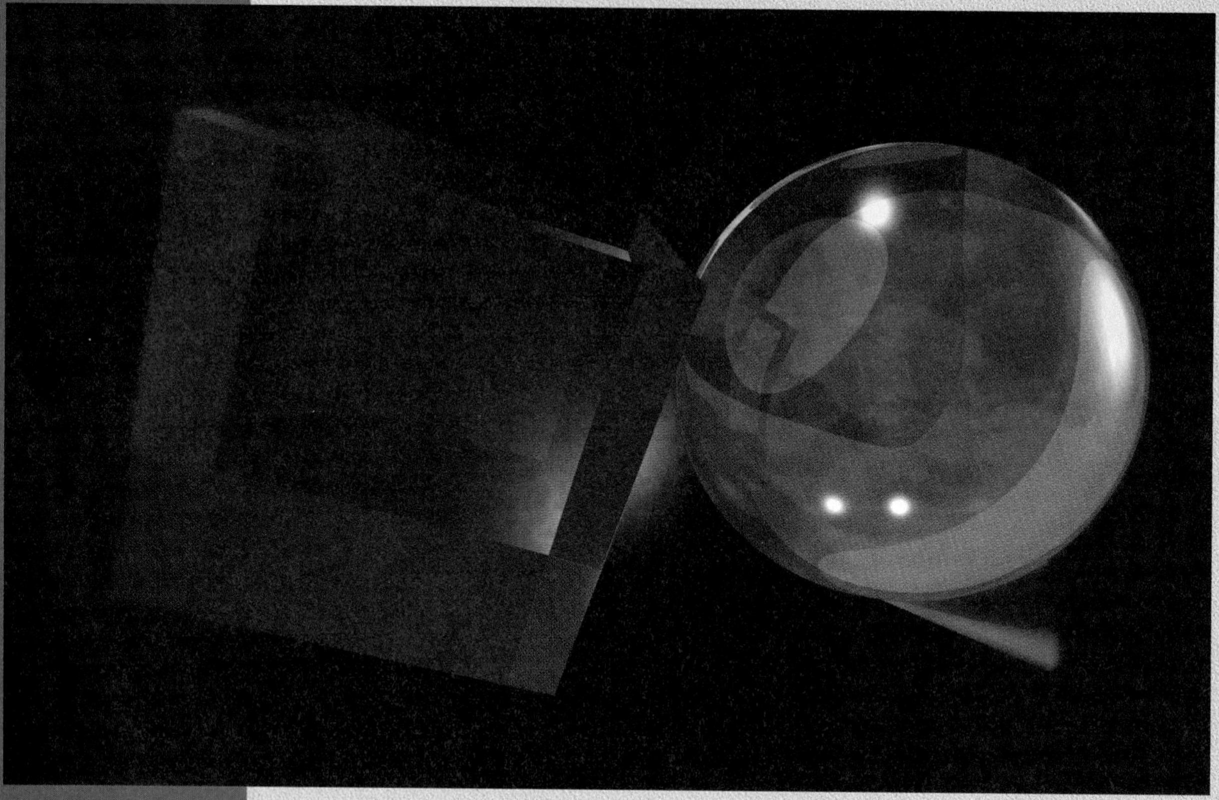

LEARNING OBJECTIVES

After studying this chapter, you should be able to:

1. Explain why using only unit-based cost drivers to assign overhead may produce distorted product costs.
2. Explain why activity-based costing produces more accurate product costs.
3. Provide a detailed description of activity-based costing, including how homogeneous sets of activities are created.
4. Explain when an activity-based cost system should be used.
5. Describe how JIT manufacturing alters the fundamental cost concepts and practices found in a conventional manufacturing environment.

Scenario

Ryan Chesser, president and owner of Sharp Paper, Inc., was reviewing the most recent financial reports. Profits had once again declined. The company had failed to achieve its targeted return for the third consecutive year. The inability of the company to improve its profits frustrated Ryan. After all, Sharp Paper had been a dominant factor in the industry for more than two decades. The company owns three paper mills, which produce coated and uncoated specialty printing papers. Customers have access to a variety of papers differing in finish, color, weight, and packages. More than 400 individual products were marketed by the company.[1]

To ascertain the reasons for the declining fortunes of the company, Ryan had asked his vice-presidents of production (Jeff Clark) and marketing (Jennifer Woodruff) to do some research. Ryan was particularly interested in knowing why the competition was winning bids on some major product lines in spite of aggressive pricing by Sharp. Four weeks after making the assignment, Ryan received the following report:

MEMO

To: Ryan Chesser, President
From: Jeff Clark and Jennifer Woodruff
Subject: Competitive Position of Sharp
Date: February 12, 1995

Our investigation has revealed some rather interesting information—information that we believe can benefit our company. We began by contacting some customers who have switched some of their purchases to competitors. We discovered that the switch usually involved our high-volume products. We have been losing bids on these products even when they are aggressively priced. Often the loss of business was to smaller competitors with less diverse product lines. Their prices were significantly lower than ours, and, in fact, seemed unrealistically low.

At first, we suspected that these businesses were pricing low simply to gain market penetration. However, after investigating in greater depth, it soon became apparent that our competitors were prospering and, in fact, earning a good return.

Our next effort was focused on determining whether competitors were employing a new technology that might provide significant cost advantages. Virtually all our small competitors use the same manufacturing processes that we use. A few of the full-line, larger competitors, however, are using just-in-time (JIT) manufacturing. As nearly as we can determine, this approach to manufacturing involves no new technology but does entail a significant shift in how inputs are organized and used. These JIT manufacturers have not only

1. The setting and the issues in this introductory case are based in part on the following three articles: James P. Borden, "Review of Literature on Activity-Based Costing," *Journal of Cost Management*, Vol. 4, No. 1 (Spring 1990); John K. Shank and Vijay Govindarajan, "Transaction-Based Costing for the Complex Product Line: A Field Study," *Journal of Cost Management*, Vol. 2., No. 2 (Summer 1988), pp. 31–38; and Robin Cooper, "Does Your Company Need a New Cost System?" *Journal of Cost Management*, Vol. 1, No. 1 (Spring 1987), pp. 45–49.

maintained their market share but also have managed to increase it over the past three years—at our expense.

Curiously, our low-volume products appear to be the most profitable. In some cases, we are the only company that produces these specialty products. At times, we even receive referrals from some of our competitors. Furthermore, some of our operational managers have urged us to drop some of these low-volume products, arguing that they're more bother than they're worth. Yet these products are being reported as highly profitable. If this is true, why are other paper companies uninterested in competing? And why do our operational managers want to drop profitable lines?

We considered a strategy of emphasizing our low-volume products more and reducing our output of high-volume products. However, when we asked the controller's office to explain why the profit margins of the low-volume products were so much greater, which seems counterintuitive given the special processes and handling required, we did not receive any logical response given our understanding of the production processes and the market. We were even told that we could increase our margin on the low-volume products by increasing prices. Recent price increases were readily accepted by customers—without any complaints.

Given the response of the controller's office and the fact that our production technology and efficiency at least match those of our smaller competitors, we have decided that we may have a major problem with the way we compute the costs of our various products. We should be making a return equal to that of our competitors on our high-volume products. We recommend that a serious evaluation of our costing procedures be conducted.

Given the ground that some of the larger competitors have gained by using JIT manufacturing, we also recommend that we hire a consultant to explore the feasibility of implementing such a system for our company. JIT manufacturing offers some potential to enhance our ability to compete.

THE LIMITATIONS OF CONVENTIONAL PRODUCT COSTING

Objective 1
Explain why using only unit-based cost drivers to assign overhead may produce distorted product costs.

The two vice-presidents of Sharp Paper identified a number of symptoms that signaled problems with the company's cost system. For example, the prices of the paper company's high-volume products are significantly higher than those of smaller, prosperous competitors. Even aggressive pricing on bids is failing to win business. Yet, the only difference between Sharp and these competitors seems to be the range of products produced. The company's low-volume specialty products are apparently quite profitable—in spite of the special processes and handling they require. In fact, the company apparently has a highly profitable niche all to itself—it is even receiving referrals from competitors. Also, the accounting system cannot explain the differences in profitability between the low-volume and high-volume products. Surprisingly, customers are not complaining about price increases on low-volume products. Could this be because the company is offering a deal too good to be true? Finally, operational managers want to drop seemingly profitable product lines. All these factors

Exhibit 19-1
Symptoms of an Outdated Cost System

1. The outcome of bids is difficult to explain.
2. Competitors' prices appear unrealistically low.
3. Products that are difficult to produce show high profits.
4. Operational managers want to drop products that appear profitable.
5. Profit margins are hard to explain.
6. The company has a highly profitable niche all to itself.
7. Customers do not complain about price increases.
8. The accounting department spends a lot of time on special projects.
9. Some departments are using their own accounting system.
10. Product costs change because of changes in financial reporting regulations.

combine to raise questions concerning the company's costing practices. These symptoms of an outdated cost system, along with a few others not mentioned in the memo, are listed in Exhibit 19-1.[2]

The vice-presidents' report also mentioned JIT manufacturing. Other large paper manufacturers with full product lines apparently are adopting this new approach to manufacturing. Over the past 10 to 20 years, a revolution has taken place in manufacturing. Innovative practices developed by the Japanese—total quality control and JIT purchasing and manufacturing—have significantly increased the competitive pressures felt by U.S. firms. Other changes, such as computer-integrated manufacturing systems, which have increased product complexity, and deregulation of service industries, have also changed the competitive environment. Thus, this new environment, referred to as the **advanced manufacturing environment,** is characterized by firms engaged in intense competition (usually on a world-wide level), continuous improvement, total quality management, total customer satisfaction, time-based competition, and sophisticated technology.

advanced manufacturing environment

As firms adopt new manufacturing strategies to achieve competitive excellence, their accounting systems must also change to keep pace. Specifically, the need for more accurate product costs has forced many companies to take a serious look at their costing procedures. Cost systems that worked reasonably well in the past may no longer be acceptable. Moreover, some of the changes have also altered the nature and mix of manufacturing costs. The advanced manufacturing environment simply demands a different approach to product costing, inventory management, quality management, and so on.

Overhead Assignment: The Source of the Problem

Sharp Paper, Inc. (unfortunately, like many other companies) is trying to operate in a highly competitive environment with an outmoded cost system, one that evidently is not producing the information management needs to make sound decisions. Over time, Sharp has added product lines until it is now producing more than 400 paper products. While having a full line of products may be a sound marketing strategy, the increased complexity apparently has made it much more difficult to determine accurate unit costs. If the vice-presidents are right that

2. The list of warning signals is based on the following article: Robin Cooper, "You Need a New Cost System When. . . . ," *Harvard Business Review* (January-February 1989), pp. 77–82.

products are being costed incorrectly, that could explain the problems the company is currently having in marketing its products. For example, if the unit costs of the high-volume products are overstated, this could lead to cost-plus prices or bids that are out of line with competitors. Similarly, if the low-volume products are undercosted, this could explain their apparent profitability.

If product costs are being distorted by Sharp's cost system, there must be a reason. Assuming that Sharp is using a traditional cost system, such as job-order costing or process costing or some blend of the two, why would this system fail to determine product costs accurately? In all likelihood, the problem is not with assigning the costs of direct labor or direct materials. These prime costs are traceable to individual products, and most traditional cost systems are designed to ensure that this tracing takes place. Assigning overhead costs to individual products, however, is another matter. Using the conventional, unit-based methods to assign overhead costs to products can produce distorted product costs.

Overhead Costing: A Single-Product Setting

The accuracy of unit-based overhead cost assignment becomes an issue only when multiple products are manufactured in a single facility. If only a single product is produced, all overhead costs are caused by it and traceable to it. The overhead cost per unit is simply the total overhead for the year divided by the number of units produced. Accuracy is not an issue. The timing of the computation may be an issue; because of this, a predetermined overhead rate is usually required. The cost calculation for a single-product setting is illustrated in Exhibit 19-2. Certainly no one would question that the cost of manufacturing the product illustrated in Exhibit 19-2 is $10 per unit. All manufacturing costs were incurred specifically to make this product. Thus, one way to ensure product-costing accuracy is to focus on producing one product. For this reason, some multiple-product firms choose to dedicate plants to the manufacture of a single product.

Such focusing may be the reason that small producers are able to compete successfully with Sharp. By focusing on only one or a few similar products, the small producers are able to calculate the cost of manufacturing their products (those that compete with Sharp's high-volume products) more accurately and price them more effectively. This observation assumes that Sharp's cost system is distorting the cost of the high-volume products.

Overhead Costing: Multiple-Product Setting with Unit-Based Cost Drivers

cost drivers

In a multiple-product setting, overhead costs are caused jointly by all products. The problem now becomes one of identifying the amount of overhead that each product consumes or causes. This is accomplished by searching for **cost drivers,**

Exhibit 19-2
Unit Cost Computation: Single Product

	Manufacturing Costs	*Units Produced*	*Unit Cost*
Direct materials	$ 600,000	100,000	$ 6
Direct labor	100,000	100,000	1
Overhead	300,000	100,000	3
Total	$1,000,000	100,000	$10

factors that measure the demands placed on overhead activities by individual products. In a conventional setting, it is normally assumed that overhead consumption is highly correlated with the number of units produced, measured in terms of direct labor hours, machine hours, or material costs. These **unit-based (volume-related) cost drivers** assign overhead to products through the use of either plant-wide or departmental rates.

unit-based (volume-related) cost drivers

To illustrate the limitation of this conventional approach, assume that Sharp has a plant that produces two products: white and blue boxwrap. Product costing data are given in Exhibit 19-3. The units are three-ream rolls. Because the quantity of blue boxwrap produced is five times greater than that of white boxwrap, we can label white boxwrap a low-volume product and blue boxwrap a high-volume product.

For simplicity, only four types of overhead costs are assumed: setup, inspection, power, and fringe benefits for direct labor. These overhead costs are allocated to the two production departments using the direct method. Assume that the four service centers do not interact. Setup costs are allocated based on the number of production runs handled by each department. Since the number is the same for both departments, each department receives 50 percent of the total setup costs. Inspection costs are allocated by the number of inspection hours used by each department. Power costs are allocated in proportion to the kilowatt hours

Exhibit 19-3
Product Costing Data

	White Boxwrap	*Blue Boxwrap*	*Total*
Units produced per year	20,000	100,000	—
Prime costs	$50,000	$250,000	$300,000
Direct labor hours	20,000	100,000	120,000
Machine hours	10,000	50,000	60,000
Production runs	20	30	50
Inspection hours	800	1,200	2,000

	Departmental Data		
	Department 1	*Department 2*	*Total*
Direct labor hours:			
White boxwrap	4,000	16,000	20,000
Blue boxwrap	76,000	24,000	100,000
Total	80,000	40,000	120,000
Machine hours:			
White boxwrap	4,000	6,000	10,000
Blue boxwrap	16,000	34,000	50,000
Total	20,000	40,000	60,000
Overhead costs:			
Setup costs	$ 44,000	$ 44,000	$ 88,000
Inspection costs	37,000	37,000	74,000
Power	14,000	70,000	84,000
Direct labor fringe benefits	52,000	26,000	78,000
Total	$147,000	$177,000	$324,000

used by each department. Finally, fringe benefit costs are allocated in proportion to the direct labor hours used.

Plant-Wide Overhead Rate. A common method to assign overhead to products is to compute a plant-wide rate using a unit-based cost driver. This approach assumes that all overhead cost variation can be explained by one cost driver. Assume that machine hours are chosen as the cost driver. (Direct labor hours would give the same assignment in this example since labor hours are used in the same proportion as machine hours.) The total overhead for the plant is $324,000, the sum of the overhead for each department ($147,000 + $177,000). Dividing the total overhead by the total machine hours yields the following overhead rate:

$$\begin{aligned}\text{Plant-wide rate} &= \$324{,}000/60{,}000\\ &= \$5.40 \text{ per machine hour}\end{aligned}$$

Using this rate and other information from Exhibit 19-3, the unit cost for each product can be calculated (see Exhibit 19-4).

Departmental Rates. Based on the distribution of labor hours and machine hours in Exhibit 19-3, Department 1 is labor intensive and Department 2, machine intensive. Moreover, the overhead costs of Department 1 are less than those of Department 2. Based on these observations, it could be argued that departmental overhead rates would reflect the consumption of overhead better than a plant-wide rate. If true, product costs would be more accurate. This approach would yield the following departmental rates, using direct labor hours for Department 1 and machine hours for Department 2:

$$\begin{aligned}\text{Department 1 rate} &= \$147{,}000/80{,}000\\ &= \$1.84 \text{ per labor hour}\end{aligned}$$

$$\begin{aligned}\text{Department 2 rate} &= \$177{,}000/40{,}000\\ &= \$4.43 \text{ per machine hour}\end{aligned}$$

Using these rates and the data from Exhibit 19-3, the computation of the unit costs for each product is shown in Exhibit 19-5.

Problems with Costing Accuracy. The accuracy of the overhead cost assignment can be challenged regardless of whether the plant-wide or departmental

Exhibit 19-4
Unit Cost Computation: Plant-Wide Rate

White Boxwrap	
Prime costs ($50,000/20,000)	$2.50
Overhead costs ($5.40 × 10,000/20,000)	2.70
Unit cost	$5.20

Blue Boxwrap	
Prime costs ($250,000/100,000)	$2.50
Overhead cost ($5.40 × 50,000/100,000)	2.70
Unit cost	$5.20

Exhibit 19-5
Unit Cost Computation: Departmental Rates

White Boxwrap	
Prime costs ($50,000/20,000)	$2.50
Overhead costs [($1.84 × 4,000) + ($4.43 × 6,000)]/20,000	1.70
Unit cost	$4.20

Blue Boxwrap	
Prime costs ($250,000/100,000)	$2.50
Overhead cost [($1.84 × 76,000) + ($4.43 × 34,000)]/100,000	2.90
Unit cost	$5.40

rates are used. The main problem with either procedure is the assumption that machine hours or direct labor hours drive or cause all overhead costs.

From Exhibit 19-3, we know that blue boxwrap—with five times the volume of white boxwrap—uses five times the machine hours and direct labor hours. Thus, if a plant-wide rate is used, blue boxwrap will receive five times more overhead cost. But is this reasonable? Do unit-based cost drivers explain the consumption of all overhead? Does a product's consumption of overhead increase in direct proportion to the number of units produced?

Examination of the data in Exhibit 19-3 suggests that a significant portion of overhead costs is *not* driven or caused by the units produced. For example, setup costs are probably related to the number of production runs and inspection costs to the number of hours of inspection. Notice that blue boxwrap has only 1.5 times as many runs as the white boxwrap (30/20) and only 1.5 times as many inspection hours (1,200/800). Use of a unit-based cost driver (machine hours or labor hours) and a plant-wide rate assigns five times more overhead to the blue boxwrap than to the white. For inspection and setup costs, blue boxwrap is overcosted and the white is undercosted.[3]

The problem is only aggravated when departmental rates are used. Blue boxwrap consumes 19 times as many direct labor hours (76,000/4,000) as white boxwrap and 5.67 times as many machine hours (34,000/6,000). Thus, blue boxwrap receives 19 times more overhead from Department 1 and 5.67 times more overhead from Department 2. As Exhibit 19-5 shows, with departmental rates, the unit cost of the white boxwrap *decreases* to $4.20, and the unit cost of the blue boxwrap *increases* to $5.40. This change is in the wrong direction, which emphasizes the failure of unit-based cost drivers to reflect accurately each product's demands for setup and inspection costs.

Why Unit-Based Cost Drivers Fail

At least two major factors impair the ability of a unit-based cost driver to assign overhead costs accurately: (1) the proportion of nonunit-related overhead costs to total overhead costs and (2) the degree of product diversity.[4]

3. A more detailed discussion of the limitations of conventional product costing can be found in Robin Cooper, "The Rise of Activity-Based Costing—Part One: What Is an Activity-Based Cost System?" *Journal of Cost Management for the Manufacturing Industry,* Vol. 2, No. 2 (Summer 1988), pp. 45–54.
4. Robin Cooper, "The Rise of Activity-Based Costing—Part Three: How Many Cost Drivers Do You Need, and How Do You Select Them?" *Journal of Cost Management for the Manufacturing Industry,* Vol. 2, No. 4 (Winter 1989), pp. 34–46.

Nonunit-Related Overhead Costs. In the example under discussion, there are four overhead activities: inspection, setup, fringe benefits, and power. Two of these activities, fringe benefits and power, are related to the number of units produced. As has already been shown, however, inspection and setup costs are not driven by the number of units produced. Setup costs, for example, are a function of the number of runs, a nonunit-based cost driver. **Nonunit-based cost drivers** are factors, other than the number of units produced, that drive costs. Thus, unit-based cost drivers cannot assign these costs accurately to products.

nonunit-based cost drivers

Using only unit-based cost drivers to assign nonunit-related overhead costs can create distorted product costs. The severity of this distortion depends on what proportion of total overhead costs these nonunit-based costs represent. For our example, setup costs and inspection costs represent a substantial share—50 percent—of total overhead ($162,000/$324,000). The percentage reflected by the simple example of Sharp Paper is representative of what can happen in real manufacturing environments. Schrader Bellows and John Deere Component Works, for example, experienced nonunit-based overhead cost ratios of about 50 percent and 40 percent, respectively.[5] This suggests that some care should be exercised in assigning nonunit-based overhead costs. If nonunit-based overhead costs are only a small percentage of total overhead costs, the distortion of product costs would be quite small. In such a case, the use of unit-based cost drivers might be acceptable.

Product Diversity. When products consume overhead activities in different proportions, a firm has **product diversity.** There are several reasons that products might consume overhead in different proportions. For example, differences in product size, product complexity, setup time, and size of batches all can cause products to consume overhead at different rates. Regardless of the nature of the product diversity, product cost will be distorted whenever the quantity of unit-based input that a product consumes does not vary in direct proportion to the quantity of nonunit-based inputs consumed.[6] To illustrate, the proportion of all overhead activities consumed by both blue and white boxwrap is computed and displayed in Exhibit 19-6. The proportion of each activity consumed by a product is defined as the **consumption ratio.** If the quantity of the unit-based inputs con-

product diversity

consumption ratio

Exhibit 19-6
Product Diversity: Proportions of Consumption

Overhead Activity	*White Boxwrap*	*Blue Boxwrap*	*Consumption Measure*
Setups	0.40[a]	0.60[a]	Production runs
Inspection	0.40[b]	0.60[b]	Inspection hours
Power	0.17[c]	0.83[c]	Machine hours
Fringe benefits	0.17[d]	0.83[d]	Direct labor hours

[a]20/50 (white) and 30/50 (blue)
[b]800/2,000 (white) and 1,200/2,000 (blue)
[c]10,000/60,000 (white) and 50,000/60,000 (blue)
[d]20,000/120,000 (white) and 100,000/120,000 (blue)

5. See Robin Cooper, "Cost Classification in Unit-Based and Activity-Based Manufacturing Cost Systems," *Journal of Cost Management for the Manufacturing Industry* (Fall 1990), pp. 4–14.
6. Robin Cooper, "The Rise of Activity-Based Costing—Part Two: When Do I Need an Activity-Based Cost System?" *Journal of Cost Manufacturing Industry,* Vol. 2, No. 3 (Fall 1988).

sumed had varied in direct proportion to the quantity of nonunit-based inputs consumed, the consumption ratios would have been identical. As you can see from the exhibit, the consumption ratios for these two products differ for the unit-based and nonunit-based inputs.

Since the nonunit-based overhead costs are a significant proportion of total overhead and the consumption ratios differ between unit-based and nonunit-based input categories, product costs can be distorted if a unit-based cost driver is used. The solution to this costing problem is to use an activity-based costing approach.

ACTIVITY-BASED PRODUCT COSTING: BASIC CONCEPTS

Objective 2
Explain why activity-based costing produces more accurate product costs.

activity-based (ABC) cost system

An **activity-based cost (ABC) system** is one that first traces costs to activities and then to products. Conventional product costing also involves two stages, but in the first stage, costs are traced not to activities but to an organizational unit, such as the plant or departments. In both conventional and activity-based costing, the second stage consists of tracing costs to the product. The principal computational difference between the two methods concerns the nature and the number of cost drivers used. Activity-based costing uses both unit-based and nonunit-based cost drivers and generally the number of drivers is greater than the number of unit-based cost drivers commonly used in a conventional system. As a result, the ABC method produces increased product-costing accuracy. From a managerial perspective, however, an ABC system offers more than just accurate product cost information. It also provides information about activities and their costs. Knowing what activities are being performed and their associated costs allows managers to focus on those activities that might offer opportunities for cost savings—provided they are simplified, performed more efficiently, eliminated, and so on. The strategic insights and process improvement capabilities of an ABC system are extremely important and are explored in Chapters 23 and 26. In this chapter, however, we will focus only on ABC's product-costing dimension, beginning with a discussion of the first-stage procedure.

First-Stage Procedure: Activity Grouping and Cost Assignment

activity

In the first stage of activity-based costing, activities are identified, costs are associated with individual activities, and activities and their associated costs are divided into homogeneous sets. An **activity** is work performed within an organization.[7] An activity is also defined as an aggregation of actions performed within an organization that is useful for purposes of activity-based costing. Thus, activity identification requires a listing of all the different kinds of work, such as materials handling, inspections, process engineering, and product enhancement. A firm may have hundreds of different activities. Once an activity is defined, the cost of performing the activity is determined. At this point, the firm could determine the cost driver associated with each activity and calculate individual activity overhead rates. For the average setting, this could literally produce hundreds of overhead rates, a cumbersome method of assigning overhead to products.

7. Norm Raffis and Peter B. B. Turney, "Glossary of Activity-Based Management," *Journal of Cost Management* (Fall 1991), pp. 53–63. Other definitions from this glossary are also used throughout our discussion of activity-based costing.

To reduce the number of overhead rates required and streamline the process, activities are grouped together based on two criteria: (1) they are logically related, and (2) they have the same consumption ratios for all products. These homogeneous sets of activities should have an easy and clear physical interpretation and should correspond to manageable segments of the production process. Costs are associated with each of these sets by summing the costs of the individual activities belonging to the set. The collection of overhead costs associated with each set of activities is called a **homogeneous cost pool.** Since the activities within a homogeneous cost pool have the same consumption ratio, we know that the cost variations for this pool can be explained by a single cost driver. Once a cost pool is defined, the cost per unit of the cost driver is computed for that pool. This is called the **pool rate.** Computation of the pool rate completes the first stage. Thus, the first stage produces four outcomes: (1) activities are identified, (2) costs are assigned to activities, (3) related activities and their costs are grouped together to define homogeneous cost pools, and (4) pool (overhead) rates are computed.[8]

homogeneous cost pool

pool rate

To illustrate this process, consider once again the Sharp Paper example. Four overhead activities have been identified: setups, inspection, power, and fringe benefits for direct labor. The costs of the individual activities have been assigned and are described in Exhibit 19-3. Logical relationships also exist. Setup activities and inspection activities both occur each time a batch of products is produced. Thus, these two activities are logically related by the more general batch-level production activity. Similarly, fringe benefit and power activities occur each time a unit of product is produced. Thus, these two activities are logically related by the more general activity of producing a unit of product. Moreover, from Exhibit 19-6 we know that the setups and inspection grouping and the power and labor grouping have the same consumption ratios for both products. Thus, we are able to reduce four activities to two sets of activities. These two sets of activities can now be used to form homogeneous cost pools. Let's call the set with setups and inspections the *batch-level pool* and the set with power and fringe benefits the *unit-level pool.* The total cost associated with each pool is simply the sum of the related activities' costs. Using the data from Exhibit 19-3, the pool costs are given below:

Batch-Level Pool		*Unit-Level Pool*	
Setups	$ 88,000	Power	$ 84,000
Inspections	74,000	Fringe Benefits	78,000
	$162,000		$162,000

Now that we have identified homogeneous cost pools and determined their costs, we can assign the pool costs to each product. To do this, a pool rate must

8. This definition of the first stage in an activity-based cost system is found in H. Thomas Johnson and Robert S. Kaplan, *Relevance Lost: The Rise and Fall of Management Accounting* (Boston: Harvard Business Press, 1987), Chapter 10. A more detailed description of both the first-stage and second-stage procedures is found in the following three sources: Robin Cooper, "The Two-Stage Procedure in Cost Accounting—Part One," *Journal of Cost Management* (Summer 1987), pp. 43–51 and "The Two-Stage Procedure in Cost Accounting—Part Two," *Journal of Cost Management* (Fall 1987), pp. 39–45; and George J. Beaujon and Vinod R. Singhal, "Understanding the Activity Costs in an Activity-Based Cost System," *Journal of Cost Management* (Spring 1990), pp. 51–72. A more current description is also found in the following article: Peter B.B. Turney, "Using ABC to Support Continuous Improvement," *Management Accounting* (September 1992), pp. 46–50. Most of the discussion of the two stages of activity-based costing is based on these five sources.

be calculated based on cost drivers. For the batch-level cost pool, the number of production runs or inspection hours could be the cost driver. Since the two cost drivers produce the same consumption ratios, they will assign the same amount of overhead to both products. For the unit-level cost pool (power and labor), machine hours or direct labor hours could be selected as the cost driver. Assume for purposes of illustration that the number of production runs and machine hours are the cost drivers chosen.[9] Using data from Exhibit 19-3, the first-stage outcomes are illustrated in Exhibit 19-7.

Second-Stage Procedure: Assigning Costs to Products

In the second stage, the costs of each overhead pool are traced to products. This is done using the pool rate computed in the first stage and the measure of the amount of activity resources consumed by each product. This measure is simply the quantity of the cost driver used by each product. In our example, that would be the number of production runs and machine hours used by each boxwrap. Thus, the overhead assigned from each cost pool to each product is computed as follows:

$$\text{Applied overhead} = \text{Pool rate} \times \text{Cost driver units used}$$

To illustrate, consider the assignment of costs from the first overhead pool to white boxwrap. From Exhibit 19-7, we know that the rate for this pool is \$3,240 per production run. We also know from Exhibit 19-3 that the white wrap uses 20 production runs. Thus, the overhead assigned to white wrap from the batch-level cost pool is \$64,800 (\$3,240 × 20 runs). Similar assignments would be made for the other cost pool and for the other product.

The total overhead cost per unit of product is obtained by first tracing the overhead costs from the pools to the individual products. This total is then

Exhibit 19-7
First-Stage Procedure: Activity-Based Costing

Batch-level pool:	
Setup costs	$ 88,000
Inspection costs	74,000
Total costs	$162,000
Production runs	50
Pool rate (Cost per run):	
($162,000/50)	$3,240
Unit-level pool:	
Power cost	$ 84,000
Direct labor fringe benefits	78,000
Total costs	$162,000
Machine hours	60,000
Pool rate (Cost per machine hour):	
($162,000/60,000)	$2.70

9. You may want to recalculate pool rates using number of inspection hours and direct labor hours to prove that the choice of cost drivers does not affect the assignment of costs to the individual products.

Exhibit 19-8
Unit Costs: Activity-Based Costing

White Boxwrap		
Overhead:		
Batch-level pool: $3,240 × 20 runs	$64,800	
Unit-level pool: $2.70 × 10,000 machine hrs	27,000	
Total overhead costs		$ 91,800
Prime costs		50,000
Total manufacturing costs		$141,800
Units produced		20,000
Unit cost		$7.09
Blue Boxwrap		
Overhead:		
Batch-level pool: $3,240 × 30 runs	$ 97,200	
Unit-level pool: $2.70 × 50,000 machine hrs	135,000	
Total overhead costs		$232,200
Prime costs		250,000
Total manufacturing costs		$482,200
Units produced		100,000
Unit cost		$4.82

divided by the number of units produced. The result is the unit overhead cost. Adding the per-unit overhead cost to the per-unit prime cost yields the manufacturing cost per unit. In Exhibit 19-8, the manufacturing cost per unit is computed using activity-based costing.

Comparison of Product Costs

In Exhibit 19-9, the unit cost from activity-based costing is compared with the unit costs produced by conventional costing using either a plant-wide or departmental rate. This comparison clearly illustrates the effects of using only unit-based cost drivers to assign overhead costs. The activity-based cost reflects the correct pattern of overhead consumption and is, therefore, the most accurate of the three costs shown in Exhibit 19-9. Activity-based product costing reveals that the conventional method undercosts the white boxwrap significantly and overcosts the blue boxwrap.

Using only unit-based cost drivers can lead to one product subsidizing another. This subsidy could create the appearance that one group of products is highly profitable and adversely impacts the pricing and competitiveness of

Exhibit 19-9
Comparison of Unit Costs

	White Boxwrap	*Blue Boxwrap*	*Source*
Activity-based cost	$7.09	$4.82	Exhibit 19-8
Conventional:			
Plant-wide rate	5.20	5.20	Exhibit 19-4
Departmental rate	4.20	5.40	Exhibit 19-5

another group of products. This seems to be one of the problems facing Sharp Paper. In a highly competitive environment, accurate cost information is critical for sound planning and decision making.

ACTIVITY-BASED PRODUCT COSTING: MORE DETAIL

Objective 3
Provide a detailed description of activity-based costing, including how homogeneous sets of activities are created.

In describing activity-based product costing, the basic features have been described and illustrated with the Sharp Paper Company example. We have learned, for example, that activities must be identified, related activities grouped in sets, and costs must be assigned to the activities within each homogeneous set to form homogeneous cost pools. Once cost pools are formed, a cost driver for each pool is used to assign costs to individual products. Activity classification is a critical part of this process. Yet, so far, only the general nature of this process has been described. A more detailed understanding of how activities are classified is needed so that homogeneous pools can be formed.

Activity Classification and Homogeneous Sets

For product-costing purposes, related activities are grouped into sets that form the basis for homogeneous cost pools. Grouping activities reduces the number of overhead rates needed, simplifies the task of product costing, and decreases the overall complexity of the ABC product costing model. Activities qualify for membership in the same set provided two criteria are satisfied: (1) *activity-level criterion:* they are performed at the same general activity level (defining specifically what is meant by logically related), and (2) *driver criterion:* they use the same cost driver.[10] These two criteria serve as filters in grouping activities to create homogeneous cost pools.

Activity-Level Classification. As a first step in building sets of related activities, activities are classified into one of the following four *general* activity categories: (1) unit-level (2) batch-level (3) product-level and (4) facility-level.[11] Classifying activities into these general categories facilitates product costing because the costs of activities associated with the different levels respond to different *types* of cost drivers. The definition of the activities belonging to each general category clearly illustrates this feature. **Unit-level activities** are those that are performed each time a unit is produced. For example, power and machine hours are used each time a unit is produced. Direct materials and direct labor activities are also unit-level activities, even though they are not overhead costs. The costs of unit-level activities vary with the number of units produced. **Batch-level activities** are those that are performed each time a batch of goods is produced. The costs of batch-level activities vary with the number of batches but are fixed with respect

unit-level activities

batch-level activities

10. Finer classifications can be realized by using additional criteria. For example, we could require activities with the same purpose or objective to be classified together. Since processes are collections of activities that are linked by a common objective, this would add a process-classification criterion. While additional criteria may improve product costing, they add very little to our understanding of the basic features of activity-based costing. Thus, we will leave the study of process classification to a more advanced course. For readers who wish to explore this topic, see Michael R. Ostrenga and Frank Probst, "Process Value Analysis: The Missing Link in Cost Management," *Journal of Cost Management* (Fall 1992), pp. 4–13, and Peter B. B. Turney and Alan J. Stratton, "Using ABC to Support Continuous Improvement," *Management Accounting* (September 1992), pp. 46–50.
11. This classification and the associated definitions are taken from Robin Cooper, "Cost Classification in Unit-Based and Activity-Based Manufacturing Cost Systems."

to the number of units in each batch. Setups, inspections, production scheduling, and material handling are examples of batch-level activities. **Product-level (sustaining) activities** are those that are performed as needed to support the various products produced by a company. These activities consume inputs that develop products or allow products to be produced and sold. These activities and their costs tend to increase as the number of different products increases. Engineering changes, development of product testing procedures, maintenance of equipment, process engineering, and expediting are examples of product-level activities. **Facility-level activities** are those that sustain a factory's general manufacturing processes. These activities benefit the organization at some level but do not provide a benefit for any specific product. Examples include plant management, landscaping, support of community programs, security, property taxes, and plant depreciation.

product-level (sustaining) activities

facility-level activities

Driver Classification. Of the four general levels, the first three, unit-level, batch-level, and product-level, contain product-related activities. For these three levels, it is possible to measure the demands placed on the activities by individual products. Activities within these three levels can be further subdivided on the basis of consumption ratios. Activities with the same consumption ratios use the same cost driver to assign costs. Thus, in effect, all activities *within* each of the first three levels that have the same cost driver are grouped together. This final grouping creates a homogeneous set of activities: a collection of activities that are at the same level and use the same cost driver. Exhibit 19-10 illustrates the activity classification model that creates homogeneous sets of activities.

Exhibit 19-10
Activity Classification Model

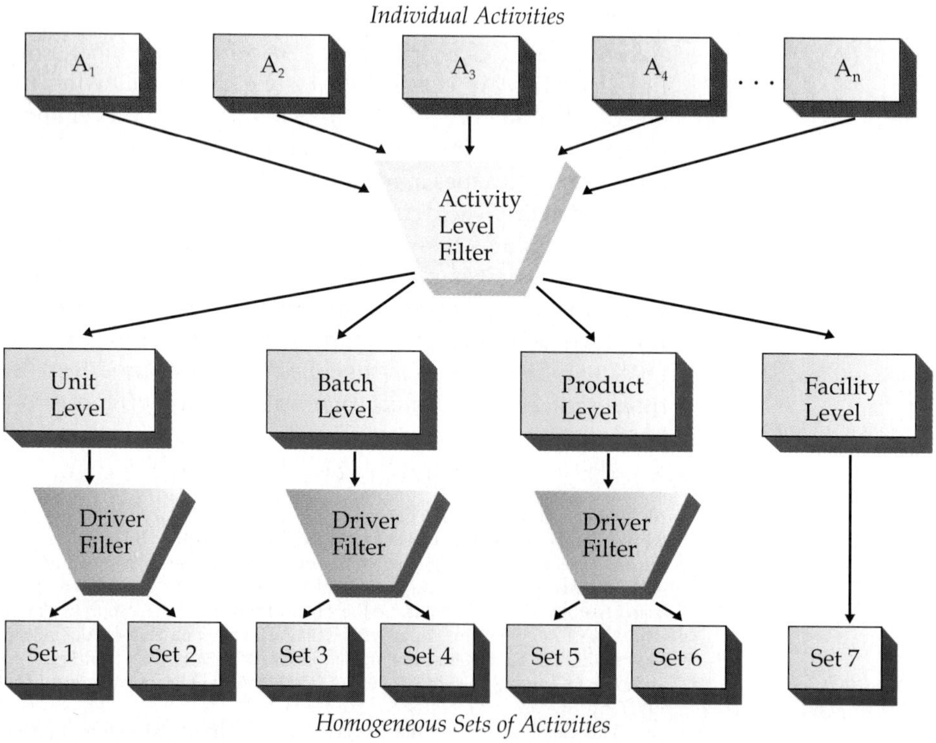

Notice that facility-level activities do not undergo the driver classification. Since it is not possible to measure the demands of individual products for facility-level activities, this finer classification is not possible. The implications of this outcome for product costing are discussed in the next section.

Cost Assignment

For product costing, the ultimate objective of activity classification is to build homogeneous cost pools so that the costs of activities can be assigned to products. Once a homogeneous set of activities is defined, a homogeneous cost pool is created by summing the costs of the individual activities that belong to the set. Then, these costs are assigned to products using carefully chosen cost drivers. Generally, this cost assignment follows the pattern illustrated by the Sharp Paper Company example; however, in a more complicated setting, there may be more than one homogeneous cost pool for each of the general activity levels. For example, the unit-level category could have labor-related and machine-related overhead pools. Notice that in Exhibit 19-10, there are two sets of homogeneous activities for each of the product-related levels. (Of course, more than two are possible.) Each homogeneous set of activities defines a homogeneous cost pool.

The fourth general category, facility-level activities, poses a problem for the ABC philosophy of tracing costs to products. Tracing activity costs to individual products depends on the ability to identify the amount of each activity consumed by a product. (Product demands for activities must be measured.) Facility-level activities (and their costs) are common to a variety of products, and it is not possible to identify how individual products consume these activities. A pure ABC system, therefore, would not assign these costs to products. They would be treated as period costs. In effect, these costs are fixed costs—costs that are not driven by any of the cost drivers found in any of the first three categories. In practice, companies adopting ABC systems usually implement a full-costing approach and allocate these facility-level costs to individual products.[12] Unit-level, batch-level, or product-level cost drivers are often used for the allocation. As a practical matter, assigning these costs may not significantly distort product costs because they are likely to be small relative to the total costs that are traced appropriately to individual products.[13]

An Illustrative Example

To illustrate the approach just described, we will build an ABC product-costing model for Marvel Components, Inc., an electronics products manufacturer. In one of its plants, Marvel produces two types of wafers: Wafer A and Wafer B. A wafer is a thin slice of silicon used as a base for integrated circuits or other electronic components. The dies on each wafer represent a particular configuration—a configuration designed for use by a particular end product. Marvel produces wafers in batches, where each batch corresponds to a particular type of wafer (A or B). Each wafer is tested to ensure that the dies inserted are not defective.

12. A study of 31 companies and 51 cost systems revealed that all companies using an ABC system allocated facility-level costs to products. See Robin Cooper, "Cost Classification in Unit-Based and Activity-Based Manufacturing Systems."

13. At least this appears to be the experience of General Motors based on its implementation of an ABC system. See Beaujon and Singhal, "Understanding the Activity Costs in an Activity-Based Cost System," pp. 51–72.

Assume that the following activities and associated costs have been identified:

Activity	*Activity Cost*
1. Developing test programs	$300,000
2. Making probe cards	160,000
3. Testing products	275,000
4. Setting up batches	120,000
5. Engineering design	130,000
6. Handling wafer lots	90,000
7. Die insertion	225,000
8. Providing utilities (heat, lighting, etc.)	20,000
9. Providing space	30,000

Applying the activity classification model of Exhibit 19-10 to the above activities produces the homogeneous cost pools illustrated in Exhibit 19-11. Notice that activities are classified into pools by level and by common driver. In this example, only activities found in the product-level category are divided into finer sets

Exhibit 19-11
Activity Level Classification and Homogeneous Cost Pools

Activities	*Cost Drivers*	*Activity Costs*
	Unit-Level Activities:	
Pool 1:		
Testing products	Number of dies	$275,000
Die insertion	Number of dies	225,000
		$500,000
	Batch-Level Activities	
Pool 2:		
Setting up batches	Number of batches	$120,000
Handling wafer lots	Number of batches	90,000
		$210,000
	Product-Level Activities	
Pool 3:		
Developing test programs	Number of products	$300,000
Making probe cards	Number of products	160,000
		$460,000
Pool 4:		
Engineering design	Number of change orders	$130,000
	Facility-Level Activities	
Pool 5:		
Providing space	Direct labor dollars	$ 20,000
Providing utilities	Direct labor dollars	30,000
		$ 50,000

by the use of cost driver analysis. Generally, the driver classification will produce more than one set for each activity level (with the exception of the facility-level category). Notice also that homogeneous cost pools are formed by adding the costs of individual activities that make up the homogeneous sets of activities. In this example, facility-level costs are allocated to products using direct labor dollars. A pure ABC model would not allocate these costs to products.

Once homogeneous cost pools are formed, pool rates are computed and overhead costs are assigned to individual products. The information for calculating pool rates and unit overhead costs is provided in Exhibit 19-12. Pool rates are also computed in this exhibit. The unit overhead cost is the sum of the unit-level, batch-level, product-level, and facility-level costs. In reporting unit-overhead costs, it is recommended that the product-cost categories be reported separately as shown in Exhibit 19-13. In this way, the facility-level component can be excluded if desired. Furthermore, it emphasizes the fact that only unit-level costs vary as the number of units changes. This last point is an important issue. Batch-level and product-level costs vary with factors other than changes in units and are assigned using nonunit cost drivers. Assigning these costs to units of product do not convert them into unit-based variable costs.

Comparison with Conventional Costing

The hierarchal classification of activities allows us to illustrate the fundamental differences between ABC and conventional cost systems. In a conventional system, the demand for overhead is assumed to be explained only by unit-based cost drivers. Thus, in a conventional system, the costs in the batch-level, product-level, and facility-level categories are fixed costs—costs that do not vary as production volume changes. Unit-based cost systems allocate fixed overhead to individual products and then add the overhead that varies with the number of units produced (variable overhead). From the perspective of activity-based costing, the

Exhibit 19-12
Activity Data and Pool Rates for Marvel Components, Inc.

Cost Drivers	*Wafer A*	*Wafer B*	*Total*
Units produced	100,000	200,000	300,000
Number of dies	600,000	1,400,000	2,000,000
Number of products	1	1	2
Number of batches	200	200	400
Number of change orders	10	30	40
Direct labor dollars	$800,000	$1,200,000	$2,000,000

Pool rates:

Unit-level pool:
Pool 1:
Rate = $500,000/2,000,000
= $0.25 per die

Product-level pools:
Pool 3:
Rate = $460,000/2
= $230,000 per product

Pool 4:
Rate = $130,000/40
= $3,250 per order

Batch-level pool:
Pool 2:
Rate = $210,000/400
= $525 per batch

Facility-level pool:
Pool 5:
Rate = $50,000/$2,000,000
= $0.025 per labor dollar

Exhibit 19-13
Unit Overhead Computation

	Wafer A	*Wafer B*
Unit-level activities:		
Pool 1 overhead:		
($0.25 × 600,000 dies)/100,000	$1.50	
($0.25 × 1,400,000 dies)/200,000		$1.75
Batch-level activities:		
Pool 2 overhead:		
($525 × 200 batches)/100,000	1.05	
($525 × 200 batches)/200,000		0.53
Product-level activities:		
Pool 3 overhead:		
($230,000 × 1 product)/100,000	2.30	
($230,000 × 1 product)/200,000		1.15
Pool 4 overhead:		
($3,250 × 10 orders)/100,000	0.33	
($3,250 × 30 orders)/200,000		0.49
Facility-level activities:		
(0.025 × $800,000)/100,000	0.20	
(0.025 × $1,200,000)/200,000		0.15
Total unit overhead cost	$5.38	$4.07

variable overhead is traced appropriately to individual products. The costs associated with unit-based cost drivers are the costs that traditionally have been labeled as variable overhead. Allocation of fixed overhead using unit-based cost drivers can be arbitrary, however, and may not reflect the activities actually being consumed by the products.

ABC systems improve product costing by recognizing that many of the so-called fixed overhead costs vary in proportion to changes other than production volume. The result of this insight is the addition of two new categories of non-unit-based cost drivers: batch level and product level. By understanding what causes these costs, they can be traced to individual products. This cause-and-effect relationship allows managers to improve product-costing accuracy, which can significantly improve decision making. Additionally, this large pool of fixed overhead costs is no longer so mysterious. Knowing the underlying behavior of many of these costs allows managers to exert more control over the activities that cause the costs.

The Choice of Cost Drivers

At least two major factors should be considered in selecting cost drivers: (1) the cost of measurement and (2) the degree of correlation between the cost driver and the actual consumption of overhead.[14]

The Cost of Measurement. In an activity-based cost system, a large number of cost drivers can be selected and used. Accordingly, where possible, it is important

14. A third factor, behavioral effects, has also been mentioned by Robin Cooper. However, discussion of this factor is reserved for Chapter 26, which discusses planning and control in the advanced manufacturing environment. See Robin Cooper, "Activity-Based Costing—Part Three."

to select cost drivers that use information that is readily available. Information that is not available in the existing system must be produced, and this production will increase the cost of the firm's information system. A homogeneous cost pool could offer a number of possible cost drivers. For this situation, any cost driver that can be used with existing information should be chosen. This choice minimizes the costs of measurement.

In the Sharp Paper example, for instance, inspection and setup costs were placed in the same cost pool, giving the choice of using either inspection hours or number of production runs as the cost driver. If the inspection hours and production runs used by the two products are already being collected by the company's information system, the choice is unimportant. Assume, however, that inspection hours by product are not tracked, but data for production runs are available. In this case, production runs should be chosen as the cost driver, avoiding the need to produce any additional information.

Indirect Measures and the Degree of Correlation. The existing information structure can be exploited in another way to minimize the costs of obtaining cost driver quantities. It is sometimes possible to replace a cost driver that directly measures the consumption of an activity with a surrogate driver—one that indirectly measures that consumption. For example, inspection hours could be replaced by the actual number of inspections associated with each product; this number is more likely to be known. This replacement works, of course, only if hours used per inspection are approximately equal for each product.

A list of potential cost drivers is given in Exhibit 19-14. Surrogate drivers indirectly measure the consumption of an activity and usually measure the number of transactions associated with that activity. Remember that it is possible to replace a cost driver that directly measures consumption with one that only indirectly measures it without loss of accuracy, provided that the quantities of activity consumed per transaction are approximately equal for each product. In such a case, the surrogate driver has a high correlation and can be used.

ABC and Service Organizations

Although most of the discussion of ABC has focused on manufacturing, ABC can also be useful to service organizations. All service organizations have activities and output that places demands on these activities. There are, however, some fundamental differences between service and manufacturing organizations. Activities within manufacturing organizations tend to be of the same type and performed in a similar way. The same cannot be said of service organizations. Imagine, for example, how dissimilar activities are for a bank and a hospital!

Exhibit 19-14
Potential Cost Drivers

Number of setups	Number of direct labor hours
Number of material moves	Number of vendors
Number of units reworked	Number of subassemblies
Number of orders placed	Number of labor transactions
Number of orders received	Number of units scrapped
Number of inspections	Number of parts
Number of schedule changes	Number of machine hours

Another basic difference between service and manufacturing organizations is output definition. For manufacturing firms, output is easily defined (the tangible products that are manufactured) but for service organizations output definition is more difficult.[15] Output for service organizations is less tangible. Yet output must be defined so that it can be costed.

Consider, for example, a hospital. What is the output of a hospital? The product of a hospital is commonly defined as a patient's stay and treatment. If we accept this definition, it immediately becomes obvious that a hospital is a multiproduct firm because there are many different kinds of "stays and treatments." During the stay, a patient will consume many different services. To the extent that this consumption of services is homogeneous, product groups can be defined. For example, all maternity patients without complications would stay about the same time in the hospital and consume essentially the same services.

To illustrate the potential of activity-based costing, we will focus on one type of service provided to each patient: daily care. Daily care is made up of three activities: occupancy, feeding, and nursing. We will define output as patient days (the "stay" part of the output only). Hospitals have traditionally assigned the cost of daily care by using a daily rate (a rate per patient day). There are actually different kinds of daily care and rates are structured to reflect these differences. For example, a higher daily rate is charged for an intensive care unit than for a maternity care unit.

Within units, however, the daily rates are the same for all patients. Under the traditional approach, the daily rate is computed by dividing the annual costs of occupancy, feeding, and nursing of a unit by the unit's capacity expressed in patient days. A single cost driver (patient days) is used to assign the costs of daily care to each patient.

But what if the costs of the three care activities are consumed in different proportions by patients? This would imply product diversity and a possible requirement to use more than one cost driver to assign daily care costs accurately to patients. To illustrate, assume that the demands for nursing care vary within the maternity unit, depending on the severity of a patient's case. Specifically, demand for nursing services per day increases with severity. Assume that within the maternity unit there are three levels of increasing severity: normal patients, Caesarian patients, and patients with complications. Now suppose that a hospital has provided the following activity and cost information:

Activity	*Annual Cost*	*Cost Driver*	*Annual Quantity*
Occupancy and feeding	$1,100,000	Patient days	11,000
Nursing care	$1,100,000	Hours of nursing care	55,000

The activity pool rates are $100 per patient day and $20 per nursing hour.

To see how activity costing can affect patient charges, assume that the three types of patients have the following annual demands:

15. For a more complete discussion on ABC and potential applications to service organizations see John Antos, "Activity-Based Management For Service, Not-For Profit, and Governmental Organizations," *Journal of Cost Management* (Summer 1992), pp. 13–23; William Rotch, "Activity-Based Costing in Service Industries," *Journal of Cost Management* (Summer 1990), pp. 4–14. The discussion in this chapter is based on these two articles.

Patient Type	*Patient Days Demanded*	*Nursing Hours Demanded*
Normal	8,000	30,000
Caesarian	2,000	13,000
Complications	1,000	12,000
Total	11,000	55,000

The traditional approach for charging daily care would produce a rate of $200 per patient day ($2,200,000/11,000)—the total cost of care divided by patient days. Every maternity patient—regardless of type—would pay the daily rate of $200. Using the pool rates for each activity, however produces a different daily rate for each patient—a rate that reflects the different demands for nursing services:

Patient	*Daily Rate*[a]
Normal	$175
Caesarian	230
Complications	340

[a][($100 × 8,000) + ($20 × 30,000)]/8,000; [($100 × 2,000) + ($20 × 13,000)]/2,000; [($100 × 1,000) + ($20 × 12,000)]/1,000

This example illustrates that ABC can produce significant product costing improvements in service organizations that experience product diversity. Although ABC has not yet had the same reception in service organizations compared to manufacturing organizations, it has been adopted by some. Examples of service organizations that have adopted an ABC approach include Union Pacific, Amtrak, and Armistead Insurance Company.[16]

WHEN TO USE AN ABC SYSTEM

Objective 4
Explain when an activity-based cost system should be used.

An ABC system offers significant benefits, including the following: greater product-costing accuracy, improved decision making, enhanced strategic planning, and better ability to manage activities. These benefits, however, are not obtained without costs. An ABC system is more complex, and it requires a significant increase in measurement activity—and measurement can be costly. Although each manager will have to assess the benefits and costs associated with implementing an ABC system, there are some reasonably good guidelines that can be followed.

Two fundamental requirements must be met before an ABC system is even considered as a possibility. First, the nonunit-based costs should be a significant percentage of total overhead costs. If they are immaterial, it simply doesn't matter how they are allocated to individual products. Second, the consumption ratios of unit-based and nonunit-based activities must differ. If products consume all overhead activities in roughly the same ratios, it doesn't matter if unit-based cost

16. William Rotch, "Activity-Based Costing in Service Industries."

drivers are used to allocate all overhead costs to individual products. The same cost assignment will be produced by either a conventional or an ABC system. Thus, firms with product homogeneity (low product diversity) may be able to use a conventional system without any problems.

Assuming that the nonunit-based costs are significant and that product diversity is high, should a manager implement an ABC system? Not necessarily. In deciding whether to implement an ABC system, a manager must assess the tradeoff between the cost of measurement and the cost of errors.[17] **Measurement costs** are the costs associated with the measurements required by the cost system. **Error costs** are the costs associated with making poor decisions based on inaccurate product costs. An **optimal cost system** is the one that minimizes the sum of measurement costs and error costs. Note, however, that the two costs conflict. More complex cost systems produce lower error costs but have higher measurement costs. This tradeoff is illustrated graphically in Exhibit 19-15. The message is clear. For some organizations, the optimal cost system may not be an ABC system even though it is a more accurate system. Depending on the tradeoffs, the optimal cost system may very well be a simpler, traditional, unit-based system. This could explain, in part, why most firms still maintain a conventional system.

There are, however, some changes that are taking place in the manufacturing environment that are increasing the attractiveness of more complex and accurate cost systems. New information technology, for example, is decreasing the cost of measurement. Computerized production planning systems and more powerful,

Exhibit 19-15
Tradeoffs Illustrated: The Optimal Cost System

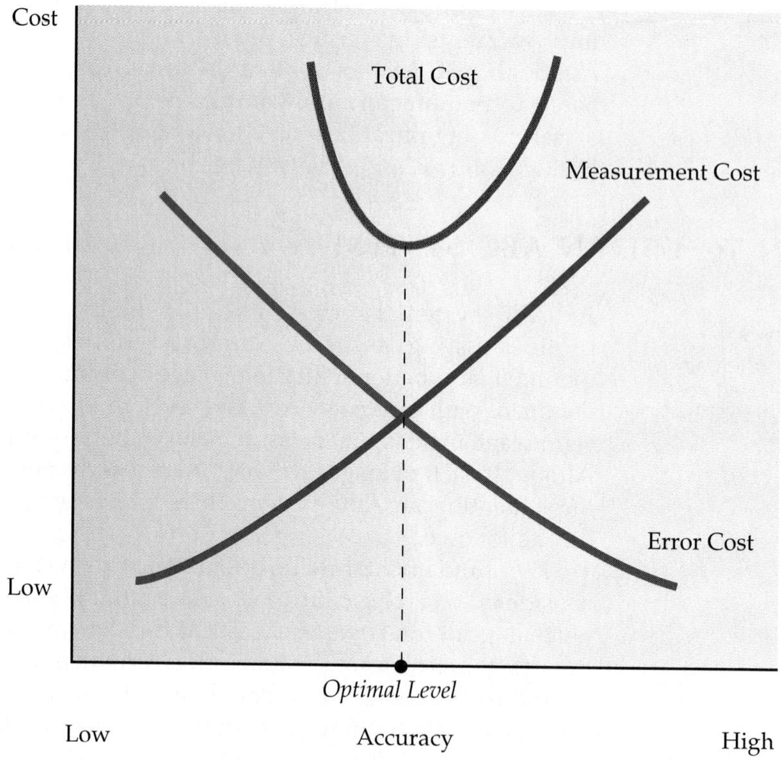

17. The discussion of these issues is based on the following article: Robin Cooper, "The Rise of Activity-Based Costing—Part Two: When Do I Need an Activity-Based Cost System?" pp. 41–48.

less expensive computers make it easier to collect data and perform calculations. As measurement costs decrease, the cost-of-the-measurement cost curve shifts downward and to the right, causing the total cost curve to shift to the right. The optimal cost system is now one that allows more accuracy.

The cost of errors has also changed for many organizations. As the degree and nature of competition changes, the cost of errors can increase. Increased competition may lead a firm to drop what appear to be unprofitable products. In the opening scenario, for example, Sharp Paper was considering the possibility of dropping its high-volume products and emphasizing the low-volume lines. If the nature of the competition changes, error costs can increase as well. For example, if focused competitors emerge, their pricing and marketing strategies will be based on more accurate cost information. The more-focused firms gain market share at the expense of the less-focused firms. Other factors, such as deregulation and JIT manufacturing (which leads to a more-focused production environment), can also increase the cost of errors. As the cost of errors increases, the error-cost curve of Exhibit 19-15 shifts upward and to the right, causing the total cost curve to again shift to the right. Thus, a more accurate cost system will become optimal.

As the cost of measurement decreases and the cost of errors increases, the existing cost system will become obsolete. A more accurate cost system is mandated. This is exactly the situation in the opening scenario that Sharp Paper was facing. The problems it was experiencing were attributable mainly to inaccurate cost information. Its cost system was no longer optimal. Furthermore, this state of affairs was being signaled. There were strong signals (symptoms) that the existing cost system was no longer useful. These symptoms of an obsolete cost system listed in Exhibit 19-1 reflect the need for a new cost system. Firms, then, should consider implementing an ABC system if they have significant nonunit-based costs and high product diversity and have experienced a decrease in measurement costs and an increase in error costs.

Although the majority of firms still use a conventional product costing system, the use of ABC is spreading and the interest in the approach is high. Firms like Hughes Aircraft, Caterpillar, Xerox, National Semiconductor, Tektronix, Dayton Extruded Plastics, Armistead Insurance, and Zytec have adopted ABC systems.[18] Furthermore, this is only a very small listing of firms that are using ABC.

JIT MANUFACTURING AND PRODUCT COSTING

Objective 5

Describe how JIT manufacturing alters the fundamental cost concepts and practices found in a conventional manufacturing environment.

In an activity-based cost system, costing accuracy is achieved by creating cost pools and identifying cost drivers that can be used to assign costs to each pool. Because of the large number of overhead activities that are shared by products, the effort and expense of an activity-based cost system can be considerable. As we noted previously, single-product firms and multiple-product firms that choose to dedicate entire facilities to the production of a single product have no problems with costing accuracy. All overhead activities are traceable directly to a single product.

Some of the same product-costing benefits found in a single-product environment are achieved by firms that install a JIT manufacturing system. These

18. See Peter B. B. Turney, "Activity-Based Management," *Management Accounting* (January 1992), pp. 20–25; Jack Hedicke and David Feil, "Hughes Aircraft," *Management Accounting* (February 1991), pp. 29–33; and Lou F. Jones, "Product Costing at Caterpillar," *Management Accounting* (February 1991), pp. 34–42.

benefits are realized because JIT manufacturing adopts a more focused approach than that found in traditional manufacturing. Installing a JIT system affects the traceability of costs, enhances product-costing accuracy, diminishes the need for allocation of service-center costs, changes the behavior and relative importance of direct labor costs, and impacts job-order and process costing systems. To understand and appreciate these effects, we need a fundamental understanding of what JIT manufacturing is and how it differs from traditional manufacturing.

JIT Compared with Traditional Manufacturing

JIT manufacturing

JIT—or just-in-time manufacturing—is a demand-pull system. The objective of **JIT manufacturing** is to produce a product only when it is needed and only in the quantities demanded by customers. Demand pulls products through the manufacturing process. Each operation produces only what is necessary to satisfy the demand of the succeeding operation. No production takes place until a signal from a succeeding process indicates a need to produce. Parts and materials arrive just in time to be used in production.

Lower Inventories. One effect of JIT is to reduce inventories to much lower levels. Contrast this with the traditional push-through system of manufacturing. In traditional manufacturing, materials are supplied and parts produced and transferred to the succeeding process without regard to the level of demand that exists downstream. In a push-through system, inventories result when production exceeds demand. Inventories are needed as a buffer when production is less than demand. Usually, the push-through system produces significantly higher levels of inventory than a JIT system.

Manufacturing Cells. In conventional manufacturing, products are moved from one group of identical machines to another. Typically, machines with identical functions are located together in an area referred to as a *department or process.* Workers who specialize in the operation of a specific machine are located in each department. This traditional pattern is often replaced with a pattern of manufacturing cells.

manufacturing cells

Manufacturing cells contain machines that are grouped in families, usually in a semicircle. The machines are arranged so that they can be used to perform a variety of operations in sequence. Each cell is set up to produce a particular product or product family. Products move from one machine to another from start to finish. Workers are assigned to cells and are trained to operate all machines within the cell. Thus, labor in a JIT, cellular manufacturing environment is interdisciplinary, not specialized. Each manufacturing cell is essentially a minifactory; in fact, cells are often referred to as a *factory within a factory.* A comparison of the physical layout of cellular manufacturing with the traditional pattern is shown in Exhibit 19-16.

One important qualification should be mentioned. Technically, JIT and cellular manufacturing can be applied independently of each other. The JIT approach can be applied to assembly line operations and even some service operations (where no cellular approach is needed). Furthermore, cellular manufacturing can be applied to job-shop environments (and other settings as well) without the use of the JIT approach. In fact, it is important to understand that cellular manufacturing by itself is an important concept and serves as the fundamental

Exhibit 19-16
Comparison of Physical Layout in Traditional and JIT Manufacturing

Traditional Manufacturing Layout

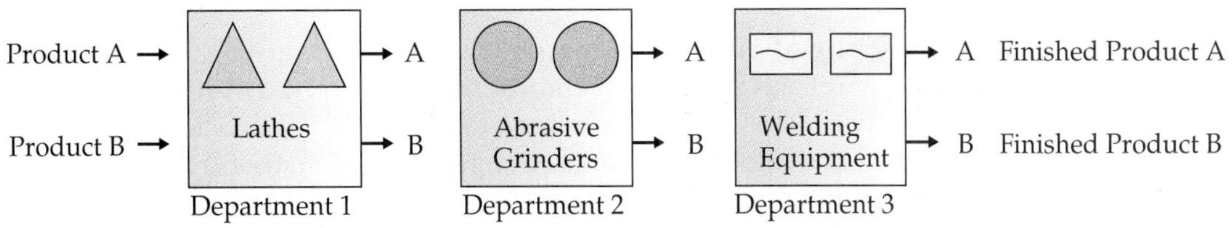

Each product passes through departments that specialize in one process. Departments process multiple products.

JIT Manufacturing Layout

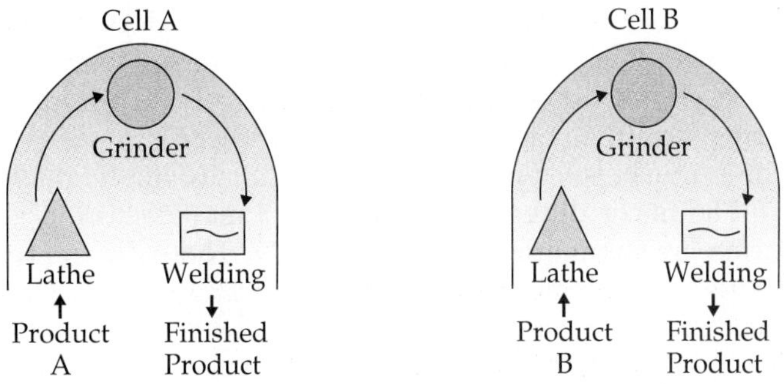

Notice that each product passes through its own cell. All machines necessary to process each product are placed within the cell. Each cell is dedicated to the production of one product or one subassembly.

building block of other advanced manufacturing processes.[19] Yet cellular manufacturing and JIT represent a potent combination; therefore, it's easy to argue that whenever possible, cellular manufacturing ought to be an integral part of JIT manufacturing.

Interdisciplinary (Multi-Task) Labor. In a conventional manufacturing environment, labor is usually specialized. Workers are trained to carry out one task, for example, the operation of one machine. In a JIT environment, workers are expected to carry out more than one task. This is viewed as a way of increasing efficiency and lowering costs. If cellular manufacturing is part of the JIT operation, workers are expected to operate several different machines as well as perform other tasks such as maintenance and inspections. But the concept of multi-task workers is not limited to cellular manufacturing. It also applies to assembly line operations. For example, in the old Henry Ford approach to mass produc-

19. An excellent discussion of cellular manufacturing and its effect on activity-based costing is provided in the following article: Dileep G. Dhavale, "Activity-Based Costing in Cellular Manufacturing Systems: A Normative Approach," forthcoming, *Journal of Cost Management*.

tion, workers on an auto assembly line performed one task. One worker would be responsible only for installing wheels and tires, another would be responsible for checking for flaws, and a third would be responsible for maintaining equipment. In the new Toyota manufacturing process, a line worker is responsible for performing *multiple tasks,* such as installing wheels and tires, checking for flaws, and maintaining equipment.[20]

A Philosophy of Total Quality Control. JIT necessarily carries with it a much stronger emphasis on quality control. A defective part brings production to a grinding halt. Poor quality cannot be tolerated in a manufacturing environment that operates without inventories. Simply put, JIT cannot be implemented without a commitment to **total quality control (TQC)**. TQC is essentially a never-ending quest for perfect quality: the striving for a defect-free manufacturing process. This approach to quality is diametrically opposed to the traditional doctrine, called **acceptable quality level (AQL)**. AQL permits or allows defects to occur provided they do not exceed a predetermined level.

total quality control (TQC)

acceptable quality level (AQL)

Decentralization of Services. JIT requires easy and quick access to support services, which means that centralized service departments must be scaled down and their personnel assigned to work directly to support production. For example, with respect to raw materials, JIT calls for multiple stock points, each one near where the material will be used. There is no need for a central stores location—in fact, such an arrangement actually hinders efficient production.

The major differences between JIT manufacturing and traditional manufacturing are summarized in Exhibit 19-17. These differences will be referred to and discussed in greater detail as the implications of JIT manufacturing for management accounting are examined.

JIT and the Traceability of Overhead Costs

In a JIT environment, many overhead activities formerly common to multiple product lines now are traceable directly to a single product. Cellular manufacturing, interdisciplinary labor, and decentralized service activities are the major features of JIT responsible for this change in traceability.[21]

In a departmental structure, many different products may be subjected to a process located in a single department (e.g., grinding). After completion of the process, the products then are transferred to other processes located in different departments (e.g., assembly, painting, and so on). Although a different set of processes usually is required for each product, most processes are applicable to more than one product. For example, three different products may need grinding. Because more than one product is processed in a department, the costs of that department are common to all products passing through and, therefore, indirectly traceable to any single product. In a manufacturing-cell structure, however, all processes necessary for the production of each product or major subassembly

20. A good discussion comparing the Toyota approach to the traditional mass production approach is given in the following article: Doron P. Levein, "Toyota Plant in Kentucky Is Font of Ideas," *New York Times,* May 5, 1992.

21. For a more detailed discussion of the costing effects of JIT, see George Foster and Charles Horngren, "JIT: Cost Accounting and Cost Management Issues," *Management Accounting* (June 1987), pp. 19–25; Robert Howell and Stephen R. Soucy, "Cost Accounting in the New Manufacturing Environment," *Management Accounting* (August 1987), pp. 42–48; and Robert D. McIlhattan, "How Cost Management Systems Can Support the JIT Philosophy," *Management Accounting* (September 1987), pp. 20–26.

Exhibit 19-17
Comparison of JIT and Traditional Manufacturing

JIT	*Traditional*
1. Pull-through system	1. Push-through system
2. Insignificant inventories	2. Significant inventories
3. Manufacturing cells	3. Departmental structure
4. Interdisciplinary labor	4. Specialized labor
5. Total quality control	5. Acceptable quality level
6. Decentralized services	6. Centralized services

are collected in one area. Thus, all the costs of operating that cell are traceable directly to the product line it serves.

Equipment formerly located in other departments, for example, is now reassigned to cells, where it is dedicated to the production of a single product or subassembly. Because of this, depreciation is now a directly traceable product cost. Interdisciplinary workers and decentralization of services also add to the effect. Workers in the cell are trained to set up the equipment in the cell, maintain it, and operate it. Additionally, cell workers may also be used to move a partially finished part from one machine to the next. These cell workers operate directly on the product and are, therefore, direct laborers. But they also perform maintenance, setups, and material handling, support functions previously done by a different set of laborers for all product lines. Thus, in a JIT environment, many costs formerly classified as indirect labor costs now are traceable directly to the product line. Exhibit 19-18 compares the traceability of some selected costs in traditional manufacturing with their traceability in the JIT environment.

Product-Costing Accuracy and JIT

One consequence of decreasing indirect costs and increasing direct costs is to increase the accuracy of product costing. Direct manufacturing costs are traceable to the product and can safely be said to belong to it. Indirect costs, however, are common to several products and must be assigned to these products using cost drivers and overhead rates. Because of cost and convenience, cost drivers that are less than perfectly correlated with the consumption of overhead activities

Exhibit 19-18
Product Cost Traceability: Traditional versus JIT Manufacturing

Manufacturing Cost	*Traditional Environment*	*JIT Environment*
Direct labor	Direct	Direct
Direct materials	Direct	Direct
Material handling	Indirect	Direct
Repairs and maintenance	Indirect	Direct
Energy	Indirect	Direct
Operating supplies	Indirect	Direct
Supervision	Indirect	Direct
Insurance and taxes	Indirect	Indirect
Building depreciation	Indirect	Indirect
Equipment depreciation	Indirect	Direct
Custodial services	Indirect	Indirect
Cafeteria services	Indirect	Indirect

may be chosen. JIT manufacturing, by reducing the pools of indirect costs and converting many of them to direct costs, diminishes the need for this difficult assessment.

For example, assume that prior to installing a JIT system, two products, a hammer and a wrench, were assigned overhead costs using an activity-based approach. One of the overhead pools contained two overhead activities: maintenance and power. The total annual costs of this pool, information concerning its cost driver (machine hours), and information pertaining to the two products are as follows:

Total maintenance and power costs	$200,000
Machine hours:	
Hammer	25,000
Wrench	25,000
Production (in units):	
Hammer	50,000
Wrench	50,000

Based on these data, the cost per unit of the cost driver is $4 ($200,000/50,000 machine hours). Using this rate, the following maintenance and power costs would be assigned to each product:

Hammer:	
Total cost assigned ($4 × 25,000)	$100,000
Cost per unit ($100,000/50,000)	$2
Wrench: Total cost assigned ($4 × 25,000)	$100,000
Cost per unit ($100,000/50,000)	$2

Now assume that the company installs JIT manufacturing and organizes a manufacturing cell for each product. Power is metered for each cell, and workers in each cell are trained to perform maintenance. The same machine hours are used for each product, and the same number of units of each product are produced. The maintenance and power costs for each cell are given below.

Cell H (produces hammers):	
Power costs	$ 50,000
Maintenance costs	30,000
Total	$ 80,000
Cell W (produces wrenches):	
Power costs	$ 60,000
Maintenance costs	60,000
Total	$120,000

Based on this information, the unit cost of each product is shown in the following table:

Hammer ($80,000/50,000)	$1.60
Wrench ($120,000/50,000)	$2.40

The unit costs under the cell structure accurately reflect the consumption of maintenance and power costs since these costs are directly traceable to each product. Focusing the manufacturing processes has increased the firm's ability to determine the costs of production. While activity-based costing offers significant improvement in product-costing accuracy, focusing offers even more potential improvement.

It should be mentioned, however, that JIT does not convert all indirect costs into direct costs. Even with JIT in place, a significant number of overhead activities remain common to the manufacturing cells. This means that activity-based costing can still be useful in tracing costs to products, but the nature of an ABC system does change. In a JIT system, the batch size is one unit of product. Thus, all batch-level activities convert into unit-level activities. Additionally, many of the batch-level activities are reduced or eliminated.[22] For example, material handling may be reduced significantly because of reorganizing from a departmental structure to a cellular structure. These changes simplify the implementation of an ABC system by significantly reducing the number of cost drivers. A pure ABC system requires the identification of cost drivers for three categories of activities: unit level, batch level, and product level. In a JIT environment, identification of cost drivers is reduced to two categories: unit level and product level. Furthermore, it is also possible that the need to use cost drivers for product-level activities may also be diminished. For example, a firm may choose to decentralize engineering activities to the cell level (and thus to the product). Engineering support, therefore, is traceable directly to the cell, and there is no need to use a cost driver to trace this cost to individual products.

cell-level activities

Also, JIT creates another category of activity: cell-level activities. **Cell-level activities** are those that sustain the cell process (e.g., supervision). These costs do not vary as the number of units increases or with product-sustaining cost drivers; however, unlike facility costs, cell-level costs are traceable to individual products. Cells also create a more logical connection with facility-level costs. It can be argued, for example, that the square footage occupied by cells drives many facility-level costs. If true, allocation of facility-level costs to cells and, thus, to products is less arbitrary. JIT and ABC together should provide significant improvements in tracing manufacturing costs to individual products.

JIT and the Allocation of Service-Center Costs

In traditional manufacturing, centralized service centers provide support to a variety of producing departments. In a JIT environment, many services are decentralized. This is accomplished by assigning people with specialized skills (e.g., industrial engineers and production schedulers) directly to product lines and by training direct laborers within cells to perform service activities formerly done by indirect laborers (e.g., maintenance). Thus, many service costs

22. See Peter B. B. Turney and James M. Reeve, "The Impact of Continuous Improvement on the Design of Activity-Based Cost Systems," *Journal of Cost Management* (Summer 1990), pp. 43–50.

now can be traced directly to a manufacturing cell and, consequently, to a specific product.

By disaggregating service costs and making them directly traceable to products, JIT gives managers a much better understanding of a product's true costs. It also creates the opportunity for managers to exercise better control over service costs through better understanding and more clearly identified responsibility. Under the traditional arrangement, service and production departments were managed by at least two different managers. Technically, in such a setting, the manager of the service department was responsible for the incurrence of service costs; however, the operating managers also had a stake in the matter since service costs affected the cost of the products over which they had responsibility. Unfortunately, operating managers were able to exercise only indirect control over service costs. Because services are decentralized in JIT, operating managers receive direct responsibility for many service costs.

JIT's Effect on Direct Labor Costs

As firms implement JIT and automate, traditional direct labor costs are reduced significantly. Moreover, as direct laborers become trained in multiple functions, the level of direct labor costs tends to stabilize as production fluctuates. For example, cell workers can be used to perform preventive maintenance during a slack period in manufacturing activity. Therefore, there are two outcomes: (1) direct labor decreases as a percentage of total manufacturing costs and (2) direct labor changes from a variable to a fixed cost.

As direct labor costs decline, the emphasis on tracking and reporting direct labor costs decreases significantly. The Milwaukee plant of Harley-Davidson, for example, found after the adoption of the JIT approach that direct labor costs were less than 10 percent of the cost of manufacturing motorcycles, yet management accountants were devoting 65 percent of their administrative efforts to tracking these costs.[23] Harley-Davidson simplified the treatment of direct labor costs by combining them with overhead costs to create a conversion cost pool on a cellular level. These conversion costs then are assigned to the product as it passes through the cell.

JIT's Effect on Inventory Valuation

One of the first accounting problems eliminated by the use of JIT manufacturing is the need to determine product costs for inventory valuation. If inventories exist, they must be valued—and valued according to a certain set of rules for financial reporting purposes (GAAP). With zero inventories (or at least insignificant levels), inventory valuation is irrelevant for financial reporting purposes. GAAP guidelines for product costing are also irrelevant, freeing up the accounting system to be more responsive to managerial needs. In fact, in a JIT environment, product costing exists only to satisfy managerial purposes. Managers need accurate product cost information for cost-plus pricing decisions, cost trend analysis, profitability analysis by product lines, comparison to competitors' costs, make-or-buy decisions, and so on. Because JIT frees up the accounting system

23. Foster and Horngren, "JIT: Cost Accounting and Cost Management Issues."

from the constraints of inventory valuation, managers are more likely to have the needed information.

JIT's Effect on Job-Order Costing

In implementing JIT in a job-order setting, first the firm should separate its repetitive business from its unique orders. Manufacturing cells then can be established to deal with the repetitive business. For those products where demand is insufficient to justify its own manufacturing cell, groups of dissimilar machines can be set up in a cell to make families of products or parts that require the same manufacturing sequence.[24]

With this reorganizing of the manufacturing layout, job orders are no longer needed to accumulate product costs. Instead, costs can be accumulated at the cellular level. Additionally, because lot sizes are now too small (as a result of reducing work-in-process and finished goods inventories), it is impractical to have job orders for each job. Add to this the short lead time of products occurring because of the demand-pull philosophy of JIT, and it becomes difficult to track each piece moving through the cell. In effect, the job environment has taken on the nature of a process costing system.[25]

Process Costing and JIT

In traditional process costing, manufacturing costs are accumulated by process for a period of time. Output is then measured for the same period of time. Unit cost for the period is computed by dividing the period's costs by its output. The unit cost is used to value work-in-process inventories and goods transferred out.

Although the unit-cost computation sounds simple, it is complicated by the presence of partially completed units in beginning and ending work in process and the costs attached to the units in beginning work in process. This complication makes it necessary to define what is meant by total output and total manufacturing costs. *Output* is defined as the equivalent units for the period, where equivalent units include an accounting for the work done on the partially finished goods in work in process. Equivalent units are computed under one of two methods: weighted average or FIFO. The former counts the work done in the prior period (found in beginning work in process) as belonging to the current period; the latter excludes this work. Similar treatment is given to prior-period costs by each method. The computation of the unit cost can become quite messy, especially for FIFO.

The computation of unit cost under process costing can become complicated because of the presence of work-in-process inventories. With JIT's zero inventories, the unit-cost computation is as simple as it sounds: divide the period's costs for a process by the number of units produced. The computation of equivalent units is no longer needed, and there is no requirement to account for prior-period costs. JIT leads to significant simplification.

24. Richard C. Walleigh, "What's Your Excuse for Not Using JIT?" *Harvard Business Review* (March-April 1986), pp. 38–54.

25. These points are based on experience. They are described by Henry J. Johansson, Thomas Volmann, and Vivian Wright in "The Effect of Zero Inventories on Cost (Just-in-Time)," *Cost Accounting for the 90s* (Montvale, NJ: National Association of Accountants, 1986), pp. 141–64.

SUMMARY OF LEARNING OBJECTIVES

1. *Explain why using only unit-based cost drivers to assign overhead may produce distorted product costs.* Overhead costs have increased significantly over time and, in many firms, represent a much higher percentage of product costs than direct labor. At the same time, many overhead activities are unrelated to the units produced. Conventional cost systems are not able to assign the costs of these nonunit-related overhead activities accurately. These overhead activities are consumed by products in different proportions than unit-based overhead activities. Because of this, assigning overhead using only unit-based drivers can distort product costs. This can be a serious matter if the nonunit-based overhead costs are a significant proportion of total overhead costs.

2. *Explain why activity-based costing produces more accurate product costs.* Overhead assignments should reflect the amount of overhead demanded (consumed) by each product. Activity-based costing recognizes that all overhead does not vary with the number of units produced. By using both unit-based and nonunit-based cost drivers, overhead can be traced more accurately to individual products. This tracing is achieved by implementing the following steps: (1) identifying the major activities, (2) determining the cost of those activities, (3) identifying what causes or drives these activity costs (cost drivers), (4) grouping activities into homogeneous cost pools, (5) calculating a pool rate, (6) measuring the demands placed on activities by each product, and (7) calculating product costs.

3. *Provide a detailed description of activity-based costing, including how homogeneous sets of activities are created.* Activities are basic units of work. Homogeneous sets of activities are collections of activities that have the same level classification and the same cost driver classification. Level classification places activities into one of four categories: unit level, batch level, product level, and facility level. Unit-level activities occur each time a unit of product is produced. Batch-level activities occur when batches of products are produced. Product-level activities are incurred to support production of each different type of product. Facility-level activities sustain a facility's general manufacturing processes. Finally, level-classified activities with the same cost driver are combined to form homogeneous sets. Summing the costs associated with activities within homogeneous sets defines homogeneous cost pools. Cost drivers are used to compute pool rates and assign costs to individual products.

4. *Explain when an activity-based cost system should be used.* An ABC system may be needed whenever nonunit-based overhead costs are a significant proportion of total overhead costs and there exists a high level of product diversity. If these two conditions are met and if a firm has experienced decreasing measurement costs or increasing error costs (or both), the likelihood of needing the more accurate ABC system is very high.

5. *Describe how JIT manufacturing alters the fundamental cost concepts and practices found in a conventional manufacturing environment.* JIT manufacturing affects product costing because it differs from traditional manufacturing on several dimensions. JIT manufacturing is a pull-through instead of a push-through approach, reduces inventories to much lower levels, uses interdisciplinary labor instead of specialized labor, uses a focused cell structure instead of departments, and decentralizes many service functions to the cellular level. The differences affect a number of product-costing practices.

For example, JIT affects the traceability and behavior of costs. Because cells are dedicated to the manufacture of a single product or subassembly, many indirect product costs are converted to direct product costs. Furthermore, because of the interdisciplinary approach, many costs formerly classified as variable (e.g., direct labor and material handling) are now fixed.

Increasing the number of costs that are traceable directly to products reduces the need to use overhead cost pools and cost drivers to assign overhead costs to products, thus increasing product-costing accuracy. Although the need for cost drivers is reduced, it is not eliminated and an ABC system can still be used to increase accuracy in a JIT setting.

JIT manufacturing also decreases the need for allocation of service-center costs; many of these costs are decentralized and located within each manufacturing cell. Job-order and process-costing systems are also affected. JIT transforms job-order systems into process systems and eliminates the need to compute equivalent units for process systems.

KEY TERMS

Acceptable quality level (AQL) 898
Activity 881
Activity-based cost (ABC) system 881
Advanced manufacturing environment 875
Batch-level activities 885
Cell-level activities 901
Consumption ratio 880
Cost drivers 876
Error costs 894

REVIEW PROBLEM

Inca Pottery Company is noted for a full line of quality vases. The company operates one of its plants in Lima, Peru. That plant produces two types of vases: Indian design and contemporary. Maria Vinueza, the president of the company, recently decided to change from a volume-based costing system to an activity-based cost system. Before making the change companywide, she wanted to assess the effect on the product costs of the Lima plant. This plant was chosen because it produces only two types of vases; most other plants produce at least a dozen.

To assess the effect of the change, the following data have been gathered. (For simplicity, costs are expressed in dollars rather than in Peruvian currency.)

Vase	*Quantity*	*Prime Costs*	*Machine Hours*	*Material Moves*	*Setups*
Indian	200,000	$700,000	50,000	700,000	100
Contemporary	50,000	150,000	12,500	100,000	50
Dollar value	—	$850,000	$250,000[a]	$300,000	$450,000

[a]The cost of maintenance.

Under the current system, the costs of maintenance, material handling, and setups are assigned to the vases on the basis of machine hours.

REQUIRED:

1. Compute the unit cost of each vase using the current unit-based approach.
2. Compute the unit cost of each vase using an activity-based costing approach.
3. Assume that Maria decides to install JIT manufacturing. Two manufacturing cells are created—one for each vase (the I-cell and the C-cell). The overhead costs traceable to each cell are as follows:

Cell	*Maintenance*	*Material Handling*	*Setups*	*Total*
I-Cell	$210,000	$260,000	$300,000	$770,000
C-Cell	40,000	40,000	150,000	230,000

Assume the same level of output and prime costs as in the current system. Compute the unit cost for each vase in the JIT system. Is this cost more accurate than the activity-based cost? Explain.

Solution

1. Total overhead is $1,000,000. The plant-wide rate is $16 per machine hour ($1,000,000/62,500). Overhead is assigned as follows:

   Indian vase: $16 × 50,000 = $800,000
   Contemporary vase: $16 × 12,500 = $200,000

   The unit costs for the two products are as follows:

   Indian vase: ($800,000 + $700,000)/200,000 = $7.50
   Contemporary: ($200,000 + $150,000)/50,000 = $7.00

2. In the activity-based approach, the consumption ratios are different for all three overhead activities, so overhead pools are formed for each activity. The overhead rates for each of these pools are as follows:

   Maintenance: $250,000/62,500 = $4 per hour
   Material handling: $300,000/800,000 = $0.375 per move
   Setup: $450,000/150 = $3,000 per setup

   Overhead is assigned as follows:

Indian vases:	
$4 × 50,000	$200,000
$0.375 × 700,000	262,500
$3,000 × 100	300,000
Total	$762,500

Contemporary vases:	
$4 × 12,500	$ 50,000
$0.375 × 100,000	37,500
$3,000 × 50	150,000
Total	$237,500

   This produces the following unit costs:

Indian vases:	
Prime costs	$ 700,000
Overhead costs	762,500
Total costs	$1,462,500
Units produced	200,000
Unit cost	$7.31
Contemporary vases:	
Prime costs	$ 150,000
Overhead costs	237,500
Total costs	$ 387,500
Units produced	50,000
Unit cost	$7.75

3. With a JIT manufacturing system, costs would be computed as follows:

Indian vases:	
Prime costs	$ 700,000
Overhead costs	770,000
Total	$1,470,000
Units produced	200,000
Unit cost	$7.35
Contemporary vases:	
Prime costs	$ 150,000
Overhead costs	230,000
Total	$ 380,000
Units produced	50,000
Unit cost	$7.60

The unit cost here is the most accurate since all costs are directly traceable to each product. This is because of the focusing effect of JIT.

QUESTIONS

1. Explain how a plant-wide overhead rate using a unit-based cost driver can produce distorted product costs.
2. What are nonunit-related overhead activities? nonunit-based cost drivers? Give some examples.
3. What is an overhead consumption ratio?
4. Explain how departmental overhead rates can produce product costs that are more distorted than those computed using a plant-wide rate.
5. What is meant by product diversity?
6. Overhead costs are the source of product cost distortions. Do you agree? Explain.
7. What is activity-based product costing?
8. What is a homogeneous cost pool?
9. What is the first-stage procedure in assigning overhead costs to products when using an activity-based system?
10. What is the second-stage procedure in assigning overhead costs to products when using an activity-based system?
11. What is an activity? a homogeneous set of activities?
12. What are unit-level activities? batch-level activities? product-level activities? facility-level activities?
13. What role does the cost of measurement have in selecting a cost driver? What about degree of correlation with indirect measures of activity?
14. Explain why some firms may choose (correctly) to continue using conventional (unit-based) cost systems.
15. How can you tell if a cost system has become obsolete? What are some of the symptoms of an outmoded cost system?
16. Explain how low-volume products can be undercosted and high-volume products overcosted if only unit-based cost drivers are used to assign overhead costs.
17. Explain how undercosting low-volume products and overcosting high-volume products can affect the competitive position of a firm.
18. What is JIT manufacturing? List four ways in which JIT manufacturing differs from traditional manufacturing.
19. What are manufacturing cells? Explain how they differ from production departments.
20. Identify four effects that a JIT environment has on traditional costs and cost concepts.
21. Explain why some indirect manufacturing costs in traditional manufacturing become direct costs in JIT manufacturing. Give some examples of costs that change in this way.
22. In JIT manufacturing, direct labor costs are less important and largely fixed in nature. Do you agree? Explain.

23. Without inventories, there is no distinction between product and period costs. Do you agree? Explain.
24. How does JIT manufacturing increase product-costing accuracy?
25. Discuss the effect JIT manufacturing has on activity-based costing.
26. How is job-order costing affected in a JIT environment? process costing?

EXERCISES

E19-1 Product-Costing Accuracy and Overhead Costs

LO 1

Gator Company has traditionally produced a handcrafted ladies' purse (sold under the label, Gator Elegant). A marketing consultant has recommended that a second purse be produced—using lower quality materials and automation so that it can be produced in larger quantities. (This purse will be sold under the label, Gator Emminent.) Gator decides to produce the second purse and buys the equipment for automated production and installs it in a currently unused part of its plant. Gator discovers that a small part of the operation associated with the handcrafted purse can be automated (using the same equipment just purchased) without compromising its claim that the purse is essentially handcrafted.

The production equipment is expected to last five years, with a capability of supplying a total of 25,000 machine hours. The costs associated with the equipment are given below:

Depreciation	$10,000[a]
Operating costs	$ 6,000

[a]Computed on a straight-line basis; book value at the beginning of the year was $50,000.

The controller has collected the expected annual prime costs for each purse, the machine hours, and the expected production.

	Elegant	*Eminent*
Direct labor	$3,000	$1,000
Direct materials	$9,000	$3,000
Units	3,000	6,000
Machine hours	500	4,500

REQUIRED:

1. Do you think that the direct labor costs and direct materials costs are traced accurately to each purse? Explain.
2. The controller has suggested that overhead costs be assigned to each product using a plant-wide rate based on direct labor costs. Machine costs are overhead costs. Calculate the machine cost per unit for each purse that would be assigned using this approach. Do you think that machine costs are traced accurately to each purse? Explain.
3. Now calculate the machine cost per unit for each purse using an overhead rate based on machine hours. Do you think machine costs are traced accurately to each purse? Explain.
4. Suppose machine hours are used to assign *all* overhead costs of the plant to the two products. Do you think this will produce an accurate cost assignment for each purse? Explain.

E19-2
Multiple versus Single Overhead Rates; Cost Drivers
LO 2

Assume that a plant has two categories of overhead: material handling and quality inspection. The costs expected for these categories for the coming year are as follows:

Material handling	$200,000
Quality inspection	$600,000

The plant currently applies overhead using machine hours and expected actual capacity. This figure is 80,000 machine hours. Linda Bixby, the plant manager, has been asked to submit a bid and has assembled the following data on the proposed job:

	Potential Job
Direct materials	$3,700
Direct labor (1,000 hours)	$7,000
Overhead	$?
Number of material moves	10
Number of inspections	5
Machine hours	900

Linda has been told that many competitors use an activity-based approach to assign overhead to jobs. Before submitting her bid, she wants to assess the effects of this alternative approach. She estimates that the expected number of material moves for all jobs during the year is 1,000; she also expects 5,000 quality inspections to be performed.

REQUIRED:

1. Compute the total cost of the potential job using machine hours to assign overhead. Assuming that the bid price is full manufacturing cost plus 25 percent, what would Linda's bid be?
2. Compute the total cost of the job using the number of material moves to allocate material handling costs and the number of inspections to allocate the quality inspection costs. Assuming a bid price of full manufacturing cost plus 25 percent, what is Linda's bid using this approach?
3. Which approach do you think best reflects the actual cost of the job? Explain.

E19-3
Multiple versus Single Overhead Rates; Cost Drivers
LO 2

Thayn Company has identified the following overhead costs and cost drivers for the coming year:

Overhead Item	*Expected Cost*	*Cost Driver*	*Practical Level*
Setup costs	$120,000	Number of setups	300
Ordering costs	$ 90,000	Number of orders	4,500
Machine costs	$ 90,000	Machine hours	18,000
Power	$ 25,000	Kilowatt hours	50,000

The following two jobs were completed during the year:

	Job 125	*Job 128*
Direct materials	$1,050	$1,750
Direct labor (50 hours per job)	$800	$800
Units completed	100	50
Number of setups	1	1
Number of orders	4	2
Machine hours	20	30
Kilowatt hours	20	40

The company's normal activity is 5,000 direct labor hours.

REQUIRED:

1. Determine the unit cost for each job using direct labor hours to apply overhead.
2. Determine the unit cost for each job using the four cost drivers.
3. Which method produces the more accurate cost assignment? Why?

E19-4
Activity-Based Costing; Homogeneous Cost Pools; Cost Drivers
LO 2, 3

Choko Manufacturing produces two types of thermometers: candy and weather. The thermometers are produced using one continuous process. Four activities have been identified: machining, setups, receiving, and packing. Costs have been assigned to each activity. The overhead activities, their costs, and the other related data are as follows:

Product	*Machine Hours*	*Setups*	*Receiving Orders*	*Packing Orders*
Candy	10,000	100	100	800
Weather	10,000	50	200	400
Costs	$200,000	$7,500	$4,500	$30,000

REQUIRED:

1. Classify the overhead activities as unit level, batch level, product level, or facility level.
2. Create homogeneous cost pools. Identify the activities that belong to each pool.
3. Identify the cost driver for each pool and compute the pool rate.
4. Assign the overhead costs to each product using the pool rates computed in Requirement 3.

E19-5
Conventional Costing; Activity-Based Costing; Pricing
LO 1, 2, 3

Swasey Company produces a variety of electronic equipment. One of its plants produces two laser printers: the deluxe and the regular. At the beginning of the year, the following data were prepared for this plant:

	Deluxe	*Regular*
Quantity	100,000	800,000
Selling price	$900	$750
Unit prime cost	$529	$482.75
Unit overhead cost	$47	$117.25

Overhead is applied using direct labor hours. Upon examining the data, the vice-president of marketing was particularly impressed with the per-unit profitability of the deluxe printer and suggested that more emphasis be placed on producing and selling this product. The plant manager objected to this strategy, arguing that the cost of the deluxe printer was understated. He argued that overhead costs could be assigned more accurately by using cost drivers—factors that reflected each product's demands for overhead activities. To convince higher management that overhead rates using cost drivers could produce a significant difference in product costs, he obtained the following projected information from the controller for the production output given above:

Pool Name[1]	*Cost Driver*	*Pool Rate*[2]	*Deluxe*	*Regular*
Setups	Number of setups	$3,000	300	200
Machine costs	Machine hours	$ 200	100,000	300,000
Engineering	Engineering hours	$ 40	50,000	100,000
Packing	Packing orders	$ 20	100,000	400,000
Providing Space	Machine hours	$ 1	200,000	800,000

[1]Pools are named according to the nature of the activities found within each pool. Providing space is a collection of all facility-level activities. Packing and setups are collections of batch-level activities. Engineering is a collection of product-level activities and machine costs is a collection of unit-level activities.
[2]Cost per unit of cost driver.

REQUIRED:

1. Using the projected data based on conventional costing, compute gross profit percentage, gross profit per unit, and total gross profit for each product.
2. Using the pool rates, compute the overhead cost per unit for each product. Using this new unit cost, compute gross profit percentage, gross profit per unit, and total gross profit for each product.
3. In view of the outcome in Requirement 2, evaluate the suggestion of the vice-president of marketing to switch the emphasis to the deluxe model.

E19-6
Two-Stage Procedure; Macro Activities; Activity-Based Costing
LO 3

Newsome Company has recently decided to convert from conventional product costing to an activity-based system. The company produces small and large alarm clocks. Information concerning these two products is given below.

	Small Clock	*Large Clock*
Quantity produced	100,000	200,000
Machine hours	50,000	50,000
Direct labor hours	100,000	100,000
Material handling (number of moves)	2,000	4,000
Engineering labor (hours)	10,000	5,000
Receiving (number of orders processed)	250	500
Setups	60	20
Maintenance (hours used)	4,000	2,000
Kilowatt hours	25,000	25,000
Inspection (number of hours)	3,000	1,000

Additionally, the following overhead costs are reported for the activities associated with the clocks:

Material handling	$120,000
Maintenance	80,000
Power	30,000
Depreciation (machines)[1]	60,000
Engineering	100,000
Receiving	30,000
Setups	96,000
Inspection	60,000

[1]Depreciation is straight line. Book value at the beginning of the year is $600,000. The remaining life of the machinery is 10 years or 1 million machine hours.

REQUIRED:

1. Group all activities into sets using activity-level and activity-driver classification criteria. Name each set based on the nature of the activities found within the set. Why is it desirable to group activities by sets?
2. Group all overhead costs into homogeneous cost pools. Select a cost driver for each cost pool and compute a pool rate.
3. Using the pool rates calculated in Requirement 2, assign all overhead costs to the two products and compute the overhead cost per unit for each.

E19-7
Classification of Activities
LO 3

Classify the following activities as unit level, batch level, product level, or facility level. Also identify a potential cost driver for each activity.

a. Setups
b. Shipments received—raw materials
c. Direct labor support
d. Shipments made
e. Ordering supplies
f. Production order activity
g. Part administration
h. Material handling
i. Processing customer orders
j. Plant-wide supervision
k. Machining
l. Plant depreciation
m. Special product testing
n. Heating and air conditioning: plant
o. Expediting
p. Product support engineering
q. Property taxes

E19-8
Selection of an ABC System
LO 4

In 1984, Sterling Company changed its cost system. It went from using a single, plant-wide overhead rate based on direct labor hours to a system using departmental overhead rates. The departmental overhead rates used direct labor hours, machine hours, and direct material dollars to assign overhead to products.

In 1994, the president of Sterling, Pamela Jones, was mulling over the possibility of changing to an ABC system. She had heard that the life of a cost system was about ten years and was worried that the current system was no longer serving the needs of the company. She was also convinced, however, that a change to ABC simply because it was a "hot" topic was not the right approach. Any change had to be in the best economic interests of the company.

REQUIRED: As a consultant to Pamela, identify the factors that should be considered in changing to an ABC system. In your discussion, include a definition of an outmoded or obsolete cost system.

E19-9
Classification of Activities; Unit-Cost Computation
LO 3

Blanding Company produces two electronic components. The two products are manufactured in the same plant. The components are boxed individually and shipped to customers who use them in producing various consumer products. The following activities have been identified for one of Blanding's plants:

	Component A	*Component B*
Quantity produced	200,000	400,000
Machine hours	200,000	200,000
Direct labor hours	50,000	50,000
Packing (number of boxes)	200,000	400,000
Setups (number of)	500	200
Engineering support (hours)	4,000	2,000
Receiving (orders processed)	300	150
Maintenance (hours used)	6,000	4,000
Material handling (number of moves)	1,500	600
Power (machine usage, kilowatt hrs)	25,000	25,000

The following overhead costs have been assigned to the various overhead activities:

Plant supervision	$ 80,000
Material handling	168,000
Maintenance	80,000
Power (machines)	100,000
Utilities (plant)[1]	20,000
Engineering	180,000
Setups	280,000
Packing	360,000
Receiving	46,000
Depreciation (plant)	50,000
Depreciation (machines)[2]	100,000

[1]These costs are in addition to those caused by machine usage and represent heating and lighting for the plant as a whole.
[2]Depreciation is calculated on a straight line basis. At the beginning of the year, book value on the equipment was $600,000. The equipment is expected to last another six years or 2,400,000 machine hours.

REQUIRED:

1. Group activities into homogeneous sets using activity-level and driver classification criteria. Name each activity set created using the nature of the activities that define the set. Explain why the use of activity sets is desirable.
2. Form homogeneous cost pools and calculate pool rates.
3. Using pool rates, calculate the overhead cost per unit for each product. In providing this calculation, prepare a report that details the cost assignment by activity level (category). In general terms, explain why reporting costs by activity category is useful to managers.

E19-10
Activity Classification; Cost Drivers
LO 2, 3

Teddy Simpson was puzzled by the recent report on the company's product-cost reduction program. The engineering department had spent considerable effort and resources to find ways to reduce the cost per setup. The recently installed ABC system was supposed to help him understand costs of activities and product costs. Based on this information, the company believed that the unit product cost could be significantly reduced by redesigning the setup procedures. The objective was to lower the cost per die since the number of dies was the cost driver for the setup activity. Yet, the reduction in cost per die was much less than expected. (A 25 percent reduction in the cost per die was expected.)

In trying to understand what happened, Teddy requested a report on the activities and costs associated with setups. The accounting department provided the following information. The percentage cost breakdown is before and after the improvements were made.

Cost driver: Number of dies (number produced: 1,000 each year)

Activities and costs assigned to the setup category:

	Setup Cost	
	Before	*After*
Die construction and repair	$300,000	$225,000
Maintaining die room machinery	100,000	100,000
Die design	100,000	75,000
Building maintenance	80,000	80,000
Bookkeeping for tooling-related costs	20,000	20,000

REQUIRED: Using the information provided by the accounting department, explain why the expected results did not materialize.

E19-11
JIT and Traceability of Costs
LO 5

Assume that a company uses JIT manufacturing. Each manufacturing cell produces a single product or major subassembly. Cell workers are responsible for manufacturing the product, setting up the machinery, and maintaining the machinery. Classify the following costs as direct or indirect product costs:

a. Inspection costs
b. Direct labor
c. Plant depreciation
d. Salary of cell supervisor
e. Oil to lubricate machinery
f. Salary of plant supervisor
g. Costs to set up machinery
h. Salaries of janitors
i. Power
j. Taxes on plant and equipment
k. Depreciation on machinery
l. Raw materials
m. Salary of industrial engineer
n. Parts for machinery
o. Pencils and paper clips for cell supervisor
p. Insurance on plant and equipment
q. Overtime wages for cell workers

E19-12
JIT and Product-Costing Accuracy
LO 5

Prior to installing a JIT system, Rumple Company used machine hours to assign maintenance costs to its three products (small, medium, and large tablecloths). The maintenance costs totaled $280,000 per year. The machine hours used by each product and the quantity of each product produced are as follows:

	Machine Hours	*Quantity Produced*
Small	30,000	7,500
Medium	30,000	7,500
Large	40,000	10,000

After installing JIT, three manufacturing cells were created, and cell workers were trained to perform maintenance. Maintenance costs for the three cells still totaled $280,000; however, these costs are now traceable to each cell as follows:

Cell, small cloths	$ 76,000
Cell, medium cloths	84,000
Cell, large cloths	120,000

REQUIRED:

1. Compute the pre-JIT maintenance cost per table cloth for each type.
2. Compute maintenance cost per unit for each type after installing JIT.
3. Explain why the JIT maintenance cost per unit is more accurate than the pre-JIT cost.

E19-13
JIT; Traceability of Costs; Product-Costing Accuracy
LO 5

The manufacturing costs assigned to Product A before and after installing JIT are given below.

	Before	*After*
Direct materials	$ 60,000	$ 60,000
Direct labor	40,000	50,000
Maintenance	50,000	30,000
Power	10,000	8,000
Depreciation	12,500	10,000
Material handling	8,000	4,000
Engineering	9,600	8,000
Setups	15,000	8,500
Building and grounds	11,800	12,400
Supplies	4,000	3,000
Supervision (plant)	8,200	8,200
Cell supervision	—	30,000
Departmental supervision	18,000	—
Total	$247,100	$232,100

In both the pre- and post-JIT setting, 100,000 units of Product A are manufactured. In the JIT setting, manufacturing cells are used to produce each product.

REQUIRED:

1. Compute the unit cost of the product before and after JIT. Explain why the JIT unit cost is more accurate.
2. Classify the costs in the JIT environment as direct or indirect product costs.

PROBLEMS

P19-1
Activity-Based Costing; Accuracy of Unit Costs; Multiple Overhead Rates Using Cost Drivers versus Single Overhead Rates; Pricing Decisions
LO 1, 2, 3

Ferguson Equipment, Inc., manufactures custom-designed manufacturing equipment. Ferguson had recently received a request to manufacture 40 units of a specialized machine at a price lower than it normally accepts. Marketing manager Emily Dorr indicated that if the order were accepted at that price, the company could expect additional orders from the same customer; in fact, if the company could offer this price in the market generally, she believed that sales of this machine would increase by 50 percent.

Cleon Skowsen, president of Ferguson, was skeptical about accepting the order. The company had a policy not to accept any order that did not provide revenues at least equal to its full manufacturing cost plus 15 percent. The price offered was $2,100 per unit. However, before a final decision was made, Cleon decided to request information on the estimated cost per unit. He was concerned because the company was experiencing increased competition, and the number of new orders was dropping. Also, the controller's office had recently researched the possibility of using activity-based multiple overhead rates instead of the single rate currently in use. The controller had promised more accurate product costing, and Cleon was curious about how this approach would affect the pricing of this particular machine.

Within 24, the controller had assembled the following data:

a. The plant-wide overhead rate is based on an expected volume of 400,000 direct labor hours and the following budgeted overhead (all figures are yearly):

Depreciation, building	$ 500,000
Depreciation, equipment	300,000
Material handling	800,000
Power (machine usage)	500,000
Rework costs	300,000
Supervision (plant-wide)	200,000
Cost of scrapped units	640,000
Other plant-wide overhead	460,000
Total	$3,700,000

b. Expected activity for selected cost drivers (for the year):

Material moves	10,000
Kilowatt hours	100,000
Units reworked	2,000
Units scrapped	1,000
Machine hours	100,000

c. Estimated data for the potential job (based on the production of 40 units):

Potential job direct labor (4,000 hours)	$20,000
Direct materials	$24,000
Number of material moves	6
Number of kilowatt hours	1,000
Number of units reworked	2
Number of units scrapped	3
Number of machine hours	1,000

REQUIRED:

1. Compute the estimated unit cost for the potential job using the current method to assign overhead on a plant-wide basis. Given this unit cost, compute the total gross profit earned by the job. Would the job be accepted under normal operating conditions?
2. Classify overhead activities as unit level, batch level, product sustaining, or facility level. Calculate pool rates using the cost drivers in Part b of the problem. The rate for facility-level overhead is based on direct labor hours.
3. Compute the estimated unit cost for the potential job using the pool rates computed in Requirement 2. Report per-unit costs by activity category. Given this cost per unit, compute the total gross profit earned by the job. Should the job be accepted?
4. Which approach—the plant-wide rate or the multiple-overhead rate with cost drivers—is the best for the company? Explain.

P19-2
Cost Drivers and Product Costing Accuracy
LO 1, 2

Indio Company for years produced only one product: bath towels. Recently, the company decided to add a line of dinner napkins. With this addition, the need to allocate service costs to the producing departments became necessary. Surprisingly, the costs to produce the towels increased and their profitability dropped.

The marketing manager and the production manager both complained about the increase in the production cost of towels. The marketing manager was concerned because the increase in unit costs led to pressure to increase the unit price of towels. She was resisting this pressure because she was certain that the increase would harm the company's market share. The production manager also was receiving pressure to cut costs; yet, he was convinced that nothing different was being done in the way the towels were produced. He was also convinced that further efficiency in the manufacture of the towels was unlikely. After some discussion, the two managers decided that the problem had to be connected with the addition of the napkin line.

Upon investigation, they were informed that the only real change in product-costing procedures was in the way overhead costs were assigned. They were informed that a two-stage procedure was used. First, the service department costs were allocated directly to the two producing departments (patterns and finishing). Second, the costs accumulated in the producing departments were allocated to the two products using direct labor hours as a base. The managers were assured that great care was taken to associate overhead costs with individual products. So that they could construct their own example of cost assignment, the controller made the following information available for one of the company's service departments (the accounting department):

	Department		
	Accounting	*Pattern*	*Finishing*
Service cost	$220,000	—	—
Transactions processed	—	40,000	60,000
Total direct labor hours	—	20,000	40,000
Direct labor hours per towel[1]	—	0.4	0.8
Direct labor hours per napkin[1]	—	0.1	0.2

[1]Hours required to produce one set, where a set has four units

The controller remarked that the cost of operating the accounting department had doubled with the addition of the new product line. The increase came because of the need to process transactions, the number of which had also doubled.

During the first year of producing napkins, the company produced and sold 30,000 sets of towels and 80,000 sets of napkins. The 30,000 sets of towels matched the prior year's output for that product.

REQUIRED:

1. Compute the amount of accounting cost assigned to each set of towels and napkins, using the two-stage allocation process described by the controller.
2. Compute the amount of accounting cost assigned to a set of towels before the napkin line was added.
3. Suppose that the company decided to allocate the accounting costs directly to the product lines using the number of transactions as the allocation base. What is the accounting cost for a set of towels? for a set of napkins?
4. Which way of assigning overhead does the best job, the conventional two-stage approach or the activity-based approach using transactions processed for each product? Explain. Discuss the benefits of using cost drivers to assign overhead costs directly to individual products. Was it necessary to form manufacturing cells to carry out the cost-driver allocation?

P19-3
Activity Classification; Activity Sets; Homogeneous Cost Pools
LO 3

Thurston Manufacturing produces two models of lawn mowers: small and large. Thurston produces all of the parts for the mowers internally. The Framing Division produces the frames for the mowers. The Framing Division takes metal sheets and cuts them into shapes that are used to form the frame of each lawn mower. Frames are produced in batches and the metal-cutting equipment must be reconfigured as the process changes from small to large frames. (Because of customer demands, the process usually produces one batch before reconfiguration.) Other components for the lawn mower are produced by other divisions of the same company and transferred to the Assembly Division. (For example, the Thurston Small Motors Division transfers the motors for the mowers.) The frame components and parts transferred in from sister divisions are used by assembly to manufacture the final product.

The management of the Framing Division has decided to implement an activity-based costing system. A special study, conducted by a team appointed by the divisional manager, revealed the following information on activities, costs, and cost drivers for its frame production plant:

Activity	*Cost*	*Cost Driver*
Setup	$ 200,000	No. of setups
Maintenance	150,000	Machine hours
Scheduling	60,000	No. of products
Machine depreciation	300,000	Machine hours
Inspection	125,000	No. of setups
Power (machine)	100,000	Machine hours
Providing space	50,000	—
Plant supervision	80,000	—
Material handling	200,000	No. of moves
	$1,265,000	

The team conducting the study recommended that facility-level costs be assigned to each product on a value-added basis (value-added is defined as the cost of direct labor plus the cost of nonfacility-level overhead).

The expected quantities of cost drivers are given below for the plant:

Activity	*Cost Driver*	*Quantity*
Setup	No. of setups	1,000
Maintenance	Machine hours	5,000
Scheduling	No. products	2
Depreciation	Machine hours	5,000

Activity	*Cost Driver*	*Quantity*
Inspection	No. of setups	1,000
Power (machine)	Machine hours	5,000
Material handling	No. of moves	10,000

In addition, the demands that each type of frame makes on activities are also given:

	Product	
Cost Driver	*Small Frame*	*Large Frame*
No. of products	1	1
Machine hours	2,000	3,000
No. of setups	300	700
No. of moves	3,500	6,500

During the year, 10,000 small frames and 15,000 large frames were produced. Total direct labor cost is $165,000 ($66,000 for the small frames and the rest for the large frames).

REQUIRED:

1. Group activities into sets based on activity-level and driver-classification criteria. Provide a name for each set based on the type of activities that belong to the set.

2. Create homogeneous cost pools and calculate pool rates.
3. Use the pool rates to compute per unit overhead costs for the small and large frames. What is the per unit cost without facility-level costs assigned? Explain why a pure ABC system would not assign facility-level costs to the two products.

P19-4 Product-Costing Accuracy; Corporate Strategy; Activity-Based Costing

LO 1, 2

Ogden Metal Manufacturing is engaged in the production of machine parts. One division specializes in the production of two machine parts: Part 12A and Part 18B. Historically, the profitability of the division had been tied to Part 12A. In the last two years, however, the division had been facing intense competition, and its sales of this part had dropped. Much of the competition was from foreign sources, and the divisional manager was convinced that the foreign producers were guilty of dumping. The following conversation between Ken Larson, divisional manager, and Martha Jones, marketing manager, reflects the concerns of the division's top management and some possible solutions that were being considered.

Martha: "I just received a call from one of our major customers concerning Part 12A. He said that a sales representative from another firm had offered the part at $20 per unit—$11 less than what we ask."

Ken: "It's costing about $21 to produce that part. I don't see how these companies can afford to sell it so cheaply. I'm not convinced that we should meet the price. Perhaps a better strategy is to emphasize producing and selling more of Part 18B. Our margin is high on this product, and we have virtually no competition for it."

Martha: "You may be right. I think we can increase the price significantly and not lose business. I called a few customers to see how they would react to a 25 percent increase in price, and they all said that they would still purchase the same quantity as before."

Ken: "It sounds promising. However, before we make a major commitment to Part 18B, I think we had better explore other possible explanations. I want to know how our production costs compare to our competitors. Perhaps we could be more efficient and find a way to earn a good return on Part 12A."

After his meeting with Martha, Ken requested an investigation of the production costs and comparative efficiency. The controller reported that as far as he could determine, the division's efficiency was similar to that of other competitors. The controller did mention the possibility of using activity-based costing, a method that might improve product costing. To assist Ken in understanding the production activities and costs associated with the two products, the controller prepared the following data:

	Part 12A	*Part 18B*
Production	50,000	10,000
Selling price	$31.86	$24.00
Overhead per unit	$12.71	$6.36
Prime cost per unit	$8.53	$6.26
Number of production runs	10	20
Receiving orders	40	100
Machine hours	12,500	6,000
Direct labor hours	25,000	2,500
Engineering hours	5,000	5,000
Material moves	50	40

Upon examining the data, Ken decided that he wanted to know more about the overhead costs since they were such a high proportion of total production costs. Ken was provided the following list of pooled overhead costs and was told that total overhead costs were assigned to products using a plant-wide rate based on direct labor hours. The controller also indicated that he had pooled the overhead costs on the basis of what he called activity level and driver classification. He indicated to Ken that it may be possible to improve product costing by assigning the costs using each activity pool instead of one grand plant-wide pool.

Overhead pool:[1]	
Setup costs	$ 24,000
Machine costs	175,000
Receiving costs	210,000
Engineering costs	200,000
Material handling costs	90,000
Total	$699,000

[1]The pools are named for the major activities found within them. All overhead costs within each pool can be assigned using a single cost driver (based on the major activity after which the pool is named).

REQUIRED:

1. Verify the overhead cost per unit reported by the controller using direct labor hours to assign overhead. Compute the per-unit gross margin for each product.
2. After learning of the activity-based costing, Ken asked the controller to compute the product cost using this approach. Recompute the unit cost of each product using activity-based costing. Compute the per-unit gross margin for each product.
3. Should the company switch its emphasis from the high-volume product to the low-volume product? Comment on the validity of the divisional manager's accusation that competitors are dumping.
4. Explain the apparent lack of competition for Part 18B. Comment also on the willingness of customers to accept a 25 percent increase in price for Part 18B.
5. Assume that you are the manager of the division. Describe what actions you would take based on the information provided by the activity-based unit costs.

P19-5
Product-Costing Accuracy; Departmental Rates; Pool Rates
LO 1, 2, 3

Maxwell Company produces two small engines for model boats (Engine A and Engine B). Both products pass through two producing departments. Engine B is by far the most popular of the two engines. The following data have been gathered for these two products:

	Product-Related Data	
	Engine A	*Engine B*
Units produced per year	30,000	300,000
Prime costs	$100,000	$1,000,000
Direct labor hours	40,000	400,000
Machine hours	20,000	200,000
Production runs	40	60
Inspection hours	800	1,200

	Departmental Data	
	Department 1	*Department 2*
Direct labor hours:		
Engine A	30,000	10,000
Engine B	45,000	355,000
Total	75,000	365,000

(continued)

	Departmental Data	
	Department 1	*Department 2*
Machine hours:		
Engine A	10,000	10,000
Engine B	160,000	40,000
Total	170,000	50,000
Overhead costs:		
Setup costs	$ 90,000	$ 90,000
Inspection costs	70,000	70,000
Power	100,000	60,000
Maintenance	80,000	100,000
Total	$340,000	$320,000

REQUIRED:

1. Compute the overhead cost per unit for each product using a plant-wide per DL hour, unit-based rate.
2. Compute the overhead cost per unit for each product using departmental rates. In calculating departmental rates, use machine hours for Department 1 and direct labor hours for Department 2. Repeat using direct labor hours for Department 1 and machine hours for Department 2.
3. Compute the overhead cost per unit for each product using activity-based costing (use overhead pools where possible).
4. Comment on the ability of departmental rates to improve the accuracy of product costing.

P19-6
ABC; Departmental Rates; Pricing Decisions
LO 1, 2, 3

(This problem is an extension of problems P16-8 and P18-9. All pertinent information is repeated here.) Alden Peterson, marketing manager for Retlief Company, was puzzled by the outcome of two recent bids. The company's policy was to bid 150 percent of full manufacturing cost. One job (Job SS) had been turned down by a prospective customer who had indicated that the proposed price was $3 per unit higher than the winning bid. A second job (Job TT) had been accepted by a customer who was amazed that Retlief could offer such favorable terms. This customer revealed that Retlief's price was $43 lower than the next lowest bid.

Alden knew that Retlief was competitive in terms of cost control. Accordingly, he suspected that the problem was related to cost assignment procedures. Upon investigating, he discovered that a plant-wide rate, based on direct labor hours, had been used to assign overhead to the jobs. With some help from the controller, the bids had been recalculated using departmental rates. Alden knew this could improve the accuracy of the cost assignment because one of the two producing departments was labor intensive and the other was machine intensive. Both jobs spent time in each department, although Job TT spent most of its time in the machine-intensive department. In calculating departmental rates, Alden decided to use two different methods to allocate service-department overhead to the producing departments: the direct method and the step method. He had heard that the step method would produce more accurate allocations. The unit bid prices for the different approaches are summarized below.

	Job SS	*Job TT*
Plant-wide rate:		
Bid price	$18.75	$ 60.00
Departmental rates:		
Bid price (direct method)	$14.67	$101.01
Bid price (step method)	$14.63	$101.45

Alden had been reading about the increased accuracy of an ABC system and convinced the controller to help in obtaining the following information (overhead costs are pooled based on activity level and common cost driver—each pool is named by the major activity found within it):

Overhead Pool	*Cost*	*Activity Category*	*Cost Driver*
Engineering support	$400,000	Product sustaining	Engineering orders
Machine costs	$735,000	Unit level	Machine hours
Setup	$200,000	Batch level	Setup hours
Material handling	$540,000	Batch level	Number of moves
General factory	$625,000	Facility level	Machine hours[1]

[1]This is an arbitrary allocation. The controller argued that machine hours used by a job would be correlated with square footage occupied by the producing departments.

The practical activity levels of the cost drivers for the year are given below.

Engineering orders	200
Machine hours	140,000
Setup hours	20,000
Number of moves	2,000

The activity data for each job are also provided.

	Job SS	*Job TT*
Machine hours	700	3,200
Engineering orders	1	2
Setup hours	20	100
Moves	2	3
Prime costs	$120,000	$50,000
Units	14,400	1,500

REQUIRED:

1. Calculate the cost of each job using activity-based costing. List the costs for each job by activity category.
2. Calculate the bid price for each job using the normal markup. How do the bid prices compare with the bids using plant-wide and departmental rates? Does this offer any real improvement? Explain.
3. Suppose that the best competing bid for Job SS was $4.20 lower than the original bid based on a plant-wide rate. Also assume that the best bid on Job TT was $30 lower than the next lowest bid. Now compare the ABC bids with the bids based on departmental rates. What does this imply about the value of ABC as price competition intensifies?
4. Discuss the importance of having the facility-level costs listed separately as the job costs are detailed. Should these costs be included in the base for calculating the bid?

P19-7
Activity-Based Costing; Service Industry
LO 1, 2, 3

Alva Hospital operates an intensive care unit. Currently, patients are charged the same rate per patient day for daily care services. Daily care services are broadly defined as occupancy, feeding, and nursing care. A recent study, however, revealed several interesting outcomes. First, the demands patients place on daily care services varies with the severity of the case being treated. Second, the occupancy activity is a combination of two activities: lodging and use of monitoring equipment. Since some patients require more monitoring than others, these activities should be separated. Third, the daily rate should reflect the difference in demands resulting from differences in patient type. To compute a daily rate that reflected the difference in demands, patients were placed in three categories according to illness severity, and the following annual data were collected:

Activity	*Cost of Activity*	*Cost Driver*	*Quantity*
Lodging	$ 900,000	Patient days	6,000
Monitoring	1,200,000	No. of monitoring devices used	10,000
Feeding	100,000	Patient days	4,000
Nursing care	945,000	Nursing hours	63,000
	$3,145,000		

The demands associated with patient severity are also provided:

Severity	*Patient Days*	*Monitoring Devices*	*Nursing Hours*
High	2,000	5,000	40,000
Medium	3,000	4,000	18,000
Low	1,000	1,000	5,000

REQUIRED:

1. Suppose that the costs of daily care are assigned using only patient days as the cost driver (which is also the measure of output). Compute the daily rate using this traditional unit-based approach of cost assignment.
2. Compute pool rates using the given cost drivers.
3. Compute the charge per patient day for each patient type using the pool rates from Requirement 2 and the demands on each activity.
4. Comment on the value of activity-based costing in service industries.

P19-8
ABC Costing and Cost Behavior
LO 3

Underwood Company produces several different models of a stereo system. The company has recently adopted an ABC system. The unit cost expected for one of the models is presented below.

Model B	
Unit-level costs (includes materials and labor)	$ 60
Batch-level costs	40
Product-sustaining costs	20
Facility-level costs	10
Total unit cost	$130

The unit cost is based on an expected volume of 10,000 units. These units will be produced in ten equal batches. The product-sustaining costs are all from engineering support. The product-sustaining costs are driven by engineering orders. The $20 cost assignment is based on five orders. Facility-level costs are allocated on the basis of direct labor hours (one hour per unit produced).

REQUIRED:

1. Calculate the total manufacturing cost to produce 10,000 units of Model B. Present the total cost for each activity category.

2. Now assume that the company has revised its forecast for Model B and expects to produce 15,000 units. A decision was made to handle the increased production by increasing batch size to 1,500 units. The increased production will not require an increase in engineering support. Calculate the total cost to produce the 15,000 units of Model B. Present the total cost for each activity category. Explain the outcome.
3. Assume that the revised forecast of 15,000 units is made. Now, however, the decision is made to handle the extra production by increasing the number of batches from 10 to 15. Also, the sale of the extra 5,000 units is possible only if an engineering modification is made. This increases the expected engineering orders from 5 to 6. Explain why the costs changed from those predicted in Requirement 2.
4. Discuss the value of classifying and reporting costs by activity category.

P19-9
JIT and Product Costing
LO 5

Surqual Company recently implemented a JIT manufacturing system. After one year of operation, the president of the company wanted to compare product cost under the JIT system with product cost under the old system. Surqual's two products are exercise springs and exercise bikes. The unit prime costs under the old system are given below.

	Springs	*Bikes*
Direct materials	$11	$42
Direct labor	3	20

Under the old manufacturing system, the company operated three service centers and two production departments. Overhead was applied using departmental overhead rates. The direct overhead costs associated with each department for the year preceding the installation of JIT are as follows:

Maintenance	$110,000
Material handling	90,000
Building and grounds	140,000
Machining	280,000
Assembly	175,000

Under the old system, the overhead costs of the service departments were allocated directly to the producing departments and then to the products passing through them. (Both products passed through each producing department.) The overhead rate for the machining department was based on machine hours and assembly was based on direct labor hours. During the last year of operations for the old system, the machining department used 80,000 machine hours, and the assembly department 20,000 direct labor hours. Each set of exercise springs required 1 machine hour in machining and 0.25 direct labor hours in assembly. Each exercise bike required 2 machine hours in machining and 0.5 hours in assembly. Bases for allocation of the service costs are given below.

	Square Feet of Space	*Number of Material Moves*	*Machine Hours*
Machining	80,000	90,000	80,000
Assembly	40,000	60,000	20,000
Total	120,000	150,000	100,000

Upon implementing JIT, a manufacturing cell for each product was created to replace the departmental structure. Maintenance and material handling were both decentralized to the cell level. Essentially, cell workers were trained to operate the machines in each cell, assemble the components, maintain the machines, and move the partially completed units from one point to the next within the cell. During the first year of the JIT system, the company produced and sold 20,000 sets of exercise springs and 30,000 exercise bikes. This output was identical to that for the last year of operations under the old system. The following costs have been assigned to the manufacturing cells:

	Springs Cell	*Bikes Cell*
Direct materials	$185,000	$1,140,000
Direct labor	66,000	660,000
Direct overhead	99,000	350,500
Allocated overhead[1]	56,000	84,000
Total	$406,000	$2,234,500

[1]Building and grounds, allocated on the basis of square footage

REQUIRED:

1. Compute the unit cost for each product under the old manufacturing system.
2. Compute the unit cost for each product under the JIT system.
3. Which of the unit costs is the more accurate? Explain. Include in your explanation a discussion of how the computational approaches differ.
4. Explain why the total overhead costs decreased.

P19-10
Cost Behavior; Traceability; Unit Costs; JIT and ABC
LO 3, 5

Benson Company, a manufacturer of toy trucks, has adopted JIT manufacturing. In implementing the system, three types of manufacturing cells were created, one for each type of toy truck produced. The manufacturing costs for the line of dump trucks are given below (expected production of 12,000 units).

Cell manufacturing costs:	
Direct materials	$60,000
Direct labor	40,000
Supplies	2,500
Power	3,500
Supervision	22,000
Depreciation	5,000
Other manufacturing costs:	
Share of plant depreciation	$ 7,000
Share of plant supervisor's salary	2,000
Engineering sustaining (4 orders)	12,000
Safety testing (10 samples)	8,000

Engineering sustaining costs are driven by engineering orders and safety testing costs by the number of samples.

REQUIRED:

1. Assume initially that all costs are strictly variable or strictly fixed with respect to units produced. Prepare a cost formula for the following costs:
   a. Direct materials
   b. Direct labor
   c. All direct manufacturing costs other than labor and materials
   d. All direct manufacturing costs

e. All indirect manufacturing costs
f. Total manufacturing costs
2. Assuming that 12,000 dump trucks are produced, compute the following:
a. Direct material costs
b. Direct labor costs
c. Direct manufacturing costs
d. Total manufacturing costs
e. Unit cost
3. Repeat Requirement 2 for 15,000 units. Which costs changed? Why?
4. Now classify costs as unit level, batch level, product sustaining, facility level or cell level. Calculate total costs for each category for 12,000 and 15,000 units. Which costs changed? Why?
5. Refer to Requirement 4. Suppose that the number of engineering orders increase from 4 to 6 and the number of samples from 10 to 15. What happens to total costs for 12,000 units? 15,000 units? Explain.

P19-11
Costs; Traditional versus JIT Environments
LO 5

Consider the following production costs before and after implementing a JIT system:

	Before	*After*
Direct labor	$ 70,000	$ 70,000
Direct materials	480,000	480,000
Material handling	100,000	20,000
Depreciation, equipment	150,000	100,000
Supplies	38,000	34,000
Rent, special equipment	10,000	10,000
Power	15,000	12,500
Salary, production supervisor	40,000	40,000
Salary, custodian	8,000	8,000
Insurance, factory	7,000	7,000
Total	$918,000	$781,500

REQUIRED:

1. Classify these costs as direct or indirect both before and after implementing JIT.
2. Explain why some indirect product costs changed to direct product costs when JIT was implemented.
3. Explain why some costs could change in amount as JIT is implemented.
4. Assume that these costs support the production of 100,000 units. Compute the unit product cost before and after implementing JIT. Which unit cost figure is more accurate? Why?

P19-12
Allocation and JIT
LO 5

Folton Company produces two types of vases (A and B). Both pass through two producing departments: molding and painting. It also has a maintenance department that services and repairs the equipment used in each producing department. Budgeted data for the three departments are given below.

	Maintenance	*Molding*	*Painting*
Overhead	$100,000	$165,000	$119,000
Maintenance hours	—	15,000	5,000
Direct labor hours	—	12,000	6,000

In the molding department, Vase A requires 1 hour of direct labor and Vase B, 2 hours. In the painting department, Vase A requires 0.5 hours of direct labor and Vase B, 1 hour. Expected production: Vase A, 4,000 units; Vase B, 4,000 units.

Immediately after preparing the budgeted data, a consultant suggests that two manufacturing cells be created: one for the manufacture of Vase A and the other for the manufacture of Vase B. Cell workers would be trained to perform maintenance; hence, the maintenance department is decentralized. The total direct overhead costs estimated for each cell are $200,000 for Cell A and $184,000 for Cell B.

REQUIRED:

1. Allocate the service costs to each department and compute the overhead cost per unit for each vase. (Overhead rates use direct labor hours.)
2. Compute the overhead cost per unit if manufacturing cells are created. Which unit overhead cost do you think is the more accurate—the one computed with a departmental structure or the one computed using a cell structure? Explain.
3. Note that the total overhead costs under each system are assumed to be the same. Would you expect the overhead costs to remain the same if the JIT manufacturing system is implemented? Explain.

DISCUSSION AND INTERPRETATION PROBLEMS

D19-1 Implementing an ABC System

Jan Booth, vice-president of finance, was reviewing the responses to her suggestion that the company's cost system be replaced with an ABC system. She had sent a detailed memo to all the company's divisional managers, outlining the proposed new system and providing a brief summary of the benefits. She had also sent a copy of the memo to the divisional controllers. In her memo, she had requested a written reaction and set a meeting to discuss the issue. All the managers and controllers had responded, but she was somewhat disappointed in the reactions. Most of the responses had been negative and unsupportive of the change. Yet, she knew the company was having problems.

Bids were being lost at a greater rate than ever before. The company was having a difficult time matching competitors' prices even with aggressive pricing. Furthermore, a recent study commissioned by the company revealed that the company was not out of line with others in terms of its overall efficiency. Also, there was the decision by one division to drop a major product line, one that had been produced successfully for years. The traditional cost system had indicated that it was the right thing to do. Yet, the profits of the division had declined dramatically the following year. Something was wrong! Based on her research, she was convinced that a major problem existed with the cost system. Her problem now was to convince these divisional types that their objections were unfounded. From the memos, she had built a list of the most common objections to the new system.[26]

a. An ABC system would be too expensive to operate.
b. An ABC system is too complicated and would be difficult to understand.
c. Improving our current system is all that's needed; for example, we can use rates based on machine hours as well as direct labor hours.
d. More accurate product costs are not needed—we know what our products cost.
e. The market sets prices—so why worry about product costs?
f. Cost systems aren't very important. Anyway, most of our manufacturing costs are fixed, and we cannot do much with fixed costs.

26. This list is taken from Peter B. B. Turney, "Ten Myths about Implementing an Activity-Based Cost System," *Journal of Cost Management* (Spring 1990), pp. 24–32.

g. Only manufacturing costs are product costs—why worry about tracing nonmanufacturing costs to products?
h. Product costs are not useful for managing overhead activities. In fact, product costs are not very useful for most managerial decisions.

REQUIRED: Prepare a memo to the divisional managers addressing each of the objections.

D19-2
Cost Drivers; Product Costing; Ethical Considerations

Consider the following conversation between Leonard Bryner, president and manager of a firm engaged in job manufacturing, and Chuck Davis, CMA, the firm's controller.

Leonard: "Chuck, as you know, our firm has been losing market share over the past three years. We have been losing more and more bids, and I don't understand why. At first, I thought other firms were undercutting simply to gain business, but after examining some of the public financial reports, I believe that they are making a reasonable rate of return. I am beginning to believe that our costs and costing methods are at fault."

Chuck: "I can't agree with that. We have good control over our costs. Like most firms in our industry, we use a normal job-costing system. I really don't see any significant waste in the plant."

Leonard: "After talking with some other managers at a recent industrial convention, I'm not so sure that waste by itself is the issue. They talked about JIT manufacturing, conversion of overhead costs to direct manufacturing costs, and the use of something called *cost drivers* to allocate overhead. They claimed that these new procedures produce more efficiency in manufacturing, better control of overhead, and more accurate product costing. Maybe our bids are too high because these other firms have found ways to decrease their overhead and to increase the accuracy of their product costing."

Chuck: "I doubt it. For one thing, I don't believe overhead costs can be made into direct manufacturing costs. That seems absurd to me. Furthermore, everyone uses some measure of production activity to assign overhead costs. I imagine that what they are calling *cost drivers* is just some new buzz word for measures of production volume. Fads in costing come and go. I wouldn't worry about it. I'll bet that our problems with decreasing sales are temporary. You might recall that we experienced a similar problem about 12 years ago—it was 2 years before it straightened out."

REQUIRED:

1. Do you agree with Chuck Davis and the advice that he gave Leonard Bryner? Explain.
2. Was there anything wrong or unethical in the behavior that Chuck Davis displayed? Explain your reasoning.
3. Do you think that Chuck was well informed—that he was aware of what the accounting implications of JIT were and that he knew what was meant by cost drivers? Should he have been? Review (in Chapter 1) the first category of the standards of ethical conduct for management accountants. Do any of these apply to Chuck's case?

D19-3
Research Assignment

Reading about applications of activity-based product costing helps us to understand the real-world advantages that the approach offers. Read the following four articles, write a brief summary of each, and comment on the value of the ABC application.

John Antos, "Activity-Based Management for Service, Not-for-Profit, and Governmental Organizations," *Journal of Cost Management*, Summer 1992, pp. 13–23.

Debbie Berlant, Reese Browning, and George Foster, "How Hewlett Packard Gets Numbers It Can Trust," *Harvard Business Review*, January-February 1990, pp. 173–183.

Lou F. Jones, "Product Costing at Caterpillar," *Management Accounting*, February 1991, pp. 34–42.

Wild Card: You find an article that describes an application.

COMPREHENSIVE CASE

C19-1 Product Costing

Confer Furniture Corporation produces sofas, recliners, and lounge chairs. It operates two plants in the same community. The fabric plant is responsible for producing the fabric that is used by the furniture plant. To produce three totally different fabrics (identified by a fabric ID code: #260, #370, and #480, respectively), the plant has three separate production operations—one for each fabric. Thus, production of all three fabrics is occurring at the same time in different locations in the plant. Each fabric's production operation has two processes: the weaving and pattern process and the coloring and bolting process. In the weaving and pattern process, yarn is used to create yards of fabric with different designs. In the next process, the fabric is dyed, cut in 25-yard sections, and divided into 25-yard bolts (the fabric is wrapped around cardboard rods). The bolts are transported by forklift to the furniture plant's receiving department. All output of the fabric plant is used by the furniture plant (to produce the sofas and chairs). For accounting purposes, the fabric is transferred at cost to the furniture plant.

The furniture plant produces orders for customers on a special order basis. The customers specify the quantity, style, fabric, and pattern. Typically, jobs are large (involving at least 500 units). The plant has two production departments: cutting and assembly. In the cutting department, the fabric and wooden frame components are sized and cut. Other components are purchased from external suppliers and removed from stores as needed for assembly. After the fabric and wooden components are finished for the entire job, they are moved to the assembly department. The assembly department takes the individual components and assembles the sofas (or chairs).

Confer Furniture has been in business for over two decades and has a good reputation. However, during the past five years, Confer has experienced eroding profits and declining sales. Bids were being lost (even aggressive bids) on the more popular models. Yet, the company was winning bids on some of the more difficult to produce items. Bill Gray, the owner and manager, was frustrated. He simply couldn't understand how some of his competitors could sell for such low prices. On a common sofa job involving 500 units, Confer's bids were running $20 per unit or $10,000 per job more than the winning bids (on average). Yet on the more difficult items, Confer's bids were running about $50 per unit less than the next closest bid. Maria Valenzuela, vice president of finance, had been assigned the task of doing a cost analysis of the company's product lines. Bill wanted to know if their costs were excessive. Perhaps they were being wasteful and production costs were higher than those of their competitors.

Maria prepared herself by reading recent literature on cost management and product costing and attending several conferences that explored the same issues. She then reviewed the costing procedures of the two plants and did a preliminary assessment of their soundness. (The fabric plant used process costing and the furniture plant used job order costing; both plants used plant-wide overhead rates based on direct labor hours.) Based on her initial reviews, she concluded that the costing procedures for the fabric plant were satisfactory. Essentially, there was no evidence of product diversity. Thus, the use of a plant-wide overhead rate based on direct labor hours was working well. Nonetheless, as part of her report to Bill, she decided to include a description of the fabric plant's costing procedures—at least for one of the fabric types. The furniture plant, however, was a more difficult matter. Product diversity was present and could be causing some distortions in product costs. She decided that additional analysis was needed so that a sound product-costing method could be recommended.

With the cooperation of each plant's controller, she gathered the following data for 1995:

Fabric Plant

Budgeted overhead: $600,000
Practical volume (direct labor hours): 60,000 hrs
Actual Overhead: $620,000

	Weaving and Pattern	*Coloring and Bolting*	*Total*
Actual hours worked:			
Fabric #260	10,000	8,000	18,000
Fabric #370	14,000	7,000	21,000
Fabric #480	13,000	9,000	22,000
	37,000	24,000	61,000

	Weaving and Pattern	*Coloring and Bolting*
Departmental data on Fabric #370:		
Beginning Inventories:		
Units (in yards)	10,000	5,000
Costs:		
Transferred-in	—	$50,000
Material	40,000	$ 2,500
Labor	9,000	$ 3,300
Overhead	11,000	$ 4,500
Current Production:		
Units started	40,000	?
Units transferred out	40,000	40,000
Costs:		
Transferred-in	—	?
Material	$160,000	$24,500
Labor	104,000	$49,700
Overhead	?	?
Percentage completion:		
Beginning inventory	30	40
Ending inventory	40	50

Note: With the exception of the cardboard bolt rods, material is added at the beginning of each process. The cost of the rods is relatively insignificant and is included in overhead.

Furniture Plant

Total budgeted plant overhead (by activity):	
Material handling	$ 300,000
Power	400,000
Maintenance	200,000
Setups	600,000
Expediting	150,000
General factory	350,000
Total	$2,000,000

(continued)

	Service Departments				*Producing Departments*	
	Material Handling	*Power*	*Maintenance*	*General Factory*	*Cutting*	*Assembly*
Departmental data (budgeted):						
Overhead	$300,000	$400,000	$200,000	$350,000	$500,000	$250,000
Machine hours	—	—	—	—	40,000	10,000
Number of moves	—	—	—	—	9,000	6,000
Square feet	1,000	5,000	4,000	—	15,000	10,000
Direct labor hours	—	—	—	—	50,000	200,000

Practical capacity for selected cost drivers:	
Direct labor hours	250,000
Number of moves	15,000
Machine hours	50,000
Number of setups	1,000
Number of expediting orders	200

After some discussion with the controller of the furniture plant, Maria decided to use machine hours to calculate the overhead rate for the cutting department and direct labor hours for the assembly department rate. (The cutting department was more automated than the assembly department.) As part of her report, she wanted to compare the effects of plant-wide rates, departmental rates, and activity pool rates on the cost of jobs. She wanted to know if overhead costing could be the source of the pricing problems the company was experiencing.

To assess the effect of the different overhead assignment procedures, Maria decided to examine two prospective jobs. Job 79P would produce 500 sofas, using a frequently requested style and fabric #370. Bids on this type of job were being lost more frequently to competitors. The second job, Job 89P, would produce 75 specially designed recliners. This job involved a new design and was more difficult for the workers to build. It involved some special cutting requirements and an unfamiliar assembly. Recently, the company seemed to be winning more bids on jobs of this type. To compute the costs of the two jobs, Maria assembled the following information on the two jobs:

	Job 79P
Direct materials:	
Fabric #370	4,500 yards @ $14
Frame components	$29,000
Direct labor:	
Cutting department	400 hours @ $10
Assembly department	1,600 hours @ $8.75
Machine time:	
Cutting department	350 machine hours
Assembly department	50 machine hours
Material moves	10
Setups	2
Expediting orders	0

Job 89P

Direct materials:	
Fabric #370	650 yards @ $14
Frame components	$3,500
Direct labor:	
Cutting department	70 hours @ $10
Assembly department	240 hours @ $8.75
Machine time:	
Cutting department	90 machine hours
Assembly department	15 machine hours
Material moves	8
Setups	4
Expediting orders	1[a]

[a]Finishing a job of this type on time almost was impossible. Customer pressure usually led to expediting activity.

REQUIRED:

1. Calculate the plant-wide overhead rate for the fabric plant.
2. Calculate the amount of under- or overapplied overhead for the fabric plant.
3. Using the weighted average method, calculate the cost per bolt for fabric #370.
4. Discuss the effect JIT manufacturing would have on the calculation in Requirement 3. Compute the cost per yard for fabric #370 in a JIT environment assuming that the *current* production data presented in the problem still hold.
5. Explain why activity-based costing would not be needed for the fabric plant.
6. Assume that the weaving and pattern process is not a separate process for each fabric. Also assume that the yarn used for each fabric differs significantly in cost. In this case, would process costing be appropriate for the weaving and pattern process? What costing approach would you recommend? Describe your approach in detail.
7. Calculate the following overhead rates for the furniture plant: (1) plant-wide rate, (2) departmental rates, and (3) activity rates. Use the direct method for assigning service costs to producing departments.
8. For each of the overhead rates computed in (7), calculate unit bid prices for Jobs 79P and 89P. Assume that an aggressive bidding policy for the company is unit cost plus 50%. Comment on the effect the plant-wide overhead cost assignment appears to have on Confer's winning or losing bids. What recommendation would you make? Explain.
9. Sam Parsons, Confer's production engineer, has made a recommendation to convert the furniture plant to JIT manufacturing (with cellular manufacturing cells). He wants to establish separate manufacturing cells for the repetitive business (business involving production and sales of the more popular lines). Additionally, one cell would be created for the nonrepetitive business. This last cell would involve reconfiguring equipment for each new job. By taking this approach, he is convinced that the cost of production can be reduced. For example, setup activity would not be required for the repetitive business cells and material handling costs would virtually vanish. He also indicated that a total quality emphasis would reduce material cost (by reducing waste) by 15%.
   a. Recalculate the bid prices for Job 79P and 89P assuming that the changes recommended by Parsons are made and that the predicted effects are realized. Comment on the competitive benefits that may be realized.
   b. Discuss other effects that switching to a JIT, cellular manufacturing approach would have on Confer's management accounting procedures (for the furniture plant only).

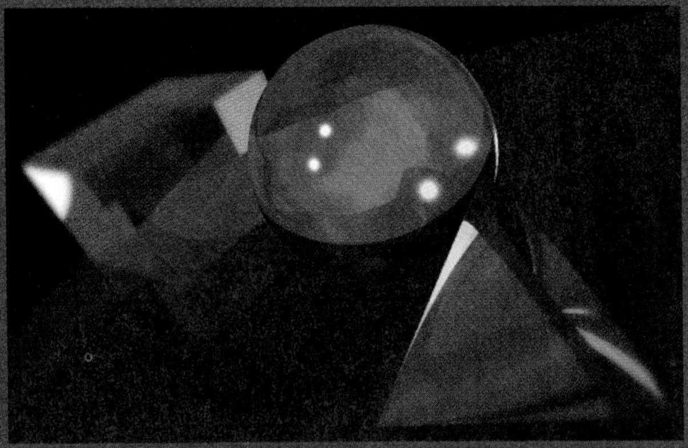

PART 7

MANAGERIAL DECISION MAKING

Consider the following scenarios:

A. *Manager:* "I have just received a request from my marketing vice-president. She tells me that if we can increase our advertising budget by $750,000 and at the same time lower our selling price by 10%, we can expand sales of our line of cereal products by 200,000 units. Should we do this?"

B. *Manager:* "Our plant is operating at 70% of capacity. We have an opportunity to produce a one-time, special order for a customer in a region of the country that we normally don't serve. The price offered, however, is less than the full cost of producing the product. What factors should I consider in deciding whether to accept or reject this order?"

C. *Manager:* "To automate or not is a critical issue. Our existing technology is certainly in good enough condition to last for years to come, and the cost of automation is high. Automation, however, offers some real savings and potential competitive advantages—better quality, more on-time deliveries, etc. Is it in the best interest of our company to automate—or should we continue with our existing technology?"

The above scenarios reveal the nature of the chapters in Section VII. All four chapters focus on the use of management accounting to make important operating and strategic decisions. Scenario A illustrates a decision that is concerned with cost-volume-profit analysis, a powerful analytical tool. This topic is covered in Chapter 20.

Scenario B illustrates a short-run decision—a decision to accept or reject a special order. Making this decision requires careful tracing of the costs and benefits associated with each alternative. How this and other short-run decisions are made is covered in Chapter 21.

Scenario C is an example of a long-run investment decision. These decisions are referred to as capital investment decisions and are the subject of Chapter 22. Techniques for making such decisions are valid in both a unit-based and an ABC environment; however, there are some issues that must be given particular attention for firms operating in an advanced manufacturing environment, and these issues are discussed in detail.

Finally, Chapter 23 expands the discussion of decision making to the advanced manufacturing environment. In addition, Chapter 23 discusses the following topics in detail: inventory decisions (traditional and JIT), strategic cost analysis, and segment analysis.

CHAPTER 20
COST BEHAVIOR AND CVP ANALYSIS

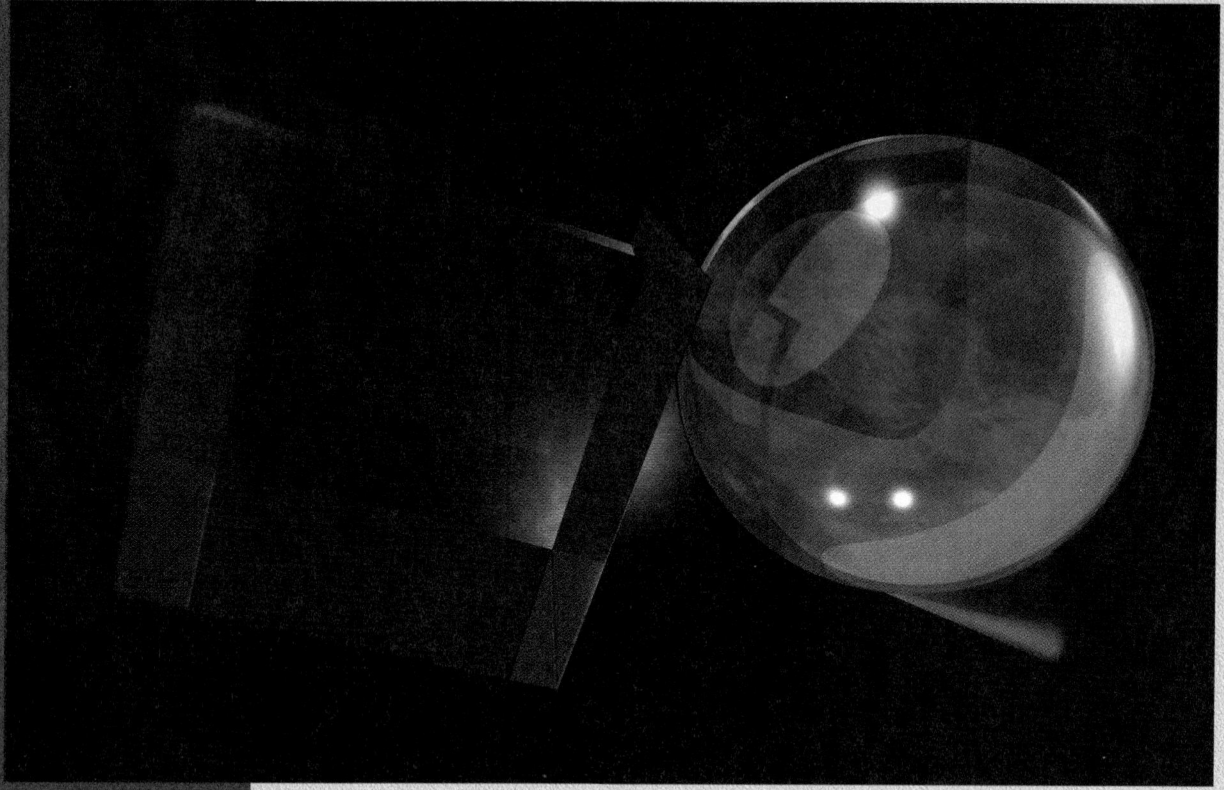

LEARNING OBJECTIVES

After studying this chapter, you should be able to:

1. Identify ways in which cost-volume-profit analysis is used in planning and decision making.
2. Compute the units that must be sold to achieve a targeted level of profit and assess the effects of changes in costs and prices on the profitability of a firm.
3. Compute the sales revenues that must be earned to achieve a targeted level of profit and assess the effects of changes in costs and prices on the profitability of a firm.
4. Prepare a profit-volume graph and a cost-volume-profit graph and explain the meaning of each.
5. Explain the significance of cost behavior and the concepts of variable, fixed, and mixed costs.
6. Separate mixed costs into their fixed and variable components using the high-low method, the scatterplot method, or the method of least squares.

Scenario

During the last month of the fourth quarter, John Kapple, manager of an electronics division, called a meeting of the division's executive committee. Members include Bill Moyes, controller; Jim Brewer, marketing manager; and Sandy Lawson, senior production manager. John had just received a preliminary report on the division's profit performance for the year, and it was gloomy. From all indications, the division was going to show a loss of $3.5 million. This would be the second straight year of significant losses.

"I felt confident at the beginning of the year that our division would at least break even," John remarked.[1] "In fact, break even was the target that I agreed upon with Kent Olsen at the head office. I suppose that we simply lost too many bids this year. It is unfortunate that the variable-costing system wasn't in place at the beginning of the year. We learned too late the importance of knowing what each job's out-of-pocket costs are—at least too late to be of any benefit this year. Fortunately, the variable-costing system became operational two weeks ago, and I understand that we now have a much better idea of what our fixed and variable costs are. In fact, this knowledge of cost behavior has already played a role in winning a major bid for next year. I think this is encouraging; however, if we expect this division to continue operating, we need at least to break even this coming year. I asked Bill to prepare a projected income statement for the coming year. Bill, what can we expect?"

"Jim and I spent a lot of time developing a sales forecast. The variable-costing system certainly has a positive effect, which we factored in when developing our forecast. Once we had a sales forecast, I calculated the sales volume needed to break even. Unfortunately, our projected sales revenue is still well below the break-even volume. As best as I can estimate, we can cut our loss from $3.5 million to $1.5 million."

"Well, given this report, I think you can all see that we have a serious problem," John said. "We cannot tolerate another operating loss of that magnitude. We must either increase revenues more or cut costs—or perhaps do both. Jim, what are the possibilities of increasing revenues beyond the projected level?"

"Not very good," Jim replied. "Our pricing strategy is to maintain full-cost plus pricing on our existing business and new small orders and use special pricing only on new large-volume orders. The competition is especially keen on large-volume orders. Our competition recognizes, as we now do, that a small contribution per unit on a large volume can produce a sizable overall profit increase. We have already built into the forecast a significant increase in sales revenue. Only a limited amount of business is available, though, and I honestly don't believe that we can capture more of it than Bill and I have estimated."

"I was afraid that you'd say that," John admitted. "This means we must focus our attention on costs in order to lower the break-even point to our projected sales volume. Somehow we must decrease costs by at least $1.5 million. Sandy, I want you to look at production and engineering. Bill, you look at

1. To *break even* means to have exactly enough sales revenues to cover all costs. *Break even* means zero profits.

accounting and administration. Jim, see what can be done with the marketing department. In two weeks, I want recommendations from each of you on how we can cut costs in those areas and still carry out the same level of projected sales activity. I want costs reduced by at least $1.5 million."

Note: This scenario is adapted from the experiences of a real company. The names have been changed to ensure confidentiality.

ISSUES ADDRESSED BY COST-VOLUME-PROFIT ANALYSIS

Objective 1
Identify ways in which CVP analysis is used in planning and decision making.

The introductory scenario is based on actual facts and describes an electronics division that decided to adopt a variable-costing accounting system for internal purposes. Knowing cost behavior apparently was having a favorable effect on pricing decisions.[2] Unfortunately, the effect was not sufficient to overcome the competitive difficulties facing the division. Knowledge of cost behavior is crucial for other areas of managerial responsibility as well. The events described in the introductory scenario also provide a good example of how cost-volume-profit analysis (or CVP analysis) can be used for managerial planning. The revenues, costs, and profits for the coming year were projected with the outcome being a predicted loss. Projected sales volume was compared with the sales volume needed to break even. The first question raised by the division manager concerned the possibility of increasing sales volume in order to reach the break-even volume. Once it was clear that this was not possible, the manager was forced to consider other measures. If sales cannot be increased to achieve the break-even volume, the next choice is to lower costs so that projected revenues become the break-even volume.

Interestingly, the division successfully cut costs. In fact, fixed overhead was reduced by $2 million, resulting in a projected profit of $500,000. How was this accomplished? To explain, we note a few examples of cost reductions made by the divisional executives. Although the list is not exhaustive, it conveys the essential flavor of the approach taken.

In production and engineering, several high-priced sustaining engineers were released. Sustaining engineers were employed to sustain products that had been sold. Their basic responsibility involved redesigning products to improve them as deficiencies and limitations were reported by users. Sustaining efforts were dropped for those products that were older and diminishing in sales, products at the end of the product life cycle. By dropping sustaining efforts for these products, less engineering time was needed, and the number of engineers employed was reduced accordingly.

In marketing, several nonproductive employees were let go. These employees poured over and analyzed masses of data that ultimately had little bearing on sales. In accounting, it was discovered that reports were being prepared that were

2. How knowledge of cost behavior can improve pricing decisions is described in Chapter 21.

never used by anyone. Many reports simply sat on desks accumulating dust, yet people were being paid to generate them. These useless reports were eliminated; as a consequence, the accounting staff was reduced by 33 percent.

A simple application of CVP analysis led to a significant increase in cost efficiency within the electronics division. In this case, CVP analysis was a valuable tool to identify the extent and magnitude of the economic trouble the division was facing and to help pinpoint the necessary solution. CVP analysis can address many other issues as well.

CVP analysis focuses on prices, revenues, volume, costs, profits, and sales mix. Most questions involving any of these six areas or combinations thereof can be addressed by CVP analysis. The following list is a sample of the types of questions that can be raised and answered by CVP analysis:

1. How many units must be sold (or how much sales revenue must be generated) in order to break even?
2. How many units must be sold to earn a before-tax profit equal to $60,000? A before-tax profit equal to 15 percent of revenues? An after-tax profit of $45,000?
3. Will overall profits increase if the unit price is increased by $2 and units sold decrease 15 percent?
4. What is the effect on profits if advertising expenditures increase by $8,000 and sales increase from 1,600 to 1,725 units?
5. What is the effect on profits if the selling price is decreased from $400 to $375 per unit and sales increase from 1,600 units to 1,900 units?
6. What is the effect on profits if the selling price is decreased from $400 to $375 per unit, advertising expenditures are increased by $8,000, and sales increase from 1,600 units to 2,300 units?
7. What is the effect on profits if the sales mix is changed?

This list is by no means complete, but it should provide you with some insight into the power of CVP analysis. So far we have not mentioned anything about how CVP analysis is executed. Since we are interested in how revenues, expenses, and profits behave as volume changes, the variable-costing (or contribution) income statement is the logical basis of CVP analysis.[3] The first step in developing the methodology of CVP analysis is to express the variable-costing income statement as a narrative equation:

Profit before taxes = Sales revenues − Variable expenses − Fixed expenses

units-sold approach
sales-revenue approach

There are two approaches to CVP analysis: the *units-sold approach* and the *sales-revenue approach*. The **units-sold approach** measures sales activity and answers CVP questions in terms of the number of units sold; the **sales-revenue approach** measures sales activity and answers CVP questions in terms of the total dollars of revenue generated. We will explore each approach assuming a single-product analysis.

3. Recall that an income statement based on cost behavior was presented in Chapter 15. You may want to review Exhibit 15-12 on page 740 to see how this type of income statement is organized.

CVP ANALYSIS: UNITS-SOLD APPROACH

Objective 2

Compute the units that must be sold to achieve a targeted level of profit and assess the effects of changes in costs and prices on the profitability of a firm.

To illustrate the units-sold approach, the narrative equation for variable-costing income must be converted to an analytical equation. We will use the following variables:

P = Selling price per unit
X = Units sold
V = Variable cost per unit sold
F = Total fixed costs
I = Income (or profit) before taxes

Using the above notation, sales revenue is expressed as PX (the unit selling price times the units sold), and total variable costs are VX (the unit variable cost times units sold). With these expressions, the units-sold form of the variable-costing income statement is expressed as:

$$I = PX - VX - F \tag{20.1}$$

Suppose you were asked how many units must be sold in order to earn a before-tax profit of I. You could answer the question by solving Equation 20.1 for X. To solve, factor out X to get:

$$I = (P - V)X - F$$

Rearrange as:

$$(P - V)X = F + I$$

and divide by $P - V$ to isolate X.

$$X = (F + I)/(P - V) \tag{20.2}$$

What is the meaning of $P - V$? P is the selling price per unit, and V is the variable cost per unit. Recall that the difference between revenues and variable expenses is called the *contribution margin*. Thus, $P - V$, the difference between unit revenue and unit variable cost, is the *contribution margin per unit*. Knowing this, the narrative version of Equation 20.2 can be stated as follows:

Units sold = (Fixed costs + Profits before taxes)/(Unit contribution margin)

Sample Application: Break-Even Analysis

Assume that Reston Company manufactures an economy-line woodburning stove. For the coming year, the controller has prepared the following projected income statement:

Sales (1,000 units @ \$400)	\$400,000
Less: Variable expenses	(325,000)
Contribution margin	\$ 75,000
Less: Fixed expenses	(45,000)
Profit before taxes	\$ 30,000

A considerable amount of information can be extracted from the income statement. For example, the income statement is based on sales of 1,000 units; the selling price (*P*) is \$400 per unit; the variable cost per unit (*V*) is \$325 (\$325,000/1,000); and total fixed expenses (*F*) are \$45,000. The contribution margin per unit can be computed in one of two ways. One way is to divide the total contribution margin by the units sold for a result of \$75 per unit (\$75,000/1,000). A second way is to compute $P - V$. Doing so yields the same result, \$75 per unit (\$400 − \$325).

break-even point

For the first application, the **break-even point** will be computed. Recall that the break-even point is where total revenues equal total costs, the point of zero profits. The units-sold approach identifies the number of units that must be sold to break even. Setting $I = 0$ in Equation 20.2, the following result is obtained for Reston Company:

$$\begin{aligned} X &= (F + I)/(P - V) \\ &= (\$45{,}000 + \$0)/(\$400 - \$325) \\ &= \$45{,}000/\$75 \text{ per unit} \\ &= 600 \text{ units} \end{aligned}$$

Reston must sell exactly 600 woodburning stoves in order to break even. An income statement based on the sale of 600 stoves can be prepared to check the accuracy of this statement.

Sales (600 units @ \$400)	\$240,000
Less: Variable expenses	(195,000)
Contribution margin	\$ 45,000
Less: Fixed expenses	(45,000)
Profit before taxes	\$ 0

Sample Application: Profit Targets

Consider the following three questions:

1. How many woodburning stoves must be sold to earn a before-tax profit of \$60,000?
2. How many woodburning stoves must be sold to earn a before-tax profit equal to 15 percent of sales revenue?
3. How many woodburning stoves must be sold to earn an after-tax profit of \$45,000 assuming that the corporate tax rate is 40 percent?

To answer the first question, set $I = \$60{,}000$ and solve the following equation:

$$\begin{aligned} X &= (F + I)/(P - V) \\ &= (\$45{,}000 + \$60{,}000)/(\$400 - \$325) \\ &= \$105{,}000/\$75 \\ &= 1{,}400 \text{ woodburning stoves} \end{aligned}$$

Reston must sell 1,400 stoves to earn a before-tax profit of \$60,000. The following income statement verifies this outcome:

Sales (1,400 units @ $400)	$560,000
Less: Variable expenses	(455,000)
Contribution margin	$105,000
Less: Fixed expenses	(45,000)
Profit before taxes	$ 60,000

Another way to check this number of units is to use the break-even point. As was just shown, Reston must sell 1,400 stoves—800 more than the break-even volume of 600 units—to earn a profit of $60,000. The contribution margin per stove is $75. Multiplying $75 by the 800 stoves above break even produces the profit of $60,000 ($75 × 800). This outcome demonstrates that contribution margin per unit for each unit above break even is equivalent to profit per unit. Since the break-even point had already been computed, the answer to the first question in the list above could have been calculated by dividing the unit contribution margin into the target profit and adding the resulting amount to the break-even volume.

In general, assuming that fixed costs remain the same, the impact on a firm's profits resulting from a change in the number of units sold can be assessed by multiplying the unit contribution margin by the change in units sold. For example, if 1,500 stoves instead of 1,400 are sold, how much more profit will be earned? The change in units sold is an increase of 100 stoves, and the unit contribution margin is $75. Thus, profits will increase by $7,500 ($75 × 100).

The second question requires that we determine the number of stoves that must be sold in order to earn a profit equal to 15 percent of sales revenue. Sales revenue is represented by PX. Thus, before-tax profit is 15 percent of PX (0.15 PX). Since P is $400 per unit, before-tax profit (I) can be expressed as 60X$ (or 0.15 × 400X$). Notice that the profit target is a function of X. Whenever the profit target involves X, using Equation 20.1, or $I = PX - VX - F$, is better than using Equation 20.2, $X = (I + F)/(P - V)$, since less algebraic manipulation is needed. Substituting I = 60X$ into the first equation and solving for X yields the following:

$$I = PX - VX - F$$
$$\$60X = \$400X - \$325X - \$45{,}000$$
$$\$60X = \$75X - \$45{,}000$$
$$\$15X = \$45{,}000$$
$$X = 3{,}000 \text{ units}$$

Does a volume of 3,000 stoves achieve a profit equal to 15 percent of sales revenue? For 3,000 stoves, the total revenue is $1.2 million ($400 × 3,000). The profit can be computed without preparing a formal income statement. Remember that above break even, the contribution margin per unit is the profit per unit. The break-even volume is 600 stoves. If 3,000 stoves are sold, then 2,400 (3,000 − 600) stoves above the break-even point are sold. The before-tax profit, therefore, is $180,000 ($75 × 2,400), which is 15 percent of sales ($180,000/$1,200,000).

Some additional development is needed to answer the third question on page 939. This question expresses the profit target in after-tax terms, but the profit target in Equations 20.1 and 20.2 is expressed in before-tax terms. Therefore, to use either equation, the after-tax profit target must first be converted to a before-tax profit target. If t represents the tax rate, then the tax paid on a before-tax profit of I is tI. The after-tax profit is computed by subtracting the tax from the before-tax profit.

$$\begin{aligned}\text{After-tax profit} &= \text{Before-tax profit} - \text{Taxes}\\ &= I - tI\\ &= (1 - t)I\end{aligned}$$

Now divide both sides of the equation by $(1 - t)$

$$I = (\text{After-tax profit})/(1 - t)$$

Thus, to convert the after-tax profit to before-tax profit, simply divide the after-tax profit by $(1 - t)$.

The third question gives an after-tax profit target of $45,000 and states that the tax rate is 40 percent. To convert the after-tax profit target into a before-tax profit target, divide it by 0.6 (1 − 0.4). Thus, the before-tax profit is $75,000 ($45,000/0.6). With this conversion, Equation 20.2 can now be used:

$$\begin{aligned}X &= (F + I)/(P - V)\\ &= (\$45{,}000 + \$75{,}000)/\$75\\ &= \$120{,}000/\$75\\ &= 1{,}600 \text{ units}\end{aligned}$$

To verify the accuracy of the analysis, an income statement based on sales of 1,600 stoves has been prepared.

Sales (1,600 units @ $400)	$640,000
Less: Variable expenses	(520,000)
Contribution margin	$120,000
Less: Fixed costs	(45,000)
Profit before taxes	$ 75,000
Less: Taxes (40% tax rate)	(30,000)
Profit after taxes	$ 45,000

Sample Application: Changes in Costs and Prices

Reston Company recently conducted a market study that revealed three possible outcomes: (1) if advertising expenditures increase by $8,000, sales will increase from 1,600 units to 1,725 units; (2) a price decrease from $400 per stove to $375 per stove would increase sales from 1,600 units to 1,900 units; and (3) decreasing prices to $375 and increasing advertising expenditures by $8,000 will increase sales from 1,600 units to 2,600 units. Should Reston maintain its current price and advertising policies, or should it select one of the three alternatives described by the marketing study?

Consider the first alternative. What is the effect on profits if advertising costs increase by $8,000 and sales increase by 125 units? This question can be answered without using the equations but by employing the contribution margin per unit.

We know that the unit contribution margin is $75. Since units sold increase by 125, the incremental increase in total contribution margin is $9,375 ($75 × 125 units). However, since fixed costs increase by $8,000, the incremental increase in profits is only $1,375 ($9,375 − $8,000). Exhibit 20-1 summarizes the effects of the first alternative. Notice that we need to look only at the incremental increase in total contribution margin and fixed expenses to compute the increase in total profits.

For the second alternative, fixed expenses do not increase. Thus, it is possible to answer the question by looking only at the effect on total contribution margin.

Exhibit 20-1
Summary of the Effects of the First Alternative

	Status Quo	*Proposed Price Change*
Units sold	1,600	1,725
Unit contribution margin	× $75	× $75
Total contribution margin	$120,000	$129,375
Less: Fixed costs	(45,000)	(53,000)
Profit	$ 75,000	$ 76,375

Incremental Effect	
Change in sales volume	125
Unit contribution margin	× $75
Change in contribution margin	$ 9,375
Less: Increase in fixed expenses	(8,000)
Increase in profits	$ 1,375

For the current price of $400, the contribution margin per unit is $75. If 1,600 units are sold, the total contribution margin is $120,000 ($75 × 1,600). If the price is dropped to $375, the contribution margin drops to $50 per unit ($375 − $325). If 1,900 units are sold at the new price, the new total contribution margin is $95,000 ($50 × 1,900). Dropping the price results in a profit decline of $25,000 ($120,000 − $95,000). The effects of the second alternative are summarized in Exhibit 20-2.

The third alternative calls for a decrease in the unit selling price and an increase in advertising costs. Like the first alternative, the profit impact can be assessed by looking at the incremental effects on contribution margin and fixed expenses. The incremental profit change can be found by (1) computing the incre-

Exhibit 20-2
Summary of the Effects of the Second Alternative

	Status Quo	*Proposed Price Change*
Units sold	1,600	1,900
Unit contribution margin	× $75	× $50
Total contribution margin	$120,000	$95,000
Less: Fixed expenses	(45,000)	(45,000)
Profit	$ 75,000	$50,000

Incremental Effect	
Change in contribution margin ($95,000 − $120,000)	($25,000)
Less: Change in fixed expenses	—
Change in profits	($25,000)

mental change in total contribution margin, (2) computing the incremental change in fixed expenses, and (3) adding the two results.

As shown, the current total contribution margin (for 1,600 units sold) is $120,000. Since the new unit contribution margin is $50, the new total contribution margin is $130,000 ($50 × 2,600 units). Thus, the incremental increase in total contribution margin is $10,000 ($130,000 − $120,000). However, to achieve this incremental increase in contribution margin, an incremental increase of $8,000 in fixed costs is needed. The net effect is an incremental increase in profits of $2,000. The effects of the third alternative are summarized in Exhibit 20-3. Of the three alternatives identified by the marketing study, the one that promises the most benefit is the third. It increases total profits by $2,000. The first alternative increases profits by only $1,375, and the second actually decreases profits by $25,000.

All these examples are based on a units-sold approach. Sales volume is measured in units sold. Variable costs and contribution margin are also expressed on a units-sold basis. It is also possible to express sales volume in another way, using revenues rather than units sold. In this approach, variable costs and contribution margin are seen as a percentage of revenues. This method will be explored next.

CVP ANALYSIS: SALES-REVENUE APPROACH

Objective 3

Compute the sales revenues that must be sold to achieve a targeted level of profit and assess the effects of changes in costs and prices on the profitability of a firm.

In some cases when using CVP analysis, managers may prefer to use sales revenues as the measure of sales activity instead of units sold. A units-sold measure can be converted to a sales-revenue measure simply by multiplying the unit sales price by the units sold. For example, the break-even point for Reston Company was computed to be 600 woodburning stoves. Since the selling price for each stove is $400, the break-even volume in revenues is $240,000 ($400 × 600). Any answer expressed in units sold can be easily converted to one expressed in sales revenues, but the answer can be computed more directly by developing a separate formula for the sales-revenue case.

Exhibit 20-3
Summary of the Effects of the Third Alternative

	Status Quo	*Proposed Price Change*
Units sold	1,600	2,600
Unit contribution margin	× $75	× $50
Total contribution margin	$120,000	$130,000
Less: Fixed expenses	(45,000)	(53,000)
Profit	$ 75,000	$ 77,000

Incremental Effect	
Change in contribution margin ($130,000 − $120,000)	$10,000
Less: Change in fixed expenses ($53,000 − $45,000)	(8,000)
Change in profits	$ 2,000

This formula uses the following variables:

$R = PX$ (Price × Units sold)
$vr = (V/P)$ or (Variable costs/Sales revenues)
$F =$ Total fixed costs
$I =$ Profit before taxes

The sales-revenue form of variable-costing income is expressed as follows:

$$I = R - F - (vr)R \tag{20.3}$$

Some immediate differences between the sales-revenue approach and the units-sold approach should be mentioned. First, sales activity is defined as sales revenues instead of units sold. Second, variable costs are defined as a percentage of sales rather than as an amount per unit sold. Logically, if costs vary in total with the units sold, the same costs should vary in total with sales in dollars. For example, assume that variable costs are $6 per unit sold and 100 units are sold for $10 each. Using the units-sold approach, total variable costs are $600 ($6 × 100 units sold). Alternatively, since each unit sold earns $10 of revenue, we would say that for every $10 of revenue earned, $6 of variable costs are incurred, or, equivalently, 60 percent of each dollar of revenue earned is attributable to variable cost ($6/$10). Thus, using the sales-revenue approach, we would expect total variable costs of $600 for revenues of $1,000 (0.60 × $1,000).

variable cost ratio

The parameter *vr* is called the **variable cost ratio.** It is simply the proportion of each sales dollar that must be used to cover variable costs. Alternatively, *vr* can be thought of as the variable cost per sales dollar. The variable cost ratio can be computed by using either total data or unit data. If total data are used, the variable cost ratio is total variable costs divided by total sales revenues. In the case of a single product, unit data can be used. Then the variable cost ratio is unit variable cost divided by unit revenue. In the latter case, $vr = V/P$, where V is the variable cost per unit sold and P is the unit selling price.

Equation 20.3 can be solved for R to determine the sales revenues needed to earn a profit target of I. First, factor out R:

$$I = (1 - vr)R - F$$

rearrange as:

$$(1 - vr)R = F + I$$

and divide both sides by $(1 - vr)$:

$$R = (F + I)/(1 - vr) \tag{20.4}$$

What is the meaning of $(1 - vr)$? Since vr equals V/P, $1 - vr$ equals $1 - V/P$, which equals $(P - V)/P$. As you know, $(P - V)$ is the unit contribution margin, and P is the unit selling price. Thus, $(P - V)/P$ is the **contribution margin ratio,** the proportion of each sales dollar available to cover fixed costs and provide for profit. It makes sense that the complement of the variable cost ratio, $(1 - vr)$, is the contribution margin ratio. After all, the proportion of the sales dollar left after variable costs are covered should be the contribution margin component.

contribution margin ratio

The contribution margin ratio can be computed in two ways. One way is to calculate the variable cost ratio (vr) and then subtract this number from one $(1 - vr)$. The second way is to divide the contribution margin by the sales revenue (either on a total basis or on a per-unit basis).

Given the definition of $(1 - vr)$, the narrative version of Equation 20.4 can be expressed as follows:

$$R = (\text{Fixed costs} + \text{Profit before taxes})/(\text{Contribution margin ratio}) \quad (20.4)$$

Sample Application: Break-Even Point

Since answers using the units-sold approach can be easily converted to sales revenues, only a couple of simple examples will be used to illustrate the direct application of the sales-revenue approach. The same data as for the earlier examples will be used. Recall that Reston Company projected the following variable-costing income for the coming year:

Sales (1,000 units @ \$400)	\$400,000
Less: Variable expenses	(325,000)
Contribution margin	\$ 75,000
Less: Fixed costs	(45,000)
Profit before taxes	\$ 30,000

From this income statement, the information needed to carry out CVP analysis under the sales-revenue approach can be easily extracted. The variable cost ratio is 0.8125 (\$325,000/\$400,000), and fixed costs are \$45,000. The contribution margin ratio is 0.1875 (computed either as 1 − 0.8125, or \$75,000/\$400,000).

Given the information in this income statement, how much sales revenue must Reston earn to break even? Setting $I = 0$ in Equation 20.4, the following result is obtained:

$$\begin{aligned} R &= (F + I)/(1 - vr) \\ &= (\$45{,}000 + 0)/0.1875 \\ &= \$240{,}000 \end{aligned}$$

Thus, Reston must earn revenues totaling \$240,000 in order to break even.

Sample Application: Profit Target

Consider the following question: How much sales revenue must Reston generate to earn a before-tax profit of \$60,000? (This question parallels one asked for the units-sold approach but phrases the question directly in terms of sales revenue.) To answer the question, set I to equal \$60,000 and solve Equation 20.4:

$$\begin{aligned} R &= (F + I)/(1 - vr) \\ &= (\$45{,}000 + \$60{,}000)/0.1875 \\ &= \$105{,}000/0.1875 \\ &= \$560{,}000 \end{aligned}$$

Reston must earn revenues equal to \$560,000 to achieve a profit target of \$60,000. Since break even is \$240,000, additional sales of \$320,000 (\$560,000 − \$240,000) must be earned above break even. Notice that multiplying the contribution margin ratio by revenues above break even yields the profit of \$60,000 (0.1875 × \$320,000). Above break even, the contribution margin ratio is a profit ratio; therefore, it represents the proportion of each sales dollar assignable to profit. For this example, every sales dollar earned above break even increases profits by \$0.1875.

In general, assuming that fixed costs remain unchanged, the contribution margin ratio can be used to find the profit impact of a change in sales revenue. To obtain the total change in profits from a change in revenues, simply multiply the contribution margin ratio times the change in sales. For example, if sales revenues are \$540,000 instead of \$560,000, how will the expected profits be affected? A decrease in sales revenues of \$20,000 will cause a decrease in profits of \$3,750 (0.1875 × \$20,000).

Comparison of the Two Approaches

For a single-product setting, converting the units-sold answers to sales-revenue answers is simply a matter of multiplying the unit sales price by the units sold. Then, why bother with a separate formula for the sales revenue approach? For a single-product setting, neither approach has any real advantage over the other. Both offer essentially the same level of conceptual and computational difficulty. Each approach does supply a different view of CVP analysis, though. Because each approach supplies different insights and different concepts (the concepts of unit contribution margin and contribution margin ratio), it is worthwhile to study both approaches.

In a multiple-product setting, however, CVP analysis is more complex. In this situation, the sales-revenue approach assumes a significant computational advantage. This approach maintains essentially the same computational requirements found in the single-product setting, whereas the units-sold approach becomes more difficult. The study of CVP analysis in a multiple-product setting is deferred to a more advanced accounting course.

GRAPHICAL REPRESENTATION OF CVP RELATIONSHIPS

Objective 4
Prepare a profit-volume graph and a cost-volume-profit graph and explain the meaning of each.

CVP analysis can offer additional insight by graphing the relationships implied by Equation 20.2 or 20.4. A visual portrayal of concepts always seems to enrich one's understanding. Charts and graphs of CVP problems are also useful in presenting an analysis to management. For example, in the case described at the beginning of the chapter, the controller could have enhanced his report to the divisional manager by preparing a graph that portrayed the division's current CVP relationships.

The Profit-Volume Graph

profit-volume graph

A **profit-volume graph** visually portrays the relationship between profits and sales volume. The profit-volume graph is the graph of the linear equation $I = PX - VX - F$, with I as the dependent variable and X as the independent variable. Usually, values of the independent variable are measured along the horizontal axis and values of the dependent variable along the vertical.

To make this discussion more concrete, a simple set of data will be used. Assume that Tyson Company produces a single product with the following cost and price data:

Total fixed costs	\$100
Variable costs per unit	5
Selling price per unit	10

Using these data, the profit-volume equation can be expressed as:

$$I = \$10X - \$5X - \$100$$
$$I = \$5X - \$100$$

The graph of $I = \$5X - \$100$ is the profit-volume graph for the Tyson Company example. Units sold will be plotted along the horizontal axis and profit (or loss) along the vertical axis. Two points are needed to graph a linear equation. While any two points will do, the two points often chosen are those that correspond to zero sales volume and zero profits. Setting $X = 0$ results in $I = -\$100$. The point corresponding to zero sales volume, therefore, is (0, −\$100). In other words, when no sales take place, the company suffers a loss equal to its total fixed costs. Setting $I = \$0$ results in $X = 20$. The point corresponding to zero profits (break even) is (20, \$0). These two points, plotted in Exhibit 20-4, define the profit graph shown in the same figure.

The graph in Exhibit 20-4 can be used to assess Tyson's profit (or loss) at any level of sales activity. For example, the profit associated with the sale of 40 units can be read from the graph by (1) drawing a vertical line from the horizontal axis to the profit line and (2) drawing a horizontal line from the profit line to the vertical axis. As illustrated in Exhibit 20-4, the profit associated with sales of 40 units is \$100. The profit-volume graph, while easy to interpret, fails to reveal how

Exhibit 20-4
Profit-Volume Graph

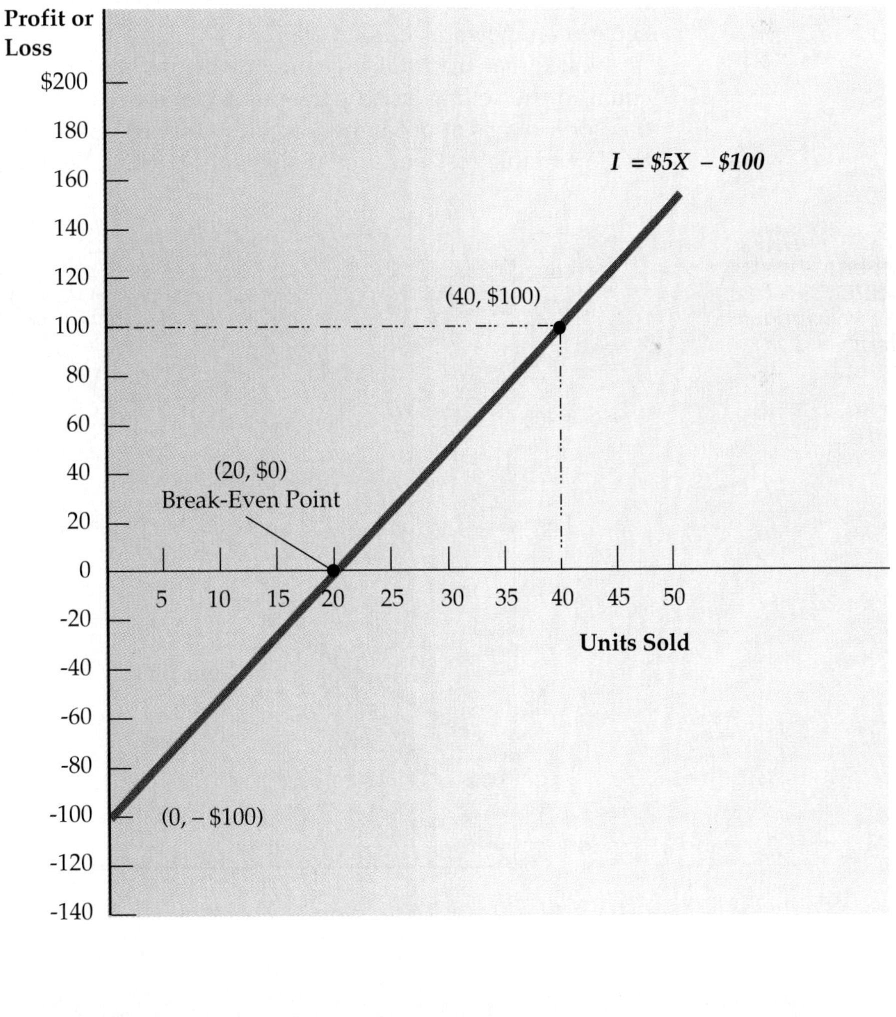

costs change as sales volume changes. An alternative approach to graphing can provide this detail.

The Cost-Volume-Profit Graph

cost-volume-profit graph

The **cost-volume-profit graph** depicts the relationships among cost, volume, and profits. To obtain the more detailed relationships, it is necessary to graph two separate lines: the total revenue line and the total cost line. These two lines are represented, respectively, by the following two equations:

$$R = PX$$
$$TC = F + VX$$

Using the Tyson Company example, the revenue and cost equations are:

$$R = \$10X$$
$$TC = \$100 + \$5X$$

To portray both equations in the same graph, the vertical axis is measured in dollars and the horizontal axis in units sold.

Two points are needed to graph each equation. We will use the same X-coordinates used for the profit-volume graph. For the revenue equation, setting $X = 0$ results in $R = \$0$; setting $X = 20$ results in $R = \$200$. Therefore, the two points for the revenue equation are (0, \$0) and (20, \$200). For the cost equation, $X = 0$ and $X = 20$ produce the points (0, \$100) and (20, \$200). The graph of each equation appears in Exhibit 20-5.

Notice that the total revenue line begins at the origin and rises with a slope equal to the selling price per unit (a slope of 10). The total cost line intercepts the vertical axis at a point equal to total fixed costs and rises with a slope equal to the variable cost per unit (a slope of 5). When the total revenue line lies below

Exhibit 20-5
Cost-Volume-Profit Graph

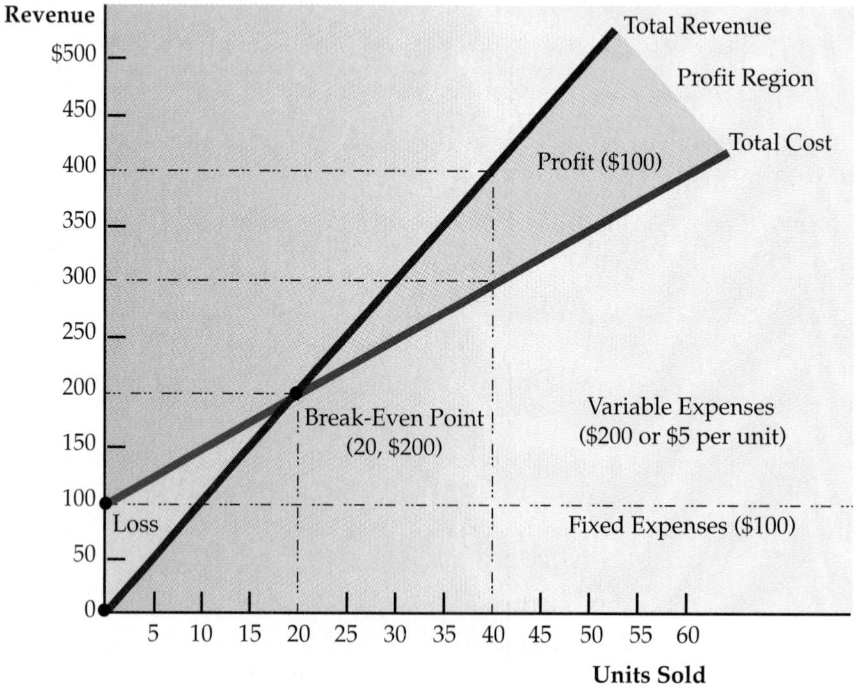

the total cost line, a loss region is defined. Similarly, when the total revenue line lies above the total cost line, a profit region is defined. The point where the total revenue line and the total cost line intersect is the break-even point. To break even, Tyson Company must sell 20 units and receive $200 total revenues.

Now let's compare the information available from the CVP graph to that available from the profit-volume graph. To do so, consider the sale of 40 units. Recall that the profit-volume graph revealed that selling 40 units produced profits of $100. Examine Exhibit 20-5 again. The CVP graph also shows profits of $100, but it reveals more as well. The CVP graph discloses that total revenues of $400 and total costs of $300 are associated with the sale of 40 units. Furthermore, the total costs can be broken down into fixed costs of $100 and variable costs of $200. The CVP graph provides revenue and cost information not provided by the profit-volume graph. Unlike the profit-volume graph, some computation is needed to determine the profit associated with a given sales volume. Nonetheless, because of the greater information content, managers are likely to find the CVP graph a more useful tool.

Limitations of CVP Analysis

A number of limitations are commonly mentioned with respect to CVP analysis.

1. The analysis assumes a linear revenue function and a linear cost function.
2. The analysis assumes that what is produced is sold.
3. The analysis assumes that fixed and variable costs can be accurately identified.
4. The selling prices and costs are assumed to be known with certainty.

Criticisms 1 through 3 pose fewer problems than does the fourth criticism. It is virtually impossible to predict with certainty the selling prices and the costs for an upcoming period. However, with the capabilities of spread-sheet analysis, the sensitivity of variables to changes in predicted values can be readily assessed. Furthermore, there are formal ways of explicitly building uncertainty into the CVP model. Exploration of these issues, however, is left to a more advanced course of study. We will, however, explore the issue of identifying fixed and variable costs. Knowing how costs behave is critical for CVP analysis.

COST BEHAVIOR

Objective 5
Explain the significance of cost behavior and the concepts of variable, fixed, and mixed costs.

cost behavior

Cost behavior is the general term for describing whether a cost is fixed or variable in relation to changes in the level of activity. A cost that remains the same in total as activity increases or decreases is a fixed cost. A variable cost is one that increases with an increase in activity and decreases with a decrease in activity. Theoretically, separating fixed and variable costs is no problem. In fact, most economics textbooks assume that the cost separation has been accomplished and proceed from there. It is the management accountant who must bring cost separation from theory to reality by considering the type of decision to be made as well as the reasons for making it. In analyzing cost behavior, it helps to consider the specific concepts of time horizon and activity-level measure.

Time Horizon

Determining whether a cost is fixed or variable depends crucially on the time horizon. We know from economics that in the long run, all costs are variable; in the short run, at least one cost is fixed. But how long is the short run? Different costs have different-length short runs. Direct materials, for example, are relatively easy to adjust. For all practical purposes, the firm may treat direct materials as strictly variable even though for the next few hours the amount of materials already purchased may be fixed. Depreciation on the plant, however, is more difficult to adjust. It could take months, or even years, to sell or expand the plant. Thus, this cost is typically seen as fixed. The length of the short-run period depends to some extent on management judgment and the purpose for which cost behavior is being estimated. For example, for some bids the short run might consist of just a month or so—long enough to obtain the bids and produce the order. Other types of decisions, such as product discontinuance or product mix decisions, may involve a much longer period of time. Thus, the costs that must be considered are long-run variable costs, including product design, development, market development, and market penetration. It is important to realize that short-run costs do not reflect adequately all the costs necessary to design, produce, market, distribute, and support a product.

Activity-Level Measures

Variable costs move in total with changes in activity level. Often the activity level is the volume of production. Tracing costs to each unit produced ranges from relatively easy (for example, direct materials) to virtually impossible (for example, janitorial services or property taxes on the factory building). For service firms, tracing costs to their units of production may be even more troublesome. Is the appropriate unit an hour of service or the performance of a particular task? Additionally, some units of service may be provided by more experienced personnel. For example, a law firm will cost (and price) an attorney's time on a case differently from a paralegal's time.

The determination of an appropriate measure of activity, or cost driver, is made easier by considering that we are trying to find out what the cost varies with. In other words, ideally the activity/cost driver relationship will be strictly variable. For example, electrical cost may be a function of machine hours, shipping expense may be a function of units sold, and hospital laundry cost may be a function of patient days. The choice of cost driver is tailored not only to the particular firm but also to the particular cost being measured.

We have defined cost drivers as causal factors that explain the consumption of activities. In general, cost drivers fall into four categories. Unit-level cost drivers increase cost every time a unit is produced. Direct materials, power to run production machinery, and direct labor can be thought of as unit-level cost drivers. Batch-level cost drivers increase cost when the number of batches increases. Examples of batch-level cost drivers include setups, scheduling, inspection, and materials moves. Product-level cost drivers increase costs as the number of products increases. They pertain to product development, production, and sales. Product-level cost drivers include engineering hours, expediting orders, and number of bills of materials (the list of materials specified to manufacture a product). Finally, at the facility level, we have general overhead, which might be thought of as a capacity cost.[4]

4. At the facility level, there is no cost driver in the short run because all facility costs are strictly fixed. Facility costs can vary only in the long run. We might think of the long-run situation as involving a shift in strategy, product obsolescence, or new technology. Any of these changes may require changes to be made in plant facilities.

We now take a closer look at variable and fixed costs. If the cost-behavior pattern of an item is strictly variable or fixed, that cost can be assigned to the appropriate category. However, what if the item displays a mixed cost pattern? For mixed cost items, we must break out their variable and fixed components so that each component can be assigned to the correct category. Assigning costs to either a variable or a fixed category may not correspond exactly to how costs actually behave. What we hope is that the cost-behavior assignment approximates reality well enough to be useful. Finally, we should note that the emphasis in the remainder of the chapter on cost behavior is on unit-level cost drivers. Thus, the analysis is primarily oriented towards conventional cost systems; however, the procedures discussed can be applied to other categories of cost driver.

Mixed Costs

As we know, mixed costs have a fixed and a variable component. As an example, assume that a firm leases a photocopier. The agreement calls for a payment of \$250 per month plus \$0.025 per copy. The behavior of this cost is expressed by the following equation:

$$Y = \$250 + \$0.025X$$

where Y = Total cost
X = The number of copies per month

The fixed charge of \$250 makes the copying capacity available, but use of that capacity also produces a cost. In fact, for every copy produced, the company must pay an additional \$0.025. The more copies made, the more the company must pay. If 1,000 copies are made during a month, the total cost is \$275 [\$250 + (\$0.025 × 1,000)]. If 5,000 copies are produced, total cost is \$375 [\$250 + (\$0.025 × 5,000)]. Total cost increases as the activity increases, but regardless of how many copies are made, the company must pay at least \$250. Exhibit 20-6 displays the mixed cost relationship. Notice that at zero units of activity, there is some cost. As activity level increases, total cost increases.

What the Accounting Records Reveal. Sometimes, as in the photocopier example, it is easy to identify the variable and fixed components of a mixed cost. Many times, however, the only information available is the total cost and a measure of the activity level (the variables Y and X). For example, the accounting system will usually record both the total cost of maintenance for a given period and the number of units produced during that period. How much of the total maintenance cost represents a fixed charge and how much represents a variable charge is not revealed by the accounting records. (In fact, the accounting records may not even reveal the breakdown of costs in the photocopier example.) Often, the total cost is simply recorded with no attempt to segregate the fixed and variable costs.

Need for Decomposition. Since accounting records typically reveal only the total cost and the associated activity of a mixed cost item, it is necessary to decompose the total cost into its fixed and variable components. Only through decomposition can all costs be classified into the appropriate categories.

If mixed costs are a very small percentage of total costs, however, decomposition may be more trouble than it's worth. In this case, mixed costs could be assigned to either the fixed- or variable-cost category without much concern for

Exhibit 20-6
Mixed Cost

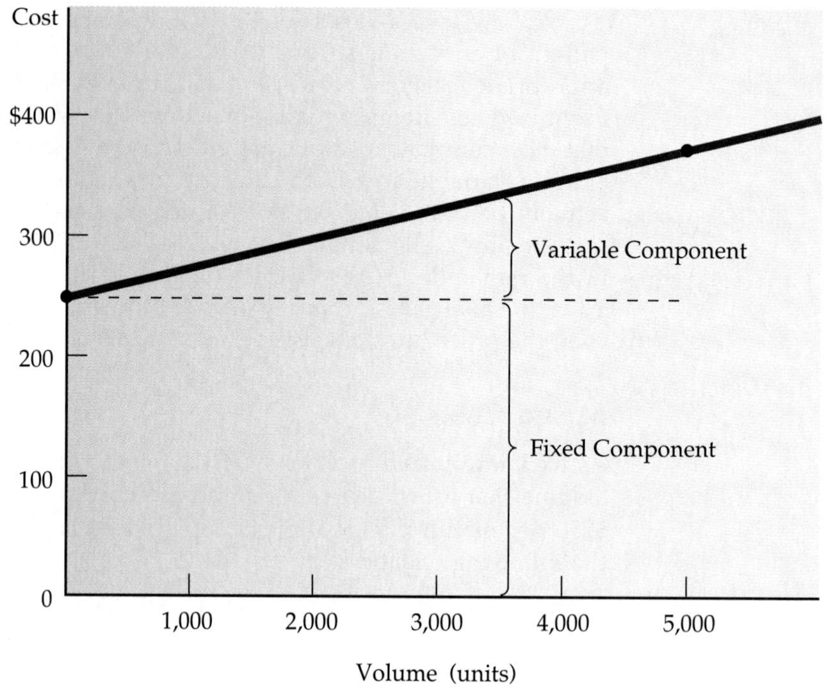

the classification error or its effect on decision making. Alternatively, the total mixed cost could be arbitrarily divided between the two cost categories. This option is seldom available, though. Mixed costs for many firms are large enough to warrant decomposition. Given the need for decomposition, how is it done?

METHODS FOR DECOMPOSING MIXED COSTS

Objective 6
Separate mixed costs into their fixed and variable components using the high-low method, the scatterplot method, or the method of least squares.

Mixed costs are assumed to follow a linear relationship:

$$Y = F + VX$$

where Y = Total mixed cost (the dependent variable)
F = Fixed cost component (the intercept parameter)
V = Variable cost per unit of activity (the slope parameter)
X = Activity level (the independent variable)

dependent variable
independent variable
intercept parameter
slope parameter

The **dependent variable** is a variable whose value depends on the value of another variable. In the above equation, total mixed cost is the dependent variable; it is the cost we are trying to predict. The **independent variable** is a variable whose value does not depend on the value of the dependent variable. In the above equation, the activity level (e.g., units produced) is the independent variable. The **intercept parameter** corresponds to fixed cost. Graphically, the intercept parameter is the point at which the mixed cost curve intercepts the vertical axis. The **slope parameter** corresponds to the variable cost per unit of activity. Graphically, this represents the slope of the mixed cost curve.

Since the accounting records reveal only X and Y, those values must be used to estimate the parameters F and V. With estimates of F and V, the fixed and variable components can be estimated and the behavior of the mixed cost can be predicted as activity changes. Three methods will be described for estimating F

and V. These methods are the high-low method, the scatterplot method, and the method of least squares.

The same data will be used with each method so that comparisons among them can be made. Assume that the accounting records of Larson, Inc., disclosed the following utility costs and associated production activity for the past five months:

Month	*Utilities Cost*	*Units Produced*
June	$1,000	100
July	1,250	200
August	2,250	300
September	2,500	400
October	3,750	500

The High-Low Method

From basic geometry, we know that two points are needed to determine a line. Once we know two points on a line, its equation can be determined. Recall that F, the fixed cost component, is the intercept of the total cost line, and that V, the variable cost per unit, is the slope of the line. Given two points, the slope and the intercept can be determined. The **high-low method** preselects the two points that will be used to compute the parameters F and V. Specifically, the method uses the high and low points. The high point is defined as the point with the highest activity level. The low point is defined as the point with the lowest activity level.

high-low method

Letting (X_1, Y_1) be one point, say the low point, and (X_2, Y_2) be the second point, the high point, the equations for determining the slope and intercept are, respectively:

$$\begin{aligned} V &= \text{Change in cost/Change in activity} \\ &= (Y_2 - Y_1)/(X_2 - X_1) \end{aligned}$$

and

$$\begin{aligned} FC &= \text{Total mixed cost} - \text{Variable cost} \\ &= Y_2 - VX_2 \end{aligned}$$

or

$$FC = Y_1 - VX_1$$

Notice that the fixed cost component is computed using the total cost at either (X_1, Y_1) or (X_2, Y_2).

For Larson, the high point is \$3,750 of utilities when 500 units were produced, or (500, \$3,750). The low point is \$1,000 of utilities cost when 100 units were produced, or (100, \$1,000). Once the high and low points are defined, the values of F and V can be computed.

$$\begin{aligned} V &= (Y_2 - Y_1)/(X_2 - X_1) \\ &= (\$3{,}750 - \$1{,}000)/(500 - 100) \\ &= \$2{,}750/400 \\ &= \$6.875 \end{aligned}$$

$$\begin{aligned} F &= Y_2 - VX_2 \\ &= \$3{,}750 - (\$6.875 \times 500) \\ &= \$312.50 \end{aligned}$$

The cost formula using the high-low method is:

$$Y = \$312.50 + \$6.875X$$

If production for December is expected to be 350 units, this cost formula will predict a total cost of $2,718.75, with fixed costs of $312.50 and variable costs of $2,406.25.

The high-low method has the advantage of objectivity. That is, any two people using the high-low method on a particular data set will arrive at the same answer. In addition, the high-low method allows a manager to get a quick fix on a cost relationship using only two data points. For example, a manager may have only two years of data. Sometimes this will be enough to get a crude approximation of the cost relationship.

The high-low method is usually not as good as the other methods. Why? First, the high and low points often can be what are known as outliers. They may represent atypical cost-activity relationships. If so, the cost formula computed using these two points will not represent what usually takes place. The scatterplot method can help a manager avoid this trap by selecting two points that appear to be representative of the general cost-activity pattern. Second, even if these points are not outliers, other pairs of points may clearly be more representative. Again, the scatterplot method allows the choice of the more representative points.

Scatterplot Method

scattergraph

The first step in applying the scatterplot method is to plot the data points so that the relationship between utility costs and activity level can be seen. This plot is referred to as a **scattergraph** and is shown in Exhibit 20-7. The vertical axis is total mixed cost and the horizontal axis is activity level or volume (utility cost and units produced, respectively, for the example).

Inspecting Exhibit 20-7 gives us increased confidence that the assumption of a linear relationship between utility costs and units produced is reasonable for the indicated range of activity. Thus, one purpose of a scattergraph is to assess the validity of the assumed linear relationship. Additionally, inspecting the scattergraph may reveal several points that do not seem to fit the general pattern of behavior. Upon investigation, it may be discovered that these points (the outliers) were due to some irregular occurrences. This knowledge can provide justification for their elimination and perhaps lead to a better estimate of the underlying cost function.

scatterplot method

A scattergraph can help a manager gain a better feel for the relationship between cost and activity. In fact, a manager can visually fit a line to the points on the scattergraph. In doing so, the manager should choose a line that he or she believes fits the points the best. In making that choice, the manager is free to use past experience with the behavior of the cost item. That is, the manager's experience may provide a good intuitive sense of how utility costs behave; the scattergraph then becomes a useful tool to quantify this intuition. Fitting a line to the points in this way is how the **scatterplot method** works.[5]

5. Keep in mind that the scattergraph and the other statistical aids are tools that can help managers improve their judgment. Using the tools does not restrict the manager from using judgment to alter any of the estimates produced by formal methods.

Exhibit 20-7
Scattergraph for Larson, Inc.

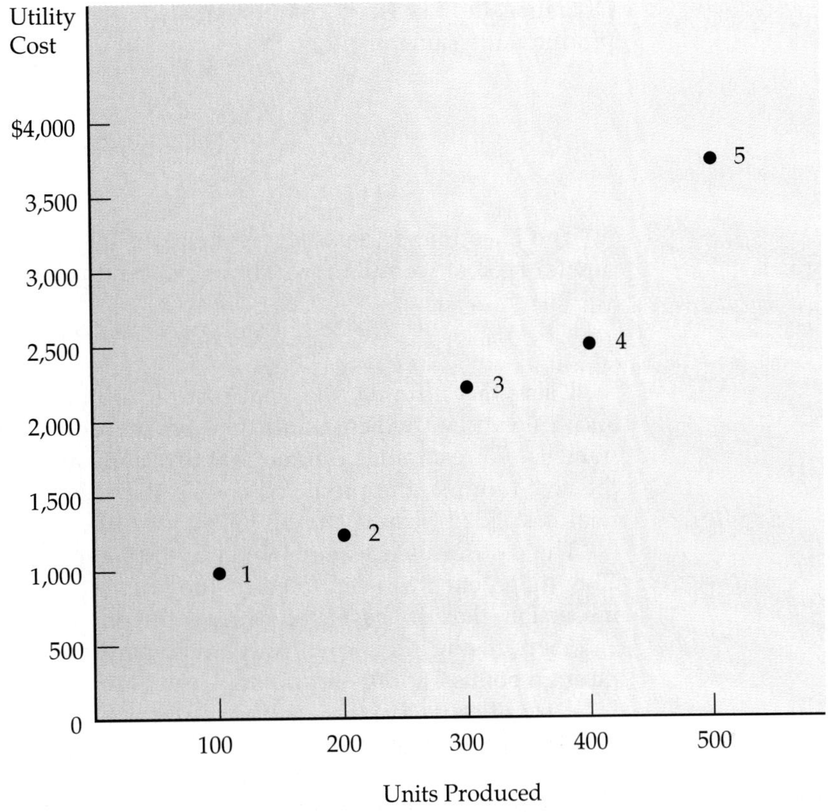

Examine Exhibit 20-7 carefully. Based only on the information contained in the graph, how would you fit a line to the points in it? Suppose that a manager decides that a line passing through points 1 and 3 provides the best fit. If so, how could this decision be used to compute the parameters *F* and *V* so that the fixed and variable cost components can be estimated?

Assuming your choice of the best-fitting line is the one passing through points 1 and 3, the variable cost per unit can be computed in the following way. First let point 1 be designated by $X_1 = 100$, $Y_1 = \$1,000$ and point 3 by $X_2 = 300$, $Y_2 = \$2,250$. (This designation is arbitrary—it really doesn't matter which point is designated (X_1, Y_1) and which one is designated (X_2, Y_2).) Next, use these two points to compute the slope:

$$\begin{aligned} V &= (Y_2 - Y_1)/(X_2 - X_1) \\ &= (\$2,250 - \$1,000)/(300 - 100) \\ &= \$1,250/200 \\ &= \$6.25 \end{aligned}$$

Thus, the variable cost per unit produced is \$6.25. Given the variable cost per unit, the final step is to compute the fixed-cost component using (X_2, Y_2) in the intercept equation:

$$\begin{aligned} F &= Y_2 - VX_2 \\ &= \$2,250 - (\$6.25 \times 300) \\ &= \$375 \end{aligned}$$

Of course, the fixed-cost component also can be computed using (X_1, Y_1), which produces the same result.

$$\begin{aligned} F &= Y_1 - VX_1 \\ &= \$1{,}000 - (\$6.25 \times 100) \\ &= \$375 \end{aligned}$$

cost formula

The fixed and variable components of the utility cost have now been identified. The **cost formula** for utilities can be expressed as:

$$Y = \$375 + \$6.25X$$

Using this formula, the total cost of utilities for activity levels between 100 and 500 can be predicted and then broken down into fixed and variable components. For example, assume that 350 units are planned for December. Using the cost formula, the predicted cost is \$2,562.50 [\$375 + (\$6.25 × 350)]. Of this total cost, \$375 is fixed and \$2,187.50 variable.

The cost formula was obtained by fitting a line to points 1 and 3 in Exhibit 20-8. Judgment was used to select the line. Whereas one person may decide, by inspection, that the best-fitting line is the one that passes through points 1 and 3, others, using their own judgment, may decide that the line should pass through points 2 and 4—or points 1 and 5. An unlimited number of choices exist.

A significant advantage of the scatterplot method is that it affords a manager the opportunity to inspect the data visually. Exhibit 20-8 illustrates cost behavior situations that are not appropriate for the straightforward application of the high-low method. Graph A shows a nonlinear relationship between overhead cost and activity level. An example of this might be a volume discount given on direct materials or evidence of learning by workers (e.g., as more hours are worked, the total cost increases at a decreasing rate due to the increased efficiency of the workers). Graph B indicates that there is an upward shift in cost if more than X_1 units are made—perhaps this could mean that an additional supervisor must be hired or a second shift run. Graph C shows outliers that are not representative of the overall cost relationship.

The scatterplot method suffers from the lack of any objective criterion for choosing the best-fitting line. The quality of the cost formula depends on the quality of the subjective judgment of the analyst. The high-low method removes the subjectivity in the choice of the line. Regardless of who uses the method, the same line will result.

	Fixed Cost	*Variable Rate*	*Utilities Cost at 350 Units*
High-Low	\$312.50	\$6.875	\$2,718.75
Scatterplot	375.00	6.250	2,562.50

Let's compare the results of the scatterplot method with those of the high-low method. There is a large difference between the fixed cost components and the variable rates. The predicted cost of utilities at 350 units is \$2,562.50 according to the scatterplot method and \$2,718.75 according to the high-low method. Which is "right"? Since the two methods can produce vastly different cost formulas, the question of which method is the best naturally arises.

Exhibit 20-8

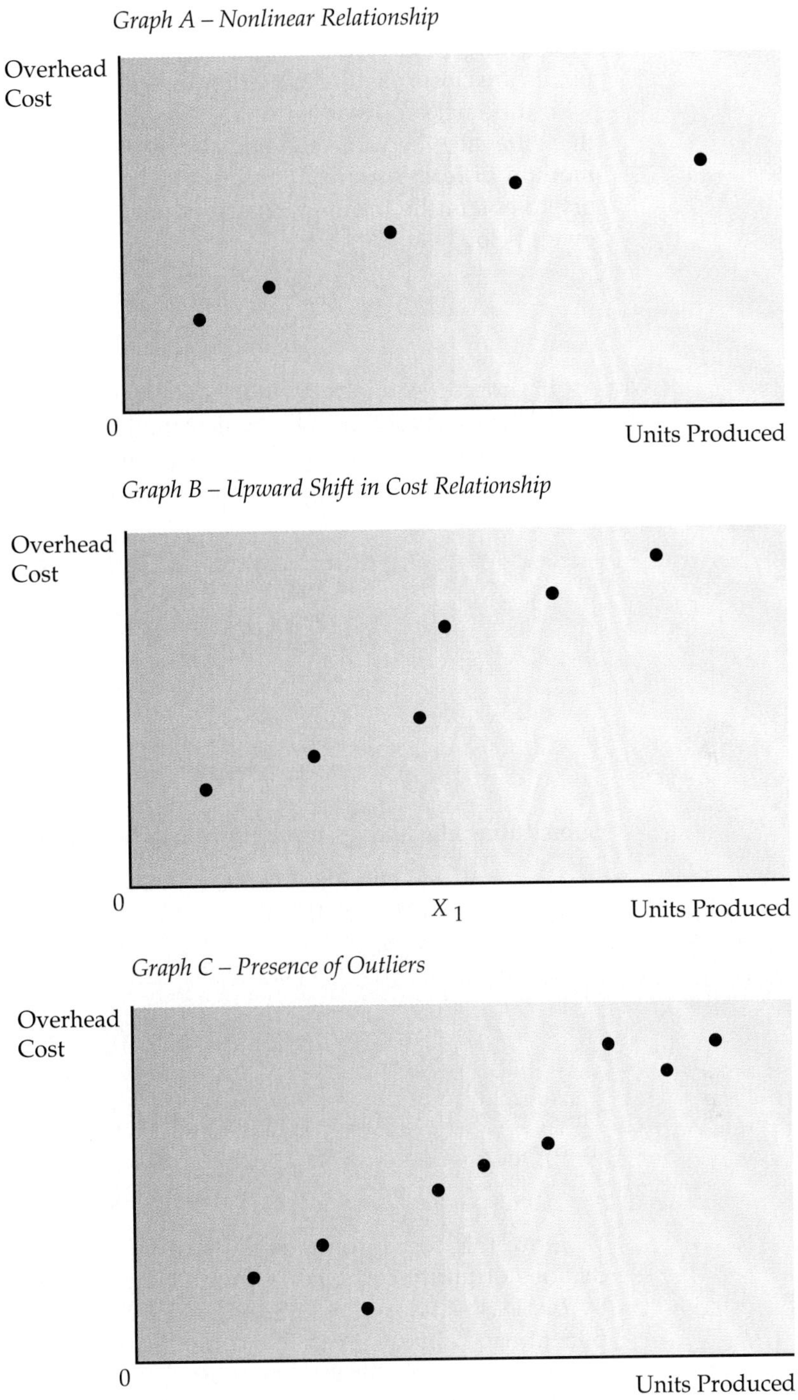

The Method of Least Squares

Ideally, a method that is objective and, at the same time, produces the best-fitting line is needed. The method of least squares defines *best-fitting* and is objective in the sense that using the method for a given set of data will produce the same

best-fitting line

deviation

method of least squares

cost formula. The line that fits the points better than any other line is called the **best-fitting line.** Intuitively, the best fitting line is the one to which the data points are closer than to any other line. But what is meant by closer? It is the line with the smallest (least) sum of squared deviations, where a **deviation** is simply the difference between the actual cost and the cost predicted by the line. The **method of least squares** identifies the best-fitting line. We rely on statistical theory to obtain the formulas that produce the best-fitting line. These formulas are given below.

$$V = [\sum XY - \sum X \sum Y/n]/[\sum X^2 - (\sum X)^2/n] \quad (20.5)$$

$$F = (\sum Y/n - v(\sum X/n) \quad (20.6)$$

In order to compute V and F, five inputs are needed: n, $\sum X$, $\sum Y$, $\sum XY$, and $\sum X^2$. The first input, n, is the easiest to obtain—simply count the number of data points in the data set. For the Larson, Inc., example, there are five data points. The other four inputs are computed as follows:

$\sum X$	$\sum Y$	$\sum XY$	$\sum X^2$
100	$ 1,000	$ 100,000	10,000
200	1,250	250,000	40,000
300	2,250	675,000	90,000
400	2,500	1,000,000	160,000
500	3,750	1,875,000	250,000
1,500	$10,750	$3,900,000	550,000

Substituting the above summations ($\sum$) into Equations 20.7 and 20.8, we obtain:

$$\begin{aligned} V &= [3{,}900{,}000 - (1{,}500 \times 10{,}750)/5]/[550{,}000 - (1{,}500)^2/5] \\ &= 675{,}000/100{,}000 \\ &= 6.75 \end{aligned}$$

and

$$\begin{aligned} F &= \$10{,}750/5 - [\$6.75(1{,}500/5)] \\ &= \$125 \end{aligned}$$

Thus, the cost formula for the method of least squares can be expressed as follows:

$$Y = \$125 + \$6.75X$$

Since this cost formula is the best-fitting line, it should produce better predictions of utility costs. For a production level of 350, the utility cost predicted by the least-squares line is $2,487.50 [$125 + ($6.75 × 350)], with a fixed component of $125 plus a variable component of $2,362.50. Using this prediction as a standard, the scatterplot line most closely approximates the least-squares line.

If the least-squares line is the best-fitting line, why worry about the other two methods? Because the other two methods involve simpler computations, they can provide quick estimates of the fixed and variable components of mixed costs. The computational complexity of the least-squares method is not high, however, and calculators or software packages are available to do the computation with the simple requirement of inputting the data points. Thus, the method of least squares is generally recommended over the other two methods. Remember, however, that the use of a scattergraph may result in the detection of nonlinearity and outliers, in which case that method may produce a better cost formula.[6] Furthermore, the method of least squares requires a large number of data points for reliable estimates. In those settings where only a small number of data points are available, the scatterplot method may be more suitable.

SUMMARY OF LEARNING OBJECTIVES

1. *Identify ways in which cost-volume-profit analysis is used in planning and decision making.* CVP analysis focuses on prices, revenues, volume, costs, profits, and sales mix. Most questions regarding one or more of these areas can be answered using CVP analysis.

2. *Compute the units that must be sold to achieve a targeted level of profit and assess the effects of changes in costs and prices on the profitability of a firm.* To compute the units required to achieve a targeted level of profit, simply add the targeted before-tax profit to fixed costs and divide by the unit contribution margin. If the target profit is expressed in after-tax profit, convert to before-tax profit by dividing the after-tax profit by $1 - t$, where t is the tax rate. The effects of changes in costs and prices on profitability can be assessed by examining the change in contribution margin.

3. *Compute the sales revenues that must be earned to achieve a targeted level of profit and assess the effects of changes in costs and prices on the profitability of a firm.* To compute the sales revenues required to achieve a targeted before-tax income, add the targeted profit to total fixed expenses and divide by the contribution margin ratio. As with the units-sold approach, the effects of changes in costs and prices can be assessed by examining the change in contribution margin.

4. *Prepare a profit-volume graph and a cost-volume-profit graph and explain the meaning of each.* The profit-volume graph portrays the relationship between profits and sales volume. Typically, profit or loss is measured on the vertical axis, and units sold are on the horizontal axis. A cost-volume-profit graph illustrates the relationships among cost, volume, and profits. In this graph, there is a total revenue line and a total cost line. The point at which the total revenue line crosses the total cost line is the break-even point.

5. *Explain the significance of cost behavior and the concepts of variable, fixed, and mixed costs.* Cost behavior is the way in which a cost changes in response to changes in activity level. Knowledge of how specific costs behave is important in many management decisions. A fixed cost remains the same in total as activity increases or decreases. A variable cost increases and decreases with increases and decreases in activity. Many costs are mixed; that is, they have both fixed and variable components.

6. *Separate mixed costs into their fixed and variable components using the high-low method, the scatterplot method, or the method of least squares.* In order to classify mixed costs into fixed and variable categories, it is necessary to break out, or decompose, the fixed and variable components. Since the accounting records normally reveal only the total mixed cost and the associated activity level, a separate methodology must be used to accomplish this decomposition. Three such methods are the high-low method, the scatterplot method, and the method of least squares.

Both the high-low and scatterplot methods involve selecting two data points, with each data point representing total mixed cost at a particular level of activity. The high-low method uses the point with the highest activity level and the point with the lowest activity level. The scatterplot method involves inspecting a scattergraph (a plot showing total mixed cost at various activity levels) and selecting two points that seem best to represent the relationship between cost and activity. Since two points determine a line, the points selected can be used to determine the intercept and the slope of the line on which they lie. The intercept gives an estimate of the fixed-cost component and the slope an estimate of the variable cost per unit of activity.

The high-low method is objective and easy. However, if either the high or low point is not representative of the true cost relationship, the relationship will be misestimated. The scatterplot method is a good way to identify nonlinearity, the presence of outliers, and the presence of a shift in the cost relationship. Its disadvantage is that it is subjective.

The method of least squares uses all of the data points (except outliers) on the scattergraph and produces a line that best fits all of the points. The line is best fitting in the sense that it is closest to all the points as measured by the sum of the squared deviations of the points from the line. Of the three methods, the method of least squares produces the line that best fits the data points and is, therefore, recommended over the other two methods.

6. If they represent unusual events that are unlikely to reoccur, outliers should be excluded before using the method of least squares.

KEY TERMS

REVIEW PROBLEMS

I. Henders Company's projected profit for the coming year is as follows:

	Total	*Per Unit*
Sales	$200,000	$ 20
Less: Variable costs	(120,000)	$(12)
Contribution margin	$ 80,000	$ 8
Less: Fixed expenses	(64,000)	
Net income	$ 16,000	

REQUIRED:

1. Compute the break-even point in units.
2. How many units must be sold to earn a profit of $30,000?
3. Compute the contribution margin ratio. Using that ratio, compute the additional profit that Henders would earn if sales were $25,000 more than expected.
4. Suppose Henders would like to earn a profit equal to 20 percent of sales revenue. How many units must be sold for this goal to be realized? Prepare an income statement to prove your answer.

Solution

1. The break-even point is $(F + I)/(P - V)$ = ($64,000 + $0)/($20 − $12) = $64,000/$8 = 8,000 units.
2. The number of units that must be sold to earn a profit of $30,000 is $(F + I)/(P - V)$ = ($64,000 + $30,000)/$8 = $94,000/$8 = 11,750 units.
3. The contribution margin ratio is $8/$20 = 0.40. With additional sales of $25,000, the additional profit would be 0.40 × $25,000 = $10,000.
4. To find the number of units sold for a profit equal to 20 percent of sales, let $I = 0.20 \times PX$ = 0.2 x $20X = $4X. To solve for X:

$$I = PX - VX - FX$$
$$\$4X = \$20X - \$12X - \$64{,}000$$
$$\$4X = \$64{,}000$$
$$X = 16{,}000 \text{ units}$$

The income statement is as follows:

Sales (16,000 × $20)	$320,000
Less: Variable expenses (16,000 × $12)	(192,000)
Contribution margin	$128,000
Less: Fixed expenses	(64,000)
Net income	$ 64,000

Net income/Sales = $64,000/$320,000 = 0.20, or 20 percent.

II. Kim Wilson, controller of Max Enterprises, has decided to estimate the fixed and variable components associated with the company's setup costs. She has collected the following data for the past six months:

Number of Setups	*Total Setup Costs*
10	$ 800
20	1,100
15	900
12	900
18	1,050
25	1,250

REQUIRED:

1. Estimate the fixed and variable components for setup costs using the high-low method. Using the cost formula, predict the total cost of setups if 14 setups are planned for the coming month.
2. Estimate the fixed and variable components using the method of least squares. Using the cost formula, predict the total cost of setups if 14 setups are planned for the coming month.

Solution

1. The estimate of fixed and variable costs using the high-low method, where Y = total cost and X = number of setups, is as follows:

$$\begin{aligned} V &= (Y_2 - Y_1)/(X_2 - X_1) \\ &= (\$1{,}250 - \$800)/(25 - 10) \\ &= 450/15 \\ &= \$30 \text{ per setup} \end{aligned}$$

$$\begin{aligned} F &= Y_2 - VX_2 \\ &= \$1{,}250 - (\$30 \times 25) \\ &= \$500 \end{aligned}$$

$$\begin{aligned} Y &= \$500 + \$30X \\ &= \$500 + (\$30 \text{ x } 14) \\ &= \$920 \end{aligned}$$

2. The calculation using the method of least squares is as follows:

$\sum X^2$	$\sum X$	$\sum Y$	$\sum XY$
100	10	$ 800	$ 8,000
400	20	1,100	22,000
225	15	900	13,500
144	12	900	10,800
324	18	1,050	18,900
625	25	1,250	31,250
1,818	100	$6,000	$104,450

$$\begin{aligned} V &= [\sum XY - \sum X \sum Y/n]/[\sum X^2 - (\sum X)^2/n] \\ &= [104{,}450 - (100 \times \$6{,}000/6)]/[1{,}818 - (100 \times 100/6)] \\ &= \$4{,}450/151.33 \\ &= \$29.41 \text{ per setup} \end{aligned}$$

$$\begin{aligned} F &= \sum Y/n - V\sum X/n \\ &= \$6000/6 - (29.41 \times 100/6) \\ &= \$509.83 \end{aligned}$$

$$Y = \$509.83 + \$29.41X$$
$$= \$509.83 + (\$29.41 \times 14)$$
$$= \$921.57$$

QUESTIONS

1. Why is knowledge of cost behavior important for managerial decision making? Give an example to illustrate your answer.
2. Explain how CVP analysis can be used for managerial planning.
3. Describe the difference between the units-sold approach to CVP analysis and the sales-revenue approach.
4. Define the term *break-even point*.
5. Explain why contribution margin per unit becomes profit per unit above the break-even point.
6. If the contribution margin per unit is $7 and the break-even point is 10,000 units, how much profit will a firm make if 15,000 units are sold?
7. What is the variable cost ratio? The contribution margin ratio? How are the two ratios related?
8. Suppose a firm has fixed costs of $20,000 and a contribution margin ratio equal to 0.4. How much sales revenue must the firm have in order to break even?
9. Suppose a firm with a contribution margin ratio of 0.3 increased its advertising expenses by $10,000 and found that sales increased by $30,000. Was it a good decision to increase advertising expenses?
10. Wilson Company has a contribution margin ratio of 0.6. The break-even point is $100,000. During the year, Wilson earned total revenues of $200,000. What was Wilson's profit?
11. How does the length of the time horizon affect the classification of cost as fixed or variable? What is the meaning of short run? Long run?
12. Why do mixed costs pose a problem when it comes to classifying costs into fixed and variable categories?
13. Why is a scattergraph a good first step in decomposing mixed costs into their fixed and variable components?
14. Describe how the scatterplot method breaks out the fixed and variable costs from a mixed cost. Now describe how the high-low method works. How do the two methods differ?
15. What are the advantages of the scatterplot method over the high-low method? The high-low method over the scatterplot method?
16. Describe the method of least squares. Why is this method better than either the high-low method or the scatterplot method?
17. What is meant by the best-fitting line?

EXERCISES

E20-1
Units Sold; After-Tax Profit
LO 2

Crunchy Morsels, Inc., manufactures and sells corn chips. Currently, Crunchy produces only one type of corn chip. The chips are packaged in 11-ounce bags and sold to retailers for $1.50 per bag. The variable costs per bag are as follows:

Corn	$0.70
Vegetable oil	0.10
Miscellaneous ingredients	0.03
Selling	0.17

Fixed manufacturing costs total $300,000 per year. Administrative costs (all fixed) total $100,000.

REQUIRED:

1. Compute the number of bags of corn chips that must be sold for Crunchy to break even.
2. How many bags of corn chips must be sold for Crunchy to earn a before-tax profit of $150,000?

3. Assuming a tax rate of 60 percent, how many bags of corn chips must be sold to earn an after-tax profit of $284,000?

E20-2 Contribution Margin; Unit Amounts
LO 2, 3

Information on four independent companies is given below. Calculate the correct amount for each question mark.

	A	*B*	*C*	*D*
Sales	$5,000	?	?	$9,000
Total variable cost	(4,000)	(11,700)	(9,750)	?
Contribution margin	$1,000	$ 3,900	?	?
Total fixed cost	?	(4,000)	?	(750)
Net income	$ 500	$?	$ 400	$2,850
Units sold	?	1,300	125	90
Price/Unit	$5	?	$130	?
Variable cost/Unit	?	$9	?	?
Contribution margin/Unit	?	$3	?	?
Contribution margin ratio	?	?	60%	?
Break-even in units	?	?	?	?

E20-3 CVP
LO 3

Stevenson Company's break-even point is 1,000 units. Variable cost per unit is $150; total fixed costs are $80,000 per year.

REQUIRED: What price does Stevenson charge?

E20-4 Contribution Margin; CVP; Net Income
LO 2, 3

Sweet Sue, Inc., produces a particularly rich praline fudge. Each 10-ounce box sells for $5.50. Variable unit costs are as follows:

Pecans	$0.75
Sugar	0.35
Butter	1.75
Other ingredients	0.24
Box, packing material	0.76
Selling commission	0.55

Fixed overhead cost is $24,000 per year. Fixed selling and administrative costs are $9,000 per year. Sweet Sue sold 35,000 boxes last year.

REQUIRED:

1. What is the contribution margin per unit for a box of praline fudge? What is the contribution margin ratio?
2. How many boxes must be sold to break even? What is the break-even sales revenue?
3. What was Sweet Sue's net income last year?
4. Suppose that Sweet Sue, Inc., raises the price to $6 per box but that anticipated sales will drop to 31,500 boxes. What will the new break-even point in units be? Should Sweet Sue raise the price? Explain.
5. Suppose that Sweet Sue has the capacity to produce 50,000 boxes of candy per year. An opportunity exists to bid on an order for a large retail firm. This order would produce sales of 10,000 boxes and will be a one time order only. What is the bid that will allow Sweet Sue to break even on the order? Also, compute the bid that will allow Sweet Sue to earn a profit of $5,000 on the order.

E20-5
Sales-Revenue Approach; Variable-Cost Ratio; Contribution Margin Ratio
LO 3

Lambert produces and sells an economy line of ski parkas. The budgeted income statement for the coming year is

Sales	$ 600,000
Less: Variable expenses	(400,000)
Contribution margin	$ 200,000
Less: Fixed expenses	(120,000)
Profit before taxes	$ 80,000
Less: Taxes	(24,000)
Profit after taxes	$ 56,000

REQUIRED:

1. What is Lambert's variable cost ratio? Its contribution margin ratio?
2. Suppose Lambert's actual revenues are $60,000 more than budgeted. By how much will before-tax profits increase? Give the answer without preparing a new income statement.
3. How much sales revenue must Lambert earn in order to break even?
4. How much sales revenue must Lambert generate to earn a before-tax profit of $100,000? An after-tax profit of $84,000? Prepare a contribution income statement to verify the accuracy of your last answer.

E20-6
CVP Analysis with Target Profits
LO 2, 3

Tom Flannery has developed a new recipe for fried chicken and plans to open a take-out restaurant in Oklahoma City. His father-in-law has agreed to invest $500,000 in the operation provided Tom can convince him that profits will be at least 20 percent of sales revenues. Tom estimated that total fixed expense would be $24,000 per year and that variable expense would be approximately 40 percent of sales revenues.

REQUIRED:

1. How much sales revenue must be earned to produce profits equal to 20 percent of sales revenue? Prepare a contribution income statement to verify your answer.
2. If Tom plans on selling 12-piece buckets of chicken for $10 each, how many buckets must he sell to earn a profit equal to 20 percent of sales? 25 percent of sales? Prepare a contribution income statement to verify the second answer.
3. Suppose Tom's father-in-law meant that the after-tax profit had to be 20 percent of sales revenue. Under this assumption, how much sales revenue must be generated by Tom's chicken business? (Assume that the tax rate is 40 percent.)

E20-7
Contribution Analysis
LO 1, 3

Fox Company produces a deluxe pen-and-pencil set. The selling price of the set is $50. The variable cost per set is $30. Total fixed costs are $2.5 million. Expected sales for the coming year are 150,000 sets. Management is unhappy with the expected profits and is trying to find ways to increase overall performance. The marketing manager has proposed two alternatives: (1) increase advertising by $100,000, which should produce additional sales of 10,000 units, or (2) decrease the selling price to $45 per set, which should boost sales from 150,000 sets to 165,000 sets.

REQUIRED:

1. Prepare an income statement that reflects expected sales for the coming year. Ignore the proposals by the marketing manager.
2. Without preparing income statements, assess the impact on profits of each of the marketing manager's proposals. Which would you recommend?
3. Prepare income statements for the two proposals to verify your analysis in Requirement 2.

E20-8
CVP and Profit-Volume Graphs
LO 4

Lotts Company produces and sells one product. The selling price is $10, and the unit variable cost is $6. Total fixed costs are $10,000.

REQUIRED:

1. Prepare a CVP graph with units sold as the horizontal axis and dollars as the vertical axis. Label the break-even point on the horizontal axis.
2. Prepare CVP graphs for each of the following scenarios:
   a. Fixed costs increase by $5,000.
   b. Unit variable cost increases to $7.
   c. Unit selling price increases to $12.
   d. Assume both *a* and *b*.
3. Prepare a profit-volume graph using the original data. Repeat, following the scenarios in Requirement 2.
4. Which of the two graphs do you think provides the most information? Why?

E20-9
CVP; Before- and After-Tax Targeted Net Income
LO 2, 3

CF Company produces a line of peach chutney. Currently, CF charges a price of $3.50 per jar. Variable costs are $1.40 per jar and fixed costs are $50,000. The tax rate is 33 percent. Last year, 27,300 jars were sold.

REQUIRED:

1. What is CF's net income after taxes for last year?
2. What is CF's break-even revenue?
3. Suppose CF wants to earn before-tax net income of $13,000. How many units must be sold?
4. Suppose CF wants to earn after-tax net income of $13,000. How many units must be sold?

E20-10
Scatterplot Method
LO 6

Betty Yeager has been operating a dental practice for the past five years. As part of her practice, she provides a dental hygiene service. She has found that her costs for this service increase with patient load. Costs for this service over the past seven months are as follows:

Month	*Patients Served*	*Total Cost*
May	320	$2,000
June	480	2,500
July	600	3,000
August	200	1,900
September	720	4,500
October	560	2,900
November	630	3,400
December	300	2,200

REQUIRED:

1. Prepare a scattergraph based on the above data. Use cost for the vertical axis and number of patients for the horizontal. Based on an examination of the scattergraph, does there appear to be a linear relationship between the cost of dental hygiene services and patients served?
2. Fit a line to the data points that you believe best describes the relationship between costs and activity. Determine the equation of this line.
3. Assume that 450 patients are expected to receive dental hygiene services in January. Using the equation you found in Requirement 2, what is the predicted cost of dental hygiene services for that month?

E20-11
High-Low Method
LO 6

Refer to the data in Exercise 20-10. (*Note:* Either do Exercise 20-10 before this exercise or exclude Requirement 3.)

REQUIRED:

1. Compute the cost formula for dental hygiene services using the high-low method.
2. Calculate the predicted cost of dental hygiene services for January for 450 patients using the formula from Requirement 1.
3. Which cost formula—the one you computed using the scatterplot method or the one using the high-low method—do you think is the best? Explain.

E20-12
Method of Least Squares
LO 6

Refer to the data in Exercise 20-10.

REQUIRED:

1. Compute the cost formula for dental hygiene services using the method of least squares.
2. Using the formula computed in Requirement 1, what is the predicted cost of dental hygiene services for January for 450 patients?

E20-13
Method of Least Squares; Pricing
LO 3, 6

Quincy Medical Center recently began operations as a community health center. The principal objective of the medical center is to provide family-centered health services with an emphasis on preventive medicine. During the first six months of operations, the need for annual physical exams was stressed in the community. Special rates of $50 were offered for physicals, and the response was enthusiastic.

The director of QMC was not certain that it could continue to offer physicals at the same price. Some staff physicians, however, insisted that the rate be maintained for at least another six months. They believed that the low price encouraged many individuals who otherwise would not do so to have a physical. The director believed that continuance of the program might be feasible provided that QMC covered at least its variable costs. Those costs were not obvious, however; the accountant had recorded only the number of exams per month along with the total cost associated with these exams.

Month	*Number of Exams*	*Operating Costs*
February	100	$ 6,500
March	150	8,500
April	200	12,000
May	225	13,000
June	175	10,000
July	300	16,500

REQUIRED:

1. Determine the variable cost per physical exam using the method of least squares.
2. Can the medical center continue offering the $50 price and still cover its variable costs?
3. Assume 250 physical exams are administered in August. What is the total expected cost of these physical exams? How much revenue would be needed to cover the variable costs? What is the full cost per patient in August?

PROBLEMS

P20-1
Basic CVP Concepts
LO 1, 2, 3

Topper Company produces a variety of glass products. One division makes windshields for compact automobiles. The division's projected income statement for the coming year is as follows:

Sales (150,000 units @ $50)	$7,500,000
Less: Variable expenses	(3,500,000)
Contribution margin	$4,000,000
Less: Fixed expenses	(3,200,000)
Net income	$ 800,000

REQUIRED:

1. Compute the contribution margin per unit and calculate the break-even point in units. Repeat using the contribution margin ratio.
2. The divisional manager has decided to increase the advertising budget by $100,000 and cut the selling price to $45. These actions will increase sales revenues by $1 million. Will the division be better off?
3. Suppose sales revenues exceed the estimated amount on the income statement by $540,000. Without preparing a new income statement, by how much are profits underestimated?
4. Refer to the original data. How many units must be sold to earn an after-tax profit of $1.254 million? Assume a tax rate of 34 percent. Repeat the analysis assuming that the after-tax profit target is 10 percent of sales revenues.
5. Suppose that the division is capable of producing 200,000 windshields per year. Now assume that the division has the opportunity to bid on a special, one-time order. The size of the order is 30,000 units. Compute the following: (a) the bid price required to break even on the order, (b) the bid price required to earn an after-tax profit of $240,000 (assume a tax rate of 40%), and (c) the before-tax profit on the order if the division bid $38 and won the bid.

P20-2
CVP Equation; Basic Concepts; Solving for Unknowns
LO 1, 2, 3

Azucar Company produces a chocolate almond bar. Each bar sells for $0.40. The variable costs for each bar (sugar, chocolate, almonds, wrapper, labor, and so on) total $0.25. The total fixed costs are $60,000. During the most recent year, 1 million bars were sold. The president of Azucar, not fully satisfied with the profit performance of the chocolate bar, was considering the following options to increase the bar's profitability: (1) increase advertising; (2) increase the quality of the ingredients and, simultaneously, increase the selling price; (3) increase the selling price; (4) a combination of the three. (Ignore income taxes for all requirements.)

REQUIRED:

1. The sales manager is confident that an advertising campaign could double sales volume. If the company president's goal is to increase this year's profits by 50 percent over last year's, what is the maximum amount that can be spent on advertising?
2. Refer to the original data and assume that the company increases the quality of its ingredients, thus increasing variable costs to $0.30. Answer the following questions:
   a. How much must the selling price be increased to maintain the same break-even point in units?
   b. What will the new price be if the company wants to increase the old contribution margin ratio by 50 percent?
3. Refer to the original data. The company has decided to increase its selling price to $0.50. The sales volume drops from 1 million to 800,000 bars. Was the decision to increase the price a good one? Compute the sales volume that would be needed at the new price for the company to earn the same profit as last year.
4. Refer to the original data. The sales manager is convinced that by increasing the quality of the ingredients (increasing variables costs to $0.30) and by advertising the increased quality (advertising dollars would be increased by $100,000), sales volume could be doubled. He has also indicated that a price increase would not affect the ability to double sales volume as long as the price increase is not more than 20 percent of the current

selling price. Compute the selling price that would be needed to achieve the goal of increasing profits by 50 percent. Is the sales manager's plan feasible? What selling price would you choose? Why?

P20-3
Basics of the Sales-Revenue Approach
LO 1, 2, 3

Kiltop Company produces a toy dart gun. The projected income statement for the coming year follows:

Sales	$480,000
Less: Variable costs	(249,600)
Contribution margin	$230,400
Less: Fixed costs	(180,000)
Net income	$ 50,400

REQUIRED:

1. Compute the contribution margin ratio for the toy gun.
2. How much revenue must Kiltop earn in order to break even?
3. What volume of sales must be earned if Kiltop wants to earn an after-tax income equal to 8 percent of sales? Assume that the tax rate is 34 percent.
4. What is the effect on the contribution margin ratio if the unit selling price and unit variable cost each increase by 10 percent?
5. Suppose that management has decided to give a 3 percent commission on all sales. The projected income statement does not reflect this commission. Recompute the contribution margin ratio assuming that the commission will be paid. What effect does this have on the break-even point?
6. If the commission is paid as described in requirement 5, management expects sales revenues to increase by $80,000. Is it a sound decision to implement the commission? Support your answer with appropriate computations.
7. Refer to the original data. Compute the safety margin and the operating leverage. Compute the percentage change in profits if sales increase by 15 percent.

P20-4
CVP Analysis: Sales-Revenue Approach; Pricing; After-Tax Profit Target
LO 3

Kline Consulting is a service organization that specializes in the design, installation, and servicing of mechanical, hydraulic, and pneumatic systems. For example, some manufacturing firms with machinery that cannot be turned off for servicing need some type of system to lubricate the machinery during use. To deal with this type of problem for a client, Kline designed a central lubricating system that pumps lubricants intermittently to bearings and other moving parts.

The operating results for the firm in 1993 are as follows:

Sales	$802,429
Less: Variable costs	(430,000)
Contribution margin	$372,429
Less: Fixed expenses	(154,750)
Net income	$217,679

In 1994, Kline expects variable costs to increase by 5 percent and fixed costs by 4 percent.

REQUIRED:

1. What is the contribution margin ratio for 1993?
2. Compute Kline's break-even point for 1993 in dollars.

3. Suppose that Kline would like to see a 6 percent increase in net income in 1994. By what percentage (on average) must Kline raise its bids to cover the expected cost increases and obtain the desired net income? Assume that Kline expects the same mix and volume of services in 1994 as in 1993.
4. In 1994, how much revenue must be earned for Kline to earn an after-tax profit of $175,000? Assume a tax rate of 34 percent.

P20-5
Multiplant Break Even
LO 2

The PTO Division of the Galva Manufacturing Company produces power take-off units for the farm equipment business. The PTO Division, headquartered in Peoria, has a newly renovated plant in Peoria and an older, less automated plant in Moline. Both plants produce the same powertake-off units for farm tractors that are sold to most domestic and foreign tractor manufacturers.

The PTO Division expects to produce and sell 192,000 power take-off units during the coming year. The division production manager has the following data available regarding the unit costs, unit prices, and production capacities for the two plants.

	Peoria		*Moline*	
Selling price		$150.00		$150.00
Variable manufacturing cost	$72.00		$88.00	
Fixed manufacturing cost	30.00		15.00	
Commission (5%)	7.50		7.50	
General and administrative expense	25.50		21.00	
Total unit cost		135.00		131.50
Unit profit		$ 15.00		$ 18.50
Production rate per day		400 units		320 units

All fixed costs are based on a normal year of 240 working days. When the number of working days exceeds 240, variable manufacturing costs increase by $3 per unit in Peoria and $8 per unit in Moline. Capacity for each plant is 300 working days.

Galva Manufacturing charges each of its plants a per-unit fee for administrative services such as payroll, general accounting, and purchasing because Galva considers these services to be a function of the work performed at the plants. For each of the plants, a fee of $6.50 represents the variable portion of the general and administrative expense.

Wishing to maximize the higher unit profit at Moline, PTO's production manager has decided to manufacture 96,000 units at each plant. This production plan results in Moline's operating at capacity and Peoria's operating at its normal volume. Galva's corporate controller is not happy with this plan; he wonders if it might be better to produce relatively more at the automated plant in Peoria.

REQUIRED:

1. Determine the annual break-even units for each of PTO's plants.
2. Calculate the operating income that would result from the division production manager's plan to produce 96,000 units at each plant.
3. Calculate the operating income that would result from sales of 192,000 power take-off units if 120,000 of them were produced at the Peoria plant and the remainder at the Moline plant.

(CMA adapted)

P20-6
CVP Analysis and Assumptions
LO 1, 3

Marston Corporation manufactures pharmaceutical products that are sold through a network of sales agents located in the United States and Canada. The agents currently are paid an 18 percent commission on sales, and this percentage was used when Marston prepared the following pro forma income statement for the fiscal year ending June 30, 1994.

Marston Corporation
Pro Forma Income Statement
For the Year Ending June 30, 1994
($000 omitted)

Sales		$26,000
Cost of goods sold		
Variable	$11,700	
Fixed	2,870	14,570
Gross profit		$11,430
Selling and administrative costs		
Commissions	$ 4,680	
Fixed advertising cost	750	
Fixed administrative cost	1,850	7,280
Operating income		$ 4,150
Fixed interest cost		650
Income before income taxes		$ 3,500
Income taxes (40%)		1,400
Net income		$ 2,100

Since the completion of the above statement, Marston has learned that its agents are requiring an increase in the commission rate to 23 percent for the upcoming year. As a result, Marston's president has decided to investigate the possibility of hiring its own sales staff in place of the network of sales agents and has asked Tom Ross, Marston's controller, to gather information on the costs associated with this change.

Ross estimates that Marston will have to hire eight salespeople to cover the current market area, and the annual payroll cost of each of these employees will average $80,000, including fringe benefit expense. Travel and entertainment expense is expected to total $600,000 for the year, and the annual cost of hiring a sales manager and sales secretary will be $150,000. In addition to their salaries, the eight salespeople will each earn commissions at the rate of 10 percent on the first $2 million in sales and 15 percent on all sales over $2 million. For planning purposes, Ross expects that all eight salespeople will exceed the $2 million mark and that sales will be at the level previously projected. Ross believes that Marston should also increase its advertising budget by $500,000.

REQUIRED:

1. Calculate Marston Corporation's break-even point in sales dollars for the fiscal year ending June 30, 1994, if the company hires its own sales force and increases its advertising costs.
2. If Marston Corporation continues to sell through its network of sales agents and pays the higher commission rate, determine the estimated volume in sales dollars for the fiscal year ending June 30, 1994, that would be required to generate the same net income as that projected in the pro forma income statement presented above.
3. Describe the general assumptions underlying break-even analysis that might limit its usefulness in this case.

(CMA adapted)

P20-7
Cost Behavior; High-Low Method; Pricing Decision
LO 2, 3, 5, 6

Hinckley Medical Clinic offers a number of specialized medical services, one of which is psychiatric care. Because of the reputation the clinic has developed over the years, demand for these services is strong. As a result, Hinckley recently opened a 100-bed psychiatric hospital near the clinic. The hospital facility itself is leased on a long-term basis. All equipment within the facility is owned by the clinic.

Since the clinic had no experience with in-patient psychiatric services, it decided to operate the hospital for two months before determining how much to charge per patient day on an ongoing basis. As a temporary measure, the clinic adopted a patient-day charge of $75, an amount equal to the charges made by a psychiatric hospital in a nearby city.

This initial per-day charge was quoted to patients entering the hospital during the first two months with assurances that if the actual operating costs of the new hospital justified it, the charge could be less. In no case would the charges be more. A temporary policy of billing after sixty days was adopted so that adjustments could be made if necessary.

The hospital opened on January 1. During January, the hospital had 2,100 patient days of activity. During February, the activity was 2,250 patient days. Costs for these two levels of activity are as follows:

	2,100 Patient Days	*2,250 Patient Days*
Salaries, nurses	$ 5,400	$ 5,400
Aides	1,200	1,200
Laboratory	25,000	26,500
Pharmacy	30,000	31,000
Lease	10,000	10,000
Laundry	16,800	18,000
Administration	12,000	12,000
Depreciation	30,000	30,000

REQUIRED:

1. Classify each cost as fixed, variable, or mixed.
2. Use the high-low method to separate the mixed costs into their fixed and variable components.
3. Tom Krance, the hospital's administrator, has estimated that the hospital will average 2,000 patient days per month. If the hospital is to be operated as a nonprofit organization, how much will it need to charge per patient day? How much of this charge is variable? How much is fixed?
4. Suppose the hospital averages 2,500 patient days per month. How much would need to be charged per patient day for the hospital to cover its costs? Explain why the charge per patient day decreased as the activity increased.

P20-8
Scattergraph; High-Low Method; Method of Least Squares
LO 6

Nickles Company has gathered data on its overhead costs and activity for the past ten months. Tina Paulsen, a member of the controller's department, has convinced management that overhead costs can be better estimated and controlled if the fixed and variable components are known. Tina is convinced that variation in overhead costs can be explained by variation in direct labor hours. The data she collected are as follows:

Month	*Direct Labor Hours*	*Total Overhead*
1	1,000	$13,000
2	800	11,000
3	1,500	19,000
4	1,200	17,000
5	1,300	16,000
6	1,100	13,000
7	1,600	21,000
8	1,400	16,000
9	1,700	22,000
10	900	10,000

REQUIRED:

1. Prepare a scattergraph, plotting the overhead costs against direct labor hours. Use the vertical axis for costs and the horizontal for hours.
2. Select two points which make the best fit and compute a cost formula for overhead costs.
3. Using the high-low method, prepare an overhead cost formula.
4. Using the method of least squares, prepare an overhead cost formula.
5. Compare the costs predicted by each formula for the odd data points (months 1, 3, and so on). Do you believe that least squares is better than either the high-low method or the scatterplot method? Explain.

P20-9 Scattergraph; High-Low Method; Method of Least Squares

LO 6

The management of Fernelius Company has decided to adopt variable costing for internal purposes. Fernelius uses a highly automated manufacturing process, and its power costs are significant. Management has decided that power costs are mixed; thus, they must be decomposed into their fixed and variable elements to implement the variable-costing system. The following data for the past eight quarters have been collected:

Quarter	*Machine Hours*	*Power Cost*
1	20,000	$26,000
2	25,000	38,000
3	30,000	42,500
4	22,000	37,000
5	21,000	34,000
6	18,000	29,000
7	24,000	36,000
8	28,000	40,000

REQUIRED:

1. Prepare a scattergraph by plotting power costs against machine hours. Fit a line to the data set; select two points and determine the cost formula for power.
2. Using the high and low points, compute a power cost formula.
3. Use the method of least squares to compute a power cost formula.
4. Compute the expected cost for 23,000 machine hours using each of the three formulas. Which cost formula would you recommend? Explain.

P20-10 Method of Least Squares; Pricing and Cost Recovery

LO 3, 6

A major source of revenues for many hospitals is treatment of Medicare patients. Currently, Medicare treatments are reimbursed on the basis of diagnostic related groups (DRGs). A DRG is an illness classification—a reason for going to the hospital for treatment—for which the government pays a fixed amount. If the costs of the treatment are greater than the DRG reimbursement, the hospital loses money. If, however, the costs of the treatment are less than the reimbursement, the hospital gains money. Knowing how much a treatment costs is important because it enables the hospital to estimate how much it will make or lose on each service. It may also enable hospitals to build a case for increasing a DRG rate. Thus, estimating the costs of the various services provided is essential for managerial planning.

For example, the Respiratory Therapy Department of a local community hospital offers a number of services, such as oxygen, ABG analysis, aeromed treatment, and CPT treatment. ABG analysis requires the use of supplies, technical labor, capital equipment, and maintenance. The total costs of ABG analysis for the past eight months are as follows:

Month	*Number of Treatments*	*Total Cost*
1	250	$3,250
2	260	3,400
3	280	3,600
4	300	3,700
5	270	3,400
6	230	3,200
7	240	3,250
8	255	3,400

REQUIRED:

1. Prepare a cost formula for ABG analysis using the method of least squares.
2. For the coming month, the hospital expects to supply 280 ABG analyses, 50 percent for Medicare patients. If the DRG reimbursement is $12 per analysis, how much will the hospital need to charge the remaining patients per treatment to cover all its costs for supplying ABG analyses? Suppose that the hospital charges non-Medicare patients the expected cost for each ABG analysis. How much will the hospital gain (or lose) on ABG analyses?

P20-11
High-Low Method; Scatterplot
LO 5, 6

Gainsville Regional Hospital has collected data on all of its departments for the past seven months. Data for Radiology follow:

	Cost	*Number of Procedures*
September 1993	$69,500	1,700
October 1993	64,250	1,550
November 1993	52,000	1,200
December 1993	66,000	1,600
January 1994	83,000	1,800
February 1994	66,550	1,330
March 1994	79,500	1,700

REQUIRED:

1. Using the high-low method, calculate the variable rate per procedure and the fixed cost for Radiology.
2. Prepare a scatterplot for Radiology using the above data. (*Hint:* Use one symbol, perhaps an "x," for observations occurring in 1993, and another symbol for observations occurring in 1994.)
3. Upon looking into the events that happened in Radiology at the end of 1993, you find that the department bought a Magnetic Resonance Imaging (MRI) machine. Monthly depreciation on the machine amounts to $10,000. Now, using the scatterplot from Requirement 2, calculate the fixed cost and variable rate applicable to October 1993; calculate the fixed cost and variable rate applicable to March 1994. Discuss your findings. Which cost formula should be used to budget radiology expense for the remainder of 1994?

DISCUSSION AND INTERPRETATION PROBLEMS

D20-1
Ethics and a CVP Application

Danna Lumus, the marketing manager for a division that produces a variety of paper products, was considering the divisional manager's request for a sales forecast for a new line of paper napkins. The divisional manager was gathering data so that he could choose between two different production processes. The first process would have a variable cost of $10 per case produced and fixed costs of $100,000. The second process would have a variable cost of $6 per case and fixed costs of $200,000. The selling price would be $30 per case. Danna had just completed a marketing analysis that projected annual sales of 30,000 cases.

Danna was reluctant to report the 30,000 forecast to the divisional manager. She knew that the first process was labor intensive, whereas the second was largely automated with little labor and no requirement for an additional production supervisor. If the first process were chosen, Jerry Johnson, a good friend, would be appointed as the line supervisor. If the second process were chosen, Jerry and an entire line of laborers would be laid off. After some consideration, Danna revised the projected sales downward to 22,000 cases.

She believed that the revision downward was justified. Since it would lead the divisional manager to choose the manual-oriented system, it showed a sensitivity to the needs of current employees—a sensitivity that she was afraid her divisional manager did not possess. He was too focused on quantitative factors in his decision making and usually ignored the qualitative aspects.

REQUIRED:

1. Compute the break-even point for each process.
2. Compute the sales volume for which the two processes are equally profitable. Identify the range of sales for which the manual process is more profitable than the automated process. Identify the range of sales for which the automated process is more profitable than the manual process. Why did the divisional manager want the sales forecast?
3. Discuss Danna's decision to alter the sales forecast. Do you agree with it? Did she act ethically? Was her decision justified since it helped a number of employees retain their employment? Should the impact on employees be factored into decisions? In fact, is it unethical not to consider the impact of decisions on employees?
4. Even though Danna is not a management accountant, do any of the ethical standards for management accountants listed in the appendix to Chapter 1 apply? Explain.

D20-2
Cost Behavior; Break-Even Analysis; CVP Analysis for Evaluation and Decision Making

Reinert Moving and Storage was established in 1962 by Allen Reinert in Lincoln, Nebraska. In 1978, the company achieved million-dollar booking status. The company experienced modest growth for the next two years; however, after the deregulation of the transportation industry in 1980, the company's growth accelerated significantly for several years. Unfortunately, by the end of 1993, the company actually experienced a drop in revenues. During the next two years, the revenues earned matched those of 1993. The revenues reported at the end of 1995 totaled $5.493 million. An income statement for 1995 follows:

Revenues:			
Local	$1,433,500		
Intrastate	510,000		
Interstate	2,490,500		
Containers	333,000		
Packing	437,000		
Storage	289,000		
Total revenues			$5,493,000
Less expenses:			
Outside vehicle repair		$ 220,000	
Fuel		352,000	
Sales commissions		102,000	
Tires, oil, lube		20,500	
Wages (driver and helper)		1,584,000	

(continued)

Internal maintenance	293,000	
Advertising	88,000	
Equipment rental	422,000	
Packing materials	557,000	
Salaries	821,000	
Cargo loss claims	234,000	
Utilities	16,700	
Insurance	44,000	
Fuel taxes and tariffs	132,000	
Bad debt	193,000	
Depreciation	205,000	
Total expenses		(5,284,200)
Income before taxes		$ 208,800
Less: Taxes (state and federal: 42%)		(87,696)
Net income		$ 121,104

Upon reviewing the income statement for 1995, Allen Reinert called a meeting to discuss the financial status of the company. He invited sales manager Heidi Jackson and controller Eric Bilodeau.

Allen: "Our before-tax income has dropped from a high of 12 percent of sales to about 4 percent this last year. I know that both of you are aware of our problem and have some suggestions on how we can improve the situation."

Heidi: "Allen, competition has become quite intense in our industry. I have two suggestions to help improve sales. First, we need to increase our advertising budget. We have a good reputation, and I think we need to capitalize on it. I suggest that we emphasize our expertise in crating electronic equipment and other sensitive instruments. Our losses in this area are minuscule. We have a much better record than any of our competitors, and we need to let customers and potential customers know about the quality of our services."

Allen: "This sounds good. How much more do you need for advertising and what kind of increase in sales would you predict?"

Heidi: "To do it right, I would need to double our current advertising budget. I would guess that sales would increase by 20 percent. I also have another suggestion. I think we should look at the international goods and freight-moving market. Many firms ship goods internationally, and I believe that they would switch to us if we entered that market. My preliminary analysis reveals that we could pick up $500,000 of sales during the first year."

Allen: "Both suggestions seem to offer some potential for improving our profitability. Eric, would you gather the data needed to estimate the effect of each of these two alternatives on our profits?"

Eric: "Sure. I have a suggestion also—I plan to install a cost accounting system. At this point, we have no real idea how much each of our services is costing. I believe that there is some hope to reduce costs without affecting the quality of our services."

Allen: "I'm all for reducing costs where possible. However, keep in mind that I don't want to lay off any employees yet. I like the idea of providing security to our employees. I would rather see everyone take a pay cut before we reduce our work force. So far we have been able to keep everyone even with the drop in sales we've had. I think it's a good policy. If these two ideas of Heidi's work out, no new hires may be necessary, and we have trained, loyal employees ready for the new business."

REQUIRED:

1. Classify all expenses in the 1995 income statement as either variable or fixed. Assume that each expense is strictly variable or strictly fixed with respect to sales revenue. Once the classification is completed, prepare a variable-costing income statement.

2. Using the information obtained in Requirement 1, compute the revenue that Reinert Moving and Storage needs to generate to break even. Now compute the revenue that is needed to earn a profit equal to 12 percent of sales revenue.
3. What is the maximum amount that Reinert can spend on additional advertising assuming profits remain unchanged for 1996 and sales will increase by 20 percent, as predicted by Heidi? Suppose that Heidi spends the amount she requested and sales increase by 20 percent—what is the change in profits? Should the suggestion be adopted?
4. Suppose that the directly traceable fixed expenses associated with entry into the international market are $200,000. Assume that the variable cost ratio for this segment is the same as that computed in the 1995 income statement prepared in Requirement 1. How much revenue must be generated from international shipping for this segment to break even? What is the expected margin of safety? Would you recommend entry into the international market? Why?
5. Suppose that Allen Reinert decides both to increase advertising and enter the international market. Assume that actual sales increased by 10 percent, and $340,000 of the increase came from international sales and the remainder from the increased advertising. Using data from the case in Requirements 1 and 4, answer the following questions:
   a. How much did before-tax profits change because of these two decisions?
   b. What is the profit change attributable to the advertising campaign? the international market? What is your recommendation for the coming year? Should the company continue these two strategies? or should it do only one or neither? Explain.
   c. Suppose that the company achieved its target profit of 12 percent of sales in spite of the less-than-expected increase in profits from the advertising campaign and the international market. The remaining increase in profits was achieved by cutting variable costs. What is the new variable cost ratio?

D20-3 Research Assignment

Interview the owner or manager of a small service business (e.g., dry cleaners, shoe repair, CPA) about the revenue to break even. Have they calculated this amount? Do they have a feel for their variable and fixed costs? Write up the results of your interview.

CHAPTER 21
RELEVANT COSTS FOR SPECIAL DECISIONS INCLUDING SEGMENT ANALYSIS

LEARNING OBJECTIVES

After studying this chapter, you should be able to:

1. Define and explain the concept of relevant costs.
2. Use a relevant-costing decision model as an aid in choosing among competing alternatives.
3. Apply the relevant-costing model to a variety of business situations.
4. Choose the optimal product mix when faced with one constrained resource.

Scenario

Tidwell Products, Inc., manufactures potentiometers. A potentiometer is a device that adjusts electrical resistance. Potentiometers are used in switches and knobs, for example, to control the volume on a radio or to raise or lower the lights using a dimmer switch. Currently, all parts necessary for the assembly of the products are produced internally. The firm, in operation for five years, has a single plant located in Wichita, Kansas. The facilities for the manufacture of potentiometers are leased, with five years remaining on the lease. All equipment is owned by the company. Because of increases in demand, production has been expanded significantly over the five years of operation, straining the capacity of the leased facilities. Currently, the company needs more warehousing and office space, as well as more space for the production of plastic moldings. The current output of these moldings, used to make potentiometers, needs to be expanded to accommodate the increased demand for the main product.

Leo Tidwell, owner and president of Tidwell Products, has asked his vice-president of marketing, John Tidwell, and his vice-president of finance, Linda Thayn, to meet and discuss the problem of limited capacity. This is the second meeting the three have had concerning the problem. In the first meeting, Leo rejected Linda's proposal to build the company's own plant. He believed it was too risky to invest the capital necessary to build a plant at this stage of the company's development. The combination of leasing a larger facility and subleasing the current plant was also considered but was rejected; subleasing would be difficult, if not impossible. At the end of the first meeting, Leo asked John to explore the possibility of leasing another facility comparable to the current one. He also assigned Linda the task of identifying other possible solutions. As the second meeting began, Leo asked John to give a report on the leasing alternative.

"After some careful research," John responded, "I'm afraid that the idea of leasing an additional plant is not a very good one. Although we have some space problems, our current level of production doesn't justify another plant. In fact, I expect it will be at least five years before we need to be concerned about expanding into another facility like the one we have now. My market studies reveal a modest growth in sales over the next five years. All this growth can be absorbed by our current production capacity. The large increases in demand that we experienced the past five years are not likely to be repeated. Leasing another plant would be an overkill solution."

"Even modest growth will aggravate our current space problems," Leo observed. "As you both know, we are already operating three production shifts. But, John, you are right—except for plastic moldings, we could expand production, particularly during the graveyard shift. Linda, I hope that you have been successful in identifying some other possible solutions. Some fairly quick action is needed."

"Fortunately," Linda replied, "I believe that I have two feasible alternatives. One is to rent an additional building to be used for warehousing. By transferring our warehousing needs to the new building, we will free up internal space for offices and for expanding the production of plastic moldings. I have located a building within two miles of our plant that we could use. It has the capacity to handle our current needs and the modest growth that John mentioned. The second alternative may be even more attractive. We currently produce all the parts that we use to manufacture potentiometers, including shafts and bushings. In the last several months, the market has been flooded with these two parts. Prices have tumbled as a result. It might be better to buy shafts and bushings instead of making them. If we stop internal production of shafts and bushings, this would free up the space we need. Well, Leo, what do you think? Are these alternatives feasible? Or should I continue my search for additional solutions?"

"I like both alternatives," responded Leo. "In fact, they are exactly the types of solutions we are looking for. All we have to do now is choose the one best for our company. A key factor that must be examined is the cost of each alternative. Linda, you're the financial chief—prepare a report that details the costs that impact this decision."

Note: This scenario is based on the experiences of a real company. The names have been changed to preserve confidentiality.

RELEVANT COSTS DEFINED

Objective 1
Define and explain the concept of relevant costs.

Linda identified two alternatives: (1) make all parts internally and rent a warehouse and (2) buy shafts and bushings (metal linings used as bearings for the shafts) from external suppliers and stop internal production of these parts. Both alternatives solve the space limitation problem faced by Tidwell Products. A significant input in choosing among the two alternatives is cost. All other things being equal, the alternative with the lower cost should be chosen. But what is meant by lower cost? How do we identify and define the costs that affect the decision?

relevant costs

In choosing between the two alternatives, only the costs relevant to the decision should be considered. **Relevant costs** are future costs that differ across alternatives. All decisions relate to the future; accordingly, only future costs can be relevant to decisions. However, to be relevant, a cost must not only be a future cost, but also it must differ from one alternative to another. If a future cost is the same for more than one alternative, it has no effect on the decision. Such a cost is an *irrelevant* cost. The ability to identify relevant and irrelevant costs is an important decision-making skill.

Relevant Costs Illustrated

To illustrate the concept of relevant costs, consider Tidwell's make-or-buy alternatives. Assume that the cost of direct labor used to produce shafts and bushings is $150,000 per year (based on normal volume). Should this cost be a factor in the decision? Is the direct labor cost a future cost that differs across the two alternatives? It is certainly a future cost. To produce the shafts and bushings for another year requires the services of direct laborers, who must be paid. But does it differ across the two alternatives? If shafts and bushings are purchased from an external supplier, no internal production is needed. The services of the direct laborers can be eliminated, reducing the direct labor cost for shafts and bushings under this alternative to zero. Thus, the cost of direct labor differs across alternatives ($150,000 for the make alternative and $0 for the buy alternative). It is, therefore, a relevant cost.

Implicit in this analysis is the use of a past cost to estimate a future cost. The most recent cost of direct labor for normal activity was $150,000. This past cost was used as the estimate of next year's cost. Although past costs are never relevant, they often are used to predict what future costs will be.

Illustration of an Irrelevant Past Cost

Tidwell Products uses machinery to manufacture shafts and bushings. This machinery was purchased five years ago and is being depreciated at an annual rate of $125,000. Is this $125,000 a relevant cost? In other words, is depreciation a future cost that differs across the two alternatives?

sunk cost

Depreciation, in this case, represents an allocation of a cost already incurred. It is a **sunk cost**, an allocation of a past cost. Thus, regardless of which alternative is chosen, the acquisition cost of the machinery cannot be avoided. It is the same across both alternatives. Although we allocate this sunk cost to future periods and call that allocation *depreciation*, none of the original cost is avoidable. Sunk costs are past costs. They are always the same across alternatives and are, therefore, always irrelevant.

In choosing between the two alternatives, the acquisition cost of the machinery used to produce shafts and bushings and its associated depreciation should not be a factor. What was paid for the machinery in the past has no bearing on what Tidwell Products should do now. All that matters is how the two alternatives differ in their future costs.

Illustration of an Irrelevant Future Cost

Assume that the cost to lease the plant—$120,000—is allocated to different production departments, including the department that produces shafts and bushings, which receives $12,000 of the cost. Is this $12,000 cost relevant to the make-or-buy decision facing Tidwell?

The lease payment is a future cost since it must be paid during each of the next five years. But does the cost differ across the make-and-buy alternatives? Whatever option Tidwell chooses, the lease payment must be made—it is the same across both alternatives. The amount of the payment allocated to the remaining departments may change if production of shafts and bushings is stopped, but the level of the total payment is unaffected by the decision. It is, therefore, an irrelevant cost.

The example illustrates the importance of identifying allocations of common fixed costs. Allocations of common fixed costs can be safely classified as irrelevant since any choice usually does not affect the level of cost. The only effect may be a reallocation of those common fixed costs to fewer cost objects or segments.

We can now look at all three cost examples for the production of shafts and bushings to see which are relevant in deciding whether or not to continue production. Of the three, only direct labor cost is relevant, since it is the only one that occurs if production continues but stops if production stops.

	Cost to Make	− *Cost Not to Make*	= *Relevant Cost*
Direct labor	$150,000	—	$150,000
Depreciation	125,000	$125,000	—
Allocated lease	12,000	12,000	—
	$287,000	$137,000	$150,000

The same concepts apply to benefits. One alternative may produce a different amount of future benefits than another alternative (for example, differences in future revenues). If future benefits differ across alternatives, they are relevant and should be included in the analysis.

How should managers use this information about costs and benefits in making decisions? The rest of the chapter describes a recommended decision-making approach, identifies the limitations of the approach, and offers several examples of how relevant costing is used for special decisions. Additionally, special decisions relating to how a company should utilize scarce resources are considered.

DECISION-MAKING APPROACH

Objective 2
Use a relevant-costing decision model as an aid in choosing among competing alternatives.

Identifying relevant costs is only part of the overall decision process that a manager should undertake—and it is not the first step. Four steps precede this one and three steps follow it. The eight steps describing the recommended decision-making process are as follows:

1. Recognize and define the problem.
2. Identify alternatives as possible solutions to the problem.
3. Eliminate alternatives that are clearly not feasible.
4. Identify the costs and benefits associated with each feasible alternative.
5. Classify costs and benefits as relevant or irrelevant and eliminate irrelevant ones from consideration.
6. Express all relevant costs and benefits on a periodically recurring basis.
7. Total the relevant costs and benefits for each alternative.
8. Select the alternative with the greatest overall benefit.

decision model

The eight steps define a simple decision model. A **decision model** is a set of procedures that, if followed, will lead to a decision. The first step is to recognize and define a specific problem. For example, the members of Tidwell's management team all recognized the need for additional space for warehousing, offices, and the production of plastic moldings. The amount of space needed, the reasons for the need, and how the additional space would be used are all important dimensions of the problem; however, how the additional space should be acquired is the central question that must be answered.

Step 2 is to list and consider possible solutions. Tidwell Products identified the following possible solutions:

1. Build its own facility with sufficient capacity to handle current and immediately foreseeable needs.
2. Lease a larger facility and sublease its current facility.
3. Lease an additional, similar facility.
4. Lease an additional building that would be used for warehousing only, thereby freeing up space for expanded production.

5. Buy shafts and bushings externally and use the space made available (previously used for producing these parts) to solve the space problem.

The next step (Step 3) is to eliminate those alternatives that are not feasible. The first alternative was eliminated because it carried too much risk for the company. The second alternative was not considered feasible because subleasing was not a viable option. The third was eliminated because it went too far in solving the space problem, and, presumably, was too expensive. The fourth and fifth alternatives were feasible. Both were perceived as being within the cost and risk constraints as well as being able to solve the space needs of the company.

Once the feasible set of alternatives is identified, the decision model calls for a cost-benefit analysis of each one. This analysis encompasses Steps 4 through 8. In identifying the total relevant costs associated with each alternative, it is important that these costs be expressed on a periodically recurring basis. To compare the relevant costs of each alternative, the same relationships must hold period after period for the time span being considered. This allows the comparison to be meaningful.

For example, assume that Tidwell Products cannot sell the machinery used to produce shafts and bushings if these parts are purchased externally. If the total relevant cost to make shafts and bushings and lease a warehouse is $480,000 per year, and the total relevant cost to buy the two parts is $500,000 per year, the make alternative is superior to the buy alternative. But this is true only if these same relationships hold over the entire time frame being considered. Suppose the lease on the warehouse is ten years, with the following costs for the make-and-purchase options:

Year	*Make Alternative*	*Buy Alternative*
1	$480,000	$500,000
2	480,000	500,000
.	.	.
.	.	.
10	480,000	500,000

In this case, the make alternative is more desirable than the buy alternative.[1]

But what if Tidwell Products can sell the machinery it uses to make the shafts and bushings for $180,000? How do we deal with this one-time benefit? It is relevant; it will occur in the future and will occur only for the buy alternative. It could be used to reduce the total relevant cost of the buy alternative in Year 1. In this case, the total relevant cost is $320,000 ($500,000 − $180,000) for the first year and $500,000 per year thereafter. The annual total relevant costs for each alternative now appear as follows:

Year	*Make Alternative*	*Buy Alternative*
1	$480,000	$320,000
2	480,000	500,000
.	.	.
.	.	.
10	480,000	500,000

1. For the make alternative to dominate, the cost to make must be less than the cost to buy for each year of the ten-year horizon. The pattern given is only one of many that could hold. Relevant cost analysis compares the costs for only one point in time, but it assumes that the relative cost relationships will continue to hold for future periods affected by the decision.

Including one-time costs or benefits can distort the analysis. Which of the two alternatives is better? In Year 1, the buy alternative is, but for subsequent years, the make alternative is superior. Is the difference from Years 2 through 10 enough for the make alternative to overcome the $180,000 benefit that the buy alternative experiences in Year 1? Over ten years, the make alternative's total cost is $4.8 million; the buy alternative's total cost is $4.82 million. Does this indicate that the make alternative is superior?

Summing costs for each alternative over the ten years ignores the time value of money. Under the buy alternative, Tidwell Products will receive $180,000 at the beginning of the first year from selling the machinery. We must assume that the company will use the money productively. A reasonable assumption is that the money will be invested by the company in a ten-year project that produces a stream of equal annual payments. Assume that Tidwell Products invests the $180,000 in a project with a ten-year life that produces a recurring benefit of $30,000 per year. This recurring benefit reduces the cost of the buy alternative to $470,000 per year ($500,000 − $30,000). Since the cost of the make alternative is $480,000 per year, the buy alternative is now superior in every year. Comparability in annual costs is reestablished by assessing the periodic effects that the one-time benefit produces. The integrity of the relevant-costing model is restored.

It should be mentioned that when the cash flow patterns become complicated for competing alternatives, it becomes difficult to produce a stream of equal cash flows for each alternative. In such a case, more sophisticated procedures can and should be used for the analysis. These procedures are discussed in Chapter 22, which deals with the long-run decisions referred to as *capital investment decisions*.

Qualitative Factors

In the scenario, the buy alternative is less costly and would be chosen. However, actual decisions usually involve other factors besides cost, which receives so much emphasis in the decision model depicted. Even given the favorable quantitative position of buying versus making, it is still possible that the make alternative would be chosen.

Relevant cost analysis can and should be viewed as only one input for the final decision. A number of qualitative factors can significantly affect a manager's decision making. For example, in the make-or-buy decision facing Tidwell Products, Leo Tidwell likely would be concerned with such qualitative considerations as the quality of the shafts and bushings purchased externally, the reliability of supply sources, the expected stability of prices over the next several years, labor relations, community image, and so on. To illustrate the possible impact of qualitative factors on the make-or-buy decision, consider the first two factors, quality and reliability of supply.

If the quality of shafts and bushings is significantly less if purchased externally than what is available internally, the quantitative advantage from purchasing may be more fictitious than real. Settling for lower-quality materials may affect adversely the quality of the potentiometers, thus harming sales. Because of this, Tidwell Products may choose to continue to produce the parts internally.

Similarly, if supply sources are not reliable, production schedules could be interrupted, and customer orders could arrive late. These factors can increase labor costs and overhead and hurt sales. Again, depending on the perceived tradeoffs, Tidwell products may decide that internal production of the parts is better than purchasing them, even if relevant cost analysis gives the initial advantage to purchasing.

While relevant cost analysis plays a key role in decision making, it does have its limitations. Relevant cost information is not all the information a manager should consider. Other information is often needed to make an informed decision. If the qualitative factors are essentially equal across alternatives, however, relevant costs become the deciding factor instead of being just one input among several.

ILLUSTRATIVE EXAMPLES OF RELEVANT COST APPLICATIONS

Objective 3
Apply the relevant-costing model to a variety of business situations.

Relevant costing is useful in various kinds of business decisions, and some of the more common applications are illustrated in this section. The basic concepts presented here can also be applied in many other types of management decisions.

Make-or-Buy Decisions

make-or-buy decisions

Managers are often faced with the decision of whether to make or buy components used in manufacturing. Indeed, management periodically should evaluate past decisions concerning production. Conditions upon which prior decisions were based may have changed and, as a result, a different approach may be required. Periodic evaluations, of course, are not the only source of these **make-or-buy decisions**. Frequently, as with Tidwell Products, the decision is motivated by an indirectly related, underlying problem.

To illustrate more fully the cost analysis of a make-or-buy problem, assume that Swasey Manufacturing currently produces an electronic component used in one of its printers. In one year, Swasey will switch production to another type of printer and the electronic component will not be used. However, for the coming year, Swasey must produce 10,000 of these parts to support the production requirements for the old printer. The costs associated with the production of these 10,000 parts are as follows:

	Total Cost	*Unit Cost*
Rental of equipment	$12,000	$1.20
Equipment depreciation	2,000	0.20
Direct materials	10,000	1.00
Direct labor	20,000	2.00
Variable overhead	8,000	0.80
General fixed overhead	30,000	3.00
Total	$82,000	$8.20

Most of the equipment is rented. However, one specialized piece of machinery had to be custom made and was purchased. Rental equipment can be returned at any time without penalty; the company is charged only for the time the equipment is held. The specialized machinery will not be fully depreciated at the end of the year; however, the company plans to scrap it, since it cannot be sold. The company recently purchased sufficient materials for 5,000 components. There is no alternative use for the materials. Variable overhead is applied to the electronic component at $0.40 per direct labor dollar. General fixed overhead for the plant totals $1 million. General fixed overhead is assigned to products based on the space occupied by each product. The manufacturing facilities for the component under consideration occupy 6,000 of the plant's 200,000 square feet. Thus, $30,000 of the general fixed overhead is allocated to the electronic component (0.03 × $1,000,000).

Swasey has been approached by a potential supplier of the component. The supplier will build the electronic component to Swasey's specifications for $4.75 per unit. Should Swasey Manufacturing make or buy the component?

At first glance, the opportunity to buy the component seems very attractive—$4.75 per unit is considerably less than the full manufacturing cost of $8.20 per unit. However, as we already know, some of the manufacturing costs should not be considered in the decision.

The problem and the feasible alternatives are both readily identifiable. Since the horizon for the decision is only one period, there is no need to be concerned about periodically recurring costs. Relevant costing is particularly useful for short-run analysis. We simply need to identify the relevant costs, total them, and make a choice (assuming no overriding qualitative concerns).

Of the cost items listed, depreciation can be eliminated; it is a sunk cost. Since the direct materials already purchased have no alternative use, half of the cost of total direct materials is also a sunk cost. General overhead is not relevant either. The $30,000 is an allocation of a common fixed cost that will continue even if the component is purchased externally.

All other costs are relevant. The cost of renting the equipment is relevant, since it will not be needed if the part is bought externally. Similarly, direct labor, the remaining 5,000 units of direct materials, and variable overhead are all relevant; they would not be incurred if the component is bought externally. Of course, the purchase cost also is relevant. If the component is made, this cost would not be incurred. A listing of the total relevant costs for each alternative follows:

	Alternatives	
	Make	*Buy*
Rental of equipment	$12,000	—
Direct materials	5,000	—
Variable overhead	8,000	—
Direct labor	20,000	—
Purchase cost	—	$47,500
Total relevant costs	$45,000	$47,500

The analysis shows that making the product is $2,500 cheaper than buying it. The offer of the supplier should be rejected.

The same analysis can be done on a unit-cost basis. Once the relevant costs are identified, relevant unit costs can be compared. For this example, these costs are $4.50 ($45,000/10,000) for the make alternative and $4.75 for the buy alternative. Identifying the relevant unit cost for the make alternative permits a direct comparison with the quoted outside unit price.

Keep-or-Drop Decisions

keep-or-drop decisions

Often a manager needs to determine whether or not a segment, such as a product line, should be kept or dropped. Segmented reports prepared on a variable-costing basis provide valuable information for these **keep-or-drop decisions**. Both the segment's contribution margin and its segment margin are useful in evaluating the performance of segments. However, while segmented reports provide useful information for keep-or-drop decisions, relevant costing describes how the information should be used to arrive at a decision.

To illustrate, consider Norton Materials, Inc., which produces concrete blocks, bricks, and roofing tile. The controller has prepared the following estimated income statement for 1995 (in thousands of dollars):

	Blocks	*Bricks*	*Tile*	*Total*
Sales revenue	$ 500	$ 800	$ 150	$1,450
Less: Variable expenses	(250)	(480)	(140)	(870)
Contribution margin	$ 250	$ 320	$ 10	$ 580
Less direct fixed expenses:				
Salaries	$ (37)	$ (40)	$ (35)	$ (112)
Advertising	(10)	(10)	(10)	(30)
Depreciation	(53)	(40)	(10)	(103)
Total	$(100)	$ (90)	$ (55)	$ (245)
Segment margin	$ 150	$ 230	$ (45)	$ 335
Less: Common fixed expenses				(125)
Net income				$ 210

The projected performance of the roofing tile line shows a negative segment margin. This would represent the third consecutive year of poor performance for that line. The president of Norton Materials, Tom Blackburn, concerned about this poor performance, is trying to decide whether to drop or keep the roofing tile line.

His first reaction is to take steps to increase the sales revenue of roofing tiles. He is considering an aggressive sales promotion coupled with an increase in the selling price. The marketing manager thinks that this approach would be fruitless; however, the market is saturated and the level of competition too keen to hold out any hope for increasing the firm's market share. An increase in the selling price would almost certainly result in a decrease in sales revenue.

Increasing the product line's profitability through cost cutting is not feasible either. Costs were cut the past two years to reduce the loss to its present anticipated level. Any further reductions would lower the quality of the product and adversely affect sales.

With no hope for improving the profit performance of the line beyond its projected level, Tom has decided to drop it. He reasons that the firm will lose a total of $10,000 in contribution margin but save $45,000 by dismissing the line's supervisor and eliminating its advertising budget. (The depreciation cost of $10,000 is not relevant since it represents an allocation of a sunk cost.) Thus, dropping the product line has a $35,000 advantage over keeping it. Before finalizing the decision, Tom decided to notify the marketing manager and the production supervisor. The following memo was sent to both individuals:

MEMO

TO: Karen Golding, Marketing, and Larry Olsen, Production
FROM: Tom Blackburn, President
SUBJECT: Tentative Decision Concerning the Production of Roofing Tiles
DATE: March 14, 1995

Since there is no realistic expectation of improving the profitability of the roofing tile line, I have reluctantly decided to discontinue its production. I realize that this decision will have a negative impact on the community since our work force will need to be reduced. I am also sympathetic about the disruption this may cause in the personal lives of many employees.

However, we must be prepared to take actions that are in the best interests of the firm. By eliminating the roofing tile line, we can improve the firm's cash position by $35,000 per year. To support this decision, I am including the following analysis (focusing only on the tile segment):

	Keep	*Drop*
Sales	$150	$—
Less: Variable expenses	(140)	—
Contribution margin	$ 10	$—
Less: Advertising	(10)	—
Less: Cost of supervision	(35)	—
Total relevant benefit (loss)	$ (35)	$ 0

I have included only future costs and benefits that differ across the two alternatives. Depreciation on the tile equipment is not relevant since it is simply an allocation of a sunk cost. Also, the level of common fixed costs is unchanged regardless of whether we keep or drop the tile line.

At this point, I view the decision as tentative and welcome any response. Perhaps I am overlooking something that would affect the decision. Please respond as soon as possible.

Keep or Drop with Complementary Effects. In response to the memo, the marketing manager wrote that dropping the roofing tile line would lower sales of blocks by 10 percent and bricks by 8 percent. She explained that many customers buy roofing tile at the same time they purchase blocks or bricks. Some will go elsewhere if they cannot buy both products at the same location.

Shortly after receiving this response, Tom Blackburn decided to repeat the analysis, factoring in the effect that dropping the tile line would have on the sales of the other two lines. He decided to use total firm sales and total costs for each alternative. As before, depreciation and common fixed costs were excluded from the analysis on the basis of irrelevancy.

Dropping the product line reduces total sales by $264,000: $50,000 (0.10 × $500,000) for blocks, $64,000 (0.08 × $800,000) for the bricks, and $150,000 for roofing tiles. Similarly, total variable expenses are reduced by $203,400: $25,000 (0.10 × $250,000) for blocks, $38,400 (0.08 × $480,000) for bricks, and $140,000 for tile. Thus, total contribution margin is reduced by $60,600 ($264,000 − $203,400). Since dropping the tile line saves only $45,000 in supervision costs and advertising, the net effect is a disadvantage of $15,600 ($45,000 − $60,600). The following is a summary of the analysis using the new information (in thousands):

	Keep	*Drop*	*Difference*
Sales	$1,450	$1,186.0	$264.0
Less: Variable expenses	(870)	(666.6)	(203.4)
Contribution margin	$ 580	$ 519.4	$ 60.6

(continued)

	Keep	*Drop*	*Difference*
Less: Advertising	(30)	(20.0)	(10.0)
Less: Cost of supervision	(112)	(77.0)	(35.0)
Total	$ 438	$ 422.4	$ 15.6

Tom was pleased to find the outcome favoring production of the roofing tile. The unpleasant task of dismissing some of his work force was no longer necessary. However, just as he was preparing to write a second memo announcing his new decision, he received Larry Olsen's written response to his first memo.

Keep or Drop with Alternative Use of Facilities. The production supervisor's response was somewhat different. He agreed that roofing tile should be eliminated but suggested that it be replaced with the production of floor tile. He gave assurances that existing machinery could be converted to produce this new product with little or no cost. He had also contacted the marketing manager about the marketability of floor tile and included this assessment in his response.

The marketing manager saw the market for floor tile as stronger and less competitive than for roofing tile. However, the other two lines would still lose sales at the same rate; producing floor tile does not change that result. The following estimated financial statement for floor tile was also submitted (in thousands of dollars):

Sales	$100
Less: Variable expenses	(40)
Contribution margin	$ 60
Less: Direct fixed expenses	(55)
Segment margin	$ 5

Tom Blackburn was now faced with a third alternative: replacing the roofing tile with floor tile. Should the roofing tile line be kept or should it be dropped and replaced with the floor tile?

From his prior analysis, Tom knows that dropping the roofing tile decreases the firm's contribution margin by $60,600. Producing the floor tile will generate $60,000 more in contribution margin according to the estimate. Dropping the roofing tile line and replacing it with floor tile, then, will cause a $600 net decrease in total contribution margin ($60,600 − $60,000). The same outcome can be developed by directly comparing the relevant benefits and costs of the two alternatives (dollars expressed in thousands).

	Keep	*Drop and Replace*	*Difference*
Sales	$1,450	$1,286.0[a]	$164.0
Variable expenses	(870)	(706.6)[b]	(163.4)
Contribution margin	$ 580	$ 579.4	$(0.6)

[a]$1,450 − $150 − $50 − $64 + $100
[b]$870 − $140 − $25 − $38.4 + $40

The Norton Materials example again illustrates the decision process underlying relevant costing. First, a problem was identified and defined (the poor performance of the roofing tile product line). Next, possible solutions were listed and those that were not feasible were eliminated. For example, increasing sales or further decreasing costs were both rejected as feasible solutions. Three feasible solutions were examined: (1) keeping the product line, (2) dropping it, and (3) dropping the product line and replacing it with another product. An analysis of the costs and benefits of the feasible alternatives led to the selection of the preferred alternative (keeping the product line).

The example provides some insights beyond the simple application of the relevant costing decision model. The initial analysis, which focused on two feasible alternatives, led to a tentative decision to drop the product line. Additional information provided by the marketing manager led to a reversal of the first decision. Before that decision could be implemented, the manager was made aware of a third feasible alternative, which required additional analysis.

Often managers do not possess all the information necessary to make the best decision. They also may not be able to identify all feasible solutions. Managers benefit from gathering all the information available before finalizing a decision. They should also attempt to identify as many feasible solutions as possible. As the example clearly illustrates, limited information can result in poor decisions. Also, if the set of feasible solutions is too narrow, the best solution may never be selected simply because the manager has not thought of it. Managers can benefit from obtaining input from others who are familiar with the problem. By so doing, both the set of information and the set of feasible solutions can be expanded. The result is improved decision making.

Special-Order Decisions

special-order decisions

Price discrimination laws require that firms sell identical products at the same price to competing customers in the same market. These restrictions do not apply to competitive bids or to noncompeting customers. Bid prices can vary to customers in the same market, and firms often have the opportunity to consider special orders from potential customers in markets not ordinarily served. **Special-order decisions** focus on whether a specially priced order should be accepted or rejected. These orders often can be attractive, especially when the firm is operating below its maximum productive capacity.

Suppose, for example, that an ice-cream company is operating at 80 percent of its productive capacity. The company has a capacity of 20 million half-gallon units. The company produces only premium ice cream. The total costs associated with producing and selling 16 million units are as follows (in thousands of dollars):

	Total	*Unit Cost*
Variable costs:		
Dairy ingredients	$11,200	$0.70
Sugar	1,600	0.10
Flavoring	2,400	0.15
Direct labor	4,000	0.25
Packaging	3,200	0.20
Commissions	320	0.02
Distribution	480	0.03
Other	800	0.05
Total variable costs	$24,000	$1.50

(continued)

	Total	*Unit Cost*
Fixed costs:		
Salaries	$ 960	$0.060
Depreciation	320	0.020
Utilities	80	0.005
Taxes	32	0.002
Other	160	0.010
Total fixed costs	$ 1,552	$0.097
Total costs	$25,552	$1.597
Wholesale selling price	$32,000	$2.00

An ice-cream distributor from a geographic region not normally served by the company has offered to buy 2 million units at $1.55 per unit, provided its own label can be attached to the product. The distributor has also agreed to pay the transportation costs. Since the distributor approached the company directly, there is no sales commission. As the manager of the ice-cream company, would you accept this order or reject it?

The offer of $1.55 is well below the normal selling price of $2.00; in fact, it is even below the total unit cost. Nonetheless, accepting the order may be profitable for the company. The company does have idle capacity, and the order will not displace other units being produced to sell at the normal price. Additionally, many of the costs are not relevant; fixed costs will continue regardless of whether the order is accepted or rejected.

If the order is accepted, a benefit of $1.55 per unit will be realized that otherwise wouldn't be. However, all of the variable costs except for distribution ($0.03) and commissions ($0.02) also will be incurred, producing a cost of $1.45 per unit. Therefore, the company will see a net benefit of $0.10 ($1.55 − $1.45). For an order of 2 million half gallons, the company's profits would increase by $200,000 ($0.10 × 2,000,000). The relevant cost analysis can be summarized as follows:

	Accept	*Reject*	*Differential Benefit to Accept*
Revenues	$3,100,000	—	$ 3,100,000
Dairy ingredients	(1,400,000)	—	(1,400,000)
Sugar	(200,000)	—	(200,000)
Flavorings	(300,000)	—	(300,000)
Direct labor	(500,000)	—	(500,000)
Packaging	(400,000)	—	(400,000)
Other	(100,000)	—	(100,000)
Total	$ 200,000	$ 0	$ 200,000

Decisions to Sell or Process Further

joint products

split-off point

Joint products have common processes and costs of production up to a split-off point. At that point, they become distinguishable. For example, certain minerals, such as copper and gold, may both be found in a given ore. The ore must be mined, crushed, and treated before the copper and gold are separated. The point of separation is called the **split-off point**. The costs of mining, crushing, and treatment are common to both products.

sell or process further

Often joint products are sold at the split-off point. Sometimes it is more profitable to process a joint product further, beyond the split-off point, prior to selling it. Determining whether to **sell or process further** is an important decision that a manager must make.

To illustrate, consider Appletime Corporation. Appletime is a large corporate farm that specializes in growing apples. Each plot produces approximately one ton of apples. The trees in each plot must be sprayed, fertilized, watered, and pruned. When the apples are ripened, workers are hired to pick them. The apples are then transported to a warehouse, where they are washed and sorted. The approximate cost of all these activities (including processing) is $300 per ton per year.

Apples are sorted into three grades (A, B, and C) determined by size and blemishes. Large apples without blemishes (bruises, cuts, wormholes, and so on) are sorted into one bin and classified as Grade A. Small apples without blemishes are sorted into a second bin and classified as Grade B. All remaining apples are placed in a third bin and classified as Grade C. Every ton of apples produces 800 pounds of Grade A, 600 pounds of Grade B, and 600 pounds of Grade C.

Grade A apples are sold to large supermarkets for $0.40 per pound. Grade B apples are packaged in five-pound bags and sold to supermarkets for $1.30 per bag. (The cost of each bag is $0.05.) Grade C apples are processed further and made into applesauce. The sauce is sold in 16-ounce cans for $0.75 each. The cost of processing is $0.10 per pound of apples. The final output is 500 16-ounce cans. Exhibit 21-1 summarizes the process.

A large supermarket chain recently requested that Appletime supply 16-ounce cans of apple pie filling for which the chain was willing to pay $0.90 per can. Appletime determined that the Grade B apples would be suitable for this purpose and estimated that it would cost $0.20 per pound to process the apples into pie filling. The output would be 500 16-ounce cans.

In deciding whether to sell Grade B apples at split-off or to process them further and sell them as pie filling, the common costs of spraying, pruning, and so on, are not relevant. The company must pay the $300 per ton for these activi-

Exhibit 21-1
Appletime's Joint Process

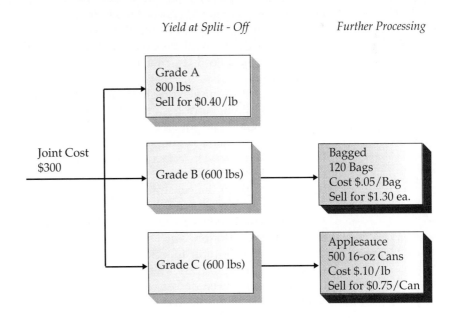

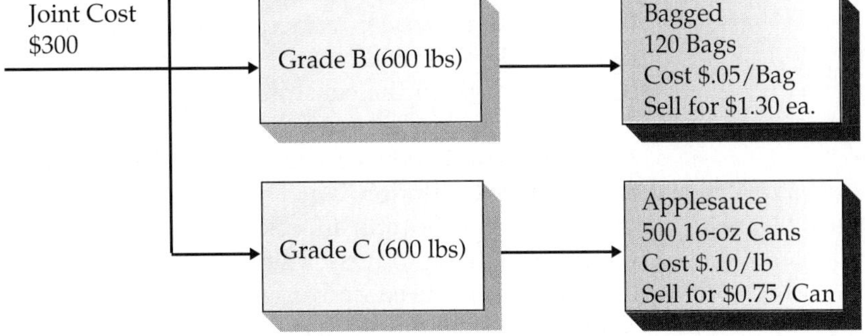

ties regardless of whether it sells at split-off or processes further. However, the revenues earned at split-off are likely to differ from the revenues that would be received if the Grade B apples were sold as pie filling. Therefore revenues are a relevant consideration. Similarly, the processing costs occur only if further processing takes place. Hence, processing costs are relevant.

Since there are 600 pounds of Grade B apples at split-off, Appletime sells 120 five-pound bags at a net per-unit price of $1.25 ($1.30 − $0.05). Thus, the total net revenues at split-off are $150 ($1.25 × 120). If the apples are processed into pie filling, the total revenues are $450 ($0.90 × 500). Therefore, the incremental revenues from processing further are $300 ($450 − $150). The incremental costs of processing are $120 ($0.20 × 600 pounds). Since revenues increase by $300 and costs by only $120, the net benefit of processing further is $180. Thus, Appletime should process the Grade B apples into pie filling. The analysis is summarized as follows:

	Sell	*Process Further*	*Difference*
Revenues	$150	$450	$300
Processing cost	—	(120)	(120)
Total	$150	$330	$180

PRODUCT MIX DECISIONS

Objective 4
Choose the optimal product mix when faced with one constrained resource.

In the example above, of every 2,000 pounds of apples harvested, 800 were Grade A, 600 were Grade B, and 600 were Grade C. Although the relative amounts of each type of apple can be influenced to some extent by the procedures followed in spraying, watering, fertilizing, and so on, the mix of apples is largely beyond Appletime's control. However, many organizations have total discretion in choosing their product mix. Moreover, decisions about product mix can have a significant impact on an organization's profitability.

Each mix represents an alternative that carries with it an associated profit level. A manager should choose the alternative that maximizes total profits. Since fixed costs do not vary with activity level, the total fixed costs of a firm would be the same for all possible mixes and, therefore, are not relevant to the decision. Thus, a manager needs to choose the alternative that maximizes total contribution margin.

Assume, for example, that Jorgenson Company produces two types of gears: X and Y, with unit contribution margins of $25 and $10, respectively. If the firm possesses unlimited resources and the demand for each product is unlimited, the product mix decision is simple—produce an infinite number of each product. Unfortunately, every firm faces limited resources and limited demand for each product. These limitations are called **constraints**. A manager must choose the optimal mix given the constraints found within the firm.

constraints

Assuming that Jorgenson can sell all that is produced, some may argue that only Gear X should be produced and sold—it has the larger contribution margin. However, this solution is not necessarily the best. The selection of the optimal mix can be significantly affected by the relationships of the constrained resources to the individual products. These relationships affect the quantity of each product that can be produced and, consequently, the total contribution margin that can be earned. This point is most vividly illustrated with one resource constraint.

One Constrained Resource

Assume that each gear must be notched by a special machine. The firm owns eight machines that together provide 40,000 hours of machine time per year. Gear X requires two hours of machine time, and Gear Y requires one half hour of machine time. Assuming no other constraints, what is the optimal mix of gears? Since each unit of Gear X requires two hours of machine time, 20,000 units of Gear X can be produced per year (40,000/2). At $25 per unit, Jorgenson can earn a total contribution margin of $500,000. On the other hand, Gear Y requires only 0.5 hours of machine time per unit; therefore, 80,000 (40,000/0.5) gears can be produced. At $10 per unit, the total contribution margin is $800,000. Producing only Gear Y yields a higher profit level than producing only Gear X—even though the unit contribution margin for Gear X is 2.5 times larger than that for Gear Y.

The contribution margin per unit of each product is not the critical concern. The contribution margin per unit of *scarce resource* is the deciding factor. The product yielding the highest contribution margin per machine hour should be selected. Gear X earns $12.50 per machine hour ($25/2), but Gear Y earns $20 per machine hour ($10/0.5). Thus, the optimal mix is 80,000 units of Gear Y and none of Gear X.

Multiple Constrained Resources

The presence of only one constrained resource is unrealistic. All organizations face multiple constraints: limitations of raw materials, limitations of labor inputs, limited demand for each product, and so on. The solution of the product mix problem in the presence of multiple constraints is considerably more complicated and requires the use of a specialized mathematical technique known as *linear programming*. The study of linear programming is beyond the scope of this text.

SUMMARY OF LEARNING OBJECTIVES

1. Define and explain the concept of relevant costs. Managers are often faced with the need to choose among competing alternatives, such as whether a component should be produced internally or purchased from an external supplier. In making this type of decision, only those costs and benefits that impact the decision should be considered. These are referred to as *relevant* costs and benefits. They are those future costs and benefits that differ across alternatives. Irrevelant costs are sunk costs (past outlays) or are costs that are incurred no matter which alternative is chosen.

2. Use a relevant-costing decision model as an aid in choosing among competing alternatives. The decision-making model described in this chapter consists of eight steps: problem recognition, alternative identification, elimination of unfeasible alternatives, determination of costs/benefits of each alternative, classification of costs/benefits as relevant or irrelevant, expression of all relevant costs/benefits on a periodically recurring basis, totaling relevant costs and benefits for each alternative, and selection of the alternative with the greatest benefit. In using cost analysis to choose among alternatives, managers should take steps to ensure that all important feasible alternatives are being considered and that all relevant costs and benefits are identified. Additionally, managers should use cost analysis as only one input. Often, qualitative factors will override the formal cost analysis.

3. Apply the relevant-costing model to a variety of business situations. Several examples illustrating the application of the relevant-costing model were given within the chapter. Applications were illustrated for make-or-buy decisions, keep-or-drop decisions, special-order decisions, and sell-or-process-further decisions. Product-mix decisions were also discussed. The list of applications is by no means exhaustive but was given to illustrate the scope and power of relevant-costing analysis.

4. Choose the optimal product mix when faced with one

constrained resource. In dealing with a resource constraint, it is important to phrase the product contribution margin in terms of contribution margin per unit of constrained resource. The product with the highest contribution per unit of constrained resource should be produced.

KEY TERMS

REVIEW PROBLEM

Rianne Company produces a light fixture with the following unit cost:

Direct materials	$2
Direct labor	1
Variable overhead	3
Fixed overhead	2
Unit cost	$8

The production capacity is 300,000 units per year. Because of a depressed housing market, the company expects to produce only 180,000 fixtures for the coming year. The company also has fixed selling costs totaling $500,000 per year and variable selling costs of $1 per unit sold. The fixtures normally sell for $12 each.

At the beginning of the year, a customer from a geographic region outside the area normally served by the company offered to buy 100,000 fixtures for $7 each. The customer also offered to pay all transportation expenses. Since there would be no sales commissions involved, this order would not have any variable selling expenses.

REQUIRED: Should the company accept the order? Provide both qualitative and quantitative justification for your decision. Assume that no other orders are expected beyond the regular business and the special order.

Solution

The company is faced with a problem of idle capacity. Accepting the special order would bring production up to near capacity. There are two options: accept or reject the order. If the order is accepted, the company could avoid laying off employees and would enhance and maintain its community image. However, the order is considerably below the normal selling price of $12. Because the price is so low, the company needs to assess the potential impact of the sale on its regular customers and the profitability of the firm. Considering the fact that the customer is located in a region not usually served by the company, the likelihood of an adverse impact on regular business is not high. Thus, the qualitative factors seem to favor acceptance.

The only remaining consideration is the profitability of the special order. To assess profitability, the firm should identify the relevant costs and benefits of each alternative. This analysis is as follows:

	Accept	*Reject*
Revenues	$700,000	—
Direct materials	(200,000)	—
Direct labor	(100,000)	—
Variable overhead	(300,000)	—
Total benefits	$100,000	$0

Accepting the order would increase profits by $100,000 (the fixed overhead and selling expenses are all irrelevant since they are the same across both alternatives). Conclusion: The order should be accepted since both qualitative and quantitative factors favor it.

QUESTIONS

1. What is a relevant cost? A relevant revenue?
2. Explain why depreciation on an existing asset is always irrelevant.
3. Give an example of a future cost that is not relevant.
4. Explain why relevant costs need to be expressed on a periodically recurring basis.
5. Relevant costs always determine which alternative should be chosen. Do you agree? Explain.
6. Can direct materials ever be irrelevant in a make-or-buy decision? Explain.
7. Discuss the importance of complementary effects in a keep-or-drop decision.
8. What are some ways a manager can expand his or her knowledge of the feasible set of alternatives?
9. Suppose that a product can be sold at split-off for $5,000 or processed further at a cost of $1,000 and then sold for $6,400. Should the product be processed further?
10. Give an example of a fixed cost that is relevant.
11. What is the difference, if any, between a relevant cost and a differential cost?
12. Should joint costs be considered in a sell-or-process-further decision? Explain.
13. When, if ever, is depreciation a relevant cost?
14. What role do past costs play in relevant costing decisions?
15. When can a firm legally offer different prices for the same product?
16. Why would a firm ever offer a price on a product that is below its full cost?
17. Why are fixed costs never relevant in a product mix decision?
18. Suppose that a firm produces two products. Should the firm always place the most emphasis on the product with the largest contribution margin per unit? Explain.

EXERCISES

E21-1
Lease Decision; Relevance of Book Value
LO 1, 2

The manager of a plant is trying to decide whether to lease a new forklift or continue using the one already owned. With careful maintenance, the old forklift will last another five years. The lease on the new forklift is also for five years, at the end of which it will be returned to the lessor. Information on the forklift owned by the company is given below:

Original cost	$15,000
Accumulated depreciation	7,500
Annual depreciation	1,500
Annual operating costs	2,800
Annual maintenance	1,200

Cost information for the new forklift is as follows:

Annual lease payment	$4,200
Annual operating costs	1,200
Annual maintenance	—

If the decision is to lease, the old forklift will be sold for an amount just sufficient to pay off a five-year note that requires annual payments of $1,320.

REQUIRED:

1. What are the alternatives being considered by the plant manager?
2. Identify the relevant costs and benefits of each alternative. Should the plant manager lease the new forklift?
3. What is the most that the plant manager would be willing to pay per year for a leased forklift?

E21-2
Keep or Buy; Sunk Costs
LO 1, 2, 3

Shane Gasser purchased a 1974 Fiat Spider in 1989 for $1,900. Since purchasing the car, he has spent the following amounts on parts and labor:

Fuel pump	$ 30
Canvas top	165
Master cylinder	45
Disk brakes	32
Hoses, plugs	28
Labor	100
Total	$400

Shane is not totally satisfied with the Fiat. To bring the car to a condition that he feels it should be, he anticipates the following costs of restoration:

Rebuilt engine	$ 500
New paint job	500
Tires	300
New interior	300
Miscellaneous maintenance	300
Total	$1,900

In a visit to a used car dealer, Shane has found a one-year-old Yugo in mint condition for $2,850. Shane has advertised and found that he can sell the Fiat for only $1,200. If he buys the Yugo, Shane will pay cash, but he would need to sell the Fiat.

REQUIRED:

1. In trying to decide whether to restore the Fiat or buy the Yugo, Shane is distressed because he already has spent $2,300 on the Fiat. The investment seems too much to give up. How would you react to Shane's concern?
2. Assuming that Shane would be equally happy with the Fiat or the Yugo, should he buy the Yugo or should he restore the Fiat?

E21-3
Make or Buy
LO 2, 3

Swift Company is currently manufacturing Part 6785, producing 5,000 units annually. The part is used in the production of several products made by Swift. The cost per unit for 6785 is as follows:

Direct materials	$3.00
Direct labor	2.00
Variable overhead	1.00
Fixed overhead	1.50
Total	$7.50

Of the total fixed overhead assigned to 6785, $1,500 is direct fixed overhead and the remainder is common fixed overhead. An outside supplier has offered to sell the part to Swift for $7.05. There is no alternative use for the facilities currently used to produce the part.

REQUIRED:

1. Should Swift Company make or buy Part 6785?
2. What is the most Swift would be willing to pay an outside supplier?

E21-4
Keep or Drop; Product Substitutes
LO 2, 3

Ernest Golding, president of Golding Corporation, has just received the following variable-costing income statement:

	Product A	*Product B*
Sales	$ 100,000	$ 250,000
Less: Variable expenses	(50,000)	(145,000)
Contribution margin	$ 50,000	$ 105,000
Less: Fixed expenses	(80,000)	(110,000)
Net income (loss)	$ (30,000)	$ (5,000)

Golding was distressed since this was the fifth consecutive quarter that both products had shown a loss. Upon careful review, Golding discovered that $70,000 of the total fixed costs were common to both products; the common fixed costs are allocated to the individual products on the basis of sales revenues. Golding also was told that the products were substitutes for each other. If either product is dropped, the sales of the other product will increase; Product A's by 50 percent if B is dropped and B's by 10 percent if A is dropped.

REQUIRED:

1. Prepare a segmented income statement in proper form for the past quarter.
2. Assume that Golding will choose among one of the following alternatives:
   a. Keep both products
   b. Drop both products
   c. Drop Product A
   d. Drop Product B

   Which is the best alternative? Provide computational support.

E21-5
Special-Order Decision; Qualitative Aspects
LO 2, 3

Cindy Burnson, the manager of Fondike Company, was agonizing over an offer for an order requesting 7,000 boxes of birthday cards. Fondike was operating at 70 percent of its capacity and could use the extra business; unfortunately, the order's offering price of $7.75 per box was below the cost to produce the cards. The controller was opposed to taking a loss on the deal. However, the personnel manager argued in favor of accepting the order even though a loss would be incurred; it would avoid the problem of layoffs and would help maintain the community image of the company. The full cost to produce a box of birthday cards is as follows:

Direct materials	$2.00
Direct labor	3.00
Variable overhead	1.50
Fixed overhead	2.50
Total	$9.00

The order is from a customer in a region not ordinarily serviced by the company. No variable selling or administrative expenses would be associated with the order.

REQUIRED:

1. Assume that the company would accept the order only if it increases total profits. Should the company accept or reject the order? Provide supporting computations.
2. Consider the personnel manager's concerns. Discuss the merits of accepting the order even if it decreases total profits.

E21-6
Sell or Process Further; Basic Analysis
LO 2, 3

A division of Triple Products produces three products from a common input. The joint costs for a typical quarter are described below.

Direct materials	$20,000
Direct labor	30,000
Overhead	15,000

The revenues from each product are as follows: Product A, $43,000; Product B, $32,000; and Product C, $25,000.

Management is considering processing Product A beyond the split-off point, which would increase the sales value of Product A to $76,000. However, to process Product A further means that the company must rent some special equipment costing $17,500 per quarter. Additional materials and labor also needed would cost $12,650 per quarter.

REQUIRED:

1. What is the gross profit earned by the three products for one quarter?
2. Should the division process Product A further or sell Product A at split-off? What is the effect of the decision on quarterly gross profit?

E21-7
Product Mix Decision; Single Constraint
LO 4

Olsen Company produces two products that use the same material input. Product A uses two pounds of the material for every unit produced, and Product B uses five pounds. Currently, Olsen has 6,000 pounds of the material in inventory. All of the material is imported. For the coming year, Olsen plans to import 6,000 pounds to produce 1,000 units of Product A and 2,000 units of Product B. The detail of each product's unit contribution margin is given below.

	Product A	*Product B*
Selling price	$81	$139
Less variable expenses:		
Direct materials	(20)	(50)
Direct labor	(21)	(14)
Variable overhead	(10)	(15)
Contribution margin	$30	$ 60

Olsen Company has received word that the source of the material has been shut down by embargo. Consequently, the company will not be able to import the 6,000 pounds it planned to use in the coming year's production. There is no other source of the material.

REQUIRED:

1. Compute the total contribution margin that the company would earn if it could import the 6,000 pounds of the material.
2. Determine the optimal usage of the company's inventory of 6,000 pounds of the material. Compute the total contribution margin for the product mix that you recommend.

E21-8
Buy or Keep; Identification of Relevant Costs and Benefits
LO 2, 3

Warren Company is currently using manufacturing machinery that some company officers believe is outdated. They are urging the president to acquire the latest computerized equipment, maintaining that output will increase and operating costs decrease. The company president has commissioned a report that compares costs and revenues of the existing equipment with that of the new equipment. The report is as follows:

	Old	*New*
Cost of acquisition	$250,000	$540,000
Accumulated depreciation[1]	100,000	—
Annual operating cost	60,000	30,000
Annual maintenance	6,000	4,000
Salvage value[2]	—	—
Output	100,000	120,000
Output selling price	100	100

[1]Using the straight-line method. Expected life for both machines is six years.
[2]At the end of the coming six years. Currently, the old machinery does have market value, and if it is sold now a six-year note will be paid off, saving the company annual payments of $16,222.

REQUIRED: Identify all costs and benefits relevant to the decision to keep or buy. Ignore taxes.

E21-9
Keep or Drop; Complementary Effects
LO 2, 3

Dutson Company manufactures running shoes and tennis shoes. The president of the company is considering dropping the running shoes. However, if the line is dropped, sales of tennis shoes will drop by 10 percent.

The projected income statements for the two products are shown on the following page.

REQUIRED:

1. Should the company drop or keep the line of running shoes? Provide supporting computations.
2. Assume that increasing the advertising budget by $10,000 will increase sales of running shoes by 5 percent and tennis shoes by 3 percent. Prepare a segmented income statement that reflects the effect of increased advertising. Should advertising be increased?

	Running Shoes	*Tennis Shoes*
Sales	$ 450,000	$ 750,000
Less: Variable costs	(270,000)	(300,000)
Contribution margin	$ 180,000	$ 450,000
Less: Direct fixed expenses	(200,000)	(220,000)
Segment margin	$ (20,000)	$ 230,000
Less: Common fixed costs (allocated)	(50,000)	(75,000)
Net income (loss)	$ (70,000)	$ 155,000

E21-10
Special Order
LO 2, 3

The Killian Company manufactures two skin care lotions, Liquid Skin and Silken Skin, out of a joint process. The joint (common) costs incurred are $420,000 for a standard production run that generates 180,000 gallons of Liquid Skin and 120,000 gallons of Silken Skin. Additional processing costs beyond the split-off point are $1.40 per gallon for Liquid Skin and $0.90 per gallon for Silken Skin. Liquid Skin sells for $2.40 per gallon while Silken Skin sells for $3.90 per gallon.

The Overnight Hotel Chain has asked the Killian Company to supply it with 240,000 gallons of Silken Skin at a price of $3.65 per gallon. Overnight plans to have the Silken Skin bottled in 1.5-ounce personal-use containers that are supplied in each of its hotel rooms as part of the complimentary personal products for guest use.

If Killian accepts the order, it will save $0.05 per gallon in packaging of Silken Skin. There is sufficient excess capacity for the order. However, the market for Liquid Skin is saturated, and any additional sales of Liquid Skin would take place at a price of $1.60 per gallon.

REQUIRED:

1. What is the profit normally earned on one production run of Liquid Skin and Silken Skin?
2. Should Killian accept the special order? Explain.

(CMA adapted)

E21-11
Product Mix Decision; Single Constraint
LO 4

Carstairs Company manufactures three types of floppy diskette storage units. Each of the three types requires the use of a special machine that has total operating capacity of 10,000 hours per year. Information on the three types of storage units is as follows:

	Basic	*Standard*	*Deluxe*
Selling price	$10.00	$15.00	$25.00
Variable cost	5.00	7.00	12.00
Machine hours required	0.10	0.25	0.75

Carstairs Company's marketing director has assessed demand for the three types of storage units and believes that the firm can sell as many units as it can produce.

REQUIRED:

1. How many of each type of unit should be produced and sold to maximize the company's contribution margin? What is the total contribution margin for your selection?
2. Now suppose that Carstairs Company believes that it can sell no more than 30,000 of each of the three types at the prices estimated. What product mix would you recommend and what would be the total contribution margin?

E21-12
Make or Buy
LO 2, 3

Laughlin Company produces automatic coffee makers. Laughlin manufactures all parts necessary for the assembly of the coffee makers, including the tempered glass pots. Recently, Laughlin has received a proposal from Katz Glass Works to produce the tempered glass pots and to sell them for $2.45 each. Laughlin requires 30,000 pots per year, and Katz Glass Works has promised to supply that level of demand.

Internal data on the manufacture of glass pots are as follows:

Direct materials	$1.00
Direct labor	0.80
Factory overhead (25% variable)	2.40
Full manufacturing cost	$4.20

REQUIRED:

1. Should Laughlin accept Katz Glass Works' offer? Explain.
2. Independent of your answer to Requirement 1, give two qualitative reasons that Laughlin might reject the offer. Give two qualitative reasons that Laughlin might accept it.

PROBLEMS

P21-1
Make or Buy; Qualitative Considerations
LO 2, 3

Gray Dentistry Services is part of an HMO that operates in a large metropolitan area. Currently, Gray has its own dental laboratory to produce porcelain and gold crowns. The unit costs to produce the crowns are as follows:

	Porcelain	*Gold*
Raw materials	$ 60	$ 90
Direct labor	20	20
Variable overhead	5	5
Fixed overhead	22	22
Total	$107	$137

Fixed overhead is detailed as follows:

Salary (supervisor)	$30,000
Depreciation	5,000
Rent (lab facility)	20,000

Overhead is applied on the basis of direct labor hours. The rates above were computed using 5,500 direct labor hours.

A local dental laboratory has offered to supply Gray all the crowns it needs. Its price is $100 for porcelain crowns and $132 for gold crowns; however, the offer is conditional on supplying both types of crowns—it will not supply just one type for the price indicated. If the offer is accepted, the equipment used by Gray's laboratory would be scrapped (it is old and has no market value), and the lab facility would be closed. Gray uses 1,500 porcelain crowns and 1,000 gold crowns per year.

REQUIRED:

1. Should Gray continue to make its own crowns or should they be purchased from the external supplier? What is the dollar effect of purchasing?
2. What qualitative factors should Gray consider in making this decision?
3. Suppose that the lab facility is owned rather than rented and that the $20,000 is depreciation rather than rent. What effect does this have on the analysis in Requirement 1?
4. Refer to the original data. Assume that the volume of crowns is 3,000 porcelain and 2,000 gold. Should Gray make or buy the crowns? Explain the outcome.

P21-2
Sell or Process Further
LO 2, 3

Godfrey Drug Corporation buys three chemicals that are processed to produce 2 types of ingredients for popular over-the-counter drugs. The purchased chemicals are blended for 2 to 3 hours and then heated for 15 minutes. The results of the process are 2 separate chemicals, X and Y, which are sent to a drying room until their moisture content is reduced to 6 to 8 percent. For every 1,100 pounds of chemicals used, 500 pounds of each chemical is produced. After drying, X and Y are sold to companies that process them into their final form. The selling prices are $10 per pound for X and $25 per pound for Y. The costs to produce 500 pounds of each chemical are as follows:

Chemicals	$5,500
Direct labor	4,500
Overhead	3,500

The chemicals are packaged in 25-pound bags and shipped. The cost of each bag is $0.75. Shipping costs $0.10 per pound.

Godfrey Company could process X further by grinding it into a fine powder and then molding the powder into tablets. The tablets can be sold directly to retail drug stores as a generic brand. If this route is taken, the revenue received per bottle of tablets would be $3.00, with 5 bottles produced by every pound of X. The costs of grinding and tableting total $2.50 per pound of X. Bottles cost $0.20 each. Bottles are shipped in boxes that hold 25 at a shipping cost of $1.00 per box.

REQUIRED:

1. Should Godfrey sell X at split-off or should X be processed and sold as tablets?
2. If Godfrey normally sells 180,000 pounds of X per year, what will be the difference in profits if X is processed further?

P21-3
Keep or Drop
LO 2, 3

SoundEasy is a retailer of radios, stereos, and televisions. The store carries two portable sound systems that have radios, tape players, and speakers. System A, of slightly higher quality than System B, costs $20 more. With rare exceptions, the store also sells a headset when a system is sold. The headset can be used with either system. Variable-costing income statements for the three products are shown below.

	System A	*System B*	*Headset*
Sales	$ 45,000	$ 32,500	$ 8,000
Less: Variable expenses	(20,000)	(25,500)	(3,200)
Contribution margin	$ 25,000	$ 7,000	$ 4,800
Less: Fixed costs[1]	(10,000)	(18,000)	(2,700)
Net income	$ 15,000	$(11,000)	$ 2,100

[1]Includes common fixed costs totaling $18,000, allocated to each product in proportion to its revenues.

The owner of the store is concerned about the profit performance of System B and is considering dropping it. If the product is dropped, sales of System A will increase by 30 percent and sales of headsets will drop by 25 percent.

REQUIRED:

1. Prepare segmented income statements for the three products using a better format.
2. Prepare segmented income statements for System A and the headsets assuming that System B is dropped. Should System B be dropped?
3. Suppose that a third system, System C, with a similar quality to System B, could be acquired. Assume that with System C the sales of System A would remain unchanged; however, System C would produce only 80 percent of the revenues of System B and sales of the headsets would drop by 10 percent. The contribution margin ratio of C is 50 percent, and its direct fixed costs would be identical to those of System B. Should System B be dropped and replaced with System C?

P21-4
Accept or Reject a Special Order
LO 2, 3

Patrick Sjoblom, manager of an electronics division, was considering an offer by Kelly Vargas, manager of a sister division. Kelly's division was operating below capacity and had just been given an opportunity to produce 10,000 units of one of its products for a customer in a market not normally served. The opportunity involves a product that uses an electrical component produced by Patrick's division. Each unit that Kelly's department produces requires two of the components. However, the price the customer is willing to pay is well below the price usually charged. To make a reasonable profit on the order, Kelly needed a price concession from Patrick's division. Kelly had offered to pay full manufacturing cost for the parts. So that Patrick would know that everything was aboveboard, Kelly had supplied the following unit-cost and price information concerning the special order, excluding the cost of the electrical component:

Selling price	$30
Less costs:	
Direct materials	(15)
Direct labor	(7)
Variable overhead	(2)
Fixed overhead	(3)
Gross profit	$ 3

The normal selling price of the electrical component is $1.60 per unit. Its full manufacturing cost is $1.20 ($1.00 variable and $0.20 fixed). Kelly had argued that paying $1.60 per component would wipe out the gross profit and result in her division showing a loss. Patrick was interested in the offer because his division was also operating below capacity (the order would not use all the excess capacity).

REQUIRED:

1. Should Patrick accept the order at a selling price of $1.20 per unit? By how much will his division's profits be changed if the order is accepted? By how much will the profits of Kelly's division change if Patrick agrees to supply the part at full cost?
2. Suppose that Patrick offers to supply the component at $1.40. In offering the price, Patrick says that it is a firm offer not subject to negotiation. Should Kelly accept this price and produce the special order? If Kelly accepts the price, what is the change in profits for Patrick's division?
3. Assume that Patrick's division is operating at full capacity and that Patrick refuses to supply the part for less than the full price. Should Kelly still accept the special order? Explain.

P21-5
Keep or Drop a Division
LO 2, 3

Lee Wright, president and general manager of Fossett Company, was concerned about the future of one of the company's largest divisions. The division's most recent quarterly income statement is as follows:

Sales	$3,680,000
Less: Cost of goods sold	(2,800,000)
Gross profit	$ 880,000
Less: Selling and administrative	(1,000,000)
Net profit (loss)	$ (120,000)

Lee is giving serious consideration to shutting down the division since this is the ninth consecutive quarter that it has shown a loss. To help him in his decision, the following additional information has been gathered:

a. The division produces one product at a selling price of $100 to outside parties.
b. The division sells 50 percent of its output to another division within the company for $84 (full manufacturing cost plus 20 percent). The internal price is set by company policy. If the division is shut down, the user division would buy the part externally for $100 per unit.
c. The fixed overhead assigned per unit is $20.
d. There is no alternative use for the facilities if shut down. The facilities and equipment would be sold and the proceeds invested to produce an annuity of $100,000 per year.
e. Of the fixed selling and administrative expenses, 30 percent represent allocated expenses from corporate headquarters.
f. Variable selling expenses are $5 per unit sold for units sold externally. These expenses are avoided for internal sales. There are no variable administrative expenses.

REQUIRED:

1. Prepare an income statement that more accurately reflects the division's profit performance.
2. Should the president shut down the division? What would be the effect on the company's profits if the division were closed?

P21-6
Plant Shutdown or Continue to Operate; Qualitative Considerations
LO 2, 3

GianAuto Corporation manufactures automobiles, vans, and trucks. Among the various GianAuto plants around the United States is the Denver cover plant, where vinyl covers and upholstery fabric are sewn. These are used to cover interior seating and other surfaces of GianAuto products.

Pam Vosilo is the plant manager for Denver cover. The plant was the first GianAuto plant in the region. As other area plants were opened, Vosilo, in recognition of her management ability, was given the responsibility to manage them. Vosilo functions as a regional manager although the budget for her and her staff is charged to the Denver plant.

Vosilo has just received a report indicating that GianAuto could purchase the entire annual output of the Denver cover plant from outside suppliers for $30 million. Vosilo was astonished at the low outside price because the budget for Denver cover's operating costs was set at $52 million. Vosilo believes that Denver cover will have to close down operations in order to realize the $22 million in annual cost savings.

The budget (in thousands) for Denver cover's operating costs for the coming year follows:

Materials		$12,000
Labor:		
Direct	$13,000	
Supervision	3,000	
Indirect plant	4,000	20,000

(continued)

Overhead:		
Depreciation—Equipment	$ 5,000	
Depreciation—Building	3,000	
Pension expense	4,000	
Plant manager and staff	2,000	
Corporate allocation	6,000	20,000
Total budgeted costs		$52,000

Additional facts regarding the plant's operations are as follows:

a. Due to Denver cover's commitment to use high-quality fabrics in all its products, the purchasing department was instructed to place blanket orders with major suppliers to ensure the receipt of sufficient materials for the coming year. If these orders are canceled as a consequence of the plant closing, termination charges would amount to 15 percent of the cost of direct materials.
b. Approximately 700 plant employees will lose their jobs if the plant is closed. This includes all direct laborers and supervisors as well as the plumbers, electricians, and other skilled workers classified as indirect plant workers. Some would be able to find new jobs, but many others would have difficulty. All employees would have difficulty matching Denver cover's base pay of $9.40 per hour, the highest in the area. A clause in Denver cover's contract with the union may help some employees; the company must provide employment assistance to its former employees for 12 months after a plant closing. The estimated cost to administer this service would be $1 million for the year.
c. Some employees would probably elect early retirement because Denver cover has an excellent pension plan. In fact, $3 million of next year's pension expense would continue whether Denver cover is open or not.
d. Vosilo and her staff would not be affected by the closing of Denver cover. They would still be responsible for administering three other area plants.
e. Denver cover considers equipment depreciation to be a variable cost and uses the units-of-production method to depreciate its equipment; Denver cover is the only GianAuto plant to use this depreciation method. However, Denver cover uses the customary straight-line method to depreciate its building.

REQUIRED:

1. Prepare a quantitative analysis to help in deciding whether or not to close the Denver cover plant. Explain how you treated the nonrecurring relevant costs.
2. Consider the analysis in Requirement 1 and add to it the qualitative factors that you believe are important to the decision. What is your decision? Would you close the plant? Explain.

(CMA adapted)

P21-7
Keep or Drop; Product Mix
LO 2, 3, 4

Olat Corporation produces three gauges. These gauges measure density, permeability, and thickness and are known as *D-gauges, P-gauges,* and *T-gauges.* For many years, the company has been profitable and has operated at capacity (which is 82,000 direct labor hours). In the last two years, however, prices on all gauges were reduced and selling expenses increased to meet competition and keep the plant operating at full capacity. Third-quarter results (in thousands), as shown below, are representative of recent experience.

	D-gauge	*P-gauge*	*T-gauge*	*Total*
Sales	$ 900	$ 1,600	$ 900	$ 3,400
Less: Cost of goods sold	(770)	(1,048)	(950)	(2,768)
Gross profit	$ 130	$ 552	$ (50)	$ 632
Less: Selling and administrative	(185)	(370)	(135)	(690)
Net income (loss)	$ (55)	$ 182	$(185)	$ (58)

Mel Carlo, president of Olat, is concerned about the results of the pricing, selling, and production policies. After reviewing the third-quarter results, he asked his management staff to consider the following three-point course of action:

a. Discontinue production of the T-gauge. T-gauges would not be returned to the line of products unless the problems with the gauge can be identified and resolved.
b. Increase quarterly sales promotion by $100,000 on the P-gauge to increase sales volume by 25 percent.
c. To accommodate the increased demand of P-gauges, cut production of the D-gauge by 50 percent and reduce traceable advertising and promotion costs for this line by $20,000 each quarter.

George Spears, controller, suggested that a more careful study of the financial relationships be made to determine the possible effects on the company's operating results as a consequence of these proposed actions. The president agreed, and JoAnn Brower, assistant controller, was given the assignment. She gathered the following information:

a. All three gauges are manufactured with common equipment and facilities.
b. The quarterly general selling and administrative expenses are allocated to the three product lines in proportion to their dollar sales volumes.
c. Special selling expenses (advertising and shipping) are incurred on each gauge as follows:

	Advertising[1]	*Shipping*[2]
D-gauge	$100,000	$ 4
P-gauge	210,000	10
T-gauge	40,000	10

[1]Per quarter
[2]Per unit

d. The unit manufacturing costs for the three products are as follows:

	D-gauge	*P-gauge*	*T-gauge*
Raw materials	$17	$ 31	$ 50
Direct labor[1]	20	40	60
Variable overhead	30	45	60
Fixed overhead	10	15	20
Total	$77	$131	$190

[1]The wage rate averages $10 per hour.

The unit sales prices for the three products are $90 for the D-gauge, $200 for the P-gauge, and $180 for the T-gauge.

The company is manufacturing at capacity and selling all that it produces.

REQUIRED:

1. Prepare a variable-costing segmented income statement for the three product lines. Make sure that you separate direct fixed expenses from common fixed expenses.
2. Should the T-gauge line be dropped as the president suggests? Explain.
3. Evaluate the remaining two suggestions of the president (combined with the first). Was the president correct in promoting the P-gauge rather than the D-gauge? Explain.

(CMA adapted)

P21-8
Make or Buy
LO 2, 3

Henderson Company produces two products, A and B. The segmented income statement for a typical quarter is as follows:

	Product A	*Product B*	*Total*
Sales	$150,000	$80,000	$230,000
Less: Variable expenses	(80,000)	(46,000)	(126,000)
Contribution margin	$ 70,000	$34,000	$104,000
Less: Direct fixed expenses[1]	(20,000)	(38,000)	(58,000)
Segment margin	$ 50,000	$(4,000)	$ 46,000
Less: Common fixed expenses			(30,000)
Net income			$ 16,000

[1]Includes depreciation.

Product A uses a subassembly that is purchased from an external supplier for $25 per unit. Each quarter, 2,000 subassemblies are purchased. All units produced are sold, and there are no ending inventories of subassemblies. Henderson is considering making the subassembly rather than buying it. Unit variable manufacturing costs are as follows:

Direct materials	$2
Direct labor	3
Variable overhead	2

Two alternatives exist to supply the productive capacity:

a. Lease the needed space and equipment at a cost of $27,000 per quarter for the space and $10,000 per quarter for a supervisor. There are no other fixed expenses.
b. Drop Product B. The equipment could be adapted with virtually no cost and the existing space utilized to produce the subassembly. The direct fixed expenses, including supervision, would be $38,000, $8,000 of which is depreciation on equipment. If Product B is dropped, there will be no effect on the sales of Product A.

REQUIRED:

1. Should Henderson Company make or buy the subassembly? If it makes the subassembly, which alternative should be chosen? Explain and provide supporting computations.
2. Suppose that dropping Product B will decrease sales of Product A by 6 percent. What effect does this have on the decision?
3. Assume that dropping Product B decreases sales of Product A by 6 percent and that 2,800 subassemblies are required per quarter. As before, assume that there are no ending inventories of subassemblies and that all units produced are sold. Assume also that the per-unit sales price and variable costs are the same as in Requirement 1. Include the leasing alternative in your consideration. Now what is the correct decision?

P21-9
Make or Buy
LO 2, 3

Sportway, Inc., is a wholesale distributor supplying a wide range of moderately priced sporting equipment to large chain stores. About 60 percent of Sportway's products are purchased from other companies while the remainder of the products are manufactured by Sportway. The company's plastics department is currently manufacturing molded fishing tackle boxes. Sportway is able to manufacture and sell 8,000 tackle boxes annually, making full use of its direct labor capacity at available work stations. Following are the selling price and costs associated with Sportway's tackle boxes.

Selling price per box		$86.00
Costs per box:		
Molded plastic	$ 8.00	
Hinges, latches, handle	9.00	
Direct labor ($15/hour)	18.75	
Manufacturing overhead	12.50	
Selling and administrative	17.00	65.25
Profit per box		$20.75

Because Sportway believes it could sell 12,000 tackle boxes if it had sufficient manufacturing capacity, the company has looked into the possibility of purchasing the tackle boxes for distribution. Maple Products, a steady supplier of quality products, would be able to provide up to 9,000 tackle boxes per year at a price of $68 per box delivered to Sportway's facility.

Bart Johnson, Sportway's product manager, has suggested that the company could make better use of its plastics department by manufacturing skateboards. To support his position, Johnson has a market study that indicates an expanding market for skateboards and a need for additional suppliers. Johnson believes that Sportway could expect to sell 17,500 skateboards annually at a price of $45 per skateboard. Johnson's estimate of the costs to manufacture the skateboards is presented below:

Selling price per skateboard		$45.00
Costs per skateboard:		
Molded plastic	$5.50	
Wheels, hardware	7.00	
Direct labor ($15/hour)	7.50	
Manufacturing overhead	5.00	
Selling and administrative cost	9.00	34.00
Profit per skateboard		$11.00

In the plastics department, Sportway uses direct labor hours as the application base for manufacturing overhead. Included in the manufacturing overhead for the current year is $50,000 of factorywide, fixed manufacturing overhead that has been allocated to the plastics department. For each unit of product that Sportway sells, regardless of whether the product has been purchased or is manufactured by Sportway, an allocated $6 fixed overhead cost per unit for distribution is included in the selling and administrative costs for all products. Total selling and administrative costs for the purchased tackle boxes would be $10 per unit.

REQUIRED:

1. In order to maximize the company's profitability, prepare an analysis based on the data presented that will show which product or products Sportway, Inc., should manufacture and/or purchase and will show the associated financial impact. Support your answer with appropriate calculations.
2. Discuss some qualitative factors that might impact on Sportway's decision.

(CMA adapted)

DISCUSSION AND INTERPRETATION PROBLEMS

D21-1
Make or Buy; Ethical Considerations

Pamela McDonald, CMA and controller for Murray Manufacturing, Inc., was having lunch with Roger Branch, manager of the company's power department. Over the past six months, Pamela and Roger had developed a romantic relationship and were making plans for marriage. To keep company gossip at a minimum, Pamela and Roger had kept the relationship very quiet, and no one in the company was aware of it. The topic of the luncheon conversation centered on a decision concerning the company's power department that Larry Johnson, president of the company, was about to make.

Pamela: "Roger, in our last executive meeting, we were told that a local utility company offered to supply power and quoted a price per kilowatt hour that they said would hold for the next three years. They even offered to enter into a contractual agreement with us."

Roger: "This is news to me. Is the bid price a threat to my area? Can they sell us power cheaper than we make it? And why wasn't I informed about this matter? I should have some input. This burns me. I think I should give Larry a call this afternoon and lodge a strong complaint."

Pamela: "Calm down, Roger. The last thing I want you to do is call Larry. Larry made us all promise to keep this whole deal quiet until a decision had been made. He did not want you involved because he wanted to make an unbiased decision. You know that the company is struggling somewhat, and they are looking for ways to save money."

Roger: "Yeah, but at my expense? And at the expense of my department's workers? At my age, I doubt that I could find a job that pays as well and has the same benefits. How much of a threat is this offer?"

Pamela: "Jack Lacy, my assistant controller, prepared an analysis while I was on vacation. It showed that internal production is cheaper than buying, but not by much. Larry asked me to review the findings and submit a final recommendation for next Wednesday's meeting. I've reviewed Jack's analysis and it's faulty. He overlooked the interactions of your department with other service departments. When these are considered, the analysis is overwhelmingly in favor of purchasing the power. The savings are about $300,000 per year."

Roger: "If Larry hears that, my department's gone. Pam, you can't let this happen. I'm three years away from having a vested retirement. And my workers—they have home mortgages, kids in college, families to support. No, it's not right. Pam, just tell him that your assistant's analysis is on target. He'll never know the difference."

Pamela: "Roger, what you're suggesting doesn't sound right either. Would it be ethical for me to fail to disclose this information?"

Roger: "Ethical? Do you think it's right to lay off employees that have been loyal, faithful workers simply to fatten the pockets of the owners of this company? The Murrays already are so rich that they don't know what to do with their money. I think that it's even more unethical to penalize me and my workers. Why should we have to bear the consequences of some bad marketing decisions? Anyway, the effects of those decisions are about gone, and the company should be back to normal within a year or so."

Pamela: "You may be right. Perhaps the well-being of you and your workers is more important than saving $300,000 for the Murrays."

REQUIRED:

1. Should Pamela have told Roger about the impending decision concerning the power department? In revealing this information, did Pamela violate any of the ethical standards described in Chapter 1?
2. Should Pamela provide Larry with the correct data concerning the power department? Or should she protect its workers? What would you do if you were Pamela?

D21-2 Centralize versus Decentralize

Central University, a Midwestern university with approximately 13,000 students, was in the middle of a budget crisis. For the third consecutive year, state appropriations for higher education remained essentially unchanged (the university is currently in its 1994-95 academic year). Yet, utilities, social security benefits, insurance, and other operating expenses have increased. Moreover, the faculty were becoming restless, and some members had begun to leave for other, higher-paying opportunities.

The president and the academic vice-president had announced their intention to eliminate some academic programs and to reduce others. The savings that result would be used to cover the increase in operating expenses and for raises for the remaining faculty. Needless to say, the possible dismissal of tenured faculty aroused a great deal of concern throughout the university.

With this background, the president and academic vice-president called a meeting of all department heads and deans to discuss the budget for the coming year. As the budget was presented, the academic vice-president noted that Continuing Education, a separate, centralized unit, had accumulated a deficit of $504,000 over the past several years, which must be eliminated during the coming fiscal year. The vice-president noted that allocating the deficit equally among the seven colleges would create a hardship on some of the colleges, wiping out all of their operating budget except for salaries.

After some discussion of alternative ways to allocate the deficit, the head of the accounting department suggested an alternative solution: decentralize Continuing Education, allowing each college to assume responsibility for its own continuing education programs. In this way, the overhead of a centralized continuing education department could be avoided.

The academic vice-president responded that the suggestion would be considered, but it was received with little enthusiasm. The vice-president observed that Continuing Education was now generating more revenues than costs—and that the trend was favorable.

A week later, at a meeting of the Deans' Council, the vice-president reviewed the role of Continuing Education. He pointed out that only the dean of Continuing Education held tenure. If Continuing Education were decentralized, her salary ($50,000) would continue; however, she would return to her academic department, and the university would save $20,000 of instructional wages since fewer temporary faculty would be needed in her department. All other employees in the unit were classified as staff. Continuing Education had responsibility for all noncredit offerings. Additionally, it had nominal responsibility for credit courses offered in the evening on campus and for credit courses offered off-campus. However, all scheduling and staffing of these evening and off-campus courses were done by the heads of the academic departments. What courses were offered and who staffed them had to be approved by the head of each department. According to the vice-president, one of the main contributions of the Continuing Education Department to the evening and off-campus programs is advertising. He estimated that $30,000 per year is being spent.

After reviewing this information, the vice-president made available the following information pertaining to the department's performance for the past several years (the 1994-95 data were projections). He once again defended keeping a centralized department, emphasizing the favorable trend revealed by the accounting data. (All numbers are expressed in thousands.)

	1990–91	*1991–92*	*1993–94*	*1994–95*
Tuition revenues:				
Off-campus	$ 300	$ 400	$ 400	$ 410
Evening	—[1]	525	907	1,000
Noncredit	135	305	338	375
Total	$ 435	$ 1,230	$ 1,645	$ 1,785

(continued)

	1990–91	*1991–92*	*1993–94*	*1994–95*
Operating costs:				
Administration	$(132)	$ (160)	$ (112)	$ (112)
Off-campus				
Direct[2]	(230)	(270)	(270)	(260)
Indirect	(350)	(410)	(525)	(440)
Evening	(—)[1]	(220)	(420)	(525)
Noncredit	(135)	(305)	(338)	(375)
Total	$(847)	$(1,365)	$(1,665)	$(1,712)
Income (loss)	$(412)	$ (135)	$ (20)	$ 73

[1]In 1990–91, the department had no responsibility for evening courses. Beginning in 1995, it was given the responsibility to pay for any costs of instruction incurred when temporary or adjunct faculty were hired to teach evening courses. Tuition revenues earned by evening courses also began to be assigned to the department at the same time.
[2]Instructional wages.

The dean of the College of Business was unimpressed by the favorable trend identified by the academic vice-president. The dean maintained that decentralization still would be in the best interests of the university. He argued that although decentralization would not fully solve the deficit, it would provide a sizable contribution each year to the operating budgets for each of the seven colleges.

The academic vice-president disagreed vehemently. He was convinced that Continuing Education was now earning its own way and would continue to produce additional resources for the university.

REQUIRED: You have been asked by the president of Central University to assess which alternative, centralization or decentralization, is in the best interest of the school. The president is willing to decentralize provided that significant savings can be produced and the mission of the Continuing Education Department will still be carried out. Prepare a memo to the president that details your analysis and reasoning and recommends one of the two alternatives. Provide both qualitative and quantitative reasoning in the memo.

D21-3 Research Assignment

"Dumping" is an accusation that is often made against foreign companies. Japanese automobile companies, for example, have been accused of this practice.

REQUIRED: Go to the library and find out the following:

1. What is "dumping"?
2. Why do international trade agreements usually prohibit dumping? Do you agree that its prohibition is good for the American consumer? Explain.
3. Explain how the relevant costing principles learned in this chapter relate to dumping.
4. Provide several examples of companies accused of dumping. See if you can determine the outcome of an accusation made against some company. Why do you suppose that international companies pursue dumping even though it's prohibited? What are the ethical implications?

CHAPTER 22
CAPITAL BUDGETING

LEARNING OBJECTIVES

After studying this chapter, you should be able to:

1. Explain what a capital investment decision is and distinguish between independent and mutually exclusive projects.
2. Compute the payback period and accounting rate of return for a proposed investment and explain their role in capital investment decisions.
3. Use net present value analysis for capital investment decisions involving independent projects.
4. Use the internal rate of return to assess the acceptability of an independent project.
5. Explain why NPV is better than IRR for capital investment decisions involving mutually exclusive projects.
6. Convert gross cash flows to after-tax cash flows.
7. Describe capital investment in the advanced manufacturing environment.

Scenario

Tasty Food Corporation, a large food-store chain, is considering investing in an automated deposit processing system for all of its stores.[1] An investment of $2 million would provide the system for all 150 existing stores as well as for the 30 stores to be opened by the beginning of the following year. The president of TastyFood assigned the responsibility to assess the investment to a special capital acquisitions committee. The first act of the committee was to design a pilot study to test such a system in seven stores for a period of nine months.

At the end of the nine months, Maryanne Wise, chair of the capital acquisitions committee and vice-president of finance, scheduled a committee meeting to evaluate the outcome of the pilot study. Besides Maryanne, the committee included Stan Miller, controller; Ron Thomas, vice-president of operations; and Paula Summers, area supervisor for the seven stores where the pilot study was conducted.

"As you recall," Maryanne remarked, "we met more than nine months ago and agreed to implement a pilot study before committing ourselves to an automated deposit system. Because of her close scrutiny of the project, Paula has agreed to give us a summary of the benefits observed in the pilot study."

"I'm extremely pleased with the results of the pilot study," Paula replied, "as I think you will be. To quantify the financial impact of this project, I have classified the benefits into four categories: immediate, near term, indirect, and potential for future. Immediate benefits are those that are available in a store as soon as the equipment is operational. Near-term benefits are those that will be realized only after the local system is connected to the store computer. Indirect benefits are those that accrue from the project but are more difficult to quantify. Potential future benefits can result from the ability of the system to interface directly with the accounting system. Here is a handout that describes some of the specific benefits found in each category."

SPECIFIC BENEFITS BY CATEGORY

Immediate Benefits:

1. *Bank Charge Reduction.* An automated deposit processing system reduces the charges for processing checks since it encodes the dollar amount on all checks prior to depositing them.
2. *Productivity Gains.* Automation of the system reduces the amount of additional payroll required during the busy season.
3. *Forms Cost Reduction.* Automation of the system eliminates nearly 3 million documents used per year to process deposits manually.

Near-Term Benefits:

Reduction of Cash Shortages. Once the system is connected to the store computer, a cash variance analysis can be provided the next day. Currently,

1. The facts of this case are based on an actual food-store chain; however, the name of the chain has been disguised.

this analysis is performed manually at headquarters and is several weeks old by the time it arrives in the store. The ability to respond more quickly to cash shortages should reduce annual losses.

Indirect Benefits:

1. *Greater Data Integrity.* By reducing manual calculations, greater data integrity will result. This will decrease time spent on making corrections to incorrect deposit information.
2. *Lower Training Costs.* Since the system is simpler and has fewer forms, new cashiers and new store openings should require less training time.

Potential for future benefits:

Interfacing Abilities. By processing data through the store computer to the host computer in headquarters, an interface program at the host can provide savings in time to both the sales audit and cash/banking calculations by eliminating manual entries and expediting bank reconciliations.

"After seeing these benefits, I'm convinced that automatic deposits are a good idea," observed Ron Thomas. "In fact, I wonder why we weren't smart enough to do this years ago. Since I'm also convinced that committees are notorious for wasting time and resources, I move that we attach Paula's handout to a recommendation to implement the automated system for the entire company. Then, we can get back to more pressing matters."

"Wait a minute!" interjected Stan. "While the description of the benefits of the automated system is impressive, we shouldn't be too hasty in our decisions. After all, we are talking about investing $2 million. We need to be certain that this is a sound investment."

"But that's the whole point, Stan. The benefits make it clear that the investment is sound. Why waste any more time deliberating over an obvious conclusion? We could spend hours discussing a matter that is already clearly decided. What do you say, Maryanne? Can we vote on this matter and adjourn?"

"Well, Ron, we can—if you will first answer the following questions. How much will this investment increase the profits of the firm? What effect will it have on our overall value? Will the investment earn at least the return required by company policy? How long will it take for us to recover the investment through the savings alluded to in Paula's handout? Only when we know the answers to some of those questions can we accurately assess the soundness of the investment. The pilot study provides us with the fundamental information we need to estimate the future cash savings associated with automation. Once we have these estimates, we can use some financial models to assess the merits of the proposed investment. Stan, for our next meeting, please bring estimates of the cash flows over the life of the proposed system. I will come prepared to discuss some of the financial models that will help us assess the financial merits of the investment."

TYPES OF CAPITAL INVESTMENT DECISIONS

Objective 1
Explain what a capital investment decision is and distinguish between independent and mutually exclusive projects.

capital investment decisions

The problem of whether to invest or not invest in an automated deposit processing system is an example of a capital investment decision. **Capital investment decisions** are concerned with the process of planning, setting goals and priorities, arranging financing, and using certain criteria to select long-term assets. The acquisition of long-term assets usually involves a significant outlay of funds, often referred to as *capital outlays.* As the case at the opening of the chapter illustrates, estimating a project's cash flows and using them to assess the project's soundness are critical steps in a capital investment decision. How cash flows can be used to evaluate the merits of a proposed project is the focus of this chapter and the next. We will study some of the financial models that Maryanne was planning to discuss in her next committee meeting.

Because capital investment decisions place large amounts of resources at risk for long periods of time and simultaneously affect the future development of the firm, they are among the most important decisions managers make. Every organization has limited resources, which should be used to maintain or enhance its long-run profitability. Poor capital investment decisions can be disastrous. For example, the failure of the American steel industry to upgrade its production facilities has proved to be a mistake. Foreign competitors with more modern facilities have been able to produce more steel at lower costs. The current state of the American steel industry would be significantly better if the right capital investment decisions had been made years ago.

capital budgeting
independent projects

The process of making capital investment decisions is often referred to as **capital budgeting.** Two types of capital budgeting projects will be considered. **Independent projects** are projects that, if accepted or rejected, do not affect the cash flows of other projects. Suppose that the managers of the marketing and the research and development departments jointly propose the addition of a new product line that would entail making significant outlays for working capital and equipment. If no other new product lines are being considered and the new product line is not complementary with existing product lines, the decision involving the new product line stands alone. Since it is independent of other proposals, the project can be evaluated on its own merits.

mutually exclusive projects

The second type of capital budgeting project requires a firm to choose among several alternatives that will provide the same basic service. Acceptance of one option precludes the acceptance of another. Thus, **mutually exclusive projects** are those projects that, if accepted, preclude the acceptance of all other competing projects. For example, TastyFoods was considering replacing its existing manual deposit processing system with an automated system. Part of the company's deliberation would concern different types of automated systems. If three different automated systems were being considered, there are four alternatives in all—the current system plus the three potential new systems. Once one system is chosen, the other three are excluded; they are mutually exclusive.

Notice that one of the competing alternatives in the example is maintaining the status quo (the manual system). This emphasizes the fact that new investments that replace existing investments must prove to be economically superior. Of course, at times replacement of the old system is mandatory and not discretionary if the firm wishes to remain in business (e.g., equipment in the old system may be worn out, making the old system not a viable alternative). In such a situation, going out of business could be a viable alternative, especially if none of the new investment alternatives is profitable.

Capital investment decisions often are concerned with investments in long-term capital assets. With the exception of land, these assets depreciate over their lives, and the original investment is used up as the assets are employed. In general terms, a sound capital investment will earn back its original capital outlay over its life and, at the same time, provide a reasonable return on the original investment. Thus, one task of a manager is to decide whether or not a capital investment will earn back its original outlay and provide a reasonable return. By making this assessment, a manager can decide on the acceptability of independent projects and compare competing projects on the basis of their economic merits. But what is meant by reasonable return? It is generally agreed that any new project must cover the *opportunity cost* of the funds invested. Furthermore, it is usually assumed that managers should select projects that promise to maximize the wealth of the owners of the firm.

To make a capital investment decision, a manager must estimate the quantity and timing of cash flows, assess the risk of the investment, and consider the impact of the project on the firm's profits. One of the most difficult tasks is to estimate the cash flows. Projections must be made years into the future, and forecasting is far from a perfect science. Obviously, as the accuracy of cash-flow forecasts increases, the reliability of the decision improves. Although forecasting future cash flows is a critical part of the capital budgeting process, forecasting methods will not be considered here. They are best left to more advanced courses. Consequently, cash flows are assumed to be known; the focus will be on making capital investment decisions *given* these cash flows. However, the discussion will reveal the sensitivity of decisions to changes in the given cash flows.

Managers must set goals and priorities for capital investments. They also must identify some basic criteria for the acceptance or rejection of proposed investments. Another problem faced by managers is ranking acceptable investments in order of their value to the firm. In this chapter, we will study four basic methods to guide managers in accepting or rejecting potential investments. The methods include both nondiscounting and discounting decision approaches (two methods are discussed for each approach). The discounting methods are applied to investment decisions involving both independent and mutually exclusive projects.

NONDISCOUNTING MODELS

Objective 2
Compute the payback period and accounting rate of return for a proposed investment and explain their role in capital investment decisions.

nondiscounting models
discounting models

The basic capital investment decision models can be classified into two major categories: nondiscounting models and discounting models. **Nondiscounting models** ignore the time value of money, whereas **discounting models** explicitly consider it. Although many accounting theorists disparage the nondiscounting models because they ignore the time value of money, many firms continue to use these models in making capital investment decisions.[2] However, the use of discounting models has increased over the years, and few firms use only one

2. The time value of money conveys the notion that a dollar now is worth more than a dollar one period from now. The reason, of course, is that a dollar now can be invested so that one period from now we get back the dollar plus some return on the investment.

model—indeed, firms seem to use both types of models.[3] This suggests that both categories supply useful information to managers as they struggle to make a capital investment decision.

Payback Period

payback period

One type of nondiscounting model is the payback period. The **payback period** is the time required for a firm to recover its original investment. For example, if the original investment is $100,000, and the firm expects the project to generate annual cash flows at $50,000, the payback period is two years ($100,000/$50,000). When the cash flows of a project are assumed to be even, the following formula can be used to compute its payback period:

Payback period = Original investment/Annual cash inflow

If, however, the cash flows are uneven, the payback period is computed by adding the annual cash flows until such time as the original investment is recovered. If a fraction of a year is needed, it is assumed that cash flows occur evenly within each year. For example, suppose that an original investment of $100,000 has a life of five years with the following expected annual cash flows: $30,000, $30,000, $20,000, $40,000, and $50,000. The payback period for the project is 3.5 years, computed as follows: $30,000 (1 year) + $30,000 (1 year) + $20,000 (1 year) + $20,000 (0.5 year) = $100,000 (3.5 years). Notice that in the fourth year, when only $20,000 is needed and $40,000 is available, the amount of time required to earn the $20,000 is found by dividing the amount needed by the annual cash flow ($20,000/$40,000). Exhibit 22-1 summarizes this analysis.

One way to use the payback period is to set a maximum payback period for all projects and to reject any project that exceeds this level. Why would a firm use the payback period in this way? Some analysts suggest that the payback

Exhibit 22-1
Payback Analysis: Uneven Cash Flows

Year	*Unrecovered Investment (Beginning of Year)*	*Annual Cash Flow*
1	$100,000	$30,000
2	70,000	30,000
3	40,000	20,000
4	20,000[a]	40,000[a]
5	—	50,000

[a]At the beginning of Year 4, $20,000 is needed to recover the investment. Since an inflow of $40,000 is expected, only 0.5 years is needed to recover the $20,000. Thus, the payback is 3.5 years.

3. In the mid-1950s, Robichek and McDonald reported that only 9 percent of large firms were using discounting models; by 1975, Petry reported that 66 percent of large firms were using these techniques. Also in 1975, Petty, Scott, and Bird surveyed Fortune 500 firms and found that 63.4 percent of the respondents used discounting models as their primary evaluation technique, with most of the remaining firms using them as secondary techniques. The same study also found that more than half of the firms used nondiscounting models as either a primary or a secondary evaluation technique. For additional detail, see A. A. Robichek and J. G. McDonald, "Financial Planning in Transition, Long Range Planning Service," Report No. 268 (Menlo Park, Calif.: Stanford Research Institute, January 1966); G. H. Petry, "Effective Use of Capital Budgeting Tools," *Business Horizons*, Vol. 18, No. 5 (October 1975), pp. 57–65; J. W. Petty, D. F. Scott, and M. M. Bird, "The Capital Budgeting Decision Making Process of Large Corporations," *The Engineering Economist*, Vol. 20, No. 3 (Spring 1975), pp. 159–86.

period can be used as a rough measure of risk, with the notion that the longer it takes for a project to pay for itself, the riskier it is. Also, firms with riskier cash flows could require a shorter payback period than normal. Additionally, firms with liquidity problems would be more interested in projects with quick paybacks. Another critical concern is obsolescence. In some industries, the risk of obsolescence is high; firms within these industries would be interested in recovering funds rapidly.

Another reason, less beneficial to the firm, may also be at work. Many managers in a position to make capital investment decisions may choose investments with quick payback periods out of self-interest. If a manager's performance is measured using such short-run criteria as annual net income, he or she may choose projects with quick paybacks to show improved net income as quickly as possible. Consider that division managers often are responsible for making capital investment decisions and are evaluated on divisional profit. The tenure of divisional managers, however, is typically short—three to five years would be average. Consequently, the incentive is for such managers to shy away from investments that promise healthy long-run returns but relatively meager returns in the short run.

The payback period can be used to choose among competing alternatives. Under this approach, the investment with the shortest payback period is preferred over investments with longer payback periods. However, this use of the payback period is less defensible because this measure suffers from two major deficiencies: (1) it ignores the performance of the investments beyond the payback period and (2) it ignores the time value of money.

These two significant deficiencies are easily illustrated. Assume that two competing investments, A and B, each requiring an initial outlay of $100,000, have a five-year life and display the following annual cash flows:

Investment	*Year 1*	*Year 2*	*Year 3*	*Year 4*	*Year 5*
A	$80,000	$20,000	$20,000	$20,000	$20,000
B	20,000	80,000	5,000	5,000	5,000

Both investments have payback periods of two years. Thus, if a manager uses the payback period to choose among competing investments, the two investments would be equally desirable. In reality, however, A should be preferred over B for two reasons. First, A provides a much larger dollar return for the years beyond the payback period ($60,000 versus $15,000). Second, A returns $80,000 in the first year while B returns only $20,000. The extra $60,000 that A provides in the first year could be put to productive use, such as investing it in another project. It is better to have a dollar now than one year from now because the dollar on hand can be invested to provide a return one year from now.

In summary, the payback period provides to managers information that can be used as follows:

1. To help control the risks associated with the uncertainty of future cash flows
2. To help minimize the impact of an investment on a firm's liquidity problems
3. To help control the risk of obsolescence
4. To help control the effect of the investment on performance measures

However, the method suffers significant deficiencies: it ignores a project's total profitability and the time value of money. While the computation of the payback period may be useful to a manager, relying on it solely for a capital investment decision would be foolish.

Accounting Rate of Return

accounting rate of return

The accounting rate of return is the second commonly used nondiscounting model. The **accounting rate of return** measures the return on a project in terms of income, as opposed to using a project's cash flow. The accounting rate of return is computed by the following formula:

Accounting rate of return = Average income/Investment

The average income of a project is obtained by adding the net income for each year of the project and then dividing this total by the number of years. Average net income for a project can be approximated by subtracting average depreciation from average cash flow. Assuming that all revenues earned in a period are collected and depreciation is the only noncash expense, the approximation is exact.

Investment can be defined as the original investment or as the average investment. Letting I equal original investment, S equal salvage value, and assuming that investment is uniformly consumed, average investment is defined as follows:[4]

$$\text{Average investment} = (I + S)/2$$

To illustrate the computation of the accounting rate of return, assume that an investment requires an initial outlay of $100,000. The life of the investment is five years with the following cash flows: $30,000, $30,000, $40,000, $30,000, $50,000. Assume that the asset has no salvage value after the five years and all revenues earned within a year are collected in that year. The total cash flow for the five years is $180,000, making the average cash flow $36,000 ($180,000/5). Average depreciation is $20,000 ($100,000/5). The average net income is the difference between these two figures: $16,000 ($36,000 − $20,000). Using the average net income and original investment, the accounting rate of return is 16 percent ($16,000/$100,000). If average investment is used instead of original investment, the accounting rate of return would be 32 percent ($16,000/$50,000).

Often debt contracts require that a firm maintain certain financial accounting ratios, which can be affected by the income reported and by the level of long-term assets. Accordingly, the accounting rate of return may be used as a screening measure to ensure that any new investment will not adversely affect these ratios. Additionally, because bonuses to managers are often based on accounting income, they may have a personal interest in seeing that any new investment contributes significantly to net income. A manager seeking to maximize personal income will select investments that return the highest net income per dollar invested.

Unlike the payback period, the accounting rate of return does consider a project's profitability; like the payback period, it ignores the time value of money. Ignoring the time value of money is a critical deficiency in this method as well; it can lead a manager to choose investments that do not maximize profits. For

4. The average investment formula is computed using the definition of the average value of a function and requires the use of calculus. The investment consumption function is $C(t) = I + [(S - I)/t^*]t$, where t is time and t^* is the life of the investment. By integrating $C(t)$ from 0 to t^* and dividing the result by t^*, the expression $(I + S)/2$ is obtained.

example, assume that two investments, A and B, each require an outlay of \$100,000 and have no salvage value. Suppose they generate the following cash flows:

Investment	*Year 1*	*Year 2*	*Year 3*	*Year 4*	*Year 5*
A	\$80,000	\$20,000	\$20,000	\$20,000	\$20,000
B	20,000	80,000	20,000	20,000	20,000

The average cash flow is \$32,000 for each investment, the average depreciation is \$20,000, and, therefore, the average net income is \$12,000. Using original investment, the accounting rate of return for both projects is 12 percent (\$12,000/\$100,000). Using the accounting rate of return criterion, a manager would find both investments equally desirable. As before, however, A is preferable to B because it allows the firm to reinvest an extra \$60,000 one year sooner than does B.

discounted cash flows

It is because the payback period and the accounting rate of return ignore the time value of money that they are referred to as *nondiscounting models.* Discounting models use **discounted cash flows,** which are future cash flows expressed in terms of their present value.[5]

DISCOUNTING MODELS: THE NET PRESENT VALUE METHOD

Objective 3
Use net present value analysis for capital investment decisions involving independent projects.

Discounting models explicitly consider the time value of money and, therefore, incorporate the concept of discounting cash inflows and outflows. Two discounting models will be considered: *net present value* (NPV) and *internal rate of return* (IRR). The net present value method will be discussed first; the internal rate of return method is discussed in the following section.

net present value

Net present value is the difference in the present value of the cash inflows and outflows associated with a project:

$$\begin{aligned} NPV &= [\textstyle\sum CF_t/(1+i)^t] - I \\ &= [\textstyle\sum (CF_t)(df_t)] - I \\ &= P - I \end{aligned} \qquad (22.1)$$

where I = The present value of the project's cost (usually the initial outlay)
CF_t = The cash inflow to be received in period t, with $t = 1 \ldots n$
i = The required rate of return
n = The useful life of the project
t = The time period
P = The present value of the project's future cash inflows

A Defining Example

A simple, one-period example will be used to develop an understanding of net present value. Assume that Nancy Wilson is approached by a friend who offers her an opportunity to invest \$1,000 in a business venture. The friend assures Nancy that one year from now she will receive a payoff of \$1,200. Currently, Nancy has \$500 in a money market account that will earn 8-percent interest for

5. See the module at the beginning of Part 3 for a review of future and present value concepts.

the coming year. To raise the other $500, Nancy would need to borrow $500 from the local credit union at a cost of 12 percent per year. Both principal and interest will be repaid at the end of the year. Nancy is confident that she can afford to invest the $1,000 but is not certain that it would make her better off. Should she accept the friend's offer and make the investment?

Choice of a Discount Rate. In answering the question, first consider the rate of return that Nancy would require. If she removes the $500 from the money-market account, she will lose the 8 percent interest for the coming year, creating an opportunity cost of $40 (0.08 × $500). Also, if she borrows $500 from the credit union, she must pay interest of 12 percent, or $60 (0.12 × $500). Thus, to break even, she would need to recover the $1,000 invested and earn a return of $100 ($40 + $60). Any return above the $100 would increase her economic well-being and make the investment desirable. The $100 return itself represents Nancy's **cost of capital,** the weighted average of the costs of funds from all sources. The rate of return corresponding to the cost of capital would be 10 percent ($100/$1,000) and is defined as the **required rate of return.** It is also referred to as the **hurdle rate.** Exhibit 22-2 summarizes Nancy's capital requirements.

cost of capital

required rate of return

hurdle rate

Exhibit 22-2 illustrates that the cost of capital is a blend of the costs of capital from all sources. In fact, it is a weighted average of the costs from the various sources, where the weight is defined by the relative amount from each source. For our example, $500 from savings and $500 from a loan represent the sources of the total $1,000 of capital. Thus, each source contributes 50 percent ($500/$1,000) to the total capital raised. The relative weights, then, are 0.5 for savings and 0.5 for the loan. As the note in Exhibit 22-2 shows, the weighted cost of capital can also be computed by using the relative weights and the individual rates.

Net Present Value: A Measure of Profitability. For Nancy to earn a profit, her investment must return more than $1,100 one year from now (the $1,000 invested plus $100 to cover her cost of capital). Since the investment will return $1,200, Nancy will earn a profit of $100 ($1,200 − $1,100). This profit, however, is expressed in future dollars. The profit can also be expressed in *current* dollars by computing its present value. Using the discount rate of 10 percent for one year (0.90909), the present value of $100 is $90.91 ($100 × 0.90909). The profit of the investment, expressed in current dollars, is equivalent to the project's net present value. To see this, apply the definition of net present value, using the required rate of return of 10 percent.

Exhibit 22-2
Cost of Capital Illustrated

Source	Amount of Capital	Percentage Cost	Dollar Cost
Savings	$ 500	8%	$ 40
Loan	500	12%	60
Total	$1,000	10%[1]	$100

[1]This weighted average can be computed in two ways:
1. $100/$1,000 = 0.10
2. (0.5 × 0.08) + (0.5 × 0.12) = 0.10

Year	Cash Flow (CF)	Discount Factor (df)[1]	Present Value [CF (df)]
0	$(1,000)	1.00000	$(1,000.00)
1	1,200	0.90909	1,090.91
Net present value			$ 90.91

[1]From Appendix B, Table 3

If the net present value is positive, it signals that (1) the initial investment has been recovered, (2) the cost of capital has been recovered, and (3) a return in excess of (1) and (2) has been received. Thus, if NPV is greater than zero, the investment is profitable and therefore is acceptable. If NPV equals zero, the decision maker will find acceptance or rejection of the investment equal. Finally, if NPV is less than zero, the investment should be rejected. In this case, it is earning less than the required rate of return.

Summary and Discussion of Net Present Value Concepts

The Nancy Wilson example was designed to be as simple as possible in order to develop the concepts pertaining to the use of the net present value method. The following important concepts were brought out by the example:

1. Net present value (NPV) measures the profitability of an investment. If the NPV is positive, it measures the increase in wealth. For a firm, this means that the size of a positive NPV measures the increase in the value of the firm resulting from an investment.
2. To use the NPV method, a discount rate must be identified. The appropriate discount rate for NPV analysis is the firm's cost of capital. The cost of capital is a weighted average of the cost of capital from all sources.

NPV and Firm Value. Although the example was based on an investment decision faced by an individual, the concepts apply equally well to organizations. Accordingly, if the firm's goal is to maximize its market value, a manager should select a portfolio of projects that promises the highest total NPV.

Cost of Capital. For a firm, the cost of capital should reflect the returns expected by the different parties contributing funds. Essentially, the cost of capital is the opportunity cost of funds provided to the firm. Sources of funds for a firm include debt, the contributions of common stockholders, and the contributions of preferred stockholders. Thus, for a firm, the weighted average cost of capital is the after-tax cost of debt, preferred stock, and common stock. The weights are equal to the proportion of total financing that is provided by each source of capital. For example, assume that a firm used debt, common equity, and preferred stock for financing with after-tax costs of 7 percent, 14 percent, and 11 percent, respectively. The proportion of each type of financing in the firm's financial structure is 20 percent for debt, 60 percent for common equity, and 20 percent for preferred stock. Using these proportions as weights, the firm's cost of capital would be computed as follows (letting K = cost of capital):

$$\begin{aligned} K &= 0.2(0.07) + 0.6(0.14) + 0.2(0.11) \\ &= 0.12 \end{aligned}$$

How the cost of each source of capital is computed is discussed in finance texts and occasionally in advanced cost accounting texts. At this point, what should be understood is that each source of capital has a cost attached to it and contributes to the firm's overall cost of capital.

A More Realistic Example Using Net Present Value

Golden Toys Inc. has developed a new toy laser gun that it believes is superior to anything on the market. The marketing manager is excited about the new toy's prospects after completing a detailed market study that revealed expected annual revenues of $150,000. The toy has a projected life of five years. Equipment to produce the toy gun would cost $160,000. After five years, that equipment can be sold for $20,000. In addition to equipment, working capital is expected to increase by $20,000 because of increases in inventories and receivables. The firm expects to recover the investment in working capital at the end of the project's life. Annual cash operating expenses are estimated at $90,000. Assuming that the required rate of return is 12 percent, should the company manufacture the new toy laser gun?

In order to answer the question, two steps must be taken: (1) the cash flows for each year must be identified and (2) the NPV must be computed using the cash flows from Step 1. The solution to the problem is given in Exhibit 22-3.

Notice that Step 2 offers two approaches for computing NPV. Step 2A computes NPV by using discount factors from Table 3 in Appendix B. Step 2B simplifies the computation by using a single discount factor from Table 4 in Appendix B for the even cash flows occurring in Years 1–4.

DISCOUNTING MODELS: INTERNAL RATE OF RETURN

Objective 4
Use the internal rate of return to assess the acceptability of an independent project.

internal rate of return

Another discounting model is the internal rate of return (IRR) method. The **internal rate of return** is defined as the interest rate that sets the present value of a project's cash inflows equal to the present value of the project's cost. In other words, it is the interest rate that sets the project's NPV at zero. The following equation can be used to determine a project's IRR:

$$I = \sum CF_t/(1 + i)^t \quad (22.2)$$

Where $t = 1 \ldots n$

Once the IRR for a project is computed, it is compared with the firm's required rate of return. If the IRR is greater than the required rate, the project is deemed acceptable; if the IRR is equal to the required rate of return, acceptance or rejection of the investment is equal; if the IRR is less than the required rate of return, the project is rejected.

The internal rate of return is the most widely used of the capital investment techniques. One reason for its popularity may be that it is a rate of return, a concept that managers are comfortable in using. Another possibility is that managers may believe (in most cases, incorrectly) that the IRR is the true or actual compounded rate of return being earned by the initial investment. Whatever the reasons for its popularity, a basic understanding of the IRR is necessary. As with NPV, we will begin with a simple example.

Exhibit 22-3
Cash Flows and NPV Analysis

Step 1. Cash-Flow Identification

Year	*Item*	*Cash Flow*
0	Equipment	$(160,000)
	Working capital	(20,000)
	Total	$(180,000)
1–4	Revenues	$ 150,000
	Operating expenses	(90,000)
	Total	$ 60,000
5	Revenues	$ 150,000
	Operating expenses	(90,000)
	Salvage	20,000
	Recovery of working capital	20,000
	Total	$ 100,000

Step 2A. NPV Analysis

Year	*Cash Flow*[1]	*Discount Factor*[2]	*Present Value*
0	$(180,000)	1.00000	$(180,000)
1	$ 60,000	0.89286	53,572
2	60,000	0.79719	47,831
3	60,000	0.71178	42,707
4	60,000	0.63552	38,131
5	100,000	0.56743	56,743
Net present value			$ 58,984

Step 2B. NPV Analysis

Year	*Cash Flow*	*Discount Factor*[3]	*Present Value*
0	$(180,000)	1.00000	$(180,000)
1–4	60,000	3.03735	182,241
5	100,000	0.56743	56,743
Net present value			$ 58,984[3]

[1]From Step 1
[2]From Appendix B, Table 3
[3]From Appendix B, Tables 3 and 4

Single-Period Example

Recall that Nancy Wilson has the opportunity to invest $1,000 now for a return of $1,200 one year from now. Nancy is able to acquire the necessary capital by borrowing $500 from a credit union and removing $500 from her savings account. The cost of using this capital is 10 percent. The question is whether Nancy should make the investment.

Using the IRR criterion, the investment should be accepted only if the IRR is greater than 10 percent. To compute the IRR, the interest rate that equates the present value of \$1,200 to the investment of \$1,000 must be identified. Using Equation 22.2, the IRR for the investment being considered by Nancy is computed as follows:

$$
\begin{aligned}
I &= CF_t/(1+i)^t \\
\$1{,}000 &= \$1{,}200/(1 + i) \\
\$1{,}000\,(1 + i) &= \$1{,}200 \\
1 + i &= \$1{,}200/\$1{,}000 \\
1 + i &= 1.20 \\
i &= 1.20 - 1 \\
i &= 0.20
\end{aligned}
$$

Thus, the IRR is 0.20, or 20 percent.

Since the internal rate of return is 20 percent, the investment should be accepted. This rate is greater than the required rate of return, which is only 10 percent (remember that the required rate of return is equal to the cost of capital). In the special case of a one-period analysis, the IRR represents the actual or true rate of return being earned by the investment [the actual rate of return for the one period is (\$1,200 − \$1,000)/\$1,000 = 0.20]. This result, however, holds for the multiple-period case only if a project's cash inflows are reinvested to earn its internal rate of return. More will be said about this later.

Multiple-Period Setting: Uniform Cash Flows

To illustrate the computation of the IRR in a multiple-period setting, assume that Nancy has an opportunity to invest \$1,200 in order to receive \$569.67 at the end of each year for the next three years. The IRR is the interest rate that equates the present value of the three equal receipts of \$569.67 to the investment of \$1,200. Since the series of cash flows is uniform, a single discount factor from Table 4 (Appendix B) can be used to compute the present value of the annuity. Letting *df* be this discount factor and *CF* be the annual cash flow, Equation 22.2 assumes the following form:

$$I = CF(df)$$

Solving for *df*, we obtain:

$$
\begin{aligned}
df &= I/CF \\
&= \textit{Investment}/\textit{Annual cash flow}
\end{aligned}
$$

Once the discount factor is computed, go to Table 4 and find the row corresponding to the life of the project, then move across that row until the computed discount factor is found. The interest rate corresponding to this discount factor is the IRR.

For example, the discount factor for Nancy's investment is 2.10648 (\$1,200/\$569.67). Since the life of the investment is three years, we must find the third row in Table 4 and then move across this row until we encounter 2.10648. The interest rate corresponding to 2.10648 is 20 percent, which is the IRR.

Table 4 does not provide discount factors for every possible interest rate. If a discount factor is computed for a series of uniform cash flows and it falls between two discount factors found in the table, the interest rate can be approximated by using interpolation. To illustrate, assume that the annual cash inflows expected by Nancy are \$578.49 instead of \$569.67. The new discount factor is 2.07436 (\$1,200/\$578.49). Going once again to the third row in Table 4, we find that the discount factor—and thus the IRR—lies between 20 and 22 percent.

Exhibit 22-4
IRR: Approximation Using Interpolation

Interest Interval	*Discount Factor Interval*
20%	2.10648
22	2.04224
2%	0.06424

Distance of IRR into Discount Factor Interval	
Discount factor, 20%	2.10648
Discount factor, IRR	(2.07436)
Absolute distance	0.03212
Relative distance	0.03212/0.06424 = 0.5

Approximation of IRR

$$\text{IRR} \sim 0.20 + (0.5)(0.02)$$
$$\sim 0.21$$

The IRR can be approximated by defining an *interest interval* and a *discount interval* and by assuming that the IRR is the same *relative* distance into the interest interval as the discount factor is into the discount interval. This approximation of the IRR is illustrated in Exhibit 22-4. Of course, a business calculator can provide a direct assessment of the IRR and makes interpolation unnecessary.

Multiple-Period Setting: Uneven Cash Flows

If the cash flows are not uniform, Equation 22.2 must be used. For a multiple-period setting, Equation 22.2 can be solved by trial and error or by using a business calculator. To show solution by trial and error, assume a \$1,000 investment produces cash flows of \$600 and \$720 for each of 2 years. The IRR is the interest rate that sets the present value of these 2 cash inflows equal to \$1,000:

$$P = [\$600/(1 + i)] + [\$720/(1 + i)^2]$$
$$= \$1,000$$

To solve the above equation by trial and error, select a possible value for i. Given this first guess, the present value of the future cash flows is computed and compared to the initial investment. If the present value is greater than the initial investment, the interest rate is too low; if the present value is less than the initial investment, the interest rate is too high. The next guess is adjusted accordingly.

Assume the first guess to be 14 percent. Using i equal to 0.14, Table 3 (Appendix B) yields the following discount factors: 0.87719 and 0.76947. These discount factors produce the following present value for the two cash inflows:

$$P = (0.87719 \times \$600) + (0.76947 \times \$720)$$
$$= \$1,080.33$$

Since P is greater than \$1,000, the interest rate selected is too low. A higher guess is needed. If the next guess is 24 percent, we obtain the following:

$$P = (0.80645 \times \$600) + (0.65036 \times \$720)$$
$$= \$952.13$$

Since P is less than $1,000, the interest rate is too high. We now know that the IRR is between 14 and 24 percent. Once a present value above and below the investment is found, interpolation can be used to approximate the IRR, using a present value interval and an interest interval. The present value interval is ($1,080.33, $952.13) with a length of 128.20. The interest interval is (0.14, 0.24) with a length of 0.10. For the IRR, we know that P equals $1,000. The actual distance into the present value interval for the present value corresponding to the IRR is 80.33 ($1,080.33 − $1,000). The relative distance is 0.63 (80.33/128.20). Thus, IRR is approximately 20.3 percent [0.14 + (0.62 × 0.10)]. Since the closest value to 20.3 percent in Table 3 in Appendix B is 20 percent, this value becomes our next guess:

$$P = (0.83333 \times \$600) + (0.69444 \times \$720)$$
$$= \$999.99$$

Since this value is very close to $1,000, we can say that the IRR is 20 percent. (The IRR is, in fact, exactly 20 percent; the present value is slightly less than the investment because of rounding error in the discount factors found in Table 3.)

MUTUALLY EXCLUSIVE PROJECTS

Objective 5
Explain why NPV is better than IRR for capital investment decisions involving mutually exclusive projects.

Up to this point, we have focused on independent projects. Many capital investment decisions, however, involve mutually exclusive projects. How NPV analysis is used to choose among competing projects is an interesting question. An even more interesting question to consider is whether NPV and IRR differ in their ability to help managers make wealth-maximizing decisions in the presence of competing alternatives. For example, we already know that the nondiscounting models can produce erroneous choices because they ignore the time value of money. Because of this deficiency, the discounting models are judged superior. Similarly, it can be shown that the NPV model is generally preferred to the IRR model when choosing among mutually exclusive alternatives.

NPV Compared with IRR

NPV and IRR both yield the same decision for independent projects; for example, if the NPV is greater than zero, then the IRR is also greater than the required rate of return; both models signal the correct decision. However, for competing projects, the two methods can produce different results. Intuitively, we believe that for mutually exclusive projects, the project with the highest NPV or the highest IRR should be chosen. Since it is possible for the two methods to produce different rankings of mutually exclusive projects, the method that consistently reveals the wealth-maximizing project should be preferred. As will be shown, the NPV method is that model.

NPV differs from IRR in two major ways. First, NPV assumes that each cash inflow received is reinvested at the required rate of return, whereas the IRR method assumes that each cash inflow is reinvested at the computed IRR. Second, the NPV method measures profitability in absolute terms, whereas the IRR method measures it in relative terms. Since absolute measures often produce different rankings than relative measures, it shouldn't be too surprising that NPV and IRR can, on occasion, produce different signals regarding the attractiveness of projects. When a conflict does occur between the two methods, NPV produces the correct signal, as can be shown by a simple example.

Assume that a manager is faced with the prospect of choosing between two mutually exclusive investments whose cash flows, timing, NPV, and IRR are given in Exhibit 22-5 (a required rate of 8 percent is assumed for NPV computation). Both projects have the same life, require the same initial outlay, have positive NPVs, and have IRRs greater than the required rate of return. However, Project A has a higher NPV, whereas Project B has a higher IRR. The NPV and IRR give conflicting signals regarding which project should be chosen.

The preferred project can be identified by modifying the cash flows of one project so that the cash flows of both can be compared year by year. The modification, which appears in Exhibit 22-6, was achieved by carrying the Year 1 cash flow of Project B forward to Year 2. This can be done by assuming that the Year 1 cash flow of $686,342 is invested to earn the required rate of return. Under this assumption, the future value of $686,342 is equal to $741,249 (1.08 × $686,342). When $741,249 is added to the $686,342 received at the end of Year 2, the cash flow expected for Project B is $1,427,591.

As can be seen from Exhibit 22-6, Project A is preferable to Project B. It has the same outlay initially and a greater cash inflow in Year 2 (the difference is $12,409). Since the NPV approach originally chose Project A over Project B, it provided the correct signal for wealth maximization.

Some may object to this analysis, arguing that Project B should be preferred since it does provide at the end of Year 1 a cash inflow of $686,342, which can be reinvested at a much more attractive rate than the firm's required rate of return. The response is that if such an investment does exist, the firm should still invest in Project A, then borrow $686,342 at the cost of capital and invest that money in the attractive opportunity, and at the end of Year 2, repay the money borrowed plus the interest by using the combined proceeds of Project A and the other investment. For example, assume that the other investment promises a return of 20 percent. The modified cash inflows for Projects A and B are shown

Exhibit 22-5
NPV and IRR: Conflicting Signals

	Projects	
Year	*A*	*B*
0	$(1,000,000)	$(1,000,000)
1	—	$686,342
2	$1,440,000	$686,342
IRR	20%	24%
NPV	$234,080	$223,748

Exhibit 22-6
Modified Comparison of Projects A and B

	Projects	
Year	*A*	*Modified B*
0	$(1,000,000)	$(1,000,000)
1	—	—
2	1,440,000	1,427,591[a]

[a](1.08 × $686,342) + $686,342

Exhibit 22-7
Modified Cash Flows with Additional Opportunity

	Projects	
Year	Modified A	Modified B
0	$(1,000,000)	$(1,000,000)
1	—	—
2	1,522,361[a]	1,509,952[b]

[a]$1,440,000 + [1.20($686,342) − 1.08($686,342)]. This last term is what is needed to repay the capital and its cost at the end of Year 2.
[b]$686,342 + (1.20 × $686,342)

in Exhibit 22-7 (assuming that the additional investment at the end of Year 1 is made under either alternative). Notice that Project A is still preferable to Project B—and by the same $12,409.

NPV provides the correct signal for choosing among mutually exclusive investments. At the same time, it measures the impact competing projects have on the value of the firm. Choosing the project with the largest NPV is consistent with maximizing the wealth of shareholders. IRR, however, does not consistently result in choices that maximize wealth. IRR, as a *relative* measure of profitability, has the virtue of measuring accurately the rate of return of funds that remain internally invested. However, maximizing IRR will not necessarily maximize the wealth of firm owners because it cannot, by nature, consider the absolute dollar contributions of projects. In the final analysis, what counts are the total dollars earned—the absolute profits—not the relative profits. Accordingly, NPV, not IRR, should be used for choosing among competing, mutually exclusive projects or competing projects when capital funds are limited.

An independent project is acceptable if its NPV is positive. For mutually exclusive projects, the project with the largest NPV is chosen. There are three steps in selecting the best project from several competing projects: (1) assessing the cash-flow pattern for each project, (2) computing the NPV for each project, and (3) identifying the project with the greatest NPV. The following example illustrates NPV analysis for competing projects.

Example: New Product Decision

Hintley Games Corporation has decided to market a game that will allow players to display and develop their knowledge of the geography of the United States. Given the recent interest in trivia games, the company is certain that the product will prove successful. The marketing department has selected *Travel USA* as the name of the game. Two different board designs are being considered. Design B is more elaborate than design A and will require a heavier investment and greater annual operating costs; however, it will also generate greater annual revenues. The projected annual revenues, annual costs, capital outlays, and project life for each design (in after-tax cash flows) follow:

	Design A	*Design B*
Annual revenues	$120,000	$150,000
Annual operating costs	60,000	80,000
Equipment (purchased before Year 1)	180,000	210,000
Project life	5 years	5 years

Since the games are identical except for board design, management has decided to produce and sell only one of the designs. The firm must decide which to choose. Assume that the cost of capital for the company is 12 percent.

Design A requires an initial outlay of $180,000 and has a net annual cash inflow of $60,000 (revenues of $120,000 minus costs of $60,000). Design B, with an initial outlay of $210,000, has a net annual cash inflow of $70,000 ($150,000 − $80,000). With this information, the cash-flow pattern for each project can be described and the NPV computed. These are shown in Exhibit 22-8. Based on NPV analysis, Design B is more profitable; it has the larger NPV. Accordingly, the company should select Design B over Design A.

Interestingly, Designs A and B have identical internal rates of return. Since both projects have uniform cash flows, the IRR can be found by dividing the initial investment by the annual cash flow and searching Table 4 (Appendix B) for the interest rate that corresponds to this discount factor. For both designs, the discount factor is 3.0 ($180,000/$60,000 and $210,000/$70,000). From Table 4, it is easily seen that a discount factor of 3.0 and a life of 5 years yields an IRR of approximately 20 percent. Even though both projects have an IRR of 20 percent, the firm should not consider the 2 designs equally desirable. The analysis above has just shown that Design B produces a larger NPV and, therefore, will increase the value of the firm more than Design A. Design B should be chosen.

Exhibit 22-8
Cash-Flow Pattern and NPV Analysis: Designs A and B

	Cash-Flow Pattern	
Year	*Design A*	*Design B*
0	$(180,000)	$(210,000)
1	60,000	70,000
2	60,000	70,000
3	60,000	70,000
4	60,000	70,000
5	60,000	70,000

Design A: NPV Analysis

Year	*Cash Flow*	*Discount Factor*[1]	*Present Value*
0	$(180,000)	1.00000	$(180,000)
1–5	60,000	3.60478	216,287
Net present value			$ 36,287

Design B: NPV Analysis

Year	*Cash Flow*	*Discount Factor*[1]	*Present Value*
0	$(210,000)	1.00000	$(210,000)
1–5	70,000	3.60478	252,335
Net present value			$ 42,335

[1]From Table 4 in Appendix B

COMPUTATION OF CASH FLOWS

Objective 6
Convert gross cash flows to after-tax cash flows.

An important step in capital investment analysis is determining the cash-flow pattern for each project being considered. In fact, the computation of cash flows may be the most critical step in the capital investment process. Erroneous estimates may result in erroneous decisions, regardless of the sophistication of the decision models being used. Two steps are needed to compute cash flows: (1) forecasting revenues, expenses, and capital outlays; and (2) converting or adjusting these results to after-tax cash flows through a careful analysis of the relevant tax factors. Of the two steps, the more challenging is the first. Forecasting cash flows is demanding and difficult. Once gross cash flows are estimated, straightforward applications of tax law can be used to compute the after-tax flows. At this level of study, we focus only on the computation of after-tax cash flows. Forecasting cash flows is reserved for more advanced courses.

Once gross cash flows are predicted with the desired degree of accuracy, the analyst must adjust these cash flows for taxes. To analyze tax effects, cash flows are usually broken into two categories: (1) the initial cash outflows needed to acquire the assets of the project and (2) the cash inflows produced over the life of the project. Cash outflows and cash inflows adjusted for tax effects are called *net* cash outflows and inflows. Net cash flows include provisions for revenues, operating expenses, depreciation, and relevant tax implications. They are the proper inputs for capital investment decisions.

After-Tax Cash Flows: Year 0

The net cash outflow in Year 0 (the initial out-of-pocket outlay) is the difference between the initial cost of the project and any cash inflows directly associated with it. The gross cost of the project includes such things as the cost of land, the cost of equipment (including transportation and installation), taxes on gains from the sale of assets, and increases in working capital. Cash inflows occurring at the time of acquisition include tax savings from the sale of assets, cash from the sale of assets, and other tax benefits such as tax credits.

Under current tax law, all costs relating to the acquisition of assets other than land must be capitalized and depreciated over the useful life of the assets. Depreciation is deducted from revenues in computing taxable income during each year of the asset's life; however, at the point of acquisition, no depreciation expense is computed. Thus, depreciation is not relevant at Year 0. The principal tax implications at the point of acquisition are related to recognition of gains and losses on the sale of existing assets and the recognition of any investment tax credits.

Gains on the sale of assets produce additional taxes and, accordingly, reduce the cash proceeds received from the sale of old assets. Losses, on the other hand, are noncash expenses that reduce taxable income, producing tax savings; consequently, the cash proceeds from the sale of an old asset are increased by the amount of the tax savings. An investment tax credit is a direct credit against the tax liability of an organization and is usually expressed as a percentage of the net cost of the investment (e.g., 10 percent); accordingly, any appropriate investment tax credits reduce the cost of acquisition. With the Tax Reform Act of 1986, investment tax credits were repealed, but some analysts believe that because of their past popularity with the business community, they are likely to reappear.[6]

6. For example, the Clinton Administration is discussing the possibility of an investment tax credit for small corporations.

Exhibit 22-9
Corporate Income Tax Rates

Taxable Income	*Tax Rate*
$0 to $50,000	15%
$50,000–$75,000	25
$75,000–$100,000	34
$100,000–$335,000	39
Over $335,000	34

Another consequence of the Tax Reform Act of 1986 was to restructure corporate tax rates. The tax rates in effect as of 1992 are given in Exhibit 22-9.[7] Note that for income between $100,000 and $335,000, an additional 5 percent tax is imposed. The effect of this additional tax is to impose an effective flat rate of 34 percent on all income for any corporation with a taxable income over $335,000.

Corporations often have to pay state income taxes in addition to federal taxes. The rates vary by state. When state taxes are considered, we will assume that the average rate is 6%, thus yielding a total tax rate of 40% (34% + 6%) for most firms.

Let us look at an example. Currently, Jarvin Company uses two types of machines (Type A and Type B) to produce one of its products. Recent technological advances have created a single machine that can replace them. Management wants to know the net investment needed to acquire the new machine. If the new machine is acquired, the old equipment will be sold.

Disposition of Old Machines		
	Book Value	*Sale Price*
Machine A	$100,000	$130,000
Machine B	250,000	200,000

Acquisition of New Machine	
Purchase cost	$1,250,000
Freight	10,000
Installation	100,000
Additional working capital	90,000
Total	$1,450,000

The net investment can be determined by computing the net proceeds from the sale of the old machines and subtracting those proceeds from the cost of the new machine. The net proceeds are determined by computing the tax consequences of the sale and adjusting the gross receipts accordingly.

The tax consequences can be assessed by subtracting the book value from the selling price. If the difference is positive, the firm has experienced a gain and will owe taxes. Money received from the sale will be reduced by the amount of taxes owed. On the other hand, if the difference is negative, a loss is experienced—a noncash loss. However, this noncash loss does have cash implications. It can be

7. Again, it should be mentioned that there is a possibility that Congress may increase the corporate tax rate. We will use the rates in effect as of 1992 throughout the chapter.

Exhibit 22-10
Tax Effects of the Sale of Two Machines

Asset	*Gain (Loss)*
Machine A[1]	$ 30,000
Machine B[2]	(50,000)
Net gain (loss)	$(20,000)
Tax rate	0.40
Tax savings	$ 8,000

[1]Sale price minus book value is $130,000 − $100,000.
[2]Sale price minus book value is $200,000 − $250,000.

deducted from revenues and, as a consequence, can shield revenues from being taxed; accordingly, taxes will be saved. Thus, a loss produces a cash inflow equal to the taxes saved.

To illustrate, consider the tax effects of Machines A and B illustrated in Exhibit 22-10. By selling the two machines, the company receives the following net proceeds:

Sale price A	$130,000
Sale price B	200,000
Tax savings	8,000
Net proceeds	$338,000

Given these net proceeds, the net investment can be computed as follows:

Total cost of new machine	$1,450,000
Less: Net proceeds of old machines	(338,000)
Net investment (cash outflow)	$1,112,000

After-Tax Cash Flows: Life of the Project

In addition to determining the initial out-of-pocket outlay, managers must also estimate the annual after-tax cash flows expected over the life of the project. If the project generates revenue, the principal source of cash flows is from operations. Operating cash inflows can be assessed from the project's income statement. The annual after-tax cash flows are the sum of the project's after-tax profits and its noncash expenses. In terms of a simple formula, this computation can be represented as follows:

$$\text{After-tax cash flow} = \text{After-tax net income} + \text{Noncash expense}$$
$$CF = NI + NC$$

where CF = After-tax cash flow
NI = After-tax net income
NC = Noncash expenses

The most prominent examples of noncash expenses are depreciation and losses. At first glance, it may seem odd that after-tax cash flows are computed using noncash expenses. Noncash expenses are not cash flows but they do generate cash flows by reducing taxes. By shielding revenues from taxation, actual cash savings are created. The use of the income statement to determine after-tax cash flows is illustrated in the following example. The example is also used to show how noncash expenses can increase cash inflows by saving taxes.

Assume that a company plans to purchase a machine that costs $300,000. The machine will produce a new product that is expected to increase the firm's annual revenues by $300,000. Materials, labor, and other cash operating expenses will be $100,000 per year. The machine has a life of 3 years and will be depreciated on a straight-line basis. The machine will have no salvage value at the end of 3 years. The income statement for the project follows:

Revenues	$300,000
Less:	
Cash operating expenses	(100,000)
Depreciation	(100,000)
Income before taxes	$100,000
Less: Taxes (@ 40%)	(40,000)
Net income	$ 60,000

Cash flow from the income statement is computed as follows:

$$
\begin{aligned}
CF &= NI + NC \\
&= \$60{,}000 + \$100{,}000 \\
&= \$160{,}000
\end{aligned}
$$

The income approach to determine operating cash flows can be decomposed to assess the after-tax cash-flow effects of each individual category on the income statement. The decomposition approach calculates the operating cash flows by computing the after-tax cash flows for each item of the income statement:

$$
\begin{aligned}
CF = {} & [(1 - \text{Tax rate}) \times \text{Revenues}] - [(1 - \text{Tax rate}) \times \text{Cash expenses}] + \\
& (\text{Tax rate} \times \text{Noncash expenses})
\end{aligned}
$$

The first term, (1 − Tax rate) × Revenues, gives the after-tax cash inflows from cash revenues. For our example, the cash revenue is projected to be $300,000. The firm, therefore, can expect to keep $180,000 of the revenues received: (1 − Tax rate) × Revenues = 0.60 × $300,000 = $180,000. The after-tax revenue is the actual amount of after-tax cash available from the sales activity of the firm.

The second term, − (1 − Tax rate) × Cash expenses, is the after-tax cash outflows from cash operating expenses. Because cash expenses can be deducted from revenues to arrive at taxable income, the effect is to shield revenues from taxation. The consequence of this shielding is to save taxes and to reduce the actual cash outflow associated with a given expenditure. In our example, the firm has cash operating expenses of $100,000. The actual cash outflow is not $100,000 but $60,000 (0.60 × $100,000). The cash outlay for operating expenses is reduced by $40,000 because of tax savings. To see this, assume that operating expense is the only expense and the firm has revenues of $300,000. If operating expense is *not* tax deductible, then the tax owed is $120,000 (0.40 × $300,000). If the operating expense is deductible for tax purposes, then the taxable income is $200,000

(\$300,000 − \$100,000), and the tax owed is \$80,000 (0.40 × \$200,000). Because the deductibility of operating expense saves \$40,000 in taxes, the actual outlay for that expenditure is reduced by \$40,000.

The third term, Tax rate × Noncash expenses, is the cash inflow from the tax savings produced by the noncash expenses. Noncash expenses, such as depreciation, also shield revenues from taxation. For example, assume that revenues are \$300,000 and the only expense is depreciation of \$100,000. If depreciation is *not* allowed as a deduction to arrive at taxable income, taxable income is \$300,000, and the tax bill is \$120,000 (0.40 × \$300,000). If depreciation can be deducted, taxable income is \$200,000 (\$300,000 − \$100,000), and the tax bill is \$80,000 (0.40 × \$200,000). The tax bill is \$40,000 less because taxable income has been lowered by the \$100,000 depreciation deduction. The depreciation *shields* \$100,000 of revenues from being taxed and thus saves \$40,000 (0.40 × \$100,000) in taxes.

The sum of the three items is given below.

After-tax revenues	\$180,000
After-tax cash expenses	(60,000)
Depreciation tax shield	40,000
Operating cash flow	\$160,000

The decomposition approach yields the same outcome as the income approach. For convenience, the three decomposition terms are summarized in Exhibit 22-11.

One feature of decomposition is the ability to compute after-tax cash flows in a spreadsheet format. This format highlights the cash-flow effects of individual items and facilitates the use of spreadsheet software packages. The spreadsheet format is achieved by creating four columns, one for each of the three cash-flow categories and one for the total after-tax cash flow, which is the sum of the first three. For our example, this format is illustrated in Exhibit 22-12. Recall that cash

Exhibit 22-11
Computation of Operating Cash Flows: Decomposition Terms

After-tax cash revenues = (1 − Tax rate) × Cash revenues
After-tax cash expenses = (1 − Tax rate) × Cash expenses
Tax savings, noncash expenses = Tax rate × Noncash expenses

Exhibit 22-12
Illustration of the Spreadsheet Approach

Year	$(1-t)R$[1]	$-(1-t)C$[2]	tNC[3]	*CF*
1	\$180,000	\$(60,000)	\$40,000	\$160,000
2	180,000	(60,000)	40,000	160,000
3	180,000	(60,000)	40,000	160,000

[1] R = Revenues; t = tax rate; $(1-t)R = (1-0.40)\$300,000 = \$180,000$
[2] C = Cash expenses; $-(1-t)C = -(1-0.40)\$100,000 = \$(60,000)$
[3] NC = Noncash expenses; $tNC = 0.40(\$100,000) = \$40,000$

revenues were $300,000 per year for 3 years, annual cash expenses were $100,000, and annual depreciation was $100,000.

A second feature of decomposition is the ability to compute the after-tax cash effects on an item-by-item basis. For example, suppose that a firm is considering a project and is uncertain as to which method of depreciation should be used. By computing the tax savings produced under each depreciation method, a firm can quickly assess which method is most desirable.

The taxpayer can use either the straight-line method or the modified accelerated cost recovery system (MACRS) to compute annual depreciation. Current law defines MACRS as the double-declining-balance method.[8] In computing depreciation, no consideration of salvage value is required. However, under either method, a half-year convention applies.[9] If the double-declining-balance method is selected, the amount of depreciation claimed in the first year is twice that of the straight-line method. Under this method, the amount of depreciation claimed becomes progressively smaller until eventually it is exceeded by that claimed under the straight-line method. When this happens, the straight-line method is used to finish depreciating the asset. Exhibit 22-13 provides a table of depreciation rates for the double-declining-balance method for assets belonging to the three-year, five-year, and seven-year classes. The rates shown in this table incorporate the half-year convention and, therefore, are the MACRS depreciation rates.

Both the straight-line method and the double-declining-balance method yield the same total amount of depreciation over the life of the asset. Both methods also produce the same total tax savings (assuming the same tax rate over the life of the asset). However, since the depreciation claimed in the early years of a project is greater using the double-declining-balance method, the tax savings are also greater during those years. Considering the time value of money, it is preferable to have the tax savings earlier than later. Thus, firms should prefer the MACRS method of depreciation over the straight-line method.

Exhibit 22-13
MACRS Depreciation Rates

Year	*Three-Year Assets*	*Five-Year Assets*	*Seven-Year Assets*
1	33.33%	20.00%	14.29%
2	44.45	32.00	24.49
3	14.81	19.20	17.49
4	7.41	11.52	12.49
5		11.52	8.93
6		5.76	8.92
7		—	8.93
8		—	4.46

8. The tax law also allows the 150 percent declining balance method; however, we will focus on only the straight-line method and the double-declining version of MACRS.

9. The tax law requires a mid-quarter convention if more than 40 percent of personal property is placed in service during the last three months of the year. We will not illustrate this possible scenario. See Chapter 10 for a review of the basic concepts of MACRS depreciation and the half-year convention.

CAPITAL INVESTMENT: THE ADVANCED MANUFACTURING ENVIRONMENT

Objective 7
Describe capital investment in the advanced manufacturing environment.

In the advanced manufacturing environment, long-term investments are generally concerned with the automation of manufacturing. Before any commitment to automation is made, however, a company should first make the most efficient use of existing technology. Many benefits can be realized by redesigning and simplifying the current manufacturing process. An example often given to support this thesis is automation of material handling. Automation of this operation can cost millions—and it is usually unnecessary because greater efficiency can be achieved by eliminating inventories and simplifying material transfers through the implementation of a JIT system.

Once the benefits from redesign and simplification are achieved, however, it becomes apparent where automation can generate additional benefits. Many companies can improve their competitive positions by adding such features as robotics, flexible manufacturing systems, and completely integrated manufacturing systems. The ultimate commitment to automation is the construction of greenfield factories. Greenfield factories are new factories designed and built from scratch; they represent a strategic decision by a company to change completely the way it manufactures.

Although discounted cash-flow analysis (using net present value and internal rate of return) remains preeminent in capital investment decisions, the new manufacturing environment demands that more attention be paid to the inputs used in discounted cash-flow models. How investment is defined, how operating cash flows are estimated, how salvage value is treated, and how the discount rate is chosen are all different in nature from the traditional approach.[10]

How Investment Differs

Investment in automated manufacturing processes is much more complex than investment in the standard manufacturing equipment of the past. For standard equipment, the direct costs of acquisition represent virtually the entire investment. For automated manufacturing, the direct costs can represent as little as 50 or 60 percent of the total investment; software, engineering, training, and implementation are a significant percentage of the total costs. Thus, great care must be exercised to assess the actual cost of an automated system. It is easy to overlook the peripheral costs, which can be substantial.

How Estimates of Operating Cash Flows Differ

Estimates of operating cash flows from investments in standard equipment have typically relied on directly identifiable tangible benefits, such as direct savings from labor, power, and scrap. Intangible benefits and indirect savings were ignored because they were viewed as immaterial. In the new manufacturing environment, however, the intangible and indirect benefits can be material and critical to the viability of the project. Greater quality, more reliability, improved customer

10. Much of the information on investment in the new manufacturing environment is based on the following two sources: Robert A. Howell and Stephen R. Soucy, "Capital Investment in the New Manufacturing Environment," *Management Accounting* (November 1987), pp. 26–32; and Callie Berliner and James A. Brimson (eds.), *Cost Management for Today's Advanced Manufacturing* (Boston: Harvard Business School Press, 1988).

satisfaction, and an enhanced ability to maintain market share are all important intangible benefits of a JIT system. Reduction of labor in support areas such as production scheduling and stores are indirect benefits. More effort is needed to measure these intangible and indirect benefits in order to assess more accurately the potential value of investments.

An example can be used to illustrate the importance of considering intangible and indirect benefits. Consider a company that is evaluating a potential investment in a flexible manufacturing system (FMS). The choice facing the company is to continue producing with its conventional equipment, expected to last ten years, or to switch to the new system, which is also expected to have a useful life of ten years. The company's discount rate is 12 percent. The data pertaining to the investment are presented in Exhibit 22-14. Using these data, the net present value of the proposed system can be computed as follows:

Present value ($4,000,000 × 5.65022[a])	$22,600,880
Investment	(18,000,000)
Net present value	$ 4,600,880

[a]Discount factor for an interest rate of 12 percent and a life of 10 years (see Appendix B, Table 4)

Exhibit 22-14
Investment Data: Direct, Intangible, and Indirect Benefits

	FMS	*Status Quo*
Investment (current outlay):		
Direct costs	$10,000,000	—
Software, engineering	8,000,000	—
Total current outlay	$18,000,000	$ 0
Net after-tax cash flow	$ 5,000,000	$1,000,000
Less: After-tax cash flow for status quo	(1,000,000)	n/a
Incremental benefit	$ 4,000,000	n/a

Incremental Benefit Explained

Direct benefits:		
Direct labor	$ 1,500,000	
Scrap reduction	500,000	
Setups	200,000	$2,200,000
Intangible benefits:		
Quality savings:		
Rework	$ 200,000	
Warranties	400,000	
Maintenance of competitive position	1,000,000	1,600,000
Indirect benefits:		
Production scheduling	$ 110,000	
Payroll	90,000	200,000
Total		$4,000,000

The net present value is positive and large in magnitude, and it clearly signals the acceptability of the FMS. This outcome, however, is strongly dependent on explicit recognition of both intangible and indirect benefits. If those benefits are eliminated, the direct savings total $2.2 million, and the NPV is negative.

Present value ($2,200,000 × 5.65022)	$12,430,484
Investment	(18,000,000)
Net present value	$ (5,569,516)

The rise of activity-based costing has made identifying indirect benefits easier with the use of cost drivers. Once they are identified, they can be included in the analysis if they are material.

Examination of Exhibit 22-14 reveals the importance of intangible benefits. One of the most important intangible benefits is maintaining or improving a firm's competitive position. A key question that needs to be asked is what will happen to the cash flows of the firm if the investment is *not* made. That is, if the company chooses to forgo an investment in technologically advanced equipment, will it be able to continue to compete with other firms on the basis of quality, delivery, and cost? (The question becomes especially relevant if competitors choose to invest in advanced equipment.) If the competitive position deteriorates, the company's current cash flows will decrease.

If cash flows will decrease if the investment is not made, this decrease should show up as an incremental benefit for the advanced technology. In Exhibit 22-14, the company estimates this competitive benefit as $1,000,000. Estimating this benefit requires some serious strategic planning and analysis, but its effect can be critical. If this benefit had been ignored or overlooked, the net present value would have been negative, and the investment alternative would have been rejected. This calculation is shown below.

Present value ($3,000,000 × 5.65022)	$16,950,660
Investment	(18,000,000)
Net present value	$ (1,049,340)

Salvage Value

Salvage or terminal value has often been ignored in investment decisions. The usual reason offered is the difficulty to estimate it. Because of this uncertainty, the effect of salvage value has often been ignored or heavily discounted. This approach may be unwise, however, because salvage value could make the difference between investing or not investing. Given the highly competitive environment, companies cannot afford to make incorrect decisions. A much better approach to deal with uncertainty is to use sensitivity analysis. In the new manufacturing environment, being too conservative can be fatal.

To illustrate the potential effect of terminal value, assume that the after-tax annual operating cash flow of the project shown in Exhibit 22-14 is $3.1 million instead of $4 million. The net present value without salvage value is as follows:

Present value ($3,100,000 × 5.65022)	$17,515,682
Investment	(18,000,000)
Net present value	$ (484,318)

Without the salvage value, the project would be rejected. The net present value with salvage value of $2 million, however, is a positive result, meaning that the investment should be made.

Present value ($3,100,000 × 5.65022)	$17,515,682
Present value ($2,000,000 × 0.32197[a])	643,940
Investment	(18,000,000)
Net present value	$ 159,622

[a]Discount factor, 12 percent and 10 years (Appendix B, Table 3)

Discount Rates

Being overly conservative with discount rates can prove even more damaging. In theory, if future cash flows are known with certainty, the correct discount rate is a firm's cost of capital. In practice, future cash flows are uncertain, and managers often choose a discount rate higher than the cost of capital to deal with that uncertainty. If the rate chosen is excessively high, it will bias the selection process toward short-term investments.

To illustrate the effect of an excessive discount rate, consider the project in Exhibit 22-14 once again. Assume that the correct discount rate is 12 percent but that the firm uses 18 percent. The net present value using an 18 percent discount rate is calculated as follows:

Present value ($4,000,000 × 4.49409)[a]	$17,976,360
Investment	(18,000,000)
Net present value	$ (23,640)

[a]Discount rate for 18 percent and 10 years (Appendix B, Table 3)

The project would be rejected. With a higher discount rate, the discount factor decreases in magnitude much more rapidly than the discount factor for a lower rate (compare the discount factor for 12 percent, 5.65022, with the factor for 18 percent, 4.49409). The effect of a higher discount factor is to place more weight on earlier cash flows and less weight on later cash flows, which favors short-term over long-term investments. This outcome makes it more difficult for automated manufacturing systems to appear as viable projects since the cash returns required to justify the investment are received over a longer period of time.

SUMMARY OF LEARNING OBJECTIVES

1. Explain what a capital investment decision is and distinguish between independent and mutually exclusive projects. Capital investment decisions are concerned with the acquisition of long-term assets and usually involve a significant outlay of funds. There are two types of capital investment projects: independent and mutually exclusive. Independent projects are projects that, if accepted or rejected, do not affect the cash flows of other projects. Mutually exclusive projects are those projects that, if accepted, preclude the acceptance of all other competing projects.

2. Compute the payback period and accounting rate of return for a proposed investment and explain their role in capital investment decisions. Managers make capital investment decisions by using formal models to decide whether to accept or reject proposed projects. These decision models are classified as nondiscounting and discounting, depending on whether they address the question of the time value of money. There are two nondiscounting models: the payback period and the accounting rate of return.

The payback period is the time required for a firm to recover its initial investment. For even cash flows, it is calculated by dividing the investment by the annual cash flow. For uneven cash flows, the cash flows are summed until the investment is recovered. If only a fraction of a year is needed, then it is assumed that the cash flows occur evenly within each year. The payback period ignores the time value of money and the profitability of projects because it does not consider the cash inflows available beyond the payback period. However, it does supply some useful information. The payback period is useful in assessing and controlling risk, minimizing the impact of an investment on a firm's liquidity, and controlling the risk of obsolescence.

The accounting rate of return is computed by dividing the average income expected from an investment by either the original or average investment. Unlike the payback period, it does consider the profitability of a project; however, it ignores the time value of money. The payback period may be useful to managers to screen new investments to ensure that certain accounting ratios are not adversely affected (specifically accounting ratios that may be monitored to ensure compliance with debt covenants).

3. Use net present value analysis for capital investment decisions involving independent projects. NPV is the difference between the present value of future cash flows and the initial investment outlay. To use the model, a required rate of return must be identified (usually the cost of capital). The NPV method uses the required rate of return to compute the present value of a project's cash inflows and outflows. If the present value of the inflows is greater than the present value of the outflows, the net present value is greater than zero, and the project is profitable; if the NPV is less than zero, the project is not profitable and should be rejected.

4. Use the internal rate of return to assess the acceptability of an independent project. The IRR is computed by finding the interest rate that equates the present value of a project's cash inflows with the present value of its cash outflows. If the IRR is greater than the required rate of return (cost of capital), the project is acceptable; if the IRR is less than the required rate of return, the project should be rejected.

5. Explain why NPV is better than IRR for capital investment decisions involving mutually exclusive projects. In evaluating mutually exclusive or competing projects, managers have a choice of using NPV or IRR. When choosing among competing projects, the NPV model correctly identifies the best investment alternative. IRR, at times, may choose an inferior project. Thus, since NPV always provides the correct signal, it should be used.

6. Convert gross cash flows to after-tax cash flows. Accurate and reliable cash flows are absolutely critical for capital investment decisions. Managers should assume responsibility for the accuracy of cash-flow projections. At a minimum, this responsibility should entail carefully reviewing the assumptions underlying the forecast, conducting a sensitivity analysis to assess the effect of changes in cash flows on the project's performance, and adjusting cash flows to reflect inflation. Furthermore, all cash flows in a capital investment analysis should be after-tax cash flows. There are two different, but equivalent, ways to compute after-tax cash flows: the income method and the decomposition method. Although depreciation is not a cash flow, it does have cash-flow implications because tax laws allow depreciation to be deducted in computing taxable income. Straight-line and double-declining-balance depreciation both produce the same total depreciation deductions over the life of the depreciated asset. Because the latter method accelerates depreciation, however, it would be preferred.

7. Describe capital investment in the advanced manufacturing environment. Capital investment in the advanced manufacturing environment is affected by the way in which inputs are determined. Much greater attention must be paid to the investment outlays because peripheral items can require substantial resources. Furthermore, in assessing benefits, intangible items such as quality and maintaining competitive position can be deciding factors. Choice of the required rate of return is also critical. The tendency of firms to use hurdle rates that are much greater than the cost of capital should be discontinued. Also, since the salvage value of an automated system can be considerable, it should be estimated and included in the analysis.

KEY TERMS

Accounting rate of return 1019
Capital budgeting 1015
Capital investment decisions 1015
Cost of capital 1021
Discounted cash flows 1020
Discounting model 1016
Hurdle rate 1021
Independent projects 1015
Internal rate of return 1023
Mutually exclusive projects 1015
Net present value 1020
Nondiscounting models 1016
Payback period 1017
Required rate of return 1021

REVIEW PROBLEMS

1.

Bill Larson is investigating the possibility of acquiring an ice-cream franchise. To acquire the franchise requires an initial outlay of \$300,000 (the purchase includes building and equipment). To raise the capital, Bill will sell stock valued at \$200,000 (the stock pays dividends of \$18,000 per year) and borrow \$100,000. The loan for \$100,000 would carry an interest rate of 12 percent.

The franchise will produce an annual cash inflow of \$50,000. Bill expects to operate the business for 20 years, after which he will turn it over to one of his children. (Ignore income taxes in this problem.)

REQUIRED:

1. Compute the payback period.
2. Assuming that depreciation is \$14,000 per year, compute the accounting rate of return (on total investment).
3. Compute Bill's cost of capital.
4. Compute the NPV of the franchise.
5. Compute the IRR of the franchise.
6. Should Bill acquire the franchise?

Solution

1. The payback period is \$300,000/\$50,000, or 6 years.
2. The accounting rate of return is (\$50,000 − \$14,000)/\$300,000, or 12 percent.
3. The cost of capital is (2/3 × .09) + (1/3 × 0.12), or (0.06) + (0.04), or 10 percent. (The opportunity cost of the stock is \$18,000/\$200,000, or 9 percent.)
4. From Appendix B, Table 4, the discount factor for an annuity with i at 10 percent and n at 20 years is 8.51356. Thus, the NPV is (8.51356 × 50,000) − \$300,000, or \$125,678.
5. The discount factor associated with the IRR is 6.00 (\$300,000/\$50,000). From Appendix B, Table 4, the IRR is between 14 and 16 percent (using the row corresponding to period 20). The interest interval is 2 percent (0.16 − 0.14). The discount interval is 0.69429 (6.62313 − 5.92884). The distance of the IRR discount factor into the interval is 0.62313 (6.62313 − 6.00000), for a relative distance of 0.62313/0.69429 ~0.9. Thus, IRR~ 0.14 + (0.9 × 0.02), or approximately 15.8 percent.
6. Since the NPV is positive and the IRR is greater than Bill's cost of capital, the franchise is a sound investment. This, of course, assumes that the cash flow projections are accurate.

2. Blalock Manufacturing has decided to acquire a new luxury automobile for transporting clients from the airport to its sales offices. The choice has been narrowed to two models. The following information has been gathered for each model:

	Model A	*Model T*
Acquisition cost	$20,000	$25,000
Annual operating costs	$3,500	$2,000
Depreciation method	MACRS	MACRS
Expected salvage value	$5,000	$8,000

Blalock's cost of capital is 14 percent. The company plans to use the car for 5 years and then sell it for its salvage value. Assume the tax rate is 34 percent.

REQUIRED:

1. Compute the after-tax operating cash flows for each model.
2. Compute the NPV for each model and make a recommendation.

Solution

1. For automobiles, the MACRS guidelines allow a five-year life. Using the rates from Exhibit 22-13, depreciation is calculated for each model.

Year	*Model A*	*Model T*
1	$ 4,000	$ 5,000
2	6,400	8,000
3	3,840	4,800
4	2,304	2,880
5	1,152[a]	1,440[a]
Total	$17,696	$22,120

[a]Only half the depreciation is allowed in year of disposal.

The after-tax operating cash flows are computed using the spreadsheet format.

Model A

Year	*(1 − t)R*	*−(1 − t)C*	*tNC*	*Other*	*CF*
1	n/a	$(2,310)	$1,360		$ (950)
2	n/a	(2,310)	2,176		(134)
3	n/a	(2,310)	1,306		(1,004)
4	n/a	(2,310)	783		(1,527)
5	$1,779[a]	(2,310)	392	$2,304[b]	2,165

[a]Salvage value ($5,000) − Book value ($20,000 − $17,696 = $2,304) = $2,696; 0.66 × $2,696 = $1,779
[b]Recovery of Capital = Book value = $2,304. Capital recovered is not taxed—only the gain on sale. Footnote "a" illustrates how the gain is treated.

Model T

Year	(1 − t)R	−(1 − t)C	tNC	Other	CF
1	n/a	$(1,320)	$1,700		$ 380
2	n/a	(1,320)	2,720		1,400
3	n/a	(1,320)	1,632		312
4	n/a	(1,320)	979		(341)
5	$3,379[a]	(1,320)	490	$2,880[b]	5,429

[a]Salvage value ($8,000) − Book value ($25,000 − $22,120 = $2,880) = $5,120; 0.66 × $5,120 = $3,379

[b]Recovery of Capital = Book value = $2,880. Capital recovered is not taxed—only the gain on sale of the asset. Footnote "a" illustrates how the gain is treated. The nontaxable item requires an additional column for the spreadsheet analysis.

2. NPV computation:

Model A

Year	Cash Flow	Discount Factor	Present Value
0	$(20,000)	1.00000	$(20,000.00)
1	(950)	0.87719	(833.33)
2	(134)	0.76947	(103.11)
3	(1,004)	0.67497	(677.67)
4	(1,527)	0.59208	(904.11)
5	2,165	0.51937	1,124.44
Net present value			$(21,393.78)

Model T

Year	Cash Flow	Discount Factor	Present Value
0	$(25,000)	1.00000	$(25,000.00)
1	380	0.87719	333.33
2	1,400	0.76947	1,077.26
3	312	0.67497	210.59
4	(341)	0.59208	(201.90)
5	5,429	0.51937	2,819.66
Net present value			$(20,761.06)

Model T should be chosen since it has the largest NPV, indicating that it is the least costly of the two cars. Note also that the net present values are negative and we are choosing the least costly investment.

QUESTIONS

1. Explain the difference between independent projects and mutually exclusive projects.
2. Explain why the timing and quantity of cash flows are important in capital investment decisions.
3. The time value of money is ignored by the payback period and the accounting rate of return. Explain why this is a major deficiency in these two models.
4. What is the payback period? Compute the payback

period for an investment requiring an initial outlay of $80,000 with expected annual cash inflows of $30,000.

5. Name and discuss three possible reasons why the payback period is used to help make capital investment decisions.
6. What is the accounting rate of return? Compute the accounting rate of return for an investment that requires an initial outlay of $250,000 and promises an average net income of $75,000.
7. The net present value is the same as the profit of a project expressed in present dollars. Do you agree? Explain.
8. What is the cost of capital? What role does it play in capital investment decisions?
9. What is the role that the required rate of return plays for the NPV model? For the IRR model?
10. The IRR is the true or actual rate of return being earned by the project. Do you agree or disagree? Discuss.
11. Explain how the NPV is used to determine whether a project should be accepted or rejected.
12. Explain the relationship between NPV and a firm's value.
13. Explain why NPV is generally preferred over IRR when choosing among competing or mutually exclusive projects. Why would managers continue to use IRR to choose among mutually exclusive projects?
14. Suppose that a firm must choose between two mutually exclusive projects, both of which have negative NPVs. Explain how a firm can legitimately choose among two such projects.
15. Why is it important to have accurate projections of cash flows for potential capital investments?
16. What are the principal tax implications that should be considered in Year 0?
17. Explain why the MACRS method of recognizing depreciation is better than the straight-line method.
18. What is the half-year convention? What is the effect of this convention on the length of time it actually takes to write off the cost of a depreciable asset?
19. Explain the important factors to consider for capital investment in the advanced manufacturing environment.

EXERCISES

E22-1
Basic Concepts
LO 2, 3, 4

Each of the following parts is independent. Assume all cash flows are after-tax cash flows.

1. Larry Alton has just invested $200,000 as a part owner of a funeral home. He expects to receive an income of $40,000 per year from the investment. What is the payback period for Larry?
2. Kay Jones placed $20,000 in a 3-year savings plan. The plan pays 10 percent, and she cannot withdraw the money early without a penalty. Assuming that Kay leaves the money in the plan for the full 3 years, how much money will she have?
3. King Manufacturing is considering the purchase of a robotics material handling system. The cash benefits will be $120,000 per year. The system costs $680,000 and will last 10 years. Compute the NPV, assuming a discount rate of 12 percent. Should the company buy the robotics system?
4. Harry Henderson has just invested $50,000 in a company. He expects to receive $8,050 per year for the next 8 years. His cost of capital is 6 percent. Compute the internal rate of return. Did Harry make a good decision?

E22-2
Payback; Accounting Rate of Return; NPV; IRR
LO 1, 2, 3, 4

Kimmer Optics is considering an investment in equipment that will be used to grind lenses. The outlay required is $600,000. The equipment is expected to last 5 years and will have no salvage value. The expected after-tax cash flows associated with the project are given below:

Year	*Cash Revenues*	*Cash Expenses*
1	$600,000	$450,000
2	600,000	450,000
3	600,000	450,000
4	600,000	450,000
5	600,000	450,000

REQUIRED:

1. Compute the project's payback period.
2. Compute the project's accounting rate of return (a) on initial investment and (b) on average investment.
3. Compute the project's net present value, assuming a required rate of return of 10 percent.
4. Compute the project's internal rate of return.

E22-3
Payback; Accounting Rate of Return; Present Value; NPV; IRR
LO 1, 2, 3, 4

The first two parts are related; the last three are independent of all other parts. Assume all cash flows are after-tax cash flows.

1. Randy Willis is considering investing in one of the two following projects. Either project will require an investment of $10,000. The expected cash flows for the two projects are given below. Assume each project is depreciable.

Year	*Project A*	*Project B*
1	$ 3,000	$3,000
2	4,000	4,000
3	5,000	6,000
4	10,000	3,000
5	10,000	3,000

What is the payback period for each project? If rapid payback is important, which project should be chosen? Which would you choose?

2. Calculate the accounting rate of return for each project in Part 1. Which project should be chosen based on the accounting rate of return?
3. Wilma Golding is retiring and has the option to take her retirement as a lump sum of $225,000 or to receive $24,000 per year for 20 years. Wilma's required rate of return is 8 percent. Assuming Wilma will live for another 20 years, should she take the lump sum or the annuity?
4. David Booth is interested in investing in some tools and equipment so that he can do independent dry walling. The cost of the tools and equipment is $20,000. He estimates that the return from owning his own equipment will be $6,000 per year. The tools and equipment will last 6 years. Assuming a required rate of return of 8 percent, calculate the NPV of the investment. Should he invest?
5. Patsy Folson is evaluating what appears to be an attractive opportunity. She is currently the owner of a small manufacturing company and has the opportunity to acquire another small company's equipment that would provide production of a part currently purchased externally. She estimates that the savings from internal production would be $25,000 per year. She estimates that the equipment would last 10 years. The owner is asking $130,400 for the equipment. Her company's cost of capital is 10 percent. Calculate the project's internal rate of return. Should she acquire the equipment?

E22-4
NPV; Accounting Rate of Return; Payback
LO 1, 2, 3

Timtell Trucking is considering investment in loading equipment and in packaging equipment. Each project would require an investment of $100,000. The loading equipment and the packaging equipment would each last 5 years and have no expected salvage value. The after-tax cash inflows associated with each of the two independent projects are given below:

Year	*Loading Equipment*	*Packaging Equipment*
1	$60,000	$10,000
2	30,000	10,000
3	40,000	60,000
4	20,000	80,000
5	10,000	90,000

REQUIRED:

1. Assuming a discount rate of 12 percent, compute the net present value of each project.
2. Compute the payback period for each project. Assume that the manager of the company accepts only projects with a payback period of 3 years or less. Offer some reasons why this may be a rational strategy even though the NPV computed in Requirement 1 may indicate otherwise.
3. Compute the accounting rate of return for each project using (a) initial investment and (b) average investment.

E22-5
NPV: Basic Concepts
LO 3

Dyers Legal Services is considering an investment that requires an outlay of $200,000 and promises an after-tax cash inflow one year from now of $231,000. The company's cost of capital is 10 percent.

REQUIRED:

1. Break the $231,000 future cash inflow into three components: (a) the return of the original investment, (b) the cost of capital, and (c) the profit earned on the investment. Now compute the present value of the profit earned on the investment.
2. Compute the NPV of the investment. Compare this with the present value of the profit computed in Requirement 1. What does this tell you about the meaning of NPV?

E22-6
NPV; Cost of Capital; Basic Concepts
LO 4

Royal Electronics Company has an opportunity to invest in a new product line that will have a two-year life cycle. The investment requires a current $100,000 outlay. The capital will be raised by borrowing $60,000 and by raising $40,000 through the issue of new stock. The $60,000 loan will have net interest payments of $3,000 at the end of each of the two years, with the principal being repaid at the end of Year 2 (thus, the net cost of debt is 5 percent). The stock issue carries with it an expectation of a 17.5 percent return, expressed in the form of dividends at the end of each year ($7,000 in dividends will be paid each of the next two years). The sources of capital for this investment represent the same proportion and costs that the company typically has. Finally, the project will produce after-tax cash inflows of $70,000 per year for the next 2 years.

REQUIRED:

1. Compute the cost of capital for the project.
2. Compute the NPV for the project. Explain why it is not necessary to subtract the interest payments and the dividend payments from the annual inflow of $70,000 in carrying out this computation.

E22-7
NPV versus IRR
LO 5

A company is considering two different modifications to its current manufacturing process. The after-tax cash flows associated with the two investments are shown below.

Year	*Project I* $(100,000)	*Project II* $(100,000)
1	—	63,857
2	134,560	63,857

The company's cost of capital is 10 percent.

REQUIRED:

1. Compute the NPV and the IRR for each investment.
2. Show that the project with the larger NPV is the correct choice for the company.

E22-8
Computation of After-Tax Cash Flows
LO 6

Reems Airlines is considering two independent projects. One involves recycling and the other involves the acquisition of some maintenance equipment. The projected annual operating revenues and expenses are given below.

Project A (recycling project)	
Revenues	$90,000
Cash expenses	(50,000)
Depreciation	(15,000)
Income before taxes	$25,000
Taxes	(10,000)
Net income	$15,000

Project B (maintenance equipment)	
Cash expenses	$40,000
Depreciation	40,000

REQUIRED: Compute the after-tax cash flows of each project. The tax rate is 40 percent and includes federal and state assessments.

E22-9
MACRS; NPV
LO 6

A trucking company is planning to buy a set of special tools for its maintenance operation. The cost of the tools is $12,000. The tools have a three-year life and qualify for the use of the three-year MACRS. The combined federal and state tax rate is 40 percent; the cost of capital is 12 percent.

REQUIRED:

1. Calculate the present value of the tax depreciation shield, assuming that straight-line depreciation with a half-year life is used.
2. Calculate the present value of the tax depreciation shield, assuming that MACRS is used.
3. What is the benefit of using MACRS to the company?

E22-10
Lease or Buy
LO 5

A small CPA firm has decided that it needs to have regular access to a car for local errands and occasional business trips. The managing partner of the firm is trying to decide between buying or leasing the car. Purchase cost is $18,500. The annual operating costs are estimated at $3,000. If the car is leased, a five-year lease will be acquired. The lease requires a refundable deposit of $500 and annual lease payments of $5,000. Operating costs, in addition to the lease payment, total $3,000 per year. The firm's cost of capital is 10 percent and its tax rate is 40 percent. If the car is purchased, MACRS depreciation will be used.

REQUIRED: Using NPV analysis, determine whether the car should be leased or purchased.

E22-11
Various Investments
LO 5, 6

Solve each of the following independent cases:

1. A hospital laboratory has decided to purchase some new diagnostic equipment for its blood-testing function. Its old equipment will be sold for $20,000 (it has a book value of $40,000). The new equipment will cost $80,000. Assuming that the tax rate is 34 percent, compute the net after-tax cash outflow.
2. The assembly department is purchasing a new conveyor system costing $60,000. Additional cash expenses of $2,000 per year are required to operate the equipment. MACRS depreciation will be used (seven-year property qualification). Assuming a tax rate of 34 percent, prepare a schedule of after-tax cash flows for the first 4 years.
3. The projected income for a project during its first year of operation is given below:

Cash revenues	$120,000
Less: Cash expenses	(50,000)
Less: Depreciation	(20,000)
Net income before taxes	$ 50,000
Less: Taxes	(17,000)
Net income	$ 33,000

Compute the following:
a. After-tax cash flow
b. After-tax cash flow from revenues
c. After-tax cash expenses
d. Cash inflow from the shielding effect of depreciation

E22-12
Discount Rates; Advanced Manufacturing Environment
LO 7

A company is considering two competing investments. The first is for a standard piece of production equipment; the second is for some computer-aided manufacturing (CAM) equipment. The investment and after-tax operating cash flows are shown below.

Year	*Standard Equipment*	*CAM*
0	$(500,000)	$(2,000,000)
1	300,000	100,000
2	200,000	200,000
3	100,000	300,000
4	100,000	400,000
5	100,000	400,000
6	100,000	400,000
7	100,000	500,000
8	100,000	1,000,000
9	100,000	1,000,000
10	100,000	1,000,000

The company uses a discount rate of 18 percent for all of its investments. The company's cost of capital is 10 percent.

REQUIRED:

1. Calculate the net present value for each investment using a discount rate of 18 percent.
2. Calculate the net present value for each investment using a discount rate of 10 percent.
3. Which rate should the company use to compute the net present value? Explain.

E22-13
Quality; Market Share; Advanced Manufacturing Environment
LO 7

Refer to Exercise 22-12. Assume that the company's cost of capital is 14 percent.

REQUIRED:

1. Calculate the NPV of each alternative using the 14 percent rate.
2. Now assume that if the standard equipment is purchased, the competitive position of the firm will deteriorate because of lower quality (relative to competitors who did automate). Marketing estimates that the loss in market share will decrease the projected net cash inflows by 50 percent for Years 3 through 10. Recalculate the NPV of the standard equipment given this outcome. What is the decision now? Discuss the importance of assessing the effect of intangible benefits.

PROBLEMS

P22-1
Basic NPV Analysis
LO 1, 3

Richard Liddel, marketing manager, was arguing for the introduction of a new product—a stair stepper. The company was already a major player in the exercise equipment market, and he felt that the new product bearing the company's brand name would be well accepted. He knew, however, that the acceptance of the new product would depend on the economic feasibility of acquiring the equipment needed to produce the product. The equipment would cost $140,000, and its cash operating expenses would total $40,000 per year. The equipment would last for 7 years but would need a major overhaul costing $20,000 at the end of the fifth year. At the end of 7 years, the equipment would be sold for $8,000. An increase in working capital totaling $20,000 would also be needed at the beginning of the project. This would be recovered at the end of the 7 years.

The new product (exercise equipment) would sell for $150 per unit and would cost $100 per unit to produce (in addition to the operating expenses of the equipment). Richard expects to sell 1,500 units per year. The cost of capital is 10 percent.

REQUIRED:

1. Prepare a schedule of cash flows for the proposed project. Assume there are no income taxes.
2. Compute the NPV of the project. Should the new product be produced?

P22-2
NPV Analysis
LO 1, 3

Box Elder Communications Company is considering the production and marketing of a communications system that will increase the efficiency of messaging for small businesses or branch offices of large companies. Each unit hooked into the system is assigned a mailbox number, which can be matched to a telephone extension number, providing access to messages 24 hours a day. Up to 20 units can be hooked into the system, allowing the delivery of the same message to as many as 20 people. Personal codes can be used to make messages confidential. Furthermore, messages can be reviewed, recorded, canceled, replied to, or deleted, all during the same phone call. Indicators wired to the telephone blink whenever new messages are present.

To produce this product, a $1.35 million investment in new equipment is required. The equipment would last 10 years but would need major maintenance costing $100,000 at the end of its sixth year. The salvage value of the equipment at the end of 10 years is estimated to be $200,000. If this new system is produced, working capital must also be increased by $100,000. This capital will be restored at the end of the product's life cycle, estimated to be 10 years. Revenues from the sale of the product are estimated at $1.5 million per year; cash operating expenses are estimated at $1.2 million per year.

REQUIRED:

1. Prepare a schedule of cash flows for the proposed project. Ignore income taxes.
2. Assuming that Box Elder's cost of capital is 12 percent, compute the project's NPV. Should the product be produced?

P22-3
Payback; NPV; Managerial Incentives; Ethical Behavior
LO 2, 3

William ("Billy") Adams, president of a branch bank, was pleased with his bank's performance over the past 3 years. Each year the branch bank's profits had increased, and he had earned a sizable bonus (bonuses are a linear function of the bank's reported income). He had also received considerable attention from higher management. A vice-president of the corporation had told him in confidence that if his performance over the next 3 years matched his first 3, he would be given the opportunity to manage one of the larger banks.

Determined to fulfill these expectations, Billy made sure that he personally reviewed every capital budget request. He wanted to be certain that any funds invested would provide good, solid returns (the division's cost of capital is 10 percent). At the moment, he is reviewing two independent requests. Proposal A involves automating a check processing operation that is currently labor intensive. Proposal B centers on developing and marketing several new electronic tellers. Proposal A requires an initial outlay of $90,000 and B requires $130,000. Both projects could be funded given the status of the branch bank's capital budget. Both have an expected life of 6 years and have the following projected after-tax cash flows:

Year	*Proposal A*	*Proposal B*
1	$60,000	$(15,000)
2	50,000	(10,000)
3	20,000	(5,000)
4	15,000	85,000
5	10,000	110,000
6	5,000	135,000

After careful consideration of each investment, Billy approved funding of Proposal A and rejected B.

REQUIRED:

1. Compute the NPV for each proposal.
2. Compute the payback period for each proposal.
3. According to your analysis, which proposal(s) should be accepted? Explain.
4. Explain why Billy accepted only Proposal A. Considering the possible reasons for rejection, would you judge his behavior to be ethical? Explain.

P22-4
Basic IRR Analysis
LO 1, 4

Healthcare Insurance Company was approached by a local furnace company with the proposition of replacing its old heating system with a modern, more efficient unit. The cost of the new system was quoted at $50,240, but it would save $10,000 per year in fuel costs. The estimated life of the new system is 10 years, with no salvage value expected. Excited over the possibility of saving $10,000 per year and having a more reliable unit, the president of Healthcare Insurance has asked for an analysis of the project's economic viability. All capital projects are required to earn at least the firm's cost of capital, which is 10 percent. There are no income taxes to consider.

REQUIRED:

1. Calculate the project's internal rate of return. Should the company acquire the new furnace?

2. Suppose that fuel savings are less than claimed. Calculate the minimum annual cash savings that must be realized for the project to earn a rate equal to the firm's cost of capital.
3. Suppose that the life of the furnace is overestimated by 2 years. Repeat Requirements 1 and 2 under this assumption.

P22-5
NPV; IRR; Uncertainty
LO 1, 3

Eden Airlines is interested in acquiring a new aircraft to service a new route. The route would be from Dallas to El Paso. The aircraft would fly one round trip daily, except for scheduled maintenance days. There are 15 maintenance days scheduled each year. The seating capacity of the aircraft is 150. Flights are expected to be fully booked. The average revenue per passenger per flight (one-way) is $200. Annual operating costs of the aircraft are given below:

Fuel	$1,400,000
Flight personnel	500,000
Food and beverages	100,000
Maintenance	400,000
Other	100,000
Total	$2,500,000

The aircraft will cost $100,000,000 and has an expected life of 20 years. The company requires a 14 percent return. Assume there are no income taxes.

REQUIRED:

1. Calculate the NPV for the aircraft. Should the company buy it?
2. In discussing the proposal, the marketing manager for the airline believes that the assumption of 100 percent booking is unrealistic. He believes that the booking rate will be somewhere between 70 percent and 90 percent, with the most likely rate being 80 percent. Recalculate the NPV using an 80 percent seating capacity. Should the aircraft be purchased?
3. Calculate the average seating rate that would be needed so that NPV = 0.
4. Suppose that the price per passenger could be increased by 10 percent without any effect on demand. What is the average seating rate now needed to achieve a NPV = 0? What would you now recommend?

P22-6
Review of Basic Capital investment Procedures
LO 1, 2, 3, 4

Dr. Donna White had just returned from a conference in which she learned of a new procedure for performing root canals, which reduces the time for them by 50 percent. Given her patient-load pressures, Dr. White was anxious to try out the new technique. By decreasing the time on root canals, she could increase her total revenues by performing more services within a work period. Unfortunately, in order to implement the new procedure, some special equipment costing $20,000 was needed. The equipment had an expected life of 4 years, with a salvage value of $2,000. Dr. White estimated that her cash revenues would increase by the following amounts:

Year	*Revenue Increases*
1	$5,600
2	8,000
3	9,800
4	9,800

She also expected additional cash expenses amounting to $1,000 per year. The cost of capital is 12 percent. Assume there are no income taxes.

REQUIRED:

1. Compute the payback period for the new equipment.
2. Compute the accounting rate of return using both original investment and average investment.
3. Compute the NPV and IRR for the project. Should Dr. White purchase the new equipment? Should she be concerned about payback or the accounting rate of return in making this decision?
4. Before finalizing her decision, Dr. White decided to call 2 dentists who had been using the new procedure for the past 6 months. The conversations revealed a somewhat less glowing report than she received at the conference. Nearly 25 percent of the patients receiving the procedure returned with complaints about the affected tooth. A traditional rework had to be performed on these patients. Dr. White estimated that the increase in cash revenues would be cut by 33 percent because of the extra time and cost involved in rework. Furthermore, who knew what the effect on patient goodwill would be? Using this information, recompute the NPV and the IRR of the project. What would you now recommend?

P22-7
Replacement Decision; Basic NPV Analysis
LO 5, 6

Dinocare Travel Agency relies heavily on its mainframe computer to conduct daily business. The agency is considering replacing its existing mainframe computer with a new model manufactured by a different company. The information presented by the salesperson on the new model was appealing. The increased capabilities of the computer promised significant savings relative to the agency's existing computer.

The old computer, however, was only acquired 3 years ago, has a remaining life of 5 years, and will have a salvage value of $10,000. The book value is $200,000. Straight-line depreciation (with a half-year convention) is being used for tax purposes. The cash operating costs of the existing computer, including software, personnel, and other supplies, total $100,000 per year.

The new computer has an initial cost of $500,000 and will have cash operating costs of $50,000 per year. The new computer will have a life of 5 years and a salvage value of $100,000 at the end of the fifth year. MACRS depreciation will be used for tax purposes. If the new computer is purchased, the old one will be sold for $50,000. The company needs to decide whether to keep the old computer or buy the new one. The cost of capital is 12 percent. The federal tax rate is 34 percent and the state tax rate is 6 percent. State tax policies follow federal policies (e.g., the state allows the same depreciation deductions as those claimed for the federal tax return).

REQUIRED: Compute the NPV of each alternative. Should the company keep the old computer or buy the new one?

P22-8
Lease versus Buy
LO 5, 6

Moore Chiropractic Clinic is trying to decide whether it should purchase or lease a new piece of equipment that would help in the diagnosis of spinal problems. If purchased, the new equipment would cost $100,000 and be used for 10 years. The salvage value at the end of ten years is estimated at $20,000. The machine would be depreciated using MACRS over a seven-year period. The annual maintenance and operating costs would be $20,000. Annual revenues are estimated at $55,000.

If the machine is leased, the company would need to pay annual lease payments of $20,700. The first lease payment and a deposit of $5,000 are due immediately. The last lease payment is paid at the beginning of Year 10. The deposit is refundable at the end of the tenth year. In addition, under a normal contract, the company must pay for all maintenance and operating costs, although the leasing company does offer a service contract that will provide annual maintenance (on leased equipment only). The contract must be paid up front and costs $30,000. Moore estimates that the contract will reduce its annual maintenance and operating costs by $10,000. Moore's cost of capital is 14 percent. The combined federal and state tax rate is 40 percent.

REQUIRED:

1. Prepare schedules showing the after-tax cash flows for each alternative. (Prepare schedules for the lease alternative with and without the service contract; assume that the service contract is amortized on a straight-line basis for the 10 years.) Include all revenues and costs associated with each alternative.
2. Compute the NPV for each alternative, assuming that Moore does not purchase the service contract. Should the equipment be purchased or leased? For this analysis, was it necessary to include all of the costs and revenues for each alternative? Explain.
3. Compute the NPV for the lease alternative assuming that the service contract *is* purchased. Does this change your decision about leasing? What revenues and costs could be excluded without affecting the conclusion?

P22-9
Competing Investments; NPV; Basic Analysis
LO 5, 6

Allen Stice has decided to start a dry cleaning business. As part of his service, he is planning to have a pickup and delivery service. A premium will be charged for the service, and this premium is expected to cover the extra operating costs. Allen has two options for providing the service. He can buy a delivery truck and hire a driver, or he can pay an annual fee to a local agency that will provide the pickup and delivery service. Cost and other data are given below:

	Ownership Option	*Agency Option*
Initial outlay	$25,000	—
Annual premiums	20,000	$20,000
Cash expenses	10,000	9,000

The expected life of the truck is 6 years, and it will have a salvage value of $1,000. The truck qualifies as five-year property for MACRS purposes. Allen's tax rate is 40 percent. The cost of capital is 12 percent.

REQUIRED: Compute the NPV of each alternative and make a recommendation to Allen.

P22-10
Capital Investment; Advanced Manufacturing Environment
LO 6, 7

"I know that it's the thing to do," insisted Pamela Kincaid, vice-president of finance for Colgate Manufacturing. "If we are going to be competitive, we need to build this completely automated plant."

"I'm not so sure," replied Bill Thomas. "The savings from labor reductions and increased productivity are only $4,000,000 per year. The price tag for this factory—and it's a small one—is $45,000,000. That gives a payback period of more than 11 years. That's a long time to put the company's money at risk."

"Yeah, but you're overlooking the savings that we'll get from the increase in quality," interjected John Simpson, production manager. "With this system, we can decrease our waste and rework time significantly. Those savings are worth another million dollars per year."

"Another million will only cut the payback to nine years," retorted Bill. "Ron, you're the marketing manager—do you have any insights?"

"Well, there are other factors to consider, such as service quality and market share. I think that increasing our product quality and improving our delivery service will make us a lot more competitive. I know for a fact that two of our competitors have decided against automation. That'll give us a shot at their customers, provided our product is of higher quality and we can deliver it faster. I estimate that it'll increase our net cash benefits by another $6 million per year."

"Wow! Now that's impressive," Bill exclaimed, nearly convinced. "The payback is now getting down to a reasonable level."

"I agree," said Pamela, "but we do need to be sure that it's a sound investment. I know that estimates for construction of the facility have gone as high as $49.8 million. I also know that the expected residual value, after the 20 years of service we expect to get, is $5 million. Also, you're using before-tax cash flows. We need after-tax cash flows. I think I had better see if this project can cover our 14 percent cost of capital."

"Now wait a minute, Pamela," Bill demanded. "You know that I usually insist on a 20 percent rate of return, especially for a project of this magnitude."

REQUIRED:

1. Compute the NPV of the project using the original savings and investment figures. Do the calculation for discount rates of 14 percent and 20 percent. Assume straight-line depreciation with no half-year convention is used for tax purposes. The tax rate is 40 percent (includes state and federal taxes).
2. Compute the NPV of the project using the additional benefits noted by the production and marketing managers. Also, use the original cost estimate of $45 million. Again do the calculation for both possible discount rates.
3. Compute the NPV of the project using all estimates of cash flows, including the possible initial outlay of $49.8 million. Do the calculation using discount rates of 14 percent and 20 percent.
4. If you were making the decision, what would you do? Explain.

P22-11 Competing Projects

LO 5, 6

John Day, owner of an repair shop, has unused space in the building he had purchased several years ago. Initially, John had offered only basic auto repair services but since the business has grown, he is now considering the possibility of using the empty space to offer one of two additional services. Specifically, he is planning to add either an engine overhaul service or a diesel engine repair. In either case, equipment must be purchased and skilled labor hired. The revenues and costs associated with each alternative are shown below.

	Overhaul Service	*Diesel Service*
Revenues	$120,000	$250,000
Labor	(24,000)	(30,000)
Materials	(20,190)	(100,000)
Tax rate	40%	40%

To set up the overhaul service, an initial investment of $280,000 in equipment is required. The equipment investment for the diesel service is $420,000. The useful life of the equipment, in each case, is 10 years, with no salvage value expected. Straight-line depreciation with a half-year convention is being used.

The tax rate used in the income statements is the sum of the federal and the state rates. The cost of capital is 16 percent.

REQUIRED:

1. Prepare a schedule of after-tax cash flows for each alternative.
2. Compute the NPV and the IRR for each alternative. Which alternative would you recommend? Do the NPV and the IRR measures recommend the same investment? Will this always be the case?
3. Someone tells John that he should be using MACRS instead of straight-line depreciation. Recompute the NPV for the diesel service alternative using MACRS depreciation. By how much did NPV increase?

P22-12 Capital Investment; Discount Rates; Intangible Benefits; Time Horizon; Advanced Manufacturing Environment

LO 6, 7

Lacy Manufacturing, Inc., produces trash compactors, microwave ovens, and electric ranges. Because of increasing competition, Lacy is considering making an investment in an automated manufacturing system. Since competition is most keen for microwave ovens, the production process for this line has been selected for initial evaluation. The automated system for the oven line would replace an existing system (purchased one year ago for $6 million). Although the existing system will be fully depreciated in nine years, it is expected to last another ten years. The automated system would also have a useful life of ten years.

The existing system is capable of producing 100,000 microwave ovens per year. Sales and production data using the existing system are provided by the accounting department:

Sales per year (units)	100,000
Selling price	$300
Costs per unit:	
Direct materials	$80
Direct labor	90
Volume-related overhead	20
Direct fixed overhead	40[a]

[a]All cash expenses with the exception of depreciation, which is $6 per unit. The existing equipment is being depreciated using straight-line with no salvage value considered.

The automated system will cost $34 million to purchase, plus an estimated $20 million in software and implementation. (Assume that all investment outlays occur at the beginning of the first year.) If the automated equipment is purchased, the old equipment can be sold for $3 million.

The automated system will require fewer parts for production and will produce with less waste. Because of this, the direct materials cost per unit will be reduced by 25 percent. Automation will also require fewer support activities and, as a consequence, volume-related overhead will be reduced by $5 per unit and direct fixed overhead (other than depreciation) by $17 per unit. Direct labor is reduced by 66 2/3 percent. Assume, for simplicity, that the new investment will be depreciated on a pure straight-line basis for tax purposes with no salvage value. Ignore the half-life convention.

The firm's cost of capital is 12 percent, but management chooses to use 18 percent as the required rate of return for evaluation of investments. The tax rate is 40 percent.

REQUIRED:

1. Compute the net present value for the old system and the automated system. Which system should the company choose?
2. Repeat the net present value analysis of Requirement 1 using 12 percent as the discount rate.
3. Upon seeing the projected sales for the old system, the marketing manager commented: "Sales of 100,000 units per year cannot be maintained in the current competitive environment for more than one year unless we buy the automated system. The automated system will allow us to compete on the basis of quality and lead time. If we keep the old system, our sales will drop by 10,000 units per year." Repeat the net present value analysis using this new information and a 12 percent discount rate.
4. An industrial engineer for Lacy noticed that salvage value for the automated equipment had not been included in the analysis. He estimated that the equipment could be sold for $4 million at the end of 10 years. He also estimated that the equipment of the

old system would have no salvage value at the end of 10 years. Repeat the net present value analysis using this information and the information in Requirement 2.

5. Given the outcomes of the previous 4 requirements, comment on the importance of providing accurate inputs for assessing investments in automated manufacturing systems.

DISCUSSION AND INTERPRETATION PROBLEMS

D22-1
Capital Investment and Ethical Behavior

Manny Carson, CMA and controller of Wakeman Enterprises, had been given permission to acquire a new computer and software for the company's accounting system. The capital investment analysis had shown an NPV of $100,000; however, the initial estimates of acquisition and installation costs had been made on the basis of tentative costs without any formal bids. Manny now has two formal bids, one that would allow the firm to meet or beat the original projected NPV and one that would reduce the projected NPV by $50,000. The second bid involves a system that would increase both the initial cost and the operating cost.

Normally, Manny would take the first bid without hesitation. However, Todd Downing, the owner of the firm presenting the second bid, was a close friend. Manny had called Todd and explained the situation, offering Todd an opportunity to alter his bid and win the job. Todd thanked Manny and then made a counteroffer.

Todd: "Listen, Manny, this job at the original price is the key to a successful year for me. The revenues will help me gain approval for the loan I need for renovation and expansion. If I don't get that loan, I see hard times ahead. The financial stats for loan approval are so marginal that reducing the bid price may blow my chances."

Manny: "Losing the bid altogether would be even worse, don't you think?"

Todd: "True. However, I have a suggestion. If you grant me the job, I will have the capability of adding personnel. I know that your son is looking for a job, and I can offer him a good salary and a promising future. Additionally, I'll be able to take you and your wife on that vacation to Hawaii that we have been talking about."

Manny: "Well, you have a point. My son is having an awful time finding a job, and he has a wife and three kids to support. My wife is tired of having them live with us. She and I could use a vacation. I doubt that the other bidder would make any fuss if we turned it down. Its offices are out of state, after all."

Todd: "Out of state? All the more reason to turn it down. Given the state's economy, it seems almost criminal to take business outside. Those are the kind of business decisions that cause problems for people like your son."

REQUIRED: Evaluate the ethical behavior of Manny. Should Manny have called Todd in the first place? What if Todd had agreed to meet the lower bid price—would there have been any problems? Identify the standards of ethical conduct (listed in Chapter 1) that Manny may be violating, if any.

D22-2
Cash Flows; NPV; Choice of Discount Rate; Advanced Manufacturing Environment

Charles Bradshaw, president and owner of Wellington Metal Works, had just returned from a trip to Europe.[11] While there, he had toured several plants using robotic manufacturing. Seeing the efficiency and success of these companies, Charles became convinced that robotic manufacturing is the wave of the future and Wellington could gain a competitive advantage by adopting the new technology.

Based on this vision, Charles requested an analysis detailing the costs and benefits of robotic manufacturing for the material handling and merchandising equipment group.

11. This case is based, in part, on the following article: David A. Greenberg, "Robotics: One Small Company's Experience," in *Cost Accounting for the 90s* (Montvale, NJ: National Association of Accountants, 1986), pp. 57–63.

This group of products consists of such items as cooler shelving, stocking carts, and bakery racks. The products are sold directly to supermarkets.

A committee, consisting of the controller, the marketing manager, and the production manager was given the responsibility to prepare the analysis. As a starting point, the controller provided the following information on expected revenues and expenses for the existing manual system:

		Percentage of Sales
Sales	$400,000	100%
Less: Variable expenses[1]	(228,000)	57
Contribution margin	$172,000	43
Less: Fixed expenses[2]	(92,000)	23
Income before taxes	$ 80,000	20

[1]Variable cost detail (as a percentage of sales):

Direct materials	16
Direct labor	20
Variable overhead	9
Variable selling	12

[2]$20,000 is depreciation; the rest are cash expenses.

Given the current competitive environment, the marketing manager thought that the above level of profitability would likely not change for the next decade.

After some investigation into various robotic equipment, the committee settled on an Aide 900 system, a robot that has the capability to weld stainless steel or aluminum. It is capable of being programmed to adjust the path, angle, and speed of the torch. The production manager was excited about the robotic system because it eliminated the need to hire welders, which was attractive because the market for welders seemed perpetually tight. By reducing the dependence on welders, better production scheduling and fewer late deliveries would result. Moreover, the robot's production rate is four times that of a person.

It was also discovered that robotic welding is superior in quality to manual welding. As a consequence, some of the costs of poor quality could be reduced. By providing better-quality products and avoiding late deliveries, the marketing manager was convinced that the company would have such a competitive edge that it would increase sales by 50 percent for the affected product group by the end of the fourth year. The marketing manager provided the following projections for the next ten years, the useful life of the robotic equipment:

	Year 1	*Year 2*	*Year 3*	*Years 4–10*
Sales	$400,000	$450,000	$500,000	$600,000

Currently, the company employs four welders, who work 40 hours per week and 50 weeks per year at an average wage of $10 per hour. If the robot is acquired, it will need one operator, who will be paid $10 per hour. Because of improved quality, the robotic system will also reduce the cost of direct materials by 25 percent, the cost of variable overhead by 33.33 percent, and variable selling expenses by 10 percent. All of these reductions will take place immediately after the robotic system is in place and operating. Fixed costs will be increased by the depreciation associated with the robot. The robot will be depreciated using MACRS. (The manual system uses straight-line depreciation without a half-year convention and has a current book value of $200,000.) If the robotic system is acquired, the old system will be sold for $40,000.

The robotic system requires the following initial investment:

Purchase price	$380,000
Installation	70,000
Training	30,000
Engineering	40,000

At the end of ten years, the robot will have a salvage value of $20,000. Assume that the company's cost of capital is 12 percent. The tax rate is 34 percent.

REQUIRED:

1. Prepare a schedule of after-tax cash flows for the manual and robotic systems.
2. Using the schedule of cash flows computed in Requirement 1, compute the NPV for each system. Should the company invest in the robotic system?
3. In practice, many financial officers tend to use a higher discount rate than is justified by what the firm's cost of capital is. For example, a firm may use a discount rate of 20 percent when its cost of capital is or could be 12 percent. Offer some reasons for this practice. Assume that the annual after-tax cash benefit of adopting the robotic system is $80,000 per year more than the manual system. The initial outlay for the robotic system is $340,000. Compute the NPV using 12 percent and 20 percent. Would the robotic system be acquired if 20 percent is used? Could this conservative approach have a negative impact on a firm's ability to stay competitive?

D22-3 Research Assignment

The principles that drive capital investment analysis should apply to all organizational settings. Yet, some settings have characteristics that make it more difficult. For example, state and federal governments routinely make capital investment decisions. State and federal governments receive capital from taxes, fees, and debt (usually bonds). Capital funds are used to build infrastructure (highways, bridges, etc.) and to invest in such intangibles as education and research. There are some fundamental questions that need to be asked. For example, should the state and federal government use formal capital investment criteria? If so, what discount rate should be used? Furthermore, how do you deal with a situation where a project has a negative NPV but it's thought to be vital for the public well-being?

REQUIRED: Search the literature and identify articles that deal with investments that governments make. Write a paper that describes how they arrive at these decisions. Do they ever use NPV or IRR? Have these models been discussed in the literature on government investment activity? Finally, write your views on the use of these models in the government sector.

D22-4 Research Assignment

The capital expenditure approach that you have studied in this chapter relies on quantitative, financial measures such as payback, net present value, and the internal rate of return. Some have argued that these traditional capital expenditure models should only be a starting point in the analysis. Other criteria such as cycle time (the time it takes to convert materials into a finished good) and flexibility may be important considerations in a capital expenditure decision—yet these factors are not captured by IRR or NPV. In fact, there have been efforts to build formal frameworks that allow explicit consideration of multiple criteria. One of these frameworks is an analytical hierarchy process. This approach is described in the following article:

David E. Stout, Matthew J. Liberatore, and Thomas F. Monahan, "Decision Support Software for Capital Budgeting," *Management Accounting,* (July, 1991), pp. 50-53.

REQUIRED: Read the above article and write a paper that describes how the method works. In your paper offer a critique of the method. What is your opinion of the approach? Is it better than the traditional models or do you think there are ways that the traditional models can capture such things as cycle time and flexibility? Do you think that managers would really use this methodology? Explain.

CHAPTER 23
Decision Making in the Advanced Manufacturing Environment

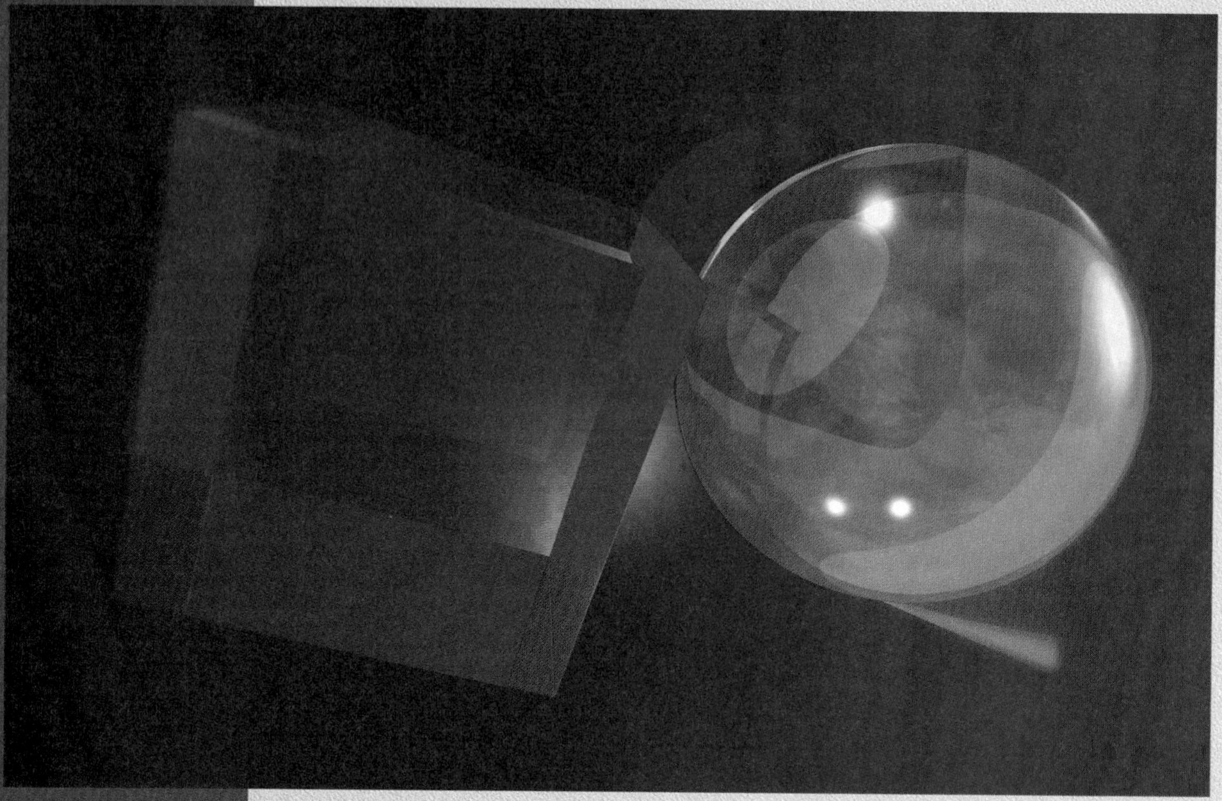

LEARNING OBJECTIVES

After studying this chapter, you should be able to:

1. Describe the traditional inventory management model.
2. Describe JIT inventory management.
3. Explain how activity-based costing facilitates strategic decision making.
4. Describe the resource usage model and its role in activity-based costing.
5. Explain the effect of activity-based costing and JIT on relevant costing.
6. Describe segment analysis in both a conventional setting and in an ABC/JIT setting.

Scenario

Michelle Anderson, president and owner of Anderson Parts Inc., had just finished reading the report prepared by Henry Jensen, a special consultant attached to the management advisory section of a national public accounting firm. The recommendations in the report were somewhat surprising, almost shocking, and Michelle was looking forward to her meeting with him to discuss them. She certainly had plenty of questions. If the report was realistic in its recommendations, hiring the consultant was one of the best decisions she had made since assuming control of the business over five years ago. Her thoughts were interrupted by Henry's arrival.

"Have a seat, Henry. I have to confess that your recommendations are intriguing. If you can convince me that they'll work, you'll have more than earned your fee."

"I think I can provide a lot of support for those recommendations. When we first met, you mentioned that your company had lost 20 percent of its market share over the past 5 years. In your industry, as in many others, much of that loss is because of the gains made by foreign competitors. Foreign producers are offering a higher-quality product at a lower price and with better delivery performance."

"I am aware of that. You remember that in our first meeting I said as much. I was certain at that time that the solution was automation, and I was prepared to sink millions into that approach. I was convinced that automating would improve quality, lower manufacturing costs, and cut down our lead time for production. Because so much money was involved, I hired you to tell us how to automate and exactly what type of equipment to buy. Instead you tell me that I shouldn't automate—at least not right away—but simplify our purchasing and manufacturing by installing something called a just-in-time system. You also indicate that we should adopt an activity-based costing system and our accounting system should ultimately be integrated with other information systems within our firm. Do you really believe that this will bring the benefits I'm seeking? Are you speaking from experience or experiment?"

"Experience. You're certainly not a guinea pig for something we haven't tried before. Case after case has shown us that 80 percent of the competitive benefits from automation can be achieved by implementing JIT— and at a significantly decreased cost. First implement JIT; then you can see where automation will be of the most benefit. Complementary to this is the concurrent development of a comprehensive, integrated information system. Your information system must supply accurate cost information. Activity-based costing has helped many firms improve the accuracy of their product costing. JIT and activity-based costing are sensible solutions. The strategy we recommend is first simplify, then automate, and, finally, integrate.[1] Of course, you should realize that JIT and activity-based costing are not an easy fix to all your prob-

1. For a detailed discussion of the strategy, see Stephen M. Hronec, "The Effects of Manufacturing Productivity on Cost Accounting and Management Reporting," *Cost Accounting for the 90s* (Montvale, NJ: Institute of Management Accountants, 1986), pp. 117–125. See also William G. Stoddard, Stephen G. Schaus, and Nolan W. Rhea, "New Guidelines for Factory Automation," *Material Handling Engineering* (May 1985), pp. 104–107.

lems. But these measures should help. I might add that they have helped some firms more than others."

"It sounds promising. But can you be more specific? What benefits have other companies experienced?"

"Well, Michelle, your firm manufactures machine parts. Another firm in your same line of business was having a difficult time competing. It needed 24 weeks to produce one of its products from start to finish while a Japanese competitor produced and delivered the same part in 6 weeks. After installing a JIT system, the American firm was able to produce the part in only 20 days."

"Henry, that's hard to believe. Yet, I know that a lot of the business we have lost is because we have such poor delivery performance compared to some of our competitors. You're telling me that we can make dramatic improvements in our lead time with our existing technology?"

"Yes—but that isn't all. Reducing lead time is only one of the benefits. A JIT purchasing and manufacturing system can reduce your inventories—raw materials, work in process, and finished goods—to much lower levels. Do you realize that U.S. industry has as much as 40 percent of its assets tied up in inventory?[2] That's a lot of nonproductive capital. The Lansing plant of GM used to carry 60,000 tons of sheet steel in inventory while consuming 900 tons a day. Now it carries 4,000 tons and consumes 1,200 tons a day. Overall, using JIT, GM has cut inventory-related costs from $8 billion to $2 billion. There are other examples. Motorola has reduced inventory by $210 million.[3] A chain saw manufacturer in Oregon has taken $15 million out of inventory through JIT."[4]

"Incredible. But what about quality?"

"JIT cannot work without adopting the concept of total quality control. Defects cannot be tolerated. JIT demands quality. For example, Hewlett-Packard's Fort Collins Division reduced scrap and rework by 60 percent. Xerox reduced its reject rate on outsourced parts from 5,000 parts-per-million one year to 1,300 parts-per-million the next."[5]

"Fascinating. Well, you've convinced me—at least about JIT. Tell me something about activity-based costing."

"Activity-based costing traces costs to activities and then to products. Products consume activities. It's a very accurate way to determine product costs. But it also provides strategic insights and should be used as a tool for decision making. It isn't simply a replacement for your existing cost accounting system."[6]

"I'm ready to start the conversion. But before I can commit our company, we need to convince some of my key executives. The lead-time and quality issues will be easy to sell. If we can convince them that our traditional inventory management practices are outmoded, they'll buy the whole package. I need their commitment and support for all of this to work. Do you agree?"

2. Ernest Raia, "Just-in-Time USA," *Purchasing* (February 13, 1986), p. 50.
3. Raia, "Just-in-Time USA."
4. Al Furst, "Spreading the Gospel at Fluke," *Electronic Business* (April 1, 1986), p. 82.
5. Both examples are in Raia, "Just-in-Time USA."
6. Richard B. Troxel and Milan G. Weber, Jr., "The Evolution of Activity-Based Costing," *Journal of Cost Management* (Spring 1990), pp. 14–22.

"Absolutely. I hope that one of those key executives is your controller. JIT manufacturing and purchasing and activity-based costing affect many traditional management accounting models. I think it would be a good idea to schedule some training seminars. In these seminars, I'll review the basics of the traditional inventory management system and discuss the JIT system. In the process, I'll point out the benefits of the new system and highlight the deficiencies of the old system. I'll also discuss how activity-based costing can improve strategic decision making."

BASICS OF TRADITIONAL INVENTORY MANAGEMENT

Objective 1
Describe the traditional inventory management model.

In a world of certainty—a world in which the demand for a product or material is known with certainty for a given period of time (usually a year)—two major costs are associated with inventory. If the inventory is a material or good purchased from an outside source, these inventory-related costs are known as *ordering costs* and *carrying costs.* If the material or good is produced internally, the costs are called *setup costs* and *carrying costs.*

ordering costs

- **Ordering costs** are the costs of placing and receiving an order. Examples include the costs of processing an order (clerical costs and documents), insurance for shipment, and unloading costs.

setup costs

- **Setup costs** are the costs of preparing equipment and facilities so they can be used to produce a particular product or component. Examples are wages of idled production workers, the cost of idled production facilities (lost income), and the costs of test runs (labor, materials, and overhead).

carrying costs

- **Carrying costs** are the costs of carrying inventory. Examples include insurance, inventory taxes, obsolescence, the opportunity cost of funds tied up in inventory, handling costs, and storage space.

Ordering costs and setup costs are similar in nature—both represent costs that must be incurred to acquire inventory. They differ only in the nature of the prerequisite activity (filling out and placing an order versus configuring equipment and facilities). Thus, in the discussion that follows, any reference to ordering costs can be viewed as a reference to setup costs.

stockout costs

If demand is not known with certainty, a third category of inventory costs—called *stockout costs*—exists. **Stockout costs** are the costs of not having sufficient inventory. Examples are lost sales (both current and future), the costs of expediting (increased transportation charges, overtime, and so on), and the costs of interrupted production.

Inventory: Why It Is Needed

Maximizing profits requires that inventory-related costs be minimized. But minimizing carrying costs favors ordering or producing in small lot sizes, whereas minimizing ordering costs favors large, infrequent orders (minimization of setup costs favors long, infrequent production runs). Thus, minimizing carrying costs encourages small or no inventories and minimizing ordering or setup costs encourages larger inventories. The need to balance these two sets of costs so that the *total* cost of carrying and ordering can be minimized is one reason organizations choose to carry inventory.

Dealing with uncertainty in demand is a second major reason for holding inventory. Even if the ordering or setup costs were negligible, organizations would still carry inventory because of stockout costs. If the demand for materials or products is greater than expected, inventory can serve as a buffer, giving organizations the abilities to meet delivery dates (thus keeping customers satisfied), to keep production flowing (avoiding the need to idle facilities while waiting for a part to arrive), and to continue supplying customers or processes with goods even if a process goes down because of a failed machine.

Although balancing conflicting costs and dealing with uncertainty are the two most frequently cited reasons for carrying inventories, other reasons, though perhaps not as major, do exist. For example, organizations may acquire larger inventories than normal to take advantage of quantity discounts or to avoid anticipated price increases.

Inventory Policy

In developing an inventory policy, two basic questions must be addressed.

1. How much should be ordered (or produced)?
2. When should the order be placed (or the setup done)?

The first question needs to be addressed before the second can be answered.

Order Quantity and Total Ordering and Carrying Costs. Assume that demand is known. In choosing an order quantity or a lot size for production, managers need be concerned only with ordering (or setup) and carrying costs. The total ordering (or setup) and carrying cost can be described by the following equation:

$$TC = PD/Q + CQ/2 \qquad (23.1)$$

$$= \text{Ordering cost} + \text{Carrying cost}$$

where TC = The total ordering (or setup) and carrying cost
P = The cost of placing and receiving an order (or the cost of setting up a production run)
Q = The number of units ordered each time an order is placed (or the lot size for production)
D = The known annual demand
C = The cost of carrying one unit of stock for one year

To illustrate, assume that the following values apply for a part used in the production of refrigerators (the part is purchased from external suppliers):

D = 10,000 units
Q = 1,000 units
P = \$25 per order
C = \$2 per unit

Dividing D by Q produces the number of orders per year, which is 10 (10,000/1,000). Multiplying the number of orders per year by the cost of placing and receiving an order ($D/Q \times P$) yields the total ordering cost of \$250 (10 × \$25).

The total carrying cost for the year is given by $CQ/2$; this expression is equivalent to multiplying the average inventory on hand ($Q/2$) by the carrying cost per unit (C). For an order of 1,000 units with a carrying cost of $2 per unit, the average inventory is 500 (1,000/2) and the carrying cost for the year is $1,000 ($2 × 500). (Assuming average inventory to be $Q/2$ is equivalent to assuming that inventory is consumed uniformly.)

Applying Equation 23.1, the total cost is $1,250 ($250 + $1,000). An order quantity of 1,000 with a total cost of $1,250, however, may not be the best choice. Some other order quantity may produce a lower total cost. The objective is to find the order quantity that minimizes the total cost. This order quantity is called the **economic order quantity (EOQ).**

economic order quantity (EOQ)

Computing the EOQ. Since the EOQ is the quantity that minimizes Equation 23.1, a formula for computing this quantity is easily derived.[7]

$$Q = \text{EOQ} = \sqrt{(2DP/C)} \quad (23.2)$$

Using the data from the example above, the EOQ can be computed using Equation 23.2:

$$\begin{aligned} \text{EOQ} &= \sqrt{(2 \times 10{,}000 \times 25)/2} \\ &= \sqrt{250{,}000} \\ &= 500 \end{aligned}$$

Substituting 500 as the value of Q in Equation 23.1 yields a total cost of $1,000. The number of orders placed would be 20 (10,000/500); thus, the total ordering cost is $500 (20 × $25). The average inventory is 250 (500/2), with a total carrying cost of $500 (250 × $2). Notice that the carrying cost equals the ordering cost. This is always true for the simple EOQ model described by Equation 23.2. Also notice that an order quantity of 500 is less costly than an order quantity of 1,000 ($1,000 versus $1,250).

Reorder Point. The EOQ answers the question of how much to order (or produce). Knowing when to place an order (or setup for production) is also an essential part of any inventory policy. The **reorder point** is the point in time a new order should be placed (or setup started). It is a function of the EOQ, the lead time, and the rate at which inventory is depleted. **Lead time** is the time required to receive the economic order quantity once an order is placed or a setup is initiated.

reorder point

lead time

To avoid stockout costs and to minimize carrying costs, an order should be placed so that it arrives just as the last item in inventory is used. Knowing the rate of usage and lead time allows us to compute the reorder point that accomplishes these objectives:

$$\text{Reorder point} = \text{Rate of usage} \times \text{Lead time} \quad (23.3)$$

To illustrate Equation 23.3, we will continue to use the refrigerator part example. Assume that the producer uses 50 parts per day and the lead time is 4 days. If so, an order should be placed when the inventory level of the refrigerator part drops to 200 units (4 × 50). Exhibit 23-1 provides a graphical illustration. Note that the inventory is depleted just as the order arrives and that the quantity on hand jumps back up to the EOQ level.

7. $d(TC)/dQ = C/2 - DP/Q^2 = 0$, where $Q^2 = 2DP/C$ and $Q = \sqrt{2DP/C}$

Exhibit 23-1
The Reorder Point

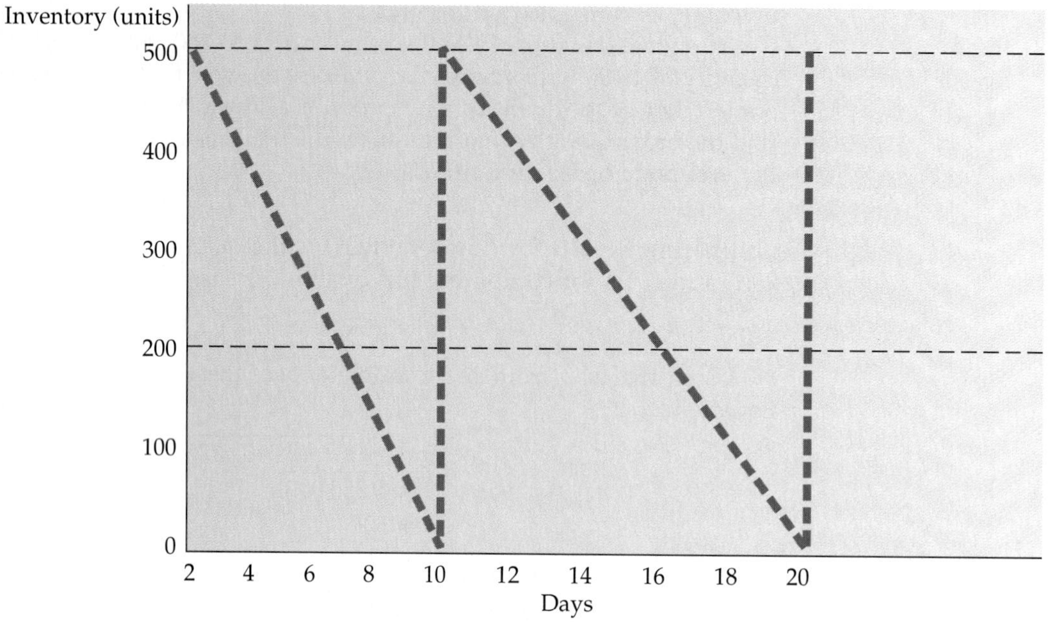

Demand Uncertainty and the Reorder Point. If the demand for the part or product is not known with certainty, the possibility of stockout exists. For example, if the refrigerator part was used at a rate of 60 parts a day instead of 50, the firm would use 200 parts after three and one-third days. Since the new order would not arrive until the end of the fourth day, some manufacturing facilities would be idled for two-thirds of a day. To avoid this problem, organizations often choose to carry safety stock. **Safety stock** is extra inventory carried to serve as insurance against fluctuations in demand. Safety stock is computed by multiplying the lead time by the difference between the maximum rate of usage and the average rate of usage. For example, if the maximum usage of refrigerator parts is 60 units per day, the average usage 50 units per day, and the lead time is 4 days, the safety stock is computed as follows:

safety stock

Maximum usage	60
Average usage	(50)
Difference	10
Lead time	× 4
Safety stock	40

With the presence of safety stock, the reorder point is computed as follows:

$$\text{Reorder point} = (\text{Average rate of usage} \times \text{Lead time}) + \text{Safety stock}$$

For the refrigerator example, the reorder point with safety stock is computed below:

$$\begin{aligned}\text{Reorder point} &= (50 \times 4) + 40 \\ &= 240 \text{ units}\end{aligned}$$

Thus, an order is automatically placed whenever the inventory level drops to 240 units.

A Comprehensive Example. Peterson Cycle is a large manufacturer of motorcycles with several plants throughout the nation. Each plant produces all subassemblies necessary to assemble a particular model. The manager of the company's largest Midwestern plant is trying to determine the size of the production runs for the gas tank fabrication area. He is convinced that the current lot size is too large and wants to identify the quantity that should be produced to minimize the sum of the carrying and setup costs. He also wants to avoid stockouts since any stockout would shut down the assembly line.

To help him in his decision, the controller has supplied the following information:

- Average demand for gas tanks: 80 per day
- Maximum demand for gas tanks: 90 per day
- Annual demand for gas tanks: 20,000
- Unit carrying cost: $3
- Setup cost: $7,500
- Lead time: 20 days

Based on the above information, the economic order quantity and the reorder point are computed in Exhibit 23-2. As the computation illustrates, the gas tanks should be produced in batches of 10,000 and a new setup should be started when the supply of gas tanks drops to 1,800.

EOQ and Inventory Management

As the preceding example illustrates, the EOQ model is very useful in identifying the optimal tradeoff between inventory carrying costs and setup costs. The historical importance of the EOQ model in many American industries can be better appreciated by understanding the nature of the traditional manufacturing environment. This environment has been characterized by the mass production of a few standardized products that typically have a very high setup cost. The pro-

Exhibit 23-2
EOQ and Reorder Point Illustrated

$$\begin{aligned} \text{EOQ} &= \sqrt{(2DP)/C} \\ &= \sqrt{(2 \times 20{,}000 \times 7{,}500)/3} \\ &= \sqrt{100{,}000{,}000} \\ &= 10{,}000 \text{ gas tanks} \end{aligned}$$

Safety stock:

Maximum usage	90
Average usage	80
Difference	10
Lead time	×20
Safety stock	200

$$\begin{aligned} \text{Reorder point} &= \text{Average usage} \times \text{Lead time} + \text{Safety stock} \\ &= (80 \times 20) + 200 \\ &= 1{,}800 \text{ units} \end{aligned}$$

duction of the gas tanks fits this pattern. The high setup cost encouraged a large batch size: 10,000 units. The annual demand of 20,000 units can be satisfied using only two batches. Thus, production runs for these firms tended to be quite long. Furthermore, diversity was viewed as being costly and was avoided. Producing variations of the product can be quite expensive, especially since additional, special features would usually demand even more expensive and frequent setups—the reason for the standardized products.

JIT AND INVENTORY MANAGEMENT: A DIFFERENT VIEW

Objective 2
Describe JIT inventory management.

The manufacturing environment for many of these traditional, large-batch, high setup cost firms has changed dramatically in the past 10 to 15 years. For one thing, the competitive markets are no longer defined by national boundaries. Advances in transportation and communication have contributed significantly to the creation of global competition. Advances in technology have contributed to shorter life cycles for products, and product diversity has increased. Foreign firms offering higher-quality, lower-cost products *with specialized features* have created tremendous pressures for our domestic large-batch, high-setup-cost firms to increase both quality and product diversity while simultaneously reducing total costs. These competitive pressures have led many firms to abandon the EOQ model in favor of the JIT approach. JIT offers increased cost efficiency and simultaneously has the flexibility to respond to customer demands for better quality and more variety. Quality, flexibility, and cost efficiency are foundation principles for world-class competition.

JIT manufacturing and purchasing represent the continual pursuit of productivity through the elimination of waste. Inventories, particularly, are viewed as representing waste. They tie up resources such as cash, space, and labor. They also conceal inefficiencies in production and increase the complexity of a firm's information system.

JIT, however, focuses on more than inventory management. It is a manufacturing approach that maintains that goods should be pulled through the system by demand rather than pushed through the system on a fixed schedule. In a JIT system, each operation produces only what is necessary to satisfy the demand of the succeeding operation. The material or subassembly arrives just in time for production to occur so that demand can be met.

JIT has two strategic objectives: to increase profits and to improve a firm's competitive position. These two objectives are achieved by controlling costs (enabling better price competition and increased profits), improving delivery performance, and improving quality.

One effect of JIT is to reduce inventories to very low levels. The pursuit of zero inventories is vital to the success of JIT. This idea of pursuing zero inventories, however, necessarily challenges the traditional reasons for holding inventories. These reasons are no longer viewed as valid.

Earlier, we offered the following reasons for holding inventories:

1. To balance ordering or setup costs and carrying costs
2. To satisfy customer demand (e.g., meet delivery dates)
3. To avoid shutting down manufacturing facilities
4. To take advantage of discounts
5. To hedge against future price increases

According to the traditional view, inventories solve some underlying problem related to each of the reasons listed above. For example, the problem of resolving the conflict between ordering or setup costs and carrying costs is solved by selecting an inventory level that minimizes the sum of these costs. If demand is greater than expected or if production is reduced by breakdowns and production inefficiencies, inventories serve as buffers, providing products to customers that may otherwise not have been available. Similarly, inventories can prevent shutdowns caused by late delivery of material, defective parts, and failures of machines used to produce subassemblies. Finally, inventories are often the solution to the problem of buying the best raw materials for the least cost through the use of quantity discounts.

JIT refuses to use inventories as the solution to problems. It offers alternative solutions that do not require inventories.

Setup and Carrying Costs: The JIT Approach

JIT takes a radically different approach to minimizing total carrying and setup costs. The traditional approach accepts the existence of setup costs and then finds the order quantity that best balances the two categories of costs. JIT, on the other hand, does not accept setup costs (or ordering costs) as a given; rather, JIT attempts to drive these costs to zero. This is accomplished by reducing the time it takes to set up (for setup costs) and by developing long-term contracts with suppliers (for ordering costs). By taking these two steps, transaction costs for acquiring inventory can be driven to an insignificant level. If setup costs and ordering costs become insignificant, the only remaining cost to minimize is carrying cost, which is accomplished by reducing inventories to very low levels. This approach explains the push for zero inventories in a JIT system.

Negotiating long-term contracts for the supply of outside materials will obviously reduce the number of orders and the associated ordering costs. Reducing setup times, however, requires a company to search for new, more efficient ways to accomplish setup. Fortunately, experience has indicated that dramatic reductions in setup times can be achieved. Upon adopting a JIT system, Harley-Davidson reduced setup time by more than 75 percent on the machines evaluated.[8] In some cases, Harley-Davidson was able to reduce the setup times from hours to minutes. Other companies have experienced similar results. Generally, setup times can be reduced by at least 75 percent.[9]

Due-Date Performance: The JIT Solution

Due-date performance is a measure of a firm's ability to respond to customer needs. In the past, finished goods inventories have been used to ensure that a firm is able to meet a requested delivery date. JIT solves the problem of due-date performance not by building inventory but by dramatically reducing lead times. Shorter lead times increase a firm's ability to meet requested delivery dates and to respond quickly to the demands of the market. Thus, the firm's competitiveness is improved. JIT cuts lead times by reducing setup times, improving quality, and using cellular manufacturing.[10]

8. Gene Schwind, "Man Arrives Just in Time to Save Harley-Davidson," *Material Handling Engineering* (August 1984), pp. 28–35.
9. William J. Stoddard and Nolan W. Rhea, "Just-in-Time Manufacturing: The Relentless Pursuit of Productivity," *Material Handling Engineering* (March 1985), pp. 70–76.
10. Cellular manufacturing is defined and discussed in detail in Chapter 19.

Manufacturing cells reduce travel distance between machines and inventory; they can also have a dramatic effect on lead time. For example, in a traditional manufacturing system, one company took two months to manufacture a valve. By grouping the lathes and drills used to make the valves into U-shaped cells, the lead time was reduced to two or three days. Oregon Cutting Systems, a chain-saw manufacturer, was able to reduce travel distance from 2,620 feet to 173 feet and lead times from 21 days to 3. Because of the reduced lead time and plans for even further reduction, the company will be filling orders directly from the factory rather than from finished goods warehouses.[11] These reductions in lead time are not unique—most companies experience at least a 90 percent reduction in lead times when they implement JIT.[12]

Avoidance of Shutdown: The JIT Approach

Most shutdowns occur for one of three reasons: machine failure, defective material or subassembly, and unavailability of a raw material or subassembly. Holding inventories is one solution to all three problems.

Those espousing the JIT approach claim that inventories do not solve the problems but cover up or hide them. JIT proponents use the analogy of rocks in a lake. The rocks represent the three problems and the water represents inventories. If the lake is deep (inventories are high), then the rocks are never exposed and managers can pretend they do not exist. By reducing inventories to zero, the rocks are exposed and can no longer be ignored. JIT solves the three problems by emphasizing total preventive maintenance and total quality control and by building the right kind of relationship with suppliers.

total preventive maintenance

Total Preventive Maintenance. Zero machine failures is the goal of **total preventive maintenance.** By paying more attention to preventive maintenance, most machine breakdowns can be avoided. This objective is easier to attain in a JIT environment because of the interdisciplinary labor philosophy. It is not uncommon for a cell worker to be trained in maintenance of the machines he or she operates. Because of the pull-through nature of JIT, it is also not unusual for a cell worker to have idle manufacturing time. Some of this time, then, can be used productively by having the cell workers involved in preventive maintenance.

Total Quality Control. The problem of defective parts is solved by striving for zero defects. Because JIT manufacturing does not rely on inventories to replace defective parts or materials, the emphasis on quality for both internally produced and externally purchased materials increases significantly. The outcome is impressive: the number of rejected parts tends to fall by 75-90 percent.[13]

Kanban system

The Kanban System. To ensure that parts or materials are available when needed, a system called the **Kanban system** is employed. This is an information system that controls production through the use of markers or cards. The Kanban

11. Richard Schonberger, "Just-in-Time Production Systems: Replacing Complexity with Simplicity in Manufacturing Management," *Industrial Engineering* (October 1984), pp. 52–63. For an excellent description of the savings realized by Oregon Cutting Systems, read the article by Jack Bailes and Ilene K. Kleinsorge, "Cutting Waste with JIT," *Management Accounting* (May 1992), pp. 28–32.
12. See Stoddard and Rhea, "Just-in-Time Manufacturing," p. 76.
13. Stoddard and Rhea, "Just-in-Time Manufacturing."

system is responsible for ensuring that the necessary products (or parts) are produced (or acquired) in the necessary quantities at the necessary time. It is the heart of the JIT inventory management system.

A Kanban system uses cards or markers, which are plastic, cardboard, or metal plates measuring 4 inches by 8 inches. The Kanban is usually placed in a vinyl sack and attached to the part or a container holding the needed parts.

A basic Kanban system uses three cards: a *withdrawal Kanban,* a *production Kanban,* and a *vendor Kanban.* The first two control the movement of work among the manufacturing processes, while the third controls movement of parts between the processes and outside suppliers. A **withdrawal Kanban** specifies the quantity that a subsequent process should withdraw from the preceding process. A **production Kanban** specifies the quantity that the preceding process should produce. A **vendor Kanban** is used to notify suppliers to deliver more parts; it also specifies when the parts are needed. The three Kanbans are illustrated in Exhibits 23-3, 23-4, and 23-5, respectively.

withdrawal Kanban

production Kanban

vendor Kanban

Exhibit 23-3
Withdrawal Kanban

Item No.	**15670T07**	Preceding Process
Item Name	**Circuit Board**	**CB Assembly**
Computer Type	**TR6547 PC**	
Box Capacity	**8**	Subsequent Process
Box Type	**C**	**Final Assembly**

Exhibit 23-4
Production Kanban

Item No.	**15670T07**	Process
Item Name	**Circuit Board**	**CB Assembly**
Computer Type	**TR6547 PC**	
Box Capacity	**8**	
Box Type	**C**	

Exhibit 23-5
Vendor Kanban

Item No. **15670T08**	Name of Receiving Company
Item Name **Computer Casing**	**Electro PC**
Box Capacity **8**	Receiving Gate
Box Type **A**	**75**
Time to Deliver **8:30 A.M., 12:30 P.M., 2:30 P.M.**	
Name of Supplier **Gerry Supply**	

Discounts and Price Increases: JIT Purchasing Versus Holding Inventories

Traditionally, inventories are carried so that a firm can take advantage of quantity discounts and hedge against future price increases of the items purchased. The objective is to lower the cost of inventory. JIT achieves the same objective without carrying inventories. The JIT solution is to negotiate long-term contracts with a few chosen suppliers located as close to the production facility as possible and to establish more extensive supplier involvement. Suppliers are not selected on the basis of price alone. Performance—the quality of the component and the ability to deliver as needed—and commitment to JIT purchasing are vital considerations.

Every effort is made to establish a partners-in-profits relationship with suppliers. Suppliers need to be convinced that their well-being is intimately tied to the well-being of the buyer.

To help reduce the uncertainty in demand and establish the mutual confidence and trust needed in such a relationship, JIT manufacturers emphasize long-term contracts. Other benefits of long-term contracts exist. They stipulate prices and acceptable quality levels. Long-term contracts also reduce dramatically the number of orders placed, which helps to drive down the ordering cost.

One effect of JIT purchasing is to lower the cost of purchased parts by 5 to 20 percent.[14] Another effect is to reduce the supplier base dramatically. One company decreased the number of suppliers it uses by 4,700 in one year. Another company decreased the supplier base from 820 to 180 within two years. By reducing the number of suppliers and working closely with those that remain, the quality of the incoming materials can be improved significantly—a crucial outcome for the success of JIT. As the quality of incoming materials increases, some quality-related costs can be avoided or reduced. For example, the need to inspect incoming materials disappears and rework requirements decline.

JIT: Some General Observations

JIT directly addresses such issues as plant layout, process design, quality standards, and inventories. Simplification and efficiency are the primary criteria for

14. Stoddard and Rhea, "Just-in-Time Manufacturing."

plant layout and process design. The JIT quality standard of zero defects is actively pursued. Doing it right the first time is a critical feature of a system that makes no allowances for rework. Inventories are viewed as evil, and every effort is made to lower them to insignificant levels.

Implementing JIT means changing the plant layout and the traditional processing design: switching from a departmental, functional layout with a centralized stores area to a cellular manufacturing layout with materials and components located adjacent to the work area itself. It means switching from a specialized labor orientation to an interdisciplinary labor orientation. Workers in a JIT system are trained to perform a variety of tasks.

The pursuit of zero defects and zero inventories requires a commitment to continuous improvement of efficiency. The principles of continuous improvement and elimination of waste are fundamental to the JIT approach.

STRATEGIC DECISION MAKING

Objective 3
Explain how activity-based costing facilitates strategic decision making.

The JIT approach to manufacturing is reshaping the manufacturing environment and also reshaping management accounting practices. JIT manufacturing and purchasing, however, are not the only forces impacting management accounting. Robotics, flexible manufacturing, computer-aided manufacturing, and activity-based costing are also changing traditional approaches. This is happening because the conventional management accounting system fails to provide the right kind of information for sound decisions in this new, advanced manufacturing environment. This is especially true for strategic decisions. Furthermore, many of the traditional control features (e.g., variance analysis) may actually encourage inappropriate behavior. Consequently, management accounting is evolving and adapting to meet the needs of the new manufacturing environment.

Traditional management accounting has three major objectives: (1) to determine the cost of services or products, (2) to provide information for decision making, and (3) to provide information for planning and control. Product costs are needed to value inventories, prepare financial statements, and provide managers with the ability to plan and make decisions. Control and management of costs is essential for implementing plans and realizing the firm's objectives. All three objectives of management accounting are affected by the philosophy of continuous improvement, activity-based costing, and automation, producing significant changes in the approach required of the management accounting system.

Product costing in the advanced manufacturing environment has already been discussed (see Chapter 19). The impact on planning and control is discussed in Chapter 26. So far in this chapter, we have discussed the impact of the advanced manufacturing environment on inventory management. Other decision-making models are also affected. Decision making tends to be more broadly focused—it is more concerned with the explicit consideration of the strategic elements. Management accounting's role should be concerned with helping the firm to achieve a competitive advantage. Moreover, the value of management accounting is directly related to its ability to help an organization be successful.

Strategic Costing

strategic decision making

Strategic decision making involves choosing among alternative strategies with the goal of selecting a strategy or strategies that provide a company with reasonable assurance of long-term growth and survival. The key to achieving this

strategic cost analysis

goal is to gain a competitive advantage. **Strategic cost analysis** is the use of cost data to develop and identify superior strategies that will produce a sustainable competitive advantage.[15]

Assigning a strategic role for a management accounting system requires a shift in attitude and orientation. Part of this shift has to do with switching from a short-term to a long-term focus. For example, virtually all product-related decisions are long term in focus. Yet many of the management accounting models dealing with such product-related decisions as pricing and product discontinuance (keep or drop decisions) are short term in focus. For example, in Chapter 21, we learned about contribution-margin pricing—a short-term pricing strategy designed to take advantage of excess capacity and increase profits—in the short run. But there are dangers associated with short-term incremental pricing. Managers, content with the increase in profits received from special orders, may fail to search for a long-term solution to the idle capacity. They may continue the practice of accepting orders that offer short-term benefits. This pattern of short-term decisions itself becomes a strategy and has long-term consequences. In the long term, all costs must be covered.

Making sure that the long run is considered—even for so-called short-run decisions—is only one aspect of strategic cost analysis. Another dimension is identifying the strategic elements present in a decision. For example, selling a medium-level quality product to low-end dealers for a special, low price because of idle capacity could threaten the main channels of distribution for the product. This is true even if the dealers apply their own private labels to the product. Why? Because selling the product to low-end dealers creates a direct competitor for its regular, medium-level dealers. Potential customers of the regular retail outlets could switch to the lower-end outlets because they can buy the same quality for a lower price. And what if the regular outlets deduce what has happened?[16]

The Role of Activity-Based Costing

We have already learned that activity-based costing (ABC) can offer a significant contribution by producing more accurate product costs—input that is critical for firms operating in the advanced manufacturing environment. In fact, product profitability is itself a strategic issue; therefore, product costs must be accurately measured. Pricing decisions, product mix, new product introduction decisions, and decisions on how to respond to competitors' products are all strategic product-related decisions. Distorted product costs can induce managers to make poor—perhaps even disastrous—decisions. For a firm with product diversity, it is common for a unit-based cost system to overcost high-volume products and undercost low-volume products. This phenomenon has been blamed for the American giveaway of high volume industries to foreign competitors such as VCRs and memory chips.[17] Another example relating to product mix is the case of the Schrader Bellows Division of Scovill Manufacturing Company. This division was producing 2,500 products, all allegedly profitable under a unit-based costing system. The use of activity-based costing, however, identified only 550

15. As defined by John K. Shank and Vijay Govindarajan, *Strategic Cost Analysis: The Evolution from Managerial to Strategic Accounting* (Homewood, Ill.: Richard D. Irwin, 1989).
16. A complete case study—the Baldwin Bicycle Case—concerning these kinds of strategic issues is presented and analyzed in Shank and Govindarajan, *Strategic Cost Analysis: The Evolution from Managerial to Strategic Accounting.*
17. Shank and Govindarajan, *Strategic Cost Analysis: The Evolution from Managerial to Strategic Accounting.*

products as profitable.[18] Poor product costing contributed, in part, to a proliferation of products. It's also easy to imagine the bad pricing decisions associated with this large group of products.

Activity-based costing, however, provides benefits beyond accurate product costing. The reason is simple and compelling. Costs are caused by activities and activities are driven by strategic choices.[19] Different strategies produce different activities. For example, switching to a JIT manufacturing strategy increases quality-related activities and decreases material-handling activities. The costs of these activities are also different from the costs in a conventional environment. By identifying the activities and their associated costs, the costs of competing strategic choices can be calculated (e.g., comparing the costs of a conventional manufacturing strategy with those of a JIT strategy). This information, then, allows managers to make better strategic decisions—selecting the strategic choices that provide the greatest economic benefit to the organization.

Another strategic benefit of activity-based costing is its ability to include postplant, customer-level activities. Expanding cost analysis to include marketing and distribution activities can enhance strategic decision making. Suppose, for example, that a company has one customer that provides 60 percent of the business and a large number of other customers that supply 40 percent of the business. The large customer places orders twice yearly and smaller customers place frequent small orders. All customers are billed on a cost-plus basis (cost includes selling expenses). Currently, sales administration costs are allocated to customers on the basis of sales volume. Thus, the large customer receives 60 percent of this cost. Now assume that this customer complains about the magnitude of the selling costs being billed and threatens to take its business elsewhere. An investigation indicates that the number of sales orders being processed is the cost driver for the sales administration activity. Using this information, it's obvious that the large customer should receive virtually none of the sales administration costs because it generates only two sales orders per year. Recognizing this, management can reassign the sales administration cost, increasing the price of the goods for the smaller customers and decreasing the price for the larger customer. Furthermore, the activity information can be used, if necessary, to explain the price changes, and price discounts can be offered for larger orders.

These postplant and customer-related benefits are particularly important for companies that have adopted a JIT approach. JIT eliminates most of the batch-related activities and locates many product-sustaining activities within the manufacturing cell. Thus, many of the benefits offered by ABC in the manufacturing area are captured by the reorganization. Postplant and customer-related activities, however, still offer significant opportunities for improvement by evaluating customers and customer segments as well as specific marketing activities associated with particular products. The example concerning the assignment of sales administration costs illustrates the potential for activity-based costing to be useful further down the value chain.[20]

Products and services, along with their characteristics, define the output strategy for an organization. This output strategy in turn defines processes, activities,

18. Robin Cooper, *Schrader Bellows Cases*, 186–272 (Harvard Business School, 1986).

19. William Rotch, "Activity-Based Costing in Service Industries," *Journal of Cost Management* (Summer 1990), pp. 4–14. The discussion linking ABC with strategies is largely based on this article.

20. The benefits of ABC in a JIT environment are more fully discussed in Peter B. B. Turney and James M. Reeve, "The Impact of Continuous Improvement on the Design of Activity-Based Cost Systems," *Journal of Cost Management* (Summer 1990), pp. 43–50.

and the associated activity costs. Understanding processes and the associated activities leads to better decisions. This can be illustrated by examining the impact ABC has on two popular management accounting decision models: relevant costing and segment analysis. As will be shown, the effect of ABC is to improve overall decision quality. However, before we discuss the effect of ABC on decision making, we need to develop some additional understanding of the linkages between activities, resource spending, and resource usage.

ACTIVITY-BASED COSTING, RESOURCE SPENDING, AND RESOURCE USAGE

Objective 4
Describe the resource usage model and its role in activity-based costing.

activity capacity
resource spending
resource usage

Activity-based costing systems provide a key insight: resource spending and resource usage can differ.[21] To understand resource spending and usage, we first need to understand activity capacity. **Activity capacity** is simply the ability to perform activities. To perform an activity, capacity must be acquired. Thus, an organization must identify the level of performance required for each activity. This level should correspond to practical capacity. **Resource spending** is the cost of *acquiring* capacity to perform an activity. **Resource usage** is the *amount* of activity capacity used in producing an organization's output. In an activity-based costing system, only the amount of resource capacity used should be actually charged to products or customers. The unused activity capacity is the cost of doing business for the period in question and is *not* assigned to products. The distinction between resource spending and resource usage is best illustrated with a simple example.

Resource Spending vs. Resource Usage

Suppose, for example, that a company hires three sustaining engineers—engineers who are responsible for redesigning existing products to meet customer requirements. By hiring the engineers, the company has acquired the ability to perform an activity: engineering redesign. The salaries paid the engineers represent the cost of acquiring the engineering redesign capacity and the number of engineering changes that can be *efficiently* processed by the three engineers is a quantitative measure of that capacity. This capacity level corresponds to what has been previously defined as practical capacity. Assume the engineers are each paid an annual salary of $50,000 and each engineer can process 2,500 engineering change orders per year. The company has acquired the capacity to process 7,500 (3 × 2,500) change orders per year at a total cost of $150,000 (3 × $50,000). Given this information, the cost per unit of activity, the *activity rate*, can be computed. The **activity rate** is the resource expenditure divided by the practical capacity: $150,000/7,500 = $20 per change order (the activity rate is basically a pool rate where the pool consists of a single activity).

activity rate

During the year, however, the company may not actually process 7,500 orders—that is, all of the available order processing capacity may not be used.

21. The concepts presented in this section draw heavily from the following two articles: Alfred M. King, "The Current Status of Activity-Based Costing: An Interview with Robin Cooper and Robert S. Kaplan," *Management Accounting* (September 1991), pp. 22–26, and Robin Cooper and Robert S. Kaplan, "Activity-Based Systems: Measuring the Costs of Resource Usage," *Accounting Horizons* (September 1992), pp. 1–13.

Resource usage is the number of change orders *actually* processed. Assume that 6,000 change orders were processed during the year. The **cost of resource usage** is the activity rate × the actual activity usage: \$20 × 6,000 = \$120,000. Further, the **cost of unused activity** is the activity rate × the unused activity: \$20 × 1,500 = \$30,000. Note that the cost of unused capacity occurs because the resource (engineering redesign) must be acquired in lump (whole) amounts. Even if the company had anticipated the need for only 6,000 change orders, it would have been difficult to hire the equivalent of 2.4 engineers (6,000/2,500).

cost of resource usage

cost of unused activity

The example illustrates that there is a difference between the *resources supplied* and the *resources used (demanded)* to perform activities. Typically, the traditional accounting system provides information only about the cost of the resources supplied. An ABC system, on the other hand, tells us how much of the activity is used and the cost of its usage. Furthermore, the relationship between resources supplied and resources demanded is expressed by either of the following two equations:

$$\text{Activity availability} = \text{Activity usage} + \text{Unused capacity} \quad (23.4)$$

$$\text{Cost of activity supplied} = \text{Cost of activity used} + \text{Cost of unused activity} \quad (23.5)$$

Equation 23.4 expresses the relationship between supply and demand in physical units while Equation 23.5 expresses it in financial terms.

For the engineering order example, the relationships appear as follows:

Physical units (Equation 23.4):

$$\text{Available orders} = \text{Orders used} + \text{Orders unused}$$
$$7{,}500 \text{ orders} = 6{,}000 \text{ orders} + 1{,}500 \text{ orders}$$

Financial terms (Equation 23.5):

$$\text{Cost of orders supplied} = \text{Cost of orders used} + \text{Cost of unused orders}$$
$$\$150{,}000 = \$120{,}000 + \$30{,}000$$

Activities, Resources, and Cost Behavior

Resources are supplied in one of two ways: (1) as used (and needed), and (2) in advance of usage. **Resources supplied as used and needed** are those that are acquired from outside sources, where the terms of acquisition do not require any long-term commitment for any given amount of the resource. Thus, the organization is free to buy only the quantity of resource needed.

resources supplied as used and needed

As a result, the quantity of the resource supplied equals the quantity demanded. There is no unused capacity for this category of resources. **Resources supplied in advance of usage** are those acquired by the use of either an explicit or implicit contract to obtain a given quantity of resource, regardless of whether the quantity of the resource available is fully used or not. Resources supplied in advance may exceed the demand for their usage; thus, unused capacity is possible.

resources supplied in advance of usage

Resources Supplied as Needed and Cost Behavior. Since the cost of the resources supplied as needed equals the cost of resources used, the total cost of the resource increases as demand for the resource increases. Thus, generally, we can treat the cost of resources supplied as needed as a variable cost. For example, in a JIT environment, materials are acquired and used as needed. Using units produced as the cost driver, it is clear that as the units produced increases, the usage (and cost) of raw materials would increase proportionately. Similarly, power is acquired and used as needed. Using kilowatt hours as the cost driver, as the demand for power increases, the cost of power increases.

Resources Supplied in Advance and Cost Behavior. Many resources are acquired before the actual demands for the resource are realized. There are two examples of this category of resource acquisition. First, organizations acquire many *multiperiod service capacities* by paying cash up front or by entering into an explicit contract that requires periodic cash payments. Buying or leasing buildings and equipment are examples of this form of advance resource acquisition. The annual expense associated with the multiperiod category is independent of actual usage of the resource; thus, these expenses can be defined as fixed expenses. Essentially, they correspond to **committed fixed expenses**—costs incurred that provide long-term activity capacity. A second and more important example concerns organizations that acquire resources in advance through implicit contracts—usually with its salaried and hourly employees. The implicit understanding is that the organization will maintain employment levels even though there may be temporary downturns in the quantity of activity used. This outcome implies that the expense associated with this category of resources is independent of the quantity used—at least in the short run. Thus, in the short-run, the amount of resource expense remains unchanged even though the quantity used may vary, and this resource cost category can be treated (cautiously) as a fixed expense. Essentially, resource spending for this category corresponds to **discretionary fixed expenses**—costs incurred for the acquisition of short-term activity capacity. Hiring three sustaining engineers for $150,000 who can supply the capacity of processing 7,500 change orders is an example of implicit contracting. Certainly, none of the three engineers would expect to be laid off if only 5,000 change orders were actually processed—unless, of course, the downturn in demand is viewed as being permanent.

committed fixed expenses

discretionary fixed expenses

Activities and Cost Behavior. Since it is possible that activities may have resources associated with them that are acquired in advance and resources that are acquired as needed, activity costs can display a mixed cost behavior.[22] For example, assume that a plant has its own power department. In this case, the plant has acquired long-term capacity for supplying power by investing in building and equipment (resources acquired in advance). The plant also acquires fuel to produce power as needed (resources acquired as needed). The cost of building and equipment is independent of the kilowatt hours produced, but the cost of fuel increases as the demand for kilowatt hours increases. The activity of supplying power has both a fixed cost component and a variable cost component, using kilowatt hours as the cost driver. Thus, in a mixed cost setting, a need exists

22. This view of activity costs differs from that found in Robin Cooper and Robert S. Kaplan, "Activity-Based Systems: Measuring the Costs of Resource Usage." They essentially argue that activity costs are either strictly fixed or strictly variable. They do not consider the possibility that activities could have both kinds of resources assigned to them. For a study that argues for mixed activity costs, see Y. T. Mak and Melvin L. Roush, "Flexible Budgeting and Variance Analysis in an ABC Environment," Unpublished Working Paper, December, 1992, Victoria University of Wellington.

to compute both a *fixed activity rate* and a *variable activity rate.* These activity rates are computed using practical capacity. The *cost of unused activity,* however, is the fixed activity rate × the unused capacity.

Implications for Decision Making and Control. The activity-based resource usage model just described can improve both managerial control and decision making. A well-designed activity-based costing system encourages managers to pay more attention to controlling resource usage and spending. For example, an activity-based costing system allows managers to assess the changes in resource demands that will occur from new product mix decisions. Adding new, customized products may increase the demands for batch-level and product-level activities; and, if sufficient unused activity capacity does not exist, resource spending must increase. Similarly, if activity management brings about excess activity capacity (by finding ways to reduce resource usage), managers must carefully consider what is to be done with the excess capacity. Eliminating the excess capacity may decrease resource spending and thus improve overall profits. Alternatively, using the excess capacity to increase output could increase revenues without a corresponding increase in resource spending. How resource usage and spending is affected by managing activities is more fully explored in Chapter 26.

The activity-based resource usage model also allows managers to calculate the changes in resource supply and demand resulting from implementing such decisions as make or buy, accept or reject special orders, and keep or drop product lines. This feature offers significant benefits for the relevant costing decision model.

RELEVANT COSTING: ADVANCED MANUFACTURING ENVIRONMENT

Objective 5
Explain the effect of activity-based costing and JIT on cost-volume-profit analysis.

The relevant costing model continues to be applicable in the advanced manufacturing environment. The utility and power of the model, however, are enhanced by the strategic insights provided by activity-based costing. This enhancement is achieved by the use of both unit- and nonunit-based cost drivers and by recognizing the interrelationships of activities, resource supply, and resource demand. The power of the relevant costing model is further increased for firms that have adopted JIT manufacturing. JIT manufacturing creates a more focused environment by redesigning and simplifying the manufacturing process. Many costs formerly common to several products are now directly traceable to specific products. This change in traceability increases managers' ability to identify costs that will change across alternatives. The increased decision power can be illustrated by an example comparing relevant costing analysis in a conventional system with that in an ABC system.

Conventional Analysis

Assume that Sweeney Manufacturing currently produces all of the components used in its line of printers (several types are produced). Sweeney is currently using a traditional, unit-based cost system. An outside supplier has offered to sell Part 678, an electro-mechanical component, for $4.75 per unit. The company normally produces 100,000 units per year. Each component requires 0.25 direct labor hours. The costs associated with the production of these 100,000 components are given below.

Direct materials	$ 50,000
Direct labor	200,000
Variable overhead[1]	80,000
Fixed overhead:	
Direct fixed:	
Supervision	50,000
Rental of special equipment	70,000
Common fixed[2]	300,000
Total	$750,000
Unit cost ($750,000/100,000)	$7.50

[1]Assigned using a variable overhead rate of $3.20 per direct labor hour
[2]Assigned using a fixed overhead rate of $12 per direct labor hour

The conventional make-or-buy analysis is shown in Exhibit 23-6. Based on the analysis, the company should continue producing the component. Notice that common fixed overhead is excluded from the analysis since it is assumed to be irrelevant. Common fixed overhead is excluded because reducing output is assumed to have no effect on this cost, which does not vary with direct labor hours. Variable overhead, however, is relevant, as it varies with direct labor hours.

ABC Analysis

The conventional analysis classified all costs as variable or fixed. In reality, in a setting in which product diversity exists, much of the common fixed overhead cost pool is made up of costs driven by factors other than production volume. Many of these costs are caused by the activities that are consumed by the individual products. Thus, eliminating a product may reduce resource demands for some of these activities and eventually lead to a reduction in resource spending. By using activity-based costing, a much clearer picture of resource demands emerges and the accuracy of the relevant costing analysis can be improved.

Assume, for illustrative purposes, that the activities included in variable overhead are power and labor fringe benefits, and the activities included in common fixed overhead are inspection, engineering, material handling, setups, and plant depreciation. In an ABC framework, power and labor fringe benefits would be classified as unit-level activities; inspection, material handling, and setups would be classified as batch-level activities; engineering support as a product-level activity; and plant depreciation as a facility-level activity.

Exhibit 23-6
Conventional Make-or-Buy Analysis

Cost Item	Make Alternative	Buy Alternative
Direct materials	$ 50,000	—
Direct labor	200,000	—
Variable overhead	80,000	—
Supervision	50,000	—
Rental of equipment	70,000	—
Purchase cost	—	$475,000
Total relevant cost	$450,000	$475,000

Of these four overhead activity categories, only the facility-level category containing plant depreciation can immediately be identified as irrelevant. Of the remaining three categories, assume that only the unit-level activities, labor benefits and power, have resources associated with them that are acquired as needed. The other two categories of activities only have resources acquired in advance of usage (of the short-term variety). The following activity rates are computed for these three overhead categories, using practical capacities for each activity:

	Cost Driver	*Rate per Unit Activity of Driver*
Unit-level:		
Power	Machine hours	$ 3
Benefits	Direct labor hours	1
Batch-level:		
Materials handling	Number of moves	20
Inspection	Inspection hours	15
Setups	Setup hours	10
Product-sustaining:		
Engineering support	Number of engineering orders	2,500

Assume that the component uses the following amounts of each cost driver:

Machine hours	30,000
Direct labor hours	25,000
Number of moves	2,000
Inspection hours	5,000
Setup hours	6,000
Engineering orders	10

Using the activity rates and the activity data for the component, a more complete relevant costing analysis is possible. Of the seven activities, power and direct labor benefits represent resources that are acquired as needed. Thus, for these two activities, resource spending will decrease by the reduction in the cost of resource usage ($3 × 30,000 and $1 × 25,000). For the remaining four activities, the *cost of resource usage* for each activity is reduced by the following amounts:

Material handling	$40,000	($20 × 2,000 moves)
Inspections	75,000	($15 × 5,000 hours)
Setups	60,000	($10 × 6,000 setup hrs)
Engineering	25,000	($2,500 × 10 orders)

Of course, for the relevant costing decision, what we need to know is how much *resource spending* can be reduced because of the ability to reduce resource usage. If we purchase the component instead of making it, excess capacity is created for each of the four activities. How this excess capacity is managed is the key to the analysis. It may not be possible to reduce resource spending by the reduction in the cost of resource usage. In fact, upon investigation, we find that because of the excess capacity we can reduce spending by the following amounts:

Material handling	$30,000	(one salaried employee)
Inspections	70,000	(two salaried employees)
Setups	60,000	(three wage employees)
Engineering	0	

The revised ABC make-or-buy analysis is given in Exhibit 23-7. The analysis now favors the purchase alternative. In the conventional analysis, use of a unit-based cost driver to describe the behavior of costs gave the impression that all common fixed costs were irrelevant. In reality, the production of the component was responsible for causing some of these so-called fixed costs. By not making the component, the resource demands on the activities of several support departments (inspection, material handling, engineering, and setups) could be reduced, creating some savings (reduced resource spending).

Strategic Issues. But is the analysis really complete? Should Sweeney buy the part instead of making it? The ABC analysis provides a more accurate picture of what it costs to make the product, but it also raises some questions. Why is the outside supplier able to offer the part for $120,000 per year less than it costs Sweeney to make it? The decision to make the part carried with it some activities and their associated costs that are hidden by conventional analysis but revealed by an ABC analysis. Will the decision to purchase the outside part also create some internal activities—activities that are costly? Changing from internal production to external sourcing is a definite strategic shift, creating a dependence that formerly didn't exist. Is this a good idea? Will the supplier deliver the part on time—in the right quantities and at the right level of quality?

Suppose that Bruce Shaver, president of Sweeney, requested his management team to address these issues and to make a recommendation. After two weeks of analysis, he received the following memo:

MEMO
TO: Bruce Shaver, President
FROM: Management Team
SUBJECT: Make or Buy: Part 678

Our recommendation is to continue internal production of Part 678. With our increased interest in providing high-quality products that will be delivered on a

Exhibit 23-7
Revised Make-or-Buy Analysis: Activity Based

Cost Item	*Make Alternative*	*Buy Alternative*
Direct materials	$ 50,000	—
Direct labor	200,000	—
Rental of equipment	70,000	—
Power	90,000	
Fringe benefits	25,000	—
Material handling	30,000	—
Inspections	70,000	—
Setups	60,000	—
Purchase of parts	—	$475,000
Total relevant cost	$595,000	$475,000

timely basis, we believe that maintaining control of the components used in the printer line is essential. This objective is also supported by pursuing a strategy that will allow us to lower the cost of producing Part 678 below the level that it would cost us to purchase it externally.

First, we discovered that purchasing the part carried with it costs in addition to the purchase cost. Given the work load of the receiving department, it would have to add an additional employee to handle the incoming parts (including inspection). This would cost an extra $30,000 per year. There would also be a material handling cost of about $5,000 per year. These additional activities reduce the benefit of buying from $120,000 to $85,000—still a very favorable outcome.

We believe, however, that we can overcome this difference. The ABC analysis revealed that this part is consuming activities that are costly—activities that can be reduced or eliminated. As you know, we plan to implement JIT on a trial basis, selecting one or two products initially so that all the bugs can be worked out before we go with the entire operation. We recommend that one of these products be Part 678. Using a manufacturing cell for Part 678, we can virtually eliminate material handling costs, saving $30,000. Setup costs can also be reduced to about $10,000, saving $50,000. Improvements in quality will decrease materials cost and inspection costs. We estimate that within a year, we can save another $20,000 to $30,000 from quality improvements—and more as we gain experience.

In total, the analysis favors internal production. It would be bad timing, given our new attitude of continuous improvement and waste reduction, to go to an outside supplier.

The example illustrates the power of activity-based costing for strategic analysis. The ABC analysis identified the activities that were being consumed by Part 678. By buying the part, many of the costs of these activities could be reduced or eliminated. These activity costs, however, could also be reduced or eliminated in another way—by adopting a JIT approach. And, as it turns out, the second approach is more in harmony with the company's desire to maintain full control of individual components, a desire related to the firm-wide strategy of supplying quality products on a timely basis.

SEGMENTED REPORTING BY COST BEHAVIOR

Objective 6

Describe segment analysis in both a conventional setting and in an ABC/JIT setting.

segmented reporting

Reporting the profit contributions of activities or other units within an organization is called **segmented reporting.** To evaluate many different activities within a firm, a manager needs more than the summary information appearing in a firm's income statement. For example, in a company with several divisions operating in different markets, the manager would certainly want to know how profitable each division has been. This knowledge may lead to greater overall profit by eliminating unprofitable divisions, giving special attention to problem divisions, allocating additional investment capital to the more profitable divisions, and so on.

Divisional income statements, however, are not all that a good management accounting system should supply. Even finer segmentation is needed for managers to properly carry out their responsibilities. Divisions are made up of different plants; thus, knowledge of plant profitability is needed, for the same reasons as divisional profitability. Plants produce products, and information on product profitability is also critical. Some products may be profitable—some may not be. Similarly, profit information on sales territories, special projects, individual salespersons, and so on, is important.

segment

Managers need to know the profitability of various segments within a firm to be able to make evaluations and decisions concerning each segment's continued existence, level of funding, and so on. A **segment** is any profit-making entity within the organization; it may be a part of the organization or an activity within the organization. A segment report can provide valuable information on costs controllable by the segment manager. Controllable costs are costs whose level can be influenced by a manager. Thus, a manager who has no responsibility for a cost should not be held accountable for that cost. For example, divisional managers have no power to authorize corporate level costs such as research and development and salaries of top managers. Therefore, they should not be held accountable for the incurrence of those costs. If noncontrollable costs are included in a segment report, they should be separated from controllable costs and labelled as noncontrollable. For example, fixed costs common to two or more plants within a division would not be allocated to each plant, but instead shown as a common cost for the two plants.

Conventional Segmented Reporting

In a conventional environment, segmented income statements are usually prepared using a variable costing approach. Segmented income statements using variable costing, however, have one additional feature. Fixed expenses are broken down into two categories: *direct fixed expenses* and *common fixed expenses.* This additional subdivision highlights controllable versus noncontrollable costs, and enhances the manager's ability to properly evaluate each segment's contribution to overall firm performance.

direct fixed expenses

Direct fixed expenses are fixed expenses that are directly traceable to a segment (e.g., a product line). These are sometimes referred to as *avoidable fixed expenses* because they vanish if the segment is eliminated. These fixed expenses are caused by the existence of the segment itself. For example, depreciation on equipment used to produce a product and the salary of the production supervisor of the production line associated with the product are examples of direct fixed expenses.

common fixed costs

Common fixed costs are indirectly traceable to any one segment. They are caused by more than one segment. These costs persist even if one of the segments to which they are common is eliminated. For example, in a plant that produces more than one product, plant depreciation and the salary of the sales supervisor are common fixed costs (where products are defined as the segments). Elimination of a product line would not eliminate the plant and its associated depreciation or the salary of the sales supervisor.

segment margin

The profit contribution each segment makes towards covering a firm's common fixed costs is called the **segment margin.** The segment margin is a meaningful measure of performance for the segment. A segment should at least be able to cover both its variable costs and its direct fixed costs. If it cannot consistently produce a positive segment margin, it is consistently dragging down the firm's total profit. It becomes time to consider dropping the product. Ignoring any effect a segment may have on the sales of other segments, the segment margin measures the change in a firm's profits that would occur if the segment were eliminated.

Exhibit 23-8 shows a segmented income statement for a conventional manufacturing setting. Segments are defined as products: pocket watches and wrist-

Exhibit 23-8
Segmented Income Statement: Conventional Setting

	Pocket Watches	Wristwatches	Total
Sales	$475,000	$840,000	$1,315,000
Less variable costs:			
Direct materials	(150,000)	(200,000)	(350,000)
Direct labor	(105,000)	(105,000)	(210,000)
Maintenance	(45,000)	(45,000)	(90,000)
Power	(17,500)	(17,500)	(35,000)
Commissions	(15,000)	(20,000)	(35,000)
Contribution margin	$142,500	$452,500	$ 595,000
Less direct fixed costs:			
Advertising	(40,000)	(30,000)	(70,000)
Product margin	$102,500	$422,500	$ 525,000
Less common fixed expenses:			
Depreciation (machinery)			(50,000)
Depreciation (plant)			(80,000)
Setups			(100,000)
Personnel			(75,000)
General administration			(90,000)
Materials handling			(70,000)
Sales administration			(40,000)
Income before taxes			$ 20,000

watches. The statement indicates that both pocket watches and wristwatches are providing positive product margins. It is unlikely, based on the information here, that the company would drop either product line. Yet, overall profitability for the company is not impressive—barely above the break-even point. An important issue—in fact, a critical issue in segmented analysis—is the ability to trace costs to individual segments. Improved traceability is offered by ABC classifications. A JIT environment offers even greater traceability.

Segmented Reporting: Effects of ABC and JIT

Exhibit 23-9 presents a segmented statement using an activity-based costing classification. The same example used for conventional segmented reporting is used to illustrate the potential for increased accuracy in segmented reporting. Machine depreciation, a resource acquired in advance and treated as a unit-level cost, is traced to each segment using machine hours to measure usage. Two batch level costs—setups and material handling—are assigned to products using batch-level cost drivers (number of setups and moves). Assume that investigation reveals that these two batch-level activities have both resources acquired in advance and resources acquired as needed. Resources acquired as needed vary with a cost driver and is labeled as a nonunit variable expense. The cost of resources acquired in advance is a fixed expense, divided into two categories: **activity fixed expenses,** representing the cost of fixed resource usage (fixed activity rate × expected activity usage) and unused activity expenses. Unused activity expenses are common to each segment. There are also two product-level costs—personnel and sales administration—assigned to products using the number of employees

activity fixed expenses

Exhibit 23-9
Segmented Income Statement: Activity-Based Costing

	Pocket Watches	*Wristwatches*	*Total*
Sales	$475,000	$840,000	$1,315,000
Less unit-level variable expenses:			
Direct materials	(150,000)	(200,000)	(350,000)
Direct labor	(105,000)	(105,000)	(210,000)
Maintenance	(45,000)	(45,000)	(90,000)
Power	(17,500)	(17,500)	(35,000)
Commissions	(15,000)	(20,000)	(35,000)
Contribution Margin	$142,500	$452,500	$ 595,000
Less traceable expenses:			
Machine depreciation			
Activity fixed	(25,000)	(25,000)	(50,000)
Setups			
Nonunit variable	(10,000)	(5,000)	(15,000)
Activity fixed	(40,000)	(25,000)	(65,000)
Material handling			
Nonunit variable	(5,000)	(7,000)	(12,000)
Activity fixed	(35,000)	(13,000)	(48,000)
Personnel			
Activity fixed	(22,500)	(37,500)	(60,000)
Sales administration			
Activity fixed	(25,000)	(15,000)	(40,000)
Advertising			
Direct fixed	(40,000)	(30,000)	(70,000)
Product margin	$(60,000)	$295,000	$235,000
Less common expenses:			
Unused activity:			
Setups			(20,000)
Material handling			(10,000)
Personnel			(15,000)
Facility-level:			
Plant depreciation			(80,000)
General administration			(90,000)
Income before taxes			$ 20,000

and number of sales orders. Resources associated with these two activities are all acquired in advance of usage and are labeled as activity fixed expenses. It could also be argued that advertising is a product-level activity (the cost increases as the number of products increases). There is no need, however, to use a cost driver to assign advertising costs to each product line. Advertising is traceable directly to each product line and, therefore, is labeled a direct fixed cost in the traditional sense.

The ABC segmented statement provides a much different view of product profitability than the conventional, variable-costing segmented statement. First, we see that the company is paying for resources that are not being used, totaling $45,000. Second, the pocket watches are unprofitable—and are causing a significant drain on company resources. Thus, the ABC segmented income statement reveals three possible ways of increasing income: (1) reducing resource spending by exploiting the current unused activity capacities, (2) eliminating the unprofitable product line, and (3) a combination of (1) and (2).

Exploiting excess capacity to increase income depends to a large extent on the nature of the involved resources. If resources must be acquired in whole units rather than fractional units, exploiting excess capacity is more difficult—at least in the short run. For example, assume that personnel costs consist of the salaries of two employees: a personnel manager ($40,000) and an assistant personnel manager ($35,000). Costs are assigned based on the number of employees, measured at practical capacity (assume this capacity is 150 employees). Thus, the activity rate for personnel is $500 per employee ($75,000/150). Presumably, each personnel manager can handle 75 employees. Currently, 120 employees are being serviced, leaving an unused capacity of 30, and a cost of unused capacity of $15,000 ($500 × 30). In practical terms, the only way to capture the cost of the excess capacity (as savings) would be to lay off the assistant manager and hire a part-time employee. The viability of this action depends on the skills needed for the position and those that would be supplied by a part-time employee. Similar analyses would be necessary for the other activities with excess capacity.

The remaining two alternatives consider the possibility of dropping the pocket watch line. Before making a decision about eliminating the unprofitable line, the manager needs to know how much resource spending will change. First, all unit and nonunit variable expenses will vanish, as will direct fixed expenses. Note, however, that machine depreciation—even though unitized—is not relevant to the decision (depreciation is an allocation of a sunk cost). Dropping the unprofitable line would increase the cost of unused resources from $45,000 to $167,500 (the total increases by the sum of the activity fixed expenses, excluding advertising). The key to the analysis is assessing how much of the cost of unused capacity can be eliminated. For example, dropping the pocket watch line increases personnel's cost of unused capacity from $15,000 to $37,500. Since the salary of the assistant personnel manager is $35,000, resource spending for the personnel activity would decrease by this amount (only $35,000 of the cost of unused capacity can be captured). Notice that because of the whole-unit (lump sum) nature of personnel costs, the savings are $12,500 more than the personnel costs traced to the pocket watch line.

Of course, it is possible that some activity fixed expenses will not vanish. For example, if the costs of sales administration coincide with the salary of the marketing manager, dropping the product line will not produce any reduction in resource spending. This outcome is again attributable to the lump sum nature of this activity's costs. Finally, assume that resource spending for fixed activity expenses can be decreased exactly by the amount assigned for the setup and material handling activities. The complete analysis is given in Exhibit 23-10. As the analysis shows, dropping the pocket watch line will increase total profitability by $22,500.

Segmented Reporting and JIT

But should the pocket watches be eliminated? Other alternatives may exist—particularly when strategic elements are considered. For example, adopting a JIT approach may increase the profitability of both lines—to the point that keeping the pocket watches is the right decision. Assume that the segmented income statement is projected as shown in Exhibit 23-11 after the installation of a JIT

Exhibit 23-10
Keep or Drop Analysis

	Keep Alternative	Drop Alternative
Contribution Margin	$142,500	0
Setups[a]		
Nonunit variable	(10,000)	0
Activity fixed	(40,000)	0
Material handling[b]		
Nonunit variable	(5,000)	0
Activity fixed	(35,000)	0
Personnel[b]		
Activity fixed	(22,500)	0
Unused capacity	(15,000)	$(2,500)
Advertising		
Direct fixed	(40,000)	0
Total	$ (25,000)	$(2,500)

[a]Assumes that these expenses can be avoided if product is dropped
[b]Activity fixed expenses plus unused capacity allows a $35,000 reduction in resource spending (salary of assistant manager). This leaves $2,500 of unused capacity that cannot be eliminated.

Exhibit 23-11
Segmented Income Statement: JIT and ABC Classification

	Pocket Watches	Wristwatches	Total
Sales	$475,000	$840,000	$1,315,000
Less variable costs:			
Direct materials	(150,000)	(200,000)	(350,000)
Power	(17,500)	(17,500)	(35,000)
Commissions	(15,000)	(20,000)	(35,000)
Contribution margin	$292,500	$602,500	$ 895,000
Less traceable expenses:			
Activity fixed:			
Personnel	(22,500)	(37,500)	(60,000)
Sales administration	(25,000)	(15,000)	(40,000)
Direct fixed:			
Advertising	(40,000)	(30,000)	(70,000)
Direct labor	(140,000)	(140,000)	(280,000)
Machine depreciation	(20,000)	(30,000)	(50,000)
Product margin	$ 45,000	$350,000	$ 395,000
Less common expenses:			
Unused capacity:			
Personnel			(15,000)
Facility level:			
Plant depreciation			(80,000)
General administration			(90,000
Income before taxes			$ 210,000

system. Notice that the batch-level activities are eliminated. Also, the maintenance function is now absorbed by the cell workers (direct labor). The extra duties may cause an increase in total direct labor cost. The remaining nonunit-based costs are product-level costs.

The consequences on the segmented income statement are dramatic. The number and magnitude of variable costs have decreased as direct labor, maintenance, and materials handling have become fixed. Direct fixed costs, however, have increased in number and magnitude. Because of the JIT system and activity-based costing, management now has a much better understanding of individual product performance. Both products are performing at a higher level. If increased profit performance is desired beyond the projected levels, management could look at the possibility of changing the selling price of one or both products.

Notice the applicability of CVP analysis in this situation. For the option to increase the selling price, the selling price that is needed to break even or reach some other targeted segmented margin can be found. Thus, the increase in product-costing accuracy has enhanced the utility of some traditional management accounting decision models.

The benefits of improved traceability were achieved primarily through the JIT system. However, activity-based costing is also an important component. Personnel costs were disaggregated and assigned to each product. By treating the nonunit-based assignments as traceable costs, it is possible to continue using the variable-costing format as a useful managerial tool.

In addition to improving the usefulness of variable costing in decision making, JIT manufacturing also simplifies its use. Recall that variable and absorption costing differ in the way they treat fixed overhead. Absorption costing treats fixed overhead as a product cost, whereas variable costing treats it as a period cost. Under absorption costing, if production exceeds sales, some of the period's fixed overhead can be inventoried and is not expensed until a later period; if production is less than sales, fixed overhead attached to inventory units from prior periods is expensed in addition to the current period's fixed overhead. How fixed overhead is treated by each method, then, leads to differences in the valuation of finished goods inventory and reported income.

In a pure JIT environment, finished goods inventories are reduced to insignificant levels. All manufacturing costs are expensed in the period. Product costs, including fixed overhead, assume the nature of period costs. No fixed overhead costs are inventoried; thus, absorption-costing income and variable-costing income are always the same. Inventory valuation is irrelevant. The only difference between income statements using the two systems is how expenses are presented on the income statement: absorption costing classifies costs by function, and variable costing classifies them by cost behavior.

SUMMARY OF LEARNING OBJECTIVES

1. Describe the traditional inventory management model. In a traditional manufacturing environment, inventory management focuses on minimizing inventory-related costs to maximize total profits. Some inventory must be held to achieve this objective. For example, inventory must be held to balance ordering (or setup) and carrying costs and to minimize stockout costs. Holding inventory helps a firm to satisfy customer demand, to keep production moving smoothly, to take advantage of quantity discounts, and to hedge against future price increases.

If demand is known with certainty, an optimal inventory policy can be developed by identifying the order (or setup) quantity that minimizes total ordering (or setup) and carrying costs and by determining when to place an order. This optimal order quantity is referred to as the *economic order quantity.* This quantity is computed using Equation 23.2.

If demand uncertainty exists, the inventory policy is altered to include provision for safety stock. Safety stock prevents significant stockout costs such as lost sales and interrupted production. Safety stock is determined by the average rate of usage, the maximum rate of usage, the economic order quantity, and the lead time. The reorder point is when an order should be placed so that the raw materials arrive just as the inventory is depleted. The reorder point is determined by the rate of usage, the economic order quantity, and the lead time.

2. *Describe JIT inventory management.* JIT inventory management rejects the traditional inventory model and views inventories as wasteful—as cash traps. JIT inventory management is part of an overall JIT purchasing and production system. In this system, the emphasis is on reducing waste, on finding more efficient and productive ways to do things. By reorganizing manufacturing into cells, using a demand-pull approach to production, developing a partners-in-profit relationship with suppliers, and emphasizing total quality and total preventive maintenance, JIT manufacturers have reduced inventories to insignificant levels.

3. *Explain how activity-based costing facilitates strategic decision making.* Activity-based costing traces costs to activities and then to products that consume activities. Different strategies cause different activities. By knowing these activities and their associated costs, the costs of different strategic choices can be assessed. This, in turn, helps a manager to select superior strategies—those that will establish a competitive advantage for the firm.

4. *Describe the resource usage model and its role in activity-based costing.* Activity-based analysis emphasizes the difference between resource spending and resource usage. Resource spending is the cost of acquiring capacity to perform an activity. Resource usage is the quantity of activity resource consumed in producing an organization's output. An activity rate is the resource expenditure divided by the practical capacity of an activity. It is used to compute the cost of resource usage and the cost of unused activity. Resources can be supplied in one of two ways: (1) as needed, and (2) in advance of usage. Both types of resources can be associated with a particular activity. Generally, the first category of resources corresponds to variable cost behavior and the second with fixed cost behavior. Knowledge of resource supply, usage, and the relationship with activities allows managers to improve decision making and control activities.

5. *Explain the effect of activity-based costing and JIT on relevant costing.* ABC and JIT both increase traceability of costs to various cost objects. Increased traceability enhances the ability to identify and use relevant costs. It also reduces the number of special studies that must be done to provide the needed information for relevant-costing decisions. Furthermore, by identifying activities and accurately tracing costs to activities and the products that consume the activities, greater strategic insights are provided. For relevant costing, this usually means a longer-term focus with more attention paid to the strategic implications.

6. *Describe segment analysis in both a conventional setting and in an ABC/JIT setting.* Reporting the profit contributions of profit-making entities (segments) within an organization is called segmented reporting. Traditional segmented reporting uses a variable-costing approach with one added feature—the separation of fixed expenses into direct and common categories. Direct fixed expenses are defined as those that are traceable to a segment and that vanish whenever the segment vanishes. Common fixed expenses are not traceable to any one segment. ABC and JIT improve segmented reporting by increasing the ability to trace costs—particularly those classified as common—to individual segments.

KEY TERMS

REVIEW PROBLEMS

I ABC, JIT, and Segmented Reporting

The following unit cost information is provided for a product for three different cost systems: conventional, activity based, and JIT. The conventional system assigns overhead using unit-based cost drivers. The activity-based system assigns overhead using both unit-based and nonunit-based cost drivers. The JIT system uses a focused approach to trace costs and activity-based costing for costs not directly associated with a manufacturing cell. The company produces 1,000 units of this product each year.

	Cost System		
	Conventional	*Activity Based*	*JIT*
Direct materials	$100	$100	$100
Direct labor	20	20	30[a]
Unit-based variable overhead	40	40	10
Nonunit-based variable overhead	—	20	10
Activity fixed overhead[b]	—	30	8
Direct fixed costs	10	10	10
Common fixed overhead	60	10	10
Total	$230	$230	$178

[a]Cell labor, including maintenance, materials handling, and packing
[b]Nonunit fixed costs assigned using a cost driver. In the short run, these costs do not vary with the level of the associated cost driver. Assume that all of the activity fixed overhead is avoidable and there are no unused activity capacity costs.

REQUIRED:

1. Assume that the product is a subassembly. What is the maximum amount, according to each cost system, that should be paid for the subassembly to an outside supplier? Explain why the amounts differ.
2. Assume that the product is a finished good that can be sold to a consumer for $200 per unit. For each cost system, prepare a product income statement that shows contribution margin and product margin assuming sales of 1,000 units. How do you think a manager would react to the product performance reported by the conventional system? The activity-based system? The JIT system? What are the strategic cost implications?

Solution

1. *Conventional cost system*—For the conventional cost system, variable manufacturing costs and direct fixed costs are usually assumed to be avoidable should the company decide to buy the assembly instead of making it. Thus, the avoidable costs would be $170, which is the most the company would pay an external supplier of the subassembly.
   Activity-Based cost system—The activity-based cost system defines avoidable costs as unit-based variable costs, nonunit-based variable costs, and direct fixed expenses (such as product advertising). Depending on the lumpy nature of the costs, activity fixed expenses may also be avoidable. ABC improves the traceability of the costs; therefore, the avoidable costs are more easily identified. For this problem, the maximum price signaled by activity-based costing is $220. The difference between the conventional and the activity-based costing prices reveals some potential problems with decision making in a conventional environment.
   JIT cost system—The avoidable costs (all but common fixed overhead) signal a maximum price of $168. The JIT system produces a lower cost than activity-based costing because JIT manufacturing and purchasing reduces or eliminates many overhead costs

(e.g., all batch-level costs are virtually eliminated). Because of greater efficiency, JIT makes it less likely to switch from internal production to external acquisition.

2. The income statements are as follows:

	Conventional	*Activity Based*	*JIT*
Sales	$200,000	$200,000	$200,000
Less: Variable expenses	(160,000)	(160,000)	(110,000)
Contribution margin	$ 40,000	$ 40,000	$ 90,000
Less: Traceable expenses			
Nonunit-based variable	—	(20,000)	(10,000)
Activity fixed	—	(30,000)	(8,000)
Direct fixed expenses	(10,000)	(10,000)	(40,000)
Product margin	$ 30,000	$ (20,000)	$ 32,000

Conventional costing provides a statement indicating a profitable product. Activity-based costing gives a truer, less rosy view of the product's performance than the conventional approach. In fact, the activity-based costing statement indicates that management needs to take steps to improve profitability or drop the product. The JIT outcome reveals that one possible solution is installing a JIT system to increase efficiency. Note that JIT has converted some costs (e.g., direct labor) to direct fixed costs. Dropping a product or keeping it and improving its profitability are strategic decisions. Changing the way activities are done by using a JIT approach is a strategy that may produce a profitable product and maintain the needed competitive advantage.

II ABC, Strategic Costing, and Relevant Costing

Thomas Company has idle capacity. Recently, Thomas received an offer to sell 2,000 units of one of its products to a new customer in a geographic region not normally serviced. The offering price is $9.50 per unit. The product normally sells for $13.50. The activity-based accounting system provides the following information:

	Cost Driver	*Unused Capacity*	*Quantity Demanded*[1]	*Activity Rate*	
				Fixed	*Variable*
Direct materials	Units	0	2,000	—	$3
Direct labor	Direct Labor hours	0	400	—	7
Setups	Setup hours	0	25	$50	8
Machining	Machine hours	6,000	4,000	4	1

[1]This only represents the amount of resources demanded by the special order being considered.

Although the fixed activity rate for setups is $25 per hour, any expansion of this resource must be acquired in whole units. Each whole unit provides an additional 100 hours of setup servicing and is priced at the fixed activity rate.

REQUIRED:

1. Compute the change in income for Thomas Company if the order is accepted. Comment on whether the order should be accepted or not. (In particular, discuss the strategic issues.)
2. Suppose that the setup activity had 50 hours of unused capacity. How does this affect the analysis?

Solution

1. The relevant costs are those that change if the order is accepted. These costs would consist of the variable activity costs (resources acquired as needed) plus any cost of

acquiring additional activity capacity (resources acquired in advance of usage). The income will change by the following amount:

Revenues ($9.50 × 2,000 units)	$19,000
Less increase in resource spending:	
Direct materials ($3 × 2,000 units)	(6,000)
Direct labor ($7 × 400 DL hrs)	(2,800)
Setups ($50 × 100 hrs) + ($8 × 25 hrs)	(5,200)
Machining ($1 × 4,000 machine hrs)	(4,000)
Income change	$ 1,000

Special orders need to be examined carefully before acceptance. This order offers an increase in income of $1,000, but it does require expansion of the setup activity capacity. If this expansion is short-run in nature, it may be worth it. If it entails a long-term commitment, the company would be exchanging a one-year benefit of $1,000 for an annual commitment of $5,000. In this case the order should be rejected. Even if the commitment is short term, other strategic factors need to be considered. Will this order affect any regular sales? Is the company looking for a permanent solution to its idle capacity or are special orders becoming a habit—a response pattern that may eventually prove disastrous?

2. If 50 hours of excess setup capacity exists, no additional resource spending for additional capacity would be required. Thus, the profitability of the special order would be increased by $5,000 (the increase in resource spending that would have been required). Thus, total income would increase by $6,000 if the order is accepted.

QUESTIONS

1. What are ordering costs? Provide examples.
2. What are setup costs? Illustrate with examples.
3. What are carrying costs? Illustrate with examples.
4. Explain why, in the traditional view of inventory, carrying costs increase as ordering costs decrease.
5. Discuss the traditional reasons for carrying inventory.
6. What are stockout costs?
7. Explain how safety stock is used to deal with demand uncertainty.
8. Suppose that a raw material has a lead time of 3 days and that the average usage of the material is 12 units per day. What is the reorder point? If the maximum usage is 15 units per day, what is the safety stock?
9. What is the economic order quantity?
10. What approach does JIT take to minimize total inventory costs?
11. One reason for inventory is to prevent shutdowns. How does the JIT approach to inventory management deal with this potential problem?
12. Explain how long-term contractual relationships with suppliers can reduce the acquisition cost of raw materials.
13. What are the three major objectives of traditional management accounting?
14. What is strategic decision making?
15. What is strategic cost analysis?
16. Explain why activity-based costing is especially useful for strategic cost analysis.
17. Explain the difference between resource spending and resource usage.
18. What is an activity rate?
19. What is the relationship between resources supplied as needed and cost behavior?
20. What is the relationship between resources supplied in advance of usage and cost behavior?
21. How does a JIT manufacturing approach increase product-costing accuracy?
22. How are relevant-costing decisions affected by activity-based costing and JIT?
23. Explain why there are more directly traceable costs

in a JIT manufacturing environment (or for a firm that uses activity-based costing).

24. The information supplied by ABC segmented income statements is superior to that provided by variable-costing income statements. Do you agree? Explain.
25. Segmented income statements are more meaningful in a JIT manufacturing environment. Do you agree? Explain.

EXERCISES

E23-1
Ordering and Carrying Costs
LO 1

Chamer Company uses 12,000 small motors each year in its production of Go Carts. The cost of placing an order is $250. The cost of holding one unit of inventory for one year is $6. Currently, Chamer places 8 orders of 1,500 motors per year.

REQUIRED:

1. Compute the annual ordering cost.
2. Compute the annual carrying cost.
3. Compute the cost of Chamer's current inventory policy.

E23-2
Economic Order Quantity
LO 1

Refer to the data in E23-1.

REQUIRED:

1. Compute the economic order quantity.
2. Compute the ordering cost and the carrying cost for the EOQ.
3. How much money does using the EOQ policy save the company over the policy of purchasing 1,500 brushes per order?

E23-3
Economic Order Quantity
LO 1

Groff Company uses 30,000 pounds of aluminum each year. The cost of placing an order is $12, and the carrying cost for one pound of aluminum is $0.50.

REQUIRED:

1. Compute the economic order quantity for aluminum.
2. Compute the carrying cost and ordering cost for the EOQ.

E23-4
Reorder Point
LO 1

Golding Company manufactures tractors. One part it orders from an outside supplier is a specially designed carburetor. Information pertaining to this carburetor is as follows:

Economic order quantity	600 units
Average daily usage	25 units
Maximum daily usage	40 units
Lead time	5 days

REQUIRED:

1. What is the reorder point, assuming no safety stock is carried?
2. What is the reorder point assuming that safety stock is carried?

E23-5
EOQ with Setup Costs
LO 1

Kiddy Manufacturing produces bicycles. In order to produce the frames, special equipment must be set up. The setup cost per production run is $40. The cost of carrying frames in inventory is $1.25 per frame per year. The company produces 40,000 bikes per year.

REQUIRED:

1. Compute the number of frames that should be produced per setup to minimize total setup and carrying costs.
2. Compute the total setup and carrying costs associated with the economic order quantity.

E23-6
Safety Stock
LO 1

Airwing Manufacturing produces a component used in its production of small two-passenger helicopters. The time to set up and produce a batch of the components is 6 days. The average daily usage is 200 components and the maximum daily usage is 240 components.

REQUIRED: Compute the reorder point assuming that safety stock is carried by Airwing Manufacturing. How much safety stock is carried by Airwing?

E23-7
Reasons for Carrying Inventory
LO 1, 2

The following reasons have been offered for holding inventories:

a. To balance setup (or ordering) and carrying costs
b. To meet delivery dates
c. To avoid shutting down production
d. To take advantage of discounts
e. To hedge against future price increases

REQUIRED: Explain how the JIT approach refutes each of these reasons and, consequently, argues for zero inventories.

E23-8
Kanban Cards
LO 2

Explain the use of each of the following markers or cards in the Kanban system:

a. The withdrawal Kanban
b. The production Kanban
c. The vendor Kanban

E23-9
ABC and Strategic Decision Making
LO 3

Bailey Manufacturing produces several types of potentiometers. The products are produced in batches according to customer order. Historically, the costs of order entry, sales, and marketing activities were expensed and not traced to individual products. Recently, the company decided to trace these costs to individual products using the number of customer orders as the cost driver. As a result of the tracing, the marketing manager recommended the imposition of a charge per customer order. The president of the company concurred. The outcome of the decision was an increase in the size of customer orders.

REQUIRED:

1. Consider the following claim: By expensing the marketing costs, all products were undercosted; furthermore, products ordered in small batches are significantly undercosted. Do you agree? Explain.
2. Explain why linking output (products) with activities (order entry and other marketing activities) changed the marketing strategy for Bailey Manufacturing. Do you think the change in strategy was good? Explain. If so, what does this have to say about the conventional costing system?

E23-10
ABC and Strategic Decision Making
LO 3

Medtech, Inc., has a traditional, unit-based cost system. The company produces a variety of high-tech medical products. The following cost equation is used to describe the total manufacturing costs:

$$Y = \$3{,}000{,}000 + \$25X \text{ where } X = \text{Direct labor hours}$$

The variable rate of $25 is broken down as follows:

Direct labor	$ 8
Variable overhead	10
Direct materials	7

Because of competitive pressures, product engineering was given the charge to redesign products to reduce the total cost of manufacturing. Using the above relationships, product engineering adopted the strategy of redesigning to reduce direct labor content. As each design was completed, an engineering change order was cut, triggering a series of events such as design approval, vendor selection, bill of material update, redrawing of schematic, test runs, changes in setup procedures, development of new inspection procedures, and so on.

After one year of design change, the normal volume of direct labor was reduced from 120,000 hours to 100,000 hours, with the same number of products being produced. Fixed overhead, however, increased from $3,000,000 to $3,500,000.

REQUIRED:

1. Using normal volume, compute the manufacturing cost per labor hour before the year of design changes.
2. Using normal volume after the one year of design changes, compute the manufacturing cost per hour.
3. What do you think is the most likely explanation for the failure of the design changes to reduce manufacturing costs?
4. Explain how an ABC system could have improved the design strategy taken by product engineering.

E23-11
ABC; Resource Supply and Usage; Activity Rates
LO 4

Rinkle Manufacturing Company has three salaried clerks to process purchase orders. Each clerk is paid a salary of $28,000 and is capable of processing 5,000 purchase orders per year (if the clerk works efficiently). In addition to the salaries, Rinkle spends $7,500 per year for forms, postage, etc. (assuming 15,000 purchase orders are processed). During the year, 12,500 orders were processed.

REQUIRED:

1. Calculate the activity rate for the purchase ordering activity. Break the activity rate into fixed and variable components.
2. Compute the total activity availability and break this into activity usage and unused activity.
3. Calculate the total cost of resource supplied and break this into the cost of activity used and the cost of unused activity.
4. How much of the total cost of processing purchase orders will be assigned to the products manufactured by the firm? If there is a residual cost, how is it treated?

E23-12
Resource Usage Model and Cost Behavior
LO 4

For the following activities and their associated resources, identify the following: (1) a cost driver (2) resources acquired as needed, (3) resources acquired in advance of usage (long-term), and (4) resources acquired in advance of usage (short-term). Also, label each resource as one of the following with respect to the cost driver: (1) variable, (2) committed fixed, and (3) discretionary fixed.

Activity	*Resource Description*
Power (internally produced)	Equipment, labor, fuel
Inspection	Test equipment, inspectors (each inspector can inspect five batches per day), units inspected (process requires destructive sampling[1])
Packing	Materials, labor, (each packer places five units in a box), conveyor belt
Payable Processing	Clerks, materials, equipment and facility

[1]Destructive sampling occurs whenever it is necessary to destroy the unit in order to test it.

E23-13
ABC; Make or Buy
LO 5

Shaw Manufacturing, Inc. has just received an offer from a supplier to buy 3,000 units of a component used in its main product. The component is a gear that is currently produced internally. The supplier has offered to sell the gear for $22 per gear. Shaw is currently using a conventional, unit-based cost system that allocates overhead to jobs on the basis of direct labor hours. Accounting has estimated the full cost of producing the gear:

Direct materials	$10
Direct labor	5
Variable overhead	5
Fixed overhead	16

Prior to making a decision, the president of the company commissioned a special study to see whether there would be any decrease in the fixed overhead costs. The results of the study revealed the following:

a. Two setups—$2,500 each. (The setups would be avoided and total spending could be reduced by $2,500 per set up.)
b. One less inspector needed, $28,000.
c. Engineering work: 500 hours, $15/hr. (Although the work decreases by 500 hours, the engineer assigned to the gear line also spends time on other products.)

REQUIRED:

1. Ignore the special study and determine whether the gear should be produced internally or purchased from the supplier.
2. Now, using the special study data, repeat the analysis.
3. Consider this claim: The use of special cost studies is a symptom of an outmoded cost system. Comment on this observation and discuss the need for the special study if an ABC system had been in place.

E23-14
ABC; Special Order
LO 5

Patterson Machining is operating at 90% of capacity. An offer to produce 3,000 units of a specially designed tool has just been received. The offering price is $10.00 per unit. The product normally sells for $13.50. The activity-based accounting system provides the following information:

	Activity Driver	*Unused Capacity*	*Quantity Demanded*[1]	*Activity Rate* *Fixed*	*Activity Rate* *Variable*
Direct materials	Units	0	3,000	—	$5.00
Direct labor	Direct labor hours	0	500	—	7.00
Setups	Setup hours	30	50	$100.00	8.00
Machining	Machine hours	6,000	4,000	5.00	1.50

[1]This only represents the amount of resources demanded by the special order being considered.

Expansion of activity capacity for setups or machining must be done in whole units. For setups, each whole unit provides an additional 25 hours of setup activity and is priced at the fixed activity rate. For machining, the capacity is expanded by 2,000 machine hours per year and the cost is $10,000 per year (the required lease payment for an additional machine).

REQUIRED:

1. Compute the change in income for Patterson Machining if the order is accepted. Comment on whether the order should be accepted or not (in particular, discuss the strategic issues).
2. Suppose that the setup activity has 60 hours of unused capacity. How is the analysis affected?
3. Suppose that the setup activity has 60 hours of unused capacity and that the machining activity has 3,000 hours of unused capacity. How is the analysis affected?

E23-15
Segmented Income Statements; Product Performance
LO 7

Carter Inc., produces two types of peanut butter: Crunchy and Smooth. Of the two, Smooth is the more popular. Data concerning the two products follow:

	Smooth	*Crunchy*	*Excess[1] Capacity*
Expected sales (in cases)	50,000	10,000	—
Selling price per case	$100	$80	—
Direct labor hours	40,000	10,000	—
Machine hours	10,000	2,500	—
Receiving orders	50	25	25
Packing orders	100	50	50
Material cost per case	$50	$48	—
Direct labor cost per case	$10	$8	—
Advertising costs	$200,000	$60,000	—

[1]Based on practical activity capacity.

Annual overhead costs are listed next. These costs are classified as fixed or variable with respect to the appropriate cost driver.

	Fixed	*Variable[b]*
Direct labor benefits	—	$200,000
Machine costs	$200,000[a]	250,000
Receiving department	200,000	22,500
Packing department	100,000	45,000
Total costs	$500,000	$517,500

[a]All depreciation
[b]These costs are for the actual levels of the cost driver.

REQUIRED:

1. Prepare a conventional segmented income statement for the two products. Machine depreciation, receiving, and packing are treated as common fixed overhead. Overhead is assigned to products using direct labor hours.
2. Prepare a revised segmented income statement, using activity-based costing to trace costs to product lines. (Assume the company chooses to continue treating machine depreciation as a common fixed cost.)

3. Assess the performance of the two products based on the two segmented income statements. Which statement do you think is the most useful? Explain.

E23-16
Product-Line Performance; Impact of JIT Manufacturing
LO 7

Refer to the activity data given in E23-15. Two manufacturing cells are created, one for each type of peanut butter. Cell laborers operate the machinery, perform maintenance, and do all the packing for the cell product. The receiving department was abolished and replaced with just-in-time delivery adjacent to the cells themselves. Inspection of incoming materials was eliminated because of careful supplier selection—only suppliers that could produce the needed quality were retained. Because of the interdisciplinary nature of the cell labor, the company was able to reduce its packing costs by 60 percent and machine costs (specifically maintenance) by 20 percent. The direct costs (except for raw materials) of the two cells are given below.

	Smooth Cell	*Crunchy Cell*
Cell labor[1]	$730,000	$108,000
Machine costs[2]	280,000	120,000

[1]Includes fringe benefits and packing (all fixed)
[2]50 percent fixed for each cell

REQUIRED:

1. Prepare a segmented income statement for Carter Inc. with segments defined as products.
2. Based on the information contained in Requirement 1, evaluate the performance of each product. If you have worked E23-15, explain why the outcomes in the two exercises differ. What does this suggest concerning the potential role of JIT in improving the competitive ability of individual products?

PROBLEMS

P23-1
EOQ and Reorder Point
LO 1

Italia Pizzeria is a popular pizza restaurant near a college campus. Brandon Thayn, an accounting student, works for Italia Pizzeria. After several months at the restaurant, Brandon began to analyze the efficiency of the business, particularly inventory practices. Brandon noticed that the owner had more than 50 items regularly carried in inventory. Of these items, the most expensive to buy and carry was cheese. Cheese was ordered in blocks at $17.50 per block. Annual usage totals 14,000 blocks.

Upon questioning the owner, Brandon discovered that the owner did not use any formal model for ordering cheese. It took 5 days to receive a new order when placed, which was done whenever the inventory of cheese dropped to 200 blocks. The size of the order was usually 400 blocks. The cost of carrying one block of cheese is 10 percent of its purchase price. It costs $40 to place and receive an order.

Italia Pizzeria stays open 7 days a week and operates 50 weeks a year. The restaurant closes for the last 2 weeks of December.

REQUIRED:

1. Compute the total cost of ordering and carrying the cheese inventory under the current policy.
2. Compute the total cost of ordering and carrying cheese if the restaurant were to change to the economic order quantity. How much would the restaurant save per year by switching policies?
3. If the restaurant uses the economic order quantity, when should it place an order? (Assume that the amount of cheese used per day is the same throughout the year.) How does this compare with the current reorder policy?

4. Suppose that storage space allows a maximum of 600 blocks of cheese. Discuss the inventory policy that should be followed with this restriction.
5. Suppose that the maximum storage is 600 blocks of cheese and cheese can be held for a maximum of 10 days. The owner will not hold cheese any longer in order to ensure the right flavor and quality. Under these conditions, evaluate the owner's current inventory policy.

P23-2
EOQ with Safety Stock
LO 1

Parry Chiropractic Clinic uses an EOQ model to order supplies. Lately, several chiropractors have been complaining about the availability of X-ray film. During the past three months, the clinic has had to place five rush orders because of stockouts. Because of the problem, the supply officer has decided to review the current inventory policy. The following data have been gathered:

Cost of placing and receiving an order	$60
Cost of carrying one package	$2
Average usage per day	5 packages
Maximum usage per day	7 packages
Lead time for an order	6 days
Annual demand	1,500 packages

The clinic currently does not carry any safety stock. The clinic operates 300 days each year.

REQUIRED:

1. Compute the economic order quantity and the reorder point. What is the total ordering and carrying cost for the clinic's current inventory policy?
2. Assume that the clinic has decided to carry safety stock. Compute how much should be carried to ensure no stockouts. Compute the total ordering and carrying cost for this policy. Will the reorder point change? If so, what is it?

P23-3
ABC and Strategic Costing
LO 3

Bruce Norton, owner of Wellington Works, a machining company, once again was disappointed in the year-end income statement. Profits had again dropped. The performance was particularly puzzling given that the shop was operating at 100 percent capacity and had been for two years—ever since it had landed a Fortune 500 firm as a regular customer. This firm currently supplies 40 percent of the business—a figure that had grown over the two years. Convinced that something was wrong, Bruce called Daryl Jenkins, a CPA with a large regional firm. Daryl agreed to look into the matter.

A short time later, Daryl made an appointment to meet with Bruce. Their conversation is recorded below.

Daryl: "Bruce, I think I have pinpointed your problem. I think your major difficulty is bad pricing—you're undercharging your major customer. It's getting high-precision machined parts for much less than the cost to you. And I bet that you have been losing some of your smaller customers."

Bruce: "You're right about losing some of our smaller customers. But their business has been replaced with more orders from our large one. But how can the large buyer be getting a great deal like you've described? It has the same markup as our regular jobs—cost plus 25 percent."

Daryl: "I have prepared a report illustrating the total overhead costs for a typical quarter. This report details your major activities and their associated costs. It also provides a comparison of a typical job for your small customers and the typical job for your large customer. Given that you assign overhead costs using machine hours, I think you'll find it quite revealing."

Report
Regional CPA Firm

I. Major Activities and Their Costs

Activity	*Costs*
Setups	$104,500
Engineering	75,600
NC programming	65,200
Machining	50,000
Rework	50,700
Inspection	11,500
Sales support	40,000

II. Job Profiles

Resources Used	*Small Customer Job*	*Fortune 500*
Job setup hours	3	10
Engineering hours	2	6
Programming hours	1	8
Defective units	20	10
Inspection hours	2	2
Machine hours	2,000	200
Prime costs	$7,000	$800
Other data:		
Job size	1,000 parts	100 parts
Quarterly jobs	15	100
Overhead rate	$7.15 per machine hour	$7.15 per machine hour

REQUIRED:

1. Without any calculation, explain why the machining company is losing money. Discuss the strategic insights provided by knowledge of activities, their costs, and their linkage to output.
2. Compute the unit price currently being charged each customer type.
3. Compute the unit price that would be charged each customer assuming that overhead is assigned using an ABC approach. Was the CPA right? Is the large customer paying less than the cost of producing the unit? How is this conclusion affected if the sales support activity is traced to jobs? (Use orders (jobs) as the cost driver.)
4. What change in strategy would you recommend?

P23-4
ABC; Resource Supply and Usage; Activity Rates
LO 4

Cushing Memorial Hospital has 5 medical technicians who are responsible for conducting sonogram testing. Each technician is paid a salary of $36,000 and is capable of processing 1,000 tests per year. The sonogram equipment is new and was purchased for $150,000. It is expected to last 5 years. In addition to the salaries and equipment, Cushing spends $10,000 per year for forms, paper, power, and other supplies needed to operate the equipment (assuming 5,000 tests are processed). During the year, 4,000 sonogram tests were run.

REQUIRED:

1. Classify the resources associated with the sonogram activity into one of the following: (1) long-term resources supplied in advance, (2) short-term resources supplied in advance, and (3) resources supplied as needed.
2. Calculate the activity rate for the sonogram testing activity. Break the activity rate into fixed and variable components.

3. Compute the total activity availability and break this into activity usage and unused activity.
4. Calculate the total cost of resources supplied and break this into the cost of activity used and the cost of unused activity.
5. How much of the total cost of running the tests should be assigned to the patients using them? If there is a residual cost, how should it be treated? Would your view hold for both not-for-profit and profit hospitals?

P23-5
ABC; Resource Usage Model; Make or Buy
LO 4, 5

Dizzyworld Company manufactures roller skates. With the exception of the rollers, all parts of the skates are produced internally. Neeta Booth, president of Dizzyworld, is seriously considering making the rollers instead of buying them from external suppliers. The rollers are purchased in sets of 4 and cost $2.00 per set. Currently, 100,000 sets of rollers are purchased annually.

Skates are produced in batches, according to shoe size. Production equipment must be reconfigured for each batch. The rollers could be produced using an available area within the plant. Prime costs will average $1.00 per set. However, equipment for production of the rollers would need to be leased ($25,000 per year lease payment). Additionally, it would cost $0.50 per machine hour for power, oil, and other operating expenses. The equipment will provide 60,000 machine hours per year. Since only one type of roller would be produced, there would be no additional demands made on the setup activity. However, other overhead activities (besides machining and setups) would be affected. The company's ABC system provides the following information about the current status of the overhead activities that would be affected. (The lump sum quantity indicates how much capacity must be purchased should any expansion of activity supply be needed. The purchase cost (per unit) is the fixed activity rate. These activities do not have any significant variable costs.)

Activity	*Cost Driver*	*Supply*	*Usage*	*Lump Sum Quantity*	*Fixed Rate*
Purchasing	Orders	25,000	22,000	5,000	$ 5.00
Inspection	Hours	10,000	9,000	2,000	15.00
Material handling	Moves	4,500	4,300	500	30.00

The demands that *production* of rollers would place on the overhead activities is given below:

Activity	*Resource Demands*
Machining	50,000 machine hours
Purchasing	2,000 purchase orders (associated with raw materials)
Inspection	750 inspection hours
Material handling	500 moves

If the rollers are made, the purchase of the rollers from outside suppliers will cease. If the rollers are not purchased, purchase orders (associated with their purchase) will decrease by 5,000. Similarly, the moves for the handling of incoming rollers will decrease by 200.

REQUIRED:

1. Should Dizzyworld make or buy the rollers?
2. Explain how the ABC resource usage model helped in the analysis. Also, comment on how a conventional approach would have differed.

P23-6
Variable and Absorption Costing in a JIT Environment
LO 6

Schultz Company, a manufacturer of two different types of disk drives for personal computers, has installed a JIT purchasing and manufacturing system. After several years of operation, Schultz has succeeded in reducing inventories to insignificant levels. During the coming year, Schultz expects to produce 200,000 drives: 150,000 of Model 144 and 50,000 of Model 720. The drives are produced in manufacturing cells. The expected output represents 80 percent of the capacity for the Model 144 cell and 100 percent of capacity for the Model 720 cell. (This capacity includes time for cell workers to perform maintenance and materials handling.) The selling price for Model 144 is $60 and for Model 720, it is $70.

The relevant data for next year's expected production are as follows:

	Cell 144	*Cell 720*
Direct materials	$3,500,000	$1,000,000
Labor[1]	$900,000	$315,000
Power	$250,000	$100,000
Depreciation	$805,000	$300,000
Number of runs	100	100
Number of cell workers	20	5
Square footage	20,000	10,000

[1]Responsible for production, maintenance, and materials handling

The following overhead costs are common to each cell:

Plant depreciation	$900,000
Production scheduling	300,000
Cafeteria	100,000
Personnel	150,000

These costs are assigned to the cells using cost drivers selected from the cell activity data given above.

In addition to the overhead costs, the company expects the following nonmanufacturing costs:

Commissions (2% of sales)	$250,000
Advertising:	
Model 144	400,000
Model 720	200,000
Administrative (all fixed)	500,000

REQUIRED:

1. Compute the unit cost under absorption costing and under variable costing.
2. Prepare an absorption-costing income statement for the company as a whole.
3. Prepare a variable-costing income statement for the company as a whole.
4. In a JIT environment, will variable-costing income and absorption-costing income ever differ? Explain.

P23-7
Segmented Income Statements; Special-Order Decision; JIT and Activity-Based Costing; Strategic Considerations
LO 3, 5, 6

Refer to P23-6. The president of Schultz Company is concerned about the profit performance of each model. She wants to know the effect on the company's profitability if Model 720 is dropped. At the same time this request was made, the company was approached by a customer in a market not normally served by the company. This customer offered to buy 30,000 units of Model 144 at $30 per unit. The order was requested on a direct contact basis and no commissions will be paid. The president was inclined to reject the offer since it was half the model's normal selling price. However, before making the decision, she wanted to know the effect of accepting the offer on the company's profits.

To help decide on the two issues, the following additional data have been made available:

Activity	*Cost Driver*	*Supply*	*Usage*	*Lump Sum Quantity*[1]	*Fixed Rate*
Scheduling	Runs	250	200	25	$1,200
Cafeteria	Cell workers	45	25	15	1,800
Personnel	Cell workers	40	25	20	3,750

[1]Lump sum quantity is the amount of resource that would be acquired (saved) if the *capacity* of the activity is expanded (reduced); assume for simplicity that the fixed rate represents the per unit cost (savings).

Of the three activities, the cafeteria activity is the only one with a variable activity rate. This rate is $760 per cell worker.

REQUIRED:

1. Prepare an ABC segmented income statement for Schultz Company using products as segments. Can the unused activity be exploited to increase overall profits? Explain.
2. By how much will profits be affected if Model 720 is dropped?
3. Prepare an analysis that shows what the effect on company profitability would have been if the special order had been accepted. Was the president correct in her feelings concerning the special order?
4. Now assume that the disk drives are sold to companies that produce medium- to high-level quality PCs. The special-order customer will use the disk drive in a low-end PC and plans to advertise the fact that the low-end PC can be purchased at a lower price with the same quality as a so-called higher-quality brand. Given this information and the results of Requirement 2, should the order be accepted? Explain.

P23-8
Make-or-Buy; Conventional versus Activity-Based Costing; Impact of JIT
LO 5

Pratt Company produces gas-powered generators. The manufacturing process includes 5 different subassemblies, which are then assembled in the final processing department. Recently, an outside supplier has offered to supply Subassembly A for $37 per unit, provided at least 80,000 units are purchased. The plant normally produces 100,000 units of Subassembly A per year. The accounting department supplied the following information on the cost of manufacturing one unit of Subassembly A:

Direct materials	$20
Direct labor	10
Variable overhead	8
Fixed overhead	12
Total	$50

The plant uses departmental overhead rates. In the Subassembly A department, the only direct overhead costs are the salary of the supervisor ($50,000) and equipment depreciation ($50,000). Plant depreciation accounts for $2 per unit of the subassembly's fixed overhead rate. The remaining fixed overhead assigned to the subassembly represents costs allocated from the plant's service departments using the step-down method.

Recently, an outside consultant suggested that an activity-based costing system be used. To illustrate the utility of the new system, she developed the following overhead costing system:

Overhead Cost Pool	*Cost Driver*	*Pool Rate*
Power and maintenance	Machine hours	$8
Material handling	Number of moves	100
Receiving	Number of orders	40
Engineering	Number of hours	20
Setups	Number of runs	500
Plant depreciation	Square footage	200
Equipment depreciation	Machine hours	1[a]

[a]There is a cost pool for the equipment in each department. This pool is for the Subassembly A department.

With the exception of the depreciation cost pools, the consultant claims that the costs of each pool essentially vary with the level of the cost driver.

Subassembly A uses the following amounts of each cost driver:

Machine hours	50,000
Number of material moves	200
Number of orders received	200
Number of engineering hours	2,000
Number of runs	50
Square footage	1,000

The consultant also recommended the installation of a JIT manufacturing and purchasing system. Assume that the company does so. A manufacturing cell is created to produce Subassembly A. After a short period, the company succeeds in driving setup costs to insignificant levels. Cell labor is trained to perform maintenance, making total cell labor (including maintenance) $2 million per year. Power costs, metered for each cell, total $300,000 per year for Subassembly A. By reorganizing the plant layout, materials handling costs for the subassembly are reduced by 50 percent; these costs are assigned on the basis of material moves. An engineer with a salary of $35,000 per year is assigned to the cell. Finally, receiving costs are decreased by 80 percent by having materials delivered adjacent to the cell on a just-in-time basis.

REQUIRED:

1. Using the conventional cost assignments, prepare an analysis that shows whether the company should make or buy Subassembly A.
2. Using the activity-based costing system, prepare an analysis that shows whether the company should make or buy Subassembly A.
3. Using the JIT system, prepare an analysis that shows whether the company should make or buy Subassembly A.
4. Comment on the impact that activity-based costing has on make-or-buy analysis. Also comment on the impact JIT has on make-or-buy analysis.

DISCUSSION AND INTERPRETATION PROBLEMS

D23-1
Ethical Issues

Martin Whitmer, controller of Cowdery Company and a CMA, was preparing a report for Bill Cowdery, the owner. The report would contain a recommendation on the make-or-buy decision for a subassembly. Martin, however, was faced with a dilemma. More than two months earlier, he had worked as a consultant for Brandon Day, owner of the supplier that had offered to sell the subassembly to Cowdery Company. Martin's opportunity to work as a consultant for Brandon had materialized during their weekly luncheon appointment.

Brandon and Martin had been friends since high school and usually met weekly for lunch. During these luncheons, Martin discovered that Brandon's company was struggling. He turned down an offer to assume the controllership of Brandon's company. Financial security was too much of an issue. Brandon, however, had offered to pay Martin a handsome consulting fee if he would do some basic financial analysis for his company. Martin had accepted this offer and had become involved with the company on a part-time basis. With Martin's help, Brandon's company began to recover.

During his consulting activity, Martin discovered that Brandon's company could produce a subassembly at a much lower cost than Cowdery Company. He suggested to Brandon that he place a bid with Cowdery Company, and he helped construct the bid. Since Brandon's company had done business with Cowdery in the past, Martin knew that the bid would be taken seriously. Bill Cowdery had always been satisfied with the quality of the products.

Martin knew that winning the bid was important to the continued recovery of Brandon's company. Martin's initial analysis had shown that Cowdery Company should definitely buy the subassembly. Based on this analysis, Martin had given some preliminary assurances to Brandon that the order would be secured. However, some recent input from a consultant hired by Bill Cowdery had muddied the waters. The consultant had introduced activity-based costing, which changed the economic outcome to favor continued internal production of the subassembly. Of course, Bill Cowdery would rely on Martin's judgment, so the possibility still existed to go with the recommendation based on the current cost system. After all, the current system had worked well for years.

REQUIRED: Evaluate the propriety of Martin Whitmer's actions (and reasoning), including his acceptance of the consulting job with Brandon Day. Does Martin really have a dilemma? (In addressing the issues, consider the ethical standards for management accountants in Chapter 1.)

D23-2
Research Assignment

Knowing how strategic cost analysis is applied in real-world settings should help you appreciate the power and utility of the methodology. Read the two articles listed below and then write a short two to three page paper that addresses the following issues:

1. How relevant cost analysis is affected by strategic analysis.
2. How cost analysis is used in identifying strategic positions of different products.
3. How cost data can be used to help develop superior strategies.
4. The steps that should be followed in strategic cost analysis.
5. The role of activity-based costing and value-chain analysis in strategic cost management.
6. Your personal assessment of how strategic cost analysis differs from conventional cost analysis.

Articles to read:

John K. Shank, Vijay Govindarajan, and Eric Spiegel, "Strategic Cost Analysis: A Case Study," *Journal of Cost Management,* Fall 1988, pp. 25–33.

Vijay Govindarajan and John K. Shank, "Strategic Cost Analysis: The Crown Cork and Seal Case," *Journal of Cost Management,* Winter 1989, pp. 5–15.

COMPREHENSIVE CASE

C23-1 Managerial Decision Making

John Thomas, president of Scholls Bike Company, had just received a report from the controller's office projecting a loss of $1.5 million for the coming year. The report indicated that the company had common fixed costs of $2,000,000. The report also provided the following budgeted data for the company's two products: tricycles and small dirt bikes.

	Tricycles	*Dirt Bikes*
Sales (units)	100,000	100,000
Selling price	$50	$100
Variable manufacturing cost (per unit)	$39	$58
Commissions (per unit)	1	2
Direct fixed expenses	$1,500,000	$2,000,000

Concerned with this year's financial performance and the projected loss for next year, John called an executive meeting. Attending the meeting were: Mike Jordan, production manager; Angie Dickison, marketing manager; and Luke Skywalker, controller. The following conversation was recorded by John's executive secretary.

John: "Scholls has been a significant role player in the small bike market for years. Until last year, we have always shown a respectable profit. With our expected performance this year and the projections for next year, we will have losses reported for three consecutive years. I'd like to know why this is occurring and what we can do—if anything—to return to a more profitable state. Otherwise, we may be seeing the demise of our company."

Angie: "We've been facing some pretty stiff competition for our tricycle line. Our competitors keep dropping prices. Right now we really should be selling for $45—not $50. Our projected sales are half what the actual sales were two years ago. If we could drop our price to $45, we could double sales. If we could drop the price by another $5, we could quadruple next year's projected sales."

Luke: "Dropping the sales price by $10 would produce no contribution margin for the tricycle line. Dropping by $5 wouldn't change our projected profits—even if sales doubled. Maybe we should just drop the entire line. Dropping the line would increase profits by $500,000."

Angie: "I wouldn't be so sure about that. After all, many of our dirt bike customers are those who have owned one of our tricycles and have looked for the same brand name. If the tricycle line is dropped we would see a 15% decline in our dirt bike sales. I wonder what that would do with our overall profitability?"

Luke: "It would produce an additional decrease of $100,000. Perhaps we need to drop the tricycles and add a larger bike line. I know we have talked about adding a new line in the past."

Mike: "Yes, we have. But you should recall that adding the line of bikes you suggest would require some new production equipment. As I remember the cost of this equipment was $2,000,000. I also have a copy of the projected revenues and expenses associated with the project. I'll pass it around so that you can review it."

Projected revenues and expenses, new bike line:

Sales	$ 6,000,000
Variable expenses	(4,250,000)
Contribution margin	$ 1,750,000
Direct fixed expenses	(1,500,000)[a]
Segment Margin	$ 250,000

[a]Includes only direct fixed cash expenses; does not include depreciation on the new equipment. The new equipment would be depreciated using five year MACRS. The equipment has a life of six years; the tax rate is 40%. The cost of capital is 10%.

John: "Even if this new line is a good investment I'm not sure that we can raise the capital needed for the project. We already have too much debt. I'm skeptical, however, that we can do as well as the projections indicate. We have little marketing experience and we would have to develop some new retail outlets. Besides, the equipment we have for the tricycle production line is good for at least another six years. I wonder if there are other means of improving the profitability of our current lines."

Luke: "Well, there is another possibility. I have been attending some seminars lately that have emphasized a new cost accounting approach called activity-based costing. I've learned, for example, that many of our so-called fixed costs actually are affected by what are called nonunit cost drivers. Focusing on activities within an organization offers many opportunities for cost reduction. For example, the warranty and repair costs make up 30% of the direct fixed costs of the two lines. Clearly, the cost of the warranty and repair activity is driven by the number of defective bikes that we produce. We could reduce costs by reducing the number of bad bikes that we produce."

Angie: "Not only could we reduce the cost of repair but if our bikes work better, then we could sell more. Quality is a critical competitive factor. Many of our competitors' bikes have developed a better quality reputation than ours over the past several years."

Luke: "I have been collecting data for the past several weeks on the common fixed cost category. These costs, with some potential cost drivers, are listed on a handout I have brought. With the exception of the power activity, I was able to use my experience to assess directly the fixed and variable activity costs. For the power activity, I collected several months of data so that I could estimate the variable and fixed components. Traditionally, we have treated power as a fixed cost because the total amount paid is about the same from year to year. I am not convinced that this is the right way to do it; however, I didn't have time to do the analysis before this meeting. I also estimated the demand each product places on each activity. Well, here's the handout:

		Activity Rate	
Activity	*Cost Driver*	*Fixed Rate*[a]	*Variable Rate*
Purchasing	Number of orders	$12.50	—
Inspection	Inspection hours	15.00	—
Shipping	Shipping hours	16.00	$5.00
Material handling	Number of moves	6.00	—
Facility	—	—	—

[a]The fixed rate is based on the following practical activity capacities (available activity quantities):

Purchasing: 8,000 orders (2,000 orders = whole unit)
Inspection: 10,000 inspection hours (2,000 hours = whole unit)
Shipping: 16,000 shipping hours (1,600 hours = whole unit)
Material handling: 50,000 moves (5,000 moves = whole unit)

Note: These resources represent those acquired in advance of usage and must be purchased and disposed of in lump sum amounts. These lump sum amounts are the whole units.

Power data:

Month	*Cost*	*Kilowatt Hours Used*
July	$ 46,000	12,000
August	56,000	15,000
September	40,000	10,000
October	40,000	9,000
November	35,000	8,000
December	46,000	9,000
Totals	$263,000	63,000

Product demands for activities:

	Tricycles	*Dirt Bikes*
Purchasing	2,000	4,000
Inspection	3,000	4,800
Shipping	4,000	8,000
Material handling	15,000	25,000
Power	46,000	90,000

REQUIRED:

1. Prepare a traditional segmented income statement where the segments are defined as products.
2. Using the information from (1), calculate the following: (1) the break-even units for each product segment (the units required to cover all segment expenses), and (2) the units that must be sold of each product so that the company as a whole breaks even. What is the effect on the overall break-even point if the price of tricycles is reduced to $45?
3. Verify the following comments by Luke: "Dropping the sales price by $10 would produce no contribution margin for the tricycle line. Dropping by $5 wouldn't change our projected profits—even if sales doubled. Maybe we should just drop the entire line. Dropping the line would increase profits by $500,000." Also verify Luke's reaction to Angie's observation that dropping the tricycle line would decrease dirt bike sales by 15%: "It would produce a projected net decrease of $100,000."
4. Calculate the net present value for the new bike line. Would you recommend this investment? Explain.
5. Prepare the cost formula for the power activity using the following two methods: (a) the high-low method and (b) the method of least squares. Indicate what the total annual fixed power costs are. Assuming that the company has its own power department, identify and discuss the nature of these fixed costs, using an activity-based framework.
6. Suppose that all unused capacity that can be eliminated is eliminated (ignore power). What effect will this have on the projected income for the coming year?
7. Prepare a keep-or-drop analysis for the tricycle line, using information on resource supply, resource usage, and activities. Assume that unused activity capacity that can be eliminated will be eliminated. Does the recommendation change from the traditional analysis? Explain. What are the strategic implications of dropping the tricycle line? What recommendations would you make to solve the problems facing Scholls?

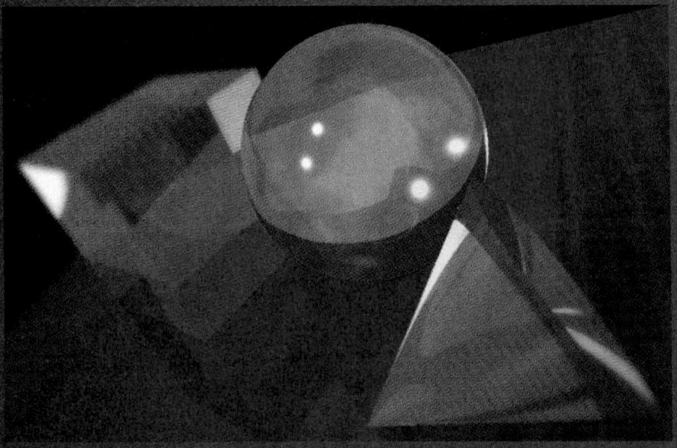

PART 8

PLANNING AND CONTROL

The management accounting systems plays a critical role in the planning and control process. Expressing plans in quantitative terms is one of the major tasks of management accountants. Ensuring that plans unfold as expected is a key managerial responsibility. Feedback, of course, is necessary to monitor the progress of plans, and management accounting has the responsibility of providing feedback to managers. Managers use the feedback to decide whether corrective action is needed or not. Managers responsible for plans are held accountable for their actions. Furthermore, the management accounting system is often used to measure the performance of individual managers. The use of accounting information for planning, control, and evaluation is referred to as responsibility accounting.

This section provides three chapters that discuss the planning and control roles of the management accounting system. The traditional responsibility accounting approach is described in Chapters 24 and 25. These chapters discuss budgeting and standard costing and describe the conventional ways in which these management accounting procedures are used.

Although budgeting and standard costing also are important in the advanced manufacturing environment, how they are used is changed dramatically. Conventional responsibility accounting may no longer apply. Chapter 26 describes the limitations of traditional responsibility accounting and introduces activity-based responsibility accounting. This chapter also discusses new areas of control emphasis: life-cycle costing, quality, and productivity.

CHAPTER 24
BUDGETING FOR PLANNING AND CONTROL

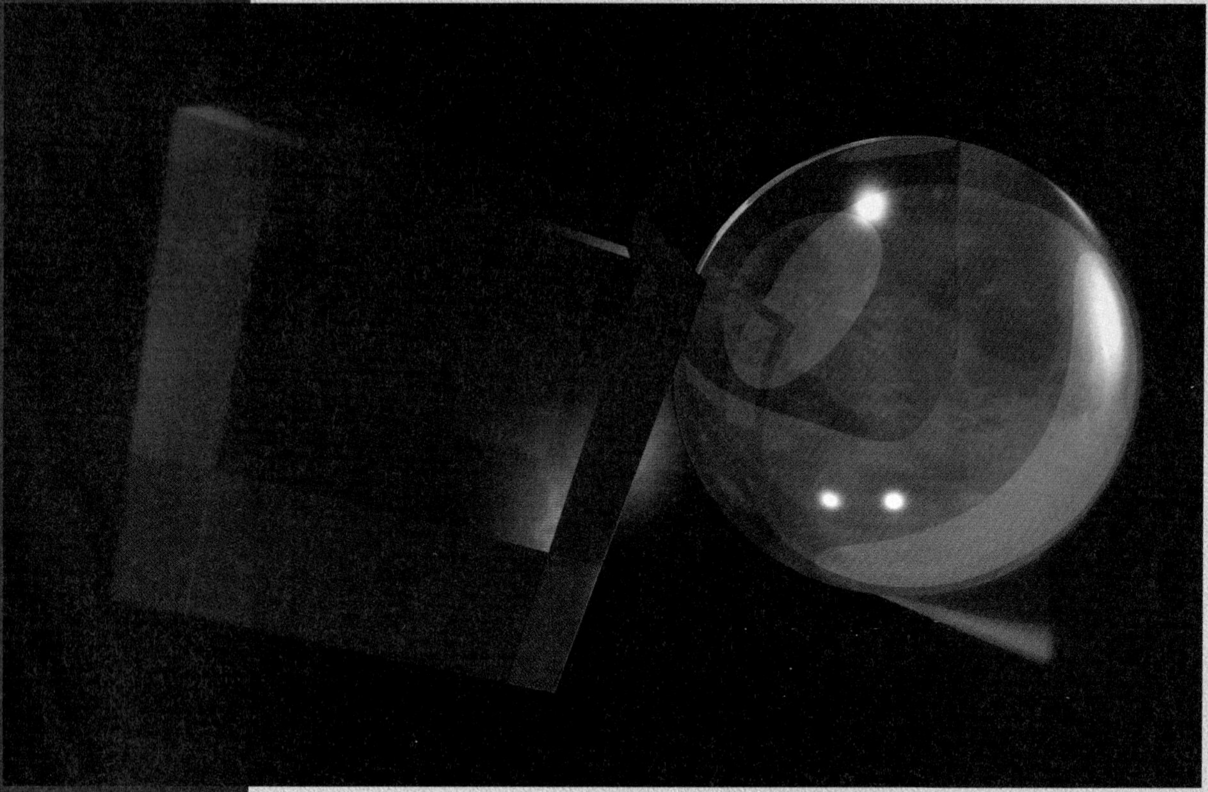

LEARNING OBJECTIVES

After studying this chapter, you should be able to:

1. Describe the role of budgeting and the structure of the master budget.
2. Prepare an operating budget including the following component budgets: sales, production, direct materials, direct labor, overhead, selling and administrative, ending finished goods, cost of goods sold, and the budgeted income statement.
3. Prepare the following two components of the financial budget: cash budget and budgeted balance sheet.
4. Identify and discuss the key features that a budgetary system should have to encourage managers to engage in goal-congruent behavior.

Scenario

By all outward appearances, Dr. Roger Jones was a successful dentist. He owned his own office building, which he leased to the professional corporation housing his dental practice. The revenues from his practice exceeded $250,000 each year, providing him with a salary of $75,000 a year. He and his family lived in a large home in a well-regarded neighborhood.

However, Dr. Jones just received a registered letter from the IRS threatening to impound his business and sell its assets for failure to pay payroll taxes for the past 6 months. Furthermore, the professional corporation was also having difficulty paying its suppliers. The corporation owed one supplier more than $100,000 and had made arrangements to pay interest payments on the bill but was missing even these payments. The corporation had experienced these kinds of difficulties repeatedly for the past five years.

In the past, Dr. Jones had solved similar problems by borrowing money on the equity in either his personal residence or his office building. Upon investigation, he discovered that sufficient equity still existed in his office building to solve the IRS problem. A visit to a local bank resulted in a refinancing agreement that produced sufficient capital to pay the back taxes and the associated penalties and interest.

This time, however, Dr. Jones was not satisfied with the short-run solution to his financial difficulties. His latest loan had exhausted his personal financial resources; further difficulties simply couldn't be tolerated. His first action was to dismiss his receptionist-bookkeeper, reasoning that a significant part of the blame was hers for failing to manage properly the financial resources of the corporation. Then, he called Lawson, Johnson, and Smith, a local CPA firm, and requested that a consultant determine the cause of his recurring financial difficulties.

Jeanette Day, a partner in the CPA firm, accepted the assignment. After spending a week examining the records of the practice and extensively interviewing Dr. Jones, Jeanette delivered the following report:

Dr. Roger Jones
1091 West Apple Avenue
Reno, Nevada

Dear Dr. Jones:

The cause of your current financial difficulties is the absence of proper planning and control. Currently, many of your expenditure decisions are made in a haphazard and arbitrary manner. Affordability is seldom, if ever, considered. Because of this, resources are often committed beyond the capabilities of the practice. To meet these additional commitments, your bookkeeper has been forced to postpone payments for essential operating expenses such as payroll taxes, supplies, and laboratory services.

The following examples illustrate some of the decisions that have contributed to your financial troubles:

1. *Salary decisions.* You have been granting 5 percent increases each year whether or not the business could successfully absorb these increases. Also, your salary is 10 percent higher than dentists with comparable practices.

2. *Withdrawal decisions.* For the past 5 years, you have withdrawn from cash receipts approximately $500 per month. These withdrawals have been treated as a loan from the corporation to you, the president of the corporation.
3. *Equipment acquisition decisions.* During the past 5 years, the corporation has acquired a van, a video recorder, a refrigerator, and a microcomputer system. Some of these items were cash acquisitions, and some are being paid for on an installment basis. None of them was essential to the mission of your corporation.

Other examples could be given, but these should suffice. These decisions have had an adverse effect on both your personal financial status and the financial well-being of the corporation. The mortgage payments for your personal residence and your office building have increased by 50 percent over the past 5 years. Additionally, the liabilities of the corporation have increased by 200 percent for the same period of time.

To prevent the recurrence of these financial problems, I recommend the installation of a formal budgetary system. A comprehensive financial plan is needed so that you know where you are going and what you are capable of doing. Each year you should develop a financial plan that details the expected revenues and associated expenditures necessary to support the mission of your corporation. Additionally, this financial plan can be used to control the use of the resources owned by your corporation.

My firm would be pleased to assist you in designing and implementing the recommended system. For it to be successful, you and your staff need to be introduced to the elementary principles of budgeting. As a part of implementation, we will offer 3 two-hour seminars on budgeting. The first will describe the basic philosophy of budgeting, the second will teach you how to prepare budgets, and the third will explore the use of budgets for planning, control, and performance evaluation.

Sincerely,

Jeanette Day

Jeanette Day, CPA

Note: This scenario is based on the experience of a dental practice. The names are changed to preserve confidentiality.

DESCRIPTION OF BUDGETING

Objective 1
Describe the role of budgeting and the structure of the master budget.

As Dr. Jones discovered, failure to plan, either formally or informally, can lead to financial disaster. Managers of businesses, whether small or large, must know their resource capabilities and have a plan that details the use of these resources. Careful planning is vital to the health of any organization.

Definition and Role of Budgeting

budgets

Jeanette Day noted that Dr. Jones's main problem was failure to plan and exercise control over his business. Her recommendation was to install a budgetary system, but what role does budgeting play in planning and control? Plans identify objectives and the actions needed to achieve them. **Budgets** are the quantitative expressions of these plans, stated in either physical or financial terms or both. Thus, a budget is a method for translating the goals and strategies of an organization into operational terms. As a plan of action, budgets can be used to control by comparing actual outcomes as they happen with the planned outcomes. If actual results differ significantly from the plan, actions can be taken to put the plans back on track if necessary.

strategic plan

Exhibit 24-1 shows the relationship between planning and control and the role that budgets play in the overall process. Before a budget is prepared, an organization should develop a **strategic plan.** The strategic plan identifies strategies for future activities and operations generally involving at least five years.

Once an organization has developed an overall strategy, the next step is to translate this strategy into long-term and short-term objectives. From these objectives, the individual units of a company create short-term plans on which to build the budget. These short-term plans should be compatible with the overall direc-

Exhibit 24-1
Planning, Control, and Budgets

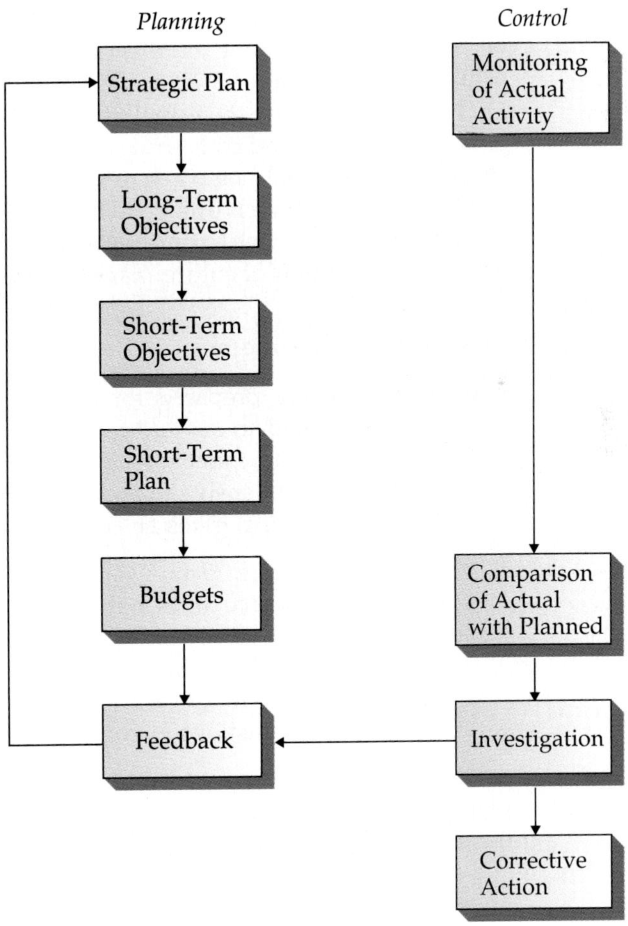

tion of the firm itself. The management of the company should develop a tight linkage between the budget and the strategic plan. In developing this linkage, however, management should take care that all attention is not focused on the short run. This is important because budgets, as one-period plans, are short run in nature.

To illustrate the process, consider again the case of Dr. Jones. (Refer to Exhibit 24-1 as you read this illustration.) Assume that Dr. Jones's strategic plan is to increase the size and profitability of his business by building a practice that has the reputation for quality and timely service. A key element in achieving this strategy is the addition of a dental laboratory to his building so that crowns, bridges, and dentures can be made in house. This is his long-term objective. This addition would increase the quality and timeliness of his services while simultaneously increasing profitability. In order to add the laboratory, he needs additional capital. His financial status dictates that the capital must be obtained by increasing revenues. After some careful calculation, Dr. Jones concludes that annual revenues must be increased by 10 percent; this is a short-term objective.

How are these long-term and short-term objectives to be achieved? Assume that Dr. Jones discovers that his fees for fillings and crowns are below the average in his community and decides that the 10 percent increase can be achieved by increasing these fees. He now has a short-term plan. A sales budget would outline the quantity of fillings and crowns expected for the coming year, the per-unit fee reflecting the increase, and the total fees expected. Thus, the sales budget becomes the quantitative expression of the qualitative plan of action needed to achieve the objective of a 10 percent increase in revenues. As the year unfolds, Dr. Jones can compare the actual revenues being received with the budgeted revenues (monitoring and comparing). If actual revenues are falling short of planned revenues, steps should be taken to find out why (investigation). Then he can take action to remedy the shortfall, such as working longer hours or increasing fees for other dental services (corrective action). The reasons for the shortfall may also lead to an alteration of future plans (feedback).

Purposes of Budgeting

Budgets are usually prepared for areas within an organization (departments, plants, divisions, and so on) and for activities (sales, production, and so on). The **master budget** is the collection of all individual area and activity budgets. It serves as the comprehensive financial plan for the organization as a whole.

master budget

A budgetary system gives an organization several advantages.

1. It forces managers to plan.
2. It provides resource information that can be used to improve decision making.
3. It aids in the use of resources and employees by setting a benchmark that can be used for subsequent evaluation of performance.
4. It improves the functions of communication and coordination.

Budgeting forces management to plan for the future. A budget or quantitative plan of action cannot be expressed unless a strategic plan exists. Budgets force managers to develop an overall direction for the organization, foresee problems, and develop future policies. If Dr. Jones had spent time planning, he would have known the capabilities of his practice and where the resources of the business should be used.

Budgets convey significant information about the resource capabilities of an organization, making better decisions possible. For example, if Dr. Jones had known the expected revenues and the costs of supplies, lab fees, utilities, salaries, and so on, he could have made more informed decisions regarding salary increases, loans, and acquisition of equipment. Knowledge of resource capabilities may have led Dr. Jones to lower the rate of salary increases, avoid borrowing money from the corporation, and limit the acquisition of nonessential equipment. These better decisions, in turn, might have prevented the financial difficulties that arose and resulted in a better financial status for both the business and Dr. Jones.

Budgets also set standards that can control the use of a company's resources and control and motivate employees. For example, if Dr. Jones knows how much amalgam should be used in a filling and what the expenditure level should be, he can evaluate his use of this resource and his own level of efficiency. If more amalgam is being used than expected, Dr. Jones may discover that he is often careless in its use and extra care will produce savings. The same principle applies to other resources used by the corporation. In total, the savings could be significant.

control

Control is fundamental to the overall success of a budgetary system. **Control** ensures that steps are being taken to achieve the objectives outlined in an organization's master plan. Control is achieved by comparing actual results with budgeted results on a periodic basis (e.g., monthly). If there is a significant deviation from planned results, that deviation is feedback revealing that the system is out of control. Steps should be taken to find out why. Once the reasons are known, corrective action can be taken.

Budgets also serve the functions of communication and coordination. Budgets formally communicate the plans of the organization to each employee. Accordingly, all employees can be aware of their role in achieving those objectives. Since budgets for the various areas and activities of the organization must all work together to achieve the stated objectives of the organization, coordination is promoted. Managers are forced to view the needs of other areas and are encouraged to subordinate their individual interests to those of the organization. The role of communication and coordination becomes more significant as an organization increases in size.

Responsibility Accounting

responsibility centers

As organizations increase in size, top management typically creates areas of responsibility, which are known as **responsibility centers,** and assigns subordinate managers to those areas. There are three major types of responsibility centers.

cost center

profit center

investment center

1. **Cost center:** A responsibility center in which a manager is responsible only for costs
2. **Profit center:** A responsibility center in which a manager is responsible for both revenues and costs
3. **Investment center:** A responsibility center in which a manager is responsible for revenues, costs, and investments

A production department is an example of a cost center. The manager of a production department has no ability to control pricing and marketing decisions; however, he or she does have the ability to control production costs. Plant managers, however, often are given the responsibility to price and market products they manufacture. These plant managers control both costs and revenues, putting them in control of a profit center. Finally, divisions are often cited as examples of investment centers. In addition to having control over costs and pricing decisions, divisional managers often have the power to make investment decisions, such as plant closings and openings, and decisions to keep or drop a product line.

Responsibility usually entails accountability. Cost center managers are accountable for controlling costs, profit center managers are accountable for profit levels, and investment center managers are accountable for profit levels and efficient use of investment resources. Accountability implies performance measurement, which, in turn, implies the existence of an expected outcome or standard against which actual outcomes can be compared. Budgets are often used to set the expected outcomes for managers of responsibility centers, which become the benchmarks to evaluate actual performance and to reward the managers.

For example, consider the use of budgets by CalBlock, a subsidiary of a large corporation located in the intermountain West. CalBlock produces concrete blocks and pipes in plants located in several Western cities. Each plant is designated as a profit center. By the beginning of the fiscal year, each plant manager must develop a budgeted income statement that is approved by higher management. At the end of the fiscal year, actual profits are compared with budgeted profits. If they exceed budgeted profits, the managers can receive a year-end bonus from 0 percent to 40 percent of salary (the maximum bonus is earned if actual profits are at least 125 percent of the budgeted profits). Additionally, promotions, salary increases, and continued employment are all affected by a plant manager's performance. Consistently poor performance can lead to dismissal or demotion. On the other hand, consistently good performance is likely to lead to promotion.

responsibility accounting

The approach described above is often referred to as **responsibility accounting** because of the key role that accounting measures and reports play in the process. The traditional system includes five aspects. First, a responsibility center is identified with the responsibility defined in accounting terms (e.g., costs or profits). Second, an accounting standard or benchmark is set, usually through budgeting. Third, a reward system is established to encourage managers to provide good performance. Fourth, a manager's performance is measured by comparing actual performance with budgeted performance. Fifth, managers are rewarded or penalized according to the policies and discretion of higher management.

The Master Budget

operating budgets

financial budgets

The master budget is a comprehensive financial plan made up of various individual budgets. A master budget can be divided into *operating* and *financial* budgets. **Operating budgets** are concerned with the income-generating activities of a firm: sales, production, and finished goods inventories. The ultimate outcome of the operating budgets is a pro forma or budgeted income statement. **Financial budgets** are concerned with the inflows and outflows of cash and with planned expenditures for capital acquisitions. The financial statements that capture planned financing (both short and long run) are the pro forma balance sheet and the pro forma statement of cash flows. Since many of the financing activities are not known until the operating budgets are known, the preparation of the operating budget should precede the preparation of the financial budget.

The Time Factor. Most of the component budgets contained in the master budget are for a one-year period usually corresponding to the fiscal year of the company. Yearly budgets are broken down into quarterly budgets, and quarterly budgets are broken down into monthly budgets. The use of smaller time periods allows managers to compare actual data with budgeted data as the year unfolds and to take corrective actions whenever necessary so that overall objectives are attained as planned. Because progress can be checked more frequently with monthly budgets, problems are less likely to become too serious.

capital budget

continuous budget

The master budget also contains a plan for acquisition of long-term assets—assets that have a time horizon much greater than the one-year operating period. Some of these assets may be purchased during the coming year; plans to purchase others may be detailed for future periods. This part of the master budget is typically referred to as the **capital budget.** Most organizations prepare the budget for the coming year during the last four or five months of the current year. However, some organizations have developed a continuous budgeting philosophy. A **continuous budget** is a moving twelve-month budget. As a month expires in the budget, an additional month in the future is added so that the company always has a twelve-month plan on hand. Proponents of continuous budgeting maintain that it forces managers to plan ahead constantly.

budget director

budget committee

Directing and Coordinating. Every organization must have someone responsible for directing and coordinating the overall budgeting process. This **budget director** is usually the controller or someone who reports to the controller. The budget director works under the direction of the budget committee. The **budget committee** has the responsibility to review the budget, provide policy guidelines and budgetary goals, resolve differences that may arise as the budget is prepared, approve the final budget, and monitor the actual performance of the organization as the year unfolds. The budget committee also has the responsibility to ensure that the budget is linked to the strategic plan of the organization. The president of the organization appoints the members of the committee, who are usually the president, vice-presidents, and the controller.

The Two Dimensions of Budgeting. The role of budgets in a responsibility accounting system reveals two dimensions to budgeting: (1) how the budget is prepared and (2) how the budget is used to implement the organization's plans. The first dimension concerns the mechanics of budget preparation.

The second involves how individuals within an organization react to a budgetary system. The use of budgets to exercise control, evaluate performance, communicate, and encourage coordination suggests that budgeting is a human activity. As such, it carries a strong behavioral dimension. Accordingly, if budgets are expected to motivate and encourage behavior consistent with organizational objectives, care must be exercised in implementing a budgetary system within an organization. In fact, the success or failure of budgeting depends on how well management considers its behavioral implications.

The remainder of this chapter is primarily concerned with these two dimensions.

PREPARATION OF THE OPERATING BUDGET

Objective 2
Prepare an operating budget including the following component budgets: sales, production, direct materials, direct labor, overhead, selling and administrative, ending finished goods, cost of goods sold, and the budgeted income statement.

The operating budget consists of a budgeted income statement accompanied by the following supporting schedules:

1. Sales budget
2. Production budget
3. Direct material purchases budget
4. Direct labor budget
5. Overhead budget
6. Selling and administrative budget
7. Ending finished goods inventory budget
8. Cost of goods sold budget

The sales forecast is the basis for the sales budget, which, in turn, is the basis for all of the other operating budgets and most of the financial budgets. Accordingly, the accuracy of the sales forecast strongly affects the soundness of the entire master budget.

Creating the sales forecast is usually the responsibility of the marketing department. One approach to forecasting sales is the *bottom-up approach.* In this approach, the chief sales executive requests that individual salespeople submit sales predictions, which are aggregated to form a total sales forecast. The accuracy of this sales forecast may be improved by considering other factors such as the general economic climate, competition, advertising, pricing policies, and so on. Other approaches also exist. Some companies supplement the bottom-up approach with other, more formal approaches, such as time-series analysis, correlation analysis, and econometric modeling.

To illustrate an actual sales forecasting approach, we consider the practices of CalBlock. Top management has discovered that sales of its concrete blocks and pipe are highly correlated with nonresidential building activity. Therefore, in developing a forecast for the coming year, the company's first action is to obtain estimates of the coming year's nonresidential construction. These estimates are available from the state government, reports published by local banks, and the local university's center for economic development.

Given this estimate, the historical correlation is used to predict next year's sales for each plant. These sales estimates are submitted to each plant manager as an initial sales forecast. Because of the strong correlation between nonresidential building and sales, plant managers are required to use this initial forecast for budgeting purposes unless they can justify a departure. Most plant managers obtain sales estimates from their individual salespeople as a cross-check on the accuracy of the forecast. Occasionally, they have been successful in revising the initial sales forecast because of superior knowledge of local conditions.

Sales Budget. Once a sales forecast is generated, a sales budget is prepared. The sales budget and the sales forecast are not necessarily synonymous. The sales forecast is merely the initial estimate. The **sales budget** is the projection approved by the budget committee that describes expected sales in units and dollars.

sales budget

The sales forecast is presented to the budget committee for consideration. The budget committee may decide that the forecast is too pessimistic or too optimistic and revise it appropriately. For example, if the budget committee decides that the forecast is too pessimistic and not in harmony with the strategic plan of the orga-

Schedule 1 (in thousands)

CalBlock, Inc.
Sales Budget
For the Year Ended December 31, 1995

	Quarter				
	1	2	3	4	Year
Units	2,000	6,000	6,000	2,000	16,000
Unit selling price	× $0.70	× $0.70	× $0.80	× $0.80	× $0.75
Sales	$1,400	$4,200	$4,800	$1,600	$12,000

nization, it may recommend specific actions to increase sales beyond the forecast level, such as increasing promotional activities and hiring additional salespeople.

Schedule 1 illustrates the sales budget for CalBlock's concrete block line. For simplicity, we assume that CalBlock has only one product: a standard block, measuring 8 × 8 × 16 inches. (For a multiple-product firm, the sales budget reflects sales for each product in units and sales dollars.)

Notice that the sales budget reveals that CalBlock's sales fluctuate seasonally. Most sales (75 percent) take place in the spring and summer quarters. Also note that the budget reflects an expected increase in selling price beginning in the summer quarter (from $0.70 to $0.80). Because of the price change within the year, an average price must be used for the column that describes the total year's activities ($0.75 = $12,000/16,000 units).

production budget

Production Budget. The **production budget** describes how many units must be produced in order to meet sales needs and satisfy ending inventory requirements. From Schedule 1, we know how many concrete blocks are needed to satisfy sales demand for each quarter and for the year. In the absence of beginning or ending inventories, the concrete blocks to be produced would correspond exactly to the units to be sold. In the JIT firm, for example, units sold equal units produced since a customer order triggers production.

Usually, however, the production budget must consider the existence of beginning and ending inventories since traditional manufacturing firms use inventories as a buffer against demand or production line fluctuations. Assume that company policy dictates that 100,000 concrete blocks be available in inventory at the beginning of the first and fourth quarters and 500,000 blocks at the beginning of the second and third quarters. The policy is equivalent to budgeting 100,000 concrete blocks as ending inventory for the third and fourth quarters and 500,000 concrete blocks as ending inventory for the first and second quarters.

To compute the units to be produced, both sales requirements and finished goods inventory information are needed.

Units to be produced = Units, ending inventory + Expected sales
− Units, beginning inventory

The formula is the basis for the production budget in Schedule 2. Notice that the production budget is expressed in terms of units.

Direct Materials Budget. After the production schedule is completed, it is possible to prepare budgets for direct materials, direct labor, and overhead. The

Schedule 2 (in thousands)

CalBlock, Inc.
Production Budget
For the Year Ended December 31, 1995

	Quarter				
	1	2	3	4	Year
Sales (Schedule 1)	2,000	6,000	6,000	2,000	16,000
Desired ending inventory	500	500	100	100	100
Total needs	2,500	6,500	6,100	2,100	16,100
Less: Beginning inventory	(100)	(500)	(500)	(100)	(100)
Units to be produced	2,400	6,000	5,600	2,000	16,000

direct materials budget

direct materials budget reveals the expected usage of materials in production and the purchasing needs of the firm. Expected usage is directly related to production requirements, but purchases depend on both expected usage and the inventories of direct materials.

The expected usage of direct materials is determined by the technological relationship existing between direct materials and output (called the *input-output relationship*). For example, a lightweight concrete block (a single unit of output) requires approximately 26 pounds of raw materials (cement, sand, gravel, shale, pumice, and water). The relative mix of these ingredients is fixed for a specific kind of concrete block. Thus, it is relatively easy to determine expected usage for each raw material from the production budget. It is simply a matter of multiplying the units of raw material needed per unit of output times the units of output.

Once expected usage is computed, the purchases (in units) can be computed as follows:

Purchases = Desired direct materials, ending inventory +
Expected usage − Direct materials, beginning inventory

The quantity of direct materials in inventory is determined by the firm's inventory policy. CalBlock's policy is to have 2,500 tons of raw materials (5 million pounds) in ending inventory for the third and fourth quarters and 4,000 tons of raw materials (8 million pounds) in ending inventory for the first and second quarters.

The direct materials budget for CalBlock is presented in Schedule 3. For simplicity, all raw materials are treated jointly (as if there were only one raw material input). In reality, a separate schedule would be needed for each kind of raw material.

direct labor budget

Direct Labor Budget. The **direct labor budget** shows the total direct labor hours needed and the associated cost for the number of units in the production budget. As with direct materials, the usage of direct labor is determined by the technological relationship between labor and output. For example, if a batch of 100 concrete blocks requires 1.5 direct labor hours, then the direct labor time per block is 0.015 hours. Assuming that the labor is used efficiently, this rate is fixed for the existing technology. The relationship will change only if a new approach to manufacturing is introduced.

Given the direct labor used per unit of output and the units to be produced from the production budget, the direct labor budget is computed as shown in

Schedule 3 (in thousands)

CalBlock, Inc.
Direct Materials Budget
For the Year Ended December 31, 1995

	Quarter 1	2	3	4	*Year*
Units to be produced (Schedule 2)	2,400	6,000	5,600	2,000	16,000
Direct materials per unit (lbs)	× 26	× 26	× 26	× 26	× 26
Production needs (lbs)	62,400	156,000	145,600	52,000	416,000
Desired ending inventory (lbs)[1]	8,000	8,000	5,000	5,000	5,000
Total needs	70,400	164,000	150,600	57,000	421,000
Less: Beginning inventory	(5,000)	(8,000)	(8,000)	(5,000)	(5,000)
Direct materials to be purchased (lbs)	65,400	156,000	142,600	52,000	416,000
Cost per pound	× $0.01	× $0.01	× $0.01	× $0.01	× $0.01
Total purchase cost	$ 654	$ 1,560	$ 1,426	$ 520	$ 4,160

[1]Follows the inventory policy of having 8 million pounds of raw materials on hand at the end of the first and second quarters and 5 million pounds on hand at the end of the third and fourth quarters.

Schedule 4. In the direct labor budget, the wage rate used ($8 per hour in this example) is the *average* wage paid the direct laborers associated with the production of the concrete blocks. Since it is an average, it allows for the possibility of differing wage rates paid to individual laborers.

overhead budget

Overhead Budget. The **overhead budget** shows the expected cost of all indirect manufacturing items. Unlike direct materials and direct labor, there is no readily identifiable input-output relationship for overhead items. Recall, however, that in a unit-level cost system overhead consists of two types of costs: costs that vary in level as activity level changes (variable overhead) and costs that remain unchanged as activity level changes (fixed overhead). These relationships can be exploited to facilitate budgeting.

Schedule 4 (in thousands)

CalBlock, Inc.
Direct Labor Budget
For the Year Ended December 31, 1995

	Quarter 1	2	3	4	*Year*
Units to be produced (Schedule 2)	2,400	6,000	5,600	2,000	16,000
Direct labor time per unit (hours)	×0.015	×0.015	×0.015	×0.015	× 0.015
Total hours needed	36	90	84	30	240
Wage per hour	× $8	× $8	× $8	× $8	× $8
Total direct labor cost	$ 288	$ 720	$ 672	$ 240	$ 1,920

Schedule 5
(in thousands)

CalBlock, Inc.
Overhead Budget
For the Year Ended December 31, 1995

	Quarter 1	Quarter 2	Quarter 3	Quarter 4	Year
Budgeted direct labor hours (Schedule 4)	36	90	84	30	240
Variable overhead rate	× $8	× $8	× $8	× $8	× $8
Budgeted variable overhead	$288	$ 720	$672	$240	$1,920
Budgeted fixed overhead[1]	320	320	320	320	1,280
Total overhead	$608	$1,040	$992	$560	$3,200

[1]Includes $200,000 of depreciation in each quarter.

Past experience can be used as a guide to determine how overhead varies with activity level. Individual items that will vary are identified (e.g., supplies and utilities), and the amount that is expected to be spent for each item per unit of activity is estimated. Individual rates are then totaled to obtain a variable overhead rate. For our example, assume that the variable overhead rate is $8 per direct labor hour.

A similar process takes place for fixed overhead. Since fixed overhead does not vary with the activity level, however, total fixed overhead is simply the sum of all amounts budgeted. Assume that fixed overhead is budgeted at $1.28 million ($320,000 per quarter). Using this information and the budgeted direct labor hours from the direct labor budget, the overhead budget in Schedule 5 is prepared.

selling and administrative expense budget

Selling and Administrative Expense Budget. The next budget to be prepared—the **selling and administrative expense budget**—outlines planned expenditures for nonmanufacturing activities. As with overhead, selling and administrative expenses can be broken into fixed and variable components. Such items as sales commissions, freight, and supplies vary with sales activity. The selling and administrative expense budget is illustrated in Schedule 6.

ending finished goods inventory budget

Ending Finished Goods Inventory Budget. The **ending finished goods inventory budget** supplies information needed for the balance sheet and also serves as an important input for the preparation of the cost of goods sold budget. To prepare this budget, the unit cost of producing each concrete block must be calculated using information from Schedules 3, 4, and 5. The unit cost of a concrete block and the cost of the planned ending inventory are shown in Schedule 7.

Budgeted Cost of Goods Sold. Assuming that the beginning finished goods inventory is valued at $55,000, the budgeted cost of goods sold schedule can be prepared using Schedules 3, 4, 5, and 7. The cost of goods sold schedule is the last schedule needed before the budgeted income statement can be prepared (see Schedule 8).

Schedule 6
(in thousands)

CalBlock, Inc.
Selling and Administrative Expense Budget
For the Year Ended December 31, 1995

	Quarter				
	1	*2*	*3*	*4*	*Year*
Planned sales in units (Schedule 1)	2,000	6,000	6,000	2,000	16,000
Variable selling and administrative expense per unit	× $0.05	× $0.05	× $0.05	× $0.05	× $0.05
Total variable expense	$ 100	$ 300	$ 300	$ 100	$ 800
Fixed selling and administrative expense:					
Salaries	$ 35	$ 35	$ 35	$ 35	$ 140
Advertising	10	10	10	10	40
Depreciation	15	15	15	15	60
Insurance	—	—	15	—	15
Travel	5	5	5	5	20
Total fixed expense	$ 65	$ 65	$ 80	$ 65	$ 275
Total selling and administrative expense	$ 165	$ 365	$ 380	$ 165	$1,075

Schedule 7
(in thousands)

CalBlock, Inc.
Ending Inventory Budget
For the Year Ended December 31, 1995

Unit cost computation:	
Direct materials (26 lbs @ $0.01)	$0.26
Direct labor (0.015 hrs @ $8)	0.12
Overhead:	
Variable (0.015 hrs @ $8)	0.12
Fixed (0.015 @ $5.33[a])	0.08
Total unit cost	$0.58

	Units	*Unit Cost*	*Total*
Finished goods: Concrete Blocks	100	$0.58	$58

[a]Budgeted fixed overhead (Schedule 5)/Budgeted direct labor hours (Schedule 4) = $1,280/240 = $5.33

Budgeted Income Statement. With the completion of the budgeted cost of goods sold schedule, CalBlock has all the operating budgets needed to prepare an estimate of operating income. This budgeted income statement is shown in Schedule 9. The eight schedules already prepared, along with the budgeted operating income statement, define the operating budget for CalBlock.

Operating income is *not* equivalent to the net income of a firm. To yield net income, interest expenses and taxes must be subtracted from operating income. The interest expense deduction is taken from the cash budget shown in Schedule 10. The taxes owed depend on the current tax laws.

Schedule 8
(in thousands)

CalBlock, Inc. Cost of Goods Sold Budget For the Year Ended December 31, 1995	
Direct materials used (Schedule 3)[a]	$4,160
Direct labor used (Schedule 4)	1,920
Overhead (Schedule 5)	3,200
Budgeted manufacturing costs	$9,280
Beginning finished goods	55
Goods available for sale	$9,335
Less: Ending finished goods (Schedule 7)	(58)
Budgeted cost of goods sold	$9,277

[a]Production needs × $0.01 = 416,000 × $0.01

Schedule 9
(in thousands)

CalBlock, Inc. Budgeted Income Statement For the Year Ended December 31, 1995	
Sales (Schedule 1)	$12,000
Less: Cost of goods sold (Schedule 8)	(9,277)
Gross margin	$ 2,723
Less: Selling and administrative expenses (Schedule 6)	(1,075)
Operating income	$ 1,648
Less: Interest expense (Schedule 10, p. 1129)	(39)
Income before taxes	$ 1,609
Less: Income taxes	(650)
Net income	$ 959

merchandise purchases budget

Operating Budgets for Merchandising and Service Firms. In a merchandising firm, the production budget is replaced with a **merchandise purchases budget.** This budget identifies the quantity of each item that must be purchased for resale, the unit cost of the item, and the total purchase cost. The format is identical to that of the direct materials budget in a manufacturing firm. The only other difference between the operating budgets of manufacturing and merchandising firms is the absence of direct materials and direct labor budgets in a merchandising firm.

In a for-profit service firm, the sales budget is also the production budget. The sales budget identifies each service and the quantity of it that will be sold. Since finished goods inventories are nonexistent, the services produced will be identical to the services sold.

For a nonprofit service firm, the sales budget is replaced by a budget that identifies the levels of the various services that will be offered for the coming year and the associated funds that will be assigned to the services. The source of the funds may be tax revenues, contributions, payments by users of the services, or some combination. For example, a state university offers various services (graduate and undergraduate programs in numerous disciplines, counseling, vocational training, and so on) and receives funds to support predetermined levels of these services from state taxes, tuition and fees, and private contributions of alumni and friends.

Both for-profit and nonprofit service organizations lack finished goods inventory budgets. However, all the remaining operating budgets found in a manufacturing organization have counterparts in service organizations. For a nonprofit service organization, the income statement is replaced by a statement of sources and uses of funds.

PREPARATION OF THE FINANCIAL BUDGET

Objective 3

Prepare the following two components of the financial budget: cash budget and budgeted balance sheet.

The remaining budgets found in the master budget are the financial budgets. The usual financial budgets prepared are:

1. The cash budget
2. The budgeted balance sheet
3. The budget for capital expenditures

The budget for capital expenditures outlines plans for investing in long-term assets such as buildings and equipment. Capital investment decisions and the capital budgeting process were discussed in Chapter 22. Accordingly, only the cash budget and the budgeted balance sheet will be illustrated here.

cash budget

Cash Budget. Knowledge of cash flows is critical to managing a business. Often a business is successful in producing and selling a product but fails because of timing problems associated with cash inflows and outflows. By knowing when cash deficiencies and surpluses are likely to occur, a manager can plan to borrow cash when needed and repay the loans during periods of excess cash. When approaching a loan officer, the manager can use the cash budget to document the ability to repay as well as the need for cash. Because cash flow is the lifeblood of an organization, the cash budget is one of the most important budgets in the master budget. The **cash budget** is, simply, the detailed plan that shows all expected sources and uses of cash. Schedules of cash receipts and cash payments are major inputs to the cash budget.

The cash budget has the following five main sections:

1. Total cash available
2. Cash disbursements
3. Cash excess or deficiency
4. Financing
5. Cash balance

The cash available section identifies the beginning cash balance and the expected cash receipts. Expected cash receipts include all sources of cash for the period being considered. However, the principal source of cash is from sales. Because a significant proportion of sales is usually on account, a major task of an organization is to determine the pattern of collection for its accounts receivable.

The cash disbursements section lists all planned cash outlays for the period except for interest payments on short-term loans (these payments appear in the financing section). All expenses not resulting in a cash outlay are excluded from the list (depreciation, for example, is never included in the disbursements section).

The cash excess or deficiency section is a function of the cash needs and the cash available. Cash needs are determined by the total cash disbursements plus the minimum cash balance required by company policy. If the total cash available is less than the cash needs, a deficiency exists. In such a case, a short-term loan will be needed. On the other hand, with a cash excess (cash available is greater than the firm's cash needs), the firm has the ability to repay loans and perhaps make some temporary investments.

In the event of a deficiency, the cash budget must show the amount to be borrowed so that the cash needs are satisfied. Also, the cash budget should reveal planned repayments. Thus, the financing section discloses the planned borrowings and repayments, including interest.

The final section of the cash budget simply reveals the planned ending cash balance. Ending cash balance is the cash available plus borrowings minus cash disbursements. This ending cash balance would be at least equal to any minimum cash balance required by company policy.

To illustrate the cash budget, assume the following for CalBlock:

a. A $100,000 minimum cash balance is required for the end of each quarter.
b. Money can be borrowed and repaid in multiples of $100,000. Interest is 12 percent per year. Interest payments are made only for the amount of the principal being repaid. All borrowing takes place at the beginning of a quarter and all repayment takes place at the end of a quarter.
c. Half of all sales are for cash, 70 percent of credit sales are collected in the quarter of sale, and the remaining 30 percent are collected in the following quarter. The sales for the fourth quarter of 1994 were $2 million.
d. Purchases of raw materials are made on account; 80 percent of purchases are paid for in the quarter of purchase. The remaining 20 percent are paid in the following quarter. The purchases for the fourth quarter of 1994 were $500,000.
e. Budgeted depreciation is $200,000 per quarter for overhead and $15,000 per quarter for selling and administration (see Schedules 5 and 6).
f. The capital budget for 1995 revealed plans to purchase additional equipment to handle increased demand at a small plant in Nevada. The cash outlay for the equipment, $600,000, will take place in the first quarter. The company plans to finance the acquisition of the equipment with operating cash, supplementing it with short-term loans as necessary.
g. Corporate income taxes are approximately $650,000 and will be paid at the end of the fourth quarter (Schedule 9).

Given the above information, the cash budget for CalBlock is shown in Schedule 10 (all figures are rounded to the nearest thousand).

Much of the information needed to prepare the cash budget comes from the operating budgets. In fact, Schedules 1, 3, 4, 5, and 6 all supply essential input. However, these schedules by themselves do not supply all of the needed information. The collection pattern for revenues and the payment pattern for materials must be known before the cash flow for sales and purchases on credit can be found.

Look at the revenues from credit sales for the second quarter, for example. Remember that for a given quarter, credit sales equal cash sales but that only 70 percent of credit sales are collected in that quarter. Thus, second quarter credit sales are $2.1 million (the same as cash sales), but only $1.47 million is received in the second quarter (0.70 × $2,100,000). The remaining $630,000 (0.30 × $2,100,000) is received in the following quarter. Similarly, the second quarter includes revenues from first-quarter credit sales. Total first-quarter sales of $1.4 million are multiplied by 0.5 to yield the amount of first-quarter credit sales ($700,000). This amount is multiplied by 0.3 to find the portion not collected until the second quarter, which is $210,000. As a check on the quarterly sales figures in Schedule 10, add the cash sales and the credit sales for one quarter to the credit sales collected in the next quarter that appear on the "prior quarter" line. The result is the total sales revenue for the quarter as shown in Schedule 1.

Schedule 10
(in thousands)

CalBlock, Inc.
Cash Budget
For the Year Ended December 31, 1995

	Quarter 1	2	3	4	*Year*	*Source*[1]
Beginning cash balance	$ 120	$ 141	$ 102	$1,421	$ 120	
Collections:						
Cash sales	700	2,100	2,400	800	6,000	c, 1
Credit sales:						
Current quarter	490	1,470	1,680	560	4,200	c, 1
Prior quarter	300	210	630	720	1,860	c, 1
Total cash available	$ 1,610	$ 3,921	$ 4,812	$ 3,501	$ 12,180	
Less disbursements:						
Raw materials:						
Current quarter	$ (523)	$(1,248)	$(1,141)	$ (416)	$(3,328)	d, 3
Prior quarter	(100)	(131)	(312)	(285)	(828)	d, 3
Direct labor	(288)	(720)	(672)	(240)	(1,920)	4
Overhead	(408)	(840)	(792)	(360)	(2,400)	e, 5
Selling and administrative	(150)	(350)	(365)	(150)	(1,015)	e, 6
Income taxes	—	—	—	(650)	(650)	g, 9
Equipment	(600)	—	—	—	(600)	f
Total disbursements	$(2,069)	$(3,289)	$(3,282)	$(2,101)	$(10,741)	
Minimum cash balance	(100)	(100)	(100)	(100)	(100)	a
Total cash needs	$(2,169)	$(3,389)	$(3,382)	$(2,201)	$(10,841)	
Excess (deficiency) of cash available over needs	$ (559)	$ 532	$ 1,430	$ 1,300	$ 1,339	
Financing:						
Borrowings	600	—	—	—	600	
Repayments	—	(500)	(100)	—	(600)	b
Interest[2]	—	(30)	(9)	—	(39)	b
Total financing	600	(530)	(109)	—	(39)	
Ending cash balance[3]	$ 141	$ 102	$ 1,421	$ 1,400	$ 1,400	

[1]Letters refer to the information on page 1128. Numbers refer to schedules already developed.
[2]Interest payments are 6/12 × 0.12 × $500 and 9/12 × 0.12 × $100, respectively. Since borrowings occur at the beginning of the quarter and repayments at the end of the quarter, the first principal repayment takes place after six months, and the second principal repayment takes place after nine months.
[3]Total cash available minus total disbursements plus (or minus) total financing.

Similar computations are done for purchases. In both cases, patterns of collection and payment are needed in addition to the information supplied by the schedules.

Additionally, all noncash expenses, such as depreciation, need to be removed from the total amounts reported in the expense budgets. Thus, the budgeted expenses in Schedules 5 and 6 were reduced by the budgeted depreciation for each quarter. Overhead expenses in Schedule 5 were reduced by depreciation of $200,000 per quarter. Selling and administrative expenses were reduced by $15,000 per quarter. The net amounts are what appear in the cash budget.

The cash budget shown in Schedule 10 underscores the importance of breaking the annual budget down into smaller time periods. The cash budget for the year gives the impression that sufficient operating cash will be available to finance the acquisition of the new equipment. Quarterly information, however, shows the need for short-term borrowing because of both the acquisition of the new equipment and the timing of the firm's cash flows. Breaking down the annual cash budget into quarterly time periods conveys more information. Even smaller time periods often prove to be useful. Most firms prepare monthly cash budgets, and some even prepare weekly and daily budgets.

Another significant piece of information emerges from CalBlock's cash budget. By the end of the third quarter, the firm owns a considerable amount of cash ($1,421,000). A similar amount is also owned by the end of the year. It is certainly not wise to allow this much cash to sit idly in a bank account. The management of CalBlock should consider paying dividends and making long-term investments. At the very least, the excess cash should be invested in short-term marketable securities. Once plans are finalized for use of the excess cash, the cash budget should be revised to reflect those plans. Budgeting is a dynamic process. As the budget is developed, new information becomes available and better plans can be formulated.

Budgeted Balance Sheet. The budgeted balance sheet depends on information contained in the current balance sheet and in the other budgets in the master budget. The balance sheet for the beginning of the year is given in Exhibit 24-2. The budgeted balance sheet for December 31, 1995, is given in Schedule 11 (page 1132). Explanations for the budgeted figures follow the schedule.

As we have described the individual budgets that make up the master budget, the interdependencies of the component budgets have become apparent. A diagram displaying these interrelationships is shown in Exhibit 24-3 (page 1133).

THE BEHAVIORAL DIMENSION OF BUDGETING

Objective 4
Identify and discuss the key features that a budgetary system should have to encourage managers to engage in goal-congruent behavior.

goal congruence

Budgets are often used to judge the actual performance of managers. Bonuses, salary increases, and promotions are all affected by a manager's ability to achieve or beat budgeted goals. Since a manager's financial status and career can be affected, budgets can have a significant behavioral effect. Whether that effect is positive or negative depends to a large extent on how budgets are used.

Positive behavior occurs when the goals of individual managers are aligned with the goals of the organization and the manager has the drive to achieve them. The alignment of managerial and organizational goals is often referred to as **goal congruence.** In addition to goal congruence, however, a manager must also exert effort to achieve the goals of the organization.

Exhibit 24-2

CalBlock, Inc.
Balance Sheet
December 31, 1994
(in thousands)

Assets		
Current assets:		
Cash	$120	
Accounts receivable	300	
Raw materials inventory	50	
Finished goods	55	
Total current assets		$ 525
Property, Plant and Equipment:		
Land	$2,500	
Building and equipment	9,000	
Accumulated depreciation	(4,500)	
Total property, plant and equipment		7,000
Total assets		$7,525
Liabilities and Stockholders' Equity		
Current liabilities:		
Accounts payable		$ 100
Stockholders' equity:		
Common stock, no par	$ 600	
Retained earnings	6,825	
Total stockholders' equity		7,425
Total liabilities and stockholders' equity		$7,525

dysfunctional behavior

ideal budgetary system

If the budget is improperly administered, the reaction of subordinate managers may be negative. This negative behavior can be manifested in numerous ways, but the overall effect is subversion of the organization's goals. **Dysfunctional behavior** is individual behavior that is in basic conflict with the goals of the organization. An **ideal budgetary system** is one that achieves complete goal congruence, and, simultaneously, creates a drive in managers to achieve the organization's goals. Currently, the level of knowledge necessary to design and operate an ideal budgetary system probably does not exist. However, research and practice have identified a number of key features that a budgetary system should have to promote a reasonable degree of positive behavior. These features emphasize human considerations.

1. Frequent feedback on performance
2. Flexible budgeting capabilities
3. Monetary and nonmonetary incentives
4. Participation
5. Realistic standards
6. Controllability of costs

One other principle is important to using a budgetary system. Regardless of how important a budget is in evaluating managerial performance, it should not be the only evaluation means. Multiple measures of performance should exist.

Schedule 11 (in thousands)

CalBlock, Inc.
Budgeted Balance Sheet
December 31, 1995

Assets		
Current assets:		
Cash	$1,400[a]	
Accounts receivable	240[b]	
Raw materials	50[c]	
Finished goods	58[d]	
Total current assets		$1,748
Property, plant and equipment:		
Land	$2,500[e]	
Building and equipment	9,600[f]	
Accumulated depreciation	(5,360)[g]	
Total property, plant and equipment		6,740
Total assets		$8,488
Liabilities and Stockholders' Equity		
Current liabilities:		
Accounts payable		$ 104[h]
Stockholders' equity:		
Common stock, no par	$ 600[i]	
Retained earnings	7,784[j]	
Total stockholders' equity		8,384
Total liabilities and stockholders' equity		$8,488

[a]Ending balance from Schedule 10
[b]30 percent of fourth-quarter credit sales (0.30 × $800,000)—see Schedules 1 and 10
[c]From Schedule 3
[d]From Schedule 8
[e]From the December 31, 1994, balance sheet
[f]December 31, 1994, balance ($9,000,000) plus new equipment acquisition of $600,000 (see the 1994 ending balance sheet and Schedule 10)
[g]From the December 31, 1994, balance sheet, Schedule 5, and Schedule 6 ($4,500,000 + $800,000 + $60,000)
[h]20 percent of fourth-quarter purchases (0.20 × $520,000)—see Schedules 3 and 10
[i]From the December 31, 1994, balance sheet
[j]$6,825,000 + $959,000 (December 31, 1994, balance plus net income from Schedule 9)

Frequent Feedback on Performance

Managers need to know how they are doing as the year unfolds. Providing them with frequent performance reports allows them to know how successful their efforts have been, to take corrective actions, and change plans as necessary. Frequent performance reports can reinforce positive behavior and give managers the time and opportunity to adapt to changing conditions.

In a budgetary setting, performance reports compare actual costs and revenues with budgeted costs and revenues. Deviations of actual results from planned results are computed and labeled as variances. Analysis of the significance of these variances allows managers to focus only on areas that need atten-

Exhibit 24-3
The Master Budget and Its Interrelationships

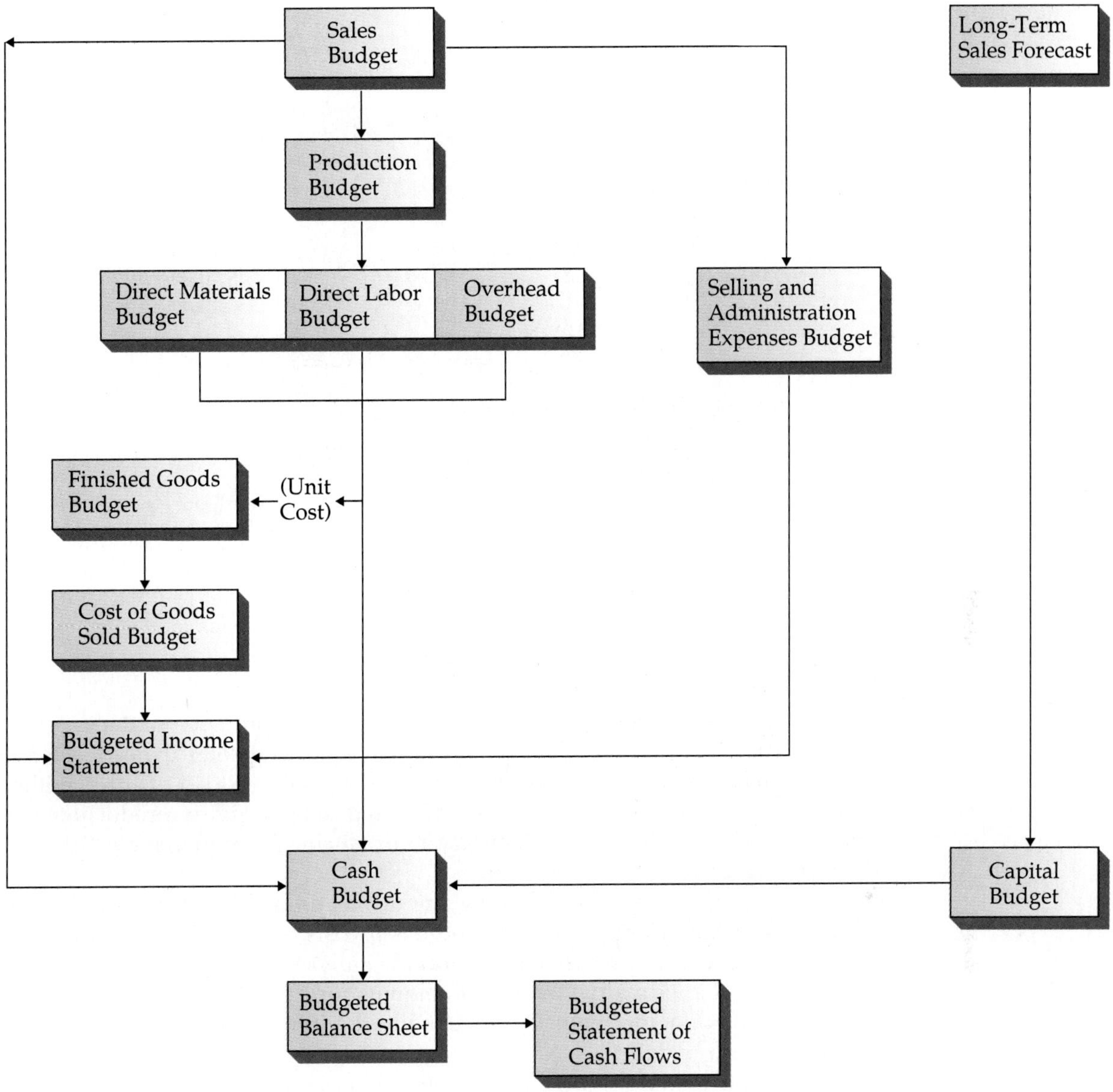

tion. This process is called *management by exception*. An example of a performance report is given in Exhibit 24-4.

Static Budgets

static budget

The budget developed for CalBlock is an example of a static budget. A **static budget** is a budget for a particular level of activity. For CalBlock, budgets were developed based on expected annual sales of 16 million units. Quarterly budgets were also developed based on particular levels of activity. Because static budgets

Exhibit 24-4
Performance Report: Quarterly Production Costs (in thousands)

	Actual	Budget	Variance
Units produced	3,000	2,400	600 F[a]
Direct materials cost	$ 927.30	$ 624.00[b]	$303.30 U[c]
Direct labor cost	360.00	288.00[d]	72.00 U
Overhead:[e]			
Variable:			
Supplies	80.00	72.00	8.00 U
Indirect labor	220.00	168.00	52.00 U
Power	40.00	48.00	(8.00) F
Fixed:			
Supervision	90.00	100.00	(10.00) F
Depreciation	200.00	200.00	0.00
Rent	30.00	20.00	10.00 U
Total	$1,947.30	$1,520.00	$427.30 U

[a]F means the variance is favorable.
[b]From Schedule 3 (62,400 lbs × $0.01).
[c]U means the variance is unfavorable.
[d]From Schedule 4.
[e]Schedule 5 provides the aggregate amount of budgeted overhead (e.g., the aggregate variable overhead is 0.015 × 2,400,000 × $8 = $288,000, and the total budgeted fixed overhead is $320,000).

depend on a particular level of activity, they are not very useful when it comes to preparing performance reports.

To illustrate, suppose that CalBlock has decided to provide quarterly performance reports. Further suppose that sales activity was greater than expected in the first quarter; 2.6 million concrete blocks were sold instead of the 2 million budgeted in Schedule 1. Because of increased sales activity, production was increased over the planned level. Instead of producing 2.4 million units (Schedule 2), CalBlock produced 3 million units.

A performance report comparing the actual production costs for the first quarter with the original planned production costs is given in Exhibit 24-4. In contrast to Schedule 5, budgeted amounts for individual overhead items are provided. Thus, the individual budgeted amounts for each overhead item are new information (except for depreciation). Usually, this information would be detailed in an overhead budget.

According to the report, unfavorable variances occur for direct materials, direct labor, all variable overhead items, and supervision. However, there is something fundamentally wrong with the report. Actual costs for production of 3 million concrete blocks are being compared with planned costs for production of 2.4 million. Because direct materials, direct labor, and variable overhead are unit-level variable costs, we would expect them to be greater at a higher activity level. Thus, even if cost control were perfect for the production of 3 million units, unfavorable variances would be produced for all variable costs.

To create a meaningful performance report, actual costs and expected costs must be compared at the *same* level of activity. Since actual output often differs from planned output, some method is needed to compute what the costs should have been for the actual output level.

Flexible Budgets

flexible budget

The budget that provides a firm with the capability to compute expected costs for a range of activity is called a **flexible budget.** Flexible budgeting has three major uses.

1. The flexible budget can be used to prepare the budget before the fact for the expected level of activity.
2. Because flexible budgeting can determine what costs should be at various levels of activity, the budget can be used after the fact to compute what costs should have been for the actual level of activity. Once expected costs are known for the actual level of activity, a performance report that compares those expected costs to actual costs can be prepared.
3. Flexible budgeting can help managers deal with uncertainty by allowing them to see the expected outcomes for a range of activity. It can be used to generate financial results for a number of plausible scenarios.

In other words, flexible budgeting is the key to providing the frequent feedback that managers need to exercise control and effectively carry out the plans of an organization.

To compute the expected cost at different levels of activity, flexible budgeting exploits the cost behavior patterns of each item in the budget. Thus, before a flexible budget can be prepared, the cost behavior of each item in the budget must be known. This means that the cost formula $Y = F + VX$ is needed for each item in the budget. In this formula, Y is the item's total cost, X is a measure of unit-level activity level, F is the item's fixed costs, and V is the item's variable cost per unit of activity.

To illustrate the power of flexible budgeting, a flexible production budget will be developed for CalBlock. Let activity level be measured by the number of concrete blocks produced. From Schedule 7, we know the variable cost formulas for direct materials ($0.26 per unit), direct labor ($0.12 per unit), and variable overhead ($0.12 per unit). To increase the detail of the flexible budget, let us assume the variable costs per unit for supplies ($0.03), indirect labor ($0.07), and power ($0.02). The three individual formulas sum to $0.12. From Schedule 5, we also know that fixed overhead is budgeted at $320,000 per quarter. Exhibit 24-5 displays a flexible budget for production costs at three levels of activity.

Notice in Exhibit 24-5 that total budgeted production costs increase as the activity level increases. Budgeted costs change because of variable costs. Because of this, flexible budgets are sometimes referred to as **variable budgets.**

variable budgets

Flexible budgets are powerful control tools because they allow management to compute what the costs should be for any level of activity. Exhibit 24-5 reveals what the costs should have been for the actual level of activity (3 million units). With this information, a performance report can be prepared that communicates useful information to management. A revised performance report that compares actual and budgeted costs for the actual level of activity is given in Exhibit 24-6.

The revised performance report in Exhibit 24-6 paints a much different picture than the one in Exhibit 24-4. By comparing budgeted costs for the actual level of activity with actual costs for the same level, a problem area can be immediately identified—expenditures for direct materials are excessive. (The other unfavorable variances seem relatively small.) With this knowledge, management can search for the causes of the excess expenditures and implement corrective measures to prevent the same problems from occurring in future quarters.

Exhibit 24-5
Flexible Production Budget (in thousands of dollars)

	Variable Cost per Unit	Range of Production (Units) 2,400	3,000	3,600
Production Costs:				
Variable:				
Direct materials	$0.26	$ 624	$ 780	$ 936
Direct labor	0.12	288	360	432
Variable overhead:				
Supplies	0.03	72	90	108
Indirect labor	0.07	168	210	252
Power	0.02	48	60	72
Total variable costs	$0.50	$1,200	$1,500	$1,800
Fixed overhead:				
Supervision		$ 100	$ 100	$ 100
Depreciation		200	200	200
Rent		20	20	20
Total fixed costs		$ 320	$ 320	$ 320
Total production costs		$1,520	$1,820	$2,120

Exhibit 24-6
Actual Versus Flexible Performance Report: Quarterly Production Costs (in thousands)

	Actual	Budget[1]	Variance
Units produced	3,000	3,000	—
Production costs:			
Direct materials	$ 927.30	$ 780.00	$147.30 U
Direct labor	360.00	360.00	0.00
Variable overhead:			
Supplies	80.00	90.00	(10.00) F
Indirect labor	220.00	210.00	10.00 U
Power	40.00	60.00	(20.00) F
Total variable costs	$1,627.30	$1,500.00	$127.30 U
Fixed overhead:			
Supervision	90.00	100.00	(10.00) F
Depreciation	200.00	200.00	0.00
Rent	30.00	20.00	10.00 U
Total fixed costs	$ 320.00	$ 320.00	0.00
Total costs	$1,947.30	$1,820.00	$127.30 U

[1]From Exhibit 24-5

flexible budget variance

Differences in the actual amount and the flexible budget amount are attributable to one of two causes: differences in the budgeted costs of the inputs, or differences in the number of inputs planned and the number actually used to produce the actual output. The first difference is referred to as a *price variance* and the second as an *efficiency variance*. The **flexible budget variance** is the sum of the price variances and the efficiency variances. (The flexible budget variance

Exhibit 24-7
Managerial Performance Report: Quarterly Production (in thousands)

	Actual Results	*Flexible Budget*	*Flexible Budget Variances*[1]	*Static Budget*	*Volume Variance*[2]
Units produced	3,000	3,000	—	2,400	600 F
Production costs:					
Direct materials	$ 927.30	$ 780.00	$147.30 U	$ 624.00	$156.00 U
Direct labor	360.00	360.00	0.00	288.00	72.00 U
Supplies	80.00	90.00	(10.00) F	72.00	18.00 U
Indirect labor	220.00	210.00	10.00 U	168.00	42.00 U
Power	40.00	60.00	(20.00) F	48.00	12.00 U
Supervision	90.00	100.00	(10.00) F	100.00	—
Depreciation	200.00	200.00	—	200.00	—
Rent	30.00	20.00	10.00 U	20.00	—
Total costs	$1,947.30	$1,820.00	$127.30 U	$1,520.00	$300.00 U

[1]Actual results minus flexible budget variances
[2]Flexible budget minus static budget

can be decomposed into price and efficiency variances; this discussion is reserved for another chapter.) Thus, the flexible budget provides the capability to assess the efficiency of a manager.

In addition to measuring the efficiency of a manager, it is often desirable to measure whether a manager accomplishes his or her goals. The static budget represented certain goals that the firm wanted to achieve. A manager is *effective* if the goals described by the static budget are achieved or exceeded. Any differences between the flexible budget and the static budget are attributable to differences in volume. They are called *volume variances.* A five-column performance report that reveals both the flexible budget variances and the volume variances can be used. Exhibit 24-7 provides an example of this report using the CalBlock data.

As the report in Exhibit 24-7 reveals, production volume was 600,000 units greater than the original budgeted amount. Thus, the manager exceeded the original budgeted goal. This volume variance is labeled *favorable* because it exceeds the original production goal. (Recall that the *reason* for the extra production was because the demand for the product was greater than expected. Thus, the increase in production over the original amount was truly favorable.) On the other hand, the budgeted variable costs are greater than expected because of the increased production. This difference is labeled unfavorable because the costs are greater than expected; however, the increase in costs is because of an increase in production. Thus, it is totally reasonable. For this particular example, the effectiveness of the manager is not in question; thus, the main issue is how well the manager controlled costs as revealed by the flexible-budget variances.

Monetary and Nonmonetary Incentives

incentives

A sound budgetary system encourages goal-congruent behavior. The means an organization uses to influence a manager to exert effort to achieve an organization's goal are called **incentives.** Incentives can be either negative or positive. Negative incentives use fear of punishment to motivate; positive incentives use the expectation of reward. What incentives should be tied into an organization's budgetary system?

Monetary Incentives. Traditional organization theory assumes that individuals are primarily motivated by monetary rewards, resist work, and are inefficient and wasteful.[1] If this view is fully accepted, budgets should be imposed from above, and a manager should be held strictly accountable for each line in the budget. In this way, top management can control a subordinate manager's tendency to shirk and be wasteful. Moreover, since a manager is primarily motivated by **monetary incentives,** this control is best achieved by relating budgetary performance to salary increases, bonuses, and promotions. The threat of dismissal is the ultimate economic sanction for poor performance.

monetary incentives

Nonmonetary Incentives. The above view of human behavior is too simplistic. Individuals are motivated by more than just external or extrinsic rewards. In fact, in addition to the economic factors, individuals are motivated by a complex set of intrinsic psychological and social factors. The satisfaction of a job well done, recognition, responsibility, self-esteem, and the nature of the work itself are examples of **nonmonetary incentives.** To be successful, a budgetary control system must not ignore the complex motivating forces affecting individuals. Monetary rewards, by themselves, are not sufficient to achieve the desired level of motivation in managers. In fact, overemphasis of monetary incentives may lead to frustration, anger, and rebellion. The budgetary system must also use nonmonetary incentives. Job enrichment, increased responsibility and autonomy, nonmonetary recognition programs, and so on, are all examples of nonmonetary incentives that can be used to enhance a budgetary control system. One way to enrich managers' jobs is to allow them meaningful participation in creating the budget by which they will be evaluated.

nonmonetary incentives

Participative Budgeting

participative budgeting

Rather than imposing budgets on subordinate managers, **participative budgeting** allows subordinate managers considerable say in how the budgets are established. Typically, overall objectives are communicated to the manager, who helps develop a budget that will accomplish these objectives. In participative budgeting, the emphasis is on the accomplishment of the broad objectives, not on individual budget items.

The budget process described earlier for CalBlock uses participative budgeting. The company provides the sales forecast to its profit centers and requests a budget that shows planned expenditures and expected profits for a given level of sales. The managers of the profit centers are fully responsible for preparing the budgets by which they will later be evaluated. Although the budgets must be approved by the president, disapproval is not common; the budgets are usually in line with the sales forecast and last year's operating results adjusted for expected changes in revenues and costs.

Participative budgeting communicates a sense of responsibility to subordinate managers and fosters creativity. Since the subordinate manager creates the budget, it is more likely that the budget's goals will become the manager's personal

1. An excellent discussion of traditional and modern views of organization theory and their implications for managerial accounting is given by Edwin H. Caplan, *Management Accounting and Behavioral Science* (Reading, Mass.: Addison-Wesley, 1971).

goals, resulting in a higher degree of goal congruence. Advocates of participative budgeting claim that the increased responsibility and challenge inherent in the process provide nonmonetary incentives that lead to a higher level of performance. They argue that individuals involved in setting their own standards will work harder to achieve them. In addition to the behavioral benefits, participative budgeting has the advantage of involving individuals whose knowledge of local conditions may enhance the entire planning process.

Participative budgeting has three potential problems that should be mentioned.

1. Setting standards that are either too high or too low
2. Building slack into the budget (often referred to as *padding the budget*)
3. Pseudoparticipation

Setting Standards. Some managers may tend to set the budget either too loose or too tight. Since budgeted goals tend to become the manager's goals when participation is allowed, making this mistake in setting the budget can result in decreased performance levels. If goals are too easily achieved, a manager may lose interest and performance may actually drop. Challenge is important to aggressive and creative individuals. Similarly, if a manager sets the budget too tight, failing to achieve the standards may frustrate him or her. This frustration, too, can lead to poorer performance. The trick is to get managers in a participative setting to set high but achievable goals.

Top management needs to know their subordinate managers well to be able to guide them properly as they set their budgets. Then, those top managers will know when the budgets reflect the right level of challenge. Furthermore, top management must have the ability to provide guidance without dictating the budget. A fine balance is needed. Top management must supply sufficient input to ensure a high but achievable level of performance, yet their input must be limited so that subordinate managers also have significant input. Participative budgeting means that budgets are not dictated—either from above or from below.

budgetary slack

Budgetary Slack. Participative budgeting also creates the opportunity for managers to build slack into the budget. **Budgetary slack** (or *padding the budget*) exists when a manager deliberately underestimates revenues or overestimates costs. Either approach increases the likelihood that the manager will achieve the budget; therefore, the risk that the manager faces is reduced. Padding the budget also unnecessarily ties up resources that might be used more productively elsewhere.

Slack in budgets can be virtually eliminated by having top management dictate lower budgets, but this approach eliminates the behavioral benefits that come from participative budgeting. The benefits gained from allowing participation may far exceed the costs associated with padding the budget. Even so, top management should carefully review budgets proposed by subordinate managers and provide input, where needed, in order to decrease the effects of building slack into the budget. Again, it should be emphasized that participation is not equivalent to complete autonomy. Both top management and lower management should have input.

Pseudoparticipation. When top management assumes total control of the budgeting process and simultaneously seeks superficial participation from lower-

pseudoparticipation

level managers, **pseudoparticipation** exists. This participation is nothing more than endorsing the budget. Top management is simply obtaining formal acceptance of the budget from subordinate managers, not seeking real input. Accordingly, none of the behavioral benefits of participation will be realized.

Realistic Standards

Budgeted objectives are used to gauge performance; accordingly, they should be based on realistic conditions and expectations. Budgets should reflect operating realities, such as actual levels of activity, seasonal variations, efficiencies, and general economic trends. Flexible budgets, for example, are used to ensure that the budgeted costs provide standards that are compatible with the actual activity level. Another factor that should be considered is that of seasonality. Some businesses receive revenues and incur costs uniformly throughout the year; thus, spreading the annual revenues and costs evenly over quarters and months is reasonable for interim performance reports. However, for businesses with seasonal variations, this practice would result in distorted performance reports.

Such factors as efficiency and general economic conditions are also important. Occasionally, top management makes arbitrary cuts in prior-year budgets with the belief that the cuts will reduce fat or inefficiencies that allegedly exist. In reality, some units may be operating efficiently and others inefficiently. An across-the-board cut without any formal evaluation may impair the ability of some units to carry out their missions. General economic conditions also need to be considered. Budgeting for a significant increase in sales when a recession is projected is not only foolish but potentially dangerous.

Controllability of Costs

controllable costs

Conventional thought maintains that managers should be held accountable only for costs over which they have control. **Controllable costs** are costs whose level a manager can influence. In this view, a manager who has no responsibility for a cost should not be held accountable for it. For example, divisional managers have no power to authorize such corporate level costs as research and development and salaries of top managers. Therefore, they should not be held accountable for the incurrence of those costs.

Many firms, however, do put noncontrollable costs in the budgets of subordinate managers. Making managers aware of the need to cover all costs is one rationale for this practice. If noncontrollable costs are included in a budget, they should be separated from controllable costs and labeled as *noncontrollable.*

Multiple Measures of Performance

myopic behavior

Often organizations make the mistake of using budgets as their only measure of managerial performance. Overemphasis on this measure can lead to a form of dysfunctional behavior called *milking the firm* or *myopic behavior.* **Myopic behavior** occurs when a manager takes actions that improve budgetary performance in the short run but bring long-run harm to the firm.

There are numerous examples of myopic behavior. To meet budgeted cost objectives or profits, managers can reduce expenditures for preventive maintenance, for advertising, and for new product development. Managers can also fail to promote promotable employees to keep the cost of labor low and choose to use lower-quality materials to reduce the cost of raw materials. In the short run, these actions will lead to improved budgetary performance, but in the long run, productivity will fall, market share will decline, and capable employees will leave for more attractive opportunities.

Managers can engage in this kind of behavior because most have a short tenure. In most cases, managers spend three to five years before being promoted or moving to a new area of responsibility. Their successors are the ones who pay the price for their myopic behavior. The best way to prevent myopic behavior is to measure the performance of managers on several dimensions, including some long-run attributes. Market share, productivity, quality, and personnel development are examples of other areas of performance that could be evaluated. Financial measures of performance are important, but overemphasis on them can be counterproductive.

SUMMARY OF LEARNING OBJECTIVES

1. Describe the role of budgeting and the structure of the master budget. Budgeting is the quantitative expression of an organization's plans, stated either in physical or financial terms or both. Thus, a budget is a method for translating the goals and strategies of an organization into operational terms. Budgeting plays a key role in planning, control, and decision making. Budgets also serve to improve communication and coordination, a role that becomes increasingly important as organizations grow in size. Responsibility accounting refers to the use of the accounting system to set standards, to measure actual outcomes, and to report the performance of responsibility centers. The three major types of responsibility centers are cost centers, profit centers, and investment centers. The master budget, the comprehensive financial plan of an organization, is made up of the operating and financial budgets. The operating budget is the budgeted income statement and all supporting schedules. The financial budget is a collection of budgets relating primarily to the balance sheet (the cash budget, the capital budget, the budgeted statement of changes in financial position).

2. Prepare an operating budget including the following component budgets: sales, production, direct materials, direct labor, overhead, selling and administrative, ending finished goods, cost of goods sold, and the budgeted income statement. The sales budget (Schedule 1) consists of the anticipated quantity and price of all products to be sold. The production budget (Schedule 2) gives the expected production in units to meet forecast sales and desired ending inventory goals; expected production is supplemented by beginning inventory. The direct materials purchases budget (Schedule 3) gives the necessary purchases during the year for every type of raw material to meet production and desired ending inventory goals. The direct labor budget (Schedule 4) and overhead budget (Schedule 5) give the amounts of these resources necessary for the coming year's production. The overhead budget may be broken into fixed and variable components to facilitate preparation of the budget. The selling and administrative budget (Schedule 6) gives the forecast costs for these functions. the finished goods inventory budget (Schedule 7) and the cost of goods sold budget (Schedule 8) detail production costs for the expected ending inventory and the units sold, respectively. The budgeted income statement (Schedule 9) outlines the net income to be realized if budgeted plans come to fruition.

3. Prepare the following two components of the financial budget: cash budget and budgeted balance sheet. The cash budget (Schedule 10) is simply the beginning balance in the cash account, plus anticipated receipts, minus anticipated disbursements, plus or minus any necessary borrowing. The budgeted (or pro forma) balance sheet (Schedule 11) gives the anticipated ending balances of the asset, liability, and equity accounts if budgeted plans hold.

4. Identify and discuss the key features that a budgetary system should have to encourage managers to engage in goal-congruent behavior. The success of a budgetary system depends on how seriously human factors are considered. To discourage dysfunctional behavior, organizations should avoid overemphasizing budgets as a control mechanism. Other areas of performance should be evaluated in addition to budgets. Budgets can be improved as performance measures by using participative budgeting and other nonmonetary incentives, providing frequent feedback on performance, using flexible budgeting, ensuring that the budgetary objectives reflect reality, and holding managers accountable for only controllable costs.

KEY TERMS

REVIEW PROBLEM

Young Products produces coat racks. The projected sales for the first quarter of the coming year and the beginning and ending inventory data are as follows:

Sales	100,000 units
Unit price	$15
Beginning inventory	8,000 units
Targeted ending inventory	12,000 units

The coat racks are molded and then painted. Each rack requires 4 pounds of metal, which costs $2.50 per pound. The beginning inventory of raw materials is 4,000 pounds. Young Products wants to have 6,000 pounds of metal in inventory at the end of the quarter. Each rack produced requires 30 minutes of direct labor time, which is billed at $9 per hour.

REQUIRED:

1. Prepare a sales budget for the first quarter.
2. Prepare a production budget for the first quarter.
3. Prepare a direct materials purchases budget for the first quarter.
4. Prepare a direct labor budget for the first quarter.

Solution:

1.

Young Products
Sales Budget
For the First Quarter

Units	100,000
Unit price	× $15
Sales	$1,500,000

2.

Young Products
Production Budget
For the First Quarter

Sales (in units)	100,000
Desired ending inventory	12,000
Total needs	112,000
Less: Beginning inventory	8,000
Units to be produced	104,000

3.

Young Products
Direct Materials
For the First Quarter

Units to be produced	104,000
Direct materials per unit (lbs)	× 4
Production needs (lbs)	416,000
Desired ending inventory (lbs)	6,000
Total needs (lbs)	422,000
Less: Beginning inventory (lbs)	(4,000)
Materials to be purchased (lbs)	418,000
Cost per pound	× $2.50
Total purchase cost	$1,045,000

4.

Young Products
Direct Labor Budget
For the First Quarter

Units to be produced	104,000
Labor: Time per unit	× 0.5
Total hours needed	52,000
Cost per hour	× $9
Total direct labor cost	$468,000

QUESTIONS

1. Define the term *budget*. How are budgets used in planning?
2. Define *control*. How are budgets used to control?
3. Explain how both small and large organizations can benefit from budgeting.
4. Discuss some of the reasons for budgeting.
5. What is a master budget? an operating budget? a financial budget?
6. Explain the role of a sales forecast in budgeting. What is the difference between a sales forecast and a sales budget?
7. All budgets depend on the sales budget. Is this true? Explain.
8. How do the master budgets differ among manufacturing, merchandising, and service organizations?
9. Why is goal congruence important?

10. Discuss the roles of monetary and nonmonetary incentives. Do you believe that nonmonetary incentives are needed? Why?
11. What is participative budgeting? Discuss some of its advantages.
12. A budget too easily achieved will lead to diminished performance. Do you agree? Explain.
13. What is the role of top management in participative budgeting?
14. Explain why a manager has an incentive to build slack into the budget.
15. Discuss the differences between static and flexible budgets. Why are flexible budgets superior to static budgets for performance reporting?
16. Explain why mixed costs must be broken down into their fixed and variable components before a flexible budget can be developed.
17. Why is it important for a manager to receive frequent feedback on his or her performance?
18. Explain how a manager can milk the firm to improve budgetary performance.
19. Identify performance measures other than budgets that can be used to discourage myopic behavior. Discuss how you would use these measures.
20. How important are the behavioral aspects of a budgetary control system? Explain.

EXERCISES

E24-1
Sales Budget
LO 2

Milan Cereal Company produces wheat flakes and corn flakes. Both products are sold in 12-ounce boxes. Wheat flakes sell for $1.50 per box and corn flakes sell for $1.30 per box. Projected sales (in boxes) for the coming four quarters are given below.

	Wheat Flakes	*Corn Flakes*
First quarter	500,000	600,000
Second quarter	600,000	600,000
Third quarter	700,000	700,000
Fourth quarter	750,000	800,000

The president of the company believes that the projected sales are realistic and can be achieved by the company.

REQUIRED: Prepare a sales budget for each quarter and for the year in total. Show sales by product and in total for each time period.

E24-2
Production Budget
LO 2

Whiskers Products, Inc., produces a variety of products for cats. Among them is a 16-ounce can of cat food. The sales budget for the first four months of the year is presented below.

	Unit Sales	*Dollar Sales*
January	100,000	$50,000
February	120,000	60,000
March	110,000	55,000
April	100,000	50,000

Company policy requires that ending inventories for each month be 20 percent of next month's sales. At the beginning of January, the inventory of cat food is 20,000 cans.

REQUIRED: Prepare a production budget for the first quarter of the year. Show the number of units that should be produced each month as well as for the quarter in total.

E24-3
Direct Materials Purchases Budget
LO 2

Dulce Company produces a 6-ounce chocolate candy bar. Each 6-ounce bar contains three ounces of sugar, which costs $0.025 per ounce. Dulce has budgeted production of the chocolate bar for the next four months as follows:

	Units
October	400,000
November	800,000
December	500,000
January	600,000

Inventory policy requires that sufficient sugar be in ending monthly inventory to satisfy 15 percent of the following month's production needs. Inventory of sugar at the beginning of October equals exactly the amount needed to satisfy the inventory policy.

REQUIRED: Prepare a direct materials purchases budget for the last quarter of the year showing purchases in units and in dollars for each month and for the quarter in total.

E24-4
Direct Labor Budget
LO 2

Refer to the production budget in Exercise 24-3. Each chocolate bar produced requires (on average) 0.01 direct labor hours. The average cost of direct labor is $9 per hour.

REQUIRED: Prepare a direct labor budget for the last quarter of the year showing the hours needed and the direct labor cost for each month and for the quarter in total.

E24-5
Purchases Budget
LO 2

Al's Auto Supply carries a variety of auto parts including oil filters. The sales budget for oil filters for the first six months of the year is presented below.

	Unit Sales	*Dollar Sales*
January	200	$ 900
February	180	810
March	220	990
April	250	1,125
May	300	1,350
June	260	1,170

Al believes that ending inventories should be sufficient to cover 30 percent of the next month's projected sales. On January 1, 84 oil filters were in inventory.

REQUIRED:

1. Prepare a purchases budget in units of oil filters for as many months as you can.
2. If oil filters are priced at 50 percent above cost, what is the dollar cost of purchases for each month of your purchases budget?

E24-6
Production Budget; Materials Purchases Budget
LO 2

Jenna Mitchell, owner of Jenna's Jams and Jellies, produces homemade-style jellies using fruits indigenous to her local area. Jenna has estimated the following sales of 16-ounce jars of fruit jelly for the rest of the year and January of next year.

September	100
October	150
November	170
December	225
January	100

Jenna likes to have 20 percent of the next month's sales needs on hand at the end of each month. This requirement was met on August 31.

Materials needed for each jar of fruit jelly are as follows:

Fruit	1 lb
Sugar	1 lb
Pectin	3 oz
Jar set	1

The materials inventory policy is to have 5 percent of the next month's fruit needs on hand as well as 50 percent of the next month's production needs for all other materials. (The relatively low inventory amount for fruit is designed to prevent spoilage.) Materials inventory on September 1 met this company policy.

REQUIRED:

1. Prepare a production budget for September, October, November, and December for fruit jelly.
2. Prepare a purchases budget for all materials used in the production of fruit jelly for the months of September, October, and November. (Round all answers to the nearest whole unit.)
3. Why can't you prepare a purchases budget for December?

E24-7
Overhead Budget; Flexible Budgeting
LO 2, 4

Toolson Manufacturing, Inc., has developed the following flexible budget for overhead for the coming year. Activity level is measured in direct labor hours.

		Activity Level (hours)		
	Variable Cost Formula	*10,000*	*15,000*	*20,000*
Variable costs:				
Maintenance	$1.50	$15,000	$22,500	$ 30,000
Supplies	0.50	5,000	7,500	10,000
Power	0.10	1,000	1,500	2,000
Total variable costs	$2.10	$21,000	$31,500	$ 42,000
Fixed costs:				
Depreciation		$ 6,000	$ 6,000	$ 6,000
Salaries		60,000	60,000	60,000
Total fixed costs		$66,000	$66,000	$ 66,000
Total overhead costs		$87,000	$97,500	$108,000

Toolson produces two different types of hammers. The production budget for April is 12,000 units for hammer A and 15,000 units for hammer B. Hammer A requires three minutes of direct labor time and hammer B requires two minutes. Fixed overhead costs are incurred uniformly throughout the year.

REQUIRED: Prepare an overhead budget for April.

E24-8
Cash Budget
LO 3

The owner of a small mining supply company has requested a cash budget for June. After examining the records of the company, you find the following:

a. Cash balance on June 1 is $1,000.
b. Actual sales for April and May are as follows:

	April	May
Cash sales	$10,000	$15,000
Credit sales	25,000	35,000
Total sales	$35,000	$50,000

c. Credit sales are collected over a three-month period: 50 percent in the month of sale, 30 percent in the second month, and 15 percent in the third month. The remaining sales are uncollectible.
d. Inventory purchases average 60 percent of a month's total sales. Of those purchases, 40 percent are paid for in the month of purchase. The remaining 60 percent are paid for in the following month.
e. Salaries and wages total $8,000 a month, including a $4,500 salary paid to the owner.
f. Rent is $1,000 per month.
g. Taxes to be paid in June are $5,000.

The owner also tells you that he expects cash sales of $20,000 and credit sales of $40,000 for June. There is no minimum cash balance required. The owner of the company does not have access to short-term loans.

REQUIRED:

1. Prepare a cash budget for June. Include supporting schedules for cash collections and cash payments.
2. Did the business show a negative cash balance for June? Assuming that the owner has no hope of establishing a line of credit for the business, what recommendations would you give the owner for dealing with a negative cash balance?

E24-9
Flexible Budget
LO 4

Roxanne Johnson, controller for Mix and Feed Company, has been instructed to develop a flexible budget for overhead costs. The company produces two fertilizers called *Ferone* and *Fertwo* that use common raw materials in different proportions. The company expects to produce 100,000 fifty-pound bags of each product during the coming year. Ferone requires 0.25 direct labor hours per bag and Fertwo requires 0.30. Roxanne has developed the following cost formulas for each of the four overhead items (X is measured in direct labor hours):

	Cost Formula
Maintenance	$10,000 + 0.3X
Power	0.5X
Indirect labor	$24,500 + 1.5X
Rent	$18,000

REQUIRED:

1. Prepare an overhead budget for the expected activity level for the coming year.
2. Prepare an overhead budget that reflects production that is 10 percent higher than expected (for both products) and one for production that is 20 percent lower than expected.

E24-10
Performance Report
LO 4

Refer to the information given in Exercise 24-9. Assume that Mix and Feed actually produced 120,000 bags of Ferone and 110,000 of Fertwo. The actual overhead costs incurred were:

Maintenance	$ 26,700
Power	34,000
Indirect labor	108,000
Rent	18,000

REQUIRED:

1. Prepare a performance report for the period.
2. Based on the report, would you judge any of the variances to be significant? Can you think of some possible reasons for the variances?

E24-11
Budgeted Cash Collections; Budgeted Cash Payments
LO 3

Information pertaining to Noskey Corporation's sales revenue is presented below.

	November 1994 (Actual)	*December 1994 (Budget)*	*January 1995 (Budget)*
Cash sales	$ 80,000	$100,000	$ 60,000
Credit sales	240,000	360,000	180,000
Total sales	$320,000	$460,000	$240,000

Management estimates that 5 percent of credit sales are uncollectible. Of the credit sales that are collectible, 60 percent are collected in the month of sale and the remainder in the month following the sale. Purchases of inventory each month are 70 percent of the next month's projected total sales. All purchases of inventory are on account; 25 percent are paid in the month of purchase, and the remainder are paid in the month following the purchase.

REQUIRED:

1. What are Noskey's budgeted cash collections in December 1994 from November 1994 credit sales?
2. What are total budgeted cash receipts in January 1995?
3. What is Noskey budgeting for total cash payments in December 1994 for inventory purchases?

(CMA adapted)

E24-12
Flexible Budgeting
LO 4

Budgeted overhead costs for two different levels of activity are given below.

	Direct Labor Hours	
	1,000	*2,000*
Maintenance	$10,000	$16,000
Depreciation	5,000	5,000
Supervision	15,000	15,000
Supplies	1,400	2,800
Power	750	1,500
Other	8,100	8,200

REQUIRED: Prepare a flexible budget for an activity level of 1,500 direct labor hours.

PROBLEMS

P24-1
Operating Budget; Comprehensive Analysis
LO 1, 2, 3

The Morgan Division of Smith Manufacturing produces a handle assembly used in the production of bows. The assembly is sold to various bow manufacturers throughout the United States. Projected sales for the coming four months are given below.

January	20,000
February	25,000
March	30,000
April	30,000

The following data pertain to production policies and manufacturing specifications followed by the Morgan Division:

a. Finished goods inventory on January 1 is 16,000 units. The desired ending inventory for each month is 80 percent of the next month's sales.
b. The data on materials used are as follows:

Direct Material	*Per-Unit Usage*	*Unit Cost*
Number 325	5	$8
Number 326	3	2

Inventory policy dictates that sufficient materials be on hand at the beginning of the month to produce 50 percent of that month's estimated sales. This is exactly the amount of material on hand on January 1.
c. The direct labor used per unit of output is two hours. The average direct labor cost per hour is $9.25.
d. Overhead each month is estimated using a flexible budget formula. (Activity is measured in direct labor hours.)

	Fixed Cost Component	*Variable Cost Component*
Supplies	—	$1.00
Power	—	0.50
Maintenance	$15,000	0.40
Supervision	8,000	—
Depreciation	100,000	—
Taxes	6,000	—
Other	40,000	1.50

e. Monthly selling and administrative expenses are also estimated using a flexible budgeting formula. (Activity is measured in units sold.)

	Fixed Costs	*Variable Costs*
Salaries	$25,000	—
Commissions	—	$1.00
Depreciation	20,000	—
Shipping	—	0.50
Other	10,000	0.30

f. The unit selling price of the handle assembly is $90.
g. All sales and purchases are for cash. Cash balance on January 1 equals $200,000. If the firm develops a cash shortage by the end of the month, sufficient cash is borrowed to cover the shortage. Any cash borrowed is repaid one month later, as is the interest due. The interest rate is 12 percent per annum.

REQUIRED: Prepare a monthly operating and financial budget for the first quarter with the following schedules:

1. Sales budget
2. Production budget
3. Direct materials purchases budget
4. Direct labor budget
5. Overhead budget
6. Selling and administrative expense budget
7. Ending finished goods budget
8. Cost of goods sold budget
9. Budgeted income statement
10. Cash budget

P24-2 Participative Budgeting; Not-for-Profit Setting

LO 1, 4

Scott Weidner, the controller in the division of social services for the state, recognizes the importance of the budgetary process for planning, control, and motivation. He believes that a properly implemented process of participative budgeting and management by exception will motivate his subordinates to improve productivity within their particular departments. Based upon this philosophy, Scott has implemented the following budgetary procedures:

1. An appropriation target figure is given to each department manager. This amount represents the maximum funding that each department can expect to receive in the next fiscal year.
2. Department managers develop their individual budgets within the following spending constraints as directed by the controller's staff:
   a. Requests for spending cannot exceed the appropriated target.
   b. All fixed expenditures should be included in the budget. Fixed expenditures include such items as contracts and salaries at current levels.
   c. All government projects directed by higher authority should be included in the budget in their entirety.
3. The controller's staff consolidates the requests from the various departments into one budget for the entire division.
4. Upon final budget approval by the legislature, the controller's staff allocates the appropriation to the various departments on instructions from the division manager. However, a specified percentage of each department's appropriation is held back in anticipation of potential budget cuts and special funding needs. The amount and use of this contingency fund is left to the discretion of the division manager.
5. Each department is allowed to adjust its budget when necessary to operate within the reduced appropriation level. However, as stated in the original directive, specific projects authorized by higher authority must remain intact.
6. The final budget is used as the basis of control for a management-by-exception form of reporting. Excessive expenditures by account for each department are highlighted on a monthly basis. Department managers are expected to account for all expenditures over budget. Fiscal responsibility is an important factor in the overall performance evaluation of department managers. Scott believes his policy of allowing the department managers to participate in the budget process and then holding them accountable for the final budget is essential, especially in times of limited resources. He further believes that the department managers will be motivated to increase the efficiency and effectiveness of their departments because they have provided input into the initial budgetary process and are required to justify any unfavorable performances.

REQUIRED:

1. Discuss the advantages and limitations of participative budgeting.
2. Identify deficiencies in Scott Weidner's outline for a budgetary process. Recommend how each deficiency identified can be corrected.

(CMA adapted)

P24-3
Cash Budgeting
LO 3

The controller of Gardner Company is gathering data to prepare the cash budget for April 1995. He plans to develop the budget from the following information:

a. Of all sales, 30 percent are cash sales.
b. Of credit sales, 60 percent are collected within the month of sale. Half of the credit sales collected within the month receive a 2 percent cash discount (for accounts paid within 10 days). Twenty percent of credit sales are collected in the following month; remaining credit sales are collected the month thereafter. There are virtually no bad debts.
c. Sales for the first six months of the year are given below. (The first three months are actual sales and the last three months are estimated sales.)

	Sales
January	$230,000
February	300,000
March	500,000
April	565,000
May	600,000
June	567,000

d. The company sells all that it produces each month. The cost of raw materials equals 20 percent of each sales dollar. The company requires a monthly ending inventory equal to the coming month's production requirements. Of raw materials purchases, 50 percent are paid for in the month of purchase. The remaining 50 percent is paid for in the following month.
e. Wages total $50,000 each month and are paid in the month of incurrence.
f. Budgeted monthly operating expenses total $168,000, of which $22,000 is depreciation and $3,000 is expiration of prepaid insurance. (The annual premium of $36,000 is paid on January 1.)
g. Dividends of $65,000, declared on March 31, will be paid on April 15.
h. Old equipment will be sold for $13,000 on April 3.
i. On April 10, new equipment will be purchased for $80,000.
j. The company maintains a minimum cash balance of $10,000.
k. The cash balance on April 1 is $12,500.

REQUIRED: Prepare a cash budget for April. Give a supporting schedule that details the cash collections from sales.

P24-4
Performance Reporting; Behavioral Considerations
LO 1, 4

Berwin, Inc., is a manufacturer of small industrial tools with annual sales of approximately $3.5 million. Sales growth has been steady during the year, and there is no evidence of cyclical demand. Production has increased gradually during the year and has been evenly distributed throughout each month. The company has a sequential processing system. The four manufacturing departments—casting, machining, finishing, and packaging—are all located in the same building. Fixed overhead is assigned using a plant-wide rate.

Berwin has always been able to compete with other manufacturers of small tools. However, its market has expanded only in response to product innovation. Thus, research and development is very important and has helped Berwin to expand as well as maintain demand.

Carla Viller, controller, has designed and implemented a new budget system in response to concerns voiced by George Berwin, president. Carla prepared an annual budget that has been divided into 12 equal segments; this budget can be used to assist in the timely evaluation of monthly performance. George was visibly upset upon receiving the May performance report for the machining department. George exclaimed, "How can they be efficient enough to produce 9 extra units every working day and still miss the budget by $300 per day?" Gene Jordan, supervisor of the machining department, could not understand "all the red ink" when he knew that the department had operated more efficiently in May than it had in months. Gene stated, "I was expecting a pat on the back and instead the boss tore me apart. What's more, I don't even know why!"

Berwin, Inc.
Machining Department Performance Report
For the Month Ended May 31, 1995

	Budget	*Actual*	*Variance*
Volume in units	3,000	3,185	185 F
Variable manufacturing costs:			
Direct materials	$24,000	$ 24,843	$ 843 U
Direct labor	27,750	29,302	1,552 U
Variable overhead	33,300	35,035	1,735 U
Total variable costs	$85,050	$ 89,180	$4,130 U
Fixed manufacturing costs:			
Indirect labor	$ 3,300	$ 3,334	$ 34 U
Depreciation	1,500	1,500	—
Taxes	300	300	—
Insurance	240	240	—
Other	930	1,027	97 U
Total fixed costs	$ 6,270	$ 6,401	$ 131 U
Corporate costs:			
Research and development	$ 2,400	$ 3,728	$1,328 U
Selling and administrative	3,600	4,075	475 U
Total corporate costs	$ 6,000	$ 7,803	$1,803 U
Total costs	$97,320	$103,384	$6,064 U

REQUIRED:

1. Review the May performance report. Based on the information given in the report and elsewhere:
   a. Discuss the strengths and weaknesses of the new budgetary system.
   b. Identify the weaknesses of the performance report and explain how it should be revised to eliminate each weakness.
2. Prepare a revised report for the machining department using the May data.
3. What other changes would you make to improve Berwin's budgetary system?

(CMA adapted)

P24-5
Master Budget; Comprehensive Review
LO 1, 2, 3

Electra Company is a high-technology organization that produces a mass-storage system. The design of Electra's system is unique and represents a breakthrough in the industry. The units Electra produces combine positive features of both floppy and hard disks. The company is completing its fifth year of operations and is preparing to build its master budget for the coming year (1995). The budget will detail each quarter's activity and the activity for the year in total. The master budget will be based on the following information:

a. Fourth quarter sales for 1994 are 55,000 units.
b. Unit sales by quarter (for 1995) are projected as follows:

First quarter	60,000
Second quarter	65,000
Third quarter	75,000
Fourth quarter	90,000

The selling price is $400 per unit. All sales are credit sales. Electra collects 85 percent of all sales within the quarter in which they are realized; the other 15 percent are collected in the following quarter. There are no bad debts.

c. There is no beginning inventory of finished goods. Electra is planning the following ending finished goods inventories for each quarter:

First quarter	13,000 units
Second quarter	15,000 units
Third quarter	20,000 units
Fourth quarter	10,000 units

d. Each mass-storage unit uses five hours of direct labor and three units of direct materials. Laborers are paid $10 per hour, and one unit of materials costs $80.

e. There are 65,700 units of direct materials in beginning inventory as of January 1, 1995. At the end of each quarter, Electra plans to have 30 percent of the raw materials needed for next quarter's unit sales. Electra will end the year with the same level of raw materials found in this year's beginning inventory.

f. Electra buys raw materials on account. One-half of the purchases are paid for in the quarter of acquisition, and the remaining half is paid for in the following quarter. Wages and salaries are paid on the 15th and 30th of each month.

g. Fixed overhead totals $1 million each quarter. Of this total, $350,000 represents depreciation. All other fixed expenses are paid for in cash in the quarter incurred. The fixed overhead rate is computed by dividing the year's total fixed overhead by the year's expected actual units produced.

h. Variable overhead is budgeted at $6 per direct labor hour. All variable overhead expenses are paid for in the quarter incurred.

i. Fixed selling and administrative expenses total $250,000 per quarter, including $50,000 depreciation.

j. Variable selling and administrative expenses are budgeted at $10 per unit sold. All selling and administrative expenses are paid for in the quarter incurred.

k. The balance sheet as of December 31, 1994, is as follows:

Assets	
Cash	$ 250,000
Accounts receivable	3,300,000
Raw Materials	5,256,000
Plant and equipment	33,500,000
Total assets	$42,306,000

Liabilities and Equity	
Accounts payable	$ 7,248,000[a]
Capital stock	27,000,000
Retained earnings	8,058,000
Total liabilities and equity	$42,306,000

[a]For purchase of materials only

l. Electra will pay quarterly dividends of $300,000. At the end of the fourth quarter, $2 million of equipment will be purchased.

REQUIRED: Prepare a master budget for Electra Company for each quarter of 1995 and for the year in total. The following component budgets must be included:

a. Sales budget
b. Production budget
c. Direct materials purchases budget
d. Direct labor budget
e. Overhead budget
f. Selling and administrative expense budget
g. Ending finished goods inventory budget
h. Cost of goods sold budget
i. Cash budget
j. Pro forma income statement (using absorption costing)
k. Pro forma balance sheet

P24-6
Flexible Budgeting
LO 4

Jean Bingham, controller of Thorpe, Inc., prepared the following budget for manufacturing costs at two levels of activity for 1995:

	Direct Labor Hours	
	100,000	*120,000*
Supervision	$ 180,000	$ 180,000
Utilities	18,000	21,000
Depreciation	25,000	25,000
Supplies	25,000	30,000
Direct labor	1,000,000	1,200,000
Direct materials	220,000	264,000
Maintenance	240,000	284,000
Rent	12,000	12,000
Other	60,000	70,000
Total manufacturing cost	$1,780,000	$2,086,000

During the year, the company worked a total of 112,000 direct labor hours and incurred the following actual costs:

Supervision	$190,000
Utilities	20,500
Depreciation	25,000
Supplies	24,640
Direct labor	963,200
Direct materials	248,000
Maintenance	237,000
Rent	12,000
Other	60,500

Thorpe applies overhead on the basis of direct labor hours. Normal volume of 120,000 direct labor hours is the activity level to compute the predetermined overhead rate.

REQUIRED:

1. Prepare a performance report for Thorpe's manufacturing costs in the year 1995. Should any cost item be given special attention? Explain.
2. Assume that the product produced by Thorpe uses two direct labor hours. Calculate the normal unit manufacturing cost.
3. Compute the total applied overhead for 1995. Compute the overhead variance for the year.

P24-7 Budgeting and Behavioral Consequences

LO 1, 4

Denny Daniels is production manager of the Alumalloy Division of WRT, Inc. Alumalloy has limited contact with outside customers and no sales staff. Most of its customers are handled by other corporate divisions. Therefore, Alumalloy is treated as a cost center rather than a profit center.

Denny perceives the accounting department as the unit that generates historical numbers but provides little useful information. The accounting department creates the budgets at the beginning of the year and then gathers the actual costs incurred by production. Denny wonders whether the accountants even understand the nature of the production process. It seems all they are concerned with are numbers—whether they mean anything or not. In his opinion, the whole accounting process is a negative motivational device that does not reflect how hard or efficiently he has worked as a production manager. Denny tried to discuss these perceptions and concerns with John Scott, the controller for Alumalloy. Denny told John, "I know I've had better production over a number of operating periods, but the cost report still says I have excessive costs. Look, I'm not an accountant, I'm a production manager. I know how to get a good quality product out. Over a number of years, I've even cut the raw materials used to do it. But the cost report doesn't show any of this. It's always negative no matter what I do. There is no way you can win with accounting or those people at corporate who use those reports."

John gave Denny little consolation. John stated that the accounting system and the cost reports generated by headquarters are just part of the corporate game and almost impossible for an individual to change. "Although these reports are the basis for evaluating the efficiency of your division and the means for corporate to determine whether you have done the job it wants, you shouldn't worry too much. You haven't been fired yet! Besides, these cost reports have been used by WRT for the last 25 years."

From talking to the production manager of the Zinc Division, Denny perceived that most of what John said was true. However, some minor cost reporting changes for Zinc had been agreed to by corporate headquarters. He also knew from the trade grapevine that the turnover of production managers was considered high at WRT, even though relatively few managers were fired. Most seemed to end up quitting, usually in disgust, out of the belief that they were not being evaluated fairly.

A recent copy of the cost report prepared by corporate headquarters for Alumalloy is shown below. Because of an unexpected increase in demand for the final product, Alumalloy produced 10,000 units more than the 40,000 originally budgeted. Denny does not like this report because he believes that it fails to reflect the division's operations properly, thereby resulting in an unfair evaluation of performance.

Alumalloy Division
Cost Report
For the Month of April 1995
(in thousands)

	Master Budget	*Actual Cost*	*Variance*
Aluminum	$ 400	$ 477	$ 77 U
Labor	560	675	115 U
Overhead	100	110	10 U
Total	$1,060	$1,262	$202 U

REQUIRED:

1. Comment on Denny's perception of:
   a. John Scott, the controller
   b. Corporate headquarters
   c. The cost report
   d. Himself as a production manager
   e. Discuss how his perception of these items affects his performance as a production manager of WRT.
2. List the deficiencies of WRT's budgetary system. Prepare a list of recommendations to improve the system so that the process and the reports produced are more useful and less threatening to the production managers.

(CMA adapted)

P24-8
Flexible Budget; Purchases Budget; Direct Labor Budget; Cash Budget
LO 3, 4

Hogan's Heroes is a hole-in-the-wall sandwich shop just off the State University campus. Customers enter off the street into a small counter area to order one of ten varieties of sandwiches and a soft drink. All orders must be taken out because there is no space for dining.

The owner of Hogan's Heroes, Paul Hogan, is attempting to construct a series of budgets. He has accumulated the following information:

a. The average sandwich (which sells for $4.25) requires 1 roll, 4 ounces of meat, 2 ounces of cheese, 0.05 head of lettuce, 0.25 of a tomato, and a healthy squirt (1 ounce) of secret sauce.
b. Each customer typically orders one soft drink (average price $1) consisting of a cup and 12 ounces of soda.
c. Use of paper supplies (napkins, bag, sandwich wrap, cup) varies from customer to customer but averages $350 per month.
d. Hogan's Heroes is open for two 8-hour shifts. The noon shift on Monday through Friday requires 5 workers earning $6 per hour (this includes fringe benefits). The evening shift is only on Friday, Saturday, and Sunday nights; the 3 evening shift employees also earn $6 per hour. There are 4.3 weeks in a month.
e. Rent is $75 per month. Other monthly cash expenses average $465.
f. Food costs are:

Meat	$5.00/lb
Cheese	$3.50/lb
Rolls	$24/gross
Lettuce	$12/box (contains 24 heads)
Tomatoes	$1.50/box (contains approximately 20 tomatoes)
Special sauce	$6/gal
Soda (syrup and carbonated water)	$2/gal

In a normal month when school is in session, Hogan sells 5,000 sandwiches. In October, State U. holds its homecoming celebration. Therefore, Hogan figures that if he adds a noon shift on Saturday and Sunday of homecoming weekend, October sales will be 30 percent higher than normal.

REQUIRED: Prepare flexible budgets for a normal school month and for the month of October.

P24-9
Flexible Budgeting
LO 4

Wilson Company employs flexible budgeting techniques to evaluate the performance of several of its activities. The selling expense flexible budgets for three representative monthly activity levels are on the following page.

Representative Monthly Flexible Budgets for Selling Expenses

Activity measures:			
Unit sales volume	400,000	425,000	450,000
Dollar sales volume	$10,000,000	$10,625,000	$11,250,000
Number of orders	4,000	4,250	4,500
Number of salespersons	75	75	75
Monthly expenses:			
Advertising and promotion	$1,200,000	$1,200,000	$1,200,000
Administrative salaries	57,000	57,000	57,000
Sales salaries	75,000	75,000	75,000
Sales commissions	200,000	212,500	225,000
Salesperson travel	170,000	175,000	180,000
Sales office expense	490,000	498,750	507,500
Shipping expense	675,000	712,500	750,000
Total	$2,867,000	$2,930,750	$2,994,500

The following assumptions were used to develop the selling expense flexible budgets:

a. The average size of Wilson's salesforce during the year was planned to be 75 people.
b. Salespersons are paid a monthly salary plus commission on gross dollar sales.
c. The travel costs are best characterized as a step-variable cost. The fixed portion is related to the number of salespersons; the variable portion tends to fluctuate with gross dollar sales.
d. Sales office expense is a mixed cost with the variable portion related to the number of orders processed.
e. Shipping expense is a mixed cost with the variable portion related to the number of units sold.

A salesforce of 80 persons generated a total of 4,300 orders resulting in a sales volume of 420,000 units during November. The gross dollar sales amounted to $10.9 million. The selling expenses incurred for November were as follows:

Advertising and promotion	$1,350,000
Administrative salaries	57,000
Sales salaries	80,000
Sales commissions	218,000
Salesperson travel	185,000
Sales office expense	497,200
Shipping expense	730,000
Total	$3,117,200

REQUIRED:

1. Explain why the selling expense flexible budgets presented above would not be appropriate for evaluating Wilson Company's November selling expenses; indicate how the flexible budget would have to be revised.
2. Prepare a selling expense report for November that Wilson Company can use to evaluate its control over selling expenses. The report should have a line for each selling expense item showing the appropriate budgeted amount, the actual selling expense, and the monthly dollar variation.

(CMA adapted)

DISCUSSION AND INTERPRETATION PROBLEMS

D24-1 Budgetary Performance; Rewards; Ethical Behavior

Linda Ellis, manager of a division that is treated as a profit center, is evaluated and rewarded on the basis of budgetary performance. She, her assistants, and the plant managers are all eligible to receive a bonus if actual divisional profits are between budgeted profits and 120 percent of budgeted profits. The bonuses are based on a fixed percentage of actual profits. Profits above 120 percent of budgeted profits earn a bonus at the 120 percent level (in other words, there is an upper limit on possible bonus payments). If the actual profits are less than budgeted profits, no bonuses are awarded. Now consider the following actions taken by Linda:

a. Linda tends to overestimate expenses and underestimate revenues. This approach facilitates the ability of the division to attain budgeted profits. Linda believes the action is justified because it increases the likelihood of receiving bonuses and helps keep the morale of the managers high.
b. Suppose that towards the end of the fiscal year, Linda saw that the division would not achieve budgeted profits. Accordingly, she instructed the sales department to defer the closing of a number of sales agreements to the following fiscal year. She also decided to write off some inventory that was nearly worthless. Deferring revenues to next year and writing off the inventory in a no-bonus year increased the chances of a bonus for next year.
c. Assume that towards the end of the year, Linda saw that actual profits would likely exceed the 120 percent limit. She took actions similar to those described in part b.

REQUIRED:

1. Comment on the ethics of Linda's behavior. Are her actions right or wrong? What role does the company play in encouraging her actions?
2. Suppose that you are the marketing manager for the division and you receive instructions to defer the closing of sales until the next fiscal year. What would you do?
3. Suppose that you are a plant manager and you know that your budget has been padded by the divisional manager. Further suppose that the padding is common knowledge among the plant managers and is generally supported because it increases the ability to achieve budget and receive a bonus. What would you do?
4. Suppose that you are divisional controller and you receive instructions from the divisional manager to accelerate the recognition of some expenses that legitimately belong to a future period. What would you do?

D24-2 Managerial Decision Case: Cash Budget

According to the analysis of a local consultant, the financial difficulties facing Dr. Roger Jones have been caused by the absence of proper planning and control.[2] Budgetary control is sorely needed. To assist you in preparing a plan of action that will help his dental practice regain financial stability, Dr. Jones has made available the following financial information that describes a typical month:

Revenues

	Average Fee	*Quantity*
Fillings	$ 50	90
Crowns	300	19
Root canals	170	8

(continued)

2. Review the introduction to the chapter for a description of the financial difficulties that Dr. Jones faces on a recurring basis.

Revenues

	Average Fee	*Quantity*
Bridges	500	7
Extractions	45	30
Cleaning	25	108
X-rays	15	150

Costs

Salaries:		
Two dental assistants	$1,900	
Receptionist/bookkeeper	1,500	
Hygienist	1,800	
Public relations (Mrs. Jones)	1,000	
Personal salary	6,500	
Total salaries		$12,700
Benefits		1,344
Building lease		1,500
Dental supplies		1,200
Janitorial		300
Utilities		400
Phone		150
Office supplies		100
Lab fees		5,000
Loan payments		570
Interest payments		500
Miscellaneous		500
Depreciation		700
Total costs		$24,964

Benefits include Dr. Jones's share of social security and a health insurance premium for all employees. Although all revenues billed in a month are not collected, the cash flowing into the business is approximately equal to the month's billings because of collections from prior months. The dental office is open Monday through Thursday from 8:30 a.m. to 4:00 p.m. and on Friday from 8:30 a.m. to 12:30 p.m. A total of 32 hours are worked each week. Additional hours could be worked, but Dr. Jones is reluctant to do so because of other personal endeavors that he enjoys.

Dr. Jones has noted that the two dental assistants and the receptionist are not fully utilized. He estimates that they are busy about 65-70 percent of the time. Dr. Jones's wife spends about five hours each week on a monthly newsletter that is sent to all patients; she also maintains a birthday list and sends cards to the patients on their birthdays.

Dr. Jones spends about $2,400 yearly on informational seminars. These seminars, targeted especially for dentists, teach them how to increase their revenues. It is from one of these seminars that Dr. Jones decided to invest in promotion and public relations (the newsletter and the birthday list).

REQUIRED:

1. Prepare a monthly cash budget for Dr. Jones. Does Dr. Jones have a significant cash flow problem? How would you use the budget to show Dr. Jones why he is having financial difficulties?
2. Using the cash budget prepared in Requirement 1 and the information given in the case, prepare some recommendations to solve Dr. Jones's financial problems. Prepare a cash budget that reflects these recommendations and demonstrates to Dr. Jones that the problems can be corrected. Do you think that Dr. Jones will accept your recom-

mendations? Do any of the behavioral principles discussed in the chapter have a role in this type of setting? Explain.

D24-3 Research Assignment

In Chapter 23, you were introduced to the concept of resource supply and resource demand. The ABC model of resource supply and usage can significantly enhance the ability of managers to build good budgets. To understand the potential of its application in budgeting, read the following article:

Robin Cooper and Robert S. Kaplan, "Activity-Based Systems: Measuring the Costs of Resource Usage," *Accounting Horizons,* (September 1992), pp. 1–13.

Once you have read the article, write a short paper describing the effects of the ABC model on budgeting. Provide a numerical example that illustrates your points.

CHAPTER 25
STANDARD COSTING: A MANAGERIAL CONTROL TOOL

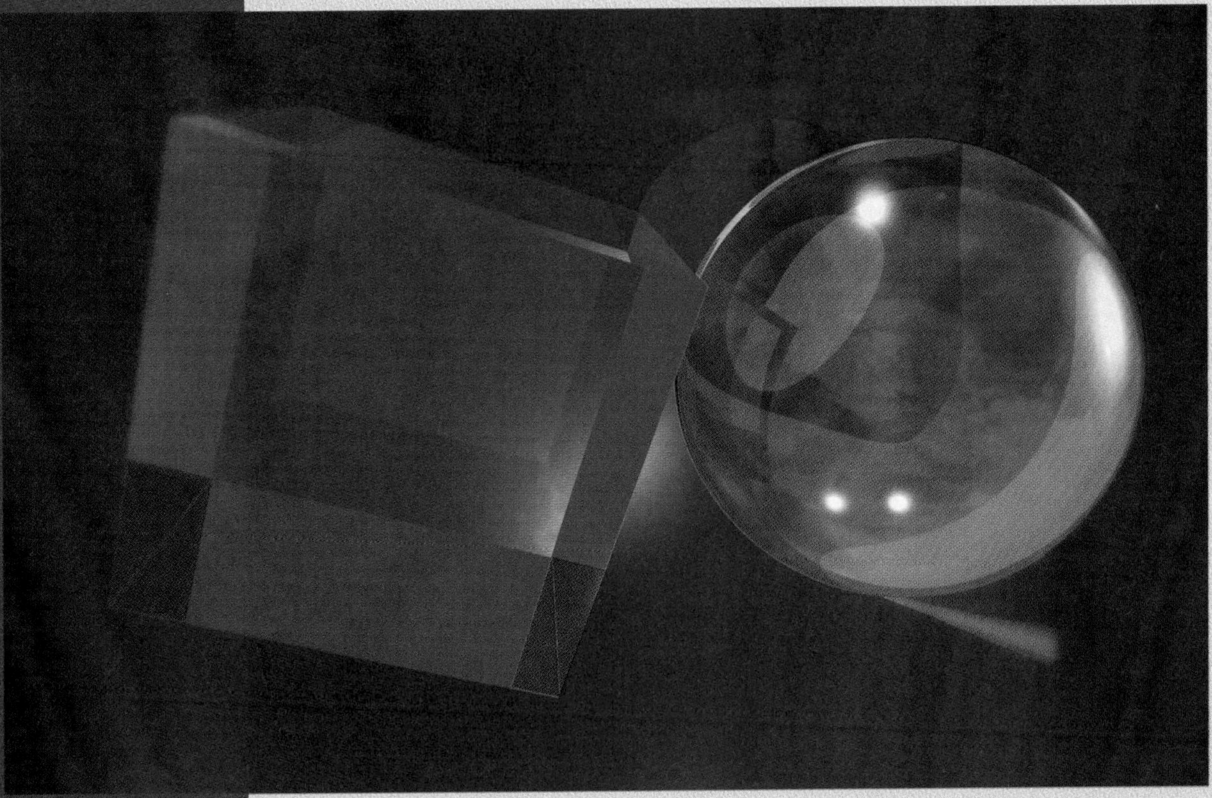

LEARNING OBJECTIVES

After studying this chapter, you should be able to:

1. Explain how unit standards are set and why standard cost systems are adopted.
2. Explain the purpose of a standard cost sheet.
3. Describe the basic concepts underlying variance analysis and explain when variances should be investigated.
4. Compute the materials and labor variances and explain how they are used for control.
5. Compute the variable and fixed overhead variances and explain their meanings.

Scenario

Millie Anderson, manager of Honley Medical's IV products division, was more than satisfied with the performance of her division last year. At the beginning of the year, the division had introduced a new line of polyurethane catheters, replacing the old teflon catheters, and sales had more than tripled. The reaction of the market to the new catheter represented a virtual replay of the company's history.

Nearly 30 years ago, Lindell Honley, the founder of Honley Medical, had perceived the need for something other than a metal needle for long-term insertion into veins. Metal needles were irritating and could damage the vein. Based on this observation, Honley had developed a catheter using teflon since it was a lubricated plastic and easy to insert into the vein. The new development was well received by the medical community and produced a new and successful company, one that had expanded its activities into a variety of medical products.

For years, because of the new technology, Honley had dominated the market. Eventually, however, the patent expired and other companies entered the market with their own teflon catheters, making competition exceptionally keen. Prices had been driven down, and profit margins were eroding.

The eroding profit margins had prompted Millie and other high-level managers to examine the continued viability of the teflon catheters. After many years, the medical profession had noted that after 24 hours of use, an infection tended to develop around the point of insertion. Researchers at Honley Medical had discovered that the problem was one of incompatibility of the blood and tissue with the teflon. Further studies showed that different plastics produced different reactions. Research began immediately on finding a material that was more biocompatible than teflon. The outcome was polyurethane catheters. The new catheter could be left in for 72 hours, compared to the 24 hours for teflon catheters.

Once again, Honley Medical was establishing a dominant position in the IV market. Millie also knew that history would repeat itself in the later stages, as well—the time would come when other firms would produce catheters with the same degree of biocompatibility. In fact, Honley's research scientists estimated that competitors would have a competing catheter on the market within three years. This time, however, Millie was determined to protect the division's market share. And better protection required a different approach. Although further research into biocompatibility was being conducted, Millie was convinced that this approach would not be as fruitful as in the past. Most patients had little need for a catheter beyond 72 hours. Thus, further improvements in biocompatibility were not likely to produce the same favorable market reaction.

In the past, because of its dominant position, the division had not been too concerned with control of manufacturing costs. Only when profit margins had begun to erode had some mention of a need for better cost control been made. Unfortunately, once the opportunity for an improved catheter was identified, the focus was again on technological dominance. Millie had decided that it was time to resurrect the cost control issue. By implementing cost control measures now, she believed that the division would be better able to compete on price when the competition resurfaced within a few years. Her conversation below with Reed McCourt, divisional controller, reflects this decision.

Millie: "Reed, as I see it, the only attempt we make to control manufacturing costs is our budgetary system. Is that right?"

Reed: "Yes. But it really isn't a very good effort. Budgets are based on last year's costs plus some allowance for inflation. At this point, we have never tried to identify what the costs *ought* to be. Nor have we really held managers responsible for cost control. Our profitability has always been good—resources have always been plentiful. My guess is that we are spending much more than necessary simply because we have been so successful."

Millie: "Well, resources wouldn't be so plentiful now if we hadn't developed the polyurethane catheter. And I'm afraid that resources won't be plentiful in the future unless we take actions now to control our manufacturing costs. Besides, if we can be more profitable now by using better cost control, we ought to use it. I want better cost control, and I want my plant and production managers to recognize their responsibilities in this area. What suggestions do you have?"

Reed: "We need to inject more formality into the budgetary system. First, budgets should reflect what costs should be, not what they have been. Second, we can encourage managers to be cost conscious by allowing them to help identify efficient levels of cost on which the budget will be based and tying their bonuses and promotions into the system as well. However, I think we can gain the cost control by going one step further and establishing a standard cost system."

Millie: "Doesn't that entail the specification of unit price and quantity standards for materials and labor?"

Reed: "That's essentially correct. Using the unit price and quantity standards, budgeted costs for labor, materials, and overhead are established for each unit produced. These unit costs are used to develop budgets and—once actual costs are in—to break down the budgetary variances into a price variance and an efficiency variance. A standard cost system provides more detailed control information than a budgetary system using normal costing. We can hold our managers responsible for meeting the standards that are established."

Millie: "I think our division needs this type of system. It's about time that our managers become cost conscious. Reed, prepare a report that provides more detail on what a standard cost system is all about."

UNIT STANDARDS

Objective 1
Explain how unit standards are set and why standard cost systems are adopted.

Millie and Reed both recognized the need to encourage operating managers to control costs. Cost control often means the difference between success and failure or between above-average profits and average or below-average profits. Millie was convinced that cost control meant that her managers had to be cost conscious and they had to assume responsibility for this important objective. Reed suggested that the way to control costs and involve managers is through the use of a formal budgetary system.

In Chapter 24, we learned that budgets set standards that are used to control and evaluate managerial performance. However, budgets are aggregate measures of performance; they identify the revenues and costs in total that an organization should experience if plans are executed as expected. By comparing the actual costs and actual revenues with the corresponding budgeted amounts at the same level of activity, a measure of managerial efficiency emerges.

Although the process just described provides significant information for control, control can be enhanced by developing standards for *unit* amounts as well as for total amounts. In fact, the groundwork for unit standards already exists within the framework of flexible budgeting. For flexible budgeting to work, the budgeted variable cost per unit of input for each unit of output must be known for every item in the budget. The budgeted variable input cost per unit of output is a unit standard. Unit standards are the basis or foundation on which a flexible budget is built.

quantity standards
price standards

To determine the unit standard cost for a particular input, two decisions must be made: (1) how much of the input should be used per unit of output (the *quantity decision*) and (2) how much should be paid for the quantity of the input to be used (the *pricing decision*). The quantity decision produces **quantity standards,** and the pricing decision produces **price standards.** The unit standard cost can be computed by multiplying these two standards.

For example, a soft-drink bottling company may decide that five ounces of fructose should be used for every 16-ounce bottle of cola (the quantity standard) and the price of the fructose should be $0.05 per ounce (the price standard). The standard cost of the fructose per bottle of cola is then $0.25 (5 × $0.05). The standard cost per unit of fructose can be used to predict what the total cost of fructose should be as the activity level varies; it thus becomes a flexible budget formula. Thus, if 10,000 bottles of cola are produced, the total expected cost of fructose is $2,500 ($0.25 × 10,000); if 15,000 bottles are produced, the total expected cost of fructose is $3,750 ($0.25 × 15,000).

How Standards Are Developed

Historical experience, engineering studies, and input from operating personnel are three potential sources of quantitative standards. Although historical experience may provide an initial guideline for setting standards, it should be used with caution. Often, processes are operating inefficiently; adopting input-output relationships from the past thus perpetuates these inefficiencies. The IV division of Honley Medical, for example, had never emphasized cost control and had operated in a resource-rich environment. Both the divisional manager and controller were convinced that significant inefficiencies existed. Engineering studies can determine the most efficient way to operate and can provide very rigorous guidelines; however, engineered standards are often too rigorous. They may not be achievable by operating personnel. Since operating personnel are accountable for meeting the standards, they should have significant input in setting standards. The same principles pertaining to participative budgeting pertain to setting unit standards.

Price standards are the joint responsibility of operations, purchasing, personnel, and accounting. Operations determines the quality of the inputs required; personnel and purchasing have the responsibility to acquire the input quality requested at the lowest price. Market forces, trade unions, and other external forces limit the range of choices for price standards. In setting price standards, purchasing must consider discounts, freight, and quality; personnel, on the other hand, must consider payroll taxes, fringe benefits, and qualifications. Accounting is responsible for recording the price standards and preparing reports that compare actual performance to the standard.

Types of Standards

ideal standards

currently attainable standards

Standards are generally classified as either *ideal* or *currently attainable.* **Ideal standards** are standards that demand maximum efficiency and can be achieved only if everything operates perfectly. No machine breakdowns, slack, or lack of skill (even momentarily) are allowed. **Currently attainable standards** can be achieved under efficient operating conditions. Allowance is made for normal breakdowns, interruptions, less than perfect skill, and so on. These standards are demanding but achievable.

Of the two types, currently attainable standards offer the most behavioral benefits. If standards are too tight and never achievable, workers become frustrated and performance levels decline. However, challenging but achievable standards tend to extract higher performance levels—particularly when the individuals subject to the standards have participated in their creation.

Why Standard Cost Systems Are Adopted

Two reasons for adopting a standard cost system are frequently mentioned: to improve planning and control and to facilitate product costing.

Planning and Control. Standard costing systems enhance planning and control and improve performance measurement. Unit standards are a fundamental requirement for a flexible budgeting system, which is a key feature of a meaningful planning and control system. Budgetary control systems compare actual costs with budgeted costs by computing variances, the difference between the actual and planned costs for the actual level of activity. By developing unit price and quantity standards, an overall variance can be decomposed into a *price variance* and a *usage or efficiency variance.*

By performing this decomposition, a manager has more information. If the variance is unfavorable, a manager can tell whether it is attributable to discrepancies between planned prices and actual prices, to discrepancies between planned usage and actual usage, or to both. Since managers have more control over the usage of inputs than over their prices, efficiency variances provide specific signals regarding the need for corrective action and where that action should be focused. Thus, in principle, the use of efficiency variances enhances operational control. Additionally, by breaking out the price variance, over which managers have little control, the system provides an improved measure of managerial efficiency.

The benefits of operational control, however, may not extend to the advanced manufacturing environment. The use of a standard cost system for operational control in an advanced manufacturing environment can produce dysfunctional behavior. Thus, the detailed computation of variances—at least at the operational level—is discouraged in this new environment. Nonetheless, standards in the advanced manufacturing environment are still useful for planning, for example, in the creation of bids. Also, variances may still be computed and presented in reports to higher-level managers so that the financial dimension can be monitored.

Finally, it should be mentioned that there are many firms operating with conventional manufacturing systems. Standard cost systems are widely used. In a recent survey, 87 percent of the firms responding used a standard cost system.[1] Furthermore, the survey revealed that significant numbers of the respondents were calculating variances at the operational level. For example, about 40 percent of the firms using a standard costing system reported labor variances for small work crews or individual workers.

Product Costing. In a standard cost system, costs are assigned to products using quantity and price standards for all three manufacturing costs: direct materials, direct labor, and overhead. In contrast, a normal cost system predetermines overhead costs for the purpose of product costing but assigns direct materials and direct labor to products by using actual costs. Overhead is assigned using a budgeted rate and actual activity. At the other end of the cost assignment spectrum, an actual cost system assigns the actual costs of all three manufacturing inputs to products. Exhibit 25-1 summarizes these three cost assignment approaches.

Standard product costing has several advantages over normal costing and actual costing. One, of course, is the greater capacity for control. Standard cost systems also provide readily available unit cost information that can be used for pricing decisions. This is particularly helpful for companies that do a significant amount of bidding and those paid on a cost-plus basis.[2]

Other simplifications are also possible. For example, if a process-costing system uses standard costing to assign product costs, there is no need to compute a unit cost for each equivalent unit-cost category. A standard unit cost would exist for each category.[3] Additionally, there is no need to distinguish between the FIFO and weighted-average methods of accounting for beginning inventory costs. Usually, a standard process costing system will follow the equivalent unit calculation of the FIFO approach. That is, *current* equivalent units of work are calculated. By calculating current equivalent work, current actual production costs can be compared with standard costs for control purposes.

Exhibit 25-1
Cost Assignment Approaches

	Manufacturing Costs		
	Direct Materials	*Direct Labor*	*Overhead*
Actual cost system	Actual	Actual	Actual
Normal cost system	Actual	Actual	Budgeted
Standard cost system	Standard	Standard	Standard

1. Bruce R. Gaumnitz and Felix P. Kollaritsch, "Manufacturing Variances: Current Practice and Trends," *Journal of Cost Management* (Spring 1991), pp. 58–64.
2. For example, the concrete and pipe company (CalBlock, Inc.) mentioned in the previous chapter conducts the vast majority of its business through bidding. This company recently adopted a standard cost system primarily to facilitate the bidding process.
3. If you have not read the chapter on process costing, the example illustrating the simplifications made possible by standard costing will not be as meaningful. However, the point being made is still relevant. Standard costing can bring useful computational savings.

STANDARD PRODUCT COSTS

Objective 2
Explain the purpose of a standard cost sheet.

standard cost per unit
standard cost sheet

The most common application of standard costing is found within manufacturing organizations.[4] Standard costs are developed for materials, labor, and overhead. Using these costs, the **standard cost per unit** is computed. The **standard cost sheet** provides the detail underlying the standard unit cost.

To illustrate, let us develop a standard cost sheet for a 16-ounce bag of corn chips produced by Crunchy Chips Company. The production of corn chips begins by steaming and soaking corn kernels overnight in a lime solution. This process softens the kernels so that they can be shaped into a sheet of dough. The dough is then cut into small triangular chips. Next, the chips are toasted in an oven and dropped into a deep fryer. After cooking, the chips pass under a salting device and are inspected for quality. Substandard chips are sorted and discarded; the chips passing inspection are bagged by a packaging machine. The bagged chips are manually packed into boxes for shipping.

Four materials are used to process corn chips: yellow corn, cooking oil, salt, and lime. The package in which the chips are placed is also classified as a direct material. Crunchy Chips has two types of direct laborers: machine operators and inspectors (or sorters). Variable overhead is made up of three costs: gas, electricity, and water; it is applied using direct labor hours. Fixed overhead is also applied using direct labor hours. The standard cost sheet is given in Exhibit 25-2. From Exhibit 25-2, note that it should cost $0.54 to produce a 16-ounce package of corn chips. Also notice that the company uses 18 ounces of corn to produce a 16-ounce package of chips. There are two reasons. First, some chips are discarded during the inspection process. The company plans on a normal amount of waste. Second, the company wants to have more than 16 ounces in each package to increase customer satisfaction with its product.

Exhibit 25-2 also reveals other important insights. The standard usage for variable and fixed overhead is tied to the direct labor standards. For variable overhead, the rate is $3.85 per direct labor hour. Since one package of corn chips uses 0.0078 direct labor hours, the variable overhead cost assigned to a package of corn chips is $0.03 ($3.85 × 0.0078). For fixed overhead, the rate is $32.05 per direct labor hour, making the fixed overhead cost per package of corn chips $0.25 ($32.05 × 0.0078). Nearly half of the cost of production is fixed, indicating a capital-intensive production effort. Indeed, much of the operation is mechanized.

standard quantity of materials allowed (SQ)
standard hours allowed (SH)

The standard cost sheet also reveals the quantity of each input that should be used to produce one unit of output. The unit quantity standards can be used to compute the total amount of inputs allowed for the actual output. This computation is an essential component in computing efficiency variances. A manager should be able to compute the **standard quantity of materials allowed** *(SQ)* and the **standard hours allowed** *(SH)* for the actual output. This computation must be done for every class of direct material and every class of direct labor. Assume, for example, that 100,000 packages of corn chips are produced during the first

4. Standard costs are also used in many nonmanufacturing organizations. The federal government, for example, is using a standard-costing system for purposes of reimbursement of Medicare costs. Based on several studies, illnesses have been classified into diagnostic related groups (DRGs) and the hospital costs that should be incurred for an average case identified. (The costs include patient days, food, medicine, supplies, use of equipment, and so on.) The government pays the hospital the standard cost for the DRG. If the cost of the patient's treatment is greater than the DRG allows, the hospital suffers a loss. If the cost of the patient's treatment is less than the DRG reimbursement, the hospital gains. On average, the hospital supposedly breaks even.

Exhibit 25-2
Standard Cost Sheet for Corn Chips

Description	*Standard Price*	*Standard Usage*	*Standard Cost*[1]	*Subtotal*
Direct materials:				
Yellow corn	$0.006	18 oz	$0.108	
Cooking oil	0.031	2 oz	0.062	
Salt	0.005	1 oz	0.005	
Lime	0.100	0.01 oz	0.001	
Bags	0.044	1 bag	0.044	
Total direct materials				$0.220
Direct labor:				
Inspection	5.00	0.0070 hrs	$0.035	
Machine operators	6.50	0.0008 hrs	0.005	
Total direct labor				0.040
Overhead:				
Variable overhead	3.85	0.0078 hrs	$0.030	
Fixed overhead	32.05	0.0078 hrs	0.250	
Total overhead				0.280
Total standard unit cost				$0.540

[1]Calculated by multiplying price times usage

week of March. How much yellow corn should have been used for the actual output of 100,000 packages? The unit quantity standard is 18 ounces of yellow corn per package (see Exhibit 25-2). For 100,000 packages, the standard quantity of yellow corn allowed is computed as follows:

$$\begin{aligned} SQ &= \text{Unit quantity standard} \times \text{Actual output} \\ &= 18 \times 100{,}000 \\ &= 1{,}800{,}000 \text{ ounces} \end{aligned}$$

The computation of standard direct labor hours allowed can be illustrated using machine operators. From Exhibit 25-2, we see that the unit quantity standard is 0.0008 hours per package produced. Thus, if 100,000 packages are produced, the standard hours allowed is as follows:

$$\begin{aligned} SH &= \text{Unit quantity standard} \times \text{Actual output} \\ &= 0.0008 \times 100{,}000 \\ &= 80 \text{ direct labor hours} \end{aligned}$$

VARIANCE ANALYSIS: GENERAL DESCRIPTION

Objective 3
Describe the basic concepts underlying variance analysis and explain when variances should be investigated.

A flexible budget can be used to identify the costs that should have been incurred for the actual level of activity. This figure is obtained by multiplying the amount of input allowed for the actual output by the standard unit price. Letting SP be the standard unit price of an input and SQ the standard quantity of inputs allowed for the actual output, the planned or budgeted input cost is $SP \times SQ$. The actual input cost is $AP \times AQ$, where AP is the actual price per unit of the input and AQ is the actual quantity of input used.

Price and Efficiency Variances

total budget variance

The **total budget variance** is simply the difference between the actual cost of the input and its planned cost. For simplicity, we will refer to the total budget variance as the *total variance.*

$$\text{Total variance} = (AP \times AQ) - (SP \times SQ)$$

price (rate) variance

usage (efficiency) variance

In a standard cost system, the total variance is broken down into price and usage variances. **Price (rate) variance** is the difference between the actual and standard unit price of an input multiplied by the number of inputs used. **Usage (efficiency) variance** is the difference between the actual and standard quantity of inputs multiplied by the standard unit price of the input. As mentioned earlier, by breaking the total budget variance down into these two components, managers can better analyze and control the total variance. They are able to identify the origin of cost increases and take appropriate corrective action.

Dividing the total variance into price and efficiency components is accomplished by subtracting and adding *SP* X *AQ* to the right-hand side of the total variance equation:

$$\begin{aligned}\text{Total variance} &= [(AP \times AQ) - (SP \times AQ)] + \\ &\quad [(SP \times AQ) - (SP \times SQ)] \\ &= (AP - SP)AQ + (AQ - SQ)SP \\ &= \text{Price variance} + \text{Usage variance}\end{aligned}$$

Exhibit 25-3 presents a three-pronged diagram that describes this process.

Usually, the total variance is divided into price and efficiency components for direct materials and direct labor. The treatment of overhead is discussed later in the chapter.

Exhibit 25-3
Variance Analysis: General Description

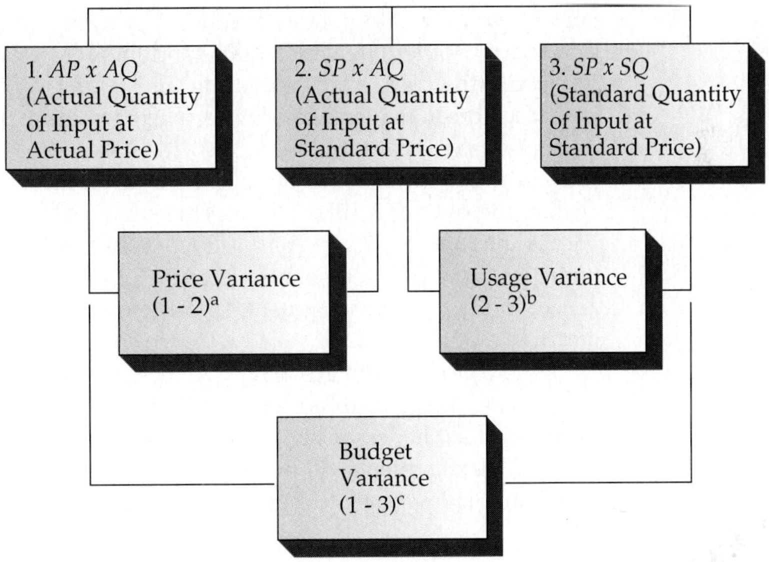

[a] Price Variance = (*AP x AQ*) - (*SP x AQ*) = (*AP - SP*)*AQ*
[b] Usage Variance = (*SP x AQ*) - (SP x SQ) = (*AP - SQ*)*SP*
[c] Budget Variance = (*AP x AQ*) - (*SP x SQ*)

unfavorable (U) variances
favorable (F) variances

Unfavorable (U) variances occur whenever actual prices or usage of inputs is greater than standard prices or usage. When the opposite occurs, **favorable (F) variances** are obtained. Favorable and unfavorable variances are not equivalent to good and bad variances. The terms merely indicate the relationship of the actual prices or quantities to the standard prices and quantities. Whether or not the variances are good or bad depends on *why* they occurred. Determining why requires managers to do some investigation.

The Decision to Investigate

Rarely will actual performance exactly meet the established standards nor does management expect it to. Random variations around the standard are expected. Because of this, management should have in mind an acceptable range of performance. When variances are within this range, they are assumed to be caused by random factors. When a variance falls outside this range, the deviation is likely to be caused by nonrandom factors, either factors that managers can control or factors they cannot control. In the noncontrollable case, managers need to revise the standard.

When to investigate variances is a critical issue. Investigating the cause of variances and taking corrective action, like all activities, have a cost associated with them. As a general principle, an investigation should be undertaken only if the anticipated benefits are greater than the expected costs. Assessing the costs and benefits of a variance investigation is not an easy task, however. A manager must consider whether a variance will recur. If so, the process may be permanently out of control, meaning that periodic savings may be achieved if corrective action is taken. But how can we tell if the variance is going to recur unless an investigation is conducted? And how do we know the cost of corrective action unless the cause of the variance is known?

Because it is difficult to assess the costs and benefits of variance analysis on a case-by-case basis, many firms adopt the general guideline of investigating variances only if they fall outside an acceptable range. They are not investigated unless they are large enough to be of concern. They must be large enough to be caused by something other than random factors and large enough (on average) to justify the costs of investigating and taking corrective action.

control limits

How do managers determine whether variances are significant? How is the acceptable range established? The acceptable range is the standard plus or minus an allowable deviation. The top and bottom measures of the allowable range are called the **control limits.** The *upper control limit* is the standard plus the allowable deviation, and the *lower control limit* is the standard minus the allowable deviation. Current practice sets the control limits subjectively: based on past experience, intuition, and judgment, management determines the allowable deviation from standard.[5]

The control limits are usually expressed both as a percentage of the standard and as an absolute dollar amount. For example, the allowable deviation may be expressed as the lesser of 10 percent of the standard amount, or $10,000. In other words, management will not accept a deviation of more than $10,000 even if that deviation is less than 10 percent of the standard. Alternatively, even if the dollar

5. Gaumnitz and Kollaritsch, "Manufacturing Variances: Current Practice and Trends," report that about 45 to 47 percent of the firms use dollar or percentage control limits. Most of the remaining use judgment rather than any formal identification of limits.

amount is less than $10,000, an investigation is required if the deviation is more than 10 percent of the standard amount.

Formal statistical procedures can also be used to set the control limits. In this way, less subjectivity is involved and a manager can assess the likelihood of the variance being caused by random factors. At this time, the use of such formal procedures has gained little acceptance.[6]

VARIANCE ANALYSIS: MATERIALS AND LABOR

Objective 4
Compute the materials and labor variances and explain how they are used for control.

The total variance measures the difference between the actual cost of materials and labor and their budgeted costs for the actual level of activity. To illustrate, consider these selected data for Crunchy Chips from the first week of March:[7]

Actual production: 48,500 bags of corn chips
Actual corn usage: 750,000 ounces
Actual price paid per ounce of corn: $0.0069
Actual hours of inspection: 360 hours
Actual wage rate: $5.35 per hour

Using the above actual data and the unit standards from Exhibit 25-2, a performance report for the first week of March can be developed (see Exhibit 25-4). As has been mentioned, the total variance can be divided into price and usage variances, providing more information to the manager. We will do so in the following sections.

Direct Materials Variances

The three-pronged approach illustrated in Exhibit 25-3 can be used to calculate the materials price and usage variances. This calculation for the Crunchy Chips example is illustrated in Exhibit 25-5. Only the price and usage variances for corn are shown. Many find this graphical approach to be easier than the use of variance formulas.

Exhibit 25-4
Performance Report: Total Variances

	Actual Costs	*Budgeted Costs*[1]	*Total Variance*
Corn	$5,175.00	$5,238.00	$ 63.00 F
Inspection labor	1,926.00	1,697.50	228.50 U

[1]The standard quantities for materials and labor are computed as follows, using unit quantity standards from Exhibit 25-2:

Materials: 18 × 48,500 = 873,000 ounces
Labor: 0.007 × 48,500 = 339.5 hours

Multiplying these standard quantities by the unit standard prices given in Exhibit 25-2 produces the budgeted amounts appearing in this column.

6. According to Gaumnitz and Kollaritsch, "Manufacturing Variances: Current Practice and Trends," only about 1 percent of the responding firms used formal statistical procedures.
7. To keep the example simple, only one material (corn) and one type of labor (inspection) are illustrated. A complete analysis for the company would include all types of materials and labor categories.

Exhibit 25-5
Price and Usage Variances: Direct Materials

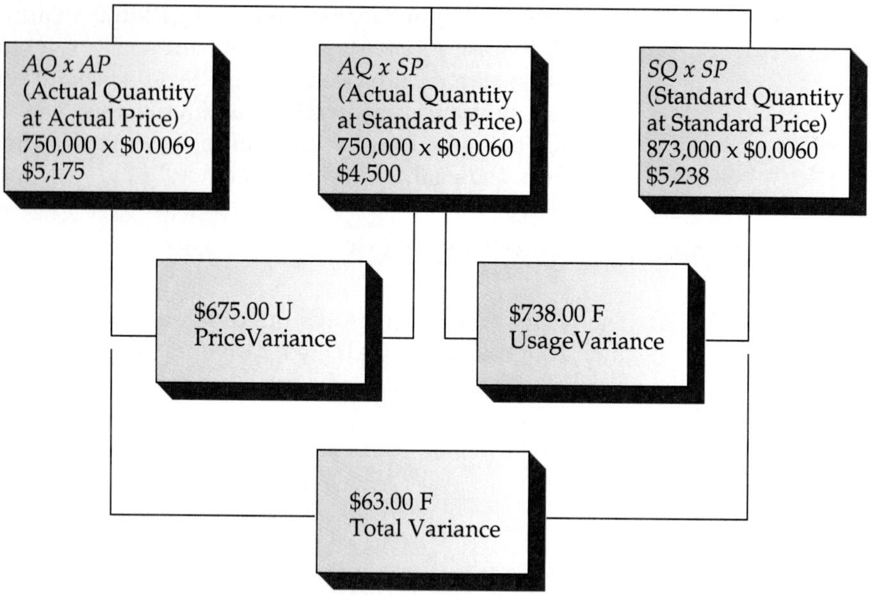

SP = $.0060 (from Exhibit 15-2)
SQ = 873,000 oz. (from Exhibit 15-4)

materials price variance

Materials Price Variance: Formula Approach. The materials price variance can be calculated separately. The **materials price variance** (*MPV*) measures the difference between what should have been paid for raw materials and what was actually paid. A simple formula for computing this variance is:

$$MPV = (AP \times AQ) - (SP \times AQ)$$

or, factoring, we have:

$$MPV = (AP - SP)AQ$$

where AP = The actual price per unit
SP = The standard price per unit
AQ = The actual quantity of material used

Computation of the Materials Price Variance. Crunchy Chips purchased and used 750,000 ounces of yellow corn for the first week of March. The purchase price was $0.0069 per ounce. Thus, *AP* is $0.0069, *AQ* is 750,000 ounces, and *SP* (from Exhibit 25-2) is $0.0060. Using this information, the materials price variance is computed as follows:

$$\begin{aligned} MPV &= (AP - SP)AQ \\ &= (\$0.0069 - \$0.0060)750{,}000 \\ &= \$0.0009 \times 750{,}000 \\ &= \$675\text{ U} \end{aligned}$$

Responsibility for the Materials Price Variance. The responsibility for controlling the materials price variance is usually the purchasing agent's. Admittedly, the price of materials is largely beyond his or her control; however, the price variance can be influenced by such factors as quality, quantity discounts, distance of the source from the plant, and so on. These factors are often under the control of the agent.

Using the price variance to evaluate the performance of purchasing has some limitations. Emphasis on meeting or beating standard can produce some undesirable outcomes. For example, if the purchasing agent feels pressured to produce favorable variances, materials of lower quality than desired may be purchased or too much inventory may be acquired to take advantage of quantity discounts.

Analysis of the Materials Price Variance. The first step in variance analysis is deciding whether the variance is significant or not. If it is judged to be insignificant, no further steps are needed. Assume that an unfavorable materials price variance of $675 is judged to be significant. The next step is to find out why it occurred.

For the Crunchy Chips example, the investigation revealed that a higher-quality corn was purchased because of a shortage of the usual grade in the market. Once the reason is known, corrective action can be taken if necessary—and possible. In this case, no corrective action is needed. The firm has no control over the supply shortage; it will simply have to wait until market conditions improve.

Timing of the Price Variance Computation. The materials price variance can be computed at one of two points: (1) when the raw materials are issued for use in production or (2) when they are purchased. Computing the price variance at the point of purchase is preferable. It is better to have information on variances earlier than later. The more timely the information, the more likely proper managerial action can be taken. Old information is often useless information.

Materials may sit in inventory for weeks or months before they are needed in production. By the time the materials price variance is computed, signaling a problem, it may be too late to take corrective action. Or, even if corrective action is still possible, the delay may cost the company thousands of dollars. For example, suppose a new purchasing agent is unaware of the availability of a quantity discount on a raw material. If the materials price variance that ignores the discount is computed when a new purchase is made, the resulting unfavorable signal would lead to quick corrective action. (In this case, the action would be to use the discount for future purchases.) If the materials price variance is not computed until the material is issued to production, it may be several weeks or even months before the problem is discovered.

If the materials price variance is computed at the point of purchase, *AQ* needs to be redefined as the actual quantity of materials *purchased*, rather than actual materials used. Since the materials purchased may differ from the materials used, the overall materials budget variance is not necessarily the sum of the materials price variance and the materials usage variance. When the materials purchased are all used in production for the period in which the variances are calculated, the two variances will equal the total variance.

Recognizing the price variance for materials at the point of purchase also means that the raw materials inventory is carried at standard cost.

materials usage variance

Direct Materials Usage Variance: Formula Approach. The **materials usage variance** (*MUV*) measures the difference between the direct materials actually used and the direct materials that should have been used for the actual output. The formula for computing this variance is:

$$MUV = (SP \times AQ) - (SP \times SQ)$$

or, factoring:

$$MUV = (AQ - SQ)SP$$

where

AQ = The actual quantity of materials used
SQ = The standard quantity of materials allowed for the actual output
SP = The standard price per unit

Computation of the Materials Usage Variance. Crunchy Chips used 750,000 ounces of yellow corn to produce 48,500 bags of corn chips. Therefore, *AQ* is 750,000. From Exhibit 25-2, we see that *SP* is $0.006 per ounce of yellow corn. Although standard materials allowed *(SQ)* has already been computed in Exhibit 25-4, the details underlying the computation need to be reviewed. Recall that *SQ* is the product of the unit quantity standard and the actual units produced. From Exhibit 25-2, the unit standard is 18 ounces of yellow corn for every bag of corn chips. Thus, *SQ* is 18 × 48,500, or 873,000 ounces. Thus, the materials usage variance is computed as follows:

$$\begin{aligned} MUV &= (AQ - SQ)SP \\ &= (750{,}000 - 873{,}000)(\$0.006) \\ &= \$738\ \text{F} \end{aligned}$$

Responsibility for the Materials Usage Variance. The production manager is generally responsible for materials usage. Minimizing scrap, waste, and rework are all ways in which the manager can ensure that the standard is met. However, at times the cause of the variance is attributable to others outside the production area, as the next section shows.

As with the price variance, using the usage variance to evaluate performance can lead to undesirable behavior. For example, a production manager feeling pressure to produce a favorable variance might allow a defective unit to be transferred to finished goods. While this avoids the problem of wasted materials, it may create customer-relations problems.

Analysis of the Variance. Investigation revealed that the favorable materials usage variance is the result of the higher-quality corn acquired by the Purchasing Department. In this case, the favorable variance is essentially assignable to Purchasing. Since the materials usage variance is favorable—and larger than the unfavorable price variance—the overall result of the change in purchasing is favorable.

If management expects the favorable usage variance to persist, the higher quality of corn should be purchased regularly and the price and quantity standards revised to reflect it. As this example reveals, standards are not static. As improvements in production take place and conditions change, standards may need to be revised to reflect the new operating environment.

Timing of the Computation of the Materials Usage Variance. The materials usage variance should be computed as materials are issued for production. To facilitate this process, many companies use three forms: a standard bill of materials, color-coded excessive usage forms, and color-coded returned-materials forms. The **standard bill of materials** identifies the quantity of materials that should be used to produce a predetermined quantity of output. A standard bill of materials for Crunchy Chips is illustrated in Exhibit 25-6.

standard bill of materials

Exhibit 25-6
Standard Bill of Materials

Product: 16-ounce bags of corn chips		*Output:* 48,500 bags
Raw Material	*Unit Standard*	*Total Requirements*
Yellow corn	18 oz	873,000 oz
Cooking Oil	2 oz	97,000 oz
Salt	1 oz	48,500 oz
Lime	0.01 oz	485 oz
Bags	1 bag	48,500 bags

The standard bill of materials acts as a materials requisition form. The production manager presents this form to the stores area and receives the standard quantity allowed for the indicated output. If the production manager has to return to requisition more materials, the excessive usage form is used. This form, different in color from the standard bill of materials, provides immediate feedback to the production manager that excess raw materials are being used. If, on the other hand, fewer materials are used than the standard requires, the production manager can return the leftover materials, along with the returned-materials form. This form also provides immediate feedback.

Direct Labor Variances

The rate (price) and efficiency (usage) variances for labor can be calculated using either the three-pronged approach of Exhibit 25-3 or a formula approach. The three-pronged calculation is illustrated in Exhibit 25-7 (for inspection at the Crunchy Chips plant). The calculation using formulas is discussed next.

Exhibit 25-7
Rate and Efficiency Variances: Direct Labor

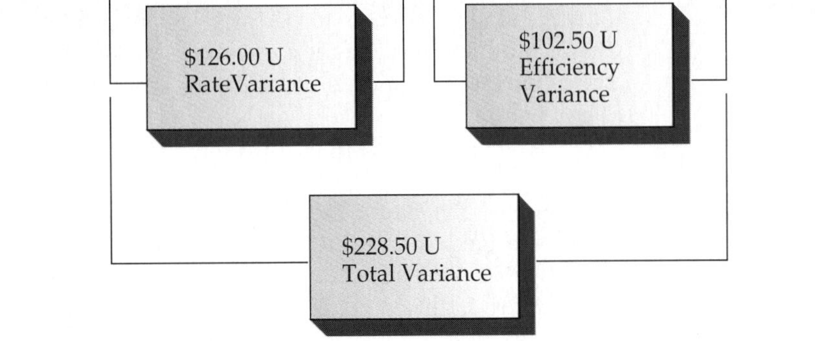

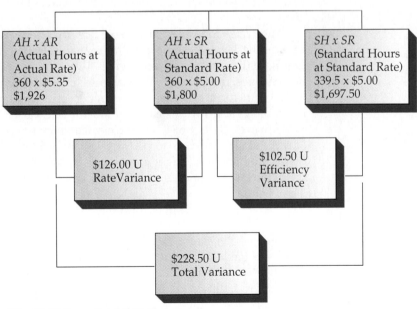

SR = $5.00 (from Exhibit 15-2)
SH = 339.5 (from Exhibit 15-4)

labor rate variance

Labor Rate Variance: Formula Approach. The **labor rate variance** *(LRV)* computes the difference between what was paid to direct laborers and what should have been paid:

$$LRV = (AR \times AH) - (SR \times AH)$$

or, factoring:

$$LRV = (AR - SR)AH$$

where AR = The actual hourly wage rate
SR = The standard hourly wage rate
AH = The actual direct labor hours used

Computation of the Labor Rate Variance. Direct labor activity for Crunchy Chips' inspectors will be used to illustrate the computation of the labor rate variance. We know that 360 hours were used for inspection during the first week in March. The actual hourly wage paid for inspection was $5.35. From Exhibit 25-2, the standard wage rate is $5.00. Thus, *AH* is 360, *AR* is $5.35, and *SR* is $5.00. The labor rate variance is computed as follows:

$$\begin{aligned} LRV &= (AR - SR)AH \\ &= (\$5.35 - \$5.00)360 \\ &= \$0.35 \times 360 \\ &= \$126\ \text{U} \end{aligned}$$

Responsibility for the Labor Rate Variance. Labor rates are largely determined by such external forces as labor markets and union contracts. The actual wage rate rarely departs from the standard rate. When labor rate variances do occur, they usually do so because an average wage rate is used for the rate standard or because more skilled and more highly paid laborers are used for less skilled tasks.

Wage rates for a particular labor activity often differ among workers because of differing levels of seniority. Rather than selecting labor rate standards reflecting those different levels, an average wage rate is often chosen. As the seniority mix changes, the average rate changes. This will give rise to a labor rate variance; it also calls for a new standard to reflect the new seniority mix. Controllability is not assignable for this cause of a labor rate variance.

However, the *use* of labor is controllable by the production manager. The use of more skilled workers to perform less skilled tasks (or vice versa) is a decision that a production manager consciously makes. For this reason, responsibility for the labor rate variance is generally assigned to the individuals who decide how labor will be used.

Analysis of the Labor Rate Variance. If the $126 unfavorable labor rate variance is judged significant, an investigation may be warranted. Assume that an investigation is conducted and the cause is found to be the use of machine operators, more highly paid and skilled, as inspectors, which occurred because two inspectors quit without formal notice. The corrective action is to hire and train two new inspectors.

labor efficiency variance

Labor Efficiency Variance. The **labor efficiency variance** (*LEV*) measures the difference between the labor hours that were actually used and the labor hours that should have been used:

$$LEV = (AH \times SR) - (SH \times SR)$$

or, factoring:

$$LEV = (AH - SH)SR$$

where AH = The actual direct labor hours used
SH = The standard direct labor hours that should have been used
SR = The standard hourly wage rate

Computation of the Labor Efficiency Variance. Crunchy Chips used 360 direct labor hours for inspection while producing 48,500 bags of corn chips. From Exhibit 25-2, 0.007 hours per bag of chips at a cost of \$5 per hour should have been used. The standard hours allowed for inspection or sorting are 339.5 (0.007 X 48,500). Thus, *AH* is 360, *SH* is 339.5, and *SR* is \$5. The labor efficiency variance is computed as follows:

$$\begin{aligned} LEV &= (AH - SH)SR \\ &= (360 - 339.5)\$5 \\ &= 20.5 \times \$5 \\ &= \$102.50\ U \end{aligned}$$

Responsibility for the Labor Efficiency Variance. Generally speaking, production managers are responsible for the productive use of direct labor. However, as is true of all variances, once the cause is discovered, responsibility may be assigned elsewhere. For example, frequent breakdowns of machinery may cause interruptions and nonproductive use of labor. But the responsibility for these breakdowns may be faulty maintenance. If so, the maintenance manager should be charged with the unfavorable labor efficiency variance.

Production managers may be tempted to engage in dysfunctional behavior if too much emphasis is placed on the labor efficiency variance. For example, to avoid losing hours and avoid using additional hours because of possible rework, a production manager could deliberately transfer defective units to finished goods.

Analysis of the Labor Efficiency Variance. The \$102.50 unfavorable variance was judged to be significant and its cause was investigated. The investigation revealed that more shutdowns of the process occurred because the duties of the machine operators were split between machine operations and inspection. (Recall that this reassignment was necessary because two inspectors quit unexpectedly.) This resulted in more idle time for inspection. Also, the machine operators were unable to meet the standard output per hour for inspection because of their lack of experience with the sorting process. The corrective action needed to solve the problem is the same as that recommended for the unfavorable rate variance—hire and train two new inspectors.

Sum of LRV and LEV. From Exhibit 25-7, we know that the total labor variance is \$228.50 unfavorable. This total variance is the sum of the unfavorable labor rate variance and the unfavorable labor efficiency variance (\$126.00 + \$102.50).

VARIANCE ANALYSIS: OVERHEAD COSTS

Objective 5
Compute the variable and fixed overhead variances and explain their meanings.

For direct materials and direct labor, total variances are broken down into price and efficiency variances. The total overhead variance—the difference between applied and actual overhead—is also broken down into component variances. How many component variances are computed depends on the method of variance analysis used. We will focus on one method only. First, we will divide overhead into categories: fixed and variable. Next we look at component variances for each category. The total variable overhead variance is divided into two components: the variable overhead spending variance and the variable overhead efficiency variance. Similarly, the total fixed overhead variance is divided into two components: the fixed overhead spending variance and the fixed overhead volume variance.

Variable Overhead Variances

To illustrate the variable overhead variances, we will examine one week of activity for Crunchy Chips Company (for the first week in March). The following data were gathered for this time period:

Variable overhead rate (standard)	\$ 3.85 per direct labor hour
Actual variable overhead costs	\$1,600
Actual hours worked	400
Bags of chips produced	48,500
Hours allowed for production	378.3[a]
Applied variable overhead	\$1,456[b]

[a].0078 × 48,500
[b]\$3.85 × 378.3 (rounded to nearest dollar; overhead is applied using hours allowed in a standard cost system).

Total Variable Overhead Variance. The total variable overhead variance is the difference between the actual and the applied variable overhead. For our example, the total variable overhead variance is computed as follows:

$$\begin{aligned}\text{Total variance} &= \$1{,}600 - \$1{,}456\\ &= \$144\text{ U}\end{aligned}$$

This total variance can be divided into spending and efficiency variances. This computation is illustrated using a three-pronged approach in Exhibit 25-8.

variable overhead spending variance

Variable Overhead Spending Variance. The **variable overhead spending variance** measures the aggregate effect of differences in the actual variable overhead rate (*AVOR*) and the standard variable overhead rate (*SVOR*). The actual variable overhead rate is simply actual variable overhead divided by actual hours. For our example, this rate is \$4 (\$1,600/400 hrs). The formula for computing the variable overhead spending variance is given below:

$$\begin{aligned}\text{Variable overhead spending variance} &= (AVOR \times AH) - (SVOR \times AH)\\ &= (AVOR - SVOR)AH\\ &= (\$4 - \$3.85)400\\ &= \$60\text{ U}\end{aligned}$$

Exhibit 25-8
Variable Overhead Variances

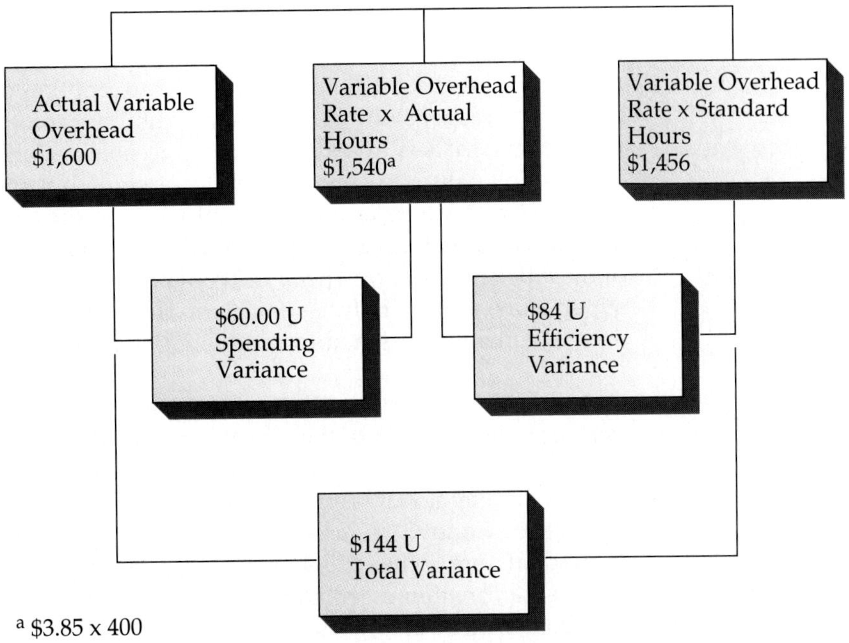

[a] $3.85 x 400

Comparison to the Price Variances of Materials and Labor. The variable overhead spending variance is similar but not identical to the price variances of materials and labor; there are some conceptual differences. Variable overhead is not a homogeneous input—it is made up of a large number of individual items such as indirect materials, indirect labor, electricity, maintenance, and so on. The standard variable overhead rate represents the weighted cost per direct labor hour that should be incurred for all variable overhead items. The difference between what should have been spent per hour and what actually was spent per hour is a type of price variance.

A variable overhead spending variance can arise because prices for individual variable overhead items have increased or decreased. Assume, for the moment, that the price changes of individual overhead items are the only cause of the spending variance. If the spending variance is unfavorable, price increases for individual variable overhead items are the cause; if the spending variance is favorable, price decreases are dominating.

If the only source of the variable overhead spending variance was price changes, then it would be completely analogous to the price variances of materials and labor. Unfortunately, the spending variance also is affected by how efficiently overhead is used. Waste or inefficiency in the use of variable overhead increases the actual variable overhead cost. This increased cost, in turn, is reflected in an increased actual variable overhead rate. Thus, even if the actual prices of the individual overhead items were equal to the budgeted or standard prices, an unfavorable variable overhead spending variance could still take place. Similarly, efficiency can decrease the actual variable overhead cost and decrease the actual variable overhead rate. Efficient use of variable overhead items contributes to a favorable spending variance. If the waste effect dominates, the net contribution will be unfavorable; if efficiency dominates, the net contribution is favorable. Thus, the variable overhead spending variance is the result of both price and efficiency.

Responsibility for the Variable Overhead Spending Variance. Many variable overhead items are affected by several responsibility centers. For example, utilities are a joint cost.[8] To the extent that consumption of variable overhead can be traced to a responsibility center, responsibility can be assigned. Consumption of indirect materials is an example of a traceable variable overhead cost.

Controllability is a prerequisite for assigning responsibility. Price changes of variable overhead items are essentially beyond the control of supervisors. If price changes are small (as they often are), the spending variance is primarily a matter of the efficient use of overhead in production, which is controllable by production supervisors. Accordingly, responsibility for the variable overhead spending variance is generally assigned to production departments.

Analysis of the Variable Overhead Spending Variance. The $60 unfavorable variance simply reveals that, in the aggregate, Crunchy Chips spent more on variable overhead than expected. Even if the variance were insignificant, it reveals nothing about how well costs of individual variable overhead items were controlled. Control of variable overhead requires line-by-line analysis for each individual item. Exhibit 25-9 presents a performance report that supplies the line-by-line information essential for proper control of variable overhead.

From Exhibit 25-9, it is clear that two of the three items present no control problems for the firm. Electricity is the only item showing an unfavorable variance; in fact, it is the cause of the overall variable overhead spending variance. If the variance is significant, an investigation may be warranted. This investigation may reveal that the power company raised the price of electricity. If so, the cause of the variance is beyond the control of the company. The correct response is to revise the budget formula to reflect the increased cost of electricity. However, if the price of electricity has remained unchanged, the usage of electricity is greater than expected. For example, the company may find that there were more startups and shutdowns of machinery than normal, causing an increased consumption of electricity.

Exhibit 25-9

Crunchy Chips, Inc.
Performance Report for the Week Ended March 8, 1995

	Cost Formula[1]	*Actual Costs*	*Budget*[2]	*Spending Variance*
Gas	$3.00	$1,190	$1,200	$10 F
Electricity	0.78	385	312	73 U
Water	0.07	25	28	3 F
Total cost	$3.85	$1,600	$1,540	$60 U

[1]Per direct labor hour
[2]The budget allowance is computed using the cost formula and an activity level of 400 actual direct labor hours.

8. If a company installs meters to measure consumption of utilities for each responsibility center, responsibility can be assigned. However, the cost of assigning responsibility can sometimes exceed any potential benefit. The alternative is allocation. Unfortunately, allocations can be arbitrary, and it is often difficult to identify accurately the amount actually consumed.

Variable Overhead Efficiency Variance. Variable overhead is assumed to vary as the production volume changes. Thus, variable overhead changes in proportion to changes in the direct labor hours used. The **variable overhead efficiency variance** measures the change in variable overhead consumption that occurs because of efficient (or inefficient) use of direct labor. The efficiency variance is computed using the following formula:

variable overhead efficiency variance

$$\begin{aligned}\text{Variable overhead efficiency variance} &= (AH - SH)SVOR \\ &= (400 - 378.3)\$3.85 \\ &= \$84\text{ U (rounded)}\end{aligned}$$

Responsibility for the Variable Overhead Efficiency Variance. The variable overhead efficiency variance is directly related to the direct labor efficiency or usage variance. If variable overhead is truly proportional to direct labor consumption, then like the labor usage variance, the variable overhead efficiency variance is caused by efficient or inefficient use of direct labor. If more (or fewer) direct labor hours are used than the standard calls for, the total variable overhead cost will increase (or decrease). The validity of the measure depends on the validity of the relationship between variable overhead costs and direct labor hours. In other words, do variable overhead costs *really* change in proportion to changes in direct labor hours? If so, responsibility for the variable overhead efficiency variance should be assigned to the individual who has responsibility for the use of direct labor: the production manager.

Analysis of the Variable Overhead Efficiency Variance. The reasons for the unfavorable variable overhead efficiency variance are the same as those offered for the unfavorable labor usage variance. More hours were used than the standard called for because of excessive idle time for inspectors and because the machine operators used as substitute inspectors were inexperienced in sorting.

More information concerning the effect of labor usage on variable overhead is available in a line-by-line analysis of individual variable overhead items. This can be accomplished by comparing the budget allowance for the actual hours used with the budget allowance for the standard hours allowed for each item. A performance report that makes this comparison for all variable overhead costs is shown in Exhibit 25-10.

From Exhibit 25-10, we can see that the cost of gas is affected most by inefficient use of labor. This can be explained by the need to keep the cooking oil hot (assuming gas is used for cooking) even though the cooking process is slowed down by the subsequent sorting process.

The column labeled *Budget for Standard Hours* gives the amount that should have been spent on variable overhead for the actual output. The total of all items in this column is the applied variable overhead, the amount assigned to production in a standard cost system. Note that in a standard cost system, variable overhead is applied using the hours allowed for the actual output *(SH)*, while in normal costing, variable overhead is applied using actual hours (see Chapter 16). Although not shown in Exhibit 25-10, the difference between actual costs and this column is the total variable overhead variance (underapplied by $143.55). Thus, the underapplied variable overhead variance is the sum of the spending and efficiency variances.

Exhibit 25-10

Crunchy Chips, Inc.
Performance Report
For the Week Ended March 8, 1995

Cost	*Cost Formula*[1]	*Budget for Actual Costs*	*Actual Hours*	*Spending Variance*[2]	*Budget for Standard Hours*[3]	*Efficiency Variance*[4]
Gas	$3.00	$1,190	$1,200	$10 F	$1,135	$65 U
Electricity	0.78	385	312	73 U	295	17 U
Water	0.07	25	28	3 F	26	2 U
Total cost	$3.85	$1,600	$1,540	$60 U	$1,456	$84 U

[1]Per direct labor hour
[2]Spending variance = Actual costs − Budget for actual hours
[3]Numbers are rounded to the nearest dollar.
[4]Efficiency variance = Budget for actual hours − Budget for standard hours

Fixed Overhead Variances

We will again use the Crunchy Chips example to illustrate the computation of the fixed overhead variances. The data needed for the example are given below:

Budgeted/Planned Items	
Budgeted fixed overhead	$749,970
Expected activity	23,400 direct labor hours[a]
Standard fixed overhead rate	$32.05[b]

[a]Hours allowed to produce 3,000,000 bags of chips: 0.0078 × 3,000,000
[b]$749,970/23,400

Actual Results	
Actual production bags of chips	2,750,000
Actual fixed overhead cost	$749,000
Standard hours allowed for actual production	21,450[a]

[a]0.0078 × 2,750,000

Total Fixed Overhead Variance

The total fixed overhead variance is the difference between actual fixed overhead and applied fixed overhead, when applied fixed overhead is obtained by multiplying the standard fixed overhead rate times the standard hours allowed for the actual output. Thus, the applied fixed overhead is:

Applied fixed overhead = Standard fixed overhead rate × Standard hours
= $32.05 × 21,450
= $687,473 (rounded)

Exhibit 25-11
Fixed Overhead Variances

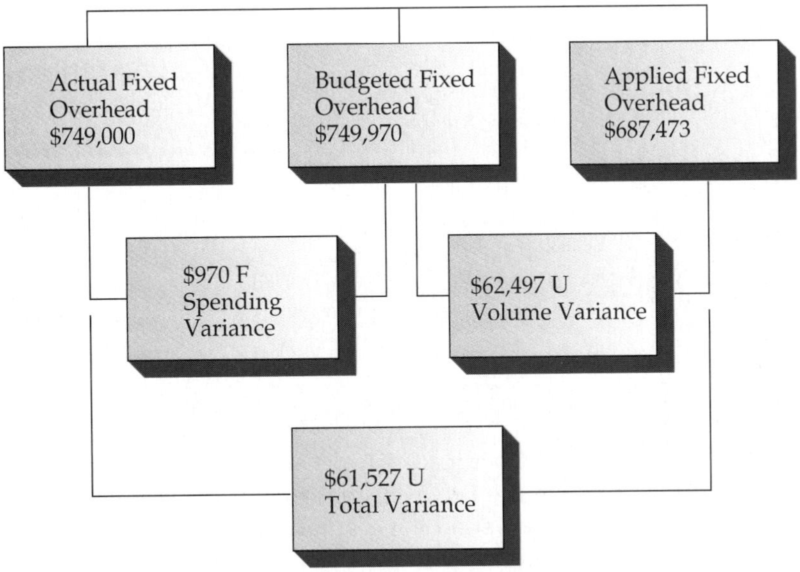

The total fixed overhead variance is the difference between the actual fixed overhead and the applied fixed overhead:

$$\text{Total fixed overhead variance} = \$749{,}000 - \$687{,}473$$
$$= \$61{,}527 \text{ underapplied}$$

To help managers understand why fixed overhead was underapplied by $61,527, the total variance can be broken into two variances: the fixed overhead spending variance and the fixed overhead volume variance. The calculation of the two variances is illustrated in Exhibit 25-11.

fixed overhead spending variance

The Fixed Overhead Spending Variance. The **fixed overhead spending variance** is defined as the difference between the actual fixed overhead and the budgeted fixed overhead. The spending variance is favorable because less was spent on fixed overhead items than was budgeted.

Responsibility for the Spending Variance. Fixed overhead is made up of a number of individual items such as salaries, depreciation, taxes, and insurance. Many fixed overhead items—long-run investments, for instance—are not subject to change in the short run; consequently, fixed overhead costs are often beyond the immediate control of management. Since many fixed overhead costs are affected primarily by long-run decisions, not by changes in production levels, the budget variance is usually small. For example, depreciation, salaries, taxes, and insurance costs are not likely to be much different than planned.

Analysis of the Spending Variance. Because fixed overhead is made up of many individual items, a line-by-line comparison of budgeted costs with actual costs provides more information concerning the causes of the spending variance. Exhibit 25-12 provides such a report. The report reveals that the fixed overhead spending variance is essentially in line with expectations. The fixed overhead spending variances, both on a line-item basis and in the aggregate, are relatively small.

Exhibit 25-12

Crunchy Chips Inc.
Performance Report for the Year Ended 1995

Fixed Overhead Items	*Actual Cost*	*Budgeted Cost*	*Variance*
Depreciation	$530,000	$530,000	$ —
Salaries	159,370	159,970	600 F
Taxes	50,500	50,000	500 U
Insurance	9,130	10,000	870 F
Total fixed	$749,000	$749,970	$970 F

fixed overhead volume variance

Fixed Overhead Volume Variance. The **fixed overhead volume variance** is the difference between budgeted fixed overhead and applied fixed overhead. The volume variance measures the effect of the actual output departing from the output used at the beginning of the year to compute the predetermined standard fixed overhead rate. To see this, let *SH(D)* represent the standard hours allowed for the denominator volume (the volume used at the beginning of the year to compute the predetermined fixed overhead rate). The standard fixed overhead rate is computed in the following way:

$$\text{Standard fixed overhead rate} = (\text{Budgeted fixed overhead})/SH(D)$$

From this equation, we know that the budgeted fixed overhead can be computed by multiplying the standard fixed overhead rate by the denominator hours.

$$\text{Budgeted fixed overhead} = \text{Standard fixed overhead rate} \times SH(D)$$

From Exhibit 25-11, we know that the volume variance can be computed as follows:

$$\begin{aligned}\text{Volume variance} &= \text{Budgeted fixed overhead} - \text{Applied fixed overhead}\\ &= \text{Standard fixed overhead rate} \times SH(D)\\ &\quad - \text{Standard fixed overhead rate} \times SH\\ &= \text{Standard fixed overhead rate} \times (SH(D) - SH)\\ &= \$32.05(23{,}400 - 21{,}450)\\ &= \$62{,}497 \text{ U (rounded down)}\end{aligned}$$

Thus, for a volume variance to occur, the denominator hours, *SH(D)*, must differ from the standard hours allowed for the actual volume, *SH*. At the beginning of the year, Crunchy expected to produce 3,000,000 bags of chips, using 23,400 direct labor hours. The actual outcome was 2,750,000 bags produced, using 21,450 standard hours. Thus, less was produced than expected and an unfavorable volume variance arises.

But what is the meaning of this variance? The variance occurs because the actual output differs from predicted output volume. At the beginning of the year, if management had used 2.75 million bags of corn chips as the denominator volume, the volume variance would not have existed. In this view, the volume variance is seen as prediction error—a measure of the inability of management to select the correct volume over which to spread fixed overhead.

If, however, the denominator volume represented the amount that management believed *could* be produced and sold, the volume variance conveys more significant information. If the actual volume is less than the denominator volume, the volume variance signals management that a loss has occurred. That loss is not equivalent, however, to the dollar value of the volume variance. The loss is equal to the lost contribution margin on the units that were not produced and sold. However, the volume variance is positively correlated with the loss. For example, suppose that the contribution margin per standard direct labor hour is $40. By producing only 2.75 million bags of chips instead of 3 million bags, the company lost sales of 250,000 bags. This is equivalent to 1,950 hours (0.0078 × 250,000). At $40 per hour, the loss is $78,000. The unfavorable volume variance of $62,497 signals this loss but understates it. In this sense, the volume variance is a measure of utilization of capacity.

Responsibility for the Volume Variance. Assuming that volume variance measures capacity utilization implies that the general responsibility for this variance should be assigned to the Production Department. At times, however, investigation into the reasons for a significant volume variance may reveal the cause to be factors beyond the control of production. In this instance, specific responsibility may be assigned elsewhere. For example, if Purchasing acquires a raw material of lower quality than usual, significant rework time may result, causing lower production and an unfavorable volume variance. In this case, responsibility for the variance rests with Purchasing, not Production.

SUMMARY OF LEARNING OBJECTIVES

1. ***Explain how unit standards are set and why standard cost systems are adopted.*** A standard cost system budgets quantities and costs on a unit basis. These unit budgets are for labor, material, and overhead. Standard costs, therefore, are the amount that should be expended to produce a product or service. Standards are set using historical experience, engineering studies, and input from operating personnel, marketing, and accounting. Currently attainable standards are those that can be achieved under efficient operating conditions. Ideal standards are those achievable under maximum efficiency—under ideal operating conditions. Standard cost systems are adopted to improve planning and control and to facilitate product costing. By comparing actual outcomes with standards, and breaking the variance into price and quantity components, detailed feedback is provided to managers. This information allows managers to exercise a greater degree of cost control than that found in a normal or actual cost system. Decisions such as bidding are also made easier when a standard cost system is in place.

2. ***Explain the purpose of a standard cost sheet.*** The standard cost sheet provides the detail for the computation of the standard cost per unit. It shows the standard costs for materials, labor, variable, and fixed overhead. It also reveals the quantity of each input that should be used to produce one unit of output. Using these unit quantity standards, the standard quantity of materials allowed and the standard hours allowed can be computed for the actual output. These computations play an important role in variance analysis.

3. ***Describe the basic concepts underlying variance analysis and explain when variances should be investigated.*** The budget variance is the difference between the actual costs and the planned costs. In a standard cost system, the budget variance is broken down into price and usage variances. By breaking the budget variances into price and usage variances, managers have more ability to analyze and control the total variance. Variances should be investigated if they are material and if the benefits of corrective action are greater than the costs of investigation. Because of the difficulty to assess cost and benefits on a case-by-case basis, many firms set up formal control limits—either a dollar amount, a percentage, or both. Others use judgment to assess the need to investigate.

4. ***Compute the materials and labor variances and explain how they are used for control.*** The materials price and usage variances are computed using either a three-pronged approach or formulas. The three-pronged approach for materials is illustrated in Exhibit 25-5. The materials price variance is the difference between what should have been paid for materials and what was paid (generally associated with the purchasing activity). The

materials usage variance is the difference in the cost of the materials that should have been used and the amount that was used (generally associated with the production activity). When a significant variance is signaled, an investigation occurs to find the cause. Corrective action is taken, if possible, to put the system back in control.

The labor variances are computed using either a three-pronged approach or formulas. The three-pronged approach for labor is illustrated in Exhibit 25-7. The labor rate variance is caused by the actual wage rate differing from the standard wage rate. It is the difference in the wages that were paid and those that should have been paid. The labor efficiency variance is the difference in the cost of the labor that was used and the cost of the labor that should have been used. When a significant variance is signaled, investigation is called for and corrective action should be taken, if possible, to put the system back in control.

5. Compute the variable and fixed overhead variances and explain their meanings. The variable overhead spending variance is the difference between the actual variable overhead cost and the budgeted variable overhead cost for actual hours worked. It therefore is a budget variance, resulting from price changes and efficient or inefficient use of variable overhead inputs. The variable efficiency variance is the difference between budgeted variable overhead at actual hours and applied variable overhead. It is strictly attributable to the efficiency of labor usage and assumes that the variable overhead items are all driven by direct labor hours.

The fixed overhead spending variance is the difference between the actual fixed overhead costs and the budgeted fixed overhead costs. Therefore, it is simply a budget variance. The volume variance is the difference between the budgeted fixed overhead and the applied fixed overhead. It occurs whenever the actual production volume is different from the expected production volume and, thus, is a measure of capacity utilization.

KEY TERMS

Control limits *1170*
Currently attainable standards *1165*
Efficiency variance *1169*
Favorable variances *1170*
Fixed overhead spending variance *1183*
Fixed overhead volume variance *1184*
Ideal standards *1165*
Labor efficiency variance *1177*
Labor rate variance *1176*
Materials price variance *1172*
Materials usage variance *1173*
Price standards *1164*
Price variance *1169*
Quantity standards *1164*
Rate variance *1169*
Standard bill of materials *1174*
Standard cost per unit *1167*
Standard cost sheet *1167*
Standard hours allowed *1167*
Standard quantity of materials allowed *1167*
Total budget variance *1169*
Unfavorable variances *1170*
Usage variance *1169*
Variable overhead efficiency variance *1181*
Variable overhead spending variance *1178*

REVIEW PROBLEM

Wangsgard Manufacturing has the following standard cost sheet for one of its products:

Direct materials (2 feet @ $5)	$10
Direct labor (0.5 hrs @ $10)	5
Fixed overhead (0.5 hrs @ $2[a])	1
Variable overhead (0.5 hrs @ $4)	2
Standard unit cost	$18

[a]Rate based on expected activity of 2,500 hours

During the most recent year, the following actual results were recorded:

Production	6,000 units
Fixed overhead	$ 6,000
Variable overhead	10,500
Direct materials (11,750 ft purchased and used)	61,100
Direct labor (2,900 hrs)	29,580

REQUIRED: Compute the following variances:

1. Materials price and usage variances
2. Labor rate and efficiency variances
3. Fixed overhead spending and volume variances
4. Variable overhead spending and efficiency variances

Solution

1. Material variances:

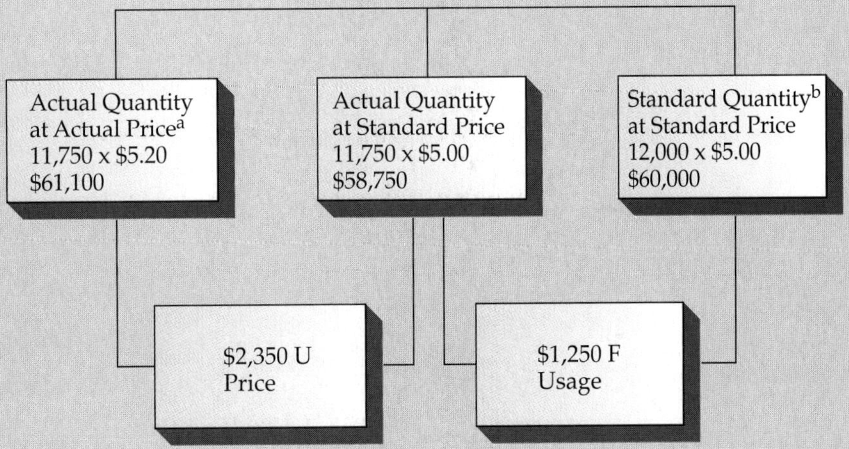

[a] $61,100/11,750 = $5.20 = Actual Price
[b] 2 x 6,000

Or, using formulas:

$$MPV = (AP - SP)AQ$$
$$= (\$5.20 - \$5.00)11{,}750$$
$$= \$2{,}350 \text{ U}$$

$$MUV = (AQ - SQ)SP$$
$$= (11{,}750 - 12{,}000)\$5.00$$
$$= \$1{,}250 \text{ F}$$

2. Labor variances:

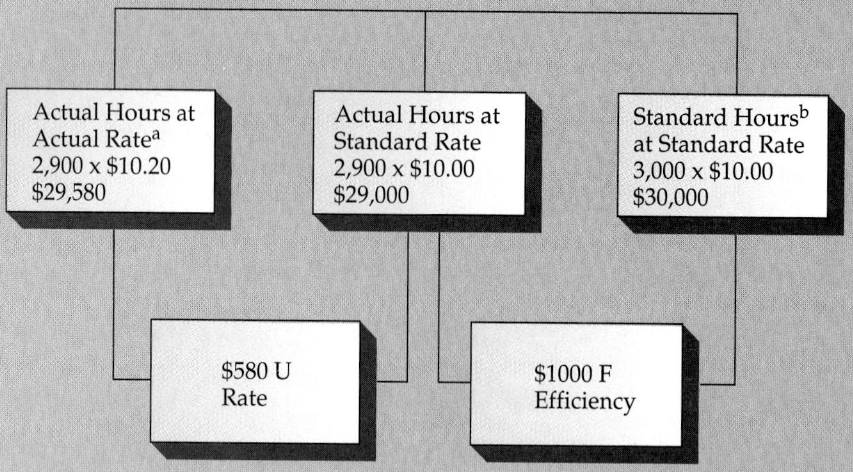

[a] $29,580/2,900 = $10.20 = Actual price
[b] 0.5 x 6,000 = 3,000 = Standard hours

Or, using formulas:

$$\begin{aligned} LRV &= (AR - SR)AH \\ &= (\$10.20 - \$10.00)2{,}900 \\ &= \$580\ \text{U} \end{aligned}$$

$$\begin{aligned} LEV &= (AH - SH)SR \\ &= (2{,}900 - 3{,}000)\$10.00 \\ &= \$1{,}000\ \text{F} \end{aligned}$$

3. Fixed overhead variances:

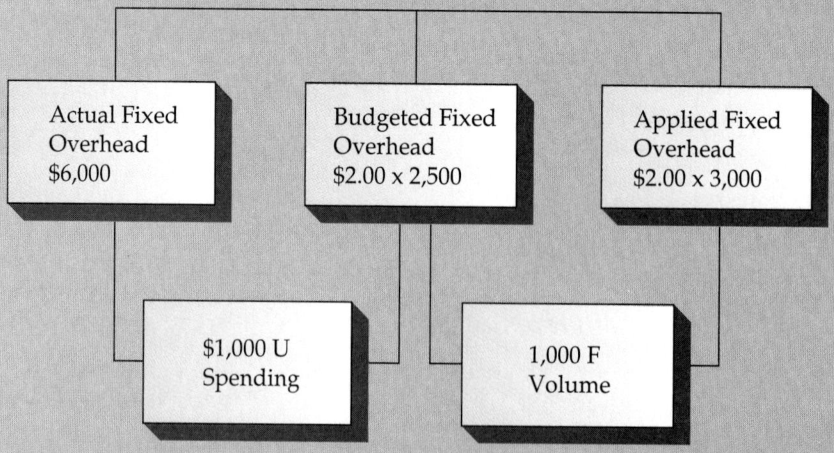

4. Variable overhead variances:

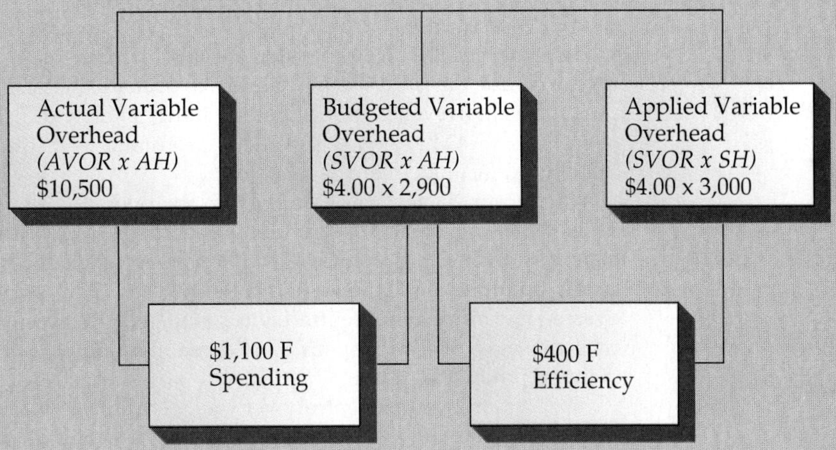

QUESTIONS

1. Discuss the difference between budgets and standard costs.
2. Describe the relationship that unit standards have with flexible budgeting.
3. What is the quantity decision? The pricing decision?
4. Why is historical experience often a poor basis for establishing standards?
5. Should standards be set by engineering studies? Why or why not?
6. What are ideal standards? Currently attainable standards? Of the two, which is usually adopted? Why?
7. How does standard costing improve the control function?
8. Discuss the differences among actual costing, normal costing, and standard costing.
9. What is the purpose of a standard cost sheet?
10. The budget variance for variable production costs is broken down into quantity and price variances. Explain why the quantity variance is more useful for control purposes than the price variance.
11. Explain why the materials price variance is often computed at the point of purchase rather than at the point of issuance.
12. The materials usage variance is always the responsibility of the production supervisor. Do you agree or disagree? Why?
13. The labor rate variance is never controllable. Do you agree or disagree? Why?
14. Suggest some possible causes of an unfavorable labor efficiency variance.
15. Explain why the variable overhead spending variance is not a pure price variance.
16. The variable overhead efficiency variance has nothing to do with efficient use of variable overhead. Do you agree or disagree? Why?
17. Explain why the fixed overhead spending variance is usually very small.
18. What is the cause of an unfavorable volume variance? Does the volume variance convey any meaningful information to managers?
19. When should a standard cost variance be investigated?
20. What are control limits and how are they set?
21. Which do you think is more important for control of fixed overhead costs: the spending variance or the volume variance? Explain.
22. Explain why standard cost systems are adopted.

EXERCISES

E25-1
Setting Standards and Assigning Responsibility
LO 1

Associated Media Graphics (AMG) is a rapidly expanding company involved in the mass reproduction of instructional materials. Ralph Boston, owner and manager of AMG, has made a concerted effort to provide a quality product at a fair price with delivery on the promised due date. Expanding sales have been attributed to this philosophy. As the business grows, however, Boston is finding it increasingly difficult to supervise personally the operations of AMG. As a result, he is beginning to institute an organizational structure that would facilitate management control.

One recent change was to designate the operating departments as cost centers, with control over departmental operations transferred from Boston to each departmental manager. However, quality control still reports directly to Boston, as do the finance and accounting functions. A materials manager was hired to purchase all raw materials and oversee inventory handling (receiving, storage, and so on) and recordkeeping. The materials manager is also responsible for maintaining an adequate inventory based upon planned production levels.

The loss of personal control over the operations of AMG caused Boston to look for a method to evaluate performance efficiently. Dave Cress, a new cost accountant, proposed the use of a standard cost system. Variances for material, labor, and overhead could then be calculated and reported directly to Boston.

REQUIRED:

1. Assume that AMG is going to implement a standard cost system and establish standards for materials, labor, and overhead.
   a. Who should be involved in setting the standards for each cost component?
   b. What factors should be considered in establishing the standards for each cost component?
2. Describe the basis for assignment of responsibility under a standard cost system.

(CMA adapted)

E25-2
Computation of Inputs Allowed; Materials and Labor
LO 2

During the year, Larson Company produced 65,000 units of a large part for a generator. Larson's material and labor standards are

Direct materials (4 lbs @ $0.80)	$3.20
Direct labor (0.5 hrs @ $11.00)	5.50

REQUIRED:

1. Compute the standard hours allowed for the production of 65,000 units.
2. Compute the standard pounds of materials allowed for the production of 65,000 units.

E25-3
Materials and Labor Variances
LO 4

Jooce Company produces fruit juices which are sold in half gallons. Recently the company adopted the following standards for one half gallon of its cranberry juice:

Direct materials (64 oz @ $0.02)	$1.28
Direct labor (0.03 hrs @ $7.00)	0.21
Standard prime cost	$1.49

During the first week of operation, the company experienced the following actual results:

a. Half gallon units produced: 8,000
b. Ounces of materials purchased: 540,000 ounces at $0.018
c. There are no beginning or ending inventories of raw materials
d. Direct labor: 250 hours at $7.50

REQUIRED:

1. Compute price and usage variances for direct materials.
2. Compute the rate variance and the efficiency variance for direct labor.

E25-4 Overhead Variances

LO 5

Pratt Inc. has gathered the following data on last year's operations:

a. Units produced: 28,000
b. Direct labor: 20,000 hours @ $10
c. Actual fixed overhead: $235,000
d. Actual variable overhead: $90,000

Pratt employs a standard cost system. During the year, the following rates were used: standard fixed overhead rate, $10 per hour; standard variable overhead rate, $4.05 per hour. The labor standard requires 0.75 hours per unit produced. (These rates were based on a standard normal volume of 22,500 direct labor hours.)

REQUIRED:

1. Compute the fixed overhead spending and volume variances.
2. Compute the variable overhead spending and efficiency variances.

E25-5 Decomposition of Budget Variances; Materials and Labor

LO 4

Fleming Corporation produces high quality leather purses. The company uses a standard cost system and has set the following standards for materials and labor:

Leather (4 strips @ $10)	$40
Direct labor (1 hr @ $12)	12
Total prime cost	$52

During the year, Fleming produced 5,000 leather purses. The actual leather purchased was 20,500 strips at $9.96 per strip. There were no beginning or ending inventories of leather. Actual direct labor was 5,200 hours at $12.50.

REQUIRED:

1. Compute the costs of leather and direct labor that should have been incurred for the production of 5,000 leather purses.
2. Compute the total budget variances for material and labor.
3. Break the total variance for materials into a price variance and a usage variance.
4. Break the total variance for labor into a rate variance and an efficiency variance.

E25-6 Overhead Application; Overhead Variances

LO 5

Reeves Metal Works is planning to produce 300,000 plumber wrenches for the coming year. Each unit requires two standard hours of labor for completion. The company uses direct labor hours to assign overhead to products. The total overhead budgeted for the coming year is $1,350,000, and the standard fixed overhead rate is $2.00 per unit produced. Actual results for the year are on the following page.

Actual production (units)	295,000
Actual direct labor hours	595,000
Actual variable overhead	$705,000
Actual fixed overhead	$580,000

REQUIRED:

1. Compute the applied fixed overhead.
2. Compute the fixed overhead spending and volume variances.
3. Compute the applied variable overhead.
4. Compute the variable overhead spending and efficiency variances.

E25-7 Investigation of Variances

LO 3

Underwood Company uses the following rule to determine whether material usage variances ought to be investigated. A materials usage variance will be investigated anytime the amount exceeds the lesser of $8,000 or 10 percent of the standard cost. Reports for the past five weeks provided the following information:

Week	*MUV*	*Standard Materials Cost*
1	$7,000 F	$80,000
2	7,800 U	75,000
3	6,000 F	80,000
4	9,000 U	85,000
5	7,000 U	69,000

REQUIRED:

1. Using the rule provided, identify the cases that will be investigated.
2. Suppose the investigation reveals that the cause of an unfavorable materials usage variance is the use of lower-quality materials than are usually used. Who is responsible? What corrective action would likely be taken?
3. Suppose the investigation reveals that the cause of a significant unfavorable materials usage variance is attributable to a new approach to manufacturing that takes less labor time but causes more material waste. Upon examining the labor efficiency variance, it is discovered that it is favorable and is larger than the unfavorable materials usage variance. Who is responsible? What action should be taken?

E25-8 Materials, Labor, and Overhead Variances

LO 4, 5

At the beginning of 1995, Britonan Company had the following standard cost sheet for one of its products:

Direct materials (5 lbs @ 1.60)	$ 8.00
Direct labor (2.0 hours @ $9.00)	18.00
Fixed overhead (2 hrs @ $2.00)	4.00
Variable overhead (2 hrs @ $1.50)	3.00
Standard cost per unit	$33.00

Britonan computes its overhead rates using practical volume, which is 72,000 units. The actual results for 1995 are:

a. Units produced: 70,000
b. Materials purchased: 372,000 pounds at $1.55
c. Materials used: 369,000 pounds
d. Direct labor: 145,000 hours at $8.95
e. Fixed overhead: $240,000
f. Variable overhead: $220,000

REQUIRED:

1. Compute price and usage variances for materials.
2. Compute the labor rate and efficiency variances.
3. Compute the fixed overhead spending and volume variances.
4. Compute the variable overhead spending and efficiency variances.

E25-9
Straightforward Computation of Variances: Materials and Labor
LO 4

Basura Company produces plastic garbage cans. The following standards for producing one unit have been established:

Direct material (5 lbs @ $0.90)	$ 4.50
Direct labor (1.5 hrs @ $7.00)	10.50
Standard prime cost	$15.00

During December, 53,000 pounds of material were purchased and used in production. There were 10,000 cans produced, with the following actual prime costs:

Direct materials	$ 42,000
Direct labor	$102,000 (for 14,900 hours)

REQUIRED: Compute the materials and labor variances, labeling each variance as favorable or unfavorable.

E25-10
Incomplete Data
LO 2, 4, 5

Reece Company uses a standard cost system. During the past quarter, the following variances were computed:

Variable overhead efficiency variance	$ 4,000 U
Labor efficiency variance	20,000 U
Labor rate variance	6,000 U

Reece applies variable overhead using a standard rate of $2 per direct labor hour allowed. Four direct labor hours are allowed per unit produced (only one type of product is manufactured). During the quarter, Reece used 20 percent more direct labor hours than should have been used.

REQUIRED:

1. What were the actual direct labor hours worked? The total hours allowed?
2. What is the standard hourly rate for direct labor? The actual hourly rate?
3. How many actual units were produced?

PROBLEMS

P25-1 Basics of Variance Analysis: Variable Inputs

LO 1, 2, 4

Ming Company manufactures a plastic toy water gun. The following standards have been established for the water gun's variable inputs:

	Standard Quantity	*Standard Price (Rate)*	*Standard Cost*
Direct materials	0.60 lbs	$ 1.00	$0.60
Direct labor	0.08 hrs	10.00	0.80
Variable overhead	0.10 hrs	2.50	0.25
			$1.65

During the first week of July, the company had the following actual results:

Units produced	40,000
Actual labor cost	$33,990
Actual labor hours	3,300
Materials purchased and used	23,000 lbs @ $1.05
Actual variable overhead costs	13,250

Other information: The purchasing agent located a new source of slightly higher-quality plastic, and this material was used during the first week in July. Also, a new manufacturing layout was implemented on a trial basis. The new layout required a slightly higher level of skilled labor. The higher-quality material has no effect on labor utilization. Similarly, the new manufacturing approach has no effect on material usage.

REQUIRED:

1. Compute the materials price and usage variances. Assuming that the material variances are essentially attributable to the higher quality of material, would you recommend that the purchasing agent continue to buy this quality? Or should the usual quality be purchased? Assume that the quality of the end product is not affected significantly.
2. Compute the labor rate and efficiency variances. Assuming that the labor variances are attributable to the new manufacturing layout, should it be continued or discontinued? Explain.
3. Refer to Requirement 2. Suppose that the industrial engineer argued that the new layout should not be evaluated after only one week. His reasoning was that it would take at least a week for the workers to become efficient with the new approach. Suppose that the production is the same the second week and that the actual labor hours were 3,000 and the labor cost was $30,900. Should the new layout be adopted? Assume the variances are attributable to the new layout. If so, what would be the projected annual savings?

P25-2 Setting Standards; Materials and Labor Variances

LO 1, 2, 4

Osgood Company is a small manufacturer of wooden household items. Ellen Rivkin, the controller, plans to implement a standard cost system for Osgood. She has the information needed to develop standards for Osgood's products.

One of Osgood's products is a wooden cutting board. Each cutting board requires 1.25 board feet of lumber and 12 minutes of direct labor time to prepare and cut the lumber. The cutting boards are inspected after they are cut. Because the cutting boards are made of a natural material that has imperfections, one board is normally rejected for each five that are accepted (the rejected boards are totally scrapped). Four rubber foot pads are attached to each good cutting board. A total of fifteen minutes of direct labor time is required to attach all four foot pads and finish each cutting board. The lumber for the cutting boards costs $3 per board foot, and each foot pad costs $0.05. Direct labor is paid at the rate of $8 per hour.

REQUIRED:

1. Develop the standard costs for the direct cost components of the cutting board. The standard cost should identify the standard quantity, standard rate, and standard cost per unit for each direct cost component of the cutting board.
2. Identify the advantages of implementing a standard cost system.
3. Explain the role of each of the following persons in developing standards:
   a. Purchasing manager
   b. Industrial engineer
   c. Cost accountant
4. Assume that the standards have been set and that the following actual results occur during the first month under the new standard cost system:
   a. Actual good units produced: 10,000
   b. Lumber purchased: 16,000 board feet @ $3.10
   c. Lumber used: 16,000 board feet
   d. Rubber foot pads purchased (and used): 51,000 @ $0.048
   e. Direct labor cost: 5,550 hours @ $8.05

Compute materials price and usage variances and labor rate and efficiency variances.

(CMA adapted)

P25-3
Setting a Direct Labor Standard; Learning Effects
LO 1, 2

Norris Company produces customized parts for industrial equipment. Although the parts are custom-made, most follow a fairly standard pattern. Recently, a potential new customer has approached the company and requested a new part, one significantly different from the usual parts manufactured by Norris. New equipment and some new labor skills will be needed to manufacture the part. The customer is placing an initial order of 15,000 units and has indicated that if the part is satisfactory, several additional orders of the same size will be placed over the next two to three years.

Norris uses a standard cost system and wants to develop a set of standards for the new part. The usage standard for direct materials is four pounds per part; the materials price standard is $3 per pound. Management has also decided on standard rates for labor and overhead: the standard labor rate is $11 per hour, the standard variable overhead rate is $6 per hour, and the standard fixed overhead rate is $2 per hour. The only remaining decision is the standard for labor usage. To assist in developing this standard, the Production Engineering Department has estimated the following relationship between units produced and average direct labor hours used:

Units Produced	*Cumulative Average Time per Unit*
20	1.000 hours
40	0.800 hours
80	0.640 hours
160	0.512 hours
320	0.448 hours

As the workers learn more about the production process, they become more efficient in manufacturing the part, and the average time needed to produce one unit declines. Engineering estimates that all of the learning effects will be achieved by the time 160 units are produced. No further improvement will be realized past this level.

REQUIRED:

1. If no further improvement in labor time per unit is possible past 160 units, explain why the cumulative average time per unit at 320 is lower than the time at 160 units.
2. What standard would you set for the per-unit usage of direct labor? Explain.
3. Using the standard you set in Requirement 2, prepare a standard cost sheet that details the standard cost per unit for the new part.
4. Given the standard you set in Requirement 2, would you expect favorable or unfavorable labor and variable overhead efficiency variances for production of the first 160 units? Explain.

P25-4 Basic Variance Analysis; Revision of Standards

LO 1, 4, 5

The Toronto plant of Clark Company's Blackwell Division produces waffle irons. The plant uses a standard cost system for production costing and control. The standard cost sheet for a waffle iron is given below.

Direct materials (3.0 lbs @ \$4.00)	\$12.00
Direct labor (0.8 hours @ \$12.50)	10.00
Variable overhead (0.8 hours @ \$6.00)	4.80
Fixed overhead (0.8 hours @ \$3.00)	2.40
Standard unit cost	\$29.20

During the year, the Toronto plant had the following actual production activity:

a. Production of waffle irons totaled 50,000 units.
b. A total of 130,000 pounds of raw materials was purchased at \$3.70 per pound.
c. There were 25,000 pounds of raw materials in beginning inventory (carried @ \$4 per pound). There was no ending inventory.
d. The company used 41,000 direct labor hours at a total cost of \$533,000.
e. Actual fixed overhead totaled \$95,000.
f. Actual variable overhead totaled \$250,000.

The Toronto plant's normal activity is 45,000 units per year. Standard overhead rates are computed based on normal activity measured in standard direct labor hours.

REQUIRED:

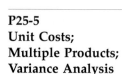

1. Compute the materials price and usage variances.
2. Compute the labor rate and efficiency variances.
3. Compute the variable overhead spending and efficiency variances.
4. Compute the fixed overhead spending and volume variances.
5. Assume that the purchasing agent for the waffle iron plant purchased a lower-quality raw material from a new supplier. Would you recommend that the Toronto plant continue to use this cheaper raw material? If so, what standards would likely need revision to reflect this decision? Assume that the end product's quality is not significantly affected.

P25-5 Unit Costs; Multiple Products; Variance Analysis

LO 3, 4, 5

Koolkare Company manufactures two types of ice makers, small and regular. The standard quantities of labor and materials per unit for 1995 are:

	Small	*Regular*
Direct materials (ounces)	12	20
Direct labor (hours)	0.2	0.30

The standard price paid per pound of direct materials is $1.60. The standard rate for labor is $8. Overhead is applied on the basis of direct labor hours. A plant-wide rate is used. Budgeted overhead for the year is given below.

Budgeted fixed overhead	$720,000
Budgeted variable overhead	960,000

The company expects to work 24,000 direct labor hours in 1995; standard overhead rates are computed using this activity level. For every small ice maker produced, the company produces two regular ice makers.

Actual operating data for 1995 are:

a. Units produced: small ice makers, 35,000; regular ice makers, 70,000.
b. Direct materials purchased and used: 112,000 pounds @ $1.55: 26,000 pounds for the small ice maker and 86,000 pounds for the regular ice maker. There were no beginning or ending raw materials inventories.
c. Direct labor: 29,600 hours: 7,200 hours for the small ice maker, and 22,400 hours for the regular. Total cost of labor: $229,400.
d. Variable overhead: $1,215,000
e. Fixed overhead: $700,000.

REQUIRED:

1. Prepare a standard cost sheet showing the unit cost for each product.
2. Compute the materials price and usage variances for each product.
3. Compute the labor rate and efficiency variances.
4. Compute the variances for fixed and variable overhead.
5. Assume that you know only the total direct materials used for both products and the total direct labor hours used for both products. Can you compute the total materials and labor usage variances? Explain.

P25-6
Incomplete Data; Overhead Analysis
LO 2, 4, 5

Watts Company produces surge protectors. To help control costs, Watts employs a standard cost system and uses a flexible budget to predict overhead costs at various levels of activity. For the most recent year, Watts used a standard overhead rate equal to $17 per direct labor hour. The rate was computed using normal activity. Budgeted overhead costs are $200,000 for 20,000 direct labor hours and $320,000 for 30,000 direct labor hours. During the past year, Watts generated the following data:

a. Actual production: 100,000 units
b. Fixed overhead volume variance: $30,000 U
c. Variable overhead efficiency variance: $12,000 F
d. Actual fixed overhead costs: $85,000
e. Actual variable overhead costs: $110,000

REQUIRED:

1. Determine the fixed overhead spending variance.
2. Determine the variable overhead spending variance.
3. Determine the standard hours allowed per unit of product.
4. If the standard labor rate is $9.25 per hour, compute the labor efficiency variance.

P25-7
Control Limits; Variance Investigation
LO 2, 3, 4, 5

Demismell Company produces a well-known cologne. The standard manufacturing cost of the cologne is described by the following standard cost sheet:

Direct materials:	
Liquids (4.2 oz @ $0.25)	$1.05
Bottles (1 @ $0.05)	0.05
Direct labor (0.2 hrs @ $12.50)	2.50
Variable overhead (0.2 hrs @ $4.70)	0.94
Fixed overhead (0.2 hrs @ $1.00)	0.20
Standard cost per unit	$4.74

Management has decided to investigate only those variances that exceed the lesser of 10 percent of the standard cost for each category or $20,000.

During the past quarter, 250,000 four-ounce bottles of cologne were produced. Actual activity for the quarter is described below.

a. A total of 1.15 million ounces of liquids were purchased, mixed, and processed. Evaporation was higher than expected (no inventories of liquids are maintained). The price paid per ounce averaged $0.27.
b. Exactly 250,000 bottles were used. The price paid for each bottle was $0.048.
c. Direct labor hours totaled 48,250 with a total cost of $622,425.
d. Variable overhead costs totaled $239,000.
e. Fixed overhead costs were $50,500.

Normal production volume for Demismell is 250,000 bottles per quarter. The standard overhead rates are computed using normal volume. All overhead costs are incurred uniformly throughout the year.

REQUIRED:

1. Calculate the upper and lower control limits for each manufacturing cost category.
2. Compute the total materials variance and then break it into price and usage variances. Would these variances be investigated?
3. Compute the total labor variance and break it into rate and efficiency variances. Would these variances be investigated?
4. Compute all overhead variances. Would any of them be investigated? Would you recommend a different approach to deal with overhead? Explain.

P25-8
Flexible Budget; Standard Cost Variances; T-Accounts
LO 1, 4, 5

Shumaker Company manufactures a line of high-top basketball shoes. At the beginning of the year, the following plans for production and costs were revealed:

Pairs of shoes to be produced and sold	55,000
Standard cost per unit:	
Direct materials	$15
Direct labor	12
Variable overhead	6
Fixed overhead	3
Total unit cost	$36

During the year, 50,000 units were produced and sold. The following actual costs were incurred:

Direct materials	$775,000
Direct labor	590,000
Variable overhead	310,000
Fixed overhead	180,000

There were no beginning or ending inventories of raw materials. The materials price variance was $5,000 unfavorable. In producing the 50,000 units, 63,000 hours were worked, 5 percent more hours than the standard allowed for the actual output. Overhead costs are applied to production using direct labor hours.

REQUIRED:

1. Using a flexible budget, prepare a performance report comparing expected costs for the actual production with actual costs.
2. Determine the following:
   a. Materials usage variance
   b. Labor rate variance
   c. Labor usage variance
   d. Fixed overhead spending and volume variances
   e. Variable overhead spending and efficiency variances

P25-9
Standard Costing: Planned Variances
LO 2, 4

As part of its cost control program, Hepler Company uses a standard cost system for all manufactured items. The standard cost for each item is established at the beginning of the fiscal year, and the standards are not revised until the beginning of the next fiscal year. Changes in costs, caused during the year by changes in material or labor inputs or by changes in the manufacturing process, are recognized as they occur by the inclusion of planned variances in Hepler's monthly operating budgets.

Presented below is the labor standard that was established for one of Hepler's products effective June 1, 1995, the beginning of the fiscal year:

Assembler A labor (5 hours @ $10 per hour)	$ 50
Assembler B labor (3 hours @ $11 per hour)	33
Machinist labor (2 hours @ $15 per hour)	30
Standard cost per 100 units	$113

The standard was based on the labor being performed by a team consisting of five persons with Assembler A skills, three persons with Assembler B skills, and two persons with machinist skills; this team represents the most efficient use of the company's skilled employees. The standard also assumed that the quality of materials that had been used in prior years would be available for the coming year.

For the first seven months of the fiscal year, actual manufacturing costs at Hepler have been within the standards established. However, the company has received a significant increase in orders, and there is an insufficient number of skilled workers to meet the increased production. Therefore, beginning in January, the production teams will consist of eight persons with Assembler A skills, one person with Assembler B skills, and one person with machinist skills. The reorganized teams will work more slowly than the normal teams; and, as a result, only 80 units will be produced in the same time period in which 100 units would normally be produced. Faulty work has never been a cause for units to be rejected in the final inspection process, and it is not expected to be a cause for rejection with the reorganized teams.

Furthermore, Hepler has been notified by its material supplier that lower quality materials will be supplied beginning January 1. Normally, one unit of raw materials is required for each good unit produced, and no units are lost due to defective material. Hepler estimates that 10 percent of the units manufactured after January 1 will be rejected in the final inspection process due to defective material.

REQUIRED:

1. Determine the number of units of lower-quality material that Hepler Company must enter into production in order to produce 54,000 good finished units.

2. How many hours of each class of labor must be used to manufacture 54,000 good finished units?
3. Determine the amount that should be included in Hepler's January operating budget for the planned labor variance caused by the reorganization of the labor teams and the lower-quality material.

(CMA adapted)

P25-10
Incomplete Data; Variance Analysis; Standard Cost Sheet
LO 2, 4, 5

Emerson Company had recently acquired Madera Inc., a small manufacturing firm located in the Midwest. Unfortunately, Madera had very poor internal controls and a master disk with some fundamental cost data for the past year was accidently erased. No backup existed. Kathy Shorts, an internal auditor for Emerson, was assigned to Madera and given the task of reconstructing some of the cost records. At first, she was discouraged with the assignment, but became excited when she discovered part of a computer printout that contained some information about last year's operations. The information pertained to Madera's cost accounting system and is presented below.

Selected Actual Results

- Direct materials: 5,000 lbs. purchased and used, costing $25,500
- Production: 10,000 units
- Labor cost: 2,200 hours totaling $17,160
- *FOH* cost: $11,500
- *VOH* cost: $23,000

Variances	
MPV	$ 500 U
MUV	5,000 F
LEV	1,500 U
Volume variance	2,000 U
Variable overhead efficiency	2,000 U
Variable overhead spending	1,000 U
Underapplied fixed overhead	1,500 U

Kathy also interviewed Madera's controller and discovered that overhead rates are based on expected actual activity. Madera calculates two variances for variable overhead and two for fixed overhead. However, before Kathy could analyze the information she had gathered, she had to take emergency leave because of a family crisis. You have been given the task of performing the analysis described by the following requirements.

REQUIRED:

1. Prepare a standard cost sheet in good form. Show fixed and variable overhead as separate items.
2. Compute the fixed overhead spending variance.
3. Compute the labor rate variance.
4. Determine the expected actual activity used to compute the predetermined fixed overhead rate.

DISCUSSION AND INTERPRETATION PROBLEMS

D25-1
Standard Costing

Mark Wright Inc. (MWI) is a specialty frozen-food processor located in the midwestern states. Since its founding in 1982, MWI has enjoyed a loyal clientele that is willing to pay premium prices for the high-quality frozen food it prepares from specialized recipes. In the last two years, the company has experienced rapid sales growth in its operating region and has had many inquiries about supplying its products on a national basis. To meet this growth, MWI expanded its processing capabilities, which resulted in increased production and distribution costs. Furthermore, MWI has been encountering pricing pressure from competitors outside its normal marketing region.

Because MWI desires to continue its expansion, Jim Condon, CEO, has engaged a consulting firm to assist MWI in determining its best course of action. The consulting firm recommended the institution of a standard cost system that would also facilitate a flexible budgeting system to better accommodate the changes in demand that can be expected when serving an expanding market area.

Condon met with his management team and explained the recommendations of the consulting firm. Condon then assigned the task of establishing standard costs to his management team. After discussing the situation with the respective staffs, the management team met to review the matter.

Jane Morgan, purchasing manager, advised that meeting expanded production would necessitate obtaining basic food supplies from other than MWI's traditional sources. This would entail increased raw material and shipping costs and might result in lower-quality supplies. Consequently, these increased costs would need to be made up by the Processing Department if current costs are to be maintained or reduced.

Stan Walters, processing manager, countered that the need to accelerate processing cycles to increase production, coupled with the possibility of receiving lower-grade supplies, can be expected to result in a slip in quality and a greater product rejection rate. Under these circumstances, per-unit labor utilization cannot be maintained or reduced, and forecasting future unit labor content becomes very difficult.

Tom Lopez, production engineer, advised that if the equipment is not properly maintained and thoroughly cleaned at prescribed daily intervals, it can be anticipated that the quality and unique taste of the frozen-food products will be affected. Jack Reid, vice president of sales, stated that if quality cannot be maintained, MWI cannot expect to increase sales to the levels projected.

When Condon was apprised of the problems encountered by his management team, he advised them that if agreement could not be reached on the appropriate standards, he would arrange to have them set by the consulting firm and everyone would have to live with the results.

REQUIRED:

1. List the major advantages of using a standard cost system.
2. List disadvantages that can result from the use of a standard cost system.
3. Identify those who should participate in setting standards and describe the benefits of their participation in the standard setting process.
4. What characteristics of a standard cost system make it an effective tool for cost control?
5. What could be the consequences if Jim Condon, CEO, has the standards set by the outside consulting firm?

(CMA adapted)

D25-2 Standard Costing and Ethical Behavior

Pat James, the purchasing agent for a local plant of the Oakden Electronics Division, was considering the possible purchase of a component from a new supplier. The component's purchase price, $0.90, compared favorably with the standard price of $1.10. Given the quantity that would be purchased, Pat knew that the favorable price variance would help offset an unfavorable variance for another component. By offsetting the unfavorable variance, his overall performance report would be impressive and good enough to help him qualify for the annual bonus. More importantly, a good performance rating this year would help him secure a position at divisional headquarters at a significant salary increase.

Purchase of the part, however, presented Pat with a dilemma. Consistent with his past behavior, Pat made inquiries regarding the reliability of the new supplier and the part's quality. Reports were basically negative. The supplier had a reputation for making the first two or three deliveries on schedule but being unreliable from then on. Worse, the part itself was of questionable quality. The number of defective units was only slightly higher than that for other suppliers, but the life of the component was 25 percent less than what normal sources provided.

If the part were purchased, no problems with deliveries would surface for several months. The problem of shorter life would cause eventual customer dissatisfaction and perhaps some loss of sales, but the part would last at least eighteen months after the final product began to be used. If all went well, Pat expected to be at headquarters within six months. He saw very little personal risk associated with a decision to purchase the part from the new supplier. By the time any problems surfaced, they would belong to his successor. With this rationalization, Pat decided to purchase the component from the new supplier.

REQUIRED:

1. Do you agree with Pat's decision? Why or why not? How important do you think Pat's assessment of his personal risk was in the decision? Should it be a factor?
2. Do you think that the use of standards and the practice of holding individuals accountable for their achievement played major roles in Pat's decision?
3. Review the ethical standards for management accountants in Chapter 1. Even though Pat is not a management accountant, identify the standards that might apply to his situation. Should every company adopt a set of ethical standards that apply to their employees, regardless of their specialty?

D25-3 Research Assignment

The usefulness of standard costing has been challenged in recent years. Some claim that its use is an impediment to the objective of continuous improvement (an objective that many feel is vital in today's competitive environment). Write a short paper that analyzes the role and value of standard costing in today's manufacturing environment. In writing this paper, address the following questions:

1. What are the major criticisms of standard costing?
2. Will standard costing disappear? Or is there still a role for it in the new manufacturing environment? If so, what is the role?
3. Given the criticisms, can you explain why its use continues to be so prevalent? Will this use eventually change?
4. If standard costing is no longer completely suitable for some manufacturing environments, what control approaches are being used to supplement (replace?) the traditional control model?

In preparing your paper, the following references may be useful; however, do not restrict your literature search to these references. These references are simply to help you get started.

1. Robin Cooper and Robert S. Kaplan, "Activity-Based Systems: Measuring the Costs of Resource Usage," *Accounting Horizons* (September 1992), pp. 1–13.
2. Forrest B. Green and Felix E. Amenkhienan, "Accounting Innovations: A Cross-Sectional Survey of Manufacturing Firms," *Journal of Cost Management* (Spring 1992), pp. 58–64.
3. Bruce R. Gaumnitz and Felix P. Kollaritsch, "Manufacturing Variances: Current Practice and Trends," *Journal of Cost Management* (Spring 1991), pp. 58–64.
4. Robert S. Kaplan, "Limitations of Cost Accounting in Advanced Manufacturing Environments," in Robert S. Kaplan (ed.), *Measures for Manufacturing Excellence* (Boston: Harvard Business School Press, 1990).
5. George Foster and Charles Horngren, "JIT: Cost Accounting and Cost Management Issues," *Management Accounting* (June 1987), pp. 19–25.

CHAPTER 26
Planning and Control: The Advanced Manufacturing Environment

LEARNING OBJECTIVES

After reading this chapter, you should be able to:

1. Explain why many traditional control measures are not suitable for an advanced manufacturing environment.
2. Explain activity-based management and how it differs from traditional responsibility accounting.
3. Explain life-cycle cost management and why it is important for the advanced manufacturing environment.
4. Describe how quality costs are measured and controlled.
5. Explain what productivity is and differentiate between partial and total measures of productivity.

Scenario

Michelle Anderson, president and owner of Anderson Parts, Inc., was not totally satisfied with the results of the company's new JIT purchasing and manufacturing system. True, inventories had been reduced, but they were still well above the levels that had been predicted by Henry Jensen, the consultant from a national public accounting firm who recommended the JIT system, along with some other major initiatives. (Henry had called the entire approach an activity-based management system.) Furthermore, although lead times had been reduced, they, too, were still higher than projected. Significant problems with quality, delivery, excessive scrap, and machine performance were persisting. Before she became too concerned, however, she wanted to hear what Jensen had to say. He had come to provide a progress report and additional recommendations for changes.

"Glad to see you again, Henry. I'm anxious to hear what you have to say about our new activity-based management system and what can be done to continue improving our efficiency. It appears that we still haven't realized many of the benefits you predicted six months ago."

"Well, that's certainly true. Change does take time, but actually your company is making the transition from conventional manufacturing to JIT much more easily than other firms I've had as clients. You've already shown some significant improvement—more so than usual for this stage of development."

"That's encouraging. How much longer will it take to realize the full benefits? What else do we need to do?"

"You have to realize that JIT and the other initiatives I recommended, such as activity-based costing, total quality control, total customer satisfaction, time-based competition, and cellular manufacturing are more than just a set of techniques. These initiatives represent a totally new view of business processes and have continuous improvement as their central objective. In fact, taken together, these initiatives define a fundamentally different business process from what you have traditionally followed. We call this new business process activity-based management. The levels of improvement that I predicted should be achieved within a year. After that, I would expect to see additional improvement each year. To achieve the short-term and long-term goals possible, you must have a system of performance measurement in place. Good evaluation and control are critical to the success of this new business process."

"Henry, we do have a good system for evaluating and controlling our operations. We have a standard costing system and budgetary control of all our major responsibility centers. We also have good incentive pay schemes in place to encourage both labor and managerial productivity."

"Michelle, measuring and controlling performance is fundamental—but performance measurement must be compatible with the concept of continuous improvement. Otherwise, the measures used can actually limit the efficiency made possible by these initiatives. Unfortunately, some of the traditional control measures you mentioned are no longer suitable for your advanced manufacturing environment."

"Explain. I don't see why our performance measures are so bad."

"The traditional approach concerns managing costs, but costs can't be managed—only the activities that cause the costs can be. The typical accounting report produces variances, and these variances are supposed to signal problems, if any exist. This approach encourages reactive decision making and is essentially backward-looking management. After all, the events that caused the costs are past, and we can't change those events.[1]

"True, but an investigation may reveal that the event that caused the problem persists and can be corrected to avoid future problems."

"I agree, but it seems more sensible to have your information system structured so that the cause of the costs is revealed without extensive investigation. Simply put, activity analysis and management is an essential part of control in an advanced manufacturing environment—it's fundamental to continuous improvement. There are other problems as well. Using variance analysis at the operational level can create some perverse incentives—encouraging behavior that is contrary to achieving continuous improvement. Also, an emphasis on total quality management really demands that you have some means of measuring and controlling quality costs. Finally, it is essential that you have a system component that measures and reports changes in productivity."

"Interesting. I really need more information about all this. Henry, prepare a report that outlines the performance and control issues for the new system. Clearly, we need to change our management accounting system to reflect the new approach to responsibility accounting, quality, and productivity measurement. Once I fully understand what needs to be done, I'll see that the necessary changes are put into place."

LIMITATIONS OF TRADITIONAL PERFORMANCE MEASURES

Objective 1

Explain why many traditional control measures are not suitable for an advanced manufacturing environment.

As the dialogue between Michelle and Henry indicates, many traditional measures used to evaluate and control workers and managers are no longer suitable for the advanced manufacturing environment. Managing activities and using an activity-based responsibility system provide a better approach for achieving continuous improvement. Furthermore, continued use of conventional cost-based performance measures actually interferes with the efficient operation of the new business process.

The traditional control mechanism of management accounting has been to compare actual costs with standard or budgeted costs. If actual costs exceed budgeted or standard costs by a material amount, managers conclude that the process is not operating as intended—that significant inefficiencies are present in the system. They then investigate the cause and take corrective actions. Furthermore, the ability to meet cost standards has been viewed as an important performance measure for managers and workers alike. Bonuses and other incentives are tied to reports that compare actual to budgeted performance.

Firms that advocate continuous improvement usually alter the role of standard costing as a managerial control tool. The new business process mentioned

1. C. J. McNair, "Interdependence and Control: Traditional vs. Activity-Based Responsibility," *Journal of Cost Management* (Summer 1990), pp. 15–24.

in the scenario emphasizes JIT, total quality control, time-based competition, total customer satisfaction, employee involvement, continuous improvement, cellular manufacturing, and zero inventories. Those espousing this new approach strongly object to the incentives present in a conventional standard cost system. They view efficiency reporting, the attendant variance analysis, and the accompanying mindset as impediments to continuous improvement.[2]

Standard costing encourages those responsible for the achievement of standards to produce favorable variances. But the pressure to meet standards may create dysfunctional behavior. For example, purchasing agents may acquire materials of low quality or in large lots in order to produce a favorable materials price variance. As a consequence, scrap, the number of defective units, and the amount of rework activity may increase, or raw materials inventories may be excessive. These outcomes run contrary to the new environment's objectives of total quality control and zero inventories.

In the advanced manufacturing environment, efficiency reporting receives considerably less emphasis. Labor efficiency variances computed at the cell level may encourage workers to produce more than needed to achieve targeted efficiency levels or to avoid an unfavorable volume variance. For example, including setup labor as part of the labor standard (as is often done) encourages large production runs and, thus, excess production; by using fewer setup hours, the actual hours reported move closer to standard. But producing more product than needed is diametrically opposed to the goal of zero inventories. In a JIT environment, idle workers (in the short run) are not necessarily viewed as bad—keeping workers active by overproducing can be much more costly than the labor services lost. Furthermore, labor becomes multidisciplinary—workers are trained to do a variety of tasks—many of which were formerly classified as indirect labor activities. Thus, in the new environment, production labor standards are less meaningful.

The computation of materials usage variances can also pose problems for the advanced manufacturing environment. Workers may pass on poor quality components to avoid an unfavorable materials usage variance. Unfortunately, defective parts disrupt production in a JIT environment. Because there are no inventories to serve as a buffer for interruptions in production, incentives that encourage defective components are not desirable. Thus, the conventional approach to control operations through efficiency reporting and variance analysis is not compatible with the advanced manufacturing environment.

Emphasis on individual overhead variances can also be detrimental. Avoiding preventive maintenance to ensure a favorable budget variance may result in equipment being unavailable for production. This behavior, however, runs counter to the JIT objective of total preventive maintenance and creates an incentive for buffer inventories.

The concept of currently attainable standards is also opposed to the objective of continuous improvement. Currently attainable standards allow for a certain level of inefficiency. All too often, in a standard costing system, those who achieve the standard believe that they have arrived and no further efforts are

2. Robert S. Kaplan, "Limitations of Cost Accounting in Advanced Manufacturing Environments," in Robert S. Kaplan (ed.), *Measures for Manufacturing Excellence* (Boston: Harvard Business School Press, 1990); McNair, "Interdependence and Control," pp. 15–23; Henry J. Johansson, Thomas Volmann, and Vivian Wright, "The Effect of Zero Inventories on Cost (Just-in-Time)," *Cost Accounting for the 90s* (Montvale, NJ: National Association of Accountants, 1986), pp. 141–164. See also Robert A. Howell and Stephen R. Soucy, "Cost Accounting in the New Manufacturing Environment," *Management Accounting* (July 1987), pp. 21–31.

Exhibit 26-1
Limitations of Conventional Control Methods: Selected Examples

Control Measure	*Limitation*	*Advanced Manufacturing Objective Violated*
Materials price variance	Encourages low quality and large lot purchases	Total quality control and zero inventories
Labor efficiency variance	Encourages overproduction	Zero inventories
Materials usage variance	Provides incentive for low quality	Total quality control
Budget variance Maintenance	Provides incentive for downtime	Total preventive maintenance
Currently attainable standards	Encourages inefficiency	Continuous improvement, zero inventories, total quality control, and total preventive maintenance

needed to improve efficiency. Of course, this is possible because the standard allows for inefficiency and is viewed as somewhat static in nature. Yet, JIT and this new business process demand that efforts be continually exerted to improve quality, improve efficiency, and find better ways to do the same task. Innovation and simplicity are encouraged and rewarded. A dynamic view of efficiency, not a static one, is characteristic of the new approach.

The conventional control measures, their limitations, and the advanced manufacturing objectives that are violated by these measures are summarized in Exhibit 26-1 for easy reference. Keep in mind that the Exhibit provides only selected examples and is in no way exhaustive. Other examples could be given. However, the selected examples are sufficient to illustrate why Henry Jensen was unimpressed with Anderson's existing control system and why he recommended a new control system that is more compatible with the advanced manufacturing system.

ACTIVITY-BASED MANAGEMENT

Objective 2
Explain activity-based management and how it differs from traditional responsibility accounting.

Responsibility accounting has been a fundamental tool of managerial control. This continues to be true in the advanced manufacturing environment. Accountability and control are fundamental principles that can be used to help implement the initiatives that define the business processes of the new environment. As we have just learned, however, conventional control systems may not be suitable. Understanding how responsibility accounting differs in the new environment requires a basic understanding of conventional responsibility accounting.

Conventional responsibility accounting is characterized by four essential elements. First, a responsibility center must be identified. This center is typically an organizational unit, such as a department or production line, or it can even be a work team or an individual. Whatever the unit is, responsibility is assigned to the individual in charge. Responsibility is defined in financial terms (e.g., costs).

Second, standards are set to serve as benchmarks for performance measurement. Budgeting and standard costing are the cornerstones of the benchmark activity. Third, performance is measured by comparing actual outcomes with budgeted outcomes. In principle, individuals are held accountable only for those items over which they have control. Fourth, individuals are rewarded or penalized according to the policies and discretion of higher management. Of course, the reward system is designed to encourage individuals to manage costs—to achieve or beat budgetary standards.

Controllability implies that costs are traced to individuals—individuals responsible for the incurrence of the costs. The emphasis of the conventional responsibility accounting system is on managing costs. The emerging consensus, however, is that management of activities—not costs—is the key to successful control in the advanced manufacturing environment.[3] To become a global competitor, managers must know what the customers want and when they want it and must be able to produce the product or service with the highest quality and lowest cost possible—and do so rapidly. Only by knowing how activities contribute value to customers and by eliminating waste can a company be successful in achieving these objectives. The realization that activities are crucial to both improved product costing and effective control has led to a new view of business processes called *activity-based management.*

activity-based management (ABM)

Activity-based management (ABM) is a system-wide, integrated approach that focuses management's attention on activities.[4] It is the cornerstone of the new business process that is emerging in the advanced manufacturing environment. Activity-based management encompasses both product costing and control features. Thus, the activity-based management model has two dimensions: a *cost dimension* and a *control dimension.* This two-dimensional model is illustrated in Exhibit 26-2.[5] The cost dimension provides cost information about resources, activities, products, and customers. As the model suggests, the cost of resources is traced to activities and then the cost of activities is assigned to products and customers. This activity-based costing dimension is useful for strategic and tactical analyses and is discussed fully in Chapters 19 and 23. The second dimension—the control dimension—provides information about why work is done and how well it is done. It is concerned with cost driver analysis, activity analysis, and performance measurement. It is this dimension that offers the connection to the concept of continuous improvement found in the advanced manufacturing environment. The control dimension, which defines activity-based responsibility accounting, focuses on accountability for activities, rather than costs, and emphasizes the maximization of system-wide performance, instead of individual performance.

3. The following all support this view: John P. Campi, "It's Not as Easy as ABC," *Journal of Cost Management,* Summer, 1992, pp. 5–12; McNair, "Interdependence and Control"; Kaplan, "Limitations of Cost Accounting"; Alfred J. Nanni, Jr., J. Robb Dixon, and Thomas E. Volmann, "Strategic Control and Measurement," *Journal of Cost Management* (Summer 1990), pp. 33–42; and H. Thomas Johnson, "Professors, Customers, and Value: Bringing a Global Perspective to Management Accounting Education," in Peter B. B. Turney (ed.), *Performance Excellence in Manufacturing and Service Organizations* (Proceedings of the Third Annual Management Accounting Symposium, March 1989), pp. 8–20.

4. The definition and subsequent discussion is taken primarily from McNair, "Interdependence and Control." See also Campi, "It's Not as Easy as ABC."

5. This model has appeared numerous times. The graphical portrayal of the model follows the form presented in Figure 1, p. 47 of the following article: Peter B. B. Turney and Alan J. Stratton, "Using ABC to Support Continuous Improvement," *Management Accounting,* September 1992, pp. 46–50. Our labeling of the model differs, however. Discussion of the model is also based on Turney and Stratton article and the following article: Norm Raffish, "How Much Does That Product Really Cost?" *Management Accounting,* March 1991, pp. 36–39.

Exhibit 26-2
The Two-Dimensional ABM Model

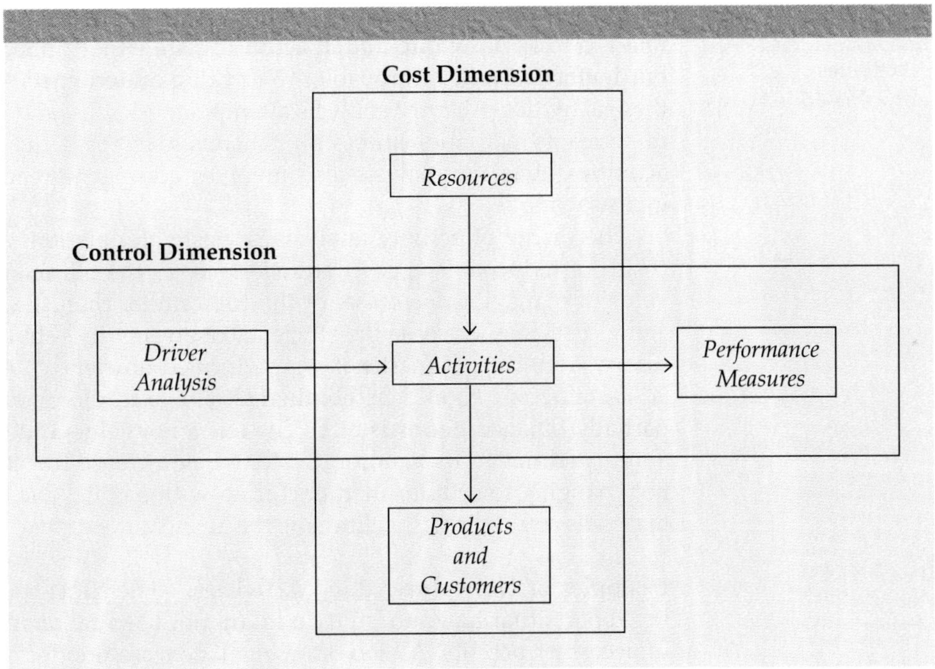

Activities cut across functional and departmental lines, are system wide in focus, and require a global approach to control. Essentially, activity-based control admits that maximizing the efficiency of individual subunits does not necessarily lead to maximum efficiency for the system as a whole. Thus, the possibility of direct laborers not continuously producing is allowed—provided that the system-wide effect is beneficial.

One key difference between the cost and control dimensions is the level of activity aggregation. For product costing, the use of homogeneous sets of activities reduces the computational complexity. These sets of activities, however, are too aggregated to provide useful insights to guide improvement efforts. More detail is needed to support activity improvement. Thus, the control dimension emphasizes the analysis and management of individual, detailed activities.

Activity Analysis

activity analysis

The heart of the control dimension is *activity analysis*. **Activity analysis** is the process of identifying, describing, and evaluating the activities an organization performs. Activity analysis should produce four outcomes: (1) what activities are done, (2) how many people perform the activities, (3) the time and resources required to perform the activities, (4) an assessment of the value of the activities to the organization, including a recommendation to select and keep only those that add value.[6] Although all four outcomes are important, the fourth outcome is the most critical (the fourth outcome is referred to as *activity management*). Because of increased competition, many firms are paying more attention to activi-

6. This definition and much of the discussion of activity analysis are derived from Johnson, "Professors, Customers, and Value." See also the glossary in Barry J. Brinker (editor), *Emerging Practices in Cost Management*, (Warren, Gorham, and Lamont: Boston, 1992).

nonvalue-added activities
nonvalue-added costs

ties that add unnecessary cost and impede performance. These activities, referred to as **nonvalue-added activities,** are either unnecessary or are necessary but inefficient and improvable.[7] **Nonvalue-added costs** are the costs caused by these activities. Activity analysis attempts to identify and eventually eliminate all unnecessary activities and, simultaneously, increase the efficiency of necessary activities. Activity analysis also involves adding new activities—activities that increase value.

The theme of activity analysis is waste elimination. As waste is eliminated, costs are reduced. The cost reduction *follows* the elimination of waste. Note the value of managing the *causes* of the costs rather than the costs themselves. Managing costs may increase the efficiency of an activity—but if the activity is unnecessary, what does it matter if it's performed efficiently? An unnecessary activity is wasteful and should be eliminated. For example, moving raw materials and partially finished goods is often cited as a nonvalue-added activity. Installing an automated materials handling system may increase the efficiency of this activity, but changing to cellular manufacturing with on-site, just-in-time delivery of raw materials could virtually eliminate the activity. It's easy to see which is preferable.

Examples of Nonvalue-Added Activities. The effort spent to produce accounting reports that have no utility and are not used by anyone is an example of an unnecessary activity. All too often, managers are flooded with reams of computer paper containing reports that are totally useless for running the company. The costs associated with producing these reports are nonvalue-added costs. By eliminating the unnecessary reports, personnel in the accounting department could be reduced and savings realized.

The activity of creating unnecessary accounting reports illustrates the important point that nonvalue-added activities can exist anywhere in the organization. In the manufacturing operation, five major activities are often cited as wasteful and unnecessary. These activities are listed and defined below.

1. Scheduling: an activity that uses time and resources to determine when different products have access to processes (or when and how many setups must be done) and how much will be produced
2. Moving: an activity that uses time and resources to move raw materials, work in process, and finished goods from one department to another
3. Waiting: an activity in which raw materials or work in process use time and resources by waiting on the next process
4. Inspecting: an activity in which time and resources are spent ensuring that the product meets specifications
5. Storing: an activity that uses time and resources while a good or raw material is held in inventory

None of these activities adds any value for the customer. Thus, the challenge of activity analysis is to find ways to produce the good without using any of these activities.

Cost Reduction. Continuous improvement carries with it the objective of cost reduction. World-class competitors must deliver products the customers want, on time, and at the lowest possible cost. This means that an organization must con-

7. This definition is found in James A. Brimson, "Improvement and Elimination of Non-Value-Added Costs," *Journal of Cost Management for the Manufacturing Industry* (Summer 1988), pp. 62–65.

tinually strive for cost improvement. Activity analysis is the key to achieving cost reduction objectives. Activity analysis can reduce costs in four ways:[8]

1. Activity elimination
2. Activity selection
3. Activity reduction
4. Activity sharing

activity elimination

Activity elimination focuses on nonvalue-added activities. Once activities that fail to add value are identified, measures must be taken to rid the organization of these activities. For example, the activity of inspecting incoming parts seems necessary to ensure that the product using the parts functions according to specifications. Use of a bad part can produce a bad final product. Yet, this activity is necessary only because of the poor quality performance of the supplying firms. Selecting suppliers that are able to supply high-quality parts or who are willing to improve their quality performance to achieve this objective eventually will allow the elimination of incoming inspection. Cost reduction then follows.

activity selection

Activity selection involves choosing among different sets of activities that are caused by competing strategies. Different strategies cause different activities. Different product design strategies, for example, can require significantly different activities. Activities, in turn, cause costs. Each product design strategy has its own set of activities and associated costs. All other things equal, the lowest-cost design strategy should be chosen. Thus, activity selection can have a significant effect on cost reduction.

activity reduction

Activity reduction decreases the time and resources required by an activity. This approach to cost reduction should be primarily aimed at improving the efficiency of necessary activities or a short-term strategy for improving nonvalue-added activities until they can be eliminated. Setup activity, for example, is a necessary activity that is often cited as an example for which less time and fewer resources need to be used. Upon adopting a JIT system, Harley-Davidson reduced setup times by more than 75 percent.[9] This usually means that costs are being reduced.

activity sharing

Activity sharing increases the efficiency of necessary activities by using economies of scale. Specifically, the quantity of the cost driver is increased without increasing the total cost of the activity itself. This lowers the per-unit cost of the cost driver and the amount of cost that is traceable to the products that consume the activity. For example, a new product can be designed to use components already being used by other products. By using existing components, the activities associated with these components already exist and the company avoids the creation of a whole new set of activities.

Performance Reporting: Value-Added and Nonvalue-Added Costs

A company's accounting system should distinguish between value-added costs and nonvalue-added costs.[10] The distinction is necessary so that management can focus on reducing and eventually eliminating nonvalue-added costs. Highlight-

8. This classification and its discussion are based on Peter B. B. Turney, "How Activity-Based Costing Helps Reduce Cost," *Journal of Cost Management* (Winter 1991), pp. 29–35.
9. Gene Schwind, "Man Arrives Just In Time To Save Harley-Davidson," *Material Handling Engineering* (August 1984), pp. 28–35.
10. Expanding cost reporting to provide visibility for nonvalue-added costs was recommended by CAM-I. See Callie Berliner and James A. Brimson (eds.), *Cost Management for Today's Advanced Manufacturing* (Boston: Harvard Business School Press, 1988).

ing nonvalue-added costs also reveals the magnitude of the waste the company is currently experiencing. Reporting nonvalue-added costs separately encourages managers to place more emphasis on controlling nonvalue-added activities. Furthermore, tracking these costs over time permits managers to assess the effectiveness of their activity-management programs. Cost reduction should follow and knowing the amount of costs saved is important for strategic purposes. For example, if an activity is eliminated, the costs saved should be traceable to individual products. These savings can produce price reductions for customers and make the firm more competitive. Changing the pricing strategy, however, requires knowledge of the cost reductions created by activity analysis. A cost reporting system, therefore, is an important ingredient in an activity-based responsibility accounting system. The activity-based cost report should include both value-added and nonvalue-added costs.

value-added activities
value-added costs

Value-added activities are necessary activities that are carried out with perfect efficiency. **Value-added costs** are the costs caused by value-added activities. These are the only costs that should be incurred in producing a product. The value-added standard calls for the complete elimination of nonvalue-added activities; the ideal would be a zero cost for these activities. This standard also calls for the complete elimination of the inefficiency of activities that are necessary but inefficiently carried out.

Ideal Standards. Value-added costs sound suspiciously like standard costs based on ideal standards; indeed, that is exactly what they are. When ideal standards were first discussed in Chapter 25, they were criticized as being difficult, if not impossible, to attain and thus would be frustrating to those workers and supervisors held responsible for achieving them. This view conflicts with the goal of continuous improvement and can create an attitude of complacency. Complacency, in turn, may prove disastrous for a firm whose competitors are pursuing a goal of continuous improvement.

Achieving a value-added (ideal) standard is frustrating only if workers are required to achieve the standard immediately. The idea of continuous improvement is to move toward the ideal, not to achieve it immediately. Workers can be rewarded for improvement. Moreover, operational performance measures, nonfinancial in nature, can be used to supplement and support the goal of eliminating nonvalue-added costs. Finally, measuring the efficiency of individual workers and supervisors is not the way to eliminate nonvalue-added activities. Remember, activities cut across departmental boundaries and are interdependent. Focusing on activities and providing incentives to find better, more efficient ways to produce are more productive approaches.

By comparing actual activity costs with value-added activity costs, management can assess the level of nonproductive activity and become informed concerning the potential for improvement. Fundamental to identifying and calculating value- and nonvalue-added costs is the identification of cost drivers for each activity. Once cost drivers are identified, then value-added standards for each cost driver can be defined. A **value-added standard** is simply the quantity of a cost driver that should be used for an activity. Value-added costs can be computed by multiplying the value-added standards by the price standard. Nonvalue-added costs can be calculated as the difference between the actual level of the cost driver and the value-added level multiplied by the unit standard cost. These formulas are presented in Exhibit 26-3. Some further explanation is needed. For resources acquired as needed, *AQ* is the actual quantity of cost driver used.

value-added standard

Exhibit 26-3
Computational Formulas for Value- and Nonvalue-Added Costs

$$\text{Value-added costs} = SQ \times SP$$
$$\text{Nonvalue-added costs} = (AQ - SQ)SP$$

where SQ = The value-added quantity level of a cost driver
SP = The standard price per unit of cost driver
AQ = The actual quantity of cost driver used (if resources are supplied as needed)
or AQ = The actual quantity of cost driver acquired (if resources are supplied in advance of usage)

For resources acquired in advance of usage, AQ represents the actual quantity of activity capacity acquired, as measured by the activity's practical capacity. This definition of AQ allows the computation of nonvalue-added costs for both variable and fixed activity costs. For fixed activity costs, SP is the budgeted activity costs divided by AQ, where AQ is practical activity capacity.

To illustrate the power of the above concepts, let's focus on the following four activities for a product manufactured in a JIT environment: material usage, power, setups, and expediting of production orders. Of the four activities, three are viewed as necessary: material usage, power, and setups; expediting is unnecessary. (In an ideal sense, orders should all be processed on a timely basis.) Furthermore, assume that the first three activities acquire resources as needed whereas expediting capacity is acquired in advance of usage (salaries are budgeted at $50,000 for two expeditors). The following data pertain to the four activities:

	Cost Driver	*SQ*	*AQ*	*SP*
Material usage	Pounds	20,000	22,000	$20.00
Power	Kilowatt hours	40,000	44,000	3.00
Setups	Setup time	—	3,000	30.00
Expediting	Number of orders	—	4,000	12.50

Notice that the value-added standard for expediting calls for its elimination; the value-added standard for setups calls for a zero setup time. As pointed out earlier, orders should be processed on a timely basis; by improving quality, changing production processes, and so on, expediting can eventually be eliminated. Setups are necessary, but in a JIT environment, efforts are made to drive setup times to zero.

Exhibit 26-4 classifies the costs for the four activities as value-added or nonvalue-added. For simplicity and to show the relationship to actual costs, the actual price per unit of the cost driver is assumed to be equal to the standard price. In this case, the value-added cost plus the nonvalue-added cost equals actual cost. Normally, it might be necessary to add a price variance column.

The cost report in Exhibit 26-4 allows managers to see the nonvalue-added costs; as a consequence, it emphasizes the opportunity for improvement. By decreasing scrap, waste, and rework, management can reduce its material cost. By reducing rework and improving labor efficiency, management can reduce kilowatt hours (the machines would be used more efficiently) and power costs.

Exhibit 26-4

Value- and Nonvalue-Added Cost Report
For the Year Ending December 31, 1994

	Costs		
Activity	*Value Added*	*Nonvalue Added*	*Actual*
Material usage	$400,000	$ 40,000	$440,000
Power	120,000	12,000	132,000
Setups	—	90,000	90,000
Expediting	—	50,000	50,000
Total	$520,000	$192,000	$712,000

Reducing setup time and reorganizing the manufacturing layout are also areas in which improvement can be realized and costs reduced.

Thus, reporting value- and nonvalue-added costs at a point in time may trigger actions to manage activities more effectively. Seeing the amount of waste may induce managers to search for ways to reduce, select, share, and eliminate activities to bring about cost reductions. Reporting these costs may also help managers improve planning, budgeting, and pricing decisions. For example, lowering the selling price to meet a competitor's price may be seen as possible if a manager can see the potential for reducing nonvalue-added costs to absorb the effect of the price reduction.

Trend Reporting. As managers take actions to reduce, eliminate, select, and share activities, do the cost reductions follow as expected? One way to answer this question is to compare the costs for each activity over time. The goal is cost reduction; therefore, we should see a decline in nonvalue-added costs from one period to the next—provided activity analysis is effective. Assume, for example, that at the beginning of 1995, the following actions are taken to manage the four activities in Exhibit 26-4:

1. Material usage activity: Statistical process control is implemented. Scrap and waste are expected to decrease.
2. Setups: The product is redesigned, creating a requirement for a simpler die. The simpler die should reduce setup time.
3. Power: The product redesign also is expected to reduce the rework and lower power consumption.
4. Expediting: Cellular manufacturing is to be implemented with the expectation that production time can be reduced for key products. Reducing the production time for products should reduce the need for the expediting activity.

Three major activity-management decisions were made: the use of statistical process control, product redesign, and cellular manufacturing. How effective were these decisions? Did a cost reduction occur as expected? Exhibit 26-5 provides a cost report that compares the nonvalue-added costs of 1994 with those that occurred in 1995 (after implementing the changes described above). The 1995 costs are assumed but would be computed the same way as shown for 1994. We assume that *SQ* is the same for both years. Comparing 1995 nonvalue-added costs directly with 1994 value-added costs requires *SQ* to be the same for both

Exhibit 26-5
Trend Report: Nonvalue-Added Costs

	Nonvalue-Added Costs		
Activity	*1994*	*1995*	*Change*
Material usage	$ 40,000	$10,000	$ 30,000 F
Power	12,000	6,000	6,000 F
Setups	90,000	45,000	45,000 F
Expediting[1]	50,000	25,000	25,000 F
Totals	$192,000	$86,000	$106,000 F

[1]During the year, cellular manufacturing decreased production time and reduced the number of late orders by 50%. Consequently, one expeditor was transferred to an open position in production.

years. If *SQ* changes, prior-year nonvalue-added costs are adjusted by simply assuming the same percentage deviation from standard in the current year as was realized in the prior year.

The trend report reveals that cost reductions followed as expected. Half of the nonvalue-added costs have been eliminated. There is still ample room for improvement, but activity analysis so far has been successful. As a note of interest, comparison of the actual costs of the two periods would have revealed the same reduction. Reporting nonvalue-added costs, however, not only reveals the reduction but also provides managers with information on how much potential for cost reduction remains. There is an important qualification, however.

Value-added standards, like other standards, are not cast in stone. New technology, new designs, and other innovations can change the nature of activities performed. Value-added activities can be converted to nonvalue-added activities, and value-added levels can change as well. Thus, as new ways for improvement surface, value-added standards can change. Managers should not become content but should continually seek higher levels of efficiency.

The Role of Currently Attainable Standards

Although value-added standards are preeminent in the advanced manufacturing environment, the use of currently attainable standards can be retained in a modified form; however, detailed reporting of deviations from these standards should not be done at the operational level. Doing so may encourage behavior that is not compatible with the objectives of the advanced manufacturing environment. The reporting of variance analysis using currently attainable standards should be at the plant level (or higher). In the new system, these reports have the primary purpose of assessing performance under existing conditions and evaluating progress towards goals. With these purposes, the definition of what is meant by a currently attainable standard is changed.

If a company is emphasizing the reduction of nonvalue-added costs, the currently attainable standards should reflect the increased efficiency expected for the year. Comparing actual costs with the currently attainable standards would then provide a measure of how well the current year's goals for improvement have been met.

This use of currently attainable standards is equivalent to emphasizing actual costs and trends in actual costs. Cost reduction targets are set; evaluations concern how well managers meet these targets. Of course, comparison of actual costs with cost reduction targets is equivalent to comparing them to a currently attainable standard provided that the currently attainable standard is defined as last year's actual costs less the targeted reduction.

For example, the value-added standard may call for 3 pounds of raw material priced at $12 each or a value-added materials cost of $36 per unit. Assume that in the prior year, the $12 price was achieved, but 3.5 pounds of material were used for each unit that was produced, yielding an actual cost of materials per unit of $42 (a nonvalue-added cost of $6 per unit). For the current year, the company has a goal to reduce the nonvalue-added cost by $1.80 per unit. This goal is to be achieved by reducing material usage by 0.15 pounds per unit (the price of materials is assumed to be the same). Thus, the currently attainable quantity standard is defined as 3.35 pounds per unit. The currently attainable standard cost of materials per unit is $40.20, the actual prior year cost less the targeted reduction ($42.00 − $1.80). For the following year, additional improvements would be sought and a new currently attainable standard defined.

target cost

Target Costing. A related, but conceptually distinct approach being used by many companies is target costs. A **target cost** is the difference between the sales price needed to capture a predetermined market share and the desired profit per unit.[11] If the target cost is less than what is currently achievable, then management must budget cost reductions that move the actual cost toward the target cost. Progress is measured by comparing actual costs with target costs.

For example, suppose that the current sales price of a product is $10 and the market share is 12 percent. The marketing manager indicates that reducing the sales price to $8.50 will increase market share from 12 percent to 20 percent. The president of the company indicates that the desired profit per unit is $2. The target cost is computed as follows:

$$\text{Target cost} = \$8.50 - \$2.00 = \$6.50$$

Suppose that it currently costs $7.75 per unit to produce the product. Thus, the cost reduction needed to achieve the target cost and desired profit is $1.25 ($7.75 − $6.50). To realize the target cost, management must build in cost reductions by judicious activity analysis and management. The idea is to achieve the reduction needed over time. Variances are computed periodically by comparing actual costs with targeted costs.

Target costs are a type of currently attainable standard. But, they are conceptually different from the modified standards discussed above. What makes them different is the motivating force. The initial modified definition of currently attainable standards was motivated by the objective of moving towards a value-added standard generated internally by industrial engineers and production managers. Target costs, on the other hand, are externally driven, generated by an analysis of markets and competitors. Regardless of motivation, the two standards generally share the common goal of cost reduction or continuous improvement.

Cost Driver Analysis: Behavioral Effects

As indicated, identifying cost drivers is a critical part of controlling nonvalue-added costs. If an individual's performance is affected by his or her ability to

11. Berliner and Brimson, *Cost Management for Today's Advanced Manufacturing*, pp. 9 and 221.

control nonvalue-added costs, the selection of cost drivers and how they are used, can affect an individual's behavior. For example, if the cost driver for setup costs is chosen as setup time, an incentive is created for workers to reduce setup time. Since the value-added standard for setup costs calls for their complete elimination, the incentive to drive setup time to zero is compatible with the company's objectives, and the induced behavior is beneficial.

Suppose, however, that the objective is to reduce the number of unique parts a company processes, thus simplifying activities such as incoming inspection, preparation of bills of materials, and vendor selection.[12] If the costs of these activities are assigned to products based on the number of parts, the incentive created is to reduce the number of parts in a product. While this behavior may be desirable to a point, it can also have negative consequences. Designers may actually reduce the marketability of the product by reducing the number of parts too greatly and adversely affect its functionality.

This type of behavior can be discouraged by the proper use of standard costing. First, if the number of parts truly drives the costs of incoming inspection, preparation of bills of materials, and vendor selection, a budgeted cost per unit of cost driver can be computed (i.e., a standard price per unit). Next, the value-added standard number of parts for each product should be identified (the standard quantity). The value-added costs are simply the product of the standard price and standard quantity ($SP \times SQ$). As before, nonvalue-added costs is the difference between the actual parts used and the standard parts allowed multiplied by the standard price $[(AQ - SQ)SP]$.

For example, assume that a company produces two machines: lathes and drills. The company has determined that activities driven by parts should cost $400 per part (*SP*). The value-added quantity and actual parts for each product are given below.

	Lathes	*Drills*
Value-added number (*SQ*)	5	10
Actual number (*AQ*)	10	15

The value-added and nonvalue-added costs for each product are presented below.

	Lathes	*Drills*
Value-added costs	$2,000	$4,000
Nonvalue-added costs	2,000	2,000

Designers should be encouraged to reduce the nonvalue-added costs by reaching the value-added standard, but indiscriminate use of cost drivers can produce dysfunctional behavior. This example illustrates the importance of setting standards. The absence of any standard can lead designers to reduce parts in order to reduce costs without any sense of direction or purpose. However, by identifying, before the fact, the number of parts each product *should* have, using

12. This example is based on the discussion concerning behavioral effects of cost drivers found in Robin Cooper, "The Rise of Activity-Based Costing—Part Three: How Many Cost Drivers Do You Need, and How Do You Select Them?" *Journal of Cost Management for the Manufacturing Industry* (Winter 1989), pp. 34–46.

the number of parts as a cost driver can encourage reduction of only nonvalue-added costs. The standard has provided a concrete objective and defined the kind of behavior that the incentive allows.

LIFE-CYCLE COST MANAGEMENT

Objective 3
Explain life-cycle cost management and why it is important for the advanced manufacturing environment.

product life cycle
life-cycle costs

The example just given illustrates the impact design can have on costs. In fact, 90 percent or more of the costs associated with a product are *committed* during the development stage of the product's life cycle.[13] **Product life cycle** is simply the time a product exists—from conception to abandonment. **Life-cycle costs** are all costs associated with the product for its entire life cycle. These costs include development (planning, design, and testing), production (conversion activities), and logistics support (advertising, distribution, warranty, and so on). The product life cycle and the associated cost commitment curve are illustrated in Exhibit 26-6.[14]

whole-life cost

Because total customer satisfaction has become a vital issue in the new business setting, *whole-life cost* has emerged as the central focus of life-cycle cost management. **Whole-life cost** is the life-cycle cost of a product plus post-purchase costs that consumers incur, including operation, support, maintenance, and dis-

Exhibit 26-6

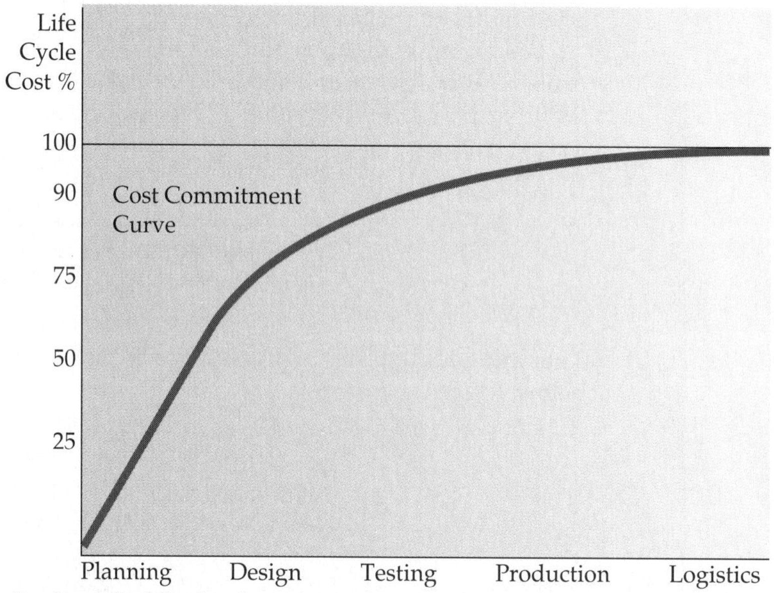

By the end of the development stage, at least 90 percent of the life-cycle costs are *committed (but not incurred).*

13. See John P. Campi, "Corporate Mindset: Strategic Advantage or Fatal Vision," *Journal of Cost Management* (Spring 1991), pp. 53–57. Also see Berliner and Brimson, *Cost Management for Today's Advanced Manufacturing.* The section on life-cycle costing is based on these two sources, with particular emphasis on the second source.
14. Life cycle can be viewed from a production or marketing perspective. We have adopted a production perspective, with stages of the life cycle defined by changes in the types of activities performed: development activities, production activities, and logistical activities. The marketing perspective, on the other hand, focuses on sales demand and has the following four stages: start-up, growth, maturity, and decline.

posal.[15] Since the costs a purchaser incurs *after* buying a product can be a significant percentage of whole-life costs and, thus, an important consideration in the purchase decision, managing activities so that whole-life costs are reduced can provide an important competitive advantage. Notice that *cost reduction* not cost control is the emphasis. Moreover, cost reduction is achieved by judicious analysis and management of activities. Whole-life costing emphasizes management of the entire *value chain*. The **value chain** is the set of activities required to design, develop, produce, market, and service a product (or service). Thus, **life-cycle cost management** focuses on managing value-chain activities so that a long-term competitive advantage is created. To achieve this goal, managers must balance a product's whole-life cost, method of delivery, innovativeness, and various product attributes including performance, features offered, reliability, conformance, durability, aesthetics, and perceived quality.

value chain

life-cycle cost management

Cost Reduction

Since 90 percent or more of a product's costs are committed during the development stage, it makes sense to emphasize management of activities during this phase of a product's existence. Studies have shown that every dollar spent on premanufacturing activities saves \$8–\$10 on manufacturing and postmanufacturing activities.[16] The real opportunities for cost reduction occur before manufacturing begins! Managers need to invest more in premanufacturing assets and dedicate more resources to activities in the early phases of the product life cycle so that overall whole-life costs can be reduced.

Yet, in spite of this observation, the traditional emphasis has been on controlling costs *during* the production stage (when much less can be done to influence them). Furthermore, product cost has been narrowly defined as production costs; development and logistics costs have been treated as period costs and have been virtually ignored when computing product profitability. Additionally, little attention has been given to the effect of the customer's post-purchase costs. While this practice may be acceptable for external reporting, it is not acceptable for managerial product costing. In the highly competitive environment of today, world-class competitors need comprehensive product cost information.

Whole-life Product Cost. From a whole-life point of view, product cost is made up of four major elements: (1) nonrecurring costs (planning, designing, and testing), (2) manufacturing costs, (3) logistic costs, and (4) the customer's post-purchase costs. Measuring, accumulating, and reporting all of a product's whole-life costs allows managers to better assess the effectiveness of life-cycle planning and build more effective and sophisticated marketing strategies. Life-cycle costing also increases their ability to make good pricing decisions and improve the assessment of product profitability.

15. It can be argued that whole-life cost is an alternative definition of life-cycle cost—one that includes the customer's perspective as well as the production point of view. For an excellent treatment of life-cycle costing, see Michael D. Shields and S. Mark Young, "Managing Product Life Cycle Costs: An Organizational Model," *Journal of Cost Management*, Fall 1991, pp. 39–52. Many of the concepts presented in this section are based on this article.

16. See Mark D. Shields and S. Mark Young, "Managing Product Life Cycle Costs: an Organizational Model; R. L. Engwall, "Cost Management Systems for Defense Contractors," in *Cost Accounting for the 90s, Responding to Technological Change* (Montvale, NJ, National Association of Accountants, 1988).

Role of Target Costing. Life-cycle cost management emphasizes cost reduction, not cost control. Thus, target costing becomes a particularly useful tool for establishing cost reduction goals. Toyota, for example, calculates the lifetime target profit for a new car model by multiplying a target profit ratio times the target sales. They then calculate the estimated profit by subtracting the estimated costs from target sales. Usually, (at this point), target profit is greater than estimated profit. The cost reduction goal is defined by the difference between the target profit and the estimated profit. Toyota then searches for cost reduction opportunities through better design of the new model. Toyota's management recognizes that more opportunities exist for cost reduction during product planning than in actual development and production.[17]

Short Life Cycles

Although life-cycle cost management is important for all manufacturing firms, it is particularly important for firms that have products with short life cycles. Products must recover all life-cycle costs and provide an acceptable profit. If a firm's products have long life cycles, profit performance can be increased by such actions as redesigning, changing prices, cost reduction, and altering the product mix. In contrast, firms that have products with short life cycles usually do not have time to react in this way and so their approach must be proactive. Thus, for short life cycles, good life-cycle planning is critical and prices must be set properly to recover all the life-cycle costs and provide a good return. Activity-based costing can be used to encourage good life-cycle planning. By careful selection of cost drivers, design engineers can be motivated to choose cost-minimizing designs.[18] (This is a proactive strategy—how this can be done was discussed in a previous section on cost driver analysis.)

Life-Cycle Costing: An Example

Murphy Company produces electronic products that typically have about a twenty-seven-month life cycle. At the beginning of the last quarter of 1994, a new component was proposed. Design engineering believed that the product would be ready to produce by the beginning of 1995. To produce this and other similar products, resistors had to be inserted into a circuit board. Management had discovered that the cost of the circuit board was driven by the number of insertions. Knowing this, design engineering produced the new component using fewer insertions than the products in the past had employed.

The budgeted costs and profits for the product over its two-year life cycle are illustrated in Exhibit 26-7. Notice that the life-cycle unit cost is $10 per unit compared with the conventional definition of $6 (which includes only the production costs) and the whole-life cost of $12. To be viable, of course, the product must cover all of its life-cycle costs and produce an acceptable profit. The $15 price was set with this objective in mind. Focusing only on the $6 cost could have led to a suboptimal pricing decision. Changing the focus requires managers to move

17. For a complete description of Toyota's approach, see Takao Tanaka, "Target Costing at Toyota," *Journal of Cost Management*, Spring 1993, pp. 4–11.
18. Robin Cooper and Peter B. B. Turney, "Internally Focused Activity-Based Cost Systems," in Kaplan (ed.), *Measures for Manufacturing Excellence*, pp. 291–305.

Exhibit 26-7
Life-Cycle Costing: Budgeted Costs and Income

Unit Cost and Price Information

Unit production cost	$ 6
Unit life-cycle cost	10
Unit whole-life cost	12
Budgeted unit selling price	15

Budgeted Costs

Item	*1993*	*1994*	*1995*	*Item Total*
Development costs	$200,000	—	—	$ 200,000
Production costs	—	$240,000	$360,000	600,000
Logistics costs	—	80,000	120,000	200,000
Annual subtotal	$200,000	$320,000	$480,000	$1,000,000
Post-purchase costs	—	80,000	120,000	200,000
Annual total	$200,000	$400,000	$600,000	$1,200,000
Units produced		40,000	60,000	

Budgeted Product Income Statements

Year	*Revenues*	*Costs*	*Annual Income*	*Cumulative Income*
1993	—	$(200,000)	$(200,000)	$(200,000)
1994	$600,000	(320,000)	280,000	80,000
1995	900,000	(480,000)	420,000	500,000

Note: the post-purchase costs are costs incurred by the customer and so would not be included in the budgeted income statements.

away from the traditional, financially driven definition of product cost. Conventional cost systems do not directly identify development costs with the product being developed. The whole-life cost provides even more information—information that could prove vital for the company's life-cycle strategy. For example, if competitors sell a similar product for the same price but with post-purchase costs of only $1 per unit, the company could be at a competitive disadvantage. Given this information, actions can be considered that can eliminate the disadvantage (e.g., redesign of the product to lower the post-purchase costs).

Feedback on the effectiveness of life-cycle planning is also helpful. This information can help future new product planning as well as be useful for assessing how design decisions affect operational and support costs. Comparing actual costs with the budgeted costs can provide useful insights. Exhibit 26-8 illustrates a simple life-cycle cost performance report. As can be seen, production costs were greater than expected. Investigation revealed that costs are driven by total number of insertions, not just insertions of resistors. Further analysis also revealed that by reducing the total number of insertions, post-purchase costs could be reduced. Thus, future design work on similar products can benefit by the assessment.

Exhibit 26-8
Performance Report: Life-Cycle Costs

Year	*Item*	*Actual Costs*	*Budgeted Costs*	*Variance*
1993	Development	$190,000	$200,000	$10,000 F
1994	Production	300,000	240,000	60,000 U
	Logistics	75,000	80,000	5,000 F
1995	Production	435,000	360,000	75,000 U
	Logistics	110,000	120,000	10,000 F

Analysis: Production costs were higher than expected because insertions of diodes and integrated circuits also drive costs (both production and post-purchase costs).
Conclusion: The design of future products should try to minimize total insertions.

QUALITY COSTS: MEASUREMENT AND CONTROL

Objective 4
Describe how quality costs are measured and controlled.

In the advanced manufacturing environment, quality is a critical competitive tool. Focusing on customer wants—total customer satisfaction—is absolutely essential for a world-class competitor. Moreover, paying more attention to quality can produce significant savings. In a tightly competitive market, these savings along with customer satisfaction can mean the difference between surviving and thriving. For example, Tennant Company, a manufacturer of floor maintenance products, over an eight-year period (1980–88) reduced its costs of quality from about 17% of sales to about 2.5% of sales. Based on sales of $136 million, annual savings from improved quality totaled approximately $19.7 million.[19] It should be pointed out that these savings are not confined to manufacturing firms. In 1980, the banking industry spent $435 million on rework because of faulty magnetic-ink character recognition codes; this is nearly one-half of all check processing costs. (When the recognition codes are faulty, the computer rejects the checks as unreadable, and they must be processed by hand.)[20] Imagine the savings possible if banks worked with the printers of checks to improve the reliability of their product.

As these examples illustrate, the costs of quality can be substantial and a source of significant savings. In fact, studies indicate that costs of quality for American companies are typically 20% to 30% of sales.[21] Yet, quality experts maintain that the optimal quality level should be about 2.5 percent of sales. Tennant Company's success indicates that the 2.5% goal is achievable.

In the last two decades, U.S. firms have faced increased competition from foreign firms in both world and domestic markets. Quality has become an important competitive dimension. Often foreign firms have been selling higher-quality products at lower prices. Consequently, many U.S. firms have lost market share. In an effort to combat this stiff competition, U.S. firms have begun to pay increasing attention to quality and productivity, especially because of the potential to reduce costs and improve product quality simultaneously. The senior management of IBM Corporation, for example, has identified poor quality as the root cause of its recent problems. In an effort to solve some of these problems, the

19. Lawrence P. Carr and Thomas Tyson, "Planning Quality Cost Expenditures," *Management Accounting*, October 1992, pp. 52–56.
20. William J. Latzko, "Quality Control for Banks," *The Banker's Magazine* (Autumn 1981), pp. 64–70.
21. Ostrenga, Michael R., "Return on Investment Through the Cost of Quality," *Journal of Cost Management* (Summer 1991), pp. 37–44.

company has implemented a quality program called "Market Driven Quality." The Chairman of IBM, John Akers, indicated very simply that quality improvement was a survival issue.[22] Other American companies are following suit and are striving to meet consumer quality expectations. Some are even calling this push for increased quality a "second industrial revolution."[23]

As companies like IBM implement quality improvement programs, a need arises to monitor and report on the progress of these programs. Managers need to know what quality costs are and how they are changing over time. Who should be responsible for measuring and reporting quality costs? As the introductory case indicates, the accounting department is ideally suited for this task. By having the accounting department measure and report quality costs, the performance of the quality department can be assessed more objectively. Moreover, it seems eminently reasonable that the department responsible for cost systems ought to be responsible for developing and operating the quality cost system.

Measuring the Costs of Quality

Managers must be able to monitor their firm's progress in achieving objectives for quality improvement and maintaining quality levels. Reporting and measuring quality performance is absolutely essential to the success of an ongoing quality improvement program. A fundamental prerequisite for this reporting is measuring the costs of quality. But to measure those costs, an operational definition of quality itself is needed.

Quality Defined. The typical dictionary definition of *quality* is the degree or grade of excellence; in this sense, quality is a relative measure of goodness. But how does this translate into day-to-day business realities? Operationally, a *quality product* is a product that conforms to customer expectations. Generally, two types of quality are recognized: quality of design and quality of conformance.

quality of design

Quality of design is a function of a product's specifications. For example, the function of watches is to allow an individual to tell what time it is. Yet, one watch may have a steel casing, require winding, have a leather strap, and be engineered to lose no more than two minutes per month. Another may have a gold-plated casing, be battery operated, have a gold-plated back, and be engineered to lose no more than one minute per year. Obviously, the design qualities are different. Most would agree that the gold watch is the higher quality of the two: Higher design quality is usually reflected in higher manufacturing costs and higher selling prices.

quality of conformance

Quality of conformance is a measure of how a product meets its requirements or specifications. If the product meets all of the designed specifications, it is fit for use. For example, a customer buying a steel-plated watch expects that the watch will function for a reasonable period of time. Suppose that the first time the customer winds the watch, the stem breaks off or that the watch consistently loses 20 minutes per day. What type of quality assessment will the customer make? On the other hand, a competitor's watch at the *same* design level may rarely experience problems with the stem or with keeping time. What is the quality assessment of this watch?

22. See Lawrence Carr and Thomas Tyson, "Planning Quality Cost Expenditures," p. 55.
23. James B. Simpson and David L. Muthler, "Quality Costs: Facilitating the Quality Initiative," *Journal of Cost Management* (Spring 1987), pp. 25–34.

Of the two types of quality, quality of conformance should receive the most emphasis. It is nonconformance to requirements that creates the most problems for companies. When quality experts speak of improving quality, they mean reducing the incidence of nonconformance. To them, the word *quality* is synonymous with conformance to requirements—doing it right the first time. The product should be produced as the design specifies it; requirements should be followed. If the product is not good, the design needs to be changed. Throughout the remainder of this chapter, whenever you see the word *quality*, think of it as quality of conformance.

costs of quality

Costs of Quality Defined. The **costs of quality** are the costs that exist because poor quality may or does exist.[24] Thus, quality costs are the costs associated with the creation, identification, repair, and prevention of defects. These costs can be classified into four categories: prevention costs, appraisal costs, internal failure costs, and external failure costs. Because things may go wrong, a company incurs prevention and appraisal costs (control costs). When things do go wrong, a company experiences failure costs.

prevention costs

Prevention costs are incurred to prevent defects in the products or services being produced. As prevention costs increase, we would expect the costs of failure to decrease; thus, prevention costs are incurred in order to decrease the number of nonconforming units. Examples of prevention costs are quality engineering, quality training programs, quality planning, quality reporting, supplier evaluations, quality audits, quality circles, and design reviews.

appraisal costs

Appraisal costs are incurred to determine whether products and services are conforming to their requirements. Examples include inspecting and testing raw materials, packaging inspection, supervising appraisal activities, product acceptance, process acceptance, supplier verification, and field testing. Two of these terms require further explanation.

Product acceptance involves sampling from batches of finished goods to determine whether they meet an acceptable quality level; if so, the goods are accepted. *Process acceptance* involves sampling goods while in process to see if the process is in control and producing nondefective goods; if not, the process is shut down until corrective action can be taken. The main objective of the appraisal function is to prevent nonconforming goods from being shipped to customers.

internal failure costs

Internal failure costs are incurred because nonconforming products and services are detected prior to being shipped to outside parties. These are the failures detected by appraisal activities. Examples of internal failure costs are scrap, rework, downtime (due to defects), reinspection, retesting, and design changes. These costs disappear if no defects exist.

external failure costs

External failure costs are incurred because products and services fail to conform to requirements after being delivered to customers. Of all the costs of quality, this category can be the most devastating. For example, Firestone spent approximately $135 million in a 1977 recall of 7.5 million steel-belted radial tires.[25] Other examples include lost sales because of poor product performance, returns and allowances because of poor quality, warranties, repair, product liability, and complaint adjustment. External failure costs, like internal failure costs, disappear if no defects exist.

24. This is the definition in Morse, Roth, and Poston, *Measuring, Planning, and Controlling*, p. 19.
25. Robert M. Reece, "QC As an Inflation Fighter," *Quality Progress* (August 1980), pp. 24–25.

Exhibit 26-9

Prevention Costs	*Appraisal Costs*
Quality engineering	Inspection of raw materials
Quality training	Packaging inspection
Quality planning	Product acceptance
Quality audits	Process acceptance
Design reviews	Field testing
Quality circles	Supplier verification
Internal Failure Costs	*External Failure Costs*
Scrap	Lost sales (performance related)
Rework	Returns/allowances
Downtime (defect related)	Warranties
Reinspection	Repair
Retesting	Product liability
Design changes	Complaint adjustment

Exhibit 26-9 summarizes the four quality cost categories and lists specific examples of costs within each category.

Reporting Quality Cost Information

A quality cost reporting system is essential if an organization is serious about improving and controlling quality costs. The first and simplest step in creating such a system is an assessment of current actual quality costs. A detailed listing of actual quality costs by category can provide two important insights. First, it reveals the magnitude of the quality costs in each category, allowing managers to assess their financial impact. Second, it shows the distribution of quality costs by category, allowing managers to assess the relative importance of each category.

Quality Cost Reports

The financial significance of quality costs can be assessed more easily by expressing these costs as a percentage of actual sales. Exhibit 26-10, for example, reports the quality costs of Jensen Products for fiscal 1995.[26] According to the report, quality costs represent almost 12 percent of sales. Given the rule of thumb that quality costs should be no more than about 2.5 percent, Jensen Products has ample opportunity to improve profits by decreasing quality costs. Understand, however, that reduction in costs should come through improvement of quality. Reduction of quality costs without any effort to improve quality could prove to be a disastrous strategy.

26. The quality cost report given in Exhibit 26-10 parallels the format used by ITT except for several minor differences. First, the ITT report combines the internal and external categories into one failure category. Second, the ITT report has a third column allowing the reporting unit to express quality costs as a percentage of a measure other than sales. For more detail, see Morse, Roth, and Poston, *Measuring, Planning, and Controlling*, pp. 78–81.

Exhibit 26-10

Jensen Products Quality Cost Report For the Year Ended March 31, 1995			
	Quality Costs		*Percentage of Sales*[a]
Prevention costs:			
Quality training	$35,000		
Reliability engineering	80,000	$115,000	4.11%
Appraisal costs:			
Materials inspection	$20,000		
Product acceptance	10,000		
Process acceptance	38,000	68,000	2.43
Internal failure costs:			
Scrap	$50,000		
Rework	35,000	85,000	3.04
External failure costs:			
Customer complaints	$25,000		
Warranty	25,000		
Repair	15,000	65,000	2.32
Total quality costs		$333,000	11.90%[b]

[a] Actual sales of $2,800,000
[b] $333,000/$2,800,000 = 11.89 percent. Difference is rounding error.

Additional insight concerning the relative distribution of quality costs can be realized by constructing a pie chart. Exhibit 26-11 provides such a chart, using the quality costs reported in Exhibit 26-10. Managers, of course, have the responsibility to assess the optimal level of quality and to determine the relative amount that should be spent in each category. There are two views concerning optimal quality costs: the traditional view, calling for an *acceptable quality level,* and the

Exhibit 26-11
Pie Chart: Quality Costs

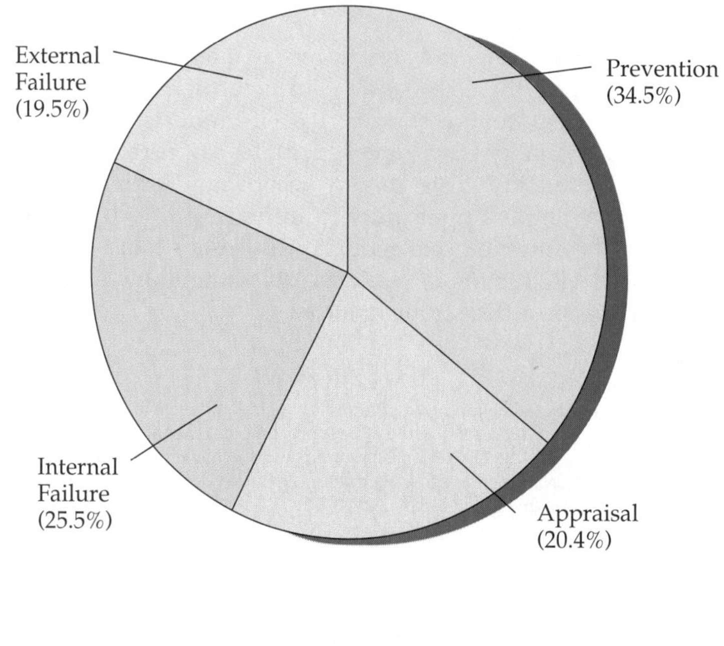

view being adopted by world-class firms referred to as *total quality control.* Each view offers managers insights about how quality costs ought to be managed.

Optimal Distribution of Quality Costs: Traditional View. Many quality experts believe that an optimal balance exists between prevention and appraisal costs and the internal and external failure costs. As control costs (prevention and appraisal costs) increase, failure costs should decrease. As long as the decrease in failure costs is greater than the corresponding increase in control costs, a company should continue increasing its efforts to prevent or detect nonconforming units. Eventually a point is reached at which any additional increase in this effort costs more than the corresponding reduction in failure costs. Without any change in technology, this point represents the minimum level of total quality costs. It is the optimal balance between control costs and failure costs. This theoretical relationship is illustrated in Exhibit 26-12.

In Exhibit 26-12, two cost functions are assumed: one for control costs and one for failure costs. It is also assumed that the percentage of defective units increases as the amount spent on prevention and appraisal activities decreases; failure costs, on the other hand, increase as the number of defective units increases. From the total quality cost function, we see that total quality costs decrease as quality improves up to a point. After that, no further improvement is possible. An optimal level of defective units is identified and the company works to achieve this level. This level of allowable defective units is defined as the **acceptable quality level (AQL).**

acceptable quality level (AQL)

Optimal Distribution of Quality Costs: World-Class View. For firms operating in an advanced manufacturing environment, competition is intense and quality can offer an important competitive advantage. If the conventional view is wrong, firms that recognize this error can capitalize on it by decreasing the number of

Exhibit 26-12
Traditional Quality Cost Graph

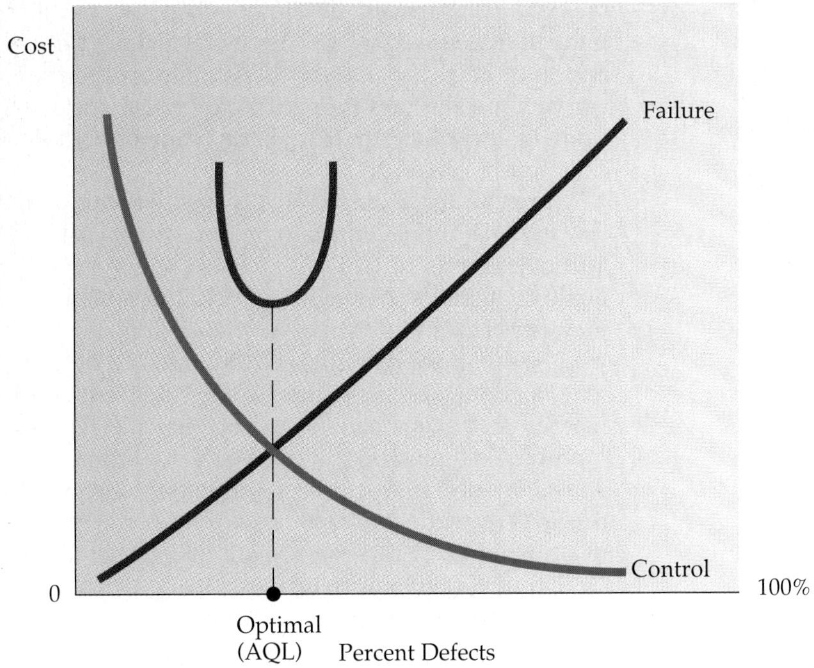

Exhibit 26-13
Zero-Defect Graph

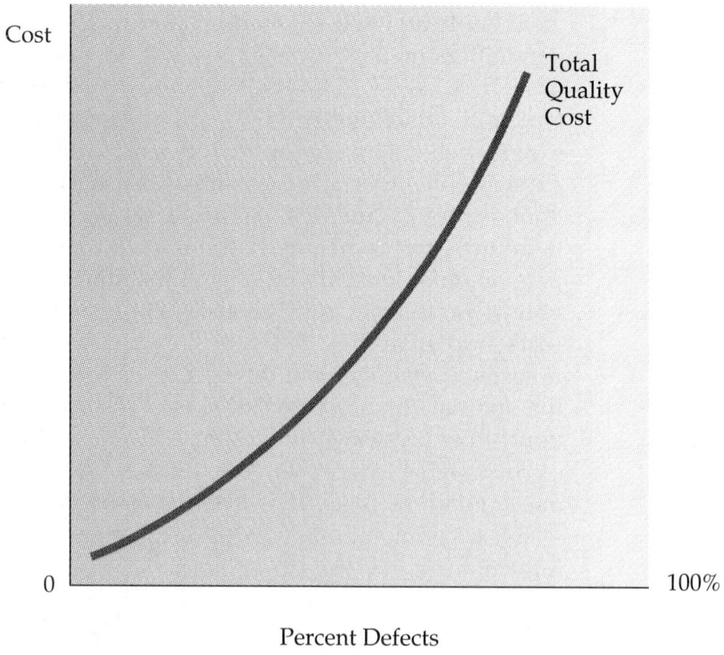

defective units while simultaneously decreasing their total quality costs. This is exactly what has happened, and it is changing the approach to quality cost management. The optimal level for quality costs is where zero defects are produced. Exhibit 26-13 illustrates the zero-defect view of the total quality cost function.

Quality Costs and Tradeoffs. The discovery that tradeoffs among quality cost categories can be managed differently than what is implied by the relationships portrayed in Exhibit 26-12 is analogous to the discovery that inventory cost tradeoffs can be managed differently than the traditional inventory model (EOQ) implied. Essentially, what happens is that as firms increase their prevention and appraisal costs and reduce their failure costs, they discover that they can then cut back on the prevention and appraisal costs. What initially appears to be a tradeoff turns out to be a permanent reduction in costs for all quality cost categories.

Suppose, for example, that a firm has decided to improve the quality of its raw material inputs through the implementation of a supplier selection program. The objective is to identify and use suppliers who are willing to meet certain quality standards. As the firm works to implement this program, additional costs may be incurred (e.g., review of suppliers, communication with suppliers, contract negotiations, and so on). And, initially, other prevention and appraisal costs may continue at their current levels. However, once the program is fully implemented and evidence is surfacing that the failure costs are being reduced (for example, less rework, fewer customer complaints, and fewer repairs), the company may decide to cut back on inspections of incoming raw materials, reduce the level of product acceptance activities, and so on. The net effect is a reduction in *all* quality cost categories. And quality has increased!

This ability to reduce total quality costs dramatically in all categories is borne out by real-world experiences. Tennant Company, for example, has reduced its costs of quality from 17% of sales in 1980 to 2.5% of sales in 1988, and, at the same time, has significantly altered the relative distribution of the quality cost categories. In 1980, failure costs accounted for 50% of the total costs of quality (8.5% of sales) and control costs 50% (8.5% of sales). In 1988, failure costs accounted for only 15% of the total costs of quality (.375% of sales) and control costs had increased to 85% of the total (2.125% of sales). Tennant increased quality, reduced quality costs in every category and in total, and shifted the distribution of quality costs to the control categories, with the greatest emphasis on prevention. This outcome argues strongly against the traditional quality cost model portrayed in Exhibit 26-12. According to the model in Exhibit 26-12, total quality costs can be decreased only by trading off control and prevention costs (increasing one while decreasing the other). Further support for the total quality control model is provided by Westinghouse Electric Company. Similar to Tennant, Westinghouse found that profits continue to improve until control costs account for about 70% to 80% of total quality costs.[27] Based on these two companies' experiences, we know it is possible to reduce total quality costs significantly—in all categories—and that the process radically alters the relative distribution of the quality cost categories.

Activity-Based Management and Optimal Quality Costs. Activity-based management classifies activities as value-added and nonvalue-added and keeps only those that add value. This principle can be applied to quality-related activities. Internal and external failure activities and their associated costs are nonvalue-added and should be eliminated. Prevention activities—performed efficiently—can be classified as value-added and should be retained. Initially, however, prevention activities may not be performed efficiently and activity reduction and activity selection (and perhaps even activity sharing) can be used to achieve the desired value-added state. Appraisal activities are more difficult to assess. The initial reaction may be to classify all appraisal activities as nonvalue-added. However, in reality, some of these activities—at some level—may be needed to prevent backsliding. Quality audits, for example, may serve a value-added objective. Similarly, it seems unrealistic to totally eliminate supplier verification. Conditions change, and without any monitoring, suppliers may also backslide.[28]

Once the activities are identified for each category, cost drivers can be used to improve cost assignments to the individual activities. Cost drivers can also be used to help managers understand what is causing the costs of the activities. This information can then be used to select ways of reducing quality costs to the level revealed by Exhibit 26-13. In effect, activity-based management supports the zero-defect view of quality costs. There is no optimal trade-off between control and failure costs. Failure costs are nonvalue-added costs and should be reduced to zero. Control activities may be performed inefficiently and the costs caused by the inefficiency are nonvalue-added. Thus, costs for these categories may also be reduced to lower levels.

27. These factual observations are based on those reported by Lawrence P. Carr and Thomas Tyson, "Planning Quality Cost Expenditures."

28. In Michael Ostrega, "Return on Investment Through the Cost of Quality," it is suggested that activity-based costing can be used to help managers understand the nature of quality costs. In this article, failure and appraisal activities are labeled as nonvalue-added. Only prevention activities were classified as value-added.

Controlling Quality Costs

Reporting quality costs is not sufficient to ensure that they are controlled. Proper control requires standards and a measure of actual outcomes so that performance can be gauged and corrective actions can be taken when necessary. Quality cost performance reports have two essential elements: actual outcomes and standard or expected outcomes. Any deviations of actual outcomes from the expected outcomes are used to evaluate managerial performance and provide signals concerning possible problems. Performance reports provide essential feedback so that managers can evaluate their own behavior and take corrective action when needed.

Performance reports are essential to quality improvement programs. A report like the one shown in Exhibit 26-10 forces managers to identify the various costs that should appear in a performance report, to identify the current quality performance level of the organization, and to begin thinking about the level of quality performance that should be achieved. Identifying the quality standard is a key element in a quality performance report.

Choosing the Quality Standard: The Traditional Approach. In the traditional approach, the appropriate quality standard is an acceptable quality level (AQL). An AQL is simply an admission that a certain number of defective products will be produced and sold. For example, the AQL may be set at 3 percent. In this case, any lot of products (or production run) that has no more than 3 percent defective units will be shipped to customers. Typically, the AQL reflects the current operating status, not what is possible if a firm has an excellent quality program. As the basis for a quality standard, AQL has the same problems as historical experience does for materials and labor usage standards: it may perpetuate past operating mistakes.

Unfortunately, AQL has additional problems. Setting a three-percent AQL is a commitment to deliver defective products to customers. Out of every 1 million units sold, 30,000 will yield dissatisfied customers. Why plan to make a certain number of defective units? Why not plan instead to make the product according to its specifications? Is there not a matter of integrity involved here? How many customers would accept a product if they knew that it was defective? How many people would consult a surgeon if they knew that the surgeon planned to botch three of every one hundred operations?

The Zero-Defects Approach. These questions reflect a new attitude toward quality being popularized by a number of quality experts. These experts suggest that a more sensible standard is to produce products as they were intended to be. This standard is often referred to as the *zero-defects concept.* **Zero defects** is a performance standard that calls for products and services to be produced and delivered according to requirements. It reflects a philosophy of total quality control. Recall that the need for total quality control is inherent in a JIT manufacturing approach. Thus, the movement toward total quality control is being sustained by the firms adopting JIT. JIT, however, is not a prerequisite for moving towards total quality control. This philosophy can stand by itself.

zero defects

Admittedly, the zero defects standard is one that may not be completely attainable; however, evidence exists that it can be closely approximated. Defects are caused either by lack of knowledge or by lack of attention. Lack of knowledge can be corrected by proper training, lack of attention by effective leadership. Note also that the zero-defects concept implies the ultimate elimination of failure costs. Those believing in zero defects will continue to search for new ways to improve quality costs. Thus, implicit in the standard is the capability to move down the total cost curve shown in Exhibit 26-13.

Some may wonder whether zero defects is a realistic standard. Consider the following anecdote. An American firm placed an order for a particular component with a Japanese firm. In the order, the American firm specified that 1,000 components should be delivered with an AQL of 5 percent defects. When the order arrived, it came in two boxes—one large and one small. A note explained that the large box contained 950 good components and the small one fifty defective components; the note also asked why the firm wanted fifty defective parts (implying the capability of delivering no defective parts).

Consider another case. A firm is engaged in a significant volume of business through mailings. On average, 15 percent of the mailings were sent to the wrong address. Returned merchandise, late payments, and lost sales all resulted from this error rate. In one case, a tax payment was sent to the wrong address. By the time the payment arrived, it was late, causing a penalty of $300,000. Why not spend the resources (surely less than $300,000) to get the mailing list right and have no errors? Is a mailing list that is 100 percent accurate really impossible to achieve? Why not do it right the first time?

Quantifying the Quality Standard. Quality can be measured by its costs; as the costs of quality decrease, higher quality results—at least up to a point. Even if the standard of zero defects is achieved, a company must still have prevention and appraisal costs. A company with a well-run quality management program can get by with quality costs that are no more than 2.5 percent of sales. (If zero defects are achieved, this cost is for prevention and appraisal.) This 2.5 percent standard is accepted by many quality control experts and many firms that are adopting aggressive quality improvement programs.

The 2.5 percent standard is for total costs of quality. Costs of individual quality factors, such as quality training or materials inspection, will be less. Each organization must determine the appropriate standard for each individual factor. Budgets can be used to set spending for each standard so that the total budgeted cost meets the 2.5 percent goal.

Behavior of Quality Costs. To make the 2.5 percent standard work, the cost behavior of individual quality factors must be identified. Some quality costs vary with sales; others do not. For performance reports to be useful, quality costs must be classified as variable or fixed with respect to sales. For variable quality costs, improvements in quality are reflected by reductions in the variable cost ratios. The beginning and ending variable cost ratios for a period can be used to compute the actual dollar savings (or actual increased costs). Budgeted and actual ratios can also be used to gauge the progress towards the period's goals. For fixed costs, quality improvements are best reflected by absolute dollar changes.

If maintaining a zero-defects standard requires a 1.5 percent variable cost ratio, meeting the overall goal of costs at 2.5 percent of sales limits fixed quality costs to 1 percent of sales. This budget for fixed quality costs would be set at the beginning of the year.

Fixed quality costs are evaluated by comparing actual costs with the budgeted costs. The dollars actually spent on these costs are what is compared. Comparing these costs using a percentage of sales, rather than actual dollars spent, is not useful. Since budgeted sales may not equal actual sales, the actual percentage could be greater or less than the budgeted percentage even if the actual fixed costs were exactly equal to the budgeted fixed costs.

Variable quality costs, on the other hand, can be compared using either percentages of sales or actual dollars or both. Since managers are accustomed to dealing with dollar amounts, the best approach is comparing absolute dollars and supplementing that measure with percentages. Furthermore, computing the overall percentage, using both variable and fixed costs, is also recommended. This will provide management with an idea of how well the overall 2.5 percent standard is being met.

Use of Interim Standards. For most firms, the standard of zero defects is a long-range goal. The ability to achieve this standard is strongly tied to supplier quality. For most companies, materials and services purchased from outside parties make up a significant part of the cost of the product. For example, more than 65 percent of the product cost for Tennant Company was from materials and parts purchased from more than 500 different suppliers. To achieve the desired quality level, Tennant had to launch a major campaign to involve its suppliers in similar quality improvement programs. Developing the relationships and securing the needed cooperation from suppliers takes time—in fact, it takes years. Similarly, getting people within the company itself to understand the need for quality improvement and to have confidence in the program can take several years.

interim quality standards

Because improving quality to the zero-defect level can take years, yearly quality improvement standards should be developed so that managers can use performance reports to assess the progress made on an interim basis. These **interim quality standards** express quality goals for the year. Progress should be reported to managers and employees in order to gain the confidence needed to achieve the ultimate standard of zero defects. Even though reaching the zero-defect level is a long-range project, management should expect significant progress on a yearly basis. For example, Tennant cut its quality costs from 17 percent of sales in 1980 to 8 percent of sales in 1986—an average reduction of more than 1 percent per year. Furthermore, once the 2.5 percent goal is reached, efforts must be expended continuously to maintain it. Performance reports, at this stage, assume a strict control role.

Types of Quality Performance Reports

Quality performance reports should measure the progress realized by an organization's quality improvement program. Two types of progress reports will be discussed:

1. Progress with respect to a current-period standard or goal (an interim standard report)
2. Progress with respect to last year's quality performance (a one-period trend report)

The interim standard report is a traditional approach to cost control, whereas the one-year trend report is more consistent with the new emphasis on tracking trends in actual costs. As will be seen, both reports provide important information for managers.

Interim Standard Report. As noted above, the organization must establish an interim quality standard each year and make plans to achieve this targeted level. Since quality costs are a measure of quality, the targeted level can be expressed in dollars budgeted for each category of quality costs and each cost item within the category. At the end of the period, the **interim quality performance report** compares the actual quality costs for the period against the budgeted costs. This report measures the progress achieved within the period relative to the planned level of progress for that period.

interim quality performance report

Exhibit 26-14 illustrates such a report. For variable costs, the budgeted figures are based on actual sales using variable cost ratios, which were obtained by dividing budgeted variable costs by budgeted sales. The original budgeted amounts are used for fixed costs.

The interim report reveals the within-period quality improvement relative to specific objectives as reflected by the budgeted figures. For Jensen Products, the overall performance is close to what was planned: total actual quality costs differ

Exhibit 26-14

Jensen Products
Interim Standard Performance Report: Quality Costs
For the Year Ended March 31, 1995

	Actual Costs	*Budgeted Costs*[a]	*Variance*
Prevention costs:			
Fixed:			
Quality training	$ 35,000	$ 30,000	$ 5,000 U
Reliability engineering	80,000	80,000	0
Total prevention	$115,000	$110,000	$ 5,000 U
Appraisal costs:			
Variable:			
Materials inspection	$ 20,000	$ 28,000	$ 8,000 F
Product acceptance	10,000	15,000	5,000 F
Process acceptance	38,000	35,000	3,000 U
Total appraisal	$ 68,000	$ 78,000	$10,000 F
Internal failure costs:			
Variable:			
Scrap	$ 50,000	$ 44,000	$ 6,000 U
Rework	35,000	36,500	1,500 F
Total internal failure	$ 85,000	$ 80,500	$ 4,500 U
External failure costs:			
Fixed:			
Customer complaints	$ 25,000	$ 25,000	$ 0
Variable:			
Warranty	25,000	20,000	5,000 U
Repair	15,000	17,500	2,500 F
Total external failure	$ 65,000	$ 62,500	$ 2,500 U
Total quality costs	$333,000	$331,000	$ 2,000 U
Percentage of actual sales[b]	11.89%	11.82%	0.07% U

[a] Based on actual sales
[b] Actual sales of $2,800,000

by only $2,000 from total budgeted quality costs and the actual costs, a mere 0.07 percent as a percentage of sales.

one-year quality performance report

One-Year Trend. Additional insight can be realized by comparing the current year's performance with what the cost of quality would have been using the prior year's quality costs. The vehicle for doing so is a **one-year quality performance report**. To make this comparison, the prior year's actual variable cost ratio is used to compute the variable quality costs expected under the prior year's cost structure by multiplying the ratio by this year's actual sales. For example, if the prior year's actual variable cost ratio for materials inspection was 1.2 percent, then $33,600 (0.012 × $2,800,000) would have been spent for materials inspection this year. The prior year's actual fixed quality costs are compared directly with this year's fixed quality costs. This report allows managers to assess the short-run trend of its quality improvement program.

The one-year performance report in Exhibit 26-15 shows that Jensen Products made significant progress in reducing its quality costs from 1994 to 1995. Overall,

Exhibit 26-15

Jensen Products
Performance Report: Quality Cost, One-Year Trend
For the Year Ended March 31, 1995

	Actual Costs 1995[a]	*Actual Costs 1994*	*Variance*
Prevention costs:			
Fixed:			
Quality training	$ 35,000	$ 36,000	$ 1,000 F
Reliability engineering	80,000	120,000	40,000 U
Total prevention	$115,000	$156,000	$41,000 F
Appraisal costs:			
Variable:			
Materials inspection	$ 20,000	$ 33,600	$13,600 F
Product acceptance	10,000	16,800	6,800 F
Process acceptance	38,000	39,200	1,200 F
Total appraisal	$ 68,000	$ 89,600	$21,600 F
Internal failure costs:			
Variable:			
Scrap	$ 50,000	$ 48,000	$ 2,000 U
Rework	35,000	40,000	5,000 F
Total internal failure	$ 85,000	$ 88,000	$ 3,000 F
External failure costs:			
Fixed:			
Customer complaints	$ 25,000	$ 33,000	$ 8,000 F
Variable:			
Warranty	25,000	23,000	2,000 U
Repair	15,000	16,400	1,400 F
Total external failure	$ 65,000	$ 72,400	$ 7,400 F
Total quality costs	$333,000	$406,000	$73,000 F
Percentage of actual sales (current year)	11.89%	14.5%	2.61% F

[a] Based on actual current sales of $2,800,000

quality costs are $73,000 less than what they would have been had Jensen continued to spend at the 1994 level (2.61 percent less as a percentage of sales). The report also provides detailed information concerning the areas in which the gains have been made. For example, the cost of reliability engineering has dropped by $40,000. This drop could be explained by a reduction in staff—one engineer was released because of quality gains made in prior years. Similarly, the drop in the cost of product acceptance could be explained by a gradual phaseout of this activity as management gains assurance that product defects are decreasing.

PRODUCTIVITY: MEASUREMENT AND CONTROL

Objective 5
Explain what productivity is and differentiate between partial and total measures of productivity.

While quality improvements offer significant economic benefits, a firm can increase its financial well-being even more by simultaneously focusing on improving productivity. Quality and productivity improvements are compatible and, in fact, are critical strategic issues for the advanced manufacturing environment. Continual striving for improvement in both quality and productivity is mandated.

Productivity Measurement Defined

productivity

Productivity concerns producing output efficiently and specifically addresses the relationship of output and the inputs used to produce the output. Usually, different combinations or mixes of inputs can be used to produce a given level of output. **Total productive efficiency** is the point at which two conditions are satisfied: (1) for any mix of inputs that will produce a given output, no more of any one input is used than necessary to produce the output and (2) given the mixes that satisfy the first condition, the least costly mix is chosen. The first condition is driven by technical relationships and, therefore, is referred to as **technical efficiency**. The second condition is driven by relative input price relationships and, therefore, is referred to as **price efficiency**. Productivity improvement programs involve moving toward a state of total productive efficiency. Productivity improvement, for example, can be achieved by using fewer of all inputs to produce the same output or by producing more output using the same inputs. Exhibit 26-16, Part A, illustrates these two ways to achieve an improvement in technical efficiency. Productivity improvement can also be achieved by trading off more costly inputs for less costly inputs. Exhibit 26-16, Part B, illustrates the possibility of improving productivity by increasing price efficiency.

total productive efficiency

technical efficiency

price efficiency

productivity measurement

Productivity measurement concerns measuring productivity changes so that efforts to improve productivity can be evaluated. Measurement can also be prospective and serve as input for strategic decision making. Productivity measures can be developed for each input separately or for all inputs jointly. Measuring productivity for one input at a time is called partial productivity measurement. Measuring productivity for all inputs at once is called **total productivity measurement**.

total productivity measurement

Partial Productivity Measurement

Productivity of a single input is typically measured by calculating the ratio of the output to the input:

$$\text{Productivity ratio} = \text{Output/Input}$$

Exhibit 26-16
Illustration of Productivity Improvement

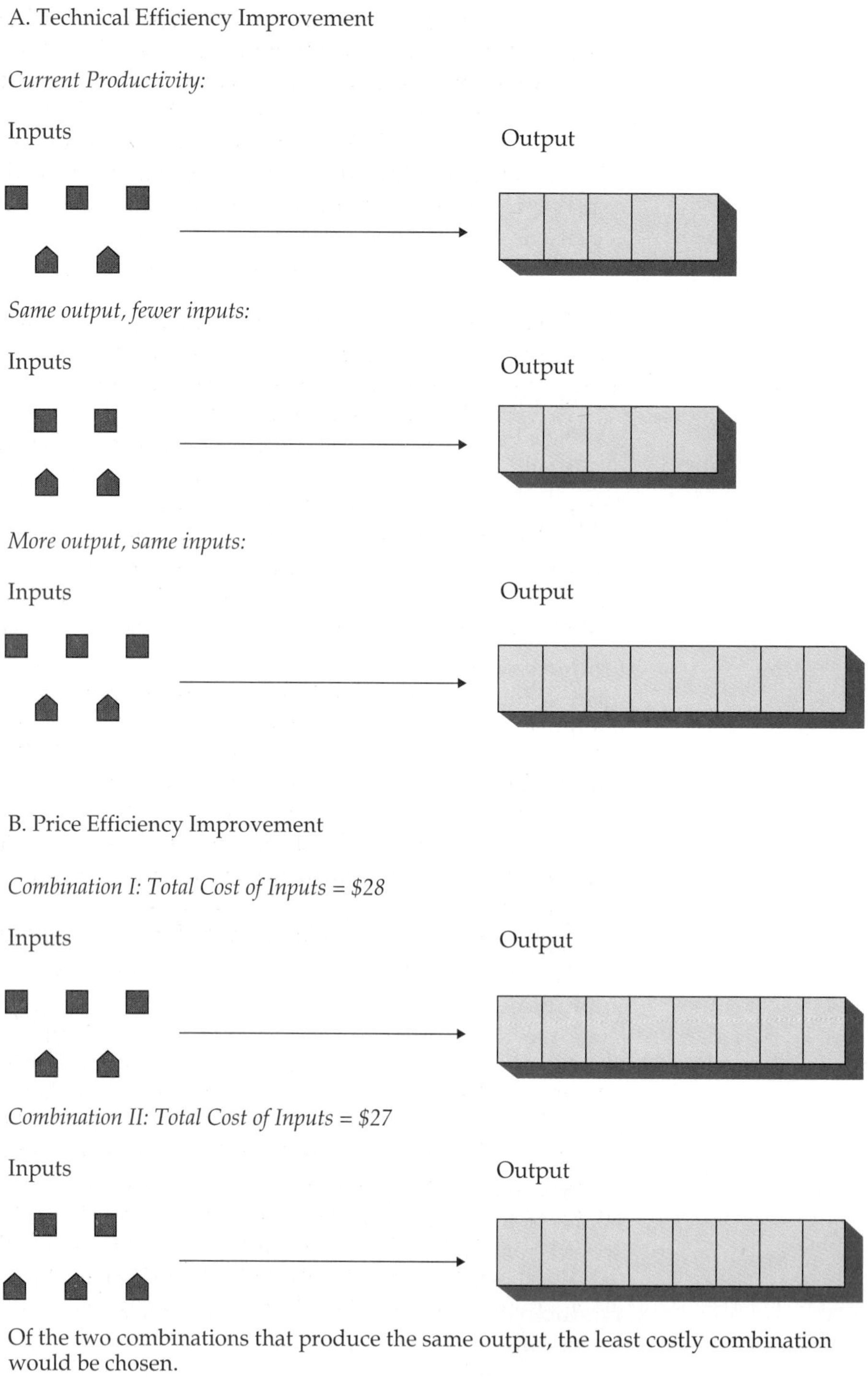

partial productivity measure

Because the productivity of only one input is being measured, the measure is called a **partial productivity measure**. If both output and input are measured in physical quantities, we have an **operational productivity measure**. If output or input is expressed in dollars, we have a **financial productivity measure**.

operational productivity measure
financial productivity measure

Assume, for example, that in 1994, Hotkumfurt Company produced 11,000 space heaters and used 1,100 hours of labor. The labor productivity ratio is ten space heaters per hour (11,000/1,100). This is an operational measure since the units are expressed in physical terms. If the selling price of each heater is $25 and the cost of labor is $10 per hour, output and input can be expressed in dollars. The labor productivity ratio, expressed in financial terms, is $25 of revenue per dollar of labor cost ($275,000/$11,000).

Partial Measures and Measuring Productivity Changes

The labor productivity ratio of ten heaters per hour measures the 1994 productivity experience of Hotkumfurt. By itself the ratio conveys little information about productive efficiency or whether the company has improving or declining productivity. It is possible, however, to make a statement about increasing or decreasing productivity efficiency by measuring *changes* in productivity. To do so, the actual current productivity measure is compared with the productivity measure of a prior period. This prior period is referred to as the **base period** and serves to set the benchmark or standard for measuring changes in productive efficiency. The prior period can be any period desired. It could, for example, be the preceding year, the preceding week, or even the period during which the last batch of products was produced. For strategic evaluations, the base period is usually chosen as an earlier year.

base period

To illustrate, assume that 1994 is the base period and the labor productivity standard, therefore, is ten heaters per hour. Further assume that late in 1994, Hotkumfurt decided to try a new procedure for assembling the heaters with the expectation that the new procedure would use labor more efficiently. In 1995, 110,000 heaters were produced, using 10,000 hours of labor. The labor productivity ratio for 1995 is eleven heaters per hour (110,000/10,000). The *change* in productivity is a one-unit per hour *increase* in productivity (from ten units per hour in 1994 to eleven units per hour in 1995). The change is a significant improvement in labor productivity and provides evidence supporting the efficacy of the new assembly process.

Advantages of Partial Measures. Partial measures allow managers to focus on the use of a particular input. Furthermore, partial operational measures are easy to use for assessing productivity performance of operating personnel. Laborers, for instance, can relate to units produced per hour or units produced per pound of material. Thus, partial operational measures provide feedback that operating personnel can relate to and understand—measures that deal with the specific inputs over which they have control. Furthermore, for operational control, the standards for performance are often very short-run in nature. For example, standards can be the productivity ratios of prior batches of goods. Using this standard, productivity trends within the year itself can be tracked.

Disadvantages of Partial Measures. Partial measures, used in isolation, can be misleading. A decline in the productivity of one input may be necessary to increase the productivity of another. Such a tradeoff is desirable if overall costs decline, but the effect would be missed by using either partial measure. For example, changing a process so that direct laborers take less time to assemble a product may increase scrap and waste while leaving total output unchanged. Labor productivity has increased but productive use of materials has declined.

If the increase in the cost of waste and scrap outweighs the savings of the decreased labor, overall productivity has declined.

Two important conclusions can be drawn from this example. First, the possible existence of tradeoffs mandates a total measure of productivity for assessing the merits of productivity decisions. Only by looking at the total productivity effect of all inputs can managers accurately draw any conclusions about productivity performance. Second, because of the possibility of tradeoffs, a total measure of productivity must assess the aggregate financial consequences, and, therefore, should be a financial measure.

Total Productivity Measurement

Producing a product involves numerous inputs such as labor, materials, capital, and energy. A total measure would assess the effect of all inputs. For simplicity, our discussion of total measurement will use only two inputs: labor and materials. Let's return to the Hotkumfurt Company example. As before, Hotkumfurt implements a new assembly process in 1995. Only now let's assume that the new assembly process affects both labor and materials. Initially, let's look at the case for which the productivity of both inputs moves in the same direction. The following data for 1994 and 1995 are available:

	1994	*1995*
Number of heaters produced	110,000	110,000
Labor hours used	11,000	10,000
Materials used (lbs)	110,000	88,000
Unit selling price (heaters)	$25	$25
Wages per labor hour	$10	$10
Cost per pound of material	$5	$5

Exhibit 26-17 provides a summary of the productivity ratios for each input for each year. Notice that productivity increased for both labor and materials (from 10 to 11 for labor and from 1.00 to 1.25 for materials). The two ratios provide enough information so that a manager can conclude that the new assembly process has definitely improved overall productivity. The *value* of this improvement, however, is not revealed by the ratios. Knowing the value of the productivity change is important for assessing the economic impact of the decision to change the assembly process. Furthermore, by valuing the productivity change, we obtain a total measure of productivity.

Assessing the effects of productivity changes on current profits is one way to value productivity changes. Profits change from the base period to the current period. Some of that profit change is attributable to productivity changes. Assess-

Exhibit 26-17
Total Productivity Measurement: No Input Tradeoffs

A. Operational Productivity Ratios

	1994[a]	*1995*[b]
Labor productivity ratio	10.00	11.00
Material productivity ratio	1.00	1.25

[a] Labor: 110,000/11,000; Materials: 110,000/110,000
[b] Labor: 110,000/10,000; Materials: 110,000/88,000

profit-linked productivity measurement

ing the amount of profit change attributable to productivity change is defined as **profit-linked productivity measurement**.[29]

Profit-Linked Productivity Measurement. A direct way to value the productivity changes is to assess their effect on current-period profits. Knowing this effect will help managers understand the economic importance of productivity changes. Linking productivity changes to profits is described by the following rule:

Profit-Linkage Rule

For the current period, calculate the cost of the inputs that would have been used in the absence of any productivity change and compare this cost with the cost of the inputs actually used. The difference in costs is the amount by which profits changed because of productivity changes.

To apply the linkage rule, the inputs that would have been used for the current period in the absence of a productivity change must be calculated. Let PQ represent this productivity-neutral quantity of input. To determine the productivity-neutral quantity for a particular input, divide the current-period output by the input's base-period productivity ratio:

$$PQ = \text{Current output/Base-period productivity ratio}$$

For our example, current output is 110,000 heaters. The productivity-neutral quantity for each input is computed below.

$$PQ \text{ (labor)} = 110{,}000/10 = 11{,}000 \text{ hrs}$$
$$PQ \text{ (materials)} = 110{,}000/1 = 110{,}000 \text{ lbs}$$

Since output quantity did not change from 1994 to 1995, the inputs that would have been used in 1995, assuming no productivity change, would have been the inputs used in 1994, which is what we obtained. What the cost would have been for these productivity-neutral quantities in 1994 is computed by multiplying each individual input quantity (PQ) by its current price (P) and adding:[30]

Cost of labor: $PQ \times P = 11{,}000 \times \$10 =$	$110,000
Cost of materials: $PQ \times P = 110{,}000 \times \$5 =$	550,000
Total PQ cost	$660,000

29. Several profit-linked productivity measures have been developed and used by firms. The American Productivity Center has developed a profit-linked measure described in J. G. Belcher Jr., *The Productivity Management Process* (Houston: The American Productivity Center, 1984). D. M. Miller developed and used a profit-linked measure while working for Ethyl Corporation. It is described in D. M. Miller, "Profitability = Productivity + Price Recovery," *Harvard Business Review* (May–June 1984), pp. 145–153. A third profit-linked measure is described in R. D. Banker, S. M. Datar, and R. S. Kaplan, "Productivity Measurement and Management Accounting," *Journal of Accounting, Auditing, and Finance* (1989). The profit-linked measure described in this text is essentially a modification of the three measures above. The modification increases the accuracy of profit-linked measurement and allows a connection to the operational and partial measures of productivity. It also establishes an equivalency among the three measures. See Don R. Hansen, Maryanne Mowen, and Lawrence Hammer, "Profit-Linked Productivity Measurement," *Journal of Management Accounting Research* (Fall 1992), pp. 79–98.

30. Base-period input prices are frequently used to value productivity changes. It has been shown, however, that current input prices should be used for accurate profit-linked productivity measurement. See Hansen, Mowen, and Hammer, "Profit-Linked Productivity Measurement."

The actual cost of inputs is obtained by multiplying the actual quantity (*AQ*) by current input price (*P*) for each input and adding:

Cost of labor: $AQ \times P = 10{,}000 \times \$10 =$	$100,000
Cost of materials: $AQ \times P = 88{,}000 \times \$5$	440,000
Total current cost	$540,000

Finally, the productivity effect on profits is computed by subtracting the total current cost from the total *PQ* cost.

$$\begin{aligned}\text{Profit-linked effect} &= \text{Total } PQ \text{ cost} - \text{Total current cost}\\ &= \$660{,}000 - \$540{,}000\\ &= \$120{,}000 \text{ increase in profits}\end{aligned}$$

The calculation of the profit-linked effect is summarized in Exhibit 26-18.

The summary in Exhibit 26-18 reveals that the profit-linked productivity effects can be assigned to individual inputs. Labor, for example, accounts for only $10,000 of the total improvement. Most of the improvement, $110,000, came from a reduction in materials usage. Thus, the profit-linked measure provides partial measurement effects as well as a total measurement effect. The total profit-linked productivity measure is the sum of the individual partial measures. This property makes the profit-linked measure ideal for assessing tradeoffs.

Total Productivity Measurement: Tradeoffs Considered. The value of profit-linked productivity measurement is more fully appreciated when the tradeoffs among inputs are caused by the implementation of a new productivity program. In this case, looking at the change in productivity ratios will not provide any clear indication of whether the change is good or bad. The profit-linked measure, however, provides the overall effect and reveals the value of the tradeoffs among inputs. To illustrate this, let's revise the Hotkumfurt data to allow for tradeoffs.

	1994	*1995*
Number of heaters produced	110,000	120,000
Labor hours used	11,000	10,000
Materials used (lbs)	110,000	126,000
Unit selling price (heaters)	$25	$25
Wages per labor hour	10	10
Cost per pound of material	5	5

Exhibit 26-18
Profit-Linked Productivity Measurement: No Tradeoffs

	(1)	(2)	(3)	(4)	(2) − (4)
Input	*PQ*[a]	*PQ* × *P*	*AQ*	*AQ* × *P*	(*PQ* × *P*) − (*AQ* × *P*)
Labor	11,000	$110,000	10,000	$100,000	$ 10,000
Materials	110,000	550,000	$88,000	440,000	110,000
		$660,000		$540,000	$120,000

[a] Labor: 110,000/10; Materials: 110,000/1

Exhibit 26-19
Operational Productivity Ratios: Tradeoffs Present

	1994[a]	1995[b]
Labor	10.00	12.00
Materials	1.00	0.95

[a]Labor: 110,000/11,000; Materials: 110,000/110,000
[b]Labor: 120,000/10,000; Materials: 120,000/126,000

Exhibit 26-20
Profit-Linked Productivity Measurement

	(1)	(2)	(3)	(4)	(2) − (4)
Input	*PQ*[a]	*PQ* × *P*	*AQ*	*AQ* × *P*	(*PQ* × *P* − *AQ* × *P*)
Labor	12,000	$120,000	10,000	$100,000	$ 20,000
Materials	120,000	600,000	126,000	630,000	(30,000)
		$720,000		$730,000	$(10,000)

[a]Labor: 120,000/10 = 12,000; Materials: 120,000/1 = 120,000

The productivity ratios for each input are calculated in Exhibit 26-19. For this scenario, notice that labor productivity has increased (from 10 to 12) but that material productivity has decreased (from 1.00 to 0.95). The partial operational measures provide mixed signals about the new assembly process. The profit-linked productivity measure, however, is a total measure of productivity—one that assesses the overall effect and values the tradeoffs of the individual inputs. The computation of the profit-linked measure is illustrated in Exhibit 26-20.

From Exhibit 26-20, we obtain a clear picture of the productivity consequences of the new assembly process. Under this scenario, labor is reduced, saving $20,000, but waste and scrap apparently increase, causing materials cost to jump by $30,000. The net effect is a $10,000 drop in profits. Unless the scrap and waste can be brought under better control, the company ought to return to the old assembly process.

price-recovery component

Price-Recovery Component. The profit-linked measure computes the amount of profit change from the base period to the current period attributable to productivity changes. This generally will not be equal to the total profit change between the two periods. The difference between the total profit change and the profit-linked productivity change is called the **price-recovery component**. This component is the change in revenue less a change in the cost of inputs, *assuming no productivity changes*. It therefore measures the ability of revenue changes to cover changes in the cost of inputs, assuming no productivity change. The second review problem at the end of the chapter allows you to compute this factor.

SUMMARY OF LEARNING OBJECTIVES

1. Explain why many traditional control measures are not suitable for an advanced manufacturing environment. The control procedures used in conventional manufacturing environments are not directly transferable to an advanced environment. Detailed variance analysis, based on currently attainable standards, can provide incentives that are not compatible with the operating objectives found in an advanced environment. Using materials price variances as a measure, for example, can encourage purchase of larger lots than desirable in order to take advantage of quantity discounts or purchase of lesser quality. This behavior encourages inventories of raw materials and low-quality materials, both of which are in opposition to the objectives of zero inventories and total quality control.

2. Explain activity-based management and how it differs from traditional responsibility accounting Activity-based management is a system-wide, integrated approach that focuses on managing activities rather than the costs. It recognizes that activities cause costs and that management of activities will produce more efficient outcomes. There are two dimensions that define activity-based management: the cost dimension and the control dimension. The cost dimension is concerned with accurate assignment of activity costs to cost objects—particularly products. The second dimension—the control dimension—provides information about why work is done and how well it is done. It is concerned with cost driver analysis, activity analysis, and performance measurement. It is this dimension that offers the connection to the concept of continuous improvement. A key element of activity-based control is activity analysis. Activity analysis is the process of identifying and describing a firm's activities, assessing their value to the organization, and selecting only those that are of value. Cost reduction is realized by decreasing, eliminating, selecting, and sharing activities. Emphasis is placed on identifying nonvalue-added costs and eliminating them. These costs are the result of unnecessary activities and inefficiencies found in necessary activities.

3. Explain life-cycle cost management and why it is important for the advanced manufacturing environment. Life-cycle costing is accumulating costs for a product over its entire life cycle. Life-cycle cost management emphasizes analysis and management of activities during the development stage in which more than 90 percent of the life-cycle costs are committed. Life-cycle cost management is important because of the ability to assess the effectiveness of life-cycle planning and identify product profitability more accurately. It is especially important for firms that have products with short life cycles.

4. Describe how quality costs are measured and controlled. To understand quality costs, it is first necessary to understand what is meant by quality. There are two types of quality: quality of design and quality of conformance. Quality of design concerns quality differences that arise for products with the same function but different specifications. Quality of conformance, on the other hand, concerns meeting the specifications required by the product. Quality costs are those costs that are incurred because products may or actually fail to meet design specifications (and are therefore associated with quality of conformance). There are four categories of quality costs: prevention, appraisal, internal failure, and external failure. Prevention costs are those incurred to prevent poor quality. Appraisal costs are those incurred to detect poor quality. Internal failure costs are those incurred because products fail to conform to requirements and this lack of conformity is discovered before an external sale. External failure costs are those incurred because products fail to conform to requirements after an external sale is made.

Quality cost information is needed to help managers control quality performance and to serve as input for decision making. It can be used to evaluate the overall performance of quality improvement programs. It can also be used to help improve a variety of managerial decisions, for example, strategic pricing and cost-volume-profit analysis. Perhaps the most important observation is that quality cost information is fundamental in a company's pursuit of continual improvement. Quality is one of the major competitive dimensions for world-class competitors.

A quality cost report is prepared by listing costs for each item within each of the four major quality cost categories. Two performance reports are mentioned in the chapter: (1) an interim report, and (2) a one-year trend report. These reports help managers assess the progress made in reducing quality costs to a level corresponding to zero defects.

5. Explain what productivity is and differentiate between partial and total measures of productivity. Productivity concerns how efficiently inputs are used to produce the output. Partial measures of productivity evaluate the efficient use of single inputs. Total measures of productivity assess efficiency for all inputs. Profit-linked productivity effects are calculated by using the linkage rule. Essentially, the profit effect is computed by taking the difference between the cost of the inputs that would have been used without any productivity change and the cost of the actual inputs used. Because of the possibility of input tradeoffs, it is essential to value productivity changes. Only in this way can the effect of productivity changes be properly assessed.

KEY TERMS

Acceptable quality level (AQL) 1227
Activity analysis 1209
Activity elimination 1211
Activity-based management (ABM) 1208
Activity reduction 1211
Activity selection 1211
Activity sharing 1211
Appraisal costs 1224
Base period 1237
Costs of quality 1224

REVIEW PROBLEMS

1 Value-Added and Nonvalue-Added Cost Reports; Currently Attainable Standards

Ludlow Manufacturing has developed value-added standards for labor usage, receiving, and packing. The value-added levels of the inputs for each of the activities, their actual levels achieved, and the standard prices are as follows:

	Cost Driver	*SQ*	*AQ*	*SP*
Labor usage	Labor hours	12,000	15,000	$ 8
Receiving	Purchase orders	400	500	100
Packing	Sales orders	600	800	80

The actual prices paid for the inputs equal the standard prices.

REQUIRED:

1. Prepare a cost report that details value- and nonvalue-added costs.
2. Suppose that the company wants to reduce nonvalue-added costs by 30 percent in the coming year. Prepare currently attainable standards that can be used to evaluate the company's progress towards this goal.

Solution

1.

	Costs		
	Value Added	*Nonvalue Added*	*Total*
Labor usage	$ 96,000	$24,000	$120,000
Receiving	40,000	10,000	50,000
Packing	48,000	16,000	64,000
Totals	$184,000	$50,000	$234,000

2.

	Currently Attainable Standard	
	Quantity	*Cost*
Labor usage	14,100	$112,800
Receiving	470	47,000
Packing	740	59,200

2 Quality

At the beginning of 1995, Kare Company initiated a quality improvement program. Considerable effort was expended to reduce the number of defective units produced. By the end of the year, reports from the production manager revealed that scrap and rework had both decreased. The president of the company was pleased to hear of the success but wanted some assessment of the financial impact of the improvements. To make this assessment, the following financial data were collected for the current and preceding year:

	Preceding Year (1994)	*Current Year (1995)*
Sales	$10,000,000	$10,000,000
Scrap	400,000	300,000
Rework	600,000	400,000
Product inspection	100,000	125,000
Product warranty	800,000	600,000
Quality training	40,000	80,000
Materials inspection	60,000	40,000

REQUIRED:

1. Classify the costs as preventive, appraisal, internal failure, and external failure.
2. Compute quality cost as a percentage of sales for each of the two years. By how much has profit increased because of quality improvements? Assuming that quality costs can be reduced to 2.5 percent of sales, how much additional profit is available through quality improvements (assume that sales revenues will remain the same)?
3. Prepare a one-year trend performance report.

Solution

1. Appraisal costs: quality training and materials inspection; prevention costs: product inspection; internal failure costs: scrap and rework; external failure costs: warranty.
2. *Preceding year*—Total quality costs: $2,000,000; percentage of sales: 20 percent ($2,000,000/$10,000,000). *Current year*—Total quality costs: $1,545,000; percentage of sales: 15.45 percent ($1,545,000/$10,000,000). Profit has increased by $455,000. If quality costs drop to 2.5 percent of sales, another $1,295,000 of profit improvement is possible ($1,545,000 − $250,000).
3.

Kare Company
Interim Quality Performance Report
For the Year Ended, December 31, 1995

	Actual Costs	*Budgeted Costs*[a]	*Variance*
Prevention costs:			
Quality training	$ 80,000	$ 40,000	$ 40,000 U
Appraisal costs:			
Product inspection	$ 125,000	$ 100,000	$ 25,000 U
Materials inspection	40,000	60,000	20,000 F
Total prevention	$ 165,000	$ 160,000	$ 5,000 U
Internal failure costs:			
Scrap	$ 300,000	$ 400,000	$100,000 F
Rework	400,000	600,000	200,000 F
Total internal failure	$ 700,000	$1,000,000	$300,000 F
External failure costs:			
Product warranty	$ 600,000	$ 800,000	$200,000 F
Total quality costs	$1,545,000	$2,000,000	$455,000 F
Percentage of sales	15.45%	20%	4.55% F

[a]Based on actual results for 1994.

3 Productivity

Bearing Company made some changes at the end of 1994 that it hoped would favorably affect the efficiency of the input usage. Now, at the end of 1995, the president of the company wants an assessment of the changes on the company's productivity. The data needed for the assessment are given below.

	1994	*1995*
Output	5,000	6,000
Output prices	$10	$10
Materials (lbs)	4,000	4,200
Materials unit price	$3	$4
Labor (hrs)	2,500	2,400
Labor rate per hour	$8	$8
Power (kwh)	1,000	1,500
Price per kwh	$2	$3

REQUIRED:

1. Compute the partial operational measures for each input for both 1994 and 1995. What can be said about productivity improvement?
2. Prepare an income statement for each year and calculate the total change in profits.
3. Calculate the profit-linked productivity measure for 1995. What can be said about the productivity program?
4. Calculate the price-recovery component. What does this tell you?

Solution

1. Partial Measures:

	1994	*1995*
Material	5,000/4,000 = 1.25	6,000/4,200 = 1.43
Labor	5,000/2,500 = 2.00	6,000/2,400 = 2.50
Power	5,000/1,000 = 5.00	6,000/1,500 = 4.00

Productive efficiency has increased for materials and labor and decreased for power. The outcome is mixed and no statement about overall productivity improvement can be made without valuing the tradeoff.

2. Income statements:

	1994	*1995*
Sales	$50,000	$60,000
Cost of inputs	34,000	40,500
Income	$16,000	$19,500

Total change in profits: $19,500 − $16,000 = $3,500 increase

3. Profit-linked measurement:

	(1)	*(2)*	*(3)*	*(4)*	*(2) − (4)*
Input	*PQ*[a]	*PQ × P*	*AQ*	*AQ × P*	*(PQ × P − AQ × P)*
Materials	4,800	$19,200	4,200	$16,800	$2,400
Labor	3,000	24,000	2,400	19,200	4,800
Power	1,200	3,600	1,500	4,500	(900)
		$46,800		$40,500	$6,300

[a]Materials: 6,000/1.25; Labor: 6,000/2; Power: 6,000/5

The value of the increases in efficiency for materials and labor more than offsets the increased usage of power. Thus, the productivity program should be labeled successful.

4. Price recovery:

   Price recovery component = Total profit change − Profit-linked productivity change
   Price recovery component = \$3,500 − \$6,300 = (\$2,800)

   This says that without the productivity improvement, profits would have declined by \$2,800. The \$10,000 increase in revenues would not have offset the increase in the cost of inputs. From the solution to Requirement 3, the cost of inputs without a productivity increase would have been \$46,800 (column (2)). The increase in the input cost without productivity would have been \$46,800 − \$34,000 = \$12,800. This is \$2,800 more than the increase in revenues. Only because of the productivity increase did the firm show an increase in profitability.

QUESTIONS

1. Explain how materials price/usage variances can work against the JIT objectives of zero inventories and total quality control.
2. What are the two dimensions of the activity-based management model? How do they differ?
3. What is activity-based responsibility accounting? How does it differ from traditional responsibility accounting?
4. What is activity analysis? Why is this approach compatible with the goal of continuous improvement?
5. Identify and define four different ways to manage activities. Explain how each can reduce costs.
6. What are nonvalue-added costs? value-added costs? Give an example of each.
7. Explain how trend reports of nonvalue-added cost can be used.
8. In controlling nonvalue-added costs, explain how cost drivers can induce behavior that is either beneficial or harmful. How can value-added standards be used to reduce the possibility of dysfunctional behavior?
9. What are target costs?
10. What is life-cycle costing? life-cycle cost management? whole-life costs?
11. Explain why life-cycle cost management is especially important for firms with products that have short life cycles.
12. What is the difference between quality of design and quality of conformance?
13. Why are quality costs the costs of doing things wrong?
14. Identify and discuss the four kinds of quality costs.
15. What is the difference between an AQL standard and a zero-defects standard?
16. Many quality experts maintain that quality is free. Do you agree? Why or why not?
17. Describe the two types of quality performance reports. How can managers use each report to help evaluate their quality improvement programs?
18. Define *total productive efficiency*.
19. Explain the difference between partial and total measures of productivity.
20. Discuss the advantages and disadvantages of partial measures of productivity.
21. What is profit-linked productivity measurement? Explain why it is important.

EXERCISES

E26-1
Labor Efficiency Variance; Ethical Issues; Incentives
LO 1

Ken Keeton, production supervisor, was given the charge to produce 2,000 units of a subassembly used in the manufacture of the company's main product. He had two weeks to produce the units. The job took priority over several other jobs that were less urgent. Each subassembly required two hours of direct labor. After producing a unit, the subassembly was inspected and rejected if defective. Defective units had no salvage value; because of the nature of the process, rework was not possible.

At the end of the first week, Ken had produced 1,000 units and used 2,150 direct labor hours, 150 hours more than the standard allowed. Ken knew that a performance report would be prepared when the batch of 2,000 subassemblies was completed. This report would compare the materials used with the materials allowed. He also knew that any variance in excess of 5 percent of standard would be investigated, possibly resulting in a poor performance rating for him. Accordingly, at the beginning of the second week, Ken directed that no inspections be done because production had to be accelerated so that the other jobs could be completed on time. He temporarily assigned his inspector to the production line's material handling activity.

REQUIRED:

1. Explain why Ken stopped inspections on the current job and reassigned his inspector to material handling. Was his behavior ethical?
2. What likely effect would Ken's actions have on the quality of the final product? On the ability of subsequent processes to meet its production schedule?
3. What implications does Ken's behavior have for a firm using JIT manufacturing? Explain.

E26-2 Conventional Control Measures and JIT

LO 1

For each action below, describe which JIT objective is being violated (more than one may be involved).

1. Cheaper, lower quality parts were acquired by the purchasing department.
2. A large lot of raw materials is purchased to take advantage of a quantity discount.
3. To reduce the amount of rework, inspection labor was temporarily transferred to material handling.
4. Production is increased so that idle time for direct laborers is minimized.
5. The maintenance supervisor refuses to buy a critical piece of diagnostic equipment in order to meet budget. As a result, maintenance workers are forced to focus more on repair and less on preventive care.

E26-3 Activity Versus Traditional Responsibility Accounting

LO 2

For each of the following situations, identify which characteristic is descriptive of activity-based responsibility accounting and which is descriptive of traditional responsibility accounting. Provide a brief commentary on the differences between the two systems for each situation, addressing the advantages of the ABC view over the traditional view. Characteristics of each situation are labeled *A* and *B*.

Situation 1:
A: Assumes that activities can be collected into independent subgroups.
B: Assumes that activities are linked.

Situation 2:
A: The focus is the organization.
B: The focus is individuals.

Situation 3:
A: The control emphasis is costs.
B: The control emphasis is activities.

Situation 4:
A: Standards are engineered and tend to be static.
B: Standards are ideal/historical trends.

Situation 5:
A: The goal is continuous improvement.
B: The goal is to meet standard.

Situation 6:
A: Control is financial.
B: Control is financial and operational.

E26-4
Activity-Based Management
LO 2

Consider the following comments concerning activity-based management:

a. "The control dimension of activity-based management deals with detailed activities whereas the cost dimension deals with aggregate collections of activities."
b. "The control dimension of activity-based management is the main linkage of activity-based management to the world of continuous improvement."
c. "Costs cannot be managed—only activities can."
d. "The primary purpose of activity analysis is to identify value-added and nonvalue-added activities."

REQUIRED: Comment on the validity of each statement, giving examples (where appropriate) to support your position.

E26-5
Identification of Nonvalue-Added Activities and Costs
LO 2

Identify the nonvalue-added activities from those listed below and provide an estimate of the nonvalue-added cost caused by each activity.

1. It takes 15 minutes to produce a product. A time and motion study revealed that it should take 10 minutes. The cost per labor hour is $12.
2. With its original design, a product requires three hours of setup time. Redesigning the product could reduce the setup time to an absolute minimum of 30 minutes. The cost per hour of setup time is $200.
3. A product currently requires five moves. By redesigning the manufacturing layout, the number of moves can be reduced from five to one. Because of the redesign, the cost per move drops from $500 to $100.
4. Expediting time for a plant is 6,000 hours per year. The cost of expediting consists of a 50% overtime labor premium for each expediting hour plus the salary of one person (an expeditor) who works in scheduling. The wage rate is $10 per hour and the salary is $27,000.
5. Each unit of a product requires 5 components. The average number of components is 5.3 due to component failure, requiring rework and extra components. By developing relations with the right suppliers and increasing the quality of the purchased component, the average number of components can be reduced to 5 components per unit. The cost per component is $600.

E26-6
Calculation of Value-Added and Nonvalue-Added Costs; Unused Capacity
LO 2

Stice Entertainment Products produces a variety of plastic toys. The company uses a conventional, departmental structure. After a careful study, the company decided that the number of purchase orders was a good cost driver for receiving costs. During the last year, the company incurred fixed receiving costs of $96,000 (salaries of four employees), and also spent an average of $4 per purchase order for variable receiving costs. Management decided that the value-added standard number of purchase orders is 8,000. The fixed costs provide a capacity of processing 16,000 orders (4,000 per employee at practical capacity). Assume that the actual receiving orders processed were 14,000. Also assume that the cost formula above is a perfect predictor of receiving costs.

REQUIRED:

1. Calculate the cost of unused capacity for receiving.
2. Calculate the value-added and nonvalue-added costs for receiving.
3. Prepare a report that presents value-added, nonvalue-added, and actual costs. Explain why highlighting the nonvalue-added costs is important.

E26-7
Cost Report; Value-Added and Nonvalue-Added Costs
LO 2

Lemmons Company has developed value-added standards for four activities: purchasing, labor, materials, and maintenance. The activities, the cost driver, the standard and actual quantities, and the price standards are given below for 1994.

Activities	*Cost Driver*	*SQ*	*AQ*	*SP*
Purchasing	Orders	500	700	$300
Labor	Hours	8,000	8,500	10
Materials	Pounds	60,000	66,000	6
Maintenance	Machine hours	20,000	25,000	5

The actual prices paid per unit of each cost driver were equal to the standard prices.

REQUIRED: Prepare a cost report that lists the value-added costs, nonvalue-added costs, and actual costs for each activity.

E26-8 Trend Report: Nonvalue-Added Costs

LO 2

Refer to Exercise 26-7. Suppose that Lemmons Company used an activity analysis program during 1995 in an effort to reduce nonvalue-added costs. The value-added standards, actual quantities, and prices for 1995 are given below.

	Cost Driver	*SQ*	*AQ*	*SP*
Purchasing	Orders	500	600	$300
Labor	Hours	8,000	7,800	10
Materials	Pounds	60,000	62,000	6
Maintenance	Machine hours	20,000	26,000	5

REQUIRED:

1. Prepare a report that compares the nonvalue-added costs for 1994 with those of 1995.
2. Comment on the value of a trend report.

E26-9 Target Costing and Nonvalue-Added Costs

LO 2

Wellkare Products manufactures a line of hospital beds. The regular model sells for $450. Sales volume averages 10,000 units per year. Recently, its largest competitor reduced the price of a similar model to $400. Wellkare's marketing manager indicated that the price must be matched or sales will drop dramatically. The president of Wellkare indicated that the current profit per unit must be maintained and wants to know what the cost per unit must be to achieve this goal. He also wants to know how the company can achieve the cost reduction. The controller has assembled the following data for the most recent year. The actual cost of inputs, their value-added (ideal) quantity levels, and the actual quantity levels are provided (for production of 10,000 units). Assume there is no difference between actual prices of activity units and standard prices.

	SQ	*AQ*	*Actual Cost*
Materials (lbs)	237,500	250,000	$2,000,000
Labor (hrs)	95,000	100,000	1,000,000
Setups (hrs)	—	4,000	280,000
Material handling (moves)	—	10,000	120,000
Warranties (no. repaired)	—	10,000	600,000
Total			$4,000,000

REQUIRED:

1. Calculate the target cost for maintaining current market share and profitability.
2. Calculate the nonvalue-added cost per unit. Assuming that nonvalue-added costs can be reduced to zero, can the target cost be achieved?

E26-10
Life-Cycle Costing
LO 3

Larry Savage, president of Limited Cycle, Inc., had just completed examining the two-year profit summary for two products that had completed their life cycle. Both had been conceived, developed, produced, and sold at the same time. Each product's life cycle was two years. The profit performance of the two items produced a return on sales of 10 percent—less than the 16 percent rate set by company standards. From the statements below, it appeared to Larry that the culprit was Circuit 12B—its gross profit percentage was much lower than that of Circuit 12A. Circuit 12B simply did not contribute enough to help cover the period costs.

	Circuit 12A	*Circuit 12B*	*Total*
Sales	$2,000,000	$2,000,000	$4,000,000
Cost of goods sold	(1,000,000)	(1,400,000)	(2,400,000)
Gross profit	$1,000,000	$ 600,000	$1,600,000
Research and development expenses			(1,000,000)
Selling expenses			(200,000)
Profit before taxes			$ 400,000

REQUIRED:

1. Explain why Larry Savage may be wrong in his assessment of the relative performances of the two products. What change in the company's management accounting system would you suggest?
2. Suppose that 80 percent of the R & D and selling expenses are traceable to Circuit 12A. Prepare life-cycle income statements for each product and calculate the return on sales. What does this tell you about the importance of accurate life-cycle costing? Managerial product costing?
3. Explain why whole-life cost may be a better measure of managerial product cost than life-cycle cost. What is the connection of life-cycle cost management to the value chain?

E26-11
Quality Cost Classification
LO 4

Classify the following quality costs as prevention costs, appraisal costs, internal failure costs, or external failure costs:

1. Downgrading because of defects
2. Receiving inspection
3. Scrap
4. Product recalls
5. Product liability suits
6. Design verification and review to evaluate the quality of new products
7. Training program for new personnel
8. Work stoppage to correct process malfunction (discovered using statistical process control procedures)
9. Settlement of a product liability suit
10. Reinspection of rework
11. Lost sales because of incorrect product labeling
12. Internal audit
13. Engineering design changes
14. Purchase order changes
15. Replacement of defective product
16. Test labor
17. Field service personnel
18. Software correction
19. Supplier evaluations
20. In process inspection
21. Consumer complaint department

22. Prototype inspection and testing
23. Retest work

E26-12
One-Year Trend Report
LO 4

In 1995, Minot Frozen Foods Inc. instituted a quality improvement program. At the end of 1995, the management of the corporation requested a report to show the amount saved by the measures taken during the year. The actual sales and actual quality costs for 1994 and 1995 are:

	1994	*1995*
Sales	$1,000,000	$1,200,000
Scrap	30,000	30,000
Rework	40,000	20,000
Training program	10,000	12,000
Consumer complaints	20,000	10,000
Lost sales, incorrect labeling	16,000	—
Test labor	24,000	16,000
Inspection labor	50,000	48,000
Supplier evaluation	30,000	26,000

REQUIRED:

1. Classify each cost as variable or fixed with respect to sales and compute the variable cost ratio. Be careful—costs may change because of quality improvement, not cost behavior.
2. Prepare the one-year trend report that corporate management requested. How much did profits increase because of quality improvements made in 1995 (assume that all reductions in quality costs are attributable to quality improvements)?

E26-13
Interperiod Measurement of Productivity; Basic Computations
LO 5

The following data pertain to the last two years of operation of Chelsey Inc.

	1994	*1995*
Output	16,000	20,000
Power (quantity used)	2,000	2,000
Materials (quantity used)	4,000	4,500
Unit price (Power)	$1.00	$2.00
Unit price (Materials)	$4.00	$5.00
Unit selling price	$2.00	$2.50

REQUIRED:

1. Compute the partial operational productivity ratios for each year. Did productivity improve? Explain.
2. Compute the profit-linked productivity measure. By how much did profits increase due to productivity?
3. Calculate the price-recovery component for 1995. Explain its meaning.

E26-14
Productivity Measurement: Technical and Price Efficiency Illustrated
LO 5

The manager of Dowson Company was reviewing two competing proposals for the Machining Department. The fiscal year was coming to a close and the manager wanted to make a decision concerning the proposed process changes so that they could be used, if beneficial, during the coming year. The process changes would affect the department's input usage. For the year just ending, the Accounting Department provided the following information about the inputs used to produce 50,000 units of output:

	Quantity	*Unit Prices*
Materials	90,000 lbs	$ 8
Labor	40,000 hrs	10
Energy	20,000 kwh	2

Each proposal offers a different process design than the one currently used. And neither proposal would cost anything to implement. Both proposals project input usage for producing 60,000 units (the expected output for the coming year).

	Proposal A	*Proposal B*
Materials	90,000 lbs	100,000 lbs
Labor	40,000 hrs	30,000 hrs
Energy	20,000 kwh	20,000 kwh

Input prices are expected to remain the same for the coming year.

REQUIRED:

1. Compute the operational partial productivity measures for the most recently completed year and each proposal. Does either proposal improve technical efficiency? Explain. Can you make a recommendation about either proposal using only the physical measures?
2. Calculate the profit-linked productivity measure for each proposal. Which proposal offers the best outcome for the company? How does this relate to the concept of price efficiency? Explain.

PROBLEMS

P26-1 JIT; Control and Performance Measurement

LO 1

Richardson Manufacturing is installing a JIT purchasing and manufacturing system; management wants to use performance measures that are compatible with the objectives of its new system. The following is a list of measures being considered for use:

a. Materials price variances
b. Cycle time
c. Comparison of actual product costs with target costs
d. Materials quantity or efficiency variances
e. Comparison of actual product costs over time (trend reports)
f. Comparison of actual overhead costs, item by item, with the corresponding budgeted costs
g. Comparison of product costs with competitors' product costs
h. Percentage of on-time deliveries
i. Quality reports
j. Reports of value-added and nonvalue-added costs
k. Labor efficiency variances
l. Machine utilization rates
m. Days of inventory
n. Downtime
o. Manufacturing cycle efficiency (MCE)

REQUIRED:

1. Describe how each of the above measures would impact the objectives associated with JIT manufacturing and purchasing.

2. Classify the measures into operational and financial categories. Explain why operational measures are better for control at the shop level (production floor) than financial measures. Should any financial measures be used at the operational level?

P26-2
Activity-Based Management; Nonvalue-Added Costs; Target Costs
LO 2

Danna Martin, president of Mays Electronics, was concerned about the end-of-the year marketing report that she had just received. According to Mike O'Brien, marketing manager, a price decrease for the coming year was again needed to maintain the company's annual sales volume of integrated circuit boards (CBs). This would make a bad situation worse. The current selling price of $18 per unit was producing a $2 per-unit profit—half the customary $4 per-unit profit. Foreign competitors kept reducing their prices. To match the latest reduction would reduce the price from $18 to $14. This would put the price below the cost to produce and sell it. How could these firms sell for such a low price?

Determined to find out if there were problems with the company's operations, Danna decided to hire a consultant to evaluate the way in which the CBs were produced and sold. After two weeks, the consultant had identified the following activities and costs:

Batch-level activities:	
Setups	$ 125,000
Material handling	180,000
Inspection	122,000
Product-sustaining activities:	
Engineering support	$ 120,000
Customer complaints	100,000
Warranties	170,000
Storing	80,000
Expediting	75,000
Unit-level activities:	
Material usage	$ 500,000
Power	48,000
Manual insertion labor[a]	250,000
Other direct labor	150,000
Total costs	$1,920,000[b]

[a]Diodes, resistors, and integrated circuits are inserted manually into the circuit board.
[b]This total cost produces a unit cost of $16 for last year's sales volume.

The consultant indicated that some preliminary activity analysis shows that per-unit costs can be reduced by at least $7. Since the marketing manager had indicated that the market share (sales volume) for the boards could be increased by 50 percent if the price could be reduced to $12, Danna became quite excited.

REQUIRED:

1. What is activity-based management? What phases of activity analysis were provided by the consultant? What else remains to be done?
2. Identify as many nonvalue-added activities as possible. Compute the cost savings per unit that would be realized if these activities were eliminated. Was the consultant correct in his preliminary cost reduction assessment? Discuss actions that the company can take to reduce/eliminate the nonvalue-added activities.
3. Compute the target cost required to maintain current market share, while earning a profit of $4 per unit. Now compute the target cost required to expand sales by 50 percent. How much cost reduction would be required to achieve each target?

4. Assume that further activity analysis revealed the following: switching to automated insertion would save $60,000 of engineering support and $90,000 of direct labor. Now what is the total potential cost reduction per unit available from activity analysis? With these additional reductions, can Mays achieve the target cost to maintain current sales? To increase it by 50 percent? What form of activity analysis is this: reduction, sharing, elimination, or selection?
5. Calculate income based on current sales, prices, and costs. Now calculate the income using a $14 price and a $12 price, assuming that the maximum cost reduction possible is achieved (including Requirement 4's reduction), what price should be selected?

P26-3
Life-Cycle Cost Management
LO 3

Boyce Productions manufactures products with life cycles that average three years. The first year of the three years involves product development, and the remaining two years concern production and sales. A budgeted life-cycle income statement has been developed for two proposed products and is presented below. Each product will sell 200,000 units. The price has been set to yield a 50 percent gross margin ratio.

	Product A	*Product B*	*Total*
Sales	$4,000,000	$5,000,000	$9,000,000
Cost of goods sold	(2,000,000)	(2,500,000)	(4,500,000)
Gross margin	$2,000,000	$2,500,000	$4,500,000
Period expenses:			
Research and development			(2,000,000)
Marketing			(1,150,000)
Life cycle income			$1,350,000

Upon seeing the budget, Rick Moss, president of Boyce Production, called in LeeAnn Gordon, marketing manager, and Art Cummings, design engineer.

Rick: "These two products are earning only a 15 percent return on sales. We need 20 percent to earn an acceptable return on our investment. Can't we raise prices?"

LeeAnn: "I doubt the market would bear any increase in prices. However, I will do some additional research and see what's possible. The gross-profit ratio is already high. The problem appears to be with R & D. Those expenses seem higher than normal."

Art: "These products are more complex than usual and we need to have the extra resources—at least if you want to have a product that functions as we are claiming it will. Also, we are charting some new waters with the features these products are offering. Specifically, our design is intended to reduce the post-purchase costs that consumers incur, including operation, support, maintenance, and disposal. LeeAnn, if you recall, you mentioned to us a year ago that our competitors were providing products that had lower post-purchase costs. This new design was intended to make us market leaders in this area. At any rate, in the future, we can probably get by on less—after we gain some experience. But it wouldn't be much less—perhaps $50,000."

Rick: "That would still allow us to earn only about 15.6 percent—even after you get more proficient. Maybe we ought to stay with our more standard features."

LeeAnn: "Before we abandon these new lines, perhaps we ought to look at each product individually. Maybe one could be retained. These new features will give us an edge in the market. Also, I'll bet Art could redesign the product so that production costs could be lowered—if he knew what was driving those costs. I'm concerned that our competitors will exploit their post-purchase cost advantage. We really need to be leaders in this post-purchase area—our reputation is at stake. If we're not careful, we could begin losing market share."

REQUIRED:

1. What specific improvements would you suggest to Rick to improve Boyce's life-cycle cost management system?
2. Assume that the "period" expenses are traceable to each product. Product A is responsible for 60 percent of R & D costs and 50% of marketing costs. Prepare a revised income statement for each product. Based on this analysis, should either product be produced?
3. Based on the revised income statements of Requirement 2, how much must production costs be reduced to make each product acceptable? Discuss how activity analysis can help achieve this outcome. Explain why this should occur now, not after the products are in production.
4. According to Art, the motivation for the new design was to reduce the post-purchase costs of the new products. Explain why whole-life cost should be the focus of life-cycle cost management.

P26-4
Cost Report; Value-Added and Nonvalue-Added Costs; Target Costs; Activity-Based Management
LO 2

For 1995, Muzik Company is expecting to produce and sell 100,000 portable radio and disk players: 90,000 units of its budget model and 10,000 units of its luxury model. This expected output is identical to the output of the year just completed. The actual quantities of activities used and actual costs associated with the production of the budget and luxury models in 1994 are as follows:

	Actual Usage		
Activity	*Luxury*	*Budget*	*Actual Cost*
Plastic components	56,000	364,000	$ 3,360,000
Electronic components	57,000	363,000	4,200,000
Labor (hours)	30,000	270,000	3,000,000
Power (kilowatt hours)	10,000	90,000	300,000
Receiving (orders)	5,000	18,000	750,000
Setups (setup time)	2,000	4,000	240,000
Materials handling (moves)	4,000	16,000	480,000
Maintenance (maintenance hours)	6,000	30,000	756,000
Warranty (number of defectives)	500	5,600	549,000
Total			$13,635,000

Of the nine activities, five have strictly variable activity costs (representing only resources acquired as needed): plastic components, electronic components, labor, power, and warranty. Receiving, setups, materials handling, and maintenance use only resources acquired in advance of usage (representing fixed short-run costs). The available capacity (actual capacity acquired for the year) of these four activities is listed below with each activity's resource block size:

	Practical Capacity	*Block size*[1]
Receiving	25,000 orders	1,000
Setups	8,000 setup hours	2,000
Materials handling	24,000 moves	1,200
Maintenance	37,800 hours	1,800

[1]Block size is defined as the number of units of the activity that must be purchased at a time, e.g., for receiving, one employee can process 1,000 orders per year, thus, receiving capability must be acquired in units of 1,000.

The actual price paid per unit of input in 1994 is equal to the standard price for that year. The value-added quantities of each activity that should have been used in producing the budget and luxury models are also known.

	Value-added Quantities		
	Luxury Model	*Budget Model*	*Total*
Plastic components	50,000	360,000	410,000
Electronic components	50,000	360,000	410,000
Labor (hours)	27,000	253,000	280,000
Power (kilowatt hours)	9,000	81,000	90,000
Receiving (orders)	1,000	4,000	5,000
Setups (setup time)	0	0	0
Materials handling (moves)	500	1,900	2,400
Maintenance (machine hours)	5,400	27,000	32,400
Warranty (defectives)	0	0	0

The selling price per unit of the luxury model is $216. The largest competitor sells a comparable unit for $190. Jeanette Day, the marketing manager for Muzik, has estimated that the company could increase its current sales from 10,000 to 15,000 units (increasing its share of the market by 50 percent) by dropping its price to $180. William Mozart, the president of Muzik, is willing to drop the price immediately if the company can increase the total profits it currently is earning on the luxury model by 10 percent. William, however, is only willing to implement the price reduction if the target profit can be reached by the end of 1996.

REQUIRED:

1. Prepare a cost report that details the total value- and nonvalue-added costs for 1994.
2. Compute the actual cost of producing one unit of the luxury model in 1994, excluding the unused activity capacity costs. Should unused activity capacity costs be excluded in calculating unit product cost? Explain.
3. Compute the value-added cost per unit for the luxury model.
4. What is the unit target cost for the luxury model assuming the price is lowered to $180 and the 10% increase in profits is required?
5. Refer to Requirement 4. Suppose that all cost reductions will come by eliminating nonvalue-added costs. Is it possible for the company to reach the targeted cost? To answer this question, compute the value-added unit cost for 1996, assuming an output of 15,000 units. Explain how activity-based management would be helpful in achieving this target.

P26-5 Identifying Nonvalue-Added Activities and Costs

LO 2

For each of the following activities, estimate the nonvalue-added costs:

1. A company currently purchases a component used in production for $30 per unit. If the component is produced internally, the cost would be $22. There are 12,000 components used annually.
2. A company has five days of raw materials inventories on hand. Carrying costs of the inventories average $100,000 per day.
3. Machine-operator error produces one defective unit for every 50 produced. The unit can be made functional by installing a new component and rerunning the machine operation. The cost of rework is $30. The company produces 300,000 units per year.
4. Design engineers produce a bill of materials as part of the design process. Later, manufacturing engineers, during process planning, produce their own bill of materials for the same product. The time required to prepare a bill of materials is two hours. Design engineers earn an average of $30 per hour. Manufacturing engineers average $25 per hour. The company is a job operation and averages 600 product designs per year.

5. A company spends $5 million per year on repair and warranty work.
6. Inspection costs for incoming raw materials are $150,000.
7. A time and motion study revealed that packing should ideally take 30 minutes per case. The actual time averages 45 minutes per case. Labor cost is $12 per hour.
8. Downtime for critical machinery (bottleneck category) averages 1,000 hours per year (involving 10 machines). During the downtime, the partially completed units are outsourced, costing an extra $30 per unit. Each unit requires 0.25 hours of bottleneck machine time.
9. The expediting activity has 4,000 available labor hours per year, costing $8 per hour.
10. There are 10,000 hours of machine operator time available, costing $15 per hour. This year, only 9,000 hours were used. Machine operator time must be purchased in blocks of 2,000 hours. Machining for this company is regarded as an efficient activity.

P26-6
Value-Added Costs; Nonvalue-Added Costs; Currently Attainable Standards; Activity-Based Responsibility Accounting
LO 2, 4

Rexburn Company produces 400,000 units of a cordless telephone each year. At the beginning of 1994, Rexburn developed value-added standards for the inputs used to produce the phone. At the end of the year, the value-added quantities of these inputs, the actual quantities, and the standard prices were made available.

Activity	*Cost Driver*	*SQ*	*AQ*	*SP*
Materials usage	Components	800,000	880,000	$ 50
Labor usage	Labor hours	125,000	160,000	10
Engineering	Engineering hours	25,000	30,000[a]	25
Maintenance	Machine hours	60,000	70,000[a]	20
Warranties	Number of defectives	—	6,000	110
Materials handling	Number of moves	400,000	800,000[a]	4
Setups	Setup time	—	4,000[a]	15
Other	Machine hours	60,000	70,000	12

[a]These are practical capacities (actual activity quantities available). With the exception of handling, activity quantities acquired in advance of usage are purchased in blocks (whole units) of 2,000 units. Handling must be purchased in blocks of 40,000.

Assume that the actual prices paid for the inputs are equal to the standard prices. All activity costs are either strictly fixed (representing resources acquired in advance of usage) or strictly variable (representing resources acquired as used). In 1994, all available activity capacity is used.

REQUIRED:

1. Calculate the actual cost per phone for 1994, including warranty costs.
2. Calculate the standard cost per phone for 1994.
3. Prepare a cost report that presents value-added, nonvalue-added, and actual costs for each of the inputs. Explain why setup costs and warranty costs are both classified as nonvalue-added costs.
4. For 1995, the company again expects to produce 400,000 units of the phone. Management has set a goal of reducing nonvalue-added quantities by 25 percent (for each input). Prepare currently attainable standards for 1995. Explain how these standards would be used and discuss why they would be compatible with activity-based responsibility accounting. Explain how currently attainable standards differ from the conventional definition.
5. Assume that the reductions in activity quantities envisioned for 1995 were achieved. Indicate the cost reductions that would be realized in 1996 because of 1995's success. The company will again produce 400,000 units in 1996.

P26-7
Quality Cost Summary
LO 4

Barbara Bush, the president of Wayne Company, has recently returned from a conference on quality and productivity. At the conference she was told that many American firms have quality costs totaling 20% to 30% of sales. She, however, was skeptical about this statistic. But even if the quality gurus were right, she was sure that her company's quality costs were much lower—probably less than 5%. On the other hand, if she was wrong, she would be passing up an opportunity to improve profits significantly and simultaneously strengthen her competitive position. The possibility was at least worth exploring. She knew that her company produced most of the information needed for quality cost reporting—but there never was a need to bother with any formal quality data gathering and analysis.

This conference, however, had convinced her that a firm's profitability can increase significantly by improving quality—provided the potential for improvement exists. Thus, before committing the company to a quality improvement program, Barbara requested a preliminary estimate of the total quality costs currently being incurred. She also indicated that the costs should be classified into four categories: prevention, appraisal, internal failure, and external failure costs. She has asked you to prepare a summary of quality costs and to compare the total costs to sales and profits. To assist you in this task, the following information has been prepared from the past year, 1995:

a. Sales revenue: $10,000,000; net income: $1,000,000.
b. During the year, customers returned 30,000 units needing repair. Repair cost averages $7 per unit.
c. Six inspectors are employed, each earning an annual salary of $25,000. These six inspectors are involved only with final inspection (product acceptance).
d. Total scrap is 30,000 units. All scrap is quality related. The cost of scrap is about $15 per unit.
e. Each year, approximately 150,000 units are rejected in final inspection. Of these units, 80 percent can be recovered through rework. The cost of rework is $3.00 per unit.
f. A customer canceled an order that would have increased profits by $250,000. The customer's reason for cancellation was poor product performance. The accounting and marketing departments agree the company loses at least this much each year for the same reason.
g. The company employs five full-time employees in its complaint department. Each earns $20,000 a year.
h. The company gave sales allowances totaling $130,000, due to substandard products being sent to the customer.
i. The company requires all new employees to take its three-hour quality training program. The estimated annual cost of the program is $80,000.
j. Inspection of the final product requires testing equipment. The annual cost of operating and maintaining this equipment is $120,000.

REQUIRED:

1. Prepare a simple quality cost report classifying costs by category. Comment on the quality cost-sales ratio.
2. Prepare a pie chart for the quality costs. Discuss the distribution of quality costs among the four categories. Are they properly distributed? Explain.
3. Discuss how the company can improve its overall quality and at the same time reduce total quality costs.
4. Suppose Wayne Company decides a six year program will reduce quality costs to 2.5% of sales and that control costs will be 80% of total quality costs. Calculate the income increase that will occur if sales remain at $10,000,000. Also, calculate the total amount spent on control and failure costs.

P26-8 Quality Cost Report; Interim Performance Report

LO 4

In September of 1994, Olson Company received a report from an external consulting group on its quality costs. The consultants reported that the company's quality costs total about 25 percent of its sales revenues. Somewhat shocked by the magnitude of the costs, Frank Roosevelt, president of Olson Company, decided to launch a major quality improvement program. This program was scheduled for implementation in January of 1995. The program's goal was to reduce quality costs to 2.5% by the end of the year 2000 by improving overall quality.

In 1995, it was decided to reduce quality costs to 22 percent of sales revenues. Management felt that the amount of reduction was reasonable, and the goal could be realized. To improve the monitoring of the quality improvement program, Frank directed Pamela Golding, the controller, to prepare quarterly performance reports comparing budgeted and actual quality costs. He told Pamela that improving quality should reduce quality costs by one percent of sales for each of the first three quarters and two percent in the last quarter. Sales are projected to be $5,000,000 per quarter. Based on the consulting report and the targeted reductions, Pamela prepared the budgets for the first two quarters of the year:

	Quarter 1	*Quarter 2*
Sales	$5,000,000	$5,000,000
Quality costs:		
Warranty	$300,000	$250,000
Scrap	150,000	125,000
Incoming materials inspection	25,000	50,000
Product acceptance	125,000	150,000
Quality planning	40,000	60,000
Field inspection	30,000	0
Retesting	50,000	40,000
Allowances	65,000	50,000
New product review	10,000	10,000
Rework	130,000	100,000
Complaint adjustment	60,000	20,000
Downtime (defective parts)	50,000	40,000
Repairs	50,000	35,000
Product liability	85,000	60,000
Quality training	30,000	70,000
Quality engineering	0	40,000
Design verification	0	20,000
Process control measurement	0	30,000
Total budgeted costs	$1,200,000	$1,150,000
Quality costs-sales ratio	24%	23%

After completing the first quarter, the following actual sales and actual quality costs were reported:

Sales	$6,000,000
Quality costs:	
Warranty	$350,000
Scrap	170,000
Incoming materials inspection	25,000

(continued)

Product acceptance	165,000
Quality planning	42,000
Field inspection	33,000
Retesting	65,000
Allowances	70,000
New product review	10,000
Rework	150,000
Complaint adjustment	60,000
Downtime	64,000
Repairs	50,000
Product liability	95,000
Quality training	30,000

REQUIRED:

1. Assume that Olson Company reduces quality costs as indicated. What will quality costs be as a percent of sales for the entire year? For the end of the fourth quarter? Will the company achieve its goal of reducing quality costs to 22% of sales?
2. Reorganize the quarterly budgets so that quality costs are grouped in one of four categories: appraisal, prevention, internal failure, and external failure (that is, prepare a budgeted cost of quality report). Also identify each cost as variable or fixed. (Assume that none are mixed costs.)
3. Compare the two quarterly budgets. What do they reveal about the quality improvement plans of Olson Company?
4. Prepare a performance report for the first quarter that compares actual costs with budgeted costs. Use a flexible budget to make the comparison. Comment on the company's progress in improving quality and reducing its quality costs.

P26-9
Quality Cost Performance Reporting: One-Year Trend; Long-Range Analysis
LO 4

In 1995, Randall Company initiated a full-scale quality improvement program. At the end of the year, the president noted with some satisfaction that the defects per unit of product had dropped significantly compared to the prior year. She was also pleased that relationships with suppliers had improved and defective raw materials had declined. The new quality training program was also well accepted by employees. Of most interest to the president, however, was the impact of the quality improvements on profitability. To help assess the dollar impact of the quality improvements, the actual sales and the actual quality costs for 1994 and 1995 are given as follows by quality category:

	1994	*1995*
Sales	$20,000,000	$25,000,000
Appraisal costs:		
Product inspection	800,000	750,000
Raw material inspection	100,000	70,000
Prevention costs:		
Quality training	10,000	100,000
Quality reporting	5,000	50,000
Quality improvement projects	5,000	250,000
Internal failure costs:		
Scrap	700,000	600,000
Rework	900,000	800,000
Yield losses	400,000	250,000
Retesting	500,000	400,000

(continued)

	1994	*1995*
External failure costs:		
Returned materials	400,000	400,000
Allowances	300,000	350,000
Warranty	1,000,000	1,100,000

All prevention costs are fixed (by discretion). All other quality costs are variable.

REQUIRED:

1. Compute the relative distribution of quality costs for each year (pie charts may be helpful). Do you believe that the company is moving in the right direction in terms of the balance among the quality-cost categories? Explain.
2. Prepare a one-year trend performance report for 1995. How much have profits increased because of the quality improvements made by Randall Company?
3. Estimate the additional improvement in profits if Randall Company ultimately reduces its quality costs to 2.5 percent of sales revenues (assume sales of $25 million).

P26-10 Productivity Measurement: Partial and Total Measures; Price Recovery

LO 5

The battery division of Chalmur Company has recently engaged in a vigorous effort to increase productivity. Over the past several years, competition has become very intense, and the divisional manager knew that a significant price decrease for its batteries was in order. Otherwise, the division would lose at least 50 percent of its market share.

To maintain its market share, Chalmur had to decrease its per-unit price by $2.50 by the end of 1995. Decreasing the price by $2.50, however, absolutely required a similar increase in cost efficiency. If divisional profits dropped by $2.50 per unit, the continued existence of the division would be in question. To assess the outcome of the productivity improvement program the following data were gathered:

	1994	*1995*
Output	400,000	500,000
Input quantities:		
Materials	100,000	100,000
Labor	400,000	200,000
Capital	$4,000,000	$10,000,000
Energy	100,000	300,000
Input prices:		
Materials	$2.00	$ 3.00
Labor	8.00	10.00
Capital	0.15	0.10
Energy	2.00	2.00

REQUIRED:

1. Calculate the partial productivity ratios for each year. Can you say that productivity has improved? Explain.
2. Calculate the profit change attributable to productivity changes.
3. Calculate the cost per unit for 1994 and 1995. Was the division able to decrease its per-unit cost by at least $2.50? Comment on the relationship of competitive advantage and productive efficiency.

P26-11 Quality and Productivity; Interaction; Use of Operational Measures

LO 5

Andy Confer, production-line manager, had arranged a visit with Will Keating, plant manager. He had some questions about the new operational measures that were being used.

Andy: "Will, my questions are more to satisfy my curiosity than anything else. At the beginning of the year, we began some new procedures that require us to work toward increasing our output per pound of material and decreasing our output per labor hour. As instructed, I've been tracking these operational measures for each batch we've produced so far this year. Here's a copy of a trend report for the first five batches of the year. Each batch had 10,000 units in it."

Batches	*Material Usage*	*Ratio*	*Labor Usage*	*Ratio*
1	4,000 lbs	2.50	2,000 hrs	5.00
2	3,900 lbs	2.56	2,020 hrs	4.95
3	3,750 lbs	2.67	2,150 hrs	4.65
4	3,700 lbs	2.70	2,200 hrs	4.55
5	3,600 lbs	2.78	2,250 hrs	4.44

Will: "Andy, this report is very encouraging. The trend is exactly what we hoped for. I'll bet we meet our goal of getting the batch productivity measures. Let's see, those goals were 3.00 units per pound for materials and 4.00 units per hour for labor. Last year's figures were 5.00 for labor and 2.50 for materials. Things are looking good. I guess tying bonuses and raises to improving these productivity stats was a good idea."

Andy: "Maybe so—but I don't understand why you want to make these tradeoffs between labor and materials. Labor costs $10 per hour and the materials cost only $5 per pound. It seems like you're simply increasing the cost of making this product."

Will: "Actually, it may seem that way, but it's not so. There are other factors to consider. You know we've been talking quality improvement. Well, the new procedures you are implementing are producing products that conform to the product's specification. More labor time is needed to achieve this and as we take more time, we do waste fewer materials. But the real benefit is the reduction in our external failure costs. Every defect in a batch of 10,000 units costs us $1,000—warranty work, lost sales, a customer service department, and so on. If we can reach the labor and material productivity goals, our defects will drop from twenty per batch to five per batch."

REQUIRED:

1. Discuss the advantages of using only operational measures of productivity for controlling shop-level activities.
2. Assume that the batch productivity statistics are met by the end of the year. Calculate the change in a batch's profits from the beginning of the year to the end attributable to changes in labor and materials productivity.
3. Now assume that three inputs are to be evaluated: materials, labor, and quality. Quality is measured by the number of defects per batch. Calculate the change in a batch's profits from the beginning of the year to the end attributable to changes in productivity of all three inputs. Do you agree that quality is an input? Explain.

P26-12 Productivity; Tradeoffs; Price Recovery

LO 5

Connie Baker, president of Fleming Chemicals, had just concluded a meeting with two of her plant managers. She had told each that the product being produced was going to have a 50 percent increase in demand—next year—over this year's output (which is expected to be 10,000 gallons). A major foreign source of the raw material had been shut down because of civil war. It would be years before the source would be available again. The result was two-fold. First, the price of the raw material was expected to quadruple. Second, many of the less efficient competitors would leave the business, creating more demand and higher output prices—in fact, output prices would double.

In discussing the situation with her plant managers, she had reminded them that the automated process now allowed them to increase the productivity of the raw material. By using more machine hours, evaporation could be decreased significantly (this was a recent development and would be operational by the beginning of the new fiscal year). There were, however, only two other feasible settings beyond the current setting. The current usage of inputs for the 10,000 gallon output (current setting) and the input usage for the other two settings are given below. The input usage for the remaining two settings is for an output of 15,000 gallons. Inputs are measured in gallons for the material and in machine hours for the equipment.

	Current	*Setting A*	*Setting B*
Input quantities:			
Material	25,000	15,000	30,000
Equipment	6,000	15,000	7,500

The current prices for this year's inputs are $3 per gallon for materials and $12 per machine hour for the equipment. The materials price will change for next year as explained, but the $12 rate for machine hours will remain the same. The chemical is currently selling for $20 per gallon. Based on separate productivity analyses, one plant manager chose setting A and the other chose setting B.

The manager who chose setting B justified his decision by noting that it was the only setting that clearly signaled an increase in both partial measures of productivity. The other manager agreed that setting B was an improvement but that setting A was even better.

REQUIRED:

1. Calculate the partial measures of productivity for the current year and the two settings. Which of the two settings signals an increase in productivity for both inputs?
2. Calculate the profits that will be realized under each setting for the coming year. Which setting provides the greatest profit increase?
3. Calculate the profit change for each setting attributable to productivity changes. Which setting offers the greatest productivity improvement? By how much? Explain why this happened. (*Hint:* Look at tradeoffs.)

DISCUSSION AND INTERPRETATION PROBLEMS

D26-1 Ethical Considerations

Tim Ireland, controller of Roberts Electronics Division, was having lunch with Jimmy Jones, chief design engineer. Tim and Jimmy were good friends, having belonged to the same fraternity during their college days. The luncheon, however, was more business than pleasure.

Jimmy: "Well, Tim, you indicated this morning that you have something important to tell me. I hope this isn't too serious. I don't want my weekend ruined."

Tim: "Well, the matter is important. You know that at the beginning of this year, I was given the charge to estimate post-purchase costs for new products. This is not an easy task."

Jimmy: "Yeah. I know. That's why I had our department supply you engineering specs on the new products—stuff like expected component life."

Tim: "This new product you've been developing has a problem. According to your reports, there are two components which will wear out within about 14 months. According to your test runs, the product starts producing subpar performance during the 13th month."

Jimmy: "Long enough to get us past the 12 month warranty. So why worry? There are no warranty costs for us to deal with."

Tim: "Yes—but the customer then must incur substantial repair costs. And the product will have to be repaired once again before its useful life is ended. The estimated repair costs, when added to the normal life cycle costs, puts the whole-life cost above the target cost. According to the new guidelines, we are going to have to scrap this new product—at least if its current design is used. Perhaps you can find a new design that avoids the use of these two components—or find ways that they won't be so stressed so that they last much longer."

Jimmy: "Listen, Tim. I don't have the time or the budget to redesign this product. I have to come under budget, and I have to meet the targeted production date or I'll have the divisional manager down my throat. Besides, you know that I'm up for the engineering management position at headquarters. If this project goes well, it'll give me what I need to edge out Thompson Division's chief engineer. If I do the redesign, my opportunity for the job is gone. Help me out on this. You know how much this opportunity means to me."

Tim: "I don't know what I can do. I have to file the whole-life cost report and I'm required to supply supporting documentation from marketing and engineering."

Jimmy: "Well, that's easy to solve. Linda, the engineer who ran the tests on this product owes me a favor. I'll get her to redo the tests so that the data produce a 24 month reliability period for the components. That should cut your estimated repair costs in half. Would that be enough to meet the targeted whole-life costs?"

Tim: "Yes, but . . ."

Jimmy: "Hey, don't worry. If I tell Linda that I'll push her for chief divisional engineer, she'll cooperate. No sweat. This is a one time thing. How about it? Are you a player?"

REQUIRED:

1. Assume you are Tim. What pressures does he have to comply with Jimmy's request? Do you think he should comply? Would you, if you were Tim? If not, how would you handle the situation?
2. Assume that Tim cooperates with Jimmy and covers up the design deficiency. What standards of ethical conduct for management accountants were violated? (See the IMA code described in Chapter 1).
3. Suppose that Tim refuses to cooperate. Jimmy then gets Linda to rerun the tests anyway, with the new, more optimistic results. He then approaches Tim with the tests and indicates that he is sending a copy of the latest results to the divisional manager. Jimmy then indicates that he will challenge any redesign recommendations that Tim recommends. What should Tim do?

D26-2 Research Assignment

You are a newly employed accountant working for a medium-sized manufacturing firm. This firm is facing intense competition from foreign and domestic competitors. You have been asked by your supervisor, Kathy Bumstead, to research the use of nonfinancial performance measures. Use your library resources and pay particular attention to articles appearing in the following journals: *Management Accounting, Journal of Cost Management, and Harvard Business Review.* Once you have collected what you can on the topic, write a memo to Kathy that addresses the following issues:

1. What has brought about the rise of nonfinancial measures?
2. What are the deficiencies of the traditional accounting performance measures?
3. What nonfinancial measures should be used and why? In particular, what are the firms trying to measure?
4. How can control be achieved through the use of nonfinancial measures?
5. What problems or limitations are associated with nonfinancial measures?
6. What is your recommendation concerning the use of nonfinancial measures?

Kathy also wants you to list the sources for the views that you articulate in your memo. She also is willing for you to address any other substantive issues that you encounter in your research. However, the memo must be no longer than two pages.

COMPREHENSIVE CASE

C26-1 Planning and Control

Supermo Company produces lawn mowers of various sizes and capabilities. It has three divisions, two that are located in the United States and one that is located in England. The small motors division is located in El Paso, Texas. The other two divisions are frame and assembly divisions. The U.S. frame and assembly division is located in Las Cruces, New Mexico, and the British division is located in London. The small motors division produces five different small motors, one of which is the 3.8 horsepower motor. The motors are sold both internally and externally. The frame and assembly divisions manufacture the frames and other mower parts and buy the motors from the motors division (they also have the freedom to buy comparable motors from other suppliers). The base of each mower is assembled and then the components are boxed with instructions for final assembly by the consumer. All three divisions are treated as investment centers.

Supermo uses a standard costing system in all three of its divisions. The following standard cost sheet is provided for the 3.8 horsepower (HP) motor produced by the small motors division:

Materials (20 lbs @ $1.50)	$30.00
Labor (1.5 hrs @ $8.00)	12.00
Fixed overhead (1.5 hrs @ $5.00)	7.50
Variable overhead (1.5 hrs @ $3.00)	4.50
Standard unit cost	$54.00

The small motors division has the capacity of producing and selling 50,000 units of the 3.8 HP motors, but demand for the motors has softened due to intense competition, and the division plans on selling 40,000 units for the coming year. A similar drop in demand is also being experienced for the other motors produced by the division. A recent market analysis indicated that foreign competitors were selling small motors for a lower price with higher performance quality. The market share for the motors and the lawn mowers was eroding in both the U.S. and England.

Because of the challenges facing Supermo, a CPA firm was hired to evaluate the productive efficiency of the small motors division. If significant improvements were possible, the consulting engagement would be expanded to include the other two divisions. After a two-month analysis, the CPA firm made several observations and recommendations. According to the report, it was imperative that the small motors division decrease its prices to match (or even beat) those of the foreign competitors. Lowering prices, however, was not sufficient. Costs had to be reduced also so that reasonable profits could be earned. In addition, quality performance had to be improved. In fact, according to the consultants, improving quality would also reduce costs. They also indicated that further cost reductions could be had through productivity improvements. By eliminating nonvalue-added activities, less inputs would be needed. An activity-based management system was recommended. To help management understand its potential, information was gathered on activities, their budgeted supply (practical capacity), budgeted costs, and budgeted demands placed on the activities by the 3.8 HP motor. This information is presented on the following page.

Cost Drivers	*Activity Availability*	*Budgeted Activity Usage*
Quality related:		
Inspection hours	21,000	16,000
Quality training hours	2,000	2,000
Pounds of scrap	100,000	100,000
Rework hours	7,500	7,500
Warranty hours	50,000	40,000
Hours of field testing	1,000	1,000
Nonquality related:		
Machine hours	400,000	400,000
Setup hours	30,000	30,000
Receiving orders	10,000	7,000
Direct labor hours	200,000	200,000

Activities[a]	*Budgeted Costs*[b]
Inspection (final product)	$410,000
Quality training	40,000
Scrap creation	150,000
Rework	60,000
Warranty work	400,000
Field testing	50,000
Machining	540,000[c]
Setup	300,000
Receiving	100,000

[a]For calculation of the direct-labor hour overhead rates (fixed and variable), scrap, rework, and machining costs (less depreciation) are treated as variable costs. From an activity-based perspective, inspection, quality training, and receiving all are strictly fixed activity costs (resources acquired in advance of usage only); scrap and rework are strictly variable activity costs (resources acquired as needed); 20% of warranty, field testing, and setup costs represent resources acquired as needed, with the residual representing resources acquired in advance of usage; machine depreciation is a resource acquired in advance of usage with the remaining machine costs representing resources acquired as needed.

[b]Budgeted costs are computed using activity-based cost formulas.

[c]$140,000 is machine depreciation (straightline, ten years of depreciation remaining with no salvage value anticipated).

REQUIRED:

1. Suppose that the small motors division has 12,000 units of the 3.8 HP motor in beginning finished goods inventory. The division sells this motor for $70 per unit. Because of the consultant's report, the division plans on implementing a JIT manufacturing system. As part of this plan, inventories will be reduced. For the coming year, the division hopes to have finished goods inventories of the 3.8 motor reduced to 2,000 units. The beginning raw materials inventory supporting the production of the 3.8 HP motors has 80,000 lbs. Because of supplier JIT delivery agreements, the division expects to reduce this inventory to 8,000 lbs. Using this information, the standard cost sheet for the 3.8 motor, and any other information needed, prepare the following budgets for the 3.8 HP motor:
   a. A production budget
   b. A sales budget
   c. A raw materials purchases budget
   d. A direct labor budget
   e. A variable overhead budget

f. A cost of goods sold budget

Discuss how standard costing helped in the preparation of the budget. Does this role disappear in the advanced manufacturing environment? Explain.

2. Suppose that the units of the 3.8 HP motor actually produced are equal to budgeted production (Requirement 1). Also assume that the following actual results were obtained: purchases, 528,000 lbs @ $1.60; material usage, 610,000 lbs; labor, 50,000 hours @ $7.90.

   Compute the following variances:
   a. Materials price variance
   b. Materials usage variance
   c. Labor rate variance
   d. Labor efficiency variance

   Discuss the role, if any, that these variances would have in the advanced manufacturing environment.
3. Prepare a quality cost report for the small motors division. Discuss the current distribution of quality costs. Can you estimate the potential savings from quality improvements, assuming that the small motors division has total sales of $6,000,000?
4. Prepare a budgeted value-added and nonvalue-added cost report. Assume the following:
   a. The actual prices of resources equal standard prices
   b. Sales total $6,000,000 and value-added quality costs are 2.5% of sales, equally divided among value-added quality activities
   c. Value-added machine costs (excluding depreciation) are 80% of the total budgeted amount
   d. The division expects to operate a JIT purchasing and manufacturing system.
5. The following activities are acquired in blocks (whole units) as indicated:

Activity	*Block*
Inspection	2,100 hours
Quality training	2,000 hours
Field testing	1,000 hours
Warranty work	2,500 hours

   Compute the unused capacity and volume variance for each activity. Explain the difference in meaning for each variance. How can each be used by management? Assume a total sales of $6,000,000 for the division.
6. Suppose that the total investment of the small motors division is $20,000,000. Calculate the increase in ROI if all nonvalue-added costs are eliminated. How much of this increase would be attributable to achieving a zero-defects state?
7. Assume that management is considering a new manufacturing process for the 3.8 HP motor. The new process would increase the labor content but would reduce scrap so that the total materials usage drops. The projected effects of the process compared with last year's inputs are provided below (output for last year was 40,000 units; usage is projected based on an expected output of 50,000 units):

	Last Year Usage	*Projected Usage*
Labor hours	60,000	80,000
Pounds of materials	800,000	950,000

   Calculate the partial productivity ratios for each input and the effect on profits if the process is implemented (use standard input prices for the computation of the profit-linked productivity measure). Should the new process be implemented? Discuss the value of profit-linked productivity measurement.

APPENDIX A
ANNUAL REPORT OF ALBERTSON'S, INC.

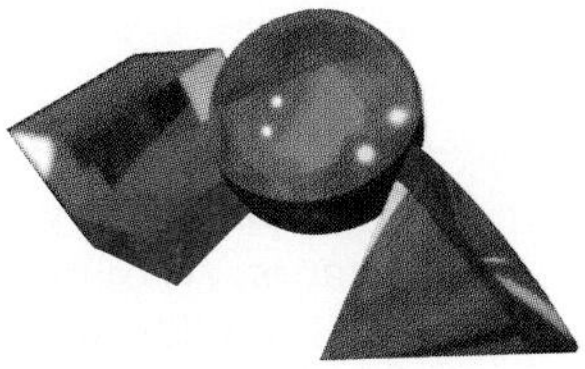

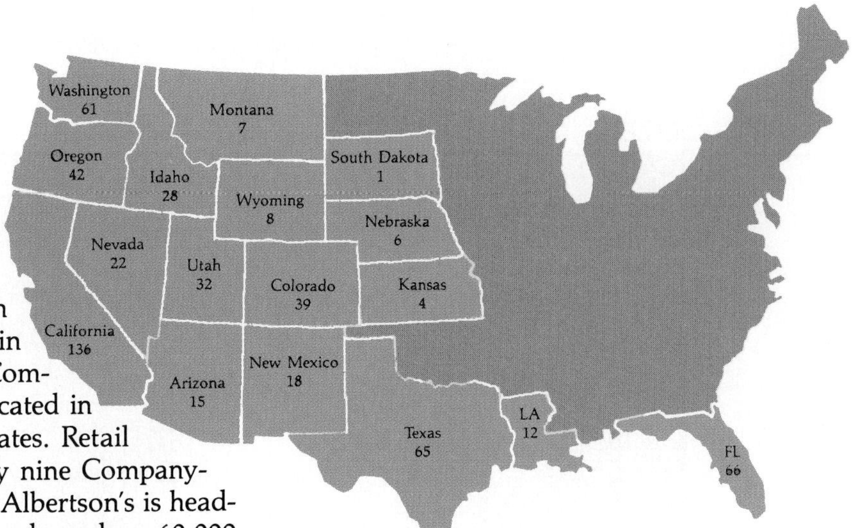

The Company

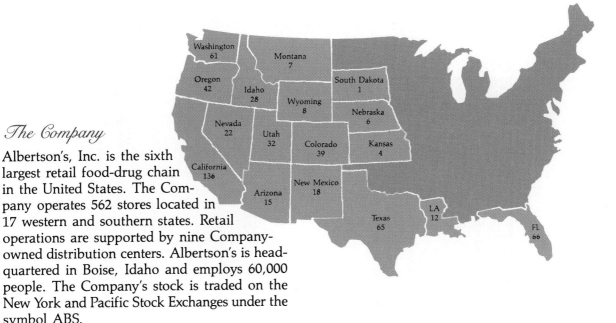

Albertson's, Inc. is the sixth largest retail food-drug chain in the United States. The Company operates 562 stores located in 17 western and southern states. Retail operations are supported by nine Company-owned distribution centers. Albertson's is headquartered in Boise, Idaho and employs 60,000 people. The Company's stock is traded on the New York and Pacific Stock Exchanges under the symbol ABS.

Management's Discussion And Analysis Of Results Of Operations And Financial Condition

Results of Operations

The Company has reported record sales and earnings for 22 consecutive years. Sales for 1991 were $8.7 billion compared to $8.2 billion in 1990 and $7.4 billion in 1989. Sales percentage increases were 5.6% in 1991, 10.7% in 1990 and 11.6% in 1989 after adjusting for the 53rd week of 1988. Increases in sales are attributable to identical store sales exceeding inflation, the continued expansion of net square footage and inflation. Identical store sales, stores that have been in operation for two full fiscal years, increased 1.1% in 1991, 5.5% in 1990 and 4.7% in 1989. Management estimates that inflation accounted for approximately 0.7% of the 1991 sales increase, compared to 3.5% in 1990 and 4.0% in 1989. During 1991, the Company opened 39 stores, 8 of which were acquired, remodeled 29 stores and closed 8 stores for a net square footage increase of 1,767,000 square feet, or 7.8%.

During 1991, gross margin increased to 23.98% as compared to 23.42% in 1990 and 22.91% in 1989. This increase was due primarily to improvements in general merchandise sales and continued benefits realized from the expansion and utilization of Company-owned distribution facilities. During 1991, the Company's distribution system provided 65% of all products purchased by retail stores as compared to 63% in 1990 and 56% in 1989. Increased volume and aggressive purchasing programs through these centers have enabled the Company to better control product costs and product distribution. The LIFO adjustment, as a percent to sales, reduced gross margin by .13% in 1991, .28% in 1990 and .31% in 1989.

Operating and administrative expenses, as a percent to sales, increased to 19.21% in 1991 as compared to 18.85% in 1990 and 18.61% in 1989. Increases in labor and related expenses exceeded price inflation in food sales during 1991. The Company continues to emphasize cost containment and job safety programs as well as increased productivity in an effort to reduce operating expenses. In addition, the Company's continued expansion of retail automation will add operating efficiencies in the future.

Operating profit, gross profit less operating and administrative expenses, increased as a percent to sales to 4.77% in 1991, as compared to 4.57% in 1990 and 4.31% in 1989.

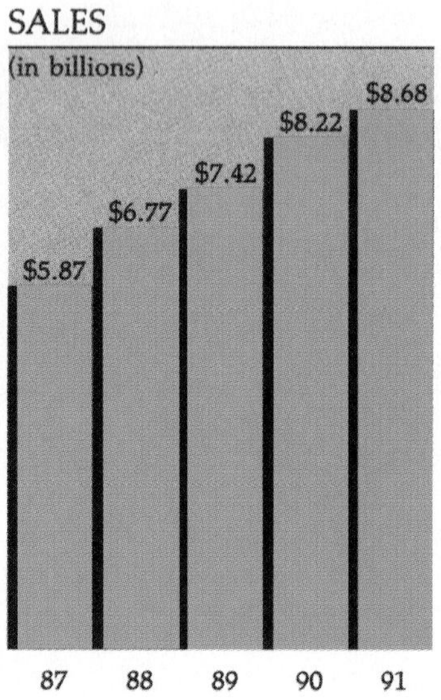

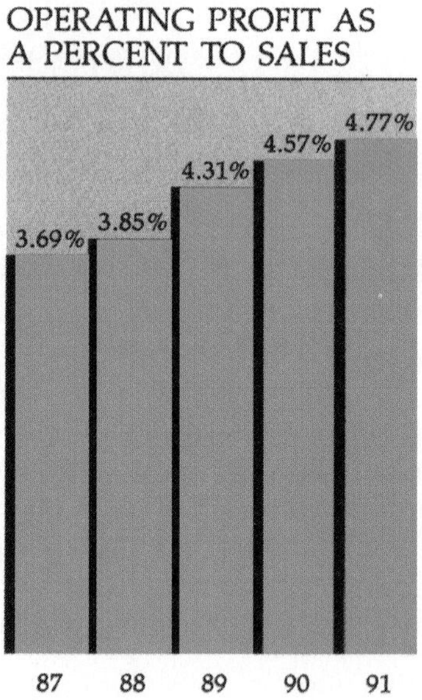

Net earnings were $257.8 million in 1991 compared to $233.8 million in 1990 and $196.6 million in 1989.

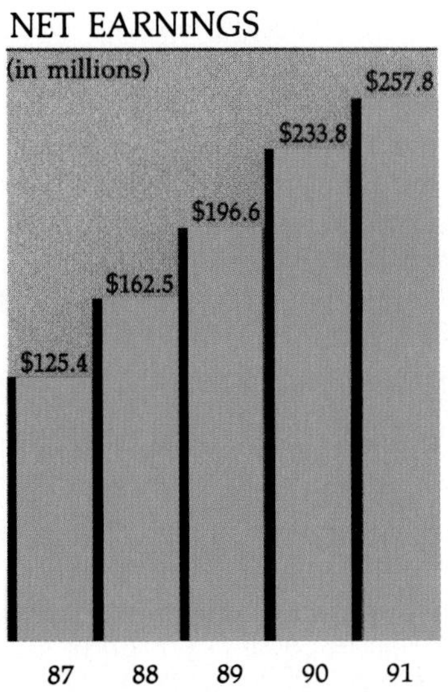

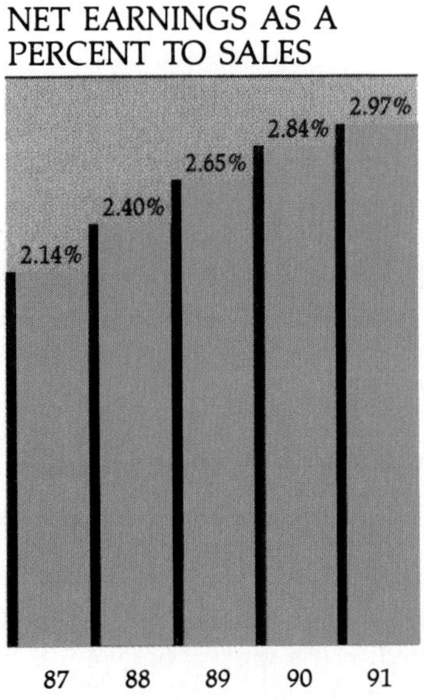

In February 1992, the Company entered into a definitive agreement with American Stores Company to acquire 74 Jewel Osco combination food-drug stores, a general merchandise warehouse in Ponca City, Oklahoma and related assets, including potential store locations (the Acquisition). The stores are located in Texas, Oklahoma, Florida and Arkansas and will add approximately 4.3 million square feet or 17.6% to the Company's existing square footage at January 30, 1992. The Acquisition which is subject to the customary conditions is expected to close in April 1992.

The majority of the stores being acquired are located in existing operating areas of the Company, which should increase efficiencies in overhead costs, including advertising, general and division office expenses and distribution. The Company will incur additional interest costs beginning in 1992 resulting from related financing.

In December 1990, the Financial Accounting Standards Board prescribed changes relating to the way the Company will be required to account for post-retirement benefits other than pensions and in February 1992, prescribed changes relating to the way the Company will be required to account for income taxes. These new requirements are discussed in the Notes to Consolidated Financial Statements. The Company must adopt the provisions of both statements no later than 1993. Implementation of the requirements of either statement is not expected to have a material impact on the Company's future financial results.

1991 SALES DOLLAR ANALYSIS

Liquidity and Capital Resources

The Company's excellent operating results enhanced its financial position and ability to complete its 1991 expansion program without additional long-term financing. The primary source of liquidity continues to be cash generated from operations. Cash provided by operating activities during 1991 was $408 million as compared to $371 million in 1990 and $292 million in 1989. These amounts have enabled the Company to fund its capital expansion program, pay dividends and purchase shares of its common stock on the open market. During 1991, the Company spent $269 million for capital expansion, $74 million for payment of dividends (which represents 28.9% of current net earnings) and $80 million for purchases of shares of its common stock. Since 1987, the Company has purchased and retired an equivalent of 6,220,644 shares of its common stock for $156,155,000. The Company continues to retain ownership of real estate when possible and long-term financing has been minimal for several years as demonstrated by the following leverage ratios:

	January 30, 1992	January 31, 1991	February 1, 1990
Long-term debt (including obligations under capital leases) to equity	12.6%	14.6%	23.5%
Long-term debt (including obligations under capital leases) to total assets	6.8%	7.9%	11.7%

Since 1987, the Company has achieved favorable returns on average stockholders' equity and on average assets as indicated in the graphs below.

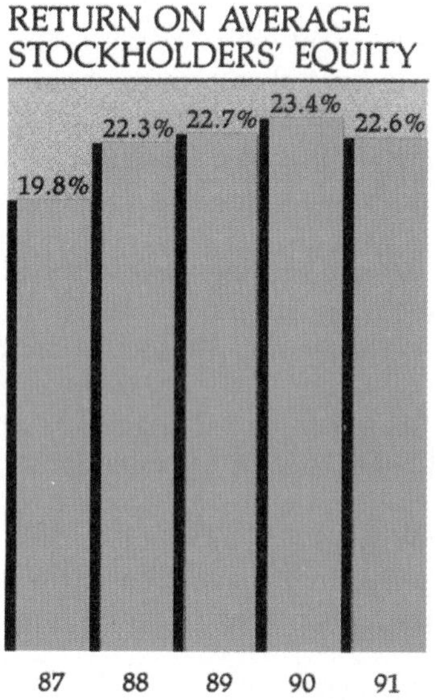

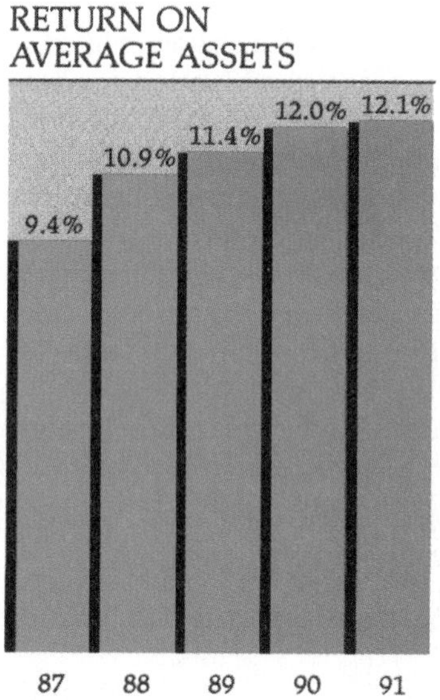

Capital expenditures for 1992 are expected to be $650 million which includes the Acquisition and an expansion of the Fort Worth, Texas Distribution Center to serve most of the acquired stores. The purchase price is based on the book value of fixed assets and cost of inventories. The Company intends to finance the 1992 capital expansion program from cash provided by operating activities and new borrowings. New borrowings of approximately $450 million will include commercial paper, senior unsecured medium-term notes and senior unsecured underwritten notes with a maturity of five years or less. A portion of the proceeds of the new borrowings will be utilized to refinance, at more favorable rates, approximately $35 million of debt existing at January 30, 1992. The Company intends to repay all new borrowings within a five year period thus minimizing the related impact on interest expense. Short-term borrowings will be used periodically to supplement cash needs. The Company had available lines of credit of $105 million at January 30, 1992.

During 1991, the Company opened 25 superstores and 14 combination units. The average size of these stores, 49,700 square feet, increased the Company's average store size to 43,600 square feet. At January 30, 1992, 85% of the Company's square footage consisted of stores 35,000 square feet or larger. Square footage has also increased because of the Company's remodel program. In 1991, 11 of the 29 remodeled stores were expanded in size.

New stores and remodeling will continue to be a significant part of planned capital expenditures. The Company is committed to keeping its stores up-to-date. In the last three years the Company has opened and remodeled 212 stores representing 9.7 million square feet.

During the past five years the Company has invested approximately $275 million (including inventory) in its distribution operations and has added over two million square feet of new or expanded facilities. In 1989, the Company opened new distribution centers in Fort Worth, Texas and Sacramento, California and completed an expansion of the Brea, California Distribution Center. During 1990, the Company began supplying health and beauty care items to its Texas Division stores and pharmaceutical items to all divisions from the Fort Worth center. During 1991, expansions were completed on the Brea and Sacramento distribution centers. During 1992, construction will begin on full-line distribution centers in Florida and Arizona in addition to the expansion of the Fort Worth center.

The following is a summary of capital expenditures, including capital leases and assets acquired with related debt for the last four fiscal years, as well as projected amounts for 1992 (in thousands):

	1992 (Projected)	1991	1990	1989	1988
New and acquired stores	$480,000	$163,072	$169,170	$157,433	$169,262
Remodels	73,000	55,803	49,277	53,137	42,409
Equipment replacement	12,000	8,341	8,814	6,133	10,632
Distribution facilities and equipment	76,000	27,465	9,115	76,826	86,980
Other	9,000	18,315	21,200	9,883	17,971
	$650,000	$272,996	$257,576	$303,412	$327,254

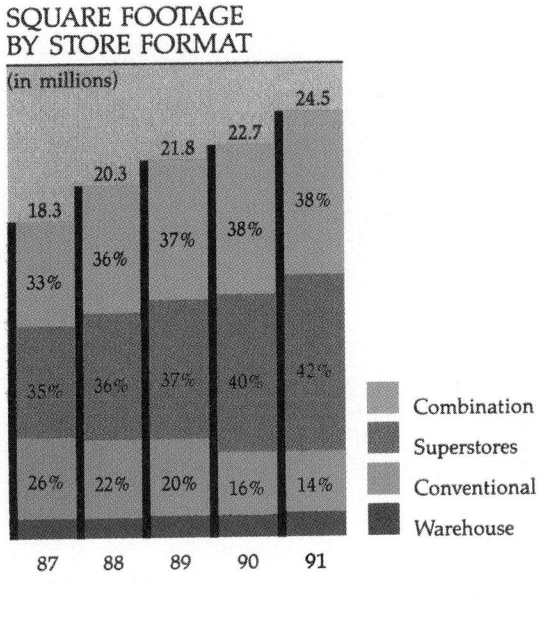

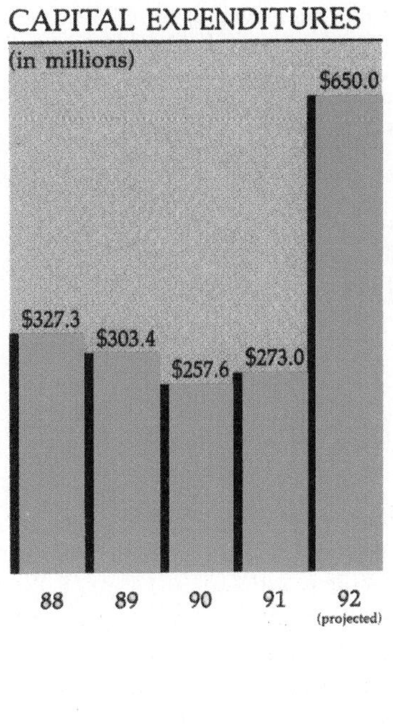

Albertson's, Inc.
Consolidated Earnings
(in thousands except per share data)

	52 Weeks January 30, 1992	52 Weeks January 31, 1991	52 Weeks February 1, 1990
Sales	**$8,680,467**	$8,218,562	$7,422,663
Cost of sales	**6,598,950**	6,293,881	5,722,036
Gross profit	**2,081,517**	1,924,681	1,700,627
Operating and administrative expenses	**1,667,355**	1,549,061	1,381,017
Operating profit	**414,162**	375,620	319,610
Other (expenses) income:			
Interest, net	**(23,106)**	(24,812)	(18,898)
Other, net	**15,338**	15,201	9,064
Earnings before income taxes	**406,394**	366,009	309,776
Income taxes	**148,600**	132,235	113,225
NET EARNINGS	**$ 257,794**	$ 233,774	$ 196,551
EARNINGS PER SHARE	**$1.94**	$1.75	$1.47
Average number of shares outstanding	**133,169**	133,777	134,136

See Notes to Consolidated Financial Statements.

Albertson's, Inc.
Consolidated Cash Flows
(in thousands)

	52 Weeks January 30, 1992	52 Weeks January 31, 1991	52 Weeks February 1, 1990
CASH FLOWS FROM OPERATING ACTIVITIES:			
Net earnings	**$257,794**	$233,774	$196,551
Adjustments to reconcile net earnings to net cash provided by operating activities:			
Depreciation and amortization	**132,813**	122,185	105,920
Net deferred income tax benefits	**(12,912)**	(5,302)	6,040
Changes in operating assets and liabilities:			
Receivables and prepaid expenses	**(2,572)**	(9,226)	(2,427)
Inventories	**(50,520)**	(18,037)	(112,354)
Refundable income taxes			5,748
Accounts payable	**8,572**	(4,352)	45,642
Other current liabilities	**19,541**	15,369	12,511
Self-insurance	**14,890**	22,346	19,500
Unearned income	**31,667**	5,459	1,825
Other long-term liabilities	**8,747**	8,785	12,904
Net cash provided by operating activities	**408,020**	371,001	291,860
CASH FLOWS FROM INVESTING ACTIVITIES:			
Increase in other assets	**(4,618)**	(19,793)	(8,543)
Capital expenditures excluding noncash items	**(268,500)**	(254,858)	(296,147)
Proceeds from disposals of land, buildings and equipment	**12,696**	11,387	5,010
Net cash used in investing activities	**(260,422)**	(263,264)	(299,680)
CASH FLOWS FROM FINANCING ACTIVITIES:			
Net proceeds from line of credit borrowings	**20,000**	10,000	
Proceeds from long-term borrowings			50,000
Payment on long-term borrowings	**(10,403)**	(62,628)	(12,558)
Proceeds from stock options exercised	**8,028**	8,312	10,846
Cash dividends	**(74,446)**	(64,215)	(53,615)
Stock purchases	**(79,806)**	(19,481)	(24,786)
Net cash used in financing activities	**(136,627)**	(128,012)	(30,113)
NET INCREASE (DECREASE) IN CASH AND CASH EQUIVALENTS	**10,971**	(20,275)	(37,933)
CASH AND CASH EQUIVALENTS AT BEGINNING OF YEAR	**23,433**	43,708	81,641
CASH AND CASH EQUIVALENTS AT END OF YEAR	**$ 34,404**	$ 23,433	$ 43,708

See Notes to Consolidated Financial Statements.

Albertson's, Inc.
Consolidated Balance Sheets
(in thousands)

ASSETS	January 30, 1992	January 31, 1991	February 1, 1990
CURRENT ASSETS:			
Cash and cash equivalents	$ 34,404	$ 23,433	$ 43,708
Accounts and notes receivable	55,835	52,274	44,103
Inventories	613,233	562,713	544,676
Prepaid expenses	10,602	11,591	10,536
Deferred income tax benefits	37,212	27,380	25,082
TOTAL CURRENT ASSETS	751,286	677,391	668,105
OTHER ASSETS	72,283	67,665	47,872
LAND, BUILDINGS AND EQUIPMENT:			
Land	289,526	259,897	215,407
Buildings	721,280	637,225	546,644
Fixtures and equipment	835,592	763,645	696,573
Leasehold improvements	180,034	158,054	142,872
Assets under capital leases	139,773	140,623	143,725
	2,166,205	1,959,444	1,745,221
Less accumulated depreciation and amortization	773,527	690,990	598,509
	1,392,678	1,268,454	1,146,712
	$2,216,247	$2,013,510	$1,862,689

See Notes to Consolidated Financial Statements.

LIABILITIES AND STOCKHOLDERS' EQUITY	January 30, 1992	January 31, 1991	February 1, 1990
CURRENT LIABILITIES:			
Accounts payable	$ 400,417	$ 391,845	$ 396,198
Notes payable	30,000	10,000	
Salaries and related liabilities	80,719	70,967	68,122
Taxes other than income taxes	37,807	30,743	26,698
Income taxes	9,589	9,443	2,768
Self-insurance	47,238	40,460	32,591
Unearned income	16,429	3,955	1,033
Other current liabilities	20,826	18,247	16,443
Current maturities of long-term debt	3,588	4,481	6,008
Current obligations under capital leases	5,634	5,426	5,122
TOTAL CURRENT LIABILITIES	652,247	585,567	554,983
LONG-TERM DEBT	52,510	56,056	111,503
OBLIGATIONS UNDER CAPITAL LEASES	99,159	103,039	106,949
OTHER LONG-TERM LIABILITIES AND DEFERRED CREDITS:			
Deferred compensation	24,755	22,013	18,807
Deferred income taxes	9,219	12,299	15,303
Deferred rents payable	66,575	62,021	53,333
Self-insurance	80,075	71,963	57,486
Unearned income	22,791	3,598	1,060
Other	9,464	9,072	13,773
	212,879	180,966	159,762
STOCKHOLDERS' EQUITY:			
Common stock	132,131	133,820	66,960
Capital in excess of par value	718	2,131	22,346
Retained earnings	1,066,603	951,931	840,186
	1,199,452	1,087,882	929,492
	$2,216,247	$2,013,510	$1,862,689

Albertson's, Inc.
Consolidated Stockholders' Equity
(in thousands)

	Common Stock $1.00 Par Value	Capital in Excess of Par Value	Retained Earnings	Total
BALANCE AT FEBRUARY 2, 1989	$ 66,929	$36,317	$ 697,250	$ 800,496
Exercise of stock options	521	6,369		6,890
Tax benefits related to stock options		3,956		3,956
Cash dividends, $.40 per share			(53,615)	(53,615)
Stock purchases	(490)	(24,296)		(24,786)
Net earnings			196,551	196,551
BALANCE AT FEBRUARY 1, 1990	66,960	22,346	840,186	929,492
Exercise of stock options	503	3,544		4,047
Tax benefits related to stock options		4,265		4,265
Cash dividends, $.48 per share			(64,215)	(64,215)
Stock purchases	(530)	(12,582)	(6,369)	(19,481)
Two-for-one stock split	66,887	(15,442)	(51,445)	
Net earnings			233,774	233,774
BALANCE AT JANUARY 31, 1991	133,820	2,131	951,931	1,087,882
Exercise of stock options	395	3,097		3,492
Tax benefits related to stock options		4,536		4,536
Cash dividends, $.56 per share			(74,446)	(74,446)
Stock purchases	(2,084)	(9,046)	(68,676)	(79,806)
Net earnings			257,794	257,794
BALANCE AT JANUARY 30, 1992	$132,131	$ 718	$1,066,603	$1,199,452

See Notes to Consolidated Financial Statements.

Albertson's, Inc.
Notes To Consolidated Financial Statements

Summary of Significant Accounting Policies

Fiscal Year End

The Company's fiscal year ends on the Thursday nearest to January 31 in each year. Unless the context otherwise indicates, reference to a fiscal year of the Company refers to the calendar year in which such fiscal year commences.

Consolidation

The consolidated financial statements include the results of operations, account balances and cash flows of the Company and its wholly-owned subsidiaries. All material intercompany balances have been eliminated.

Cash and Cash Equivalents

The Company considers all highly liquid investments with a maturity of three months or less at the time of purchase to be cash equivalents.

Inventories

The Company values inventories at the lower of cost or market. Cost of substantially all inventories is determined on a last-in, first-out (LIFO) basis. Cost of the remaining inventories is determined on a first-in, first-out (FIFO) basis.

Capitalization, Depreciation and Amortization

Land, buildings and equipment are recorded at cost. Depreciation is provided on the straight-line method over the estimated useful life of the asset.

The costs of major remodeling and improvements on leased stores are capitalized as leasehold improvements. Leasehold improvements are amortized over the shorter of the life of the applicable lease or the useful life of the asset. Capital leases are recorded at the lower of fair market value or the present value of future minimum lease payments. These leases are amortized over their primary term.

Upon disposal of fixed assets, the appropriate property accounts are reduced by the related costs and accumulated depreciation. The resulting gains and losses are reflected in the consolidated earnings.

Store Opening and Closing Costs

Noncapital expenditures incurred in opening new stores or remodeling existing stores are expensed in the year in which they are incurred. When a store is closed the remaining investment in fixtures and leasehold improvements, net of expected salvage value, is expensed. The present value of any remaining liability under the lease, net of expected sublease recovery, is also expensed.

Self-Insurance

The Company is primarily self-insured for property loss, workers' compensation and general liability costs. Self-insurance liabilities are based on claims filed and estimates for claims incurred but not reported.

Stock Options

Proceeds from the sale of newly issued stock to employees under the Company's stock option plans are credited to common stock to the extent of par value and the excess to capital in excess of par value. With respect to nonqualified stock options, the difference between the option exercise price and market value of the stock at date of grant is charged to operations over the vesting period. Income tax benefits attributable to stock options exercised are credited to capital in excess of par value.

Income Taxes

The Company provides for deferred income taxes resulting from timing differences in reporting certain income and expense items for income tax and financial accounting purposes. The major timing differences and their net effect are shown in the income taxes note.

The tax provisions were computed in accordance with Accounting Principles Board Opinion No. 11 and do not reflect the impact of adopting Statement of Financial Accounting Standards No. 109, "Accounting for Income Taxes."

Investment tax credits have been deferred and are being amortized over the remaining useful life of the related asset.

Earnings Per Share

Earnings per share are computed by dividing consolidated net earnings by the weighted average number of shares outstanding. Equivalent shares in the form of stock options are excluded from the calculation since they are not materially dilutive.

Reclassifications

Certain reclassifications have been made in prior years' financial statements to conform to classifications used in the current year.

Accounts and Notes Receivable

Accounts and notes receivable consist of the following (in thousands):

	January 30, 1992	January 31, 1991	February 1, 1990
Trade accounts receivable	$54,832	$50,732	$43,828
Trade notes receivable	1,658	2,280	757
Less allowance for doubtful accounts	(655)	(738)	(482)
	$55,835	$52,274	$44,103

Inventories

Approximately 96% of the Company's inventories are valued using the last-in, first-out (LIFO) method. If the first-in, first-out (FIFO) method had been used, inventories would have been $172,470,000, $160,877,000 and $137,804,000 higher at the end of 1991, 1990 and 1989. Net earnings would have been higher by $7,354,000 ($.06 per share) in 1991, $14,477,000 ($.11 per share) in 1990 and $14,660,000 ($.11 per share) in 1989. The replacement cost of inventories valued at LIFO approximates FIFO cost.

Indebtedness

Long-term debt includes the following (in thousands):

	January 30, 1992	January 31, 1991	February 1, 1990
Notes payable, unsecured:			
Notes payable to insurance companies	$12,870	$15,624	$ 19,932
Revolving credit agreement			50,000
Miscellaneous	386	408	1,684
	13,256	16,032	71,616
Mortgage notes	24,252	25,360	26,270
Industrial revenue bonds	18,590	19,145	19,625
	56,098	60,537	117,511
Less current maturities	(3,588)	(4,481)	(6,008)
	$52,510	$56,056	$111,503

The notes payable to insurance companies are payable in varying quarterly and annual installments through 1998. Interest on these notes is payable quarterly and semiannually at $9\frac{1}{4}$% to $9\frac{8}{10}$%. The loan agreements contain certain restrictions, including limitations on the payment of cash dividends and on purchase of stock. Under the most restrictive of the agreements, approximately $705,000,000 of retained earnings plus 75% of net earnings after January 30, 1992, are free of restrictions; and consolidated working capital, as defined, shall not be less than $30,000,000.

The Company has pledged real estate with a cost of $38,131,000 as collateral for the mortgage notes, which are payable monthly, quarterly and annually, including interest at $7\frac{1}{2}$% to $12\frac{1}{2}$%. The notes mature from 1992 to 2015.

The industrial revenue bonds are payable in varying annual installments through 2011, with interest to be paid semiannually at $4\frac{3}{4}$% to $10\frac{7}{8}$%.

A summary of scheduled maturities of all long-term debt for the next five years is as follows:

1992	$3,588,000
1993	3,742,000
1994	4,336,000
1995	4,126,000
1996	4,164,000

During 1991, 1990 and 1989, the Company acquired assets by incurring directly related liabilities in the amount of $25,000, $670,000 and $3,783,000, respectively. These transactions are considered noncash items and, accordingly, are not included in the consolidated cash flows.

In October 1988, the Company entered into a revolving credit agreement with several banks, whereby the Company may borrow principal amounts up to $100,000,000 at varying interest rates any time prior to October 28, 1993. In accordance with this agreement, the Company's consolidated tangible net worth, as defined, shall not be less than $500,000,000. As of January 30, 1992, $30,000,000 was outstanding under the revolving credit agreement which has been classified as current notes payable.

In addition to the revolving credit agreement, the Company had lines of credit from banks at prevailing interest rates in the amount of $35,000,000 at January 30, 1992. The cash balances maintained at these banks are not legally restricted. Outstanding letters of credit at year end amounted to $43,082,000.

Interest expense, net was as follows (in thousands):

	1991	1990	1989
Obligations under capital leases	$12,278	$11,786	$13,162
Debt	10,876	13,549	12,197
Capitalized interest	(5,013)	(4,198)	(6,940)
Interest expense	18,141	21,137	18,419
Net bank service charges	4,965	3,675	479
Interest expense, net	$23,106	$24,812	$18,898

Cash payments for interest, net of amounts capitalized, were $15,037,000 in 1991, $23,332,000 in 1990 and $14,264,000 in 1989.

Capital Stock

On March 2, 1987, the Board of Directors adopted a stockholder rights plan, which was amended on August 31, 1987, November 28, 1988 and September 6, 1989. Under the plan, stockholders of record on March 23, 1987, received a dividend distribution of one nonvoting right for each share of common stock. Subject to certain exceptions, one right has been or will be issued with each share of common stock issued after March 23, 1987. The rights are attached to all common stock certificates and no separate rights certificate will be distributed. Each right entitles the holder to purchase one share of the Company's common stock at a price of $65. The rights are exercisable for shares of common stock upon the earlier of the tenth business day following (i) the public announcement that a person or group acquired, or has obtained the right to acquire, beneficial ownership of 20 percent or more of the outstanding common stock, or (ii) the commencement of, or public announcement of an intention to make, a tender offer or exchange offer if, upon consummation, such person or group would be the beneficial owner of 20 percent or more of the then outstanding common stock.

Additionally, if any person or group becomes the beneficial owner of more than 20 percent of the outstanding common stock, each right will entitle its holder, other than such person or group, upon payment of the $65 exercise price, to purchase common stock with a deemed market value of twice the exercise price. The purchase rights for common stock will not be exercisable if the 20 percent acquisition is made pursuant to a tender or exchange offer for all outstanding common stock which a majority of certain directors of the Company deem to be in the best interests of the Company and its stockholders. If there is a merger with an acquirer of 20 percent or more of the Company's common stock and the Company is not the surviving corporation, or more than 50 percent of the Company's assets or earning power is transferred or sold, each right will entitle its holder, other than the acquirer, to purchase, or in certain instances to receive the cash value of, the acquiring company's common stock with a deemed market value of twice the exercise price.

All of the rights may be redeemed by the Board of Directors, and under certain circumstances, with the approval of a majority of the continuing directors (as defined in the plan), at a price of $.0125 per right until the earlier of (i) ten business days after the public announcement that a person or group has acquired beneficial ownership of 20 percent or more of the outstanding common stock or (ii) the date the stockholder rights plan expires. The rights, which are not entitled to dividends, expire on March 23, 1997.

Since 1987, the Board of Directors has continuously adopted or renewed plans under which the Company is authorized, but not required, to purchase shares of its common stock on the open market. The current plan was adopted by the Board on March 2, 1992 and authorizes the Company to purchase up to 6,700,000 shares through March 31, 1993. The Company has purchased and retired an equivalent of 6,220,644 shares under these plans.

At January 30, 1992, there were 600,000,000 shares of common stock and 10,000,000 shares of preferred stock authorized, of which 132,130,528 shares of common stock were issued and outstanding.

Income Taxes

Income tax expense consists of the following (in thousands):

	1991	1990	1989
Current:			
Federal	$139,793	$119,603	$ 93,272
State	22,778	19,526	16,094
	162,571	139,129	109,366
Deferred:			
Federal	(11,270)	(4,842)	5,250
State	(1,642)	(460)	790
	(12,912)	(5,302)	6,040
Amortization of deferred investment tax credits	(1,059)	(1,592)	(2,181)
	$148,600	$132,235	$113,225
Deferred results from:			
Unearned income	$ (13,198)	$ (2,210)	$ 65
Accelerated depreciation	4,834	4,336	15,322
Provision for self-insurance	(5,457)	(7,410)	(4,715)
Other	909	(18)	(4,632)
	$ (12,912)	$ (5,302)	$ 6,040

The reconciliations between the federal statutory tax rate and the Company's effective tax rates are as follows (in thousands):

	1991	%	1990	%	1989	%
Taxes computed at statutory rate	$138,174	34.0	$124,443	34.0	$105,324	34.0
State income taxes net of federal income tax benefit	14,047	3.5	12,770	3.5	11,211	3.6
Amortization of deferred investment tax credits	(1,059)	(.3)	(1,592)	(.5)	(2,181)	(.7)
Other	(2,562)	(.6)	(3,386)	(.9)	(1,129)	(.3)
	$148,600	36.6	$132,235	36.1	$113,225	36.6

Cash payments for income taxes were $158,377,000 in 1991, $128,428,000 in 1990 and $97,150,000 in 1989.

In February 1992, the Financial Accounting Standards Board issued Statement of Financial Accounting Standards No. 109, "Accounting for Income Taxes." Effective for fiscal years beginning after December 15, 1992, this new statement requires changes in the method of accounting for income taxes. It may be implemented either on a cumulative basis or through restatement of prior years' results. Implementation of Statement No. 109 is not expected to have a material impact on the Company's future financial results.

Stock Options

The Company has options outstanding under plans adopted in 1986, 1982 and 1975. The 1986 plan authorized the granting of options with respect to 4,000,000 shares of the Company's common stock. The 1982 plan expired on February 29, 1992, and the 1975 plan expired on April 6, 1985. Expiration of the 1982 plan and 1975 plan did not affect the rights of optionees for any options outstanding and not exercised in full.

The changes in the number of shares reserved for outstanding options under the plans are summarized as follows:

	Option Price Per Share	Number of Shares
Balance at February 2, 1989	$ 1.00 to $17.38	3,219,040
Granted	27.13 to 28.57	462,000
Exercised	1.00 to 11.82	(1,065,774)
Forfeited	1.75 to 27.13	(122,400)
Balance at February 1, 1990	1.25 to 28.57	2,492,866
Granted	17.38 to 33.13	197,000
Exercised	1.25 to 11.81	(616,766)
Forfeited	1.75 to 27.13	(35,200)
Balance at January 31, 1991	1.75 to 33.13	2,037,900
Granted	33.75 to 45.25	740,000
Exercised	1.75 to 27.13	(396,300)
Forfeited	3.75 to 45.25	(185,900)
Canceled	45.25 to 45.25	(79,500)
Balance at January 30, 1992	$ 1.75 to $45.25	2,116,200

Options on 139,400 shares were exercisable at January 30, 1992. In addition, there were 2,270,000 shares of common stock under the 1986 plan and 3,020,000 shares of common stock under the 1982 plan reserved for the granting of additional options.

Employee Benefit Plans

Substantially all employees working over 20 hours per week are covered by retirement plans. Union employees participate in multi-employer retirement plans under collective bargaining agreements. The Company sponsors two plans, Albertson's Salaried Employees Pension Plan and Albertson's Employees Corporate Pension Plan, which are defined benefit, noncontributory plans for eligible employees who are 21 years of age with one or more years of service and (with certain exceptions) are not covered by collective bargaining agreements. Benefits paid to retirees are based upon age at retirement, years of credited service and average compensation. The Company's funding policy for these plans is to contribute amounts deductible for federal income tax purposes.

Assets of the two Company plans are invested in directed trusts. Assets in the directed trusts are invested in common stocks (including $21,565,000, $21,359,000 and $14,434,000 of the Company's common stock in 1991, 1990 and 1989, respectively), U.S. Government obligations, corporate bonds, real estate and money market funds.

During 1988 the Company began sponsoring an unfunded Executive Pension Makeup Plan. The plan is nonqualified and provides certain key employees defined pension benefits which supplement those provided by the Company's other retirement plans.

Net periodic pension cost for the Company plans was as follows (in thousands):

	1991	1990	1989
Service cost - benefits earned during the period	$ 8,560	$ 7,612	$ 6,128
Interest cost on projected benefit obligations	8,956	7,644	6,483
Actual return on assets	(17,668)	(13,471)	(9,846)
Net amortization and deferral	6,076	4,076	2,209
Net periodic pension cost	$ 5,924	$ 5,861	$ 4,974

The following table sets forth the funding status of Albertson's Salaried Employees Pension Plan and Albertson's Employees Corporate Pension Plan and the amount included in other assets in the Company's consolidated balance sheets (in thousands):

	January 30, 1992	January 31, 1991	February 1, 1990
Plan assets at fair value	$150,603	$123,083	$103,264
Actuarial present value of:			
Vested benefits	91,924	78,205	64,485
Nonvested benefits	5,136	4,150	7,032
Accumulated benefit obligation	97,060	82,355	71,517
Effect of projected future salary increases	25,475	17,414	15,495
Projected benefit obligation	122,535	99,769	87,012
Plan assets in excess of projected benefit obligation	28,068	23,314	16,252
Unrecognized net gain	(15,077)	(14,246)	(11,147)
Unrecognized prior service cost	8,154	4,690	5,133
Unrecognized net assets at January 30, 1987	(1,545)	(1,732)	(1,919)
Prepaid pension cost	$ 19,600	$ 12,026	$ 8,319

The following table sets forth the status of the unfunded Executive Pension Makeup Plan and the amount included in other long-term liabilities in the Company's consolidated balance sheets (in thousands):

	January 30, 1992	January 31, 1991	February 1, 1990
Actuarial present value of:			
Accumulated benefit obligation (fully vested)	$ 4,614	$ 3,608	$ 3,436
Effect of projected future salary increases	2,684	2,505	2,251
Projected benefit obligation	7,298	6,113	5,687
Actuarial present value of projected benefit obligations in excess of plan assets	(7,298)	(6,113)	(5,687)
Unrecognized net gain	458	86	85
Unrecognized prior service cost	1,326	1,421	1,516
Unrecognized net liability	2,050	2,230	2,411
Additional minimum liability	(1,150)	(1,232)	(1,761)
Accrued pension cost	$(4,614)	$(3,608)	$(3,436)

Assumptions used in the computation of net periodic pension cost for all Company-sponsored plans were as follows:

	1991	1990	1989
Weighted-average discount rate	8½%	8%	8%
Annual salary increases	5½%	5½%	5½%
Expected long-term rate of return on assets	9%	9%	9%

The Company also contributes to various plans under industry-wide collective bargaining agreements which provide for pension benefits. Total contributions to these plans were $17,705,000 for 1991, $18,411,000 for 1990 and $22,645,000 for 1989.

The Company has bonus plans for store management personnel and other key management personnel. Amounts charged to earnings under all bonus plans were $36,205,000 for 1991, $37,090,000 for 1990 and $32,530,000 for 1989.

In December 1990, the Financial Accounting Standards Board issued Statement of Financial Accounting Standards No. 106 "Employers' Accounting for Postretirement Benefits Other Than Pensions" effective for fiscal years beginning after December 15, 1992. This new statement requires an accrual of postretirement benefits (such as health care benefits) during the years an employee provides services. The costs of these benefits are currently expensed on a pay-as-you-go basis and are not material. Implementation of Statement No. 106 is not expected to have a material impact on the Company's future financial results.

Leases

The Company leases a portion of its real estate. The typical lease period is 25 to 30 years and most leases contain renewal options. Exercise of such options is dependent on the level of business conducted at the location. In addition, the Company leases certain equipment. Some leases contain contingent rental provisions based on sales volume at retail units or miles traveled for trucks.

Assets under capital leases are capitalized using interest rates appropriate at the inception of each lease. Contingent rents associated with capital leases were $2,570,000 in 1991, $2,571,000 in 1990 and $3,115,000 in 1989. Following is an analysis of the Company's assets under capital leases (in thousands):

	January 30, 1992	January 31, 1991	February 1, 1990
Real estate	$138,116	$138,618	$141,980
Equipment	1,657	2,005	1,745
	$139,773	$140,623	$143,725
Accumulated amortization	$ 70,058	$ 67,601	$ 66,113

Future minimum lease payments for assets under capital leases at January 30, 1992 are as follows (in thousands):

	Real Estate	Equipment	Total
1992	$ 16,226	$ 326	$ 16,552
1993	15,971	261	16,232
1994	15,783	233	16,016
1995	15,667	225	15,892
1996	15,291	175	15,466
Remainder	115,530	33	115,563
Total minimum obligations	194,468	1,253	195,721
Less executory costs	(61)		(61)
Net minimum obligations	194,407	1,253	195,660
Less interest	(90,612)	(255)	(90,867)
Present value of net minimum obligations	103,795	998	104,793
Less current portion	(5,402)	(232)	(5,634)
Long-term obligations at January 30, 1992	$ 98,393	$ 766	$ 99,159

Minimum obligations have not been reduced by minimum capital sublease rentals of $6,508,000 receivable in the future under noncancelable capital subleases. Executory costs include such items as property taxes and insurance.

Rent expense under operating leases was as follows (in thousands):

	1991	1990	1989
Minimum rent	$56,664	$55,714	$55,653
Contingent rent	4,335	4,984	3,889
	60,999	60,698	59,542
Less sublease rent	(14,372)	(11,548)	(12,050)
	$46,627	$49,150	$47,492

Future minimum lease payments for all noncancelable operating leases and related subleases having a remaining term in excess of one year at January 30, 1992 are as follows (in thousands):

	Real Estate	Equipment	Subleases
1992	$ 52,337	$ 74	$(11,855)
1993	53,609	49	(9,439)
1994	53,313		(7,125)
1995	52,771		(6,447)
1996	52,974		(4,855)
Remainder	660,849		(20,433)
Total minimum obligations (receivables)	$925,853	$123	$(60,154)

Capital lease obligations incurred and capital lease obligations terminated are considered noncash items and, accordingly, are not reflected in the consolidated cash flows. The following table summarizes these transactions (in thousands):

	1991	1990	1989
Capital lease obligations incurred	$4,471	$2,048	$3,482
Capital lease obligations terminated	2,203	670	3,296

The present value of minimum rent payments under operating leases is approximately $400,000,000 at January 30, 1992.

Legal Proceedings

The Company is involved in routine litigation incidental to operations. In the opinion of Management, it is unlikely that any exposure from these actions will have a material affect on the Company's future financial results.

Subsequent Events

In February 1992, the Company entered into a definitive agreement with American Stores Company for the purchase of 74 Jewel Osco combination food-drug stores in Texas, Oklahoma, Florida and Arkansas, a general merchandise warehouse in Ponca City, Oklahoma and related assets, including potential store locations (the Acquisition). The purchase price is based upon the book value of fixed assets and cost of inventories. The Acquisition which is subject to the customary conditions is expected to close in April 1992. The Company expects to finance the Acquisition through new borrowings. The majority of the stores being acquired are located in existing operating areas of the Company, which should increase efficiencies in overhead costs, including advertising, general and division office expenses and distribution.

In conjunction with debt financing associated with the Acquisition, the Company plans to refinance, at more favorable rates, approximately $35,000,000 of existing mortgage notes and unsecured notes payable to insurance companies. On March 10, 1992 notes in the amount of $9,750,000 were repaid pursuant to this plan.

Total new debt is anticipated to be approximately $450,000,000 and will consist of a combination of commercial paper, senior unsecured medium-term notes and senior unsecured underwritten notes with a maturity of five years or less. The Company intends to repay all new debt within a five year period.

Responsibility For Financial Reporting

The Management of Albertson's, Inc. is responsible for the preparation and integrity of the consolidated financial statements of the Company. The accompanying consolidated financial statements have been prepared by the Management of the Company, in accordance with generally accepted accounting principles, using Management's best estimates and judgment where necessary. Financial information appearing throughout this Annual Report is consistent with that in the consolidated financial statements.

To help fulfill its responsibility, Management maintains a system of internal controls designed to provide reasonable assurance that assets are safeguarded against loss or unauthorized use and that transactions are executed in accordance with Management's authorizations and are reflected accurately in the Company's records. The concept of reasonable assurance is based on the recognition that the cost of maintaining a system of internal accounting controls should not exceed benefits expected to be derived from the system. The Company believes that its long-standing emphasis on the highest standards of conduct and ethics, set forth in comprehensive written policies, serves to reinforce its system of internal controls.

Deloitte & Touche, independent auditors, audited the consolidated financial statements in accordance with generally accepted auditing standards to independently assess the fair presentation of the Company's financial position, results of operations and cash flows.

The Audit Committee of the Board of Directors, comprised entirely of outside directors, oversees the fulfillment by Management of its responsibilities over financial controls and the preparation of financial statements. The Committee meets with internal and external auditors at least three times per year to review audit plans and audit results. This provides internal and external auditors direct access to the Board of Directors.

Management recognizes its responsibility to conduct Albertson's business in accordance with high ethical standards. This responsibility is reflected in key policy statements that, among other things, address potentially conflicting outside business interests of Company employees and specify proper conduct of business activities. Ongoing communications and review programs are designed to help ensure compliance with these policies.

Gary G. Michael
Chairman of the Board and
Chief Executive Officer

A. Craig Olson
Senior Vice President, Finance and
Chief Financial Officer

Independent Auditors' Report

The Board of Directors and Stockholders of Albertson's, Inc.:

We have audited the accompanying consolidated balance sheets of Albertson's, Inc. and subsidiaries as of January 30, 1992, January 31, 1991 and February 1, 1990, and the related consolidated statements of earnings, stockholders' equity and cash flows for the years then ended. These financial statements are the responsibility of the Company's management. Our responsibility is to express an opinion on these financial statements based on our audits.

We conducted our audits in accordance with generally accepted auditing standards. Those standards require that we plan and perform the audit to obtain reasonable assurance about whether the financial statements are free of material misstatement. An audit includes examining, on a test basis, evidence supporting the amounts and disclosures in the financial statements. An audit also includes assessing the accounting principles used and significant estimates made by management, as well as evaluating the overall financial statement presentation. We believe that our audits provide a reasonable basis for our opinion.

In our opinion, the consolidated financial statements referred to above present fairly, in all material respects, the financial position of Albertson's, Inc. and subsidiaries at January 30, 1992, January 31, 1991 and February 1, 1990, and the results of their operations and their cash flows for the years then ended in conformity with generally accepted accounting principles.

Deloitte & Touche

Boise, Idaho — March 18, 1992

APPENDIX B
PRESENT AND FUTURE VALUE TABLES

APPENDIX CONTENTS

This appendix contains the following tables:

1. Future value of a single amount
2. Present value of a single amount
3. Future value of a single annuity
4. Present value of a single annuity

Table 1
Future Value of a Single Amount

(n) Period	2.00%	2.50%	3.00%	4.00%	5.00%	6.00%	7.00%	8.00%
1	1.02000	1.02500	1.03000	1.04000	1.05000	1.06000	1.07000	1.08000
2	1.04040	1.05062	1.06090	1.08160	1.10250	1.12360	1.14490	1.16640
3	1.06121	1.07689	1.09273	1.12486	1.15763	1.19102	1.22504	1.25971
4	1.08243	1.10381	1.12551	1.16986	1.21551	1.26248	1.31080	1.36049
5	1.10408	1.13141	1.15927	1.21665	1.27628	1.33823	1.40255	1.46933
6	1.12616	1.15969	1.19405	1.26532	1.34010	1.41852	1.50073	1.58687
7	1.14869	1.18869	1.22987	1.31593	1.40710	1.50363	1.60578	1.71382
8	1.17166	1.21840	1.26677	1.36857	1.47746	1.59385	1.71819	1.85093
9	1.19509	1.24886	1.30477	1.42331	1.55133	1.68948	1.83846	1.99900
10	1.21899	1.28008	1.34392	1.48024	1.62889	1.79085	1.96715	2.15892
11	1.24337	1.31209	1.38423	1.53945	1.71034	1.89830	2.10485	2.33164
12	1.26824	1.34489	1.42576	1.60103	1.79586	2.01220	2.25219	2.51817
13	1.29361	1.37851	1.46853	1.66507	1.88565	2.13293	2.40985	2.71962
14	1.31948	1.41297	1.51259	1.73168	1.97993	2.26090	2.57853	2.93719
15	1.34587	1.44830	1.55797	1.80094	2.07893	2.39656	2.75903	3.17217
16	1.37279	1.48451	1.60471	1.87298	2.18287	2.54035	2.95216	3.42594
17	1.40024	1.52162	1.65285	1.94790	2.29202	2.69277	3.15882	3.70002
18	1.42825	1.55966	1.70243	2.02582	2.40662	2.85434	3.37993	3.99602
19	1.45681	1.59865	1.75351	2.10685	2.52695	3.02560	3.61653	4.31570
20	1.48595	1.63862	1.80611	2.19112	2.65330	3.20714	3.86968	4.66096
21	1.51567	1.67958	1.86029	2.27877	2.78596	3.39956	4.14056	5.03383
22	1.54598	1.72157	1.91610	2.36992	2.92526	3.60354	4.43040	5.43654
23	1.57690	1.76461	1.97359	2.46472	3.07152	3.81975	4.74053	5.87146
24	1.60844	1.80873	2.03279	2.56330	3.22510	4.04893	5.07237	6.34118
25	1.64061	1.85394	2.09378	2.66584	3.38635	4.29187	5.42743	6.84848
30	1.81136	2.09757	2.42726	3.24340	4.32194	5.74349	7.61226	10.06266
32	1.88454	2.20376	2.57508	3.50806	4.76494	6.45339	8.71527	11.73708
34	1.96068	2.31532	2.73191	3.79432	5.25335	7.25103	9.97811	13.69013
36	2.03989	2.43254	2.89828	4.10393	5.79182	8.14725	11.42394	15.96817
40	2.20804	2.68506	3.26204	4.80102	7.03999	10.28572	14.97446	21.72452

9.00%	10.00%	12.00%	14.00%	16.00%	18.00%	20.00%	22.00%	(n) Period
1.09000	1.10000	1.12000	1.14000	1.16000	1.18000	1.20000	1.22000	1
1.18810	1.21000	1.25440	1.29960	1.34560	1.39240	1.44000	1.48840	2
1.29503	1.33100	1.40493	1.48154	1.56090	1.64303	1.72800	1.81585	3
1.41158	1.46410	1.57352	1.68896	1.81064	1.93878	2.07360	2.21533	4
1.53862	1.61051	1.76234	1.92541	2.10034	2.28776	2.48832	2.70271	5
1.67710	1.77156	1.97382	2.19497	2.43640	2.69955	2.98598	3.29730	6
1.82804	1.94872	2.21068	2.50227	2.82622	3.18547	3.58318	4.02271	7
1.99256	2.14359	2.47596	2.85259	3.27841	3.75886	4.29982	4.90771	8
2.17189	2.35795	2.77308	3.25195	3.80296	4.43545	5.15978	5.98740	9
2.36736	2.59374	3.10585	3.70722	4.41144	5.23384	6.19174	7.30463	10
2.58043	2.85312	3.47855	4.22623	5.11726	6.17593	7.43008	8.91165	11
2.81266	3.13843	3.89598	4.81790	5.93603	7.28759	8.91610	10.87221	12
3.06580	3.45227	4.36349	5.49241	6.88579	8.59936	10.69932	13.26410	13
3.34173	3.79750	4.88711	6.26135	7.98752	10.14724	12.83918	16.18220	14
3.64248	4.17725	5.47357	7.13794	9.26552	11.97375	15.40702	19.74229	15
3.97031	4.59497	6.13039	8.13725	10.74800	14.12902	18.48843	24.08559	16
4.32763	5.05447	6.86604	9.27646	12.46768	16.67225	22.18611	29.38442	17
4.71712	5.55992	7.68997	10.57517	14.46251	19.67325	26.62333	35.84899	18
5.14166	6.11591	8.61276	12.05569	16.77652	23.21444	31.94800	43.73577	19
5.60441	6.72750	9.64629	13.74349	19.46076	27.39303	38.33760	53.35764	20
6.10881	7.40025	10.80385	15.66758	22.57448	32.32378	46.00512	65.09632	21
6.65860	8.14027	12.10031	17.86104	26.18640	38.14206	55.20614	79.41751	22
7.25787	8.95430	13.55235	20.36158	30.37622	45.00763	66.24737	96.88936	23
7.91108	9.84973	15.17863	23.21221	35.23642	53.10901	79.49685	118.20502	24
8.62308	10.83471	17.00006	26.46192	40.87424	62.66863	95.39622	144.21013	25
13.26768	17.44940	29.95992	50.95016	85.84988	143.37064	237.37631	389.75789	30
15.76333	21.11378	37.58173	66.21483	115.51959	199.62928	341.82189	580.11565	32
18.72841	25.54767	47.14252	86.05279	155.44317	277.96381	492.22352	863.44413	34
22.25123	30.91268	59.13557	111.83420	209.16432	387.03680	708.80187	1285.15025	36
31.40942	45.25926	93.05097	188.88351	378.72116	750.37834	1469.77157	2847.03776	40

Table 2
Future Value of an Annuity

(n) *Period*	*2.00%*	*2.50%*	*3.00%*	*4.00%*	*5.00%*	*6.00%*	*7.00%*	*8.00%*
1	1.00000	1.00000	1.00000	1.00000	1.00000	1.00000	1.00000	1.00000
2	2.02000	2.02500	2.03000	2.04000	2.05000	2.06000	2.07000	2.08000
3	3.06040	3.07562	3.09090	3.12160	3.15250	3.18360	3.21490	3.24640
4	4.12161	4.15252	4.18363	4.24646	4.31013	4.37462	4.43994	4.50611
5	5.20404	5.25633	5.30914	5.41632	5.52563	5.63709	5.75074	5.86660
6	6.30812	6.38774	6.46841	6.63298	6.80191	6.97532	7.15329	7.33593
7	7.43428	7.54743	7.66246	7.89829	8.14201	8.39384	8.65402	8.92280
8	8.58297	8.73612	8.89234	9.21423	9.54911	9.89747	10.25980	10.63663
9	9.75463	9.95452	10.15911	10.58280	11.02656	11.49132	11.97799	12.48756
10	10.94972	11.20338	11.46388	12.00611	12.57789	13.18079	13.81645	14.48656
11	12.16872	12.48347	12.80780	13.48635	14.20679	14.97164	15.78360	16.64549
12	13.41209	13.79555	14.19203	15.02581	15.91713	16.86994	17.88845	18.97713
13	14.68033	15.14044	15.61779	16.62684	17.71298	18.88214	20.14064	21.49530
14	15.97394	16.51895	17.08632	18.29191	19.59863	21.01507	22.55049	24.21492
15	17.29342	17.93193	18.59891	20.02359	21.57856	23.27597	25.12902	27.15211
16	18.63929	19.38022	20.15688	21.82453	23.65749	25.67253	27.88805	30.32428
17	20.01207	20.86473	21.76159	23.69751	25.84037	28.21288	30.84022	33.75023
18	21.41231	22.38635	23.41444	25.64541	28.13238	30.90565	33.99903	37.45024
19	22.84056	23.94601	25.11687	27.67123	30.53900	33.75999	37.37896	41.44626
20	24.29737	25.54466	26.87037	29.77808	33.06595	36.78559	40.99549	45.76196
21	25.78332	27.18327	28.67649	31.96920	35.71925	39.99273	44.86518	50.42292
22	27.29898	28.86286	30.53678	34.24797	38.50521	43.39229	49.00574	55.45676
23	28.84496	30.58443	32.45288	36.61789	41.43048	46.99583	53.43614	60.89330
24	30.42186	32.34904	34.42647	39.08260	44.50200	50.81558	58.17667	66.76476
25	32.03030	34.15776	36.45926	41.64591	47.72710	54.86451	63.24904	73.10594
30	40.56808	43.90270	47.57542	56.08494	66.43885	79.05819	94.46079	113.28321
32	44.22703	48.15028	52.50276	62.70147	75.29883	90.88978	110.21815	134.21354
34	48.03380	52.61289	57.73018	69.85791	85.06696	104.18375	128.25876	158.62667
36	51.99437	57.30141	63.27594	77.59831	95.83632	119.12087	148.91346	187.10215
40	60.40198	67.40255	75.40126	95.02552	120.79977	154.76197	199.63511	259.05652

9.00%	10.00%	12.00%	14.00%	16.00%	18.00%	20.00%	22.00%	(n) Period
1.00000	1.00000	1.00000	1.00000	1.00000	1.00000	1.00000	1.00000	1
2.09000	2.10000	2.12000	2.14000	2.16000	2.18000	2.20000	2.22000	2
3.27810	3.31000	3.37440	3.43960	3.50560	3.57240	3.64000	3.70840	3
4.57313	4.64100	4.77933	4.92114	5.06650	5.21543	5.36800	5.52425	4
5.98471	6.10510	6.35285	6.61010	6.87714	7.15421	7.44160	7.73958	5
7.52333	7.71561	8.11519	8.53552	8.97748	9.44197	9.92992	10.44229	6
9.20043	9.48717	10.08901	10.73049	11.41387	12.14152	12.91590	13.73959	7
11.02847	11.43589	12.29969	13.23276	14.24009	15.32700	16.49908	17.76231	8
13.02104	13.57948	14.77566	16.08535	17.51851	19.08585	20.79890	22.67001	9
15.19293	15.93742	17.54874	19.33730	21.32147	23.52131	25.95868	28.65742	10
17.56029	18.53117	20.65458	23.04452	25.73290	28.75514	32.15042	35.96205	11
20.14072	21.38428	24.13313	27.27075	30.85017	34.93107	39.58050	44.87370	12
22.95338	24.52271	28.02911	32.08865	36.78620	42.21866	48.49660	55.74591	13
26.01919	27.97498	32.39260	37.58107	43.67199	50.81802	59.19592	69.01001	14
29.36092	31.77248	37.27971	43.84241	51.65951	60.96527	72.03511	85.19221	15
33.00340	35.94973	42.75328	50.98035	60.92503	72.93901	87.44213	104.93450	16
36.97370	40.54470	48.88367	59.11760	71.67303	87.06804	105.93056	129.02009	17
41.30134	45.59917	55.74971	68.39407	84.14072	103.74028	128.11667	158.40451	18
46.01846	51.15909	63.43968	78.96923	98.60323	123.41353	154.74000	194.25350	19
51.16012	57.27500	72.05244	91.02493	115.37975	146.62797	186.68800	237.98927	20
56.76453	64.00250	81.69874	104.76842	134.84051	174.02100	225.02560	291.34691	21
62.87334	71.40275	92.50258	120.43600	157.41499	206.34479	271.03072	356.44323	22
69.53194	79.54302	104.60289	138.29704	183.60138	244.48685	326.23686	435.86075	23
76.78981	88.49733	118.15524	158.65862	213.97761	289.49448	392.48424	532.75011	24
84.70090	98.34706	133.33387	181.87083	249.21402	342.60349	471.98108	650.95513	25
136.30754	164.49402	241.33268	356.78685	530.31173	790.94799	1181.88157	1767.08134	30
164.03699	201.13777	304.84772	465.82019	715.74746	1103.49598	1704.10946	2632.34386	32
196.98234	245.47670	384.52098	607.51991	965.26979	1538.68781	2456.11762	3920.20061	34
236.12472	299.12681	484.46312	791.67288	1301.02703	2144.64890	3539.00937	5837.04658	36
337.88245	442.59256	767.09142	1342.02510	2360.75724	4163.21303	7343.85784	12936.53527	40

Table 3
Present Value of a Single Amount

(n) Period	2.00%	2.50%	3.00%	4.00%	5.00%	6.00%	7.00%	8.00%
1	0.98039	0.97561	0.97087	0.96154	0.95238	0.94340	0.93458	0.92593
2	0.96117	0.95181	0.94260	0.92456	0.90703	0.89000	0.87344	0.85734
3	0.94232	0.92860	0.91514	0.88900	0.86384	0.83962	0.81630	0.79383
4	0.92385	0.90595	0.88849	0.85480	0.82270	0.79209	0.76290	0.73503
5	0.90573	0.88385	0.86261	0.82193	0.78353	0.74726	0.71299	0.68058
6	0.88797	0.86230	0.83748	0.79031	0.74622	0.70496	0.66634	0.63017
7	0.87056	0.84127	0.81309	0.75992	0.71068	0.66506	0.62275	0.58349
8	0.85349	0.82075	0.78941	0.73069	0.67684	0.62741	0.58201	0.54027
9	0.83676	0.80073	0.76642	0.70259	0.64461	0.59190	0.54393	0.50025
10	0.82035	0.78120	0.74409	0.67556	0.61391	0.55839	0.50835	0.46319
11	0.80426	0.76214	0.72242	0.64958	0.58468	0.52679	0.47509	0.42888
12	0.78849	0.74356	0.70138	0.62460	0.55684	0.49697	0.44401	0.39711
13	0.77303	0.72542	0.68095	0.60057	0.53032	0.46884	0.41496	0.36770
14	0.75788	0.70773	0.66112	0.57748	0.50507	0.44230	0.38782	0.34046
15	0.74301	0.69047	0.64186	0.55526	0.48102	0.41727	0.36245	0.31524
16	0.72845	0.67362	0.62317	0.53391	0.45811	0.39365	0.33873	0.29189
17	0.71416	0.65720	0.60502	0.51337	0.43630	0.37136	0.31657	0.27027
18	0.70016	0.64117	0.58739	0.49363	0.41552	0.35034	0.29586	0.25025
19	0.68643	0.62553	0.57029	0.47464	0.39573	0.33051	0.27651	0.23171
20	0.67297	0.61027	0.55368	0.45639	0.37689	0.31180	0.25842	0.21455
21	0.65978	0.59539	0.53755	0.43883	0.35894	0.29416	0.24151	0.19866
22	0.64684	0.58086	0.52189	0.42196	0.34185	0.27751	0.22571	0.18394
23	0.63416	0.56670	0.50669	0.40573	0.32557	0.26180	0.21095	0.17032
24	0.62172	0.55288	0.49193	0.39012	0.31007	0.24698	0.19715	0.15770
25	0.60953	0.53939	0.47761	0.37512	0.29530	0.23300	0.18425	0.14602
26	0.59758	0.52623	0.46369	0.36069	0.28124	0.21981	0.17220	0.13520
27	0.58586	0.51340	0.45019	0.34682	0.26785	0.20737	0.16093	0.12519
28	0.57437	0.50088	0.43708	0.33348	0.25509	0.19563	0.15040	0.11591
29	0.56311	0.48866	0.42435	0.32065	0.24295	0.18456	0.14056	0.10733
30	0.55207	0.47674	0.41199	0.30832	0.23138	0.17411	0.13137	0.09938
32	0.53063	0.45377	0.38834	0.28506	0.20987	0.15496	0.11474	0.08520
34	0.51003	0.43191	0.36604	0.26355	0.19035	0.13791	0.10022	0.07305
36	0.49022	0.41109	0.34503	0.24367	0.17266	0.12274	0.08754	0.06262
40	0.45289	0.37243	0.30656	0.20829	0.14205	0.09722	0.06678	0.04603

9.00%	10.00%	12.00%	14.00%	16.00%	18.00%	20.00%	22.00%	(n) Period
0.91743	0.90909	0.89286	0.87719	0.86207	0.84746	0.83333	0.81967	1
0.84168	0.82645	0.79719	0.76947	0.74316	0.71818	0.69444	0.67186	2
0.77218	0.75131	0.71178	0.67497	0.64066	0.60863	0.57870	0.55071	3
0.70843	0.68301	0.63552	0.59208	0.55229	0.51579	0.48225	0.45140	4
0.64993	0.62092	0.56743	0.51937	0.47611	0.43711	0.40188	0.37000	5
0.59627	0.56447	0.50663	0.45559	0.41044	0.37043	0.33490	0.30328	6
0.54703	0.51316	0.45235	0.39964	0.35383	0.31393	0.27908	0.24859	7
0.50187	0.46651	0.40388	0.35056	0.30503	0.26604	0.23257	0.20376	8
0.46043	0.42410	0.36061	0.30751	0.26295	0.22546	0.19381	0.16702	9
0.42241	0.38554	0.32197	0.26974	0.22668	0.19106	0.16151	0.13690	10
0.38753	0.35049	0.28748	0.23662	0.19542	0.16192	0.13459	0.11221	11
0.35553	0.31863	0.25668	0.20756	0.16846	0.13722	0.11216	0.09198	12
0.32618	0.28966	0.22917	0.18207	0.14523	0.11629	0.09346	0.07539	13
0.29925	0.26333	0.20462	0.15971	0.12520	0.09855	0.07789	0.06180	14
0.27454	0.23939	0.18270	0.14010	0.10793	0.08352	0.06491	0.05065	15
0.25187	0.21763	0.16312	0.12289	0.09304	0.07078	0.05409	0.04152	16
0.23107	0.19784	0.14564	0.10780	0.08021	0.05998	0.04507	0.03403	17
0.21199	0.17986	0.13004	0.09456	0.06914	0.05083	0.03756	0.02789	18
0.19449	0.16351	0.11611	0.08295	0.05961	0.04308	0.03130	0.02286	19
0.17843	0.14864	0.10367	0.07276	0.05139	0.03651	0.02608	0.01874	20
0.16370	0.13513	0.09256	0.06383	0.04430	0.03094	0.02174	0.01536	21
0.15018	0.12285	0.08264	0.05599	0.03819	0.02622	0.01811	0.01259	22
0.13778	0.11168	0.07379	0.04911	0.03292	0.02222	0.01509	0.01032	23
0.12640	0.10153	0.06588	0.04308	0.02838	0.01883	0.01258	0.00846	24
0.11597	0.09230	0.05882	0.03779	0.02447	0.01596	0.01048	0.00693	25
0.10639	0.08391	0.05252	0.03315	0.02109	0.01352	0.00874	0.00568	26
0.09761	0.07628	0.04689	0.02908	0.01818	0.01146	0.00728	0.00466	27
0.08955	0.06934	0.04187	0.02551	0.01567	0.00971	0.00607	0.00382	28
0.08215	0.06304	0.03738	0.02237	0.01351	0.00823	0.00506	0.00313	29
0.07537	0.05731	0.03338	0.01963	0.01165	0.00697	0.00421	0.00257	30
0.06344	0.04736	0.02661	0.01510	0.00866	0.00501	0.00293	0.00172	32
0.05339	0.03914	0.02121	0.01162	0.00643	0.00360	0.00203	0.00116	34
0.04494	0.03235	0.01691	0.00894	0.00478	0.00258	0.00141	0.00078	36
0.03184	0.02209	0.01075	0.00529	0.00264	0.00133	0.00068	0.00035	40

Table 4
Present Value of an Annuity

(n) Period	2.00%	2.50%	3.00%	4.00%	5.00%	6.00%	7.00%	8.00%
1	0.98039	0.97561	0.97087	0.96154	0.95238	0.94340	0.93458	0.92593
2	1.94156	1.92742	1.91347	1.88609	1.85941	1.83339	1.80802	1.78326
3	2.88388	2.85602	2.82861	2.77509	2.72325	2.67301	2.62432	2.57710
4	3.80773	3.76197	3.71710	3.62990	3.54595	3.46511	3.38721	3.31213
5	4.71346	4.64583	4.57971	4.45182	4.32948	4.21236	4.10020	3.99271
6	5.60143	5.50813	5.41719	5.24214	5.07569	4.91732	4.76654	4.62288
7	6.47199	6.34939	6.23028	6.00205	5.78637	5.58238	5.38929	5.20637
8	7.32548	7.17014	7.01969	6.73274	6.46321	6.20979	5.97130	5.74664
9	8.16224	7.97087	7.78611	7.43533	7.10782	6.80169	6.51523	6.24689
10	8.98259	8.75206	8.53020	8.11090	7.72173	7.36009	7.02358	6.71008
11	9.78685	9.51421	9.25262	8.76048	8.30641	7.88687	7.49867	7.13896
12	10.57534	10.25776	9.95400	9.38507	8.86325	8.38384	7.94269	7.53608
13	11.34837	10.98318	10.63496	9.98565	9.39357	8.85268	8.35765	7.90378
14	12.10625	11.69091	11.29607	10.56312	9.89864	9.29498	8.74547	8.24424
15	12.84926	12.38138	11.93794	11.11839	10.37966	9.71225	9.10791	8.55948
16	13.57771	13.05500	12.56110	11.65230	10.83777	10.10590	9.44665	8.85137
17	14.29187	13.71220	13.16612	12.16567	11.27407	10.47726	9.76322	9.12164
18	14.99203	14.35336	13.75351	12.65930	11.68959	10.82760	10.05909	9.37189
19	15.67846	14.97889	14.32380	13.13394	12.08532	11.15812	10.33560	9.60360
20	16.35143	15.58916	14.87747	13.59033	12.46221	11.46992	10.59401	9.81815
21	17.01121	16.18455	15.41502	14.02916	12.82115	11.76408	10.83553	10.01680
22	17.65805	16.76541	15.93692	14.45112	13.16300	12.04158	11.06124	10.20074
23	18.29220	17.33211	16.44361	14.85684	13.48857	12.30338	11.27219	10.37106
24	18.91393	17.88499	16.93554	15.24696	13.79864	12.55036	11.46933	10.52876
25	19.52346	18.42438	17.41315	15.62208	14.09394	12.78336	11.65358	10.67478
26	20.12104	18.95061	17.87684	15.98277	14.37519	13.00317	11.82578	10.80998
27	20.70690	19.46401	18.32703	16.32959	14.64303	13.21053	11.98671	10.93516
28	21.28127	19.96489	18.76411	16.66306	14.89813	13.40616	12.13711	11.05108
29	21.84438	20.45355	19.18845	16.98371	15.14107	13.59072	12.27767	11.15841
30	22.39646	20.93029	19.60044	17.29203	15.37245	13.76483	12.40904	11.25778
32	23.46833	21.84918	20.38877	17.87355	15.80268	14.08404	12.64656	11.43500
34	24.49859	22.72379	21.13184	18.41120	16.19290	14.36814	12.85401	11.58693
36	25.48884	23.55625	21.83225	18.90828	16.54685	14.62099	13.03521	11.71719
40	27.35548	25.10278	23.11477	19.79277	17.15909	15.04630	13.33171	11.92461

9.00%	10.00%	12.00%	14.00%	16.00%	18.00%	20.00%	22.00%	(n) Period
0.91743	0.90909	0.89286	0.87719	0.86207	0.84746	0.83333	0.81967	1
1.75911	1.73554	1.69005	1.64666	1.60523	1.56564	1.52778	1.49153	2
2.53129	2.48685	2.40183	2.32163	2.24589	2.17427	2.10648	2.04224	3
3.23972	3.16987	3.03735	2.91371	2.79818	2.69006	2.58873	2.49364	4
3.88965	3.79079	3.60478	3.43308	3.27429	3.12717	2.99061	2.86364	5
4.48592	4.35526	4.11141	3.88867	3.68474	3.49760	3.32551	3.16692	6
5.03295	4.86842	4.56376	4.28830	4.03857	3.81153	3.60459	3.41551	7
5.53482	5.33493	4.96764	4.63886	4.34359	4.07757	3.83716	3.61927	8
5.99525	5.75902	5.32825	4.94637	4.60654	4.30302	4.03097	3.78628	9
6.41766	6.14457	5.65022	5.21612	4.83323	4.49409	4.19247	3.92318	10
6.80519	6.49506	5.93770	5.45273	5.02864	4.65601	4.32706	4.03540	11
7.16073	6.81369	6.19437	5.66029	5.19711	4.79322	4.43922	4.12737	12
7.48690	7.10336	6.42355	5.84236	5.34233	4.90951	4.53268	4.20277	13
7.78615	7.36669	6.62817	6.00207	5.46753	5.00806	4.61057	4.26456	14
8.06069	7.60608	6.81086	6.14217	5.57546	5.09158	4.67547	4.31522	15
8.31256	7.82371	6.97399	6.26506	5.66850	5.16235	4.72956	4.35673	16
8.54363	8.02155	7.11963	6.37286	5.74870	5.22233	4.77463	4.39077	17
8.75563	8.20141	7.24967	6.46742	5.81785	5.27316	4.81219	4.41866	18
8.95011	8.36492	7.36578	6.55037	5.87746	5.31624	4.84350	4.44152	19
9.12855	8.51356	7.46944	6.62313	5.92884	5.35275	4.86958	4.46027	20
9.29224	8.64869	7.56200	6.68696	5.97314	5.38368	4.89132	4.47563	21
9.44243	8.77154	7.64465	6.74294	6.01133	5.40990	4.90943	4.48822	22
9.58021	8.88322	7.71843	6.79206	6.04425	5.43212	4.92453	4.49854	23
9.70661	8.98474	7.78432	6.83514	6.07263	5.45095	4.93710	4.50700	24
9.82258	9.07704	7.84314	6.87293	6.09709	5.46691	4.94759	4.51393	25
9.92897	9.16095	7.89566	6.90608	6.11818	5.48043	4.95632	4.51962	26
10.02658	9.23722	7.94255	6.93515	6.13636	5.49189	4.96360	4.52428	27
10.11613	9.30657	7.98442	6.96066	6.15204	5.50160	4.96967	4.52810	28
10.19828	9.36961	8.02181	6.98304	6.16555	5.50983	4.97472	4.53123	29
10.27365	9.42691	8.05518	7.00266	6.17720	5.51681	4.97894	4.53379	30
10.40624	9.52638	8.11159	7.03498	6.19590	5.52773	4.98537	4.53762	32
10.51784	9.60857	8.15656	7.05985	6.20979	5.53557	4.98984	4.54019	34
10.61176	9.67651	8.19241	7.07899	6.22012	5.54120	4.99295	4.54192	36
10.75736	9.77905	8.24378	7.10504	6.23350	5.54815	4.99660	4.54386	40

GLOSSARY

A

absorption-costing income income computed by following a functional classification. Expenses are segregated according to function and then deducted from revenues to arrive at income before taxes.

accelerated depreciation methods depreciation methods allocating a greater portion of an asset's cost to the early years of its useful life and, consequently, less to later years.

acceptable quality level (AQL) a quality standard that allows a prespecified number of defects.

account a record summarizing all the transactions that affect a particular category of asset, liability, or stockholders' equity.

account form of balance sheet the balance sheet format in which assets are listed on the left and the liabilities and stockholders' equity on the right.

accounting the business discipline concerned with: (1) the selection, observation, and identification of significant variables of an organization's activities, (2) the measurement of these selected variables, (3) the analysis and processing of data to identify relevant information for long-term and operating decision making, and (4) the disclosure of the information to the various decision makers.

accounting cycle the standard set of accounting procedures performed in sequence each accounting period.

accounting equation Assets = Liabilities + Owners' equity.

accounting information system the interrelated parts and procedures used to process accounting transactions and provide useful information to decision makers.

accounting rate of return the rate of return obtained by dividing the average accounting net income by the original investment (or by average investment).

accounting system that part of an organization's overall information system which includes the principles, methods, and procedures used to record, classify, and summarize financial information to be distributed to decision makers.

accounts payable system an accounting system that records and controls current liabilities.

accrual an adjusting entry that records revenue or expense before cash is received or paid.

accrual basis of accounting the method of accounting where revenues, expenses, and other changes in assets, liabilities, and owners' equity are accounted for in the period in which the economic event takes place and not in the period in which cash is received or paid.

accrued expenses expenses incurred in one accounting period but paid in a subsequent accounting period.

accrued revenue revenue that is earned over time but for which the corresponding cash is received periodically.

activity a basic unit of work within an organization.

activity analysis the process of identifying, describing, and evaluating the activities an organization performs.

activity-based cost (ABC) system a cost system that first traces costs to activities and then traces costs from activities to products.

activity-based management (ABM) a system-wide, integrated approach that focuses management's attention on activities.

activity capacity the ability to perform activities.

activity elimination the process of eliminating non-value-added activities.

activity fixed expenses the costs of fixed resource usage (fixed activity rate × expected activity usage).

activity rate the resource expenditure for an activity divided by the practical activity capacity.

activity reduction decreasing the time and resources required by an activity.

activity selection the process of choosing among sets of activities caused by competing strategies.

activity sharing increasing the efficiency of necessary activities by using economies of scale.

actual cost system a cost measurement system in which actual manufacturing costs are assigned to products.

additional paid-in capital the amount invested by owners in excess of the par value of the stock that they have purchased.

additions asset enlargements, such as the addition of a new wing to an existing operation.

adjunct account an account that increases the balance in another related account. An adjunct account does the opposite of a contra account.

adjusted cost of goods sold normal cost of goods sold adjusted to include overhead variance.

adjusted trial balance a trial balance prepared after adjusting entries have been posted.

adjusting entries journal entries prepared at the end of an accounting period to recognize transactions in the proper accounting period.

administrative costs the costs of general administration that cannot be reasonably assigned to the marketing or manufacturing categories.

advanced manufacturing environment an environment characterized by intense competition (usually worldwide), sophisticated technology, total quality control, and continuous improvement.

aging method a method of estimating the balance in the account Allowance for Uncollectible Accounts by analyzing the age of each accounts receivable account.

allowance method a method of estimating uncollectible accounts expense for the period and matching that expense against the sales for that period.

American Accounting Association (AAA) a professional association of accountants, principally academics and practicing accountants, concerned with accounting education and research.

American Institute of Certified Public Accountants (AICPA) the professional organization of CPAs.

amortization the allocation of the cost of intangible assets to the period in which the enterprise receives the benefits from those assets.

annuity a series of equal payments or receipts at regular intervals.

application controls controls that have been tailored to reduce specific risks in a given system.

applied overhead the overhead assigned to production using a predetermined overhead rate.

appraisal costs costs incurred to determine if products and services conform to requirements.

appropriation of retained earnings transfer of a portion of the retained earnings account to a separate retained earnings account. Appropriations are made by the board of directors for some specific purpose, and appropriate retained earnings are not available for payment as dividends.

articulation the relationships among the financial statements tying them together.

assets the economic resources a firm owns or controls that represent a current or future benefit to the firm.

audit the objective and independent third-party examination of an organization's financial statements.

audit report the formal report of the CPA that contains the auditor's opinion of the fairness of the financial statements being audited.

audit through the system an approach to auditing computer-based accounting systems by testing controls and processes within the system.

auditor's opinion an auditor's conclusion, expressed in the audit report, about whether a firm's financial statements present fairly its financial position, results of operations, and cash flow.

auditor's report an external auditor's opinion on the fairness of financial statements.

available-for-sale securities debt and equity securities that are not classified as either held-to-maturity or trading.

average collection period a statistic that shows, on average, how long an account is outstanding.

average cost a cost flow assumption that attaches an average cost to both the cost of goods sold and the ending inventory.

B

balance sheet a financial statement presenting the financial position of a firm at a particular point in time.

base period a prior period used to set the benchmark for measuring productivity changes.

batch-level activities those activities performed each time a batch is produced.
best-fitting line the line fitting a set of data points the best in the sense that the sum of the squared deviations of the data points from the line is the smallest.
betterments improvements to existing assets.
board of directors a group of individuals, elected by stockholders, who establish broad corporate policy and hire top management.
bond a written agreement between a borrower and a lender in which the borrower agrees to repay a stated sum on a future date and in most cases to make periodic interest payments at specified dates.
bond indentures written covenants that are part of the bond agreement.
book value per share the equity that one share of stock has in the net book value (assets minus liabilities) of the assets of a corporation.
break-even point the point where total sales revenue equals total costs; the point of zero profits.
budget committee a committee responsible for setting budgetary policies and goals, reviewing and approving the budget, and resolving any differences that may arise in the budgetary process.
budget director the individual responsible for coordinating and directing the overall budgeting process.
budgetary slack the process of padding the budget by overestimating costs and underestimating revenues.
budgets a plan of action expressed in financial terms.
business entity an economic unit whose transactions are kept separate from those of its owner and whose existence is independent of the owner.
business entity assumption the concept that a business is independent and distinct from its owners.

C

call premium the difference between the call price and the par value of preferred stock.
callable preferred stock preferred stock that may be called or repurchased at the option of the corporation.
capital budget a financial plan outlining the acquisition of long-term assets.
capital budgeting the process of planning, setting goals and priorities, arranging financing, and identifying criteria for making long-term investments.
capital expenditure an expenditure resulting in the acquisition of an operating asset.
capital investment decisions the process of planning, setting goals and priorities, arranging financing, and identifying criteria for making long-term investments.
capital leases a type of lease that is essentially a financing agreement to purchase an asset.
capital stock the stockholder's equity account reporting owners' investment in the stock of a corporation.
capitalizing retained earnings converting retained earnings into permanent capital, usually through the issuance of stock dividends. Capitalized retained earnings are unavailable for future cash dividends.
carrying costs the costs of holding inventory.
cash basis of accounting the method of accounting where revenues and expenses are recorded when cash is received or paid.
cash budget a detailed plan that outlines all sources and uses of cash.
cash equivalents short-term liquid investments that can usually be converted into cash without loss of principal. Examples include commercial paper, money market accounts, and treasury notes.
causal factor activities or variables that invoke service costs. Generally, it is desirable to use causal factors as the basis for allocating service costs.
cell-level activities activities sustaining the cell process but not varying with cost drivers of other activity categories.
certified internal auditor (CIA) an accountant who has passed the CIA exam and has met experience and other special requirements.
certified management accountant (CMA) an accountant who has passed the CMA exam and has met experience and other special requirements.
certified public accountant (CPA) an accountant licensed by individual states to practice accounting after having met a number of education and experience requirements and passing the uniform CPA exam.
change in accounting estimate a firm's change in a particular estimate, such as an asset's depreciable life, as a result of new information that was not available when the original estimate was made.
change in accounting method a firm's change from one generally accepted accounting principle or method to another generally accepted one.
chart of accounts a list of all of the general ledger accounts used by a firm.
check register a report prepared by a cash disbursements system listing each check printed, by number, the payee name, the check amount, and the invoices that were paid by each check.
classified financial statements financial statements with subcategories for each of the major reporting categories.
closing entries journal entries made at the end of the period to (1) update the retained earnings balance to reflect the results of operations, and (2) eliminate the balances in the revenue and expense accounts so

that the income statement accounts begin the subsequent period with zero balances.

committed fixed expenses fixed expenses that cannot be directly traced to individual segments and that are unaffected by the elimination of any one segment.

common stock a class of capital stock issued by all corporations. Common stockholders have voting rights and thus can contest the corporation.

common-dollar statements financial statements expressed in percentages where the appropriate figure is set to 100% and other items are expressed as a percentage of that figure.

comparability a characteristic of information which exists when the similarities and differences between two sets of economic events can be understood.

comparative balance sheet a balance sheet that shows account balances at two or more different points in time.

compensated absences absences for which the employee is paid.

completed-contract method a revenue recognition method where all of the revenue earned from the contract is recognized in the year that the project is 100% completed.

compliance audits audits that determine whether employees are following managements' policies and procedures.

compliance controls controls that provide a reasonable assurance that an enterprise complies with local, state, and federal regulations.

compound interest interest computed on the principal, plus any previously accrued interest.

conservatism a convention that results in prudence in financial reporting because of the uncertainty surrounding business and economic activities.

consistency a characteristic of information which is present when the same accounting procedures and policies are used from one period to another.

consolidated financial statements financial statements of a parent company and its subsidiaries presented as if the separate organizations were one economic entity.

constraint a mathematical expression that expresses a resource limitation.

consumption ratio the proportion of an overhead activity consumed by a product.

contingent liabilities potential future liabilities whose existence is contingent upon some future event.

continuous budget a moving twelve-month budget with a future month added as the current month expires.

contra account an account that partially or wholly offsets the balance in another account.

contributed capital legal capital plus any additional capital contributed by the owners.

contribution margin sales revenue less all variable expenses. It represents the amount available to cover fixed expenses and provide for profit.

contribution margin ratio contribution margin divided by sales revenue. It is the proportion of each sales dollar available to cover fixed costs and provide for profit.

control the process of setting standards, receiving feedback on actual performance, and taking corrective action whenever actual performance deviates significantly from planned performance.

control environment the organizational climate and structure within which the accounting and control systems operate.

control limits the maximum allowable deviation from a standard.

control procedures the transaction processing steps established by management to provide reasonable assurance that the firm's objective will be met.

controllable costs costs that can be significantly influenced by a manager.

conventional cost system a cost system that uses only unit-based cost drivers to describe cost behavior and trace costs to products.

conversion cost the sum of direct labor cost and overhead cost.

convertible bonds bonds that can be exchanged, at some future specified date, for a firm's common stock.

convertible preferred stock preferred stock that can be converted into common stock at a stated rate and time.

corporation a business entity that is viewed legally as being separate and distinct from its owners, who are stockholders.

corrective controls controls designed to facilitate the correction of an error or an irregularity after it has been detected.

cost the cash or cash equivalent value sacrificed for goods and services that are expected to bring a current or future benefit to the firm.

cost assignment the process of associating manufacturing costs with the units produced.

cost behavior the way in which a cost changes in relation to changes in the level of an activity.

cost center a responsibility center in which a manager has responsibility for the costs incurred.

cost drivers factors that measure the demand placed on overhead activities by individual products.

cost flows the process of accounting for a cost from the point of incurrence to its expiration on the income statement.

cost formula a linear function, $Y = F + VX$, where Y = Total mixed cost, F = Fixed cost, V = Variable cost per unit of activity, and X = Activity level.

cost measurement the process of assigning dollar values to cost items.

cost method a method of accounting for investments where the investment is reported at the lower of cost or market.

cost object any objective or activity to which costs are assigned.

cost of capital the cost of investment funds, usually viewed as a weighted average of the costs of funds from all sources.

cost of goods manufactured the cost of direct materials, direct labor, and overhead attached to the units produced in a period.

cost of goods sold the cost of direct materials, direct labor, and overhead attached to the units sold.

cost of resource usage the activity rate times the actual activity usage.

cost of unused activity the activity rate (fixed) times the unused activity.

cost reconciliation determining whether the costs assigned to units transferred out and to units in ending work in process are equal to the costs in beginning work in process plus the manufacturing costs incurred in the current period.

costs of quality costs incurred because poor quality may exist or because poor quality does exist.

cost-volume-profit graph a graph depicting the relationships among costs, volume, and profits. It consists of a total revenue line and a total cost line.

credit an entry on the right side of an account. Credits increase liability and stockholders' equity account balances and decrease asset account balances.

credit memorandum a business form that documents sales return and allowance transactions.

current assets cash and other assets that are expected to be converted into cash or sold or consumed during the normal operating cycle of a business or within one year, whichever is shorter.

current cost an item's current acquisition cost.

current liabilities liabilities that will be paid in cash or liquidated through the use of another current asset within one year or the normal operating cycle, whichever is shorter.

currently attainable standards standards reflecting an efficient operating state; are rigorous but achievable.

current portion of long-term debt that portion of long-term debt which is scheduled to be paid within one year or the normal operating cycle, whichever is shorter.

current ratio a measure of liquidity computed by dividing current assets by current liabilities.

D

data base management system a program that accesses data for other application programs and users and manages the physical storage of the data.

data elements individual attributes that help define an entity.

data record a set of related attributes that define a single entity.

date of record the date that stockholders are entitled to receive their dividends.

debit an entry on the left side of an account. Debits increase asset account balances and decrease liability and stockholders' equity account balances.

debt ratio a ratio measuring the proportion of assets provided by debt holders and calculated by dividing total liabilities by total assets.

debt securities long-tern notes, bonds, and other liabilities.

debt-to-equity ratio a measure of the use of financial leverage computed by dividing total liabilities by total stockholders' equity.

debt-to-total-assets ratio a measure of long-term financial strength computed by dividing total liabilities by total assets.

decision model a specific set of procedures that, when followed, produces a decision.

decision support system (DSS) flexible computer-based systems that help individuals analyze quantitative data in complex decision situations.

declaration date the date that dividends are declared by the board of directors.

declining-balance depreciation a depreciation method in which yearly depreciation is calculated by applying an operating percentage rate to an asset's remaining book value at the beginning of each year.

deferred income taxes income tax payments whose balance has been postponed to a future period.

denomination the face value of a bond.

dependent variable a variable whose value depends on the value of another variable. For example, Y in the cost formula $Y = F + VX$ depends on the value of X.

depletion the allocation of the cost of natural resources to the period in which the enterprise receives the benefits from those assets.

depreciable cost (base) the difference between an asset's acquisition cost and its estimated residual value.

depreciation the systematic allocation of the cost of an asset to the time periods that derive benefits from the use of the asset.

depreciation register a report listing the current depreciation expense as computed for each operating asset.

detective controls controls designed to detect errors and irregularities after they have occurred.

deviation the difference between the cost predicted by a cost formula and the actual cost. It measures the distance of a data point from the cost line.

differential cost the amount by which cost differs between two alternatives.

direct access file a file that stores records in a way that permits immediate access to a specific record.

direct costs costs that are easily traceable to a cost object.

direct data entry procedures procedures and devices that allow input to be entered directly from source documents, with minimal human intervention.

direct labor cost of workers who transform raw materials into a finished product.

direct labor budget a budget showing the total direct labor hours needed and the associated cost for the number of units in the production budget.

direct manufacturing costs those manufacturing costs that can be easily traced to the product being manufactured.

direct materials materials that become part of the product and can be easily traced to it.

direct materials budget a budget that outlines the expected usage of materials production and purchases of the direct materials required.

direct method a method allocating service costs directly to producing departments. This method ignores any interactions that may exist among service departments.

discounted cash flows future cash flows expressed in present value terms.

discounting model any capital investment model that explicitly considers the time value of money in identifying criteria for accepting or rejecting proposed projects.

discretionary fixed expenses fixed expenses that are directly traceable to a given segment without the use of a cost driver and, consequently, disappear if the segment is eliminated.

dividends a return to the stockholders of some of the assets that have increased because of the profits earned.

dividends in arrears accumulated unpaid dividends on cumulative preferred stock.

double-entry accounting the system of accounting where every transaction is represented by equal debits and credits.

dual-read control a hardware control that detects errors when a computer reads data from a disk.

dysfunctional behavior individual behavior conflicting with the goals of the organization.

E

early extinguishment of debt the redemption of a bond prior to its maturity date.

earnings per share (EPS) a measure of profitability, computed by dividing net income by the the average number of common shares outstanding during a year.

economic order quantity (EOQ) the amount that should be ordered (or produced) to minimize the total ordering (or setup) and carrying costs.

edits detective controls that identify and reject input that appears to be erroneous.

effective interest rate the interest rate at which a bond is issued.

effective-interest method a method of determining periodic interest whereby the effective interest rate is applied to the carrying value of the note or bond at the beginning of the period.

efficiency variance *see* **usage variance.**

ending finished goods inventory budget a budget describing planned ending inventory of finished goods in units and dollars.

equity method a method of accounting for investments where the investments are first recorded at acquisition cost and subsequently adjusted to reflect changes in balance sheet value of the firms invested in.

equity ratio a ratio measuring the proportion of total assets supplied by shareholders and calculated by dividing total stockholders' equity by total assets.

equity securities preferred and common stock.

equivalent units of output the whole units that could have been produced in a period given the amount of manufacturing inputs used.

error the unintentional misstatement of financial information.

error costs costs incurred from making bad decisions because of inaccurate product costs.

estimated (useful) economic life the service potential that the current user may expect from the asset.

expectation gap the difference in perceived responsibilities between accountants and auditors and the general public.

expected activity level the level of production activity expected for the coming period.

expenditure the payment of an asset or the incurrence of a liability in exchange for another asset or for a service rendered.

expenditure cycle the systems and procedures used to process transactions related to the acquisition and use of goods and services.

expenditures outflows of cash or other assets or increases in liabilities which may not represent expenses.

expenses costs that have expired or been used up in the production of revenues; these appear as deductions on the income statement.

external failure costs costs incurred because products fail to conform to requirements after being sold to outside parties.

extraordinary items gains and losses that result from transactions both unusual in nature and infrequent in occurrence.

extraordinary repairs the major reconditioning or overhaul of existing assets.

F

facility-level activities those activities that sustain a facility's general manufacturing process.

favorable variances variance produced whenever the actual amounts are less than the budgeted or standard allowances.

FICA (Federal Insurance Contributions Act) or social security taxes a combination of old age survivors and disability insurance (OASDI) and Medicare insurance.

fields *see* **data elements.**

FIFO costing method a unit-costing method that excludes prior-period work and costs in computing current-period unit work and costs.

file a group of records with the same data-element format.

file labels controls that physically and logically identify computer files.

financial accounting the study of concepts and procedures used to prepare financial information for external users.

financial accounting information system a subsystem of the accounting information system. The main objective of this system is to prepare financial statements for external users. This subsystem follows legally mandated rules for identifying and processing inputs (economic events).

Financial Accounting Standards Board (FASB) an independent body that has the responsibility to set accounting standards and principles.

financial budget that portion of the master budget that includes the cash budget, the budgeted balance sheet, the budgeted statement of cash flows, and the capital budget.

financial cycle a collection of systems that process transactions and events involving the acquisition and use of capital resources.

financial instruments cash, evidence of an ownership interest in an entity, or a contract between companies to deliver or exchange cash or other financial instruments (e.g., accounts receivable, accounts payable, debt, etc.).

financial productivity measure a productivity measure in which inputs and outputs are expressed in dollars.

financial reporting controls controls that provide a reasonable assurance that financial records and reports are reliable.

financial reporting system an information system that uses the accounting data that has been collected and summarized in ledgers to produce financial reports and statements.

financial statement analysis the set of techniques including horizontal, vertical, and ratio analysis designed to provide relevant data to decision makers.

financial statements concise reports that summarize specific transactions for a particular period. These reports show the financial position of the firm as well as the results of its operation.

financing activities nonoperating activities, such as selling stock or issuing bonds, that provide cash.

finished goods inventory stores of fully completed goods ready for sale to customers.

first-in, first-out (FIFO) a cost flow assumption whereby the costs attached to the first goods sold are the costs of the first goods purchased.

fixed costs those costs, in total, that are constant within the relevant range as the level of the cost driver varies.

fixed overhead spending variance the difference between actual fixed overhead and applied fixed overhead.

fixed overhead volume variance the difference between budgeted fixed overhead and applied fixed overhead; a measure of capacity utilization.

flexible budget a budget that can specify costs for a range of activity.

flexible budget variance the sum of price variances and efficiency variances in a performance report comparing actual costs to expected costs predicted by a flexible budget.

Foreign Corrupt Practices Act an act requiring that publicly traded companies establish an adequate accounting system and internal controls.

fraudulent financial reporting the intentional misstatement of financial reports.

freight-in the cost of freight for goods purchased for resale.

freight-out freight charges paid by the seller.

full disclosure the assumption that all relevant information must be disclosed to users for that information to be useful.

full-costing income *see* **absorption-costing income.**

future value of a single amount the amount of a current single amount taken to a future date at a specified interest rate.

future value of an annuity the amount of a series of payments or receipts taken to a future date at a specified interest rate.

G

gains increases in equity (net assets) from activities other than revenues and investments by owners of the firm during a period.

general controls pervasive global controls that affect all system users.

general ledger the book of final entry. This record contains a specific account for each item listed on the financial statements.

general ledger system a manual or computer-based accounting system that accepts journal entry input and posts those entries to a general ledger.

generally accepted accounting principles (GAAP) the concepts and standards underlying accounting for financial reporting purposes.

goal congruence the alignment of a manager's personal goals with those of the organization.

going concern assumption the assumption that a firm will continue to operate indefinitely.

goods in public warehouses goods a firm owns but stores in a public warehouse, rather than a warehouse that the firm owns.

goods in transit goods purchased but not yet received by the purchaser.

goods on consignment goods held by a firm for resale but title remains with the manufacturer of the product.

goodwill the difference between the cost of the net assets acquired in a purchase and the fair market value of those assets.

governmental accounting the practice of accounting within a governmental entity.

gross method of accounting for sales discounts a method of recording a sale and receivable at the gross amount before any discount.

gross method of recording purchase discounts a method of recording the purchase of merchandise inventory and the payable at the gross amount before any discount.

gross profit (margin) on sales the difference between net sales and cost of goods sold.

gross profit percentage a measure of profitability, computed by dividing gross profit on sales by sales.

H

hardware controls general controls that operate whenever the computer hardware is used.

held-to-maturity securities debt securities that management intends to hold to maturity.

high-low method a method for fitting a line to a set of data points using the high and low points in the data set. For a cost formula, the high and low points represent the high and low activity levels. It is used to break out the fixed and variable components of a mixed cost.

historical cost convention the practice of recording assets and liabilities in the accounting system at their original, or historical, cost and not adjusting the amounts for subsequent changes in value.

holding gain profit that is caused by the increase in the acquisition price of the inventory between the time that the firm purchased the item and when it was sold.

homogeneous cost pool a collection of overhead costs associated with activities that have the same level and can use the same cost driver to assign costs to products.

horizontal analysis the focus on the dollar and percentage changes in accounts from year to year.

hurdle rate *see* **required rate of return.**

I

ideal budgetary system a budgetary system that simultaneously achieves goal congruence and induces a manager to exert effort toward achieving the organization's goals.

ideal standards standards reflecting perfect operating conditions.

incentives the positive or negative measures taken by an organization to induce a manager to exert effort toward achieving the organization's goals.

income from continuing operations income including all of the recurring and usual transactions that a firm enters into as it produces its goods and services.

income statement the financial statement reporting the results (profit or loss) of a firm's operations over a period.

income summary account a temporary holding account used in the closing process.

independent projects projects that, if accepted or rejected, will not affect the cash flows of another project.

independent registrar an individual or firm who represents the stockholders in stock transactions.

independent trustee an individual or organization, usually a bank, who performs transaction processing functions for a bond issue.

independent variable a variable whose value does not depend on the value of another variable. For example, in the cost formula $Y = F + VX$, the variable X is an independent variable.

indexed sequential file a structure that combines the attributes of sequential and direct access file structures.

indirect costs costs common to several cost objects and not traceable to any single cost object.

indirect labor labor used in manufacturing that is not part of transforming the raw materials into the product.

indirect materials all materials used in production that do not become part of the product. Includes insignificant direct materials.

indirect method a method established by FASB to convert an accrual-basis income statement into a cash-based statement to determine cash flow from operations by adjusting items not affecting cash flows.

input controls controls designed to prevent or detect and correct erroneous input.

Institute of Management Accountants (IMA) the professional organization for management accountants.

intangible assets assets having no physical substance; rather, they give the enterprise the right of ownership or use.

integrity controls corrective controls that minimize losses from data and system destruction.

intercept parameter the fixed cost, representing the point where the cost formula intercepts the vertical axis. In the cost formula $Y = F + VX$, F is the intercept parameter.

interest rate the annual percentage rate of interest charged on a loan.

interim quality performance report a comparison of current actual quality costs with short-run budgeted quality targets.

interim quality standard a standard based on short-run quality goals.

interim statements financial statements prepared at times other than the end of a firm's fiscal year.

internal auditor an individual who performs an audit function within an organization and who is not independent of the organization.

internal control the practices and procedures used by an enterprise to reduce the risk of errors and irregularities in an accounting system.

internal control structure the environment, accounting system, and control procedures used to provide a reasonable assurance that management's objectives are met.

internal failure costs costs incurred because products and services fail to conform to requirements where lack of conformity is discovered prior to external sale.

internal rate of return the rate of return that equates the present value of a project's cash inflows with the present value of its cash outflows (i.e., it sets the NPV equal to zero). Also, the rate of return being earned on funds that remain internally invested in a project.

interperiod income tax allocation the reporting of the tax effects of temporary differences in the balance sheet as assets and liabilities.

intraperiod income tax allocation allocation of income taxes in such a way that the total income tax expense for the period is related to the proper component that caused the income.

inventories items held for resale to customers in the normal course of business or items that are to be consumed in producing or manufacturing goods or rendering services.

inventory profits profits that are realized when current revenue is matched with low historical inventory costs that do not approximate the current replacement cost of inventory.

inventory turnover a ratio that indicates how quickly a firm is able to sell its inventory.

investing activities activities through which plant and equipment are acquired.

investment center a responsibility center in which a manager is responsible for revenues, costs, and investments.

invoice a business document billing a customer for one purchase transaction.

irregularity the intentional misstatement of financial information.

J

JIT manufacturing a manufacturing approach that produces only what is necessary to satisfy the demand of the succeeding process (a demand-pull system).

job-order cost sheet a document or record used to accumulate manufacturing costs for a job.

job-order costing system a cost accumulation method that accumulates manufacturing costs by job.

joint products products inseparable prior to a split-off point. All manufacturing costs up to the split-off point are joint costs.

journal the book of original entry. The record where transactions are initially recorded in chronological order.

journal entry balance edit an edit ensuring that debits equal credits in every journal entry.

K

kanban system an information system that controls production on a demand-pull basis through the use of cards or markers.

keep-or-drop decision a relevant costing analysis that focuses on keeping or dropping a segment of a business.

key data element a data element that can be used to uniquely identify an entity.

L

labor efficiency variance the difference between the actual direct labor hours used and the standard direct labor hours allowed multiplied by the standard hourly wage rate.

labor rate variance the difference between the actual hourly rate paid and the standard hourly rate multiplied by the actual hours worked.

last-in, first-out (LIFO) an inventory valuation method that assumes that the costs attached to the last purchases made are the costs of the first items sold.

lead time for purchasing, the time to receive an order after it is placed. For manufacturing, the time to produce a product from start to finish.

lease a contractual agreement between the lessor and the lessee which gives the lessee the right to use the lessor's property for a specified period in exchange for stipulated cash payments.

ledger a book or computerized record of specific accounts where the effects of all transactions which affect a specific account are recorded.

legal (stated) capital the minimum amount that can be reported as contributed capital, usually equal to the par or stated value of all of the capital stock issued.

lessee the person who leases and uses the leased property.

lessor the owner of the property leased to the lessee.

leverage the amount of resources raised by borrowing or by issuing preferred stock.

liabilities the financial obligations of a firm to its creditors.

life-cycle cost management an approach that focuses on managing value-chain activities so that a long-term competitive advantage is created.

life-cycle costs costs associated with the product for its entire life cycle.

LIFO liquidation the sale of prior year inventory layers.

limit test a control that rejects transactions that include amounts either less than or greater than a predetermined limit.

limited liability an attribute of corporations. Stockholders' liability is limited to the extent of their investment in the corporation.

liquidity the ease with which an item can be turned into cash.

location list a report identifying each asset and its corresponding custodian and location.

long-term investments assets not available for current use.

loss a cost that expires without producing a revenue benefit.

losses decreases in equity (net assets) from activities affecting the firm during the period other than expenses and distributions to its owners.

lower of cost or market (LCM) a conservative approach to inventory valuation which reports inventory at the lower of historical acquisition cost or current market value.

M

make-or-buy decision relevant costing analysis that focuses on whether a component should be made internally or purchased externally.

management accountant an accountant who works for a single firm and is responsible for collecting, processing, and reporting financial information.

management accounting the system and procedures related to providing information for managerial activities.

management accounting information system a subsystem of the accounting information system. The main objective of this system is to produce accounting information (reports) for managerial use.

manual input symbol a systems flowchart symbol that is used to document the data entry process where human-readable information is key-entered into a computer system using a keyboard.

manufacturing cells a collection of machines dedicated to the production of a single product or subassembly.

manufacturing costs those costs necessary to make a product. They include the costs of direct materials, direct labor, and overhead.

manufacturing overhead all manufacturing costs other than direct labor and direct materials.

market the current purchase price or replacement cost of an inventory item.

market interest rate the interest rate being paid in the marketplace. This rate may differ from the stated or face interest rate.

master budget the collection of all area and activity budgets representing a firm's comprehensive plan of action.

master file a file containing relatively permanent information about an entity.

matching convention the concept that expenses incurred in one time period to earn the revenues of that period should be offset against those revenues.

materiality the relative importance or significance of an item to an informed decision maker.

materials price variance the difference between the actual price paid per unit of materials and the standard price allowed per unit multiplied by the actual quantity of materials purchased.

materials requisition form a document used to identify the cost of raw materials assigned to each job.

materials usage variance the difference between the direct materials actually used and the direct materials allowed for the actual output multiplied by the standard price.

maturity date the date when a loan becomes due and payable.

maturity value the total amount to be paid on a loan at its maturity date. This amount is normally the sum of the principal amount of a loan plus interest on the loan.

measurement costs costs incurred from measurements required by a cost system.

merchandise purchases budget a budget that details the quantity of each item that must be purchased for resale, the unit cost of each item, and the total purchase cost.

method of least squares a statistical method to find a line that best fits a set of data. It is used to break out the fixed and variable components of a mixed cost.

mixed costs those costs that have both a fixed and a variable component.

monetary assets cash or the right to receive a specific amount of cash, such as a receivable.

monetary incentives the use of economic rewards to motivate managers.

monetary liabilities obligations payable in a fixed sum of money.

mortgage a promissory note secured by an asset whose title is pledged to the lender.

mutually exclusive projects projects that, if accepted, preclude the acceptance of competing projects.

myopic behavior managerial actions that improve budgetary performance in the short run at the expense of the long-run welfare of the organization.

N

natural resources physical substances that, when taken from the ground, produce revenues for a firm.

net assets Assets − Liabilities = Net assets.

net book value the difference between the historical cost of an asset and its accumulated depreciation.

net income (net loss) the difference between revenues and expenses in an accounting period.

net method of accounting for sales discounts a method of recording a sale and receivable after deducting the allowable discount.

net method of recording purchase discounts a method of recording the purchase of merchandise and the accounts payable net of the allowable discount.

net present value the difference between the present value of a project's cash inflows and the present value of its cash outflows.

net realizable value the net amount that a firm expects to receive from a sale after deducting taxes and discounts.

no-par stock stock that does not have a stated or par value.

nominal (temporary) accounts accounts zeroed at the end of an accounting period. Revenue and expense accounts are examples.

noncash activity a business activity that does not provide or use cash. Depreciation is an example.

noncontrollable cost a cost that cannot be significantly influenced by a manager.

nondiscounting models capital investment models that identify criteria for accepting or rejecting projects without considering the time value of money.

nonmanufacturing costs the costs associated with selling and general administration.

nonmonetary assets assets that do not represent future claims to fixed amounts of cash.

nonmonetary incentives the use of psychological and social rewards to motivate managers.

nonmonetary liabilities liabilities reduced by the performance of a service or delivery of goods, not by a cash payment. Unearned revenue is an example.

nonmonetary liabilities obligations to provide fixed amounts of goods and services.

nonunit-based cost drivers factors, other than the number of units produced, that explain the consumption of overhead.

nonvalue-added activities any activities either unnecessary or necessary but inefficient and improvable.

nonvalue-added costs costs caused by nonvalue-added activities.

normal activity level the average activity level that a firm experiences over more than one fiscal period.

normal cost of goods sold the cost of goods sold figure obtained when the per-unit normal cost is used.

normal costing system a cost measurement system in which the actual costs of direct materials and direct labor are assigned to production and a predetermined rate is used to assign overhead costs to production.

O

objectivity a characteristic of information that is reliable, verifiable, and not subject to different interpretations.

obsolescence the process of becoming outdated, outmoded, or inadequate.

off-balance-sheet financing the use of financing instruments that are not recorded as liabilities on the balance sheet.

one-year quality performance report a report that compares current-year quality costs with prior-year quality costs based on current-year sales.

on-page connector symbol a systems flowchart symbol that is used to connect two flowchart symbols when a connector line cannot be easily used.

operating activities transactions and events other than financing or investing activities.

operating assets assets used to conduct business operations.

operating budgets budgets associated with the income-producing activities of an organization.

operating cycle the time it takes a firm to go from cash back to cash.

operating expenses the normal operating expenses of an enterprise.

operating leases leases that do not meet the FASB's criteria to be considered financing leases.

operating profit the difference between gross profit on sales and operating expenses.

operating-asset ledger a report listing each operating asset and its corresponding acquisition date, cost, book value, salvage value, depreciation method, and life.

operation costing a costing system that uses job-order costing to assign materials costs and process costing to assign conversion costs.

operational audits audits that assess the efficiency and effectiveness of operations within an organizational unit.

operational productivity measures measures expressed in physical terms.

operations controls controls that provide a reasonable assurance that business activities are performed in accordance with management's authorizations.

opportunity cost the benefit sacrificed or foregone when one alternative is chosen over another.

optimal cost system a cost system that minimizes the sum of error costs and measurement costs.

ordering costs the costs of placing and receiving an order.

organization costs the costs incurred to start a business, including legal costs, filing and incorporation fees, promotion costs, printing and engraving costs.

other revenues (income) and expenses revenue and expenses earned and incurred from nonbusiness operations.

out-of-pocket cost a cost that involves a current cash outlay.

output controls controls designed to prevent or detect and correct output errors and irregularities.

overapplied overhead the overhead variance resulting when applied overhead is greater than the actual overhead cost incurred.

overhead budget a budget that reveals the planned expenditures for all indirect manufacturing items.

overhead variance the difference between the actual overhead and the applied overhead.

owners' equity owners' residual interest in the assets of a firm.

P

par value an amount designated by the articles of incorporation or board of directors and printed on the stock certificates.

parallel processing a method of process manufacturing in which subunits pass through different sequential processes before being brought together in a final process.

parent company the corporation owning the majority of stock in another corporation.

parity checks hardware controls that detect data errors when information is transferred into a computer.

partial productivity measurement a ratio measuring productive efficiency for one input.

participative budgeting an approach to budgeting that allows managers who will be held accountable for budgetary performance to participate in the budget's development.

partnership a business entity owned by two or more individuals but not legally independent of the owners.

password protection a general control that restricts access to computer systems to authorized system users.

patent an exclusive right to use, manufacture, process, or sell a product.

payback period the time required for a project to return its investment.

payment date the date that a dividend is actually paid.

pension an agreement in which an employer promises to make certain payments to employees after they retire.

percentage-of-completion method a revenue recognition method that recognizes revenue during construction in proportion to the amount of work completed on the project.

percentage-of-net-sales method a method of determining the amount of uncollectible accounts expense by analyzing the relationship between net credit sales and uncollectible accounts expense of prior years.

period costs costs related to periods of time rather than units of output and expensed each period.

period expenses expenses that cannot be directly related to a product or service and consequently are expensed in the period in which they are incurred.

periodic inventory system an approach to maintaining inventory data without keeping continuous track of inventories and cost of goods sold.

permanent differences statutory differences between GAAP and the IRC that result in differences between accounting income and taxable income.

perpetual inventory system an approach to maintaining inventory data that keeps a running balance of both inventory on hand and the cost of goods sold.

physical flow schedule a schedule that accounts for all units flowing through a department during a period.

physical inventory the counting of end-of-period inventory to determine the quantity on hand.

physical security controls general controls that prevent unauthorized access to or destruction of a computer facility.

pool rate the overhead costs for a homogeneous cost pool divided by the practical quantity of cost drivers associated with the pool.

pooling of interests method a consolidation method that assumes that the subsidiary's stockholders are now stockholders of the parent company.

post-closing trial balance a trial balance prepared after the closing entries have been posted.

posting the process of transferring recorded transaction data from a journal to a ledger.

post-retirement health care costs the insurance costs that the employer agrees to pay for health and similar insurance on behalf of the employee.

practical activity level the output a firm can achieve if it is operating efficiently.

predetermined overhead rate estimated overhead divided by the estimated level of production activity. It is used to assign overhead to production.

preferred stock stock that has preferential rights over and above those of common stock.

prepaid assets nonmonetary assets whose benefits affect more than one accounting period.

present value the concept that the value of money is affected by time.

present value of a single amount the value of a future promise to pay or receive a single amount at a specified interest rate.

present value of an annuity present value of a series of future promises to pay or receive an annuity at a specified interest rate.

pretax accounting income income based on generally accepted accounting principles before income tax expense is deducted.

prevention costs costs incurred to prevent defects in products or services being produced.

preventive controls controls designed to prevent the occurrence of errors or irregularities.

price-earnings (P-E) ratio the current market price of a stock divided by its earnings per share.

price efficiency the least-cost, technically efficient mix of inputs.

price recovery component the difference between the total profit change and the profit-linked productivity change.

price standard the price that should be paid per unit of input.

price variance the difference between standard price and actual price multiplied by the actual quantity of inputs used.

prime cost the sum of the cost of direct materials and direct labor.

principal the amount of money borrowed on a loan.

prior period adjustments transactions that relate to an earlier accounting period but which were not determinable in the earlier period. Specifically limited by the FASB.

process controls controls designed to prevent or detect and correct processing errors.

process costing system a cost accumulation method that accumulates costs by process or department.

producing departments units within an organization responsible for producing the products or services sold to customers.

product costs costs attached to a product and inventoried and expensed only when the product is sold.

product diversity the situation when products consume overhead in different proportions.

product-level (sustaining) activities those activities performed to support the production of each different type of product.

production budget a budget that shows how many units must be produced to meet sales needs and satisfy ending inventory requirements.

production Kanban a card or marker that specifies the quantity that the preceding process should produce.

production report a report that summarizes the manufacturing activity for a department during a period and discloses physical flow, equivalent units, total costs to account for, unit cost computation, and costs assigned to goods transferred out and to units in ending work in process.

productivity producing output efficiently, using the least quantity of inputs possible.

productivity measurement assessment of productivity changes.

product life cycle the time a product exists—from conception to abandonment.

profit center a responsibility center in which a manager is responsible for revenues and costs.

profit-linked productivity measurement an assessment of the amount of profit change—from the base period to the current period—attributable to productivity changes.

profit margin percentage a profitability measure computed by dividing net income by sales.

profit-volume graph a graphical portrayal of the relationship between profits and sales activity.

proxy a legal document, signed by a stockholder, giving another person the right to vote the shares in the manner they deem best.

pseudoparticipation a budgetary system in which top management solicits inputs from lower-level managers and then ignores those inputs. Thus, in reality, budgets are dictated from above.

public accounting the field of accounting providing a variety of accounting services to clients for a fee.

publicly owned corporation a corporation whose stock is bought and sold by the public often on exchanges such as the New York or American Stock Exchange.

purchase discounts price reductions offered by vendors to customers.

purchase method a consolidation method that assumes that the company's shareholders have sold out their interest to the parent company.

purchase order a formal, external request for the purchase of goods or services.

purchase returns and allowances transactions that result when goods are returned to vendors or when vendors offer price reductions on goods which have been purchased.

purchasing system a transaction processing system that maintains adequate inventory stock levels by generating purchase orders when the quantity-on-hand plus the quantity-on-order is less than the reorder point.

Q

quality of conformance conforming to the design requirements of the product.

quality of design quality differences that arise for products with the same function but different specifications.

quality of earnings a qualitative measure of the extent to which reported earnings are the result of economic events rather than the result of accounting principles.

quantifiability the convention that financial statements only represent the effects of economic events which can be represented in numerical (primarily monetary) terms.

quantity discounts reductions from the list price based on quantity purchases.

quantity standards the quantity of input allowed per unit of output.

questionable reporting practices reporting practices considered legal but deceptive—perhaps unethical or at least questionable.

R

range test a control that rejects transactions that include an amount not falling within an allowable range.

rate variance *see* **price variance.**

ratio analysis a method of expressing relationships among various items in a company's financial statements.

raw materials inventory stores of materials, usually purchased from outside suppliers, that are eventually converted into finished goods.

read-after-write control a hardware control that detects errors when data is recorded on a magnetic disk.

real (permanent) accounts accounts that maintain a running balance extending beyond an accounting period. Balance sheet accounts are real accounts.

realization principle the principle accountants follow to determine when revenue should be recognized.

receipts inflows of cash or other assets, which may not always represent revenues.

receivable turnover an accounts receivable performance ratio computed by dividing credit sales by the average accounts receivable for the period.

receiving report a report showing the quantity of goods received from a vendor.

receiving system a transaction processing system that controls and records goods as they are received from vendors.

recovery and restart procedures corrective controls that aid the resumption of processing after abnormal program termination.

redeemable preferred stock preferred stock that can be callable and that can be returned by the stockholder to the corporation under certain circumstances.

register a report that lists all of the transactions processed by a system.

relational data base a data base in which data is stored in tabular form.

relevance a characteristic of accounting information capable of making a difference in a decision because it has predictive and/or feedback value.

relevant costs future costs that change across alternatives.

relevant range the range of activity over which cost behavioral relationships are valid.

reliability a characteristic of information that actually represents what it purports to represent.

remittance advice a business document returned by a customer which identifies their account number and the amount being paid on their account.

reorder point the stock level at which additional units of an inventory item should be purchased to meet expected demand.

repair or maintenance an expenditure that maintains the asset's expected level of service or output and neither extends its useful life nor increases the quantity or quality of its output.

report form of balance sheet the vertical balance sheet format with liabilities and stockholders' equity listed below the assets.

required rate of return the minimum rate of return that a project must earn in order to be acceptable. Usually corresponds to the cost of capital.

research and development costs costs and expenditures incurred in discovering, planning, designing, and implementing a new product or process.

residual (salvage) value an estimate of what the asset will be worth at the end of its life.

resource spending the cost of acquiring capacity to perform an activity.

resources supplied as used (needed) resources acquired from outside sources, where the terms of acquisition do not require any long-term commitment.

resources supplied in advance of usage resources acquired by the use of either an explicit or implicit contract to obtain a given quantity of resource, regardless of whether the resource available is fully used or not.

resource usage the amount of activity used in producing an organization's output.

responsibility accounting the use of the accounting system to set standards, measure actual outcomes, and report the performance of responsibility centers.

responsibility centers an area or unit within an organization over which a manager is assigned responsibility for a specific activity or set of activities.

retained earnings the portion of stockholders' equity (resulting from the cumulative profitable operations) that has not been distributed to owners.

retained earnings statement a financial statement explaining the change in retained earnings from the beginning to the end of an accounting period.

return on assets a measure of management effectiveness computed by dividing net income by average total assets.

return on stockholders' equity a measure of management effectiveness computed by dividing net income by average stockholders' equity.

revenue cycle the set of systems and procedures that processes transactions related to the sale of goods and services.

revenue expenditures the purchase of goods or services whose benefits are consumed in the current period.

revenues the price of goods sold or services rendered by a firm to others in exchange for cash or other assets or to satisfy liabilities.

S

safety stock extra inventory carried to serve as insurance against fluctuations in demand.

sales allowances reduction in the actual sales price, occurring when an item purchased does not perform to expectations or when there are other defects in the product.

sales budget a budget that describes expected sales in units and dollars for the coming period.

sales discount a cash reduction offered to customers who purchase merchandise on account and pay for the goods within a specific time period.

sales return a transaction that results when a customer returns an item for a cash refund or a credit on account.

sales-revenue approach an approach to CVP analysis that uses sales revenue to measure sales activity. Variable costs and contribution margin are expressed as percentages of sales revenue.

scattergraph a plot of (X, Y) data points. For cost analysis, X is activity level and Y is the associated cost at that activity level.

scatterplot method a method to fit a line to a set of data using two points that are selected by judgment. It is used to break out the fixed and variable components of a mixed cost.

segment a component of an entity whose activities represent a separate major line of business or class of customer.

self-constructed assets a building or piece of equipment constructed by the enterprise.

sell or process further relevant costing analysis that focuses on whether a product should be processed beyond the split-off point.

selling and administrative expense budget a budget that outlines planned expenditures for nonmanufacturing activities.

selling costs those costs incurred to market and distribute a firm's products or services.

sequential file a file structure that stores records in key data element sequence.

sequential (or step) method a method that allocates service costs to user departments in a sequential manner. It gives partial consideration to interactions among service departments.

sequential processing a method of process manufacturing in which units flow from one process to another in a sequential pattern.

serial bonds bonds payable on various dates.

service departments units within an organization that provide essential support services for producing departments.

setup costs the costs of preparing equipment and facilities so that they can be used for production.

shipping notice a business document that informs the customer that the goods have been shipped.

simple interest interest amount for one or more periods, assuming that the amount on which interest is computed stays the same.

sinking fund a collection of cash or other assets such as marketable securities set apart to be used for a specific purpose, such as bond repayment.

slope parameter the variable cost per unit of activity, represented by V in the cost formula $Y = F + VX$.

sole proprietorship a business entity owned by one individual and not legally independent of the owner.

special-order decision relevant costing analysis that focuses on whether a specially priced order should be accepted or rejected.

specifically identifiable intangible assets intangible assets whose costs can easily be identified as part of the cost of the asset and whose benefits generally have a determinable life.

specific-identification method an inventory valuation method that determines the actual acquisition cost of each individual item in the ending inventory.

split-off point the point at which products become distinguishable after passing through a common process.

standard bill of materials a listing of the type and quantity of materials allowed for a given level of output.

standard cost per unit the per-unit cost that should be achieved given materials, labor, and overhead standards.

standard cost sheet a listing of the standard costs and standard quantities of direct materials, direct labor, and overhead that should apply to a single product.

standard hours allowed the direct labor hours that should have been used to produce the actual output (Unit labor standard × Actual output).

standard quantity of materials allowed the quantity of materials that should have been used to produce the actual output (Unit materials standard × Actual output).

stated interest rate the interest rate stated on the face of the bond at the time of sale.

statement of cash flows a required financial statement disclosing the effects of operating, financing, and investing activities on a firm's cash flows.

statement of stockholders' equity a financial statement that explains the change in total stockholders' equity from the beginning to the end of a reporting period.

static budget a budget for a particular level of activity.

stock dividend a proportional distribution of a corporation's own stock to its shareholders.

stock split an increase in the number of shares of stock outstanding with a proportional decrease in the par or stated value of the stock.

stockholders' equity owners' residual interest in the assets of a corporation.

stock-out costs the costs of insufficient inventory.

straight-line depreciation a depreciation method that assumes that depreciation is a constant function of time and results in an equal allocation of the asset's cost to each accounting period during its estimated service life.

strategic cost analysis the use of cost data to develop and identify superior strategies that will produce a sustainable competitive advantage.

strategic decision making the process of choosing among alternative strategies, with the goal of selecting a strategy or strategies that provide a company with a reasonable assurance of long-term growth and survival.

strategic plan the long-term plan for future activities and operations, usually involving at least five years.

subsidiary a corporation wholly or partially owned by another corporation.

subsidiary ledger a detailed record of the effects of all transactions on a specific entity within a general ledger account.

sum-of-the-years-digits an accelerated depreciation method in which the asset's depreciable base (cost less salvage value) is multiplied by a declining rate.

sunk cost a cost for which the outlay has already been made and that cannot be affected by a future decision.

surge protector a hardware control installed on many computer systems to prevent hardware failures caused by sudden fluctuations in electrical power.

system flowchart a diagram depicting the flows into and out of an information system.

system security controls general controls that prevent unauthorized access to or destruction of system resources.

systems development procedures general controls that ensure that application systems are properly designed and installed.

T

t account a short-hand representation of an individual ledger account.

tangible assets assets having physical substance and capabilities.

target cost the difference between the sales price needed to achieve a projected market share and the desired per-unit profit.

technical efficiency point at which for any mix of inputs that will produce a given output, no more of any one input is used than is absolutely necessary.

temporary differences differences between accounting and tax income that result from the fact that some transactions affect taxable income and accounting income in different periods.

term bonds bonds whose entire principal is due in one payment.

test data transactions prepared to test the adequacy of controls and processes in a system.

theoretical activity level the maximum output possible for a firm under perfect operating conditions.

time period assumption the division of a firm's life into time periods.

time ticket a document used to identify the cost of direct labor for a job.

times interest earned the ratio of the income that is available for interest payments to the annual interest expense; calculated by dividing income before interest and taxes (operating income) by the annual interest expense.

total budget variance the difference between the actual cost of an input and its planned cost.

total preventive maintenance a program of preventive maintenance that has zero machine failures as its standard.

total productive efficiency the point at which technical and price efficiency are achieved.

total productivity measurement an assessment of productive efficiency for all inputs combined.

total quality control (TQC) a quality standard that demands perfection (zero defects).

trade discounts price reductions offered to a certain class of buyers.

trading securities debt and equity securities that are purchased and held primarily for sale in the near term.

transaction cycle the sequence of related steps used to process a transaction.

transaction file a file containing information used to update a master file.

transaction review and authorization controls controls that prevent the submission of data containing errors or that is unauthorized.

transactions business events of a particular enterprise which are measured in monetary terms and recorded in its financial records.

transfer agent one who maintains a record of all of the stockholders, updates the record when stock is traded, issues new shares of stock to new owners, cancels certificates when they are sold, and pays dividends to the stockholders.

transferred-in costs the costs of goods transferred in from a prior process.

transportation-in *see* **freight-in.**

treasury stock a corporation's own stock that it has repurchased.

trend analysis horizontal analysis that includes more than a single change from one year to the next.

trial balance a list of all general ledger accounts and their corresponding account balances at a point in time. A trial balance is used to test the equality of the accounting equation.

U

unadjusted trial balance a trial balance prepared before adjusting journal entries have been recorded and posted.

uncollectible accounts receivables that the firm is unable to collect in full from the customer.

uncollectible accounts expense the amount of current period sales that are not expected to be collected.

underapplied overhead the overhead variance resulting when the actual overhead cost incurred is greater than the applied overhead.

underwriters brokerage firms or groups of firms that, for a stated price, purchase an entire stock issue and assume the risks involved in marketing the stock to their clients.

unearned revenue a liability recognizing an obligation when cash is received in advance of performing some service or providing some good.

unfavorable variances variances produced whenever the actual input amounts are greater than the budgeted or standard allowances.

unit-based (volume-related) cost drivers factors that increase in direct proportion to the number of units produced and that explain the consumption of unit-based overhead costs.

unit-level activities activities performed each time a unit is produced.

units-of-production a depreciation method that assumes that the primary depreciation factor is use rather than the passage of time.

units-sold approach an approach to CVP analysis that uses units sold to measure sales activity. Variable costs and contribution margin are expressed on a units-sold basis.

unsecured bonds (debentures) bonds issued without any security to back them.

update a file operation that changes the contents of a master file.

usage variance the difference between standard quantities and actual quantities multiplied by standard price.

useful life or economic life a measure of the service potential that the current user may expect from the asset.

V

value-added activities necessary, perfectly efficient activities.

value-added costs costs caused by value-added activities.

value-added standard the quantity of a cost driver that should be used for an activity.

value chain the set of activities required to design, develop, produce, market, and service a product (or service).

variable budgets *see* **flexible budget.**

variable cost of goods manufactured the cost of direct materials, direct labor, and variable overhead attached to the units produced in a period.

variable cost of goods sold the total variable manufacturing costs attached to the units sold.

variable cost ratio variable costs divided by sales revenues. It is the proportion of each sales dollar needed to cover variable costs.

variable costs those costs, in total, that vary as a cost driver (activity level) changes.

variable-costing income income remaining after fixed costs have been deducted from contribution margin. A product-costing approach that treats all fixed expenses, including fixed overhead, as period expenses.

variable overhead efficiency variance the difference between the actual direct labor hours used and the standard hours allowed multiplied by the standard variable overhead rate.

variable overhead spending variance the difference between the actual variable overhead and the budgeted variable overhead based on actual hours used to produce the actual output.

vendor Kanban a card or marker that signals to a supplier the quantity of materials that need to be delivered and the time of delivery.

verifiability the concept that data related to a transaction or event must be available and that two or more qualified persons would reach the same conclusions about the proper accounting treatment of the transaction or event if they examined the data.

vertical analysis an analysis that evaluates the relationships within a single financial statement in which the appropriate total figure in the financial statement is set to 100% and other items are expressed as a percentage of that figure.

W

weighted average costing method a unit-costing method that merges prior-period work and costs with current-period work and costs.

whole life cost the life cycle cost of a product plus costs that consumers incur, including operation, support, maintenance, and disposal.

withdrawal Kanban a marker or card that specifies the quantity that a subsequent process should withdraw from a preceding process.

work in process all partially completed units found in production at a given point in time.

work-in-process file a collection of open job-order cost sheets or job-order cost records.

work in process inventory stores of partially completed goods.

working capital a measure of short-term liquidity computed as the difference between current assets and current liabilities.

Y

yield rate the actual rate at which the bond is issued.

Z

zero-coupon bonds bonds that do not pay interest periodically.

zero defects a quality performance standard requiring all products and services to be produced and delivered according to specifications.

Company Index

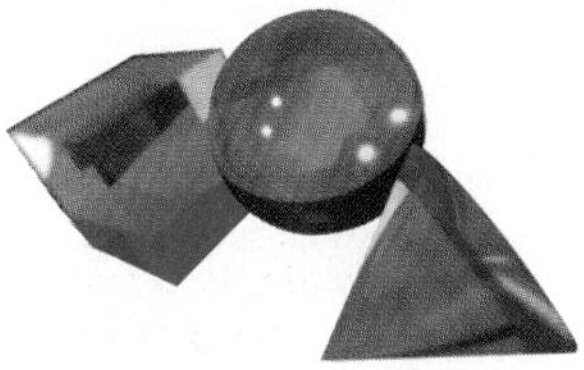

Subject Index

A

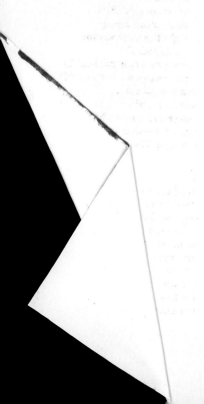